These newspapers
are on microfilm
and are located in
the first drawer
in the microfilm
area.

BIRTH OF AMERICA
THE YEAR IN REVIEW
1763—1783

NEW YORK, *June* 23, 1769.

To the PUBLICK.

AS I have juftly incurred the Refentment of my Fellow Citizens, from my Behaviour, as fet forth in an Advertifement, *Of great Importance to the Publick* ; I beg Leave to implore the Pardon of the Publick, affuring them that I am truly forry for the Part I have acted ; declare and pro-mife that I never will again attempt an Act contrary to the true Intereft and Refolutions of a People zea-lous in the Caufe of *Virtue* and *Liberty* ; and by my future Conduct, not only convince them of my Contrition, but make it my whole Study to main-tain inviolate the Refolutions they have entered into,---befeeching the Public in general to believe me,   Their ready devoted, and moft

Obedient Humble Servant,

ALEXANDER ROBERTSON.

I Alfo declare, That the Goods were returned back to Philadelphia by the Stage laft Monday, and that a Certificate of the fame fhall be produced to the Publick.

☞The laft four Lines
fworn to before me, } *Elias Defbroffes.*

See p. 26, June - December,   Broadside: June 23.

BIRTH OF AMERICA
THE YEAR IN REVIEW
1763—1783

A Chronological Guide and Index
to the Contemporary Colonial Press

By Thomas W. Jodziewicz

NYT **Microfilming Corporation of America**
A New York Times Company
21 Harristown Road, Glen Rock, New Jersey 07452

Birth of America: The Year in Review 1763-1783 is a combined printed guide – microfilm collection. Information on the availability of microfilm reels containing the approximately 4,000 newspaper issues referred to in this guide may be obtained by writing or calling

Microfilming Corporation of America
21 Harristown Road
Glen Rock, New Jersey 07452
Telephone: (201) 447-3000 Ext. 216

Library of Congress Cataloguing in Publication data

Jodziewicz, Thomas W
    Birth of America.

    Includes index.
    1. United States – History – Colonial Period, ca. 1600-1775 – Sources – Indexes. 2. United States – History – Revolution, 1775-1783 – Sources – Indexes. 3. American newspapers – Indexes. 4. Newspapers on microfilm – Indexes. I. Title.
Z1237.J63   [E187]   016.9732   76-50542
ISBN 0-667-00288-X

Table of Contents

Preface

Any project as large as this has numerous acknowledgments to make. Such is the case here, although the customary and obligatory nature of these short notations hardly suffices in the present instance. The following libraries supplied newspapers to be filmed and/or films of newspapers: the New Hampshire Historical Society, the Connecticut Historical Society, the New York Historical Society, the Maryland Historical Society, the Library of Congress, the Virginia State Library, the Institute for Colonial History and Culture at Williamsburg, the Library Society of Charleston (which has been around a while! See 1773 Topical Chronology under Natural History), and the Georgia Historical Society.

Especial thanks go to Mr. Bernard A. Bernier, Jr., Head of the Reference Section of the Serial Division of the Library of Congress where the bulk of the filming was done. In addition the periodic wrestling with the process of selecting citations was eased by my unlimited access to the Library's important collection of colonial newspapers and by Mr. Bernier's, and his staff's, cheerful assistance. The selection of the papers included here was also helped considerably by Director Thad Tate's ready loan of any of the Institute of Early American History and Culture's microfilmed colonial newspapers for reading in Williamsburg and, in particular, at the University of Richmond. Both he and the University made that part of the task much simpler than it might otherwise have been. And my frequent trips to the Virginia State Library to read Virginia's colonial newspapers were likewise profitable and pleasant.

I am pleased to acknowledge also Mrs. Jeanne Koster's fine index and her careful reading of the text. Ed Reno's official designation as Vice President-Editorial of the Microfilming Corporation of America is singularly misleading. His vision, philosophical and critical; his attention to detail; his marshaling of the filming process – all are major contributions to the following. (As were his handy red tape-cutting scissors, unworthy of an administrator.)

Lastly, I thank Janet and Tom, who had absolutely nothing to do with the project that might be put on a library catalogue card. They knew, and did, better.

T. W. J.

Introduction

Revolution – and Everyday Life

The present *Year in Review* project is an effort to gain a sense of immediacy with the momentous events in colonial America between 1763-1783; the principal medium is the colonial newspaper. During the era of the American Revolution, the colonial press served to convey patriot and, for a time, non-patriot sentiments within the colonies from New Hampshire to Georgia, as well as to instruct colonists in how to dress and what to buy. The newspapers publicized shipping schedules and the appearance of runaway slaves, and catered to the numerous other everyday concerns of the English colonists who lived in America. It is precisely the newspapers' function as a means of information – be it political or social or economic or decidedly pedestrian, mundane information – that entitles the variety of the colonial press to especial consideration. The slice of life quality of the newspapers, their juxtapositions of cadenced political rhetoric regarding natural rights with a definitive way to deal with pesty caterpillars, encourages a reader to see the Revolutionary period in a rather new light.

The semi-mythical machinations of a Patrick Henry or Adams, Samuel and John, or a Benjamin Franklin acquire a perhaps different perspective when exposed side-by-side with other contemporary causes, anxieties, activities, and frivolities. The value of the colonial newspaper lies not in its use as the only historical source for the Revolutionary period. Rather its value is precisely as a primary source touched by the usual, the common.

Descriptive and Topic Chronologies

The present publication is composed of an extended Descriptive Chronology for the years 1763-1783 that is accompanied by a listing of microfilmed colonial newspapers that are consciously selected to illustrate the chronological text with a cross-section of contemporary description and documentation from the American colonies. Added also are a small number of broadsides that supplement the information provided by the newspapers and deal more graphically with specific events. While the newspaper citations after each part of the chronology are by a precise page in a certain issue, the particular newspaper issue in its entirety is available in the microfilmed collection. The complete issue presents the reader with historical material beyond the primary chronological entry.

In this latter connection, an additional Topical Chronology follows the Descriptive Chronology text for each year. This Topical Chronology concentrates on sampling the 'peripheral' subjects. For instance, the 1763 Descriptive Chronology deals with the Treaty of Paris, George Grenville's accession to the office of Prime Minister, Pontiac's Rebellion, the Proclamation of 1763, and the (Virginia) Parson's Cause. The specific newspaper citations after each entry deal with these topics. The Topical Chronology citations for 1763 touch on such matters as piracy, lotteries, slavery, small-pox, and the desertion of British sailors in New Hampshire.

A Representative Selection of Newspapers and Broadsides

The fifty-two newspapers included in this *Year in Review* project offer a representative selection of the mid-eighteen-century colonial American press. With the exception of Delaware which had no newspaper of its own during the period, the remaining twelve mainland colonies are each represented through at least two (usually (weekly) newspapers. Certain colonies – North Carolina and New Jersey, for example – offered little difficulty in a selection of newspapers in this period, since there was very little choice either of any newspaper(s) published or of any newspaper(s) extant between 1763-1783. Other colonies, particularly the larger ones with the major colonial cities — Massachusetts (Boston), New York (New York City), and Pennsylvania (Philadelphia) — presented more perplexing decisions because of the number of newspapers appropriate to the period of the present work. Availability was also an important consideration. The choices in the latter colonies were made with the intention of adequately portraying colonial sentiment, whether patriot or loyalist, radical or moderate, as well as with a view toward the historical significance of the particular newspaper.

Review of the Sources Included

The following is a concise colony-by-colony description of the newspapers included in the project. It is to be noted that shortened and modernized titles are used for the newspapers. For example, James Rivington's first newspaper was published in New York City in 1773 and carried the grand title of *Rivington's New-York Gazetteer; or the Connecticut, New-Jersey, Hudson's River, and Quebec Weekly Advertiser.* Here it appears as *Rivington's New York Gazetteer* or in the citations as *Riv. N.Y. Gazetteer.* The colonial penchant for hyphenation, as in New York and New Jersey above, is also eliminated for place names but maintained in double nouns whose modernization would alter the title much too substantially. Examples are *Post-Boy* instead of *Postboy; News-Letter* rather than *Newsletter.* (See below for a complete listing of the fifty-two newspapers and the abbreviation of each newspaper's title used in the citations to the issues microfilmed for the 1763-1783 period.)

New Hampshire. Easily the most bibliographically troublesome colonial newspapers are from the northernmost clime. When the anti-independence stance of the *New Hampshire Gazette* in its January 9, 1776 issue proved too unpalatable for patriot sensibilities, the Portsmouth publication abruptly ended its operations. In late May of the same year, the *Freeman's Journal* began operations, also in Portsmouth. Within a short time, the original publisher of the *Journal* was replaced by Daniel Fowle, the principal publisher of the suspended *Gazette.* On June 16, 1778, Daniel changed the newspaper's name and together with his brother Zechariah (continuing publisher of the *Exeter Journal*) began to bring

out the *New Hampshire Gazette or State Journal and General Advertiser.* The very same paper was printed in Portsmouth by Daniel and in Exeter by Zechariah. Beginning with the February 23, 1779 issue of this *Gazette,* the publishing was done only in Portsmouth. The October 5 issue of the *Gasette* in the same year took up the lapsed issue numbering of the original, suspended *New Hampshire Gazette.* For the next two years issues of the newspaper were published in Portsmouth and/or Exeter. Beginning September 8, 1781, the entire publishing operation was confined to Portsmouth.

In the present study the continuity sought by the eighteenth-century printers will be confirmed. Citations for any of the *New Hampshire Gazettes* — pre-1776 or post-1778, Portsmouth or Exeter — will be undifferentiated. The *Freeman's Journal* will, of course, stand by itself.

Massachusetts. As one of the larger colonies, with one of the largest colonial cities, the Bay Colony presents a variety of newspapers available and appropriate for use. The *Boston Gazette* is a ready selection as a representative patriot newspaper since many of its columns reappeared before 1775 in the colonies to the south. Indeed, the continuous influence of the Boston press before Lexington and Concord is amply demonstrated in this process of reprinting all or part of patriot Boston's news or views. The process of duplication of the news may be followed quite easily in the present study.

Loyalist sentiments were expressed in the *Massachusetts Gazette and Boston Weekly News-Letter* and the *Massachusetts Gazette and Boston Post-Boy and Advertiser,* while the *Boston Evening Post* was more impartial regarding current political events. With the beginning of the Revolutionary War in 1775-1776, the latter three newspapers went out of business. Taking their place in this project are a) the (Salem) *Essex Gazette* — with its name changed first to the (Cambridge, Boston) *New England Chronicle* and finally to the (Boston) *Independent Chronicle;* and b) the (Boston) *Continental Journal.*

Rhode Island. The patriot *Newport Mercury* covered the Rhode Island situation very well except for the period between December 1776 and January 1780 when the unfriendly British occupied Newport. During the enforced three-year silence of the *Mercury,* the *Providence Gazette* was a quite adequate expression of American sentiment.

Connecticut. The (Hartford) *Connecticut Courant* was the principal newspaper in colonial Connecticut. A number of early issues of the

New London Summary, and the subsequent *New London Gazette,* are also included.

New York. Similar to Massachusetts, New York, in particular New Your City, presents a large number of newspapers for the Revolutionary period. The *New York Mercury* and the *New York Gazette or Weekly Post-Boy* are useful for the time before the war, while the importance of John Holt's *New York Journal* is enhanced by its forced publication in Kingston and later Poughkeepsie during the British occupation of New York City (1776-1783). This territorial flexibility was shared by the *New York Packet,* which moved to Fishkill in face of the enemy's unwelcome intrusion: and the *New York Gazette and Weekly Mercury,* a continuation of the *New York Mercury,* which was moved to Newark, New Jersey during the early military maneuverings between the rebels and redcoats before New York City in September 1776. By November, however, the publisher had decided upon the Loyalist cause and returned forthwith to New York City where the *Gazette* continued to be published throughout the war.

A final group of New York newspapers of interest are those of James Rivington, an unabashed Loyalist who offended numerous patriots both before the war and during it after his return from a forced retreat to England. His efforts, in succession, were *Rivington's New York Gazetter,* the *New York Loyal Gazette,* and the (New York) *Royal Gazette.* (See the Descriptive Chronology for November 23, 1775.)

New Jersey. Although the single issue (September 21, 1765) of the (Woodbridge) *Constitutional Courant* against the Stamp Act is included, the first continuously-published New Jersey newspaper did not appear until December 5, 1777. The *New Jersey Gazette,* published for three months in Burlington and thereafter in Trenton, is quite important because of New Jersey's proximity to British-held Philadelphia (September 1777-June 1778) and New York (September 1776-November 1783).

Pennsylvania. As in Boston and New York City, so too in Philadelphia: there are a number of newspapers to choose from for the present study. The *Pennsylvania Gazette* and the *Pennsylvania Journal,* both published in Philadelphia, are obvious choices due to their acknowledged and continued prominence in the colony before 1763. During the British occupation of the American capital (late 1777-June 1778), the *Gazette* was published in York, Pennsylvania, while the *Journal* was suspended. The (Philadelphia) *Pennsylvania Chronicle* is included as

the original publisher of the very influential "Farmer's Letters." (See below the Descriptive Chronology for December 2, 1767-February 15, 1768.) Pennsylvania is represented by two other Philadelphia newspapers: the *Pennsylvania Packet,* published in Lancaster during the British presence in Philadelphia, and the short-lived *Royal Pennsylvania Gazette.* The latter took advantage of General William Howe's nine-month occupation.

Maryland. The (Annapolis) *Maryland Gazette* is included here as the principal newspaper of the Chesapeake colony's capital. The (Baltimore) *Maryland Journal* is offered primarily to cover the period from December 25, 1777 to April 30, 1779, when the publication of the *Gazette* was suspended.

Virginia. The potential confusion associated with the four (Williamsburg) *Virginia Gazettes* for this period is taken care of by notation of the publishers' name(s) after the newspaper title. Thus, the earliest *Gazette* used was published in turn by (Royle); (Purdie); (Purdie and Dixon); and (Dixon and Hunter) between 1763-1778. The second, distinct *Virginia Gazette* was published between 1766-1776 by (Rind) and by (Pinkney). The third *Virginia Gazette,* the work of (Purdie) and (Clarkson and Davis), came off the presses from 1775-1780. The final *Gazette* was published for just over a year, 1779-1780, in Williamsburg by (Dixon and Nicolson). For a subsequent year, 1780-1781, the latter two individuals continued to publish their paper in Richmond, the new Virginia capital. The final three years of the war are covered by Richmond newspapers: the *Virginia Gazette or American Advertiser,* the *Virginia Gazette and Weekly Advertiser,* and the *Virginia Gazette or Independent Chronicle.*

Two other newspapers are utilized for Virginia because of their special circumstances. The first is the (Norfolk) *Virginia Gazette* published for just over a year in 1774-1775 by John Hunter Holt, the nephew of John Holt, publisher of the *New York Journal.* The younger Holt's printing press was stolen by a British force and used to print the royal (Norfolk) *Virginia Gazette* of erstwhilte Virginia Governor Dunmore. The two extant issues of the latter paper are included in the present study. (See below the Descriptive Chronology for December 9, 1775.)

North Carolina. The newspaper situation for North Carolina, 1763-1783, is decidedly meager. The available extant issues of three newspapers (approximately one hundred issues) were examined and the appropriate issues included from the (Wilmington) *North Carolina Gazette,* the (New Bern) *North Carolina Gazette,* and the (Wilmington) *Cape Fear Mercury.*

South Carolina. The newspapers included for this colony were all published in Charleston: the patriot *South Carolina Gazette,* suspended in December 1775, and revived in April 1777 as the *Gazette of the State of South Carolina;* the *South Carolina and American General Gazette,* retitled the *Royal Gazette* between March 1781-September 1782 during the British occupation of Charleston (May 1780-December 1782); and the *South Carolina Gazette and General Advertiser.*

Georgia. Georgia's available newspapers number three, all published in Savannah: the *Georgia Gazette* between 1763-1776; the *Royal Georgia Gazette* from 1779 to June 1782; and the *Gazette of the State of Georgia* for the year of 1783. The gaps in publication total approximately three and one-half years of important news not covered by any extant Georgia newspaper.

Broadsides. In addition to the fifty-two newspapers, about sixty broadsides are included. Broadsides were often a simple extension of the newspapers of the period, responding in prompt fashion to the information needs of the moment. The broadsides in the collection were carefully selected from The Library of Congress well-known American Revolutionary Broadsides collection. They are interwoven at the appropriate places in the citations for both the Descriptive and Topical Chronologies.

Organization of the Citations and the Microfilm File

Below are the titles of the newspapers appearing in the study and short abbreviations of their titles. These abbreviations are used in the text in order to identify the appropriate microfilmed newspaper issues that illustrate each chronological entry. The listing of the newspapers follows two complementary schemes of order. First,

citations after an entry in the chronological text appear in a north-to-south geographical sequence. Thus, New Hampshire newspapers, if cited for a particular entry, will always come first while Georgia's papers, if cited, will always come last. (The Continental Congress followed such an arrangement of listing the colonies in its own proceedings and activities.) The broadsides, when cited, follow the last newspaper entry.

This same geographical basis of organization is followed in the compilation of the microfilmed newspaper collection. The filmed papers, *in toto,* are in yearly sequence — all 1763 newspaper issues are placed together before all 1764 issues; and the sequence of newspapers within the specific year adheres to the established geographical arrangement, *i.e.,* New Hampshire papers are followed by Massachusetts papers, and so on south through the Middle Atlantic colonies, Virginia, the Carolinas, and finally to Georgia, with the broadsides following Georgia.

Second, the basis for the arrangement of the different newspapers of a particular colony is according to their order of appearance in the project. That is, since the first *Boston Gazette* citation (1763) precedes the first citation from the *New England Chronicle* (1775), the *Gazette* always comes before the *Chronicle,* both after the entries in the chronologies and in the filming sequence in the microfilm collection (as for example in 1775).

A Final Note on the Microfilm Collection

The reels of 35mm microfilm in *The Birth of America: The Year in Review 1763-1783* are labelled with the year(s) of the issues they contain. From a citation in the Descriptive or Topical Chronology a user need only note the year, select the reel of microfilm which contains that year, and follow the sequence of newspapers indicated above to find the issue he wants. There are frequent colony/state and date targets on the film to assist the user.

Sequence and title abbreviations used for newspapers.

New Hampshire
New Hampshire Gazette   N. Hamp. Gaz.
Freeman's Journal   *Freeman's Journal*

Massachusetts
Boston Gazette   Bos. Gaz.
Boston Evening Post   Bos. Even. Post

Massachusetts Gazette and Boston	Mass. Gaz. and Bos.
Weekly News-Letter	Week. News-Letter
Massachusetts Gazette and Boston	Mass. Gaz. and Bos.
Post-Boy and Advertiser	Post-Boy and Adv.
Essex Gazette	Essex Gaz.
*New England Chronicle	N.E. Chron.
*Independent Chronicle	Indep. Chron.
Continental Journal	Cont. Journal

Rhode Island

Newport Mercury	Newpt. Merc.
Providence Gazette	Prov. Gaz.

Connecticut

New London Summary	N.L. Summary
*New London Gazette	N.L. Gaz.
Connecticut Courant	Conn. Courant

New York

New York Mercury	N.Y. Merc.
*New York Gazette and Weekly Mercury	N.Y. Gaz. and Week. Merc.
New York Gazette or Weekly Post-Boy	N.Y. Gaz. or Week. Post-Boy
New York Journal	N.Y. Journal
Rivington's New York Gazetteer	Riv. N.Y. Gazetteer
*New York Loyal Gazette	N.Y. Loyal Gaz.
*(New York) Royal Gazette	(N.Y.) Royal Gaz.
New York Packet	N.Y. Packet

New Jersey

Constitutional Courant	Const. Courant
New Jersey Gazette	N.J. Gaz.

Pennsylvania

Pennsylvania Gazette	Pa. Gaz.
Pennsylvania Chronicle	Pa. Chron.
Pennsylvania Journal	Pa. Journal
Pennsylvania Packet	Pa. Packet
Royal Pennsylvania Gazette	Royal Pa. Gaz.

Maryland

Maryland Gazette	Md. Gaz.
Maryland Journal	Md. Journal

Virginia

Virginia Gazette (Royle) (Purdie)	Va. Gaz. (Royle) (Purdie)
(Purdie and Dixon) (Dixon and Hunter)	(Purdie and Dixon) (Dixon
Virginia Gazette (Rind) (Pinkney)	Va. Ga. (Rind) (Pinkney)
Virginia Gazette (Purdie) (Clarkson	Va. Gaz. (Purdie) (Clarkson
and Davis)	and Davis)
(Norfolk) Virginia Gazette (Holt)	(Norfolk) Va. Gaz. (Holt)
(Norfolk) Virginia Gazette (Dunmore)	(Norfolk) Va. Gaz. (Dunmore)
Virginia Gazette (Dixon and Nicolson)	Va. Gaz. (Dixon and Nicolson)
Virginia Gazette or American Advertiser	Va. Gaz. or Amer. Adv.
Virginia Gazette and Weekly Advertiser	Va. Gaz. and Week. Adv.
Virginia Gazette or Independent Chronicle	Va. Gaz. or Indep. Chron.

North Carolina
(Wilmington) *North Carolina Gazette* (Wil.) *N.C. Gaz.*
(New Bern) *North Carolina Gazette* (N.B.) *N.C. Gaz.*
Cape Fear Mercury *Cape Fear Merc.*

South Carolina
South Carolina Gazette *S.C. Gaz.*
   **Gazette of the State of South Carolina*   *Gaz. of St. of S.C.*
South Carolina and American General Gazette *S.C. and A.G. Gaz.*
   *(Charleston) *Royal Gazette*   (Charl.) *Royal Gaz.*
South Carolina Gazette and General Advertiser *S.C. Gaz. and Gen. Adv.*

Georgia
Georgia Gazette *Ga. Gaz.*
Royal Georgia Gazette *Royal Ga. Gaz.*
Gazette of the State of Georgia *Gaz. of St. of Ga.*

*Indicates a later title of the preceding newspaper.

Illustrations

The broadsides reproduced in the text are all in the microfilm collection and are taken from the originals in the American Revolutionary Broadsides Collection at the Library of Congress, Washington, D.C.

By the King,

A PROCLAMATION.

GEORGE R.

HEREAS a Definitive Treaty of Peace and Friendſhip between Us, the Moſt Chriſtian King, and the King of *Spain*, to which the King of *Portugal* hath acceded, hath been concluded at *Paris*, on the Tenth Day of *February* laſt, and the Ratifications thereof have been exchanged upon the Tenth Day of this Inſtant *March*: In Conformity thereunto, We have thought fit hereby to command, That the ſame be publiſhed throughout all Our Dominions: And We do declare to all Our Loving Subjects Our Will and Pleaſure, That the ſaid Treaty of Peace and Friendſhip be obſerved inviolably, as well by Sea as Land, and in all Places whatſoever; ſtrictly charging and commanding all Our Loving Subjects to take Notice hereof, and to conform themſelves thereunto accordingly.

Given at Our Court at St. *James's*, the Twenty firſt Day of *March*, One thouſand ſeven hundred and ſixty three, in the Third Year of Our Reign.

God ſave the King.

L O N D O N:

Printed by *Mark Baskett*, Printer to the King's moſt Excellent Majeſty; and by the Aſſigns of *Robert Baskett*. 1763.

See p. 1, February 10, Broadside: March 21.

February 10

The Great War for the Empire Ends. The Treaty of Paris ends the Seven Years' War, or the Great War for the Empire, between a victorious Great Britain and the French-Spanish alliance. From France, Britain receives Canada and all the French territories east of the Mississippi River except the city of New Orleans; Spain turns over the area that becomes the British colonies of East and West Florida. In particular, the removal of the French presence enables the American colonies to demonstrate a latent self-interest or nationalism in their opposition to British imperial designs (1763-1775). At the same time a re-awakened British interest in its overseas colonies is shown by a decision to station regular British army regiments in America and the British West Indies for the security of British possessions.

Bos. Gaz. Jan. 11, extraordinary, p. 1; Feb. 7, pp. 1-3; May 2, p. 1; May 23, pp. 1-4.
Newpt. Merc. Mar. 7, p. 1; Mar. 21, pp. 1-2; May 23, pp. 1-3.
N.Y. Merc. Jan 24, pp. 2, 3; May 9, p. 3; May 30, p. 2.
Pa. Gaz. Jan. 27, pp. 1-2, 3; May 12, pp. 1, 4.
Md. Gaz. May 5, p. 1; Aug. 4, pp. 1, 2.
S.C. Gaz. May 7/14, pp. 1, 3.
Ga. Gaz. Apr. 7, p. 3; Apr. 21, p. 3; Apr. 28, p. 2; May 5, p. 3; May 26, p. 2.
Broadside: Mar. 21.

April 3

Grenville Succeeds Bute. George Grenville succeeds Lord Bute as prime minister.

Md. Gaz. June 9, p. 1; June 23, p. 1.
Ga. Gaz. June 30, p. 2; July 7, p. 4; Aug. 11, p. 2.

May—November

Pontiac's Rebellion. An uprising of the western Indians claims numerous English forts (Sandusky, Miami, Presque Isle) as a consequence of an influx of English settlers and the Indian policies of General Jeffrey Amherst.

Newpt. Merc. June 20, p. 3; July 11, pp. 2-3.
N.L. Summary June 24, p. 2.
N.Y. Merc. June 20, p. 2; July 18, p. 2; Dec. 12, p. 2.
Pa. Gaz. June 9, p. 3; June 16, pp. 2-3; June 30, pp. 2-3.
Md. Gaz. June 30, p. 2; July 21, p. 2; July 28, p. 2.
Ga. Gaz. July 7, pp. 3-4; July 28, pp. 2-3; Sept. 15, p. 2.

Fort Detroit withstands a seven-month siege.

Newpt. Merc. June 27, p. 3; Aug. 15, p. 3; Aug. 22, pp. 2-3; Dec. 26, p. 3.
N.Y. Merc. Sept. 5, p. 2.
Pa. Gaz. Sept. 8, p. 2; Dec. 29, p. 2.
Ga. Gaz. Oct. 20, pp. 2-3.

The siege of Fort Pitt is relieved August 10.

Newpt. Merc. Sept. 5, pp. 2-3.
N.Y. Merc. Sept. 5, p. 2.
Pa. Gaz. Aug. 25, p. 2; Sept. 1, p. 2.
Md. Gaz. Sept. 8, pp. 1, 2.
Ga. Gaz. Oct. 20, pp. 1-2.

October 7

Proclamation of 1763. Three new crown colonies are established: Canada, East Florida, and West Florida. Also, a line is drawn along the crest of the Appalachian Mountains from Canada to Florida intended to divide Indians' and colonists' lands. Numerous settlers have already penetrated beyond the line which is especially significant to colonies such as Virginia which have claimed large areas beyond the Proclamation line.

Newpt. Merc. Dec. 12, p. 2.
N.Y. Merc. Dec. 12, pp. 1-2.
Pa. Gaz. Dec. 8, p. 1.
S.C. Gaz. Dec. 3/10, p. 3.
Ga. Gaz. Dec. 8, pp. 1-2.

December 1

Parson's Cause. Patrick Henry emerges as a popular leader in Virginia and as a defender of colonial rights. He argues against the crown's right to disallow beneficial Virginia statutes. In this instance, lawyer Henry scores the disallowance of the so-called Two-Penny Act (1758) which is intended to establish a specific (low) value for tobacco, *i.e.*, two pence per pound. Times are hard in Virginia and the current value of tobacco is much higher than usual. Virginia's Anglican clergy react against the legislation since their salaries, fixed at 17,200 pounds of tobacco a year, will now decrease in value. A minority of the clergymen, upset by the situation, point out that the act is retroactive and will affect past due salaries. Henry loses the case in defense of the Fredericksburg vestry against an aggrieved cleric suing for owed salary, but the jury shows its true feelings in the matter by awarding the Reverend James Maury damages of one penny.

Customs
    Violations of in Piscataway, New Hampshire
        N.Hamp. Gaz. Dec. 2, p. 3.

Diseases
    Small-pox
        S.C. Gaz. June 11/18, p. 2; June 18/25,
           p. 2.
        Ga. Gaz. July 7, p. 5.

Lotteries
    By Rhode Island General Assembly to build
    wharf
        Newpt. Merc. Mar. 21, p. 3.

Piracy
    Narrative of act of
        Ga. Gaz. June 23, p. 2.

Sailors, British
    Deserters in New Hampshire
        N.Hamp. Gaz. Dec. 2, p. 4.

Slaves
    Runaways
        Newpt. Merc. June 20, p. 4.
        Va. Gaz. (Royle) Nov. 4, pp. 3-4.
    Sales of
        Bos. Gaz. Feb. 7, p. 3.
        Newpt. Merc. June 20, p. 4.
        Va. Gaz. (Royle) Nov. 4, pp. 3-4.

Trade
    Imported goods listed for sale
        Ga. Gaz. May 26, p. 3.

Wilkes, John
    (English radical printer and politician: see
    text, February 1770)
        N.Y. Merc. June 20, p. 2.
        Md. Gaz. June 30, pp. 1-2; July 14, p. 1;
           [July 14], postscript, p. 1; July 21, pp.
           1-2; Sept. 8, p. 1.

December 1973–February

Paxton Boys. Underrepresentation in the Pennsylvania General Assembly and vulnerability to Indian attacks induce a group of men from the western counties to attack and massacre a company of friendly Conestoga Indians. In response to an order for their arrest, these Paxton Boys march toward Philadelphia only to be turned back outside the city by the persuasive abilities of Benjamin Franklin.

N.Y. Merc. Jan. 2, p. 2; Jan. 16, pp. 2-3; Feb. 13, p. 3.
Pa. Gaz. Dec. 29 (1763), p. 1; Jan. 5, p. 2; Feb. 9, p. 2; Mar. 1, p. 2.
Md. Gaz. Jan. 5, p. 2; Feb. 16, p. 2.
Va. Gaz. (Royle) Nov. 4 (1763), p. 2.
S.C. Gaz. Jan. 7/14, p. 2.
Ga. Gaz. Nov. 17 (1763), p. 2; Jan. 19, p. 2; Feb. 9, p. 1; Mar. 15, p. 2.
Broadside: Dec. 22 (1763).

April 5

Revenue Act. Heavy postwar debts and the projected costs of maintaining elements of the British army in America cause Parliament to pass the first act specifically intended to raise monies in the American colonies for the use of the crown. Important features of the Sugar Act, as it is known in America, include a reduction of the present duty on foreign molasses from six pence to three pence per gallon and the establishment of a vice-admiralty court (without benefit of jury trial) at Halifax, Nova Scotia, with jurisdiction over all American colonies. Both measures aim at curtailing pandemic colonial smuggling: the former is intended to make it unprofitable, the latter to cause those apprehended proper discomfort for their transgression. Several new American products such as iron, hides, and potash are added to an already extensive enumerated list, *i.e.*, such goods can be exported only to England.

Bos. Gaz. May 14, p. 1; Oct. 29, p. 1.
Newpt. Merc. May 14, p. 2; June 18, pp. 1-2; June 25, pp. 1-2; July 2, pp. 1-2.
N.Y. Merc. Feb. 6, pp. 1-2; May 14, p. 3.
Pa. Gaz. May 10, p. 2.
Md. Gaz. Apr. 26, p. 1; June 7, p. 1; June 14, p. 2; June 21, p. 1.
S.C. Gaz. Oct. 1, supplement, p. 1.
Ga. Gaz. June 7, p. 3; June 14, p. 2; Nov. 8, pp. 1-2.

April 19

Currency Act. Parliament extends an existing prohibition against the issuance of paper money or legal tender by colonial legislatures to all American colonies as of September 1, in response to British merchants' complaints regarding American use of depreciated colonial currency for debts calculated in sterling silver and owed to British merchants. American merchants face a mounting foreign debt with very little means of procuring the necessary specie for proper repayment.

Newpt. Merc. July 2, p. 2.
N.Y. Merc. May 14, p. 2.
Pa. Gaz. July 12, p. 1.
Md. Gaz. July 12, p. 2; July 19, p. 1.
S.C. Gaz. Oct. 15/22, p. 1.
Ga. Gaz. July 19, p. 1.

May 24

Boston Objects Quickly. The Boston town meeting protests taxation without representation and instructs its representatives to the Massachusetts General Assembly to attempt to prevent further taxation (such as a Stamp Act).

Bos. Gaz. May 28, p. 1.
Ga. Gaz. Aug. 2, pp. 2-3.

June

Massachusetts Follows Suit. On June 13, the Massachusetts House of Representatives establishes a committee to correspond with other American colonial legislatures regarding matters of common colonial interest. Twelve days later the newly-formed Massachusetts committee of correspondence sends out a circular letter to the other American colonies urging united action in their present economic and political discontents.

Bos. Gaz. Aug. 20, p. 3; Sept. 3, p. 2.
N.Y. Merc. Aug. 13, p. 3.
Ga. Gaz. Sept. 6, p. 2.

May–December

The Specter of a Stamp Act. Official colonial reactions to the Sugar Act frequently note opposition to any proposed Stamp Act. Several colonies approve (Connecticut) or imply approval (Massachusetts, Rhode Island) of "external" taxes such as port duties but reject "internal" taxes such as stamp duties. The most forceful reaction is by the New York Assembly which claims exemption from Parliamentary taxation as a right. The Virginia Council and House of Burgesses agree that the colony cannot be virtually represented in Parliament as many English localities theoretically were, *i.e.,* represented not by a specific member but rather by the whole Commons. Moreover, the Council and Burgesses imply a rejection of any colonial representation in the House of Commons as an answer to the taxation problem. Newspaper essays join in the general displeasure with Parliament's actions.

N.Hamp. Gaz. Aug. 10, p. 1; Aug. 17, p. 1; Mar. 22 (1765), p. 1.
Bos. Gaz. Mar. 18 (1765), p. 1.
Newpt. Merc. Dec. 2, p. 3.
N.Y. Merc. Nov. 5, p. 1; Dec. 10, p. 2; Jan. 28 (1765), pp. 1-2, 4.
Pa. Gaz. May 3, p. 1.
Md. Gaz. Nov. 29, p. 2.
Ga. Gaz. Aug. 23, p. 3; Dec. 13, pp. 1, 4; Dec. 20, p. 2; Jan 3 (1765), p. 2.

August – December

Boston Sparks Colonial Reaction. Boston leads the way in a burgeoning colonial non-importation of certain British goods, encouragement of colonial manufacturing, and a staunch advocacy of colonial frugality and simplicity in attire and consumption as manifest protests against the Sugar Act.

Bos. Gaz. Oct. 1, pp. 2-3.
Newpt. Merc. Aug. 20, pp. 3, 4; Dec. 2, p. 3.
Conn. Courant Oct. 29, p. 1.
N.Y. Merc. Nov. 12, p. 2.
Pa. Gaz. Aug. 30, p. 2.
Md. Gaz. Sept. 6, p. 1; Oct. 25, p. 2.
Ga. Gaz. Nov. 8, pp. 2-3.

December

New York City Warms. The Society for the Promotion of Arts, Agriculture and Oeconomy, in the Province of New-York, in North America is established; its principal purpose is the encouragement of indigenous colonial economic development.

Bos. Gaz. Dec. 17, pp. 1-2.
N.Y. Merc. Dec. 3, p. 1; Dec. 10, p. 1; Dec. 17, p. 3; Dec. 24, p. 2; Dec. 31, p. 2; Jan. 28 (1765), p. 3; Feb. 25 (1765), p. 2; Dec. 23 (1765), p. 2.
Md. Gaz. Jan 10 (1765), pp. 2-3; Jan 17 (1765), p. 3; Jan. 24 (1765), p. 1.
Ga. Gaz. Feb. 7 (1765), p. 1.

Acadians (displaced Nova Scotians)
Pass through Savannah
Ga. Gaz. Jan. 12, p. 1.

Agriculture
American seeds sent to Scotland
N.L. Gaz. Sept. 14, p. 1.

Apprentices
Ad for runaways
Newpt. Merc. Aug. 20, p. 3.

Boundary
North Carolina-South Carolina nearly established
Ga. Gaz. Nov. 15, p. 3.

Colleges
College of New Jersey (Princeton), commencement
Pa. Gaz. Oct. 11, p. 3.
Harvard, fire at
Ga. Gaz. Mar. 15, p. 2.
Proposed for South Carolina
Ga. Gaz. Sept. 6, p. 2.
Yale non-importation efforts
Newpt. Merc. Dec. 2, p. 3.

Counterfeiting
Pa. Gaz. July 19, p. 2.

Diseases
Fevers of servants/slaves
Md. Gaz. July 12, p. 1.
Small-pox
N.Hamp. Gaz. Mar. 16, p. 1; May 4, p. 3.
Bos. Gaz. May 28, p. 1.
S.C. Gaz. Mar. 31/Aug. 25, pp. 1-2.
Ga. Gaz. June 7, p. 1; June 21, p. 1; June 28, pp. 1, 2; July 12, p. 2.

East Florida
Description of
Ga. Gaz. Dec. 27, pp. 2-3.

Hospitals
Pennsylvania Hospital: conditions in
Pa. Gaz. July 19, pp. 1-2.

Huguenots (French Protestants)
Established South Carolina town of New Bordeaux
Ga. Gaz. Sept. 20, p. 3.

Humor
Joke about miser
N.Hamp. Gaz. Aug. 3, p. 4.

Indians
Brutality of
N.Hamp. Gaz. May 4, p. 1.
Continuing wars with colonists after Pontiac peace
N.Y. Merc. Mar. 5, p. 3; Mar. 12, p. 3; Mar. 19, p. 2; Apr. 9, p. 2; May 14, p. 3; Aug. 13, p. 2; Sept. 3, p. 3; Sept. 10, p. 2; Oct. 15, p. 3; Oct. 29, p. 2; Nov. 19, p. 1; Nov. 26, p. 2; Dec. 10, p. 2.
Md. Gaz. Jan. 5, p. 2; June 7, p. 1; June 14, p. 2; June 21, pp. 1-2; June 28, pp. 1-2; July 26, p. 1; Sept. 27, p. 1; Oct. 4, p. 1.
Ga. Gaz. Jan. 19, p. 2; July 19, p. 2.
Land ownership by presents problems for purchase by colonists
N.Y. Merc. Oct. 22, pp. 1-2.

Instruction
In writing system
Newpt. Merc. Dec. 2, p. 3.

Mobile (Alabama)
Description of
Ga. Gaz. Feb. 9, pp. 1-2.

Moral Exhortation
Against snuff
N.Hamp. Gaz. Aug. 3, pp. 1-2.

Newspapers
Subscribers' accounts in arrears
N.Hamp. Gaz. July 13, p. 1.

Pennsylvania
Dispute in regarding possible change from proprietary to royal colony
Ga. Gaz. Nov. 15, p. 2.

Post Office
Act to establish monopoly in Rhode Island
Newpt. Merc. Aug. 20, p. 4.

Servants
Ad for indentured runaways
Md. Gaz. June 14, p. 3.

Shipwreck
Narrative of
Ga. Gaz. Nov. 15, pp. 2-3.

Slaves
    Freedom of movement restricted in Savannah
        Ga. Gaz. June 28, p. 2.
    Runaways
        Ga. Gaz. June 7, p. 4.
    Sales of
        N.Hamp. Gaz. Aug. 3, p. 4.
        Md. Gaz. June 14, p. 3.

Transportation
    Bridge: engineering marvel in Norwich, Connecticut

Md. Gaz. July 19, p. 2.
Lighthouse: begins operation on Sandy
Hook, New Jersey
    Md. Gaz. June 28, p. 1.

Wilkes, John
    N.Y. Merc. Feb. 20, pp. 2, 3.

Women
    Patriotism of
        N.Y. Merc. Dec. 24, p. 2.

March 22

Stamp Act. The first direct tax by Parliament on the colonies places duties on newspapers and newspaper advertisements, diplomas, licenses, bonds, wills, contracts, dice, playing cards, and almanacs. The announced purpose of the act, to take effect on November 1, is to defray part of the costs of the British military presence in America. An alarming feature of the act, to the colonists, is the proposal for the use of vice-admiralty courts (*sans* jury trials) to facilitate enforcement of the act. In a self-conscious gesture of British good will, the Stamp Act revenues are to be kept in America after their collection by American stamp agents. Opposition to the Stamp Act is immediate in the colonies.

Early notices of the Stamp Act:

N.Hamp. Gaz. Feb. 1, p. 2; May 10, p. 3; May 17, p. 3.
   May 24, p. 1; May 31, p. 2; June 21, p. 1; Sept. 6, p.
   1; Sept. 13, p. 1; Sept. 27, p. 1; Oct. 4, pp. 1-2.
Bos. Gaz. May 27, p. 2; June 3, p. 2.
Conn. Courant May 27, p. 3; Sept. 9, pp. 1-2.
N.Y. Merc. Apr. 15, p. 2; Apr. 15, supplement, pp. 1-2;
   May 6, p. 2; Oct. 21, p. 2; Oct. 28, p. 2.
Const. Courant Sept. 21, pp. 1-2.
Pa. Gaz. Apr. 18, pp. 1-2.
Md. Gaz. May 30, p. 2; June 6, p. 2.
S.C. Gaz. May 18/25, p. 3; June 22/29, p. 2.
Ga. Gaz. Apr. 25, p. 3; May 2, pp. 1-2; May 9, p. 2; June
   27, p. 2; July 11, p. 1.

March 24

Mutiny or Quartering Act. The Colonies are to supply British troops with barracks and other necessary living supplies for the next two years.

N.Hamp. Gaz. May 31, p. 2.
Bos. Gaz. May 27, p. 2.
Conn. Courant June 3, p. 2; June 17, p. 1.
Md. Gaz. June 6, p. 2.
Ga. Gaz. Aug. 15, p. 1.

May 29

Virginia Resolves. Patrick Henry of Louisa County introduces seven resolutions directed against the Stamp Act into a sparsely-attended House of Burgesses. Despite the passage of these resolutions, the House votes the following day (May 30) to reject the two most strident, the sixth and seventh. On May 31, the House also rejects the fifth resolution as too radical in its assertion of the Burgesses' exclusive right to tax Virginians. On June 1, Lieutenant Governor Francis Fauquier demonstrates his displeasure with the Resolves by dissolving the General Assembly. Certain newspapers publish these proceedings and include the three rejected Resolves,

or a portion of them, thereby offering a more radical Virginia protest as an influential example for other colonies.

N. Hamp. Gaz. July 26, pp. 2-3.
Newpt. Merc. July 22, p. 3.
Conn. Courant July 8, p. 1; July 29, pp. 1-2.
Md. Gaz. July 4, p. 3.
S.C. Gaz. Aug. 26, supplement, p. 1.
Ga. Gaz. Aug. 29, p. 2; Sept. 5, p. 2.

June 6-8

Otis Proposes a Stamp Act Congress. James Otis, a leading Massachusetts radical, presents a motion in the General Assembly for an intercolonial gathering to discuss the Stamp Act. Continuing its role as the locus of colonial discontent and leadership, the Massachusetts General Assembly sends out a circular letter on June 8 inviting other colonies to send representatives to New York City in October to participate in a meeting about the Stamp Act.

N.Hamp. Gaz. July 12, p. 2.
N.Y. Merc. July 15, p. 2.
Pa. Gaz. July 18, p. 2.
Ga. Gaz. Aug. 15, p. 2; Aug. 22, p. 2.

July 10

Rockingham Succeeds Grenville. The Grenville ministry falls because of events in England, including an alleged slight to the King's mother, and is replaced by a new administration headed by the Marquis of Rockingham.

N.Hamp. Gaz. Sept. 20, pp. 1-2.
Bos. Gaz. Sept. 16, supplement, p. 1.
N.Y. Merc. Aug. 19, p. 2; Sept. 9, pp. 2, 3.
Ga. Gaz. Oct. 10, p. 4; Oct. 17, p. 2.

August 14-26

Boston Disorders. A well-directed mob attacks the home of Provincial Secretary/Massachusetts stamp distributor Andrew Oliver (August 14), who promises to resign the latter post (August 15) when he receives his commission. Chief Justice Thomas Hutchinson's home is attacked and looted as well as those of admiralty and customs officials (August 26). Governor Francis Bernard demands the apprehension of the culprits. A Boston town meeting (August 27) registers its disapproval of violence and initiates a night watch.

N.Hamp. Gaz. Aug. 23, p. 2; Aug. 30, p. 3.
Bos. Gaz. Aug. 26, p. 3; Sept. 2, pp. 1, 2, 3.
Newpt. Merc. Sept. 2, p. 3.
N.Y. Merc. Aug. 26, p. 3.
Pa. Gaz. Aug. 29, p. 2; Sept. 12, p. 2.
Ga. Gaz. Oct. 3, pp. 2-3; Oct. 10, p. 2.

August 27—29

Newport Disorders. Augustus Johnston promises under pressure to resign his post as Rhode Island stamp distributor when he receives his commission.

N.Hamp. Gaz. Sept. 20, p. 3.
Bos. Gaz. Sept. 2, p. 3.
Newpt. Merc. Sept. 9, p. 3.
N.Y. Merc. Sept. 9, p. 2.
Pa. Gaz. Sept. 5, p. 2.
Ga. Gaz. Oct. 10, p. 3.

August 26—November 16

Stamps Prove Expensive. Other stamp distributors resign their positions under duress or expected threats:

New Hampshire
N.Hamp. Gaz. June 21, p. 3; Sept. 13, p. 3; Sept. 20, pp. 2, 3; Sept. 27, p. 3; Jan. 10 (1766), p. 3; Jan. 17 (1766), p. 1;
Pa. Gaz. Sept. 26, p. 2; Nov. 21, p. 1; Jan. 30 (1766), p. 2.
Ga. Gaz. Oct. 10, p. 3.

Connecticut
Bos. Gaz. Sept. 30, p. 4.
Conn. Courant June 10, p. 3; Sept. 2, p. 2; Sept. 23, p. 2; Jan. 20 (1766), pp. 1-2; Jan. 27 (1766), p. 3.
Pa. Gaz. Sept. 5, p. 2; Oct. 3, p. 2; Dec. 26, p. 2; Jan. 23 (1766), p. 1.
Ga. Gaz. Oct. 10, pp. 2-3; Oct. 24, p. 1.

New York
N.Hamp. Gaz. Sept. 13, p. 2.
N.Y. Merc. Aug. 19, p. 2; Sept. 2, p. 3; Dec. 2, p. 3; Dec. 9, p. 2.

New Jersey
N.Y. Merc. Sept. 9, p. 3; Jan. 13 (1766), p. 1.
Pa. Gaz. May 30, p. 3; Sept. 5, p. 2; Sept. 12, p. 3; Jan. 2 (1766), p. 3.
Ga. Gaz. Oct. 10, p. 3.

Pennsylvania—Delaware
Pa. Gaz. May 30, p. 3; Oct. 10, pp. 2-3; Nov. 21, p. 3; Dec. 19, p. 3.
Ga. Gaz. Nov. 21, p. 3.

Maryland
N.Y. Merc. Dec. 9, pp. 1-2; Dec. 23, p. 3.
N.Y. Gaz. or Week. Post-Boy Dec. 5, pp. 2-3.
Pa. Gaz. Sept. 12, p. 2.
Md. Gaz. Sept. 5, p. 2; Oct. 3, p. 2; Jan. 30 (1766), pp. 1-2.
Ga. Gaz. Oct. 10, pp. 3, 4.

Virginia
N.Hamp. Gaz. Nov. 29, p. 1.
Pa. Gaz. Nov. 21, pp. 1, 4.

Va. Gaz. (Royle) Oct. 25, supplement extraordinary, p. 3.
Ga. Gaz. Oct. 10, p. 2.

North Carolina
N.Y. Merc. Jan. 13 (1766), p. 1.
Pa. Gaz. Oct. 17, p. 2; Jan. 2 (1766), p. 2.

South Carolina
N.Hamp. Gaz. Nov. 29, p. 1.
N.Y. Merc. Jan. 13 (1766), p. 1.
S.C. Gaz. July 6/13, p. 2; Sept. 21/28, p. 3; Oct. 19/31, p. 2.
Ga. Gaz. Nov. 7, p. 2.

Georgia
Ga. Gaz. Oct. 31, p. 1; Nov. 7, p. 2; Nov. 14, p. 2; Nov. 21, p. 3.

September

Stamps Unwelcome in Boston. Stamps arrive in Boston and are placed in Castle William, located on an island in Boston Harbor, by order of Governor Bernard after he unsuccessfully solicits the advice and cooperation of the Massachusetts General Assembly.

Bos. Gaz. Sept. 9, pp. 1, 3; Sept. 30, pp. 1, 2, 3; Oct. 28, pp. 1-2.
N.Y. Merc. Sept. 16, p. 2.
Ga. Gaz. Oct. 10, p. 3.

September

Rhode Island and Pennsylvania Resolves. The Rhode Island General Assembly resolves that only it can tax Rhode Island inhabitants much less impose internal taxes. Similar resolves are passed by the Pennsylvania General Assembly (September 21).

N.Hamp. Gaz. Oct. 11, pp. 2-3.
Newpt. Merc. Sept. 16, p. 3.
N.Y. Merc. Sept. 23, p. 3; Sept. 30, p. 2.
Pa. Gaz. Sept. 26, pp. 2-3.
Ga. Gaz. Oct. 10, p. 4; Oct. 17, pp. 1-2.

September 28

Maryland Resolves. The Maryland legislature states that any tax on Maryland citizens is unconstitutional unless enacted by Maryland's representatives. It is also voted that jury trial is a right and that delegates are to be sent to the Stamp Act Congress.

Pa. Gaz. Oct. 17, p. 1.
Md. Gaz. Oct. 3, p. 1.

September—October

Local New England Opposition to Stamps. Numerous New England town meetings instruct their representatives to the various general assemblies regarding local opposition to the Stamp Act. (The author of the very influential Braintree, Massachusetts, instructions is John Adams.)

Providence, R.I.
   Md. Gaz. Sept. 5, p. 1.
Little Compton, R.I.
   Newpt. Merc. Sept. 2, p. 3.
Newport, R.I.
   Newpt. Merc. Sept. 9, p. 1.
Plymouth Mass.
   Bos. Gaz. Nov 4, supplement, p. 1.
Newburyport, Mass.
   Bos. Gaz. Nov. 4, supplement, pp. 1-2.
Ipswich, Mass.
   Bos. Gaz. Nov. 4, supplement, p. 2.
Braintree, Mass.
   N.Hamp. Gaz. Oct. 18, pp. 1-2.
Boston
   Bos. Gaz. Oct. 7, p. 1; Oct. 14, p. 1.
   Ga. Gaz. Oct. 24, pp. 2, 3.

October 7-25

Stamp Act Congress. Meeting in New York, twenty-seven delegates from nine colonies (not represented are New Hampshire, Virginia, North Carolina, and Georgia) draft a "Declaration of Rights and Grievances" (October 19). Included in the "Declaration" are resolutions that taxation without representation is unconstitutional, colonists are not and cannot be represented in Parliament, and only colonial assemblies can rightfully tax colonists.

N.Hamp. Gaz. Nov. 15, pp. 1, 2; Dec. 6, p. 2.
Bos. Gaz. Nov. 4, p. 1.
N.Y. Merc. Oct. 7, p. 2; Oct. 14, p. 2; Apr. 7 (1766), p. 2.
N.Y. Gaz. or Week. Post-Boy Dec. 5, p. 3.
Pa. Gaz. Sept. 12, p. 3; Sept. 19, p. 3; Oct. 10, pp. 2, 3; Oct. 17, p. 2; Oct. 31, p. 3.
Md. Gaz. Sept. 19, p. 2.
Va. Gaz. (Royle) Oct. 25, supplement extraordinary, p. 2.
Ga. Gaz. Nov. 14, pp. 1-2.

October 29

Massachusetts and Connecticut Claim Right of Taxation. Finally reconvened and properly encouraged by specific town instructions as well as by the actions of the Stamp Act Congress, the Massachusetts House of Representatives resolves that only the province's representatives can tax the inhabitants. Connecticut's General Assembly passes its own similar resolves in late October.

Bos. Gaz. Nov. 4, p. 3.
Conn. Courant Sept. 23, pp. 1, 2; [Nov.], pp. 2-3.

September-December

Newspaper Response to Stamp Act. Directly affected by the Stamp Act's provisions, the various colonial newspapers react to the November 1 official date for the Act's implementation in a variety of ways: use of skull and crossbones/tombstone symbols for stamps before November 1; undated issues or issues with no notice of publisher after November 1; imaginative use of title sub-headings for patriotic (American) sentiments. While certain newspapers suspend publication for limited periods of time after November 1, others continue business as usual.

N.Hamp. Gaz. Oct. 31, pp. 1-2, 3.
Bos. Gaz. Oct. 7, p. 1; Nov. 4, p. 1.
Conn. Courant [Nov.], p. 1.
N.Y. Merc. Oct. 28, pp. 1, 3; [Nov.], p. 1.
N.Y. Gaz. or Week. Post-Boy Dec. 5, pp. 1, 4.
Pa. Gaz. [Nov.], no. 1924; [Nov.], no. 1925.
Md. Gaz. Sept. 5, p. 1; Oct. 10, p. 1; Oct. 31, p. 1; [Dec. 10], p. 1.
S.C. Gaz. Oct. 31, 1765/June 2 (1766), p. 1.
Ga. Gaz. Sept. 12, p. 1; Oct. 31, p. 2; Nov. 14, p. 3; Nov. 21, p. 1.

November

Stamp Act Stirs the Colonial Imagination. A variety of colorful ceremonies and colonial observances mark the day for the Stamp Act to take effect, November 1, as well as the next few weeks of heady protest. Exeter and Portsmouth, New Hampshire experience an unanticipated result of the current 'legitimization' of illegal acts when associations of citizens are hurriedly formed to help the local peace officers: some persons have come to regard all laws at an end and are proceeding accordingly.

N.Hamp. Gaz. Nov. 8, p. 2; Nov. 15, pp. 1-2; Nov. 22, pp. 1, 2-3; Nov. 29, p. 1.
Bos. Gaz. Nov. 4, p. 1.
Newpt. Merc. Oct. 21, p. 3; Oct. 28, supplement, pp. 1, 2; Nov. 4, pp. 2-3.
N.Y. Merc. [Nov.], pp. 1, 2; Dec. 16, p. 3; Dec. 23, pp. 1, 3.
Pa. Gaz. Nov. 21, pp. 1, 3.

November

Maryland Affected? A short notice in the *Maryland Gazette* advises Maryland residents that despite conducting its business without stamped documents, the Frederick County Court's proceedings are valid.

Md. Gaz. [Dec. 10], p. 3.

November 29

South Carolina, Too? South Carolina Resolves are passed by the General Assembly of South Carolina in protest against infringements on colonial liberties.

N.Y. Merc. Dec. 30, pp. 1-2.
Pa. Gaz. Jan 2 (1766), p. 1.

November 30

Stamp Act Receives Its Last Respects. The "Stamp Act" is formally buried in Fredericktown, Maryland.

Md. Gaz. [Dec. 10], p. 4.

October-December

Sentiment Appears for Non-Importation. A movement for a policy of non-importation of English goods until the Stamp Act is repealed gathers force and direction among a growing number of colonial merchants: New York City (October 31), Philadelphia (November 14), Boston (December 9).

N.Hamp. Gaz. Nov. 29, p. 1.
Bos. Gaz. Sept. 16, supplement, p. 2; Dec. 16, p. 3.
Newpt. Merc. Nov. 18, p. 2; Nov. 25, p. 2; Dec. 16, p. 3.
N.Y. Merc. [Nov.], p. 2; Nov. 25, p. 2; Dec. 16; p. 2.
Pa. Gaz. [Nov.], no. 1924; [Nov.], no. 1925; Dec. 19, p. 1.

November-December

New Jersey and New York Resolves. The legislatures of New Jersey (November 30) and New York (December 17) pass resolutions against the Stamp Act and other British-administered injustices similar to the resolves of the other colonies.

N.Y. Merc. Dec. 2, pp. 1-2; Dec. 9, p. 3; Dec. 23, pp. 2-3.
Pa. Gaz. Dec. 5, pp. 2-3.

December 17

Massachusetts Loses a Stamp Official. Andrew Oliver formally resigns his post as Massachusetts' stamp distributor.

Bos. Gaz. Dec. 23, p. 1.
Pa. Gaz. Dec. 26, p. 2; Jan. 2 (1766), p. 2.

December 25

Rhode Island Follows Suit. Augustus Johnston "officially" resigns his post as Rhode Island stamp distributor, *again*, for the amusement of the local Sons of Liberty, although he has yet to receive his commission.

Newpt. Merc. Dec. 30, p. 3.
N.Y. Merc. Jan. 13 (1766), p. 2.

December

Stamps More Acceptable Elsewhere. News of the successful implementation of the Stamp Act in Barbados and Quebec reaches the American colonies. (Stamps are also used in Nova Scotia, Florida, Grenada, and Jamaica, as well as in Georgia for a short time.) American contempt for such proceedings is moderated by assurances that the majority of each jurisdiction's population is averse to the Stamp Act. Not all patriots distant from the thirteen mainland colonies are able to emulate the New Providence (Bahamas) stalwarts who bury their stamp officer in order to convince him to resign.

N.Hamp. Gaz. Oct. 25, p. 3; Nov. 29, p. 2; Dec. 13, p. 3.
Newpt. Merc. Dec. 23, pp. 2-3.
N.Y. Merc. Dec. 9, p. 3; Dec. 16, pp. 2-3.
Pa. Gaz. Nov. 28, p. 2; Jan. 9 (1766), p. 2.

Acadians
  Sufferings in exile
    Ga. Gaz. Apr. 25, p. 2.

Almanac
  Ad for *Poor Richard's*
    Pa. Gaz. Aug. 29, p. 4.

Boundary
  New Hampshire-New York settled
    N.Hamp. Gaz. Apr. 26, p. 2.

Church of England
  Established in North Carolina
    Newpt. Merc. July 22, pp. 2-3.
    Ga. Gaz. July 11, pp. 1-2.

Coffee
  New type discovered (rye)
    Newpt. Merc. May 20, p. 1.

Colleges
  College of New Jersey, commencement
    Pa. Gaz. Oct. 10, p. 1.
  Proposed for Georgia
    N.Hamp. Gaz. Mar. 1, p. 3.
    Ga. Gaz. Jan. 17, pp. 2-3.

Customs
  Polly seized for violations, but scuttled (Taunton, Massachusetts)
    Newpt. Merc. Apr. 22, p. 3.

East Florida
  Land grants available
    N. Hamp. Gaz. Feb. 8, p. 2.

Frostbite
  Cure for
    Md. Gaz. Jan. 24, p. 1.

George III (King of England)
  Birthday celebrated
    Ga. Gaz. June 6, p. 2.

Guy Fawkes Day
  Celebration of
    N.Hamp. Gaz. Nov. 15, p. 2.

Gwinnett, Button (Future signer of the Declaration of Independence)
  Merchant's ad of
    Ga. Gaz. Sept. 12, p. 2.

Hogarth, William (English artist)
  Memoir of
    Ga. Gaz. May 23, p. 1.

Independence, American
    Bos. Gaz. Sept. 16, p. 1.
  Denied by essayists as American goal
    Ga. Gaz. Aug. 15, pp. 1-2.

Indians
  Continuing wars with colonists after Pontiac peace
    Ga. Gaz. Jan 17, pp. 1-2; Feb. 7, p. 1; Feb. 21, p. 2; Mar. 7, p. 2.

Manufactures
  Hemp cultivation for rope industry
    Newpt. Merc. Apr. 29, p. 1.

Moral Exhortation
  For Frugality
    N.Hamp. Gaz. Feb. 1, p. 3; Feb. 8, p. 2; Feb. 15, p. 1.

Newspapers
  Freedom of press now imperilled according to essay
    N.Hamp. Gaz. July 12, p. 3.

Orphan House (Savannah)
  Operations of, funds
    Ga. Gaz. Jan. 17, p. 2; Feb. 21, p. 3.

Poetry
  "A Remarkable Dream" (regarding Stamp Act)
    N.Hamp. Gaz. Oct. 25, pp. 1-2.

Rights, American Political
  Virtual representation of America in Parliament denied
    N.Y. Gaz. or Week. Post-Boy June 27, pp. 2-3.
    Ga. Gaz. Sept. 19, pp. 1-2; Sept. 26, pp. 1-2; Oct. 3, pp. 1-2.

Slaves
  Sales of
    N.Y. Merc. Aug. 19, p. 4.

Vampires
    Conn. Courant Jan. 21, p. 1.

West Florida
    Description of
        Ga. Gaz. Jan. 10, p. 1.

Whitefield, George (English Methodist minister)
    Proposes Georgia college
        N.Hamp. Gaz. Mar. 1, p. 3.
        Ga. Gaz. Jan. 17, pp. 2-3.

To the PUBLIC.

AS I am convinced that my refusing to store my Goods, was wrong; I do promise and consent, That they shall be deposited in the public Store with other Goods which were imported contrary to the *Non-importation Agreement*;——which I hope will appease the Minds of my injured Fellow Citizens, and convince them that I do not regard sacrificing my private Interest for the *Good of the Public*.

Simeon Coley.

New-York, 21st July, 1769.
Afternoon, 2 o'Clock.

See p. 26, June-December, Broadside: July 21.

December 1765-April

Unrelenting Colonial Opposition to Stamp Act. Opposition to the unenforced Stamp Act continues in the colonies. Meanwhile, periodic reports of English opposition, constitutional and economic, and possible repeal circulate.

N.Hamp. Gaz. Dec. 13 (1765), p. 3; Dec. 27 (1765), p. 2; Jan. 10, p. 3.
Bos. Gaz. Feb. 24, p. 3; Mar. 3, p. 2.
Conn. Courant Jan. 13, p. 3; Feb. 3, p. 3; Feb. 10, pp. 1, 3, 4; Feb. 17, p. 1; Mar. 24, p. 4; Mar. 31, p. 3; Apr. 7, p. 4.
N.Y. Merc. Jan. 13, p. 3; Jan. 20, pp. 1, 2, 3; Jan. 27, pp. 1, 2-3; Feb. 17, pp. 2, 3; Feb. 20, extraordinary, p. 1; Feb. 24, p. 3; Mar. 3, p. 3; Mar. 10, p. 2; Apr. 7, pp. 1, 2, 3; Apr. 21, p. 3; May 12, p. 1.
Pa. Gaz. Jan. 9, p. 3; Jan. 23, pp. 1, 3; Jan. 30, pp. 1, 2, 3; Feb. 6, p. 3; Feb. 20, pp. 2-3; Mar. 27, pp. 1, 3; Apr. 17, pp. 2-3.
Md. Gaz. Jan. 30, p. 3; Feb. 20, p. 3; Mar. 6, pp. 1, 3; Mar. 20, p. 3; Mar. 27, p. 1; Apr. 3, p. 2.
Va. Gaz. (Purdie) Mar. 7, pp. 1-3; Mar. 14, p. 2; Mar. 21, pp. 1, 3.
Va. Gaz. (Rind) May 16, pp. 1-2.
N.C. Gaz. (Wil.) Feb. 12, p. 1; Feb. 26, pp. 2-3.
Ga. Gaz. May 21, pp. 3-4.

January

New York Buckles on Quartering Act. The New York General Assembly complies with General Thomas Gage's request (December 13, 1765) for troop provisions according to the Quartering Act.

February 11

Stamp Act Unconstitutional on Virginia's Eastern Shore. Virginia's Northampton County Court declares the Stamp Act unconstitutional and therefore not binding.

Va. Gaz. (Purdie) Mar. 21, p. 3.

January—March

Finally, Stamp Act Repealed

January 14. Parliament convenes.
January 17. London merchants petition Parliament to repeal the Stamp Act.
March 4. The House of Commons votes repeal.
March 17. The House of Lords votes repeal.
March 18. King George III assents to the repeal of the Stamp Act, to take effect May 1. He also gives his assent to the Declaratory Act which asserts Parliament's right to legislate for the colonies "in all cases whatsoever." The significance of the latter act is generally overlooked in America in the jubilation over repeal of the hated Stamp Act (April-May).

N.Hamp. Gaz. Mar. 28/Apr. 4, p. 1; Apr. 11, pp. 2, 3; Apr. 18, p 1; May 22, p. 1; July 4, p. 2.
Bos. Gaz. Apr. 21, p. 3; May 19, pp. 2, 3; May 26, p. 2; May 26, supplement, p. 1.
Newpt. Merc. May 12/19, p. 3; May 19/26, pp. 3, 4; May 26/June 2, pp. 2, 3; June 9/16, p. 3.
Conn. Courant May 26, p. 4; June 2, pp. 3, 4.
N.Y. Merc. Mar. 24, p. 2; Apr. 21, p. 3; Broadside: Apr. 26; May 5, p. 1; Broadside: May 16; May 26, p. 3; June 2, pp. 1-2; June 9, p. 2.
Pa. Gaz. Mar. 20, p. 2; Apr. 17, p. 3; May 19, supplement, p. 1.
Md. Gaz. Apr. 10, p. 2; June 12, pp. 1, 2.
Va. Gaz. (Purdie) Apr. 18, p. 3; Apr. 25, pp. 2, 3; May 2, p. 1; June 13, p. 1; June 20, pp. 1-2.
Va. Gaz. (Rind) May 16, p. 4.
S.C. Gaz. Oct. 31, 1765/June 2, 1766, p. 3; June 2/9, pp. 1, 3.
Ga. Gaz. May 21, pp. 1, 4; June 4, p. 1; June 11, p. 3; June 18, p. 2; June 25, p. 1; July 2, p. 3; July 9, p. 3; July 16, p. 3; Aug. 20, pp. 1-2; Dec. 16 (1767), p. 2; Dec. 23 (1767), p. 1.

May-June

Pitt to Be Honored by Colonists. The colonial press celebrates the colonies' champion in the repeal of the Stamp Act, William Pitt: "I rejoice that America has resisted." Statues of Pitt, the Great Commoner, are proposed in such cities as New York, Charleston, Annapolis.

N.Hamp. Gaz. Apr. 25, p. 3.
N.Y. Merc. May 5, p. 2; May 26, p. 3; June 30, p. 2.
Pa. Gaz. May 8, p. 1.
Md. Gaz. Mar. 27, p. 3; Apr. 10, p. 3.
Va. Gaz. (Purdie) May 9, pp. 1-2.
S.C. Gaz. June 2/9, p. 3.
Ga. Gaz. Jan. 7 (1767), pp. 1-2.

June 6

British Effort to Make Sugar Duties Attractive. Parliament modifies the Sugar Act (1764): the three pence duty on foreign molasses is reduced to one pence per gallon on all imported molasses, foreign or British. Scheduled to take effect on November 1, the revised act also specifies that all colonial exports to Northern Europe must pass through a British port.

Newpt. Merc. Sept. 8/15, pp. 2-4.
Pa. Gaz. Aug 21, pp. 2-3; Sept. 4, pp. 1, 4.
Va. Gaz. (Rind) Sept. 5, p. 2.
Ga. Gaz. Aug. 27, p. 1; Sept. 3, p. 1; Oct. 8, p. 2.

June-December

Colonial Compensation for Stamp Act Riots. The Massachusetts House of Representatives delays compliance with a British ministry recommendation regarding compensation for the victims of the August, 1765 Stamp Act riots in Boston until early December. The Massachusetts bill grants compensation and assumes the power to pardon all involved in the disturbances. This colonial usurpation of the crown's pardoning power is disallowed by the Privy Council (May 1767), but the entire matter is then allowed to recede from public attention. New York readily conforms to a similar ministry directive for its own disorders.

N.Hamp. Gaz. Aug. 1, p. 2; Nov. 21, p. 2; June 12 (1767), p. 2.
Bos. Gaz. July 14, p. 1.
Conn. Courant Nov. 10, p. 1; Dec. 1, pp. 1, 3; Dec. 15, p. 3; Dec. 29, p. 3.
N.Y. Merc. June 16, p. 2; June 23, pp. 1-2; Oct. 27, p. 2; Dec. 8, p. 2; Dec. 15, p. 2; Dec. 29, p. 2.
Pa. Gaz. Oct. 29 (1767), p. 2.
Md. Gaz. July 24, p. 2; Nov. 13, p. 2; Jan. 1 (1767), p. 2.
Ga. Gaz. Aug. 13, pp. 2-4; Aug. 20, pp. 2-3; Feb. 18 (1767), p. 1.

August

Chatham Replaces Rockingham. The Rockingham ministry is replaced by a ministry headed by the newly titled, but aging, Earl of Chatham (William Pitt). The new Chancellor of the Exchequer is Charles Townshend.

N.Hamp. Gaz. Sept. 26, p. 2.
Conn. Courant Sept. 22, p. 3; Sept. 29, p. 1; Oct. 6, p. 1.
Ga. Gaz. Sept. 24, p. 3; Oct. 29, p. 2.

August 10-11

New York City Liberty Poles and Fisticuffs. The continued potential for trouble between British troops and the colonists is demonstrated in New York City when an altercation between troops and the local Sons of Liberty follows the destruction of the town's Liberty Pole by a group of soldiers.

Newpt. Merc. Aug. 18/25, p. 3.
Conn. Courant July 21, p. 3; Aug. 18, p. 3.
N.Y. Merc. Aug. 18, p. 2; Aug. 25, p. 3.
Pa. Gaz. Aug. 28, p. 3.
S.C. Gaz. Sept. 8/15, p. 2.
Ga. Gaz. Oct. 15, p. 2.

December 15

New York Unbuckles on Quartering Act. The New York Assembly refuses Governor Henry Moore's request for provisions for the British troops stationed in New York City. For the assembly's failure to comply with the Quartering Act, Moore prorogues them (December 19). (See below, May 27, 1767.)

N.Hamp. Gaz. June 12 (1767), p. 2.
N.Y. Merc. Dec. 29, p. 2.
Pa. Gaz. Jan. 1 (1767), p. 2.

Colleges
Yale commencement
Conn. Courant Sept. 22, pp. 2-3.

Currency
Colonial bills of credit, possible allowance of
N.Y. Merc. Nov. 17, pp. 1-2, 3; Nov. 24, p. 2.
Md. Gaz. Nov. 20, p. 2.

Free Masons
To admit women?
Conn. Courant Sept. 15, p. 1.

Geography, American
Once part of Asia, accounts for pre-1492 inhabitants
Conn. Courant Nov. 3, pp. 1-2.

Georgia
Ongoing settlement of colony by township
Ga. Gaz. June 4, p. 3.

Jefferson, Thomas
Ad for horse he has found
Va. Gaz. (Rind) Aug. 8, p. 3.

Lee, Richard Henry
Vindicates self for attempting to be Virginia stamp officer
Va. Gaz. (Rind) Aug. 8, p. 2.

Mineral Spring (Stafford, Connecticut)
Observations on

Conn. Courant July 21, p. 4; Aug. 11, p. 3; Aug. 18, p. 1.

Pontiac
Account of life of
Conn. Courant Aug. 25, p. 1.

Servants
Convict, runaways
Va. Gaz. (Purdie) Mar. 7, p. 3.

Shipwreck
Narrative of
Ga. Gaz. Oct. 29, pp. 1-2; Nov. 5, p. 1.

Slaves
Runaways
Va. Gaz. (Purdie) June 13, pp. 3-4.

Sugar Plums
Ad for
N.Y. Merc. Aug. 25, p. 1.

Swimming
Observations on
N.Hamp. Gaz. July 4, p. 3.

Vesuvius
Eruption of in Italy
Ga. Gaz. Aug. 27, p. 2.

Women
Admittance to Free Mason lodges?
Conn. Courant Sept. 15, p. 1.

February 27

English Tax Cut Portends Colonial Tax. A cut of approximately £500,000 in British revenues brought about by a reduction in the English land tax makes a new American tax mandatory. Englishmen at home are vehemently opposed to any more taxation on themselves and feel that they are paying more than their fair share of imperial costs. The land tax cut is intended also to facilitate agriculture and thus reduce a growing shortage of English grain.

N.Hamp. Gaz. Jan. 16, p. 2; Mar. 20, p. 2; May 1, p. 2.
Md. Gaz. May 21, p. 1; May 28, p. 1.
Ga. Gaz. May 27, p. 2; July 15, p. 1.

May 27

New York's Quartering Problems Continue. Governor Henry Moore requests new provisions for troops from the New York Assembly, which finally complies on June 6 with a grant of £3000. Moore and the assembly are both unaware when Parliament in July 1767 suspends New York's legislative powers as of October 1, 1767, for the colony's extended recalcitrance regarding the Quartering Act. When Moore does learn of Parliament's measure, he declines to enforce the suspension in light of the assembly's capitulation. The Board of Trade, the British advisory agency that oversees colonial affairs, later sustains his action (May 7, 1768).

Bos. Gaz. Aug. 31, p. 3.
Conn. Courant July 27, p. 1; Sept. 7, p. 3; Oct. 5, pp. 1, 2; Nov. 2, p. 4.
N.Y. Journal June 4, p. 2; July 23, p. 2; Aug. 6, pp. 2-3; Aug. 20, pp. 2-3; Sept. 10, pp. 1-2; Oct. 29, pp. 1, 2; Dec. 3, p. 1.
Pa. Gaz. June 11, p. 2; June 18, p. 1; Dec. 3, pp. 1, 2.
Md. Gaz. Apr. 30, p. 2; June 25, p. 2; July 30, p. 1.
Ga. Gaz. May 6, p. 3; July 1, p. 1; July 8, p. 3; July 15, p. 2; July 29, p. 2; Aug. 26, p. 1; Sept. 16, p. 3; Oct. 7, p. 1.

July 2

Townshend Acts. Acting on colonial agent Benjamin Franklin's misleading (and erroneous) testimony regarding American distinctions between different types of taxation, given before Parliament (January 1766) in connection with the repeal of the Stamp Act, Chancellor of the Exchequer Charles Townshend accepts the distinction between internal and external taxes and the implication that the latter are quite acceptable to the Americans. Townshend draws up a series of "external" taxes for the colonies to take effect November 20. Small duties are placed on various colonial imports from Britain: tea, lead, glass, silk, paper, and paints. The resultant revenue is intended to remain in the colonies for colonial administration salaries. The latter disposition of funds is totally unsatisfactory to the colonists who maintain a large measure of political leverage through their hitherto exclusive control of the salaries of colonial governors as well as the colonial judiciary. A second act reorganizes the American customs service by establishing an autonomous Board of Customs Commissioners, located in Boston, that will exercise a final authority over all American customs officials. This act is designed both to cut down on unnecessary delays and financial losses occasioned by appeals to customs officers in England and to improve customs collections. The third Townshend Act is the July suspension of New York's legislative power (see above). The colonies learn of the new duties:

N.Hamp. Gaz. May 15, p. 2; June 26, pp. 2, 3; Oct. 16, pp. 1-2.
Bos. Gaz. July 6, p. 1.
Newpt. Merc. Oct. 5/12, p. 2.
Conn. Courant Aug. 24, p. 3; Sept. 7, p. 3; Oct. 26, p. 1; Nov. 2, p. 4.
N.Y. Journal Aug. 20, pp. 2-3; Sept. 3, p. 3.
Pa. Gaz. Oct. 8, p. 2.
Md. Gas. May 7, pp. 1-2; July 23, p. 1; Oct. 15, p. 2.
Va. Gaz. (Purdie and Dixon) Sept. 10, p. 2.
S.C. Gaz. July 20-27, p. 1; Aug. 10/17, p. 2.
Ga. Gaz. Sept. 2, p. 2; Sept. 9, p. 1; Oct. 7, pp. 1-2, 3; Oct. 14, p. 1.

October 28

Boston Seeks Renewal of Non-Importation. The Boston town meeting votes to renew the use of non-consumption as of December 3, 1767, as an economic weapon against British trade acts. While various luxuries such as clothing and jewelry are not to be imported from Britain, a self-conscious impetus is to be afforded home manufacturing. In the next few months there is much comment in other colonies about Boston's efforts, but the initial colonial reaction to the Townshend Acts is, in general, moderate.

N.Hamp. Gaz. Nov. 20, p. 1; Nov. 27, pp. 1, 2.
Bos. Gaz. Nov. 2, pp. 1, 2, 3.
Newpt. Merc. Nov. 2/9, p. 2.
Conn. Courant Nov. 16, p. 1; Dec. 7, pp. 1-2.
Pa. Gaz. Nov. 26, p. 2; Dec. 10, p. 2.
Md. Gaz. Nov. 19, p. 1.
Va. Gaz. (Purdie and Dixon) [Nov. 26], p. 2; Dec. 10, p. 2; Dec. 17, p. 2; Dec. 24, p. 2.
S.C. Gaz. Dec. 7/14, p. 1; Dec. 14/21, pp. 1-2.
Ga. Gaz. Dec. 2, p. 1; Dec. 16, p. 4; Dec. 30, p. 1.

December 2-4

Providence and Newport Amenable. Providence and Newport vote non-importation plans, effective January 1, 1768, in response to the Townshend Acts.

N.Hamp. Gaz. Dec. 4, p. 2; Dec. 18, pp. 2-3.
Newpt. Merc. Nov. 30/Dec. 7, p. 3; Dec. 7/14, p. 3.
Conn. Courant Nov. 30, p. 3; Dec. 7, p. 3.
Pa. Gaz. Dec. 24, p. 2.
Va. Gaz. (Purdie and Dixon) Jan. 21 (1768), p. 3.

December

Support for Non-Importation Hesitant Elsewhere. However, other American cities of importance, such as New York, are slow to respond to the challenge of the Townshend Acts.

N.Y. Journal Dec. 17, pp. 2-3.

December 2-February 15, 1768

Letters from a Farmer in Pennsylvania to the Inhabitants of the British Colonies. Appearing first in the pages of the *Pennsylvania Chronicle*, John Dickinson's twelve *Letters* are reprinted immediately in newspapers throughout the American colonies and are published as a pamphlet in both England and America in 1768. Dickinson's moderate tract makes use of precedent to establish the thesis that Parliament cannot tax the colonies internally or externally although it can regulate commerce and colonial industry. Dickinson notes that the colonies do not contemplate independence. *The Farmer's Letters* enjoys an extraordinary success in the colonies and Dickinson is widely and passionately acclaimed. (The citations to the *Pennsylvania Gazette*, following the twelve citations of the *Letters* in the *Pennsylvania Chronicle*, include various thanks to and celebrations of the Farmer as well as his replies to several of the encomiums.)

Pa. Chron. Nov. 30/Dec. 2, p. 1; Dec. 2/7, p. 1; Dec. 7/14, p. 1; Dec. 14/21, pp. 1-2; Dec. 21/28, p. 1; Dec. 28/Jan. 4 (1768), p. 1; Jan. 4/11 (1768), p. 1; Jan. 11/18 (1768), p. 1; Jan. 18/25 (1768), p. 1; Jan. 25/Feb. 1 (1768), pp. 4-5; Feb. 1/8 (1768), pp. 4-5; Feb. 8/15 (1768), pp. 4-5.
Pa. Gaz. Mar. 31 (1768), p. 2; Apr. 7 (1768), pp. 2-3; Apr. 28 (1768), p. 3; May 5 (1768), p. 2; May 12 (1768), p. 3; May 19 (1768), p. 1; June 9 (1768), p. 3; June 16 (1768), p. 3; June 23 (1768), p. 3; July 7 (1768), pp. 1, 2; July 14 (1768), p. 3; Sept. 1 (1768), pp. 2, 3; Dec. 29 (1768), p. 3.

Astronomical Phenomena
    Mars: influence on earth
        N.Hamp. Gaz. Jan. 30, p. 2.

Books
    List of titles for sale
        Conn. Courant Nov. 9, pp. 3-4.

Boston
    Fire in noted
        Md. Gaz. Feb. 26, p. 2.

Capital Punishment
    Observations on
        Ga. Gaz. Aug. 19, p. 1; Aug. 26, p. 2.

Colleges
    King's (Columbia), admission to
        N.Y. Gaz. or Week. Post-Boy June 4, p. 3.

Congregationalists
    Installation of Hartford minister narrated
        Conn. Courant Sept. 28, p. 3.

Currency
    Debate regarding possible American paper money
        Md. Gaz. June 11, pp. 1-2; June 18, pp. 1-2.

Diseases
    Small-pox
        Conn. Courant Nov. 9, pp. 1-2.

Franklin, Benjamin
    On electricity
        N.Y. Journal July 16, supplement, pp. 1, 2.
    Pseudonymous: "Benevolus" on internal-external taxes
        S.C. Gaz. July 20/27, p. 1.

Georgia
    Crackers (descriptive name of certain Georgians) noticed
        Pa. Gaz. Sept. 10, p. 2.

Imprisonment
    Hardships of observed
        N.Hamp. Gaz. Dec. 4, p. 1.
        Ga. Gaz. Aug. 19, pp. 1-2.

Indians
    Appreciate Shakespeare
        N.Y. Journal Dec. 17, p. 3.

Justice
    English judicial proceedings in Sussex, New Jersey
        N.Hamp. Gaz. Jan. 30, pp. 1-2.

Lotteries
    On individual's belongings: includes land, slaves, livestock
        Va. Gaz. (Purdie and Dixon) Sept. 10, p. 3.

Manufactures
    Hemp cultivation explained
        Ga. Gaz. Feb. 18, p. 3.

Mineral Spring (Stafford, Connecticut)
    Observations on
        Conn. Courant June 29, p. 2.

Navy, British
    Impressment of Americans for service in
        Ga. Gaz. Nov. 25, p. 2.

Rousseau, Jean-Jacques
    Noticed
        Ga. Gaz. Sept. 16, p. 2.

Slaves
    Sales of
        N.Y. Journal Aug. 20, p. 4.
    Slave trade denounced
        N.Hamp. Gaz. Apr. 10, p. 1.

Trade
    Imported goods listed for sale
        Pa. Gaz. Jan. 15, p. 1.

Vagabonds
    Law passed against in Pennsylvania
        Pa. Gaz. June 18, p. 1.

Vermont
    New Hampshire-New York dispute over area reaches British authority in England
        N.Hamp. Gaz. June 19, p. 2.

January-March

Mutual Colonial Encouragement for Non-Importation. News of various forms of colonial non-consumption, economy, and home manufacture circulates in newspapers not only as information but also as incentive, encouragement, suggestion.

N.Hamp. Gaz. Jan. 22, p. 3; Jan. 29, p. 3.
Bos. Gaz. Feb. 29, p. 2.
Newpt. Merc. Jan. 4/11, p. 3; Jan. 11/18, p. 3; Jan. 25/Feb. 1, p. 3; Feb. 15/22, p. 3; Feb. 22/29, p. 3.
Conn. Courant Jan. 4, p. 4; Jan. 11, pp. 2, 4; Mar. 21, p. 1.
N.Y. Journal Feb. 11, p. 2.
Pa. Gaz. Jan. 14, p. 3; Feb. 11, pp. 2-3; Feb. 18, p. 2; Mar. 17, p. 2.; Mar. 24, p. 1; Apr. 14, pp. 2, 3.
Va. Gaz. (Purdie and Dixon) Jan. 7, p. 3.
Ga. Gaz. Jan. 13, p. 3; Mar. 2, p. 2.

February 11

Massachusetts Circular Letter. The Massachusetts House of Representatives approves of the Massachusetts Circular Letter, drawn up by Samuel Adams, and directs its transmission to other colonies. The Letter describes Massachusetts' actions against the Townshend Acts; addresses itself to the unconstitutionality of both taxation without representation and the payment of colonial officials from customs duties; asserts the impossibility of colonial representation in Parliament; denies any provincial desire for independence; and urges united action by the colonies against the Townshend Acts. Governor Francis Bernard responds by dissolving the General Assembly, both House of Representatives and Council, on March 4.

N.Hamp. Gaz. July 8, p. 1.
Bos. Gaz. Feb. 15, p. 3; Mar. 14, p. 1.
Newpt. Merc. Feb. 22/29, p. 3.
Pa. Gaz. Mar. 31, p. 2.
Md. Gaz. Mar. 10, p. 2.
Va. Gaz. (Purdie and Dixon) Apr. 21, p. 2.

February 25-April 28

The Monitor's Letters. A series of (initially) ten letters, appears in William Rind's *Virginia Gazette*. This series complements Dickinson's *Farmer's Letters* and is a marked influence on Virginia's 1769 (non-importation) Association although the intercolonial appeal and appearance of *The Monitor's Letters* is limited to partial publication only in the *New York Journal,* the *Pennsylvania Gazette,* and the *South Carolina Gazette.* (There is no extant newspaper copy of the first and seventh numbers.)

N.Y. Journal May 26, supplement, p. 1; June 22 (1769), pp. 1, 2-3; July 6 (1769), p. 1.
Pa. Gaz. Apr. 21, p. 1.
Va. Gaz. (Rind) Mar. 3, p. 1; Mar. 10, p. 1; Mar. 17, p. 1; Mar. 24, p. 1; Mar. 31, p. 1; Apr. 14, p. 1; Apr. 21, p. 1; Apr. 28, p. 1.
S.C. Gaz. June 27, p. 1.

March

Non-Importation Lacks Unanimity. Boston merchants take the lead in employment of more stringent non-importation measures, but hinge their own actions on similar activities to be undertaken by fellow merchants in New York and Philadelphia. The spirit of urgency and united interest conspicuous in the opposition to the Stamp Act (1765-1766) is absent, however, as considerations of economic gain and intracolony divisions over the Townshend Acts negate unanimous opposition to the Acts. New York merchants do reach an agreement in April, but Philadelphia's efforts to reach a consensus on a program are ineffective (March-June).

N.Hamp. Gaz. Apr. 29, p. 2.
Newpt. Merc. May 9/16, pp. 1-2.
N.Y. Journal Apr. 21, p. 2.
Pa. Gaz. Mar. 31, p. 3; Apr. 21, pp. 2-3; Apr. 28, p. 3; May 12, pp. 1, 4; June 2, p. 3; June 16, p. 1; July 21, p. 1; Aug. 4, p. 1; Oct. 20, pp. 1, 4.
Md. Gaz. Apr. 14, p. 2; Mar. 23 (1769), p. 1.
Va. Gaz. (Purdie and Dixon) Apr. 21, p. 2.
Ga. Gaz. May 4, p. 3.

April 21

Lord Hillsborough Reacts to the Massachusetts Circular Letter. New Secretary of State for the Colonies, Lord Hillsborough, reacts very strongly to the Massachusetts Circular Letter. He sends notices to the colonial governors in which he denounces the Letter and orders that colonial assemblies are to be dissolved rather than be allowed to endorse the Circular Letter. Hillsborough's efforts are of no avail in New Hampshire, New Jersey, Connecticut, Maryland, Rhode Island, Georgia, South Carolina, and North Carolina, where the Letter is in fact endorsed. In Virginia the House of Burgesses responds with its own letter of support to the Massachusetts House of Representatives. (See below, November 24 and December 24, 1768; and December 28, 1768-January 2, 1769.)

N.Hamp. Gaz. [July 8], extraordinary, p. 1; Feb. 10 (1769), p. 2.
Bos. Gaz. June 27, pp. 1-2; Mar. 20 (1769), p. 3.
Newpt. Merc. July 11/18, p. 2.
Conn. Courant May 8 (1769), p. 2.
Pa. Gaz. Aug. 25, p. 2.

Md. Gaz. May 19, p. 1; June 30, p. 2; July 14, pp. 1, 2; July 28, pp. 1-2.
Va. Gaz. (Purdie and Dixon) May 26, p. 1; July 21, pp. 1, 2.
Ga. Gaz. Aug. 24, pp. 1, 4; Aug. 31, p. 3; Sept. 28, p. 2; Nov. 30, pp. 1, 2; Dec. 21, pp. 2-3; Feb. 22 (1769), p. 1.

May 17

Boston Customs Commissioners Uneasy. The agitated requests by the Boston Customs Commissioners for immediate protection motivate a quick reaction by the British authorities. The H.M.S. *Romney*, a fifty-gun frigate, is dispatched to assist the uneasy commissioners and arrives in Boston Harbor on May 17.

N.Hamp. Gaz. May 27, p. 2.

June 10

Liberty Seized. The sloop *Liberty*, owned by John Hancock, an eminent colonial merchant/smuggler and political radical, is seized for customs violation and anchored near H.M.S. *Romney*. The customs officials flee to the *Romney* on June 13 after they are attacked by a mob. Presently, the officials appeal for British troops. In turn the Boston town meeting asks Governor Bernard to remove the *Romney* from Boston harbor (June 14), but he denies any authority to do so.

Bos. Gaz. June 13, p. 3; June 20, pp. 1, 2.
Newpt. Merc. June 13/20, p. 3.
Pa. Gaz. June 23, p. 2.
Md. Gaz. June 30, p. 1.
Va. Gaz. (Purdie and Dixon) July 14, p. 1.
Ga. Gaz. July 27, p. 4.

June 21

Governor Bernard: "Take Back the Circular Letter." Acting under Lord Hillsborough's direct orders, Governor Bernard orders the House of Representatives to rescind the Massachusetts Circular Letter.

N.Hamp. Gaz. June 24, p. 3.
Bos. Gaz. June 27, p. 2; July 4, p. 1.
Newpt. Merc. June 27/July 4, p. 3.
Conn. Courant July 11, pp. 2-4.
Pa. Gaz. July 14, p. 1.

June 30

Massachusetts House of Representatives: "No." By a vote of ninety-two to seventeen, the Massachusetts House of Representatives refuses to rescind its Circular Letter, and Governor Bernard accordingly dissolves it on July 1.

Bos. Gaz. July 4, pp. 1-2.
Newpt. Merc. July 4/11, pp. 2-3.
Conn. Courant Aug. 1, pp. 1-2.
Pa. Gaz. July 14, p. 2.
Md. Gaz. July 21, pp. 1-2.
Va. Gaz. (Purdie and Dixon) July 28, pp. 1-2.
Ga. Gaz. July 27, p. 3; Aug. 3, pp. 1, 4.

July—October

The Glorious Ninety-Two. The ninety-two representatives who vote against rescinding the Circular Letter as well as the seventeen members who vote for rescinding it enjoy a great deal of notoriety in Massachusetts and throughout the colonies. But while the ninety-two are feted and celebrated, the seventeen are publicly reviled and specifically named in various colonial newspapers.

Bos. Gaz. July 11, p. 1; July 18, p. 3; July 25, p. 1.
Newpt. Merc. July 18/25, p. 3.
Conn. Courant July 25, p. 3; Sept. 5, p. 4; Jan. 2 (1769), p. 4.
Pa. Gaz. July 14, p. 2; July 21, p. 3.
Va. Gaz. (Purdie and Dixon) July 28, p. 2; Sept. 1, p. 2; Dec. 8, p. 1.
S.C. Gaz. Oct. 3, p. 2; Oct. 10, p. 2.

August 1

Boston Merchants Seek to Strengthen Non-Importation. Acting alone, Boston merchants draw up a plan for non-importation of the articles included in the Townshend duties (tea, glass, lead, paper, paints) to begin January 1, 1769, and to continue until said duties are repealed. The merchants agree also not to import most other British goods from January 1, 1769 to January 1, 1770.

Bos. Gaz. Aug. 15, p. 3.
Newpt. Merc. Aug. 22/29, p. 3.
Conn. Courant Aug. 22, p. 3.
Pa. Gaz. Aug. 25, p. 2.

August 27

New York Merchants Cooperate in Non-Importation. New York merchants agree not to import most British goods after November 1, 1769, until the Townshend duties are repealed.

Newpt. Merc. Sept. 12/19, p. 3.
N.Y. Journal Sept. 8, pp. 2-3.
Pa. Gaz. Sept. 15, p. 2.
Md. Gaz. Sept. 22, p. 1.
Va. Gaz. (Purdie and Dixon) Sept. 29, p. 2.
S.C. Gaz. Oct. 10, p. 1.

September 5

Non-Importation and Nationalism. New York tradesmen and mechanics reach agreement not to purchase any imported European goods and to boycott any merchants who sell such goods. Further, provision is made to publicize any merchant who continues to import said goods. The emphasis on American manufacture symbolizes an inchoate, but real and growing awareness of an American nationalism.

N.Hamp. Gaz. Sept. 30, p. 4.
Newpt. Merc. Sept. 12/19, p. 3.
N.Y. Journal Sept. 15, p. 3.
Pa. Gaz. Sept. 15, p. 2.
Md. Gaz. Sept. 22, p. 1.
S.C. Gaz. Oct. 10, p. 1.

September 12–13

British Troops for Boston? Citing rumors of the imminent arrival of British troops, the Boston town meeting passes a resolution urging Governor Bernard to issue a call for a General Assembly to convene. The town meeting contends that a standing army can only be raised and maintained by the consent of the province's representatives. Moreover, any use of the army to enforce laws would constitute, according to the town meeting, a grievance. Bernard replies that he must await King George's decision regarding the calling of a new General Assembly. The Boston town meeting reacts by (a) calling on all citizens to arm themselves because of a possible war with France, a handy and traditional pretext; and (b) issuing a circular letter to Massachusetts' towns to attend a convention at Fanueil Hall in Boston on September 22.

N.Hamp. Gaz. Sept. 23, p. 3.
Bos. Gaz. Sept. 19, pp. 1, 2.
Newpt. Merc. Sept. 19/26, p. 3.
Md. Gaz. Oct. 6, p. 2; Oct. 13, pp. 1-2.
S.C. Gaz. Oct. 10, p. 1.
Ga. Gaz. Oct. 26, pp. 1-2.

September 22–28

A Massachusetts Provincial Convention. An informal Massachusetts provincial convention of delegates from ninety-six towns meets in Boston. Governor Bernard refuses to recognize the convention or to issue a call for a new General Assembly. The convention stresses its own lack of governmental authority, but asserts its legitimate right to assemble and to seek counsel and advice regarding measures to be taken for the common peace and good.

Bos. Gaz. Sept. 26, p. 2; Oct. 3, p. 1; Oct. 10, p. 1.
Newpt. Merc. Sept. 26/Oct. 3, pp. 2-3.
N.Y. Journal Sept. 29, p. 2; Oct. 13, p. 3.
Pa. Gaz. Oct. 6, pp. 2-3.
Md. Gaz. Oct. 13, pp. 1-2.

Va. Gaz. (Purdie and Dixon) Oct. 27, pp. 2-3; Nov. 3, pp. 1-2.
S.C. Gaz. Oct. 16, p. 1.
Ga. Gaz. Nov. 16, p. 1.

September 29

British Troops Arrive in Boston. The long-expected British troops arrive aboard British warships. On October 1 the 14th and 29th regiments from Halifax, Nova Scotia, disembark under the command of Lieutenant Colonel Dalrymple. The arrival of the two regiments precipitates a dispute over whether the soldiers should be billeted in barracks in Castle William or among the populace.

Bos. Gaz. Sept. 26, p. 1; Oct. 3, p. 2; Oct. 10, p. 3; Oct. 10, supplement, p. 1.
Newpt. Merc. Oct. 3/10, p. 3.
Md. Gaz. Oct. 20, p. 3.
Va. Gaz. (Purdie and Dixon) Oct. 27, pp. 2-3.
S.C. Gaz. Oct. 24, p. 2.
Ga. Gaz. Nov. 2, p. 1; Nov. 9, p. 1.

September 28–August 1, 1769

The Occupation of Boston. Boston's predicament is vividly portrayed – and its position as the center of American resistance to British imperial strategies maintained – in a continuing diary of daily events in Boston between September 28, 1768 and August 1, 1769, published in numerous colonial newspapers and styled variously "Journal of Transactions in Boston," "Journal of the Times," "Journal of Occurrences." The "Journal" is written by an anonymous group of patriots whose primary objective is to describe the evils of military rule in Boston as well as the ongoing, attendant machinations and ill-gotten gains of the resident customs commissioners. Southern opinion is solicited by accounts of British overtures to Boston slaves to seek their freedom. Its function as propaganda is enhanced by the novelty of editorial comment, added by means of italicized remarks. The "Journal" represents the first effort in colonial newspapers to gather news specifically for widespread distribution and use in other locales. The *New York Journal* is the first newspaper to begin to print the series; gaps in the "Journal's" publication are supplied from the *Boston Evening Post*, the other colonial newspaper whose edition of the "Journal" is most widely copied by fellow journalists. (Included below are the chronological dates of the "Journal" with the matching citations from the two newspapers.)

"Journal" date	N.Y. Journal
Sept. 28-Oct. 2	Oct. 13, p. 2.
Oct. 3-9	Oct. 20, p. 2.
Oct. 10-16	Oct. 27, pp. 2-3.
Oct. 17-23	Nov. 3, p. 2.
Oct. 24-30	Nov. 10, pp. 1-3.
Oct. 31-Nov. 6	Nov. 17, pp. 2-3.
Nov. 7-13	Nov. 24, p. 2.
Nov. 14-20	Dec. 1, pp. 1-2.
Nov. 21-27	Dec. 8, pp. 1-2.
Nov. 28-Dec. 4	Dec. 15, pp. 1-2.
Dec. 5-11	Dec. 22, pp. 1-2.
Dec. 12-18	Dec. 29, pp. 1-2.
Dec. 19-25	Jan. 12 (1769), supplement, p. 2.
Dec. 26-Jan. 1 (1769)	Jan. 19 (1769), pp. 1-2.
Jan. 2-5 (1769)	Feb. 2 (1769), supplement, p. 2.
Jan. 6-8 (1769)	Feb. 2 (1769), p. 1.
Jan. 9-15 (1769)	Feb. 9 (1769), supplement, pp. 1-2.
Jan. 16-20 (1769)	Feb. 16 (1769), supplement, p. 2.
Jan. 21-22 (1769)	Feb. 16 (1769), p. 2.
	Bos. Even. Post
Jan. 23-24 (1769)	Mar. 13 (1769), p. 1.
Jan. 25-29 (1769)	Mar. 20 (1769), p. 1.
	N.Y. Journal
Jan. 30-Feb. 5 (1769)	Mar. 2 (1769), supplement, pp. 1-2.
	Bos. Even. Post
Feb. 6-9 (1769)	Apr. 3 (1769), pp. 1-2.
Feb. 10-19 (1769)	Apr. 10 (1769), pp. 1-2.
Feb. 21-25 (1769)	Apr. 17 (1769), pp. 1-2.
	N.Y. Journal
Feb. 25-Mar. 3 (1769)	Apr. 6 (1769), supplement, p. 1.
	Bos. Even. Post
Mar. 4-7 (1769)	May 1 (1769), p. 1.
Mar. 8 (1769)	May 8 (1769), p. 1.
	N.Y. Journal
Mar. 9-18 (1769)	Apr. 13 (1769), supplement, pp. 1-2.
Mar. 19-24 (1769)	Apr. 27 (1769), supplement, p. 1.
Mar. 25-27 (1769)	May 4 (1769), supplement, p. 1.
Mar. 28-Apr. 2 (1769)	May 11 (1769), supplement, p. 1.
Apr. 4-12 (1769)	May 18 (1769), supplement, p. 1.
Apr. 13-22 (1769)	June 1 (1769), supplement, p. 1.
	Bos. Even. Post
Apr. 23 (1769)	June 19 (1769), p. 1.
Apr. 28-May 2 (1769)	June 26 (1769), p. 1.
N.Y. Journal	
May 3-10 (1769)	June 22 (1769), supplement, p. 1.
May 12-19 (1769)	June 29 (1769), supplement, p. 1.
May 20-28 (1769)	July 6 (1769), supplement, p. 1.
May 29-June 12 (1769)	July 13 (1769), supplement, pp. 1-2.

June 13-25 (1769)	July 20 (1769), supplement, pp. 1-2.
June 26-July 5 (1769)	July 27 (1769), supplement, p. 1.
July 8-17 (1769)	Aug. 24 (1769), supplement, p. 1.
	Bos. Even. Post
July 18-24 (1769)	Sept. 25 (1769), p. 1.
July 25, 28-30 (1769)	Oct. 2 (1769), pp. 1-2.
	N.Y. Journal
Aug. 1 (1769)	Nov. 30 (1769), supplement, pp. 1-2.

November 24

Resistance to New York's Quartering Act. New York City's freemen instruct their four representatives to the upcoming General Assembly to exert themselves against any compliance with the Quartering Act. What is the difference, they ask rhetorically, between direct taxation by Parliament or a tax voted by the colony's representatives under compulsion? The delegates are also directed to read and answer the Massachusetts Circular Letter despite the governor's threat of consequent dissolution of the assembly.

N.Hamp. Gaz. Dec. 23, p. 2.
Newpt. Merc. Dec. 5/12, p. 3.
N.Y. Journal Dec. 1, p. 1.
Pa. Gaz. Dec. 8, p. 3.
Md. Gaz. Dec. 22, pp. 1-2.
Ga. Gaz. Jan 11 (1769), pp. 1-2.

December 24

Georgia Endorses the Massachusetts Circular Letter. Georgia's Commons House Of Assembly endorses both the Massachusetts Circular Letter and Virginia's letter of approval of the Circular Letter. The Assembly proceeds to transmit its endorsement to Massachusetts and Virginia and to compose an address to King George in support of both communications' sentiments. Governor James Wright immediately dissolves the Assembly; scoffs at the internal-external taxation dichotomy as "a distinction without a difference"; and warns the legislators that if America achieves independence, "from that day you might date the foundation of your ruin and misery."

Bos. Gaz. Feb. 13 (1769), p. 1.
N.Y. Journal Feb. 9 (1769), pp. 1-2; Oct. 26 (1769), p.2.
Pa. Gaz. Feb. 16 (1769), pp. 2-3.
Va. Gaz. (Purdie and Dixon) Feb. 2 (1769), p. 2; Mar. 9 (1769), p. 2.
Ga. Gaz. Nov. 16, p. 2; Nov. 23, pp. 2-3; Dec. 28, p. 1.

American Philosophical Society
Organization of
Pa. Gaz. Jan. 28, p. 2; Mar. 17, pp. 1, 4;
Mar. 24, p. 3; Mar. 31, p. 3.

Astronomical Phenomena
Transit of Venus
Pa. Gaz. Nov. 10, pp. 2-3.

Capital Punishment
For any type of theft?
Conn. Courant Aug. 22, p. 4.

Church of England
Speculation regarding establishment of
American episcopate
Va. Gaz. (Purdie and Dixon) Oct. 27, p. 2.

Currency
Lack of in Pennsylvania
Pa. Gaz. Jan. 14, p. 2.

Diseases
Small-pox
Va. Gaz. (Purdie and Dixon) Jan. 21, p. 3.

Drunkenness
Character of a sot
Ga. Gaz. Jan. 27, p. 3.

Georgia
Complies with Mutiny Act
Va. Gaz. (Purdie and Dixon) Jan. 7, pp.
2-3.

Guy Fawkes Day
Explanation of
Broadside: [1768]

Inventions
Furnace with self-regulating register
Pa. Gaz. July 7, p. 3.

Lightning
Strikes three boys in Pennsylvania
Newpt. Merc. Aug. 29/Sept. 5, pp. 1-2.

Mathematics
Magic square noted
Pa. Gaz. Sept. 1, p. 1.

Newspapers
Freedom of the press: essays on importance
Bos. Gaz. Mar. 14, p. 2.
Va. Gaz. (Purdie and Dixon) Jan. 7, p. 3.

Orrery (Planetarium)
Description of
Pa. Gaz. May 5, p. 1.

Rittenhouse, David (American astronomer and
mathematician)
Orrery of described
Pa. Gaz. May 5, p. 1.

Roman Catholics
Anti-Catholocism: anti-papacy reflections
Newpt. Merc. Aug. 29/Sept. 5, p. 2.

Songs
Massachusetts Song of Liberty
Bos. Gaz. Oct. 3, p. 2.

Tea
Injurious to health
Newpt. Merc. Dec. 5/12, p. 1.

Theater
Ad for
N.Y. Journal Feb. 4, p. 3.
Evils of debated
N.Y. Journal Jan. 7, p. 2; Jan. 14, p. 2;
Jan. 21, p. 1; Jan. 28, pp. 1-2; Feb. 4, p.
3; Feb. 11, p. 1; Feb. 18, pp. 1-2; Mar.
3, p. 1.

Vesuvius
Eruption of in Italy
Pa. Gaz. Mar. 31, p. 1.

December 28, 1768—January 2

New York Endorses the Massachusetts Circular Letter. New York's General Assembly answers both the Massachusetts Circular Letter and Virginia's complementary letter. The Assembly votes £1800 for the army's supplies and then proceeds to the consideration of an address to the King regarding their rights; at this point Governor Moore dissolves the Assembly.

N.Hamp. Gaz. Jan. 20, pp. 2-3.
Newpt. Merc. Jan. 9/16, p. 3.
Conn. Courant Jan. 9, p. 3.
N.Y. Journal Jan. 12, pp. 1-2; Apr. 13, p. 1.
Pa. Gaz. [Jan. 5], postscript extraordinary, p. 1.
Md. Gaz. Jan. 19, p. 2; Feb. 16, p. 2.
Ga. Gaz. Feb. 1, p. 2; Feb. 15, p. 1; Feb. 22, p. 1.

February 8

Parliament Reacts to Colonial Reactions. The House of Commons, after lengthy debate and the addition of certain amendments, concurs with strongly worded House of Lords resolutions regarding disorders and denials of parliamentary and crown authority in Massachusetts, particularly Boston. A related directive to Governor Bernard to apprehend any and all who have committed acts of treason in Massachusetts since December 17, 1767, is the occasion of angry denunciation in America because of a stipulation that said individuals are to be sent to England for trial, according to a statute of Henry VIII.

N.Hamp. Gaz. Mar. 24, pp. 2-3; Apr.14, pp. 2-3.
Newpt. Merc. Apr. 10/17, p. 1.
Conn. Courant Apr. 24, p. 3.
N.Y. Journal Mar. 23, p. 2; Apr. 28, supplement extraordinary, pp. 1-2; May 4, supplement, p. 1.
Pa. Gaz. Mar. 2, p. 3; Mar. 23, p. 2; Mar. 30, p. 2; Apr. 6, p. 2; Apr. 20, p. 2.
Md. Gaz. May 18, pp. 2-3.
Va. Gaz. (Purdie and Dixon) Mar. 23, pp. 2-3.
Ga. Gaz. May 10, p. 2; May 17, pp. 1-2; June 7, p. 1.

September 1768—May

More Reaction to Colonial Circumstances. Various English and colonial reactions to the colonies' problems, especially Boston's situation, are given widespread and eager attention in America.

N.Hamp. Gaz. Jan. 27, p. 2; Feb. 3, pp. 1-2, 3; Feb. 17, p. 1; Feb. 24, pp. 1-2; Mar. 3, pp. 1-2; Mar. 17, pp. 1-2; Mar. 24, p. 1; Apr. 7, pp. 1-2.
Conn. Courant Feb. 20, p. 3; Feb. 27, p. 1; Mar. 6, p. 1; Mar. 13, p. 1.
N.Y. Journal Sept. 29 (1768), pp. 2-3; Oct. 20 (1768), pp. 2-3; May 11, p. 1; May 25, p. 1; June 1, p. 1; July 27, p. 1.

Pa. Gaz. Oct. 13 (1768), p. 3; Nov. 24 (1768), p. 2; Dec. 8 (1768), p. 2; Jan. 5, p. 2; Feb. 2, p. 3; Feb. 9, pp. 2, 3; Feb. 16, p. 3; Feb. 23, p. 3; Mar. 30, pp. 2-3; Apr. 13, p. 3; Apr. 20, pp. 2, 3.
Md. Gaz. Feb. 2, p. 2; Mar. 2, p. 1; Mar. 9, p. 1; Mar. 16, p. 1.
Va. Gaz. (Purdie and Dixon) Oct. 6 (1768), p. 1; Feb. 9, pp. 1-2; Feb. 23, p. 2; Mar. 9, p. 1; May 25, p. 1.
Ga. Gaz. Mar. 1, p. 3; Apr. 26, p. 1; May 3, p. 3; June 7, p. 3; June 14, pp. 2, 3; June 28, p. 1; July 5, p. 1.

March 10

Philadelphia Merchants Join in Non-Importation. Philadelphia's merchants finally agree on a non-importation plan to prohibit most British goods after April 1, 1769. Criticism of their previous lack of patriotism by fellow Americans in Philadelphia and Pennsylvania, and in the other colonies, is responsible for their conversion.

N.Hamp. Gaz. Mar. 31, p. 4.
Bos. Gaz. May 22, p. 2.
Newpt. Merc. May 29, p. 2.
Pa. Gaz. Aug. 31, p. 1.
Ga. Gaz. June 14, p. 2.

June 1767—March 25, 1769

South Carolina Regulators. America's "first large-scale vigilante movement" centers in the South Carolina backcountry where grievances abound, including want of an adequate court system, lack of protection against roving outlaw gangs, and underrepresentation in the colony's General Assembly. Backcountry men of property join together in August 1767 to eliminate or "regulate" the outlaws. After a time the Regulators begin such a thoroughgoing moral rehabilitation of their society and local miscreants (both real and imagined) that by 1769 a reaction has set in against them. By late March 1769, an accommodation is reached in the backcountry, but for all their local successes the Regulators still do not enjoy county courts: the South Carolina General Assembly passes only a Circuit Court Act (1768).

Conn. Courant Sept. 14 (1767), p. 4.
Pa. Gaz. Sept. 10 (1767), p. 2; Dec. 17 (1767), p. 2; Nov. 24 (1768), p. 2; Dec. 22 (1768), p. 2.
Md. Gaz. Dec. 22 (1768), p. 1.
S.C. Gaz. July 27/Aug. 3 (1767), p. 3; Aug. 10/17 (1767), p. 3; Oct. 12/19 (1767), p. 2; Nov. 2/9 (1767), pp. 1, 3; Apr. 11/18 (1768), p. 2; June 13 (1768), p. 3; July 11 (1768), p. 2; July 25 (1768), p. 3; Aug. 8 (1768), pp. 1, 2; Aug. 15 (1768), p. 2; Aug. 22 (1768), p. 2; Sept. 12 (1768), p. 3; Sept. 26 (1768), p. 3; Oct. 10 (1768), p. 2; Oct. 17 (1768), p. 3; Oct. 31 (1768), p. 4; Dec. 8 (1768), p. 2; Mar. 16 (1769), p. 2; Mar. 23 (1769), p. 3; Apr. 6 (1769), p. 2.

Ga. Gaz. Aug. 12 (1767), p. 3; Nov. 25 (1767), p. 2; Nov. 30 (1768), pp. 1-2; Apr. 5 (1769), p. 3; July 19 (1769), p. 1.

March 30

Baltimore Merchants Agree to Non-Importation. Baltimore merchants adopt a non-importation scheme similar to Philadelphia's.

January—May

Non-Importation Requires Encouragement. Non-importation in Boston and New York requires continuous vigilance because of violations of the plan and a certain few non-subscribers who remain stubborn in the fact of various forms of pressure: public ostracism, highlighted by personal identification in the cooperative colonial newspapers; boycotts of offending merchants, under the direction of the local Sons of Liberty; and direct confrontation by subscribers and local men of prominence. Boston and New York maintain a wary eye on each other in order to ensure that neither city's merchants will subordinate the common interest to personal and/or colony gain at the expense of other merchants and colonies.

N.Hamp. Gaz. May 19, p. 2.
Bos. Gaz. Apr. 24, p. 3; May 22, p. 2.
Newpt. Merc. May 15, pp. 2-3; May 22, p. 3.
N.Y. Journal Apr. 13, p. 3; May 4, p. 3; May 25, p. 3; June 22, pp. 2-3.
Md. Gaz. June 1, p. 2.
Ga. Gaz. June 21, p. 2.

May 16-18

Virginia Resolves and Virginia Association. On May 16 the House of Burgesses votes unanimously for a series of resolutions drafted by George Mason and introduced by George Washington. The resolutions assert again the Burgesses' exclusive right to grant taxes in Virginia and attack the recent proposals in Parliament to bring colonists to England for trial. On May 17 the House reconvenes and adopts a letter to George III based on the Resolves and drawn up by Patrick Henry and Richard Henry Lee. Governor Botetourt promptly dissolves the General Assembly whereupon most of the Burgesses adjourn to the Raleigh Tavern. A proposal by George Mason for a Virginia Association is considered. On May 18 the Association, an agreement not to import a lengthy list of British and European goods after September 1, nor to import slaves after November 1, is signed by eighty-eight Burgesses. Copies circulate throughout the colony and the list of signatories grows.

N.Hamp. Gaz. June 16, p. 1.
Bos. Gaz. June 12, supplement, pp. 1-2.
N.Y. Journal June 1, pp. 2-3; July 20, supplement, pp. 1-2.
Pa. Gaz. June 1, pp. 1-2; June 22, p. 1.
Md. Gaz. May 25, pp. 2-3.
Va. Gaz. (Purdie and Dixon) May 11, supplement, pp. 1, 4; May 18, p. 2; May 25, p. 1.
S.C. Gaz. June 29, p. 3; July 20, p. 4.
Ga. Gaz. July 5, pp. 2-3.

June 22

Soon, a Maryland Association. A provincial convention meeting at Annapolis agrees upon a Maryland Association similar to the Virginia Association.

N.Hamp. Gaz. July 14, p. 1.
Newpt. Merc. July 17, p. 3.
N.Y. Journal July 6, p. 3.
Pa. Gaz. June 29, p. 2.
Md. Gaz. June 29, p. 2.
S.C. Gaz. Aug. 10, p. 2.
Ga. Gaz. July 5, p. 3; Aug. 16, p. 1.

July 19

Liberty Burned. HM sloop *Liberty* is scuttled and subsequently burned by Rhode Islanders in retaliation for the ship's participation in a recent spate of seizures of customs violators in Rhode Island waters. (For the more famous burning of the *Gaspee*, see below, June 9, 1772.)

Newpt. Merc. July 24, p. 3; July 31, p. 3; Aug. 7, p. 3.
Conn. Courant July 31, p. 3.
N.Y. Journal July 27, p. 3.
Pa. Gaz. Aug. 3, p. 2.
Ga. Gaz. Aug. 30, p. 3.

July 22

And, a South Carolina Association. Nearly two months of effort in Charleston results in a South Carolina Association acceptable to mechanics and tradesmen as well as merchants.

Bos. Gaz. Aug. 7, p. 2; Aug. 14, p. 3; Aug. 21, p. 2.
Newpt. Merc. Aug. 7, p. 2.
N.Y. Journal Aug. 24, supplement, pp. 1-2; Aug. 31, p. 2.
S.C. Gaz. June 8, p. 3; June 22, pp. 1, 4; June 29, pp. 1, 3; July 6, pp. 1, 2; July 13, p. 1; July 20, p. 4; July 27, pp. 1, 2; Aug. 3, p. 1; Aug. 10, p. 3.
Ga. Gaz. July 19, p. 2.

June—December

Non-Importation Requires Vigilance. As non-importation associations spread throughout the colonies outside the major ports of Boston, New York, and Philadelphia, these three cities especially continue to find enforcement of their own non-importation plans a matter of enduring difficulty. Aside from purely local infractions or intransigence, the unpatriotic reluctance of the Providence and Newport merchants to reach any non-importation agreement among themselves serves both as an irritant and as a possible excuse for modification or abandonment of the economic self-denial practiced willingly, or not so willingly, by other colonial merchants and citizens. Adding to the pressures on the various associations is public knowledge of a May 13 communication from Lord Hillsborough to the colonial governors in which the Colonial Secretary describes the cabinet's intention to request Parliament to rescind all the Townshend duties except that on tea.

N.Hamp. Gaz. Sept. 1, p. 2; Nov. 17, p. 3.
Bos. Gaz. July 31, pp. 1, 2; Aug. 14, p. 2; Aug. 28, p. 1; Sept. 4, p. 3; Oct. 9, p. 1; Oct. 16, p. 1; Oct. 30, pp. 2, 3; Nov. 20, p. 1.
Newpt. Merc. July 31, p. 3; Aug. 14, p. 3; Aug. 21, p. 3; Oct. 16, p. 3; Nov. 27, p. 3; Dec. 11, p. 3; Jan. 1 (1770), p. 2.
Conn. Courant Sept. 25, p. 3; Nov. 6, p. 3; Nov. 13, p. 3; Jan 1 (1770), p. 3.
N.Y. Journal June 22, p. 1; July 27, p. 2; Oct. 26, p. 1.
Pa. Gaz. July 20, p. 3; Aug. 3, p. 3; Oct. 19, p. 2; Nov. 30, p. 3.
Md. Gaz. Oct. 12, p. 2; Oct. 26, p. 2; Nov. 23, p. 1; Dec. 28, pp. 1-2.
(N.B.) *N.C. Gaz.* Nov. 10, pp. 2-3.
S.C. Gaz. Sept. 14, p. 3; Sept. 21, p. 1; Oct. 5, p. 1; Nov. 14, p. 3.
Ga. Gaz. Aug. 23, p. 3; Jan. 3 (1770), p. 3; Jan. 10 (1770), p. 3.
Broadsides: June 21; June 23; July 20; July 21; Aug. 23; Sept. 18; Dec. 6.

August 19

South Carolina Resolves and Resistance. After a consideration of the Virginia Resolves, the South Carolina Commons House of Assembly adopts its own resolutions stipulating that only itself can tax South Carolinians. Further, the House asserts that inhabitants' trials are to be held in South Carolina, not overseas, and affirms its own right to petition the crown. On the same day the House votes against provisioning British troops in the province who, the representatives contend, are supposed to be stationed in St. Augustine, East Florida.

Newpt. Merc. Oct. 2, p. 2.
Pa. Gaz. Aug. 31, p. 2.
Md. Gaz. Sept. 21, p. 2.
S.C. Gaz. Aug. 24, p. 3; Aug. 31, pp. 1-2.
Ga. Gaz. Sept. 6, p. 3.

August 28

Non-Importation in Delaware. New Castle County, Delaware, draws up a non-importation compact.

Pa. Gaz. Aug. 31, p. 3.
S.C. Gaz. Oct. 12, pp. 1-2.

September 19

Georgia Association. After Savannah merchants agree (September 16) on a plan of non-importation, a Georgia Association is created that copies the form of the South Carolina Association.

Pa. Gaz. Nov. 9, p. 1.
S.C. Gaz. Oct. 9, p. 1.
Ga. Gaz. Sept. 6, pp. 1, 3, 4; Sept. 13, p. 3; Sept. 20, p. 3.

October 18

New Jersey Endorses Non-Importation. The New Jersey House of Assembly passes a resolution that offers thanks for and an endorsement of non-importation agreements entered into by New Jersey, New York, and Pennsylvania merchants until the Parliamentary acts for revenue purposes, chiefly the Townshend duties, are repealed.

Newpt. Merc. Nov. 13, p. 3.
N.Y. Journal Oct. 26, pp. 1, 3.
Pa. Gaz. Oct. 26, p. 3; Nov. 9, p. 3.

October 24

Providence Gives in to Non-Importation. Under continuing pressure the Providence merchants reach a non-importation agreement.

Bos. Gaz. Oct. 16, p. 2.
Newpt. Merc. Oct. 30, p. 3.
Conn. Courant Nov. 13, p. 2.
Pa. Gaz. Nov. 16, p. 2.
Ga. Gaz. Nov. 29, p. 2.

October 30

Newport Follows, Hesitantly. Newport finally adopts a (weak) plan for non-importation.

Bos. Gaz. Oct. 30, p. 3.
Newpt. Merc. May 29, p. 3; Aug. 21, p. 3; Nov. 6, p. 3; Nov. 13, p. 1; Nov. 27, p. 3.
N.Y. Journal Dec. 21, p. 2.
Pa. Gaz. Nov. 16, pp. 2-3.
Ga. Gaz. Nov. 29, p. 2.

November 7

North Carolina Association. A North Carolina Association is adopted by an informal con-

New-York, September 18, 1769.

ADVERTISEMENT.

WE are forry to acquaint the Public, that *Thomas Richardfon*, Jeweller, lately from London, now living in the Houfe of Mr. *Thomas Grigg*, Cabinet Maker, has knowingly and wilfully, fubjected himfelf to the legal Refentment of every Friend to *Great-Britain* and the Colonies, by a direct and open Oppofition to the Terms of the Non-Importation Agreement. It was hoped that the Treatment fome Capital Offenders met with, would have deterred the moft obftinate and daring from attempting to imitate Examples fo inglorious and dangerous. The Particulars of his Conduct are as follows :---He brought with him, and privately introduced into this City, Jewellery, and Materials for his Bufinefs to a confiderable Amount, which he expofed to Sale at his Shop Window; the Committee being apprized of this, fent for him, and defired him to ftore his Goods; but as he urged his immediate Want of Cafh as an Argument againft his Compliance, the Committee engaged to ufe their Influence in procuring him a Sum that would have more than compenfated for the trifling Lofs he might have fuftained by fuffering in common with all who had imported or received Goods contrary to Agreement ;---a temporary Storage of them. This generous Offer he refufed to accept of, and ambitious of diftinguifhing himfelf as an Enemy to the glorious Caufe of Liberty, obftinately perfifts in refolving to difpofe of them.

See p. 26, June-December,   Broadside: Sept. 18.

vention of assemblymen after Governor William Tryon's dissolution of the assembly for its endorsement of the Virginia Resolves.

Pa. Journal Jan 18 (1770), p. 4; Jan. 25 (1770), p. 1.
Md. Gaz. Jan. 25 (1770), p. 2.
S.C. Gaz. Dec. 8, supplement, pp. 1, 4.
Ga. Gaz. Dec. 27, p. 2.

December

New York Adopts the Virginia Resolves. The New York General Assembly concurs with and adopts the Virginia Resolves.

N.Y. Journal Dec. 7, p. 3.
Ga. Gaz. Jan. 3 (1770), p. 3.

December 16

A New York Son of Liberty Protests Compliance with Quartering Act. One day after the New York General Assembly votes an appropriation of £2000 for troop supplies, Sons of Liberty leader Alexander McDougall authors a broadside to "The Betrayed Inhabitants of the City and Colony of New York." This effort and a companion work by McDougall against the compliance with the Quartering Act prompt the assembly's wrath and a search by the colony authorities for the miscreant.

Bos. Gaz. Jan. 1 (1770), pp. 2-3; Jan. 8 (1770), p. 2.
Newpt. Merc. Jan. 1 (1770), p. 3.
Pa. Gaz. Dec. 28, pp. 2-3.
Md. Gaz. Jan. 4 (1770), p. 2; Jan. 18 (1770), p. 1.
Ga. Gaz. Feb. 14 (1770), p. 3.
Broadsides: Dec. 16, 20; Dec. 20.

Astronomical Phenomena
  Comets
    N.Hamp. Gaz. Sept. 29, pp. 1-2; Oct. 6, p. 1.
    Newpt. Merc. Sept. 25, p. 3.
    Conn. Courant Sept. 4, p. 2; Sept. 11, p. 1; Sept. 18, p. 1; Oct. 16, p. 1; Oct. 23, pp. 1-2; Oct. 30, pp. 1, 3; Nov. 6, p.1.
  Transit of Mercury
    Newpt. Merc. Dec. 4, pp. 2-3.
  Transit of Venus
    Newpt. Merc. June 5, p. 3; June 19, p. 3.
    Ga. Gaz. Aug. 16, p. 1.

Boundary
  New York-New Jersey settled
    Conn. Courant Oct. 16, p. 2.

Colleges
  Harvard, home manufactures endorsed
    Bos. Gaz. Sept. 4, p. 3.
  King's commencement
    N.Y. Journal May 25, p. 3.
  Rhode Island College (Brown) commencement
    Newpt. Merc. Sept. 11, p. 3.

Crime
  Georgia grand jury presentments
    Ga. Gaz. July 19, p. 3.

Customs
  New fee schedule challenged in Newport
    Newpt. Merc. Oct. 9, p. 3.

Dueling
  Dreadful effects of
    Ga. Gaz. Oct. 25, p. 1.

Guy Fawkes Day
  Celebration of
    Newpt. Merc. Nov. 20, p. 3.

Newspapers
  Subscribers' accounts in arrears
    Conn. Courant Nov. 6, p. 3.

Orphan House (Savannah)
  Noticed in orphans' memorial
    Ga. Gaz. Apr. 5, p. 1.

Poetry
  "On Liberty Tree"
    S.C. Gaz. Sept. 21, p. 2.

Pontiac
  Death of: French blame English
    Bos. Gaz. Aug. 28, p. 3.

Slaves
  Sales of
    S.C. Gaz. Sept. 21, p. 3.

Theater
  Ad for
    Md. Gaz. Mar. 9, p. 2.

Toothache
  Cure for
    Newpt. Merc. July 24, p. 3.

Women
  Patriotism of
    S.C. Gaz. Oct. 5, p. 1.

January 13-19

Battle of Golden Hill. A prelude to the more celebrated Boston Massacre occurs in New York City on January 19 when a long simmering competition between the local Sons of Liberty and garrisoned British troops over the fate of the former's Liberty Pole results in a riot on Golden Hill. Unlike the Boston Massacre, no one is killed in the scuffle and the affair is treated in the colonial press with very little sustained interest. (See above, August 10-11, 1766.)

Bos. Gaz. Feb. 5, p. 2; Feb. 19, supplement, pp. 1-2.
N.Y. Journal Jan. 18, p. 3; Jan. 25, p. 3; Feb. 8, p. 3; Mar. 1, supplement, pp. 1-2.
Pa. Journal Jan. 25, p. 3; Feb. 1, p. 2.
Va. Gaz. (Purdie and Dixon) Feb. 22, pp. 1-2.
S.C. Gaz. Feb. 15, p. 2.
Ga. Gaz. Feb. 21, p. 2; Feb. 28, p. 2; Mar. 28, pp. 1-2; Apr. 4, pp. 2-3.

January 29-30

North Succeeds Chatham and Grafton. The Duke of Grafton resigns as First Lord of the Treasury, ending the Pitt/Chatham-Grafton ministry (1766-1770). Grafton is succeeded by Lord North whose ministry (1770-1782) is destined to oversee the dissolution of the First English Empire. (North's title is a courtesy from George II. Not until 1790 will the former prime minister become the second Earl of Guilford.)

Newpt. Merc. Apr. 23, p. 2.
Pa. Journal Apr. 26, p. 2.
Ga. Gaz. Apr. 11, p. 3; Apr. 18, p. 3.

February

Alexander McDougall, Patriot. Arrested on February 8, the radical Alexander McDougall moves quickly to fill the role of an American John Wilkes, that contemporary English printer and politician whose unrestrained criticism of King George's administration and the king himself had gained Wilkes jail, temporary exile, and notoriety on both sides of the Atlantic. (Wilkes-Barre, Pennsylvania is named in honor of John Wilkes and a champion of the colonies in the House of Commons, Colonel Isaac Barre.) McDougall's letters (February 9, 24) to the inhabitants of New York, City and County, continue his assault on the lower house of the New York General Assembly. His initial stay in jail is ended when he is released on bail, April 28, after finally entering his plea — not guilty. (The frequent allusion to the number forty-five comes from the number of Wilkes' newspaper, *The North Briton*, in which he reminded King

George of his responsibility to the people, an unappreciated admonition which resulted in Wilkes' arrest. An interesting commentary on New York's current political situation is contained in the widely-reprinted series of letters entitled "The Watchman," which are noted in the following citations.)

Bos. Gaz. (Watchman No. 1) Feb. 26, pp. 1-2; Feb. 26, supplement, p. 2; (Watchman No. 2) Mar. 19, supplement, pp. 1-2; (Watchman No. 3) Apr. 9, pp. 1, 4.
Newpt. Merc. Feb. 19, p. 3.
N.Y. Journal Feb. 15, pp. 1-2, 2-3; Mar. 8, supplement, pp. 1-2; Mar. 22, p. 3; Mar. 29, p. 3; May 3, p. 3.
Pa. Journal Feb. 1, pp. 1-2; Feb. 22, pp. 1-2.
Va. Gaz. (Purdie and Dixon) Mar. 22, p. 2.
S.C. Gaz. May 17, supplement, pp. 3-4.
Ga. Gaz. Apr. 25, p. 1.

March 5

Boston Massacre. Taunted by a jeering mob, a British army contingent under command of Captain Thomas Preston fires on the crowd, killing five and wounding others. The Boston radicals take advantage of the Massacre by depicting it as part of a deliberate plot to murder patriots. On March 6, Preston and six of his soldiers are arrested for murder. (Their trials take place in October; see below, October 24-30.) An immediate result of the Massacre is a growing unease among the mercantile elements of the other cities in the colonies about their liaison with the unruly Boston mob. The date of the Massacre itself serves the Boston patriots well as an anniversary, an occasion to be celebrated with inflammatory rhetoric and expressions of protest against British policies.

Bos. Gaz. Mar. 12, pp. 2-3; Mar. 19, pp. 2, 3; Apr. 9, p. 3; May 28, p. 3.
Newpt. Merc. Mar. 12, pp. 2-3.
Conn. Courant Mar. 19, pp. 1-3; Apr. 16, p. 3.
N.Y. Journal Mar. 15, p. 3; Apr. 5, pp. 1-2.
Pa. Journal Apr. 26, supplement, p. 2.
Md. Gaz. Apr. 5, pp. 1-2.
Va. Gaz. (Purdie and Dixon) Apr. 5, pp. 2-3.
S.C. Gaz. Apr. 5, pp. 1-2.
Ga. Gaz. Apr. 11, pp. 2, 4; Apr. 25, p. 1.
Broadside: undated poem on five victims.

January—April

Non-Importation Requires More Encouragement and Vigilance. The inherent difficulties associated with maintaining the various local non-importation agreements are compounded during the early months of the year when continuing rumors of a repeal of all the protested duties except that on tea circulate throughout the colonies. Barely submerged jealousies and mistrust between the principal American ports, especially among Boston, New York, Philadelphia, and Newport, call for continued manifestations of good will and intentions to carry on the good efforts. Numerous smaller towns pass their own resolutions of support for non-importation.

Bos. Gaz. Jan. 22, p. 3; Jan. 29, pp. 1-2; Mar. 19, supplement, p. 2; Mar. 26, pp. 1, 3.
Conn. Courant Mar. 5, p. 1.
N.Y. Journal Jan. 4, p. 3; Feb. 1, p. 3; Mar. 1, p. 1.
Pa. Journal Jan. 18, p. 3; Feb. 8, pp. 1-2; Feb. 15, pp. 2-3.
Md. Gaz. Feb. 15, p. 2; Feb. 22, p. 2; Mar. 15, pp. 2-3; Apr. 12, p. 2.
Va. Gaz. (Purdie and Dixon) Mar. 22, pp. 2-3.
S.C. Gaz. Feb. 1, p. 2; Feb. 15, p. 3; Mar. 8, p. 1; Mar. 29, p. 2; Apr. 4, supplement, p. 1.
Ga. Gaz. Feb. 14, p. 3.
Broadsides: undated Boston Sons of Liberty against importer; undated Philadelphia recantation by importers for violations.

March 5

Repeal of the Townshend Duties, Except.... On the same day as the Boston Massacre, Lord North proposes the repeal of all the Townshend duties except that on tea. (Previous duties on such as wine, sugar, and molasses are retained.) King George gives his assent to partial repeal on April 12.

Bos. Gaz. Apr. 30, p. 2.
Conn. Courant Apr. 30, p. 3.
N.Y. Journal May 10, p. 6.
Pa. Journal Apr. 19, p. 3; May 7, postscript, pp. 1-2.
Va. Gaz. (Purdie and Dixon) May 24, p. 2.
S.C. Gaz. Apr. 19, p. 1; Apr. 24, supplement, p. 3.
Ga. Gaz. May 2, p. 2.

April—September

Incomplete Repeal Accentuates Colonial Divisions. Word of the repeal of all the Townshend duties except that on tea leads to a growing division in the colonies between those who wish to retain non-importation until all revenue duties are repealed and those who would accept North's handiwork as a creditable compromise and accordingly bring the boycott of British goods to an end.

Bos. Gaz. May 14, p. 3; May 28, p. 2; June 4, p. 4; July 2, p. 2; July 16, p. 2; July 23, pp. 1-2; July 30, p. 2.
Newpt. Merc. Apr. 30, p. 3; May 21, p. 3; June 7, postscript, p. 1; July 9, pp. 2-3.
Conn. Courant June 11, p. 3; July 16, pp. 2, 4; July 30, p. 3; Aug. 13, pp. 2-3; Aug. 20, pp. 1, 2; Aug. 27, pp. 1, 3; Sept. 3, p. 3; Sept. 17, pp. 2-3.

N.Y. Journal May 17, p. 3; May 24, pp. 3, 6; June 7, p. 2; June 21, pp. 2-3; July 5, p. 3; July 19, p. 5.
Pa. Journal May 10, pp. 2, 3; May 17, p. 4; May 24, p. 2; June 7, pp. 2, 3; June 14, p. 2; June 28, p. 1.
Md. Gaz. May 3, p. 2; May 10, p. 3; May 24, pp. 2-3; June 14, p. 2; June 21, p. 2; July 12, p. 2.
Va. Gaz. (Purdie and Dixon) June 7, p. 1; June 14, p. 1.
S.C. Gaz. May 17, supplement, pp. 1-2, 4; May 24, p. 2; May 24, supplement, p. 1; May 31, pp. 1, 2; June 21, p. 3; June 28, p. 2; July 12, pp. 1-2; July 26, p. 3; Aug. 9, p. 6; Aug. 16, pp. 1, 2; Aug. 20, supplement, pp. 1-2; Aug. 23, p. 1; Aug. 30, continuation, pp. 2, 3.
Broadside: May 30.

May

Rhode Island Defections Cause Colonial Reaction. Newport and Providence merchants are the first defectors from the colonial ranks after news of the partial repeal of the Townshend duties reaches America. The response of their fellow colonies is an outpouring of rebukes, threats of ostracism, and a prohibition of intercolonial trade with Rhode Island by Boston, New York City, Philadelphia, Delaware, Maryland, Charleston, and various other colonial towns (May-June). Strenuous countermeasures among Rhode Island patriots result in a reimposition of the non-importation agreement in Newport (August 20), with the condition that all other colonies must pariticpate in the program, and a reopening of trade between Newport and Boston (September) and Newport and Charleston (October 20).

Bos. Gaz. May 28, p. 2; June 4, p. 4; June 11, p. 2; June 25, p. 2; July 23, p. 1.
Newpt. Merc. June 4, p. 3; June 11, p. 3.
Conn. Courant June 11, pp. 2, 4; July 16, p. 4; Aug. 27, p. 3; Sept. 3, p. 3.
N.Y. Journal May 31, pp. 2-3; June 7, pp. 2, 3; June 14, p. 3.
Pa. Journal May 24, p. 3; June 7, pp. 2, 3; June 14, p. 2; June 28, p. 1; Sept. 20, p. 3.
Md. Gaz. May 31, pp. 2-3; June 7, p. 2; June 14, p. 2; Sept. 20, p. 2.
Va. Gaz. (Purdie and Dixon) June 14, p. 2.
S.C. Gaz. June 21, p. 1; June 28, p. 3; July 12, p. 3; Aug. 16, p. 1; Sept. 27, p. 3; Oct. 25, p. 3.

May—June

New Hampshire and Georgia Feel Similar Reactions. New Hampshire, the only colony never to subscribe to a non-importation agreement, is specifically closed to trade in June by Boston and Connecticut. Georgia's open violations of its September 19, 1769, Association causes Charleston to end all commerce with it on June 27.

[January, 1770]
_[1773(?)]_

WILLIAM JACKSON,

an _IMPORTER_; at the

BRAZEN HEAD,

North Side of the TOWN-HOUSE,

and _Opposite_ the _Town-Pump, in_

Corn-hill, BOSTON.

It is defired that the Sons and
DAUGHTERS of _LIBERTY,_
would not buy any one thing of
him, for in fo doing they will bring
Difgrace upon _themfelves,_ and their
Pofterity, for _ever_ and _ever,_ AMEN.

See p. 30, January-April,   Broadside: Undated Boston Sons of Liberty.

N.Hamp. Gaz. June 15, pp. 2, 3; June 22, p. 3; July 6, pp. 1, 3; July 13, pp. 1, 4.
Bos. Gaz. June 25, p. 3; July 23, p. 1.
Conn. Courant June 11, p. 2; July 2, p. 3.
S.C. Gaz. May 17, supplement, pp. 1-2; June 21, p. 1; June 28, p. 3.

June—July

New York City Hedges on Non-Importation. Despite constant encouragements to hold the line on non-importation until the tea duties as well as any other revenue duties are repealed, the first major American city to compromise on the issue is New York. Sure of the duplicity of its sister colonies (especially merchants in Boston and Philadelphia), frightened of the mob violence easily orchestrated by the radicals, and faced with the continued prospect of empty coffers, the New York merchants move for a door-to-door poll of the city (July 7-9). The result is a change in the New York agreement: all goods may be imported from Great Britain except tea and any other merchandise which carries a duty for revenue. A short-lived movement for a return to non-importation in New York serves only to illustrate the divisions inherent in New York society. The reaction of New York's fellow colonies is indeed blistering: Connecticut even ends trade with New York City (August 4).

Bos. Gaz. June 25, p. 2; July 2, p. 2; July 16, pp. 2-3; July 23, pp. 1, 2, 3; July 30, pp. 1, 2, 3; Oct. 8, p. 1.
Bos. Even. Post Dec. 24, p. 2.
Newpt. Merc. May 28, p. 3; July 9, p. 3.
Conn. Courant July 16, pp. 2, 4; July 23, pp. 1-2; July 30, pp. 1-2, 4; Aug. 6, p. 3; Aug. 13, p. 3; Oct. 2, p. 4.
N.Y. Journal June 7, p. 3; June 21, p. 3; June 28, p. 1; July 5, p. 3; July 12, p. 1; July 19, pp. 1, 2-3; July 26, pp. 1, 3, 5; Aug. 2, pp. 1-2, 3; Aug. 9, p. 1.
Pa. Journal June 21, p. 3; June 28, p. 1; July 12, p. 3; July 12, postscript, p. 1.
Md. Gaz. July 19, p. 2; Aug. 9, pp. 2-3; Aug. 23, p. 2.
Va. Gaz. (Purdie and Dixon) June 7, p. 1.
S.C. Gaz. Aug. 9, p. 7; Aug. 16, pp. 2-3; Aug. 20, supplement, pp. 1-2; Aug. 23, p. 1; Aug. 30, continuation, pp. 1-2; Sept. 6, p. 1.
Broadside: July 7.

September

Philadelphia Compromises. The colonies' facade of unity continues to come apart as Philadelphia's merchants succumb to the argument (September 12, 14) that non-importation is ineffectual and should be altered. A general meeting (September 20) of the subscribers to Philadelphia's boycott of British goods votes to follow New York's example and its modified non-importation scheme. As in New York op-position in Philadelphia is quick — and itself ineffectual.

Bos. Gaz. Sept. 17, p. 2; Oct. 1, pp. 2-3.
Conn. Courant Oct. 2, p. 2.
N.Y. Journal Sept. 27, p. 2; Oct. 4, p. 6.
Pa. Journal Sept. 20, p. 3; Sept. 27, p. 3; Oct. 4, p. 3.
Md. Gaz. Oct. 11, p. 2; Nov. 1, p. 2.
S.C. Gaz. Oct. 18, p. 4; Oct. 25, pp. 1-3.
Broadsides: Sept. 24; Sept. 25; Sept. 27.

October 12

And Boston, Too, Succumbs. Unable to continue alone in its designs against British imports, Boston's merchants quietly and without significant opposition modify their non-importation policy along the same lines as New York and Philadelphia.

Bos. Gaz. Oct. 15, p. 2.
Conn. Courant Oct. 23, p. 2.
N.Y. Journal Oct. 18, p. 3.
Pa. Journal Oct. 25, p. 2.
Va. Gaz. (Purdie and Dixon) Nov. 1, p. 2.

October 24-30

Boston Massacre Trial. Captain Thomas Preston stands trial for his alleged participation in the Boston Massacre. Ably defended by two staunch patriots, John Adams, the future second President of the United States, and Josiah Quincy, Jr., Preston is acquitted of all charges. In early December Preston's command of eight soldiers is likewise tried: six are acquitted and two found guilty of manslaughter. The latter pair claim benefit of clergy — their ability to read enables them to plead they are "clerks" and thus exempt from secular jurisdiction — and suffer branding on the thumb after which they are released. Writing in the *Boston Gazette* in December 1770 and January 1771 under the pseudonym "Vindex," Sam Adams, the firebrand patriot, rakes over the testimony, finds incriminating evidence, and argues the merits of the case with "Philanthrop" (Attorney General Jonathan Sewall). The latter's counter-arguments about the trial appear in the *Boston Evening Post.*

Bos. Gaz. Nov. 5, p. 2; Dec. 10, p. 3; Dec. 17, pp. 1, 3; Dec. 24, pp. 1-2; Dec. 31, pp. 2-3; Jan. 7 (1771), pp. 1-2; Jan. 14 (1771), p. 1; Jan. 21 (1771), pp. 2-3; Jan. 28 (1771), p. 3; Mar. 4 (1771), p. 2.
Bos. Even. Post. Dec. 24, p. 1; Jan. 14 (1771), pp. 1-2; Jan. 28 (1771), p. 2; Feb. 4 (1771), pp. 1, 2; Feb. 11 (1771), p. 2; Feb. 18 (1771), pp. 1-2.
Conn. Courant Dec. 4, p. 3.
Pa. Journal Nov. 15, p. 3.
Va. Gaz. (Rind) Nov. 29, p. 1.

December 13

South Carolina Unhappily Compromises Non-Importation. Bitterly blaming Northern merchants for the termination of economic opposition to the British ministerial policies — but specifically exonerating Northern freeholders, landholders, farmers, and mechanics — South Carolina merchants follow the lead of their peers and end non-importation of all items except tea and other goods with duties attached. (Virginia does not abandon its own rather ineffective non-importation agreement until July 1771.)

S.C. Gaz. Oct. 4, p. 3; Nov. 1, p. 1; Dec. 13, p. 2; Dec. 27, p. 1.

Apprentices
   Wanted to chaise and harness maker
      Conn. Courant Apr. 9, p. 3.

Astronomical phenomena
   Aurora Borealis
      Conn. Courant Sept. 25, p. 1.
   Comets
      Conn. Courant July 16, p. 1.

Colleges
   College of New Jersey, solicitation of funds
   for
      S.C. Gaz. Feb. 15, p. 2; Mar. 8, p. 3.
   College of Philadelphia (Pennsylvania) com-
   mencement
      Pa. Journal June 14, p. 3; June 21, p. 4.
   Proposed for South Carolina
      S.C. Gaz. Mar. 8, p. 2.
   Rhode Island College
      Solicitation of funds for
         S.C. Gaz. Feb. 15, p. 2; Mar. 8, p. 3.
      Where to place?
         Newpt. Merc. Feb. 12, p. 3.

Crime
   Grand jury presentments
      S.C. Gaz. Jan. 25, p. 1.
   Murder
      Conn. Courant Oct. 23, p. 3; Oct. 30, p. 3
   Rape
      Conn. Courant Oct. 23, p. 2.
   Theft
      Conn. Courant Apr. 2, p. 4.
      S.C. Gaz. Mar. 15, p. 1.

Diseases
   Inoculations
      Conn. Courant Aug. 13, p. 3.
   Whooping-cough cure
      Conn. Courant July 16, p. 3.

Doctors
   Miracle oculist: Dr. Graham (*see also* Doctors, 1773)
      Md. Gaz. Jan. 25, p. 2.

Fables
   Regarding "True Born Son of Liberty"
   (political)
      Conn. Courant Apr. 30, p. 3.

Foundlings
      Conn. Courant Oct. 2, p. 4.

Housing
   Survey of in Philadelphia over twenty-year
   period
      Pa. Journal Jan 18, p. 3.

Humor
   Satire on importers
      Conn. Courant Aug. 20, p. 3.
   Satire on "Present State of Europe"
      Conn. Courant Nov. 6/13, p. 4.

Jefferson, Thomas
   House burns in Albermarle County, Virginia
      Va. Gaz. (Purdie and Dixon) Feb. 22, p. 3.

Jews
   Anti-Semitism: Jewish importers noted
      Bos. Gaz. May 28, p. 2.
      Pa. Journal June 7, p. 2.
   Georgia bill regarding burials of
      Ga. Gaz. Mar. 21, p. 1.

Lightning Rods
      Conn. Courant Aug. 20, p. 2; Sept. 10,
      pp. 1-2.

Marriage
   Husband announces non-support of wife; latter disputes
      Conn. Courant Sept. 10, p. 3; Sept. 25, p. 3.

Newspapers
   Paper shortage: rags desired
      Conn. Courant Mar. 19, p. 4.

Orphan House (Savannah)
   Descriptions of
      Ga. Gaz. Mar. 28, p. 3.

Pitt, William
   Statue of erected in Charleston (see text,
   May-June 1766)
      S.C. Gaz. May 24, p. 2; May 31, p. 3; July
      5, p. 3; July 10, p. 2.

Revere, Paul
   Ad as dentist
      Bos. Gaz. July 30, p. 3.

Roman Catholics
   Priest publicly exercises illegal ministry in
   Halifax, Nova Scotia
      Bos. Gaz. Nov. 19, p. 1.

Servants
    Ad for escaped
        Conn. Courant Apr. 9, p. 3.

Slaves
    Georgia bill governing
        Ga. Gaz. Mar. 21, p. 1.
    Insurrections
        N.Y. Journal Feb. 22, p. 2.

Theater
    Ad for *Tempest*
        Pa. Journal Jan. 18, p. 3.

Transportation
    Highway work protested
        Conn. Courant Oct. 30, p. 1.

Unusual Phenomena
    Child with taste for raw flesh
        Conn. Courant Aug. 27, p. 3.
    Ground sinking in Windsor, Connecticut
        Conn. Courant June 11, p. 3.

Voting
    Secret ballot protested
        N.Y. Journal Jan. 11, p. 1.

Whitefield, George
    Death of in Newburyport, Massachusetts
        N.Hamp. Gaz. Oct. 5, p. 3; Oct. 12, p. 3

Winthrop, John (Massachusetts scientist)
    On electricity
        N.Hamp. Gaz. Aug. 17, p. 2.

March 5

First Anniversary of Boston Massacre. The first anniversary of the Boston Massacre is commemorated in Boston with appropriate ceremony and oratory intended not only to remind true patriots of the sad event but also to maintain a live current of anti-British sentiment amongst the populace.

Bos. Gaz. Mar. 11, p. 1; Mar. 18, p. 3.
Conn. Courant Mar. 5/12, p. 3.

March

Permanent Salaries for Massachusetts Crown Officials? Early notice in Boston is given to the story that Governor Thomas Hutchinson and Lieutenant Governor Andrew Oliver are to receive their salaries from the crown from American revenues rather than from the Massachusetts House of Representatives. Control of the governor's and lieutenant governor's subsidies has before this given the representatives a measure of leverage over the two officials appointed by the king. To remove said subsidies from colonial hands is correctly considered to be an effort to establish a more independent executive. The ensuing dispute over the executives' (and later the Superior Court justices', see below, October-November, 1772) salaries furnishes the Boston radicals with a continuing issue during a quiet period (1771-1773) in British-American affairs.

Bos. Gaz. Mar. 11, p. 2; May 6, p. 1; May 13, p. 1.
Mass. Gaz. and Bos. Week. News-Letter May 16, p. 1.
Pa. Journal Apr. 4, p. 3.
Conn. Courant Mar. 12/19, p. 3.

January—June

Regulator Movement in North Carolina. Between 1765-1771, sectional differences in North Carolina centering on political representation and the legal system dominate Carolina attention. During this period the eastern section of North Carolina, heavily English, Highland Scotch, and Anglican, enjoys a ratio of one representative for every 1700 persons while the western parts of the colony — predominantly German, Scotch-Irish, as well as Presbyterian and Baptist — have only one representative for every 7300 persons. The anti-English bias of the west is given sharper focus by its settlement pattern of small, independent farms, while the heartily English tone of the east is sustained by its cultivation by plantations. Local officials are appointed by the governor, who is resident in the east and thereby most susceptible to the attitudes of the eastern planter. The judicial system is founded upon extortionist sheriffs and county justices beholden only to the governor. The Regulators, groups of westerners intent on "regulating" their own affairs, are most active in the period 1768-1771. Riotous proceedings by Regulators in general and attacks on attorneys at the Hillsborough Superior Court in particular, in September 1770, lead to the passage by the General Assembly of the Johnston Riot Act (January 15, 1771) which gives Governor William Tryon authorization to suppress the Regulators with military power. His force of 1400 militiamen wins the Battle of Alamance over approximately 2000 Regulators on May 16, 1771. Six Regulator leaders are hanged immediately and within six weeks over 6000 take advantage of Tryon's offer of clemency. Many Regulators thereafter move on to Tennessee and Georgia while the majority of those who remain fight on the American side in the Revolutionary War.

Bos. Gaz. June 17, p. 1; July 1, p. 2; July 15, p. 2; July 22, pp. 2-3; Aug. 26, pp. 1, 4; Oct. 21, pp. 1-2.
Mas. Gaz. and Bos. Week. News-Letter May 16, p. 2; Oct. 31, supplement, p. 1.
Mass. Gaz. and Bos. Post-Boy and Adv. July 29, pp. 2, 3; Aug. 26, p. 3; Sept. 30, pp. 1-3.
Conn. Courant Nov. 6/13 (1770), pp. 2-3; June 11/18, p. 2.
N.Y. Journal Jan. 3, pp. 2, 3; Apr. 4, p. 2; Apr. 11, p. 2; June 13, p. 3; June 27, p. 3.
Pa. Journal Apr. 25, pp. 2-3; June 13, p. 2.
Va. Gaz. (Purdie and Dixon) June 13, p. 2; July 4, p. 2.
S.C. Gaz. May 30, p. 1; June 13, p. 2; July 4, p. 1; July 18, p. 2.

October—December

Samuel Adams Disagrees with Permanent Salaries. The issue of Governor Hutchinson's and Lieutenant Governor Oliver's salaries is kept alive through the good offices — and strident rhetoric — of Samuel Adams as "Candidus" in a series of articles in the *Boston Gazette.*

Bos. Gaz. Oct. 7, p. 2; Oct. 14, p. 2; Dec. 2, p. 2; Dec. 9, p. 2; Dec. 23, p. 2.

Astronomical Phenomena
Transit of Venus
Pa. Journal Mar. 28, pp. 2-3.

Books
List of titles for sale
Va. Gaz. (Purdie and Dixon) July 18, pp. 2-3.

Charity
Monies for the Society for Relief of the Poor and Distressed Masters of Ships, Their Widows and Children
Pa. Journal Apr. 4, p. 1.

Church of England
Debate over establishment of American Episcopate
Va. Gaz. (Purdie and Dixon) June 6, p. 2; June 20, pp. 1-2; June 27, pp. 1-2; July 4, p. 2; July 11, p. 2; July 18, p. 1.

Colleges
Dartmouth
chartered
N.Hamp. Gaz. Jan. 4, p. 1.
first commencement
Bos. Even. Post Sept. 9, p. 3.
Yale students return after short AWOL
Conn. Courant Mar. 19/26, p. 3.

Diseases
Dropsy cure
Conn. Courant Jan. 1/8, p. 1.
Inoculation
Conn. Courant Mar. 19/26, p. 3.
Inoculation (Turkish)
N.Y. Journal Mar. 14, p. 1.
Whooping-cough cure
Mass. Gaz. and Bos. Post-Boy and Adv. Aug. 26, p. 4.

Doctors
Quackery
N.Y. Journal Mar. 14, p. 2.

Moral Exhortations
Against bad company
Mass. Gaz. and Bos. Week. News-Letter Dec. 23, p. 1.
Against swearing
Mass. Gaz. and Bos. Week. News-Letter Dec. 23, p. 2.

New Year's Day
New York City revelers punished for over-exuberance
N.Hamp. Gaz. Jan. 18, p. 2.

Poor House
New York City's, conditions in
N.Y. Journal Mar. 14, p. 2.

Rittenhouse, David (American scientist)
Notice of
Pa. Journal Mar. 28, pp. 2-3.

Roman Catholics
Anti-Catholicism: burlesque of Boston Catholics in support of Governor Thomas Hutchinson
Bos. Gaz. July 29, p. 2.

Slaves
Anti-slavery sentiments
Va. Gaz. (Purdie and Dixon) July 18, p. 1.

Swine
New Hampshire Hog Act
N.Hamp. Gaz. Jan. 25, p. 3.

June 9

The Gaspee *Affair.* The enthusiastic efforts (March-June) of Lieutenant William Dudingston, commander of H.M. schooner *Gaspee,* to curtail the Newport and Providence smuggling system results in a cordial hatred among the Rhode Island populace for the Britisher. Accidentally run aground off Namquit Point in Warwick while in pursuit of a smuggler on the afternoon of June 9, the *Gaspee* is boarded by local patriots that night; Dudingston is shot and harassed. The crew and the lieutenant are then set adrift in boats while the ship is burned. Despite a conscious desire not to rile the Americans, the British ministry is compelled to react to the *Gaspee's* burning with the establishment of a Commission of Inquiry (September 2) scheduled to meet in 1773. (See below, January-June 1773.)

Bos. Gaz. June 22, p. 3; Oct. 5, p. 3.
Newpt. Merc. June 1, p. 3; June 15, p. 3; Sept. 28, p. 3.
Conn. Courant Dec. 22/29, p. 2.
N.Y. Journal June 18, p. 3; June 25, p. 3.
Md. Gaz. July 2, p. 2; July 9, p. 2.
S.C. Gaz. July 30, p. 2.

June 13

Governor Hutchinson Indeed Paid by Crown. In reply to a query from the Massachusetts House of Representatives, Governor Hutchinson states that now his subsidy does come from His Majesty, King George III. Hutchinson's answer initiates a summer of discontent in Boston.

Bos. Gaz. June 15, p. 3; July 20, pp. 2-3; July 27, p. 1.
N.Y. Journal July 9, p. 5.
S.C. Gaz. July 30, p. 2; Aug. 13, p. 3.

August 20

As Is Governor Franklin. Governor William Franklin tells the New Jersey General Assembly that he will no longer require a subsidy from them: King George has graciously provided for him.

Conn. Courant Sept. 1/8, p. 3.

October–November

Boston Creates a Standing Committee of Correspondence. In response to an announcement that Massachusetts Superior Court justices will now receive their salaries from the Crown, Sam Adams calls for united Massachusetts action against such threats. The result is a November 2 Boston town meeting which creates a standing committee of correspondence of twenty-one worthies to communicate with other Massachusetts towns and "the World."

Bos. Gaz. Oct. 5, p. 3; Oct. 12, p. 3; Oct. 19, pp. 1, 2, 4; Oct. 26, p. 2; Nov. 2, pp. 1-2; Nov. 9, pp. 1, 2.
N.Y. Journal Oct. 8, p. 3; Nov. 12, pp. 2-3; Nov. 19, p. 5.
Pa. Journal Feb. 3 (1773), pp. 1-2; Mar. 3 (1773), pp. 1, 4.
Va. Gaz. (Rind) Dec. 3, p. 1; Dec. 10, p. 2.

November–February 1773

Other Massachusetts Towns Follow Boston's Lead. The Boston town meeting (November 19) approves a threefold report concerning rights of Massachusetts citizens (Sam Adams), their grievances (Dr. Joseph Warren), and the necessity of said citizens' towns to establish committees of correspondence (Dr. Benjamin Church). The statement is forwarded to Massachusetts towns and to the other American assemblies. The result in Massachusetts is a dramatic increase in the establishment of town committees of correspondence as well as a singular instance of opposition in Marblehead.

Bos. Gaz. Nov. 23, p. 3; Nov. 30, p. 1; Jan. 4 (1773), p. 3; Jan. 11 (1773), p. 3; Mar. 22 (1773), p. 2; Apr. 5 (1773), pp. 1, 4; Apr. 12 (1773), p. 1.
Bos. Even. Post Dec. 7, p. 1; Dec. 14, p. 2; Dec. 21, pp. 1, 2; Dec. 28, pp. 1, 2.
Pa. Journal Feb. 4 (1773), pp. 1-2; Mar. 3 (1773), pp. 1, 4.

Topical Chronology

Capital Punishment
  Executions
    Conn. Courant Sept. 1/8, p. 3.

Colleges
  College of New Jersey, commencement
    N.Y. Journal Sept. 17, p. 3.
  Dartmouth
    commencement
      Conn. Courant Sept. 8/15, p. 2.
    to educate Indian children
      Conn. Courant Oct. 13/20, p. 2.
  Rhode Island College
    first commencement
      Conn. Courant Sept. 8/15, p. 2.
    regarding establishment of
      Bos. Gaz. July 27, p. 1.

Crime
  Murder
    N.Y. Journal July 9, p. 5.

Diseases
  Measles
    S.C. Gaz. July 30, p. 3.

Dueling
  Against
    S.C. Gaz. Aug. 20, pp. 1-2.

Education
  Ad for academy for children
    S.C. Gaz. Dec. 10, p. 3.

Humor
  Anecdote: stiff bowl of punch
    Bos. Even. Post Dec. 14, p. 1.
  "The Character of a Loving Wife"
    S.C. Gaz. Dec. 17, supplement, p. 1.

Hurricanes
  Damages by in West Indies
    Bos. Gaz. Oct. 5, p. 2; Oct. 12, p. 2.
    S.C. Gaz. Nov. 2, extraordinary, pp. 1-2.

Independence, American
  Prospects of
    Bos. Gaz. Jan. 6, p. 1; Jan. 27, p. 1.

Indians
  Education of at Dartmouth College
    Conn. Courant Oct. 13/20, p. 2.

Marriage
  "The Character of a Loving Wife"
    S.C. Gaz. Dec. 17, supplement, p. 1.

Northwest Passage
  Major Robert Rogers to seek
    Conn. Courant July 21/28, p. 3.

Pest Control
  Caterpillars
    Conn. Courant June 9/16, p. 2.

Pilgrims
  Commemoration of
    Bos. Even. Post Dec. 28, p. 3.

Piracy
  Narrative of act of
    N.Y. Journal Nov. 26, p. 3.

Public Utilities
  Aqueduct (wooden)
    Conn. Courant Sept. 1/8, p. 3.
  Fire prevention
    S.C. Gaz. Oct. 8, p. 1.

Roman Catholics
  Clergy obituary
    Conn. Courant Sept. 8/15, p. 2.
    N.Y. Journal Sept. 10, p. 2.

  Jesuits: Protestantism's arch-enemies assessed
    S.C. Gaz. Dec. 31, supplement, p. 1.

Slaves
  Legal status of
    Va. Gaz. (Rind) Nov. 12, p. 2.
  Murder master
    N.Y. Journal July 9, p. 5.
  Status of in South Carolina
    S.C. Gaz. Aug. 27, p. 1; Sept. 17, pp. 1-2;
    Sept. 24, pp. 1-2.

Unusual Phenomena
  Giant youth described
    Bos. Even. Post Dec. 7, p. 2.

Women
  Letter to Parents on Female Education
    Conn. Courant Dec. 8/15, p. 1.

January–June

Gaspee *Investigation.* Meeting for approximately three weeks in January and again in May-June, the royal commission is able to obtain no information regarding the destruction of the *Gaspee* even though the perpetrators are well-known in Rhode Island. For his troubles, William Dudingston is promoted to Captain – a hollow triumph for His Majesty's justice.

Bos. Gaz. Jan. 4, p. 2; Jan. 11, p. 3; June 28, supplement, p. 2.
Bos. Even. Post Dec. 21 (1772), p. 2; June 7, p. 2.
Newpt. Merc. Nov. 23 (1772), p. 3; Dec. 21 (1772), pp. 2, 3; Dec. 28 (1772), p. 3; Jan. 18, pp. 2, 3; Jan. 25, p. 3; Feb. 1, p. 3; May 31, p. 3; June 21, p. 3; June 28, p. 3.
Conn. Courant Dec. 22/29 (1772), p. 2; Dec. 29 (1772)/Jan. 5, p. 3; Jan. 5/12, p. 3; Jan. 12/19, p. 2; Jan. 19/26, p. 3; June 29/July 6, p. 3.
N.Y. Journal Jan. 7, pp. 2, 5; Jan. 14, pp. 2, 3; Jan. 21, pp. 2, 3;
S.C. Gaz. Feb. 1, postscript, p. 2; July 12, p. 2.

January–June

The Unpopular Governor Thomas Hutchinson. Massachusetts continues to be the scene of the Governor Hutchinson–House of Representatives quarrel over who is to pay the judges' salaries (see above, October-November 1772). One unfortunate result of the dispute is an increasingly bitter colonial portraiture of Thomas Hutchinson as a predator upon American liberties.

Mass. Gaz. and Bos. Post-Boy and Adv. Feb. 8, p. 3.
Bos. Gaz. Mar. 1, p. 2; Mar. 8, pp. 2-3; Mar. 15, supplement, p. 1; Apr. 26, p. 2.
Pa. Journal Mar. 10, pp. 1-2, 4; Mar. 17, pp. 1-2, 4; Mar. 17, supplement, p. 1.
S.C. Gaz. Mar. 1, p. 2.

March 12

Intercolonial Committees of Correspondence. Stirred into action by the inquiry into the *Gaspee* affair and the (false) rumor that any persons indicated would be shipped to England for trial, the Virginia House of Burgesses establishes a *standing* committee of correspondence (through the leadership of Patrick Henry, Richard Henry Lee, and Thomas Jefferson) in order to transmit any information regarding British colonial measures to the other colonies. Virginia's sister colonies are invited to set up their own committees of correspondence. Within four months the four New England colonies and South Carolina have established such committees. By February 1774, all the colonies except Pennsylvania and North Carolina have complied with Virginia's suggestion. The Virginia committee includes Henry, Lee, Jefferson, and Peyton Randolph. This effort is an important step toward colonial unity and directly influences the calling of a Continental Congress in September 1774 (see below, September 5-October 26, 1774).

N.Hamp. Gaz. Apr. 23, p. 1.
Bos. Gaz. Apr. 12, p. 2; May 17, p. 2; May 31, pp. 2, 3; Aug. 9, p. 3; Nov. 8, p. 3.
Newpt. Merc. May 10, p. 3.
Conn. Courant May 11/18, p. 3; May 25/June 1, p. 2; June 1/8, p. 2; Nov. 9/16, p. 2; Feb. 15/22 (1774), p. 3.
N.Y. Journal Apr. 15, p. 3; May 20, p. 2; June 17, p. 3; Dec. 30, p. 3.
Pa. Journal Apr. 14, p. 3; June 9, pp. 2-3; June 16, p. 3; July 28, p. 2; Dec. 22, p. 3; Jan. 26 (1774), pp. 2-3; Feb. 2 (1774), p. 3.
S.C. Gaz. June 28, p. 3; July 12, p. 3; Nov. 22, p. 2.
Va. Gaz. (Rind) Mar. 18, pp. 2-3; June 3, p. 2; July 1, p. 2; July 8, p. 2; Jan. 13 (1774), p. 3.
Ga. Gaz. Feb. 2 (1774), pp. 1, 4.

April 27

Parliament Attempts Rescue of East India Company. In order to save the East India Company from bankruptcy, Parliament votes to allow a drawback of the export duty on the company's tea presently stored in England. A special license allows for the direct exportation of tea to America, further cutting the company's costs. The three pence per pound Townshend duty is still to be collected in the colonies. This reminder of Parliamentary power ignites a concerted colonial reaction later in the year when the East India Company authorizes shipments of tea to the ports of Boston, New York City, Philadelphia, and Charleston. (The inflammatory "Alarm," discoursing on the affairs of the East India Company and tea, is noted in the citations.)

Bos. Gaz. Mar. 29, p. 3; Apr. 12, p. 3.
Conn. Courant June 15/22, p. 1; July 13/20, p. 2; Aug. 17/24, p. 3.
N.Y. Journal July 22, p. 2; (Alarm No. 1) Oct. 14, pp. 1-2, 2-3; (Alarm No. 2) Oct. 21, pp. 1-2; (Alarm No. 3) Oct. 28, pp. 1-2, 3; (Alarm No. 5) Nov. 18, pp. 1-2.
Pa. Journal June 30, p. 2; Nov. 3, p. 1.
Broadside: undated Alarm No. 4.

June

The Damaging Hutchinson/Oliver – Whately Letters. Redoubtable Benjamin Franklin secures a number of letters in London (1768-1769), the most important of which are written to a member of Parliament, Thomas Whately, by then

Lieutenant Governor Thomas Hutchinson and Andrew Oliver. Allegedly intended to be read by Sam Adams to a secret session of the Massachusetts House of Representatives, the letters are edited by leading radicals, copied, and printed in various colonial newspapers. Governor Hutchinson and present Lieutenant Governor Andrew Oliver are excoriated for their apparent anti-American views. (In fact, Hutchinson is a leading proponent of American rights within the context of a British Empire.) A petition (June 23) sent to England by the Massachusetts General Assembly calling for the ouster of the Governor and Lieutenant Governor is disapproved by the Privy Council (February 1774), but Hutchinson does depart for England himself in 1774 after being replaced by General Thomas Gage. (See below for Franklin's fate, January 1774.)

Bos. Gaz. June 21, pp. 1-2, 3; June 28, pp. 1, 2-3, 4; June 28, supplement, pp. 1, 2; Aug. 2, p. 3.
Bos. Even. Post June 7, p. 3; July 5, p. 1.
Conn. Courant Nov. 9/16, p. 3.
N.Y. Journal June 17, p. 3; July 1, pp. 1-2.
Pa. Journal June 16, p. 3; June 30, pp. 1, 2; July 7, p. 1; July 14, pp. 1, 2-3, 4.
S.C. Gaz. July 5, p. 3; July 12, p. 2; July 26, p. 2; July 26, supplement, pp. 1-2; Aug. 9, p. 4; Aug. 16, supplement, pp. 1-2; Aug. 23, supplement, pp. 1-2; Aug. 30, supplement, pp. 1-2.

August 30–September 13

Freedom of the Press in South Carolina. The issue of the freedom of the press to report legislative proceedings is raised in South Carolina when Thomas Powell, temporary editor of Peter Timothy's *South Carolina Gazette*, prints a protest by two councilors against the South Carolina Council's defeat of an anti-counterfeiting bill passed by the Commons House of Assembly (August 30). Upon his refusal to apologize for his actions, Powell is jailed by direction of the Council or upper house (August 31-September 3). Powell's subsequent release by two assemblymen/justices of the peace broadens the conflict into the familiar theme of colonial upper house versus lower house dispute. Both parts of the South Carolina General Assembly petition England in hopes of ultimate vindication of their action.

Newpt. Merc. Oct. 11, pp. 1-2.
N.Y. Journal Oct. 21, p. 3.
S.C. Gaz. Aug. 30, p. 3; Sept. 2, extraordinary, pp. 1, 3; Sept. 6, supplement, p. 1; Sept. 13, pp. 1-2; Sept. 15, postscript, pp. 1-3.

October 16

Tea Unwelcome in Philadelphia. Upon word of a tea shipment intended for Philadelphia, a mass meeting at the Pennsylvania State House declares the tea duty taxation without representation and an act whose purpose is to render the colonial assemblies useless. All Americans are urged to oppose the ministerial scheme which in reality is a violent attack on American liberties; any who should receive such tea are to be accounted enemies of America. A committee is created to seek actively the resignations of the Philadelphia tea commissioners or consignees. In late November, the Committee for Tarring and Feathering produces a handbill that cautions the Delaware River pilots against helping any tea ships to reach Philadelphia.

Bos. Gaz. Oct. 11, p. 3; Nov. 1, p. 2; Nov. 8, p. 1; Dec. 13, p. 3.
Conn. Courant Oct. 19/26, p. 2; Nov. 2/9, p. 2.
N.Y. Journal Oct. 21, p. 3; Dec. 2, pp. 1-2; Dec. 16, pp. 2-3.
Pa. Journal Sept. 29, p. 3; Oct. 13, p. 1; Oct. 20, pp. 2-3; Nov. 3, pp. 1-2; Nov. 24, p. 3; Dec. 8, pp. 2-3.
Va. Gaz. (Rind) Oct. 28, p. 3; Nov. 11, supplement, p. 2; Dec. 30, pp. 2-3.
S.C. Gaz. Nov. 15, p. 3; Nov. 22, pp. 1-2; Dec. 20, p. 2.
Broadsides: two undated [Dec.] to Delaware River pilots.

October–November

New York Also Protests Tea Duty. A variety of letters and essays in the *New York Journal* protests the tea duty and warns the consignees or commissioners to resign their posts forthwith. Under pressure from the Sons of Liberty the gentlemen assert their refusal to receive or to sell the expected tea (November 30). Three weeks earlier in a handbill (November 10) subsequently printed in the *New York Journal* – "To the Stated Pilots of the Post of New-York" – "Legion" cautions against any assistance to tea ships arriving outside the New York Harbor. Earlier (October-November) a series of vitriolic and anti-Tea Act essays by an unknown author appears in the *Journal* entitled "The Alarm." Publication in other colonial newspapers is prompt.

Bos. Gaz. Oct. 11, p. 3; Nov. 1, p. 2; Dec. 13, p. 3.
Conn. Courant Dec. 7, supplement, pp. 1-2; Dec. 28/Jan. 4 (1774), p. 1.
N.Y. Journal Oct. 7, p. 3; (Alarm No. 1) Oct. 14, pp. 1-2, 2-3; (Alarm No. 2) Oct. 21, pp. 1-2, 3; (Alarm No. 3) Oct. 28, pp. 1-2, 3; Nov. 4, p. 3; Nov. 25, p. 3; Dec. 2, p. 3; Dec. 9, p. 2; Dec. 16, pp. 2, 3.
Pa. Journal Sept. 29, p. 3; Oct. 27, p. 3; (Alarm No. 5) Nov. 17, pp. 1, 2-3, 4; Nov. 24, p. 3.

T   E   A,

DESTROYED BY INDIANS.

YE GLORIOUS SONS OF FREEDOM, brave and bold,
That has stood forth----fair LIBERTY to hold ;
Though you were INDIANS, come from distant shores,
Like MEN you acted-----not like savage Moors.

CHORUS.

Bostonian's SONS keep up your Courage good,
Or Dye, like Martyrs, in fair Free-born Blood.

Our LIBERTY, and LIFE is now invaded,
And FREEDOM's brightest Charms are darkly shaded :
But, we will STAND---and think it noble mirth,
To DART the man that dare oppress the Earth.

Bostonian's SONS keep up your Courage good,
Or Dye, like Martyrs, in fair Free-born Blood.

How grand the Scene !----(No Tyrant shall oppose)
The TEA is sunk in spite of all our foes.
A NOBLE SIGHT---to see th' accursed TEA
Mingled with MUD----and ever for to be ;
For KING and PRINCE shall know that we are FREE.

Bostonian's SONS keep up your Courage good,
Or Dye, like Martyrs, in fair Free-born Blood,

Must we be still--- and live on Blood-bought Ground,
And not oppose the Tyrants cursed sound ?
We Scorn the thought----our views are well refin'd
We Scorn those slavish shackles of the Mind,
" We've Souls that were not made to be confin'd."

Bostonian's SONS keep up your Courage good,
Or Dye, like Martyrs, in fair Free-born Blood.

Could our Fore-fathers rise from their cold Graves,
And view their Land, with all their Children SLAVES ;
What would they say ! how would their Spirits rend,
And, Thunder-strucken, to their Graves descend.

Bostonian's SONS keep up your Courage good,
Or Dye, like Martyrs, in fair Free-born Blood.

Let us with hearts of steel now stand the task,
Throw off all darksome ways, nor wear a Mask.
Oh ! may our noble Zeal support our frame,
And brand all Tyrants with eternal SHAME.

Bostonian's SONS keep up your Courage good,
And sink all Tyrants in their GUILTY BLOOD.

See p. 41, December 16,   Broadside: Undated poem.

Va. Gaz. (Rind) Oct. 28, p. 3; Dec. 16, p. 3.
S.C. Gaz. Nov. 15, p. 3; Nov. 22, pp. 1-2; Dec. 20, p. 2.
Broadsides: undated Alarm No. 4; Nov. 5.

November 5-6

Boston Joins in Tea Protest. A Boston town meeting resolves to prevent the sale of any dutied tea within the town and inveighs against any who might import the East India Company's tea. Although presented with the considerations of the town, the tea consignees, which include Governor Hutchinson's sons Thomas, Jr., and Elisha, refuse to resign their commissions. They refuse again to resign during another Boston town meeting (November 18), pleading their ignorance of any such consignment of tea to themselves.

Bos. Gaz. Oct. 11, p. 3; Oct. 18, pp. 2, 3; Oct. 25, p. 3; Nov. 1, p. 2; Nov. 8, pp. 2, 3; Nov. 15, pp. 2, 3; Nov. 22, p. 2; Dec. 13, p. 1; Dec. 27, pp. 2-3.
Conn. Courant Oct. 19/26, p. 2; Nov. 2/9, p. 2; Nov. 9/16, p. 2; Nov. 23/30, p. 2.
N.Y. Journal Nov. 18, p. 2.
Pa. Journal Sept. 29, p. 3; Oct. 27, pp. 2-3; Nov. 17, p. 2; Dec. 1, pp. 2-3.
Va. Gaz. (Rind) Oct. 28, p. 3; Nov. 25, p. 3; Dec. 9, p. 1; Dec. 16, p. 3.
S.C. Gaz. Nov. 15, p. 3; Nov. 22, pp. 1-2; Dec. 20, p. 2.
Broadside: Nov. 3.

November 28

Tea Not Allowed to Land in Boston. The *Dartmouth* arrives in Boston Harbor with 114 chests of East India Company tea. The wishes of boisterous, illegal Boston town meetings (November 29-30) to send the ship immediately back to England with the tea aboard are opposed by Governor Hutchinson who demands payment of the export duty before the *Dartmouth* will be allowed to depart. Technically the ship has entered the Harbor and has thus come under the jurisdiction of the port customs collector. Moreover, Hutchinson is aware that if the ship is not unloaded within twenty days (December 17), the legal procedure is to seize and unload the cargo — with whatever force is necessary. The radicals refuse to allow the tea to be landed and stored. The same situation greets two more tea ships upon their arrival in Boston, the *Eleanor* (December 2) and the *Beaver* (December 7). A fourth tea ship bound for Boston, the *William*, runs aground on Cape Cod (December 10). Its cargo of fifty-eight chests of tea is rescued by one of the consignees who brings it safely to Castle William in Boston Harbor.

Bos. Gaz. Nov. 29, p. 2; Dec. 6, pp. 2-3, 4; Dec. 13, p. 2; Dec. 20, p. 1; Dec. 27. p. 3; Jan. 17 (1774), pp. 2, 3.
Conn. Courant Nov. 30/Dec. 7, p. 3; Dec. 7, supplement, p. 1; Dec. 14/21, p. 2.
N.Y. Journal Dec. 9, p. 3; Dec. 16, p. 2.
Pa. Journal Dec. 8, pp. 2, 3; Dec. 15, p. 2.
Va. Gaz. (Rind) Dec. 30, pp. 2-3.
Broadside: undated parody regarding a tea ship.

December 12

New Hampshire Protests Tea Duty. Resolves are passed in Portsmouth, New Hampshire, that any attempted landing of tea will be prevented; other colonies' opposition to the Tea Act will be supported; and the subscribers to the agreement will be persevering in their own opposition to ministerial efforts to enforce the Tea Act. (Other, similar New Hampshire town resolves are included.)

N.Hamp. Gaz. Nov. 26, p. 3; Dec. 24, p. 1; Jan. 7 (1774), p. 2; Jan. 14 (1774), p. 2; Jan. 21 (1774), p. 1; Feb. 4 (1774), p. 3; Feb. 11 (1774), p. 1; Feb. 18 (1774), p. 2; Feb. 25 (1774), p. 2.
Bos. Gaz. Dec. 20, p. 2; Dec. 27, p. 3.
Conn. Courant Dec. 28/Jan. 4 (1774), p. 2.
N.Y. Journal Jan. 13 (1774), p. 1.

December 16

Boston Tea Party. Upon Governor Hutchinson's refusal to grant the *Dartmouth* a pass to leave Boston without clearance from the customhouse, the celebrated "Mohawks" dump the 340 chests of tea aboard the *Dartmouth, Eleanor,* and *Beaver* into Boston Harbor. The 90,000 pounds of tea are valued at £9000. The work is quick, well-planned, and anonymously-done.

N.Hamp. Gaz. Dec. 24, p. 3.
Bos. Gaz. Dec. 13, p. 3; Dec. 20, p. 3; Dec. 27, p. 3; Dec. 27, supplement, p. 1.
Conn. Courant Dec. 21/28, p. 2; Dec. 28/Jan. 4 (1774), p. 1.
N.Y. Journal Dec. 23, pp. 2-3; Jan. 13 (1774), p. 3.
Riv. N.Y. Gazetteer Dec. 23, pp. 1-2, 3.
Pa. Journal [Dec. 22], postscript, p. 1; Dec. 29, p. 1.
Md. Gaz. Jan. 6 (1774), pp. 2-3.
Va. Gaz. (Rind) Jan. 13 (1774), p. 2; May 26 (1774), p. 2.
Va. Gaz. (Purdie and Dixon) Jan. 13 (1774), pp. 1-2.
S.C. Gaz. Jan. 17 (1774), p. 3.
Ga. Gaz. Feb. 2 (1774), p. 4.
Broadside: undated poem.

December 17

New York Tea Protest Unyielding. Referring to a November 29 association or agreement against imported, taxed tea, the New York Sons of Liberty refuse to agree to a proposal by Lieutenant Governor Cadwallader Colden that such tea be stored in New York City's Fort George when it arrives.

Bos. Gaz. Dec. 27, supplement, p. 2.
Pa. Journal [Dec. 22], postscript, p. 1.
Va. Gaz. (Purdie and Dixon) Jan. 13 (1774), pp. 2-3.
S.C. Gaz. Feb. 21 (1774), p. 1.
Broadside: Nov. 27; Nov. 29.

December 22

Charleston Patriots Victorious in Tea Protest. Upon the arrival of the *London* in Charleston (December 2) its shipment of tea is refused by the tea consignees, who value prudential judgments. The *London* is forced to remain for the twenty-day period after which the tea is landed for non-payment of the appropriate importation duties and stored in government warehouses. The tea is eventually sold in July 1776 in order to aid the American Revolutionary cause.

Bos. Gaz. Jan. 17 (1774), p. 3.
Conn. Courant Dec. 28/Jan. 4 (1774), pp. 1, 2.

N.Y. Journal Dec. 23, p. 3; Dec. 30, p. 2; Jan. 6 (1774), p. 2.
Pa. Journal Dec. 22, p. 2; Apr. 20 (1774), postscript, p. 2.
Va. Gaz. (Rind) Oct. 28, p. 3; Dec. 30, p. 2.
Va. Gaz. (Purdie and Dixon) Jan. 13 (1774), p. 2.
S.C. Gaz. Nov. 15, p. 3; Nov. 15, supplement, p. 1; Nov. 22, p. 3; Nov. 29, p. 1; Dec. 20, p. 3; Dec. 27, p. 2; Jan. 24 (1774), p. 2; Mar. 21 (1774), p. 2.
Ga. Gaz. Jan. 26 (1774), p. 2.

December 28

Philadelphia's Tea Protest Successful. The *Polly* leaves Philadelphia after three days in America. The shipment of tea remains aboard in the face of a rather vocal and popular opposition to its unloading.

Bos. Gaz. Jan. 10 (1774), p. 3; Jan. 17 (1774), p. 3.
Conn. Courant Dec. 28/Jan. 4 (1774), p. 2; Jan. 11/18 (1774), p. 2.
N.Y. Journal Dec. 30, p. 3; Jan. 6 (1774), pp. 2-3.
Pa. Journal Dec. 29, pp. 2-3.
Va. Gaz. (Purdie and Dixon) Jan. 20 (1774), pp. 2-3.
S.C. Gaz. Jan. 17 (1774), p. 3.

Almanac
  1774: descriptive ad
    N.Y. Journal Nov. 25, p. 1.

Baptists
  Protest taxation to support Massachusetts Congregationalists
    Bos. Gaz. Mar. 1, p. 1.

Boston Massacre
  Anniversary
    Bos. Gaz. Mar. 8, p. 4.

Capital Punishment
  Georgia laws modified
    N.Y. Journal Aug. 26, p. 4.
  Last words
    Conn. Courant Apr. 6/13, pp. 2-3; Apr. 13/20, pp. 2, 4.

Children
  "On the Management of Children in Infancy"
    S.C. Gaz. Nov. 1, supplement, p. 1.

Colleges
  College of New Jersey, lotteries to aid by Presbyterians
    S.C. Gaz. July 5, supplement, p. 1.
  Harvard, lottery to aid
    Bos. Gaz. Apr. 26, p. 1.

Counterfeiting
  New Jersey
    Conn. Courant July 6/13, p. 1.
    N.Y. Journal Dec. 16, p. 1.
  South Carolina
    S.C. Gaz. Apr. 12, p. 3.

Currency
  Possible use of paper, in colonies
    N.Hamp. Gaz. Oct. 15, p. 1; Oct. 29, p. 1; Nov. 12, p. 1.

Customs
  Violations: efforts of customs officer John Malcolm (see below, Vigilantes, 1774)
    Bos. Gaz. Aug. 23, p. 2; Nov. 15, p. 3.

Dentist
  Ad for surgeon-dentist
    Bos. Gaz. Aug. 9, p. 3.

Doctors
  Miracle oculist: Dr. Graham (see also Doctors, 1770)

N.Y. Journal Aug. 5, p. 4; Aug. 12, p. 3; Aug. 19, p. 3; Aug. 26, pp. 3-4; Sept. 2, p. 3.
    Md. Gaz. Sept. 16, p. 3; Sept. 30, p. 2.

Education
  Ad for French language school
    S.C. Gaz. Apr. 26, supplement, p. 2.
  Ads for grammar schools
    N.Y. Journal Aug. 19, p. 4; Oct. 21, p. 3.

Handel, George Frederick
  Concert of his music
    Bos. Gaz. July 19, p. 1.

Horseracing
  Annapolis races noticed
    Md. Gaz. Sept. 16, p. 3.

Humor
  Lampoon of statue of Earl of Hillsborough (anti-colonial colony administrator)
    S.C. Gaz. Sept. 2, extraordinary, p. 3.
  Satire on rules for reducing great empire
    Pa. Journal Dec. 15, pp. 1-2.

Hurricanes
  Damages by in northern Massachusetts
    Bos. Even. Post. Aug. 30, p. 1.

Independence, American
  Union of Great Britain and America proposed
    Bos. Gaz. Aug. 2, p. 1.

Indians
  React to new (encroaching) Ohio government
    Conn. Courant Aug. 24/31, p. 3.

Irish
  Emigration due to rent problems in Ireland
    Conn. Courant June 29/July 6, p. 3.

Jails
  Established in Simsbury, Connecticut copper-mine
    Conn. Courant Dec. 21/28, p. 1.

Locke, John
  Ad for *An Essay on Civil Government* (Part 2)
    Bos. Gaz. Mar. 1, p. 1.

Magazines
  Proposal for *Royal American Magazine or*

Universal Repository
   Conn. Courant Aug. 17/24, p. 4.

Magician
   Ad for
   S.C. Gaz. Mar. 22, p. 1.

Mississippi Country
   New Jersey packet to Natchez [Mississippi]
   for settlement
   N.Y. Journal May 27, p. 3; July 15, p. 3;
      Aug. 12, p. 3.

Natural History
   Collection of items proposed by Library Society of Charleston
   S.C. Gaz. Mar. 22, p. 3.

Newspapers
   Subscribers' accounts in arrears
   S.C. Gaz. June 14, p. 1.

Paddock, John
   Harvard student drowns; lamented
   Bos. Gaz. July 12, p. 3.
   Bos. Even. Post July 5, p. 3.

Piracy
   Trial of Ansell Nickerson (defended by John
   Adams and Josiah Quincy, Jr.)
   Bos. Gaz. Nov. 23 (1772), p. 3; Aug. 2, p.
   3; Aug. 9, p. 2.
   Bos. Even. Post Dec. 21 (1772), p. 2.

Rights, American Political
   "A Constitutional Catechism"
   N.Y. Journal Dec. 9, p.2.

Roman Catholics
   Anti-Catholicism: ad for D. Antonio Gavin's
   A Master Key to Popery
   Bos. Gaz. Feb. 1, p. 3.

Slaves
   Imported into South Carolina, 1753-1771
   S.C. Gaz. June 14, p. 1.
   License necessary for them to peddle
   S.C. Gaz. Mar. 29, p. 3.
   Massachusetts: slave sues owner for freedom
   (and wins)
   N.Y. Journal Oct. 28, p. 3.
   Ordinance requiring them to carry lantern at
   night
   N.Y. Journal Dec. 9, p. 3.

Owner regarding small-pox of his
   S.C. Gaz. Aug. 9, p. 3; Aug. 25, p. 1.
Sales of
   Bos. Gaz. Feb. 1, p. 1.
   S.C. Gaz. May 31, p. 1.

Stamp Act
   Anniversary of resignation of Boston stamp-
   collector (Aug. 14, 1765)
   Bos. Gaz. Aug. 16, p. 2; Aug. 23, p. 2.

Tea
   How to make own
   Pa. Journal Dec. 22, p. 1.
   Injurious to health
   Conn. Courant Nov. 23/30, p. 2.
   Va. Gaz. (Rind) Dec. 16. p. 3.

Theater
   Ad for commented on
   S.C. Gaz. Aug. 9, p. 3.
   Ad for *Hamlet*
   N.Y. Journal May 27, p. 3.
   Benefit performance for hospital
   N.Y. Journal July 22, p. 3.
   Defense of
   N.Y. Journal July 8, p. 3.
   Evils of
   S.C. Gaz. Aug. 25, postscript, pp. 1-2.

Transportation
   Cartage rates
   S.C. Gaz. June 14, p. 3.

Union, American
   Proposed
   Conn. Courant June 22/29, p. 3; June
      29/July 6, p. 2.

Washington, George
   Offers Ohio land for sale
   Md. Gaz. Sept. 16, p. 3.

Wheatley, Phillis (Negro Poetess)
   "Farewell to America"
   Conn. Courant May 18/25, p. 4.
   Poem to Earl of Dartmouth
   N.Y. Journal June 3, p. 4.

Women
   Sally Tickle on superiority of
   N.Y. Journal Jan. 21, p. 2.

1774

Connecticut-Pennsylvania Land Dispute. With the military phase of the American Revolution just over one year away, certain colonies are engaged in jurisdictional disputes with one another. In present northeastern Pennsylvania, Connecticut and Pennsylvania citizens press rival claims to the Wyoming Valley. Connecticut's Susquehannah Company, involved in the conflict, receives official support on January 27, 1774, when Governor Jonathan Trumbull issues a proclamation against any settlement in the disputed area without Connecticut's permission. On Febrary 28, 1774, Governor John Penn issues his own proclamation against intruders into what has always been Pennsylvania territory.

Conn. Courant July 2 (1770), pp. 1-2; Aug. 13 (1770), p. 2; Oct. 9 (1770), p. 3; Jan 25/Feb. 1, pp. 1-2; Feb. 8/15, p. 2; Mar. 15/22, p. 1.
N.Y. Journal Dec. 30 (1773), p. 3.
Riv. N.Y. Gazetteer Jan. 27, p. 2.
Pa. Journal Jan. 19, p. 3; Jan. 26, p. 2; Feb. 9, p. 3; Feb. 16, p. 3; Feb. 23, p. 2; Nov. 8 (1775), pp. 1-2, 4.

1774

Future Vermont Scene of Boundary Dispute. In present Vermont, New Yorkers, New Hampshiremen, and Massachusetts settlers contend for land granted by each colony to different individuals while Ethan Allen and his Green Mountain Boys engage in disorders calculated to eventuate in statehood (Vermont, 1791).

Conn. Courant. June 21, supplement, pp. 1-2.
N.Y. Journal Jan. 20, p. 2.
Pa. Journal Jan. 19, pp. 2-3.

1774

Virginia-Pennsylvania Dispute Ohio River Valley. Farther south, Governor Dunmore of Virginia strengthens his colony's claim to land in the Ohio River Valley by participation in a successful campaign against Chief Cornstalk and his Shawnees at Point Pleasant near the mouth of the Kanawha River (in present West Virginia) on October 10. Pennsylvania's rival claims to the area west of Fort Pitt (Pittsburgh) are pressed forward despite Virginia's success and Dunmore's proclamation denouncing Pennsylvania intrusions.

Bos. Gaz. Nov. 28, p. 2; Dec. 26, p. 1.
Conn. Courant Nov. 21, p. 3.
Pa. Gaz. Oct. 2 (1776), pp. 1-2.
Pa. Journal Oct. 19, p. 1; Nov. 16, pp. 2, 3; Nov. 30, p. 2; Dec. 21, p. 2; Jan. 4 (1775), p. 3.
Md. Gaz. Nov. 10, p. 2.
Va. Gaz. (Purdie and Dixon) Aug. 25, p. 2; Sept. 8, p. 2; Oct. 13, pp. 2-3.

Va. Gaz. (Pinkney) Nov. 17, pp. 1-2.
Ga. Gaz. Nov. 30, p. 3; Jan. 11 (1775) p. 1.

January

Poor Richard's Comeuppance. Appearing before the House of Commons in his role as colonial agent for Massachusetts, Benjamin Franklin is the chagrined but silent recipient of a severe verbal chastisement from Solicitor General Alexander Wedderburn for Franklin's part in the Hutchinson-Whately letters scandal, which has led already in England to one duel, with prospects for another. Franklin's notoriety in the colonies does not suffer, however, and is in fact enhanced by his concurrent dismissal (January 30) as Deputy Postmaster General for America. The loss of his position is sufficient to associate Franklin's fate with that of the besieged inhabitants of Boston.

Bos. Gaz. Apr. 25, pp. 1-2, 3; May 2, p. 1; May 2, supplement, pp. 1-2.
Conn. Courant Mar. 8/15, p. 3; Apr. 12/19, p. 1.
Pa. Journal Apr. 20, pp. 2-3; Apr. 20, postscript, pp. 1-2; May 4, pp. 2-3.
Va. Gaz. (Purdie and Dixon) Mar. 31, p. 3.
S.C. Gaz. Mar. 21, p. 2.
Ga. Gaz. Apr. 13, p. 2.

December 1773–March

Massachusetts Support for Boston's Course. Numerous Massachusetts towns pass resolutions in support of the Boston initiative in the matter of the tea duty, both before and after the Tea Party. Opposition to Boston's tendency for excesses is demonstrated in Marshfield (January 31) and earlier in Plymouth (December 7), but the methods and pressures of local patriots are sufficient before too long in eliciting recantations from such 'enemies of American liberties.'

Bos. Gaz. Dec. 13 (1773), p. 2; Dec. 20 (1773), p. 1; Dec. 27 (1773), p. 3; Dec. 27 (1773), supplement, p. 1; Jan. 3, pp. 2-3; Jan. 10, pp. 2, 3; Jan. 17, pp. 1-2; Jan. 31, p. 2; Feb. 7, pp. 2-3; Feb. 14, p. 3; Feb. 28, pp. 1, 3; Mar. 28, p. 2.
Bos. Even. Post Apr. 4, pp. 2, 3.

December 1773–January

Americans React to Boston Tea Party. Public reaction in the American colonies to the Boston Tea Party is generally favorable.

Bos. Gaz. Jan. 3, p. 3.
Newpt. Merc. Dec. 27 (1773), p. 3.
Pa. Journal Feb. 23, p. 1.

February–March

Massachusetts Attempt to Remove Chief Justice. Massachusetts' seemingly insatiable appetite for controversy is directed toward the removal of the Chief Justice of the Superior Court, Peter Oliver, because of the lingering dispute over salaries for colonial administrators (see above, March, October-December 1772; and June 13, October-November 1773). Despite a vote of ninety-two to eight in the House of Representatives (February 24), Oliver is given a reprieve by Governor Hutchinson's refusal to entertain the "unconstitutional" measure (February 15-March 9), his proroguing of the General Assembly (March 9), and his dissolution of the General Assembly (March 30). The issue is resurrected in the fall when protests against taking oaths as grand jurors and petit jurors are entered in Massachusetts courts because of Oliver's continued official presence.

Bos. Gaz. Feb. 7, p. 3; Feb. 14, pp. 2, 3; Feb. 28, p. 2; Mar. 7, pp. 1-2; Mar. 14, pp. 2-3; Apr. 11, p. 2; May 2, p. 3; May 9, p. 1; Sept. 5, supplement, p. 1.
Bos. Even. Post Feb. 21, pp. 1, 2; Apr. 4, p. 1.
Conn. Courant Feb. 15/22, p. 3; Feb. 22/Mar. 1, pp. 2-3; Mar. 1/8, p. 2; Mar. 8/15, p. 3.
N.Y. Journal Feb. 24, p. 3.
Va. Gaz. (Purdie and Dixon) Mar. 10, p. 2; Mar. 24, p. 1.
Ga. Gaz. Apr. 6, p. 2.

January—March

Boston Port Act. Early reports of the British reaction to the Boston Tea Party are mixed. Parliamentary intentions are soon made obvious when Lord North (March 15) proposes a bill to close the port of Boston to trade. Passed in Parliament on March 25 and given royal assent on March 31, the Boston Port Act closes Boston to shipping as of June 1 until compensation is offered for the destroyed East India Company tea and the lost tea duty.

Bos. Gaz. Apr. 25, pp. 1-2; May 2, p. 3.
Conn. Courant Apr. 12/19, p. 1; May 3/10, pp. 2-3; May 10/17, pp. 2-3.
N.Y. Journal May 12, pp. 1-3; May 26, p. 4.
Pa. Journal Apr. 20, pp. 2-3; May 11, pp. 2-3; May 14, supplement, p. 1; May 18, p. 2; May 25, p. 1.
Md. Gaz. Apr. 7, p. 1; May 19, pp. 1-3.
Va. Gaz. (Purdie and Dixon) May 5, pp. 1-2; May 19, pp. 1-2.
Va. Gaz. (Rind) May 26, p. 2.
S.C. Gaz. June 3, extraordinary, pp. 1-2.
Ga. Gaz. Apr. 13, p. 2; Apr. 27, p. 3; May 4, p. 3; June 1, p. 1; June 8, p. 1.

April 19-24

New York Tea Party. New York City holds its own Tea Party when eighteen chests of tea smuggled into the harbor by a Captain Chambers aboard the *London* are destroyed (April 22).

Chambers is quietly spirited onto the *Nancy*, returning to London with a consignment of tea under popular mandate.

Bos. Gaz. May 2, p. 3.
Conn. Courant Apr. 19/26, p. 1; Apr. 26/May 3, p. 3.
N.Y. Journal Mar. 17, p. 3; Apr. 21, p. 3; Apr. 28, p. 3.
Riv. N.Y. Gazetteer Apr. 28, p. 3; May 12, pp. 2-3.
Pa. Journal Apr. 27, pp. 2-3.
S.C. Gaz. May 16, pp. 1-2.
Ga. Gaz. May 25, p. 1.
Broadside: Apr. 19.

May 13

Boston Ready to Embargo Britain. On the same day that General Thomas Gage arrives as the new Massachusetts governor, as well as commander-in-chief of the British armed forces in America, the Boston town meeting votes to end all trade between the colonies and Great Britain and the West Indies — if the other American colonies will join with the beleagured Bostonians. Paul Revere speeds south from Boston with news of the tentative scheme for an economic response to Massachusetts' (and America's) troubles.

Conn. Courant May 10/17, pp. 2-3; May 17/24, p. 2.
N.Y. Journal May 19, p. 3; May 26, pp. 2-3.
Pa. Journal May 20, postscript, p. 1; May 25, p. 2.
Md. Gaz. May 26, p. 2.
Ga. Gaz. June 15, p. 2.

May

Proposal for Continental Congress. Most prominent in the immediate colonial reaction to the Boston Port Act and Boston's demand for an end to American-British trade are proposals — Providence (May 17), Philadelphia (May 21), New York City (May 23), and Williamsburg (May 27) — for the convening of a "continental congress" of the American colonies.

N.Hamp. Gaz. July 22, p. 3.
Bos. Gaz. May 30, p. 2; June 13, p. 2.
Newpt. Merc. June 13, supplement, p. 1.
Conn. Courant May 17/24, p. 3.
N.Y. Journal June 9, pp. 2-3.
Riv. N.Y. Gazetteer May 26, p. 3.
Pa. Journal June 8, p. 1.
Md. Gaz. May 26, p. 2; June 2, pp. 2-3.
Va. Gaz. (Rind) May 26, p. 3.
S.C. Gaz. June 13, p. 3.
Ga. Gaz. June 29, p. 3.

June 1

Boston Port Act Takes Effect. The day on which the Boston Port Act is to take effect is marked by appropriate religious observances in Philadelphia (without Quaker participation),

To the Public.

THE long expected TEA SHIP arrived laſt night at Sandy-Hook, but the pilot would not bring up the Captain till the ſenſe of the city was known. The committee were immediately informed of her arrival, and that the Captain ſolicits for liberty to come up to provide neceſſaries for his return. The ſhip to remain at Sandy-Hook. The committee conceiving it to be the ſenſe of the city that he ſhould have ſuch liberty, ſignified it to the Gentleman who is to ſupply him with proviſions, and other neceſſaries. Advice of this was immediately diſpatched to the Captain; and whenever he comes up, care will be taken that he does not enter at the cuſtom-houſe, and that no time be loſt in diſpatching him.

New-York, April 19, 1774.

See p. 46, April 19-24,   Broadside April 19.

New York City (shaky), Williamsburg and Fredericksburg, Virginia, and Connecticut. The day is fraught with appreciated symbolism in Charleston when a terrible storm marks the occasion.

Bos. Gaz. June 27, p. 2.
Conn. Courant June 7, p. 3; June 14, pp. 2, 3.
N.Y. Journal June 2, p. 3.
Riv. N.Y. Gazetteer June 2, p. 3; June 30, p. 1.
Pa. Journal June 1, p. 3; June 8, pp. 1, 3.
Va. Gaz. (Rind) May 26, pp. 2-3; June 2, p. 2.
S.C. Gaz. June 6, p. 3; June 13, p. 3.
Ga. Gaz. June 29, p. 3.

June 5

Boston's Solemn League and Covenant. The Boston Committee of Correspondence adopts an economic stratagem despite their disappointment at the moderating responses of the other colonies, especially the New York and Philadelphia calls for a congress instead of immediate trade measures. The Boston plan is a Solemn League and Covenant by which subscribers bind themselves to stop all trade with Britain and end consumption of British imports after October 1. Although the Massachusetts radicals maintain their own direction, Boston's readiness to take such extreme economic reprisals is not generally duplicated before the creation of the Continental Association by the Continental Congress in October (see below, September 5-October 26).

N.Hamp. Gaz. July 8, p. 3.
Pa. Journal June 22, postscript, p. 1.
Md. Gaz. July 14, p. 2.
Ga. Gaz. Aug. 10, p. 2.

May—June

Intolerable, or Coercive, Acts. Intent on bringing Massachusetts to heel, Parliament passes three bills which, together with the Boston Port Act, come to be known as the Intolerable, or Coercive, Acts. The Administration of Justice Act (May 20) allows for the trial of soldiers or crown officials indicted while involved in maintaining civil order in America to be held in England or another colony if, in the governor's opinion, a fair trial is impossible in Massachusetts. This act is promptly dubbed the "Murder Act" in America. The Massachusetts Government Act (May 20) effectively changes the colony's structure of government. The act (a) allows the governor to appoint his council rather than have it chosen by the lower house, subject to his veto; (b) eliminates the council's veto power over the governor's decisions; (c) authorizes the governor to forbid town meetings other

than an annual election meeting; and (d) empowers the governor to remove the provincial sheriffs, judges, attorney general, or marshal at his discretion. The Quartering Act (June 2) is a revision of the earlier, and revised, 1768 act which enlarges the possibilities for obtaining suitable quarters for troops. Hostility to these measures is widespread in America.

Bos. Gaz. June 6, pp. 2-3; Aug. 8, p. 3; Aug. 15, p. 2.
Conn. Courant June 14, pp. 1, 4; July 12, p. 2; Aug. 9, p. 2; Aug. 23, p. 2.
N.Y. Journal May 12, pp. 1-3.
Pa. Journal June 1, postscript, p. 1; June 15, postscript, pp. 1-2; Sept. 14, p. 1.
Va. Gaz. (Rind) June 9, supplement, p. 1; June 23, pp. 2-3.
Ga. Gaz. July 6, p. 4.

June 22

Quebec Act. Often included by the colonists as a fifth Intolerable Act, the Quebec Act is the British solution to the problem of their French Canadian population won in 1763. The bounds of the Province of Quebec are extended south to the Ohio River and west to the Mississippi, effectively infringing on the claims cultivated by Virginia. The French legal code is to be maintained by French-speaking inhabitants of the province, a move adjudged inimical especially by English merchants trading in the area. Government would be by a crown-appointed governor and council without a representative assembly — a fate in the offing for recalcitrant colonies? And most exercising to the American colonists, the Roman Catholic Church is recognized as the established church (publicly financed) in Quebec, an establishment particularly hateful to a people with a traditional English abhorrence for "popery."

Bos. Gaz. Aug. 22, p. 2; Aug. 29, p. 3.
Conn. Courant Aug. 16, p. 2; Aug. 23, p. 1; Aug. 30, pp. 2, 3; Sept. 6, pp. 2-3; Sept. 15, extraordinary, p. 1; Oct. 10, p. 3; Nov. 21, p. 2.
Pa. Journal July 20, postscript, p. 2; Aug. 24, p. 2; Aug. 31, pp. 2-3; Sept. 14, p. 1.
Va. Gaz. (Rind) Sept. 15, pp. 1-2.
Ga. Gaz. Sept. 28, pp. 1, 4.

May—September

Colonial Reaction to Boston's Situation. The reaction in the colonies to Boston's plight is basically revealed in numerous town/county/colony resolutions that include generally a majority of the following sentiments: (1) obedience to King George III and constitutional laws is readily pledged; (2) the various British revenue acts are described as oppressive and arbitrary, and the acts' initiators are characterized as enemies of His Majesty and the English Constitution; (3) the Boston Port Act is unconstitutional and a concern to all Americans; (4) American unanimity is necessary in order to secure American rights and relieve the Boston brethren; (5) a congress of colony representatives and some form of non-importation of Great Britain and East Indies/West Indies goods are the most proper methods available to America; (6) cooperation in such an enterprise will be forthcoming through provision for congressional delegates and an assertion to abide by any commitments made by said delegates; (7) subscriptions for Boston's relief will be initiated; and (8) committees of correspondence are established on all colonial jurisdictional levels. [Each colony is noted below with a brief description of its activities during this period. Specific resolves are indicated by the name of the town, county, or colony preceding the date of citation.]

May–September

New Hampshire. On June 25, twenty-seven chests of tea arrive in Portsmouth; on June 28 said merchandise is on its way back to England. Despite Governor John Wentworth's dissolution of the General Assembly in early July, New Hampshire delegates to the Continental Congress are chosen by an extralegal gathering of town representatives (July 14).

N.Hamp. Gaz. July 1, p. 1; July 8, p. 1; July 22, p. 3; Aug. 12, p. 4; Sept. 9, p. 3; Sept. 16, p. 3; Sept. 23, p. 3; Sept. 30, p. 1; Dec. 9, p. 4.
Bos. Gaz. July 4, p. 2.
Newpt. Merc. Aug. 8, p. 1.
Conn. Courant July 19, p. 3; Aug. 2, p. 2.
Pa. Journal July 13, p. 2; Aug. 3, p. 2.

May–September

Massachusetts. Throughout the summer, Boston is the willing recipient of gifts of food and other forms of relief from Massachusetts towns as well as from the other colonies. The activities of the Boston Committee of Correspondence, in connection with its energetic solicitation for the compliance of other Massachusetts towns in the Solemn League and Covenant, provokes opposition. Dissidence in the Boston town meeting is easily voted down (June 27-28), and General Gage's depiction of said recruitment and League as "seditious" is ignored. It is at the suggestion of the Massachusetts House of Representatives

(June 17) that the proposed congress is to be convened in Philadelphia in early September.

Bos. Gaz. (Marblehead) May 30, p. 2; July 4, pp. 2, 3; (Berkshire County) July 25, p. 1.
Bos. Even. Post June 20, p. 2.
Newpt. Merc. June 27, p. 3.
Conn. Courant June 7, pp. 2-3; June 28, pp. 2, 3; June 5 [*sic*, i.e., July 5], pp. 2-3; July 26, p. 3.
N.Y. Journal Sept. 29, pp. 1, 2.
Pa. Journal June 29, p. 2; July 13, p. 2. Sept. 7, p. 3.
Va. Gaz. (Rind) June 9, supplement, p. 2; June 23, pp. 2-3.
S.C. Gaz. June 27, p. 1.

May–September

Rhode Island. On May 17, Providence urges the convening of a colonial congress; on May 20, Newport's town meeting votes to end all trade with Great Britain and the West Indies if the other colonies will agree to do likewise. The Rhode Island General Assembly issues its own appeal for a congress (June 13). Pursuing the logic of the revolutionary rhetoric regarding natural rights, Providence proceeds against slavery and urges (successfully) the General Assembly to prohibit the importation of slaves into Rhode Island.

Bos. Gaz. May 23, p. 2; May 30, p. 2.
Newpt. Merc. May 23, pp. 2-3; June 13, supplement, p. 1; June 20, p. 3; July 4, p. 3; July 18, p. 3; Aug. 22, p. 3.
Conn. Courant May 17/24, p. 3; June 7, p. 4; June 21, p. 4; June 28, p. 3; June 5 [*sic*, i.e., July 5], p. 1.
N.Y. Journal June 2, p. 2; June 9, supplement, p. 2; June 30, p. 4.
Pa. Journal June 29, postscript, p. 1.

May–September

Connecticut. On May 12, the Connecticut General Assembly votes resolutions that include a reaffirmation of their 1662 Charter rights as well as their liberties as Englishmen and a denunciation of the Boston Port Act. During the summer months, Connecticut towns pass their own resolutions of support for Boston, express fervent dissent from British actions, and coordinate and provide for committees of correspondence. On September 15, town representatives reach agreement on non-consumption of British goods.

Conn. Courant June 7, p. 3; June 14, p. 3; (Connecticut) June 21, p. 1; (Preston, Farmington, Wethersfield, Hartford) June 21, p. 2; (Middletown, Glastonbury, Lyme, Groton, New Haven) June 28, p. 3; June 5 [*sic*, i.e., July 5], p. 3; July 12, p. 3; July 19, p. 3; July 26, p. 3; Aug. 2, p. 3; Aug. 9, p. 3; Aug. 16, p. 2;

(East Windsor, Litchfield) Aug. 23, pp. 1, 2, 3; (Connecticut) Sept. 19, p. 2.
N.Y. Journal (Connecticut) June 16, p. 2; July 28, p. 2.
Pa. Journal July 27, p. 2.

May–September

New York. The immediate response in New York City to Boston's plight is the formulation of a strategy by city merchants to counter the radicals' current control of the important committee of correspondence. A more conservatively oriented Committee of 51 is duly established (May 16) and, after a short-lived opposition, is given consent by dissident merchants and mechanics (May 23). On the same day, New York City issues a call for a colonial congress. Numerous county resolutions offer New York Colony's advocacy of the American colonial cause. On July 27, New York's delegates to the Continental Congress are chosen without the participation of any but New York City and County representatives.

Bos. Gaz. June 27, p. 3.
Conn. Courant June 21, pp. 2, 3; July 26, pp. 2-3; Aug. 9, p. 2.
N.Y. Journal May 19, p. 3; May 26, pp. 2, 3; June 9, supplement, pp. 1-2; (Easthampton) June 30, p. 3; (New York City) July 7, pp. 2-3; (Huntington) July 7, p. 3; (Orange Town) July 14, p. 3; (New York) July 21, p. 3; Aug. 4, p. 2; (Rye) Aug. 18, p. 3; Sept. 8, p. 2.
Riv. N.Y. Gazetteer May 26, p. 3.
Pa. Journal May 25, p. 3; July 13, pp. 2-3; July 6, postscript, p. 1.

May–September

New Jersey. A provincial convention is held in New Brunswick on July 21, at which allegiance to the king is proclaimed while the Boston Port Act is condemned, relief for Boston is proposed, and the concept of a colonial congress is approved. Delegates for the congress are chosen and its adoption of non-importation and non-exportation agreements is recommended by the provincial convention. Governor William Franklin, Tory son of Benjamin Franklin, is content to allow such proceedings in a studied effort at reconciliation.

Newpt. Merc. Aug. 8, p. 3.
N.Y. Journal (Essex County) June 16, pp. 2-3; (Lower Freehold) July 7, p. 3; (Morris County) July 14, supplement, p. 1; (New Brunswick) July 21, p. 3; (New Jersey) July 28, pp. 2-3.
Pa. Journal (Hunterdon County) July 13, p. 3; (Gloucester County) July 20, p. 3; (Salem County) July 20, p. 3; (Somerset County) July 20, supplement, p. 2;

(New Jersey) July 27, p. 3; (Gloucester County) Aug. 3, p. 4; Sept. 14, p. 3.

May–September

Pennsylvania. Reaction to the Boston Port Act initially comes in a Philadelphia motion for a colonial congress (May 20) and proposals for the observance of the official blockade of Boston, June 1, by a general suspension of business. The latter is successful except for the majority of Quakers who do not participate on grounds of religious principle. The remainder of the period before the convening of the Continental Congress in Philadelphia (September 5) is marked by county resolutions and Philadelphia maneuverings calculated to demonstrate Pennsylvania's opposition to the British imperial tactics. A provincial convention (July 15-21) prepares a series of resolves and instructions for the Pennsylvania General Assembly that includes a cautionary statement regarding economic sanctions against Great Britain: the coming congress may first attempt a petition for the removal of grievances, but if it does not, and the congress decides to end all trade with Great Britain, then the inhabitants of Pennsylvania will go along — if said restriction is permanent on *all* colonies (see June-July 1770). The Pennsylvanians are influenced in their comparative moderation, and intention to wait upon the decisions of the congress, by the author of the *Farmer's Letters* (see December 2, 1776-February 15, 1768), John Dickinson, who writes four widely-reprinted "Letters to the Inhabitants of the British Colonies in America" critical of British policies (text in newspapers noted below before citations).

Bos. Gaz. June 27, p. 3; (Philadelphia) July 4, p. 4; Aug. 1, p. 2.
N.Y. Journal (Letter No. 1) June 2, p. 1; (Letter No. 2) June 9, p. 1; (Chester County) June 30, p. 4; (Pennsylvania) July 28, p. 2.
Pa. Journal (Philadelphia) May 25, p. 3; June 1, p. 3; (Letter No. 3) June 8, pp. 1, 3; (Letter No. 4) June 15, pp. 1-2, 2-3; (Philadelphia, Lancaster) June 22, p. 3; (Chester) June 22, postscript, p. 1; (Berks County, York, Chester) July 6, pp. 2-3; (York County) July 13, p. 3; (Bucks County, Chester County, Cumberland County, Bedford) July 20, postscript, p. 1; (Lancaster County) July 20, supplement, p. 2; (Pennsylvania) July 23, postscript extra. [*sic*], pp. 1-2; July 27, p. 3; Aug. 31, p. 1; Sept. 14, p. 3.
Va. Gaz. (Purdie and Dixon) (Pennsylvania) Aug. 11, pp. 2-3.
Va. Gaz. (Rind) June 9, supplement, p. 2.

May–September

Delaware. The Lower Counties – New Castle, Kent, and Sussex – pass similar resolutions against the Boston Port Act and for Boston relief; establish county committees of correspondence; and request the convening of the Lower Counties' General Assembly in order to choose delegates to the proposed colonial congress. An unofficial meeting of Delaware's Assembly convenes in New Castle in August and elects three delegates who are instructed to carry colonials abroad for trial, and to seek the implementation of economic measures designed to end trade between the colonies and Great Britain. (The Lower Counties officially become "Delaware State" on September 20, 1776, with the adoption of a state constitution.)

Newpt. Merc. Aug. 15, p. 3.
Pa. Journal (New Castle) July 6, p. 3; (Lewes Town, Sussex County, Kent County) Aug. 3, pp. 1, 2; Aug. 10, p. 3.

May–September

Maryland. An Annapolis gathering of patriots (May 25) pledges itself to an end of trade with Great Britain – if the other colonies will so agree. Similar sentiments are expressed in Queen Ann's County (May 30) and Baltimore (May 31). Despite (infrequent) instances of opposition, a June 22 meeting of Maryland representatives in Annapolis voices its opinion that an end to the British trade is indeed the best colonial course of action and votes relief for suffering Boston.

Bos. Gaz. (Annapolis, Queen Ann's County) June 13, p. 2.
Conn. Courant (Queen Ann's County) June 21, p. 4.
Conn. Courant (Queen Ann's County) June 21, p. 4.
N.Y. Journal June 16, p. 3; July 7, p. 3.
Pa. Journal (Annapolis) June 1, p. 2; (Baltimore, Queen Ann's County, Chestertown, Talbot Courthouse) June 29, postscript, p. 1; Aug. 3, p. 2; Sept. 7, p. 3.
Md. Gaz. May 26, p. 2; June 2, pp. 2-3; June 9, p. 2; June 16, p. 2; June 30, pp. 2-3; Aug. 11, p. 2; Aug. 18, p. 2.
Va. Gaz. (Rind) June 9, supplement, p. 2.

May–September

Virginia. The Old Dominion's reaction to Boston's circumstances is immediately manifest when the House of Burgesses resolves (May 24) that June 1 is to be observed as a day of fasting and prayer. Governor Dunmore responds by dissolving the General Assembly (May 26), whereupon eighty-nine Burgesses meet at the Raleigh Tavern (May 27) and establish an association to boycott tea and other items imported by the East India Company. These Burgesses also declare the Boston Port Act an attack on all the colonies and call for a congress of the American colonies. The First Virginia Convention meets in Williamsburg (August 1-6) and agrees to end importation of British goods after November 1 and exportation to Great Britain after August 10, 1775, so as to enable the Virginia planters to pay their debts after the year's crops are harvested. Delegates to the Continental Congress are chosen. During this period a large number of Virginia counties and towns pass resolutions similar to those of their fellow Northern and Southern colonists.

Bos. Gaz. (Virginia) June 13, p. 2; (Fairfax County) Aug. 8, pp. 2-3; Aug. 29, supplement, p. 1.
Conn. Courant June 14, p. 2.
N.Y. Journal (Virginia) June 9, pp. 2-3; June 16, p. 3; (Prince William County, Dumfries) June 30, p. 2; (Virginia) Aug. 25, pp. 3-4; Sept. 1, supplement, pp. 1-2.
Pa. Journal (Virginia) June 8, p. 1; (Westmoreland County) July 20, supplement, p. 1; (Virginia) Aug. 24, p. 1.
Va. Gaz. (Purdie and Dixon) July 21, pp. 2-3; (Hanover County, Caroline County, Henrico County, Nansemond County) July 28, supplement, pp. 1, 2; (Virginia) Aug. 11, p. 1.
Va. Gaz. (Rind) (Virginia) May 26, pp. 2-3; June 2, p. 2; (Westmoreland County, Prince George County) June 30, p. 2; (York County, New Kent County, Essex County, Dinwiddie County, Surry County, Chesterfield County) July 21, pp. 2-3.
S.C. Gaz. (Virginia) June 13, p. 3; (Virginia) Sept. 12, p. 2.
Ga. Gaz. Aug. 24, p. 1.

May–September

North Carolina. When Governor Josiah Martin refuses to convene an assembly in time to select delegates to the proposed congress, a Wilmington meeting (July 21) issues its own call for a provincial congress at New Bern on August 25. Despite a proclamation (August 13) by the governor prohibiting the planned meeting, thirty of thirty-six counties are represented at North Carolina's First Provincial Congress (August 25-28). Resolutions are passed against Parliamentary taxation of the colonies, in support of Boston, and in reaffirmation of allegiance to the king; a non-exportation and non-importation agreement is passed; the idea of a colonial congress is endorsed; and North Carolina delegates are chosen to attend a congress of the American colonies.

N.Hamp. Gaz. Jan. 6 (1775), p. 2.
Conn. Courant (North Carolina) Sept. 19, p. 3.
N.Y. Journal (North Carolina) Sept. 29, supplement, pp. 1-2.
Pa. Journal Aug. 31, p. 3; (North Carolina) Sept. 16, postscript, pp. 1-2.
(N.B.) *N.C. Gaz.* Sept. 2, pp. 1-3.
S.C. Gaz. (Wilmington, North Carolina) Sept. 12, p. 4; Oct. 10, p. 2.

May—September

South Carolina. Acting within a month of news of the closing of Boston's harbor (which event merits black borders in Peter Timothy's June 3, extraordinary, *South Carolina Gazette*), South Carolina representatives meet (July 6-8), pass appropriate resolves against British activities and for Boston's resistance, and choose delegates for the colonial congress. An incidental example of the colony's intentions in the growing conflict occurs with the arrival of a ship with three chests of tea aboard; these symbols of tyranny are promptly stored in Charleston (July 18-19). Resentment at Northern defections from the non-importation agreements established against the Townshend Acts recedes quickly in the face of British policies (see above June-July, September, October 12, and December 13, 1770).

Bos. Gaz. (South Carolina) July 25, p. 2; (South Carolina) Aug. 15, p. 1.
Conn. Courant July 26, p. 3; Aug. 9, p. 2.
N.Y. Journal June 30, supplement, p. 1; (South Carolina) July 21, p. 1; (South Carolina) Aug. 4, p. 1.
Pa. Journal July 20, p. 2; Oct. 5, p. 2.
S.C. Gaz. June 20, p. 1; June 27, p. 1; (St. Bartholomew Parish) July 4, p. 3; (South Carolina) July 11, p. 2; July 25, p. 2; Sept. 19, p. 2.
Ga. Gaz. July 13, p. 3.

May—September

Georgia. Of the original thirteen colonies, Georgia is the only colony not to be represented at the First Continental Congress. Despite an August 5 proclamation by Governor James Wright that any assemblies convened by private summons are illegal and unconstitutional, an August 10 meeting is held in Savannah. This gathering declares itself against the Boston Port Act and the Massachusetts Government Act; states that Britain has no right to tax the unrepresented Americans; dissents from any attempt to transport colonists to Great Britain for trial; agrees to work with the other colonies in all constitutional ways; and establishes a General Committee to oversee colony actions and function as an intercolonial committee of correspon-

dence. These patriotic actions have little popular support and Georgia continues to remain outside the orbit of the twelve other colonies.

Bos. Even. Post Sept. 19, supplement, p. 1.
Pa. Journal Oct. 5, p. 2.
S.C. Gaz. Sept. 12, pp. 1, 4; Oct. 10, p. 2.
Ga. Gaz. July 27, pp. 1, 3; Aug. 3, pp. 2-3; Aug. 10, pp. 2, 4; Aug. 17, pp. 1, 2, 4; Aug. 24, pp. 1, 2, 4; Sept. 7, pp. 2, 3; Sept. 28, p. 2; Oct. 12, pp. 1-2; Oct. 19, p. 3; Oct. 26, p. 2.

September

British Raids on Charlestown and Cambridge. British troops surprise the Massachusetts patriots by quick raids which net provincial cannon and powder stored in Cambridge and Charlestown (September 1). Colonial protest is also occasioned by General Gage's efforts to fortify Boston Neck, a slim strip of land that connects the town of Boston (actually a peninsula in the eighteenth century) with Roxbury and the rest of Massachusetts.

Bos. Gaz. Sept. 12, p. 2.
Bos. Even. Post Sept. 5, p. 2.
Newpt. Merc. Sept. 5, p. 3.
Conn. Courant Sept. 12, p. 2.
N.Y. Journal Sept. 8, p. 3; Sept. 29, p. 2.
Pa. Journal Sept. 14, p. 2; Sept. 21, p. 2.
Md. Gaz. Sept. 15, pp. 2-3.
Ga. Gaz. Oct. 5, p. 1.

September 5—October 26

First Continental Congress. Chosen either by extralegal provincial conventions composed of county and town representatives and committees of correspondence members or by the colony legislature (Pennsylvania), delegates to the First Continental Congress formally convene in Philadelphia on September 5, 1774. With the arrival of the North Carolina delegates on September 12, all the colonies except Georgia are represented. Preliminary getting-acquainted is interrupted by the arrival of Paul Revere (September 17) with a series of resolves passed eight days earlier in Suffolk County, Massachusetts. These radical sentiments are endorsed by the Congress on October 8. The Suffolk Resolves state that (a) the Coercive Acts are unconstitutional and hence not to be obeyed; (b) Massachusetts taxes are to be collected by the Provincial Congress and kept away from the royal government until a constitutional government is established; (c) Massachusetts men are advised to arm themselves and form militia units to protect themselves from attack; and (d) if any patriot leaders are jailed, every official in the royal government might be imprisoned by the people.

The approval of the Suffolk Resolves, coupled with the defeat of Joseph Galloway's (Pennsylvania) conciliatory Plan of Union, its expunging from the official records (October 22), and the adoption of the Continental Association (October 20), signals the defeat of the conservative elements in the Congress. Modeled on the Virginia Association (see above, August 1-6), the Continental Association is expected to be endorsed and observed by every American locality. Its provisions include non-importation and non-consumption of goods from Great Britain, Ireland, and the British West Indies as of December 1, 1774. A date for non-exportation to British soil as of September 10, 1775, is more difficult to agree upon and compromises are reached with Virginia (one year's delay) and South Carolina (rice exportation is excepted) that nearly cause a premature dissolution of the Congress.

Other measures of the Congress include a Declaration of Rights and Resolves (October 14); a petition and remonstrance to King George III; and Addresses to the People of Great Britain, the Inhabitants of the Province of Quebec, and a letter to the American people. Finally, the delegates agree to meet again on May 10, 1775, if American grievances are still unresolved.

N. Hamp. Gaz. Sept. 30, p. 2; Nov. 11, p. 3; Dec. 9, p. 2; Dec. 16, pp. 2-3; Dec. 23, p. 2; Jan. 6 (1775), p. 2.
Bos. Gaz. Sept. 12, supplement, pp. 1-2; Sept. 26, p. 2; Oct. 3, p. 3; Oct. 24, p. 1; Oct. 31, p. 3; Nov. 7, pp. 1-2; Nov. 14, pp. 1-2; Jan. 30 (1775), p. 2.
Bos. Even. Post Sept. 19, pp. 1-2.
Newpt. Merc. Oct. 3, p. 3; Nov. 7, p. 3.
Conn. Courant Sept. 19, p. 3; Sept. 26, pp. 1-2; Oct. 17, p. 3; Oct. 24, p. 3; Nov. 7, pp. 1-2; Jan. 30 (1775), p. 4.
N.Y. Journal Sept. 8, p. 2; Sept. 22, p. 3; Oct. 6, p. 3; Oct. 13, p. 3; Nov. 3, p. 3; Jan. 26 (1775), pp. 1-2.
Pa. Journal Aug. 24, p. 3; Aug. 31, p. 3; Sept. 7, p. 3; Sept. 14, p. 3; Sept. 21, pp. 1-2; Sept. 28, pp. 1, 2, 3, 4; Nov. 2, p. 3; Mar. 15 (1775), pp. 2-3.
Md. Gaz. Nov. 3, pp. 2-3.
Va. Gaz. (Purdie and Dixon) Oct. 6, p. 2.
Va. Gaz. (Pinkney) Nov. 3, pp. 1-2; Nov. 10, pp. 1-2.
S.C. Gaz. Oct. 10, pp. 2-3; Oct. 17, pp. 1, 4; Nov. 21, pp. 2-3.
Ga. Gaz. Sept. 28, p. 3; Oct 19, pp. 1, 4; Nov. 16, p. 3; Nov. 23, pp. 1-2.

October 7

Massachusetts Provincial Congress. An illegal gathering of Massachusetts representatives, styling itself a Provincial Congress, convenes in Salem after General Gage refuses to give the oaths of office to a previously-called General Assembly. John Hancock is chosen head of a committee of safety and empowered to call out the local militia (minutemen) if necessary. The creation of the Massachusetts Provincial Congress is preceded by Middlesex County and Worcester County resolutions that urge a suspension of the legal processes of the colony (in view of the Massachusetts Government Act), stress the necessity for good order, and propose the establishment of a provincial congress.

N.Hamp. Gaz. Sept. 16, p. 2.
Bos. Gaz. Sept. 12, supplement, pp. 1-2; Oct. 17, pp. 2, 3; Oct. 24, p. 1; Oct. 31, p. 3.
Bos. Even. Post Oct. 10, pp. 1, 2.
Conn. Courant Sept. 12, pp. 2-3; Oct. 17, pp. 2-3; Oct. 24, p. 3; Oct. 31, p. 2.
Pa. Journal Sept. 21, pp. 1, 4; Oct. 19, p. 2; Oct. 26, p. 2.
Md. Gaz. Oct. 27, p. 2; Nov. 24, pp. 1-2.
Ga. Gaz. Nov. 16, supplement, p. 1; Dec. 21, p. 1.

October 19

Annapolis Tea Party. Outdoing even Boston, Annapolis patriots oversee the burning of a cargo of tea as well as its carrier, the *Peggy Stewart*, with the ready cooperation of the ship's owner.

Bos. Gaz. Nov. 7, p. 4.
Newpt. Merc. Oct. 31, p. 2.
N.Y. Journal Oct. 27, p. 2.
Pa. Journal Oct. 26, p. 2.
Md. Gaz. Oct. 20, p. 2; Oct. 27, pp. 2-3; Apr. 13 (1775), pp. 2-3.
Va. Gaz. (Purdie and Dixon) Oct. 27, p. 2.

October-April 1775

Widespread Colonial Support of Congress's Proposals. Colonial reaction to the recommendations and proceedings of the Continental Congress is demonstrated by local expressions of approval of Congressional actions, adoption of the Continental Association, and the establishment of committees to oversee the implementation and observance of the local associations. Provision is made in each colony for the choice of delegates for the reconvening of the Continental Congress (May 10). Instances of local committees' robust vigilance are printed in the colonial newspapers in the form of recantations of those caught compromising the local association or in the guise of public indictments of those with sufficient fortitude to continue unpatriotic activities. Such advertisements dramatize the colonials' determination and establish the "circumstances" necessary for a willing compliance with the dictates of American patriotism. While relief efforts for Boston continue, colonies such as Massachusetts and Connecticut begin to reorganize and refurbish their respective militia.

Opposition to the Congressional proposals is generally muted, but specific problems with the enforcement of the Association are experienced in Ridgefield, Newtown, and Fairfield County, Connecticut; in Dutchess County and Staten Island, New York; and in Farmington, Connecticut, where Solomon and Martha Cowles offer an apology for serving tea in their home. Although neither the colonies of New York nor Georgia enter the Continental Association at this moment, the work of local committees in the former reduces the value of New York City imports from Britain from £440,000 (1774) to £1200 (1775)! Georgia finds its trade with South Carolina suspended (March 8, 1775) by Carolina patriots. Georgia does not enter the Continental Association until July 4, 1775, nor does it send a full complement of delegates to the Continental Congress until September 12, 1775.

New Hampshire
N.Hamp. Gaz. Nov. 18, p. 1; Dec. 2, p. 1; Dec. 16, pp. 1, 4; Dec. 30, p. 1; Jan. 13 (1775), p. 4; Feb. 10 (1775), p. 1; Apr. 14 (1775), pp. 2-3.
Bos. Gaz. Dec. 26, p. 3; Feb. 6 (1775), supplement, p. 2; Feb. 27 (1775), supplement, p. 4.
Conn. Courant Dec. 26, p. 3;
Pa. Journal Nov. 30, p. 1; Feb. 8 (1775), p. 2; Feb. 22 (1775), p. 4.
Ga. Gaz. Mar. 22 (1775), p. 1.

Massachusetts
Bos. Gaz. Nov. 21, pp. 2, 3; Nov. 28, p. 1; Dec. 5, pp. 1, 2, 3; Dec. 12, p. 1; Jan. 16 (1775), pp. 2, 3; Jan. 23 (1775), p. 3; Jan. 30 (1775), p. 3; Feb. 13 (1775), p. 1; Mar. 13 (1775), p. 3; Mar. 20 (1775), p. 2; Mar. 27 (1775), p. 2; Apr. 3 (1775), p. 3; Apr. 17 (1775), p. 4.
N.Y. Journal Nov. 10, pp. 1-2; Dec. 29, supplement, p. 1.
Pa. Journal Dec. 21, p. 1; Feb. 22 (1775), p. 3; Mar. 22 (1775), pp. 2-3.

Connecticut
Bos. Gaz. Nov. 21, p. 3; Dec. 12, p. 1; Dec. 19, pp. 1, 4; Dec. 26, p. 3; Mar. 27 (1775), p. 2.
Conn. Courant Nov. 7, pp. 1-2, 3; Dec. 5, p. 3; Dec. 12, p. 1; Dec. 26, pp. 1, 3; Jan. 30 (1775), pp. 1, 3; Feb. 13 (1775), p. 4; Feb. 20 (1775), p. 3; Feb. 27 (1775), p. 3; Mar. 6 (1775), p. 3; Apr. 3 (1775), p. 3; May 8 (1775), p. 4; June 12 (1775), p. 3.
N.Y. Journal Dec. 29, p. 3; Dec. 29, supplement, p. 1; Jan. 19 (1775), p. 1; Feb. 9 (1775), p. 2; Mar. 9 (1775), p. 2; Apr. 6 (1775), p. 1.
Riv. N.Y. Gazetteer Feb. 23 (1775), p. 1.
Pa. Journal Nov. 16, p. 3; Nov. 30, p. 1.

Rhode Island
N.Hamp. Gaz. Nov. 28, p. 3; Dec. 12, pp. 2-3; Dec. 19, p. 3.

Bos. Gaz. Dec. 26, p. 3.
Newpt. Merc. Jan 23 (1775), p. 3; Jan. 30 (1775), p. 3.
Conn. Courant Dec. 26, p. 3.
N.Y. Journal Nov. 24, p. 2; Dec. 29, p. 3.
Pa. Journal Nov. 30, p. 1; Feb. 22 (1775), p. 2.

New York
Bos. Gaz. Dec. 12, p. 1; Dec. 26, p. 2; Feb. 6 (1775), supplement, p. 2; Mar. 27 (1775), p. 2.
Conn. Courant Mar. 6 (1775), pp. 2, 3.
N.Y. Journal Oct. 13, p. 3; Nov. 3, p. 3; Nov. 10, p. 3; Nov. 24, pp. 1, 3; Dec. 15, pp. 2, 3; Dec. 29, p. 3; Jan. 5 (1775), p. 2; Jan. 26 (1775), p. 2; Feb. 2 (1775), p. 3; Feb. 16 (1775), p. 3; Mar. 9 (1775), p. 3; Apr. 6 (1775), pp. 2, 3; Apr. 27 (1775), p. 2.
Riv. N.Y. Gazetteer Nov. 10, p. 1; Dec. 1, p. 2; Dec. 29, p. 1; Jan. 12 (1775), p. 2; Jan. 19 (1775), p. 2; Feb. 16 (1775), p. 1; Mar. 2 (1775), p. 1; Apr. 20 (1775), pp. 1, 3;
Pa. Journal Dec. 21, pp. 2-3; Feb. 22 (1775), p. 2; Mar. 15 (1775), p. 1; Mar. 22 (1775), p. 2; Apr. 26 (1775), p. 2.

New Jersey
Conn. Courant Feb. 20 (1775), p. 3; Mar. 27 (1775), p. 3.
N.Y. Journal Dec. 15, p. 2; Dec. 22, p. 2; Jan. 19 (1775), p. 1; Jan. 26 (1775), p. 1; Feb. 2 (1775), p. 2; Feb. 9 (1775), p. 3; Feb. 16 (1775), supplement, p. 1; Mar. 9 (1775), p. 3; Apr. 6 (1775), p. 1; Apr. 6 (1775), supplement extraordinary, pp. 1-2.
Pa. Journal Nov. 23, p. 3; Jan. 4 (1775), p. 3; Jan. 25 (1775), p. 3; Feb. 1 (1775), p. 3; Feb. 22 (1775), p. 3.

Pennsylvania
Bos. Gaz. Dec. 26, p. 2.
Conn. Courant Jan. 2 (1775), p. 2; May 15 (1775), pp. 1-2.
N.Y. Journal Nov. 10, p. 2; Dec. 29, p. 3.
Pa. Journal Nov. 2, p. 3; Nov. 9, p. 3; Nov. 30, p. 3; Dec. 7, p. 3; Dec. 14, p. 3; Dec. 21, pp. 1, 3; Jan. 11 (1775), p. 3; Jan. 18 (1775), p. 3; Jan 25 (1775), p. 3; Feb. 1 (1775), p. 1; Feb. 22 (1775), pp. 2, 3.

Delaware
N.Y. Journal Mar. 30 (1775), supplement extraordinary, pp. 1-2.
Pa. Journal Dec. 28, p. 3; Mar. 22 (1775), p. 3.

Maryland
Bos. Gaz. Jan. 9 (1775), p. 4.
Conn. Courant Jan. 2 (1775), p. 3.
N.Y. Journal Dec. 29, pp. 2, 3.
Pa. Journal Dec. 21, pp. 1-2.
Md. Gaz. Nov. 3, p. 3; Nov. 10, p. 2; Nov. 24, pp. 2-3; Dec. 1, p. 2; Dec. 15, pp. 1-2; Dec. 22, p. 2; Dec. 29, p. 2; Jan. 19 (1775), pp. 2-3; Feb. 2 (1775), pp. 1-2; Mar. 30 (1775), p. 2; Apr. 13 (1775), p. 3.
Ga. Gaz. Jan. 11 (1775), pp. 2-3.

Virginia
Bos. Gaz. Dec. 12, p. 1; Dec. 26, p. 1.
N.Y. Journal Dec. 8, p. 2.

Pa. Journal Nov. 30, pp. 2, 3; Dec. 14, p. 2; Apr. 12 (1775), p. 3.
Md. Gaz. Dec. 8, p. 2.
Va. Gaz. (Pinkney) Nov. 17, p. 3; Nov. 24, p. 3; Dec. 1, p. 3; Apr. 13 (1775), supplement, p. 1.

North Carolina

N.Y. Journal Apr. 27 (1775), p. 1.
Pa. Journal Apr. 19 (1775), p. 3; Apr. 26 (1775), pp. 1, 4; May 3 (1775), p. 1.
Md. Gaz. Feb. 9 (1775), p. 2.
(N.B.) *N.C. Gaz.* Apr. 7 (1775), pp. 3-4.
S.C. Gaz. Apr. 3 (1775), p. 1.

South Carolina

Bos. Gaz. Mar. 27 (1775), p. 3.
Conn. Courant Apr. 3 (1775), p. 3.
N.Y. Journal Jan. 26 (1775), p. 3; Feb. 2 (1775), supplement, p. 1; Feb. 9 (1775), p. 3; Apr. 6 (1775), p. 3.
Pa. Journal Nov. 9, p. 2; Nov. 23, p. 3; Feb. 1 (1775), p. 2; Feb. 1 (1775), supplement, p. 1; Apr. 5 (1775), p. 2.
S.C. Gaz. Oct. 17, p. 3; Oct. 31, p. 2; Nov. 21, p. 2; Jan. 23 (1775), pp. 1, 2; Jan. 30 (1775), p. 1; Mar. 6 (1775), p. 1; Mar. 27 (1775), p. 1.

Georgia

Bos. Gaz. Apr. 3 (1775), p. 3.
N.Y. Journal Jan. 5 (1775), pp. 2, 3; Apr. 6 (1775), p. 3; Apr. 13 (1775), p. 1.
Pa. Journal Mar. 8 (1775), p. 3.
S.C. Gaz. Dec. 12, p. 3; Jan. 30 (1775), p. 3; Feb. 20 (1775), p. 1.
Ga. Gaz. Nov. 23, p. 2; Nov. 30, p. 1; Dec. 7, p. 1; Dec. 14, pp. 1-2; Dec. 21, p. 3; Jan. 25 (1775), p. 1; Feb. 1 (1775), p. 1.

December 14

New Hampshire Raids British Fort. Warned by the well-traveled Paul Revere of a British plan to garrison Portsmouth, New Hampshire, local patriots led by John Sullivan break into Fort William and Mary (Portsmouth) and take away arms and gunpowder.

N.Hamp. Gaz. Dec. 23, p. 1.
Bos. Gaz. Dec. 19, p. 2; Dec. 26, p. 2;
Conn. Courant Dec, 26, p. 3.
Va. Gaz. (Pinkney) June 8 (1775), p. 1.
Ga. Gaz. Feb. 1 (1775), supplement, p. 1.

Boston Massacre
Anniversary
Conn. Courant Mar. 15/22, p. 2.

Boundary
East and West Jersey noted
Pa. Journal Feb. 16, p. 4.
Pennsylvania-Maryland to be settled
Pa. Journal Nov. 9, p. 1.

Bull-baiting
Ad for
Riv. N.Y. Gazetteer July 28, p. 4.

Church of England
Connecticut minister apologizes for non-patri-
otism: fails to conduct official colony day of
fast for American problems
Conn. Courant Sept. 19, p. 2.

Class Consciousness
Should lower discuss current politics?
Pa. Journal Oct. 5, p. 2.

Colleges
College of New Jersey commencement
Pa. Journal Oct. 12, p. 2.
Queen's College (Rutgers), first public com-
mencement
N.Y. Journal Nov. 3, p. 3.
William and Mary, plan for reorganization of
preparatory education for
Va. Gaz. (Purdie and Dixon) May 12, p. 2.

Counterfeiting
New Jersey
N.Y. Journal Jan. 6, p. 1.

Diseases
Small-pox
Pa. Journal Feb. 2, p. 3; Sept. 7, p. 3.

Education
Grammar school (headmaster Thomas Byer-
ley's grammar in ad for school is attacked —
see above,
N.Y. Journal Oct. 21 (1773)
N.Y. Journal Mar. 17, p. 3; Mar. 31, p. 3;
Apr. 28, p. 1.

First Aid
To resuscitate drowned person
Pa. Journal Dec. 7, p. 3.

Guy Fawkes Day (November 5)
Anniversary
S.C. Gaz. Nov. 21, p. 2.

Horseracing
Connecticut race
Conn. Courant May 24/31, p. 4.
Maryland races
Md. Gaz. May 26, p. 2; Oct. 20, p. 2.
Maryland races cancelled
Md. Gaz. Nov. 3, p. 3.

Humor
Lampoon of future Parliament acts to enforce
American dependence
Pa. Journal June 29, supplement, p. 1.

Indians
Creeks: possible attack on Georgia, South Car-
olina
Va. Gaz. (Purdie and Dixon) Mar. 10, p. 3;
Mar. 24, p. 1.
S.C. Gaz. Jan. 31, p. 3; Feb. 14, p. 3.
Ga. Gaz. Feb, p. 2; Feb. 16, p. 2; Mar. 2, p.
1; Mar. 9, p. 2; Mar. 16, pp. 1, 2; Mar. 30,
p. 2; Apr. 20, p. 2; Apr. 27, p. 1; May 11,
p. 3; May 25, p. 2.

Independence, American
English view of: extract from *American Inde-
pendence the Interest and Glory of Great
Britain*
Bos. Gaz. Dec. 19, p. 2.

Libraries
Library Company of Philadelphia: officers
chosen
Pa. Journal May 4, p. 3.

Locke, John
Extract from regarding right of rebellion
N. Hamp. Gaz. Oct. 21, p. 1.

Marriage
Ad for runaway wife and consort
Pa. Journal Aug. 3, p. 4.

Newspapers
Subscribers' accounts in arrears
Conn. Courant Dec. 5, p. 4.
Thoughts on freedom of press
Conn. Courant June 7, p. 2.
Pa. Journal Aug. 17, supplement, p. 1.

Verse on freedom of press
Riv. N.Y. Gazetteer Dec. 8, p. 3; Dec. 15,
p. 2.

Poetry
Against tea
N.Hamp. Gaz. July 22, p. 4.

Population
American colonies estimated September 1774
Bos. Gaz. Nov. 21, p. 3.

Post Office
American proposed
Conn. Courant May 24/31, p. 3.

Public Utilities
Street lamps: law regarding destruction of
Bos. Gaz. Feb. 28, p. 3.

Quakers
Comments on patriotism of
Md. Gaz. Sept. 29, p. 2.

Rights, American Political
America does not tax Britain: *vice versa* desirable
Conn. Courant Mar. 1/8, p. 3.

Roman Catholics
Anti-Catholicism: Quebec Act and "slaves of popery"
Conn. Courant Aug. 30, p. 2.

Russia
Russians desire American liberties
Conn. Courant Nov. 28, p. 3.

Saltwater Bathing
Plans for announced
Pa. Journal Feb. 23, p. 3.

Servants
Ad for hire of
Pa. Journal Aug. 24, p. 4.

Slaves
Anti-slavery sentiments
Newpt. Merc. June 13, p. 3.
Conn. Courant Sept. 12, p. 1; Oct. 3, p. 4;
Oct. 10, pp. 1-2; Nov. 28, p. 1.
Pa. Journal Sept. 21, p. 4;
Va. Gaz. (Rind) June 30, p. 2.

Connecticut prohibits importation of
N.Y. Journal Dec. 29, supplement, p. 1.

Georgia regulations regarding hire of
Ga. Gaz. Mar. 30, p. 1.
Providence, Rhode Island; emancipation of
Bos. Gaz. May 30, p. 2.
Conn. Courant June 21, p. 4.
N.Y. Journal June 9, supplement, p. 2.
Rhode Island prohibits importation of
Newpt. Merc. June 27, p. 3.
Conn. Courant June 5, p. 1.

Tea
Injurious to health
N.Y. Journal Jan. 13, pp. 1-2.

Theater
Contrary to Continental Association: not frugal
N.Y. Journal Dec. 15, p. 3.

Tories
Certain Anglican clergy in Connecticut raise patriot ire
Conn. Courant Oct. 17, pp. 1-2; Nov. 7, pp. 2, 3.

Transportation
Stagecoach route (Baltimore-Philadelphia)
Pa. Journal July 6, postscript, p. 1.

Vigilantes
Boston customs officer, John Malcolm, tarred and feathered for civil disturbance (see Customs, 1773)
Bos. Gaz. Jan. 31, p. 2.
Conn. Courant Jan. 25/Feb. 1, p. 3; Feb. 1/8, p. 2.

Washington, George
Ad for sale of Ohio land
Pa. Journal July 23, postscript extraordinary, p. 2.

Wheatley, Phillis
Poems: On Various Subjects, Religious and Moral
Bos. Gaz. Jan. 31, p. 1.

Women
Patriotism of
Pa. Journal Sept. 21, pp. 2-3.

December 5/12, 1774–April 17

Novanglus v. Massachusettensis. A newspaper debate in Boston pits John Adams ("Novanglus") in the *Boston Gazette* against the totally anonymous Solicitor General to the Customs Board, Daniel Leonard ("Massachusettensis") writing in the *Massachusetts Gazette and Boston Post-Boy and Advertiser.* Their dialogue ranges over a wide area of controversial political ideas and practices. Leonard argues, in particular, that the colonies must be dependent on Parliament or completely independent; Adams counters with the claim that the colonies' only tie with Great Britain is through their allegiance to King George. The series and debate are terminated by the events at Lexington and Concord, April 19, 1775 (see below).

Bos. Gaz. Jan. 23, pp. 1, 4; Jan. 30, pp. 1, 4; Feb. 6, pp. 2-4; Feb. 13, pp. 2-4; Feb. 20, pp. 1-4; Feb. 27, pp. 1-4; Mar. 6, pp. 1-4; Mar. 13, pp. 1-2; Mar. 20, pp. 1, 4; Mar. 27, pp. 1, 4; Apr. 3, pp. 1, 4; Apr. 10, pp. 1, 4; Apr. 17, pp. 1, 4.
Mass. Gaz. and Bos. Post-Boy and Adv. Dec. 5/12 (1774), pp. 1-2; Dec. 12/19 (1774), pp. 1-2; Dec. 19/26 (1774), pp. 1-2; Dec. 26 (1774)/Jan. 2, pp. 1-2; Jan. 2/9, pp. 1-2; Jan. 9/16, pp. 1-2; Jan. 16/23, pp. 1-2; Jan. 23/30, p. 1; Jan. 30/Feb. 6, p. 1; Feb. 6/13, p. 1; Feb. 13/20, p. 1; Feb. 20/27, p. 1; Feb. 27/Mar. 6, pp. 1-2; Mar. 6/13, p. 1; Mar. 13/20, pp. 1, 4; Mar. 20/27, pp. 1-2; Mar. 27/Apr. 3, p. 1.

December 1774–February

Parliament Considers Congress's Case. The petition and other communications from the First Continental Congress to King George are set before Parliament in January (see above, September 5–October 26, 1774). A motion by the Earl of Chatham (William Pitt) urging the removal of all troops from Boston and the end of all colonial taxation by Parliament for revenue without the express approval of the colonial assemblies (January 20), and a reconciliation plan introduced by him on February 1, are defeated. On February 9, both Houses of Parliament vote that Massachusetts is in rebellion and urge the king to take appropriate actions. On February 20, Lord North introduces the ministry's reconciliation scheme: any colony that voluntarily contributes a sufficient sum for imperial expenses will not be taxed by Parliament.

Bos. Gaz. Mar. 20, p. 2; Apr. 10, p. 2; Apr. 17, p. 2.
N.E. Chron. Oct. 19/26, pp. 1-2.
Newpt. Merc. Mar. 15, extraordinary, pp. 1-2; Mar. 20, p. 3.
Conn. Courant Feb. 6, p. 2; Feb. 13, pp. 2-3; Feb. 20, p. 2; Mar. 6, p. 1; Mar. 20, pp. 2-3; Mar. 27, pp. 2-3;

Apr. 10, pp. 2-3; Apr. 10, supplement, pp. 1-2; Apr. 17, pp. 1-2.
N.Y. Journal Apr. 13, p. 2.
Pa. Journal Apr. 14, postscript, pp. 1-2; Apr. 19, pp. 1, 3; Apr. 26, supplement, p. 1.
Va. Gaz. (Pinkney) Apr. 13, pp. 2-3; Apr. 28, p. 1; May 4, p. 1.
Va. Gaz. (Purdie) Apr. 28, supplement, pp. 1, 2-3; May 26, supplement, pp. 1-3.
S.C. Gaz. Apr. 10, p. 3.
Ga. Gaz. Mar. 29, p. 4.

February 26

British Raid on Salem Frustrated. British forces attempt to seize military supplies at Salem, Massachusetts (on the Sabbath), but are easily repulsed due to the good services of a lengthy delay at a drawbridge. Neighboring towns respond quickly to the threat with great numbers of armed men who arrive after the British retreat. (See above, September 1774).

Bos. Gaz. Mar. 6, supplement, p. 1; Mar. 13, p. 3.
Conn. Courant Mar. 6, pp. 2-3; Mar. 13, p. 1.
Pa. Journal Mar. 15, p. 1.
Md. Gaz. Mar. 23, p. 2.

March–April

The Restraining Acts. On March 30, Parliament passes the New England Restraining Act by which Massachusetts, New Hampshire, Connecticut, and Rhode Island (a) are to be barred from the North Atlantic fisheries (the Grand Banks in particular) after July 20, and (b) are to be prohibited from trade with any countries other than Great Britain and the British West Indies after July 1. On April 13, a second Restraining Act applies both prohibitions to New Jersey, Pennsylvania, Maryland, Delaware, Virginia, and South Carolina. Edmund Burke's famous speech for reconciliation with the colonies is given during debate on the former act in Parliament, March 22.

Bos. Gaz. Apr. 3, pp. 2-3; Apr. 17, p. 3.
Essex Gaz. Apr. 18/25, pp. 1, 4; Apr. 25/May 2, p. 3.
N.E. Chron. May 25/June 1, pp. 1-2; Aug. 10/17, pp. 1-2.
Conn. Courant Apr. 10, pp. 2-3; Apr. 10, supplement, pp. 1-2; Apr. 17, pp. 1-2; Apr. 24, pp. 2-3; May 15, p. 2.
Pa. Journal Apr. 26, p. 1; May 10, pp. 1-2; May 17, pp. 1, 3; June 7, pp. 1, 4; Aug. 30, p. 1.
Cape Fear Merc. July 28, p. 4.
Ga. Gaz. June 14, p. 1; July 12, p. 3.

April 19

Lexington and Concord. Directed to arrest patriot leaders by Lord Dartmouth, Secretary of

State for the Colonies, General Gage decides to proceed at the same time against a cache of military supplies in Concord (see above, September 1774; February 26, 1775). Forewarned principally by Williams Dawes and Paul Revere, a force of 70 American colonials faces Major John Pitcairn's 700 regulars on Lexington green. An unknown person fires his gun upon which an exchange of fire results in 8 Americans killed and 10 wounded while the British have 1 wounded soldier. After marching to Concord and destroying what supplies they are able to find, the British are met on their passage back to Boston at the North Bridge (Concord) by approximately 400 Massachusetts minutemen. A short exchange of gunfire leaves 3 Britishers dead and 9 wounded while the Americans suffer 2 killed. The British retreat to Boston is a fiasco as the Americans fire volley after volley upon the Redcoats from behind rocks, walls, trees, and buildings. Boston is immediately besieged by colonials who continue to gather outside the city through April and May.

N.Hamp. Gaz. Apr. 21, p. 1; Apr. 28, p. 2; May 26, p. 2.
Essex Gaz. Apr. 18/25, p. 3.
N.E. Chron. May 2/12, pp. 2, 3; May 12/18, p. 4; May 18/25, pp. 1-2; May 25/June 1, p. 4.
Newpt. Merc. Apr. 24, p. 3.
Conn. Courant May 1, p. 3; May 8, pp. 2-3; May 22, pp. 2, 3.
N.Y. Journal Apr. 27, p. 3; May 4, pp. 2, 3; June 1, p. 2; June 15, supplement, pp. 1-2; Oct. 5, p. 2.
Riv. N.Y. Gazetteer Apr. 27, p. 3.
Pa. Journal Apr. 26, pp. 2-3; May 3, pp. 2-3; May 17, p. 2; May 24, pp. 2, 3; May 24, supplement, p. 1; May 31, p. 1; Aug. 16, p. 1.
Md. Gaz. Apr. 27, pp. 2-3; May 4, pp. 2-3.
Va. Gaz. (Pinkney) June 22, p. 1.
Va. Gaz. (Purdie) May 5, supplement, pp. 3-4; May 26, supplement, p. 3.
(N.B.) *N.C. Gaz.* May 5, p. 3.
S.C. Gaz. Sept. 7, supplement, pp. 2-3.
Ga. Gaz. May 24, p. 1; May 31, p. 1.
Broadsides: undated "Bloody Butchery"; undated pro-British.

April—June

American Reaction to Lexington and Concord. Immediate colonial reaction to the skirmishes at Lexington and Concord is overwhelmingly hostile to Britain. American eyes now turn upon Philadelphia and the upcoming Second Continental Congress. Georgia Tories are upset by the events in Massachusetts, according to reliable reports; Connecticut's General Assembly votes to raise and pay 6000 soldiers for the defense of their colony; and Rhode Island gives notice that its forces are ready for any

eventuality. News of General Gage's excursion into the Bay Colony countryside causes New York, City and County, to enter finally into the Continental Association; across the Hudson River, New Jersey patriots confidently assert that their colony is prepared to raise troops.

N.Hamp. Gaz. May 19, p. 3.
Essex Gaz. Apr. 25/May 2, p. 3.
N.E. Chron. July 6/13, p. 3.
Conn. Courant May 8, p. 3; May 15, p. 3.
N.Y. Journal May 4, pp. 2, 3; May 11, p. 1; May 18, pp. 1-2, 3; May 25, supplement, p. 1; June 1, pp. 2, 3; June 29, p. 3.
Pa. Journal May 31, p. 2.
Md. Gaz. June 15, p. 3.
Va. Gaz. (Pinkney) May 25, p. 3; June 1, p. 3.
(N.B.) *N.C. Gaz.* July 7, p. 2.
Ga. Gaz. [May 31], supplement, p. 1; June 7, pp. 2, 3; June 14, p. 2; June 21, p. 2.
Broadside: Apr. 30.

April 21

British Seize Virginia Gunpowder. Under cover of night, royal marines take the gunpowder from the colony magazine in Williamsburg. Governor Dunmore refuses to return the powder prompting Patrict Henry to gather a force on Hanover County for a march on Williamsburg. Upon payment for the gunpowder with a bill of credit to the Virginia Convention from Virginia Receiver General, Richard Corbin, Henry disbands his troops and leaves for the Continental Congress (May 2-4).

N.E. Chron. May 2/12, p. 3; May 12/18, pp. 1-2; May 25/June 1, p. 2.
Conn. Courant May 15, p. 4.
N.Y. Journal May 4, p. 3.
Pa. Journal May 17. p. 4.
Md. Gaz. June 22, p. 2.
Va. Gaz. (Pinkney) Apr. 20, p. 2; May 11, p. 3.
Va. Gaz. (Purdie) May 5, supplement, pp. 2-3.
Ga. Gaz. June 7, p. 2.

May 10-16

American Control of Champlain River Valley. Ethan Allen (Vermont) and Benedict Arnold (Connecticut) cause embarassment to the Continental Congress's plans to depict the spreading conflict as a defensive effort when they capture Fort Ticonderoga (May 10), Crown Point (May 12), and St. John's (May 16). Firmly in control of the strategic Champlain River Valley, the major route between Canada and New York, the Congress states that a British plan to invade the colonies is thus defeated. The statement is premature by two years.

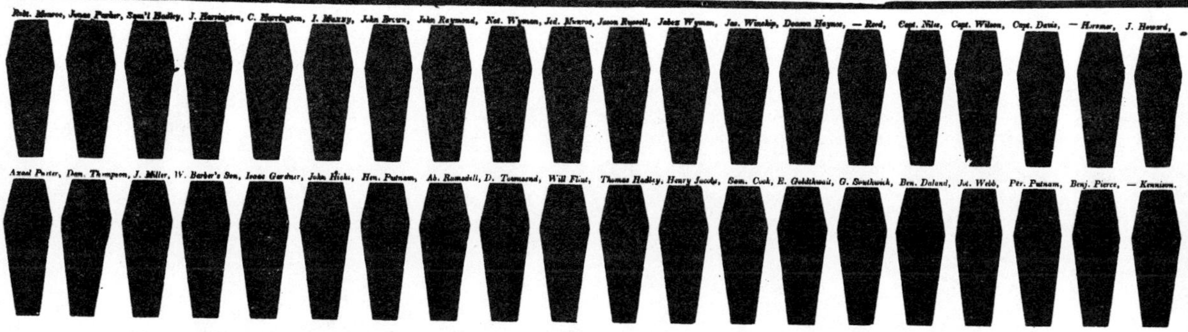
Robt. Monroe, Jonas Parker, Sam'l Hadley, J. Harrington, C. Harrington, I. Muzzy, John Brown, John Raymond, Nat. Wyman, Jed. Munroe, Jason Russell, Jabez Wyman, Jas. Winship, Deacon Haynes, — Reed, Capt. Niles, Capt. Wilson, Capt. Davis, — Hosmer, J. Howard,
Azael Porter, Dan. Thompson, J. Miller, W. Barber's Son, Isaac Gardner, John Hicks, Hen. Putnam, Ab. Ramsdell, D. Townsend, Will Flint, Thomas Hadley, Henry Jacobs, Sam. Cook, E. Goldthwait, G. Southwick, Ben. Daland, Jot. Webb, Per. Putnam, Benj. Pierce, — Kennison.

BLOODY BUTCHERY,

BY THE

BRITISH TROOPS;

OR THE

RUNAWAY FIGHT OF THE REGULARS.

Being the **PARTICULARS** of the **VICTORIOUS BATTLE** fought at and near **CONCORD**, situated Twenty Miles from Boston, in the Province of the Massachusetts-Bay, between Two Thousand Regular Troops, belonging to His Britannic Majesty, and a few Hundred Provincial Troops, belonging to the Province of Massachusetts-Bay, which lasted from sunrise until sunset, on the 19th of April, 1775, when it was decided greatly in favor of the latter. These particulars are published in this cheap form, at the request of the friends of the deceased **WORTHIES**, who died gloriously fighting in the CAUSE OF LIBERTY and their COUNTRY, and it is their sincere desire that every Householder in the country, who are sincere well-wishers to America, may be possessed of the same, either to frame and glass, or otherwise to preserve in their houses, not only as a Token of Gratitude to the memory of the Deceased Forty Persons, but as a perpetual memorial of that important event, on which, perhaps, may depend the future Freedom and Greatness of the Commonwealth of America. To which is annexed a Funeral Elegy on those who were slain in the Battle.

From E. RUSSELL's *Salem Gazette*, or *Newbury* and *Marblehead Advertiser*, published on Friday, April 21, 1775.

ON Tuesday evening the eighteenth instant, a body of soldiers under the command of Lieutenant-Colonel *Smith*, to the amount of about eight hundred men, embarked from *Barton's* Point in *Boston*, about eleven o'clock, crossed *Charles*-River, landed at *Phips's*-Farm, in *Cambridge*, and marched immediately up to *Lexington*, near twelve miles from *Boston*; at sunrise they observing between thirty and forty inhabitants exercising near the meeting-house, the Commanding-Officer ordered them to lay down their arms and disperse, which not being directly complied with, he "*damnded them for a pack of rebels*," ordered his men to fire upon them, and killed eight men upon the spot, besides wounding several more. The army then proceeded to *Concord*, drew up on the parade, near the meeting-house, during which time the inhabitants from the neighboring towns collected and took possession of the adjacent hills; about eleven o'clock the firing began on both sides, which lasted near an hour, when the regular troops began to retreat, the provincials closely pursuing them to a bridge at a small distance, which the regulars took up as they passed; they then renewed the fire, and some were slain on both sides; but the regulars still retreated, and the provincials pursued them down to *Lexington*, where the regulars, about three o'clock in the afternoon, met with a reinforcement of about twelve hundred men commanded by Earl *Percy*, with two brass field pieces; they again renewed the attack upon the provincials, but soon thought proper further to retreat towards their head-quarters, the provincials pursued them into *Charlestown*, where they arrived at 6 o'clock; taking immediately, an advantageous post on *Bunker's*-Hill, about a mile from the ferry; the provincials now discontinued the pursuit. The loss on either side we have not yet been able to ascertain, but it is said about one hundred regulars were killed and fifty wounded, among which were several officers: Two officers and a number of soldiers were taken prisoners. On the part of the province, we hear that thirty-five were slain, and several wounded. The above is as particular an account of the engagement, as can at this time be collected, in the present confused state of the province.

We hear an officer and his servant, with two pair of pistols, were yesterday taken and secured by our people, at *Roxbury*, on their way to Castle-*William*.

S A L E M, April 25.

LAST Wednesday, the nineteenth of April, the troops of his *Britannic* Majesty commenced hostilities upon the people of this province, attended with circumstances of cruelty not less brutal than what our venerable Ancestors received from the vilest savages of the wilderness. The particulars relative to this interesting event, by which we are involved in all the horrors of a civil war, we have endeavored to collect as well as the present confused state of affairs will admit.

On Thursday evening a detachment from the army, consisting, it is said, of eight or nine hundred men, commanded by Lieutenant-Colonel *Smith*, embarked at the bottom of the common in *Boston*, on board a number of boats, and landed at *Phillips's*-farm, a little way up *Charles*-River, from whence they proceeded with silence and expedition, on their way to *Concord*, about twenty miles from *Boston*. The people were soon alarmed, and began to assemble, in several towns, before day-light, in order to watch the motion of the troops. At *Lexington*, six miles below *Concord*, a company of militia, of about one hundred men, mustered near the meeting-house; the troops came in sight of them just before sunrise; and running within a few rods of them, the Commanding-Officer accosted the militia in words to this effect:—"*Disperse you rebels—Damn you throw down your arms and disperse;*" Upon which the troops huzza'd, and immediately one or two officers discharged their pistols, which were instantaneously followed by the firing of four or five of the soldiers, and then there seemed to be a general discharge from the whole body. Eight of our men were killed, and nine wounded. In a few minutes after this action the enemy renewed their march for *Concord*; at which place they destroyed several carriages, carriage-wheels, and about twenty barrels of flour, all belonging to the province. Here about one hundred men, going towards a bridge, of which the enemy were in possession, the latter fired, and killed two of our men, who then returned the fire, and obliged the enemy to retreat back to *Lexington*, where they met Lord *Percy*, with a large reinforcement, with two pieces of cannon. The enemy now having a body of about eighteen hundred men made a halt, picked up many of their dead, and took care of their wounded. At *Menotomy*, a few of the men, belonging to the detachment from *Lynn-End*, attacked a party of twelve of the enemy (carrying stores and provisions to the troops) killed two of them, wounded several, took six prisoners, shot five horses, and took possession of all their arms, stores, provisions, &c., without any loss on our side; among these who were killed was a Lieutenant, who went with the provisions for his recreation, and to view the country, the officer of the guard who generally attends on such occasions being only a serjant.—The enemy having halted one or two hours at *Lexington*, found it necessary to make a second retreat, carrying with them many of their dead and wounded, who they put into chaises and on horses that they found standing in the road. They continued their retreat from *Lexington* to *Charlestown* with great precipitation; and notwithstanding their field pieces, our people continued the pursuit, firing at them until they got to *Charlestown* neck, (which they reached a little after sunset) over which the enemy passed, proceeded up *Bunker's*-Hill, and soon afterwards went into the town, under the protection of the *Somerset* man of war of seventy-four guns.

In *Lexington* the enemy set fire to Deacon *Joseph's Loring's* house and barn, Mrs. *Mulliken's* house and shop, and Mr. *Joshua Ind's* house and shop, which were all consumed. The also set fire to several other houses, but our people extinguished the flames. They pillaged almost every house they passed by, breaking and destroying doors, windows, glasses, &c., and carrying off clothing and other valuable effects. It appeared to be their design to burn and destroy all before them; and nothing but our vigorous pursuit prevented their infernal purposes from being put in execution. But the savage barbarity exercised upon the bodies of our unfortunate brethren who fell, is almost incredible. Not content with shooting down the unarmed, aged, and infirm, they disregarded the cries of the wounded, killed them without mercy, and mangling their bodies in the most shocking manner.

We have the pleasure to say, that notwithstanding the highest provocations given by the enemy, not one instance of cruelty, that we have heard of was committed by our victorious militia; but, listened to the merciful dictates of the christian religion, they "breathed higher sentiments of humanity."

By an account of the loss of the enemy, said to have come from an officer of one of the men of war, it appears that sixty-three of the regulars, and forty-nine marines were killed, and one hundred and three of both wounded: In all two hundred and fifteen. Lieut. *Gou'd*, of the fourth regiment, who is wounded, and Lieut. *Potter*, of the marines, and about twelve soldiers, are prisoners.

Mr. *James Howard* and one of the regulars discharged their pieces at the same instant, and each killed the other.

The public most sincerely sympathize with the friends, and relations of our deceased brethren, who gloriously sacrificed their lives in fighting for the liberties of their country. By their noble, intrepid conduct, in helping to defeat the forces of an ungrateful Tyrant, they have endeared their memories to the present generation, who will transmit their virtues down to the latest posterity.

The above account is the best we have been able to obtain. We can only add, that the town of *Boston* is now invested by a vast army of our brave countrymen, who have flown to our assistance from all quarters. GOD grant them assistance in the extirpation of our cruel and unnatural enemies.

S A L E M, May 5.

ON the nineteenth of April, was killed among others, by the *British* troops, at *Menotomy*, as he was courageously defending his country's rights, the good, the pious, and friendly Mr. DANIEL TOWNSEND, of *Lynn-End*. He was a constant and ready friend to the poor and afflicted; a good adviser in case of difficulty, and an able, mild, and sincere reprover of those who were out of the way. In short, he was a friend to his country, a blessing to society, and an ornament to the church of which he was a member. He has left an amiable consort, and five young children, to bewail the loss.

Lie, valiant *Townsend*, in the peaceful shades.—We trust
Immortal honors mingle with thy dust.
What! tho' thy body struggled in the gore;
So did thy Savior's body long before!
And as he rais'd his own, by power divine;
So the same power shall also quicken thine,
And in eternal glory mayst thou shine.

On Thursday the twentieth past, the bodies of eleven of the unfortunate persons who fell in the battle, were collected together and buried at *Medford*.

And on Friday the bodies of Messrs. Henry Jacobs, Samuel Cook, Ebenezer Goldthwait, George Southwick, Benjamin Daland, Jun. Jotham Webb, and Perley Putnam, of *Danvers*, who were likewise slain fighting in the GLORIOUS CAUSE OF LIBERTY AND THEIR COUNTRY, on the nineteenth of April, were respectfully interred among their friends in the different parishes belonging to that town, their corpse being attended to the place of interment by two companies of minute-men from this place, and a large concourse of people from this and the neighboring towns; previous to that interment, an excellent and well adapted prayer was delivered by the Rev. Mr. Holt, of that place.

Same day, the remains of Messrs. Azel Porter and Daniel Thompson, *of Woburn*, who also fell victims to tyranny, were decently interred at that place, attended to the grave by a multitude of persons who assembled on the occasion from that and the neighboring towns: Before they were interred, a very suitable sermon and prayer was delivered by the Rev. Mr. Sherman.

Captain Thomas Knights, of the fifth regiment, died at Boston the next day after the engagement, of his wounds he received in the same. He was greatly regretted being esteemed one of the best officers among the King's troops.

Lieut. Hull, of the regulars, died of his wounds on Wednesday last at the provincial hospital: His remains were next day conveyed to Charlestown, attended by a company of provincials, and several officers of distinction, and there delivered to the order of General Gage. Twenty-three wounded soldiers lately died at the Castle.

Lieutenant Hawkshaw was wounded in the cheek, and it is tho't will not recover.

Lieutenant Gore was wounded in the arm: About 12 other officers are wounded.

We can assure the public, from the best authority, that our brethren, of all the colonies which we can yet have heard from, are firm and unshaken in their attachment to the common cause of *America*; and that they are now ready, with their lives and fortunes, to assist us in defeating the cruel designs of our implacable enemies.

We have received no particulars of the transactions between General Gage and the inhabitants of *Boston*. It is certain that the people have delivered up their arms; very few of them have, however been permitted to leave the town, notwithstanding the promise of the General.

The following is a list of the Provincials who were KILLED and WOUNDED.

Belonging to *L E X I N G T O N.*

K I L L E D.

1 * Mr. Robert Monroe,
2 * Mr. Jonas Parker,
3 * Mr. Samuel Hadley,
4 * Mr. Jonathan Harrington,
5 * Mr. Caleb Harrington,
6 * Mr. Isaac Muzzy,
7 * Mr. John Brown,
8 Mr. John Raymond,
9 Mr. Nathaniel Wyman,
10 Mr. Jedediah Munroe.

W O U N D E D.

1 Mr. John Robbins
2 Mr. John Tidd
3 Mr. Solomon Pierce
4 Mr. Thomas Winship
5 Mr. Nathan Parmer
6 Mr. Joseph Amee
7 Mr. Ebenezer Munroe
8 Mr. Francis Brown
9 Prince Easterbrooks (a Negro Man)

M E N O T O M Y.

K I L L E D

11 Mr. Jason Russell
12 Mr. Jabez Wyman
13 Jason Winship

MISSING, (supposed to be on board one of the men of war)

Mr. Samuel Frost
Mr. Seth Russell

S U D B U R Y.

K I L L E D

14 Deacon Haynes
15 Mr. —— Reed

C O N C O R D.

K I L L E D

16 Captain Miles

B E D F O R D.

K I L L E D

17 Captain Jonathan Willson

A C T O N.

K I L L E D

18 Captain Davis
19 Mr —— Hosmor
20 Mr. James Howard

W O B U R N.

K I L L E D

21 * Mr. Azel Porter
22 Mr. Daniel Thompson

W O U N D E D

10 Mr. George Reed
11 Mr. Jacob Bacon

C H A R L E S T O W N.

K I L L E D

23 Mr. James Miller.
24 Captain William Barber's Son, aged 14

B R O O K L I N E.

K I L L E D

25 Isaac Gardiner, Esquire

C A M B R I D G E.

K I L L E D

26 Mr. John Hicks

M E D F O R D.

K I L L E D

27 Mr. Henry Putnam.

W O U N D E D

12 Mr. William Polly.

L Y N N.

K I L L E D

28 Mr. Abednego Ramsdell
29 Daniel Townsend
30 William Flint
31 Thomas Hadley

W O U N D E D

13 Mr. Joshua Felt
14 Mr. Timothy Munroe

D A N V E R S.

K I L L E D

32 Mr. Henry Jacobs
33 Mr. Samuel Cook
34 Mr. Ebenezer Goldthwait
35 Mr. George Southwick
36 Mr. Benjamin Daland, jun.
37 Mr. Jotham Webb
38 Perley Putnam

W O U N D E D

15 Mr. Nathan Putnam
16 Mr. Dennis Wallis

S A L E M.

K I L L E D

39 Mr. Benjamin Pierce

B E V E R L Y.

K I L L E D

40 —— Kennison

W O U N D E D

17 Mr. Samuel Woodbury
18 Mr. Nathaniel Cleaves

F R A M I N G H A M.

19 Mr. —— Hemmenway.

B E D F O R D.

20 Mr. John Lane.

Those distinguished with this mark [*] were killed by the first fire of the enemy.

A F U N E R A L

ELEGY,

TO THE

IMMORTAL MEMORY

Of those WORTHIES *who were slain in the Battle of* CONCORD, *April* 19, 1775.

AID me ye nine! my muse assist,
A sad tale to relate,
When such a number of brave men
Met their unhappy fate.
At *Lexington* they met their foe
Completely all equipp'd,
Their guns & swords made glit'ring show,
But their base schemes were nipp'd.

Americans, go drop a tear
Where your slain brethren lay!
O! mourn and sympathize for them!
O! weep this very day!
What shall we say to this loud call
From the Almighty sent?
It surely bids both great and small
Seek GOD's face and repent.
Words can't express the ghastly scene
That here presents to view,
When forty of our brave countrymen
Sure bid their friends adieu.
O! think how awful it must seem,
To hear widows relent
Their husbands and their children
Who to their graves were sent.

The tender babes, nay those unborn,
O! dismal cruel death!
To snatch their fondest parents dear
And leave them thus bereft.
O! *Lexington!* your loss is great!
Alas! too great to tell;
But justice bids me to relate
What to you has befell.
Ten of your hardy, bravest sons,
Some in their prime did fall;
May we no more hear noise of guns,
To terrify us all.
Let's not forget the *Danvers* race,
So late in battle slain,
Their valor and their courage shown,
Upon this crimson'd plain.

Seven of your youthful sprightly sons
In the fierce fight were slain,
O! may your loss be all made up,
And prove a lasting gain.
Cambridge and *Medford's* loss is great,
Though not like *Acton's* town,
Where three fierce military sons
Met their untimely doom.
Menotomy and *Charlestown* met
A sore and heavy stroke,
In losing five of their towsmen
Who fell by a tyrant's yoke.
Unhappy *Lynn* and *Beverly*,
Your loss I do bemoan,
Five your brave sons in dust doth lie,
Who late were in the bloom.

Bedford, *Woburn*, *Sudbury*, all,
Have suffer'd most severe,
You miss five of your choicest chore,
On them let's drop a tear.
Concord, your Captain's fate rehearse,
His loss is felt severe,
Come, brethren, join with me in verse,
His mem'ry hence revere.
O! 'Squire *Gardiner's* death we feel,
And sympathizing mourn,
Let's drop a tear when it we tell,
And view his hapless urn.
We sore regret poor *Pierce's* death,
A stroke to *Salem* known,
Where tears did flow from every brow,
When the sad tidings come.

The groans of wounded, dying men,
Would melt the stoutest soul,
O! how it strikes thro' every vein,
My flesh and blood runs cold.
May all prepare to meet their fate
At GOD's tribunal bar,
And may war's terrible alarm,
For death us now prepare.
Your country calls you far and near,
America's sons awake,
Your helmet, buckler, and your spear,
The LORD's own arm now make.
His shield will keep us from all harm,
Tho' thousands 'gainst us rise,
His buckler we must sure put on,
If we would win the prize.

See p. 58, April 19, *Broadside: Undated "Bloody Butchery."*

N.E. Chron. May 12/18, p. 3; May 25/June 1, p. 3.
Conn. Courant July 31, p. 2; Oct. 16, pp. 1-2.
N.Y. Journal Aug. 3, pp. 1-2, 3.
Pa. Journal May 24, p. 3.
Ga. Gaz. June 14, p. 3.

May 10—August 2

Second Continental Congress. With a single Georgia delegate present representing one parish (county), the colonies' delegates assemble in Philadelphia. Dependent on the good will of the several colonies for its power, the Congress proceeds to business. Taking control of the army rapidly growing outside Boston, the Congress taps the southerner, George Washington, to be commander-in-chief of the Continental Army (June 15) which will be filled out by quotas on each colony. On June 22, $2,000,000. in bills of credit, or continental currency, are authorized to be printed in order to support the Army. Indian affairs are seen to with establishment of three departments (areas) with commissioners empowered to deal with the Indians and make treaties (July 13). The colonies are requested to set up committees of safety to oversee the implementation of Congressional recommendations and the military affairs of the particular colony (July 18). An American Post Office is created (July 26) with Benjamin Franklin the first Postmaster. The Congress also busies itself with Addresses: to Canada, soliciting aid (May 26); to King George III, the so-called Olive Branch Petition, for his help against Parliament (July 5); to the Inhabitants of Great Britain (July 8); and to the people of Ireland (July 28). On July 6, Congress adopts a Declaration of the Causes and Necessities of Taking Up Arms, written by Thomas Jefferson and John Dickinson which manfully underscores American determination to resist aggression but emphasizes the colonies' rejection of independence. Lord North's plan for reconciliation (see above, January-February) is summarily defeated (July 31) and the Continental Association is modified to enable war supplies to be imported into the colonies.

N.E. Chron. June 1/8, p. 2; June 22/29, pp. 2, 3; July 21/27, pp. 1-2; July 27/Aug. 3, pp. 1, 4; Aug. 3/10, p. 1; Aug. 10/17, p. 3; Aug. 17/24, pp. 1, 4; Aug. 24/31, p. 1; Aug. 31/Sept. 7, p. 1; Nov. 9/16, p. 1.
Conn. Courant June 26, p. 2; July 17, p. 2; July 24, pp. 1, 4; Aug. 7, Aug. 14, pp. 2-3; Nov. 6, p. 1.
N.Y. Journal June 22, p. 2; July 13, supplement, p. 2; July 27, p. 1, 3; Aug. 3, supplement, p. 2; Aug. 10, supplement, p. 1; Aug. 24, pp. 1-2; Aug. 31, p. 1.
Pa. Journal May 10, p. 3; June 21, p. 3; July 5, p. 3; July 12, p. 1; July 26, p. 3; Aug. 16, pp. 2-3; Sept. 6, p. 2.

Md. Gaz. June 22, p. 2; July 20, p. 1.
Va. Gaz. (Pinkney) July 6, p. 3; July 20, pp. 2-3.
S.C. Gaz. Sept. 7, supplement, p. 3; Sept. 19, p. 1.
Ga. Gaz. June 14, p. 2; June 21, p. 2; [July 26], supplement, p. 3; Aug. 2, pp. 1-2.
Broadside: undated Declaration of Causes.

May 31

Mecklenburg County Resolutions. In the face of uncertainties throughout the colonies regarding matters of government and the actual locus of power and authority, inhabitants of Mecklenburg County, North Carolina, meet in Charlotte Town and draw up a set of resolutions for their colony representatives at the Continental Congress. Explicitly based on Parliament's depiction of the colonies as in an actual state of rebellion (February 9), the Mecklenburg County Resolutions declare that all former laws and commissions are null and void since they are given under authority of King George and Parliament. Indeed, the former civil constitutions of these colonies, according to the resolutions, are wholly suspended. It is up to the people to provide for the military exigencies and a regular government until Congress will do so. Ahead of its fellow colonists in these revolutionary sentiments, Mecklenburg County's Resolutions are never introduced into the Continental Congress. Governor Josiah Martin of North Carolina is not pleased with the resolutions which he describes as "most traterously declaring the intire dissolution of the laws, government, and constitutions of this country" in an August 8 proclamation that includes North Carolina's Provincial Congress on his list of local vexations. Earlier, on July 20, North Carolina assures the other colonies that the Carolinians will not take advantage of their exclusion from the second Restraining Act (see above, March-April).

N.E. Chron. Aug. 10/17, p. 4; Aug. 24/31, p. 3; Sept. 21/28, p. 1.
Newpt. Merc. July 17, p. 1.
N.Y. Journal June 29, p. 2.
Pa. Journal Sept. 27, p. 2; Oct. 25, p. 2; Nov. 1, pp. 1-2; Nov. 29, p. 2.

June 12

Martial Law in Massachusetts. General Gage proclaims martial law in Massachusetts, states that any colonists in arms are to be considered traitors, and offers pardons to any persons who will renounce their offenses against the Crown — except Samuel Adams and John Hancock.

N. Hamp. Gaz. Aug. 29, p.1.
N.E. Chron. June 1/8, p. 2; June 8/15, p. 2.
N.Y. Journal July 6, pp. 1-2.
Pa. Journal June 28, p. 1.
Md. Gaz. June 29, p. 1.
Cape Fear Merc. Aug. 7, p. 3.
Ga. Gaz. July 18, pp. 3-4.

June 17

Bunker Hill. The colonials are actually driven from nearby Breed's Hill, a strategic position overlooking Boston and its harbor, by the repeated frontal charges of heavily equipped and closely packed lines of British regulars. The regulars' losses are so great that colonials claim a triumph of sorts while English viewers wryly comment that any similar British victories and there would be no one surviving and capable of carrying the news back to England. The British losses are over 1000 while the Americans lose 300 men. The victory claims one eighth of all the British officers who will be lost during the entire American Revolution and also the command of General Thomas Gage, who is replaced by General William Howe (October 10).

N.Hamp. Gaz. June 20, p. 1.
N.E. Chron. June 15/22, p. 2; June 22/29, p. 3; July 6/13, p. 3; Oct. 5/12, pp. 3, 4.
Conn. Courant June 26, p. 2; July 3, p. 3; July 31, p. 3.
N.Y. Journal June 29, p. 3; June 29, supplement, p. 1; July 27, p. 2; Oct. 5, pp. 1-2; Oct. 19, p. 1.
Riv. N.Y. Gazeteer June 29, pp. 1-2.
Pa. Journal June 28, p. 2; July 5, supplement, p. 1; Oct. 4, p. 1.
Md. Gaz. June 29, p. 1.
Va. Gaz. (Purdie) July 14, supplement, p. 1; July 21, p. 2.
(N.B.) *N.C. Gaz.* July 14, pp. 2-3
S.C. Gaz. Sept. 7, supplement, p. 3.
Ga. Gaz. [July 12], supplement, pp. 1-2; Aug. 23, pp. 1-2.

July 3

Washington Assumes Command. General George Washington takes formal command of the American troops outside Boston. Sentiment is apparent for describing the units as those of the United Colonies of North America rather than those of particular colonies. Washington is disappointed by the lack of equipment and begins his war-long battle with the Continental Congress for proper supplies, Morale, high on the American lines after the "victory" at Bunker Hill, is demonstrated further by the sustained cheering and celebrations which greet the reading to the troops of the Declaration of the Causes and Necessities for Taking Up Arms issued by the Continental Congress (July 15-18).

N.E. Chron. June 29/July 6, p. 3; July 13/21, p. 3; July 21/27, pp. 1-2.
Conn. Courant July 3, p. 3; July 17, p. 2; July 24, p. 2.
N.Y. Journal June 29, p. 3; July 13, p. 3.
Va. Gaz. (Purdie) Aug. 4, pp. 1-2.
S.C. Gaz. Sept. 7, p. 3.

June—July

English Reaction to Lexington and Concord. English popular reaction to Lexington and Concord, and American affairs, is favorable to the colonies according to the colonial press. Petitions presented to the king by London's inhabitants — John Wilkes is now the Lord Mayor — are pro-American and maintain the fiction that all problems are caused by King George's evil ministers (July 6, 11).

N.E. Chron. Aug. 31/Sept. 7, pp. 2, 4; Sept. 7/14, pp. 2, 4; Sept. 14/21, p. 1; Sept. 21/28, p. 2.
Conn. Courant May 22, p. 1; Oct. 2, p. 2.
Md. Gaz. Sept. 28, p. 3; Nov. 2, p. 1; Nov. 9, p. 3.

June—September

Colonies Begin to Arm, South of New England. Pennsylvania, South Carolina, North Carolina, and Maryland vote through their provincial congresses (Virginia through its Third Convention) to arm themselves against the common danger. Philadelphia Quakers agree to raise money and supplies for those colonials who have suffered losses in the growing conflict. New York's Provincial Congress organizes the colony's militia and makes provision for ships leaving New York City to have licenses from the Continental Congress or the local committee of inspection: too many ships are purposely allowing themselves to be captured in order to supply the British.

N.E. Chron. July 13/21, p. 2.
Conn. Courant July 31, p. 1.
N.Y. Journal June 29, p. 2; July 13, p. 2; July 20, p. 1; Aug. 10, p. 2; Aug. 31, pp. 2, 3; Sept. 7, p. 3; Sept. 14, p. 4.
Pa. Journal July 5, supplement, p. 1; July 12, p. 2; Aug. 9, pp. 2, 3; Aug. 30, pp. 2-3; Sept. 20, p. 1.
Md. Gaz. Aug. 17, p. 2; Aug. 24, pp. 1-2; Aug. 31, pp. 1-2; Sept. 7, p. 1.
S.C. Gaz. Sept. 7, p. 1; Sept. 7, supplement, p. 4; Oct. 3, p. 4; Oct. 17, p. 4; Oct. 24, p. 4.
Ga. Gaz. June 21, p. 1; July 12, pp. 1-2.

September 12

Second Continental Congress Reconvenes. The Second Continental Congress reconvenes in Philadelphia with all thirteen colonies represented by full delegations. Among its actions are the creation of a Continental Navy of four ships

(October 13, 30); a declaration that British vessels are subject to capture by American ships (November 25); and provision for a Committee of Secret Correspondence (later the Committee for Foreign Affairs) to seek contact with America's friends abroad (November 29). On November 9, Congress receives word that King George has refused to receive the Olive Branch Petition (see above, May 10-August 2) and has proclaimed that the American colonies are in open rebellion (August 23). Congress responds to King George's proclamation, which has in effect branded the delegates as traitors, on December 6 with a reiteration of the colonies' allegiance to the king, but not to Parliament.

N.E. Chron. July 13/21, p. 3; July 27/Aug. 3, p. 3; Nov. 9/16, p. 4; Nov. 16/23, p. 3; Dec. 14/21, p. 3.
Conn. Courant Nov. 13, p. 1; Nov. 20, p. 1.
N.Y. Journal Nov. 9, p. 3; Dec. 14, p. 3.
Pa. Journal Nov. 1, p. 3; Dec. 13, p. 1.
Md. Gaz. Nov. 9, p. 1.
Va. Gaz. (Purdie) Nov. 10, p. 2; Dec. 29, p. 2.
S.C. Gaz. Dec. 11, p. 3.
Ga. Gaz. [July 26], supplement, p. 3; Oct. 25, p. 2; Jan. 3 (1776), p. 4; Jan. 10 (1776), pp. 1, 2; Jan. 17 (1776), pp. 1-2.

August—December

Canadian Campaign. Turning their gaze upon the projected fourteenth colony, American forces move swiftly north under General Richard Montgomery, a former British officer, retaking St. John's (November 2), capturing Chambly, and finally Montreal (November 13). A second force, headed by Benedict Arnold, moves west through Maine with the intention of joining Montgomery before the last bastion of British control in central Canada, Quebec. Their meeting (December 3) is not to advantage: winter is hard upon them; the extraordinary hardships of Arnold's march and Montgomery's battle-exhausted troops enable the Americans to confront Sir Guy Carleton with only 1000 effective men. A night attack on Quebec (December 30-31) is a disaster for the hard-pressed colonials. Three hundred and seventy Americans are captured, Montgomery is killed, and Arnold wounded. The remainder of the American army barely endures the Canadian winter, low supplies, and a small-pox epidemic.

N.E. Chron. Aug. 10/17, p. 2; Sept. 14/21, pp. 2, 3; Sept. 21/28, p. 1; Nov. 9/16, p. 2; Nov. 16/23, p. 3; Nov. 24/30, pp. 2, 3; Dec. 7/14, p. 1; Jan. 4/11 (1776), p. 3; Jan. 18/25 (1776), p. 3.
Newpt. Merc. Dec. 4, p. 2; Jan. 1 (1776), p. 2; Jan. 22 (1776), p. 2; Feb. 5 (1776), p. 2.

Conn. Courant Sept. 25, p. 3; Oct. 2, p. 2; Oct. 9, p. 3; Oct. 16, pp. 1-2; Oct. 23, p. 2; Nov. 6, p. 2; Nov. 13, pp. 2, 3; Nov. 20, p. 2; Nov. 27, p. 3; Dec. 4, p. 3; Jan. 15, (1776), p. 3; Feb. 5 (1776), p. 3.
N.Y. Journal Sept. 7, p. 3; Sept. 14, p. 3; Sept. 21, p. 3; Sept. 28, pp. 1, 3; Oct. 5, p. 3; Oct. 12, p. 3; Oct. 19, p. 2; Oct. 26, p. 2; Nov. 2, p. 3; Nov. 9, p. 3; Nov. 23, p. 3; Dec. 7, pp. 1-2, 3; Dec. 21, pp. 2, 3; Jan. 4 (1776), p. 3; Jan. 25 (1776), pp. 2, 3; Feb. 1 (1776), p. 3; July 4 (1776), p. 1.
Pa. Gaz. Jan. 3 (1776), p. 2; Feb. 14 (1776), p. 3.
Pa. Journal Sept. 20, p. 2; Oct. 11, p. 3; Oct. 18, p. 3; Oct. 25, pp. 2-3; Nov. 8, p. 3; Nov. 15, pp. 2-3; Dec. 6, p. 3; Dec. 13, p. 3.
Md. Gaz. Nov. 30, p. 1; Feb. 1 (1776), p. 2.
Va. Gaz. (Purdie) Dec. 1, supplement, pp. 1-2.
S.C. Gaz. Nov. 21, p. 3.
S.C. and A.G. Gaz. Jan. 5/12 (1776), pp. 1-2; Feb. 2/9 (1776), p. 3.
Ga. Gaz. Jan. 3 (1776), p. 2; Feb. 7 (1776), p. 3.

October 17-18

New England Suffers British Navy Raids. British naval raids on New England towns since April culminate in the burning of Falmouth (Portland, Maine).

N.Hamp. Gaz. June 2, p. 1; Nov. 2, p. 1.
Cont. Journal Sept. 12, pp. 1-2.
Newpt. Merc. Oct. 16, p. 2; Oct. 30, p. 2.
N.Y. Journal Sept. 28, p. 3; Nov. 2, p. 3.
Pa. Journal June 21, p. 2; Sept. 20, p. 2; Nov. 8, pp. 2, 3.
Md. Gaz. Aug. 10, p. 1; Aug. 31, p. 2; Sept. 14, pp. 1-2.
Ga. Gaz. Dec. 20, p. 1.
Broadside: Oct. 24.

November 16, 29

New Jersey Not in Favor of Independence. Governor William Franklin addresses the New Jersey General Assembly (November 16) asking them to disavow openly any thought of American independence. The Assembly's answer is precise: they do not approve of notions of American independence. Indeed the assembly contends that they detest such sentiments (November 29).

N.Hamp. Gaz. Dec. 5, p. 1.
Pa. Journal Nov. 22, p. 2; Dec. 6, p. 3.
Md. Gaz. Dec. 14, p. 1; Mar. 7 (1776), p. 3.

November 23

Jemmy Rivington, Tory Propagandist. Few newspapers counter the patriot, or Whig, sentiments as effectively as *Rivington's New York Gazetteer* (1773-1775). Nor do many papers rival the fury and excitement James Rivington's Toryism incites by certain of the columns of his weekly and through his printing of Tory pamphlets. On November 23, 1775, Rivington's office is attacked, his press destroyed, and his type stolen by Connecticut soldiers led by "King" Isaac Sears, a noted New York radical, leader of mobs, and object of unflattering attention in the *Gazetteer* from time to time. In January 1776 Rivington sails for England. Upon his return to British-occupied New York City in 1777, he resumes publication of his newspaper, which after two title changes within two months is published for the remainder of the war as the (New York) *Royal Gazette*. When New York is evacuated by the British army at the end of the war (November 25, 1783), Rivington is surprisingly allowed to continue his life there, but only as a bookseller. (Evidence does exist that Rivington may have been an American spy as early as 1781.)

Conn. Courant Mar. 6, p. 2; May 8, p. 4; July 3, p. 3; Nov. 27, p. 3.
N.Y. Journal Feb. 3 (1774), p. 3; Aug. 18, (1774), pp. 2-3; Sept. 1 (1774), pp. 2-3; Oct. 6 (1774), p. 3; Oct. 27 (1774), p. 2; Nov. 17 (1774), p. 2; Nov. 24 (1774), p. 3; Dec. 8 (1774), p. 3; Dec. 15 (1774), pp. 1-2; Dec. 22 (1774), pp. 1, 2; Dec. 29 (1774), p. 1; Jan. 5, pp. 1-2; Feb. 9, p. 3; Feb. 23, p. 2; Mar. 2, pp. 1-3; Apr. 6, p. 1; Apr. 6, supplement extraordinary, pp. 1-2.
Riv. N.Y. Gazetteer Dec. 23 (1773), pp. 1-2; Jan. 27 (1774), p. 2; May 12 (1774), pp. 2-3; June 30 (1774), p. 1; Dec. 1 (1774), p. 2; Dec. 29 (1774), p. 1; Jan. 12, p. 2; Jan. 19, p. 2; Jan. 26, pp. 1-2, 3; Feb. 16, pp. 1, 3; Feb. 23, p. 2; Mar. 2, p. 1; Mar. 9, pp. 1, 3; Mar. 23, p. 1; Mar. 30, pp. 1-2; Apr. 6, p. 1; Apr. 20, p. 3; Apr. 27, p. 3.
Pa. Journal Feb. 22, p. 1; Mar. 8, p. 1.
Va. Gaz. (Purdie) Apr. 4 (1777), p. 2.
Broadside: Apr. 27.

December 9

Governor Dunmore Campaigns Against Virginia. A contingent of Governor Dunmore's British regulars is defeated at Great Bridge, Virginia, by a combined force of Virginia and North Carolina militia. Dunmore's exploits since his confiscation of the colony gunpowder in Williamsburg (see above, April 21) have not endeared him to the Virginia populace. Dunmore's raids on coastal areas are eclipsed by his "Emancipation Proclamation," issued November 7, in which he declares martial law in Virginia and frees the slaves and indentured servants owned by rebels as long as said runaways will join His Majesty's forces. Virginians are much concerned with Dunmore's ploy and make much of stories that many of these slaves are being sold to the West Indies in order to line Dunmore's own pockets.

Dunmore's explicit slave policies and their implicit potential for racial warfare give southerners pause. Many whites find rebellion preferable to the future machinations of leaders who, it is rumored, allow black regiments to march with "Liberty to Slaves" emblazoned on their coats.

An interesting sidelight to Dunmore's activities on the Virginia peninsula is the theft, on September 30, of John Hunter Holt's printing press used for his (Norfolk) *Virginia Gazette*; it is seized by a force of (unopposed) British sailors. Holt is the nephew of John Holt, publisher of the patriot *New York Journal*. Dunmore grinds out his own (Norfolk) *Virginia Gazette* aboard H.M.S. *Dunmore* until spring.

N.E. Chron. Aug. 24/31, p. 3; Oct. 26/Nov. 2, p. 3; Nov. 9/16, p. 3; Nov. 30/Dec. 7, p. 2; Dec. 21/28, pp. 2, 4; Dec. 28/Jan. 4 (1776), p. 2.
Newpt. Merc. Jan. 15 (1776), pp. 1-2.
Conn. Courant Oct. 30, p. 2; Nov. 13, p. 3.
N.Y. Journal Aug. 24, p. 1; Oct. 26, p. 2; Nov. 2, p. 2; Dec. 7, p. 2; Dec. 21, pp. 2, 3; Dec. 28, p. 2; Jan. 4 (1776), p. 2.
Pa. Journal Aug. 16, p. 2; Oct. 18, p. 2; Nov. 1, p. 2; Nov. 8, p. 2; Nov. 15, p. 3; Dec. 6, p. 2; Dec. 13, p. 2; Dec. 20, pp. 2-3; Dec. 27, p. 2.
Md. Gaz. Nov. 9, p. 2; Dec. 14, p. 2; Dec. 21, p. 2.
Va. Gaz. (Purdie) Aug. 4, p. 1; Nov. 10, pp. 3-4; Nov. 24, p. 2; Dec. 15, pp. 2-3; Dec. 22, p. 2; Dec. 29, p. 1. Jan. 12 (1776), p. 3; Feb. 23 (1776), p. 1; Mar. 22 (1776), pp. 2-3.
(Norfolk) *Va. Gaz.* (Holt) Aug. 2, p. 2; Aug. 16, p. 3; Sept. 13, p. 3; Sept. 20, p. 3.
(Norfolk) *Va. Gaz.* (Dunmore) Nov. 25, pp. 1-2, 6-7, 8; Feb. 3 (1776), p. 1.
S.C. and A.G. Gaz. Feb. 2/9 (1776), p. 1.
Ga. Gaz. Nov. 29, p. 1; Jan. 10 (1776), p. 2.

New-York, April 27, 1775.

To the PUBLIC.

AS many Publications have appeared from my Prefs which have given great Offence to the Colonies, and particularly to many of my Fellow Citizens; I am therefore led, by a moſt ſincere Regard for their favourable Opinion, to declare to the Public, that Nothing which I have ever done, has proceeded from any Sentiments in the leaſt unfriendly to the Liberties of this Continent, but altogether from the Ideas I entertained of the Liberty of the Preſs, and of my duty as a Printer. I am led to make this free and public Declaration to my Fellow Citizens, which I hope they will conſider as a ſufficient Pledge of my Reſolution, for the future, to conduct my Preſs upon ſuch Principles as ſhall not give Offence to the Inhabitants of the Colonies in general, and of this City in particular, to which I am connected by the tendereſt of all human Ties, and in the Welfare of which I ſhall conſider my own as inſeparably involved.

James Rivington.

The above will be inſerted in the next Week's New-York Gazetteer, and continued four Weeks.

See p. 62, November 23,   Broadside: April 27.

Almanac
  1776 (includes Connecticut officers in Continental Army)
    Conn. Courant Nov. 13, p. 3.

Astronomical Phenomena
  Meteor
    Conn. Courant Mar. 6, p. 4.

Boston Massacre
  Anniversary
    Conn. Courant Mar. 13, p. 1.
    Pa. Journal Mar. 22, pp. 2-3; Mar. 29, supplement, pp. 1-2.
  Joseph Warren's Address on
    Va. Gaz. (Pinkney) Apr. 13, p. 1.

China
  Novel animals and vegetables of
    N.Y. Journal Oct. 26, p. 3.

Colleges
  College of New Jersey commencement
    Pa. Journal Nov. 29, p. 1.
  Harvard
    general diploma given because students dispersed
      N.E. Chron. Oct. 12/19, p. 1.
    moves to Concord
      N.E. Chron. Aug. 31/Sept. 7, p. 3.

Currency
  New York accepts Connecticut bills of credit
    N.Y. Journal July 13, p. 3.

Diseases
  Small-pox
    Bos. Gaz. Apr. 3, p. 3.

East Florida
  Escape tumults, move here
    Ga. Gaz. Nov. 15, p. 2.

Education
  Ad for Hartford grammar school
    Conn. Courant Apr. 17, p. 4.

Franklin, Benjamin
  Poem to upon arrival in America from Europe
    N.Y. Journal May 18, p. 4.

Hancock, John (Massachusetts patriot)
  Marriage of
    N.E. Chron. Aug. 31/Sept. 7, p. 3.

Independence, American
  Denied as American goal
    Va. Gaz. (Purdie) Nov. 10, p. 3.
  Expected
    N.E. Chron. Nov. 16/24, p. 2.
  Plan of union necessary for
    Pa. Journal Dec. 27, p. 1.

Indians
  British instigate possible southern war by against colonists
    Conn. Courant July 24, p. 2.

Military Science
  Officers' manual published
    Pa. Journal Aug. 16, p. 3.

Newspapers
  Poor quality of paper
    Conn. Courant Oct. 16, p. 3.

Patriotism
  Henrico County, Virginia, counseled on
    Va. Gaz. (Pinkney) June 22, p. 1.

Poetry
  Parody on General Thomas Gage
    Va. Gaz. (Pinkney) July 20, p. 1.
  "A Song" (by Continental soldier)
    N.E. Chron. Dec. 7/14, p. 4.
  Verse ad for runaway
    Pa. Journal Sept. 20, p. 3.

Post Office
  American to be established
    Conn. Courant May 8, p. 3.

Prisoners of War
  George Washington to Thomas Gage regarding mistreatment of
    Conn. Courant Oct. 16, p. 1.

Quakers
  Contributions in lieu of military service
    Conn. Cournat Aug. 14, pp. 2-3.
  Patriotism (Boston)
    Pa. Journal Feb. 22, p. 3.

Rattlesnake
  As symbol of America explained
    Pa. Journal Dec. 27, p. 1.

Rumors (printed as authentic news)
  British ministry overthrown by John Wilkes, Edmund Burke

N.Hamp. Gaz. Aug. 29, p. 1.
N.E. Chron. Aug. 3/10, p. 3.
British regulars defeated in Boston (July 5);
Boston burned
Va. Gaz. (Purdie) July 28, p. 1.

Sabbath
British officers profane by skating
Bos. Gaz. Jan. 16, p. 2.

Saltpeter
Manufacture of
Bos. Gaz. Jan. 2, p. 2.
Pa. Journal Nov. 22, pp. 1, 2; Dec. 6, p. 2.
Md. Gaz. Nov. 30, p. 1.

Slaves
Anti-slavery sentiment
Conn. Courant Jan. 2, p. 1.
N.Y. Journal Jan. 12, pp. 1, 4.
British slave trade denounced
Pa. Journal Mar. 8, postscript, p. 1.
Va. Gaz. (Purdie) Nov. 24. p. 2.
Connecticut prohibits importation
Pa. Journal Jan. 4, p. 2.
Possible insurrections
Bos. Gaz. Feb. 27, supplement, p. 2.
N.Y. Journal Mar. 2, p. 3; Oct. 19, p. 2.
Royal governor (North Carolina) proposes
arming of against colonists
Pa. Journal Oct. 25, p. 2.
Sales of
N.Y. Journal Feb. 2, supplement, p. 2.

Soldiers, American
Discharged: individual presents certificate of
good conduct from Washington and Lee to
quell rumors
Pa. Journal Nov. 1, p. 3.
Recruiting instructions (Massachusetts)
N.E. Chron. July 27/Aug. 3, p. 3.
Reward for deserters (Boston)
Conn. Courant Sept. 25, p. 4.

Soldiers, British
An Old Soldier in letter admonishes: leave
Americans alone
N.E. Chron. July 13/21, p. 2.

Tories
Boston: belongings confiscated
Pa. Journal July 12, p. 2.

Connecticut
N.E. Chron. Nov. 30/Dec. 7, p. 3.
Conn. Courant July 3, p. 3.
N.Y. Journal Sept. 28, p. 2; Oct. 5, p. 3;
Oct. 26, p. 1; Dec. 7, p. 1.
Definition of (satirical)
Conn. Courant Feb. 13, p. 3.
Delaware: recantations of
Pa. Journal Nov. 29, p. 1.
General Thomas Gage to raise regiment of
Conn. Courant Oct. 2, p. 1.
Massachusetts: enemies of colonists noted
Conn. Courant July 3, p. 3.
Portsmouth, New Hampshire: disarmed
Pa. Journal Oct. 11, p. 2.
Rhode Island: recantation of
Pa. Journal Feb. 22, p. 2.
"The Tories' Creed" (satire)
Conn. Courant Mar. 27, p. 1.

Transylvania (Kentucky)
Ad for settlement of
Pa. Journal Nov. 15, p. 3.

Union, American
Neccessary for independence
Pa. Journal Dec. 27, p. 1.

Ventriloquism
Noticed
Ga. Gaz. Sept. 13, pp. 2-3.

Weather
Comparative temperatures recorded in December 1774 and January 1775
Conn. Courant Feb. 13, p. 3.

West Florida
Mississippi and Mobile River land available
Md. Gaz. June 1, p. 3.

Women
Patriotism of
Conn. Courant Mar. 13, p. 1.

Yankee
Etymology [questionable] of word
Conn. Courant June 12, p. 4.

"Yankee Doodle"
British aversion to song after Lexington/
Concord
Conn. Courant May 15, p. 3.

January 1-3

Burning of Norfolk. Although Dunmore's command is given complete credit for the burning of Norfolk, the British contribution of one day's bombardment (January 1) is quite superseded by the destruction perpetrated during a two-day riot (January 2-3) by disaffected colonial soldiers. The Americans, officially, complete the devastation of the town on February 6 in order to frustrate any future British design to use it as a naval base.

N.E. Chron. Jan. 25/Feb. 1, p. 1.
N.Y. Journal Jan. 25, pp. 1-2, 3; Feb. 29, p. 3.
Pa. Gaz. Jan. 17, p. 2; Feb. 21, p. 2.
Va. Gaz. (Purdie) Jan. 5, supplement, p. 2; Jan. 12, p. 3; Feb. 9, p. 3.
S.C. and A.G. Gaz. Jan. 19/26, p. 1.

January—June

Canadian Campaign. After the loss at Quebec, the American military remnant in Canada waits out the winter under terribly adverse circumstances, chief of which is small-pox. In the face of the arrival of British reinforcements for Carleton in early May, the Americans, now under the command of General John Thomas — Arnold's injury from the assault on Quebec has forced his withdrawal to Montreal — begin a retreat more appropriately termed a panic. Thomas dies of small-pox on June 2; his replacement is General John Sullivan. An American countermove on Trois Rivières (Three Rivers), June 8, ends disastrously when the supposedly small British garrison is actually in the process of receiving an 8000-man reinforcement through the good offices of the recently arrived General John Burgoyne. The Americans flee with a loss of approximately 400; the British losses are about one dozen.

An interesting sidelight of the campaign is the arrival in April of a Congressional committee sent to seek the assistance of the Canadians for the patriot cause. This rejection is suffered despite the purposeful inclusion in the American party of a Catholic priest, Father John Carroll, as well as his Catholic brother, the aristocratic Charles Carroll of Carrollton (Maryland). The presence of both is intended to assuage Catholic French Canadian fears of heretofore rabidly anti-Catholic America. (The other members of the commission are Benjamin Franklin and Samuel Chase, who, together with Charles Carroll, will sign the Declaration of Independence within less than four months.)

N.E. Chron. Mar. 21/28, p. 3; May 9, p. 3.
Newpt. Merc. Apr. 1, p. 2; Apr. 29, p. 1; May 6, p. 2; May 13, p. 2; May 20, pp. 1-2; May 27, p. 2; June 3, p. 2; June 6, extraordinary, p. 2; June 20, p. 3; June 24, p. 4; July 1, p. 4; July 18, extraordinary, p. 3; July 29, p. 2.
N.Y. Journal Feb. 15, pp. 2-3; Feb. 29, p. 3; June 20, p. 3; Aug. 1, pp. 1-2.
Pa. Gaz. Feb. 21, p. 3; Mar. 6, p. 2; June 19, p. 2; July 10, p. 2.
Pa. Journal May 8, pp. 2-3; May 22, p. 3; July 17, p. 3.
Md. Gaz. Mar. 7, p. 3; May 2, p. 3; May 9, pp. 3-4.

January 10

Common Sense. With the publication of Tom Paine's extraordinarily influential pamphlet calling for independence from Great Britain, the hitherto forbidden subject becomes a respectable topic for public discussion. Although specific objections to or denials of independence as a goal are voiced in New Jersey (see below, November 16, 29, 1775), Maryland, and in assorted newspaper letters and essays, Paine's pen transforms what is already a rational leap for a few into a reasonable step for many. Especially significant are a series of letters republished in the *Pennsylvania Gazette* against the argument of *Common Sense* by "Cato" (the Reverend William Smith, Provost of the College of Philadelphia) which are quickly answered by assorted patriots such as a mathematics tutor at the College of Philadelphia, James Cannon, who signs himself "Cassandra," and by Tom Paine himself, who writes as the "Forester." Paine also composes the pro-independence "Dialogue between the Ghost of General Montgomery Just Arrived from the Elysian Fields; and an American Delegate, in a Wood near Philadelphia" [included here in *Va. Gaz.* (Purdie), March 8, supplement, p. 1].

N.Hamp. Gaz. Jan. 9, p. 1.
N.E. Chron. Jan. 11/18, pp. 1-2; Jan. 18/25, p. 2; Mar. 21/28, pp. 1-2, 3, 4.
Newpt. Merc. Apr. 8, p. 2; Apr. 22, p. 1.
Conn. Courant Feb. 19, pp. 1-2, 4; Feb. 26, pp. 1-2, 4; Mar. 4, pp. 1-2; Mar. 11, pp. 1-2.
N.Y. Journal Dec. 21 (1775), p. 1; Feb. 1, p. 1; Feb. 29, pp. 1-2; Mar. 7, pp. 1, 3; Mar. 14, p. 1; Apr. 18, p. 1.
Pa. Gaz. Feb. 21, p. 3; Feb. 28, p. 3; Mar. 6, p. 2; Mar. 13, pp. 1, 4; Mar. 20, pp. 1, 2, 4; Mar. 27, p. 1; Apr. 3, pp. 1, 4; Apr. 10, pp. 1, 2, 4; Apr. 24, pp. 1, 2, 4; May 1, p. 4.
Pa. Journal May 1, p. 3.
Md. Gaz. Feb. 22, p. 3; Mar. 7, p. 1; Apr. 11, p. 1; Apr. 18, p. 1; Apr. 25, p. 1; May 2, p. 2; May 23, pp. 2, 3; June 20, p. 3; June 27, pp. 2, 3; July 4, pp. 2-3.
Va. Gaz. (Purdie) Feb. 2, pp. 1-2; Mar. 8, supplement, p. 1; Mar. 29, p. 1; Apr. 12, pp. 1-2; Apr. 19, pp. 2-3.

S.C. and A.G. Gaz. Apr. 3/10, p. 2; May 8/22, pp. 1-2; May 31/Aug. 2, p. 1.

February 27

Moore's Creek Bridge. After his departure from New York City in early February, General Sir Henry Clinton's pleasant expectation of arousing Loyalist sentiment – and arms – in the Carolinas is effectively frustrated when approximately 1700 Tories on their way to his standard are defeated by North Carolina militia. Clinton is forced to reembark and to leave the state for more friendly climes (see below, June 28).

N.E. Chron. Mar. 14/21, p. 3; Mar. 28/Apr. 4, p. 3.
Newpt. Merc. Apr. 1, pp. 1, 2.
Conn. Courant Apr. 1, p. 2.
N.Y. Journal Apr. 25, p. 2.
Pa. Gaz. Mar. 27, p. 3.
Md. Gaz. Mar. 14, p. 2; Mar. 21, p. 3; Mar. 28, p. 3; Apr. 4, pp. 2-3.
Va. Gaz. (Purdie) Mar. 15, supplement, p. 1; Mar. 22, pp. 1, 2; Apr. 12, pp. 2-3.
S.C. and A.G. Gaz. Feb. 9/16, p. 1.

March 4

British Evacuation of Boston. Cannon captured at Fort Ticonderoga is brought to Boston by Colonel Henry Knox. Their emplacement on Dorchester Heights on the night of March 4 by a force under Major General John Thomas gives the Americans a strong position from which to bombard Boston. General William Howe's response is an evacuation of the city on March 17. The British transports reach Halifax, Nova Scotia, with nearly a thousand Loyalists, or Tories, most of whom settle down, never to return to Massachusetts.

N.E. Chron. Feb. 29/Mar. 6, p. 3; Mar. 14/21, p. 3.
Cont. Journal Oct. 17, p. 4.
Newpt. Merc. Mar. 18, p. 2; Mar. 25, p. 2.
Conn. Courant Mar. 25, p. 3.
N.Y. Journal Mar. 14, p. 3; Apr. 25, p. 3.
Pa. Gaz. Mar. 20, p. 2; Mar. 27, p. 2; Apr. 3, p. 2.
Md. Gaz. May 9, p. 2.
Va. Gaz. (Purdie) Apr. 5, p. 2.

March 19

American Privateering Authorized. Congress authorizes privateering, *i.e.*, the use of privately-owned ships against another country. Within days the Congress begins to issue letters of marque and reprisal to the states for their disposition. (These papers serve as licenses for such maritime activities, according to international custom.) And while an infant United States Navy is able to put only a few vessels to sea, the enterprising American privateers turn a healthy, and patriotic, profit at the expense of British commerce. During the war, over 600 British ships worth $18,000,000. are captured by American privateers. The Continental Navy enjoys certain early successes such as the capture of New Providence (Nassau) in the Bahamas in March 1776 by Commander-in-Chief of the Fleet Essex Hopkins (Rhode Island).

Bos. Gaz. Apr. 8, p. 1.
N.E. Chron. Apr. 25, p. 1; May 16, p. 1.
Newpt. Merc. Apr. 29, p. 2; May 6, p. 1.
Conn. Courant Apr. 22, p. 2.
N.Y. Journal Apr. 18, pp. 2, 3; Apr. 25, p. 1.
Pa. Gaz. Mar. 27, p. 2.

April 6

America to Trade with the World. After bitter debate, Congress opens American ports to the commerce of all nations save Great Britain. This step is necessary in order for essential supplies for the American war effort to be gathered from abroad. It is also another move on the rapidly descending path to independence. The trade act includes a prohibition against the importation of slaves, a clause without meaning to the southernmost states. The Congress's action follows King George's proclamation closing American ports to any trade (December 23, 1775).

Bos. Gaz. Apr. 22, p. 2.
N.E. Chron. Apr. 25, p. 3; May 9, pp. 1-2.
Conn. Courant Mar. 18, p. 2; Mar. 25, p. 2; Apr. 22, p. 4.
N.Y. Journal Mar. 14, p. 3.
N.Y. Packet Apr. 11, p. 3.
Pa. Journal Mar. 13, pp. 1-2; Apr. 10, p. 2.
Va. Gaz. (Purdie) Apr. 16, postscript, p. 1.

May

Secret French Aid for America. King Louis XVI of France secretly directs one million livres worth of arms and munitions to the American colonies through a fictitious firm, Roderique Hortalez and Company, under the direction of the French author of the play *The Barber of Seville (Le Barbier de Seville)*, Caron de Beaumarchais. The French foreign minister, the Comte de Vergennes, is most pleased to assist the possible initiators of Britain's eventual demise. Representing the colonies in France at the moment is Silas Deane (Connecticut), who is to be joined before the end of the year by Arthur Lee (Virginia) and Benjamin Franklin. The Spanish, sharing a hatred for the British with the neighboring French, join the latter in the clandestine supply of the American military exertion. In 1776-1777, American efforts to produce gunpowder are "supplemented" by these two foreign benefactors, thirsting for revenge for the Treaty of Paris (1763), who contribute 80% of the total amount used by the colonists.

May 15

State Constitutions. Acting on Congress's recommendation (May 15) that the individual colonies should look to their internal governments in the absence of any effective authority, eleven of the thirteen colonies draw up state constitutions: 1776 – New Hampshire and South Carolina (both before May 15), Virginia, New Jersey, Delaware, Pennsylvania, Maryland, and North Carolina; 1777 – Georgia and New York; 1780 – Massachusetts. Rhode Island and Connecticut continue to use colonial charters from the mid-seventeenth century but with all mention of King George replaced by allusion to the fundamental sovereignty of the people of the state. Vermont, which in 1791 becomes the fourteenth state, ratifies its own constitution in 1777 despite continued New York and New Hampshire opposition to its separate existence (see above, 1774). Except for Massachusetts' use of a constitutional convention and an attendant provision for popular ratification, the ordinary drafting procedure is accomplished solely by special state congresses or conventions, or by sitting state legislatures. Drawing on the colonists' political heritage of royal governor/popular assembly conflict, the state constitutions provide for weak executives and legislatures with overwhelming political power. Pennsylvania and New Hampshire alone determine upon unicameral legislative bodies. Property qualifications for the suffrage and office-holding are maintained although modified in certain states. Frequent elections and an appointed judiciary to serve during good behavior are further instances of an American bent for a large measure of control over their own destinies. Virginia is the first state to adopt a Declaration, or Bill, of Rights (June 12).

(The principal reason behind Congress' May 15 resolution is a deliberate effort to replace Pennsylvania's moderate and anti-independence government with a more revolutionary, pro-independence body and government. John Adams and his cohorts are successful in this respect, but the idea of a new Pennsylvania constitution and its actual establishment and ac-

ceptance are all matters of intense dispute within the state.)

Newpt. Merc. May 27, p. 3.
Conn. Courant May 27, p. 2.
N.Y. Journal Dec. 7 (1775), p. 3.
Pa. Journal May 22, p. 1.
S.C. and A.G. Gaz. May 31/Aug. 2, p. 1.
Ga. Gaz. Jan. 10, p. 1.

New Hampshire
N.Hamp. Gaz. Aug. 17 (1779), p. 1.
N.E. Chron. Jan. 25/Feb. 1, p. 3.
Md. Gaz. Feb. 22, p. 1.

Vermont
Conn. Courant Mar. 17 (1777), p. 1; June 30 (1777), p. 1.

Massachusetts
Indep. Chron. Mar. 6 (1777), pp. 1-2; May 8 (1777), p. 3; May 29 (1777), p. 3; June 19 (1777), p. 1; Mar. 5 (1778), p. 3; Mar. 19 (1778), pp. 1, 4; Apr. 2 (1778), p. 1; Apr. 9 (1778), pp. 1, 2; Apr. 16 (1778), pp. 1-2; Apr. 30 (1778), p. 4; May 28 (1778), p. 2; June 4 (1778), pp. 3, 4; June 11 (1778), p. 2; Aug. 19 (1779), p. 2; Sept. 23 (1779), p. 1; Dec. 2 (1779), p. 1; Feb. 10 (1780), pp. 1-2; Mar. 2 (1780), p. 1; Mar. 16 (1780), supplement, p. 1; Mar. 23 (1780), p. 1; Apr. 1 (1780), p. 1; Apr. 13 (1780), p. 1; Apr. 20 (1780), p. 4; May 4 (1780), p. 1; May 18 (1780), pp. 1-2, 4; July 6 (1780), p. 4; Nov. 2 (1780), pp. 2-3, 4; Nov. 16 (1780), pp. 1-2.
N.J. Gaz. July 12 (1780), p. 2.
(N.B.) *N.C. Gaz.* Aug. 14 (1778), p. 3.

Rhode Island
N.E. Chron. May 23, p. 1.
Pa. Journal May 15, p. 3.

Connecticut
Conn. Courant Nov. 18, pp. 1-2.
Md. Gaz. Aug. 8, p. 1.

New York
N.Y. Journal June 13, pp. 1-2.
N.Y. Packet [June 11] (1778), p. 2.

New Jersey
Cont. Journal Aug. 8, p. 1.
Newpt. Merc. July 11, extraordinary, p. 2.
N.J. Gaz. Oct. 14 (1778), pp. 1-2; May 12 (1779), pp. 1, 4.
Pa. Journal July 17, pp. 2, 3; Aug. 28, p. 1.
Md. Gaz. July 25, pp. 2-3; Aug. 1, p. 3.

Pennsylvania
Newpt. Merc. July 1, p. 3.
N.J. Gaz. Jan. 6 (1779), p. 2.
Pa. Gaz. Aug. 21, pp. 2-3; Sept. 18, pp. 1, 4; Oct. 16, pp. 1, 4; Oct. 23, pp. 1, 2-3, 4; Oct. 30, p. 2; Nov. 13, p. 2.
Pa. Journal May 22, pp. 1, 3; May 29, p. 3; July 17, p. 2; Oct. 9, p. 3; Mar. 12 (1777), p. 3; Mar. 19

(1777), pp. 2-3; Mar. 26 (1777), pp. 2-3; Apr. 9 (1777), p. 1; Apr. 23 (1777), p. 1; May 14 (1777), p. 2; May 21 (1777), pp. 2-3; May 28 (1777), pp. 1-2; June 4 (1777), pp. 1-2; Feb 3 (1779), pp. 1-2; Feb. 17 (1779), p. 1; Feb. 24 (1779), pp. 1, 2; Mar. 17 (1779), pp. 1-2.

Pa. Packet Nov. 26, p. 2; Feb. 27 (1779), p. 2; Mar. 2 (1779), p. 1; Mar. 4 (1779), p. 3.

Md. Gaz. Mar. 14, p. 2; Mar. 21, p. 3; Mar. 28, pp. 2-3; Apr. 4, pp. 1-2; Apr. 11, pp. 2-3; Apr. 25, pp. 1-2; May 2, pp. 1-2; May 9, pp. 1-2.

Delaware
Newpt. Merc. July 11, extraordinary, pp. 1-2.
Pa. Gaz. July 31, p. 3; Oct. 2, p. 4.
Pa. Journal Oct. 9, pp. 1, 4.
Md. Gaz. Aug. 8, p. 2; Oct. 3, p. 1.

Maryland
Indep. Chron. Jan. 9 (1777), pp. 1-2.
Md. Gaz. July 18, pp. 2-4; Aug. 15, p. 3; Aug. 22, pp. 2-3; Aug. 29, pp. 2-3; Sept. 12, p. 3; Nov. 14, pp. 3-4; Nov. 21, pp. 1-2; Nov. 28, pp. 1-2.

Virginia
Cont. Journal Aug. 2, pp. 1-2, 3.
Pa. Journal May 22, p. 2.
Va. Gaz. (Purdie) July 5, supplement, pp. 1-2; July 5, postscript, p. 1; July 12, p. 1.

North Carolina
(N.Y.) *Royal Gaz.* July 29 (1778), p. 3.

South Carolina
Newpt. Merc. Apr. 22, p. 1.
Pa. Journal Apr. 23 (1777), p. 3.
Md. Gaz. May 16, p. 3; May 23, p. 2; May 30, p. 3; June 6, p. 3.
S.C. and A.G. Gaz. Mar. 27/Apr. 3, p. 3.

May 15

Virginia Instructs for Independence. Although chronologically first with instructions to its delegates "to concur with the delegates of the other Colonies in declaring Independency," North Carolina's Halifax Resolves (April 12) are afforded minimal coverage in the colonial press. The dramatic initiative for independence comes from the more politically important colony of Virginia. On May 15 the Virginia Convention directs its delegates to the Continental Congress "to declare the United Colonies free and independent states, absolved from all allegiance to or dependence upon the Crown or Parliament of Great Britain." On June 12 the Virginia Convention adopts the Virginia Declaration of Rights, chiefly the work of George Mason, which influences many other state declarations as well as the United States Bill of Rights (1791).

Newpt. Merc. May 20, p. 2; June 10, pp. 1-2; June 20, pp. 1-2.
Conn. Courant June 10, p. 3; July 8, p. 2.
Pa. Journal May 1, pp. 2-3; May 29, pp. 2, 3.
Md. Gaz. May 2, p. 3; May 30, p. 3; June 13, p. 3.
Va. Gaz. (Purdie) May 17, pp. 2-3; June 14, postscript to supplement, p. 1.
S.C. and A.G. Gaz. May 31/Aug. 2, p. 1.

June 28.

Charleston. Admiral Sir Peter Parker's fleet, with General Sir Henry Clinton's army, arrives off Charleston on June 4. The British plan to wrest the valuable port from the Americans and then to proceed to separate the Southern colonies from their more rebellious Northern brothers is ended when General Charles Lee's forces stubbornly resist an all-day bombardment, principally directed upon Sullivan's Island, a major part of Charleston's harbor defenses. Strategically situated Fort Sullivan is commanded by Colonel William Moultrie (for whom the fort is later renamed in honor of his role in the American victory). The British defeat is most significant as it frees the South from invasion for over two years (see below, December 29, 1778).

Cont. Journal Aug. 2, p. 1; Aug. 15, p. 1.
Newpt. Merc. July 29, pp. 1-2.
Conn. Courant July 1, p. 2; July 8, p. 2; July 29, pp. 2-3.
N.Y. Journal June 13, p. 3; July 4, p. 2; July 11, p. 2; Aug. 1, p. 1.
Pa. Gaz. June 19, p. 2; July 24, p. 1; Sept. 11, p. 2.
Pa. Journal Aug. 28, p. 2; Nov. 20, pp. 1-2.
Md. Gaz. May 16, p. 3.
Va. Gaz. (Purdie) July 12, supplement, p. 1; July 19, p. 1.
S.C. and A.G. Gaz. Jan. 12/19, p. 3; May 31/Aug. 2, p. 3; Dec. 5/12, pp. 1-2.

July 4

Declaration of Independence. On June 7, Richard Henry Lee of Virginia presents resolutions in Congress calling for independence, foreign alliances, and the establishment of a plan of colonial confederation. A three-week period is set aside for further consideration, primarily for the benefit of Pennsylvania (which finally opts on June 24 for independence if Congress should decide to declare it), Maryland, New Jersey, and New York; in all these colonies there is considerable anti-independence sentiment. During this period a five-member committee drafts an appropriate document. Thomas Jefferson (Virginia), Roger Sherman (Connecticut), John Adams (Massachusetts), Benjamin Franklin (Pennsylvania), and Robert R. Livingston (New

York) bring forth the American Declaration of Independence on June 28. On July 4, the Declaration, minus a Jefferson condemnation of King George III's neglect to end the slave trade (unacceptable to South Carolina and Georgia), is approved "unanimously" by Congress. (The New York delegation abstains because of a 'lack of instructions.' The New York legislature does approve of the Declaration on July 9.) Only John Hancock and secretary Charles Thomson, who authenticates the document, sign on July 4; no other signatures are added until August 2. The last of the fifty-six signers affixes his name in 1781. The fateful state paper is first offered to the American people on July 8 in Philadelphia. Drafted substantially by Thomas Jefferson, the Declaration of Independence is essentially a listing of twenty-seven charges against George III that lead the colonists irrevocably to revolution and independence. The more famous, but less important natural rights preamble (two paragraphs) is based largely on the ideas of such as John Locke, a seventeenth-century English political philosopher.

Cont. Journal July 11, p. 2.
Newpt. Merc. June 24, p. 2; July 18, extraordinary, pp. 2-3.
Conn. Courant July 1, p. 2; July 8, p. 2; July 15, p. 2.
N.Y. Journal July 4, p. 2; July 11, pp. 2, 3.
Pa. Gaz. June 19, pp. 2-3; June 26, p. 3; July 3, p. 2; July 10, pp. 1, 2.
Pa. Journal May 29, p. 3; June 12, pp. 1, 2-3.
Va. Gaz. (Purdie) July 19, p. 2; July 26, pp. 1-2.
S.C. and A.G. Gaz. May 31/Aug. 2, p. 4.
Broadside: July (Newport, Rhode Island)

July—August

Americans React Favorably to Declaration. American public reaction to the proclamation of the Declaration of Independence is joyous and overwhelmingly affirmative. In New York City the statue of King George III is pulled down and the residual lead is unceremoniously converted into bullets to put down the king's troops.

Newpt. Merc. July 22, pp. 3, 4; July 29, p. 2; Aug. 12, p. 3; Aug. 19, p. 1; Sept. 30, p. 3.
N.Y. Journal Aug. 8, pp. 1-2.
Pa. Journal Aug. 28, p. 1.
Md. Gaz. Aug. 22, p. 2.
Va. Gaz. (Purdie) July 26, p. 2.

July—November

Canadian Campaign. Retreating from Crown Point to Fort Ticonderoga in early July, the sick, ill-supplied, discontented colonials fortify themselves against the expected British attack.

Heroic efforts directed by Benedict Arnold counter Carleton's construction of a Lake Champlain fleet with an American fleet. Although the Americans lose first a battle (Valcour Bay, October 11) and then a battle plus their fleet (Split Rock, October 13), their struggle prevents a British move toward Albany and thence to New York City via the North, or Hudson, River where General Howe is expected to be safely established after chasing Washington into the hinterlands of New Jersey or some other suitable place. (A similar intention to divide arch-radical New England from the rest of the colonies, predicated upon British control of the Lake Champlain-Albany-Hudson River route, motivates General John Burgoyne in the ill-fated campaign of 1777: see below, June-October 1777.) Carleton ends a short occupation of Crown Point on November 3, convinced that winter is too close for a move against supposedly well-manned Fort Ticonderoga, where the Americans are now concentrated, and a further descent toward New York City. The British return to Canada.

The noted American naval historian, Alfred Thayer Mahan, later describes the late summer events in upstate New York as the necessary prelude to the British surrender at Saratoga the following year and the consequent French alliance which led directly to American victory in 1783. His praise is highest for "the indomitable energy, and . . . the indomitable courage of the traitor, Benedict Arnold."

N.Hamp. Gaz. Oct. 29, pp. 2, 3.
Freeman's Journal Nov. 19, pp. 2-3; Dec. 10, p. 2.
Cont. Journal Oct. 24, p. 3; Nov. 14, p. 3.
Newpt. Merc. July 29, p. 2; Aug. 5, pp. 1-2; Nov. 4, p. 3; Nov. 11, p. 3.
Conn. Courant Aug. 19, p. 3; Oct. 21, p. 2; Nov. 11, p. 3; Nov. 18, p. 3; Dec. 2, p. 2.
N.Y. Gaz. and Week. Merc. Oct. 26, p. 3.
Pa. Journal Nov. 20, p. 2.
Va. Gaz. (Purdie) Nov. 15, p. 2; Nov. 29, p. 1.
S.C. and A.G. Gaz. Oct. 24/Nov. 7, p. 2.

July 2

Enter the Howe Brothers. General William Howe lands forces on Staten Island, a preliminary to the long-awaited invasion of New York City. His brother, Admiral Richard Howe arrives with a fleet for his assistance July 12. Soon General Howe's forces are augmented with the arrival of General Clinton's command from the unsuccessful attempt on Charleston. Howe's troops now number over 34,000. In August a British move to initiate peace negotiations comes to no account since the Howes are authorized only to grant pardons, and nothing else. Moreover, the patriots take umbrage at the Howes' aversion to addressing exploratory letters to Washington other than to "Mr. Washington" or "George Washington, Esquire, etc. etc." (Recognition of Washington's rank will imply recognition of American statehood and independence.)

Cont. Journal Oct. 3, pp. 1-2; Oct. 10, p. 1; Oct. 17, p. 2.
Newpt. Merc. June 20, p. 4; Aug. 5, p. 3; Aug. 19, pp. 2-3.
Conn. Courant July 22, p. 2.
N.Y. Journal July 4, p. 2; Aug. 1, p. 2; Aug. 8, p. 2.
Pa. Journal Aug. 28, p. 3.
Md. Gaz. Aug. 1, pp. 1-2; Aug. 8, pp. 1-2; Sept. 26, pp. 2-3.
Va. Gaz. (Purdie) July 19, p. 2.

August 26

Long Island. General Howe finally begins his attack with New York City as the objective. His landing on Long Island surprises the Americans under General John Sullivan and leads to a British victory. Howe's customary caution allows Washington the opportunity to evacuate the remainder of the American forces from Long Island on the foggy night of August 29. Washington's stratagem, by which 9500 troops are ferried across the East River to Manhattan Island by Massachusetts fishermen under the command of General John Glover, saves the Americans and prevents a crushing British victory. Another effort by the Howe brothers, who seem genuinely disposed to conciliation, to begin peace negotiations is dismissed by Congress, whose three representatives at an early September dinner with Admiral Howe on Long Island are nonplussed. Benjamin Franklin, John Adams, and Edward Rutledge (South Carolina) find nothing new in their host's proposals for renewed allegiance and pardon.

Cont. Journal Sept. 5, p. 3; Sept. 12, p. 3; Sept. 19, pp. 3, 4; Oct. 3, p. 2.
Newpt. Merc. Sept. 23, p. 1.
Conn. Courant Sept. 2, p. 3; Sept. 2, p. 3; Sept. 9, p. 2. p. 3; Sept. 30, p. 2.
N.Y. Gaz. and Week. Merc. Sept. 21, p. 2.
N.Y. Journal Aug. 29, p. 3.
Pa. Gaz. Sept. 4, p. 2; Sept. 18, p. 2.
Pa. Journal Oct. 9, pp. 2-3; Apr. 23 (1777), p. 2.
Md. Gaz. Sept. 5, pp. 2-3; Sept. 26, p. 3.
Va. Gaz. (Purdie) Sept. 6, p. 2; Sept. 13, p. 2; Sept. 13, supplement, p. 1; Oct. 4, pp. 1-2.
S.C. and A.G. Gaz. Sept. 25/Oct. 2, p. 3.

September 15

Kip's Bay and Harlem Heights. A British landing at Kip's Bay on the east side of Manhattan Island precipitates a furious and disorderly American retreat to Harlem Heights. The unsoldierly haste prompts Washington to a rage which nearly results in his capture by a Hessian advance contingent. A short, spirited action at Harlem Heights the next day works as a salve and an encouragement to American pride so badly damaged the 15th. The characteristic Howe hesitation serves again to Washington's short-lived advantage as the British remain inside newly-won New York City for three weeks.

During this time, the British are infuriated by a fire that destroys a large section of the city (September 20-21). Perhaps in retaliation for this suspected rebel maneuver, a Connecticut schoolmaster-American spy, Nathan Hale, is summarily executed on September 22. Hale's heroism and last words are celebrated in a 1781 *Independent Chronicle* comparison with Major John André, Benedict Arnold's executed British ally in the plot to give up West Point to General Clinton (see below, September 1780): "I am so satisfied with the cause in which I have engaged, that my only regret is, that I have not more lives than one to offer in its service."

N.Hamp. Gaz. Oct. 29, pp. 2, 3.
Cont. Journal Sept. 26, pp. 1, 2; Oct. 24, p. 3; Nov. 7, pp. 1-2.
Indep. Chron. Mar. 13 (1777), p. 1; May 17 (1781), p. 1.
Newpt. Merc. Sept. 23, p. 2; Sept. 30, pp. 3, 4; Oct. 7, pp. 2, 3.
Conn. Courant Oct. 7, p. 2; Oct. 21, p. 2. Oct. 21, p. 2.
N.Y. Gaz. and Week. Merc. Sept. 28, p. 3.
Pa. Gaz. Sept. 25, p. 3.
Md. Gaz. Oct. 3, p. 3; Oct. 10, p. 3.
Va. Gaz. (Purdie) Oct. 11, p. 1; Oct. 25, p. 1.

October 28

White Plains. Skirmishes at Throg's Neck (October 12) and Pell's Point (October 18) lead to a battle between Howe, attempting to outflank the Americans on the east, and Washington, who is determined to contain the British east of the Hudson River. Unable to bring on a general engagement, Howe returns toward New York City.

Freeman's Journal Nov. 19, p. 3.
Cont. Journal Nov. 7, p. 2; Nov. 25, p. 3.
Conn. Courant Oct. 28, pp. 2-3; Nov. 4, p. 3; Nov. 11, p. 2.
N.Y. Gaz. and Week. Merc. Nov. 2, p. 3.
Pa. Journal Nov. 6, p. 3.
S.C. and A.G. Gaz. Dec. 5/12, p. 2.

November 16

Fort Washington. On the east bank of the

Hudson River, Fort Washington, along with Fort Lee across the river in New Jersey, is expected to prevent any British naval movement past the line of sunken ships and prepared fire ships between the forts. Fort Washington's position is totally untenable; its loss to a far superior enemy force quick and costly. The American army is staggered by the surrender of 2800 men. Four days later Lord Cornwallis's approach causes the evacuation and loss of Fort Lee.

Freeman's Journal Dec. 10, p. 1.
Cont. Journal Dec. 5, p. 3.
Indep. Chron. Jan. 2 (1777), p. 1.
Newpt. Merc. Nov. 25, p. 4.
Conn. Courant Nov. 18, p. 3; Nov. 25, p. 3; Dec. 2, p. 3; Dec. 23, p. 3.
Pa. Journal Nov. 20, p. 2.
Va. Gaz. (Purdie) Dec. 6, p. 1.

November—December

Retreat Across New Jersey. Washington moves southwest across New Jersey after the fall of Fort Lee with Howe's British and Hessian troops in close pursuit. On December 8 the Americans cross the Delaware River into Pennsylvania. Rumors of British designs upon the Continental capital hurries Congress from Philadelphia to Baltimore (December 12). Patriotism and self-preservation become warring sentiments with the colonial press aflame with stories of British and, more especially, Hessian atrocities upon the Jerseymen and their families.

Indep. Chron. Jan. 2 (1777), p. 3; Jan. 16 (1777), p. 2.
Pa. Packet Nov. 26, pp. 2-3; Dec. 18, pp. 1, 2; Dec. 27, p. 2.
Md. Gaz. Dec. 19, p. 2.
Va. Gaz. (Purdie) Dec. 13, p. 2; Dec. 27, pp. 1-2.
S.C. and A.G. Gaz. Jan. 16 (1777), p. 3.
Broadsides: undated Howe in New Jersey; Nov. 27; Dec. 9; Dec. 11.

December 8

Newport Occupied. Quite confident in his situation, General Howe dispatches General Henry Clinton to Rhode Island with 6000 troops. Clinton easily takes Newport and settles down for a comfortable winter. These British troops maintain their position — and remain outside of the war — for three years.

Conn. Courant Dec. 23, p. 2.
Va. Gaz. (Purdie) Feb. 7 (1777), p. 2; Feb. 28, supplement, p. 1.

December 13

General Lee Captured. General Charles Lee, a former British officer tainted with hatred for King George III and contempt for Washington and the Continental Congress, is captured at Basking Ridge, New Jersey, as he tarries on his own way toward the retreating American army. Ironically, his capture is effected by elements of a regiment he had commanded in Portugal in 1762. A daring raid on Newport, July 10, 1777, nets the British commander-in-chief of that post, General Richard Prescott, abed. The appropriate exchange of Lee and Prescott is completed (April 1778) in time for Lee, who wines and dines in New York City for the better part of a year, to participate in the Battle of Monmouth — and bring upon himself his own ruin (see below, June 18-28, 1778). Lee's captivity achieves apparent Providential dispensation when he wins $500. in the New York lottery which he promptly distributes among the American prisoners in New York City.

Indep. Chron. Mar. 13 (1777), p. 2.
Prov. Gaz. July 12 (1777), p. 3; July 19 (1777), p. 3; Aug. 23 (1777), p. 4.
Conn. Courant Dec. 23, p. 3.
N.Y. Packet Feb. 26 (1778), p. 3.
Pa. Journal July 23 (1777), p. 3.
Va. Gaz. (Purdie) Jan. 3 (1777), supplement, p. 1; Feb. 28 (1777), supplement, p. 1.

December 25—January 3, 1777

Trenton and Princeton. Almost simultaneously with the appearance of Tom Paine's first *American Crisis* paper in the colonial press — "There are the times that try men's souls" — Washington daringly crosses the Delaware River into New Jersey, completely surprises the Hessian garrison (befuddled by its Christmas celebration), and crosses back into Pennsylvania with 900 prisoners. In early January, a potentially disastrous foray into New Jersey toward New Brunswick, site of a British supply depot, ends in another American triumph at Princeton (January 3, 1777) despite Cornwallis's superior army. Washington's tactical surprise is not enough for a strategic victory, however, as Cornwallis moves hurriedly to defend New Brunswick and the exhausted Americans move into winter quarters at Morristown, New Jersey, twenty-five miles west of the British position.

Indep. Chron. Jan. 9 (1777), p. 3; Jan. 16 (1777), pp. 1, 2, 3; Jan. 23 (1777), p. 2; Feb. 13 (1777), p. 1.
Prov. Gaz. Jan. 18 (1777), pp. 2-3; Jan. 25 (1777), p. 2.
Conn. Courant Jan 6 (1777), pp. 2-3; Jan. 13 (1777), p. 3.
Pa. Journal Feb. 5 (1777), pp. 1, 3.

Pa. Packet Dec. 27, p. 1; Jan. 4 (1777), pp. 1, 2.
Md. Gaz. Jan. 9 (1777), p. 1.
Va. Gaz. (Purdie) Jan. 10 (1777), pp. 1-2; Jan. 17 (1777), pp. 1-2; Jan. 24 (1777), pp. 1-2; Feb. 7 (1777), p. 1.

Gaz. of St. of S.C. Apr. 28 (1777), pp. 1-2.
S.C. and A.G. Gaz. Jan. 30 (1777), pp. 1, 2.
Broadside: undated [1777].

Church of England
Disestablishment of debated in Virginia
Va. Gaz. (Purdie) Oct. 18, p. 1; Nov. 1, p.
1; Nov. 8, pp. 1-2; Dec. 6, p. 1.

Gunpowder
Manufacture of
N.E. Chron. Feb. 22/29, p. 1.

Newspapers
Cash for rags
Freeman's Journal Oct. 22, p. 4.

Patriotism
Child baptism "Independence"
Conn. Courant July 29, p. 3.

Poetry
"The Patriot's Prayer"
N.Y. Journal Feb. 15, p. 4.

Saltpeter
Manufacture of
Md. Gaz. Mar. 7, pp. 2-3.

Slaves
Runaways found
Va. Gaz. (Purdie) July 26, pp. 3-4.

Soldiers, German
British agreements for assistance of
Newpt. Merc. June 6, extraordinary, pp.
1-2.
Pa. Journal May 24, supplement, p. 1; May
29, p. 1.

Sugar Plums
Ad for, to destroy worms
Pa. Journal Oct. 9, p. 4.

Theater
Ad for *The Battle of Bunker Hill*
Pa. Journal Nov. 20, p. 3.

Tories
Break jail
Md. Gaz. Oct. 3, p. 3.
Child of Loyalist baptized George Washington, disastrous results
Conn. Courant Nov. 4, p. 3.
Connecticut publicizes
Conn. Courant Apr. 8, p. 1; Apr. 15, p. 1;
July 15, p. 3.
N.Y. Journal Apr. 18, p. 3; June 20, p. 1.
In New Jersey
Va. Gaz. (Purdie) July 26, p. 2.
Non-subscribers to Association
N.Y. Journal Apr. 25, p. 1.
Virginia Treason Act
Va. Gaz. (Purdie) Dec. 20, supplement,
p. 1.

Virginia
Explanation of state seal
Newpt. Merc. July 29, p. 2.

Washington, George
Receives Harvard L.L.D.
N.E. Chron. Apr. 25, p. 1.

February

American-Dutch Trade. Britain's representative to the States-General of the Netherlands, Sir Joseph Yorke, demands an end to the clandestine trade between Britian's American colonies and the Dutch. The latter's national legislature replies that Sir Joseph might do well to mind his own business. British efforts to stop the trade to and from America, so vital to the colonial war capacity, eventually lead to the formation of a European League of Armed Neutrality (see below, March 9, 1780) as well as war with the Netherlands (see below, December 20, 1780). Both events serve American interests.

Indep. Chron. June 26, p. 3.
Pa. Gaz. Apr. 24, p. 2.
Va. Gaz. (Purdie) June 20, p. 2.
Gaz. of St. of S.C. May 19, p. 3; July 14, p. 2; July 8 (1778), p. 3.

March

Eastern Shore Loyalists. A Loyalist uprising on Maryland's Eastern Shore is put down by Maryland and Virginia militia before Continental troops can be brought into the area. Indeed, a great number of the inhabitants of the Delmarva Peninsula (formed by the eastern parts of Delaware, Maryland, and Virginia), as it is now called, are disaffected toward the patriot cause.

Indep. Chron. Mar. 27, p. 3.
Pa. Packet Feb. 11, p. 3.
Va. Gaz. (Purdie) Feb. 28, supplement, p. 1; Mar. 7, supplement, p. 1; Apr. 4, p. 1.
Broadside: Feb. 13.

April 25-28

Danbury. A Continental supply depot at Danbury, Connecticut, is destroyed by a British force commanded by General William Tryon, former royal governor of both North Carolina and New York. Part of the town is also burned. The British return to their waiting ships on Long Island Sound is unlike their leisurely, and unopposed, march to their objective as Generals Benedict Arnold and David Wooster and Colonel John Lamb impose 200 casualties on the Britishers while the Americans lose 60 men.

Indep. Chron. May 2, p. 3; May 8, p. 3; June 12, p. 2.
Conn. Courant Apr. 28, p. 3; May 5, p. 3.
Pa. Journal May 14, pp. 2-3; May 21, p. 3.
Va. Gaz. (Purdie) May 16, p. 2; June 13, p. 2.
Gaz. of St. of S.C. May 19, pp. 1-2; June 9, p. 2.

June 14

American Flag. Congress formally establishes an American flag to consist of thirteen alternate red and white stripes with thirteen white stars on a blue field.

Conn. Courant. Sept. 15, p. 2.
Md. Gaz. Sept. 11, p. 1.
Va. Gaz. (Purdie) Sept. 12, p. 2.
(N.B.) *N.C. Gaz.* Oct. 3, p. 3.

June—October

Burgoyne's Plan to Win the War. In January 1777, General John Burgoyne offers a plan to King George III calculated to separate the New England colonies from their fellows. A British force (the command is given to Burgoyne as General Guy Carleton is passed over by unfriendly Colonial Secretary Lord George Germain) is to move south from Canada down Lake Champlain, take Fort Ticonderoga, and then proceed to Albany. This force is then to establish communications with British military elements from New York City by way of the Hudson River. At the same time, another British army contingent, under Colonel Barry St. Leger, is to march east from Lake Ontario and Oswego to Albany via the Mohawk River. A major difficulty arises when General William Howe is not given definitive notice of the projected invasion plan until he is on his passage to attack Philadelphia in August (see below, August 25). Howe dele- the army in New York City, to offer Burgoyne any necessary assistance from that quarter.

Va. Gaz. (Purdie) May 23, p. 2; June 20, p. 2.

July 5

Fort Ticonderoga Falls. Setting out on June 20 with a mile-long flotilla on Lake Champlain, General Burgoyne moves on Fort Ticonderoga, which he reaches June 30. General Arthur St. Clair, a former British officer, evacuates the strategic position on July 5, a decision quite unpopular with his adopted countrymen. St. Clair defends his precipitate withdrawal in the American press, but the explanation is rendered less palatable by Burgoyne's easy successes at Hubbardton, Skenesboro, and Fort Anne (July 6-7).

Indep. Chron. July 10, pp. 2, 3; July 24, pp. 1, 3; Aug. 7, pp. 1-2; Aug. 21, p. 2; Aug. 29, pp. 1-2; Sept. 25, p. 2; Nov. 27, pp. 1-2.
Prov. Gaz. July 26, pp. 1-2; Aug. 2, pp. 2, 3.
Conn. Courant July 21, p. 3.
N.Y. Journal Aug. 25, pp. 2-3; Oct. 6, pp. 1, 4.
Pa. Journal July 23, pp. 2-3; Aug. 6, p. 3; Aug. 13, p. 2.
Va. Gaz. (Purdie) July 4, p. 2; July 25, p. 2; Aug. 1, supplement, p. 1; Aug. 15, p. 2; Aug. 22, p. 2; Aug. 29, p. 2.

(N.B.)*N.C. Gaz.* Aug. 1, p. 3; Aug. 8, p. 3; Aug. 15, p. 3; Jan. 16 (1778), p. 1.
Gaz. of St. of S.C. Sept. 15, pp. 2-3.

August 3-22

Siege of Fort Stanwix. St. Leger's command invests Fort Stanwix (Fort Schuyler), the principal American defensive position in the Mohawk Valley, on August 3. Under the leadership of Colonel Peter Gansevoort, the Americans withstand the siege despite the ambush at nearby Oriskany (August 6) of an American relief force led by General Nicholas Herkimer. This surprise attack by a band of Tories and Indians is directed by Joseph Brant, a Mohawk chieftain who has studied in Connecticut and travelled to England where he dined with James Boswell and later sat for a portrait. Gansevoort's actual relief is afforded by Benedict Arnold who uses a ruse to stampede St. Leger's Indians: a report of Arnold's approach with a far superior army is spread by a half-wit, condemned fellow, Hon Yost Schuyler, whom the Indians esteem for his madness. The British besiegers are gone on the 22nd; Arnold arrives to a hero's welcome on the 24th of August.

Indep. Chron. Aug. 21, p. 3; Aug. 29, p. 3.
Prov. Gaz. Aug. 23, p. 2; Sept. 6, p. 3.
Conn. Courant Aug. 18, pp. 2-3; Aug. 25, pp. 2-3; Sept. 1, p. 3.
N.Y. Journal Sept. 8, p. 3.
Pa. Packet Aug. 19, p. 2.
Md. Gaz. Sept. 25, p. 1.
Va. Gaz. (Purdie) Sept. 5, pp. 1-2; Sept. 12, p. 2.
(N.B.) *N.C. Gaz.* Sept. 26, p. 2.
Gaz. of St. of S.C. Sept. 30, p. 3.

August 16

Bennington. "Gentleman Johnny" Burgoyne's leisurely pace south necessitates the dispatch of a foraging expedition into the New Hampshire Grants (Vermont). The German contingent sent on the mission, as well as a British relief column, are defeated at Bennington by a force of independent New Hampshiremen led by General John Stark. The Germans lose over 900 killed and wounded; Starks's losses are 70 killed and wounded. Burgoyne's loss is one seventh of his army. To add to his woes, New England is inflamed over the murder, by British-led Indians, of one Jane McCrea (July 27). Her fate comes to personalize the alternative to active resistance by the sturdy farmers of the region. The aroused New England militia swell Gates' ranks.

Freeman's Journal Aug. 23, p. 2.
Indep. Chron. Aug. 21, p. 3; Aug. 29, p. 4.

Prov. Gaz. Broadside [Aug. 23]; Aug. 30, p. 3.
Conn. Courant Aug. 11, p. 2; Aug. 25, p. 3.
N.Y. Journal Aug. 25, p. 3; Sept. 1, pp. 1, 2, 3; Sept. 15, pp. 2-3.
Pa. Packet Aug. 26, p. 2.
Va. Gaz. (Purdie) Sept. 5, p. 1.
(N.B.) *N.C. Gaz.* Sept. 12, p. 3.
Gaz. of St. of S.C. Sept. 23, pp. 1, 2.

August 25

Head of Elk. General Howe ends close to two months of American anxiety as to his next move when he lands his army at the Head of Elk, Maryland, after a thirty-three day voyage from New York City. Though Washington has expected a Howe move north toward Albany to complement Burgoyne's march south from Canada, the British intention is a quick reduction of the American capital, Philadelphia, and perhaps a division of the Southern and Middle Atlantic states just as Burgoyne is busy separating the Middle Atlantic from the New England states.

Conn. Courant Aug. 4, p. 2; Sept. 15, p. 2.
N.Y. Journal Sept. 8, pp. 2, 3.
Pa. Packet Aug. 26, p. 2.
Md. Gaz. Aug. 21, p. 3; Aug. 28, pp. 1-2.
Va. Gaz. (Purdie) July 11, pp. 2-3; Aug. 8, p. 2; Aug. 15, p. 2; Aug. 22, p. 2; Sept. 5, p. 2; Sept. 12, p. 2.
(N.B.) *N.C. Gaz.* Sept. 12, p. 3; Sept. 19, p. 3; Oct. 24, pp. 1-2; Oct. 31, p. 1.
Gaz. of St. of S.C. Sept. 15, p. 3; Sept. 30, p. 2.
Broadside: undated.

September 11

Brandywine, or Chad's Ford. Washington contests Howe's march toward Philadelphia at Chad's Ford, a crossing-place over the Brandywine River approximately twenty-five miles from the capital. A flanking movement led by Howe and Lord Cornwallis takes the Americans unaware. The loss for Washington's army is 1000; the British loss 550. Organization is restored to the colonial army at Chester, Pennsylvania, from which an orderly march is made to Germantown, just north of Philadelphia at the falls of the Schuylkill River. Washington remains in a position to meet Howe's designs on Philadelphia.

Indep. Chron. Sept. 25, pp. 1, 3; Oct. 2, p. 3.
Prov. Gaz. Sept. 20, p. 3.
Conn. Courant Sept. 22, p. 2.
Md. Gaz. Sept. 18, pp. 1, 2.
Va. Gaz. (Purdie) Sept. 19, p. 2; Sept. 26, pp. 1-2; Oct. 3, p. 2.
(N.B.) *N.C. Gaz.* Oct. 10, p. 2.
Gaz. of St. of S.C. Oct. 14, p. 3; Oct. 28, p. 3.

September 26

Philadelphia Occupied. A British bayonet attack that victimizes Anthony Wayne's position at Paoli athwart the supposed British rear (September 20-21), and a Howe feint toward Reading, a Continental supply depot north of Philadelphia, that induces Washington's hurried march to intercept the attackers; allows Howe to enter Philadelphia unmolested on September 26. Congress flees to Lancaster on September 19 and then to York, Pennsylvania, on September 30.

Prov. Gaz. Oct. 18, p. 3.
Conn. Courant Oct. 14, pp. 1-2.
Va. Gaz. (Purdie) Oct. 10, p. 2.
(N.B.) *N.C. Gaz.* Oct. 24, p. 3; Dec. 5, p. 2.

October 4

Germantown. A four-pronged American attack on the British army of 9000 encamped north of Philadelphia at Germantown is promising, at first. Fog, confusion, and faulty communication that precipitates Americans firing on Americans snatches away a victory close to the patriot grasp.

Indep. Chron. Oct. 23, pp. 2, 3.
Prov. Gaz. Oct. 25, pp. 1-2; Nov. 1, pp. 1-2.
Conn. Courant Oct. 14, pp. 1-2.
N.Y. Loyal Gaz. Nov. 22, p. 3.
N.Y. Packet Dec. 4, p. 3.
N.J. Gaz. Dec. 10, p. 2.
Md. Gaz. Oct. 16, p. 1; Oct. 23, p. 1.
Va. Gaz. (Purdie) Oct. 17, p. 2; Oct. 24, p. 2; Dec. 19, p. 2.
(N.B.) *N.C. Gaz.* Oct. 31, pp. 1-2, 3.
Gaz. of St. of S.C. Oct. 28, p. 3; Nov. 4, pp. 2-3.

September

Burgoyne in Difficulty. The retreat of St. Leger and the American victory at Bennington prompts Burgoyne's more active advance toward Albany in order to receive hoped-for assistance from New York City. His progress on the west side of the Hudson River, to which he now crosses (September 13) is to be contested by General Horatio Gates, presently entrenched in Burgoyne's path at Bemis Heights. Replacing Philip Schuyler as commander of the Northern Department on August 19, Gates has left the east bank of the Hudson unguarded since Albany, on the west bank, is much easier to approach by land than by water as the river widens farther south. The first Battle of Freeman's Farm, just north of Bemis Heights, is fought September 19. The chance for a complete American victory is lost when the inept Gates fails to reinforce a flanking movement directed by

Benedict Arnold. As it is, the British are checked and suffer 600 casualties; the Americans 300.

N.Hamp. Gaz. Apr. 22, p. 2.
Indep. Chron. Oct. 2, p. 3.
Prov. Gaz. Aug. 16, p. 3; Sept. 27, p. 3; Oct. 4, p. 3.
Conn. Courant Sept. 29, p. 3; Oct. 14, p. 2.
N.Y. Journal Oct. 6, pp. 2-3.
Pa. Journal Aug. 6, p. 3.
Md. Gaz. Oct. 2, p. 1.
Va. Gaz. (Purdie) Aug. 22, p. 2; Oct. 10, p. 2.
Va. Gaz. (Dixon and Hunter) May 8 (1778), pp. 4-5; May 15 (1778), p. 1.
(N.B.) *N.C. Gaz.* Oct. 24, p. 3.
Gaz. of St. of S.C. Nov. 4, p. 2.

October 3-16

Clinton and Burgoyne's Relief. Responding to Burgoyne's distress, General Clinton sails north to his compatriot's rescue. Two American positions on the Hudson River forty miles north of New York City, Forts Clinton and Montgomery, fall on October 6 as Clinton seeks to create a diversion in Gates' rear to persuade an American countermove and thus relieve Burgoyne of some pressure. Except for garrisoning his two conquests and ordering the burning of Esopus (Kingston), where the New York legislature's session is prematurely ended, Clinton does nothing more and returns to New York City.

Indep. Chron. Oct. 16, p. 3; Nov. 6, p. 4.
Prov. Gaz. Oct. 25, p. 2; Nov. 1, p. 3.
Conn. Courant Oct. 28, p. 1.
N.Y. Journal May 18 (1778), p. 2.
N.Y. Packet Dec. 4, pp. 1-2.
Pa. Packet Feb. 18 (1778), p. 2.
Va. Gaz. (Purdie) Oct. 31, p. 2; Nov. 14, p. 2; Dec. 5, p. 1.
(N.B.) *N.C. Gaz.* Nov. 14, p. 3.
Gaz. of St. of S.C. Nov. 11, pp. 1, 2.

October 7-17

Saratoga. The second Battle at Freeman's Farm (also variously styled the Battle of Bemis Heights, or Stillwater) is a desperation reconnoitering move by Burgoyne whose troops are discouraged, already on half-rations, and consumed with longing for the sight of Clinton's relief units. Arnold and Daniel Morgan direct the American victory that claims 600 British casualties and 150 American. With less than 4000 effective troops to oppose Gates' 11,000 Continentals and militia, Burgoyne begins a characteristically slow retreat north only to become completely surrounded near Saratoga. This great American victory is later termed one of the most decisive battles in history as it convinces the

French to bring their support of the Americans into the open with a formal alliance.

Burgoyne's surrender on October 17 is termed a Convention rather than a capitulation, *i.e.*, the British give up their arms but are free to perform soldierly duties — and free other troops for American service — upon their return to Britain. Recognizing Gates' uncommon largesse, the American Congress brings discredit upon itself by citing a lack of positive proof that King George assents to the Convention. The Convention Army, as it is called, is held for the remainder of the war by the Americans, first in Boston, then in Virginia. Burgoyne returns to England and a sceptical Parliament.

Indep. Chron. Oct. 16, p. 3; Oct. 23, p. 3; Oct. 30, pp. 2, 3; June 25 (1778), p. 3; July 23 (1778), pp. 1-2; Oct. 22 (1778), pp. 2-3; Nov. 27 (1778), p. 3.
Prov. Gaz. Oct. 25, pp. 2, 3; Nov. 1, p. 1; Dec. 6, p. 1.
Conn. Courant Oct. 28, p. 2; Nov. 4, p. 1.
N.J. Gaz. Dec. 5, p. 2; Dec. 24, p. 1; Dec. 31, p. 1; Jan. 13 (1779), p. 3.
Pa. Journal Feb. 2 (1780), p. 3.
Pa. Packet Dec. 17, pp. 1, 3, 4; Jan. 28 (1778), p. 3.
Md. Gaz. Nov. 6, p. 1.
Va. Gaz. (Purdie) Oct. 24, p. 2; Oct. 31, p. 2; Nov. 7, supplement, p. 1; Nov. 14, p. 2; Nov. 21, p. 2; Dec. 5, p. 2; Dec. 12, p. 2; Dec. 19, p. 1; Oct. 16 (1778), p. 2.
Va. Gaz. (Dixon and Hunter) Apr. 24 (1778), p. 2; May 8 (1778), pp. 4-5; May 15 (1778), p. 1; Oct. 9 (1778), pp. 1-2.
Va. Gaz. (Dixon and Nicolson) July 24 (1779), p. 2; Feb. 19 (1779), pp. 1-2; Mar. 25 (1780), p. 2.
(N.B.) *N.C. Gaz.* Nov. 7, p. 4; Nov. 7, supplement, p. 1; Nov. 14, p. 4; Dec. 26, p. 1; Jan. 2 (1778), p. 2; Mar. 13 (1778), pp. 1-2; May 1 (1778), p. 3.
Gaz. of St. of S.C. Nov. 4, p. 3; Nov. 11, p. 1; Nov. 12, extraordinary, p. 1.

October—November

Delaware River Forts. Howe's choice of the Head of Elk landing via the Chesapeake Bay rather than a quicker move upon Philadelphia by way of the Delaware River is determined by an exaggerated respect for American defensive positions and ships on the latter river. Although Fort Mercer at Red Bank, New Jersey, with a command of 400 repulses an attack by 2000 Hessians on October 22, the Americans are ill-prepared to withstand Howe's overwhelming superiority for very long. Protecting the west side of the Delaware River channel is Fort Mifflin on Mud Island. Not nearly so strong a position as Fort Mercer, Fort Mifflin succumbs grudgingly to a six-day bombardment and is evacuated November 15. Its own situation now untenable, Fort Mercer is evacuated five days later. The Delaware River is in British control.

By mid-December Washington is in uncomfortable winter quarters west of Philadelphia at Valley Forge (see below, December 18, 1777-June 18, 1778).

Indep. Chron. Nov. 21, p. 2; Dec. 4, p. 2.
Conn. Courant Dec. 2, p. 3; Jan. 13 (1778), p. 3; Feb. 17 (1778), p. 1.
N.Y. Loyal Gaz. Nov. 29, p. 2; Dec. 6, p. 3.
(N.Y.) *Royal Gaz.* Dec. 13, p. 3.
N.J. Gaz. Dec. 5, p. 1; Dec. 24, p. 3.
Pa. Packet Dec. 31, p. 3.
Md. Gaz. Dec. 4, p. 1.
Va. Gaz. (Purdie) Nov. 7, supplement, p. 1; Nov. 28, p. 2; Dec. 5, p. 2; Dec. 12, p. 2.
(N.B.) *N.C. Gaz.* Nov. 14, p. 4; Nov. 21, p. 3; Nov. 28, pp. 2-3; Dec. 12, p. 1; Dec. 26, p. 2; Jan. 30 (1778), p. 3.
Gaz. of St. of S.C. Nov. 25, p. 3.

November 15

Articles of Confederation. Richard Henry Lee's original call for a plan of colonial union (see above, June 7, 1776) is given substance after more than one year's debate as Congress adopts an amended version of John Dickinson's draft of July 12, 1776. The Articles of Confederation are essentially an appropriate elaboration of the American colonial experience. The central authority, the Congress, is granted few powers by the thirteen American "countries," and certainly not the taxing power so recently abused by Parliament. Sectional and large-small state differences over voting procedure (according to population or one vote per state?), state contributions to national coffers (to include taxation of non-white individuals?), and most importantly, have-nots versus haves as to the dispensation of the bountiful western lands claimed by sea-to-sea colonial charters and Indian grants — all combine to retard the Articles' ratification by the states for close to three and one-half years (see below, February 27, 1781).

Freeman's Journal Jan. 13 (1778), p. 1.
Bos. Gaz. Apr. 22 (1776), p. 1.
Indep. Chron. Jan. 1 (1778), p. 2; Jan. 15 (1778), pp. 1-2; Jan. 22 (1778), p. 1; Apr. 22 (1779), p. 2.
Newpt. Merc. Apr. 29 (1776), p. 1.
Conn. Courant Apr. 15 (1776), p. 1; Jan. 6 (1778), pp. 1-2; Jan. 27 (1778), pp. 2-3; Feb. 10 (1778), p. 2.
N.J. Gaz. Apr. 29 (1778), p. 1; Apr. 21 (1779), p. 2; June 23 (1779), p. 1; Sept. 22 (1779), p. 1; Oct. 6 (1779), p. 2; Dec. 15 (1779), pp. 1-2.
Pa. Journal Sept. 15 (1779), p. 3.
Pa. Packet Feb. 4 (1778), p. 3; Feb. 25 (1778), p. 2; Mar. 25 (1778), p. 2.
Md. Gaz. Aug. 15 (1776), p. 3; Aug. 22 (1776), p. 3; Oct. 31 (1776), p. 3.
(N.B.) *N.C. Gaz.* Oct. 6 (1775), p. 1.

Barbers
Ad for
Va. Gaz. (Purdie) May 16, supplement,
p. 3.

Boston Massacre
Oration on anniversary
Indep. Chron. Mar. 20, pp. 1, 4.

Colleges
Hampden-Sydney Academy lottery
Va. Gaz. (Purdie) July 4, supplement, p. 4.

Counterfeiting
Indep. Chron. June 5, p. 3.

Declaration of Independence
English find poorly written
Va. Gaz. (Purdie) Mar. 7, pp. 1-2; Mar. 14,
pp. 1-2.

Franklin, Benjamin
Triumph in Paris as American diplomat
Pa. Journal Mar. 26, p. 3; Apr. 9, p. 2;
Apr. 23, p. 2.
Va. Gaz. (Purdie) Dec. 12, p. 1.

Horseracing
Rhode Island Act prohibits
Prov. Gaz. Oct. 4, p. 1.

Humor
Lampoon of London news of war in manner
of (Tory) *New York Mercury*
Pa. Packet Feb. 18, pp. 1-2.

Indians
Georgia and South Carolina peace with Cher-
okees
Indep. Chron. Aug. 14, p. 2.

July 4th Celebrations
Charleston
Pa. Journal July 30, p. 2.
Philadelphia
Indep. Chron. July 24, p. 2.

Lottery
United States sponsors
Indep. Chron. Jan. 30, p. 1.

Monopolies (Merchants)
Massachusetts sentiment against
Indep. Chron. Jan. 30, p. 2; Apr. 24, p. 2.

New Jersey
Seeks clothing for state regiments
N.J. Gaz. Dec. 17, pp. 1-2.

Newspapers
Rags needed desperately
Conn. Courant Sept. 22, p. 1.

Opinion, British
Against war
Indep. Chron. Feb. 27, p. 3.
Earl of Chatham seeks end to war
(N.B.) *N.C. Gaz.* Nov. 7, pp. 1-2; Nov. 14,
pp. 1-2.
Va. Gaz. (Purdie) Oct. 3, p. 2.

Paine, Thomas
American Crisis II
Pa. Packet Jan. 22, p. 1; Feb. 4, p. 1; Feb.
11, p. 3; Feb. 18, p. 4.
American Crisis III
Indep. Chron. May 15, pp. 1-2; May 22,
pp. 1-2; May 29, p. 4.
American Crisis IV
N.Y. Journal Sept. 29, p. 3.

Patriotism
Virginia women refuse overtures unless from
army veterans
Indep. Chron. Aug. 7, p. 3.

Prisoners of War
Americans abused in New York City
Indep. Chron. Jan. 23, p. 3.
British abused by Americans
(N.Y.) *Royal Gaz.* Dec. 27, p. 2.

Quakers
Imprisoned in Philadelphia for pro-British
agreement
N.Y. Journal Sept. 29, p. 2.
Pro-British sentiments of
Pa. Packet Sept. 9, pp. 2-3.

Salt
Exportation of from North Carolina pro-
hibited
(N.B.) *N.C. Gaz.* Sept. 5, p. 3.

Servants
Verse ad for runaway
Pa. Journal July 9, p. 1.

Slaves
  Anti-slavery sentiments
    Broadside: Aug. 14.
  Runaway
    N.J. Gaz. Dec. 5, p. 3.

Soldiers, American
  Ad for deserters
    Prov. Gaz. July 12, p. 4.
  Clothing for received in Williamsburg
    Va. Gaz. (Purdie) Dec. 5, p. 2.
  Concerning depradations on Williamsburg
  houses
    Va. Gaz. (Purdie) May 2, supplement, p. 3.
  "Deserter" clears self
    Va. Gaz. (Purdie) Feb. 14, p. 4; Mar. 21,
      p. 1.
  Regarding their health
    Gaz. of St. of S.C. July 14, supplement,
      p. 1.

Soldiers, Russian
  Rumor of 24,000 to come as British allies
    Va. Gaz. (Purdie) Apr. 4, p. 1.

South Carolina
  Explanation of state seal
    Indep. Chron. Oct. 9, p. 2.

Tories
  Described unflatteringly
    Indep. Chron. Jan. 2, p. 2.
  Massachusetts Treason Act
    Indep. Chron. Feb. 6, p. 1; May 15, p. 2.
  New Hampshire Treason Act
    Freeman's Journal Mar. 18, pp. 2-3.
  Vermont Treason Act
    Conn. Courant Oct. 21, p. 1.
  Virginia, merchants to leave
    Va. Gaz. (Purdie) Jan. 3, p. 2; Feb. 14, pp.
      1-2; Mar. 21, supplement, p. 1.
  Virginia oath of allegiance noted
    Va. Gaz. (Purdie) July 4, pp. 1-2.

War Atrocities
  British scalp bounties in Canada
    Pa. Journal Mar. 12, p. 2.
  By British in New York City area
    N.Hamp. Gaz. Apr. 15, p. 3.
  Congressional report documents British
    Indep. Chron. May 22, p. 2; May 29, pp.
      1-2; June 5, p. 2; June 12, pp. 1-2.

Washington, George
  Encomium
    S.C. and A.G. Gaz. Feb. 20, p. 1.

Wolves
  Planter seeks their demise in area
    (N.B.) *N.C. Gaz.* Dec. 5, p. 3.

December 18, 1777–June 18

Valley Forge. Washington's ill-clad, starving remnant of an army winters at Valley Forge outside Philadelphia. American farmers prefer to sell to the triumphant British who pay with coin, not paper currency. The colonial newspapers give no hint of the army's ragged condition, especially the *New Jersey Gazette* recently established with Washington's encouragement so his men will have something to read. The General even contributes a few old tents to be used in making paper for the *Gazette*. The bogus, but talented, *Baron* von Steuben uses the time at Valley Forge to drill – to good effect – the Continentals.

Indep. Chron. Mar. 5, p. 3; May 21, p. 4; June 4, p. 2.
N.J. Gaz. Jan. 14, pp. 2, 3; May 13, p. 2.
Pa. Packet Feb. 4, p. 2; May 13, p. 3.
Md. Journal Apr. 7, p. 3.
Broadsides: (7) for 1778.

December 1777–June

French Alliance. News of Burgoyne's disaster reaches France in December 1777 and prompts the long-sought public assistance of a foreign power. On February 6, two treaties are signed in Paris between the United States and France. (The American signers are Benjamin Franklin, Silas Deane, and Arthur Lee.) By the Treaty of Amity and Commerce, the new American nation is officially recognized as a sovereign, independent state; France receives trade privileges. A Treaty of Alliance is negotiated that is not to take effect until France and Great Britain should commence hostilities (which does happen in June). By the latter document, France guarantees American independence and eschews any design on American territory east of the Mississippi River; the United States will, however, recognize any French conquests in the West Indies. What will later become a most important aspect of the agreements is the stipulation that neither of the signatories will negotiate a peace with Britain without the knowledge and consent of the other. The United States Congress receives official notice of the treaties on May 2. Quick ratification by the Congress (May 4) is the cause for widespread celebration and renewed hope in America (especially at Valley Forge). With the entrance of France into the affair, the American Revolution becomes one theater in another of the eighteenth-century's world wars as conflict erupts in the East and West Indies, and India.

Freeman's Journal June 2, p. 2.
Indep. Chron. Apr. 23, p. 3; May 21, pp. 2-3; June 4, p. 2; Aug. 27, p. 3; Dec. 10, pp. 2-4; Nov. 25 (1779), pp. 1-2.
Prov. Gaz. Apr. 25, p. 3; May 9, p. 2; May 23, pp. 1-2, 4.
Conn. Courant May 19, pp. 1-2; Sept. 29, p. 3.
N.Y. Packet May 7, pp. 1-2, 3.
(N.Y.) *Royal Gaz.* May 13, p. 3; May 20, p. 3; Sept. 19, p. 3; Oct. 10, p. 3; Oct. 14, pp. 2-3; Oct. 17, p. 2; Oct. 21, p. 2; Dec. 5, p. 3.
N.J. Gaz. May 13, p. 2; May 27, p. 2.
Pa. Packet May 6, p. 2; May 13, p. 3; May 20, p. 1; Sept. 24, pp. 1-2.
Va. Gaz. (Purdie) May 1, pp. 1-2; Aug. 21, p. 2.
Va. Gaz. (Dixon and Hunter) [May 8, supplement], pp. 1-2; May 15, pp. 2, 3.
(N.B.) *N.C. Gaz.* May 1, pp. 1, 2; May 22, pp. 3-4; May 29, p. 4; July 31, p. 4.
Gaz. of St. of S.C. June 24, pp. 2, 3; July 8, p. 2; Sept. 9, p. 2.

February 17

North Proposes Reconciliation. Alerted to the impending French-American alliance, Lord North introduces a conciliatory program into Parliament. In essence the proposals grant a pseudo-dominion status to the colonies: certain Parliamentary acts offensive to the colonies are repealed (tea duty of 1767, Massachusetts Government Act of 1774, the act excluding America from British trade in 1775); American trade and commerce are to be regulated by Parliament, but Parliament will not tax the colonists; all revenues obtained by the British in America will be spent in America. Provision is also made for a peace commission to travel to America in order to treat with the colonists. The Carlisle Commission is composed of five men: General Sir William Howe and Admiral Richard Lord Howe; the Earl of Carlisle, Frederick Howard; George Johnstone, former governor of West Florida; and William Eden, a member of the Board of Trade. The Commission is not authorized to recognize American independence or to order the British troops out of America. Indeed, Parliament must give its approval to any accommodation or agreement negotiated by the Commission.

Indep. Chron. Apr. 23, pp. 1-2; Apr. 30, pp. 1-2, 3; May 7, p. 2.
Prov. Gaz. Apr. 25, p. 2.
N.Y. Journal May 11, pp. 1-2.
(N.Y.) *Royal Gaz.* May 2, p. 1; May 13, p. 1; June 13, p. 3.
N.J. Gaz. Apr. 29, pp. 2-3; May 6, p. 1; June 17, pp. 2-3.
Pa. Packet Apr. 22, p. 2; Apr. 25, postscript, pp. 1, 2, 4.
Royal Pa. Gaz. May 5, p. 2; May 12, p. 3.
Va. Gaz. (Purdie) May 1, pp. 1-2.
Va. Gaz. (Dixon and Hunter) Jan. 23, pp. 1-2; May 8, pp. 1-4.
(N.B.) *N.C. Gaz.* May 8, pp. 2-4; May 15, pp. 1-2.

April 23-24

John Paul Jones. Terrorizing the English by his presence and daring, John Paul Jones brings the war home to the British Isles with landings at Whitehaven, England, and St. Mary's, Scotland, on April 23. On the next day he captures the *Drake*, a British warship, after a short combat and takes it to Brest, France.

Va. Gaz. (Purdie) Oct. 16, p. 2.
(N.B.) *N.C. Gaz.* July 24, p. 4; Aug. 7, p. 3.
Gaz. of St. of S.C. Aug. 12, p. 2.

May—November

British-Indian Raids in Wyoming Valley and New York. Pro-British Indians and Tories savage the American frontier, particularly Pennsylvania's Wyoming Valley. Literally hundreds of settlers are killed by such as Colonel Walter Butler, a New York Tory, and Joseph Brant, the Mohawk chieftain. A noted massacre occurs in Cherry Valley, New York, on November 11.

N.Hamp. Gaz. Dec. 1, p. 2.
Indep. Chron. July 23, p. 3; July 30, p. 3; Oct. 29, p. 2; Nov. 27, p. 3; Dec. 3, p. 3.
Prov. Gaz. Aug. 1, p. 2; Nov. 28, p. 3; Dec. 5, p. 3; Jan. 2 (1779), p. 3.
Conn. Courant Aug. 25, pp. 2-3; Sept. 29, p. 3; Oct. 13, p. 3; Oct. 27, p. 3; Dec. 1, p. 2.
N.Y. Journal July 20, pp. 1-2; Aug. 10, p. 2; Aug. 17, p. 2; Aug. 31, pp. 1-2; Sept. 28, p. 2; Oct. 19, p. 2; Nov. 9, p. 2; Nov. 23, p. 2; Dec. 14, p. 2.
(N.Y.) *Royal Gaz.* Aug. 1, p. 3; Sept. 12, p. 3; Oct. 10, p. 3; Dec. 2, p. 2; Dec. 9, p. 2; Dec. 12, p. 2.
N.J. Gaz. Dec. 2, p. 2; Dec. 31, p. 2.
Pa. Packet July 16, p. 3; July 30, pp. 1, 4; Sept. 5, p. 3; Dec. 19, p. 2.
Va. Gaz. (Purdie) Aug. 21, p. 2; Oct. 23, p. 2.
(N.B.) *N.C. Gaz.* Aug. 14, p. 3.

June—November

Carlisle Commission. Having previously resolved that any persons who might negotiate with the British should be considered enemies of America and that the expected peace commissioners must recognize American independence or withdraw the British troops from America in order to treat formally with Congress (April 22), the Congressional reaction to the Carlisle Commission's arrival in America is steadfast. When no agreement on either of the latter two points is reached in preliminary maneuverings (June 6-17), Congress washes its collective hands of the matter. Before their subsequent departure from the United States (November 27), the commissioners manage to increase American antipathy toward their mission when (a) Johnstone's attempts to bribe such as Congressman Joseph Reed (Pennsylvania) are disclosed, prompting Johnstone's resignation and (b) a Manifesto and Proclamation is issued (October 3) that threatens America with the carnage and destruction reserved usually for non-Anglos, such as Frenchman. Dissident members of the House of Lords introduce a resolution in December attacking the commissioners' ill-advised declaration.

Indep. Chron. July 2, pp. 2-3; July 9, pp. 1-2; Sept. 3, p. 3; Oct. 1, pp. 1-2; Oct. 22, pp. 2-3; Oct. 29, p. 3.
Prov. Gaz. July 4, pp. 1-3; [Apr. 10, 1779], supplement, p. 1.
Conn. Courant July 7, pp. 2-3; Nov. 10, p. 1.
N.Y. Journal June 22, p. 2; Aug. 31, p. 1.
N.Y. Packet Oct. 29, p. 1.
(N.Y.) *Royal Gaz.* Oct. 10, pp. 2, 3; Nov. 21, p. 2; Nov. 25, p. 2.
N.J. Gaz. June 10, p. 3; July 8, pp. 1-2; Aug. 5, pp. 1-2; Aug. 19, p. 2; Oct. 21, pp. 1-2; Apr. 7 (1779), p. 2; Apr. 21 (1779), pp. 1-2.
Pa. Journal Mar. 10 (1779), pp. 1-2; Mar. 17 (1779), pp. 1, 4.
Pa. Packet June 10, p. 3; June 17, p. 3; July 4, pp. 2-3; July 21, pp. 2, 3.
Va. Gaz. (Purdie) Oct. 23, p. 2; Oct. 30, pp. 1-2.
Va. Gaz. (Dixon and Hunter) Oct. 9, pp. 1-3; Oct. 16, pp. 1-2; Nov. 27, pp. 1-2; Dec. 4, p. 1.
Va. Gaz. (Dixon and Nicolson) Feb. 26 (1779), pp. 2-3; Mar. 19 (1779), p. 1.
(N.B.) *N.C. Gaz.* Oct. 16, pp. 1-2; Nov. 14, pp. 1-2.
Gaz. of St. of S.C. July 22, pp. 2-3; Aug. 26, p. 2; Nov. 18, p. 3.

June 28

Monmouth Court House. General Henry Clinton, who replaces General Howe as commander of the British army (May 8), evacuates Philadelphia on June 18 under the direct orders of the British ministry. The American army pursues Clinton across New Jersey toward New York City, a pursuit that precipitates an action near Monmouth Court House on June 28. The recently exchanged General Charles Lee, commanding the van of the American army, retreats at a moment when an American victory seems in the offing. Duly enraged, Washington has Lee arrested and (too late) assumes command. Clinton reaches New York City; the affair at Monmouth is considered a prospective victory lost for the colonials by Lee. General Lee is subsequently court-martialed at his own demand, convicted of disobeying orders, and suspended for one year from the service. Clinton and Washington settle down to a three-year stalemate in the north while the major British activity in North America comes in the South (see below, December 29). Any British preoccupation with her dissident American colonists is severely compromised now by the French, and in 1779 the Spanish, challenge.

N.Hamp. Gaz. June 23, p. 4; July 14, p. 1; July 21, pp. 2-3; July 28, pp. 2-3.
Indep. Chron. July 9, p. 3; July 16, pp. 2, 3; July 23, pp. 3, 4; Sept. 10, p. 3.
Prov. Gaz. July 18, pp. 2-3.
Conn. Courant July 7, p. 3; July 14, p. 3.
N.Y. Journal June 8, p. 2; June 29, p. 2; July 20, p. 1.
(N.Y.) *Royal Gaz.* July 4, p. 3; July 8, p. 3.
N.J. Gaz. June 24, pp. 2-3; July 8, pp. 2-3; Dec. 2, p. 1; Jan. 27 (1779), p. 3.
Pa. Packet June 10, p. 3; June 17, p. 3; July 4, p. 1; Dec. 3, pp. 2-3; Dec. 10, p. 3.
Va. Gaz. (Purdie) July 10, pp. 1, 2.
Va. Gaz. (Dixon and Hunter) July 10, p. 1; July 17, pp. 1-2.
(N.B.) *N.C. Gaz.* May 8, p. 4; June 6, p. 3; July 17, pp. 3, 4; July 24, p. 3.
Gaz. of St. of S.C. July 24, extraordinary, p. 1; Aug. 5, p. 3; Feb. 3 (1779), p. 3.

July—August

George Rogers Clark in the Old Northwest. Intent on reducing the British-Indian pressure on settlers in the western reaches of his state, Virginia Governor Patrick Henry sends Colonel George Rogers Clark into what is now Kentucky, Illinois, and Indiana. Clark's small force gains three immediate and easy victories over French settlements: Kaskaskia (July 4), Cahokia (July 6), and Vincennes (July 20). The news of the French alliance contributes significantly to these early successes. Clark's hope is to enroll the settlers as his allies against the British and their Indian allies, who move south from this area into Kentucky on their raiding ventures. The principal British culprit is Colonel Henry Hamilton, notorious to the colonists as the "Hair Buyer": he is said to pay bounties only for scalps, not prisoners.

Indep. Chron. Nov. 19, p. 3.
Pa. Packet Dec. 12, p. 2; Dec. 19, p. 2; Jan. 12 (1779), p. 2.
Va. Gaz. (Dixon and Hunter) Dec. 4, p. 2.
;

August 29

Newport. Hoping to reap immediate benefits from the French alliance, General John Sullivan cooperates in a projected land-sea attack on British-held Newport, Rhode Island. Comte Jean d'Estaing's fleet arrives off the island on which

Newport is located on July 29 after an eighteen-day flirtation with a possible attack on New York City. Sullivan's forces are in place before Newport on August 8; but a prospective naval engagement (August 10-11) between d'Estaing and Admiral Howe, who moves to assist the British garrison, is curtailed by a storm. Both fleets look to their necessary repairs, in Boston and New York City respectively, and Sullivan decides to press his attack on August 29. The result is an American retreat, precipitate and colored with anger at the seeming French non-cooperation. D'Estaing sails for the West Indies in late November (see below, July 3, 1779) and Newport remains occupied for another year.

N.Hamp. Gaz. July 28, p. 1.
Indep. Chron. Aug. 20, p. 3; Aug. 27, p. 3; Sept. 3, p. 3; Sept. 10, p. 2.
Prov. Gaz. July 18, p. 3; Aug. 8, p. 3; Aug. 15, p. 2; Aug. 22, p. 3; Aug. 29, p. 3; Sept. 5, pp. 2-3.
Conn. Courant Aug. 11, p. 3; Aug. 25, p. 2; Sept. 1, p. 3; Sept. 8, pp. 2, 3.
N.Y. Journal Aug. 17, p. 2; Aug. 24, pp. 1-2; Aug. 31, p. 2; Sept. 7, p. 2; Sept. 14, p. 3.
(N.Y.) *Royal Gaz.* Aug. 15, p. 3; Sept. 12, p. 3.
N.J. Gaz. Aug. 26, pp. 2-3; Sept. 2, p. 2; Sept. 9, pp. 2-3. 2; Sept. 7, p. 2; Sept. 14, p. 2.
Pa. Packet July 25, p. 2; Sept. 1, p. 2; Sept. 3, p. 3; Sept. 5, p. 3; Sept. 8, p. 2.
Va. Gaz. (Purdie) Aug. 21, p. 2.
(N.B.) *N.C. Gaz.* July 31, p. 4; Aug. 28, p. 3; Sept. 25, pp. 2, 3, 4.
Gaz. of St. of S.C. Aug. 12, p. 3; Sept. 16, p. 3; Sept. 23, p. 2; Oct. 7, p. 3.

December 29

Savannah. Turning to the South again after an absence of over two years, the British seek to separate the allegedly pro-British Southerners from their rebel custodians. Savannah falls quickly to a force commanded by Lieutenant Colonel Archibald Campbell.

N.Hamp. Gaz. Dec. 1, p. 2.
Indep. Chron. Nov. 12, p. 3; Feb. 18 (1779), pp. 1, 3; Mar. 4 (1779), pp. 1-2.
Prov. Gaz. Jan. 23 (1779), p. 2; Jan. 30 (1779), p. 3; Feb. 13 (1779), p. 3.
Conn. Courant Mar. 2 (1779), p. 3.
(N.Y.) *Royal Gaz.* Jan. 9 (1779), p. 3; Feb. 4 (1779), extraordinary, pp. 1-2.
N.J. Gaz. Feb. 10 (1779), p. 2.
Pa. Journal Feb. 3 (1779), pp. 2-3.
Pa. Packet Jan. 23 (1779), p. 3; Jan. 28 (1779), p. 2; Jan. 30 (1779), pp. 1-2, 3.
Va. Gaz. (Dixon and Hunter) Dec. 4, p. 2.
Gaz. of St. of S.C. Jan. 20 (1779), p. 1.

Army, Continental
    Reorganized
        Indep. Chron. July 2, p. 1.

Astronomical Phenomena
    Total solar eclipse
        (N.B.) *N.C. Gaz.* June 13, p. 3; June 26, p. 4.

Bombmakers
    Ad for employment
        N.Y. Packet May 7, p. 4.

Chatham, William Pitt (Earl of)
    Description of picture of death
        Broadside: 1781.
    Notice of death
        (N.B.) *N.C. Gaz.* Sept. 25, p. 1.

Colleges
    Queen's (Rutgers) commencement
        N.J. Gaz. Sept. 2, p. 4.
    William and Mary anniversary celebration
        Va. Gaz. (Purdie) Aug. 21, p. 2.

Counterfeiting
    British fake American currency
        Pa. Packet Jan. 28, p. 2.

Crime
    North Carolina grand jury presentment
        (N.B.) *N.C. Gaz.* Aug. 14, pp. 1-2.
Dueling
    Concerning in army
        N.Y. Packet Oct. 8, p. 1; Oct. 29, pp. 1-2.

Fashion
    Rites of decried
        Indep. Chron. Aug. 13, p. 1.

Fishing Tackle
    Ad for
        Pa. Packet July 30, p. 1.

Franklin, Benjamin
    Continues Paris triumph
        Indep. Chron. June 18, p. 2.

Humor
    Lampoon:
        "British Valour Displayed: Or, the Battle of the Kegs"
            Pa. Packet Mar. 4, p. 4.
        "On the British Commanders"
            Freeman's Journal June 2, p. 1.

Poem on Newport "Battle of the Cushions"
        Indep. Chron. Nov. 12, p. 4.

Independence, American
    Satirized in A Modern Catechism
        (N.Y.) *Royal Gaz.* May 23, p. 1.

Iredell, James (future U.S. Supreme Court Justice)
    Charge to North Carolina jury includes vindication of Declaration of Independence
        (N.B.) *N.C. Gaz.* June 6, pp. 1-2; June 13, pp. 2-3.

July 4th Celebrations
    Charleston
        Gaz. of St. of S.C. July 8, p. 3; July 15, p. 3.
    New Bern
        (N.B.) *N.C. Gaz.* July 10, p. 4.
    Portsmouth, New Hampshire
        N.Hamp. Gaz. July 14, p. 4.

Lottery
    United States sponsors
        Indep. Chron. Apr. 16, p. 3; June 25, p. 2.

Monopolies
    Of necessities, decried
        N.Y. Journal Oct. 19, p. 2.

Newspapers
    Payment for may be made in kind
        N.Y. Journal Aug. 17, p. 2.
    Price of affected by depreciation
        Indep. Chron. Mar. 12, p. 1.
    Rags needed
        N.Y. Packet Mar. 12, p. 2; Apr. 16, p. 3.
    Satire on: fourteen readers for one purchased paper
        (N.B.) *N.C. Gaz.* Jan. 23, p. 2.

North Carolina
    Act to complete Continental batallion
        (N.B.) *N.C. Gaz.* May 8, pp. 1-2.

Orange Juice
    Ad for fresh
        Indep. Chron. Oct. 15, p. 3.

Paine, Thomas
    American Crisis V
        Md. Journal Mar. 31, pp. 1-2; Apr. 7, pp. 1-2; Apr. 21, pp. 1-2.

American Crisis VII
  Gaz. of St. of S.C. Dec. 16, pp. 1-3.

Patriotism
  Appeal to Americans to continue efforts in war
  Freeman's Journal Jan. 6, p. 1.
  Twenty-first son baptized George Washington
  Pa. Packet Mar. 11, p. 2.

Poetry
  "On General Gates"
  Freeman's Journal Mar. 10, p. 4.
  "Rising Glory of America"
  Pa. Packet Apr. 8, p. 4.
  To George Washington on visit to Philadelphia
  Pa. Packet Dec. 24, pp. 2, 3.

Prisoners of War
  Americans abused
  Indep. Chron. Feb. 5, p. 2; Mar. 5, pp. 1-2.
  Americans helped in Philadelphia by free Negress
  Pa. Packet Apr. 22, p. 2.
  British-American dispute over payment for support of respective
  Pa. Packet Jan. 29, supplement, p. 1.
  Congress regulates treatment of
  N.J. Gaz. Feb. 11, pp. 1-2.

Prize Ship
  To be sold
  N.J. Gaz. Sept. 9, p. 3.

Quakers
  Concerning Pennsylvania oath of allegiance
  Pa. Packet June 17, pp. 1, 3.
  New Jersey law allows oaths by hand
  N.J. Gaz. Oct. 7, p. 2.

Religious Freedom
  In proposed Massachusetts constitution debated
  Indep. Chron. Mar. 5, p. 3; Apr. 9, p. 1;
    Apr. 16, pp. 1-2; Apr. 30, p. 4; June 4,
    p. 4; June 11, p. 2.

Ships
  Prize, to be sold
  N.J. Gaz. Sept. 9, p. 3.

Slaves
  Gradual abolition of slavery in Pennsylvania
  Pa. Packet Nov. 28, pp. 1-2.

Sale of
  N.J. Gaz. Sept. 2, p. 4.

Soldiers, American
  Ad for clothing for New Hampshire Continentals
  Freeman's Journal Mar. 10, p. 1.
  Massachusetts seeks clothing for army
  Indep. Chron. Mar. 19, pp. 2-3.
  Reward for deserters
  N.J. Gaz. Sept. 2, p. 4.

Suffrage
  Extent of debated in proposed Massachusetts constitution
  Indep. Chron. Apr. 9, p. 2.

Sugar
  To manufacture from Indian cornstalks
  Pa. Packet Sept. 3, pp. 1-2.

Swine
  Boston law to control
  Indep. Chron. Apr. 9, p. 4.

Taxation
  Massachusetts rateable estate list
  Indep. Chron. May 14, p. 2.

Theater
  Congress brands as unpatriotic diversion
  N.J. Gaz. Oct. 21, p. 2.

Tories
  Not welcome to return to Boston or Massachusetts
  Indep. Chron. Oct. 15, p. 2; Oct. 22,
    pp. 1-2.
  To arm in New York
  N.Y. Journal Oct. 12, p. 2.

Trade
  Actions against American with New York City
  N.J. Gaz. Aug. 26, p. 3.

Voltaire (François Marie Arouet)
  Would migrate to America if younger
  Indep. Chron. June 18, p. 3.

1777-1779

Inflation, Depreciation, Price-Fixing. The continued devaluation of American currency, the subsequent issuance of still more Continental paper money, and the consequent extraordinary rise in prices elicits colonial attempts to fix prices. In January 1779, the Congress establishes the value ratio of $8. Continental currency equals $1. in gold. (By the end of 1779, the ratio is forty to one.) Congress's good offices, directed at heavy state taxation, which is supposed to take the Continental currency out of circulation (and thus thwart devaluation . . .), are a failure due to the non-cooperation of the states. One humorous sidelight to America's currency woes is the striking literacy — and fatal flaw — of American counterfeiters. A warning in early 1778 regarding counterfeit $30. bills cautions that on the real bills the appropriate spelling is "Philadelpkia" while the fraudulent currency notes the governmental authority of "Philadelphia."

N.Hamp. Gaz. Aug. 10 (1776), pp. 1, 4.
Freeman's Journal June 28 (1777), p. 2.
Indep. Chron. Jan. 1 (1778), pp. 1-2; Jan. 22 (1778), pp. 1-2; Mar. 12 (1778), pp. 1-2; May 28 (1778), pp. 1-2; June 10 (1779), p. 2; June 17 (1779), p. 3; June 24 (1779), p. 4; July 22 (1779), p. 1; July 29 (1779), pp. 2-3; Aug. 19 (1779), p. 2; Sept. 16 (1779), p. 2; Oct. 7 (1779), pp. 2-3; Dec. 10 (1779), p. 2.
Newpt. Merc. Jan. 5 (1780), p. 3.
Prov. Gaz. July 3 (1779), p. 3; July 17 (1779), p. 2; July 31 (1779), pp. 1, 2, 3; Aug. 7 (1779), p. 3; [Aug. 14 (1779)], supplement, pp. 1-2; Aug. 28 (1779), p. 3; Sept. 4 (1779), p. 3; Oct. 2 (1779), p. 2; Oct. 9 (1779), pp. 1-2, 4.
Conn. Courant Aug. 4 (1778), p. 2; Aug. 25 (1778), p. 1; Oct. 20 (1778), pp. 1-2; Oct. 27 (1778), p. 1; Nov. 16 (1779), pp. 1-2.
N.Y. Journal Dec. 21 (1778), p. 1; Jan. 18 (1779), p. 2; Oct. 11 (1779), p. 2.
N.Y. Packet Apr. 16 (1778), p. 2.
(N.Y.) *Royal Gaz.* Jan. 20 (1779), p. 3; Feb. 27 (1779), p. 2.
N.J. Gaz. Dec. 24 (1777), p. 1; Dec. 31 (1777), p. 4; May 27 (1778), p. 1; Feb. 24 (1779), pp. 1-2; Mar. 10 (1779), pp. 1-2; Mar. 17 (1779), pp. 1-2; Mar. 24 (1779), pp. 1-2; Apr. 7 (1779), pp. 1-2; Apr. 14 (1779), pp. 1-2; Apr. 28 (1779), pp. 1-2; May 5 (1779), pp. 1, 4; May 12 (1779), pp. 1, 4; June 9 (1779), pp. 3, 4; June 16 (1779), p. 2; July 28 (1779), p. 3; Aug. 4 (1779), p. 3; Sept. 1 (1779), p. 1; Sept. 29 (1779), p. 2; Oct. 6 (1779), pp. 1, 3, 4; Oct. 13 (1779), p. 3; Nov. 24 (1779), p. 2; Dec. 1 (1779), pp. 1, 2, 3; Dec. 8 (1779), p. 1; Dec. 15 (1779), p. 3; Jan. 5 (1780), p. 3; Jan. 12 (1780), pp. 1, 4; Jan. 19 (1780), p. 1; Feb. 2 (1780), p. 3; Feb. 23 (1780), p. 2; Mar. 1 (1780), p. 3; Mar. 22 (1780), p. 2; Mar. 29 (1780), pp. 1-2; Apr. 5 (1780), p. 1; Apr. 19 (1780), pp. 1-2.
Pa. Journal Nov. 20 (1776), p. 3; June 2 (1779), pp. 1, 3; June 23 (1779), p. 3; July 7 (1779), pp. 1, 4; Dec. 8 (1779), p. 2; Dec. 22 (1779), pp. 1-2; Feb. 16

(1780), p. 3; Mar. 15 (1780), p. 3; Mar. 29 (1780), p. 3.
Pa. Packet Dec. 31 (1777), pp. 2, 3; Jan. 21 (1779), p. 3; Jan. 26 (1779), pp. 2-3.
Royal Pa. Gaz. Mar. 24 (1778), p. 1.
Va. Gaz. (Purdie) Sept. 26 (1777), p. 1.
Va. Gaz. (Dixon and Nicholson) Feb. 19 (1779), p. 3; Mar. 19 (1779), p. 1; June 5 (1779), p. 2; June 12 (1779), pp. 1-2, 3; June 19 (1779), pp. 1-2; July 10 (1779), p. 2; July 17 (1779), p. 3; July 24 (1779), pp. 1-2; July 31 (1779), p. 3; Aug. 7 (1779), pp. 1-3; Oct. 9 (1779), p. 1; Apr. 1 (1780), p. 1.
(N.B.) *N.C. Gaz.* Oct. 3 (1777), p. 3; Dec. 12 (1777), p. 1; Dec. 26 (1777), p. 1; Jan. 23 (1778), p. 1; Feb. 6 (1778), pp. 2-3; June 13 (1778), pp. 1-2.
Gaz. of St. of S.C. Apr. 9 (1777), p. 2; Apr. 14 (1779), p. 1; Dec. 8 (1779), pp. 1-2.

January—June

Georgia and South Carolina. The British offensive grinds along as General Augustine Prevost and Colonel Campbell enjoy successes early in the new year at the Georgia towns of Sunbury (January 6) and Augusta (January 29). Temporarily evacuated by the British on February 14 in the face of a three-pronged American assault, Augusta is recovered by General Prevost with a victory over General John Ashe (North Carolina) at Briar Creek (March 3). A renewed American offensive directed by General Benjamin Lincoln in May and June aimed at Augusta succeeds in prompting Genral Prevost to counter with a thrust against American-held Charleston, South Carolina. The latter's hesitation before the city enables Lincoln to attack the retreating British at Stono Ferry (June 20). The result is another American loss and a British occupation of Port Royal Island off the southwestern coast of South Carolina. American successes are limited to General William Moultrie's defense of Port Royal Island on February 3, which he later abandons, and Colonel Andrew Pickens' (South Carolina) victory over a force of Tories on February 14 at Kettle Creek, South Carolina. These triumphs early in the campaign serve as effective recruiting material for the American army in the South, but the military importance of the victories is of short life given the coming British control over South Carolina.

Indep. Chron. Mar. 4, pp. 1-2; Apr. 1, p. 2; Apr. 22, p. 2; Apr. 29, p. 2; June 17, p. 3; June 24, p. 3; July 1, p. 2; July 8, pp. 1, 2, 3; July 15, p. 3; July 22, p. 1; Aug. 5, p. 2.
Prov. Gaz. Apr. 3, p. 2; Apr. 10, p. 2; Aug. 7, p. 4.
N.Y. Journal [Apr. 19], pp. 1-2; July 19, p. 1.
(N.Y.) *Royal Gaz.* June 9, p. 3; July 14, p. 2; Aug. 25, p. 3.
N.J. Gaz. Mar. 17, p. 2; Mar. 24, p. 2; Apr. 14, p. 2; Apr. 21, p. 2; May 5, p. 2.
Pa. Journal Feb. 17, pp. 2-3; Mar. 17, p. 3; June 2, p. 3.

Md. Gaz. July 23, p. 2.
Va. Gaz. (Dixon and Nicolson) Apr. 2, p. 2; May 29, pp. 2-3; June 12, p. 3; July 3, p. 1; July 17, p. 3; Aug. 14, p. 2; Sept. 4, p. 1; Jan. 29 (1780), p. 1.
Gaz. of St. of S.C. Feb. 24, p. 3; Mar. 10, p. 2; Apr. 7, p. 2; Apr. 28, pp. 1, 2; May 5, p. 2; July 9, p. 1.
Royal Ga. Gaz. Feb. 11, p. 4; Mar. 11, p. 4.

February 24-25

Fort Sackville. After Colonel Henry Hamilton's bloodless recapture of Vincennes (December 17, 1778), George Rogers Clark returns to the town and forces a capitulation of the town's Fort Sackville. Hamilton is sent to Williamsburg where newly-elected Governor Thomas Jefferson keeps him under close confinement for over a year. Clark's ultimate objective is the British garrison at Detroit, which serves as the primary base for expeditions against the Americans; however, the stronghold remains secure from colonial attack for the rest of the war. Clark does achieve control of the Illinois country. (See also below, November 10, 1782.)

Indep. Chron. June 10, p. 2; June 17, p. 3; July 8, p. 2.
Conn. Courant July 20, pp. 1-2.
N.Y. Journal July 5, pp. 1-2.
N.J. Gaz. June 2, p. 3.
Va. Gaz. (Dixon and Nicolson) May 22, p. 2; June 5, pp. 2-3; June 26, pp. 1, 2, 3;

May 10-24

Virginia. A British expedition destroys over £2,000,000 worth of American supplies in a two-week devastation of tidewater Virginia. The destruction includes the burning of Portsmouth, Suffolk, and Gosport. The British encounter minimal opposition and lose not a single man.

Indep. Chron. June 10, p. 3.
(N.Y.) *Royal Gaz.* June 5, p. 3.
N.J. Gaz. May 26, pp. 2-3.
Pa. Journal June 2, pp. 2, 3.
Md. Gaz. May 28, p. 2.
Va. Gaz. (Dixon and Nicolson) May 15, p. 2; May 22, p. 2; May 29, p. 3.

June 21

Spain Declares War on Great Britain. Spain enters the war as a French, but not an American, ally. The revolt of the British colonies is considered an evil precedent for Spain's own American colonies. John Jay resigns as president of the Congress in order to travel to Spain as an American agent (September 27), lured by visions of a Spanish recognition of American independence. Jay is destined to undergo almost two and one-half difficult years in quest of his objective.

Indep. Chron. Aug. 26, pp. 3-4.
Prov. Gaz. Aug. 28, pp. 1, 2.
N.J. Gaz. Aug. 25, pp. 2, 3; Sept. 8, p. 1; Oct. 20, pp. 2-3.
Pa. Journal Sept. 8, p. 1.
Md. Gaz. Oct. 8, p. 3.
Va. Gaz. (Dixon and Nicolson) July 17, pp. 1, 2; Aug. 21, p. 2; Sept. 18, p. 2.
Gaz. of St. of S.C. Sept. 8, p. 1.

July 3

West Indies. Despite the British capture of St. Lucia (December 13, 1778), the French enjoy control of the West Indian waters with victories on Dominica (September 7, 1778), St. Vincent's (June 1779), and, most importantly, Grenada (July 3, 1779). D'Estaing's latter triumph symbolizes the pre-eminent position of the West Indian islands in French strategic plans.

Indep. Chron. July 29, p. 4; Aug. 19, p. 3; Aug. 26, pp. 1-2, 4.
N.Y. Journal Nov. 23 (1778), p. 1.
N.J. Gaz. Feb. 3, p. 3; Feb. 10, p. 1.
Va. Gaz. (Dixon and Nicolson) Aug. 21, pp. 1-2; Aug. 28, pp. 1, 2; Feb. 19 (1780), pp. 1, 2.
Gaz. of St. of S.C. Nov. 11 (1778), p. 3; Nov. 18 (1778), p. 2.

July 5-11

Connecticut Coastal Towns Burned. In retaliation for Connecticut-based vessels attacking British commerce, as well as for the state's ready provisioning of Washington's army, an expedition of British regulars, Hessians, and Loyalists terrorize Connecticut's Long Island coast. Former Governor of New York, and North Carolina, William Tryon, now a British general, commands the Loyalist regiment. New Haven, East Haven, Fairfield, Green Farms, and Norwalk are looted and many buildings destroyed. One British explanation for this savagery is that it is intended to force Washington to leave his position outside New York City and thus prompt a large-scale battle.

Indep. Chron. July 15, p. 3; July 29, p. 4; Feb. 3 (1780), pp. 1-2.
Prov. Gaz. July 10, pp. 2-3; July 17, p. 3.
Conn. Courant July 13, p. 2; Feb. 22 (1780), pp. 1-2.
N.Y. Journal July 19, p. 2.
(N.Y.) *Royal Gaz.* July 10, p. 1; July 14, p. 3.
N.J. Gaz. July 28, pp. 1-2.
Va. Gaz. (Dixon and Nicolson) July 31, p. 2; Aug. 7, p. 2.
Gaz. of St. of S.C. Aug. 25, pp. 1-2.

July 15

Stony Point. A numerically superior British force pushes up the Hudson River and takes Stony Point and Fort Lafayette at Verplanck's Point on June 1. This threat to West Point and American control of the upper Hudson River is relieved by "Mad" Anthony Wayne who directs the capture, with bayonet only, of Stony Point (July 15). Washington decides the fort will require too large a contingent of Americans for its defense and orders it evacuated on July 18 after the works are destroyed and the armament removed. British forces immediately reoccupy Stony Point and strengthen its position. Stony Point remains as a major American achievement, however, because of the manner of its taking and the capture of over 600 British regulars.

N.Hamp. Gaz. Aug. 17, p. 2.
Indep. Chron. June 17, p. 2; July 22, pp. 2, 3; July 29, p. 1; Aug. 12, pp. 1-2.
Prov. Gaz. July 24, p. 3.
Conn. Courant July 20, p. 3.
(N.Y.) *Royal Gaz.* June 5, p. 3; July 17, p. 3; July 21, p. 3.
N.J. Gaz. June 9, p. 2; June 16, p. 3; July 28, pp. 2-3.
Md. Gaz. July 23, p. 2.
Va. Gaz. (Dixon and Nicolson) July 31, p. 2.
Gaz. of St. of S.C. Aug. 25, pp. 2-3; Nov. 24, p. 2.

August 19

Paulus Hook. Major Henry "Light-Horse Harry" Lee, Jr., leads a successful action against the British position on Powles, or Paulus, Hook in New Jersey opposite New York City.

Indep. Chron. Aug. 26, p. 2.
(N.Y.) *Royal Gaz.* Aug. 21, p. 3; Aug. 25, p. 3.
N.J. Gaz. Aug. 25, p. 3.
Pa. Journal Sept. 1, p. 3.
Va. Gaz. (Dixon and Nicolson) Sept. 4, p. 2; Sept. 25, p. 1; Oct. 30, p. 1.
Gaz. of St. of S.C. Sept. 29, pp. 1-2.

August—September

Sullivan Challenges the Iroquois. General John Sullivan leads a Continental detachment against the Indians and their Tory allies in Pennsylvania and New York in order to prevent a repetition of the havoc caused the previous year (see above, May-November 1778) by this unholy combination. Unable to penetrate as far west as Fort Detroit, the British supply center for its Indian allies, and the Americans' ultimate objective, Sullivan does taste success at Newtown (Elmira), New York, on August 29 against Joseph Brant. During September Sullivan and General James Clinton march northwest, as far as the Genesee Valley, destroying Indian villages and supplies. The American accomplishment is a damper on the war-making threat of Britain's principal allies, the Iroquois.

Indep. Chron. Aug. 26, p. 2; Sept. 2, pp. 2, 3; Sept. 16, p. 3; Sept. 30, p. 2; Oct. 28, p. 2; Nov. 11, pp. 1-2, 4; Nov. 18, pp. 1-2.
Prov. Gaz. Oct. 30, pp. 1-2, 4.
N.Y. Journal Sept. 20, pp. 1-2; Oct. 11, p. 1.
(N.Y.) *Royal Gaz.* July 14, p. 3; July 17, p. 3.
N.J. Gaz. Aug. 11, pp. 2-3; Sept. 1, p. 3; Sept. 8, pp. 2-3.
Va. Gaz. (Dixon and Nicolson) July 10, p. 2; Sept. 25, p. 1; Oct. 9, p. 2.
Gaz. of St. of S.C. Nov. 24, p. 2.

September 14

Penobscot Bay. In a clash peripheral to the main colonial effort, a Massachusetts amphibious force is routed in an attempt to dislodge a British naval foothold in nearby Penobscot Bay, Maine. Massachusetts maritime interests look unfavorably on potentially more effective British incursions on Bay State trade. Colonel Paul Revere fares badly in the military disaster and is not cleared, by a court-martial, for close to three years.

Indep. Chron. Sept. 30, p. 2; Dec. 23, pp. 2-3; Jan. 6 (1780), p. 2.
N.J. Gaz. Aug. 25, p. 2; Sept. 8, p. 2; Feb. 9 (1780), p. 2.
Pa. Journal Sept. 22, pp. 1-2.
Va. Gaz. (Dixon and Nicolson) Aug. 28, p. 2.

September 23-24

Bonhomme Richard vs. H.M.S. Serapis. Continuing his naval exploits, Captain John Paul Jones wins a September 23 engagement with H.M.S. *Serapis* just off the English coast. Jones transfers to the *Serapis* on September 24 when his own ship, the *Bonhomme Richard*, sinks because of the previous day's action. During the battle, Jones is reputed to have declared, "I have not yet begun to fight," when asked to strike his colors by the British commander, Captain Pearson. Jones, a native of Scotland, is to become a Russian admiral after the American Revolution.

Indep. Chron. Feb. 17 (1780), p. 2; Mar. 16 (1780), p. 2; Apr. 13 (1780), p. 4.
Prov. Gaz. Apr. 29 (1780), p. 2.
Conn. Courant Feb. 8 (1780), p. 2.
N.J. Gaz. Dec. 22, p. 3; Jan. 26 (1780), p. 3; Feb. 2 (1780), p. 4; Mar. 8 (1780), p. 1; May 24 (1780), p. 1.
Pa. Journal Dec. 22, pp. 1-2.
Va. Gaz. (Dixon and Nicolson) Oct. 30, p. 3; Jan. 8 (1780), p. 2; Jan. 15 (1780), pp. 1-2; Feb. 12 (1780), pp. 2-3; Mar. 18 (1780), pp. 1, 2; Apr. 1 (1780), p. 1; Aug. 2 (1780), p. 1.

September–October

Savannah. A French fleet under Comte d'Estaing and an American army commanded by General Benjamin Lincoln confidently assault Savannah (October 9). Forewarned of the attack, General Augustine Prevost is waiting and the French and Americans suffer over 800 casualties. Count Casimir Pulaski, a Polish volunteer who is responsible for the development of an American cavalry, is killed; d'Estaing is wounded. The French fleet returns to France within a few weeks.

Indep. Chron. Oct. 7, p. 1; Nov. 11, p. 3; Nov. 18, p. 3; Nov. 25, pp. 2, 3; Dec. 16, pp. 2, 3.
Newpt. Merc. Jan. 5 (1780), pp. 2-3.
Conn. Courant Nov. 16, p. 2; Nov. 23, p. 2.
N.Y. Packet Nov. 25, pp. 2, 3.
N.J. Gaz. Nov. 17, pp. 2-3; June 7 (1780), p. 1.

Pa. Journal Oct. 6, pp. 2-3; Nov. 17, p. 2.
Md. Gaz. Oct. 29, p. 3; Nov. 12, p. 2.
Va. Gaz. (Dixon and Nicolson) Sept. 25, p. 2; Oct. 9, p. 2; Oct. 23, p. 2; Nov. 6, pp. 2-3; Nov. 13, p. 2; Nov. 20, p. 2.
Gaz. of St. of S.C. Sept. 15, p. 3; Oct. 6, p. 2; Oct. 27, p.1.

October 25

Newport Evacuated. The Allied threat in the South causes Clinton to order the evacuation of Newport after nearly three years of British occupation. Many of the troops are concentrated in New York City; others are destined for the renewed British offensive in South Carolina and Georgia (see below, April–May 1780).

Indep. Chron. Oct. 28, p. 2; Nov. 5, p. 3.
Prov. Gaz. Oct. 9, p. 3; Oct. 16, p. 3; Oct. 23, p. 3; Oct. 30, p. 3; Nov. 13, pp. 2, 3.
N.J. Gaz. Nov. 10, p. 2.
Va. Gaz. (Dixon and Nicolson) Nov. 20, p. 2.

Allen, Ethan
  Narrative of own captivity by British
    Indep. Chron. Dec. 10, pp. 1-2; Dec. 16,
      pp. 1-2; Dec. 23, pp. 1-2; Dec. 30, pp.
      1-2; Jan. 6 (1780), p. 4; Feb. 10
      (1780), p. 2; Feb. 17 (1780). pp. 1-2;
      Feb. 24 (1780), pp. 1-2; Mar. 9 (1780),
      pp. 1-2; Mar. 23 (1780), pp. 1-2; Mar.
      30 (1780), pp. 1-2.

Apprentice
  Ad for missing, reward
    Pa. Packet Nov. 14 (1778), p. 1.
  Response by missing apprentice
    Pa. Packet Jan. 19, p. 4.

Army, Continental
  Commissaries of, cheating?
    N.J. Gaz. Apr. 21, p. 1; May 12, p. 2; May
      26, p. 1; June 2, p. 4; June 9, p. 2; Aug.
      25, pp. 1-2; Nov. 10, p. 1.
  Rhode Island act to supply in state
    Prov. Gaz. Jan. 9, p. 1.

Backus, Isaac (Baptist minister)
  On Baptists' situation in Massachusetts, new
    state constitution
    Indep. Chron. Dec. 2, p. 1.

Colleges
  College of New Jersey, flourishing
    N.J. Gaz. May 5, p. 3.

Cook, James (Captain, English explorer)
  Notice of voyage of
    Va. Gaz. (Dixon and Nicolson) July 17,
      p. 1.

Fox-hunting
  Verse ridicules
    N.J. Gaz. Sept. 29, p. 2.

Galloway, Joseph (American Tory; former member of Congress)
  Questioned in London by British officials
    Prov. Gaz. Nov. 20, pp. 1-2; Dec. 4, p. 1;
      Dec. 11, pp. 1-2; Dec. 18, pp. 1, 4; Dec.
      25, pp. 1-2; Jan. 1 (1780), pp. 1-2.

Garrick, David (English actor)
  In memoriam
    Indep. Chron. Dec. 23, p. 1.

Horse
  Verse ad for missing
    N.J. Gaz. June 23, p. 4.

Hospital
  Small-pox, opened
    Va. Gaz. (Dixon and Nicolson) Mar. 12,
      p. 4.

Humor
  Lampoon of patriot printers need for linen
    rags
    (N.Y.) *Royal Gaz.* June 16, p. 3.

Ireland
  Benefits by American Revolution
    Indep. Chron. Sept. 30, p. 1.
  Benjamin Franklin addresses people of
    N.J. Gaz. Sept. 29, p. 2.

July 4th Celebrations
  Philadelphia
    N.Hamp. Gaz. Aug. 17, p. 1.

Newspapers
  Letter to editor regarding freedom of press
    N.J. Gaz. Dec. 29, p. 1.
  Price of reflects depreciated currency
    Va. Gaz. (Dixon and Nicolson) Nov. 27
      (1778), p. 2; June 19, p. 3; Sept. 11, p.
      3; Nov. 20, p. 2.

Patriotism
  Inspirational message to Americans from
    President John Jay
    Indep. Chron. June 17, pp. 1, 4.
  Tory answer to President Jay
    (N.Y.) *Royal Gaz.* June 16, p. 3.

Peale, Charles Willson (American painter)
  Congress commissions, to paint George Washington
    N.J. Gaz. Feb. 10, p. 1.

Prisoners of War
  British abuse Americans
    Va. Gaz. (Dixon and Nicolson) Sept. 4,
      p. 1.
  Exchange of
    Prov. Gaz. July 10, p. 4; July 17, pp. 1, 4;
      July 24, p. 4.

Quebec Act (1774)
  British purpose in passage of
    N.Y. Packet Nov. 25, pp. 1-2.

Religious Freedom
  In new Massachusetts constitution
    Indep. Chron. Dec. 2, p. 1.

In Virginia, proposed
  Va. Gaz. (Dixon and Nicolson) Aug. 14, p.
    1; Sept. 11, p. 1; Sept. 18, pp. 1-2.

Sanitation
  Philadelphia streets to be cleaned
    Pa. Packet Feb. 23, p. 4.

Seven
  Noted as lucky number for America
    N.Hamp. Gaz. Aug. 17, p. 4.

Slaves
  Gradual abolition of slavery in Pennsylvania
    N.J. Gaz. Feb. 17, pp. 2-3.
  Scheme to use against British in South, in
  exchange for freedom
    Indep. Chron. May 13, p. 3.

Soldiers, American
  Deserters: descriptions, rewards
    Va. Gaz. (Dixon and Nicolson) Mar. 12, p.
      3; Mar. 19, p. 2; May 1, p. 3; June 5, p. 2.
  Deserters: Washington pardon if return
    Va. Gaz. (Dixon and Nicolson) Apr. 2,
      p. 2.
  Thanked for good conduct in Winchester,
  Virginia

Va. Gaz. (Dixon and Nicolson June 5,
    p. 3.

Soldiers, Russian
  British seek to scare with stories of as allies
    N.J. Gaz. Jan. 27, p. 3.

Suffrage
  In new Massachusetts constitution
    Indep. Chron. Sept. 23, p. 1.

Swearing
  Washington order against in army
    N.J. Gaz. Nov. 17, p. 2.

Tories
  As criminals, captured
    N.J. Gaz. Feb. 3, p. 3.
  Forfeiture of estates to state
    N.J. Gaz. Oct. 20, pp. 1-2.
  Lord North comments on condition of
    Indep. Chron. Aug. 12, p. 1.
  Returning to Dutchess County, New York
    N.Y. Journal Jan. 11, p. 2.

Washington, George
  Birthday of celebrated in Williamsburg
    Va. Gaz. (Dixon and Nicolson) Feb. 26,
      p. 3.

March 9

League of Armed Neutrality. Catherine the Great, Czarina of Russia, displays her irritation at British intrusions upon "neutral" trade by forming the League of Armed Neutrality. Uninterested in America's situation, the Russians are desirous of maintaining their trade, which is carried principally in Dutch ships. The latter are especially subject to increased British attention in Lord North's effort to intercept war supplies meant for the Americans and their co-belligerents. The League's principles include (1) free passage by neutrals to and from belligerent ports; (2) free (neutral) ships make free goods, even if the goods are owned by or bound for belligerents (contraband of war is excluded from this provision but limited in definition to arms and military supplies since Britain's more extended definition which includes naval stores is ignored); and (3) blockades must be real and effective; not just proclaimed on paper. Within two years Russia's League is joined by Denmark, Sweden, the Netherlands, Prussia, Austria, and Portugal. The Continental Congress attempts to join the League in order to gain further recognition of American independence; but its agent, Francis Dana, is ignored by the Russians.

Indep. Chron. July 27, p. 2; Aug. 17, p. 3; Aug. 31, p. 4; Dec. 28, p. 2.
Newpt. Merc. Sept. 2, p. 4.
Prov. Gaz. Jan. 3 (1781), p. 1.
Conn Courant Mar. 6 (1781), p. 3; May 8 (1781), p. 2; May 15 (1781), p. 2; Nov. 5 (1782), p. 3.
N.Y. Packet May 10 (1781), p. 2.
N.J. Gaz. July 19, p. 2; Aug. 2, p. 1; Sept. 13, pp. 1, 4; Nov. 8, p. 2; Nov. 15, p. 2; Nov. 29, p. 2; Dec. 20, pp. 1, 3; Dec. 5 (1781), p. 3.
Pa. Journal Oct. 11, p. 2; Dec. 27, pp. 1, 2.
Md. Gaz. May 3 (1781), p. 2; Nov. 15 (1781), supplement, p. 1.
Va. Gaz. (Dixon and Nicolson) Aug. 2, p. 1.

March 18

Inflation. "Not worth a Continental" is a colonial expression appropriate to the American currency situation by 1780. By that year close to $200,000,000. worth of paper money is issued by order of the Continental Congress to pay for the American war effort. State cooperation, in the form of state taxes to be paid in Continental currency, is non-existent; the states in fact continue to issue their own money. Hence the repeated emissions of Continental money are left in circulation and come to be worth less and less. On March 18, Congress declares that $40. in Continental currency is to represent $1. in gold. Therefore, the states are

requested to retire a specific amount of the former at forty to one. Within a year this devaluation scheme does take over 60% of the Continental money out of circulation. The remainder, however, is worthless by the end of 1780. And inflation continues apace. (See above, 1779, 1777-1779.)

N.Hamp. Gaz. Apr. 16 (1781), p. 1.
Indep. Chron. Apr. 6, p. 2; May 11, pp. 1-2; July 27, p. 3.
Prov. Gaz. Apr. 8, pp. 2-3.
Conn. Courant Apr. 4, p. 3; Jan. 9 (1781), pp. 1-2; Jan. 16 (1781), pp. 1-2.
N.J. Gaz. Mar. 29, p. 3; Apr. 27, p. 3; Oct. 25, pp. 1-2; Nov. 1, pp. 1-2; May 23 (1781), p. 2; July 4 (1781), pp. 1-3, 4; July 25 (1781), p. 1.
Pa. Journal Nov. 22, p. 3; Mar. 28 (1781), p. 3; May 16 (1781), pp. 2, 3; June 27 (1781), pp. 1-2; June 30 (1781), p. 1.
Md. Gaz. June 14 (1781), p. 1; Nov. 8 (1781), p. 1.
Va. Gaz. (Dixon and Nicolson) Apr. 8, supplement, pp. 1, 2; May 23, pp. 1-2; June 28, p. 2; Sept. 13, p. 3.

April—May

Charleston. The worst American defeat of the war is the capitulation of Charleston by General Lincoln to General Henry Clinton on May 12 after a siege of approximately one and one-half months. American prisoners number over 5000 while the British lose but 250. Upon Clinton's return to New York City in early June, Lord Cornwallis is left in Charleston with 8000 troops. Vitalized by the capture of South Carolina's capital, the perennial British strategy of cutting the South off from the rest of the United States will now proceed under Cornwallis's direction. With Colonel Banastre Tarleton's massacre of an American force under Colonel Abraham Buford at Waxhaws, South Carolina (May 29), the latter state joins Georgia as effectively-controlled British territory. The next three months are marked by patriot-loyalist clashes, or, more specifically, civil war in North Carolina.

N.Hamp. Gaz. May 13, p. 2; June 24, p. 2; July 1, p. 2.
Indep. Chron. Jan. 13, p. 2; Mar. 30, p. 3; Apr. 13, p. 2; June 8, pp. 1-2, 3; June 22, pp. 1-2, 3; June 29, pp. 1, 3, 4; July 21, p. 3.
Prov. Gaz. June 10, pp. 2, 3; June 24, pp. 1-2, 3.
Conn. Courant May 30, p. 3; June 6, p. 3; Aug. 8, p. 1.
N.J. Gaz. Jan. 5, p. 3; Mar. 22, p. 3; June 7, p. 3; June 21, p. 4; July 19, p. 2; Sept. 27, p. 2.
Pa. Journal Mar. 22, p. 3; May 3, p. 3; May 31, p. 3; June 14, pp. 2-3.
Md. Gaz. Mar. 10, p. 4; Mar. 17, p. 4; Apr. 28, p. 4; June 9, p. 2; June 16, p. 2.
Va. Gaz. (Dixon and Nicolson) Jan. 29, p. 2; Mar. 18, p. 3; Apr. 8, p. 2; May 9, p. 2; May 16, p. 3; May 23, p. 2; June 7, pp. 2-3; June 21, p. 2; July 5, pp. 1, 2, 3; July 19, p. 1.

Broadside: [Mar. 2, 1780] regarding attack upon Charleston.

June

New Jersey. A British force of 5000 crosses into New Jersey from Staten Island and sets Connecticut Farms to the torch (June 6-7). At the approach of the Continentals the British, commanded by General Wilhelm von Knyphausen, retire to Elizabethtown. A small American detachment under Nathanial Greene establishes itself at Springfield in order to watch the intruders. On June 23 the British march on Springfield and burn a number of buildings. A spirited resistance by the numerically inferior Americans checks what is potentially a damaging situation for the New Jerseyites, who are suffering from the effects of America's currency problems, and the Continentals, who are down due to their still elusive back pay, and reduced in numbers because of the end of enlistment terms. Indeed, a May 25 mutiny by Connecticut troops in New Jersey is stopped — barely — by the persuasive abilities of their officers.

Indep. Chron. June 22, p. 3; June 29, pp. 2-3; July 21, p. 1.
Prov. Gaz. June 24, p. 3; July 8, p. 3.
Conn. Courant June 20, pp. 2-3; July 4, p. 3; July 11, p. 3.
N.J. Gaz. June 14, p. 3; June 21, pp. 3, 4; June 28, p. 3; July 5, pp. 1, 3; July 26, p. 1.
Md. Gaz. June 16, p. 2; June 30, pp. 2-3.
Va. Gaz. (Dixon and Nicolson) June 28, pp. 2-3; July 12, pp. 2-3; July 19, p. 2.

August 16

Camden. Under the overall command of General Horatio Gates, a hastily formed army of Continentals and militia proceeds south to contest Cornwallis's progress. The Battle of Camden is a singular American defeat as Baron de Kalb, a Bavarian volunteer, falls with his American command while Gates and the majority of the militia flee in a disorganized and disorderly rout. The British loss is approximately 300 while the Americans lose over 600 killed and wounded. Over 1000 Americans are taken prisoners. Gates is able to re-form only 700 of his original 4000-man army. Two days later "Bloody" Tarleton falls upon General Thomas Sumter's American force in retreat after hearing of Gates' defeat. The ensuing British victory at Fishing Creek is total as over 400 Americans are killed or captured while Tarleton's command loses 16 men. North Carolina lies open to a British invasion.

N.Hamp. Gaz. Sept. 23, p. 1.
Indep. Chron. Sept. 21, p. 3; Sept. 28, pp. 1-2; Oct. 5, pp. 1-2.
Newpt. Merc. Sept. 9, p. 3.
Prov. Gaz. Jan. 24 (1781), p. 1.
Conn. Courant Sept. 19, p. 2; Sept. 26, pp. 2-3.
(N.Y.) *Royal Gaz.* Oct. 21, p. 3.
N.Y. Packet Sept. 14, p. 2.
N.J. Gaz. Sept. 13, p. 2; Sept. 27, p. 3; Dec. 27, p. 1.
Pa. Journal Sept. 6, p. 3; Sept. 13, pp. 2-3.
Va. Gaz. (Dixon and Nicolson) July 12, p. 3; Aug. 23, p. 2; Sept. 6, p. 2; Sept. 27, p. 2.
S.C. and A.G. Gaz. Aug. 23, pp. 2, 3; Aug. 30, pp. 1-2; Sept. 6, pp. 2-3.

September

Benedict Arnold. Though smarting from an official reprimand (April 6) of his conduct as commander of the American forces in Philadelphia after Clinton's evacuation (June 18, 1778) and a persistent belief that his talents are not properly rewarded, especially with rank, General Benedict Arnold retains Washington's confidence and seeks command of West Point. Washington, the dispenser of the reprimand, agrees; and Arnold assumes command of the strategic fort in early August. Driven by financial and professional frustrations, Arnold is already corresponding with General Clinton regarding the surrender of both Washington and West Point. The capture (September 23) of Major John André, Clinton's adjutant-general and Arnold's personal contact in his treachery, hastens Arnold's flight to the British (September 25). Americans vilify Arnold and pay honor to the unfortunate André, who is hanged as a spy on October 3.

N.Hamp. Gaz. Oct. 14, pp. 2, 3.
Indep. Chron. Mar. 4 (1779), p. 2; Oct. 5, p. 3; Oct. 12, p. 3; Oct. 26, p. 3; Nov. 9, pp. 1-2; Nov. 16, pp. 2-3; Nov. 23, pp. 1-2; Nov. 30, p. 2; Dec. 8, p. 1; Dec. 14, pp. 1-2.
Newpt. Merc. Nov. 23, pp. 1-2.
Prov. Gaz. Nov. 15, p. 3; Dec. 6, pp. 1-2; Feb. 24 (1781), p. 2.
Conn. Courant Oct. 10, pp. 2, 3; Nov. 7, pp. 1-2; Sept. 25 (1781), pp. 2, 3.
(N.Y.) *Royal Gaz.* June 10 (1778), p. 2; Feb. 17 (1779), p. 3.
N.Y. Packet Oct. 12, pp. 1-2; Oct. 19, p. 2; Oct. 26, pp. 2-3.
N.J. Gaz. Oct. 4, p. 2; Nov. 1, p. 3; Nov. 8, pp. 1-2.
Pa. Journal Oct. 4, pp. 2-3; Oct. 18, pp. 1-2; Oct. 25, pp. 1, 4.
Pa. Packet Feb. 27 (1779), p. 3; Mar. 4 (1779), p. 2.
Md. Gaz. Oct. 6, p. 2.
Va. Gaz. (Dixon and Nicolson) Oct. 11, p. 2; Oct. 18, pp. 1-2; Nov. 4, p. 2; Nov. 11, pp. 1-2; Dec. 2, p. 2.
S.C. and A.G. Gaz. Oct. 11, p. 2; Oct. 14, p. 2.
Broadside: Feb. 3, 1779.

In COUNCIL.

Philadelphia, February 3d, 1779.

PRESENT, His Excellency JOSEPH REED, Esq. President, Hon. GEORGE BRYAN, Esq. Vice President, Col. *Joseph Hart*, *John Macky*, *James McLene*, *James Read*, *John Hambright*, and *Thomas Scott*, Esquires.

THIS Board having maturely considered the general tenor and course of the military command exercised by Major General *Arnold*, in this City and State; and divers transactions which have appeared to this Board, during his command, do *Resolve*, unanimously,

First, That the same hath been in many respects oppressive to the faithful subjects of this State, unworthy of his rank and station, highly discouraging to those who have manifested their attachment to the liberties and interests of America, and disrespectful to the Supreme Executive Authority of the State.

Wherefore *Resolved* unanimously,

Second, That nothing but the most urgent and pressing necessity can justify or induce this Board to call forth any waggons or militia, or otherwise subject the good people of this State, to the power of the said General *Arnold* within the State, should he resume it upon his return.

Third, *Ordered*, That the Attorney General do prosecute the said General *Arnold*, for such illegal and oppressive conduct as is cognizable in the Courts of Law.

And that this Board may not be supposed capable of passing the above resolves upon mere general grounds, and more especially in the case of one who has formerly distinguished himself in public service, they think proper to declare that the consideration last mentioned, has hitherto restrained them from taking proper notice of General *Arnold*, hoping that every unworthy transaction would be the last, or that a becoming sense of such improprieties, would effect an alteration of conduct; but finding that tenderness has only led to insult and farther oppression, duty to the State, regard to the interests and happiness of the good people thereof, who must be affected by all abuses of power, oblige us thus to take notice thereof, and farther declare, that the said Resolves are founded upon the following articles, in which they have sufficient grounds to esteem General *Arnold* culpable.

1. That while in the camp of General *Washington* at *Valley-Forge*, last spring, he gave permission to a vessel belonging to persons then voluntarily residing in this city with the enemy, and of disaffected character, to come to a port of the United States, without the knowledge of the authority of the State, or of the Commander in Chief, though then present.

2. In having shut up the stores and shops on his arrival in the city, so as even to prevent officers of the army from purchasing, while he privately made considerable purchases for his own benefit, as is alledged and believed.

3. In imposing menial offices upon the sons of freemen of this State, when called forth by the desire of Congress to perform militia duty, and when remonstrated to hereupon, justifying himself in writing upon the ground of having power so to do, for that, " when a citizen assumed the character of a soldier, the former was intirely lost in the latter, and that it was the duty of " the militia to obey *every* order of his Aids (not a breach of the laws and constitution) as his (the General's) without judging of " the propriety of them."

4. For that when a prize was brought into this port by the Convention brig of this State, whereon a dispute arose respecting the capture, which would otherwise, in great probability, have been amicably adjusted between the claimants, General *Arnold* interposed by an illegal and unworthy purchase of the suit, at a low and inadequate price, as he has been publicly charged by a reputable citizen, to which may in some degree be ascribed the delay of justice in the Courts of Appeals, and the dispute in which the State may probably be involved with Congress hereupon.

5. The appropriating the waggons of this State when called forth upon a special emergency last Autumn, to the transportation of private property, and that of persons who voluntarily remained with the enemy last winter, and were deemed disaffected to the interests and independence of America.

6. In that Congress by a resolve of the 21st of August last, having given to the executive powers of every state, an exclusive power to recommend persons desirous of going within the enemy's lines, to the officer there commanding; General *Arnold* in order, as may reasonably be inferred, to elude the said resolve, wrote a letter, as appears by comparison of hands, and the declaration of the intended bearer, recommendatory for the above purpose, and caused his Aid du Camp, Major *Clarkson*, to sign the same; but the said device not taking effect, through the vigilance of the officers at *Elizabeth-town*, General *Arnold*, without disclosing any of the above circumstances, applied to Council for their permission, which was instantly refused; the connections, character, and situation of the party being well known, and deemed utterly improper to be indulged with such permission; thereby violating the resolve of Congress, and usurping the authority of this Board.

7. This Board having, upon the complaint of several inhabitants of Chester county, through the late Waggon-Master General, *requested* of the said General *Arnold* to state the said transaction respecting the waggons, in order that they might satisfy the complainants, or explain the same without farther trouble, received, in return, an indecent and disrespectful refusal of any satisfaction whatsoever.

8. The discouragement and neglect manifested by General *Arnold* during his command, to civil, military, and other characters, who have adhered to the cause of their country---with an entire different conduct towards those of another character, are too notorious to need proof or illustration; and if this command has been, as is generally believed, supported at an expence of four or five thousand pounds per annum, to the United States, we freely declare we shall very unwillingly pay any share of expences thus incurred.

On consideration, *Ordered*, That as the waggons sent by General *Arnold* to *Egg-Harbour*, were drawn forth under the law of the State, and the waggoners not being able to procure payment, either from the Quarter-Master's department, or from General *Arnold*, who is departed from this city while the complaint against him was depending, and they being in great necessity, this Board ought to relieve them so far as to advance four hundred and fifty pounds, until they can procure farther redress. And that *Jesse Jordan* the Waggon-Master, give a special receipt to be accountable therefor.

Extract from the Minutes,

T. MATLACK, *Secretary.*

PHILADELPHIA: Printed by FRANCIS BAILEY, in Front-Street.

October 7

King's Mountain. Cornwallis's move into North Carolina (September 8) is pointed toward Hillsboro. By early October his main force is in Charlotte while a 1300-man flanking force under Major Patrick Ferguson moves northward on Cornwallis's left. Ferguson's Tory command is completely defeated by patriot militia and mountainmen whose chief motive is revenge for British atrocities such as Tarleton's conduct at the Waxhaws on May 29 (see above, April–May). The American victory is most important as it hurries Cornwallis back into South Carolina (October 14) where he winters at Winnsboro. The British offensive for 1780 is checked. The loss also aborts a British invasion of the Virginia peninsula as the British troops are diverted to reinforce Cornwallis. At this moment the newly appointed commander of the American army in the South, on Washington's recommendation, is on his way south. Nathaniel Greene will more than hold his own in the coming campaign.

Indep. Chron. Nov. 9, p. 3; Nov. 30, p. 3; Dec. 14, p. 3.
Newpt. Merc. Nov. 23, p. 2.
Conn. Courant Nov. 7, p. 4.
N.Y. Packet Nov. 2, pp. 2, 3.
N.J. Gaz. Oct. 25, p. 3; Nov. 8, pp. 2-3; Nov. 15, p. 3; Nov. 22, pp. 2, 3; Nov. 29, p. 3; Dec. 6, p. 3; Dec. 13, p. 2.
Pa. Journal Oct. 11, p. 2; Oct. 25, p. 3; Nov. 15, pp. 2-3; Dec. 20, p. 2.
Md. Gaz. Nov. 10, p. 2.
Va. Gaz. (Dixon and Nicolson) Oct. 18, p. 2; Nov. 4, pp. 2-3; Nov. 18, pp. 2, 3; Nov. 25, p. 2.
S.C. and A.G. Gaz. Nov. 22, p. 2; Nov. 29, p. 2; Dec. 20, p. 3.

December

Britain Declares War on the Netherlands. Irritated beyond measure by Dutch supply of the Americans with war materials, Great Britain declares war. The first target of the British is the "neutral" Dutch West Indian island of St. Eustatius, principal entrepôt for Dutch and other neutral goods into eager American hands (see above, February 1777). Admiral George Rodney's fleet takes the island and its approximately £3,000,000 worth of prizes, on Febraury 3, 1781. A large portion of the confiscated booty is English since that kingdom's merchants, or a goodly number of them, seek continued American profits during the war — despite such a pursuit's seeming lack of patriotism. Rodney's exertion nets him lawsuits by the injured English merchants — which the latter win!

Indep. Chron. Nov. 11 (1779), p. 2.
Conn. Courant Mar. 6 (1781), p. 3; Mar. 20 (1781), p. 2; Apr. 10 (1781), p. 2; May 8 (1781), p. 2; May 15 (1781), p. 2; May 22 (1781), pp. 1-2; Aug. 28 (1781), pp. 1-2; Nov. 5 (1782), p. 3.
(N.Y.) *Royal Gaz.* Apr. 11 (1781), p. 3.
N.Y. Packet Mar. 22 (1781), p. 3.
N.J. Gaz. May 12 (1779), p. 2; Apr. 12 (1780), p. 2; May 24 (1780), p. 3; Mar. 21 (1781), p. 3.
Pa. Journal Feb. 28 (1781), p. 2; Mar. 7 (1781), p. 3; Mar. 21 (1781), p. 2; Apr. 18 (1781), p. 2; July 14 (1781), pp. 2-3.
Pa. Packet Feb. 25 (1779), p. 2.
Md. Gaz. May 3 (1781), p. 2.
Va. Gaz. (Dixon and Nicolson) July 3 (1779), p. 1; Apr. 1 (1780), p. 1; June 28 (1780), p. 1; Aug. 2 (1780), p. 1; Nov. 18 (1780), p. 2; Mar. 24 (1781), p. 1; Mar. 31 (1781), p. 1; Apr. 7 (1781), p. 1; Apr. 14 (1781), p. 1; May 19 (1781), p. 1.
Gaz. of St. of S.C. Sept. 8 (1779), p. 2.

American Philosophical Society
Incorporated
Pa. Journal May 24, p. 2.
Seeks weather information
Pa. Journal Mar. 22, p. 3.

Army, Continental
Proposed to use against states that refuse to supply quota of provisions for
Newpt. Merc. Nov. 23, p. 2.

Backus, Isaac
Defends Baptists in Massachusetts
Indep. Chron. Apr. 20, p. 4.

Boston Massacre
Commemorated
Indep. Chron. Mar. 9, p. 2.
Last victim of dies
Indep. Chron. Apr. 20, p. 3.
Pa. Journal May 10, p. 3.

Colleges
College of New Jersey, how to prepare for
N.J. Gaz. Mar. 15, p. 1.
College of Philadelphia, commencement
Pa. Journal July 12, pp. 1, 4.
William and Mary, board offered to students
Va. Gaz. (Dixon and Nicolson) Feb. 19, p. 3.

Cook, James (Captain)
Death of
N.J. Gaz. Apr. 27, p. 2.
Voyage of
Indep. Chron. Jan. 13, p. 1.

Crime
Murder: narrative of
Prov. Gaz. June 10, pp. 1, 4.

Drowning Victim
Apparent, revived
Pa. Journal Aug. 9, p. 1.

Gambling
Virginia act to suppress excessive
Va. Gaz. (Dixon and Nicolson) Feb. 26, p. 1.

Gordon, George (English peer)
Precipitates anti-Catholic, anti-administration riots in London
N.Hamp. Gaz. Sept. 9, p. 2.
Indep. Chron. Aug. 17, p. 3; Aug. 31, pp. 1-2, 3.

Newpt. Merc. Sept. 9, p. 2.
N.J. Gaz. May 10, p. 1; Sept. 20, pp. 1, 4; Nov. 15, p. 2.
Pa. Journal Nov. 29, p. 2.

Horseracing
Ad for Maryland
Pa. Journal Sept. 20, p. 3.

Hurricane
Damages West Indies
Indep. Chron. Dec. 14, pp. 2, 3.
N.J. Gaz. Dec. 6, p. 3; Dec. 20, pp. 2, 3, 4.

Ireland
Seeks own freedom from British
N.Hamp. Gaz. Aug. 26, p. 1.
Indep. Chron. Mar. 2, p. 3; Mar. 16, supplement, p. 4.
Conn. Courant Mar. 14, p. 2.
N.J. Gaz. Apr. 5, p. 2; Apr. 12, pp. 1, 2, 4; May 3, pp. 1, 2; May 10, pp. 2, 3; May 24, p. 2.
Va. Gaz. (Dixon and Nicolson) May 23, p. 2; May 31, pp. 2-3; June 7, p. 1.

July 4th Celebrations
College of New Jersey
N.J. Gaz. July 12, p. 3.
Portsmouth, New Hampshire
N.Hamp. Gaz. July 8, p. 3.
St. Eustastius, West Indies
Newpt. Merc. Aug. 12, p. 3.

Laurens, Henry (American diplomat)
Held in Tower of London
N.Y. Packet Dec. 21, p. 2.

Martial Law
Power of granted to Pennsylvania authorities
Pa. Journal June 7, p. 3; June 21, p. 3.

Mathematics
Geometrical problem offered to readers
Va. Gaz. (Dixon and Nicolson) Mar. 18, p. 3.

Navy, Continental
Congress encourages recruitment for
Pa. Journal Aug. 2, p. 3.

Opinion, British
Scourge: harsh essays protest Britain's current political, social, economic circumstances

Prov. Gaz. Sept. 9, pp. 3-4; Sept. 23, p. 1; Oct. 4, p. 1.
Conn. Courant Aug. 15, pp. 1-2; Aug. 22, pp. 1, 4; Aug. 29, pp. 1-2; Sept. 5, pp. 1-2; Sept. 12, pp. 3-4;
N.J. Gaz. Sept. 20, p. 1.

Prisoners of War
American, brutalized
Va. Gaz. (Dixon and Nicolson) Sept. 6, pp. 2-3.
American, escape narrative
Va. Gaz. (Dixon and Nicolson) Sept. 13, pp. 1-2.

Religious Freedom
In new Massachusetts constitution, debated
Indep. Chron. Feb. 10, pp. 1-2; Mar. 2, p. 1; Mar. 16, supplement, p. 1; Mar. 23, p. 1; Apr. 6, p. 1; Apr. 13, p. 1; May 18, pp. 1-2.
Proposed in Virginia
Prov. Gaz. May 13, p. 1.
N.Y. Packet Oct. 26, p. 1.

Slaves
Act for Gradual Abolition of Slavery in Pennsylvania
N.J. Gaz. May 17, p. 1.
Pa. Journal Sept. 20, p. 1.
Anti-slavery sentiments
N.J. Gaz. Sept. 20, p. 2.
Individual, sues for freedom
N.J. Gaz. Mar. 1, p. 3.
Manumission now? debated
N.J. Gaz. Oct. 4, p. 1; Nov. 8, p. 1.
Sales of
N.J. Gaz. July 19, p. 4.
Virginia taxation protested: heaviest on slave-owners
Va. Gaz. (Dixon and Nicolson) Mar. 4, p. 1.

Soldiers, American
Virginia Desertion Act
Va. Gaz. (Dixon and Nicolson) July 26, p. 1.

Soldiers, German
Ad for British army deserters: welcome to join French army
N.J. Gaz. Sept. 27, p. 3.

Tories
Situation in New York City
Va. Gaz. (Dixon and Nicolson), Jan. 29, p. 2.

Trade
American with British in New York City noted
N.J. Gaz. Dec. 6, p. 3; Dec. 27, pp. 2-3, 4.

Unusual Phenomena
Dark Day
Prov. Gaz. May 20, p. 3; May 27, p. 2; June 3, p. 2.
Broadside: May 19,

Washington, George
Birthday celebrated in Williamsburg
Va. Gaz. (Dixon and Nicolson) Feb. 19, p. 2.
English sketch of life of
N.J. Gaz. Dec. 6, p. 1.
Picture of, ad for sale of
Pa. Journal Dec. 27, p. 2.

Women
Patriotism must continue
Va. Gaz. (Dixon and Nicolson) Aug. 9, p. 1.

Wood
Scarce: share
Newpt. Merc. Jan. 5, p. 4.

January

Pennsylvania and New Jersey Lines Mutiny. Soldierly frustration brought on by their insistence that their enlistments are over, and compounded by the usual aggravations of back pay and lack of supplies, leads to mutinies by the Pennsylvania Line (Continentals) in Morristown (January 1) and New Jersey regulars in Pompton, New Jersey (January 20). Both mutinies are ended peacefully enough: the former when one-half of the men are allowed to leave the service, the latter when General Robert Howe disarms the mutineers (January 27) and hangs two of the leaders. Another Pennsylvania mutiny in May is also stopped quickly. The problems affecting the soldiers are due primarily to the chaotic financial situation presided over by Congress.

N.Hamp. Gaz. Jan. 22, p. 2; Feb. 12, p. 1.
Indep. Chron. Feb. 8, p. 3.
Conn. Courant Feb. 6, p. 2; Feb. 13, pp. 2, 3; Feb. 20, pp. 1-2; June 12, p. 3; Aug. 14, pp. 1, 2.
(N.Y.) *Royal Gaz.* Jan. 31, p. 3.
N.Y. Packet Jan. 11, p. 3; Feb. 8, p. 2.
N.J. Gaz. Jan. 17, p. 3; Jan. 31, p. 3; Feb. 7, p. 2; Feb. 14, p. 2.
Pa. Journal Feb. 5, p. 2; July 4, pp. 1-2; July 7, p. 2.
Md. Gaz. Feb. 15, p. 1.
(Charl.) *Royal Gaz.* Mar. 3/7, p. 3; Apr. 4/7, pp. 1-2.
Broadside: Jan. 22.

January

Arnold in Virginia. Newly appointed General Benedict Arnold arrives in Virginia with 1200 men, intent on destroying war materials and preventing American reinforcements from joining Greene's army in North Carolina. The British burn much of Richmond (January 5-6) and then retreat to winter quarters at Portsmouth.

N. Hamp. Gaz. Feb. 12, p. 1.
Indep. Chron. Dec. 21 (1780), p. 3; Feb. 1, p. 3.
Prov. Gaz. Feb. 24, p. 3.
Conn. Courant Feb. 6, p. 2; Feb. 13, p. 2; Feb. 27, p. 2; Mar. 20, p. 2.
(N.Y.) *Royal Gaz.* Jan. 27, p. 3; Feb. 7, pp. 2-3; Oct. 28, p. 1.
N.Y. Packet Mar. 8, p. 3.
N.J. Gaz. Jan. 31, p. 2.
Pa. Journal Jan. 17, p. 3; Mar. 28, p. 2.
Va. Gaz. (Dixon and Nicolson) Mar. 31, p. 2.
S.C. and A.G. Gaz. Jan. 31, p. 2; Feb. 24, p. 2.

January 17

Cowpens. Contrary to the accepted principles of war, General Nathaniel Greene divides his small army. While he proceeds south from Charlotte, North Carolina, toward Cornwallis in Winnsboro, South Carolina, General Daniel Morgan moves southwest against the British. Morgan's victory over the hated Lieutenant Colonel Tarleton in a North Carolina field used for coralling cattle is extraordinary. The British lose 90% of their 1100-man force; the American loss is 72 of 1040 men. More importantly, Greene's plan, to preserve the American army, never risking an all-out battle unless plainly superior to the enemy, is given a recruiting lift. Cornwallis marches into North Carolina after the slowly retiring Greene.

Indep. Chron. Feb. 22, p. 3; Mar. 8, p. 3.
Conn. Courant Feb. 20, p. 2; July 10, pp. 1-2.
N.J. Gaz. Feb. 14, p. 2.
Pa. Journal Feb. 14, p. 3.
Va. Gaz. (Dixon and Nicolson) Feb. 3, p. 1.
S.C. and A.G. Gaz. Jan. 27, p. 3.

March 1

Articles of Confederation Ratified. Virginia follows the recent examples of New York (February 1780) and Connecticut (October 1780) by ceding its land claims north of the Ohio River, except for land previously granted to individuals, to the United States on January 1, 1781. (Congress does not accept the cession until September 1783 because of Virginia specifications regarding ownership of land south of the Ohio River — Kentucky — and Virginia conditions concerning previous purchases by individuals from Indians of Ohio lands.) Maryland, alone in its refusal to ratify the Articles of Confederation until Virginia's cession, votes ratification on February 27. Two days later the "United States in Congress assembled" celebrates the completed forging of a federal union. The American union established by the Articles of Confederation suffers from inherent difficulties (see above, November 15, 1777) and is replaced by the Constitution of 1787.

An interesting sidelight is the election in November of John Hanson (Maryland) as the first duly-elected President of the Confederation Congress — and of the United States. Hanson succeeds Samuel Huntington of Connecticut (president in 1781 until July 6) and Thomas McKean of Delaware (interim president from July 6 to November 1). In his turn President Hanson is followed for one year terms by Elias Boudinot (New Jersey) and Thomas Mifflin (Pennsylvania).

N.Hamp. Gaz. Mar. 26, p. 1.
Indep. Chron. Mar. 22, p. 3.
Prov. Gaz. Feb. 24, p. 3;

Conn. Courant Feb. 1 (1780), p. 3; Feb. 27, p. 2; Mar. 20, p. 3.
N.Y. Packet July 12, p. 1; July 19, p. 1; Aug. 30, p. 1.
N.J. Gaz. Apr. 21 (1779), p. 2; June 23 (1779), p. 1; Sept. 22 (1779), p. 1; Oct. 6 (1779), p. 2; Dec. 15 (1779), pp. 1-2; Oct. 18 (1780), p. 2; Feb. 14, p. 3.
Pa. Journal Jan. 31, p. 2; Mar. 7, p. 3; Nov. 7, p. 3; Nov. 6 (1782), p. 2; Nov. 5 (1783), p. 3.
Md. Gaz. Oct. 8 (1779), p. 3; Mar. 22, p. 1; July 26, p. 2; Nov. 15, p. 2; Nov. 20 (1783), p. 2.
Va. Gaz. (Dixon and Nicolson) Feb. 24, p. 1.
Va. Gaz. or Amer. Adv. Mar. 20 (1784), p. 2.
Gaz. of St. of S.C. Nov. 27 (1783), p. 2.

March 15

Guilford Court House. Cornwallis catches up with the strengthened American army in northern North Carolina. Although Greene retreats from Guilford Court House, Cornwallis' "victory" is hard on the British who suffer over 500 casualties to their 1900-man army. The 4400-man American army, 2600 of them militia from North Carolina and Virginia, loses 250. Desperately short of supplies, Cornwallis proceeds painfully to Wilmington, North Carolina, two hundred miles distant, where a British supply magazine is located (April 7). With his 1400 troops, Cornwallis next decides to move into Virginia in order to join with General William Phillips, now in command of the British forces in that state.

N.Hamp. Gaz. Apr. 23, p. 2.
Conn. Courant Mar. 27, p. 2; Apr. 10, pp. 2, 3; Apr. 17, pp. 1-2; Apr. 24, pp. 2, 3; May 15, p. 2.
N.J. Gaz. Mar. 28, p. 3; Apr. 4, p. 3; Apr. 11, p. 3.
Pa. Journal Mar. 21, p. 3; Mar. 28, p. 3; Apr. 11, p. 3.
Md. Gaz. Apr. 5, p. 2.
Va. Gaz. (Dixon and Nicolson) Mar. 31, p. 2; Apr. 14, pp. 1-2.
S.C. and A.G. Gaz. Feb. 10, p. 3.

April 25

Hobkirk's Hill. Greene loses to Lord Francis Rawdon at Hobkirk's Hill just north of Camden, South Carolina. Greene's tactics are secure as he retreats with his own army intact; the British win but suffer heavier casualties and see their effective control in the South pushed ever closer to the seacoast and the ready encouragement of British naval strength. In Greene's words: "We fight, get beat, rise and fight again."

N.Hamp. Gaz. June 11, p. 1.
Conn. Courant June 5, pp. 1-2; June 12, p. 1.
Pa. Journal May 30, p. 3.
Md. Gaz. May 24, p. 2.
Va. Gaz. (Dixon and Nicolson) May 19, p. 2.
(Charl.) Royal Gaz. Apr. 28/May 2, p. 2; May 5/9, p. 2.

March—May

Virginia Suffers in the Cause. Arnold's force at Portsmouth is increased by 2600 with the arrival of General William Phillips (March 26) who takes over command of the entire 3800-man army until his death at Petersburg, May 13. (Americans are quick to claim Phillips is poisoned by Arnold.) A British contingent moves in late April up the James River to Petersburg destroying and burning American ships, tobacco, and military supplies. Lafayette's arrival (April 29) in Richmond, Virginia's capital for the past year, with 1200 Continental troops is not enough to offset Virginia's lack of preparedness. The British armies — Cornwallis's and Arnold's, after Phillips' death — come together in Petersburg on May 20. Within a few days reinforcements arrive from New York City, and Cornwallis' strength reaches 7200. With reinforcements of his own, Lafayette's army numbers only 3000.

Indep. Chron. Mar. 22, p. 3; May 31, p. 3.
Conn. Courant May 22, p. 2; May 29, p. 2; June 19, p. 2.
Va. Gaz. (Dixon and Nicolson) May 19, p. 2.
(Charl.) Royal Gaz. Oct. 10/13, p. 2.

May 22—June 19

Siege of Ninety-six. The fall of Forts Motte (May 12) and Grandby (May 15), coupled with the further American conquests of Camden, Fort Watson, Nelson's ferry, and Orangeburg, all in South Carolina, leave the British with few positions in the South. In Georgia only Savannah and Augusta are held for King George III; in South Carolina only Charleston, Georgetown, and Ninety-six are still in British hands. (Within a month Georgetown and Augusta are both taken by the Americans.) Greene promptly invests Ninety-six, an important post for British communications with their Indian allies, a protection for neighborhood Tories, and a hindrance to American settlements west of the fort. The 550 Tory defenders commanded by Lieutenant John Cruger successfully withstand Greene's approximately 1000 besiegers, with the "assistance" of Rawdon's expected arrival with 2000 reinforcements.

Indep. Chron. June 28, p. 1; Aug. 9, p. 3.
Conn. Courant June 12, p. 1; June 26, p. 2; July 24, p. 2; July 31, p. 2; Aug. 7, p. 2.
N.Y. Packet June 21, p. 3.
Pa. Journal July 18, pp. 2-3.
Va. Gaz. (Dixon and Nicolson) Apr. 21, p. 1.

June–August 2

Lafayette, von Steuben, and Wayne vs. Cornwallis. Throughout June and into July, the Americans and British spar in Virginia. Tarleton nearly captures Governor Thomas Jefferson and the entire General Assembly meeting in Charlottesville (June 4), yet the various military actions are anything but definitive. With Lafayette's army growing to 5200 men through reinforcements, Cornwallis moves finally toward the area of Virginia supposedly most open to British influence. By July 14, Cornwallis is in Portsmouth, a port suited to the exercise of British naval power. On August 2, the British begin to fortify Yorktown for use as a naval base because of its superior potential.

Indep. Chron. July 26, p. 2; Aug. 30, p. 3.
Prov. Gaz. Sept. 8, p. 2.
Conn. Courant July 3, p. 2; July 10, p. 2; July 24, p. 2; July 31, p. 3; Aug. 7, pp. 1, 2; Aug. 14, p. 2; Sept. 4, p. 2.
N.J. Gaz. Sept. 5, p. 3.
Pa. Journal July 21, pp. 2-3; July 25, p. 3.

September 6

New London Burned. Returned from his southern excursion in June, Benedict Arnold plans an attack on Connecticut calculated to force Washington to divert some troops northward instead of south to Virginia. New London is chosen as the objective due to its store of military supplies. A massacre inflicted on the garrison of Fort Griswold as well as the burning of most of New London and nearby Groton end the war in the North and signalize for Americans once again the perfidy of Benedict Arnold.

N.Hamp. Gaz. Sept. 22, p. 1; Sept. 29, p. 4.
Conn. Courant July 3, p. 2; Sept. 11, p. 3; Sept. 18, p. 3; Sept. 25, pp. 2, 3.
(N.Y.) Royal Gaz. Sept. 19, p. 3.
N.Y. Packet June 21, p. 3; Sept. 27, p. 3.
N.J. Gaz. June 20, p. 3; July 25, p. 3; Sept. 26, pp. 2-3; Oct. 3, pp. 2, 3.
Pa. Journal Sept. 22, p. 3; Sept. 26, pp. 1-2.

September 8

Eutaw Springs. The last large-scale battle of the war in the deep South is considered a victory by both sides. Greene's "victory" seems more appropriate as the action at Eutaw Springs, South Carolina, marks the retreat of the British to enclaves about Charleston and Savannah in the South. Moreover, both Georgia and South Carolina state governments are reestablished. The stage is set for the final act, to be played in Virginia at Yorktown.

Prov. Gaz. Oct. 20, p. 2.
Conn. Courant July 17, p. 3; Aug. 28, p. 2; Sept. 18, p. 2; Oct. 9, p. 2; Oct. 16, p. 2; Oct. 23, p. 2; Oct. 30, pp. 2-3; Nov. 6, p. 2; Dec. 18, p. 1.
N.Y. Packet Oct. 11, p. 3.
N.J. Gaz. Aug. 15, p. 3.
Pa. Journal Oct. 10, p. 2; Oct. 17, pp. 2-3.
Md. Gaz. Oct. 4, p. 2; Oct. 18, pp. 1-2.
(Charl.) Royal Gaz. Sept. 8/12, p. 3; Sept. 15/19, p. 3; Sept. 26/29, p. 1.

September 5-9

DeGrasse in the Chesapeake. After an unsuccessful attempt on St. Lucia (May) and a more successful venture on Tobago (June 2), both in the West Indies, Admiral de Grasse sails north in response to messages from General Rochambeau and the French minister to the United States, Chevalier de Luzerne. The communications are about the developing situation in Virginia. De Grasse's ability to prevent Admiral Thomas Graves from entering Chesapeake Bay in support of the beleaguered Cornwallis is actually the final blow to the latter's chances for survival.

N.Hamp. Gaz. Oct. 6, p. 4.
Indep. Chron. July 26, p. 3; Sept. 20, p. 3.
Prov. Gaz. Sept. 29, p. 1.
Conn. Courant July 10, p. 3; July 24, p. 3; July 31, p. 3; Sept. 11, p. 3; Sept. 18, p. 2; Sept. 25, p. 2; Oct. 2, p. 2; Oct. 9, p. 2.
(N.Y.) Royal Gaz. Sept. 5, p. 3; Sept. 22, pp. 2, 3.
N.Y. Packet Sept. 13, p. 3; Sept. 27, p. 3; Oct. 4, pp. 2-3; Oct. 11, pp. 2-3.
N.J. Gaz. Sept. 19, p. 3; Sept. 26, p. 3.
Pa. Journal Sept. 8, pp. 2-3; Sept. 19, p. 2; Sept. 26, p. 3.
Md. Gaz. Sept. 6, p. 1; Sept. 20, p. 1; Oct. 4, p. 2.
Royal Ga. Gaz. Jan. 3 (1782), pp. 1, 4.

August–September

Cornwallis Attracts Attention. Seizing the moment, Washington moves secretly south from New York with Rochambeau on August 21. A plan to attack New York City, agreed upon by the two allied generals in late May in Wethersfield, Connecticut, is scrubbed. The American and French troops are intended to join Lafayette's besieging army at Yorktown in time to cooperate with Admiral de Grasse who is expected in Chesapeake Bay in late August. De Grasse states that he will remain only until October 15, a deadline that necessitates Washington's hurry toward Virginia. De Grasse is also bringing 3000 French troops for the projected campaign. By September 6, the Americans are at the Head of Elk, Maryland, and by September 28 they are in Yorktown. With Rochambeau's army, de Grasse's reinforcements, American militia, and Continentals, Washington commands approximately 16,000 troops. Cornwallis' army numbers about 6000. De Grasse's successful action with Graves (see above, September 5-9) prevents any British escape by the sea. The allied armies now cut off any hope of escape on the Virginia peninsula.

N. Hamp. Gaz. Sept. 8, p. 2.
Indep. Chron. May 31, p. 3.
Prov. Gaz. Sept. 29, p. 3.
Conn. Courant May 29, p. 3; July 3, p. 3; Sept. 25, p. 2; Oct. 2, p. 3; Oct. 16, p. 2.
N.Y. Packet July 5, p. 3; Sept. 27, p. 3.
N.J. Gaz. July 18, p. 4; Oct. 3, p. 3.
Pa. Journal Sept. 1, p. 3; Sept. 8, pp. 2-3; Oct. 10, p. 2.
Md. Gaz. Sept. 13, p. 1; Sept. 20, p. 2.
(Charl.) *Royal Gaz.* Sept. 22/26, p. 3.

October 19

Yorktown. A well-executed allied siege and a final, unsuccessful British attempt to strike out for the safety of New York City by reinforcing their position across the York River at Gloucester preparatory to a general retreat (October 16-17) end the British dream of reconquering their colonies. Truly, the traditional British martial tune played as the British surrender on October 19 is appropriate: "The World Turned Upside Down." America is jubilant and triumphant. Clinton's arrival off the Chesapeake Capes on October 24 with 7000 reinforcements adds a touch of irony to the defeat. In December the British evacuate their naval base at Wilmington, North Carolina.

N.Hamp. Gaz. Oct. 20, p. 3;
Indep. Chron. Nov. 1, p. 3; Nov. 8, p. 3; Feb. 21 (1782), p. 3; Mar. 28 (1782), pp. 1-2.
Prov. Gaz. Oct. 27, p. 3; Nov. 3, p. 3; Nov. 10, pp. 1, 2; Nov. 17, pp. 1-2; Mar. 16 (1782), pp. 1-2; Mar. 30 (1782), pp. 1-2.
Conn. Courant Oct. 16, p. 3; Oct. 23, p. 3; Nov. 6, pp. 2-3; Nov. 13, pp. 1-2, 3; Nov. 20, pp. 1-2, 3, 4; Nov. 27, pp. 1-2; Dec. 4, p. 1; Dec. 11, pp. 2-3; Dec. 18, p. 2; Dec. 25, pp. 3, 4; Feb. 26 (1782), p. 1; May 14 (1782), p. 1; July 9 (1782), pp. 1-2.

(N.Y.) *Royal Gaz.* Oct. 10, p. 3; Oct. 13, p. 3; Oct. 17, p. 3.
N.Y. Packet Oct. 25, pp. 2-3; Nov. 1, pp. 1, 3; Nov. 15, p. 3.
N.J. Gaz. Oct. 17, pp. 2-3; Oct. 24, p. 3; Oct. 31, p. 3; Nov. 7, p. 3; Dec. 12, pp. 2-3; Dec. 19, p. 2.
Pa. Journal Oct. 17, p. 3; Oct. 24, p. 3; Oct. 27, pp. 1-3; Oct. 31, pp. 1, 3; Nov. 7, p. 3; Nov. 10, p. 1; Nov. 21, p. 2; Nov. 28, p. 3; Dec. 1, p. 3.
Md. Gaz. Oct. 25, p. 2; Nov. 1, pp. 1-2; Nov. 29, p. 2.
(Charl.) *Royal Gaz.* Dec. 1/5, p. 3.
Royal Ga. Gaz. Mar. 21 (1782), p. 1; May 30 (1782), p. 2.

December 31

Bank of North America. Chartered on the last day of 1781 by the Congress, the Bank of North America is one of a number of positive economic actions initiated by Robert Morris. Morris, a wealthy Philadelphia merchant, is named Superintendent of Finance in February as the American union is about to become a reality and as the American financial situation is about to reach new depths. With the establishment of a national bank (first approved by Congress in May) intended to issue notes acceptable for taxes, trade duties, and American debt — of which there is a bit — the United States gains a measure of or direction toward fiscal stability. This objective is materially aided by French (May) and Dutch (November) loans. Despite an aversion to dispensing back pay to soldiers too quickly, Morris does junk the less than happy state requisition system of army supply. Private contract supply proves more adequate.

N.Hamp. Gaz. Sept. 29, pp. 2, 3; May 25 (1782), p. 3.
Indep. Chron. Mar. 1, p. 1; June 21, pp. 1-2.
Conn. Courant Apr. 17, p. 3; June 12, p. 2; Aug. 7, p. 1.
(N.Y.) *Royal Gaz.* May 12, p. 2.
N.J. Gaz. June 6, pp. 1-2; Jan. 9 (1782), pp. 1-2.
Pa. Journal May 30, p. 2; July 7, p. 1; July 11, p. 2; Nov. 13 (1782), p. 1.
Va. Gaz. or Amer. Adv. Jan. 26, p. 3.

Alliance: French-American
Commented on by French newspaper
Prov. Gaz. Apr. 28, pp. 1-2.

Army, Continental
Market places for supply of regulated, protection offered
N.Y. Packet July 19, p. 3.

Barry, John (Captain, American naval officer)
Exploits of
Conn. Courant June 12, p. 3; June 19, pp. 2-3.

Gordon, Lord George
Treason trial
Conn. Courant May 15, p. 1; May 29, pp. 1-2; June 5, p. 1.

Humor
Lampoon of British war efforts
Conn. Courant Nov. 27, p. 2.
Last will and testament of Congress
(N.Y.) *Royal Gaz.* Jan. 31, p. 3.
Parody on Congress by means of altered Declaration of Independence
(Charl.) *Royal Gaz.* Dec. 19/22, p. 3.
Satire of British recruiter and Hesse (German state) peasant
Pa. Journal Jan. 31, pp. 1-2; Feb. 5 [*i.e.,* 7], p. 1.

Jones, John Paul
Honored by French, Congress
Conn. Courant July 24, p. 2.
Pa. Journal July 7, p. 3.

July 4th Celebration
Amsterdam, Holland
N.Hamp. Gaz. Sept. 29, p. 1.

Laurens, Henry
Held in Tower of London
Conn. Courant Feb. 6, pp. 1, 3.

Massachusetts Medical Society
Incorporated
Indep. Chron. Dec. 14, p. 1.

Newspapers
Observations on freedom of press
N.J. Gaz. June 6, p. 4.

Peale, Charles Willson
Philadelphia show, includes patriotic works
N.J. Gaz. Dec. 12, pp. 2-3.

Peddlers
New York act restrains
N.Y. Packet Apr. 26, p. 1.

Quakers
War conduct attacked
Pa. Journal Oct. 10, p. 1.

Sanitation
Keep streets clean for health reasons
Pa. Journal July 11, p. 3; Oct. 24, p. 1.

Slaves
Manumission debated
N.J. Gaz. Jan. 10, p. 1; Feb. 14, p. 1; Mar. 14, p. 1; Mar. 21, p. 1; Apr. 11, p. 2.
Pa. Journal Jan. 31, p. 2; Feb. 5 [*i.e.,* 7], p. 1; Feb. 21, p. 1; Apr. 4, pp. 1-2.
Regarding abolition of slavery in land ceded to Pennsylvania from Virginia
Pa. Journal Apr. 25, p. 1.

Tories
Admonished in letter
Pa. Journal Sept. 19, p. 1.

War Atrocities
British, in Charleston
N.Hamp. Gaz. Sept. 3, p. 1.
Va. Gaz. (Dixon and Nicolson) May 19, p. 2.

Washington, George
Rhode Island county changes name from King's to Washington County
Prov. Gaz. Nov. 10, p. 1.

1782

Vermont. During the American Revolution, the controversy over the New Hampshire Grants area, or Vermont, continues between New York, New Hampshire, and a group of indigenous inhabitants who follow the lead of the Allen brothers in a quest to become an American state. The Vermont state constitution established in 1777 (see above, May 15, 1776) is considered an effrontery by New York and New Hampshire authorities and dispossessed landowners; but its unpopularity is outdistanced in the early 1780's by rumors of Vermont/Allen flirtations with the British. Empowered to settle the matter in September 1779, Congress succumbs to a not so unusual inertia that is facilitated by jealousies of a possible fifth New England vote as well as of the precedent of dismembering former colonies. Not until 1791 does Vermont become the fourteenth state. (See also above, 1774.)

N.Hamp. Gaz. Nov. 24 (1781), pp. 1-2; Feb. 2 (1782), p. 1; Feb. 9 (1782), p. 1.
Prov. Gaz. Feb. 9 (1782), pp. 1-2; Apr. 20 (1782), p. 3; Jan. 4 (1783), pp. 2-3.
Conn. Courant Aug. 18 (1777), pp. 1-2; Sept. 4 (1781), p. 3; Feb. 5 (1782), pp. 1-2; Feb. 12 (1782), pp. 1-2; July 9 (1782), p. 4; Dec. 24 (1782), p. 3.
N.Y. Journal July 5 (1779), p. 2.
N.Y. Packet Feb. 14 (1782), p. 2.
N.J. Gaz. June 23 (1779), p. 4; Dec. 15 (1779), p. 2.
Pa. Journal Aug. 13 (1777), p. 1; Dec. 11 (1782), p. 3.
Gaz. of St. of S.C. Sept. 3 (1783), p. 3.
(Charl.) *Royal Gaz.* Mar. 3/7 (1781), p. 3.

February—March

Britain Abandons the War. On February 27 a motion in the House of Commons against further prosecution of the war is carried by nineteen votes. In the face of King George's stubborn refusal to agree, a March 4 resolution in the Commons condemns as enemies to their country any who counsel or pursue continuation of the American war effort. On March 20 Lord North finally resigns and two days later the Marquess of Rockingham returns as prime minister after an absence of almost sixteen years (see below, August 1766). The new prime minister and the Secretary of State for the Colonies, the Earl of Shelburne, are ready to recognize America's independence.

N.Hamp. Gaz. May 18, p. 3; June 1, p. 1.
Indep. Chron. May 16, pp. 1-6; Apr. 4, p. 2.
Prov. Gaz. Apr. 6, pp. 1-3.
Conn. Courant Apr. 9, p. 1; Apr. 16, pp. 1-2; Apr. 23, p. 2; Apr. 30, pp. 1-2; May 14, pp. 2, 3; May 21, pp. 1-2; May 28, pp. 1-2.
N.J. Gaz. May 8, p. 3; May 15, p. 2.

Pa. Journal May 8, pp. 1, 2, 3, 4; May 11, p. 2.
Va. Gaz. or Amer. Adv. May 18, pp. 1-2; May 25, pp. 2, 3.
Royal Ga. Gaz. May 30, pp. 1, 4.

April 9-12

Battle of the Saints. The loss at Yorktown is only one piece of bad news for the British in the winter of 1781-1782. St. Eustatius and St. Martin's are recaptured by the French in late November 1781; earlier in the same year (May 1781) Pensacola in West Florida is lost to the Spanish; the strategically important western Mediterranean island of Minorca falls to the French on February 5, 1782; the ubiquitous de Grasse takes the West Indian islands of St. Kitts (St. Christopher's) and Nevis in February 1782; and an expected Spanish-French assault on Jamaica is dreaded for its possible result and disruption of British trade. British prospects and the circumstances of any peace negotiations are dramatically altered in April when Admiral Rodney defeats de Grasse off Les Saintes, a group of French islands northwest of Martinique in the West Indies. With Jamaica safe and Gibralter holding out despite a Spanish distraction regarding its return, and even with the British position in India still precarious given French incursions, the Battle of the Saints enables the British to bargain for peace from a position of relative strength at the upcoming Paris negotiations.

Prov. Gaz. Mar. 9, p. 3; Mar. 23, p. 3; Mar. 30, pp. 2-3.
Conn. Courant Dec. 11 (1781), p. 3; Jan. 15, pp. 2-3; Jan. 22, p. 1; Apr. 2, p. 2; May 7, p. 3; May 21, p. 2; May 28, p. 2; June 11, pp. 1, 2; July 2, pp. 1-2; Dec. 10, pp. 2-3; Dec. 24, p. 3.
(N.Y.) *Royal Gaz.* June 1, pp. 1-2.
N.Y. Packet Jan. 17, p. 3.
Pa. Journal June 13 (1781), p. 3; July 18 (1781), pp. 1-2; July 21 (1781), p. 1; May 15, p. 3; May 18, p. 3; May 29, pp. 2, 3.
Md. Gaz. Mar. 21, p. 2.
Va. Gaz. or Amer. Adv. Jan. 26, p. 3; Feb. 9, p. 3; Aug. 3, p. 3.
Royal Ga. Gaz. May 23, p. 1; May 30, p. 4; June 6, pp. 1, 4.

April 19

Netherlands Recognizes American Independence. John Adams is received as minister plenipotentiary of the United States (April 22) by Their High Mightinesses the States General of the Netherlands after a year's worth of doughty diplomacy. A very important Dutch loan (June 11) and the prospect for more aid for America's financial condition is followed by a treaty of commerce and friendship (October 8) between the two countries.

N.Hamp. Gaz. May 25, p. 2.
Prov. Gaz. Oct. 20 (1781), pp. 1-2; Oct. 19, pp. 1-2; Feb. 8 (1783), p. 3.
Conn. Courant May 28, p. 3; Aug. 6, p. 2; Aug. 20, p. 3.
N.Y. Packet Feb. 14, p. 3.
N.J. Gaz. June 5, p. 2; Feb. 26 (1783), pp. 1-2; Mar. 5 (1783), pp. 2-3.
Pa. Journal June 22, p. 3.
Md. Gaz. July 25, p. 2.
Va. Gaz. or Amer. Adv. Aug. 3, p. 2.
Va. Gaz. and Week. Adv. Sept. 28, pp. 2-3; Dec. 21, pp. 1-2; Dec. 28, pp. 1-2.

May 5

Carleton Arrives in New York City. Named to succeed Clinton and commissioned to open peace talks with the Americans, if possible, General Carleton reaches his new command. His orders include plans for the evacuation of Savannah, Charleston, and New York City, and a redeployment of British troops to meet the French and Spanish threat, especially in the West Indies. Carleton's peace efforts, and primary design of cracking the French-American alliance, are rebuffed – real negotiations are to proceed in Europe – while his announced intentions regarding a British farewell to United States territory are welcomed.

Conn. Courant May 21, p. 3; June 18, p. 2; Aug. 13, p. 3; Dec. 3, p. 3; Dec. 24, pp. 1-2.
Pa. Journal May 11, p. 2.
Va. Gaz. or Amer. Adv. May 25, pp. 2, 3.
Va. Gaz. and Week. Adv. Dec. 21, p. 3.

July 1

Shelburne Succeeds Rockingham. Rockingham's death results politically in the emergence of the Earl of Shelburne as the new prime minister.

Conn. Courant Sept. 10, p. 3; Sept. 17, pp. 1-2, 3; Sept. 24, pp. 1-2; Nov. 5, p. 3.
Pa. Journal Sept. 11, p. 2; Nov. 6, p. 1.

July 11

Evacuation of Savannah. Savannah is evacuated by the British.

Indep. Chron. Sept. 19, p. 3.
Prov. Gaz. Aug. 17, p. 2.
Conn. Courant Aug. 13, p. 2; Aug. 27, p. 2; Sept. 24, p. 4.
Pa. Journal Aug. 3, p. 3.
Va. Gaz. or Amer. Adv. Aug. 3, p. 3.
(Charl.) Royal Gaz. July 24/27, p. 3.

October 4

American Peace Commissioners Tied to French Designs. The Continental Congress reiterates its earlier pronouncements that its negotiators are to proceed solely with the advice and under the direction of the French, except on the matter of American independence. Various localities and states subscribe to the same naive sentiments (1782-1783). Jay, Franklin, and Adams wisely disregard the intent of Congress's admonitions (see below, November 30).

N. Hamp. Gaz. June 29, p. 2.
Prov. Gaz. Oct. 26, p. 2.
Conn. Courant July 16, p. 3; Oct. 22, pp. 2-3; Oct. 29, p. 3; Feb. 18 (1783), p. 2.
N.J. Gaz. May 29, pp. 2-3.

November 1

Rhode Island Vetoes an American Trade Duty. Exercising its Confederation veto, the Rhode Island General Assembly votes down any Congressional power to collect a five per cent *ad valorem* tax on American imports. The authority is first requested by Congress in February 1781. Contrary-minded Little Rhody's action is indicative of the strong element of localism, or states' rights, alive and well in early America.

Indep. Chron. Jan 9 (1783), p. 3.
Prov. Gaz. Mar. 2, p. 1; Mar. 9, p. 4; Mar. 16, pp. 1, 2; Mar. 23, pp. 1, 2; Mar. 30, pp. 1, 2; Apr. 6, p. 3; Apr. 13, pp. 1-2, 4; Apr. 20, pp. 1-2; Apr. 27, pp. 1-2; July 20, p. 1; Aug. 3, pp. 1-2; Aug. 10, pp. 1-2; Aug. 17, p. 1; Aug. 24, p. 2; Sept. 21, pp. 1-2; Oct. 19, supplement, p. 1; Oct. 26, pp. 1-2, 3; Nov. 2, p. 3; Nov. 9, p. 2; Dec. 21, p. 1; Dec. 28, pp. 1-2; Jan. 4 (1783), pp. 1-2; Jan. 11 (1783), pp. 1-2; Jan. 18 (1783), pp. 1-2, 3; Feb. 1 (1783), pp. 1-2; Feb. 8 (1783), pp. 2-3, 4; Feb. 15 (1783), p. 2; Feb. 22 (1783), p. 2; June 21 (1783), pp. 1-2, 4; June 28 (1783), pp. 1-2, 4; Sept. 27 (1783), p. 3; Oct. 11 (1783), pp. 1, 3.
Conn. Courant Oct. 22, pp. 1-2; Dec. 10, p. 1; Jan. 7 (1783), p. 3; Mar. 11 (1783), pp. 2-3; June 24 (1783), p. 3; Aug. 5 (1783), pp. 2, 3.
N.Y. Packet July 4, pp. 1-2.
N.J. Gaz. Mar. 21 (1781), p. 2; July 25 (1781), p. 4; July 9 (1783), p. 1.
Pa. Journal Nov. 20, pp. 2-3; June 11 (1783), p. 3.
Md. Gaz. July 18, p. 1.
Gaz. of St. of Ga. June 19 (1783), pp. 1, 4.

November 10

Chillicothe. General George Rogers Clark leads a force of riflemen against the Shawnee in one of the last actions of the war. Chillicothe and five other Indian towns are destroyed partly in response to American military disasters in the

Sandusky Valley (Ohio) on June 4 and 5, and the Lower Blue Licks (Kentucky) on August 19, in which latter battle Daniel Boone serves well. Although Detroit, the ultimate American objective in the West, is not gained, Clark's exploits in this area are responsible, at least in part, for its cession to the United States by the Treaty of Paris (see below, November 30).

Conn. Courant Aug. 13, p. 2; Nov. 19, p. 2; Jan. 21 (1783), p. 2.
Va. Gaz. or Amer. Adv. July 20, p. 3; Aug. 3, p. 3.

November 30

The Treaty of Paris. The preliminary articles of peace are signed in Paris after two months of formal, private talks between Great Britain and the United States. The prior recognition of American independence is a diplomatic victory for the principal American negotiators, John Jay and Benjamin Franklin. (Of the three other American diplomats appointed by Congress, John Adams arrives from the Netherlands in late October (see above, April 19), Henry Laurens in November, after his short stay in the Tower of London in October-December 1780 (see below, Laurens in additional citations), and Thomas Jefferson never does travel to Europe.) The American cause is aided by the death in July of the Marquess of Rockingham and the new Shelburne ministry's preoccupation with the diplomatic isolation of France. Spanish and French desires to continue the war in search of conquests at British expense — and, by the way, to keep the United States weak — are effectively circumvented by the American delegates' disregard of Congressional instructions to govern themselves wholly in the negotiations by French advice.

The independent Unites States' boundaries are fixed as the Mississippi River on the west and Florida (which eventually goes to Spain from Britain) and the southernmost portions of present-day Alabama, Mississippi, and Louisiana on the south. The British agree (but fail) to evacuate their Great Lakes forts although the American northern boundary remains somewhat fuzzy — owing much to inferior maps and geographical knowledge. New Englanders are pleased by a provision allowing them to fish off Newfoundland and to land at uninhabited spots in order to dry and cure their catch. Congress agrees not to impede collection of American debts owed to British subjects and to "recommend" a full restoration of loyalist losses.

Britain regains its West Indian islands from France, except for Tobago; France regains trad-

ing posts in India and two North Atlantic islands; Spain acquires both East and West Florida and keeps conquered Minorca; Holland is left with a big bill.

Indep. Chron. Nov. 21, p. 1; Feb. 20 (1783), p. 3; Mar. 6 (1783), p. 3; Mar. 13 (1783), pp. 1-3.
Prov. Gaz. Apr. 12 (1783), p. 2.
Conn. Courant Aug. 20, p. 2; Sept. 10, pp. 1-2; Nov. 19, p. 2; Dec. 10, p. 4; Dec. 24, p. 1; Dec. 31, p. 3; Jan. 7 (1783), p. 2; Feb. 4 (1783), pp. 1, 2; Feb. 18 (1783), p. 2; Feb. 25 (1783), p. 2; Mar. 4 (1783), p. 2; Mar. 18 (1783), pp. 2-3; Mar. 15 (*sic*) (1783), pp. 1-2, 3; Apr. 1 (1783), p. 3; Apr. 8 (1783), p. 2.
(N.Y.) *Royal Gaz.* Mar. 26 (1783), p. 1.
N.Y. Packet May 9, p. 3; May 16, p. 3; Oct. 24, p. 3; Jan. 30 (1783), p. 3; Feb. 20 (1783), p. 2.
Pa. Journal Oct. 26, p. 2; Oct. 30, p. 3; Nov. 9, p. 2; Jan. 11 (1783), p. 2; Jan. 25 (1783), pp. 2-3; Feb. 12 (1783), p. 3; Feb. 15 (1783), p. 1; Mar. 8 (1783), p. 2; Mar. 15 (1783), p. 3.
Va. Gaz. or Amer. Adv. Aug. 3, p. 2; Feb. 22 (1783), p. 3; Mar. 22 (1783), p. 3.
Va. Gaz. and Week. Adv. Aug. 24, p. 3; Oct. 12, p. 3.
Royal Ga. Gaz. May 30, pp. 1-2.
Gaz. of St. of Ga. Mar. 17, extraordinary, p. 1.

December 14

Evacuation of Charleston. Charleston is evacuated by the British.

N. Hamp. Gaz. Jan. 25 (1783), p. 3.
Indep. Chron. Dec. 26, p. 3.
Conn. Courant Jan. 7 (1783), p. 3; Jan. 21 (1783), p. 3; Feb. 4 (1783), p. 2; May 20 (1783), p. 2.
(N.Y.) *Royal Gaz.* Jan. 4 (1783), p. 2.
N.Y. Packet Jan. 30 (1783), p. 2.
N.J. Gaz. Jan. 8 (1783), p. 3.
Pa. Journal Jan. 18 (1783), p. 3.
Va. Gaz. or Amer. Adv. Jan. 11 (1783), p. 3.
Va. Gaz. and Week. Adv. Dec. 7, p. 3; Dec. 28, p. 3.

December 30

Settlement of the Connecticut-Pennsylvania Land Controversy. Convening in Trenton, New Jersey, from November 12 to December 30, the five commissioners appointed by the Continental Congress decide in Pennsylvania's favor in the Susquehannah Company conflict (see above, 1774). The ruling regards jurisdictional rights, though, and disputes over private land rights within Pennsylvania's Wyoming Valley continue for a number of years.

Prov. Gaz. Oct. 5, p. 3.
Conn. Courant Feb. 5, p. 2; Oct. 1, p. 2; Oct. 8, p. 3; Dec. 3, p. 3; Dec. 31, p. 3; Jan. 14 (1783), p. 2; Jan. 28 (1783), p. 1.
N.J. Gaz. Nov. 20, p. 3; Jan. 1 (1783), p. 3.
Pa. Journal Dec. 18, p. 3; Jan. 4 (1783), p. 3; Jan. 11 (1783), p. 3; Feb. 1 (1783), p. 2.
Gaz. of St. of Ga. Mar. 6 (1783), p. 4.

Army, Continental
Congress, not states, responsible for back pay
Conn. Courant Nov. 5, p. 2.

Arnold, Benedict
Great friends with King George
Conn. Courant May 7, p. 3.
Rumored execution of in London — for horse-stealing
Prov. Gaz. July 20, p. 2.

Chatham, William Pitt (Earl of)
Honored in memoriam
Pa. Journal May 25, p. 3.

Colleges
Washington College, Maryland, established
Pa. Journal Dec. 21, pp. 2-3.

Franklin, Benjamin
Prints bogus *Independent Chronicle* in Europe, contains British atrocities
Conn. Courant Jan. 14 (1783), p. 1.
N.J. Gaz. Dec. 18, p. 1.

Horseracing
Ad for Annapolis
Md. Gaz. Oct. 17, p. 2.

Ireland
Notice of Irish Declaration of Rights
Conn. Courant Aug. 13, pp. 1-2.

July 4th Celebration
New London
Prov. Gaz. July 13, p. 3.

Navy, Continental
Favored for American world commerce
Prov. Gaz. Sept. 14, pp. 1-2.

Peace
Caution expressed as to immediate
Indep. Chron. May 30. p. 3.

Population
Comparative New Jersey: 1737-38; 1745; 1781
N.J. Gaz. Feb. 27, p. 3.

Purple Heart
Awarded for "singular meritorious action"
Va. Gaz. and Week. Adv. Sept. 14, p. 3.

Religious Freedom
Essay against official establishment of religion
N.Hamp. Gaz. July 13, pp. 1-2.

Slaves
British said to arm in Charleston
Conn. Courant May 7, p. 2.
British said to dance with in Charleston
N.Hamp. Gaz. Apr. 27, p. 3.
Manumission debated
Va. Gaz. and Week. Adv. Aug. 31, p. 1; Sept. 14, p. 1.
Observations on slavery
Pa. Journal Aug. 7, p. 1.
Virginia act for recovery of property lost during war
Va. Gaz. or Amer. Adv. Aug. 3, p. 1.

Tories
Address to King George, in England
Prov. Gaz. Aug. 24, pp. 1, 4.

War Atrocities
British dig up Huntington, New York graveyard, while fortifying area
Va. Gaz. and Week. Adv. Dec. 21, p. 3.
By Americans in evacuated Wilmington, North Carolina
(Charl.) *Royal Gaz.* Feb. 16/20, p. 3.
Franklin prints European issue of bogus *Independent Chronicle*, includes stories of British
Conn. Courant Jan. 14 (1783), p. 1.
N.J. Gaz. Dec. 18, p. 1.

Western Lands
Observation that all states should own
Prov. Gaz. Nov. 30, p. 1.

American Loyalists. The remainder of approximately 80,000 loyalists who leave the United States during the American Revolution are harassed out of the country, primarily to Nova Scotia in Canada, by the prospect of British withdrawal from the States. Their flight is also recommended by the increasing clamor in localities and states for (a) further confiscation of Tory property and (b) a prohibition against the re-entry of any "enemies" of the United States within specific local or state boundaries.

N.Hamp. Gaz. Aug. 5 (1780), p. 2; May 11 (1782), p. 1; July 26 (1783), p. 1.
Prov. Gaz. Aug. 24 (1782), pp. 1, 4.
Conn. Courant Dec. 24 (1782), p. 2; Jan. 14 (1783), p. 2; May 6 (1783), p. 3; Aug. 12 (1783), p. 3; Aug. 26 (1783), p. 2.
(N.Y.) *Royal Gaz.* Mar. 29 (1783), p. 1.
N.J. Gaz. Jan. 20 (1779), pp. 1-2; Mar. 15 (1780), p. 3; Apr. 23 (1783), p. 3.
Pa. Journal Oct. 25 (1780), p. 3; Jan. 29 (1783), p. 2; June 7 (1783), p. 3; June 28 (1783), p. 2; July 2 (1783), p. 2; July 12 (1783), p. 3; July 23 (1783), p. 2; Oct. 22 (1783), p. 2; Oct. 29 (1783), p. 2; Nov. 8 (1783), p. 1.
Md. Gaz. Feb. 11 (1780), pp. 1-4; Feb. 18 (1780), pp. 1-4; Feb. 25 (1780), pp. 1-4; Mar. 3 (1780), pp. 1-3; Mar. 10 (1780), pp. 1-4; Apr. 21 (1780), pp. 3-4; Apr. 28 (1780), pp. 1-2.
Va. Gaz. (Dixon and Nicolson) July 3 (1779), p. 3; July 19 (1780), pp. 2-3.
S.C. and A.G. Gaz. Feb. 21 (1781), p. 3.
(Charl.) *Royal Gaz.* July 10/13 (1782), pp. 1-3.
Gaz. of St. of S.C. Oct. 15 (1783), p. 1.
S.C. Gaz. and Gen. Adv. July 16 (1783), pp. 3-4.
Royal Ga. Gaz. Jan. 3 (1782), p. 2.
Gaz. of St. of Ga. May 8 (1783), pp. 2, 3; Oct. 9 (1783), pp. 2-3.

January 20

Peace Proceeds Between Great Britain, France, and Spain. Great Britain exchanges preliminary peace treaty signings at Versailles with France and Spain.

Prov. Gaz. Apr. 19, pp. 1-2.
Conn. Courant Apr. 1, p. 3; Apr. 8, pp. 2-3; May 6, pp. 1-2.
Pa. Journal Apr. 12, pp. 1-2.

March 15

Officers Threaten Reactions to Congressional Neglect. Angered by Congress's seeming insensitivity to their complaints about back pay, clothing and food accounts, and an unfulfilled three-year-old promise for half-pay for life for incapacitated and retired officers; Continental officers hint at some kind of revolt or action against the American government. Washington's appearance at a March 15 gathering in New-

burgh, New York, headquarters of the American army, and his words against the proceedings are followed by a repudiation of the offensive sentiments and implications by the officers.

Congress's reaction is to change a 1780 promise of half-pay for life for officers to five years full pay. Americans, none too keen on officers' pensions (too aristocratic), are rankled by the new settlement. Indeed it is not until 1908 that Continental Army claims for pay and pensions — $70,000,000. worth — are completely ended.

Prov. Gaz. Apr. 26, pp. 1-2, 4.
Conn. Courant Apr. 15, pp. 1-2, 3, 4; May 13, p. 3; June 3, pp. 1-2; June 24, p. 1; Aug. 12, pp. 1-2; Aug. 19, pp. 1-2; Aug. 26, p. 3; Sept. 2, pp. 1, 2, 3, 4; Sept. 9, pp. 3, 4.
Gaz. of St. of S.C. Aug. 6, p. 2.
S.C. Gaz. and Gen. Adv. May 10, pp. 3-4; May 13, pp. 3-4; June 21, p. 4.
Gaz. of St. of Ga. July 3, p. 3.

April 15

Congress Ratifies the Provisional Treaty. On April 11, Congress formally proclaims an end to hostile actions, one month after receiving a copy of the preliminary peace treaty (March 12) and just over two months after King George III issues his own proclamation to cease hostilities (February 4). Four days later (April 15) Congress approves the handiwork of the Paris commissioners. Great Britain ratifies the preliminary articles on August 6.

N.Hamp. Gaz. May 3, p. 3; June 7, p. 3.
Indep. Chron. Mar. 20, p. 3; May 16, p. 3.
Prov. Gaz. Apr. 26, p. 3; May 24, p. 1.
Conn. Courant Apr. 15, p. 3; Apr. 22, pp. 2, 3; Apr. 29, p. 3; May 6, p. 3.
(N.Y.) *Royal Gaz.* Mar. 22, pp. 2-3; Mar. 26, p. 3.
N.J. Gaz. Mar. 26, p. 3; Apr. 16, p. 3.
Pa. Journal Apr. 2, p. 3; Apr. 12, pp. 1, 3; Apr. 19, p. 2.
Va. Gaz. or Amer. Adv. Apr. 5, p. 3; Apr. 12, p. 3.
S.C. Gaz. and Gen. Adv. Apr. 12, p. 4; Apr. 16, p. 1; Apr. 26, p. 4.
Gaz. of St. of Ga. Apr. 17, p. 2; May 1, pp. 1, 2-3, 4; May 8, pp. 2, 3.

June

Soldiers March on Philadelphia — and the Continental Army Melts Away. The perennial soldier discontents result in a march on Philadelphia by a small group that eventually totals nearly 300. On June 21, a demonstration is held before Independence Hall, meeting-place of the Pennsylvania government as well as the United States Congress. Within a few days the latter is meeting in Princeton, and the demonstrators are gone. In spite of attempted Congressional formalities regarding furloughs, pay, and regular discharges, the Continental Army rapidly disappears as the soldiers return home to their plows by merely walking away from camp.

N.Hamp. Gaz. Aug. 2, p. 2; Aug. 9, p. 1; Aug. 23, p. 1.
Prov. Gaz. July 12, p. 3; Aug. 9, pp. 1-2; Oct. 11, p. 2.
Conn. Courant July 15, pp. 1, 2; July 22, pp. 2, 3; July 29, pp. 2-3.
N.J. Gaz. July 16, pp. 1-2.
Pa. Journal June 28, pp. 2-3; July 2, p. 3; July 12, pp. 1-2, 3.
Va. Gaz. or Amer. Adv. July 12, p. 2; July 19, p. 2.
S.C. Gaz. and Gen. Adv. July 19, p. 4.
Gaz. of St. of Ga. Nov. 27, p. 3.
Broadside: June 24.

July 2

British-American Trade. A British order-in-council dampens the enthusiasm building for renewed (free) trade between Great Britain and its erstwhile colonies. The condition for commerce between the Americans and the British West Indies is that ships engaged in the trade, in either direction, must be British-built and British-owned. Despite this setback, the end of the war gives new life to old habits, and Americans are soon deeply involved in trade with Great Britain.

N.Hamp. Gaz. June 7, p. 3.
Conn. Courant May 20, p. 2; July 8, pp. 1-2; Aug. 19, p. 2.
Pa. Journal May 7, p. 3; May 10, p. 3; June 4, p. 3; June 18, p. 1; July 17, pp. 1-2; Aug. 20, pp. 2, 3; Sept. 13, p. 3; Oct. 4, p. 3; Oct. 15, p. 3; Oct. 25, p. 2; Oct. 29, p. 3; Nov. 15, p. 3; [Dec. 3], supplement, p. 1; Dec. 6, pp. 2, 3; Dec. 13, p. 2.

September 3

Treaty of Paris. The definitive treaty, the same as the preliminary treaty, is signed officially in Paris between the United States and Great Britain and, on the same day, in Versailles between Britain and France and Spain. In turn Congress ratifies the final treaty for the United States on January 14, 1784; the ratifications are exchanged on May 12, 1784.

Indep. Chron. Jan. 22 (1784), p. 3; Feb. 12 (1784), p. 3.
Pa. Journal Sept. 10, p. 2; Nov. 5, p. 3; Nov. 8, p. 2; Dec. 3, p. 1; Jan. 21 (1784), pp. 2-3.
Va. Gaz. or Amer. Adv. Jan. 17 (1784), p. 2; Jan. 31 (1784), pp. 2-3; Feb. 7 (1784), p. 3; Feb. 21 (1784), p. 2.
Va. Gaz. or Indep. Chron. Nov. 22, pp. 2, 3.
Gaz. of St. of Ga. Nov. 20, p. 2; Dec. 25, p. 1; Jan. 8 (1784), p. 2; Jan. 15 (1784), pp. 1, 4; Jan. 22 (1784), pp. 2-3; Jan. 29 (1784), p. 3.

October 21

Congress Chooses Capitals. The search for a new capital prompts eager offers from Esopus (Kingston), New York; Annapolis; Williamsburg; and New Jersey, which offers space anywhere within the state as well as the necessary building funds. Philadelphia quietly invites Congress to return there. On October 21, Congress votes to have alternating capitals: one is to be built near Lamberton (Lambertville), New Jersey, northwest of Trenton on the Delaware River; the other on the Potomac River near Georgetown, Maryland. Until their completion, the capital is to alternate between Trenton and Annapolis.

Prov. Gaz. Sept. 27, pp. 1-2.
Conn. Courant July 8, p. 2; Aug. 19, p. 3.
Pa. Journal June 25, p. 3; Aug. 9, p. 3; Sept. 3, p. 3; Oct. 11, p. 3; Oct. 25, p. 3.
Va. Gaz. or Amer. Adv. Oct. 25, p. 2; Nov. 1, p. 2; Nov. 8, p. 3.

November 25

British Evacuation of New York City. The British leave the city on November 25 and Staten Island and Long Island on December 4. The final British offensive is a greased flag pole — and a cut flag halliard — at Fort George which causes a short delay before the American flag can be raised.

Indep. Chron. Dec. 18, p. 3.
Prov. Gaz. Dec. 6, pp. 2-3; Dec. 13, pp. 1-2.
Conn. Courant June 3, p. 3; Aug. 19, p. 3; Sept. 9, p. 3.
Pa. Journal Nov. 29, pp. 2-3; Dec. 3, p. 3.
Va. Gaz. or Amer. Adv. Dec. 13, p. 2.
Gaz. of St. of S.C. Feb. 12 (1784), p. 2.
Gaz. of St. of Ga. Jan. 1 (1784), p. 2; Jan. 8 (1784), p. 1.

December 4

Washington Begins to Take His Leave. Washington takes leave of his officers at Fraunces Tavern in New York City. Earlier, from his headquarters at Rocky Hill, New Jersey, Washington pens his Farewell Orders to the Armies of the United States (November 2).

Indep. Chron. Dec. 18, p. 3.
Pa. Journal Nov. 5, p. 3; Dec. 13, p. 3.
Va. Gaz. or Indep. Chron. Nov. 15, p. 2.
Gaz. of St. of S.C. Jan. 1 (1784), p. 2.
Gaz. of St. of Ga. Nov. 27, p. 4.

By His EXCELLENCY

Elias Boudinot, Efquire,

Prefident of the United States in Congrefs Affembled.

A   PROCLAMATION.

WHEREAS a body of armed Soldiers in the fervice of the United States, and quartered in the Barracks of this City, having mutinoufly renounced their obedience to their Officers, did, on Saturday the Twenty-Firft Day of this inftant, proceed, under the direction of their Serjeants, in a hoftile and threatning manner, to the Place in which Congrefs were affembled, and did furround the fame with Guards: And whereas Congrefs in confequence thereof, did on the fame Day, refolve "That the Prefident and Supreme Executive Council of this State "fhould be informed, that the authority of the United States having been, that Day, groffly infulted by the "diforderly and menacing appearance of a body of armed Soldiers, about the Place within which Congrefs were affem- "bled; and that the Peace of this City being endangered by the mutinous Difpofition of the faid Troops then in the "Barracks; it was, in the Opinion of Congrefs, neceffary, that effectual Meafures fhould be immediately taken for "fupporting the public Authority:" And alfo whereas Congrefs did at the fame Time appoint a Committee to con- fer with the faid Prefident and Supreme Executive Council on the practicability of carrying the faid Refolution in o due effect: And alfo whereas the faid Committee have reported to me, that they have not received fatisfactory Affurances for expecting adequate and prompt exertions of this State for fupporting the Dignity of the fœderal Government: And alfo whereas the faid Soldiers ftill continue in a ftate of open Mutiny and Revolt, fo that the Dignity and Authority of the United States would be conftantly expofed to a repetition of Infult, while Congrefs fhall continue to fit in this City. I do therefore, by and with the Advice of the faid Committee, and according to the Powers and Authorities in me veft- ed for this Purpofe, hereby fummon the honourabe the Delegates compofing the Congrefs of the United States, and every of them, to meet in Congrefs on Thurfday the Twenty-Sixth Day of June inftant, at Princeton, in the ftate of New-Jerfey, in order that further and more effectual Meafures may be taken for fuppreffing the prefent Revolt, and maintaining the Dignity and Authority of the United States, of which all Officers of the United States, civil and military, and all others whom it may concern, are defired to take Notice and govern themfelves accordingly.

GIVEN under my Hand and Seal at Philadelphia, in the ftate of Pennfylvania, this Twenty-Fourth Day of June, in the Year of Our Lord One Thoufand Seven Hundred and Eighty-Three, and of the Sovereignty and Inde- pendence, the feventh.

ELIAS BOUDINOT.

Atteft.

SAMUEL STERETT, *Private Secretary.*

See p. 106, June,   Broadside: June 24.

December 23

Washington Resigns His Commission. Prior to his departure for Mount Vernon (and a short-lived retirement from public life), General George Washington pauses at Annapolis, present seat of the Continental Congress, to return his commission: ". . . the great events on which my resignation depended having at length taken place."

Indep. Chron. Jan. 22 (1784), p. 3.
N.J. Gaz. Dec. 9, p. 3; Dec. 16, p. 2.
Md. Gaz. Dec. 25, p. 2.
Gaz. of St. of Ga. Feb. 5 (1784), p. 2.

Army, Continental
Congressional propositions for settlement of a western state (Ohio area) by individuals of *Gaz. of St. of Ga.* Sept. 4, p. 1.

Arnold, Benedict
Refuses Bermuda governorship: fearful of New Englanders
Conn. Courant July 29, p. 3.

Arnold, Jonathan (Connecticut sergeant)
Connecticut General Assembly allows to change name to Stuben
Conn. Courant Feb. 11, p. 3.
N.Y. Packet Feb. 27, p. 3.

Colleges
Dickinson, Pennsylvania, established
Pa. Journal Sept. 6, pp. 2-3.
Rhode Island College commencement
Prov. Gaz. Sept. 6, p. 3.
Washington College first commencement
Pa. Journal July 17, p. 1; July 23, pp. 1-2.

Copyright Laws
Connecticut
Conn. Courant Feb. 25, p. 1.
New Hampshire
N.J. Gaz. Dec. 16, p. 3.
Pennsylvania
Pa. Journal Nov. 19, p. 1.

Cowboy
Long Island, wins duel
Conn. Courant Aug. 5, p. 3.

Crime
Augusta grand jury presentments
Gaz. of St. of Ga. Apr. 10, p. 2.

Dueling
Sentiments against
Conn. Courant Aug. 12, p. 4.

Herschel, William (English astronomer)
Discovers new planet [Uranus], Mar. 13, 1781
Indep. Chron. Dec. 18, p. 2; Jan. 22 (1784), p. 3.

Humor
Lampoon: British troops, cannon auctioned off
Conn. Courant Aug. 19, p. 4.

Lampoon of ad for Anglican minister, Bristol, Virginia
Va. Gaz. or Indep. Chron. Nov. 15, p. 3; Nov. 22, p. 1.
Lampoon of attack on George Washington, Congress, American independence
Conn. Courant Aug. 19, p. 2.
Lampoon of Fairfax, Virginia, and Torrington, Connecticut, resolves against Congressional power
Conn. Courant Aug. 5, p. 2.

Independence, State
Comments against, for union
S.C. Gaz. and Gen. Adv. April 12, p. 3.

Indians
Congressional proclamation against trespass on their land
Pa. Journal Oct. 15, p. 3.

July 4th Celebration
Boston: Oration by Dr. John Warren
Indep. Chron. Dec. 4, pp. 1-2; Dec. 12, pp. 1-2.
Charleston
S.C. Gaz. and Gen. Adv. July 5, p. 4.

Mad Dog
Recipe for bite of
Prov. Gaz. July 19, p. 3.

New Hampshire
Revised constitution considered
N.Hamp. Gaz. May 10, p. 3; June 28, pp. 1-2; Aug. 30, pp. 1-2; Oct. 4, p. 1; Oct. 25, p. 1.

New York Flying Machines
Ad for
Pa. Journal Aug. 9, p. 4.

Newspapers
Observation on freedom of press
Prov. Gaz. Jan. 25, p. 3.

Philadelphia
Incorporated
Pa. Journal Sept. 10, p. 3.

Poetry
"On Peace"
Prov. Gaz. Apr. 19, p. 4.

"The Tory's Soliloquy"
Gaz. of St. of S.C. Jan. 8 (1784), p. 3.

Prisoners of War
In New York: American and French noted, described
(N.Y.) *Royal Gaz.* Mar. 5, p. 3.

Slaves
Anti-slavery expressions
Prov. Gaz. Sept. 20, p. 1; Dec. 20, p. 1.
Observations on slavery: "all created equal"
Prov. Gaz. Aug. 30, p. 1.
Rhode Island act against slavery
Prov. Gaz. Jan. 10 (1784), p. 3.
Sales of
Va. Gaz. or Indep. Chron. Nov. 15, pp. 3-4.
South Carolina act against holding, other property not true owner of
S.C. Gaz. and Gen. Adv. Mar. 25, p. 1.

Snakes
Battle of black and rattler attracts Baltimore spectators
Conn. Courant July 15, p. 3.

Society of the Cincinnati (American officers)
Establishment of
Gaz. of St. of S.C. Oct. 1, p. 3; Oct. 8, p. 3; Oct. 15, p. 3.

Suicide
Accomplished
Conn. Courant July 15, p. 3.
Observations on
Indep. Chron. Jan. 30, pp. 1-2; Mar. 20, p. 1.

Theater
Observations against
Pa. Journal Nov. 12, p. 3; Nov. 15, p. 3.

Warning
To Americans: must pay French back
(N.Y.) *Royal Gaz.* Feb. 2, p. 2.

Washington, George
Birthday celebrated in Milton
Indep. Chron. Feb. 13, p. 3.
"Circular Letter to the Governors of All the States" (June 8)
Conn. Courant Sept. 9, pp. 1-2.
Congress proposes equestrian statue of
Prov. Gaz. Sept. 20, p. 3.

INDEX

How to Use the Index

The following name and subject index covers both the Descriptive Chronology and the Topical Chronology. The key to its use is in understanding the form of the *citations*. There are basically two types: 1) citations to the dates in the Descriptive Chronology, and 2) citations to the dates in the Topical Chronology. Citations are in *no* case to pages in the text.

1) **Descriptive Chronology Citations.** Each of these begins with a two digit number which indicates the year in the Descriptive Chronology where the item referred to may be found: e.g., 65 = 1765, 66 = 1766, etc. If the year is followed by no other punctuation, letters, or numbers, the citation is for an entry in the Descriptive Chronology which is similarly undated as to month and day(s): e.g., in the entry "Allen, Ethan – Vt. Statehood, 74;82," the "74" and "82" mean there are references to Vermont's statehood under entries in the Descriptive Chronology that begin, simply, "1774" and "1782." When the year is followed by punctuation, letters (see below on "Abbreviations"), and (sometimes) numbers, these latter parts of the citation refer to the month(s) and day(s) which mark the entries in the Descriptive Chronology: e.g., the entry "Adams, John – Braintree, Mass., protest against Stamp Act, 65:S-O" means the discussion referred to is found in the Descriptive Chronology of 1765 in the entry marked "September-October." Where there is simply a month abbreviation by itself, or a month and day abbreviation by itself, the year for this reference is the first one reading back to the left: e.g., in the entry "Adams, John – Paris peace negotiations, 82:O 4, N 30," the "N 30" is for the "November 30" 1782 entry in the Descriptive Chronology.

2) **Topical Chronology Citations.** These citations follow the same principle for indicating the year as do those for the Descriptive Chronology. They differ primarily in that the "T" after the year indicates that the reference is to the Topical Chronology: e.g., in the entry "Acadians, 64:T; 65:T," the citations mean there is an entry under Acadians in both the 1764 and 1765 Topical Chronology. Where there is a term in parentheses following the "T," e.g., "Adams, John – Nickerson, defense of, 73:T (Piracy)," the term in parentheses indicates the heading under which the entry in the Topical Chronology will be found. A "T" or a "T(——)" by itself has its year as the first one to its left.

Referring citations to the text. Citations may be referred back to the main text by simply following the dated running heads which indicated immediately where one is in either the Descriptive or the Topical Chronology. One note of caution: there will occasionally be more than one entry in the Descriptive Chronology for a given year with the same date: e.g., there are two entries for "September" 1765, one concerning Massachusetts, the following one concerning Rhode Island. The index does not discriminate between such multiple entries for the same date – usually they are back to back. So if a reference is not located under the first occurrence of a date, check immediately before or after this occurrence. This is particularly true for 1774, where there is a colony by colony series of entries for May – September on the reaction to the closing of the Port of Boston.

Abbreviations. Standard abbreviations are used throughout the index, and here it need only be noted that the months are: Ja, F, Mr, Ap, My, Je, Jl, Ag, S, O, N, D; N.Y.C. is New York City; and the abbreviations for the colonies/states are obvious.

SUBJECT INDEX

George III, alleged friendship with — 82:T
treason — 76:S 15; 80:S
Va., British command in — 81:Ja, Mr-My
Arnold, Jonathan (Conn. sergeant)
changes name to Stuben — 83:T
Arouet, François Marie.
See Voltaire
Articles of Confederation
adoption by Congress — 77:N 15
ratification — 81:Mr 1
Arts
See also
Hogarth
Music
Poetry
Peale
Theater
Society for the Promotion of Arts, Agriculture, and
Oeconomy in the Province of N.Y. — 64:D
Ashe, John (Gen.)
Battle of Briar Creek, Ga. — 79:Ja-Je
Asia
See also
China
India
America once part of — 66:T (Geography)
Assembly, Right of
asserted by Mass. provincial convention — 68:S 22-28
Astronomical Phenomena
Aurora Borealis — 70:T
comets — 69:T; 70:T
Mars, influence on earth — 67:T
Mercury, transit of — 69:T
meteor — 75:T
solar eclipse — 78:T
Venus, transit of — 68:T; 69:T; 71:T
Astronomy
orrery of Rittenhouse — 68:T (Orrery)
Uranus, discovery of by Herschel — 83:T (Herschel)
Atrocities
See War Atrocities
Augusta, Ga.
See also Battles
grand jury presentments — 83:T (Crime)
southern campaign, importance in — 81:My 22-Je 19
Aurora Borealis
See Astronomical Phenomena
Austria
League of Armed Neutrality — 80:Mr 9

B

Backus, Isaac
Baptists under Mass. state constitution — 79:T; 80:T
Baltimore, Md.
Congress moves to — 76:N-D
Intolerable Acts, reaction to — 74:My-S
non-importation — 69:Mr 30
snake fight — 83:T (Snakes)
Bank of North America — 81:D 31

Baptists
Mass. state constitution, effect of on — 79:T (Backus);
80:T (Backus)
N.C. — 71:Ja-Je
tax to aid Congregationalists, protest of — 73:T
Barbados, West Indies
successful implementation of Stamp Act — 65:D
Barbers
ad for — 77:T
Barre, Isaac (Col.)
champion of colonies — 70:F
Barry, John (Capt.)
exploits of — 81:T
Basking Ridge, N.J.
capture of Gen. Charles Lee — 76:D 13
Battles, Revolutionary War
For battles in other wars or between hostile parties
other than British or their allies and Americans, *see*
battle locations by name
Augusta, Ga. — 79:Ja-Je
Bennington, Vt. — 77:Ag 16, S
Bonhomme Richard v. HMS *Serapis* — 79:S 23-24
Boston Massacre — 70:Ja 13-19
Briar Creek, Ga. — 79:Ja-Je
Bunker (Breed's) Hill, Boston — 75:Je 17, Jl 3; 76:T
    (Theater)
Cahokia, Ill. — 78:Jl-Ag
Camden, S.C. — 80:Ag 16; 81:My 22-Je 19
Chad's Ford, Pa. — 77:S 11
Chambly, Que. — 75:Ag-D
Charleston, S.C. — 76:Je 28; 80:Ap-My
Chillicothe, O. — 82:N 10
Cowpens, N.C. — 81:Ja 17
Crown Point, N.Y. — 75:My 10-16
Danbury, Conn. — 77:Ap 25-28
Eutaw Springs, S.C. — 81:S 8
Fishing Creek, S.C. — 80:Ag 16
Fort Anne, N.Y. — 77:Jl 5
Fort Clinton, N.Y. — 77:O 3-16
Ft. Grandby, S.C. — 81:My 22-Je 19
Ft. Lafayette, N.Y. — 79:Jl 15
Ft. Mercer, N.J. — 77:O-N
Ft. Mifflin, Pa. — 77:O-N
Ft. Montgomery, N.Y. — 77:O 3-16
Ft. Motte, S.C. — 81:My 22-Je 19
Ft. Stanwix (Schuyler), N.Y. — 77:Ag 3-22
Ft. Sullivan, S.C. — 76:Je 28
Ft. Ticonderoga, N.Y. — 75:My 10-16; 77:Jl 5
Ft. Watson, S.C. — 81:My 22-Je 19
Freeman's Farm, N.Y. 77:S, O 7-17
Georgetown, S.C. — 81:My 22-Je 19
Germantown, Pa. — 77:O 4
Golden Hill, N.Y.C. — 70:Ja 13-19
Gosport, Va. — 79:My 10-24
Great Bridge, Va. — 75:D 9
Guilford Court House, N.C. — 81:Mr 15
Harlem Heights, N.Y. — 76:S 15
Hobkirk's Hill, S.C. — 81:Ap 25
Hubbardton, N.Y. — 77:Jl 15
Kaskaskia, Ill. — 78:Jl-Ag

Boston Massacre — 70:Mr 5

commemoration — 71:Mr 5; 73:T; 74:T; 75:T; 77:T; 80:T

last victim of dies — 80:T

prelude: Battle of Golden Hill — 70:Ja 13-19

trail of alleged participants in — 70:O 24-30

Warren, Joseph, address on by — 75:T

Boston Neck

fortification of — 74:S

Boston Port Act — 74:Ja-Mr, My, Je 1, My-Je, My-S

Boston Tea Party — 73:D 16, D-74:Mr; 73:D-74: Ja, Ja-Mr

Boston Town Meeting

American-British trade, vote to end — 74:My 13, My, My-S

circular letter invitation to Faneuil Hall convention and call to arms — 68:S 12-13

HMS *Romney*, request for removal of — 68:Je 10

salaries of officials from customs revenues, objection to — 72:O-N, N-73:F

Stamp Act, protest against — 64:My 24; 65:Ag 14-26

tea duty protest — 77:N 5-6, N:28

Townshend Acts, vote to renew non-importation as protest against — 67:O 28

Boswell, James — 77: 3-22

Botetourt, Norborne Berkeley, Baron de (Gov.)

dissolution of Virginia House of Burgesses — 69:My 16-18

Boudinot, Elias

presidency under Articles of Confederation — 81:Mr

Boundary Dispute and Settlement

See also Articles of Confederation

East and West Jersey — 74:T

N.H.-N.Y. — 65:T

N.Y.-N.J. — 69:T

N.C.-S.C. — 64:T

Ohio and Miss. Rivers as Quebec boundaries — 74:Je 22

Pa.-Md. settlement — 74:T

Proclamation of 1763 — 63:O 7

Treaty of Alliance — 77:D-78:Je

Treaty of Paris (1763) — 63:F 10

Treaty of Paris (1783) — 82:N 30

Vt., disputed jurisdiction over — 67:T (Vt.); 74; 76:My 15; 82

Va.: claims in Ohio River Valley — 74, Je 22; 81:Mr 1

Va.-Pa. dispute — 74

Wyoming Valley, Conn.-Pa. dispute over — 74; 82:D 30

Bounties

See Scalp Bounties

Braintree, Massachusetts

protest against Stamp Act — 65:S-O

Brandywine River

See Battles — Chad's Ford

Brant, Joseph (Mohawk chieftan) — 77:Ag 3-22; 78:My-N; 79:Ag-S

Brest, France

Jones takes the *Drake* to — 78:Ap 23-24

Bribery

See Johnstone, George

Bridges

See also Battles — Moore's Creek Bridge and Great Bridge

North Bridge, Concord, Battle of — 75:Ap 17

Norwich, Conn. — 64:T (Transportation)

British Empire

See also

British Empire, Constitution of the

Treaty of Paris (1763)

Treaty of Paris (1783)

names of British colonies and territorial possessions

dissolution of First English Empire under Lord North — 70:Ja 29-30

rules for reducing: satire — 73:T (Humor)

British Empire, Constitution of the

Boston Port Act, unconstitutionality of — 74:My-S

Coercive Acts declared unconstitutional by Suffolk Resolves — 74:S 5-O 26

"Constitutional Catechism, A" — 73:T (Rights, American Political)

constitutional laws, colonies pledge upholding of — 74:My-S

legislation for colonies, Parliament's right of — 64:My-D; 65:O 7-25, T (Rights); 66:Mr 18

Mass. governor's refusal to entertain dismissal of Oliver — 74:F- Mr

pardon power — 66:Je-D

salaries of colonial administrators — 68:F 11

Stamp Act, constitutionality of — 65:D-66:Ap, F 11

taxation, power of — 64:My-D; 65:S 28, O 7-25, O 29; 67:D 2-68; F 15, F 11, N 24; 69:My 16-18

Brown (University)

See Rhode Island College

Buford, Abraham (Col.)

Waxhaws, S.C., defeat at — 80:Ap-My

Bullbaiting

ad for — 74:T

Burgoyne, John (Gen.)

campaign to cut off New England — 76:Jl-N; 77:Je-O, Jl 5, Ag 16, Ag 25, S, O 3-16

Saratoga surrender — 77:O 7-17, D-78:Je

Trois Rivieres, Battle of — 76:Ja-Je

Burial

See

Huntington, N.Y.

Jews

Burke, Edmund

reconciliation with colonies, speech urging — 75:Mr-Ap

rumored overthrow of British ministry by — 75:T (Rumor)

Burning

See also Fire

Conn. coastal towns — 79:Jl 5-11

Conn. Farms, N.J. — 80:Je

Danbury, Conn. — 77:Ap 25-28

Esopus (Kingston), N.Y. — 77:O 3-16

Falmouth, Me. — 75:O 17-18

Gaspee — 72:Je 9

HMS *Liberty* — 69:Je 19

reconciliation with colonies, plan for — 74:D-75:F
Stamp Act repeal — 66:My-Je
statue of in Charleston — 70:T

Cherokees
See Indians

Cherry Valley, N.Y.
British-Indian massacre of Americans — 78:My-N

Chesapeake Bay
de Grasse blockade of to cut off Cornwallis — 81:S
5-9, Ag-S
Howe's route to Philadelphia — 77:O-N

Chesapeake Capes, Va.
too-late arrival at of reinforcements for Cornwallis —
81:O 19

Chester, Pa.
Washington camp after Chad's Ford — 77:S 11

Children
academy, ad for — 72:T (Education)
charity for — 71:T (Charity)
giant youth described — 72:T (Unusual Phenomena)
Indian children at Dartmouth — 72:T (Colleges)
management of — 73:T
named George Washington — 76:T (Tories); 78:T (Patriotism)
taste for raw flesh in child — 70:T (Unusual Phenomena)

China
novel animals and vegetables of — 75:T

Church, Benjamin (Dr.)
Boston Town Meeting: establishment of committees of
correspondence — 72:N-73:F

Church of England
See also
Clergy
Religious Freedom
ad for minister, lampoon of — 83:T (Humor)
American episcopate, establishment of — 68:T; 71:T
disestablishment in Va. — 76:T
N.C. — 65:T; 71:Ja-Je
Parson's Cause — 63:D 1
unpatriotic clergy in Conn. — 74:T, T (Tories)

Churches
See
Christian denominations by name
Religion
Religious Freedom

Cincinnati, Society of the (American officers) — 83:T
Circuit Court Act (S.C., 1768) — 69:Mr 5
Civil War
patriot-Tory conflict in N.C. — 80:Ap-My

Clark, George Rogers
campaign in Northwest — 78:Jl-Ag; 79:G 24-25;
82:N 10

Class Consciousness
example of — 74:T

Clemency
to N.C. Regulators — 71:Ja-Je

Clergy
See also
Religious Freedom
names of Christian denominations

Boston Massacre participants plead benefit of — 70:O
24-30
salaries in tobacco in Va. — 63:D 1

Clinton, Sir Henry (Gen.)
campaign to cut off New England, role in — 77:Je-O,
O 3-16, O 7-17
Carleton replaces in command — 82:My 5
Carolina Tories defeated en route to join — 76:F 27
Charleston, defeat at — 76:Je 28
N.Y.C., invasion of — 76:Jl 2
Newport evacuation — 79:O 25
Newport occupation — 76:D 8; 78:Ag 29
Phila. evacuation — 78:Je 28; 80:S
reinforcement for Cornwallis at Yorktown too late —
81:O 9
southern campaign, role in — 76:Je 28; 79:O 25;
80:Ap-My; 81:O 19
West Point, Arnold's plot to betray — 76:S 15; 80:S

Clinton, James (Gen.)
expedition against Tory-Indian alliance — 79:Ag S

Coercive (Intolerable) Acts
See also Quebec Act
colonial support for Boston after — 74:My-S
passage of and initial American reaction — 74:My-Je

Coffee
new type — 65:T

Colden, Cadwallader (Lt.-Gov.)
proposal to store rejected tea at Ft. George, N.Y. —
73:D 17

Colleges
See also entries of individual colleges
Dartmouth — 71:T; 72:T
Dickinson — 83:T
Georgia — 65:T
Hampden-Sydney Academy — 77:T
Harvard — 64:T; 69:T; 73:T, T (Paddock); 75:T; 76:T
(Washington)
King's College (Columbia) — 67:T; 69:T
New Jersey (Princeton) — 64:T; 65:T; 70:T; 72:T;
73:T; 74:T; 75:T; 79:T; 80:T
Philadelphia — 70:T, 80:T
Queen's College (Rutgers) — 74:T; 78:T
Rhode Island — 69:T; 70:T; 72:T; 83:T
South Carolina — 64:T; 70:T
Washington College — 82:T; 83:T
William and Mary — 74:T; 78:T; 80:T
Yale — 64:T; 66:T; 71:T

Colonial Union
See
Articles of Confederation
Continental Congress entries
Union, American
United Colonies of North America

Columbia (University)
See King's College

Comets
See Astronomical Phenomena

Commerce
See Trade

***Common Sense,* by Thomas Paine** — 76:Ja 10

Dickinson College

establishment of — 83:T (College)

Dickinson, John

Articles of Confederation, draft of — 77:N 15

Declaration of the Causes and Necessities of Taking Up Arms, authorship of — 75:My 10-Ag 2

Letters from a Farmer in Pennsylvania — 67:D 2-68:F 15; 74:My-S

"Letters to the Inhabitants of the British Colonies in America" — 74:My-S

Diplomacy, American

See

Foreign Relations, American

Treaty entries

American diplomats by name

names of countries maintaining relations with the Revolutionary government

Diseases

dropsy cure — 71:T

fevers of servants, slaves — 64:T

inoculations — 70:T; 71:T

mad dog bite — 83:T

measles — 72:T

small-pox — 63:T; 64:T; 67:T; 68:T; 73:T (Slaves); 74:T; 75:Ag-D, T; 76:Ja-Je; 79:T

whooping cough cure — 70:T; 71:T

Doctors

See also

Dentists

Warren, John

Warren, Joseph

miracle oculist: Dr. Graham — 70:T; 73:T

quackery — 71:T

Dogs

See Mad Dog

Dominica, West Indies

French control of — 79:Jl 3

Dorchester Heights, Boston

Ft. Ticonderoga cannon emplaced for Boston bombardment — 76:Mr 4

Drake, **the (ship)**

capture by John Paul Jones — 78:Ap 23-24

Drowning — 70:T (First Aid); 73:T (Paddock); 80:T

Drunkenness

character of a sot — 68:T

Dudingston, William (Lt.)

Gaspee affair — 72:Je 9; 73:Ja-Je

Dueling

against — 69:T

army — 78:T

cowboy wins duel — 83:T (Cowboy)

occasioned by Hutchinson-Whately letters scandal — 74:Ja

Dunmore, **HMS**

(Norfolk) *Va. Gazette* printed aboard — 75:D 9

Dunmore, John Murray, Earl of (Gov.)

dissolution of House of Burgesses for protest against Intolerable Acts — 74:My-S

gunpowder seized by royal marines, refusal to return — 75:Ap 21

land disputes — 74

Norfolk bombardment — 76:Ja 1-3

prints *Va. Gazette* aboard HMS *Dunmore* — 75:D 9

slave policies designed to thwart Revolutionary cause — 75:D 9

Dutchess County, N.Y.

Tories return to — 79:T (Tories)

Duty

See

Customs

Non-Importation

Stamp Act

Sugar Act

Townshend Acts

Trade Duty, American

names of goods subject to customs duties

E

East Florida

See also Florida

crown colony status — 63:O 7

description of — 64:T

freedom from tumults — 75:T

land grants available in — 65:T

Treaty of Paris (1763), ceded to Britain under — 63:F 10

Treaty of Paris (1783), ceded to Spain under — 82:N 30

East Haven, Conn.

looted by British — 79:Jl 5-11

East India Company

compensation for Boston Tea Party — 74:Ja-Mr

tea export privileges — 73:Ap 27, N 5-6

tea refused at Boston Harbor — 73:N 28

East Indies

colonial boycott of merchandise from — 74:My-S

war between France and Britain — 77:D-78:Je

Eclipse

See Astronomical Phenomena

Economic Conditions, British — 80:T (Opinion, British)

Economic Development, American

See also Manufacturing

Bank of North America — 81:D 31

encouragement of — 64:Ag-D, D

Eden, William

Carlisle Commission — 78:F 17

Education

See also Colleges

advertisement for academy — 72:T

grammar in ad for school attacked — 74:T

Hartford grammar school, ad for — 75:T

Indian children at Dartmouth — 72:T (Colleges)

women — 72:T (Women)

writing system, instruction in — 64:T (Instruction)

Eleanor, **the (ship)**

Boston Tea Party — 73:D 16

prevented from unloading tea — 73:N 28

Elections

See also

Office, State Elective

Suffrage

Foreign Relations, American
>*See also*
>>Continental Congress entries
>>Trade
>>Treaty entries
>>names of American diplomats
>>names of countries maintaining diplomatic relations with Revolutionary government

Canada — 76:Ja-Je

Committee of Secret Correspondence (Committee for Foreign Affairs) — 75:S 12

France — 68:S 12-13; 76:My, Jl-N; 77:O 7-17, D-78:Je, F 17, Jl-Ag; 81:D 3, T (Alliance); 82:My 5, O 4, N 30

Netherlands — 77:F; 80:Mr 9; 81:D 31; 82:Ap 19

League of Armed Neutrality — 77:F; 80:Mr 9

Lee calls for foreign alliances — 76:Jl 4

Russia — 74:T (Russia); 81:Mr 9

Spain — 79:Je 21

"Forester, the"
>*See* Pseudonymous Writing

Fort
>*See* specific Fort names
>*See also* Great Lakes Forts. Forts noted solely as Revolutionary War battle sites are also indexed under Battles

Fort Detroit — 63:My-N; 79:F 24-25, Ag-S; 82:N 10

Fort George, N.Y.

British leave greased flag pole for Americans — 83:D 4

storage of rejected tea at, proposal for — 73:D 17

Fort Griswold, Conn.

massacre of Americans by Arnold — 81:S 6

Fort Lee, N.J.

American evacuation of — 76:N 16

Fort Miami, Ohio

captured by Indians — 63:My-N

Fort Pitt, Pa. — 63:My-N; 74

Fort Presque Isle (now Mich.)

captured by Indians — 63:My-N

Fort Sandusky, Ohio

captured by Indians — 63:My-N

Fort Ticonderoga, N.Y.
>*See also* Battles

American retreat to — 76:Jl-N

campaign to cut off New England, importance in — 77:Je-O

cannon captured at used to bombard Boston — 76:Mr 4

Fort William and Mary, N.H.

raid by N.H. patriots — 74:D 14

Fox-hunting

verse ridicules — 79:T

France
>*See also*
>>Army, French
>>Franklin, Benjamin
>>French entries

aid to American Revolution (pre-alliance) — 76:My; Jl-N

alliance with Americans — 77:O 7-17, D-78:Je, F 17, Jl-Ag, Ag 29; 79:S-O; 81:S 5-9, Ag-S, T (Alliance)

American peace negotiators reject French direction — 82:O 4

Britain, war with — 68:S 12-13; 77:D-78:Je, F 17, Je 28; 79:Jl 3; 81:S 5-9; 82:Ap 9-12, My 5, N 30

John Paul Jones honored by — 81:T (Jones)

loan to U.S. to promote fiscal stability — 81:D 31

navy in Western Hemisphere — 78:Ag 29; 79:Jl 3, S-O; 81:S 5-9

Shelburne ministry attempts diplomatic isolation of — 82:N 30

Spain, alliance with against British — 79:Je 21

Treaty of Paris (1763) — 63:F 10; 76:My

warning to Americans: must repay French — 83:T (Warning)

Franklin, Benjamin

Canada, Congressional mission to solicit aid from — 76:Ja-Je

Declaration of Independence, drafting of — 76:Jl 4

electricity — 67:T

England, secret contact with — 76:My

France, diplomatic mission to — 76:My; 77:T, D-78:Je

Independent Chronicle, bogus edition of — 82:T

Ireland, address to the people of — 79:T (Ireland)

letters of Hutchinson and Oliver, securing of — 73:Je; 74:Ja

Paris peace negotiations, disregard of Congressional instruction — 82:O 4, N 30

Paxton Boys, confrontation with — 63:D-64:F

peace proposals by British, rejection of — 76:Ag 26

poem to upon return from Europe — 75:T

postmaster — 75:My 10-Ag 2

Stamp Act, testimony before Parliament on — 67:Jl 2

taxes: internal v. external, pseudonymous article on — 67:T

Tory son William Franklin — 74:My-S

Franklin, William (Gov.)

American independence, asks N.J. disavowal of — 75:N 16, 29

N.J. provincial convention in response to Intolerable Acts, permission for — 74:My-S

salary paid from customs revenues — 72:Ag 20

Fraunces Tavern

Washington takes leave of officers at — 83:D 4

Frederick County, Md., Court

defiance of Stamp Act — 65:N

Fredericksburg, Va.

religious observance, effective date of Boston Port Act — 74:Je 1

Fredericktown, Maryland

"burial" of Stamp Act — 65:N 30

Free Masons

admission of women — 66:T

Freedom
>*See*
>>Declaration entries
>>Independence, American
>>Ireland
>>Newspapers
>>Religion
>>Rights entries
>>States' Rights

slaves, regulation of — 70:T (Slaves)
Stamp Act, successful implementation of — 65:D
stamp distributors, resignation of — 65:Ag 26-N 16
state government, reestablishment of — 81:S 8
Tories upset by Lexington and Concord — 75:Ap-Je
township, settlement by — 66:T
Georgia (non-importation) Association — 69:S 19
Georgia Commons House of Assembly (lower house of General Assembly). *Use* Georgia General Assembly
Georgia General Assembly
burial of Jews — 70:T (Jews)
Mass. Circular Letter, endorsement — 68:Ap 21, D 24
state constitution — 76:My 15
state government, reestablishment of after Battle of Eutaw Springs — 81:S 8
Germain, Lord George (Colonial Secretary)
chooses Burgoyne over Carleton — 77:Je-O
Germans
See also
Hessians
Kalb, Johann de
Soldiers, German
Steuben, Baron von
western N.C. — 71:Ja-Je
Germantown, Pa.
See also Battles
Washington camps at — 77:S 11
Gibraltar
defense of against Spanish — 82:Ap 9-12
Glass
non-importation — 68:Ag 1
Townshend Act duty on — 67:Jl 2
Gloucester, Va.
British reinforcement of for attempted retreat after Yorktown — 81:O 19
Glover, John (Gov.)
evacuation of American troops from Long Is. — 76:Ag 26
Gordon, Lord George
precipitates riots in London — 80:T
treason trial — 81:T
Governors, Colonial
See also
Arnold, Benedict
Bernard (Mass.)
Botetourt (Va.)
Dunmore (Va.)
Franklin, William (N.J.)
Gage (Mass.)
Hutchinson (Mass.)
Martin (N.C.)
Moore (N.Y.)
Penn (Pa.)
Trumbull (Conn.)
Tryon (N.C. and N.Y.)
Wentworth (N.H.)
Wright (Ga.)
power of under Mass. Government Act — 74:My-Je
Quebec Act, appointment of under — 74:Je 22

salaries from customs revenues — 67:Jl 2; 68:F 11, 71:Mr, O-D; 72:Je 13
Grafton, Augustus Henry Fitzroy, Third Duke of
resignation ends Pitt/Chatham-Grafton ministry — 70:Ja 29-30
Graham, Dr.
miracle oculist — 70:T (Doctors)
Grain
shortage in England — 67:F 27
Grammar
school ad criticized for — 74:T (Education)
Grand Banks
Restraining Acts bar colonial fishermen from — 75:Mr-Ap
Grand Jury
See Crime
Grasse, Francois Joseph Paul, Comte de (Adm.)
prevents Adm. Graves from aiding Cornwallis — 81:S 5-9; Ag S
West Indies actions against British — 82:Ap 9-12
Graves, Thomas (Adm.)
de Grasse prevents from aiding Cornwallis — 81:S 5-9, Ag-S
Great Lakes Forts
Treaty of Paris (1783) provisions concerning — 82:N 10, N 30
Great War for the Empire (Seven Years War) — 63:F 10
Green Farms, Conn.
looted by British — 79:Jl 5-11
Green Mountain Boys — 74
Greene, Nathaniel (Gen.)
resistance to British invasion of N.J. — 80:Je
southern campaign, role in — 80:O 7; 81:Ja, Ja 17, Mr 15, Ap 25, My 22-Je 19, S 8
Grenada, West Indies
French control — 79:Jl 3
Grenville, George (Prime Min.)
accession to office — 63:Ap 3
succeeded by Rockingham — 65:Jl 10
Groton, Conn.
burning by Arnold to divert American troops from South — 81:S 6
Guilford, Frederick, Lord North, Second Earl of (Prime Min.)
Boston Port Act, proposal of — 74:Ja-Mr
military supplies for America, interception of — 80:Mr 9
reconciliation with American colonies, proposal for — 74:D-75:F, My 10-Ag 2; 78:F 17
resignation as prime minister — 82:F-Mr
succeeds Grafton as prime minister — 70:Ja 29-30
Tories, comment on condition of — 79:T (Tories)
Townshend duties, asks partial repeal of — 70:Mr 5, Ap-S
Gunpowder
See
Manufacturing, American
Military Supplies
Guy Fawkes Day — 65:T; 68:T; 69:T; 74:T
Gwinnett, Button — 65:T (Gwinnett, Button)

H

Hale, Nathan
execution — 76:S 15
Halifax (N.C.) Resolves
N.C. instructs for independence — 76:My 15
Halifax, Nova Scotia
priest exercises illegal ministry — 70:T (Roman Catholics)
Tories evacuated from Boston flee to — 76:Mr 4
vice-admiralty court seat — 64:Ap 5
Hamilton, Henry (Col.)
capture by Clarke — 79:F 24-25
scalp bounties — 78:Jl-Ag
Hamlet
ad for performance — 73:T (Theater)
Hampden-Sydney Academy
lottery — 77:T (Colleges)
Hancock, John
Declaration of Independence signing — 76:Jl 4
Liberty seized for customs violations — 68:Je
marriage — 75:T
Mass. Committee of Safety — 74:O 7
pardon by Gage, excepted from — 75:Je 12
Handel, George Frederick
concert of his music — 73:T (Handel)
Hanging
See Executions
Hanover County, Va.
protest of gunpowder seizure at Williamsburg, Patrick Henry raises troops for — 75:Ap 21
Hanson, John (Pres.)
presidency under Articles of Confederation — 81:Mr 1
Hartford, Conn.
grammar school in — 75:T (Education)
Congregationalist minister installed — 67:T (Congregationalists)
Harvard College
fire — 64:T (Colleges)
general diploma given — 75:T (Colleges)
home manufacture endorsed — 69:T (Colleges)
lottery to aid — 73:T (Colleges)
moves to Concord — 75:T (Colleges)
student drowns — 73:T (Paddock)
Washington awarded degree — 76:T (Washington)
Head of Elk, Md.
Americans reach en route to Yorktown — 80:Ag-S
Howe's landing at — 77:Ag 25, O-N
Health
See
Diseases
Doctors
Medicine
Sanitation
Soldiers, American
Tea
Hemp — 65:T (Manufactures); 67:T (Manufactures)
Henrico County, Va.
counseled on patriotism — 75:T (Patriotism)
Henry, Patrick
Clark mission to Northwest — 78:Jl-Ag

committees of correspondence leadership — 73:Mr 12
letter to George III based on Va. Resolves — 69:My 16-18
Parson's Cause — 63:D 1
Va. Resolves — 65:My 29
Williamsburg gunpowder seizure, protest of — 75:Ap 21
Henry VIII, King of England
statute: traitors liable to trial in England — 69:F 8
Herkimer, Nicholas (Gen.)
Oriskany, N.Y., ambushed at — 77:Ag 3-22
Herschel, William
discovery of Uranus — 83:T
Hessians
See also Soldiers, German
atrocities by, rumor of — 76:N-D
Conn. coast, terrorizing of — 79:Jl 5-11
Ft. Mercer, repulsed at — 77:O-N
satire on — 81:T (Humor)
Trenton, surprised by Washington at — 76:D 25-77:Ja 3
Washington, near capture of — 76:S 15
Hides
export of — 64:Ap 5
Hillsborough, Lord (Sec. of State for the Colonies)
lampoon of statue of — 73:T (Humor)
Townshend duties, communique on rescinding of — 69:Je-D
Mass. Circular Letter, reaction to — 68:Ap 21
Hillsborough, N.C.
Cornwallis objective in 1780 offensive — 80:O 7
N.C. Regulators riot at — 71:Ja-Je
Hogarth, William — 65:T (Hogarth)
Holt, John
patriot publisher of *N.Y. Journal* — 75:D 9
Holt, John Hunter
press stolen — 75:D 9
Hopkins, Essex (Cdr.-in-Chief of the Fleet)
New Providence, capture of — 76:Mr 19
Horse
ad for missing — 79:T
Horseracing
Conn. — 74:T
Md. — 73:T; 74:T; 80:T; 82:T
R.I. prohibition of — 77:T
Hortalez, Roderique, and Company (fictitious firm) — 76:My
Hospital
Pa. — 64:T
small-pox — 79:T
theater benefit for — 73:T (Theater)
House of Commons
See also Parliament
Barre: champion of colonies — 70:F
Franklin reprimanded and dismissed from office for Hutchinson-Whately letters scandal — 73:Ja
Mass. disorders, resolutions against — 69:F 8
Stamp Act repeal — 66:Mr 4
vote to abandon war in America — 82:F-Mr

House of Lords
   See also Parliament
   Carlisle Commission Manifesto, attack on — 78:Je-N
   Mass. disorders, resolutions against — 69:F 8
   Stamp Act Repeal — 66:Mr 17
Housing
   See also Quartering Act
   survey of in Phila. over 20-year period — 70:T
Howe, Richard (Adm.)
   d'Estaing, aborted naval battle with — 78:Ag 29
   N.Y.C. invasion — 76:Jl 2
   reconciliation with Americans, attempted — 78:F 17
Howe, Robert (Gen.)
   disarms Continental Army mutineers — 81:Ja
Howe, William (Gen.)
   Boston evacuation — 76:Mr 4
   campaign to cut off New England — 77:Je-O, Ag 25
   Chad's Ford, Battle of — 77:S 11
   Clinton, dispatch of to R.I. — 76:D 8
   Clinton, replacement by — 78:Je 28
   Delaware River forts, assault on — 77:O-N
   Gage, assumes command from — 75:Je 17
   Head of Elk, Md., landing at — 77:Ag 25, O-N
   N.Y.C. invasion — 76:Jl-N, Jl 2, Ag 26, S 15
   reconciliation with Americans, attempted — 76:Ag 26;
     78:F 17
   Washington, pursuit of across N.J. — 76:N-D
   White Plains, Battle of — 76:O 28
Hudson River
   British campaign to cut off New England, importance
     in — 76:Jl-N; 77:S, O 3-16
   containment of British east of — 76:O 28
   West Point important to American control of — 79:Jl
     15
Huguenots — 64:T
Humor
   Anglican minister, lampoon of ad for — 83:T
   anecdote: stiff bowl of punch — 72:T
   attack on Washington, Congress, American indepen-
     dence: lampoon — 83:T
   British Army — 78:T; 81:T; 83:T
   British war efforts: lampoon — 81:T
   "Character of a Loving Wife, The" — 72:T
   Congress — 81:T
   Europe, state of — 70:T
   future Parliamentary acts — 74:T
   Gage, parody on — 75:T (Poetry)
   Hillsborough statue, lampoon — 73:T
   importers — 70:T
   independence, American — 78:T (Independence); 83:T
   miser, joke about — 64:T
   Newport, Battle of — 78:T
   newspapers, satire on — 78:T
   patriot printers' need for rags — 79:T
   resolves against congressional power, lampoon of —
     83:T
   rules for reducing empire, satire — 73:T
   Tories — 75:T (Tories)
   Tory newspaper — 77:T

Huntington, N.Y.
   British dig up graveyard at — 82:T (War Atrocities)
Huntington, Samuel
   presidency under Articles of Confederation — 81:Mr 1
Hurricanes
   Mass. — 73:T
   West Indies damage — 72:T; 80:T
Hutchinson, Elisha
   refusal to resign tea commission — 73:N 5-6
Hutchinson, Thomas (Chief Justice; Gov.)
   anti-Catholicism used in ridicule of — 71:T (Roman
     Catholics)
   home attacked in Stamp Act riots — 65:Ag 14-26
   judges' salaries — 73:Ja-Je; 74:F-Mr
   letters to Whately secured by Franklin: scandal —
     73:Je; 74:Ja
   non-importation of tea, attempted obstruction of —
     73:N 28, D 16
   salary from customs revenues — 71:Mr, O-D; 72:Je 13
   sons as tea commissioners — 73:N 5-6
Hutchinson, Thomas, Jr.
   refusal to resign tea commission — 73:N 5-6

I

Illinois
   See also Battles
   Clark mission to Northwest — 78:Jl-Ag; 79:F 24-25
Importation
   See also
     Continental Association
     Customs
     Merchants entries
     Non-Importation
     Smuggling
     Sugar Act
     Trade
     imported goods by name
   Jewish importers noted — 70:T (Jews)
   satire on importers — 70:T (Humor)
   slaves — 73:T (Slaves); 74:My-S, T (Slaves); 75:T
     (Slaves); 76:Ap 6
Impressment of Americans into British Navy — 67:T
   (Navy, British)
Imprisonment and Jailing
   See also
     Jail
     Prisoners of War
   hardships of — 67:T
   Laurens in Tower of London — 81:T (Laurens)
   Powell, Thomas: for criticizing S.C. Council — 73:Ag
     30-S 13
   Quakers: for pro-British agreement — 77:T (Quakers)
   Suffolk Resolves threaten royal officials with — 74:S
     5-O 26
   Tories break jail — 76:T (Tories)
   Wilkes and Barre — 70:F
Independence, American
   See also
     Declaration of Independence

July 4th Celebration
Nationalism
Union, American
attack on lampooned — 83:T (Humor)
Carlisle Commission not authorized to recognize — 78:F 17, Je-N
Common Sense influences sentiment for — 76:Ja 10
Congressional opening of ports important to — 76:Ap 6
disavowal of by Americans — 65:T; 67:D 2-68:F 15, F 11; 75:My 10-Ag 2, N 16, 29, T; 76:Ja 10, My 15, Jl 4
English view of — 74:T
expected — 75:T
foreign recognition of — 76:Jl 2; 79:Je 21; 80:Mr 9; 82:F-Mr, Ap 19
French guarantee of — 77:D-78:Je
non-negotiable item in Paris Peace talks — 82:O 4
"Novanglus" v. "Massachusettensis" — 74:D 5/17-75:Ap 17
prospects of — 72:T
satire on — 78:T
states instruct for — 76:My 15
union necessary for — 75:T
union of Great Britain and America proposed — 73:T
warning against pursuit of — 68:D 24

Independence Hall
soldiers' protest demonstration before — 83:Je

Independence, State
See also States' Rights
comments against — 83:T

Independent Chronicle
bogus printing by Franklin — 82:T (Franklin)

India
Treaty of Paris (1783) settlement — 82:N 30
war between French and British — 77:D-78:Je; 82:Ap 9-12

Indiana
Clark mission to Northwest — 78:Jl-Ag

Indians
alliance with British against Americans — 75:T; 77:Ag 3-22, Ag 16; 78:My-N, Jl-Ag; 79:Ag-S; 81:My 22-Je 19; 82:N 10
Asian origin of — 66:T (Geography)
brutality of — 64:T
Cherokees: peace in Ga., S.C. — 77:T
Continental Congress departments of Indian affairs — 75:My 10-Ag 2
Creeks: possible attack on Ga., S.C. — 74:T
education at Dartmouth — 72:T (Colleges)
land purchase from — 81:Mr 1
land rights of — 63:O 7; 64:T; 77:N 15; 83:T
McCrea, Jane, murder of — 77:Ag 16
Ohio government, reaction to — 73:T
Pontiac, life of — 66:T (Pontiac)
Shakespeare appreciated by — 67:T
Shawnees defeated in Ohio River Valley — 74
wars with colonists — 63:My-N, D-64:F, T; 65:T

Inflation
See Currency

Inoculations
See Diseases

Instruction
See
Education
Independence — states instruct for

Intolerable Acts
See Coercive Acts

Inventions
See also N.Y. Flying Machines
furnace with self-regulating register — 68:T

Iredell, James (future U.S. Supreme Court Justice)
Declaration of Independence, vindication of — 78:T

Ireland
See also
Irish
Declaration of Rights (Irish)
American Revolution, benefit to from — 79:T
Continental Association ban on trade with — 74:S 5-O 26
Continental Congress address to people of — 75:My 10-Ag 2
Franklin addresses people of — 79:T
freedom from Britain sought — 80:T
rent problems cause emigration — 73:T (Irish)

Irish
See also
Ireland
Declaration of Rights (Irish)
emigration due to rent problems — 73:T

Iron
export of — 64:Ap 5

Iroquois
See Indians — alliance with British

J

Jail
See also Imprisonment and Jailing
Conn. Copper mine as jail — 73:T

Jamaica
saved from French in Battle of the Saints — 82:Ap 9-12

James River
British move up to take Petersburg — 81:Mr-My

Jay, John
Paris peace negotiations, disregard of congressional instructions — 82:O 4, N 30
patriotic message to Americans — 79:T (Patriotism)
Spain, diplomatic mission to — 79:Je 21

Jefferson, Thomas
committee of correspondence leadership — 73:Mr 12
Declaration of Independence — 76:Jl 4
Declaration of the Causes and Necessities of Taking Up Arms — 75:My 10-Ag 2
horse found by, ad for — 66:T
house burns, Albemarle County, Va. — 70:T
Paris peace negotiation, absence from — 82:N 30
Tarleton, near capture by — 81:Je-Ag 2
Va. governorship — 79:F 24-25; 81:Je-Ag 2

Language
French language school — 73:T (Education)
etymology of *Yankee* — 75:T (Yankee)

Laurens, Henry (American Diplomat)
held in Tower of London — 80:T; 81:T
Paris peace negotiations — 82:N 30

Law and Legislation
See also
    Articles of Confederation
    Constitution entries
    Continental Congress entries
    Courts
    Crime
    French Legal Code
    Justice and Judicial System
    Lawsuit
    Martial Law
    Parliament
      also
    legislative bodies (general assemblies) of colonies/
      states
    specific laws by name
    subjects of legislation
colonial laws considered null and void or suspended
    due to British unconstitutional acts — 65:N; 74:O
    7; 75:My 31; 76:My 15

Lawsuit
British merchants supplying Americans v. Adm. Rod-
    ney — 80:D
slaves sue for freedom — 73:T (Slaves); 80:T (Slaves)

Lead
non-importation — 68:Ag 1
Townshend Act duty on — 67:Jl 2

League of Armed Neutrality — 77:F; 80:Mr 9, D

Lee, Arthur
mission to France — 77:D-78:Je

Lee, Charles (Gen.)
capture and exchange for Prescott — 76:D 13
Charleston, S.C., victory — 76:Je 28
court-martial — 78:Je 28

Lee, Henry ("Light-Horse Harry"), Jr. (Maj.)
Battle of Paulus Hook, N.J. — 79:Ag 19

Lee, Richard Henry
certificate of good conduct from as soldier's discharge
    — 75:T (Soldiers, American)
colonial union, proposal for — 76:Jl 4; 77:N 15
committee of correspondence leadership — 73:Mr 12
independence, presents resolutions for — 76:Jl 4
letter to George III — 69:My 16-18
stamp officer, vindication of attempt to be — 66:T

Legislative Power
See Constitution entries

Leonard, Daniel (Solicitor General to Customs Board)
"Novanglus" v. "Massachusettensis" — 74:D
    5/17-75:Ap 18

Les Saintes, Battle of — 82:Ap 9-12

Letters
Boston Town Meeting to Mass. towns urging conven-
    tion — 68:S 12-13
Common Sense occasions letters for and against inde-
    pendence — 76:Ja 10

Continental Congress to the American people — 74:S
    5-O 26
female education, letter to parents on — 72:T
    (Women)
Hutchinson and Oliver letters to Whately secured by
    Franklin — 73:Je; 74:Ja
McDougall to the citizens of N.Y. — 70:F
marque and reprisal — 76:Mr 19
Mass. Circular Letter — 68:F 11, Ap 21, Je 21, Je 30,
    Jl-O, N 24, D 24, D 28-69:Ja 2
Mass. House of Representatives to colonist urging
    united action — 64:Je
Monitor's Letters, The — 68:F 25-Ap 28
old soldier advises leaving Americans alone — 75:T
    (Soldiers, British)
press freedom, letter to editor on — 79:T (News-
    papers)
Tories, admonition of — 81:T (Tories)
Va. approval of Mass. Circular Letter — 68:Ap 21, D
    24, D 28-69:Ja 2
Va. House of Burgesses to George III — 69:My
Washington to Gen. Gage on prisoner of war treatment
    — 75:T (Prisoners of War)
Washington to governors of all states — 83:T (Washing-
    ton)
"Watchman, The" — 70:F

Letters from a Farmer in Pennsylvania to the Inhabitants
    of the British Colonies —67:D 2-68:F 15; 74:My-S

"Letters to the Inhabitants of the British Colonies in
    America" — 74:My-S

Liberty, HMS
burned to retaliate for customs seizures — 69:Jl 19

Liberty, the (ship)
seized for customs violation — 68:Je 10

Liberty Poles — 66:Ag 10-11; 70:Ja 13-19

Library Company of Philadelphia
officers chosen — 74:T (Libraries)

Library Society, Charleston, S.C.
proposes natural history collection — 73:T (Natural
    History)

Licensing
East India Co., for direct export of tea to America —
    73:Ap 27
marque and reprisal, letters of — 76:Mr 19
ships leaving N.Y.C. — 75:Je-S
slaves, for peddling — 73:T (Slaves)

Lighthouse
Sandy Hook, N.J. — 64:T (Transportation)

Lightning
strikes three in Phila. — 68:T

Lightning Rods — 70:T

Lincoln, Benjamin (Gen.)
Augusta and Stono Ferry, Battles of — 79:Ja-Je
Charleston, defeat at — 80:Ap-My
Savannah, losses at — 79:S-O

Livestock
See also
    Cows
    Swine
lottery on — 67:T (Lotteries)

Livingston, Robert R.
Declaration of Independence, drafting of — 76:Jl 4

Locke, John
   Declaration of Independence, influence on — 76:Jl 4
   Essay on Civil Government, ad for — 73:T
   rebellion, right of — 74:T
London, England
   See also Tower of London
   anti-Catholic, anti-administration riots — 80:T (Gordon)
   pro-American sentiment after Lexington and Concord — 75:Je-Jl
London, the (ship)
   tea cargo refused and confiscated at Charleston — 73:D 22
   tea cargo destroyed in N.Y.C. Tea Party — 74:Ap 19-24
Long Island
   See also Battles
   British evacuation of — 83:N 25
   Conn. coastal towns burned — 79:Jl 5-11
Lotteries
   Hampden-Sydney Academy — 77:T (Colleges)
   Harvard — 73:T (Colleges)
   individuals' belongings — 67:T
   New Jersey, College of — 73:T (Colleges)
   N.Y. lottery won by Gen. Charles Lee — 76:D 13
   R.I. — 63:T
   U.S. sponsors — 77:T; 78:T
Louis XVI, King of France
   aid to American Revolution — 76:My
Louisiana
   U.S. boundary under Treaty of Paris (1783) — 82:N 30
Lower Counties
   See Delaware
Loyalists
   See Tories
Luzerne, the Chevalier de
   summons de Grasse to prevent Adm. Graves from aiding Cornwallis — 81:S 5-9

M

McCrea, Jane
   murder of — 77:Ag 16
McDougall, Alexander
   "Betrayed Inhabitants of the City and Colony of New York, The" — 69:D 16
   jailed for further letters to New Yorkers — 70:F
McKean, Thomas
   presidency under Articles of Confederation — 81:Mr 1
Mad Dog
   bite treatment — 83:T
Magazines
   Royal American Magazine, proposal for — 73:T
Magician
   ad for — 73:T
Mahan, Alfred Thayer (American naval historian)
   significance of Arnold campaign in upstate N.Y. — 76:Jl-N

Maine
   See also
      Battles
      Burning
   Arnold's march through on Canadian campaign 75:Ag-D
Malcolm, John
   efforts as customs officer — 73:T (Customs)
Manhattan Island, N.Y.
   evacuation of Long Island troops to — 76:Ag 26
Manifesto and Proclamation (of the Carlisle Commission) — 78:Je-N
Manufacturing, American
   encouragement of — 64:Ag-D, D; 67:O 28; 68:Ja-Mr, S 5; 69:T (Colleges)
   gunpowder — 76:My, T (Gunpowder)
   hemp cultivation — 65:T; 67:T
   saltpeter — 75:T (Saltpeter); 76:T (Saltpeter)
   silk — 72:T (Silk)
   sugar from cornstalks — 78:T (Sugar)
Marblehead, Mass.
   opposition to establishment of committee of correspondence — 72:N-73:F
Marque and Reprisal, Letters of — 76:Mr 19
Marriage
   "Character of a Loving Wife, The" — 72:T
   Hancock, John — 75:T (Hancock)
   non-support dispute — 70:T
   wife, ad for — 80:T
   wife, runaway, ad for — 74:T
Mars.
   See Astronomical Phenomena
Marshals
   Mass. gov. authorized to remove — 74:My-Je
Marshfield, Mass.
   opposition to Boston excesses in protest — 73:D-74:Mr
Martial Law
   Dunmore declares in Va. — 75:D 9
   Gage declares in Mass. — 75:Je 12
   Pa. — 80:T
Martin, Josiah (Gov.)
   Mecklenburg County Resolutions, displeased by — 75:My 31
   refusal to convene N.C. General Assembly — 74:My-S
   slaves, proposal to arm against colonists — 75:T (Slaves)
Martinique, West Indies
   importance in war between France and Britain — 82:Ap 9-12
Maryland
   See also
      Horseracing
      Md. place names
      Militia
   independence, resistance to — 76:Ja 10, Jl 4
   Intolerable Acts, reaction to — 74:My-S

license for slaves to peddle — 73:T (Slaves)

monopoly — 77:T (Monopolies)

non-importation, failure to support — 69:Mr 10, Je-D; 70:Je-Jl, D 13

poll in N.Y. on maintenance of non-importation — 70:Je-Jl

Merchants, British

American paper money, complaints about — 64:Ap 19

Continental Army supply — 80:D

French legal code, objections to use of — 74:Je 22

Stamp Act, petition for repeal of — 66:Ja 17

Mercury

See Astronomical Phenomena

Meteors

See Astronomical Phenomena

Middlesex County, Mass.

resolutions protesting Mass. Government Act — 74:O 7

Mifflin, Thomas

presidency under Articles of Confederation — 81:Mr 1

Military Science

officers' manual published — 75:T

Military Supplies

See also Manufacturing, American

British merchants supply to Continental Army — 80:D

bullets made from statue of George III — 76:Jl-Ag

Cambridge depot, British raid on — 74:S

Canadian campaign, American shortage during — 75: Ag-D; 76:Jl-N

Concord, British seizure of cache at — 75:Ap 19

Conn. supply of Washington — 79:Jl 5-11

Continental Association allows importation of — 75:My 10-Ag 2

Danbury, Conn., American depot destroyed — 77:Ap 25-28

Detroit as British suppy center for Indian allies — 79:Ag-S

Dutch-American trade in — 77:F; 80:D

French contribution to Americans — 76:My

licensing of ships to stop supply to British — 75:Je-S

market places for regulated, protection offered — 81:T (Army, Continental)

N.H. patriots raid Ft. William and Mary for — 74:D 14

New London, Conn., burned due to storage of — 81:S 6

Petersburg, Va., British burn American supplies at — 81:Mr-My

ports, opening of essential for American cause — 76: Ap 6

R.I. supply of Continental Army — 79:T (Army, Continental)

Salem, Mass., attempted British seizure at — 75:F 26

Spanish contribution to Americans — 76:My

Tidewater, Va., American loss of in — 79:My 10-24

Washington requests additional — 75:Jl 3

Williamsburg, Va., royal marines seize gunpowder at — 75:Ap 21

Wilmington, N.C., British supply center at — 81:Mr 15

Militia

See also Minutemen

Conn. — 74:O-75:Ap

Gates, militiamen fighting with — 77:Ag 16, O 7-17; 80:Ag 16

Lexington and Concord precipitate readiness of — 75:Ap-Je

Md. Tories put down — 76:Mr

Mass. raises — 74:S 5-O 26, O 7, O-75:Ap

N.C. — 75:D 9; 76:F 27; 80:O 7; 81:Mr 15

provincial congresses raise — 75:Je-S

Va. — 75:D 9; 81:Mr 15

Yorktown participation — 81:Ag-S

Mineral Spring

Stafford, Conn. — 66:T; 67:T

Ministry, British

See also names of individual ministers

blamed for American troubles by Londoners — 75: Je-Jl

rumored overthrow by Wilkes and Burke — 75:T (Rumor)

Minorca

captured by French — 82:Ap 9-12

ceded to Spain, Treaty of Paris (1783) — 82:N 30

Minutemen

Hancock empowered to call up — 74:O 7

Lexington and Concord, Battles of — 75:Ap 19

Mississippi

land available — 75:T (West Fla.)

settlement of — 73:T

U.S. boundary under Treaty of Paris (1783) — 82:N 30

Mississippi River

boundary under Quebec — 74:Je 22

boundary under Treaty of Alliance — 77:D-78:Je

boundary under Treaty of Paris (1763) — 63:F 1-O

boundary under Treaty of Paris (1783) — 82:N 30

Mobile, Ala. — 64:T; 75:T (West Fla.)

Mohawk Indians

See also

Brant, Joseph

Indians — alliance with British

Boston Tea Party participants disguised as — 73:D 16

Mohawk River

British campaign to cut off New England, importance in — 77:Je-O

Mohawk Valley

British campaign to cut off New England, importance in — 77:Ag 3-22

Molasses

See Sugar Act

Money

See

Army, Continental — back pay

Counterfeiting

Currency entries

Paper Money, American

Parson's Cause

Revenues, British

"Monitor's Letters, The"

influence on Va. Association — 68:F 25-Ap 28

Monopolies

Post office, R.I. — 64:T (Post Office)

sentiment against — 77:T; 78:T

Montgomery, Richard (Gen.)

Canadian Campaign and death — 75:Ag-D

"Dialogue between the Ghost of General Montgomery . . . and an American Delegate . . ." — 76:Ja 10

Montreal, Quebec
Arnold withdraws to with injury — 76:Ja-Je
Montgomery wins in Canadian campaign — 75:Ag-D

Moore, Henry (Gov.)
dissolution of N.Y. General Assembly for Mass. Circular Letter endorsement — 68:D 28-69:Ja 2
Quartering Act, conflict with General Assembly over — 66:D 15; 67:My 27

Moral Exhortation
bad company, against — 71:T
frugality, for — 65:T
snuff, against — 64:T
swearing, against — 71:T

Morgan, Daniel (Gen.)
Cowpens, S.C., victory over Tarleton at — 81:Ja 17
Freeman's Farm, Second Battle of — 77:O 7-17

Morris, Robert
fiscal policies initiated by — 81:D 31

Morristown, N.J.
mutiny, Continental Army — 81:Ja
winter quarters, Washington's troops — 76:D 25-Ja 3

Moultrie, William (Col.)
Ft. Sullivan (Charleston) victory — 76:Je 28
Port Royal Is., S.C., defense of — 79:Ja-Je

Mount Vernon, Va.
Washington retires to — 83:D 23

Mountainmen
against British in N.C. — 80:O 7

Mud Island
See Battles — Ft. Mifflin

Murder
See Crime

Murder Act
See Administration of Justice Act

Music
See also Songs
concert of Handel music — 73:T (Handel)

Mutiny
See Continental Army

Mutiny Act
See Quartering Act

N

Namquit Point, R.I.
Gaspee run aground at — 72:Je 9

Nancy, the (ship)
Captain Chambers spirited aboard for return to London — 74:Ap 19-24

Natchez, Miss.
settlement — 73:T (Mississippi Country)

National Debt, U.S.
Bank of North America notes for payment of — 81:D 31

Nationalism, American
See also
Independence, American
Manufacturing, American
Union, American

growth of tied to movement for indigenous manufacturing — 68:S 5

Natural History
collection proposed, Charleston — 73:T

Naval Stores
See also Military Supplies
League of Armed Neutrality rule for trade in — 80:Mr 9

Navy, British
de Grasse blocks naval aid to Cornwallis — 81:S 5-9, Ag-S
impressment of Americans — 67:T
New England raids and burning of Falmouth, Me. — 75:O 17-18
printing press of *Va. Gazette* stolen by — 75:D 9
HMS *Romney* sent to protect Boston Customs Commissioners — 68:My 17
St. Eustatius, capture of to cut off Dutch supplies to Americans — 80:D
southern campaign, role in — 81:Ap 25, Je-Ag 2, S 5-9, Ag-S
Williamsburg, gunpowder seizure at — 75:Ap 21

Navy, Continental
See also
Barry, John
Jones, John Paul
American world commerce, favored to carry on — 82:T
creation of — 75:S 12
early successes — 76:Mr 19
French aid — 78:Ag 29
Jones incursions in Britain — 78:Ap 23-24
recruitment — 80:T

Negroes
See also
Non-Whites
Slaves
freed woman helps American prisoners — 78:T (Prisoners of War)
Wheatley, Phillis — 73:T (Wheatley); 74:T (Wheatley)

Netherlands
American-Dutch trade, British protest of — 77:F
July 4th celebration — 81:T (July 4th)
League of Armed Neutrality — 80:Mr 9
loan to U.S. — 81:D 31; 82:Ap 19
Treaty of Paris (1783) — 82:N 30
treaty with U.S. and recognition of American independence — 82:Ap 19
war with Britain — 80:D 8

Neutral Nations
See League of Armed Neutrality

Nevis, West Indies
French capture of — 82:Ap 9-12

New Bern, N.C.
July 4th celebration — 78:T (July 4th)
site of N.C. provincial congress — 74:My-S

New Brunswick, N.J.
defense of by Cornwallis — 76:D 25
N.J. provincial convention at — 74:My-S

New Castle County, Del.
　　Continental Congress delegate selection — 74:My-S
　　non-importation agreement — 69:Ag 28
New England
　　See also
　　　　North Atlantic Fisheries
　　　　other New England entries
　　inflamed over murder of Jane McCrea — 77:Ag 16
　　British campaign to cut off from other states — 77:
　　　　Je-O, Jl 5, Ag 3-22, Ag 16, S, O7-17; 78:Je 28
New England Restraining Act — 75:Mr-Ap
New England Town Meetings
　　See also
　　　　Boston Town Meeting
　　Boston tea protest, support for — 73:D-74:Mr
　　Intolerable Acts, reaction to — 74:My-S
　　Mass. Government Act curbs on — 74:My-Je
　　Stamp Act protest — 65:S-O
　　tea non-importation resolves — 73:D 12
New Englanders
　　Benedict Arnold afraid of — 83:T (Arnold)
New Hampshire
　　See also
　　　　Battles
　　　　Governors, Colonial
　　　　New Hampshire place names
　　boundary dispute settlement — 65:T (Boundary); 67:T
　　　　(Vt.); 74; 76:My 15; 82
　　clothing for army — 78:T (Soldiers, American)
　　Continental Congress delegate selection — 74:My-S
　　copyright laws — 83:T (Copyright Laws)
　　customs violations — 63:T (Customs)
　　New England Restraining Act, subject to — 75:Mr-Ap
　　sailors, desertion of in — 63:T (Sailors, British)
　　Stamp Act protest — 65:N
　　Stamp Act Congress, not represented at — 65:O 7-25
　　stamp distributor, resignation of — 65:Ag 26-N 16
　　tea, town resolves against landing of — 73:D 12
　　trade with closed by Boston and Conn. for failure to
　　　　support non-importation — 70:My-Je
New Hampshire General Assembly
　　dissolution by Gov. Wentworth — 74:My-S
　　Hog Act — 71:T (Swine)
　　Mass. Circular Letter endorsement — 68:Ap 21
　　state constitution — 76:My 15; 83:T (N.H.)
　　Treason Act — 77:T (Tories)
New Hampshire Grants
　　See Vermont
New Haven, Conn.
　　looted by British — 79:Jl 5-11
New Jersey
　　See also
　　　　Battles
　　　　Governors, Colonial
　　　　N.J. place names
　　American retreat across — 76:N-D
　　anti-independence sentiment — 76:Ja 10, Jl 4
　　boundary settlement — 69:T (Boundary); 74:T (Boun-
　　　　dary)
　　clothing for state regiments — 77:T
　　Continental currency, problems with — 80:Je

counterfeiting — 73:T (Counterfeiting); 74:T (Counter-
　　feiting)
Intolerable Acts, provincial convention responds to —
　　74:My-S
Knyphausen, British invasion under — 80:Je
lighthouse at Sandy Hook — 64:T (Transportation)
militia — 75:Ap-Je
non-importation, merchants thank for — 69:O 18
oath by hand — 78:T (Quakers)
population, comparative — 82:T (Population)
Restraining Act, subject to — 75:Mr-Ap
stamp distributor, resignation of — 65:Ag 26-N 16
Tories — 76:T (Tories)
U.S. capital, offer of land and funds for — 83:O 21
Washington crosses the Delaware into — 76:D 25-77:Ja
　　3
New Jersey, College of (Princeton)
　　commencement — 64:T (Colleges); 65:T (Colleges):
　　　　72:T (Colleges); 74:T (Colleges); 75:T (Colleges)
　　flourishing of — 79:T (Colleges)
　　funds solicitation — 70:T (Colleges); 72:T (Colleges)
　　July 4th celebration — 80:T (July 4th)
　　lottery to aid — 73:T (Colleges)
　　preparation for — 80:T (Colleges)
New Jersey Gazette
　　encouraged by Washington — 77:D 18-78:Je 18
New Jersey General Assembly
　　American independence, disavowal of — 75:N 16, 19
　　Mass. Circular Letter endorsement — 68:Ap 21
　　non-importation, resolution thanks merchants for —
　　　　69:O 18
　　salary of governor, payment of from customs revenues
　　　　— 72:Ag 20
　　state constitution — 76:My 15
**New Jersey House of Assembly (lower house of General
　　Assembly)**
　　See New Jersey General Assembly
New London, Conn.
　　burning by Arnold to divert Americans from South —
　　　　81:S 6
New Orleans
　　Treaty of Paris (1763) provision for — 63:F 10
New Providence (island), Bahamas
　　Stamp Act, protest against — 65:D
New Providence (town on Island of New Providence)
　　Continental Navy capture of — 76:Mr 19
New Year's Day
　　New York City revelers punished — 71:T
New York
　　See also
　　　　Battles
　　　　Governors, Colonial
　　　　N.Y. place names
　　boundary disputes — 65:T (Boundary); 69:T (Boun-
　　　　dary); 74; 76:My 15; 81:Mr 1; 82
　　British-Indian raids — 78:My-N; 79:Ag-S
　　Conn. bills of credit accepted — 75:T (Currency)
　　Continental Association — 74:O-75:Ap, Ap-Je
　　Declaration of Independence, slow approval of — 76:Jl
　　　　4
　　economic development, encouragement of — 64:D

Stamp Act, response to — 65:O-D

Sugar Act, response to — 64:Ag-D, D, T (Colleges)

Townshend Acts, response to — 67:O 28, D 2-4, D; 68:Ja-Mr, F 11, F 25-Ap 28, Mr, Ag 1, Ag 27, S 5; 69:Mr 10, Mr 30, My 16-18, Je 22, Jl 22, Ag 28, S 19, O 18, O 24, O 30; 70:Ja-Ap

Townshend Duties, partial repeal of occasions dispute over maintenance of — 70:Ap-S, My; 74:My-S

trade closed with colonies for failure to support — 70:Je-Jl, S, O 12, D 13

Non-Whites

See also

Indians

Negroes

Slaves

taxation of under Articles of Confederation — 77:N 15

Norfolk, Va.

burning of — 76:Ja 1-3

North Atlantic Fisheries

Americans barred from — 75:Mr-Ap

New England fishermen allowed use of — 82:N 30

North Carolina

See also

Battles

Governors, Colonial

Militia

N.C. place names

boundary settlement — 64:T (Boundary)

Church of England, establishment of in — 65:T (Church of England)

Continental Army Battalion — 78:T

independence, Halifax Resolves instruct for — 76:My 15

Mecklenburg County Resolutions: advanced revolutionary sentiments — 75: My 31

militia — 75:D 9; 76:F 27; 80:O 7; 81:Mr 15

patriot-Loyalist civil war — 80:Ap-My

provincial congress at New Bern — 74:My-S; 75:Je-S

Salt export prohibited — 77:T (Salt)

sectional differences in — 71:Ja-Je

Second Restraining Act, exclusion from — 75:My 31

slaves, proposal to arm against colonists — 75:T (Slaves)

southern campaign, importance in — 80:Ag 16, O 7; 81:Ja, Ja 17, Mr 15

Stamp Act Congress, not represented at — 65:O 7-25

stamp distributor, resignation of — 65:Ag 26-N 16

North Carolina (non-importation) Association — 69:N 7

North Carolina General Assembly

committee of correspondence, failure to form — 73: Mr 12

Continental Congress delegate selection, governor refuses to convene in time for — 74:My-S

dissolution for endorsement of Va. Resolves — 69:N 7

Johnston Riot Act — 71:Ja-Je

Mass. Circular Letter endorsement — 68:Ap 21

state constitution — 76:My 15

North Carolina Regulators — 71:Ja-Je

North, Frederick, Lord (Prime Min.)

See Guilford

North River

See Hudson River

Northwest

See also place names in Northwest

Clark mission to — 78:Jl-Ag; 79:F 24-25; 82:N 10

Treaty of Paris (1783) provisions concerning — 82:N 10

Northwest Passage

Rogers to seek — 72:T

Norwalk, Conn.

looted by British — 79:Jl 5-11

Nova Scotia

See also Halifax

Loyalist flight to — 76:Mr 4; 83

"Novanglus"

See Pseudonymous Writing

O

Oath by Hand — 78:T (Quakers)

Oath of Office

Gage refuses to administer to Mass. General Assembly — 74:O 7

Oculist

See Doctors

Office, State Elective

elections, qualifications — 76:My 15

Ohio

Indians react to new government — 73:T (Indians)

land for sale by Washington — 73:T (Washington); 74:T (Washington)

settlement of by army veterans proposed — 83:T (Army, Continental)

Va. land claims in — 74; Je 22; 81:Mr 1

Ohio River

boundary under Articles of Confederation — 81:Mr 1

boundary under Quebec Act — 74:Je 22

Oliver, Andrew (Lt.-Gov.)

letters to Whately secured by Franklin — 73:Je

resignation as stamp distributor — 65:Ag 14-26, D 17

salary from customs revenues — 71:Mr, O-D

Oliver, Peter (Chief Justice of Superior Court)

Mass. pressure for dismissal of — 74:F-Mr

Opinion, British

See also Pro-American Sentiment

against war — 77:T

Chatham seeks end to war — 77:T

English reaction to colonial problems — 68:S-69:My

London petitions to King blame ministers for American conflict — 75:Je-Jl

Scourge: essays on Britain's political, social, economic conditions — 80:T

Orange Juice

ad for — 78:T

Oriskany, N.Y.

ambush of Americans at — 77:Ag 3-22

Orphan House (Savannah) — 65:T; 69:T; 70:T

Orrery (planetarium) — 68:T

Oswego, N.Y.

importance in campaign to cut off New England — 77:Je-O

Peale, Charles Willson
commissioned to paint Washington — 79:T
patriotic works — 81:T

Peddlers
N.Y. restraints on — 81:T
slaves as — 73:T (Slaves)

Peggy Stewart, the (ship)
burning of — 74:O 19

Penn, John (Gov.)
Wyoming Valley land dispute — 74

Pennsylvania
See also
Battles
Governors, Colonial
Pa. place names
Quakers
boundary dispute with Md. — 74:T (Boundary)
boundary dispute with Va. — 74
British-Indian raids — 78:My-N; 79:Ag-S
copyright laws — 83:T (Copyright Laws)
hospital — 64:T (Hospitals)
independence, resistance to — 76:My 15, Jl 4
Intolerable Acts, reaction to — 74:My-S
martial law in — 80:T (Martial Law)
non-importation — 69:O 18; 74:My-S
Paxton Boys — 63:D-64:F
proprietary colony status — 64:T
provincial congress votes to arm — 75:Je-S
Restraining Act, subject to — 75:Mr-Ap
slavery, gradual abolition of — 78:T (Slaves); 79:T
(Slaves); 80:T (Slaves)
stamp distributor, resignation of — 65:Ag 26-N 16
Washington retreats to from N.J. — 76:N-D
Wyoming Valley, dispute with Conn. over — 74; 82:D
30

Pennsylvania Chronicle
publication of Dickinson's *Letters from a Farmer* —
67:D 2-68:F 15

Pennsylvania General Assembly
committee of correspondence, failure to form — 73:Mr
12
independence, resistance to — 76:My 15
non-importation, Pa. provincial convention instructs
regarding — 74:My-S
Pa. Resolves protesting taxation — 65:S
state constitution — 76:My 15
vagabonds, law against — 67:T (Vagabonds)

Pennsylvania State House
mass protest against tea duty — 73:O 16

Pensacola, West Fla.
Spanish capture of — 82:Ap 9-12

Pest Control
caterpillars — 72:T

Petersburg, Va.
British occupation — 81:Mr-My

Petition of the Crown
by Continental Congress (First) — 74:S 5-O 26, D-75:F
by Continental Congress (Second) — 75:My 10-Ag 2, S
12
by Mass. General Assembly for ouster of Hutchinson
and Oliver — 73:Je

by pro-American Londoners — 75:Je-Jl
by S.C. General Assembly in Powell jailing dispute —
73:Ag 30-S 13
right to — 69:Ag 19

Phenomena
See
Astronomical Phenomena
Unusual Phenomena

Philadelphia
Arnold command after British evacuation — 80:S
Boston Port Act, religious observance on effective date
of — 74:Je i, My-S
continental congress, proposal for — 74:My
Congress moves from to Baltimore — 76:N-D
evacuation by British — 78:Je 28; 80:S
housing survey — 70:T (Housing)
Howe's campaign to capture — 77:Je-O, Ag 25, S 11,
O-N
incorporation of — 83:T
July 4th celebration — 77:T (July 4th); 79:T (July
4th)
Library Company officers chosen — 74:T (Libraries)
non-importation — 65:O-D; 68:Mr; 69:Mr 10
non-importation, difficulty of enforcing — 69:Je-D;
70:Ja-Ap, Je-Jl
non-importation, dispute over maintenance of after
partial Townshend duty repeal — 70:My, S, O 12
occupation by British — 77:S 26
Peale: show of paintings — 81:T (Peale)
Quakers imprisoned for pro-British agreement — 77:T
(Quakers)
sanitation — 79:T (Sanitation); 81:T (Sanitation)
site of Continental Congress — 74:My-S, S 5-O 26
soldiers' protest march on — 83:Je
tea duty protest — 73:O 16, D 28
U.S. capital, offered as — 83:O 21

Philadelphia, College of
"Cato" v. "Cassandra" on Paine's *Common Sense* —
76:Ja 10
commencement — 70:T (Colleges); 80:T (Colleges)

"Philanthrop"
See Pseudonymous Writing

Phillips, William (Gen.)
Cornwallis joins in Va. — 81:Mr 15
death at Petersburg, Va. — 81:Mr-My

Philosophical Society, American — 68:T; 80:T

Pickens, Andrew (Col.)
victory at Kettle Creek, S.C. — 79:Ja-Je

Pilgrims
commemoration of — 72:T

Piracy — 63:T; 72:T; 73:T

Pitcairn, John (Maj.)
Lexington and Concord, command of British troops at
— 75:Ap 19

Pitt, William (Prime Min.)
See Chatham

Plantations
See Agriculture, American

Plymouth, Mass.
opposition to excesses in Boston tea duty protest —
73:D-74:Mr

Property

See also

Land

Slaves

Tories

qualification for holding state office — 76:My 15

Va. act for recovery of that lost during war — 82:T (Slaves)

Protestantism

Jesuits as enemies of — 72:T (Roman Catholics)

Providence, R.I.

continental congress, proposal for — 74:My, My-S

non-importation, dispute over maintenance of after partial Townshend duty repeal — 70:My

non-importation, protest against Townshend Acts — 67:D 2-4; 69:Je-D, O 24

slaves — 74:My-S, T (Slaves)

smuggling — 72:Je 9

Pseudonymous Writing

Benevolus (B. Franklin) on internal v. external taxes — 67:T (Franklin)

Candidus (S. Adams) on officials' salaries from customs revenues — 71:O-D

Cassandra (J. Cannon) for *Common Sense* — 76:Ja 10

Cato (W. Smith) against *Common Sense* — 76:Ja 10

Forester, the (T. Paine), for *Common Sense* — 76:Ja 10

Novanglus (J. Adams) v. Massachusettensis (D. Leonard) on American political issues — 74:D 5/12-75:Ap 17

Vindex (S. Adams) and Philanthrop (Sewall) on Boston Massacre trail — 70:O 24-30

Public Utilities

aqueduct — 72:T

fire prevention — 72:T

street lamps, law against destruction of — 74:T

Pulaski, Count Casimir

killed at Savannah — 79:S-O

Purple Heart Award — 82:T

Provincial Congresses and Conventions

delegate selection for Continental Congress — 74:S 5-O 26

Intolerable Acts, reaction to — 74:My-S

Mass. congress in lieu of General Assembly — 74:O 7

N.C. congress vexes Gov. Martin — 75:My 31

N.Y. asks licensing of ships leaving N.Y.C. — 75:Je-S

vote to arm by — 75:Je-S

Prussia

League of Armed Neutrality — 80:Mr 9

Q

Quakers

contributions in lieu of military service — 75:T

money for colonials suffering losses — 75:Je-S

non-participation in demonstrations against Boston Port Act — 74:Je 2

oath by hand, N.J. — 78:T

oath of allegiance, Pa. — 78:T

patriotism of — 74:T; 75:T

pro-British — 77:T

war conduct attacked — 81:T

Quartering Act (Mutiny Act)

effective — 65:Mr 24

N.Y. General Assembly compliance with — 66:Ja; 67:My 27; 69:D 16

N.Y. General Assembly resistance to — 66:D 15; 68:N 24

revision of included in Intolerable Acts — 74:My-Je

Sons of Liberty, N.Y., resistance to — 69:D 16

S.C. defiance of — 69:Ag 19

Quebec Act — 74:Je 22, T (Roman Catholics); 79:T

Quebec, Province of

See also

Canada

Quebec Act

Quebec place names

Canadian campaign under Montgomery and Arnold — 75:Ag-D; 76:Ja-Je, Jl-N

French legal code — 74:Je 22

Stamp Act, successful implementation of — 65:D

Queen Ann's County, Md.

sentiment for the end of trade with Britain — 74:My-S

Queen's College (Rutgers)

commencement — 74:T (Colleges); 78:T (Colleges)

Quincy, Josiah, Jr.

Boston Massacre trial — 70:O 24-30

defense of Ansell Nickerson — 73:T (Piracy)

R

Raleigh Tavern

Va. Burgesses adjourn to — 69:My 16-18; 74:My-S

Randolph, Peyton

Va. committee of correspondence membership — 73:Mr 12

Rape

See Crime

Rattlesnake

symbol of America explained — 75:T

Rawdon, Lord Francis

Hobkirk's Hill, S.C., defeat of Greene at — 81:Ap 25

reinforcement for Cruger, Ninety-six, S.C. — 81:My 22-19

Reading, Pa.

Howe feint toward on march to Phila. — 77:S 26

Reconciliation, British-American

Burke plan — 75:Mr-Ap

Chatham plan — 74:D-75:F

North plan — 78:F 17

Reed, Joseph (Congressman)

attempted bribery of — 78:Je-N

Regulators

See

North Carolina Regulators

South Carolina Regulators

Relief

See

Charity

Subscriptions

Religion

See also

Clergy

Rhode Island College (Brown)

commencement — 69:T (Colleges); 72:T (Colleges);
   83:T (Colleges)
establishment of — 72:T (Colleges)
funds solicitation — 70:T (Colleges)
location — 70:T (Colleges)

Rhode Island General Assembly

anti-slavery act — 83:T (Slaves)
continental congress, proposal for — 74:My-S
lottery to build wharf — 63:T (Lotteries)
Mass. Circular Letter endorsement — 68:Ap 21
militia readied — 75:Ap-Je
opposition to British taxation — 64:My-D; 65:S
post office — 64:T (Post Office)
state constitution — 76:My 15
supply of Continental Army — 79:T (Army, Continental)

Rice

S.C. compromise on non-exportation of — 74:S 5-O 26

Richmond, Va.

British burning of — 81:Je
Lafayette's arrival in — 81:Mr-My

Rights, American Political

See also
   British Empire, Constitution of the
   Declaration entries
   Newspapers
   Rights of Man, Natural
   States' Rights
   Voting
assembly, right of — 68:S 22-28
Conn. affirmation of — 74:My-S
"Constitutional Catechism, A" — 73:T
Hutchinson as proponent of — 73:Je
necessity of colonial unity for securing — 74:My-S
pardon, power of — 66:Je-D
Parliamentary representation of colonies — 64:My-D;
   65:O 7-25; T; 66:Mr 18
petition of Crown — 69:Ag 19
rebellion, Locke on right of — 74:T (Locke)
Russians encourage — 74:T (Russia)
taxation power — 64:My-D; 65:S, S 28, O 7-25, O 29;
   67:D 2-68:F 15, F 11, N 24; 69:My 16-18, Ag 19;
   74:T; 77:N 15
tea duty called violent attack on — 73:O 16
veto power — 74:My-Je

Rights, Natural

See also
   Locke, John
   Declaration entries
   Religious Freedom
   Slaves
Declaration of Independence, preamble to — 76:Jl 4
R.I. prohibition of slave trade as affirmation of —
   74:My-S, T (Slaves)

Riots

Johnston Riot Act — 71:Ja-Je
London anti-Catholic, anti-administration riots — 80:T
   (Gordon)
Norfolk, Va., colonial soldiers in — 76:Ja 1-3
Stamp Act Riots — 65:Ag 14-26, Ag 27-29; 66:Je-D

Rittenhouse, David (American Scientist) — 68:T; 71:T

River Pilots

warned against guiding tea ships — 73:O 16, O-N

Rivington, James ("Jemmy")

Tory propagandist — 75:N 23

Rochambeau, Jean Baptiste, Comte de (Gen.)

summons de Grasse to prevent Graves from aiding
   Cornwallis — 81:S 5-9
Yorktown, joins Washington en route to — 81:Ag-S

Rockingham, Charles Watson Wentworth, Second Marquis of (Prime Min.)

accession to office of prime minister — 65:Jl 10
death — 82:Jl 1, N 30
return as prime minister — 82:F-Mr
succeeded by Pitt — 66:Ag

Rocky Hill, N.J.

Washington's farewell orders — 83:D 4

Rodney, George (Adm.)

capture of St. Eustatius — 80:D
defeats de Grasse at Les Saintes — 82:Ap 9-12

Rogers, Robert (Maj.)

Northwest Passage — 72:T

Roman Catholics

See also Jesuits
anti-Catholicism, examples of — 68:T; 71:T; 73:T;
   74:Je 22, T; 76:Ja-Je; 80:T (Gordon)
Carroll Brothers on congressional committee sent to
   ask Canadian aid — 76:Ja-Je
clergy obituary — 72:T
priest exercises illegal ministry — 70:T

Romney, HMS

protection of Boston Customs Commissioners —
   68:My 17, Je 10

Rousseau, Jean-Jacques — 67:T

Royal American Magazine or Universal Repository,

proposal for — 73:T (Magazines)

Royal Colonies

See Crown Colonies

Rumors

Arnold, Benedict, execution of — 82:T (Arnold)
atrocities by British Army — 76:N-D
Boston, British defeat at — 75:T
British ministry overthrown by Wilkes, Burke — 75:T
emancipated slaves sold in West Indies by Dunmore —
   75:D 9
Phila., British plan for capture — 76:N-D
quelled by soldier's certificate of good conduct — 75:T
   (Soldiers, American)
Russian alliance — 77:T (Soldiers, Russian)
Vermont Allen Brothers flirtation with British — 82

Russia

See also
   League of Armed Neutrality
   Soldiers, Russian
encouragement of American liberties — 74:T
John Paul Jones becomes admiral in service of — 79:S
   23-24

Rutgers (University)

See
   Queen's College

S

Sabbath
British officers profane by skating — 75:T

Safety, Committees of
Hancock chosen head of in Mass. — 74:O 7
recommendation of Second Continental Congress — 75:My 10-Ag 2

Sailors, British
deserters in N.H. — 63:T

St. Augustine, East Fla.
station for British troops — 69:Ag 19

St. Christopher's
See St. Kitts

St. Clair, Arthur (Gen.)
evacuation of Ft. Ticonderoga — 77:Jl 5

St. Eustatius, West Indies
British capture — 80:D
French recapture — 82:Ap 9-12
July 4th celebration — 80:T (July 4)

St. Kitts, West Indies
French capture of — 82:Ap 9-12

St. Leger, Barry (Col.)
campaign to cut off New England, role in — 77:Je-O Ag 3-22, S

St. Lucia, West Indies
Adm. de Grasse attacks — 81:S 5-9

St. Martin's, West Indies
recapture by French — 82:Ap 9-12

St. Mary's, Scotland
John Paul Jones lands at — 78:Ap 23-24

St. Vincent's, West Indies
French control — 79:Jl 3

Saints, the (Les Saintes), Battle of — 82:Ap 9-12

Salaries of Colonial Officials (payment of from customs revenues)
Mass. protest — 68:F 11; 71:Mr, O-D; 72:Je 13; 73: Ja-Je; 74:F-Mr
N.J. announcement of — 72:Ag 20
Townshend Acts provide for — 67:Jl 2

Salem, Mass.
Mass. Provincial Congress — 74:O 7
military supplies, British attempt to seize — 75:F 26

Salt
export prohibited — 77:T

Saltpeter
manufacture of — 75:T; 76:T

Saltwater Bathing — 74:T

Sanitation
Phila. streets — 79:T; 81:T

Satire
See Humor

Savannah, Ga.
See also Battles
committee of correspondence — 74:My-S
final British evacuation of — 82:My 5, Jl 11
non-importation, merchants agree on — 69:S 19
southern campaign, importance in — 81:My 22-Je 19, S 8

Scalp Bounties — 77:T (War Atrocities); 78:Jl-Ag

Schools
See Education

Schuyler, Hon Yost
Ft. Stanwix, role in relief of — 77:Ag 3-22

Schuyler, Philip
replaced by Gen. Gates — 77:S

Scotch-Irish
western N.C. — 71:Ja-Je

Scottish
western N.C. — 71:Ja-Je

Scourge
essays on Britain's political, social, economic conditions — 80:T (Opinion, British)

Sears, "King" Isaac
leads destruction of Tory printing press — 75:N 23

Secret Ballot
See Voting

Secret Correspondence, Committee of
See Foreign Affairs, Committee for

***Serapis*, HMS**
clash with *Bonhomme Richard* — 79:S 23-24

Servants
ad for hire of — 74:T
fevers of — 64:T (Diseases)
runaways — 64:T; 66:T; 70:T; 77:T
Va. indentured servants emancipated to join British forces — 75:D 9

Settlement
See
Boundary Dispute and Settlement
Land

Seven
noted as lucky number for Americans — 79:T

Seven Years' War
See Great War for the Empire

Sewall, Jonathan (Atty. Gen.)
"Philanthrop" on Boston Massacre trial — 70:O 24-30

Shakespeare
ad for *Hamlet* — 73:T (Theater)
ad for *The Tempest* — 70:T (Theater)
Indians' appreciation of — 67:T

Shawnees
defeat of at Point Pleasant — 74

Shelburne, William Petty Fitzmaurice, Earl of (Prime Min.)
American independence, recognition of — 82:F-Mr
diplomatic isolation of France — 82:N 30
succeeds Rockingham as prime minister — 82:Jl 1

Sheriffs
corrupt in N.C. — 71:Ja-Je
Mass. governor authorized to remove — 74:My-Je

Sherman, Roger
drafting of Declaration of Independence — 76:Jl 4

Ships and Shipping
See also
Navy entries
Privateering
British ownership of required in British-American West Indies trade — 83:Jl 2
British vessels declared open to capture by Americans — 75:S 12
burned by British at Petersburg — 81:Mr-My

Shipwreck

licensing of to prevent supplies reaching British —
75:Je-S

prize ship to be sold — 78:T

Shipwreck

narrative of — 64:T; 66:T

Silk

Townshend Act duty on — 67:Jl 2

Simsbury, Conn.

jail in copper mine — 73:T (Jails)

Slaves

See also

Negroes

Non-Whites

anti-slavery sentiments — 71:T; 74:T; 75:T; 77:T;
80:T; 83:T

arming of by British — 75:D 9, T; 82:T

British said to dance with in Charleston — 82:T

Declaration of Independence: rejected condemnation
of slave trade — 76:Jl 4

emancipation of — 74:T; 75:D 9; 80:T; 81:T; 82:T

freedom suit by — 73:T; 80:T

Ga. regulation of — 64:T; 70:T; 74:T

illness of — 64:T; 73:T

insurrection — 68:S 28-69:Ag 1; 70:T; 75:T

legal status of — 72:T

license for slaves to peddle — 73:T

lottery on — 67:T (Lotteries)

murder of master — 72:T

non-importation — 69:My 16-18; 73:T; 74:My-S, T;
75:T; 76:Ap 6

observations on slavery — 82:T

ordinance requiring them to carry lantern at night —
73:T

Pa., abolition of slavery in — 78:T; 79:T; 80:T; 81:T

popery as slavery — 74:T (Roman Catholics)

R.I. act against slavery — 83:T

runaways — 63:T; 64:T; 66:T; 76:T; 77:T

sales of — 63:T; 64:T; 65:T; 67:T; 69:T; 73:T; 75:T;
78:T; 80:T; 83:T

scheme to use against British in South — 79:T

S.C., status in — 72:T

trading in denounced — 67:T; 75:T; 76:Jl 4

Va. act for recovery of — 82:T

Small Pox

See Diseases

Smith, Rev. William ("Cato")

against Paine's *Common Sense* — 76:Ja 10

Smuggling

See

Customs

Export

Gaspee Affair

Importation

Sugar Act

names of goods smuggled

Snakes

battle between — 83:T

rattlesnake as symbol of America — 75:T (Rattlesnake)

Snuff — 64:T

Social Conditions, British — 80:T (Opinion, British)

Soldiers, American

See also

Army, Continental

Battles

Militia

clothing for — 77:T; 78:T

depredations on houses, Williamsburg — 77:T

deserters — 75:T; 77:T; 78:T; 79:T; 80:T

discharge: certificate of good conduct — 75:T

health of — 77:T

recruiting instructions — 75:T

riot at Norfolk — 76:Ja 1-3

song by soldier — 75:T (Poetry)

thanked for good conduct in Winchester, Va. — 79:T

Soldiers, British

See also

Army, British

old soldier advises leaving Americans alone — 75:T

Soldiers, German

See also Hessians

Bennington, heavy losses at — 77:Ag 16

British agreements for assistance of — 76:T

deserters invited to join French Army — 80:T

Soldiers, Russian — 77:T; 79:T

Songs

See also Poetry

"Mass. Song of Liberty" — 68:T

"World Turned Upside Down, The" played at British
surrender, Yorktown — 81:O 19

"Yankee Doodle" — 75:T

Sons of Liberty

See also McDougall, Alexander

altercations with British troops, N.Y. — 66:Ag 10-11

boycott of non-importation violators — 69:Ja-My

force resignation of stamp distributor — 65:D 5

non-importation of tea, pressure for — 73:O-N, D 17

Quartering Act, resistance to — 69:D 16

South Carolina

See also

Battles

S.C. place names

backcountry grievances — 69:Mr 25

boundary settlement — 64:T (Boundary)

Cherokees, peace with — 77:T (Indians)

college proposed — 64:T (Colleges); 70:T (Colleges)

counterfeiting — 73:T (Counterfeiting)

Creeks, possible attack by — 74:T (Indians)

Declaration of Independence condemnation of slave
trade unacceptable to — 76:Jl 4

Ga., trade with cut off — 74:O-75:Ap

Huguenots — 64:T (Huguenots)

non-importation, resentment of northern defections
from — 70:Je-Jl, S, O 12, D 13; 74:My-S

provincial congress votes to arm — 75:Je-S

Restraining Act, subject to — 75:Mr-Ap

rice, compromise in non-exportation of — 74:S 5-O 26

slavery — 72:T (Slaves); 73:T (Slaves); 76:Jl 4; 82:T

state government, reestablishment of after Battle of
Eutaw Springs — 81:S 8

state seal — 77:T

tea, seizure of by S.C. patriots — 74:My-S

South Carolina (non-importation) Association — 69:Jl 22, S 19; 70:D 13

South Carolina Commons House of Assembly (lower house of General Assembly).
Use South Carolina General Assembly

South Carolina General Assembly
Mass. Circular Letter endorsement — 68:Ap 21
Powell jailing: challenge to freedom of press — 73:Ag 30-S 13
provision of British troops, refusal — 69:Ag 19
resolves protesting infringement of colonial liberties — 65:N 29
state constitution — 76:My 15
state government reestablished — 81:S 8
Va. Resolves endorsement — 69:Ag 19

South Carolina Regulators — 69:Mr 25

Spain
See also Treaty of Paris (1783)
aid to American cause — 76:My
Treaty of Paris (1763) — 63:F 10; 76:My
war with Britain — 78:Je 28; 79:Je 21; 82:Ap 9-12, N 30

Spies
See Espionage

Stafford, Conn.
mineral spring — 66:T (Mineral Spring); 67:T (Mineral Spring)

Stagecoach Travel
See Transportation

Stamp Act
See also
Stamp Act Congress
Stamp Distributors
compensation of Stamp Act Riot victims — 66:Je-D
newspapers' defiance of — 65:S-D
non-importation to protest — 65:O-D, N-D, D 17, D 25, D, D-66:Apr
opposition to, before effective date — 64:My 24, My-D; 65:Mr 22, My 29, Je 6-8, Ag 14-26, Ag 27-29, Ag 26-N 16, S, S 28, S-O, O 7-25, O 29
opposition to, effective date and after — 65:N 29, N 30
opposition to, English — 65:D-66:Apr, Ja 17
poem about — 65:T (Poetry)
protest against contrasted with protest against Townshend Acts — 68:Mr
repeal of — 66:Mr 4, Mr 17, Mr 18, My-Je, 67:Jl 2
successful implementation of — 65:D
unconstitutionality of — 65:S 28, O 7-25, N; 66:F 11

Stamp Act Congress — 65:Je 6-8, S 28, O 7-25, O 29

Stamp Distributors
anniversary, resignation of Boston Stamp official — 73:T (Stamp Act)
forced resignation of — 65:Ag 14-26, Ag 22-29, Ag 26-N 16
Lee, Richard Henry, vindication of attempt to be distributor — 66:T (Richard Henry Lee)

Stark, John (Gen.)
Bennington, defeat of British at — 77:Ag 16

Staten Island, N.Y.
evacuation by British — 83:N 25
landing by British preliminary to N.Y.C. invasion — 76:Jl 2
N.J., British invasion of from — 80:Je

States' Rights
Articles of Confederation — 77:N 15
local resolves against congressional power — 83:T (Humor)
R.I. veto of American trade duty — 82:N 1
state independence, comments against — 83:T (Independence, State)

Statues
George III, statue of pulled down — 76:Jl-Ag
Hillsborough statue, lampoon of — 73:T (Humor)
Pitt statue, Charleston — 70:T (Pitt)
Washington statue proposed by Congress — 83:T (Washington)

Steuben, Baron Friedrich Wilhelm Ludolf Gerhard Augustin von
drill of Continentals at Valley Forge — 77:D 18-78:Je 18
Va. action against Cornwallis — 81:Je-Ag 2

Subscriptions
taken up by colonies for Boston relief — 74:My-S

Suffolk County, Mass.
resolves approved by Continental Congress — 74:S 5-O 26

Suffrage
See also Voting
qualifications for in state constitutions — 76:My 15; 78:T; 79:T

Sugar
See also
Molasses
Sugar Act
duty on — 70:Mr 5
manufacture from cornstalks — 78:T

Sugar Act
colonial opposition to — 64:My-D, Ag-D
description of — 64:Ap 5
modification of — 66:Je 6

Sugar Plums
ad for — 66:T
to destroy worms — 76:T

Suicide — 83:T

Sullivan, John (Gen.)
British-Indian alliance, challenge to — 79:Ag-S
Canadian campaign — 76:Ja-Je
defeat on Long Island — 76:Ag 26
Ft. William and Mary raid — 74:D 14
Newport, unsuccessful attack on — 78:Ag 29

Sumter, Thomas (Gen.)
defeat, Fishing Creek, S.C. — 80:Ag 16

Susquehannah Company
land claim, Wyoming Valley, Pa. — 74; 82:D 30

Sussex, N.J.
English judicial proceedings — 67:T (Justice)

Swearing
See also Oath entries

Sweden

Washington order against in army — 79:T

exhortation against — 71:T (Moral Exhortation)

Sweden

League of Armed Neutrality — 80:Mr 9

Swimming

observations on — 66:T

Swine

Boston law to control — 78:T

N.H. Hog Act — 71:T

T

Tarleton, Banastre (Lt.-Col.)

Charlottesville, near capture of Jefferson and Va. General Assembly at — 81:Je-Ag 2

Cowpens, N.C., loss at — 81:Ja 17

Fishing Creek, S.C., victory — 80:Ag 16

Waxhaws, S.C., massacre of Americans at — 80:Ap-My, O 7

Tarring and Feathering, Committee for

cautions river pilots not to help tea ships — 73:O 16

Taxation

See also

Customs

Revenue entries

Stamp Act

Sugar Act

Taxation, American Protest Against

Townshend Acts

ad valorem tax on imports requested by Congress — 82:N 1

Articles of Confederation provisions for — 77:N 15

Bank of America notes for payment of taxes — 81:D 31

English land tax reduction necessitates American taxes — 67:F 27

internal (direct) v. external (indirect) — 64:My-D; 65:Mr 22, S; 67:Jl 2, D 2-68:F 15; 67:T (Franklin); 68:D 24

Mass. rateable estate list — 78:T

reconciliation with America on issue of, proposals for — 74:D-75:F; 78:F 17

right of reserved by colonies — 64:My-D; 65:S, S 28, O 7-25, O 29; 69:My 16-18

slaves in Va. — 80:T (Slavery)

state taxation, effect of on Continental currency — 79 (77-79); 80:Mr 18

Taxation, American Protest Against

See also

Customs

Non-Importation

Stamp Act

Sugar Act

Tea

Townshend Acts

Baptists protest aid to Congregationalists — 73:T (Baptists)

Boston Town Meeting — 64:My 24

Congress — 74:My-S

Conn. Courant article — 74:T (Rights, American Political)

Dickinson's *Letters from a Farmer* — 67:D 2-68:F 15

Md. Resolves — 65:S 28

Mass. Circular Letter — 68:F 11

N.Y. General Assembly — 64:My-D; 68:N 24

N.C. First Provincial Congress resolution — 74:My-S

Pa. Resolves — 65:S

R.I. Resolves — 65:S

Savannah illegal meeting — 74:My-S

S.C. Resolves — 69:Ag 19

Stamp Act Congress — 65:O 7-25

Suffolk Resolves — 74:S 5-O 26

Va. Resolves and Va. Association — 69:My 16-18

Tea

See also Non-Importation

Annapolis, tea ship and cargo burned in — 74:O 19

Boston protest against tea duty (including Boston Tea Party) — 73:N 5-6, N 28, D 16, D-74:Mr, Ja-Mr

Charleston confiscation of — 73:D 22; 74:My-S

Continental Association infringements — 74:O-75:Ap

East India Company special privileges — 73:Ap 27

how to make own — 73:T

injurious to health — 68:T; 73:T; 74:T

N.Y. protest against duty on — 73:O-N, D 17; 74:Ap 17-24

non-importation, maintenance of after partial Townshend Act repeal — 70:Je-Jl, D 13

non-importation to protest Townshend duty — 68:Ag 1

Phila. protest against duty on — 73:O 16, D 28

poem against — 74:T (Poetry)

Portsmouth, N.H., protest against duty on — 73:D 12; 74:My-S

repeal of duty on under North reconciliation plan — 78:F 17

Townshend Act duty on — 67:Jl 2; 69:Je-D; 70:Ja-Ap, Mr 5, Ap-S; 73:Ap 27

Tea Commissioners

pressure for resignation of — 73:O 16, O-N

refusal of Hutchinson to resign Boston commission — 73:N 5-6

rescue of tea cargo from the *William* — 73:N 28

Tennessee

N.C. Regulators move to — 71:Ja-Je

Theater

ad for — 68:T; 69:T; 73:T

ad for *The Battle of Bunker Hill* — 76:T

ad for *Hamlet* — 73:T

ad for *The Tempest* — 70:T

against — 66:T; 73:T; 74:T; 78:T; 83:T

defense of — 73:T

Garrick, David — 79:T

hospital benefit performance — 73:T

Theft

See Crime

Thomas, John (Gen.)

Boston, bombardment of — 76:Mr 4

Canadian campaign, death in — 76:Ja-Je

Thomson, Charles

signer, Declaration of Independence — 76:Jl 4

Thornton, Matthew

last to sign Declaration of Independence — 76:Jl 4

Greene, recommendation of for southern command —
80:O 7

Hessian capture, avoidance of — 76:S 15

Howe, expectation of northward move by — 77:Ag 25

Hudson River, containment of British east of — 76:O
28

Lee, Gen. Charles, relations with — 76:D 13

officers' protest for back pay and pensions, disapproval of — 83:Mr 15

Ohio land for sale by — 73:T; 74:T

pardon for deserters — 79:T (Soldiers, American)

Peale portrait of — 79:T (Peale)

Phila., loss of — 77:S 26

picture of for sale — 80:T

poem about — 78:T (Poetry)

prisoners of war, letter to Gage on mistreatment of —
75:T (Prisoners of War)

rank not recognized by British — 76:Jl 2

resignation of commission — 83:D 23

statue of proposed — 83:T

Stony Point, N.Y., decision to evacuate — 79:Jl 15

supplied by Conn. — 79:Jl 5-11

swearing, order against — 79:T (Swearing)

Trenton and Princeton, victories at — 76:D 25-77:Ja 3

Valley Forge winter quarters — 77:O-N, D 18-78:Je 18

Va. Resolves, introduction of — 69:My 16-18

Yorktown, Battle of — 81:S 6, Ag-S, O 19

"Watchman, The"

series of letters by McDougall — 70:F

Wayne, Anthony (Gen.)

Paoli, Battle of — 77:S 26

Stony Point, Battle of — 79:Jl 15

Va., southern campaign — 81:Je-Ag 2

Weather

See also Hurricanes

comparative temperatures — 74:D and 75:Ja, 75:T

information on sought by American Philosophical Society — 80:T (American Philosophical Society)

Wedderburn, Alexander (Solicitor General)

reprimand of Franklin before House of Commons —
74:Ja

Wentworth, John (Gov.)

dissolution of N.H. General Assembly — 74:My-S

West Florida

See also West Fla. place names

ceded to Britain by Treaty of Paris (1763) — 63:F 10

ceded to Spain by Treaty of Paris (1783)

crown colony status — 63:O 7

description of — 65:T

Mississippi and Mobile River land available — 75:T

West Indies

See also

Hurricanes

New England Restraining Act

Sugar Act

West Indian place names

British troops stationed in — 63:F 10

colonial boycott of merchandise from — 74:My 13,
My-S, S 5-O 26

Dunmore's selling of emancipated slaves in, rumor of
— 75:D 9

Franco-British hostilities in — 77:D-78:Je, Ag 29,
79:Jl 3; 80:D; 81:S 5-9; 82:My 5, 82:Ap 9-12

post-Revolutionary War British-American trade in —
83:Jl 2

Treaty of Paris (1783) provisions for — 82:N 30

West Point, N.Y.

Arnold's plot to give up — 76:S 15; 80:S

importance to American control of Hudson — 79:Jl 5

Western Lands

See also

Articles of Confederation

Boundary Dispute and Settlement

Indiana

Illinois

Kentucky

Land

Northwest

observation that all states should own — 82:T

Ohio settlement by army vets proposed — 83:T
(Army, Continental)

Wethersfield, Conn.

Rochambeau and Washington meet at to plan N.Y.C.
attack — 81:Ag-S

Whately, Thomas (M.P.)

letters from Hutchinson and Oliver — 73:Je; 74:Ja

Wheat

See

Agriculture, American

Grain

Wheatley, Phillis

poems by — 73:T; 74:T

Whigs

N.Y. General Assembly — 70:F

sentiments countered by Tory propagandist Rivington
— 75:N 23

Whitefield, George

Ga. college, proposal for — 65:T

death of — 70:T

Whitehaven, England

John Paul Jones lands at — 78:Ap 23-24

Whooping Cough

See Diseases

Widows

charity for — 71:T (Charity)

Wife

See Marriage

Wilkes, John — 63:T; 64:T

Lord Mayor of London — 75:Je-Jl

newspaper: *The North Briton* — 70:F

rumored overthrow of British ministry by — 75:T (Rumor)

William and Mary, College of

anniversary of — 78:T (Colleges)

boarding at — 80:T (Colleges)

preparatory education for — 74:T (Colleges)

William, the (ship)

tea cargo rescued and brought to Castle William —
73:N 28

Williamsburg, Va.

American soldiers in — 77:T (Soldiers, American)

Wilmington, N.C.

Boston Port Act, religious observance on effective date
   of — 74:Je 1, My-S

continental congress, proposal for — 74:My

First Va. Convention meeting — 74:My-S

gunpowder, seizure of by royal marines — 75:Ap 21

U.S. capital, offered as — 83:O 21

Washington's birthday celebration — 79:T (Washington); 80:T (Washington)

Wilmington, N.C.

American atrocities — 82:T (War Atrocities)

British supply magazine at — 81:Mr 15

evacuation, British — 81:O 19

proposal for provincial congress — 74:My-S

Winchester, Va.

American soldiers thanked for good conduct in — 79:T
   (Soldiers, American)

Windsor, Conn.

ground sinking — 70:T (Unusual Phenomena)

Wine

duty on — 70:Mr 5

Winnsboro, S.C.

Cornwallis winter quarters at — 80:O 7; 81:Ja 17

Winthrop, John

on electricity — 70:T

Wolves — 77:T

Women

ad for wife — 80:T (Marriage)

"Character of a Loving Wife, The" — 72:T (Humor)

education, letter to parents on — 72:T

Free Masons, admission to — 66:T (Free Masons)

non-support dispute — 70:T (Marriage)

patriotism of — 64:T; 69:T; 74:T; 75:T; 77:T (Patriotism); 80:T

runaway wife, ad for — 74:T (Marriage)

superiority of, Sally Tickle on — 73:T

Wood

scarcity — 80:T

Wooster, David (Gen.)

battle with British returning from Danbury — 77:Ap
   25-28

Worcester County, Mass.

resolutions protesting Mass. Government Act — 74:O 7

Wright, James (Gov.)

declares private protest assemblies illegal — 74:My-S

dissolves Ga. General Assembly — 68:D 24

Wyoming Valley

British-Indian raids — 78:My-N

Pa.-Conn. jurisdictional dispute — 74; 82:D 30

Y

Yale College

AWOL students — 71:T (Colleges)

commencement — 66:T (Colleges)

non-importation — 64:T (Colleges)

Yankee

etymolgy of word — 75:T

"Yankee Doodle" — 75:T

York, Pa.

Congress flees to — 77:S 26

Yorke, Sir Joseph

protest of Dutch trade with America — 77:F

Yorktown

See also Battles

Continental Army assembles under Washington —
   81:Ag-S

fortification for British naval base — 81:Je-Ag

NEW
CATHOLIC
ENCYCLOPEDIA

SUPPLEMENT 2009

NEW CATHOLIC ENCYCLOPEDIA

SUPPLEMENT 2009

VOLUME 2
J-Z

INDEX

in association with

THE CATHOLIC UNIVERSITY OF AMERICA • WASHINTON, D.C.

GALE
CENGAGE Learning

Detroit • New York • San Francisco • New Haven, Conn • Waterville, Maine • London

New Catholic Encyclopedia Supplement 2009

Robert L. Fastiggi, Executive Editor

© 2010 by The Catholic University of America. Published by Gale, a part of Cengage Learning.

For product information and technology assistance, contact us at
Gale Customer Support, 1-800-877-4253.
For permission to use material from this text or product,
submit all requests online at **www.cengage.com/permissions.**
Further permissions questions can be emailed to
permissionrequest@cengage.com

While every effort has been made to ensure the reliability of the information presented in this publication, Gale, a part of Cengage Learning, does not guarantee the accuracy of the data contained herein. Gale accepts no payment for listing; and inclusion in the publication of any organization, agency, institution, publication, service, or individual does not imply endorsement of the editors or publisher. Errors brought to the attention of the publisher and verified to the satisfaction of the publisher will be corrected in future editions.

EDITORIAL DATA PRIVACY POLICY: Does this product contain information about you as an individual? If so, for more information about our editorial data privacy policies, please see our Privacy Statement at www.gale.cengage.com.

Gale
27500 Drake Rd.
Farmington Hills, MI, 48331-3535

LIBRARY OF CONGRESS CATALOGING-IN-PUBLICATION DATA

New Catholic encyclopedia supplement 2009 / Robert L. Fastiggi, executive editor.
   p. cm.
   Includes bibliographical references and index.
   ISBN 978-1-4144-7526-4 (set) — ISBN 978-1-4144-7527-1 (v. 1) — ISBN 978-1-4144-7528-8 (v. 2)
   1. Catholic Church—Encyclopedias. I. Fastiggi, Robert L.

BX841.N44 Suppl. 2010
282.03—dc22   2009031096

ISBN-13: 978-1-41-447526-4 (set)   ISBN-10: 1-41-447526-8 (set)
ISBN-13: 978-1-41-447527-1 (vol. 1)   ISBN-10: 1-41-447527-6 (vol. 1)
ISBN-13: 978-1-41-447528-8 (vol. 2)   ISBN-10: 1-41-447528-4 (vol. 2)

This title is also available as an e-book:
ISBN-13: 978-1-41-447526-4 ISBN-10: 1-41-446413-4
Contact your Gale, a part of Cengage Learning sales representative for ordering information.

Printed in the United States of America
1 2 3 4 5 6 7 13 12 11 10 09

EDITORIAL AND PRODUCTION STAFF

PROJECT EDITORS

Thomas E. Carson
Douglas A. Dentino

**EDITORIAL TECHNICAL
SUPPORT**

Mike Lesniak
Amanda D. Sams

MANUSCRIPT EDITORS

Judith Clinebell
Tony Coulter
Laurie J. Edwards
Peter Jaskowiak
Christine Kelley
Michael Levine
Pamala Revitzer
Ann Shurgin

PROOFREADERS

Tony Coulter
Amy Francis
Heather Price

INDEXER

Lynne Maday

PRODUCT DESIGN

Pamela A.E. Galbreath

IMAGING

John Watkins

GRAPHIC ART

Pre-PressPMG

PERMISSIONS

Dean Dauphinais
Margaret Abendroth

COMPOSITION

Gary Leach

EDITORIAL DIRECTOR

John Fitzpatrick

**DIRECTOR, NEW
PRODUCT DEVELOPMENT**

Hélène Potter

PUBLISHER

Jay Flynn

CONTENTS

FOREWORD

In its *Decree, Inter mirifica*, Vatican II recognized the inherent right of the Church to employ all instruments of social communication "for the instruction of Christians" and "the welfare of souls" (no. 3). When this decree was issued in 1963, the electronic medium of the Internet had yet to be developed, but who can doubt the importance of electronic means of communication in the world today. In keeping with the spirit of *Inter mirifica*, the Church today has embraced electronic means of communicating: from the Vatican website to the various sites of Catholic schools, dioceses, religious congregations and parishes.

The New Catholic Encyclopedia (NCE) was originally published in print form in 1967, and supplemental volumes were issued in 1974, 1979, 1989, and 1996. A Jubilee Volume honoring the papacy of Pope John Paul II was published in 2001 as a transition to the Second Edition, which appeared in 2003. In light of the present context of electronic communication, I am very pleased that the Second Edition of the NCE is available in electronic form and that supplements will appear regularly in the same medium. In today's world of instant communication, it is essential that the *New Catholic Encyclopedia* keep pace with new developments in the life of the Church in the electronic medium. It is also important that there be an electronic means of accessing the many articles of the NCE that have already appeared, as well as those that are new, revised and updated. At the same time, it is good to know that the editors and publisher of the NCE recognize that the world of print is still with us, and that they will issue print editions of this and future supplements, especially for those who are not comfortable with reading in the electronic medium.

I am happy that the partnership formed some years ago between The Catholic University of America and the Gale Group (now a division of Cengage Learning) still continues with this supplement to the NCE. I am also pleased that the editors of the NCE — Dr. Robert Fastiggi, Fr. Joseph Koterski, S.J. and Dr. Frank Coppa — have committed themselves to the same standards of objectivity, accuracy and balance that have marked previous editions. These yearly supplements will not only provide new updates and articles on general Catholic topics; they will also focus on yearly themes, such as "science and faith," "Catholic history," "literature and the arts," and "philosophy and ethics" to insure that Catholic contributions and perspectives related to these fields are thoroughly covered.

I wish to thank the project editors of Gale, Cengage Learning as well as Dr. David McGonagle, the Director of the Catholic University of America Press, for their commitment to the NCE. I am confident that the *New Catholic Encyclopedia*, will continue to be a preeminent source of Catholic scholarship and information for many years to come.

Very Rev. David M. O'Connell, C.M., J.C.D.
President,
The Catholic University of America

PREFACE

The present volume represents a new phase in the development of the *New Catholic Encyclopedia* [NCE]. For the first time since the original 15-volume edition of 1967, a supplement is being published not only in print but also in electronic form. In today's world of information, this makes eminent sense since students and scholars are more and more relying on electronic means of communication. An electronic format has several advantages: those seeking articles from the present or previous two publications of the NCE (2001 and 2003) have easy and almost immediate access to them. In addition, in this e-publication environment, the shackles of page count do not apply. In the past, it was often the case that some older entries would be dropped from a print encyclopedia in order to make room for new topics. They were victims of "page count." Such sacrifices no longer need to be made. It is also now possible to retain all of the previous versions of a revised, updated or rewritten entry as the NCE moves forward with each successive supplemental release. The result is that those who subscribe to the Jubilee Volume, the Second Edition and all forthcoming supplements will have access, in electronic form, to an ever-expanding archive of Catholic content and perspective readily available, making their research more efficient and fruitful. Future supplements, however, will continue to be published in print form for the benefit of libraries as well as those who are more comfortable with a traditional print format.

The Catholic University of America Press first published the *New Catholic Encyclopedia* in 15 volumes in 1967, followed by four supplemental volumes published irregularly between 1972 and 1995. In 2001, a Jubilee Volume was issued marking the year 2000, which was published by the Gale Group of Farmington Hills, Michigan in editorial partnership with the Catholic University of America Press. This Jubilee Volume covered the people, issues and events of the Catholic Church since the Second Vatican Council with a special focus on the pontificate of Pope John Paul II. It also prepared the way for the second edition of the NCE, which was published in 2003. This second edition included many new articles and revisions of the original entries from the 1967 volumes.

In the summer of 2006, planning for new supplements of the NCE began with an eye towards an electronic format. Cengage Learning (the successor to the Gale Group), together with the Catholic University of America Press, decided to combine the thematic approach of the 2001 Jubilee Volume with the necessary updating and revision of prior entries, along with addition of many new entries. A commitment was made to publish annual supplements in order to facilitate more frequent updating and revisions than the prior periodic print supplements allowed. Annual supplements also support the inclusion of more new topics that touch on Catholic life, thought and practice.

In reviewing the contents of the second edition of the NCE, the editorial board found a number of thematic areas in need of greater coverage and expansion, especially in the light of contemporary developments. The editors, therefore, decided that each of the annual supplements should focus special attention on certain themes, beginning with Science and the Church in 2009, followed by Modern History and the Church (2010), Literature and the Arts (2011) and Philosophy and Ethics (2012).

The concept behind the thematic focus is the need for a systematic plan of ongoing revision of existing entries. This enables the editors to concentrate their attention on certain areas of scholarship for each yearly supplement. The present volume (2009) covers scientific and bioethical topics that have received increased attention since the 2003 edition of the NCE. New articles, for example, are included on the "Anthropic Principle," "Intelligent Design," "Brain Death," "Assisted Nutrition and Hydration," and "Condoms and HIV Protection." Other topics that were covered indirectly or partially in the 2003 edition are now treated with articles of their own: for example, "Big Bang," "Cloning," and "Reproductive Technology." There are likewise entries that have revised, expanded and updated articles from the second edition: e.g. "Creationism" and "Evolution."

In addition to these thematic articles, the editors realized that the ongoing life of the Catholic Church necessitates coverage of new ecclesial documents, personalities and matters of emerging interest. Thus, new entries are included in the present volume, for example, on the encyclicals of Pope Benedict XVI (*Deus caritas est* and *Spe salvi*), the recently deceased Cardinal Avery Dulles, S.J. and "the Internet and the Church." (All together these "new" entries make up roughly 40% of this volumes content.)

The editors believe that yearly supplements enable more frequent updating of the statistics and events of the Catholic Church in the different states and archdioceses. The rapid growth of new ethnic populations (e.g. Hispanics) and local ecclesial responses to the various sex abuse cases make such updating even more important. In addition to the expanded coverage of focused themes and the updating on states and archdioceses, the 2009 supplement includes entries that have revised, expanded or replaced certain entries from the 2003 volume: e.g. *Humani generis*, the History of Moral Theology, and the Catholic University of America. (These revised and updated entries make up the remaining 60% of the content in this volume.)

Having yearly electronic as well as print supplements enables the NCE to be more dynamic, inclusive and contemporary. The goal is to provide readers with access to solid information from a Catholic perspective about the life of the Church and emerging topics of interest and discussion. These yearly supplements will also provide revisions and expansions of earlier material, reflecting new developments in research and scholarship. By covering topics of historic as well as contemporary interest, the *New Catholic Encyclopedia* strives to be faithful to the Church herself, which is "ever ancient" and "ever new."

Robert L. Fastiggi
Executive Editor

Editorial Note: In an effort to focus on topics that are of interest to our readers, we have created a mailbox where you can email us your ideas for topics that you would like us to cover, or comment on those we have already published. We welcome your participation in the re-forging of the New Catholic Encyclopedia. The mailbox address is: Gale.new.catholic@Cengage.com

ABBREVIATIONS

The system of abbreviations used for the works of Plato, Aristotle, St. Augustine, and St. Thomas Aquinas is as follows: Plato is cited by book and Stephanus number only, e.g., Phaedo 79B; Rep. 480A. Aristotle is cited by book and Bekker number only, e.g., Anal. post. 72b 8—12; Anim. 430a 18. St. Augustine is cited as in the Thesaurus Linguae Latinae, e.g., C. acad. 3.20.45; Conf. 13.38.53, with capitalization of the first word of the title. St. Thomas is cited as in scholarly journals, but using Arabic numerals. In addition, the following abbreviations have been used throughout the encyclopedia for biblical books and versions of the Bible.

Books

Acts	Acts of the Apostles
Am	Amos
Bar	Baruch
1—2 Chr	1 and 2 Chronicles (1 and 2 Paralipomenon in Septuagint and Vulgate)
Col	Colossians
1—2 Cor	1 and 2 Corinthians
Dn	Daniel
Dt	Deuteronomy
Eccl	Ecclesiastes
Eph	Ephesians
Est	Esther
Ex	Exodus
Ez	Ezekiel
Ezr	Ezra (Esdras B in Septuagint; 1 Esdras in Vulgate) Gal Galatians
Gn	Genesis
Hb	Habakkuk
Heb	Hebrews
Hg	Haggai
Hos	Hosea
Is	Isaiah
Jas	James
Jb	Job
Jdt	Judith
Jer	Jeremiah
Jgs	Judges
Jl	Joel
Jn	John
1—3 Jn	1, 2, and 3 John
Jon	Jonah
Jos	Joshua
Jude	Jude
1—2 Kgs	1 and 2 Kings (3 and 4 Kings in Septuagint and Vulgate)
Lam	Lamentations
Lk	Luke
Lv	Leviticus
Mal	Malachi (Malachias in Vulgate)
1—2 Mc	1 and 2 Maccabees
Mi	Micah
Mk	Mark
Mt	Matthew
Na	Nahum
Neh	Nehemiah (2 Esdras in Septuagint and Vulgate) Nm Numbers
Ob	Obadiah
Phil	Philippians
Phlm	Philemon
Prv	Proverbs
Ps	Psalms

1—2 Pt	1 and 2 Peter
Rom	Romans
Ru	Ruth
Rv	Revelation (Apocalypse in Vulgate)
Sg	Song of Songs Sir Sirach (Wisdom of Ben Sira; Ecclesiasticus in Septuagint and Vulgate)
1—2 Sm	1 and 2 Samuel (1 and 2 Kings in Septuagint and Vulgate)
Tb	Tobit
1—2 Thes	1 and 2 Thessalonians
Ti	Titus
1—2 Tm	1 and 2 Timothy
Wis	Wisdom
Zec	Zechariah
Zep	Zephaniah

Versions

Apoc	Apocrypha
ARV	American Standard Revised Version
ARVm	American Standard Revised Version, margin
AT	American Translation
AV	Authorized Version (King James)
CCD	Confraternity of Christian Doctrine
DV	Douay-Challoner Version
ERV	English Revised Version
ERVm	English Revised Version, margin
EV	English Version(s) of the Bible
JB	Jerusalem Bible
LXX	Septuagint
MT	Masoretic Text
NAB	New American Bible
NEB	New English Bible
NIV	New International Version
NJB	New Jerusalem Bible
NRSV	New Revised Standard Version
NT	New Testament
OT	Old Testament
RSV	Revised Standard Version
RV	Revised Version
RVm	Revised Version, margin
Syr	Syriac
Vulg	Vulgate

J

JIHĀD

The Muslim term *jihād*, which means "to strive," must be understood in its historical context, rather than defining it based solely on one historical moment. The text of Sūrah IX:20, a late portion of the *Qur'ān*, states: "Those who believed, and suffered displacement, and *strove perseveringly* in God's cause, with their possessions and their lives, are highly ranked in the sight of God: These people will succeed." This Sūrah clarifies the difference between those who behaved well and those who did not during a conflict on the border of Syria. Earliest ISLAM distinguished between acts of aggression and justifiable defensive warfare. In addition, Sūrahs 16:90, 7:33, and 10:23 warn against aggression. However, Sūrah IX clearly advocates justifiable warfare. Indeed, verses 38 and 39 make justifiable warfare a moral obligation. In the social context of early Islam, this obligation referred to the defense of the community of believers.

The majority of early Muslim jurists maintained that the obligation to undertake *jihād* was to be understood in terms of warfare. However, the term *jihād* can also mean any form of striving that involves a determined effort. The objective of military *jihād* was political; that is, it was meant to establish Muslims as the rulers of a territory and to fulfill the moral imperative of Sūrah 3:104 to establish goodness and justice. Aggressive warfare outside the boundaries of Arabia was considered justifiable because of perceived threats from the surrounding empires. *Jihād* was not to be undertaken to convert others, since the *Qur'ān* states that there can be no compulsion in religion (Sūrah 2:256).

It was not until centuries later, when Muslims had been fighting not only unbelievers but also one another, that a *hadīth* (an account of a deed or saying of MUHAMMAD or his companions) emerged in Sufi circles claiming that striving in the cause of God is to be articulated in two categories: the greater *jihād* and the lesser *jihād*. The greater *jihād* is one's inner struggle against evil inclinations and temptations; the lesser *jihād* is warfare. This distinction is not found in early collections of *hadīth* that form the basis of Muslim jurisprudence. However, with the widespread influence of Sufism in premodern Islam, this *hadīth* gained wide credibility and continues to influence the way the term *jihād* is understood today.

At about the same time, Ibn Taymīyah (1263–1328) advocated a stricter notion of active *jihād* as an indispensable feature of legitimate Muslim rule. He believed that failure to pursue *jihād* was a moral defect, and his views continue to influence activist Muslims in the modern period.

Since the seventeenth century, Muslims have had to confront the challenge of colonialism. With the defeat of the Indian Mutiny in 1857, Muslims in South Asia developed new perspectives on *jihād*. Sir Sayyid Ahmad Khan (1817–1898) argued that *jihād* meant only defensive war and could not justify further resistance to British rule, as long as the British did not actively interfere with the practice of Islam. This argument became a way by which Muslims could articulate a humane, modernist understanding of *jihād*, and it influenced attempts to rationalize early Islamic history. To this end, The *Qur'ān* was interpreted by a cautious consensus of noted late nineteenth and early twentieth-century South Asian and Arab reformist Muslim leaders to require peace treaties with adversaries who wish to live in peace. Thus, Muslim law (*Sharī'ah*) could be reconciled with international law.

Sayyid Abū Al-A' Lā Mawdūdī (1903–1979), the Indo-Pakistani modernist political philosopher, claimed that *jihād* is not merely warfare to expand Islamic political dominance, but that it is also undertaken to establish a just rule, one that includes freedom of religion. Thus, Islam was presented as an instrument by which justice can be established for all, even for non-Muslims, and indeed even for persons who are not "people of the Book," such as Hindus and Buddhists.

Nonmodernist Muslim thinkers, including Hasan al-Banna (1906–1949) and Sayyid Qutb (1906–1966), emphasized the establishment of a truly Islamic government through *jihād*. Following the medieval theorist Ibn Taymīyah, they advocated the overthrow of governments that fail to enforce *Sharī'ah*, making the case for legitimate revolution in a morally deficient Islamic state. As in other modernist movements that have taken a radical turn, *jihād* took center stage in defining the faith for these theorists. Understood as armed action to set things right in the political order, *jihād* is the heart of Islam. From this perspective, it is the neglect of *jihād* that has caused the current depressed state of Islam in the world.

Most ominously for Muslims and non-Muslims alike is the spectacle of educated, gainfully employed Muslims planning and executing acts of terrorism. The idea that such terrorism is obligatory *jihād* presents a profound challenge to Islam. Many governments are increasingly under pressure to identify potential adherents of terrorist groups of all kinds. As a result, the idealism of Islam as a religion of peace has been gravely compromised. Authentic Islam seems unable to prevent the spread of rhetoric that presents *jihād* as a courageous response to a hostile world. A possible solution requires collaboration among all Islamic sectarian movements, many of whom are working to dissuade those who are convinced that terrorism is an obligatory form of *jihād*.

SEE ALSO ISLAMIC LAW; ISLAMIC TRADITIONS (ḤADĪTH); QUR'ĀN.

BIBLIOGRAPHY

Akbar Ahmed, *Journey Into Islam: The Crisis of Globalization* (Washington, D.C. 2007).

John L. Esposito, *What Everyone Needs to Know about Islam* (Oxford, U.K. 2002).

M. Fethullah Gülen, *Prophet Muhammad as Commander* (London 1996).

Douglas E. Streusand, "What Does *Jihād* Mean?" *Middle East Quarterly* 4, no. 3 (1997); pp.1–6.

Rev. Francis V. Tiso
Associate Director
Secretariat for Ecumenical and Interreligious Affairs,
United States Conference of Catholic Bishops (2009)

JOHN PAUL II, POPE

The first Slavic POPE ever and the first non-Italian elected to the See of Peter in four and a half centuries, John Paul II's personality, pastoral method, and magisterium left indelible marks on world Catholicism. As the Council of Trent and the Counter-Reformation popes defined the Church's relationship to an emerging modern world, the Second Vatican Council as authoritatively interpreted by John Paul II may well define Catholicism's relationship to whatever follows in the twenty-first century and beyond.

PRE-PAPAL YEARS

Early Life. Karol Józef Wojtyła was born on May 18, 1920, in Wadowice, a provincial Galician town near Kraków. His father, Karol, was a retired army officer; his mother, Emilia Kaczorowska, had previously borne another son, Edmund, and a daughter who died shortly after birth. Emilia Wojtyła died in 1929; young Karol, *Lolek* to his family and friends, was just finishing the third grade. Three and a half years later, his brother Edmund, a doctor, died of scarlet fever contracted from a patient. Lolek and his father lived by themselves for the next nine years. The son would later write that his father's piety, austerity, and interest in Polish literature and history constituted "my first seminary."

Wojtyła received an excellent classical elementary and secondary education in Wadowice, where he was a star student and a fine athlete and outdoorsman. During high school he immersed himself in the classics of Polish Romantic literature and became deeply involved in the theater under the influence of an avant-garde director, Mieczysław Kotlarczyk.

In 1938 Wojtyła moved with his father to Kraków to begin studies in Polish PHILOLOGY at the Jagiellonian University. His undergraduate career was interrupted by the Second World War. Shortly after conquering Poland, the Nazis closed the university and shipped many of its professors to the Sachsenhausen concentration camp. Polish cultural life went underground for the duration of the war.

The War Years. From 1939 to 1945 Wojtyła was heavily engaged in various forms of cultural resistance to the German Occupation of his homeland. He continued his studies when the Jagiellonian University reconstituted itself underground. With his mentor, Mieczysław Kotlarczyk, he founded the Rhapsodic Theatre, a clandestine troupe whose experimental productions of Polish classics helped keep alive the national memory the Nazis were determined to erase. He joined UNIA, a broad-based, clandestine resistance movement which included armed cadres and a unit devoted to saving Polish Jews from the HOLOCAUST (SHOAH); UNIA worked to lay the cultural, social, and political foundations for a postwar Christian democratic Poland. Young Wojtyła also took an active role in his parish, leading one of the original Living Rosary groups of young men; here he encountered the lay mystic Jan Tyranowski (1901–1947), who introduced him to the writings of St. JOHN OF THE CROSS and St. TERESA OF AVILA. As all these activities were strictly banned by the Occupation, Wojtyła lived for more than five years at the daily risk of his life.

From 1940 to August of 1944 Wojtyła was also a manual laborer, first as a quarryman and blaster and later as a worker in the Solvay chemical factory on the outskirts of Kraków; the experience marked him for life. After his father's death in February 1941, Karol struggled to discern his vocation, torn between his love for the theater and the academic life and an increasing sense that he was being called to the priesthood. After a period of intense REFLECTION (during which he explored the possibility of entering the CARMELITES, only to be told that they were accepting no new novices during the war), it became clear to him that GOD intended him for the priesthood. The heroic Archbishop of Kraków, Adam Stefan SAPIEHA, accepted him as a candidate, and for two years Wojtyła lived a double life, continuing his manual work and his resistance activities while beginning his PHILOSOPHY and THEOLOGY studies in the clandestine seminary that Sapieha had created in defiance of the Occupation.

In August 1944 when the Gestapo attempted to arrest the young men of Kraków to forestall a repetition of the Warsaw Uprising, Sapieha took his clandestine seminarians into his home, which functioned as an underground seminary, until the Soviet Army drove the Germans from Kraków in January 1945. Daily life with the "prince-archbishop," as Sapieha (son of a noble Polish-Lithuanian family) was known, provided Wojtyła with his model of the priest and bishop as *defensor hominis*, the defender of the rights of his people.

The Young Priest. On November 1, 1946, Cardinal Sapieha ordained Wojtyła to the priesthood and then sent him to ROME to obtain his doctorate in theology at the Pontifical University of St. Thomas Aquinas, the "Angelicum." After living at the Belgian College for two years and exploring the Belgian and French worker-priest experiments during vacations, Wojtyła completed a dissertation on *The Doctrine of Faith According to St. John of the Cross* under the direction of Réginald GARRIGOU-LAGRANGE, O.P. Garrigou's single criticism of the dissertation, that Wojtyła did not use the phrase "divine object" of God, indicated that the young Polish

priest-scholar was beginning to move beyond the Neoscholasticism then dominating Catholic intellectual life.

After six months of service in the country parish at Niegowić, Father Wojtyła was assigned by Cardinal Sapieha to St. Florian's Church in Kraków, a parish frequented by Catholic intellectuals and professionals. His task was to form a new chaplaincy for the students of the Jagiellonian University, the Kraków Academy of Fine Arts, and the Kraków Polytechnic: a front-line post in the struggle with Poland's new communist regime for the SOUL of Polish youth. Father Wojtyła became an immensely successful student chaplain and a pastoral pioneer. He encouraged his students to participate actively in the Mass; he formed choirs, directed theatrical groups, and provided off-campus opportunities for philosophical and theological studies that were difficult or impossible in the Marxist-dominated academic environment of Kraków. Defying both clerical convention and communist restrictions on organizing youth groups, he took young men and women into the countryside for skiing, hiking, camping, and kayaking trips that were also opportunities for pastoral care. His young friends called him *Wujek* (Uncle), a kind of Stalin-era *nom de guerre*; as the circle of students expanded, they called themselves Wojtyła's *Środowisko*, or *milieu*. The friendships formed in these years endured throughout Wojtyła's life. As he formed young professionals into mature Christians, they were forming him into one of the most dynamic priests of his generation and igniting his interests in modern problems of sexual ETHICS, marriage, and family life.

Amidst this intense pastoral activity, Father Wojtyła wrote numerous essays and poems (the latter published pseudonymously) for the independent Kraków Catholic newspaper *Tygodnik Powszechny* (Universal Weekly). He also composed a play, *Our God's Brother*, which explored the temptations of revolutionary violence through Kotlarczyk's *inner theater* dramatic method. The play was loosely based on the life of Albert CHMIELOWSKI, a Polish painter who founded a religious community dedicated to the homeless.

Scholar and Bishop. In 1953 Wojtyła completed his habilitation doctorate under instructions from Archbishop Eugeniusz Baziak (1890–1962). His dissertation explored the moral philosophy of the German phenomenologist, Max SCHELER, and marked the beginning of Wojtyła's intellectual combination of THOMISM and PHENOMENOLOGY. One of the dissertation readers, Professor Stefan Swieżawski (1907–2004), encouraged the young philosopher to join the faculty of the Catholic University of Lublin (KUL), the only Catholic institution of higher education behind the iron curtain.

Archbishop Baziak approved the arrangement, and Karol Wojtyła was appointed instructor in philosophical ethics at KUL, where he later occupied the Chair of Ethics. Wojtyła maintained his relationship to KUL for decades, participating in a distinctive philosophical project in which the truth of reality and morals were probed through a disciplined reflection on the human person. The KUL philosophers proposed to challenge Marxism and other distorted modern ideologies on their own intellectual ground: What is authentic human liberation? On this basis Wojtyła eventually developed a complex philosophical anthropology rooted in an analysis of human moral agency.

While commuting weekly to KUL, where he was a magnetic teacher, CONFESSOR, and counselor; Father Wojtyła continued his pastoral work in Kraków, adding a ministry to healthcare professionals to his ongoing work with students and teaching social ethics in the Kraków seminary. In 1958 Pope PIUS XII appointed him TITULAR BISHOP of Ombi and Auxiliary Bishop of Kraków. After Wojtyła was ordained bishop in Wawel Cathedral on September 29, 1958, he added a new load of episcopal duties to his academic work at KUL and his pastoral activities. In conversation with his graduate students and other lay friends, Bishop Wojtyła prepared his first book, *Love and Responsibility*, in which he discussed sexual ethics and the beauty of sexual love with a frankness startling in its time and place.

The Second Vatican Council. When the Ante-Preparatory Commission appointed by Pope JOHN XXIII wrote the world's bishops inviting suggestions for the agenda of the Second Vatican Council, Bishop Wojtyła, the forty-year-old auxiliary of Kraków, responded with a philosophical essay urging that the council propose Christian HUMANISM as the Church's response to the civilizational crisis of the mid-twentieth century. Defective ideas of the human person, Wojtyła argued, were at the root of a century of fear that had already produced two world wars, three totalitarian systems, unprecedented slaughter, and the greatest persecution of the Church in history. Reconstituting the Church as an evangelical movement proclaiming the truth about the human person was, in his judgment, the crucial intellectual and pastoral task of the Council—a vision congruent with John XXIII's historic opening address to the bishops on October 11, 1962. That vision would guide Wojtyła's participation in and implementation of Vatican II for more than forty years.

Wojtyła attended all four periods of the Council, taking an increasingly active role. Entering the council as a very junior auxiliary bishop, he participated in the third and fourth periods (and the crucial intercession between the third and fourth periods) as the archbishop of Kraków, a post to which he was nominated by Pope PAUL VI on December 30, 1963. His formal interventions at the council were on themes he had stressed during his priestly ministry: the universal call to HOLINESS, the baptismal dignity of all Christians, the lay vocation in the world as an expression of the triple *munus* of CHRIST, and religious freedom as the first of human rights. Wojtyła's largest contribution to Vatican II came in helping draft and then defend *Gaudium et spes*, the Pastoral Constitution on the Church in the Modern World. Work on this document during the early 1965 intercession and the fourth period of Vatican II brought Wojtyła into contact with important Western theologians, including Yves Marie-Joseph CONGAR and Henri de LUBAC; the latter became a good friend.

During the later periods of the council, Wojtyła began work on *Osoba y czyn* (Person and Act), his major philosophical work, which was intended to provide a secure philosophical foundation for the council's anthropology and teaching on religious freedom. In it, he utilized the resources of both a renewed Thomism and phenomenology.

Archbishop of Kraków. With the entire Polish Church Wojtyła celebrated the millennium of Polish Christianity in 1966. In 1970 after completing a guidebook to the Vatican Council's sixteen documents, *Sources of Renewal*, he began planning an extensive implementation of Vatican II, aimed at enabling his entire archdiocese to relive the conciliar experience. After two years of preparation the Synod of Kraków began in May 1972 and was completed in June 1979. Five hundred discussion groups brought religious, clergy, and laity together to learn the council's teaching and apply it to the pastoral life of the archdiocese.

Named CARDINAL in 1967, Wojtyła's priorities as archbishop included a vigorous defense of religious freedom, which involved an ongoing battle with the communist regime over the construction of new churches and the public expression of Catholic faith; the development of the seminary and a faculty of theology to replace the theology faculty of the Jagiellonian University, which had been closed by the regime in 1954; support for family life, including the establishment of an Institute of Family Life and diocesan-wide marriage-preparation programs; youth ministry; outreach to intellectuals; a broad-ranging ministry of CHARITY; and extensive parish visitations. In carrying out these projects, Wojtyła exemplified the local bishop as pastor, teacher, and defender of the rights of his people.

Cardinal Wojtyła collaborated closely with Cardinal Stefan WYSZYNSKI, Primate of Poland. The two men had different sensibilities, and Wojtyła's ECCLESIOLOGY was more reflective of Vatican II than Wyszyński's. But the communist regime was completely unsuccessful in its ongoing attempts to drive a wedge between the two Polish cardinals, both of whom were determined to maintain the Church's unity against an implacable foe. Wojtyła also did what he could to support the hard-pressed Church in Czechoslovakia; he and one of his auxiliary bishops clandestinely ordained priests for service underground in Czechoslovakia.

During his fourteen years as archbishop of Kraków, Wojtyła became one of the best-known and most highly respected churchmen in the world. In addition to his work as a cardinal with various dicasteries of the Roman Curia, he participated in the meetings of the SYNOD OF BISHOPS in 1969, 1971, 1974, and 1977, serving as *relator* of the 1974 synod on evangelization. Wojtyła was also elected by his episcopal peers as a member of the Synod Council. In 1968 a Kraków-based theological commission organized by Cardinal Wojtyła sent a lengthy memorandum on the Church's marital ethic to Pope Paul VI, who was then preparing the ENCYCLICAL *Humanae vitae*; the memorandum proposed a thoroughly humanistic understanding of human sexuality as the foundation for the Church's sexual ethic and teaching on CONTRACEPTION.

Wojtyła visited the United States and Canada in 1969 and returned to the United States in 1976 for the International Eucharistic Congress. He also led the Polish delegation to the 1973 International Eucharistic Congress in Australia. In April 1974 he gave a major philosophical paper at the International Thomistic Congress in Italy, drawing the admiration of the German philosopher Joseph Pieper (1904–1997), among others. Paul VI invited Cardinal Wojtyła to deliver the 1976 Lenten retreat for the pope and his closest Curial collaborators; Wojtyła's retreat conferences were later published as a book, *Sign of Contradiction*.

The Year of Three Popes. Paul VI died on Aug. 6, 1978; Wojtyła traveled to Rome with Cardinal Wyszyński for the conclave that elected Albino Luciani of Venice as Pope JOHN PAUL I on August 25. On September 29, after celebrating his twentieth episcopal anniversary with friends, Wojtyła received the news of John Paul I's death the previous night. Over the next several days Wojtyła wrote "Stanislaw," a poetic meditation on the first martyr-bishop of Kraków. On October 8 at the church of St. Stanislaw in Rome he preached at a memorial Mass for John Paul I, citing John 21:15 and the capacity for a greater love of Christ as the prime requisite of Peter's successor.

On October 16, the second day of the second CONCLAVE of 1978, Karol Wojtyła was elected the 263rd successor to St. Peter. Taking the name John Paul II, he immediately broke precedent by receiving the first homage of the College of Cardinals standing, rather than sitting on a faldstool as tradition dictated. Like John Paul I, he declined coronation with the tiara. The HOMILY at his installation Mass on October 22 was punctuated by the ANTIPHON, "Be not afraid! Open the doors to Christ!"—a proclamation of robust faith and a call to a new Christian humanism that would characterize his pontificate for more than two decades.

JOHN PAUL II AND THE WORLD

Pope John Paul II had a greater impact on contemporary history than any pope in centuries. Yet his capacity to shape the world of his times was not mediated through the normal instruments of power. Rather, his PAPACY embodied a new, post–Constantinian approach to politics that was anticipated by the Second Vatican Council. The council's Declaration on Religious Freedom had broken the Church free from the embrace of political authority by asserting that the Catholic Church would no longer accept coercive state power as a buttress for its truth claims or as a support for its evangelical mission. This new vision of the Church's relationship to the worlds of power—an ecclesiology of public engagement in which the Church sought to teach the nations, not rule the nations—had a decisive influence on the pontificate of John Paul II, and through him, on the history of the late twentieth century.

The Framework. The intellectual framework for John Paul II's public witness and diplomacy and his distinctive view of the history of his times may be found in his two addresses to the General Assembly of the United Nations. In his first UN address on October 2, 1979, John Paul characteristically began his analysis of world politics with the dignity of the human person: Any legitimate politics, he proposed, "comes *from man*, is exercised *by man*, and is *for man*." Human progress was to be measured, not only by material standards, but in the realm of the human spirit; that was why the 1948 Universal Declaration of Human Rights was a "milestone on the long and difficult path of the human race." Violations of human rights, not weapons stockpiles, were at the root of the world's division into Cold War camps and were the primary threat to world peace. The cause of peace was thus the cause of human rights, and the first of human rights was religious freedom. To deny anyone the freedom to search for the truth, to adhere to it, and to express it publicly was profoundly dehumanizing, because the search for truth was of the very essence of humanity. Religious believers, agnostics, and atheists should be able to agree on this as a matter of shared humanistic conviction. Rightly understood, religious freedom was not a sectarian matter.

John Paul II: The Early Years of His Papacy. *In 1979, John Paul II became the first pope to ever visit a communist-ruled country when he returned to his homeland, Poland.* © TRINITY MIRROR / MIRRORPIX / ALAMY

In this 1979 address, which challenged both communist regimes and the instrumental view of politics frequently encountered in the West, John Paul II explicitly committed the Catholic Church to the cause of human freedom and the defense of basic human rights as the primary goals of its engagement with world politics, a commitment that had been implicit in Pope John XXIII's 1963 encyclical *Pacem in terries* and in Vatican II's "Declaration on Religious Freedom." Sixteen years later, on October 8, 1995, the pope deepened that commitment in a second address to the UN General Assembly, which was marking its fiftieth anniversary in a world dramatically changed from 1979.

In that address John Paul II vigorously defended the universality of human rights, a concept then being challenged by authoritarian regimes in Asia, by Islamic activists, and by some western intellectuals. The universal reach of the quest for freedom, the pope argued, was a key to understanding this quest as "one of the great dynamics of human history." Moreover, the global character of the human striving for freedom bore empirical witness that there is a universal human nature and a universal moral law; this moral logic built into human beings was the basis for a genuine dialogue between individuals, nations, and cultures. The "universal moral law written on the human heart is precisely [the] kind of 'grammar' which is needed" if the world was to engage in a serious conversation about the human future: if a "century of violent coercion," as the pope put it, was to

be followed by a "century of persuasion." The world had yet to learn to "live with diversity"; yet difference was enriching, for "different cultures are but different ways of facing the question of the meaning of human existence." If humanity could learn "not [to] be afraid of man," then men and women would eventually come to see that "the tears of this century have prepared the ground for a new springtime of the human spirit."

The Challenge to Communism. As his 1979 UN address made clear, John Paul II intended to be a global public defender of human rights: He would challenge the material power of totalitarian and authoritarian regimes with the weapons of the human spirit and of culture, those products of man's spiritual nature that create national identities. This "culture first" strategy of change was first tested in the pope's native east central Europe.

The Soviet authorities quickly discerned that the election of a Polish pope created a profound challenge to the post–Yalta order in Europe. As restive and persecuted Catholic minorities in Lithuania and Ukraine asserted themselves more vigorously in the wake of John Paul's election and, as the pope ignited a revolution of conscience in Poland that spread throughout the Soviet external empire, the Kremlin's worst fears were realized.

John Paul II's epic nine-day pilgrimage to Poland in June 1979 was a primary, even decisive, catalyst in the decade-long process that led to the collapse of European communism ten years later. In some forty homilies and addresses, John Paul returned to his Polish countrymen their authentic history and culture, giving them tools of resistance that communism could not blunt. One-third of the Polish nation saw the pope in person, and virtually everyone else saw him on television or heard him on radio. The visit, a moment of catharsis for a people oppressed since 1939, was also a moment of moral clarification in which tens of thousands of people made the personal decision to resist the communist culture of the lie and to take the "risk of freedom," as the pope would call it at the United Nations in 1995.

The results of that revolution of conscience came swiftly. SOLIDARITY, a free-trade union movement that was also a de facto political opposition, was born in August 1980 in Gdańsk. In December 1980 the Soviet Union was on the verge of launching an invasion of Poland to crush the new independent union and execute its leaders. On December 16, 1980, having been made aware of this threat through his own informants and through United States intelligence sources, John Paul II wrote an unprecedented personal letter to Soviet president Leonid Brezhnev (1906–1982), urging full respect for the integrity of Poland and the rights of its people and signaling his nonnegotiable support for Solidarity. It seemed to many observers that there was an obvious connection between the pope's relationship to Solidarity and the attempt on his life that took place on May 13, 1981, in St. Peter's Square, when he was shot by a professional assassin with links to Warsaw Pact intelligence services.

John Paul condemned the imposition of martial law in Poland on December 13, 1981, which included the mass arrests of Solidarity leaders. During his 1983 pilgrimage to his homeland, he urged the Polish authorities to enter a dialogue with the Solidarity leadership as the precondition to national renewal. In 1987 as the Polish economy and regime slowly crumbled, John Paul returned to Poland to help lay the moral foundations for the free society whose emergence he anticipated, an expectation that was vindicated two years later when Solidarity swept the available seats in the first semi-free elections in Poland in decades.

During the 1980s the pope urged Catholic leaders throughout east central Europe to be vigorous defenders of religious freedom and other basic human rights. His support had a marked effect on Cardinal František TOMÁŠEK of Prague, who was transformed from a rather mute figure into the grand old man of the democratic resistance to communism in Czechoslovakia. John Paul also inspired a revitalized Catholic resistance in Slovakia, where numerous Catholic clergy and laity emerged from underground to take leading roles in the resistance. As these events were unfolding, the Lithuanian Catholic Committee for the Defense of Believers Rights intensified its activity despite harsh Soviet repression, and activists for religious freedom became more vocal among the Greek Catholics of Ukraine. John Paul's apostolic letter of December 31, 1980, *Egregiae virtutis*, naming Ss. Cyril and Methodius, apostles of the Slavs, as co-patrons of Europe was an unmistakable signal to Catholics throughout central and eastern Europe that the pope would bend every effort to re-link the two halves of Catholic Europe. The pope's increasing prestige as a global moral leader brought him into contact with Soviet dissidents in the mid-1980s. In 1985 human rights activist Elena Bonner (1923–) left a secret meeting with John Paul in the VATICAN in tears, saying "He's the most remarkable man I have ever met. He is all light. He is a source of light." Some three years later, John Paul counseled Bonner's husband, Soviet physicist and human rights campaigner Andrei Sakharov (1921–1989), as he tried to clarify his political responsibilities in the USSR.

Mikhail Gorbachev (1931–), the last leader of the Soviet Union, visited John Paul II in the Vatican on December 1, 1989, symbolically marking the end of seventy years of fierce Soviet anti–Catholic PROPAGANDA and persecution. In the mid-1990s Gorbachev publicly conceded what was obvious to the Catholic people of central and eastern Europe throughout the 1980s: that John Paul II had been the pivotal figure in the complex events that led to the collapse of communist regimes in 1989. That the pope did this not by issuing anathemas or by calling princes to REPENTANCE in the snow but by igniting a revolution of conscience that ultimately produced a nonviolent political revolution demonstrated in action the morally driven approach to world politics that he had outlined to the United Nations in 1979.

John Paul II was less successful in engaging communist regimes in Asia. More than two decades of efforts to open a line of dialogue with the People's Republic of China were largely frustrated, although diplomatic contacts between the HOLY SEE and the PRC took place. In November 1983 the pope wrote a private letter to Chinese leader Deng Xiaoping (1904–1997), underscoring the Church's respect for Chinese culture and requesting a formal dialogue; Deng Xiaoping never answered, and his successors persistently blocked the pope's efforts to visit any part of China. Holy See relations with Vietnam were also difficult during the pontificate, although some progress was made in the 1990s on the appointment of bishops.

The Challenge to Free Societies. John Paul II quickly discerned that the quest for human freedom had not been completely vindicated, much less secured, by the Revolution of 1989. On May 1, 1991, his third social encyclical, *Centesimus annus*, analyzed the dramatic events of the recent past while scouting the terrain of public life in the democracies of the future. Describing the free and virtuous society as an interlocking complex of three parts—democratic polity, free economy, public moral culture—the pope argued that the last was the foundation of the entire edifice. DEMOCRACY and the free economy were not machines that could run by themselves. Absent the disciplines and direction given by a vibrant public moral culture, democracy and the free economy would self-destruct; as the pope explained in perhaps the most controversial sentence of the encyclical, "a democracy without values easily turns into open or thinly disguised totalitarianism."

The totalitarianism John Paul had in mind was not a recrudescence of FASCISM or communism, but a gross utilitarianism that drove genuine moral discourse out of public life. A democracy without transcendent moral reference points would have to resolve its differences on the basis of power alone, the pope warned. And that would spell the end of democracy. In his 1992 encyclical *Veritatis splendor*, the pope deepened his challenge to free societies, arguing that a mutual recognition of the obligations of the moral law was the most secure foundation on which to build democratic equality and to safeguard the rights of the less powerful. John Paul returned to this theme in the encyclical *Evangelium vitae* (1995), chastising democracies that erect moral wrongs into "rights" as "tyrant states." The democratic future was profoundly threatened, the pope wrote, if those whom the strong deemed weak, inconvenient, or burdensome could be put beyond the boundaries of legal protection through the legalization of ABORTION and EUTHANASIA.

The urgency of these life issues for the democratic future was underlined by the World Conference on Population and Development held in Cairo in September 1994. The U.S. government and several of its European allies, coordinating their efforts with the UN Fund for Population Activities and the International Planned Parenthood Federation, intended that the Cairo conference would declare abortion as a basic human right on par with religious freedom or freedom of speech. John Paul II, amidst the difficulties caused by a broken femur and hip-replacement surgery in April 1994, led a worldwide effort against this proposal, deploying all the assets of Vatican diplomacy while conducting a vigorous public campaign through the media in defense of the rights of women and the rights of the unborn. It was a striking example of the pope's enduring conviction that the word of truth, spoken clearly and forcefully enough, can bend the shape of history in humane directions. The Cairo conference refused to endorse the notion of abortion as a basic human right. Few doubted that it would

have done so absent the intervention of John Paul II exercising the power of moral witness.

John Paul II and Latin America. When John Paul was elected in 1978, Latin America was both the demographic center of world Catholicism and an arena of turmoil, confusion, and violence. During his first pilgrimage abroad in January of 1979, the pope spoke to the Third General Conference of the Conference of Latin American Bishops Conferences (CELAM) in Puebla, Mexico. In a lengthy address he criticized those aspects of LIBERATION THEOLOGY which portrayed Jesus as the "subversive man of Nazareth." A Church fully engaged in the struggle for JUSTICE in Latin America was an evangelical imperative; a partisan Church, the pope insisted, was an evangelical impossibility. These themes were later developed in two instructions from the Congregation for the Doctrine of the Faith, on "Certain Aspects of the Theology of Liberation" (1984) and on "Christian Freedom and Liberation" (1987). The pope's 1979 visit to Mexico, which had been governed as a secularist one-party state for decades, gave the local Church an unprecedented opportunity to express itself publicly. Tremendous popular support set in motion a process in which the Church was gradually freed to assume the kind of culture-forming role that John Paul II had urged at Puebla. In 2000 one-party rule in Mexico ended, and a new future for Mexican Catholicism opened up.

The pope's sharpest personal confrontation with certain distorted theologies of liberation came in Nicaragua in 1983. There, the Marxist Sandinista government (which included two priests) attempted to disrupt the pope's Mass in Managua and to drown out his homily. The pope's efforts were vindicated, however, in the democratic transitions in Central America of the late 1980s. Those transitions, effected through popular votes, put an end to the civil wars in Nicaragua and El Salvador, which had led to a crude persecution of the Church in the former and the murder of the Archbishop Oscar ROMERO in the latter.

The problems of democratic transition also framed John Paul's important pilgrimage to Chile in 1987. Chile had been ruled for fourteen years by a military dictatorship led by General Augusto Pinochet (1915–2006). Human rights abuses were widespread; the Chilean Church had responded by creating a Vicariate of Solidarity, which sought to rebuild civil society in the country. Beginning in 1978 the Holy See, at John Paul II's initiative, had successfully mediated a border dispute between Chile and Argentina that threatened to result in war, and the pope had considerable credibility with both the Pinochet regime (which included many serious Catholics) and the Chilean democratic opposition. The pope and his Chilean collaborators designed a pilgrimage built around the theme of civil reconciliation. During the pilgrimage John Paul defended the Church's role as promoter of human rights, signaling to both the government and the democratic opposition that a nonviolent transition to democracy was imperative. The pilgrimage was marred by a violent demonstration that threatened to disrupt the pope's Mass in Santiago; the pope refused to leave the venue and the Mass was completed, despite the riot, in which the government seemed not entirely innocent. Eighteen months after the pilgrimage, a national plebiscite rejected continuing military rule and set Chile firmly on the road to democracy.

A year later John Paul defied the efforts of Paraguayan dictator Alfredo Stroessner (1912–2006) to block his meeting with that country's democratic dissidents. As in Chile, the pope stressed the moral cleansing of society as the foundation of building authentic democracy. Less than nine months after the pope's visit, General Stroessner was overthrown in a military coup, which led to general elections in 1989 and a democratic transition that the local Church supported throughout the 1990s, despite difficult political and economic conditions.

As with Poland in 1979, John Paul's epic pilgrimage to Cuba in January of 1998 sought to restore to a hard-pressed people their authentic history and culture. This reclamation of national culture would, it was hoped, create the foundations of civil society and enable Cuba to move beyond communist dictatorship and re-enter the community of the western hemisphere. The Castro regime was reasonably cooperative during the papal visit, which saw the first public display of the national Marian ICON, Our Lady of Charity of El Cobre, in forty years. In the years immediately following the papal pilgrimage, however, change in Cuba was much slower than either the Holy See or the local Church had anticipated.

In 1978 when John Paul II was elected pope, virtually all of Latin America was ruled by authoritarian regimes of one sort or another; economic stagnation was epidemic; and Central America was beset by chaos and war. Within two decades Latin America had made a remarkable transition to democratic governments and free economies, although widespread POVERTY and some political instability remained. While the changes in Latin America had multiple causes, it was clear that John Paul's ability to inspire an engaged Church that was not a partisan Church had had a considerable impact on Latin American public life.

Papal Diplomacy Under John Paul II. Even as John Paul II explored the possibilities of a post–Constantinian papacy that engaged the world of power through moral witness and argument, the diplomacy of the Holy See continued. By 2000 the Holy See had formal diplomatic relations at the ambassadorial level with 172 countries and was represented at the United Nations, the European Community, and a host of other international agencies and organizations. John Paul's annual New Year's meetings with the diplomatic corps accredited to the Holy See provided an opportunity to drive home the message that all politics, including international politics, had an irreducible moral component.

A singularly dramatic accomplishment of John Paul II's diplomacy was the completion of a "Fundamental Agreement" between the Holy See and the State of IS-RAEL on December 30, 1993; they exchanged ambassadors the following year. The Fundamental Agreement was the result of a complex eighteen-month-long negotiation in which the pope's personal commitment to full diplomatic relations between the Holy See and the Jewish state played a decisive role.

John Paul's diplomacy also suffered frustrations. Through both formal and informal means, the pope tried to help create conditions for a peaceful resolution of the crisis of Yugoslavia. These efforts did not meet with notable success. John Paul was determined to go to Sarajevo as a witness for peace when the city was being destroyed by shelling, but a scheduled 1994 visit was canceled because of the threat of violence against pilgrims. When the pope did manage to get to shattered Sarajevo in 1997, officials discovered and defused a bomb, evidently intended to destroy his motorcade, along the road into the city.

In 1982 the pope was confronted by a diplomatic conundrum: Could he make a long-planned pilgrimage to Great Britain during the Falklands/Malvinas War, which was being fought against Argentina, a Catholic country? John Paul's solution was instinctively pastoral: to fulfill his commitment to Great Britain, to go on pilgrimage to Argentina the following month, and to urge peace and reconciliation in both countries. The 1989–1990 Gulf crisis and the period before and during the Iraq War that commenced in 2003 were trying times for the pope, who urged a negotiated diplomatic resolution, first to Iraq's invasion and subjugation of Kuwait and subsequently to the threat posed by the Saddam Hussein regime. In 1992 addressing the UN Food and Agricultural Organization in Rome, John Paul spoke of a duty of humanitarian intervention in situations where GENOCIDE was impending or underway; the pope did not specify on whom this duty fell or how it was to be carried out. As with the Gulf War and the Iraq War, the question of a papal development of the Church's traditional just-war doctrine was, evidently, being left for a future pontificate. In Ireland in 1979, in Latin America throughout the 1980s, and in the Philippines in 1985–1986, the pope had urged a "preferential option for nonviolence" in resolving sectarian conflict and in effecting democratic transitions. The relationship of this option to the Church's traditional approach to interstate conflict, in which the restoration of justice was the primary imperative, was also a topic for future theological development.

Throughout his pontificate John Paul II, whose contempt for the Yalta division of Europe into Cold War camps dated back to the late 1940s, spoke frequently about the urgency of rebuilding a Europe that could breathe with both its "lungs," east and west. This personal passion matched the Holy See's longstanding commitment to European unification through such instruments as the Common Market and the European Union (EU). In later years, however, the pope sharply criticized the tendency of EU bureaucracies and the European Parliament to enshrine a host of dubious lifestyle rights in European law; the Holy See also grew increasingly concerned about the way in which issues of abortion, euthanasia, and the technological means of human reproduction were being resolved in western European states. During the 2003–2004 debate over a new European constitutional treaty, John Paul II, without success, urged Europe's political leaders to acknowledge formally the Christian sources that had, over the centuries, helped inform contemporary European commitments to human rights and democracy. These concerns and contentions raised questions about the future of the Holy See's relationship to European integration.

John Paul II also dealt with the worlds of power through an unprecedented informal diplomacy. With the pope's encouragement, although without any formal linkage to the Holy See, the Sant' Egidio Community, a Rome-based Catholic renewal movement, successfully mediated the Mozambican civil war in a series of negotiations during the 1990s. Similar Sant' Egidio efforts took place in Algeria and the Balkans, although without measurable success. John Paul II also sent Cardinal Roger ETCHEGARAY, the French president of the Pontifical Council for Justice and Peace, as a personal, unofficial representative to conflict situations in Africa, Latin America, Asia, and Oceania. The cardinal described this informal diplomacy, aimed at getting conflicted parties in conversation with one another, as a "politics of presence" that was a "reinforcement and extension of the spiritual mission" of the pope.

THE POPE AND THE CHURCH

Immediately after his election John Paul announced that the program of his pontificate would be the full implementation of the Second Vatican Council. Like Pope John XXIII, John Paul II believed that the council was a "new Pentecost" in which the Holy Spirit was preparing the Church for a "springtime of evangelization" in its third millennium. That conviction set the framework for the pope's governance of the Church, his magisterium, and his distinctive papal style.

An Evangelical Church. The most visible expression of John Paul's vision of the Church as a dynamic evangelical movement proposing to the world the truth of the human condition was his wide-ranging program of pastoral pilgrimages, of which there were 104 between 1979 and 2004. The pope took seriously the injunction of Luke 22:32, that Peter's distinctive mission was to strengthen his BRETHREN in the faith. Interpreting this mandate literally while marrying it to the modern transportation and communications revolutions, John Paul II traveled to virtually every corner of the planet (as well as making 146 pastoral visits within Italy and visiting almost 300 Roman parishes). His global evangelism drew two of the largest crowds in human history, in Manila in 1995 and in Mexico City in 2002. By the end of the pontificate, John Paul II, having traveled more than 720,000 miles, had been seen in person by more human beings than any man who ever lived. The impact of this new style of papal witness was multiplied by the broadcast media, as radio and television brought the Successor of Peter into billions of homes.

In line with his evangelical priorities John Paul moved quickly to address one of the most deeply contentious issues in post–conciliar Catholicism, devoting 129 general audience addresses between 1979 and 1984 to an innovative "theology of the body" which sought to explain the Church's sexual ethic (and meet the challenge of the sexual revolution) on the basis of a humanistic reading of human sexuality and a fresh analysis of biblical texts. In a similarly conflicted area John Paul worked to open a new dialogue between the Church and natural science. In 1981 he established a papal commission to re-examine the Galileo case; the commission report, issued in 1992 and endorsed by the pope, openly admitted that the Church had made an "objective error" in the Galileo controversy.

The pope's commitment to Vatican II teaching on the "universal call to holiness" impelled him to restructure the process of BEATIFICATION and canonization in 1983. The APOSTOLIC CONSTITUTION *Divinus perfectionis magister* shifted the paradigm of the process from legal procedure to scholarly historical investigation. The result was an unprecedented number of beatifications (1,338) and canonizations (482) during the pontificate, as the pope sought to give public expression to the Church's teaching that sanctity was available to everyone.

World Youth Days, which drew millions of young people from all over the planet for a week of catechesis and liturgical celebrations with the Bishop of Rome,

Way of the Cross. *Pope John Paul II hugs a cross as he watches from his Vatican apartment via television the "Via Crucis" (Way of the Cross) procession at Rome's ancient Colosseum, March 25, 2005. Pope John Paul, whose illness prevented him from leaving the Vatican, on Friday night used a video link to join a traditional Via Crucis (Way of the Cross) procession in Rome. It was the first time in his papacy, then in its 27th year, that the 84–year-old Pope had missed the procession around Rome's ancient Colosseum which commemorates the last hours in Christ's life.* © **ARTURO MARI/OSSERVATORE ROMANO/POOL/REUTERS/CORBIS**

were another John Paul II innovation and quickly became a signature event in the pontificate. The first international WORLD YOUTH DAY, held in Buenos Aires in 1987, was followed by similar meetings in Santiago de Compostela (1989), Czestochowa (1991), Denver (1993), Manila (1995), Paris (1997), Rome (2000), and Toronto (2002). The Rome WYD, which drew two million young people to its closing Mass, was the largest pilgrimage in European history. The pope's magnetic attraction for the young, which involved a profound challenge to lead lives of moral heroism, continued even as he aged.

John Paul's leadership in more traditional Church events should also be understood in an evangelical and conciliar framework. The sixteen general, regional, and local Synods of Bishops he summoned and attended, like the post–synodal apostolic exhortations he wrote as a reflection on the deliberations of a Synod general assembly, were intended to provide interpretive keys to the renewal of Catholic life as proposed by Vatican II. The Extraordinary Synod of 1985, marking the twentieth anniversary of the Council, was of particular importance for its stress on the Council's COMMUNION ecclesiology, its critique of political and ideological interpretations of Vatican II, and its commissioning of the CATECHISM OF THE CATHOLIC CHURCH. Of special note as well were the Synods (and subsequent apostolic exhortations) on the family, the priesthood, the sacrament of reconciliation, the lay vocation in the world, the priesthood, and the CONSECRATED LIFE. While few, including the pope, were entirely satisfied with the Synod process, the pontificate unmistakably established the Synod of Bishops as a permanent feature of Catholic life.

John Paul's was also one of the most important legislative pontificates in history. Following the intentions of John XXIII, he completed a thorough reform of canon law, issuing the new Code of Canon Law for Latin-rite Catholicism in 1983. The apostolic constitution promulgating the new code, *Sacrae disciplinae leges*, stressed its incorporation of the ecclesiology of Vatican II. A new Code of Oriental Canon Law for Eastern Catholic Churches was issued in 1990. In addition to these legislative accomplishments, the pope also reorganized the Roman Curia to reflect the council's concerns in the 1988 apostolic constitution *Pastor bonus*. In 1996 he issued *Universi dominici gregis*, which reformed the process for the election of a pope by suppressing election by acclamation and delegation, stressing the personal responsibility of the cardinal-electors, and providing for election by simple majority after two weeks of inconclusive voting under the traditional two-thirds majority rule (a provision that would be rescinded by his successor, who restored the two-thirds rule while retaining John Paul's attempt to limit on the number of

ballots by narrowing the field after thirty-four failed ballots).

In another apostolic constitution, *Ex corde ecclesiae* (1990), John Paul sought to strengthen the Catholic identity of all Catholic institutions of higher education, as he had done in *Sapientia christiana*, a 1979 apostolic constitution regulating pontifical universities and pontifical faculties in the sacred sciences. *Ex corde ecclesiae* caused considerable controversy in the United States, even as the pope changed the terms of debate over the distinctive character of CATHOLIC COLLEGES AND UNIVERSITIES. *Sapientia chistiana* and *Ex corde ecclesiae* were important moments in the pope's continuous effort to strengthen Catholic intellectual life as an integral part of what he came to call, in the 1990s, the "new evangelization," which put considerable emphasis on the evangelization of culture.

The pope's reform of Vatican press relations was also evangelically inspired. John Paul II recognized the crucial importance of the media. His 1984 decision to appoint Joaquín NAVARRO-VALLS, a Spanish layman and veteran foreign correspondent, as papal spokesman and head of the Holy See Press Office helped move the Vatican into the modern communications age. An online Vatican Information Service began transmitting daily bulletins in 1991. According to Navarro, John Paul II saw the "dialectic with world opinion" available through the media as an instrument for reforming the Church and shaping the world political agenda, as in the months before the Cairo world population conference in 1994.

The multiple strands of John Paul's effort to get the Church to experience itself as a vibrant evangelical movement were woven into a complex tapestry during the Great Jubilee of 2000, which the Pope frequently described as the interpretive key to his pontificate. After opening the Holy Door of St. Peter's on Christmas Eve 1999, John Paul undertook an extensive biblical pilgrimage in several phases to Mount Sinai, the Holy Land, Athens, and Damascus. The Iraqi government made it impossible for the pope to begin this pilgrimage in UR, home of Abraham, the Church's "father in faith," so John Paul celebrated a day of recollection in honor of Abraham in the Vatican audience hall. Symbolizing the universal call to holiness, there were special jubilee days in Rome for consecrated RELIGIOUS MEN AND WOMEN, the sick, health-care workers, artists, permanent deacons, the Roman Curia, craftsmen, priests, scientists, migrants and itinerants, journalists, prisoners, young people, intellectuals, the elderly, bishops, families, athletes, parliamentarians and government workers, agricultural workers, the armed forces and police, laity, the disabled, and the entertainment world. In June 2000 Rome hosted the forty-seventh International Eucharistic Congress. On the First Sunday of LENT during the JUBILEE YEAR, the pope, presiding at a Mass in St. Peter's Basilica, publicly asked God's forgiveness for the sins Christians had committed against the GOSPEL and against their neighbors in the first two millennia—a "cleansing of the Church's conscience" which John Paul believed essential to preparing for the twenty-first-century springtime of evangelization. The Christian witnesses of the twentieth century, the greatest century of persecution in history, were honored at a special ecumenical service at the Roman Coliseum on May 7. During the Jubilee the pope beatified a host of martyrs (from Brazil, the Philippines, Poland, Thailand, Mexico, and Vietnam), two popes (Pope PIUS IX and John XXIII), and two of the child visionaries of Fatíma (Francisco and Jacinta Marto). The first saint canonized during the jubilee was Sister Faustina KOWALSKA, the Polish mystic whose devotion to the merciful Christ had spread throughout the world. In October 2000 John Paul canonized 120 martyrs of China, the Philadelphia heiress and foundress Katherine DREXEL, and Josephine BAKHITA, a former Sudanese slave.

The Great Jubilee of 2000, which drew an estimated twenty-seven million pilgrims to Rome, was solemnly closed on January 6, 2001. As John Paul had intended, it had been a celebration of the evangelical future, not simply a commemoration of the past.

Magisterium. Unlike previous councils, Vatican II had provided no interpretive keys to its teaching through doctrinal definitions, creeds, canons, or anathemas. The extensive magisterium of John Paul II, which marks his as one of the great teaching pontificates in history, offered the Church keys for the authentic interpretation of Vatican II and its implementation.

In addition to issuing seven APOSTOLIC CONSTITUTIONS, John Paul II wrote fourteen encyclicals and fifteen apostolic exhortations, touching virtually every major issue on the post–Vatican II Catholic agenda. His inaugural encyclical, *Redemptor hominis*, was the first encyclical ever on Christian anthropology and offered the Church and the world a set of program notes for the pontificate to follow; *Redemptor hominis* was also the first panel in a Trinitarian triptych of encyclicals that came to include *Dives in misericordia* and *Dominum et vivificantem*. Two encyclicals, *Veritatis splendor* and *Fides et ratio*, defended the human capacity to know the truth of things, including the moral truth of things. The pope's social doctrine was developed in three encyclicals: *Laborem exercens*, *Sollicitudo rei socialis*, and *Centesimus annus*. *Ut unum sint* was the first encyclical ever devoted entirely to ecumenism. *Redemptoris missio* recommitted the Church to the mission *ad gente* in a distinctively

dialogical mode: "The Church proposes; she imposes nothing." *Evangelium vitae* was a passionate defense of the right to life from conception until natural death. Other encyclicals honored SS. Cyril and Methodius (*Slavorum apostolic*) and the Blessed Virgin at the end of the 1986–87 Marian Year (*Redemptoris mater*), while the pope's final encyclical, *Ecclesia de eucharistia*, reminded the Church that the vital center of its life and mission is the Holy Eucharist.

Following the lead of Paul VI in *Evangelium nuntiandi*, John Paul sought to complete the work of general assemblies of the Synods of Bishops with post–synodal apostolic exhortations addressing key issues of the post–Vatican II period: *Catechesi tradendae* (catechetics), *Familiaris consortio* (marriage and family life), *Reconciliatio et paenitenti* (the sacrament of PENANCE), *Christifideles laici* (the lay vocation in the world), *Pastores dabo vobis* (the ministerial priesthood and priestly formation), and *Vita consecrate* (consecrated life). John Paul also issued apostolic exhortations after the pre-jubilee regional synods for Africa, Asia, North and South America and after two synods to consider the Church's condition in Europe.

The Pope also wrote a large number of apostolic letters, among the most important of which were *Dominicae cenae* (the Eucharist), *Salvifici doloris* (redemptive SUFFERING), *Euntes in mundum* (the millennium of Christianity among the eastern Slavs), *Mulieris dignitatem* (women in the modern world), *Tertio millennio adveniente* (announcing the Great Jubilee of 2000), *Dies Domini* (on sanctifying time and the Lord's Day), and *Novo millennio ineunte* (concluding the Great Jubilee of 2000). Among some Catholics in North America and western Europe, the apostolic letter *Ordinatio sacerdotalis*, which reaffirmed that the Church was not authorized to ordain women to the ministerial priesthood, caused controversy.

John Paul II also devised new forms of the papal magisterium, writing extensive letters to families, children, artists, and the elderly. John Paul's theology of the body should also be considered among the most important developments in his papal magisterium. In addition to his formal magisterium, John Paul II created a new method of papal dialogue with the world by publishing an international best-seller (*Crossing the Threshold of Hope*), two volumes of memoirs (*Gift and Mystery*, *Arise–Let Us Be on Our Way*), a philosophical dialogue (*Memory and Identity*), and a three-paneled set of poems (*Roman Triptych*).

Ecumenism and Interreligious Dialogue. With the pontificate of John Paul II, the Catholic Church entered fully into the ECUMENICAL MOVEMENT and in doing so reconfigured the world movement for Christian unity.

The pope laid particular emphasis on ecumenism with the Christian East, in the HOPE that the wounds of a millennium of Christian division (formally opened in 1054), could be healed on the threshold of the third millennium of Christian history. While the pope did not bring that great dream of ecclesial reconciliation to fruition, in part because of the reluctance (and, in some cases, hostility) of Orthodox leaders and theologians, he did advance Catholic ecumenism (*ad orientem*) in numerous ways: visiting Ecumenical Patriarch Dimitrios I (1914–1991) at the Phanar in 1979 and hosting Dimitrios in Rome in 1987 and his successor Bartholomew I (1940–) in 1995; through his PILGRIMAGES to Romania (1999), the Holy Land (2000), Greece and Damascus (2001) and Ukraine (2001); and in the encyclical *Ut unum sint*, which seemed to propose a return to the status quo before 1054. The difficulties of dialogue with ORTHODOXY were amplified by the post-communist resurgence of the once-heavily-persecuted Eastern Catholic Churches in the former Soviet Union and its satellites.

More tangible progress was made during the pontificate with the Oriental Orthodox churches (sometimes known as Monophysite or pre-Chalcedonian churches), as the pope signed or re-affirmed common Christological declarations with the Armenian Apostolic Church, the Coptic Orthodox Church, and the Syrian Orthodox Church, and also with the ASSYRIAN CHURCH OF THE EAST. John Paul II formed a close spiritual friendship with the Armenian Católicos, Karekin I Sarkissian, who died in 1999.

John Paul also bent considerable efforts toward closing breaches in western Christianity dating back to the reformation. At the pope's insistence, a meeting with other Christian leaders and an ecumenical PRAYER service were part of virtually every papal pilgrimage throughout the world. The once-promising Anglican-Roman Catholic dialogue ran into considerable difficulties, however, when parts of the ANGLICAN COMMUNION decided to admit women to the ministerial priesthood, a decision that raised questions about Anglican understandings of APOSTOLICITY and sacramentality. The pontificate saw some advances in the Lutheran-Catholic dialogue, including a historic "Joint Declaration on Justification by Faith" in 1999, but without the cause of full ecclesial communion being much advanced. John Paul's global evangelism and his vigorous defense of the right to life created new possibilities for ecumenical dialogue with evangelical and pentecostal Protestantism, even as the Catholic insistence on the centrality of the life issues to contemporary Christian witness created further ecumenical difficulties with liberal Protestant communities.

In 1995 the general secretary of the WORLD COUNCIL OF CHURCHES told a Roman audience that a new ecumenical paradigm was needed, in which the various Christian communities would abandon the quest for a common CREED, a common baptism, and a common Eucharist while working together on issues of the environment, peace, and world poverty. Thus John Paul's insistence that Christian unity must be unity in the truth that Christ bequeathed his Church made the Catholic Church the principal institutional defender of the classic goals that had launched the modern ecumenical movement in 1910.

Building on Vatican II's declaration *Nostra aetatae*, Catholic-Jewish relations entered a new phase with the pontificate of John Paul II. The pope's historic 1986 visit to the SYNAGOGUE of Rome, his steady condemnations of the sin of anti–semitism, the establishment of diplomatic relations between the Holy See and the State of Israel, and the pope's Holy Land pilgrimage laid the foundation for what some observers saw as a new, theologically oriented Catholic-Jewish dialogue in the twenty-first century.

In 1985 at the invitation of King Hassan II (1929–1999), John Paul addressed a large gathering of Muslim young people in Casablanca. During his jubilee pilgrimage to Damascus in 2001, he became the first pope to visit a MOSQUE. The dialogue with ISLAM, however, was made more difficult because of Muslim persecution of Christians in the Holy Land, Asia, and Africa, which the pope sharply challenged during a visit to Sudan in 1993, and by the threat posed in the last years of his pontificate by the rising violence of global jihadism. The pope also met on several occasions with the Dalai Lama, and was enthusiastically received by Hindus in India in 1986.

On October 27, 1986, the pope gathered several dozen world religious leaders at Assisi for an unprecedented World Day of Prayer for Peace. "Being together to pray," John Paul insisted, was not syncretism. Criticism of the event from some curial elements continued long afterwards.

Internationalizing the Curia. The pope drew his closest collaborators in Rome from throughout the world Church, accelerating the internationalization of the Roman Curia that had begun under Paul VI. Among the pope's closest advisers were a German (Cardinal Joseph RATZINGER, prefect of the Congregation for the Doctrine of the Faith from November 1981), an African (Cardinal Bernardin GANTIN of Benin, prefect of the Congregation for Bishops from 1984 to 1998), a Slovak (Cardinal Jozef TOMKO, general secretary of the Synod of Bishops from 1979 to 1985, and prefect of the Congregation for the Evangelization of Peoples [*Propaganda fidei*] from 1985 until 2001). A Spaniard (Eduardo MARTÍNEZ SOMALO), an Australian, (Edward CASSIDY), an Italian (Giovanni Battista Re [1934–]), and an Argentine (Leonardo Sandri [1943–]) served the Pope in the crucial post of Sostituto (Deputy for Ordinary Affairs of the Secretariat of State), in effect the papal chief-of-staff. In 1998 an American, James Harvey (1949–), was named Prefect of the Papal Household; by 2001 nineteen of the twenty-four heads of Roman dicasteries were non-Italians.

After Paul VI's Secretary of State, the Frenchman Jean VILLOT, died in 1979, two Italian papal diplomats were appointed to this most senior post in the Roman Curia: Agostino CASAROLI (1979–1990) and Angelo SODANO (from 1990). The pope's choice of Casaroli, architect of the *Ostpolitik* (Eastern Politics) of Paul VI (about which Cardinal Wojtyła had had serious doubts), surprised some. But the Polish pope, with his vigorous public defense of religious freedom, and the Italian curialist, devoted to the discretions of diplomacy, made an effective team in confronting European communism. Two Italians (Achille Silvestrini [1923–], later Prefect of the Congregation for the Oriental Churches, and Giovanni Lajolo [1935–]) and a Frenchman (Jean-Louis Tauran[1920–], later Librarian and Archivist of the Holy Roman Church, and named cardinal in 2003) served John Paul as Secretary for Relations with States, or foreign minister of the Holy See. Father Roberto Tucci, S.J. (1921–), the president of Vatican Radio, played an important role as impresario of the pope's foreign travels for more than fifteen years.

The pope's willingness to go against the grain of bureaucratic convention led to several distinctive episcopal appointments during his pontificate: a convert from JUDAISM as archbishop of Paris (Jean-Marie LUSTIGER); a former US Navy chaplain, who had been a diocesan bishop for just a few months, as archbishop of New York (John O'CONNOR); and, in the latter years of the pontificate, intellectually accomplished and publicly assertive younger bishops who had not followed the conventional career path as leaders of major sees.

Between 1979 and 2003 John Paul II created 231 cardinals (including one whose name remained *in pectore*). On six occasions he called the College of Cardinals into extraordinary CONSISTORY to discuss various problems of Catholic life, a practice that had lain fallow for 400 years. By the time of his death John Paul had created more than 90 percent of the electorate that would choose his successor.

Controversies. Ecumenical Councils have always been followed by controversy, and the pontificate of John Paul II, an expression of Vatican II, was no exception. In 1982 the pope intervened in the governance of the

Society of Jesus, appointing a personal delegate to lead the Society after the incapacitation of its general, Father Pedro ARRUPE. Father Arrupe's successor, Father Peter-Hans Kolvenbach (1928–), was elected in 1983; opinions differed widely on whether the papal intervention had led to a successful reformation of the Church's largest and most prestigious male religious order.

The situation of post–conciliar Catholic theology was another arena of controversy. On December 15, 1979, at the order of the Congregation for the Doctrine of the Faith, Father Hans KÜNG's ecclesiastical mandate to teach as a professor of Catholic theology was withdrawn; in 1987 CDF wrote the Chancellor of The CATHOLIC UNIVERSITY OF AMERICA that Father Charles Curran was to be considered no longer suitable to teach Catholic theology. In both cases, action followed extensive and public DISSENT by the theologians in question and lengthy consultations with Vatican officials. Public action was taken against less than a dozen theologians during the pontificate, and the pope's theological critics remained in control of many theological faculties in the West, suggesting that frequently heard charges of repression were over-wrought.

John Paul II and Cardinal Ratzinger made considerable efforts to reconcile Archbishop Marcel LEFEBVRE and his followers. In 1984 the pope granted an indult allowing more widespread use of 1962 Roman Missal of John XXIII. But the core of the Lefebvrist dissent was not liturgical, but rather theological: Among other matters, the French archbishop disdained the Council's ecclesiology and refused to accept Vatican II's *Declaration on Religious Freedom*. His refusal to be mollified by the 1984 indult made clear that he considered Vatican II an act of infidelity of which liturgical change was but one manifestation. Dissent became crisis when, on June 30, 1988, Lefebvre, after lengthy and fruitless negotiations and a plea from the pope, ordained four new bishops without authorization. On July 1 Cardinal Gantin signed a decree stating that, as Lefebvre had committed a schismatic act, he, the four bishops he ordained, and the retired bishops who had taken part in the ordinations had automatically incurred EXCOMMUNICATION. Any Catholic supporting Lefebvre would also incur excommunication. On July 2 the pope issued an apostolic letter, *Ecclesia Dei*, creating a commission to reconcile those of Lefebvre's supporters who did not wish to follow the Frenchman into SCHISM.

While criticism of the pope from self-styled progressive Catholics received extensive media attention, John Paul II was also criticized, if less vocally, by Catholics who welcomed his strong evangelical presence and his vigorous exercise of the papal magisterium, but who thought him lax in his governance of the Church: too willing to countenance theological dissent and insuf-

John Paul II's Funeral Mass. *A general view of the pilgrims gathered in St. Peter's Square during Pope John Paul II's funeral on April 8, 2005, in Vatican City.* **DARIO MITIDIERI/GETTY IMAGES**

ficiently energetic in reforming the episcopate, the priesthood, and the religious orders. The pope, committed to what he termed the "method of persuasion," had, it seems, a different ecclesiological vision and a different strategy, based on the conviction that what was true to the vision of Vatican II would endure and flourish, while what was false would wither and eventually die of its own implausibility.

A Different Kind of Pope. Determined to remain himself, John Paul II gave a distinctive personal stamp to the Office of Peter. Until the summer before his death, he hosted an annual seminar at CASTEL GANDOLFO, the papal summer residence, for humanities scholars or scholars in the natural sciences; some participants were agnostics or atheists. With the exceptions of those times when he was in hospital or on vacation (two more innovations: a pope being treated in a hospital and a pope spending time hiking in the Italian Alps), he invited guests for lunch or dinner every day, drawing information about the Church and the world from a diverse set of personalities. The pope also maintained an extensive, informal correspondence, outside official channels, with

interlocutors throughout the world. Friends and colleagues became accustomed to unexpected phone calls announcing that "the Holy Father would like to speak with you."

John Paul also reorganized the procedures for the quinquennial *Ad limina* visit that all diocesan bishops make to Rome in order to spend more time with the bishops individually and in national or regional groups. *Ad limina* visits under Paul VI gave the visiting bishop one opportunity to meet the pope; John Paul II met each bishop four times: in a private session, at Mass, over a meal, and by delivering a discourse to the bishop's national or regional group (the discourse was given to each bishop individually in written form after 1995). By one knowledgeable estimate, forty percent of the pope's official schedule was devoted in any given year to meetings with bishops. John Paul II also took his title as Primate of Italy with greater seriousness than any pope in centuries, and by the end of the pontificate Italy showed measurable signs of increased Catholic practice.

The pope's determination that the Vatican itself should reflect the realities of the world Church was manifest in the vast number of audiences he granted to an extraordinary range of groups, including chefs, hairdressers, and kayakers. John Paul changed the ambience of the Vatican in other ways. In 1994 he opened a CONVENT for contemplative nuns inside Vatican City, a new feature of Vatican life that demonstrated the pope's conviction that prayer must be at the heart of the ministry of service exercised by the APOSTOLIC SEE. In 1988 John Paul dedicated a shelter for the homeless within the walls of the Vatican. During his pontificate the pope also created two new PONTIFICAL ACADEMIES—the Pontifical Academy for the Social Sciences and the Pontifical Academy for Life.

From 1994 on John Paul suffered from an increasing number of physical burdens. He was most visibly affected by a form of Parkinson's disease and a hip replacement that left him walking with pain. Yet the pope's charisma did not diminish, as the jubilee year amply demonstrated. In a world tempted to think of the elderly and disabled as disposable, the pope's witness to the dignity of human life was magnified by his evident physical suffering.

That the world was deeply touched by that witness became evident during Lent of 2005, much of which John Paul II spent in the Policlino Gemelli or in a sickbed in the papal apartment in the Vatican. Immediately after his death on April 2, 2005, millions of pilgrims poured into Rome, effectively doubling the population of the city in the days before the papal funeral Mass, which was celebrated in St. Peter's Square on April 8 before a vast congregation that included more than seventy heads of state, the ecumenical patriarch of CONSTANTINOPLE, representatives of a vast array of other religious communities, ordinary Romans, and several dozen members of Karol Wojtyła's *Środowisko*, themselves now well advanced in middle age, who came to Rome to say goodbye to the man they still called *Wujek*. An estimated two billion people participated in John Paul II's funeral by television and witnessed a sight not seen since the funeral of Pope St. GREGORY I in 604: the sponatneous acclamation by the congregation that the deceased pope should be called "great."

The cause for the beatification of John Paul II was opened in Rome later in 2005. Having received testimony from both formal witnesses and thousands of people who spontaneously wrote letters of thanks, the local (diocesan) process was completed on the second anniversary of the late pope's death, April 2, 2007. The cause was then sent to the Congregation for the Causes of Saints.

Enduring Accomplishments. As he led the Church into the third millennium of its history, ten enduring accomplishments of the pontificate of John Paul II could

be identified. He had revitalized the papacy as an office of evangelical witness. He had secured the legacy of Vatican II in its fullness as an epic spiritual event at which the Church, guided by the Holy Spirit, had engaged modernity through an enriched sense of its own unique nature and mission. He had been the pivotal figure in the collapse of European communism. He had identified the moral challenges facing free societies in the twenty-first century. He had put ecumenism at the heart of the Church's CONSCIOUSNESS. He had created the possibility of a new religious dialogue between Catholicism and living Judaism. He had modeled a truth-centered method of interreligious dialogue, demonstrating that humanity's deepest convictions could be in conversation rather than in conflict, and he had re-ignited the Church's dialogue with the sciences. He had proposed a compelling Christian response to the sexual revolution in his theology of the body. He had made clear in the *Catechism of the Catholic Church* that the Church could still advance a comprehensive account of its faith and hope, and he had positioned the Catholic Church as the principal institutional defender of the claims of human reason. He had given inspiration to tens, perhaps hundreds, of millions of human beings. His inaugural call, "Be not afraid!" had changed the course of world history by changing the direction of individual lives.

In light of these accomplishments, it was frequently suggested that history would know him as "John Paul the Great."

SEE ALSO AD LIMINA VISIT; APOSTOLIC EXHORTATION; BODY, THEOLOGY OF; CANON LAW, 1983 CODE; CANONIZATION OF SAINTS (HISTORY AND PROCEDURE); CATECHESI TRADENDAE; CENTESIMUS ANNUS; CHRISTIFIDELES LAICI; COLD WAR AND THE PAPACY; CURIA, ROMAN; DIES DOMINI; DIVES IN MISERICORDIA; DOCTRINE OF THE FAITH, CONGREGATION FOR THE; DOMINUM ET VIVIFICANTEM; EASTERN SCHISM; ECCLESIA DEI; EDUCATION, CATHOLIC (HIGHER) IN THE UNITED STATES; EUCHARISTIC CONGRESSES; EUNTES IN MUNDUM; EUROPEAN UNION AND THE PAPACY; EVANGELIUM VITAE; EVANGELIZATION, NEW; EVANGELIZATION OF PEOPLES, CONGREGATION FOR THE; EX CORDE ECCLESIAE; FAMILIARIS CONSORTIO; FIDES ET RATIO; FROM ROME TO CAIRO AND BEIJING: JOHN PAUL II ON FAMILY AND HUMAN RIGHTS; GALILEI, GALILEO; GOD IN THE WORLD: A TRINITARIAN TRIPTYCH; HOLINESS, UNIVERSAL CALL TO; HUMANAE VITAE; HUMANISM, CHRISTIAN; JEWISH-CATHOLIC RELATIONS; JOHN PAUL II AND INTERRELIGIOUS DIALOGUE; JOHN PAUL II INSTITUTE ON MARRIAGE AND FAMILY; JOHN PAUL II'S ECONOMIC TEACHING: A CALL FOR SPIRITUAL, MORAL, AND STRUCTURAL CONVERSION; JUSTIFICATION, JOINT DECLARATION ON; KAROL WOJTYŁA: EARLY YEARS; KAROL WOJTYŁA: POET, PLAYWRIGHT, PHILOSOPHER, AND PATRIOT; LABOREM EXERCENS; LATIN RITE; LUBLIN, CATHOLIC UNIVERSITY OF; MARTYR; MISSAL, ROMAN; MONOPHYSITISM; MULIERIS DIGNITATEM; NEOSCHOLASTICISM AND NEOTHOMISM; ORDINATIO SACERDOTALIS; ORTHODOX AND ORIENTAL ORTHODOX CHURCHES; PACEM IN TERRIS; PAPACY: 1978–1988; PAPACY: 1988–1994; PAPACY: 1995–2000; PASTOR BONUS; PASTORES

BIBLIOGRAPHY

Rocco Buttiglione, *Karol Wojtyła: The Thought of the Man Who Became Pope John Paul II* (Grand Rapids, Mich. 1997).

Pope John Paul II, *Crossing the Threshold of Hope*, translated by Jenny McPhee and Martha McPhee (New York 1994).

Pope John Paul II, *Man and Woman He Created Them: A Theology of the Body*, edited with an introduction by Michael M. Waldstein (Boston 2006).

Kenneth L. Schmitz, *At the Center of the Human Drama: The Philosophical Anthropology of Karol Wojtyła/Pope John Paul II* (Washington, D.C. 1993).

George Weigel, *Witness to Hope: The Biography of Pope John Paul II* (New York 1999; rev. ed. 2000, 2005), contains bibliography.

The ecclesial writings of John Paul II can be found on the official Vatican Web site, available from http://www.vatican.va/holy_father/john_paul_ii/index.htm (accessed March 21, 2008).

George Weigel
Distinguished Senior Fellow
William E. Simon Chair in Catholic Studies
Ethics and Public Policy Center, Washington, D.C. (2009)

JUDAS, GOSPEL OF

The *Gospel of Judas* is a Gnostic tractate in *Codex Tchacos*, which contains three other Gnostic works. Discovered in middle EGYPT around 1978, *Codex Tchacos* deteriorated substantially before coming into the hands of scholars in 2001. A restoration process led to the publication of *Judas* in 2006. Immediate popular attention focused on the GOSPEL's portrayal of Judas as the favored disciple who betrays Jesus with Jesus' encouragement. Thorough analysis, however, reveals that most of the text contains ideas and motifs familiar from other Gnostic works.

The manuscript of the *Gospel of Judas* dates from the late third to early fourth century AD. Although the manuscript is written in Sahidic, a dialect of Coptic, the *Gospel of Judas* was originally composed in Greek. St. IRENAEUS of Lyon, writing around AD 180, mentions a *Gospel of Judas* (*Adversus Haer.* 1.31.1). His brief description of the gospel suggests that it is the same gospel found in *Codex Tchacos*. The original Greek version of *Judas* was, therefore, probably composed around AD 150.

As a product of mid-second century GNOSTICISM, the *Gospel of Judas* is of no value for historical reconstructions of Jesus or Judas. Rather, it provides further witness to the ways some Gnostics reinvented the Christian narrative to express their worldview. The last week of Jesus' life serves as the setting for *Judas*. The gospel consists of conversations between Jesus and his disciples, especially Judas.

The earlier dialogue sections contain harsh polemics against the orthodox Church. Jesus laughs at the twelve disciples as they give thanks over bread, for they serve a lesser god. Only Judas recognizes that Jesus is from one of the highest heavenly realms and not the son of the disciples' god. The twelve disciples later report a DREAM in which they witness twelve priests guilty of sins, from homosexual acts to child sacrifice, offering sacrifice at the altar in the Temple. Jesus reveals that these twelve priests represent the twelve disciples, and the sacrifices are the people they will lead astray by their service to the lesser god. Their successors will continue to be immoral and to lead people astray.

In the second half of the gospel, Jesus bequeaths to Judas the secrets of the cosmos and its origins. The Spirit is the highest existing BEING and dwells in an invisible realm transcending material reality. *Autogenes* (or the *Self-Generated*), the offspring of the Spirit, creates numerous aeons. A luminary rules each aeon, and numerous ANGELS serve the ruler. Heavens containing their own luminaries appear within the aeons, and the cosmos emerges according to numerical patterns rooted in ancient astronomy, NUMEROLOGY, and ASTROLOGY. Autogenes also creates Adamas, the archetype of human beings, within a cloud in the highest aeon. The generation of Seth, the spiritual seed of Adamas, is created soon thereafter.

Twelve angels come forth to rule the underworld, and they in turn create twelve angels, and to each of these twelve they apportion a segment of the material heavens to rule. The angel Saklas (meaning *fool*), along with other angels, creates earthly human beings. Human beings are thus trapped under the detrimental influence of the stars, which are associated with these deviant cosmic rulers. "God," an ambivalent celestial figure, merely loans spirit to human beings. The Spirit, however, gives to Seth's generation the permanent gift of spirit, and only they can ascend to the realm of the Spirit.

Toward the end of the gospel, Jesus reassures Judas, "you will sacrifice the man who bears me" (*Judas* 56:19–20, Meyer and Gaudard 2007). Thereby, Judas will surpass the other disciples, despite the infamy that will be attached to his name. As the thirteenth disciple, Judas is led by his own star and is beyond the reach of the rulers allotted the twelve segments of heaven. Judas betrays Jesus to the scribes, and the gospel ends, without any account of the CRUCIFIXION or Resurrection.

Other texts that claim Seth as a spiritual forefather and contain similar theologies and cosmogonies have enabled scholars to designate one strand of Gnosticism as Sethian Gnosticism. Affinities between theses texts and the cosmological section of *Judas* lead some scholars to interpret *Judas* in light of Sethian Gnosticism. James Robinson, however, suggests that the cosmological section has been inserted into the dialogues, because the dialogues have distinct concerns and contain less Sethian terminology (2007).

Other tensions await explanation. The Spirit approves the creation of most of the ruling heavenly luminaries. The stars of the material cosmos, however, wield a negative influence on human beings, and Jesus predicts their destruction. Although a star leads Judas and helps him to surpass the other disciples, this star also leads him down the wrong path. Seth appears as both a spiritual progenitor in an upper aeon and a lower angel, identified with Christ. The fragmentary state of *Judas*, the combination of sources, or indifference to logical coherence might explain these tensions.

SEE ALSO APOCRYPHA; DEAD SEA SCROLLS; DISCIPLES; GNOSTICISM; GOSPEL; HERMAS, SHEPHERD OF; HEAVEN (IN THE BIBLE); JESUS CHRIST (IN THE BIBLE); JUDAS ISCARIOT.

BIBLIOGRAPHY

Rodolphe Kasser and Gregor Wurst, eds., *The Gospel of Judas: Together with the Letter of Peter to Philip, James, and a Book of Allogenes from Codex Tchacos: Critical Edition*, translated by Rodolphe Kasser, Marvin Meyer, Gregor Wurst, and François Gaudard (Washington, D.C. 2007).

Rodolphe Kasser, Marvin Meyer, and Gregor Wurst, eds., *The Gospel of Judas from Codex Tchacos* (Washington, D.C. 2006).

Elaine Pagels and Karen L. King, *Reading Judas: The Gospel of Judas and the Shaping of Christianity* (New York 2007).

James M. Robinson, *The Secrets of Judas: The Story of the Misunderstood Disciple and His Lost Gospel* (New York 2007).

John D. Turner, *Sethian Gnosticism and the Platonic Tradition* Bibliothèque Copte de Nag Hammadi Section Études 6 (Québec 2001).

Tom Wright, *Judas and the Gospel of Jesus: Understanding a Newly Discovered Ancient Text and Its Contemporary Significance* (London 2006).

James B. Wallace
Ph.D. Candidate, Graduate Division of Religion
Emory University, Atlanta, Ga. (2009)

K

KANSAS, CATHOLIC CHURCH IN

Part of the Louisiana Purchase, the area that is now Kansas was annexed to the United States in 1803. Having been part of the Missouri Territory until 1821, it remained unorganized until formation of the Indian Territory in 1832. The Kansas-Nebraska Act (1854) established the territories of Kansas and Nebraska, and on January 29, 1861, Kansas became the thirty-fourth state to enter the Union. Its 81,815 square miles are at the geographic center of the continental United States, with Nebraska to the North, Missouri to the East, Oklahoma to the South, and Colorado to the West.

At the time of the Louisiana Purchase, Shawnee, Osage, Potawatomi, Quivira, Kaw (Kansa), Ottawa, Cherokee, and many other Native American tribes occupied the territory. During the nineteenth century, thousands of Native Americans were relocated to Kansas, and then to Oklahoma. When Kansas attained statehood, it held a population of about 110,000—mostly settlers from the South and New England and immigrants from Germany, Russia, Sweden, and England. By that time nearly all Native Americans had been pushed into Oklahoma. In the year 2006 Kansas had a total population of 2,764,065, of whom 89.1 percent were white, 8.6 percent Hispanic, 6.0 percent black, 2.2 percent Asian, and only 1.0 percent Native American (U.S. Census Bureau 2008).

Early History. On June 29, 1541, Franciscan Friar Juan de PADILLA (c. 1490–1542) crossed the Arkansas River near present-day Dodge City with Spanish conquistador Francisco Vásquez de Coronado (c. 1510–1554). After celebrating the first Mass in what is now the United States, he separated from Coronado and began evangelizing the Quivira. A monument stands near Saint Rose's Church, Council Grove, at the site believed to be the place where he became the protomartyr of the United States at the hands of a rival tribe.

Father Charles DE LA CROIX (1792–1869) made the next attempt to evangelize Kansas when he traveled to the Neosho River and converted many of the Osage (1822), but it was the JESUITS who established a lasting presence. Beginning in 1827, Father Charles VAN QUICKENBORNE, S.J. (1788–1837), journeyed repeatedly from St. Louis to evangelize the Native Americans of northeast Kansas—primarily the Osage, Peoria, Wea, and Pienkishaw. He established Saint Francis Xavier mission for the Kickapoo near Leavenworth in 1836, but abandoned it in 1847. Father Christian Hoecken, S.J. (1851), established a mission for the Pottawatomie at Sugar Creek (1839), where Saint Rose Philippine DUCHESNE (1769–1852) and the Religious of the Sacred Heart founded a school for girls (1841). In 1847, when the Pottawatomie moved to their new reservation west of present-day Topeka, the missionaries followed and established Saint Mary's Jesuit Mission with Saint Mary's College, which they operated until 1967, then in 1978 sold to the schismatic Society of Saint Pius X. In 1846 the Jesuits established a mission for soldiers at Fort Scott, and then in 1847 Fathers John Schoenmakers, S.J. (1807–1883), and John Bax, S.J. (1817–1852), along with three lay brothers, established Osage Mission at St. Paul; both missions were located in southeast Kansas. Osage Mission included Saint Ann's Academy for girls, run by the Sisters of LORETTO from Kentucky.

PIUS IX established the Vicariate Apostolic East of the Rocky Mountains to Missouri in 1851. He gave care of this territory to Bishop Jean-Baptiste MIÈGE (1851–1874), who resided at Saint Mary's Mission. With more than one million square miles of land, the territory stretched from the Rocky Mountains to the Missouri

Our Lady of Lourdes Catholic Church in Pittsburg, Kan. *A rainbow forms near this church Thursday evening, Oct. 18, 2007, as showers moved through the area.* AP PHOTO/THE MORNING SUN, SEAN STEFFEN

River, and from Texas to Canada. A year after the Kansas-Nebraska Act allowed white immigration, Miège established Leavenworth as his episcopal city. There were 700 Catholics, 6 complete churches, 3 under construction, 11 stations, and 8 priests. Pius IX divided the vicariate in 1857, leaving Miège with just the Kansas Territory. Even in this smaller territory, covering the vast land remained a considerable challenge. To this end, Father Philip Colleton (1821–1876) organized a circulating library of 250 volumes, and Miège brought various RELIGIOUS orders to Kansas, including Benedictine monks (Atchison, 1858), Sisters of Charity (Leavenworth, 1858), Benedictine Sisters (Atchison, 1863), and Carmelite priests (Leavenworth, 1864). These religious men and women established schools and took of the care of parishes and missions. Bishop Miège consecrated the Leavenworth Cathedral of the Immaculate Conception (1868) and attended the First Vatican Council (1869–1870) before he resigned in 1874.

Louis Fink. Bishop Louis Mary FINK (1877–1904) succeeded Miège and promoted Catholic immigration to Kansas, bringing German, Polish, Croatian, Slovak, Slovenian, Lithuanian, and Irish immigrants who established ethnic parishes. The Homestead Act (1862)—granting 160 acres of land to each settler—and the building of railroads led to a tripling of the Kansas population from 107,206 in 1860 to 364,399 in 1870. In the aftermath of the Civil War, the African-American population also rose, and Holy Epiphany parish was established in Leavenworth as the first African-American parish west of St. Louis (1874). At Fink's request, the HOLY SEE established Leavenworth as a DIOCESE on May 22, 1877, a suffragan of St. Louis. At the time, it included 45,000 Catholics, 60 priests, 80 churches and chapels, 1 ABBEY, 7 colleges, 20 parochial schools, an orphanage, and a hospital.

Fink's vision was to establish a system of Christian forts throughout Kansas following the military model.

These would be places of refuge for Catholics and especially the clergy who often traveled long distances in their ministerial activities. He brought Franciscan FRIARS to Emporia (1878) and Ursuline sisters to Scipio (1896). The most notable example of these was, however, Saint Fidelis Friary at Victoria, established in 1878 by Capuchin friar Anastasius Joseph Mueller (d. 1878), who died two months after founding the friary. The Capuchins expanded the friary to include the Capuchin school of PHILOSOPHY (1903), Hays Catholic College (1908), Saint Anthony's Hospital in Hays (1909), and the nationally known Cathedral of the Plains (1912). The friary with the CATHEDRAL still stands as a landmark for travelers on Interstate 70. The Capuchin friars of Missouri, Kansas, and Colorado formed the Mid-American Province of Saint Conrad (1977), with a novitiate in Victoria.

At Fink's request, the Holy See divided the diocese in 1887, establishing the Dioceses of Concordia in northwest Kansas under Bishop Richard Scannell (1887–1890) and Wichita, which occupied the southern half of the state, under James O'Reilly (d. 1887), who died before his installation, and who was replaced by Bishop John Joseph Hennessy (1888–1897). The Church of Our Lady of Perpetual Help was made the cathedral in Concordia, and in Wichita, Saint Aloysius church was designated the pro-cathedral until the dedication of the Cathedral of the Immaculate Conception (1912). The last Indian raid in Kansas occurred that year, and the railroads flourished. Quarantine laws had stopped the cattle drives from Texas in 1885, and harsh winters in 1886 and 1887 had disastrous effects on cattle. Land values had risen 400 percent from 1881 to 1887, so a crash in 1887 drove many settlers from the land, making room for immigrants. These immigrants came largely from around the Great Lakes, especially Illinois and Ohio, and from Germany. Unlike in most other states, women in Kansas could vote in municipal, school, and bond elections, and Susanna Medora Salter (1860–1961) served in Argonia, Kansas, as the first woman mayor in America.

Twentieth Century. When Scannell was transferred to Omaha, Bishop Henessey of Wichita was named administrator of Concordia until the 1897 appointment of Thaddeus Butler (1833–1897), who died in ROME before his installation. John Francis Cunningham (1898–1919) was then named the second bishop of Concordia. Immigration continued through the turn of the century, bringing more challenges for the Church. As communities grew and moved due to flooding, railroads, or changes in county seats, churches were needed that could hold larger congregations and withstand the Kansas weather. Many of the earlier wooden buildings had since been destroyed by fire, flood, or wind, so new churches were built of stone, many of which remained in use into the early twenty-first century, especially in rural communities.

Father Francis Clement Kelly, pastor of Immaculate Conception parish, Lapeer, Michigan, and later bishop of Oklahoma City and Tulsa (1924–1948), gave a lecture to Catholics at Argonia in southwestern Kansas. The following day, moved by their inability to build a church, he addressed Bishop Hennessy who suggested that he form an extension society to collect money for needy parishes. Therefore, in 1904 Father Kelly established the Catholic Church Extension Society of the United States of America (CCES). One of the earliest society projects was Saint Anthony's chapel car, a seventy-two-foot railroad car with a chapel that seated fifty and contained sleeping quarters for the missionaries and a porter, a kitchen with refrigerator, and a library. On June 22, 1907, it left Wichita on its first missionary journey, stopping first in Wellington, Kansas, the following day; Father Tom McKernan (1881–1959) celebrated a Mass at which Bishop Hennessy preached. Those two, along with organist George Hennessey (no relation to the bishop), a representative of the CCES, and a porter traveled throughout the Diocese of WICHITA administering the sacraments, praying VESPERS, and leading various devotions. They made a tour through the South before leaving the chapel car in New Orleans with the CCES. The overwhelming success prompted the Extension Society to construct a second, larger car, but it did not serve in Kansas due to new anti–pass laws that prevented the pass courtesy that the chapel car had previously enjoyed from the railroads.

Due in part to the great demand for wheat in Europe, the 1910s and 1920s were a time of economic prosperity for Kansas. Bishops Thomas F. Lillis (1904–1910) and John Ward (1911–1929) of Leavenworth; Hennessy, and August J. Schwertner (1921–1939) of Wichita; and Cunningham and Francis J. Tief (1921–1938) of Concordia placed great emphasis on education. In addition to the high schools these bishops established throughout the state, Tief founded Marymount College at Salina in 1922, which, four years later, was the first school in the state to offer degrees to women; Ward founded Saint Mary's College at Leavenworth in 1923.

However prosperous times may have been in the first two decades of the century, the following decade brought disaster. In 1929 the Great Depression reduced the demand for crops, while production remained high. The following year brought dust storms in which violent winds at times carried the fertile Kansas soil more than 100 miles before dropping it, covering roads, railroad tracks, and farm machinery. Hot summers, cold winters, floods, and grasshopper swarms devastated Kansas agriculture throughout the 1930s. During the depression, the emphasis on education continued with Bishop

Cunningham establishing Saint Joseph's College and Military Academy at Hays in 1931. Bishop Schwertner established 16 religious vocation schools in 1929, with 737 students, and 19 more in 1930, with a total of 1,469 students. He also established religious correspondence schools for children who lived far from a church, and in 1929 the Sisters College, a branch of the University of Wichita, opened at the cathedral to train teachers, with 129 sisters enrolled. The following year radio station KFH aired the Catholic Radio Hour to further these educational efforts, and in the 1930s the CONFRATERNITY OF CHRISTIAN DOCTRINE (CCD) was begun in all three dioceses.

Expansion and Change. Because of its location on the Missouri River and the presence of railroad lines, Kansas City grew rapidly. As a result, Bishop George Donnelly (1947–1950) moved his see from Leavenworth to Kansas City, Kansas, in 1947, shortly after his installation. He made Saint Peter's church his cathedral.

Clyde Cessna (1879–1954), during the winter of 1916 to 1917, and Walter Beech (1891–1951), in 1932, began constructing planes on assembly lines in Wichita, setting the stage for a great turning point in state history. With the entry of the United States into World War II (1939), the demand for military aircraft brought thousands of workers to Wichita from surrounding rural areas and other states; in the 1940s, the population of Wichita grew from 114,966 to 168,279. Further growth came for Wichita with the activation of McConnell Air Force Base in 1951. While at the beginning of World War II only eight parishes existed in the city, by 1960 there were seventeen. In that same time, only seven parishes were established elsewhere within the 1960 diocesan boundaries, three of which were near the Air Force base. Expansion of Fort Riley infantry camp and Air Force bases in Salina and Walker brought rapid growth to those towns. The Kansas population, and by consequence, the Church, became more and more urban.

As populations grew and shifted, Bishop Frank A. Thill (1938–1957) moved his see from Concordia to the larger Salina, where better access to railroads facilitated travel for himself and his priests; he named Sacred Heart church his new cathedral. Bishop Frederick W. Freking (1957–1965) in 1962 dedicated the current Sacred Heart Cathedral, built in a grain elevator motif. Also due to this rapid growth, Bishop Mark K. Carroll of Wichita (1947–1963) petitioned that the Diocese of Wichita be split. The Holy See granted his request and in 1951 established the Diocese of DODGE CITY with Bishop John B. Franz (1951–1960) as its first ordinary. In 1961, under Bishop Marion F. Forst, Dodge City became the first diocese in the United States and the second in the western hemisphere to honor Mary as its patroness under the title of Our Lady of GUADALUPE, and the Cathedral

of Our Lady of Guadalupe was dedicated in 2001. A year after the establishment of the Diocese of Dodge City, Kansas was made an ecclesiastical province with Kansas City as its metropolitan see.

In 1954 Bishop Carroll announced the project he considered to be his greatest ambition, the establishment of Chaplain Kapaun Memorial High School in Wichita, which he opened two years later. A priest of the Diocese of Wichita from Pilsen, Kansas, Chaplain Emil Kapaun (1916–1951) had served as an army chaplain in both World War II and the Korean Conflict. He died in a prisoner of war camp hospital in Pyoktong, Korea. In 1971, at the direction of Bishop David M. Maloney, the high school merged with Mount Carmel Academy to form Kapaun-Mount Carmel High School. In 1965 Archbishop Edward J. Hunkeler (1951–1969) opened Savior of the World Minor Seminary in Kansas City with sixty-six freshmen and thirty-one sophomores from various dioceses. The early years of the high school seminary saw increased enrollments. However, decreasing enrollments beginning in the mid-1970s coupled with the shortage of priests to serve on its faculty forced Archbishop Ignatius J. Strecker (1969–1993) to close the seminary in 1987. The facility was then converted into Savior Pastoral Center, an archdiocesan retreat and meeting facility, and the archdiocesan offices.

With the rapid cultural changes that came about in the 1950s and 1960s, the dioceses of Kansas felt the need to reevaluate their ministries. Dodge City held its first synod in 1957. Wichita held a synod the following year, its first since 1898, and Salina held its first in 1962. Diocesan Councils of Catholic Women were established in Wichita and Salina in 1958 and in Dodge City in 1962. As the number of priests in all four dioceses decreased in the years following the Second Vatican Council (1962–1965), new efforts were made to meet the spiritual needs of the FAITHFUL. In Salina in 1975 Bishop Cyril J. Vogel (1965–1979) began "Team Ministry," a group of three priests who together staffed six parishes (though each retained canonical responsibility for two of them). The model was continued, though individual priests were transferred into and out of the team. Eventually, women religious were included, thus initiating their role as pastoral associates in the diocese. In Dodge City Bishop Eugene J. Gerber (1976–1982) began a permanent diaconate program in 1978 that produced seven deacons, ordained in the winter of 1983 to 1984 by Bishop Stanley G. Schlarman (1983–1998). Bishop Ronald M. Gilmore (1998–) reestablished the program in 1999, and in December 2000 ordained six Hispanic men to the diaconate to meet the growing demand for Hispanic MINISTRY that arose as Mexican laborers immigrated to the area to work in meat packing plants. In addition, priests were recruited for ministry in the state from Burma, Vietnam, the Philippines, India, Ghana, Kenya, Nigeria, Mexico, and Colombia.

Wichita received international attention in 1991 when the pro-life organization Operation Rescue organized the *Summer of Mercy*, a six-week series of demonstrations, rallies, and protests. Operation Rescue leaders arrived in Wichita on July 15 and immediately began protesting in front of the three Wichita ABORTION clinics by praying, singing, and physically blocking entrances. Those six weeks saw more than 2,000 arrests and cost local and county governments more than $500,000. The Summer of Mercy culminated on August 24 with a rally at which Bishop Gerber encouraged the 40,000 people present to continue their peaceful efforts against abortion. At the same time the National Organization for Women held a counter-rally drawing a mere 5,000 pro-choice advocates. As the counter-rally disbanded, a group calling themselves *Rural America For Life* jammed Wichita traffic for three hours as their *tractorcade* moved through the city with 300 farm vehicles sporting pro-life signs. The Summer of Mercy breathed new life into the pro-life movement in Wichita, throughout the state, and other parts of the country. The diocese saw lasting effects as the abortion issue remained a source of unity, drawing adults and especially youth to greater participation in the life of the Church.

Catholic healthcare in Kansas has been led by the Sisters of the Sorrowful Mother of the Third Order of Saint Francis, who started Saint Francis Hospital in Wichita in 1889. By 1969, with 860 beds, it had become the second largest Catholic hospital in the nation. In 1995 the hospital merged with Saint Joseph's Hospital (for which the Sister's of SAINT JOSEPH had assumed responsibility in 1925) to form the Via Christi Regional Medical Center with more than 1,500 beds at the two campuses. In addition the Sisters of Charity of Leavenworth continued to serve as leaders and innovators in the healthcare industry through their hospitals located in Topeka, Leavenworth, and Kansas City. During the 1980s and 1990s, many smaller hospitals operated by individual orders closed their doors due to increased competition by larger and better-funded public institutions. St. Mary's Hospital in Emporia, which remained competitive with the public county hospital through the early 1980s, is one such example; it ceased operation in 1990.

After Vatican Council II. Since the Second Vatican Council, all four dioceses, in keeping with the teachings of the council, placed great emphasis on the universal call to HOLINESS. Bishop Gerber, while in Dodge City, introduced RENEW (1981) to promote family and small group PRAYER and scripture study. Later, in that same diocese, Bishop Stanley G. Schlarman (1983–1998) promoted Teens Encounter Christ and the CURSILLO

MOVEMENT. Catholics in the diocese participated in Cursillo weekends in Texas beginning in 1962 until 1988, when the first weekend was held in the diocese at Lakin. Though normally conducted in Spanish, the diocese has also held weekends in English. Bishop George K. Fitzsimons (1984–2004) established a RENEW Office (1985) and an Office of Lay Ministry (1986) for the Diocese of Salina, and Archbishop Strecker directed every parish in the Archdiocese of KANSAS CITY to establish a parish council and finance committee to promote greater lay involvement. In addition Archbishop Strecker established the archdiocesan Call-to-Share program, a stewardship initiative which, while also financial in nature, commenced with a study of parish life and the pastoral needs of the laity. The program has continued for more than thirty years and remains a strong part of the life of the archdiocese, supporting parish initiatives and providing needed funding to an extensive diocesan ministry. The archdiocese also became home to a large number of active Serra Clubs, an international organization that supports vocations. Programs in youth ministry and family life were also established in each of the dioceses from the late 1980s through 1990s that provide applied ministries, support, and resources to both parish programs and individual young people and families.

After being transferred to the Diocese of Wichita in 1982, Bishop Gerber promoted various programs to deepen spirituality among the laity, including Teens Encounter Christ, an intensive retreat program for high school students, and the *Totus Tuus* summer catechetical program that has served all four dioceses of Kansas as well as parishes in Colorado, Nebraska, Oklahoma, Missouri, Georgia, and Wisconsin since its beginning in 1987; it recruits and trains young adults to serve as parish catechists during week-long, all-day sessions. Bishop Gerber, Bishop Thomas J. Olmsted of Wichita (2001–2003), and Archbishop James P. Keleher of Kansas City (1993–2005) made a priority of promoting and fostering parish EUCHARISTIC DEVOTION, efforts that were enthusiastically received in parishes throughout their respective dioceses. In addition all four dioceses in the state reinvigorated their efforts toward nurturing, recruiting, and supporting priestly vocations. These efforts resulted in a substantial increase in the number of seminarians and ordinations to the priesthood, the most dramatic surge occurring in Salina under Bishop Paul S. Coakley (2004–) whose seminarians increased in three years from one to more than fifteen. In 2006 the Archdiocese of Kansas City in Kansas, under Archbishop Joseph F. Naumann (2005–), established its first-ever program of studies and formation leading to the permanent diaconate, the first class of permanent deacons scheduled to be ordained in early 2011.

In the 2004 and 2008 presidential elections, the bishops of Kansas were especially vocal in their instruction of the faithful regarding the importance of voting according to the moral CONSCIENCE of the Church. Although Kansas had always traditionally embraced political conservatism, signs indicated that understanding and support of the Church's teachings regarding abortion, embryonic stem-cell research, and EUTHANASIA among the faithful were perhaps waning somewhat. The election of a pro-choice Catholic governor, Kathleen Sibelius, exacerbated the political situation. Bishops Gilmore, Coakley, Michael O. Jackels of Wichita (2005–), and Archbishop Naumann published a joint pastoral letter that clarified the Church's teachings on the primacy of human life in the late spring of 2008. Archbishop Naumann, after privately meeting repeatedly with Governor Sibelius about her opposition to legislation restricting late-term abortions, publicly called for her to refrain from presenting herself for Holy Communion at her parish in Topeka.

The Catholic Church in Kansas continues to respond to the demographical, cultural, and societal changes affecting the state population. These changes include the continued movement of the populace from rural to urban life; the increased cultural and racial diversity of the population; the rise in immigration, both documented and undocumented, to the state; and the increased chasm between modern American political values and the social and moral teachings of the Church's Magisterium.

SEE ALSO BENEDICTINE NUNS AND SISTERS; BENEDICTINES; CARMELITES; CATECHIST; COLORADO, CATHOLIC CHURCH IN; CONVERTS AND CONVERSION; DEACON; EMBRYOLOGY, HUMAN; HOLINESS, UNIVERSAL CALL TO; MARTYR; MARYMOUNT COLLEGES AND UNIVERSITIES; MISSION AND MISSIONS; MISSOURI, CATHOLIC CHURCH IN; NATIONAL COUNCIL OF CATHOLIC WOMEN (NCCW); PIUS X, POPE, ST.; SERRA INTERNATIONAL; TEACHING AUTHORITY OF THE CHURCH (MAGISTERIUM); URSULINES; VATICAN COUNCIL I; VATICAN COUNCIL II.

BIBLIOGRAPHY

The Archdiocese of Kansas City in Kansas, *The Archdiocese of Kansas City in Kansas: 150 Years of Faith, 1850–2000* (Strasbourg, France 2000).

Mary Paul Fitzgerald, S.C.L., *Beacon on the Plains* (Leavenworth, Kans. 1939).

Mary Frances Lahey, *Harvest of Faith: History of the Diocese of Salina, 1887–1987* (Dallas, Tex. 1987).

John M. Moeder, *History of the Diocese of Wichita* (Wichita, Kans. 1963).

Ignatius J. Strecker, *The Church in Kansas 1850–1905: A Family Story* (2000)

Arthur Tonne, *The Story of Chaplain Kapaun: Patriot Priest of the Korean Conflict* (Emporia, Kans. 1954).

U.S. Census Bureau, *Kansas Quickfacts*, available from: http://quickfacts.census.gov/qfd/states/20000.html (accessed November 12, 2008).

Timothy F. Wenzl, *A Legacy of Faith: A History of the Diocese of Dodge City* (Newton, Kans. 2001).

David Thomas Marstall
Pontifical College Josephinum
Columbus, Ohio

Michael Podrebarac
Archdiocesan Archivist
Archdiocese of Kansas City, Kan. (2009)

KANSAS CITY, ARCHDIOCESE OF

Metropolitan see embracing 21 counties in the northeastern part of Kansas, an area of 12,524 square miles, with the dioceses of Dodge City, Salina, and Wichita, all in Kansas, as suffragan sees. The Archdiocese of Kansas City (Kansanopolitana) was established as the Diocese of Leavenworth on May 22, 1877, was changed to Kansas City on May 10, 1947, and became an ARCHDIOCESE on August 9, 1952. In 2008, Catholics comprised 17 percent of the total population (*The Official Catholic Directory* 2008, p. 616).

Early History. Catholicism in Kansas dates from 1541, when the Coronado expedition arrived, accompanied by the Franciscan Juan de PADILLA, who lost his life while preaching to Native American tribes. In 1820, Sans Nerf, head chief of the Osage, appealed to Bishop Louis William DUBOURG of St. Louis to visit or send them missionaries. Reverend Charles DE LA CROIX was sent in 1822. That same year Dubourg went to Washington to ask the U.S. government to subsidize four missionaries whom he proposed to send to the Osage. His proposal was approved by Secretary of War John C. Calhoun (1782–1850), then in charge of Native American affairs, who promised an annual subsidy of $800.

Although the Kickapoo mission, founded in 1835 by Charles Van Quickenborne, S.J., lasted only four years, it became the center from which the two focal missions were later established among the Osage and the Pottawatomie. From Osage Mission School, founded by John Schoenmakers, S.J., in 1847, and from St. Mary's Pottawatomie mission, founded by Christian Hoecken, S.J., in 1848, the JESUITS first ministered to surrounding Indian tribes and later sought out scattered white frontiersmen. Their itinerant circuits covered most of what is now Kansas. As secular priests arrived to assume responsibility for established parishes, the Jesuits gradually withdrew from the mission field. However, the zeal of Fathers John Bax, Paul Ponziglione, Philip Colleton, and Louis Dumortier had opened the frontier to the Catholic Church, making it known and respected not only by Catholics but also by non-Catholics.

The Religious of the SACRED HEART OF MARY, including Mother Rose Philippine DUCHESNE, opened a school for Native American girls among the Pottawatomie in 1841. The Sisters of LORETTO arrived at Osage mission in 1847 to establish the first permanent boarding school on Kansas soil.

At the request of the Seventh Provincial Council of Baltimore, Pope PIUS IX, on July 19, 1850, erected the Vicariate APOSTOLIC of Indian Territory East of the Rocky Mountains, which included the present states of Kansas, Nebraska, Oklahoma, Wyoming, Montana, Colorado, and parts of North and South Dakota west of the Missouri River. John Baptist MIÈGE, S.J., professor of MORAL THEOLOGY at ST. LOUIS UNIVERSITY, was consecrated bishop of Messine and first vicar apostolic of the new jurisdiction. He made St. Mary's Mission in Kansas his residence, and the log cabin church there served as his cathedral until August 1855, when he moved to Leavenworth, a promising city in the newly organized Kansas Territory. On horseback or by wagon, Miège visited the Native American villages, military forts, trading posts, and growing towns of his vast mission, which was reduced in size in 1857 when Nebraska was organized into a separate vicariate.

Miège invited the Benedictine and Carmelite fathers, the Benedictine sisters, and the Sisters of Charity to the mission fields in his vicariate. The Sisters of Charity opened the first orphanage in Kansas (1863) and the first hospital in Leavenworth (1869). Among the first secular priests to enter the apostolate in Kansas were Theodore Heimann, a German priest who later joined the CARMELITES, J. H. Defourri from France, and Ambrose T. Butler from Ireland. Daniel Hurley, the first Native American ordained in Kansas (1877), exerted an important influence on the growth of the Church there.

Ecclesiastical Administration. In 1871, Louis M. FINK, O.S.B., was consecrated bishop of Eucarpia and auxiliary to Bishop Miège, whom he succeeded on Miège's resignation in 1874. When Leavenworth was elevated to the status of DIOCESE in 1877, Fink administered the entire state of Kansas, which then included 65 priests, 88 churches, 3 "colleges," 4 academies, 1 hospital, 1 orphanage, and 13 parochial schools with 1,700 pupils. During the next ten years, the building of roads and railroads, generous government land policies, and the settlement of the Native American issue on the frontier attracted immigrants. Irish, Germans, Belgians, and French established colonies throughout the diocese. The German-Russians who settled in Ellis and Rush counties

in the late 1890s left an enviable cultural heritage to the Church in Kansas. Those who worked among them included the Capuchin Fathers, Sisters of St. Agnes, and Sisters of ST. JOSEPH of Concordia. Meanwhile, the BENEDICTINES (men and women), Franciscans, Jesuits, URSULINES, Sisters of Charity, and other smaller orders developed institutions in the eastern parts of the diocese.

At Fink's suggestion, the Diocese of Leavenworth was divided on August 2, 1887, and the western section constituted the dioceses of Concordia and Wichita. The areas of the three dioceses were redistributed in 1897 when boundaries were adjusted. Fink continued to administer Leavenworth until his death in 1904, when he was succeeded by Thomas F. Lillis, who was consecrated on December 27, 1904, and governed the see until his transfer to the Diocese of Kansas City, Missouri, in 1910. John Ward, consecrated third bishop of Leavenworth on February 22, 1911, ruled until his death in 1929, when his coadjutor, Francis Johannes, succeeded to the see, which he headed until his death in 1937. Paul C. Schulte's administration, begun in 1937, was terminated by his transfer to the Archdiocese of INDIANAPOLIS in 1946, when George J. Donnelly succeeded him in Leavenworth. A year later the see was changed to Kansas City, where, following Donnelly's death in 1950, Edward J. Hunkeler became bishop (1951) and archbishop (1952). When Hunkeler retired in 1969, he was succeeded by Ignatius J. Strecker, bishop of Springfield-Cape Girardeau, who was archbishop of Kansas City from 1969 until his retirement in 1993. In 1976, the retired bishop of Dodge City, Kansas, Marion F. Forst, was appointed auxiliary bishop to Archbishop Strecker. He served as auxiliary bishop until his retirement in 1986, but he remained active in both diocesan administration and pastoral ministry until just a few years before his death in 2007 at age 96. Forst was the oldest living bishop in the United States and one of the few remaining bishops to have participated in VATICAN COUNCIL II, before his death. In 1993, James P. Keleher, bishop of Belleville, was installed as Strecker's successor. In 2004, Joseph F. Naumann, auxiliary bishop of St. Louis, was named coadjutor archbishop; he succeeded Archbishop Keleher in 2005.

Institutional Development. In the expansion of its parochial and secondary school systems, the Archdiocese of Kansas City was a pioneer in the central Catholic high school movement in the United States in the early twentieth century. Catholic institutions of higher learning in the archdiocese included Donnelly College (Kansas City); St. Mary College (Leavenworth); and Benedictine College (Atchison), established July 1, 1971, as a merger between St. Benedict's College, directed by the Benedictine monks, and Mt. St. Scholastica College, directed by the Benedictine sisters. All three colleges,

Sunday Mass. *Young U.S. Army soldiers attend a Sunday morning Catholic service, February 2, 2003 on base at Fort Levinworth in Kansas.* CHARLES OMMANNEY/GETTY IMAGES

which offer bachelor's degrees (Benedictine and St. Mary also offer some master's degree programs) have grown and have seen an increased need for their services to both Catholic and non-Catholic populations. Benedictine College has been credited as being both an excellent liberal arts college and an institution with a pronounced Catholic identity, demonstrating exceptional fidelity to the Church's intended mission and purpose of Catholic higher education.

The archdiocese continued to lead by example in the development and growth of Catholic elementary and secondary education. At a time when numerous dioceses throughout the nation were scaling back parochial and secondary educational facilities and services, under Archbishop Keleher the number of schools and enrolled students continued to climb though the first decade of the new millennium. Beginning with Archbishop Strecker, the archdiocese also became a leader in the area of Catholic campus ministry for students attending state universities. The University of Kansas at Lawrence, Emporia State University in Emporia, Washburn Municipal College in Topeka, and Haskell Indian Nations University in Lawrence all enjoy the services of established and active campus ministry programs.

The demographics of the archdiocese began to shift in the mid-1960s, with increased population moves to the suburbs of Kansas City, Kansas, and a decline of urban and rural populations. Most of the historic ethnic parishes of Kansas City began to decline in population and no longer served their original purpose. The consolidation of many of these parishes—along with the rapid growth of the Hispanic population of Kansas City during the 1990s and the first decade of the new millennium—led to diocesan directives aimed at revitalizing Catholic community life in the urban core. The directives also emphasized serving the needs of new immigrants who, like those 100 years before, came to the region seeking work and the opportunity for a better life for themselves and their children. At the same time, diocesan attention toward changes in rural life resulted in the consolidation and clustering of rural parishes, in some cases meaning that two or more small parishes began being served by a single pastor. The growth of new parishes and schools has attempted to keep pace with the explosive growth and expansion of suburban communities to the south of Kansas City.

The decline of religious and priestly vocations has also had an impact on the archdiocese. In 1993, the Franciscan fathers and brothers of Cincinnati, Ohio, ended their nearly 125 years of service to the archdiocese. In 2007, the Ursuline sisters of Paola announced their plans to merge with another Ursuline community in Kentucky, thus beginning the end of their nearly 150 years of service to the archdiocese. However, the archdiocese renewed its active promotion of religious vocations in the mid-1990s and has invited a number of women's religious orders to serve in schools and other institutions. The men's and women's Benedictine monasteries at Atchison remain a vital part of archdiocesan life, as do the Sisters of Charity of Leavenworth (especially in educational and hospital work) and the Sisters, SERVANTS OF MARY in their service to the sick and dying. The Priestly Fraternity of St. Peter began service to the archdiocese in the early 1990s to meet the needs of those attached to the TRIDENTINE MASS; two communities, one in Kansas City and one serving the faithful in Topeka and Maple Hill, remain strong. Since 1998, the number of seminarians and ordinations to the priesthood have largely kept pace with the retirement and death of diocesan priests. The permanent diaconate was instituted in the archdiocese for the first time in 2006, with the first class of permanent deacons to be ordained in 2011 to assist both in parochial and archdiocesan ministries and services.

In the Jubilee Year of 2000, the Archdiocese of Kansas City in Kansas celebrated the sesquicentennial of the erection of the Vicariate Apostolic of Indian Territory East of the Rocky Mountains, which marked the beginning of the Church's institutional history in Kansas and much of the Great Plains.

SEE ALSO DODGE CITY, DIOCESE OF; EDUCATION, CATHOLIC (HIGHER) IN THE UNITED STATES; KANSAS, CATHOLIC CHURCH IN; ST. AGNES, CONGREGATION OF SISTERS OF; SISTERS OF CHARITY, FEDERATION OF; WICHITA, DIOCESE OF.

BIBLIOGRAPHY

Archdiocese of Kansas City Official Web site, available from: http://www.archkck.org (accessed December 18, 2008).

Peter Beckman, *The Catholic Church on the Kansas Frontier, 1850–1877* (Washington, D.C. 1943).

Richard Joseph Bollig, *History of Catholic Education in Kansas, 1836–1932* (Washington, D.C. 1933).

William Whites Graves, *Life and Letters of Fathers Ponziglione, Schoenmakers and Other Early Jesuits at Osage Mission* (St. Paul, Kans. 1916).

Todd Habiger, *The Archdiocese of Kansas City in Kansas: 150 Years of Faith, 1850–2000* (Strasbourg, France 2000).

Thomas H. Kinsella, *A Centenary of Catholicity in Kansas 1822–1922* (Kansas City, Kans. 1921).

The Official Catholic Directory, 2008 (New Providence, N.J. 2008).

M. Evangeline Thomas, *Footprints on the Frontier* (Westminster, Md. 1948).

Sister Mary Evangeline Thomas CSJ
Chairman, Department of History, and Director of College Relations
Marymount College, Salina, Kan.

Michael Podrebarac
Archdiocesan Archivist
Archdiocese of Kansas City, Kan. (2009)

KENTUCKY, CATHOLIC CHURCH IN

In 2008 the Catholic population in the state of Kentucky (382,521 in 302 parishes) constituted almost 10 percent of the population (*The Official Catholic Directory* 2008, p. 2081). In addition to the Holy Land area near Bardstown, the greater numbers of these live in cities along the Ohio River that received a significant inflow of German and Irish immigrants in the nineteenth century. They are concentrated in Louisville, Owensboro, Covington, Henderson, Paducah, and Lexington. In many other areas of Kentucky, especially in the south and east, it is not uncommon to find only one Catholic congregation per county. There are four Catholic jurisdictions in the state: the Archdiocese of LOUISVILLE, founded as the Diocese of Bardstown in 1808, and the Dioceses of Covington (1853), Owensboro (1937), and Lexington (1988).

Early History. The early Catholics in Kentucky were a resourceful group of pioneers. Initially without priests, their earliest parishes were gathered by laity. Their first seminary (St. Thomas) had its beginnings on a flatboat coming down the Ohio River. One of their first colleges (St. Mary's) began life in an old distillery building. One of their pioneer priests was Stephen BADIN, the first priest ordained in the United States.

In 1808 Pope PIUS VII established America's first inland DIOCESE at Bardstown in Nelson County, Kentucky. Nelson, Marion, and Washington counties came to be known as the Kentucky "Catholic Holy Land." The designation results both from the history of the area as well as from its ongoing institutions—such as St. Joseph's Proto-Cathedral, numerous parishes, three large motherhouses of sisters, and the Abbey of GETHSEMANI. The sizable population of Catholics in the area is something of a rarity in the rural South.

The first Catholics in Kentucky came almost entirely from Maryland, including the William Coomes (1712–1783) family and Dr. George Hart, who settled at Harrodsburg in 1775. Dr. Hart was one of the first physicians, and Mrs. Coomes conducted the first elementary school in Kentucky. The first Catholic colony, consisting of twenty-five families led by Basil Hayden (c. 1743–1804), came in the spring of 1785 to establish the Pottinger Creek settlement, a few miles from Bardstown. Before Kentucky was admitted to the Union in 1792, at least six distinct colonies had settled on the creeks in an arc around Bardstown. The first priest to be assigned to Kentucky by Bishop John CARROLL was an Irish Franciscan, Charles WHELAN, who, in the fall of 1787, accompanied a group from Maryland. A controversy over his salary, leading to a court case, forced Whelan to leave Kentucky after two-and-a-half years of service. In 1791 Reverend William de Rohan arrived with a group from North Carolina. Under his direction the Pottinger Creek Catholics built a log chapel, named variously Holy Cross and Sacred Heart, which was the first Catholic place of WORSHIP in Kentucky. However, his MINISTRY, unauthorized by Carroll, soon met with many difficulties, and de Rohan was deprived of his faculties. Thereafter, he taught in various Catholic settlement schools and resided at St. Thomas Seminary, where he died in 1832.

In 1793 Reverend Stephen T. Badin, the first priest to be ordained in the United States, with Reverend Michael Barrieres (b. 1747) arrived in Kentucky from Baltimore. On the first Sunday in ADVENT, Badin said Mass in the home of Denis McCarthy at Lexington; he remained in the Scott County settlement for more than a year before moving to Pottinger's Creek. Three miles from the chapel at Holy Cross, he purchased a farm, which he named St. Stephen's. From this place (later the site of the motherhouse of the Sisters of LORETTO), Badin directed Catholic life for the next fifteen years. Among the 70,000 Kentuckians in 1793, Badin estimated there were about 300 Catholic families, to whom he alone ministered until February 1797, when Carroll sent Reverend Michael Fournier to his aid. Two years later Reverend Anthony Salmon joined them, and shortly after, Reverend John THAYER of Boston was added to the group. However, Salmon was killed by a fall from his horse in 1799, and in 1803 Fournier died and Thayer departed, leaving Badin alone once again.

In 1805 help arrived in the person of the Belgian priest, Charles NERINCKX, who soon began the erection of Holy Mary, the first of ten churches he built in less than ten years. The Dominican, Edward D. FENWICK, also arrived that spring to look for land; a year later he returned with three English confreres, Samuel T. Wilson, William R. Tuite, and Robert A. Angier, to establish the first foundation of the Dominican order in the United States at Springfield. By 1807 they had enrolled twelve boys in their seminary, and two years later they dedicated St. Rose Church, a brick structure. In 1809 the DO-

MINICANS opened St. Thomas College, the first Catholic college in the West, which for twenty years provided a classical education for many prominent Southerners, including Jefferson Davis (1808–1889). A group of Trappist monks, led by Dom Urbain Guillet, had also come to Kentucky with Nerinckx in 1805. After a short stay with Badin, the monks moved to a farm on Pottinger's Creek and finally bought land on the Green River in Casey County, where they began a free school for boys, the first Catholic school in Kentucky. In 1809 Dom Urbain transferred the group to the Illinois country after seven priests and eight brothers died in the attempt to found the community in Kentucky.

Diocese. As early as October 1804, Carroll asked Badin for a report on the possibility of establishing a diocese in Kentucky; every year thereafter Badin discussed the idea with the BISHOP. In 1807 the missionary recommended that the see be located at Bardstown and the first incumbent be Benedict FLAGET. Among the names submitted to ROME by Carroll were Flaget, Badin (whom some, including the Dominicans, feared might be selected), Wilson, and Nerinckx. In 1808 Rome finally acted, creating Baltimore an ARCHDIOCESE with suffragan sees at Boston, New York, Philadelphia, and Bardstown.

Flaget, shocked by his nomination to Bardstown, tried to refuse the office, going to France to plead with his Sulpician superiors for support in his stand. However, when the POPE ordered him to accept, he gave up his resistance and spent his time in France gathering recruits for his new diocese. Upon their return, Archbishop Carroll consecrated Flaget on November 4, 1810, in Fells Point, Maryland, and the following May the new bishop set out for Kentucky.

Immediately after his installation in Bardstown on June 9, 1811, Flaget began a visitation of the Kentucky congregations organized by Badin and Nerinckx. On December 21, 1811, Flaget ordained Chabrat at St. Rose, the first ordination in Kentucky and in the West. Three miles from Bardstown, on the Thomas Howard plantation, he established St. Thomas Seminary, and by 1816 erected a brick church there. In 1812 two distinctly American sisterhoods were founded: the Sisters of Loretto and the Sisters of Charity of Nazareth, both of which flourished; the sisters staffed schools, orphanages, and hospitals throughout the diocese and the country. In 1822 another native Kentuckian sisterhood, the Dominican Sisters of St. Catharine, was formed by Wilson at St. Rose, Springfield. The order later spread to conduct hospitals, a college, and grade and high schools.

Flaget called the first diocesan synod on February 20, 1812; five seculars and three Dominican priests attended. This period also marked the beginning of the

St. Mary Cathedral-Basilica of the Assumption, Covington, KY. *Pictured here is the interior of the Cathedral-Basilica. Construction began in 1894 and ended in 1915, though the building has yet to be fully completed. Still, it is one of only 35 basilicas in the U.S.* © WALTER BIBIKOW/CORBIS

dispute between Badin and Flaget over church lands. Title to practically all land was held by Badin, who had purchased many acres with his own money or funds he had personally borrowed. The bishop thought that Badin should turn over to him all titles, with no conditions; Badin argued that Flaget should at least assume the outstanding debts. Because canon law was not clear on the subject and Carroll would make no decision, the matter went unsettled and was partly the cause of Badin's departure for Europe in 1819. On his return nine years later, Badin performed missionary work in various states, returning frequently to Kentucky, where in later years he was again invested with the title of vicar general. The land question was evidently settled when Badin made the transfer in his will.

During his long episcopate, Flaget's visitations took him to Catholic settlements throughout a vast territory that ultimately embraced not only Kentucky, but also Tennessee, Indiana, Missouri, Ohio, Illinois, Wisconsin, and Michigan. He administered CONFIRMATION, settled disputes over TRUSTEEISM, negotiated with Indian commissioners, and directed the progress of the Church. In 1816 Flaget blessed the cornerstone of St. Joseph's Cathedral in Bardstown, which was dedicated on August 8, 1819. The first CATHEDRAL west of the Alleghenies, it has been named a national monument by the federal government. A seminary was opened next to the cathedral, and the seminarians moved from St. Thomas to Bardstown. In the fall of 1819 Reverend George ELDER founded St. Joseph's College in the basement of the seminary, and within a year another building was necessary to accommodate the students. In 1821 Reverend William BYRNE founded St. Mary's College near Lebanon on property acquired by Nerinckx, who had intended it for the establishment of a brotherhood. As there were only two members for the proposed community, the college remained there and in 1833 was entrusted to JESUITS Peter Chazelle and Nicholas Petit. Four years later the state granted it a charter, and the next year a novitiate was opened there. The Jesuits kept this college until 1846, when they left to accept St. John's College, Fordham, New York City, on the invitation of John HUGHES, later ARCHBISHOP of New York. Two years later a group of Jesuits from Missouri entered the diocese; they served in Bardstown and established a free school and St. Aloysius College in Louisville. In 1868 the Jesuits again left the diocese.

In 1832 when Flaget resigned his see, Rome designated his coadjutor, John DAVID, whom he had consecrated in 1819, as his successor. However, the uproar that ensued in Catholic Kentucky led the HOLY SEE to reverse the action, and the see was returned to Flaget. On July 20, 1834, when Chabrat was consecrated as the second coadjutor of Bardstown, many of the priests, especially the faculty of St. Joseph College, were opposed to this promotion. Although there remained a great deal of unrest and dissatisfaction, Chabrat made no major blunders and satisfactorily directed the diocese during the several years Flaget was in Europe. Failing eyesight caused Chabrat to retire to France in 1846; he died at Mauriac, November 21, 1868.

When Flaget made his first *ad limina* visit to Rome in 1836, he petitioned for the removal of the see from Bardstown to Louisville. This was done in 1841, four years after the boundaries of the diocese had been reduced to the single state of Kentucky. Bishop David died July 12, 1841, in Nazareth, Kentucky, and was buried there.

Soon after Martin J. SPALDING's return from Rome in 1834 he joined the faculty of the seminary and the college in Bardstown and initiated the publication of the first Catholic periodical of Kentucky, a monthly literary magazine, the *St. Joseph College Minerva*. After a year it was succeeded by a weekly newspaper, the *Catholic Advocate* under Benjamin J. Webb, and it lasted fifteen years before merging with the Cincinnati paper.

Flaget's invitation to the French sisters of the Institute of the Good Shepherd was accepted in 1843, and they established a house in Louisville. In December 1848 a colony of forty TRAPPISTS purchased 1,600 acres in Nelson County from the Sisters of Loretto. This foundation of Gethsemani, which was raised to the rank of ABBEY in July 1850, gave the diocese seven religious communities. Flaget consecrated Martin J. Spalding coadjutor bishop of Louisville on September 10, 1848. The following year the cornerstone of the new Cathedral of the Assumption in Louisville was blessed. When Flaget died on February 11, 1850, at the age of 87, he had been a priest for sixty-two years and a bishop for almost forty. Buried first in the garden of the Good Shepherd CONVENT, his remains were later transferred to the crypt of the cathedral in Louisville.

Flaget was succeeded by his coadjutor, Bishop Martin John Spalding, who served until 1864, when he was transferred to Baltimore. In 1853 the Diocese of COVINGTON was erected by separating the eastern part of Kentucky from Louisville with George A. Carrell (1853–1868), S.J., consecrated as its first bishop by Archbishop John B. PURCELL of Cincinnati, Ohio.

The Civil War took its toll on Catholic institutions in the state. The colleges and academies of the Holy Land were especially hard hit in their enrollments. St. Joseph's College in Bardstown had to close and was commandeered for a military hospital. Train accommodations were in such short supply that Bishop Martin John Spalding was once required to ride back to Louisville in a baggage car with soldiers' corpses.

In the years after the war, the turbulent administration of Bishop William George MCCLOSKEY began

(1868–1909). At Rome during the Vatican Council, he long opposed the declaration of papal INFALLIBILITY as inopportune, but eventually joined the large number who accepted it. At home he quarreled frequently and publicly with his priests as well as with many of the religious communities in the diocese. He once placed the motherhouse of the Sisters of Loretto under INTERDICT over an insurance issue. During these disputes a number of priests left the diocese, perhaps the best known was the intellectual John Lancaster SPALDING (1840–1916), nephew of Bishop Martin John Spalding and later first bishop of Peoria.

In the late nineteenth and early twentieth centuries, the state was home to a group of lively and talented Catholic laity: Colonel Patrick Henry CALLAHAN (1866–1941), an early national figure in furthering SOCIAL JUSTICE issues as elucidated by papal social ENCYCLICALS; poet Elvira Sydnor Miller (1860–1937); writer Charles T. O'Malley (1851–1910); John Whallen (1850–1913) and James Whallen (1851–1930), brothers who ran the Democratic political machine in Louisville; and Colonel Matt Winn (1861–1941), who turned the Kentucky Derby into an international event. Additionally, in this era Daniel Rudd (1854–1933), a national black lay leader, helped to bring together congresses of African-American Catholics in the 1890s. He grew up in the area, moved away, but was buried at Bardstown.

In 1937 the Diocese of Louisville was elevated to a metropolitan see, and the Diocese of Owensboro was created out of the western third of the state of Kentucky, including thirty-two counties and approximately 12,500 square miles. Father Francis Cotton (1937–1960), chancellor to Bishop John Alexander Floersh (bishop 1923–1937; archbishop 1937–1968), the sixth bishop of Louisville, was named the first bishop of Owensboro.

The latter part of the twentieth century was a time of change and challenge for the Church in Kentucky. As the Church embraced the Second Vatican Council, it also began to deal with the realities of changing demographics, declining numbers of ordained clergy, and the call to be good stewards, especially in the primal see of Louisville. In 1995 and again in 2006, the Archdiocese of Louisville merged and closed parishes, while establishing new parishes and ministries in areas of growth. The Church in Kentucky also responded to the growing ethnic diversity of the Commonwealth, reaching out to immigrants and migrants through refugee resettlement programs and pastoral ministry. As a result the Archdiocese of Louisville established one Vietnamese parish, and forty other parishes throughout the state celebrate liturgies in Spanish.

The Church in Kentucky faced serious challenges from the SEX ABUSE CRISIS. The Archdiocese of Louisville paid $25.7 million to 243 plaintiffs in a 2003 settlement, and the Diocese of Covington agreed to a class action settlement that created a $120 million fund in 2005. As of January 2008, 400 claims and 243 awards had been made totaling $79 million. In 2006 the Sisters of Charity of Nazareth paid $1.5 million to 45 plaintiffs for sexual abuse by a priest and nuns at schools and an orphanage run by the order.

Education. The Catholic Church in Kentucky has a long, venerable tradition with academic institutions. As of 2008 the four dioceses had more than 120 Catholic elementary and secondary schools with nearly 41,000 students. Five Catholic higher education centers stand proudly in the Commonwealth. Spalding University opened in 1920 in Louisville as Nazareth College, continuing an educational tradition of the Sisters of Charity of Nazareth dating back to 1814. St. Catharine Junior College at Springfield, later St. Catharine College, was founded by the DOMINICAN SISTERS in 1931 as a women's academy and junior college. Bellarmine College in Louisville, established in 1950, merged with Ursuline College in 1968. Archbishop John A. Floersh chose Father Alfred F. Horrigan, known as a human rights advocate, to serve as Bellarmine's founding president in 1949. Bellarmine, a university since 2000, hosts the international Thomas Merton Studies Center and the International Thomas Merton Society. It houses fifty thousand Merton-related materials and is the official location of the artistic estate of Merton including thirteen hundred photographs and nine hundred drawings in addition to his writings. Covington is home to Thomas More College, originally founded as Villa Madonna in 1921 by the Benedictine Sisters of Covington. Before becoming a diocesan institution in 1929, it was operated by the Sisters of NOTRE DAME, the Congregation of Divine Providence, and the Benedictine Sisters. With its origins as the Mount Saint Joseph Junior college for Women, which opened in 1925, Brescia University in Owensboro was founded in 1950.

Health Care. Catholic health-care ministry in Kentucky continues to grow, primarily through the expansion of Catholic Health Initiatives headquartered in Colorado. In 2008 the state had seventeen Catholic acute care hospitals, thirty-two nursing facilities, and other Catholic-sponsored service organizations including hospice, home health, assisted living, and senior housing.

Public Policy. In 1968 the bishops of the Commonwealth established the Catholic Conference of Kentucky (CCK) to speak for the Church in matters of public policy, to serve as liaison with the government and the legislature, and to coordinate communications and activities between the church and secular agencies and among the four dioceses. The bishops of the dioceses of Kentucky constitute CCK's Board of Directors. Through the years, the CCK has influenced many laws dealing with ABORTION, the death penalty, health care, housing, education, and other social justice issues.

In 1988 the Diocese of Lexington was created in the eastern portion of the state out of forty-three counties previously in the Diocese of Covington and seven counties previously in the Archdiocese of Louisville. This new diocese covers 16,423 square miles. A priest from the Archdiocese of Louisville, James Kendrick Williams (1988–2002), was consecrated the first bishop of Lexington.

Archdiocese of Louisville. Bishops of the twentieth century for the Archdiocese of Louisville included:

Bishop Denis O'Donaghue (1910–1924)

Archbishop John Alexander Floersh (1924–1967)

Archbishop Thomas J. McDonough (1967–1982)

Archbishop Thomas C. Kelly, O.P. (1982–2007)

Archbishop Joseph E. Kurtz (2007–)

Bishop O'Donaghue was called to shepherd the flock during some very difficult days, including World War I and an influenza epidemic. He was an able and gentle man, but he became incapacitated by 1924 and was replaced by Nashville native John A. Floersh, who is known for his piety, caution, and planning abilities. In 1924 Floersh began an episcopate that endured for more than forty years and helped shape the diocese profoundly during the middle years of the twentieth century.

In 1967 Philadelphia-born cleric Thomas J. McDonough succeeded Archbishop Floersh. Archbishop McDonough called himself a "Vatican II bishop," and he shepherded the local Church through its most intensive period of activity and change since the days of the early Church in Kentucky. Archbishop McDonough resigned in 1981 and was succeeded by Archbishop Thomas C. Kelly, O.P. This Dominican cleric had served as the general secretary of the National Conference of Catholic Bishops before coming to Louisville. He served the archdiocese for twenty-five years and established a strategic planning process that guided many initiatives in the areas of social services, evangelization, lay ministry, multicultural ministry, pastoral care, and education/ formation.

Installed in 2007, Archbishop Joseph Kurtz was bishop of Knoxville before coming to Louisville. He became active on many national committees, including Catholic Relief Services; the UNITED STATES CONFERENCE OF CATHOLIC BISHOPS (USCCB) Committee on Laity, Marriage, Family, and Youth (including chair of the subcommittee on Marriage and Family); the Bishops'

Committee for Pro-Life Activities; and the Bishops Committee on Budget and Finance. In November 2008 he became treasurer of the United States Conference of Catholic Bishops and went on to serve on the executive and administrative committees of that body. Archbishop Kurtz's priorities include spiritual renewal, increasing vocations to the priesthood, evangelization, Catholic education, and parish vitality. He embarked in 2008 on the first parish share capital campaign in diocesan history and in 2009 on the fourth revision of the archdiocesan strategic plan.

Diocese of Covington. In 1853 the Diocese of Covington was erected by separating the eastern part of Kentucky from Louisville. George A. Carrell, S.J., was consecrated as its first bishop by Archbishop John B. Purcell of Cincinnati, Ohio. Bishop Carrell was an excellent administrator, but he found the administrative responsibilities difficult. Bishop Carrell was followed by Bishop Augustus Maria Toebbe (bishop from 1869–1884), who is credited with establishing the diocesan school system. The third bishop, Camillus Paul MAES (1884–1915), oversaw the construction of the Cathedral Basilica of the Assumption in Covington. Twentieth-century bishops included Bishop Ferdinand Brossart (1915–1923), remembered for his heroism as a priest during the cholera and smallpox epidemics of the 1880s; Bishop Francis William HOWARD (1923–1944), a noted scholar on Catholic education who helped establish and lead the NATIONAL CATHOLIC EDUCATION ASSOCIATION (NCEA); Bishop William Theodore Mulloy (1944–1959), whose accomplishments touched every aspect of Catholic life in the diocese; Bishop Richard Henry Ackerman (1960–1979), who guided the diocese through the changes in the Church after the Second Vatican Council; Bishop William Anthony Hughes (1979–1995), a leader in education and parish renewal efforts; and Kentucky native Bishop Robert William Muench, who led a successful effort to build an education endowment for tuition assistance and renovated the Cathedral Basilica of the Assumption during his brief tenure from 1996 to 2001. Bishop Roger Joseph Foys was installed in July 2002. After becoming the tenth bishop of Covington, Bishop Foys focused on increasing vocations to the priesthood and conducting a diocesan synod process as well as ministering to victims of employee and clergy sexual abuse, resolving litigation, and implementing the U.S. Bishops "Charter for the Protection of Children and Young People."

Diocese of Lexington. The first bishop of Lexington, J. Kendrick Williams, is remembered for his efforts in establishing the diocese, building lay leadership, and promoting ecumenical initiatives. When Bishop Williams resigned in 2002 after accusations of sexual abuse. Bishop Ronald W. Gainer, a native of Pennsylvania, became the second bishop of Lexington. Bishop Gainer is a member of the USCCB Canonical Affairs Committee and the Committee on Higher Education. He serves as the USCCB moderator for Catholic Campus Ministry Association and is a liaison with the North American Forum on the CATECHUMENATE. Bishop Gainer has been instrumental in promoting healing in the diocese after the resignation of its first bishop. During the first six years of his episcopacy, Bishop Gainer oversaw the restructuring of diocesan offices into five secretariats, promoted an increase in vocations to the priesthood and the permanent diaconate, expanded services to the needy in Eastern Kentucky, and began a successful annual appeal exceeding $1 million for the first time in the diocese's twenty-year history. Bishop Gainer also initiated more rigorous marriage preparation and began the popular annual Bishop's Cathedral Lecture Series.

Diocese of Owensboro. The first bishop of Covington, Francis Cotton, is remembered as an intelligent and hardworking bishop whose business and architectural skills greatly benefited the new western Kentucky diocese. After Bishop Cotton's sudden death in 1960, Bishop Henry Joseph Soenneker of Minnesota was consecrated bishop in 1961. Bishop Soenneker attended the Second Vatican Council and planted the seeds of renewal and carefully guided the changes in the liturgy. He established the first diocesan Liturgical Commission in 1964, which ushered in a greater involvement of the laity in the life of the local church. Bishop Soenneker retired in 1982 and remained in Owensboro until his death in 1987. John J. McRaith was consecrated the third bishop of Owensboro in 1982. His involvement on several committees of the United States Catholic Conference of Bishops (USCCB) included the Ad Hoc Committee on Stewardship, which was responsible for authoring the bishops' pastoral letter, "Stewardship: A Disciples' Response." In 1986 Bishop McRaith wrote a pastoral letter for the Diocese of Owensboro on the AIDS crisis titled "Go and Do Likewise." Bishop McRaith's priorities included establishing diocesan consultative councils, encouraging spiritual renewal, increasing evangelization, and instituting long-range planning.

SEE ALSO AFRICAN-AMERICAN CATHOLICS IN THE UNITED STATES (HISTORY OF); BALTIMORE, ARCHDIOCESE OF; BENEDICTINE NUNS AND SISTERS; CANON LAW, HISTORY OF; ILLINOIS, CATHOLIC CHURCH IN; INDIANA, CATHOLIC CHURCH IN; MICHIGAN, CATHOLIC CHURCH IN; MISSOURI, CATHOLIC CHURCH IN; OHIO, CATHOLIC CHURCH IN; SISTERS OF DIVINE PROVIDENCE OF KENTUCKY; SULPICIANS; TENNESSEE, CATHOLIC CHURCH IN; UR-SULINES; VATICAN COUNCIL II; WISCONSIN, CATHOLIC CHURCH IN.

BIBLIOGRAPHY

Archdiocese of Louisville Official Web site, available from: http://www.archlou.org (accessed December 12, 2008).

Bellarmine University Official Web site, available from http://www.bellarmine.edu/ (accessed December 12, 2008).

J. A. Boone, ed., *The Roman Catholic Diocese of Owensboro, Kentucky* (Owensboro, Ky. 1995).

Brescia University Official Web site, available from http://www.brescia.edu/ (accessed December 12, 2008).

Catholic Conference of Kentucky Official Web site, available from http://www.ccky.org (accessed December 12, 2008).

Thomas Dionysius Clark, *A History of Kentucky* (Lexingtonz, Ky. 1977).

Clyde F. Crews, *An American Holy Land: A History of the Archdiocese of Louisville* (Wilmington, Del. 1987).

Diocese of Covington Official Web site, available from: http://www.covingtondiocese.org (accessed December 12, 2008).

Diocese of Lexington Official Web site, available from: http://www.cdlex.org (accessed December 12, 2008).

Diocese of Owensboro Official Web site, available from: http://www.owensborodio.org (accessed December 12, 2008).

Timothy Fitzgerald, "'Let Your Light Shine—Bishop Foys Celebrates First Five Years Shepherding the Diocese of Covington," *The Messenger* (July 27, 2007).

Lowell H. Harrison and James C. Klotter, *A New History of Kentucky* (Lexington, Ky. 1997).

Judy Hayden, ed., *This Far by Faith: The Story of Catholicity in Western Kentucky* (Owensboro, Ky. 1987).

Dale E. Jones et al., "Religious Congregations & Membership in the United States, 2000: An Enumeration by Region, State, and County Based on Data Reported for 149 Religious Bodies" (Nashville, Tenn. 2002).

Mary Ramona Mattingly, *The Catholic Church on the Kentucky Frontier, 1785–1812* (Washington, D.C. 1936).

The Official Catholic Directory, 2008 (New Providence, N.J. 2008).

James Ott, *Seekers of the Everlasting Kingdom: A Brief History of the Diocese of Covington* (Covington, Ky. 2002).

Paul E. Ryan, *History of the Diocese of Covington, Kentucky, On the Occasion of the Centenary of the Diocese, 1853–1953* (Covington, Ky. 1954).

J. Herman Schauinger, *Cathedrals in the Wilderness* (Milwaukee, Wisc. 1952).

Peter Smith, "Supporters Praise Williams for Building Diocese." *The Courier-Journal* (June 12, 2002).

Martin John Spalding, *Sketches of the Early Catholic Missions of Kentucky* (Louisville, Ky. 1844).

Spalding University Official Web site, available from http://www.spalding.edu/ (accessed December 12, 2008).

St. Catharine College Official Web site, available from http://www.sccky.edu/ (accessed December 12, 2008).

Thomas More College Official Web site, available from http://www.thomasmore.edu (accessed December 12, 2008).

Ben J. Webb, *The Centenary of Catholicity in Kentucky* (Louisville, Ky. 1884).

Rev. Vincent de Paul McMurry
Prefect of Discipline
St. Thomas Seminary, Louisville, Ky.

Rev. Clyde F. Crews OFM Conv
Professor of Theology
Bellarmine University, Louisville, Ky.

Ed Monahan
Former Executive Director
Catholic Conference of Kentucky
Public Advocate
Department of Pulic Advocacy (2009)

Cecelia H. Price
Chief Communications Officer
Archdiocese of Louisville (2009)

L

LATIN AMERICA, CHURCH IN

The impact of the Catholic Church upon the history of Latin America has been profound. Five centuries of history have shaped the cultural, economic, and social fabric of the region. Beginning with Columbus's era and the first evangelization to the establishment of the Church in the colonial period and concluding with its contemporary manifestations, it has been a major player in the destinies of Latin Americans. The purpose here is to highlight significant historical developments that have shaped the Latin American Church throughout its history. These developments show an institution, at times, with different voices, even conflictive ones, but with a great ability to adapt to historical circumstances and transformations, which together with its cohesiveness and vitality have made the Church so influential and long lasting.

The Colonial Period (1492–1824). One of the most important characteristics of the Catholic Church in Latin America is its colonial nature. The Church arrived as part of a series of institutions imposed by the Spanish and Portuguese colonial governments. In many respects the colonial nature of the Church limited the ways in which the evangelization process took place. For the conquistadores and Spanish colonial officials evangelization was not a priority. On the contrary, the conquest was a violent affair which systematically plundered and exhausted native communities. War, labor exploitation, epidemic diseases and other factors took a heavy toll on indigenous populations. In this sense, the conquest represented a dark shadow over the goal of spreading the Gospel and Christian values. Despite these constraints, missionaries, especially members of the religious orders, were able to accomplish crucial gains, especially the

creation of a legal system which indigenous populations used to defend themselves from abuses and enable their accommodation and survival throughout the colonial period.

The Royal Patronage. The beginnings of the Catholic Church in Latin America are closely tied to two important historical events during the sixteenth century: the hegemony of Imperial Spain in Europe and the discovery and colonization of large sections of America by the Spanish monarchy. The Spanish monarchy prevailed over other European monarchies, making its control over the newly discovered territories virtually exclusive. Under these historical circumstances, Pope AL-EXANDER VI issued a series of bulls in 1493 that conceded unprecedented rights—a Royal Patronage in the terminology of the time—to the Spanish king to oversee the Christianization of the new territories. Significantly, at the time the bulls were issued, Alexander VI had only the Caribbean Islands in mind. He did not anticipate the extensive territories that later were discovered.

The pope requested that the Spanish monarchs spend large portions of their resources to guarantee the successful functioning of the Church in the Indies. As a result, the Spanish king was granted collection of the ecclesiastical tax or tithe to finance the missionary enterprise. In addition, the Royal patronage granted other sets of rights to the Spanish crown, such as the right to appoint bishops, parish priests, or any other ecclesiastical officers (*beneficio*), as well as authorization to erect churches and other buildings (e.g., hospitals).

The interpretation and implementation of the Royal Patronage by the colonial authorities created conflict among the archbishops and viceroys (the latter constituting the supreme royal authority in the colonies) over legal jurisdiction and other matters. Throughout the colonial period, archbishops and bishops demanded more autonomy in decision making and in directing their clergy, while the viceroys and other colonial bureaucrats pressured for more direct supervision of Church personnel and activities.

Establishing the Church Structure. Once the conquest wars ended in New Spain (Mexico) and Peru, the Church began a systematic effort to create its institutional infrastructure. One of the first steps was the division of territory into archdioceses and dioceses. During the sixteenth and early seventeenth centuries, five archdioceses were created: Mexico (1546), Santo Domingo (1546), Lima (1546), Santa Fe de Bogotá (1564), and La Plata (1609). Under these Episcopal sees, twenty-six suffragan dioceses were also created.

At the same time, the Church formed appropriate ecclesiastical legislation to support and guide the activities of Church personnel in the new territories. Several provincial councils were celebrated by the hierarchy during the first years of the conquest, and important norms emerged. The ecumenical council of TRENT in Europe signified a turning point for Church law and pastoral practices in the European Church as well as the Church in the Americas. The convocation of two councils, the Third Council in Lima (1582–1583) and the Third Council in Mexico (1585) marked a historical watershed in the history of the Church in Latin America and provided the hierarchy with indispensable tools for a long-term planning process of Christianization in the new territories. In these church meetings, bishops and theologians discussed general pastoral strategies of evangelization. Among the strategies was the publication of catechisms in native languages such as Nahuatl, Quechua, and Aymara. A manual for confession and other catechetical materials was also published, and priests were required to learn and use the native languages. Both councils made an effort on behalf of faith inculturation, especially the Third Council of Lima, at which the ideas of José de ACOSTA, a Jesuit priest, were highly influential.

The Struggle for Justice. The constant struggle in defense of human rights of the native populations in which the Church, under the guidance of churchmen such as Fray Bartolomé de LAS CASAS, O.P., and others, played a crucial role, has been well documented. Las Casas was the foremost voice in the denunciation of the abuses committed by the colonizers, abuses that devastated the native populations and undermined the efforts of Christianization. In addition, in the sixteenth century in particular, theologians and bishops went to great efforts to emphasize the dignity of native populations and the respect and value of their culture. Members

of religious orders undertook extensive study of native culture and religion. However, this early missionary attitude was not held to in the following two centuries of colonial domination.

Spiritual Conquest and Accommodation. Scholars who have studied the process of Christianization in Latin America, relying mainly on Spanish sources, argue that the early missionary efforts were effective. Native people embraced Christianity with great interest and rejected their native religious beliefs. In recent years, however, scholarly research based mainly on local records and native sources is challenging this conclusion and describes the complexities of native peoples' reactions to the process of Christianization.

Accommodation is a suitable word to describe the complexities of their response. Native peoples of the Americas accommodated their native beliefs to the new religion. From their polytheistic understanding of religion, there was no conflict between adopting Christianity and keeping their native beliefs. The practice of adopting a new religion was not a new phenomenon in the Andes or Mesoamerica. Rather, accepting the religion of the victor was a recurrent pattern of the history of expansionist states. However, the adoption of the Christian God did not translate into the exclusiveness worship of this God in the minds of the natives.

The best example of this attitude occurred in the Andes during the early seventeenth century. On April 23, 1613, the archbishop of Lima, Lobo Guerrero (1546–1622), writing to King Philip III (1578–1621), reported that to his dismay, the majority of natives continued to be idolaters (unchristian) as they were before the conquest and blamed those who were supposed to take care of them, the parish priests, as responsible for the failure to convert them. The discovery of the natives' IDOLATRY convinced the bishops of the need for a more systematic plan to effectively convert them to Christianity. Consequently, a plan was devised, called the Campaigns of Extirpation of Idolatry. As a result, between 1610 and 1650, especially in the archdiocese of Lima, the hierarchy implemented a systematic, brutal, and violent campaign to eradicate native beliefs, which included inspections, arrests, interrogation and torture of native priests, and the physical destruction of *wakas* (native sacred places).

Through the use of both violent evangelism and more peaceful and persuasive methods, Catholic missionaries eventually succeeded in making Catholic Christianity the formal religious expression of indigenous groups in the Americas. This religious expression brought together two religious systems: Christianity and native religion. The Cult to the Saints, the Virgin Mary, and Jesus Christ were reshaped—often mixed with elements of the worship of native gods—becoming the cornerstone of the emerging Latin American Catholicism. An important aspect of this new religious expression was the rise of regional devotions. Some of these devotions, although based on apparitions that took place in the sixteenth century, became more popular and widespread in the late colonial period due to the support of the Church structure and the colonial government. The devotion of the Virgin of Guadalupe in Mexico and the Lord of Miracles in Peru are two examples of this historical evolution.

Conflicts among the Clergy. The image of the Catholic Church as a monolithic institution fails to recognize the varieties of spiritualities and pastoral practices that were, at times, conflictive, among the members of Catholic clergy. The history of the Catholic Church in Latin America provides many examples of how the conflicts among Catholic clergy over the varieties of spiritualities and pastoral practices impacted upon the fabric of colonial society. The conflict between the regular (religious order) and secular (diocesan) clergy best illustrates this point.

Regular clergy were the first to be responsible for the conversion and spiritual growth of the native populations. On May 9, 1522, Pope ADRIAN VI issued a bull, titled *Omnímoda*, that granted a series of rights to the religious orders to function as parish priests. After a brief period of almost total control by the religious orders over the process of Christianization, secular clergy slowly regained control of the evangelization enterprise. The legislation created by the provincial councils and regional synods consolidated secular clergy's control over the Church structure but did not completely nullify the activities of the regular clergy. In certain areas of the viceroyalties of Peru and Mexico, the conflict between the regular and secular clergy for control of souls assumed disproportional dimensions. Ironically, one of the new orders, the Jesuits, became important collaborators of the secular clergy and were the only order suppressed by the Spanish Bourbon monarchy in the eighteenth century as part of a general ecclesiastical reform.

The Church's Economic Role. Diocesan clergy and religious orders participated actively in the colonial economy. They owned textile workshops, cattle ranches, landholdings, and other economic entities. In addition to these enterprises, clergymen profited from the sale of the tithe. They used their authority to coerce natives to work on their properties and then abused them as laborers. Religious orders such as the Dominicans, Mercedarians, Augustinians, and especially the Jesuits owned large landholdings (*haciendas*) in the viceroyalties of New Spain and Peru. The Jesuit haciendas were famous for their productivity and profitability to the point of becoming a threat to the colonial government. Eventu-

ally, the order was suppressed by the colonial government and its properties were confiscated. After the confiscation, the colonial government rented the Jesuits' estates and later sold them in public auctions.

The Church and Independence. Most Catholic bishops supported the royalist cause during the wars of independence to the point of considering any kind of independence discourse sinful. The Catholic hierarchy viewed its destiny as connected to the Spanish Crown and the colonial establishment. As a result, the Church as an institution lost a great deal of influence during the independence struggle and its aftermath. Parish priests, however, reacted differently than bishops. In the case of Mexico, many rural priests were organizers in the struggle for independence. Enlightened priests such as Miguel Hidalgo (1753–1811) and José María Morelos (1765–1815), both of whom were profoundly progressive-minded for their time, are good examples of the dramatic turn that led many priests to fight for independence from Spain. The emergence of insurgent priests caused the viceroy to abolish ecclesiastical privileges and authorize royal army officials to execute priests. Between 1810 and 1813, the Spanish royal authorities executed 125 priests.

The leaders of the Latin American revolution believed that in order to create the new republics, it was necessary to undermine the power of the Church. As a consequence, after independence the diocesan and regular clergy lost many of their privileges. During the first years after independence, in countries such as Mexico and Peru, the landholdings and other possessions of the religious orders were systematically expropriated.

In Europe, the Enlightenment and the French Revolution unleashed a massive wave of anticlericalism and secularization that made the Catholic Church defensive and protective of its privileges. In this historical context, obviously, the reaction of the HOLY SEE to the struggle for independence was negative. The Holy See, or the VATICAN, opposed Latin Americans' demands for independence because the independence movements were perceived as anticlerical and looking to undermine the power of the Church. This resistance on the part of the Vatican created a gap between Latin Americans and the Church that republican leaders used to gain control over the national Church. At the same time, once the wars of independence ended, the Holy See was forced to accept the new republics and establish diplomatic relations. It sent personnel to fill vacancies in many episcopacies and provided parish priests for the overwhelmingly Catholic populations of Latin America.

The Republican Period (1825–2007). Independence from Spain meant a new beginning for the Catholic

Church in Latin America. The history of the Church became intertwined with the history of the new nations of Latin America. In some cases, the relations between the state and the Church were cordial and respectful, but in others, the relations were precarious and profoundly conflictive.

The Liberal Offensive. During the second half of the nineteenth century, liberal parties gained control of governments in many Latin American countries. In nations like Colombia, the Church's influence was undermined by the reforms made during the administration of Tomas Cipriano de Mosquera in 1845–1849 and 1866–1868. The government's attempt to secularize public education was opposed by the Church, which eventually led to a Catholic-Conservative counterrevolution in 1876 and subsequently to a civil war in 1876 and 1877. The outcome of this civil war brought profound political changes in Colombia such as the collapse of the liberal state and the beginning of an era called the Regeneration, an era dominated by a Conservative and highly centralized state. During this period the Church regained power and in 1887 signed a Concordat with the Colombian state that restored much of its privileges.

In Mexico the liberal offensive encountered great resistance. The Conservatives took the side of the Church and defended Church prerogatives. In the end, the conflict was resolved by war (1858–1860), a war the Church lost. Under the leadership of Benito Juárez (1806–1872), a politician of American Indian background, the Mexican government abolished clerical immunity and dictated the expropriation and nationalization of Church properties. The government also decreed civil marriage, the suppression of all male religious orders, and the secularization of public schools, hospitals, and charity institutions. Years later, under the long dictatorship of Porfirio Díaz (1830–1915), the Church was able to regain many of its privileges, establishing new schools and many religious orders. New dioceses were also created and the number of parishes and priests increased. The crowning moment was the coronation of the Virgin of Guadalupe as patroness of Mexico in 1895.

During the period of the Mexican Revolution (1910–1930), the Church faced a new set of challenges. The Mexican Constitution of 1917 contained a series of anti–clerical measures which aimed at suppressing the Church's influence on Mexican society. These measures included the secularization of public education, the outlaw of religious orders, the prohibition of public religious worship outside of the churches, restrictions on the right of religious organizations to own property, a ban on clergy wearing religious garb in public, and a ban on their right to vote and make comments against the government.

Under the leadership of Plutarco Elias Calles, an atheist, these measures were harshly applied and triggered a general rebellion in the Church. This rebellion has been coined The Cristero Rebellion because of its cry: "Viva Cristo Rey" and lasted from 1926 to 1929. At first, the Church hierarchy supported a boycott against Calles's laws. On July 1926, Mexican bishops announced the suspension of all public worship but this measure was not widely embraced by all Catholics. Pope Pious XI ordered the Mexican episcopate to work with the government to amend the anti–clerical articles of the Constitution but this task proved to be unsuccessful. Quickly the conflict turned violent and on January 1, 1917, the formal armed rebellion began. The rebellion was more intense in the central and western states of Mexico; the leadership was composed mainly of laymen and those who were involved considered their participation an act of religious loyalty. Eventually the diplomatic intermediation of the U.S. ambassador to Mexico Dwight Whitney Morrow, who mediated between both the Mexican State and the Mexican Episcopate, was crucial to finding a peaceful solution to the conflict.

After three years of war the Church lost ninety thousand members of the Cristero army. Many priests also gave their lives for the cause. Other clergy emigrated or were expatriated. By 1934, there were only 334 priests in Mexico to serve fifteen million people.

Brazil went through a process of independence promoted by its monarchy and did not experience serious conflicts with the Church. However, by the 1880s, Dom Pedro II (1825–1891), the second Brazilian monarch, challenged the Church's influence and favored the formation of a secular Brazil. He did not systematically attempt to undermine Church power, but as Brazil slowly moved toward the formation of a secular state, the Church lost ground. The sudden liberal capture of power in 1889, which astonished Brazilians and international opinion, struck a powerful blow to the Church's privileges. In 1890, one of the first decrees of the New Republic was to declare the separation of church and state. Paradoxically, the period that followed this separation witnessed a reorganization and restructuring of the Church under the leadership of the archbishop of Olinda, Sebastiaō LEME DA SILVEIRA CINTRA, who sought to make the Brazilian Church a more modern and influential institution.

Participation of the Laity. In the 1930s the Catholic Church witnessed greater participation on the part of the laity. The most important development in that respect during these years was the emergence of Catholic Action (Acción Católica), an international organization that originated in Europe. In Europe Acción Católica focused on inactive Catholics, while in Latin America the emphasis was on the concrete participation of lay

Catholics in specific social actions. In countries including Cuba, Argentina, Colombia, Costa Rica, and Peru, this lay organization experienced significant membership growth.

The Progressive Church. For centuries, the Church hierarchy in Latin America served the establishment, supporting and blessing the actions of the ruling classes. However, this changed dramatically during the 1950s and 1960s. A new image emerged, the image of a Church committed to the poor. Countries like Brazil and Chile were in the forefront of these changes in the 1950s. A historical landmark that explains this new period is the Conference of Bishops in Medellín, Colombia, in 1968. Under the leadership of progressive bishops, the Medellín Conference applied VATICAN COUNCIL II to Latin America realities and made crucial, and some would say revolutionary, statements regarding the Church's option for the poor, social justice, and peace. Medellín was followed by another major meeting in Puebla, Mexico, in 1973 in which the influence of LIBERATION THEOLOGY in Church discourse was evident. The documents that came from this meeting touched on crucial issues in Latin America, such as the participation of Catholics in politics, the denunciation of poverty and inequality, the preferential option for the poor, and the formation of base communities.

Liberation Theology was the underlying theological perspective that directed this change of attitude. Father Gustavo Gutierrez, a Peruvian theologian, defined Liberation Theology as reflection on praxis, which is to say, learning by reflecting on experience. Liberation Theology dialogues with the social sciences, an interaction that, in the opinion of liberation theologians, illuminates our understanding of Latin American countries and their issues. Gutierrez and other theologians acknowledged the influence of Marxism as a methodological tool in their new way of doing theology.

The Church Magisterium, through the Sacred Congregation for the DOCTRINE OF THE FAITH, issued two documents in 1984 and 1986 concerning Liberation Theology. In the first document, called "Instruction on Certain Aspects of the 'Theology of Liberation'," the Church acknowledged the urgent need for action among Christians to improve the lives of people in Latin America and throughout the world who unjustly are condemned to live in extreme conditions of poverty and under repressive political systems. But at the same time, the Church also drew attention "to the deviations and the risks of deviation" of "certain forms of Liberation Theology which use, in an insufficiently critical manner, concepts borrowed from various currents of Marxist thought" (Congregation for the Doctrine of the Faith 1984).

In the second document, titled "Instruction on Christian Freedom and Liberation," the Magisterium clarified the Church's understanding of crucial theological concepts such as liberation and FREEDOM. According to this document, it is important to remind the faithful that the Church is a community of faith built on love and communion. An authentic liberation goes beyond the transformation of historical and sociological realities of current societies. An authentic liberation is the construction of a "civilization of love" (Congregation for the Doctrine of the Faith 1986).

The rise of Base Communities (Comunidades Cristianas de Base), in particular, gave Liberation Theology a popular foundation. Most Base Communities were formed by ten to twenty members who once a week gathered to read the Bible, pray and discuss social and religious matters pertinent to the parish and greater community. In countries like Brazil, Chile, and Panama, Base Communities have been greatly influential.

The impact of Liberation Theology on the life of the Catholic Church in Latin America declined significantly after the fall of dictatorial regimes in Latin America and the collapse of the Soviet Union in 1991. The fall of the Soviet Union discredited the Marxist theory and practice that had inspired Liberation Theology. While its influence in lay groups was localized and limited, its terminology has been incorporated into the language of Church theologians and the documents of Latin American episcopacies.

The Struggle for Human Rights. A separate issue that deserves special attention was the commitment of the Church in the struggle for human rights, especially after Vatican Council II. The background to these actions was the cold war. The U.S. applied cold war principles in its adversarial relationship with the left-wing Sandinista government in Nicaragua, which took power in a 1979 revolution. On the other hand, the United States supported repressive right-wing governments fighting the so-called Communist threat and supervised the application of the strategies of national security. In countries such as Chile, El Salvador, Nicaragua, and Argentina, many priests, nuns, and lay workers faced repressive governments. The most shocking example was in El Salvador, where the Church took a serious and profound stand to defend social justice and strongly denounced injustices toward the poor. Many Church workers lost their lives in their commitment to social justice. Among them was Archbishop Oscar Romero, who was murdered in 1980 by paramilitary soldiers while celebrating Mass. This was followed by the rape and murder of three American nuns and a lay worker during the same year. While the Church was still recovering from these shocks, six Jesuit priests and two lay helpers were brutally assassinated by the Salvadoran military in 1989.

The Church's struggle for social justice in Latin America has not ceased and continues not only through its denunciation of human rights violations, but also through the lives of martyrs. The ever-lengthening list of martyrs includes Bishop Juan Gerardi of Guatemala, beaten to death in 1998, and Sister Dorothy Mae Stang, an American nun who worked in the Brazilian rainforest, shot to death in 2005.

Trends since Vatican II. The participation of the laity in the life of the Church is one of the most important developments since Vatican Council II. Among the most important lay ecclesial movements in Latin America are the Cursillos de Cristiandad (Short Courses in Christianity), the Catholic CHARISMATIC RENEWAL, and Base Communities. Other lay movements such as the Neo-Cathecumenal and OPUS DEI, along with the influence of Pope JOHN XXIII, have made inroads among Latin American Catholics.

Cursillos de Cristiandad is a movement that originated in Spain in the 1930s and was later successfully transplanted to Latin America. The Cursillo movement starts its potential members with a four-day retreat experience that is followed by weekly meetings called Ultreyas. Although the Cursillo became an important movement after Vatican Council II, its spirituality is profoundly traditional. It is the oldest among these movements that still has a sizable following. In historical terms the Cursillo is important because it formed an entire generation of lay leaders committed to the participation of lay people in the life of the Church.

The Catholic Charismatic Renewal is one the fastest-growing lay movements in the Latin America's Catholic Church and in the rest of the Catholic world. Its growth is explained in part by the global growth of PENTECOSTALISM, a great spiritual hunger in society, and the support it has received from the popes and the Magisterium. Charismatic spirituality is centered on prayer, healing, and music. Leaders of the Catholic Charismatic Renewal are active members of the Church and very often assume positions of leadership in their parish communities.

Base Communities had a period of growth and apogee during the 1970s and 1980s. Especially after the Puebla gathering in 1973, the Church hierarchy supported the initiative, guiding its functioning and blessing its theological priorities. However, in only some countries, including Brazil and Chile, have Base Communities matured to become an important lay organization. Base Communities are not as numerous early in the twenty-first century as they were in the 1970s and 1980s. However, they still exist, and their late 1990s resurgence of communities in countries such as Brazil is proof of their continued vitality and a sign of the Church's commitment to social issues and to community life.

Latin American societies are rapidly changing. Beginning in the late twentieth century, the impact of globalization created a new cultural atmosphere dominated by pluralism, cultural relativism, and economic neoliberalism. In this context "a single image of the world, of the human being and God, which used to offer guidance for everyday life is disappearing" (5th General Conference of the Latin American and Caribbean Bishops 2007). In other words, the Church is but one voice amidst many others. This represents a major challenge for the Church and has led Latin American bishops to call for an evangelization of culture. In addition, the Church has been challenged in what it has called its sense of authority. It now has to compete with other institutions in society and make its positions rationally sound in order to maintain its relevance.

Fifth General Conference, 2007. Following the contributions of the previous General Conferences at Rio (1958), Medellín (1968), Puebla (1973), and Santo Domingo (1992), the Latin American episcopacies met in Aparecida, Brazil, in 2007 with a new set of pastoral concerns. The priority of the conference was evangelization, framed in the new social climate shaped by a Latin American reality defined by globalization trends. The first documents made available by the bishops were characterized by the humble and reflective tone of the Conference's contributions and made clear the awareness among the hierarchy of the challenges that the Church faces and the weaknesses of the institutional Church. Particularly interesting is the section called "some deficiencies to correct in the Church." Among the deficiencies mentioned are clericalism; lack of self-criticism; moralizing, "which weakens the centrality of Jesus Christ"; weakness of the preferential option for the poor; discrimination against many women and other human groups; insufficient support for lay people in tasks of public service; evangelization with scant ardor and lacking in new methods and expressions of faith inculturation; an emphasis on the sacraments to the neglect of other pastoral tasks; individualistic spirituality; a slowness in committing to democracy; and, finally, "the persistence of languages that do not mean much to contemporary culture and that sometimes do not seem to take into account the pluralistic character of society and culture" (5th General Conference of the Latin American and Caribbean Bishops 2007).

Although in the meeting in Aparecida, the Latin American bishops acknowledged these serious challenges to the life of the Church, it is also important to note that the Latin American Church, compared to the

Charismatic Movement. *Padre Zeca sings to thousands during the "Deus e Dez," (God is a Ten) show on the Ipanema Beach of Rio de Janeiro, Brazil, Sunday, November 15, 1999. Zeca, known as the "Surfing Priest," is part of a new generation of clerics who belong to the Catholic Church's charismatic movement.* **AP IMAGES**

Church in Europe and even the United States, is a vibrant and dynamic community of believers. For these believers, Catholic identity and imagery is still relevant for their lives and societies.

SEE ALSO Consejo Episcopal Latinoamericano (Celam); Guadalupe, Our Lady of; Latin America; Mission in Postcolonial Latin America; Papal Volunteers for Latin America.

BIBLIOGRAPHY

David C. Bailey, *!Viva Cristo Rey! The Cristero Rebellion and the Church-State Conflict in Mexico* (Austin, Tex. 1982).

Pedro Borges, ed. *Historia de la Iglesia en Hispanoamérica y Filipinas (Siglos XV–XVI)*, vol 1, *Aspectos Generales* (Madrid 1992).

Edward L. Cleary, *Crisis and Change: The Church in Latin America Today* (Maryknoll, N.Y. 1985).

Congregation for the Doctrine of the Faith, *Libertatis nuntius*, On Certain Aspects of the "Theology of Liberation" (Instruction, August 6, 1984), available from http://www.vatican.va/roman_curia/congregations/cfaith/documents/rc_con_cfaith_doc_19840806_theology-liberation_en.html (accessed March 3, 2008).

Congregation for the Doctrine of the Faith, *Libertatis conscientia*, On Christian Freedom and Liberation (Instruction, March 22, 1986), available from http://www.vatican.va/roman_curia/congregations/cfaith/documents/rc_con_cfaith_doc_19860322_freedom-liberation_en.html (accessed March 3, 2008).

Enrique Dussel, *A History of the Church in Latin America: Colonialism to Liberation (1492–1979)* (Grand Rapids, Mich. 1981).

Enrique Dussel, ed. *Historia General de la Iglesia en América Latina*, 7 vols. (Salamanca, Spain 1982–1989).

5th General Conference of the Latin American and Caribbean Bishops, "Synthesis of Contributions," 2007, available from http://en.celam.info/

Anthony Gill, *Rendering unto Caesar: The Catholic Church and the State in Latin America* (Chicago 1998).

Elisa Luque Alcaide and Josep-Ignasi Saranyana, *La Iglesia Católica y América* (Madrid 1992).

John Lynch, "The Catholic Church in Latin America, 1830–1930," in *Cambridge History of Latin America*, ed. Leslie Bethell, vol. 4 (Cambridge, U.K. 1984).

Jean A. Meyer, *Historia de los Cristianos en America Latina: Siglos XIX and XX*, translated by Tomás Segovia (Mexico, D.F. 1989).

Jean A. Meyer, *The Cristero Rebellion: The Mexican People between Church and State, 1926–1929* (Cambridge, U.K. 1976).

John Schwaller, ed. *The Church in Colonial Latin America* (Wilmington, Del. 2000).

Miguel A. León
Assistant Professor, Department of History
State University of New York at Oneonta (2009)

LOS ANGELES, ARCHDIOCESE OF

Historical commentators are quick to observe that almost everything in Southern California has been imported—plants, flowers, shrubs, trees, water, and even religion. More than three decades ago, the late Carey McWilliams (1905–1980) pointed to the unprecedented influx of peoples—a factor that in the twenty-first century accounts for the ethnic diversity of the onetime *Pueblo de Nuestra Señora de los Angeles*. Native Americans were the first to inhabit the area. And though they were mostly gone by the twenty-first century, they left behind an indelible mark in such names as Cahuenga, Malibu, Mugu, and Pacoima. Then came the Catholic *pobladores* from Sonora who laid out the original plaza on a bluff above the river named by Fray Juan Crespi (1721–1782) to honor Our Lady of the Angels. For a while after the war with Mexico and the discovery of gold, Los Angeles remained a small and insignificant town. But that soon changed.

Statehood came in 1850, and then, following the Civil War, the railroads reached out to touch Los Angeles, bringing newcomers from the South and Midwest, many of them lured westward by the well-publicized sunshine. The roots of the BIBLE were solidly transplanted by this great midwestern migration. Los Angeles remains predominantly Protestant, though the importance of the Catholic FAITH was attested to in 1953, when the ARCHBISHOP of Los Angeles became the first CARDINAL in the western United States. Though the city is famous for its revivalists and cultists, they have probably drawn attention out of proportion to their numbers. Studies indicate that the great majority of churchgoers belong to the traditional faiths.

The Chinese and Japanese arrived; French, Poles, and German Jews also, and many of the beach areas became popular resort meccas for British tourists. Early in the twenty-first century, the Mexican population rose again, this time forming the bulk of the migratory work force. The African Americans, who in 2008 constituted 12.5 percent of the population, first arrived in 1900. And the waves of immigration continue. In the late 1990s, Vietnamese and Koreans, with their distinctive contributions, flooded into Los Angeles to join dozens of other Asiatic groups, such as the Samoans, more of whom live in Los Angeles than reside on the island of American Samoa itself.

The people thronging to the area have generally been an adventurous and inventive lot. In Hollywood, for example, creative minds have entertained and informed the whole world, reflecting both America's manifold problems and its unique promise. A major port city, Los Angeles expanded its aircraft and electronics industries to meet the challenges of World War II and then transitioned to handle contemporary transportation and communication needs.

As it welcomed Pope JOHN PAUL II, the Vicar of Christ, in 1987, this largest of the world cities dedicated to Our Lady provided a haven for its perpetual transplants. It amazes, amuses, and eventually absorbs. New arrivals are confronted with culture shock—the climate, the freeways, the lifestyles, and the ethnic mix.

The Pueblo. The *Pueblo de Nuestra Señora de los Angeles* was established on September 4, 1781, within the parochial confines of San Gabriel Mission, with a contingent of eleven families, or forty-four people. Four square leagues of land, good for planting all kinds of grains and seeds, about three-fourths of a mile west of the river on a ledge rising above the present Alameda Street, were set aside for the farthest extension in the presidial district of San Diego de Alcala.

Fray Junípero SERRA first visited the pueblo on March 18, 1782, seven months after its foundation, enroute to San Gabriel. He referred to the town endearingly as *La Porciuncula*, though he did not describe it. His biographer relates that the inhabitants of those days worked in the fields; ate tortillas, beans, and tamales; and, for recreation, played cards.

Though Serra and his confreres harbored serious reservations about the expediency of establishing the *Pueblo de Nuestra Señora de los Angeles*, the foundation, like its sister metropolis to the north, San Francisco, bears that distinctively seraphic imprint of the earliest penetrators into this far-away Province of California.

Franciscan influence in Los Angeles reflects, at the local level, what the FRIARS accomplished along the whole expanse of the Pacific Slope. Even Governor Pedro Fages (1734–1794), whose relationship with Serra was anything but cordial, admitted in 1789 "that the rapid, pleasing, and interesting progress both in spiritual and temporal matters; ...are the glorious effect of the apostolic zeal, activity, and indefatigable labors of these missionaries" (Priestly 1937).

That viewpoint has been generally sustained, even by the most hostile of observers. The openly antagonistic Frances Fuller Victor (1826–1902), for example, once remarked that "the spectacle of a small number of men, some of whom certainly were men of ability and scholarship, exiling themselves from their kind, to spend their lives in contact with a race whom it was impossible in a lifetime to bring anywhere near their level, excites our sympathy and commendation." The early Franciscan heritage endured into the twenty-first century. Indeed, Fray Junípero Serra's biographer stated that "nowhere else does Serra have so conspicuous a location today" as he does in contemporary Los Angeles (Geiger 1959, vol. 2, p. 273).

The handsomely sculptured bronze statue of the *presidente*, prominently enshrined in the Old Plaza area of the city, embodies one of the most meaningful national tributes to a religious founder. Fray Junípero is also remembered in the names of numerous streets, schools, plaques, buildings, institutions, and even the national capital.

The Franciscan influence has been manifested rather consistently since the earliest days. One creditable author acknowledges that until 1854, the only organization in Los Angeles upholding any standard of MORALITY "whatever was the Roman Catholic church. It erected houses of worship, hospitals and schools; it was the pioneer in all good works" (Weber 1974). Little wonder that a renewed interest was stimulated in the work that Serra and his band of Franciscan collaborators accomplished in Southern California, the more so when one recalls that Los Angeles in the 2000s is second only to Mexico City in the number of inhabitants who carry the blood and speak the beautiful tongue of the old vice-royalty of New Spain.

A Metropolitan District. The geographical derivation of the 8,762 square miles comprising the Archdiocese of Los Angeles (*Archidioecesis Angelorum*) can be traced to April 27, 1840, when Pope GREGORY XVI created the parent jurisdiction from the already-established See of Sonora and named Fray Francisco GARCIA DIEGO Y MORENO (1840–1846) the proto-bishop.

Boundaries for the gigantic Diocese of Both Californias were the Colorado River in the east, the forty-second degree of north latitude (Oregon line), the Pacific Ocean in the west, and south to all of Baja California. The title was officially changed to the Diocese of Monterey in 1849. The subsequent transfer of sovereignty in California made a further delineation of boundaries imperative. On April 17, 1853, Archbishop Joseph Sadoc ALEMANY (1850–1853) received word that the Sacred Congregation of Propaganda Fide had removed peninsular California from its attachment to the Diocese of Monterey.

Several months later, on July 29, Pope PIUS IX created a metropolitan district at San Francisco. The southern parallel of the parish at San Jose was fixed as the demarcation between the new Archdiocese of San Francisco and the larger, but suffragan, Diocese of Monterey. The Monterey jurisdiction, which encompassed all of Southern California, remained territorially intact for the next seven decades. On July 8, 1859, Bishop Thaddeus AMAT (1853–1878) was authorized to move his episcopal seat to Los Angeles. At that time he was also permitted to add the city name to the diocesan title.

Cathedral of Our Lady of the Angels, Los Angeles. *Opened in 2002, this 12–story cathedral serves the nation's largest Roman Catholic archdiocese.* © **GOPLACES** / **ALAMY**

During the subsequent years, there were a number of proposals for dividing the large and unwieldy Diocese of Monterey-Los Angeles. As early as 1866 Bishop Amat confided to a friend that he expected within a few years to see another bishopric formed in the southland. While no official action was taken by Amat, his successor, Bishop Francis Mora (1878–1896), petitioned the HOLY SEE several times for a reduction of his jurisdiction. The proposal was shelved temporarily in 1894, when Mora was given a coadjutor in the person of Bishop George T. Montgomery (1896–1903). Rumors of a division were revived after the death of Bishop Thomas J. CONATY (1903–1915) and were sustained by the long interregnum that ensued before the appointment of John J. CANTWELL (1917–1947).

Early in 1922 Bishop Cantwell asked that the 90,000–square-mile Diocese of Monterey-Los Angeles be dismembered, with twelve counties formed into a separate jurisdiction. Pope PIUS XI acquiesced and in June created the new Diocese of Monterey-Fresno. The larger area, known as the Diocese of Los Angeles-San Diego, embraced the remaining southland counties and stretched to the Mexican border. The penultimate

alteration in the southland occurred on July 11, 1936, with the erection of a second metropolitan district in California at Los Angeles. Simultaneously, the four southernmost counties were fashioned into the Diocese of San Diego. Included in the newly formed Province of Los Angeles were the suffragan Sees of Monterey-Fresno, San Diego, and Tucson.

In January of 1948 the APOSTOLIC DELEGATE informed officials at Los Angeles that to avoid confusion with the older Archdiocese of *Puebla de Los Angeles* in Mexico, the southland jurisdiction would henceforth be known officially as the Archdiocese of Los Angeles in California. The archdiocese retained its geographical integrity from 1936 until June 18, 1976, when Pope PAUL VI created a new DIOCESE for Orange County. Remaining in the parent see were the counties of Los Angeles, Ventura, and Santa Barbara.

The assertion made in 1903 that the glory of California "lies not in the fact that her wilderness was conquered, nor that her priceless treasures were unearthed, but in the propagation and marvelous growth of religious faith" (Lummis 1903) has lost none of its force, even with the passage of eight decades.

The Archdiocese of Los Angeles, largest of the twelve state ecclesial divisions, encompasses an area of 8,762 square miles, or the totality of Los Angeles, Ventura, and Santa Barbara counties. Ranking first among the 183 national juridic units, the ARCHDIOCESE in 2008 provided for the spiritual needs of 4,212,887 Catholics with 1,155 priests serving 287 parishes. To facilitate its apostolic mandate of spreading the GOSPEL message, the educational system in the Archdiocese of Los Angeles enrolled 56,888 youngsters in 219 elementary schools, 30,604 teenagers in 50 secondary schools, and 11,845 students in 5 colleges and universities. Statistics indicated an annual enrollment of 270,000 public school youngsters in the various programs operated by the Office of Religious Education. Students ranging from kindergarten to twelfth grade were engaged in pedagogical pursuits in after-school, Saturday, and Sunday sessions. Teacher-training courses were also available throughout the archdiocese (*The Official Catholic Directory* 2008, pp. 697–698).

The extensive involvement of the Church in the active apostolate is exemplified by its network of thirteen general hospitals, which accommodated 1,820,256 patients in the 2008 statistics. An additional seven special hospitals or *sanitaria* looked after the physical needs of numerous other persons. Although these and other statistics have been described as the "dry bones" of history, one can easily perceive that ecclesial accomplishments in the Archdiocese of Los Angeles indicate a vibrant and healthy Catholic populace, firmly dedicated to the furthering of Christian ideals.

Largest U.S. Ecclesial Jurisdiction. Since 1983, the Archdiocese of Los Angeles has been the largest ecclesial district in the United States. Interestingly enough, the runner-up to Los Angeles in California is the Diocese of Orange, which was only severed from its parent jurisdiction in 1976. The figures are based on those reported by the thirty-five national Latin and Eastern Rite archdioceses and 150 Latin and Eastern Rite dioceses as enumerated in the *The Official Catholic Directory*.

Naturally, the Church's growth reflects the civil structure. The metropolitan area of Los Angeles continues to grow at a phenomenal rate. Its 34,000 square miles encompass an area larger in population than all the states except California, New York, and Texas. It has the largest Latino market, with 27 percent of the population of Latino heritage as well as the largest Asian Pacific Islander market, with 8.2 percent of the population of Asian origin.

There are 157 separate incorporated cities in the district, ranging in size from Los Angeles (3.3 million people) to Vernon (90 people). It is first in manufacturing shipments, as compared to second-place Chicago. (The Archdiocese of CHICAGO was formerly the largest

in the nation.) More than one hundred million tourists come every year, many of them to shop in an area which is fourth in production of apparel after New York, California, and Pennsylvania. Ranking third in the manufacture of furniture, Los Angeles and its metropolitan area is a major market for imported cars; yet the area is not all highways either, but ranks just behind Washington and Oklahoma in the quantity of land devoted to agriculture.

Financially, the area has a firm base. The savings and loan capital of the United States, it had eleven of the fifty largest such institutions headquartered there. As of 2008, savings deposits total 104.4 billion, nearly twice that of second-ranked Chicago. In addition, 120 foreign banks were located in the area. In terms of gross national product, the metropolitan area of Los Angeles ranks tenth among the nations of the world. The 2008 figures of the GNP (Gross National Product) placed it at 275 billion, putting it ahead of Brazil, India, Mexico, Australia, Spain, the Netherlands, and Switzerland.

In 1968 James Francis Cardinal MCINTYRE (1948–1970) predicted that "Los Angeles would become a world center with an orientation to the Pacific" (Weber 1997). His Eminence may not have been a PROPHET in the scriptural sense, but he was exceedingly shrewd at reading the signs of the times. His successor was no less astute. Timothy Cardinal MANNING (1970–1985) likened Los Angeles to Ellis Island, a multi-cultural archdiocese, destined to take its rightful place as the flagship of the American Church.

When Pope John Paul II came to the archdiocese in September 1987, he found the Church experiencing what Archbishop Roger MAHONY (1985–) described as "a New Pentecost, a vigorous growth in faith and in diversity of peoples, a renewal of spirit and joy in our Lord Jesus Christ and in the tradition of Fray Junípero Serra" (John Paul II 1987).

Reaching to the Future. Even those outside her fold must accord the Catholic Church a special historical preeminence during the earliest days of Los Angeles. The Catholic presence in the present-day city of Los Angeles actually pre-dates the city by a dozen years. The very name derives from the diary of Fray Juan Crespi, who introduced the Feast of the *portiuncula* into Californian vocabulary.

On January 17, 1837, a year and a half after Los Angeles had been raised to the status of a city, the *ayuntamiento* or council passed, without a dissenting voice, a resolution declaring that "the Roman Catholic apostolic religion shall prevail throughout this jurisdiction" (Weber 1992). Although no evidence exists that this expressed, but never enforced, establishment of religion benefitted Catholics, it did provide adherents with a unique distinction in Western Americana historical annals.

Plans were unveiled to open a Catholic school in the city in 1849, and two years later the institution opened its doors with twenty-six scholars. Bishop Joseph Sadoc Alemany entrusted the administration of the school to the Picpus Fathers. As late as 1853 Harris Newmark (1834–1916) said that "nearly all the population was Catholic"(Newmark 1916). And while it all changed following the onrush of the gold seekers, Los Angeles continued through the decades to be a unique haven for religious-minded peoples of all creeds. In a survey of local history published in 1967, Christopher Rand observed that "there are probably more religions in Los Angeles than in the whole previous history of mankind" (Rand 1967). And it all started with the Catholic Church in 1781.

Religious Patronage. On June 8, 2006, the Vatican Prefect of the Congregation for DIVINE WORSHIP AND THE DISCIPLINE OF THE SACRAMENTS notified Catholics in the California southland that Our Lady of the Angels had been named principal patroness of the Archdiocese of Los Angeles, a decision approved by Pope BENEDICT XVI. The earliest ecclesiastical patronage in California dates from January 4, 1843, when the first bishop, Francisco Garcia Diego y Moreno, placed his jurisdiction under the spiritual protection of Our Lady, Refuge of Sinners. When the diocese was divided in 1853, the archbishop of San Francisco adopted another heavenly intercessor while the southland retained its earlier allegiance. On September 1, 1856, Pope Pius IX gave the Diocese of Monterey Vibiana as its patroness, a saint unearthed in the Roman CATACOMBS a few years earlier.

The term *Los Angeles* had been a part of the episcopal title since 1859, but that appellation, a shortened form of *Nuestra Señora de los Angeles*, never figured in the original religious patronage of Southern California. Roman authorities suggested that a transfer of patronage to Our Lady of the Angels would be highly appropriate for the Archdiocese of Los Angeles. Possibly the late Archbishop John J. Cantwell had that in mind when he had plans drafted for a CATHEDRAL by that name in the 1940s. That the title of the archdiocese had no connection with its patronage, however, is not without precedent in the United States, where only four of the twenty-eight archdioceses identify title and patron.

Fray Juan Crespi recorded in his diary that late in the afternoon of July 31, 1769, the expeditionary force of Gaspar de Portola (1716–1770) crossed an *arroyo* of muddy water and stopped a little farther on in a wide clearing. He stated that the following day was set aside to celebrate the jubilee of Our Lady of the Angels de Porciuncula. The next morning on the vigil of the feast,

the party continued its journey and came through a pass between two hills into a broad valley abounding in poplar and elder trees. A beautiful brook crossed the valley and later curved around a hill to the south. After traveling another twenty miles, the Spaniards camped along a river, which they fittingly named in honor of *Nuestra Señora de los Angeles de Porciuncula*, a title derived from the liturgical calendar for that day.

According to canonical procedures, the patron of a place is the saint honored as the special protector of that locale. In the case of Los Angeles, this distinction was accorded to Our Lady of the Angels when the name given to the *Rio Porciuncula* was extended in its alternate form to the *pueblo* founded in the fall of 1781.

Because the feast of Our Lady of the Angels of the Porciuncula was not observed in the universal liturgical schema, the patronage of Mary under that title could not be applied to the pueblo as a formal ecclesiastical patron except by privilege and even then only after consultation with the clergy and laity of the place. In this, as in other similar cases, the practice of the Holy See has been to bestow as the titular feastday that of Mary's Assumption into HEAVEN. Hence as early as 1814, Fray Luis Gil of San Gabriel spoke of laying the cornerstone of the church at Los Angeles on the fifteenth of August, on which day the pueblo celebrates its titular feast.

Thus, until 2006 religious patronage in the Archdiocese of Los Angeles had no connection with that of the City of Our Lady of the Angels, which proudly saluted its patroness each year on August 15 under her original title, *Nuestra Señora de los Angeles*. The feastday for Our Lady of the Angels, which some years ago was moved to coincide with the anniversary of the establishment of the city, continues to be observed on September 4.

Bishop Francisco Garcia Diego y Moreno. Francisco Garcia Diego y Moreno was born on September 17, 1785, at Lagos de Moreno, Mexico, the son of Francisco and Ana Maria (Moreno) Garcia Diego. Invested with the religious habit of the Order of Friars Minor at the College of Nuestra Señora de Guadalupe on November 26, 1801, Francisco was ordained a priest on November 14, 1808, by Bishop Prime Feliciano Marin de Porras of Linares.

Upon completion of his service as novice master for the Franciscan community at Zacatecas, Fray Francisco Garcia Diego was elected *comisario prefecto* of the missions attached to the Apostolic College. In 1832 he led a contingent of friars to peninsular California and then north to Alta California, arriving at Santa Clara Mission where he labored for several years.

On April 27, 1840, Pope Gregory XVI erected the Diocese of Both Californias naming Fray Francisco Garcia Diego as the proto bishop of the new jurisdiction. The friar was ordained (consecrated) by the Right Reverend Antonio Maria de Jesus Campos on October 4, 1840, at the National Shrine of Our Lady of GUADA-LUPE just outside the Mexican Distrito Federal.

Upon his return to Alta California, Bishop Garcia Diego took up residence at Santa Barbara Mission where he lived for the relatively few years of his episcopal tenure. Beyond opening a seminary at Santa Ines Mission, the PRELATE was frustrated in bringing his other objectives to completion because of the economic, political, and religious challenges in the region. The bishop succumbed on April 30, 1846, probably from tuberculosis. He is buried in a vault on the epistle side of the sanctuary at Santa Barbara Mission.

Archbishop Joseph Sadoc Alemany. Joseph Alemany was born July 13, 1814, at #9 Rambla del Paseo in the ancient town of Vich, Spain, the third youngster of Antonio Alamany and Micaela de los Santos Cunill. In 1830 Joseph Alemany (he preferred and always used the *e* rather than the *a*) entered the Priory of Santo Domingo and, on September 23, 1831, took solemn vows as a member of the Order of Preachers (DOMINICANS) at which time he was given the name *Sadoc.*

After philosophical studies at Tremp's Priory of San Jaime de Pillars and theological training at the Gerona Priory of Our Lady's Annuntiation, Alemany completed his sacerdotal preparations at the Viterbo Priory of Santa Maria dei Gradi. He was ordained to the priesthood by Bishop Gaspar Bernardo Pianetti (1780–1862) on March 11, 1837, at the Viterbo Cathedral of San Lorenzo. Following reception of a lectorate in THEOLOGY and extensive courses in English at the Urban College of Propaganda Fide, Father Alemany was sent to the United States. Arriving on April 2, 1840, he was assigned to Saint Joseph's Priory in Somerset, Ohio.

Naturalized as an American citizen on April 15, 1841, Father Alemany served at Zanesville, Nashville, and Memphis. He was elected master of novices in 1847, and the following year he was named major superior for Saint Joseph's Province in which capacity he attended the Seventh Provincial Council of Baltimore.

Appointed bishop of Monterey on May 31, 1850, by Pope Pius IX, Alemany was consecrated (ordained) on June 30 in Rome at the Church of San Carlos al Corso by Giacomo Cardinal Fransoni (1775–1856), assisted by Archbishop Giovanni Stefanelli and Patriarch Guiseppe Valerga (1813–1872). Disembarking at San Francisco on December 6, 1850, the newly appointed Bishop of Monterey immediately journeyed to Santa Barbara, where he presented himself to the vicar capitular of the vacant jurisdiction, Fray Jose Maria Gonzalez Rubio. He was formally installed on January 28th. While in Santa Barbara, Alemany issued his first pastoral letter

in which he exhorted Catholics in California to a greater "purity of morals" in the practice of their faith.

By the end of the following year, Alemany had established himself at Monterey where he designated the presidio Chapel of San Carlos Borromeo as his cathedral. On December 21, 1851, at Alemany's request, the Diocese of Monterey was separated from its attachment to the Metropolitan District of Mexico City. Alemany also took steps to establish a vicariate for peninsular California. He invoked a diocesan synod, which was held in San Francisco on March 19–23, 1852. While attending the First Plenary Council of Baltimore, Bishop Alemany initiated proceedings for the recovery of the PIOUS FUND of the Californias, a legal action that remained prominent in American juridical annals until its ultimate resolution in 1967. On July 17, 1853, Alemany laid the cornerstone of Saint Mary's Cathedral in San Francisco.

On July 29, 1853, Pope Pius IX created the Metropolitan District of San Francisco with Alemany as its first archbishop, a distinction bestowed on only six other districts during the longest pontifical reign in history. On November 18, 1855, Alemany was invested with the sacred PALLIUM by his suffragan, Bishop Thaddeus Amat, C.M., of Monterey.

Death claimed the prelate on April 14, 1888, in the city of Valencia, where he was endeavoring to re-establish his order's ancient Province of Aragon. He was interred on the epistle side of the main altar in the chapel of Santo Domingo. Alemany's remains were disinterred in January of 1965 and returned to San Francisco where, after services conducted in old Saint Mary's Cathedral, he was placed in a vault alongside his successors at Holy Cross Mausoleum in Colma.

Bishop Thaddeus Amat y Brusi, C.M. Thaddeus Amat, C.M., born December 31, 1811, at Barcelona, Spain, the son of Pedro and Martha (Brusi) Amat, was received into the Congregation of the Mission (VINCENTIANS) on January 4, 1832. Ordained a priest on December 23, 1837, by Hyacinthe Louis de Quelen (1778–1839) of Paris. Amat arrived in New Orleans on October 9, 1838. He served at posts in Perryville, Cape Girardeau, and Saint Louis until 1847, when he became rector of Saint Charles Seminary in Philadelphia. He attended the Seventh Provincial Council of Baltimore. Consecrated (ordained) bishop of Monterey on March 12, 1854, by Giacomo Cardinal Fransoni in the chapel of Propaganda Fide, Rome, Amat arrived in California with the RELICS of Saint Vibiana, under whose patronage he erected a cathedral in 1876. He was installed at Monterey on November 25, 1855.

Amat issued his first pastoral letter in 1854 and authored a catechism on matrimony (1864), which was used widely throughout the United States. He moved to Southern California and had the name of the diocese changed to Monterey-Los Angeles in 1859. Amat attended the sessions of VATICAN COUNCIL I and brought to an end the first phase of the settlement for the Pious Fund of the Californias (1875). Later, he engaged in a protracted canonical dispute with the Franciscans at Santa Barbara.

Bishop Amat died at Los Angeles on May 12, 1878, and was interred beneath the main altar in Saint Vibiana's Cathedral. In 1962 his remains were moved to the episcopal vault at Calvary Mausoleum and then reinterred in the new Cathedral of Our Lady of the Angels in 2004.

Bishop Francis Mora. The fourth southland bishop, Francis Mora, was born on November 25, 1827, in the 12,414–square-mile Principality of Catalonia, in the northeastern corner of the Iherian peninsula. Christened on the day of his birth at Gurb, Francisco was enrolled on the parochial roster of the fifth century church of San Andres. He entered the Conciliar Seminary of San Joachim as a student for the bishopric of Vich. After several years there he was accepted as a divinity student by Bishop Thaddeus Amat, the newly consecrated bishop of Monterey-Los Angeles.

Raised to the priesthood on March 19, 1856, his initial assignment was to the presidio chapel of San Carlos Borromeo at Monterey. Later he served at San Juan Bautista Mission and then became pastor of the parish of the Immaculate Heart of Mary in Pajaro Valley, Watsonville. For a while he also functioned at San Luis Obispo Mission. Mora was called to Los Angeles and the pastorate of the old Plaza Church of Nuestra Señora de los Angeles in 1863, a position he held for the following fifteen years.

On July 25, 1866, Mora was named vicar general for the Diocese of Monterey-Los Angeles and, when the health of Bishop Thadeus Amat declined, Mora was appointed coadjutor bishop of the diocese. He was consecrated on August 3, 1873. He became the residential bishop of the 75,984–square-mile Diocese of Monterey-Los Angeles on May 12, 1878.

During his episcopal tenure, Mora encouraged the formation of a Catholic newspaper, selected the sites of several cemeteries, combated the local activities of the AMERICAN PROTECTIVE ASSOCIATION, and expanded diocesan services and outreach programs. He also oversaw a modest expansion of educational services, the establishment of several teaching communities of women, and the convocation of a synod.

After sustaining a carriage accident, Bishop Mora asked for and was given a coadjutor in the person of George Montgomery. With Montgomery's elevation,

Mora handed over his crozier and returned to Spain, where he lived for the final years of his life. Mora died on the thirty-second anniversary of his episcopal consecration in 1905. He was interred in the local cemetery at Sarria until 1962, when his remains were returned to Los Angeles. He is now entombed in the Cathedral of Our Lady of the Angels.

Bishop George Montgomery. When Bishop George Montgomery (1847–1907) succeeded Bishop Francis Mora on June 10, 1896, anti–Catholic bigotry in the guise of the American Protective Association (APA) was rampant. The need for vigorous leadership to defend the Church was fully met in this able prelate. Chancellor of the Archdiocese of San Francisco, he was consecrated April 8, 1894, shortly after Bishop Mora's request for a coadjutor had been approved. Immediately he assumed almost complete administration of the Diocese of Monterey and Los Angeles for the ailing Bishop Mora. That year the APA showed alarming power in the Los Angeles city elections. Bishop Montgomery acted promptly and decisively, organizing a branch of the Catholic Truth Society and instituting a series of popular lectures on Catholic DOCTRINE. By the end of the century the wave of bigotry had subsided. When Bishop Mora's precarious health compelled him to resign and he returned to his native Spain, Bishop Montgomery continued his vigorous program of establishing Catholic prestige in Southern California and at the same time providing for the spiritual needs of an expanding population.

Montgomery was the first American-born bishop of the diocese. Born in Daviéss County, Kentucky, December 30, 1847, he had been ordained to the priesthood by James Cardinal GIBBONS, archbishop of Baltimore on December 20, 1879. On February 3, 1903, Bishop Montgomery left Los Angeles to become coadjutor archbishop of San Francisco. But his life was cut short by appendicitis, from which he died after a week-long illness on January 10, 1907. He was mourned throughout the entire state, for he had proved himself not only a dynamic churchman, but also a great civic leader and an outstanding American.

During nearly nine years of residence in the southland, Bishop Montgomery achieved widespread respect through his numerous associations and activities not only for himself but for all Catholics. He was a fearless and convincing speaker. An inscribed plaque to his memory was placed on the pulpit in the Cathedral of St. Vibiana. Bishop Montgomery High School in the South Bay area is named for him.

Bishop Thomas J. Conaty. In his younger days, Thomas James Conaty, second rector of The CATHOLIC UNIVERSITY OF AMERICA, was described in terms as realistic as they were poetic: "We can easily imagine him a Peter waking up Europe to the crusades, but would find it hard to see in him the same Peter in a hermit's cell. God made him an active man, and in every agitation for the people's health he is the angel who, stronger than the rest, can best stir the waters" (Weber 1969b, p. 31).

Conaty was born in Kilnaleck, County Cavan, Ireland, on August 1, 1847, the son of Patrick and Alice Lynch Conaty. Two years later the infant was brought to the United States by his parents who settled in Taunton, Massachusetts. He grew up in the Old Colony State and after attending the local public schools, he entered Montreal College on December 30, 1863, then transferred four years later to Holy Cross in Worcester. Under the patronage of a cousin, Conaty returned to Montreal in 1869 and enrolled at the Grand Seminaire. He was ordained for the Diocese of Springfield on December 21, 1872, by the Most Reverend Ignatius Bourget (1799–1885).

The following spring Father Conaty was named curate at Saint John's Church in Worcester, and in 1880, when the parochial boundaries were adjusted, Conaty was given charge of the newly erected parish of the Sacred Heart. A school, rectory, convent, gymnasium, and finally a church were built and within a few years the parish had no less than sixteen societies to coordinate its many-phased apostolate.

With the completion of his term in Washington, Conaty was named Bishop of Monterey-Los Angeles in 1903. In California, Conaty became involved with a host of activities. He purchased a newspaper for the diocese, took an active interest in all manner of laity groups, and was a pioneer in charitable and hospital works and educational expansion. He brought a number of religious women to the diocese, worked closely with Saint Vincent College, and even tried, unsuccessfully, to build a cathedral. Conaty interacted well with ethnic groups and was a close collaborator with movements to better the conditions of Native Americans. A noted preacher, he was involved in ecumenical activities. He died at the seaside town of Coronado on September 18, 1915. He is now interred in the Cathedral of Our Lady of the Angels.

Archbishop John J. Cantwell. John Cantwell was one of seven California prelates from the Emerald Isle. Born in Limerick, he was baptized in Saint Michael's Church on December 7, 1874, the only one of Patrick and Ellen Cantwell's ten children not initiated into the Mystical Body at the ancestral city of Fethard. Sent at the age of six to the Patrician Monastery National School and later to the nearby Classical Academy, young Cantwell prepared early for the clerical life he was to share with three of his brothers in the archdiocese of San Francisco.

From Fethard, John went to Sacred Heart College in Limerick near the home of his grandparents on George Street. He entered in 1892 Saint Patrick's College at Thurles, one of the renowned missionary seminaries in Ireland, and spent the following seven years preparing for his ordination. He was raised to the priesthood on June 18, 1899, at the hands of Robert Browne (1844–1935), bishop of Cloyne, in the nineteenth-century Cathedral of the Assumption.

Soon after his ordination, Father Cantwell arrived in San Francisco and served for the next five years at Saint Joseph's Church in Berkeley. An enthusiastic promoter of educational activities, he helped to organize the Newman Club at the University of California and taught classics at Saint Joseph's Presentation Convent. In 1905 he became secretary to Archbishop Patrick W. RI-ORDAN and nine years later was promoted to vicar general under Archbishop Edward J. HANNA. He was named to the long vacant Diocese of Monterey-Los Angeles in 1917, after he refused an appointment to Salt Lake City some years earlier. The staggering problems facing the young bishop on his arrival in Los Angeles were manifold, but he took as his yardstick the sage advice of his longtime friend Father Peter C. Yorke (1864–1925): "Don't start by building a cathedral ...get the little ones to love Christ ...concentrate on Christian education of the youth and you will be a great success in the eyes of the Lord."(Peter Yorke quoted in Weber 1971).

During an episcopate that stretched over three full decades, Cantwell saw his original diocese divided twice, first in 1922 when the Monterey-Fresno area was detached and again in 1936 when San Diego became a distinct ecclesiastical jurisdiction. In the latter year Los Angeles became a metropolitan see, thus making California the only state in the Union with two separate provinces until Galveston-Houston was elevated to archdiocesan status in 2004, making Texas also a state with two separate provinces.

The first archbishop of Los Angeles was a man of vision. Reading well the signs of potential and real growth for Southern California, he boldly proposed to the Holy Father the need for establishing a metropolitan district for Los Angeles. By the time of his death on October 30, 1947, Archbishop Cantwell had developed a bustling, sprawling archdiocese of a few churches and schools into one of the major provinces in the nation.

Though the people of later eras probably associate him mostly with the high school bearing his name, John J. Cantwell left his mark, and a prominent one at that, in the Catholic annals of the California southland. In fact he was a pioneer whose stature contrasts favorably with the great missionary founders of the Golden State. The prelate's accomplishments were as spiritually profitable to the FAITHFUL of his day as they are statistically phenomenal to those of succeeding generations. As noted by his long-time friend and collaborator, the archbishop "was a worthy successor to the prelates who preceded him. He piloted the Church of Los Angeles from a frontier rim of the Christian world to the edge of greatness in the family of American jurisdictions" (Manning 1971). He is interred in the Cathedral of Our Lady of the Angels.

James Francis Cardinal McIntyre. Fulton J. SHEEN once credited the second archbishop of Los Angeles with being the greatest spiritual inspiration of his life, "not because of what he told me about the priesthood, but because of the way he lived it" (Weber 1997).

James Francis Aloysius McIntyre was born on June 25, 1886, in mid-Manhattan, the son of James and Mary (Pelley) McIntyre. After the death of his mother in 1896, he was reared by a cousin, Mrs. Robert F. Conley. He spent several years in the employ of H. L. Horton and Company, an investment house on the New York Stock Exchange. Young McIntyre took night courses at New York City College and Columbia and, following the demise of his father in 1915, he entered the preparatory seminary for the Archdiocese of New York. The next year he enrolled in Saint Joseph's Seminary at Dunwoodie, where he spent five years until May 21, 1921, when he was advanced to the priesthood by Patrick Cardinal HAYES.

Immediately after ordination, Father McIntyre was appointed assistant to the pastor of Saint Gabriel's Church where he remained until September 1923, when he was named vice chancellor and liaison officer between Cardinal Hayes and the curial staff. He became chancellor in 1934, and on December 27th of that year was designated a private chamberlain by Pope Pius XI. Two years later, on November 12, 1936, he was promoted to the domestic prelacy.

After the arrival of Archbishop Francis J. SPELLMAN in 1939, Monsignor McIntyre became a member of the Board of Consultors for the Archdiocese of New York. On November 16, 1940, Pope PIUS XII appointed him auxiliary bishop of New York. He was consecrated by Archbishop Spellman in Saint Patrick's Cathedral on January 8, 1941. Bishop McIntyre was made vicar general of the archdiocese on January 27, 1945, and, eighteen months later, on July 20, 1946, the Holy Father advanced the prelate to coadjutor archbishop of New York. On February 7, 1948, Archbishop McIntyre was transferred to Los Angeles.

Shortly after his installation at Los Angeles, Archbishop McIntyre reorganized the archdiocesan curia, erected a new chancery, and refurbished Saint Vibiana's Cathedral—all of which he deemed necessary to the efficient management of a jurisdiction encompassing an area of 9,508 square miles with a steadily increasing Catholic population. Pope Pius XII elevated Archbishop J. Francis A. McIntyre to the cardinalate, presenting him with the scarlet *galero* in ST. PETER'S BASILICA on January 12, 1953, making him the twelfth American member of the Sacred College.

Undoubtedly Cardinal McIntyre's greatest contribution was his program for expanding Catholic educational facilities. In the first fifteen years of his tenure, Catholic schools tripled from 141 to 347, an average of one a month. In addition to serving a significant role in the Central Preparatory Commission for VATICAN COUNCIL II, the cardinal attended all the sessions of the council and was active in its deliberations.

After his retirement, Cardinal McIntyre spent the final nine years of his life serving as a parish priest at Saint Basil's in midtown Los Angeles. By the time of his demise on July 16, 1979, he was the acknowledged "Elder Statesman of the American Hierarchy." He is interred in the Cathedral of Our Lady of the Angels.

Timothy Cardinal Manning. Trained in the noble tradition of the Cantwell years, seasoned in the expansionary complexities of the McIntyre archepiscopate, and steeped in the spirit of Vatican Council II; Timothy Cardinal Manning left an impressive imprint on the pilgrim Church of Our Lady of the Angels.

One of the four children of Cornelius and Margaret (Cronin) Manning, Timothy was born on November 14, 1909, at Ballingeary, County Cork, Ireland. In 1915 he enrolled at the local National School and seven years later advanced to the educational facilities operated at nearby Cork by the Christian Brothers. His preparation for the priesthood began in 1923 at Mungret College, a secondary school staffed by the Society of Jesus for the foreign missions. The youthful clerical aspirant was attracted to California by an appeal on behalf of the Diocese of Los Angeles-San Diego. Leaving Ireland in October 1928, he traveled to Menlo Park where he joined the student body of St. Patrick's Seminary.

He was ordained to the priesthood by Bishop John J. Cantwell on June 16, 1934, in Saint Vibiana's Cathedral. His initial assignment was that of curate at Immaculate Conception Church in Los Angeles. The following year, Father Manning was sent to Rome for postgraduate studies at the Pontifical Gregorian University, where he received the doctorate in Canon Law in 1938. Upon his return to Southern California, Father Manning was named secretary to Archbishop Cantwell, a post he occupied for eight years. In 1943 he was made a papal chamberlain and, two years afterwards, was promoted by Pope Pius XII to the domestic prelacy.

On August 17, 1946, Monsignor Manning was appointed TITULAR BISHOP of Lesvi and auxiliary of Los

Angeles. Episcopal orders were bestowed on October 15, by Bishop Joseph T. McGucken (1902–1983), then apostolic administrator for the Diocese of Monterey-Fresno. At the time and for a goodly while thereafter, Bishop Manning was the "Benjamin of the American Hierarchy." With the appointment to Los Angeles in 1948 of Archbishop J. Francis A. McIntyre, Manning was named chancellor. From 1953 to 1967 he also occupied the pastorate of Saint Gregory's, a parish on the western rim of downtown Los Angeles. On November 29, 1955, he became vicar general of the archdiocese.

A popular speaker and writer, Bishop Manning published a chapter of his doctoral thesis dealing with clerical education in major seminaries, a fifty-page treatise called *The Grey Ox*, and the entry for the "Archdiocese of Los Angeles" in the *New Catholic Encyclopedia* (1967). A number of his sermons and addresses appeared in various ecclesiastical journals. The bishop served the commonweal in several capacities during his tenure as auxiliary of Los Angeles, including a fifteen-year stint on the Los Angeles City Library Commission and a lengthy term as a director for El Pueblo de Los Angeles Commission.

Upon realignment of ecclesial boundaries in Central California, Bishop Manning was named to the newly erected Diocese of Fresno on October 24, 1967. His work in the eight counties of the San Joaquin Valley was described as "a servanthood of justice and reconciliation." In eighteen brief but intensely fruitful months, he created a diocesan housing commission, established four new parishes and five missions, approved the formation of a priests' senate, authorized a task force to marshal resources for inner city and minority groups, shared the bitter anguish of the Delano labor dispute (1965–1970), and visited each of the eighty parishes scattered through the 35,239–square-mile jurisdiction.

Bishop Manning was recalled from Fresno to the scene of his earlier priestly labors on May 6, 1969, as coadjutor to James Francis Cardinal McIntyre. Assigned to the titular See of Capri, Archbishop Manning was renamed vicar general and given the pastorate of Saint Brendan's Church. Upon the retirement of Cardinal McIntyre on January 21, 1970, Archbishop Manning became chief shepherd of the Church of Los Angeles. He received the *pallium*, symbolic of the metropolitan office, on June 17, 1970.

In addition to pursuing administrative and expansionary policies, Archbishop Manning established a priests' senate, an inter-parochial council, and a clerical personnel board. He energetically supported a host of ecumenical involvements and warmly endorsed and participated in the CURSILLO MOVEMENT. He personally chaired the Commission for Liturgy, established a spirituality house, and erected an archival center, to mention but a few of his many activities.

Manning made a solemn pilgrimage to the Mexico City National Shrine of Our Lady of Guadalupe, where it all began for California, to thank the Mexican people for their role in being the bedrock of the faith along the Pacific Slope. Also in 1971 the archbishop was elected proto-president of the newly created California Catholic Conference. In his concern for and identification with the archdiocesan founded and sponsored Lay Mission Helpers, Manning visited missionaries in South Africa, Rhodesia, Ghana, Kenya, Malawi, and Uganda. While enroute to another segment of that far-flung apostolate early in 1973, he received word that Pope Paul VI once again had honored the people of God at Los Angeles, by naming him to the College of Cardinals.

Though the Catholics of Orange County were given their own diocese in 1974, Los Angeles continued to expand and, by 1984, was acknowledged as the largest ecclesial jurisdiction in the United States. Manning died in Los Angeles on June 23, 1989, and is buried in the Priest's Plot at Calvary Cemetery.

Roger Cardinal Mahony. Catholics in the California southland rejoiced when word reached them that one of their own was returning to be the fourth archbishop in 1985. Their new prelate was the fourth native of Los Angeles and the twenty-third Californian called to the episcopate.

Roger Michael Mahony's ecclesial pedigree is deeply imbedded in the area's heritage. His relationship to Timothy Cardinal Manning, for example, went back almost forty years. Their kinship began in the pages of *The Tidings* on October 18, 1946. That issue describes Manning's consecration as auxiliary bishop of Los Angeles and carries a picture of ten-year-old Roger and his twin brother, Louis. Thirteen years later, Bishop Manning conferred the minor orders of LECTOR and PORTER on Mr. Mahony and, the following year, those of ACOLYTE and exorcist. In 1967 when Bishop Manning was named to the Diocese of Fresno, young Father Mahony served as chief liaison between the new ordinary and retiring Bishop Aloysius J. Willinger (1886–1973).

Roger Michael Mahony was born to Victor James and Loretta Marie (Baron) Mahony on February 27, 1936. His entire elementary training was acquired at St. Charles School in North Hollywood, where he fell under the pastoral tutelage of the late Monsignor Harry Meade. In 1950 he entered Los Angeles College, the preparatory seminary for the Archdiocese of Los Angeles. He was among the initial enrollees at Mission Hills Queen of Angels Seminary in 1954. Upon completing his collegiate courses at St John's Seminary, Camarillo, young Mahony asked for and received incardination as a clerical aspirant for the Diocese of Monterey-Fresno. He received priestly ordination at the hands of the Most Reverend Aloysius Willinger on May 1, 1962. A few days later, he was assigned to a curacy at Saint John's Cathedral, Fresno. In the following fall, Bishop Willinger asked Father Mahony to take further studies at the National Catholic School of Social Service in Washington, D.C.

Soon after returning to Central California in 1964, Father Mahony was named diocesan Director for Catholic Charities and Social Service, an assignment he held for six years. In September 1964 he became administrator (and later pastor) of Saint Genevieve's Parish, Fresno. Among other positions occupied by the tireless priest during the late 1960s were executive director for both the Catholic Welfare Bureau and the Infant of Prague Adoption Service, as well as chaplain of the diocesan Saint Vincent de Paul Society. He also found time to teach during those years at Fresno State University and Coalinga College. Long interested in the apostolate to Hispanic peoples, Father Roger Mahony served a term on the board of directors for the West Coast Office of the Bishops' Committee for the Spanish Speaking. He was also been active as Secretary for the United States Catholic Bishops *ad hoc* Committee on Farm Labor.

He made time for civic responsibilities too. Father Mahony was affiliated with the Fresno County Economic Opportunities Commission, the Alcoholic Rehabilitation Committee, the United Crusade, the Community Worship, the Urban Coalition, and the Fresno Redevelopment Agency. Those manifold duties prompted the Junior Chamber of Commerce to proclaim Father Mahony "Young Man of the Year for 1967." In that year also he was named honorary chaplain to His Holiness Pope Paul VI.

In 1970, shortly after the transfer of the Most Reverend Hugh A. Donohoe (1905–1987) to Fresno, Monsignor Mahony was appointed diocesan chancellor, a position he continued to hold after his episcopal consecration on March 19, 1975, as titular bishop of Tamascani. He became pastor of Saint John's Cathedral in 1973. Bishop Mahony was transferred to Stockton as residential ordinary in 1980 and presided over the pastoral needs of that 10,023–square-mile, six-county diocese. Transferred to Southern California as archbishop of Los Angeles on September 5, 1985, Mahony became a cardinal priest on June 28, 1991.

During Cardinal Mahony's tenure in Los Angeles, he launched numerous new apostolates and ministries, including forming an ad hoc Womens' Task Force (1985), launching five pastoral regions with an auxiliary bishop in charge of each, starting the *Tercero Encuentro Hispano*, introducing new immigration policies and initiatives, establishing the Catholic Education Foundation, organizing annual cardinals' awards, publishing a Spanish language newspaper (*Vida Nueva*), inaugurating an annual appeal for poor parishes and schools (Together

in Mission), forming a Clergy Misconduct Oversight Board, acquiring a central Archdiocesan Catholic Center, installing Catholic Mortuaries at archdiocesan cemeteries, and erecting the largest cathedral in the United States (Our Lady of the Angels) to mention but a few. The Archdiocese of Los Angeles welcomed Pope John Paul II in 1987, when the Holy Father paid the first papal visit ever to a California mission (San Fernando, Rey de España).

Clergy Misconduct Oversight Board. In 1994 the cardinal formed a Sexual Abuse Advisory Board. Its purpose was to provide advice to the vicar for clergy in dealing with complaints of abuse and in refining policies and practices. The board consisted of pastors as well as priests, psychologists, social workers, attorneys, and victims or parents of victims. The vicar for clergy presented the factual situations to the board using pseudonyms for the accused priests and victims. The board discussed each case and offered its wisdom, usually by consensus, but did not make a formal recommendation. Instead, the advice of the various members of the board was conveyed by the vicar to the archbishop. The question of a priest's return to ministry remained the archbishop's judgment based on the recommendations of therapists, the board's suggestions, and the ability of the archdiocese to monitor the priest's activities.

Eight years later, Cardinal Mahony established a Clergy Misconduct Oversight Board headed by retired presiding Superior Court Judge Richard Byrne. Expanding the functions of the earlier advisory panel, the new board, composed of thirteen members representing a broad spectrum of the community, was given new authority to review and strengthen all existing programs to end sexual abuse. The board, directly answerable to the archbishop, provides formal written recommendations. All cases of sexual misconduct by clergy are presented to the board. The board meetings and records, including its recommendations, are strictly confidential. When an allegation is received, the accuser is directed to the archdiocesan Coordinator for Victim Assistance. Civil authorities are notified, and the accused is informed of the allegation. The case is brought before the board, which receives a report of each allegation lodged against a priest or DEACON. The board reviews all the relevant information and may request additional information as necessary. Among other things the board makes written recommendations to the archbishop concerning:

- Compliance with California child sexual abuse reporting laws;
- whether the needs of the victim or victims are being addressed and pastoral outreach has been extended to every victim and his or her family; and

- the type of notice to be given to the parish staff and community.

As of February 1, 2004, the board had twenty-eight meetings. It reviewed thirty-seven cases of reported abuse of minors, the vast majority of which happened before 1987. Board recommendations were instrumental in the decision-making of the cardinal and other archdiocesan officials. Policies on sexual abuse remain under regular review, with an eye to the best practices around the country that could enhance those in the archdiocese. In the early 2000s three former FBI special agents were hired to assist the archdiocese with investigations.

Safeguarding the Children Program. As a response to what future historians will surely classify as the worst SCANDAL ever in the Catholic Church in the United States, the Archdiocese of Los Angeles adopted a Safeguarding the Children Program in 2002, whereby victims harmed by sexual abuse at the hands of priests, religious, deacons, or other ministers of the Church could obtain therapy and spiritual direction. Though the scandal touched most areas of the Catholic Church in the United States, it affected the Archdiocese of Los Angeles more severely than many other places because of the sheer numbers of people comprising the largest ecclesial jurisdiction in the country. The files for the archdiocese contain a mountain of materials tracing the scandal as it unfolded in the newspapers, magazines, journals, radio reports, and television commentaries. Future sociologist-historians will be able to study what transpired and how it affected the nation as a whole and the archdiocese in particular. Even in the early 2000s, norms adopted and implemented by the National Conference of Catholic Bishops took hold so that the Church could deal aggressively with this problem.

Even a single case is reprehensible, but the problem is not as rampant as newspaper and television reports indicate. Statistics are few, but one survey of 2,400 priests in the Archdiocese of Chicago over a forty-year period puts the percentage rate for all kinds of sexual misbehavior at 1.8 percent, considerably lesser than the number of incidences in the general population. Priests are human beings and, as such, they reflect all the traits, good and bad, that enhance or taint human nature. Gary Schoener, a nationally recognized expert on sexual abuse, expressed a widely accepted opinion that "true pedophilia is very rare among all clergy, and now there is no evidence that it is more common among clergy than laypersons" (Sipe 2003).

Sexual abuse of young people is not just a Catholic problem. *The Christian Science Monitor* reported on April 5, 2002, that most American churches being hit with the child sexual abuse allegations are Protestant, and most of the alleged abusers are not members of the clergy or staff, but church volunteers. Though comparative data is not readily available, indications are that this is not a problem only in the church. For example, the Gallup Organization reported that 1.3 million children were assaulted in 1995. Most abuse takes place in families, where it remains a hidden, but very real, problem. According to Dr. Garth A. Rattray, "about eighty-five percent of the offenders [of child sexual abuse] are family members, babysitters, neighbors, family friends, or relatives" (Rausch 2004, p. 14).

A second and troublesome aspect of this scandal has been the attempts by bishops and others to cover up the whole matter. To some extent, that is true. Until the first decade of the 2000s, most psychologists believed that pedophilia was treatable; now experts say there is no cure. Prior to that, acting on the best available medical and psychological advice, a number of pedophiles were sent to treatment, and then a few were put back into active service. Belatedly, the bishops are better informed and have adopted a zero tolerance for these cases. The critics, however, will keep regurgitating the well-intentioned mistakes of the past.

Unfortunately, down through the ages, scandals, indiscretions, and outright crimes have been perpetrated by the clergy in almost every century. The twenty-first century scandals, bad as they are, are simply the latest manifestations of the power of evil in the world. The French king once took Cardinal Richelieu to task for not complying with one of his directives.

Christians are reminded that from arid deserts will come streams of running water, and out of the deepest darkness will come the light of God's peace and good news. Darkness gives place to sunlight in the early hours of every day. This horrible scandal will pass, but it may take a long time for wounds to heal because communications are immediate and universal. The Lord has promised to be with His poor, mud-splattered Church until the end of time. Forgive your priests, pray for them, and encourage vocations. In the plan of Divine Providence, priests are designated ministers of the sacraments, which are the normal means for communicating God's graces to His people. God has chosen to publicize the sins of His chosen people from the time of David, the King. Even among Christ's innermost apostolic family, one of the twelve denied Him, another doubted Him, and a third betrayed Him. But the early Church was strengthened by the scar tissue of those unpleasantries.

Over the past decades, the archdiocese settled various lawsuits with insurance funds and archdiocesan funds, totaling some $10.5 million. In November 2006 the archdiocese settled forty-five lawsuits for $60 million, with $40 million of that coming from reserve investment funds of the archdiocese. These cases had occurred prior to 1950, when no insurance policies could be located, or after 1986, when insurance for this misconduct was no longer available.

In July 2007 the archdiocese reached a global settlement in principle for the 508 remaining civil lawsuits for $660 million. To reach this amount, the archdiocese contributed $250 million, the insurance companies $225 million, religious orders and other defendants $60 million, and other defendants $125 million. (This latter amount is guaranteed by the archdiocese, but was not due immediately, and a large portion of this amount is to be obtained from remaining defendants who chose not to participate in the global settlement.)

SEE ALSO ASSUMPTION OF MARY; BALTIMORE, COUNCILS OF; CALIFORNIA, CATHOLIC CHURCH IN; CATECHISMS; CATHOLIC CHARITIES USA; CONVERTS AND CONVERSION; FEASTS, RELIGIOUS; IRISH CHRISTIAN BROTHERS; MEXICO, COLONIAL; MISSION AND MISSIONS; PALLIUM; PATRON SAINTS; PORTIUNCULA; RICHELIEU, ARMAND JEAN DU PLESSIS DE; SAN FRANCISCO, ARCHDIOCESE OF; SEX ABUSE CRISIS; ST. VINCENT DE PAUL, SOCIETY OF; UNITED STATES CONFERENCE OF CATHOLIC BISHOPS (USCCB).

BIBLIOGRAPHY

Archdiocese of Los Angeles Official Web site, available from: http://www.archdiocese.la/ (accessed November 13, 2008).

Maynard J. Geiger, O.F.M., *The Life and Times of Fray Junipero Serra, O.F.M.* (Washington, D.C. 1959), vol. 2, 273.

Pope John Paul II, "Address at San Carlos Borromeo Mission" (Carmel, Calif. 1987).

Charles F. Lummis, *The Landmarks Club* (Los Angeles 1903).

Timothy Manning, "Preface," in *John Joseph Cantwell: His Excellency of Los Angeles*, by Francis J. Weber (Hong Kong 1971).

Harris Newmark, *Sixty Years in Southern California, 1853–1913, Containing the Reminiscences of Harris Newmark* (New York 1916).

The Official Catholic Directory, 2008 (New Providence, N.J. 2008).

H. I. Priestly, *A Historical, Political, and Natural Description of California by Pedro Fages, Soldier of Spain* (Berkeley, Calif. 1937).

Christopher Rand, *Los Angeles, The Ultimate City* (New York 1967).

Thomas P. Rausch "Where Do We Go from Here?" *America* 191 (October 18, 2004): 14.

"The Report to the People Of God: Clergy Sexual Abuse in the Archdiocese of Los Angeles 1930–2003" (Los Angeles 2004), available from http://www.archdiocese.la/ (accessed November 13, 2008).

A. W. Richard Sipe, *A Secret World: The Search for Celibacy* (London 1990).

A. W. Richard Sipe, *Celibacy in Crisis: A Secret World Revisted* (London 2003).

Francis J. Weber, *California's Reluctant Prelate, The Life and Times of Right Reverend Thaddeus Amat, C.M. (1811–1878)* (Los Angeles 1964).

Francis J. Weber, *George Thomas Montgomery, California Churchman* (Los Angeles 1966).

Francis J. Weber, *Francisco Mora, Last of the Catalans* (Los Angeles 1967).

Francis J. Weber, *Thomas James Conaty, Pastor-Educator-Bishop* (Los Angeles 1969a).

Francis J. Weber, "Rum, Romanism and Thomas J. Conaty" in *Holy Cross Quarterly* II (Spring, 1969b), 31.

Francis J. Weber, *John Joseph Cantwell; His Excellency of Los Angeles* (Hong Kong 1971).

Francis J. Weber, *Francis Garcia Diego, California's Transition Bishop* (Los Angeles 1972).

Francis J. Weber, *Joseph Sadoc Alemany; Harbinger of a New Era* (Los Angeles 1973).

Francis J. Weber, *The Franciscans and Los Angeles* (Los Angeles 1974).

Francis J. Weber, *Century of Fulfillment: The Roman Catholic Church in Southern California, 1840–1947* (Mission Hills, Calif. 1990; repr. Los Angeles 1996).

Francis J. Weber, *Past Is Prologue: Some Historical Reflections, 1961–1991* (Los Angeles 1992).

Francis J. Weber, *His Eminence of Los Angeles: James Francis Cardinal McIntyre*, 2 vols. (Mission Hills, Calif. 1997).

Francis J. Weber, *Magnificat: The Life and Times of Timothy Cardinal Manning* (Mission Hills, Calif. 1999).

Francis J. Weber, *A History of the Archdiocese of Los Angeles and Its Precursor Jurisdictions in Southern California, 1840–2007* (Strasbourg, France 2006).

Msgr. Francis J. Weber
Archivist, Archdiocese of Los Angeles
Director, San Fernando Mission
Mission Hills, Calif. (2009)

LOUISIANA, CATHOLIC CHURCH IN

Located in the southcentral United States, Louisiana was admitted to the Union as the eighteenth state on April 30, 1812. The area now comprising the state was once part of the immense Louisiana Territory claimed in 1682 by Robert Cavelier, Sieur de LA SALLE, for France and was under the successive control of Antoine Crozat (1712–1717), John Law's Company of the West (1717–1731), and the French Crown (1731–1762); it then became a Spanish possession (1762–1801), was returned to France (1800–1803), and was sold to the United States and governed as a territory (1804–1812). Baton Rouge is the capital, and New Orleans is the largest city.

In 2008 Catholics numbered 1,188,798, slightly more than twenty-eight percent of the total state population of 4,230,295 (*The Official Catholic Directory* 2008, p. 2083). The ecclesiastical province of New Orleans coincides with the state boundaries. New Orleans is the metropolitan see, and the other six Louisiana dioceses—

Alexandria, Baton Rouge, Houma-Thibodaux, Lafayette, Lake Charles, and Shreveport—are its suffragans. Catholics are concentrated mainly in the southern part of the state. Lafayette has a higher proportion of Catholics (fifty-six percent) than any other DIOCESE in the United States and with New Orleans has one of the highest populations of African-American Catholics in the nation.

Colonization and Missionary History. The discovery, colonization, settlement, history, and economic growth of the territory and state are associated with its waterways, principally the Mississippi River. Hernando De Soto (c.1496/1500–1542) discovered it in 1541; La Salle went down the Mississippi from Illinois in 1682; Pierre LeMoyne (1661–1706), Sieur de Iberville, sailed up the river from the Gulf of Mexico in 1699; and his brother, Jean-Baptiste LeMoyne (1680–1767), Sieur de Bienville, in 1722 transferred the capital of French Louisiana from New Biloxi on the Gulf Coast to a bend of the river that gives to New Orleans its sobriquet of *Crescent City.* The 1718 plans of the city, laid by Adrien de Pauger (d. 1726), provided for a church and presbytery, but divine services were held only in improvised and inadequate quarters until April 1727, when the first substantial St. Louis parish church was finally completed.

Franciscan recollects, Zénobe Membré and Anastase Douay, were with La Salle when he reached the mouth of the Mississippi, and the territory was placed under the ecclesiastical jurisdiction of the BISHOP of Quebec. Priests of the Quebec Seminary, connected with the Seminary of Foreign Missions in Paris, worked among the Native Americans of lower Louisiana in the late 1600s and early 1700s. François de Montigny, Antoine Davion, and Jean François Buisson de St. Cosmé were outstanding pioneer missionaries. Buisson, regarded as the first American-born missionary MARTYR, was killed in 1706 by a party of Chitimacha tribe members a few miles below Donaldsonville on the Mississippi River. In 1717 the Franciscan Antonio MARGIL offered the first Mass in Natchitoches, the oldest Louisiana town (1715), and ministered to its French settlers and Native American inhabitants. In 1724 three years before New Orleans had its own substantial church building, a CHAPEL was erected about thirty-five miles upstream at present-day Killona on the German Coast (Les Allemands). The first Louisiana chapel was built in 1700 by the Bayagoula tribe under the supervision of Father Paul du Ru at the site of present-day Bayou Goula in Iberville Parish (county), which the Jesuit missionary had reached via the Mississippi.

Catholicism made little progress during the five years when Antione Crozat, a French financier, attempted to exploit the region. In 1717 the Council of the Marine recommended turning the colony over to John Law's Company of the West and its successor, the Company of the Indies (or Mississippi Company). In accordance with the charter issued by the regent PHILIP II, duke of Orleans, religious affairs were included in the activities of the Company of the West from 1717 to 1731. Occasionally, concession chaplains, JESUITS, CAPUCHINS, CARMELITES, and other missionaries traveled up and down the river during the early years of colonization. The first Capuchins were Bruno de Langres, who arrived in New Orleans toward the end of 1722, and Plilibert de Vianden, who took charge of the district from the Chapitoulas. The district extended a few miles above the original boundaries of the city to Pointe Coupée. It included Les Allemands, the German Coast, and the intervening concessions. Les Allemands had a chapel, dedicated to St. John, on the west bank of the Mississippi as early as 1724. Most land grants were along the Mississippi River, Bayou St. John, and Lake Pontchartrain. On the Mississippi the land grants stretched from Chapitoulas to Point Coupee about 140 miles upstream. From the parochial centers established along the river, priests plied the waterways or pushed into the interior to build chapels and start missions from which emerged the later parishes. At the confluence of the Mississippi River and Bayou Lafourche, Capuchins and, later, VINCENTIANS, descended in pirogues from the Plattenville Assumption Church (1793) and Seminary (1838) to lay the foundation of bayou parishes. In 1722 the Jesuits, who contributed notably to the spiritual and economic well-being of the area, undertook the spiritual jurisdiction of the natives in the colony, a responsibility entrusted to them by Bishop Louis DUPLESSIS-MORNAY of Quebec. Their endeavors were mainly supported by an extensive indigo and sugar plantation adjacent to New Orleans. In July 1763, while Michel Baudouin (1691–1768) was superior, the Jesuits were dispossessed of their property and banished from Louisiana. Their departure, some ten years before the society was suppressed, seriously hampered the growth of the Church in colonial Louisiana.

Arrival of the Acadians. The French-speaking Acadians, expelled from Nova Scotia in the mid-1750s, were a boon to the state and a blessing to the Church in Louisiana. As early as 1758 Acadians reached Louisiana by way of Georgia, the Carolinas, and Maryland. During the following years several hundred—including groups from New England, the Antilles, and French ports—migrated to the state. They settled in St. Martinville (Les Attakapas) on Bayou Têche, in the Poste des Opelousas, and along the Mississippi below Baton Rouge. At St. Gabriel, Iberville Parish, they deposited the precious parish registers of St. Charles Church, Grand Pré (1688–1755). Those who settled along Les

The Cathedral-Basilica of St. Louis King of France overlooking Jackson Square. *This Cathedral-Basilica is one of the most recognized buildings in the United States, and it is the oldest Catholic cathedral in continual use in the country.* **MEDIOIMAGES/PHOTODISC /GETTY IMAGES**

Allemands soon intermarried with the descendants of the original settlers—almost all Catholics—from Switzerland, Alsace Lorraine, and the Rhineland. Most French-speaking Louisianians retained their Catholic FAITH, despite a dire shortage of priests and churches. With other settlers, they formed a cluster of parishes in St. Martinville (1765); Opelousas (1777); Grand Coteau (1819); Lafayette, formerly Vermilionville (1821); and New Iberia (1838). In the central and northern areas of the state, the Church made smaller gains than elsewhere. Except in the civil parishes of Natchitoches, Avoyelles, and Rapides, the inhabitants were and still are mostly Protestants of Anglo-Saxon descent.

Spanish Interlude. In 1769 Spanish troops took control of New Orleans and the Louisiana Territory, which was ceded to Spain by the Treaty of Fontainbleau. After 1776 Church affairs in New Orleans were greatly influenced by the Spanish. Cirilo de Barcelona, chaplain of the Spanish expedition against the British in West Florida, was consecrated auxiliary bishop for the Louisiana colony on March 6, 1785. Shortly before leaving for his consecration in Cuba, he appointed his assistant, Antonio de SEDELLA, temporary pastor of St. Louis. For decades thereafter, Sedella, known as Père Antoine, was the center of controversy in the area.

Church Expansion. When the Diocese of Louisiana and the Floridas was created in 1793, Luis Ignacio de PEÑALVER Y CÀRDENAS was consecrated as first ordinary. He arrived in New Orleans on July 17, 1795, marking the beginning of home government in Church affairs. Peñalver noted in a report to the Spanish government, that of the 11,000 Catholics in New Orleans, only about 400 had performed their Easter duty. He instituted a number of necessary reforms, combated religious indifference and Voltaireanism, and established parishes in the Poste des Avoyelles, Many (Nuestra Señora de Guadalupe at Bayou Scie), and Monroe. Meanwhile, the parish church in use since 1727 was destroyed in the great fire of 1788, and a new structure, the future Cathedral of St. Louis, was completed in 1794. Although renovated several times, it remains substantially the same building, still in use as the CATHE-DRAL into the twenty-first century. In December 1964 it became a minor BASILICA.

In 1801 Peñalver was transferred to the Archdiocese of Guatemala, and jurisdictional quarrels, interdiction, and threats of SCHISM marked the next fifteen years in New Orleans. Père Antoine was at odds with Father Patrick Walsh and Canon Thomas Hasset, who administered the diocese during the episcopal vacancy. When Hasset died on April 24, 1804, the last canonical link of the Louisiana Church with Spain was extinguished. Walsh claimed to be vicar general of Louisiana, which precipitated a two-year schism between his followers and those of Père Antoine, who was "elected" pastor of St. Louis Cathedral the following year by the majority of

New Orleans citizens under the direction of the church wardens (*marguilliers*). To complicate matters further, Spain ceded Louisiana back to France, which in turn, sold it to the United States in 1803.

Transfer to United States. Aware of the territorial transfer, the HOLY SEE did not send Bishop-elect Francisco Porro y Peinado to Louisiana, and on September 1, 1805, placed it temporarily under the spiritual supervision of Bishop John CARROLL of Baltimore. Carroll, in time, named the chaplain of the URSULINES, Jean Olivier, his vicar general, but the latter's authority was openly challenged by Père Antione and the cathedral wardens. Finally, on August 18, 1812, Father Louis William DUBOURG was named administrator apostolic by Archbishop Carroll. DuBourg, complying with Andrew Jackson's request, officiated at a *Te Deum* in St. Louis Cathedral following the U.S. victory over the British at the Battle of New Orleans on January 8, 1815. An all-night vigil before Our Lady of Prompt Succor was held at the Ursuline CONVENT chapel before the battle; Jackson personally thanked the nuns for their prayers at the thanksgiving service presided over by DuBourg.

On September 24, 1815, DuBourg was consecrated in ROME, and Louisiana finally had a bishop after an interregnum of nearly fifteen years. DuBourg, however, remained in Europe for the next two years enlisting the help of priests and seminarians. He successfully acquired the services of St. Rose Philippine DUCHESNE, who visited New Orleans, and the Religious of the Sacred Heart and helped form what later became the Pontifical Society for the PROPAGATION OF THE FAITH. Upon arriving in the United States, DuBourg went to St. Louis, Missouri, and did not return to New Orleans until late 1820. The next year he called a synod, attended by twenty priests. On March 25, 1824, Joseph ROSATI, C.M., was consecrated as DuBourg's coadjutor, but supervised at a distance, because he resided in St. Louis. The Sisters of Charity from Emmitsburg, Maryland, arrived to staff the Poydras Asylum in New Orleans, the first of numerous educational, social, and healthcare facilities in Louisiana, including Hôtel Dieu. DuBourg resigned in mid-1826 and returned to France, where he died in 1833, as ARCHBISHOP of Besançon. A further division of the old diocese took place when St. Louis, Missouri, became the see of the northern area, and the Diocese of New Orleans became co-extensive with the Louisiana state boundaries. DuBourg's resignation left the lower end of the Mississippi Valley without a resident bishop, which caused further disorder. Although Rosati visited the area, he could not completely control the see. Rosati, appointed bishop of St. Louis in 1827, recommended a fellow Vincentian for the See of New Orleans, and Leo de Neckère (1800–1833) was

consecrated in St. Louis Cathedral on June 24, 1830, at the age of twenty-nine. His episcopate was brief, for he was stricken with yellow fever and died on September 5, 1833. A few months before, he had established New Orleans's second parish, St. Patrick's, to accommodate the Irish immigrants and other English-speaking people of the city.

Expansion of New Orleans. A period of church expansion coincided with the growing importance of New Orleans as a center of commerce. The city emerged as the fourth largest in the nation; its population increased from 29,737 in 1830 to 102,193 in 1840. The diocese covered the entire state and had a total population approaching 300,000, served by twenty-six churches and twenty-seven priests when Antoine BLANC became fourth bishop on November 22, 1835. During the twenty-five years Blanc administered the see, the number of churches increased to seventy-three and the number of priests to ninety-two. He established Assumption Seminary on Bayou Lafourche, two colleges, nine academies and schools, four orphanages, a hospital, and a home for girls. Under the guidance of Etienne Rousselon, vicar general, the Sisters of the HOLY FAMILY were founded in 1842 by a free African-American woman, Henriette Delille (1813–1862). It was a community commited to teaching, caring for orphans, and tending to elderly African Americans. The Redemptorist Fathers established themselves (1843) in Lafayette and New Orleans where German, Irish, and French immigrants had settled. Of the REDEMPTORISTS, Blessed Francis Xavier SEELOS died and was buried in New Orleans in 1865. In 1836, while abroad recruiting priests and religious for his diocese, Blanc persuaded the Father General of the Jesuits in Rome to release eight members of the society for service in Louisiana, guaranteeing the return of a Jesuit presence to the area after nearly three-quarters of a century. In 1837 they established themselves in Grand Coteau, building St. Charles College for their novitiate. They also took charge of Sacred Heart Church and parish, which embraced a wide territory in the west. The Jesuit Fathers opened the College of the Immaculate Conception in 1849 on a plot of ground, part of the plantation of which they had been defrauded in 1763. The Congregation of the HOLY CROSS came in 1849 to stabilize St. Mary's Orphan Boys's Home, which had been opened by Father Adam Kindelon, first pastor of St. Patrick's. Father Cyril de la Croix organized the first conference of the Society of ST. VINCENT DE PAUL after a layman, William Blair Lancaster, brought a manual of the society to New Orleans (1852).

Blanc called two diocesan synods and two provincial councils. The death of Abbé Louis Moni, pastor of St. Louis Cathedral in 1842, precipitated a three-year struggle between Blanc and the wardens of the cathedral over the right to appoint clergy; the controversy, which caused the withdrawal of the clergy from the cathedral, eventually was settled in the Louisiana supreme court in favor of the bishop and shaped the pattern of parish establishment for several decades by abolishing the trustee system.

Diocesan Developments. In 1850 Pope PIUS IX (POPE 1846–1878) raised New Orleans to the rank of an ARCHDIOCESE and created the Province of New Orleans which included all of Louisiana, Mississippi, Arkansas, Alabama, Texas, and part of Indian Territory (Oklahoma). Three years later the upper part of Louisiana state was erected into the Diocese of Natchitoches with Auguste M. Martin (bishop 1853–1875) as its first bishop. The new diocese had only five priests and five churches to serve the Catholic population of about 25,000, spread throughout the entire northern half of Louisiana. After Blanc's death on June 20, 1860, the archdiocese was administered by Rousselon until the arrival of Archbishop-elect Jean Marie ODIN from Galveston, Texas.

Civil War and Aftermath. Archbishop Odin took possession of his see only a few days after the bombardment of Fort Sumter on April 12, 1861. Louisiana had already seceded from the Union and joined the Confederacy. During the Civil War, the archbishop's position was an extremely delicate one, calling for infinite tact and diplomacy; Pope Pius IX appointed Odin and Archbishop HUGHES of New York his personal intermediaries to effect a reconciliation between the North and South. The city was occupied by federal troops on May 1, 1862. Union forces wrought considerable damage on church properties in such places as Vermilionville (Lafayette), Pointe Coupée, and Donaldsonville. In addition, the war years disrupted religious and educational work. Reconstruction was no less trying, but Odin continued his predecessor's expansion program. In 1863 Odin went to Europe in search of religious and money for his diocese. He convinced the MARIST FATHERS to come to Louisiana. In 1867 the OBLATE SISTERS OF PROVIDENCE, a Baltimore community of African-American nuns, began staffing a home for dependent children of the newly freed slaves. The LITTLE SISTERS OF THE POOR opened their home for the aged poor after a committee of pious women, called Les Dames de la Providence, asked for their help in maintaining another home for the aged founded in 1840. The Brothers of the Sacred Heart came to New Orleans from Mobile, Alabama, in 1869. The first Benedictine convent in the archdiocese was opened (1870) in the German national parish of Holy Trinity, New Orleans (1847). The nuns arrived from Covington, Kentucky, and later established a motherhouse in Covington, Lousiana. After numerous

requests for assistance, Odin obtained a coadjutor with right of succession, Napoleon Joseph Percheé (1805–1883), who had been chaplain of the Ursulines for many years, founder of the first Catholic newspaper in Louisiana, *Le Propagateur Catholique* (1842), and vicar general of the archdiocese. He was consecrated in St. Louis Cathedral on May 1, 1870, and succeeded to the see when Odin died in France on May 25, 1870, after attending the First Vatican Council with Bishop Martin of Natchitoches.

Like his predecessors, Percheé invited several communities to the archdiocese: the SISTERS OF THE MOST HOLY SACRAMENT (formerly Perpetual Adoration), who arrived at Waggaman in 1872; the Sisters of CHRISTIAN CHARITY, who established themselves at St. Henry's Convent, New Orleans, in 1873; and the Discalced Carmelite Nuns, who arrived in 1877. In addition, Archbishop Perché approved the founding of a diocesan community, the Sisters of the Immaculate Conception, organized on July 11, 1874, in Labadieville with Elvina Vienne as first superior. Soon after his installation as head of the see, Perché also inaugurated a costly program of church building, school construction, and parish foundations that contrasted sharply with the record of his predecessor. These expenses, plus financial aid to families impoverished by the Civil War, increased archdiocesan debt. Weakened by age and infirmities and overwhelmed by the tremendous debt, the archbishop asked for a coadjutor. The Holy See appointed François Xavier Leray (1825–1887) of Natchitoches, who became archbishop upon Perché's death on December 27, 1883. Bishop Leray was succeeded in Natchitoches by Bishop Antoine Durier (1883–1904), who was instrumental in establishing a Catholic school board and Catholic schools near every church in his diocese. Leray's chief concern as coadjutor and as ordinary was reducing archdiocesan debt, so he began few building or expansion programs. The only new community established in the archdiocese was that of the Poor Clare Nuns (1885). Upon his death on September 23, 1887, Leray was succeeded by Francis Janssens (1843–1897), the Dutch-born bishop of Natchez.

Turn of the Century. The new archbishop received the PALLIUM from Cardinal James GIBBONS on May 8, 1889, although he took possession of the archdiocese on September 16, 1888. He invited the BENEDICTINES of St. Meinrad's Abbey in Indiana to open a seminary to train native priests. Father Luke Grüwe, O.S.B., established in 1890 what later became St. Joseph Abbey and Seminary at St. Benedict, Lousiana. Janssens dedicated the seminary on September 3, 1891. The archbishop welcomed St. Frances Xavier CABRINI to New Orleans and encouraged her in 1892 to establish a school and orphanage to assist the children of Italian immigrants; thousands were entering the city. In 1893 he asked the Sisters of the Holy Family to care for dependent or neglected African-American boys, and thus started the present Lafon Home for Boys, one of several institutions named for the local African-American philanthropist Thomy Lafon (1810–1893).

Janssens was greatly esteemed throughout the archdiocese, which numbered 341,613 in the centennial year of 1893. The celebration that year attracted many dignitaries to Louisiana, including Cardinal Gibbons of Baltimore. Janssens encouraged spiritual ministrations to patients at the leprosarium at Carville, Louisiana. When the hurricane of 1893 swept the Louisiana Gulf Coast, Janssens went among the Italian, Spanish, and Malay fishermen in the island settlements to comfort them; he later helped rebuild their homes. He promoted DEVOTION to Our Lady under the title of Prompt Succor. The structure of the parishes was determined in 1894 when each was legally incorporated with the archbishop, the vicar general, the pastor, and two lay directors as board members. Janssens was the first ordinary to promote native vocations on a large scale. His predecessors depended on priests and seminarians from Europe and leaned heavily on religious to staff new parishes. He sponsored the Catholic Winter School, opened parochial schools, and launched a dozen new parishes. Alarmed at the defections from the faith among African Americans, he established St. Katherine's as an African-American parish, but on a temporary basis, because he did not want to promote racial segregation. He died on June 9, 1897, while traveling to Europe on behalf of the archdiocese.

Placide Louis CHAPELLE, sixth archbishop of New Orleans, was transferred from Santa Fe, New Mexico, in February 1898. Concerned about archdiocesean debt, he ordered an annual contribution of twelve percent of the revenues of each parish for five years. This measure liquidated longstanding debt, but aroused the displeasure of some pastors. Chapelle's relationship with priests in the diocese was strained. Many were upset by his extended, though necessary, absences as APOSTOLIC DELEGATE to Cuba and Puerto Rico, and later as apostolic delegate extraordinary to the Philippines, where he negotiated ecclesiastical problems arising from the Spanish-American War (1898). He needed an auxiliary; thus, the pastor of Annunciation Church in New Orleans, Gustave Rouxel (1840–1908), was consecrated on April 9, 1899.

Twentieth-Century Developments. Archbishop Chapelle opened a theological seminary (1900) with the Vincentian Fathers as professors. He established some twelve parishes and missions, and the Dominicans began their MINISTRY in the archdiocese (1903). Chapelle died a victim of yellow fever on August 9, 1905. The next

ordinary, James Hubert Blenk (1856–1917), S.M., was well known to the archdiocese long before his appointment on April 20, 1906. He had served as bishop of Puerto Rico, former auditor and secretary to the apostolic delegation to the West Indies, rector of Holy Name of Mary Church, and president of Jefferson College, Convent, Louisiana. Blenk, an ardent promoter of Catholic education, set up in 1908 the first archdiocesan school board and appointed the first superintendent of schools. In 1914 he hosted the NATIONAL CATHOLIC EDUCATION ASSOCIATION (NCEA) convention in New Orleans, the first major convention held in Louisiana. The Benedictine Fathers of St. Joseph Abbey took over the preparatory seminary again, but theological courses were discontinued in 1907. Most major seminarians matriculated at Kenrick Seminary in St. Louis or St. Mary's Seminary in Baltimore or studied abroad. In September 1904 the Jesuits started a small college in New Orleans, which in 1911 was amalgamated with the College of the Immaculate Conception and became Loyola University, receiving state charter as a university in 1912. Blenk designated St. Mary's the normal school for women religious engaged in teaching in the archdiocese. In time, St. Mary's Dominican College became an accredited Catholic women's college.

French Benedictine nuns, forced to leave their country in 1906, settled in Ramsay under the guidance of Paul Schaeuble, O.S.B., first ABBOT of St. Joseph Abbey since 1903. The Sisters Servants of Mary, having left Mexico during the Carranza revolution, found refuge also in the archdiocese and in 1914 began their ministrations among the sick and the bedridden in the city. The sisters of the Society of ST. TERESA OF JESUS, likewise refugees from Mexico, began teaching at St. Louis Cathedral School in 1915. That same year, the archbishop urgently requested St. Katharine DREXEL, foundress of the Sisters of the BLESSED SACRAMENT, to undertake the education of African-American youth. Accordingly, in 1915 the sisters opened Xavier High School and ten years later opened Xavier College, the oldest continuing African-American Catholic university in the United States. In 1911 the BROTHERS OF CHRISTIAN SCHOOLS purchased St. Paul's College, Covington, from the Benedictine Fathers. In 1912 the Ursulines, under the supervision of their chaplain, François Racine, moved from their third convent building to a new site on State Street where ten years later, the national SHRINE of Our Lady of Prompt Succor was erected.

Early in his administration, Blenk strengthened lay groups. He organized the state board of Holy Name Societies in 1906, the Louisiana State Federation of Catholic Societies in 1909, and the Federation of Catholic Societies of Women of Louisiana. He promoted the Catholic Order of Foresters, the KNIGHTS OF CO-LUMBUS, and the KNIGHTS OF PETER CLAVER.

The growth of the population in the archdiocese, especially in Acadian (Cajun) southwest Louisiana, made a division expedient. Shortly before Archbishop John William Shaw (1863–1934) was promoted to the New Orleans see on January 11, 1918, Pope BENEDICT XV established the Diocese of LAFAYETTE, comprising western Louisiana. He also appointed Jules Benjamin Jeanmard (1879–1957) administrator of the archdiocese following the death of Blenk on April 15, 1917. Jeanmard became the first native Louisianian to be raised to the episcopate, its founding bishop.

In New Orleans Archbishop Shaw invited the OB-LATES OF MARY IMMACULATE, with whom he had worked closely in San Antonio, Texas, to administer St. Louis Cathedral and take charge of the churches and missions in Livingston parish. In 1919 the Sisters of Charity of the INCARNATE WORD from San Antonio came to teach at St. Francis de Sales parochial school. In 1920 Archbishop Shaw, with his chancellor, August J. Bruening, laid plans for a financial campaign to erect a major seminary. In September 1923 the Notre Dame Seminary opened and was staffed by the Marist Fathers. That same year the Sisters of St. Francis of Calais opened Our Lady of the Lake Hospital in Baton Rouge. Franciscan Fathers returned to the archdiocese on July 21, 1925, to take charge of the newly established parish of St. Mary of the Angels in the city and the missions of the Lower Coast. The Sisters of the Holy Ghost and Mary Immaculate arrived from San Antonio in September 1926 to teach the African-American children of St. Luke's School in Thibodaux. Shaw encouraged the endeavors of Catharine Bostick and Zoé Grouchy to establish the Eucharistic Missionaries of St. Dominic, an organization that provided religious instruction to children in public schools and offered social relief work. In 1928 the Society of the DIVINE WORD took over the mission stations along the lower Mississippi River. In 1931 the Jesuits purchased the old Jefferson College in Convent and converted it into Manresa House for laymen's retreats.

Father (later Bishop) Maurice Schexnayder (1895–1981) began Newman Club work in 1929 at Louisiana State University, one-third of whose student body was Catholic. Monsignor Peter M. H. Wynhoven established (1925) Hope Haven for orphaned and abandoned boys, later placed under the direction of the Salesian Fathers of St. John Bosco. Opposite Hope Haven, Madonna Manor for small boys replaced St. Mary's and St. Joseph's Orphanages. Wynhoven also reorganized the social services of the archdiocese under Associated Catholic Charities in 1924. In 1922 Shaw convoked the sixth synod, the first in thirty-three years. In 1932 he launched the official diocesan paper, the *Catholic Action*

of the South, and acted as first editor in chief. It replaced the *Morning Star*, published between 1878 and 1930. Shaw's last years were burdened by the Depression of the 1930s. Some archdiocesan funds were frozen in local banks, and several parishes struggled to meet the high interest due on monies borrowed during the 1920s. Nevertheless, thirty-three new parishes opened between 1919 and 1934. After a brief illness Shaw died on November 2, 1934, and Jean Marius Laval (1854–1937), auxiliary to Blenk, became administrator.

In 1935 Joseph Francis RUMMEL of Omaha, Nebraska, was transferred to the Archdiocese of NEW ORLEANS as thirteenth ordinary and ninth archbishop. Rummel accelerated existing movements; proposed and promoted new projects; sponsored the eighth National Eucharistic Congress in 1938, the largest public demonstration of Catholic faith ever seen in the city to that time; and endorsed numerous regional and national conventions. He also issued authoritative statements on social problems, such as the 1953 letter, "Blessed are the Peacemakers," which deplored racism. Two years later he ordered the planned desegregation of Catholic schools in the archdiocese. Rummel also launched a series of successful financial campaigns, insisted on a sound fiscal policy for each parish and institution, reorganized and expanded archdiocesan administration, and promptly implemented decrees of the Holy See.

Post–World War II Developments. When Rummel was appointed to New Orleans, the Catholic population was estimated at 361,882, out of a total population of nearly one million. At that time, there were 132 resident parishes, ninety-seven missions, and 451 secular and religious priests. By 1960 the entire population (Catholic and non-Catholic) had increased by about sixty-six percent. The number of parishes had grown by forty percent, and the number of priests had increased by twenty-five percent. Insufficient vocations to the priesthood prevented the archbishop from establishing more parishes, although a growing population brought an increased demand for churches, schools, and other institutions, especially in suburban areas. Nevertheless, well over $100 million worth of building contracts were signed, the majority after World War II, and at least half were for schools, convents, and school-allied buildings. The Youth Progress Program was launched on January 21, 1945, for the expansion of high schools for boys, recreational facilities, and a boy's protectory. Twelve years later, the oversubscribed Diocesan Campaign of Progress made possible the construction of a $2 million seminary at St. Benedict to accommodate 400 students, a new central administration (chancery) building, four centers for Newman Clubs at state and private colleges and universities, and a projected home for the aged. Between these two campaigns, carried out by volunteer laymen under the guidance of their pastors, parishes of the archdiocese memorialized Rummel's golden jubilee as a priest in 1952 by contributing $1 million for the erection of St. Joseph Hall of Philosophy, which raised the capacity of Notre Dame Seminary to 150.

In twenty-five years the Catholic school population more than doubled, reaching 90,546 in 1961. Contributions to missions totaled $3.6 million from 1935 to 1960. Under the leadership of Monsignor Edward C. J. Prendergast, Father (later Bishop) Robert E. Tracy (1909–1980), and (after 1945) Monsignor (later Bishop) Gerard L. Frey (1914–2007), the CONFRATERNITY OF CHRISTIAN DOCTRINE (CCD) became one of the most dynamic forces in the archdiocese, as did the Cana and pre-Cana conferences to which Rummel gave impetus in 1957.

New communities of men entering the archdiocese were Missionaries of Our Lady of LA SALETTE (1938), Maryknoll Fathers (1944), and Brothers of the Good Shepherd (1955). Communities of women included the Religious of the PRESENTATION OF THE BLESSED VIRGIN MARY (1949), Poor Sisters of St. Francis Seraph of the Perpetual Adoration (1951), Daughters of Jesus (1952), Oblate Sisters of Providence (1958), and Religious of Our Lady of the Retreat in the Cenacle (1958), who opened Maria Immaculata Retreat House. Rummel organized the Archdiocesan Council of Catholic Men, later the Archdiocesan Union of Holy Name Societies. The Archdiocesan Council of Catholic Women was even more successful as the CATHOLIC DAUGHTERS OF THE AMERICAS, and the St. Margaret's Daughters augmented their courts and circles. Organizations established since 1935 included Serra Clubs, Catholic Committees for Boy and Girl Scouts, Catholic Youth Organizations, Catholic Physicians and Nurses Guilds, Ozanam Inn, and St. Vincent de Paul Store.

In addition to the curial posts, diocesan administration included an appreciably expanded ecclesiastical tribunal; commissions for sacred music, ecclesiastical ART, and the LITURGY; a diocesan building commission, appointed at the time of the seventh diocesan synod in 1949; a Catholic Bureau of Information; directors for the Legion of Decency; the deaf apostolate and hospitals; and a Catholic Council on Human Relations, an organization of Catholic laymen designed to promote justice and CHARITY, which held its first meeting in March 1961.

Through the years, Rummel was a staunch champion of the underprivileged and a promoter of SOCIAL JUSTICE. He opposed right-to-work bills introduced in the state legislature during the sessions of 1948 and 1954; led a movement to maintain reasonable rent controls after World War II; accepted African-American applicants at both minor and major seminaries; racially integrated the archdiocesan school board, the Councils of Catholic Men and Women, the Sodalities, and the Holy Name Societies; recommended African-American laypersons for papal honors; and spoke out vehemently against segregation, upholding the Supreme Court decision of May 17, 1954, which ruled segregation in public schools unconstitutional. Regrettably, his stand on these socio-moral issues proved unpopular among many Catholic laymen.

On August 14, 1961, Pope JOHN XXIII (pope 1958–1963) named Bishop John P. CODY of Kansas City-St. Joseph, Missouri, coadjutor archbishop with right of succession and erected the Diocese of BATON ROUGE. He also appointed Robert E. Tracy, formerly auxiliary of Lafayette, its first bishop. The Louisiana bishops departed for Rome in 1962 to attend the Second Vatican Council. Tracy, who later published his well-received council diary, formed his diocese according to the norms of the council, thereby, making Baton Rouge a model for other dioceses in establishing post–conciliar administrative structure and consultative process. He placed particular emphasis on liturgical renewal and modern catechetical efforts.

On the sixtieth anniversary of his ordination to the priesthood, May 24, 1962, Archbishop Rummel announced that Archbishop Cody had been appointed apostolic administrator of New Orleans. Cody succeeded to the see at Rummel's death on November 8, 1964. Archbishop Cody was transferred to Chicago, Illinois, on June 16, 1965, and his successor, Philip M. Hannan (1913–), auxiliary bishop of Washington, D.C., was installed in New Orleans on October 13. Prior to this time, Hannan had been helping the victims of the devastating Hurricane Betsy. The following year, Harold R. Perry (1916–1991), the first African-American bishop since 1875, was consecrated as New Orleans auxiliary on January 6.

During Hannan's administration the Vatican Pavilion at the New Orleans World Exposition was erected in 1984. The treasures of Catholic art assembled in the pavilion drew hundreds of thousands of visitors to the site. Three years later New Orleans received its first visit by a reigning PONTIFF. From September 11 to September 13, 1987, Pope JOHN PAUL II made a pastoral visit to New Orleans, highlighted by a PRAYER service in the cathedral, a visit with the young people of the area at the Superdome, a Mass on the grounds of the University of New Orleans, and an address on education at Xavier University. On December 13, 1988, Archbishop Hannan announced that his resignation had been accepted by the Holy See. His twenty-four years as ordinary was marked by an impressive increase in social services rendered by the archdiocese. During his tenure three new diocese were created: Houma-Thibodaux (1977) was carved out of the Archdiocese of New

Blessing of the Fleet. *Father John Ryan (2nd-R) of Saint Anthony's Catholic Church tosses holy water on a passing shrimp boat during the annual "Blessing of the Fleet" before the start of shrimp season April 30, 2006 in Lafitte, Louisiana.* **MARIO TAMA/GETTY IMAGES**

Orleans with Bishop Warren Boudreaux (1918–1997) as its founding ordinary. The Diocese of Lake Charles was created from the Diocese of Lafayette (1980) with Bishop Jude Speyrer (1929–) as ordinary. In 1986 the Diocese of Alexandria-Shreveport was divided. Bishop William B. Friend (1931–) became the first bishop of the new Diocese of Shreveport. On April 19, 1986, Albany native Harry J. Flynn (1933–) was appointed coadjutor bishop of Lafayette to Bishop Gerard L. Frey. On June 16, 1986, New Orleans native John C. Favalora (1935–) was appointed ninth bishop of Alexandria. Three years later on March 14, 1989, Favalora was appointed third bishop of St. Petersburg, Florida, and, later that year, Frey retired as bishop of Lafayette (May 13th), at which point Flynn automatically became the fourth bishop of that diocese. Favalora was replaced as bishop of Alexandria when Sam G. Jacobs (1938–) was appointed tenth bishop of that see on July 1, 1989.

On February 14, 1989, Philadelphia native, Francis Bible Schulte (1926–), was installed as twelfth archbishop of New Orleans after serving as bishop of Wheeling-Charleston, West Viginia. Alfred C. Hughes (1932–), appointed in 1993 fourth bishop of Baton Rouge to replace Stanley J. Ott (1927–1992), who had died on November 28, 1992, was named coadjutor with right of succession to Archbishop Schulte on February 16, 2001.

The founding Bishop of Houma-Thibodeaux, Warren L. Boudreaux, retired on December 29, 1992, and was succeeded by Lafayette native C. Michael Jarrell (1940–), who received ordination as the second Bishop of Houma-Thibodeaux on March 4, 1993. After eight years in Lafayette, on February 24, 1994, Flynn was named coadjutor archbishop of St. Paul-Minneapolis and was replaced when St. Louis native Edward J. O'Donnell (1931–) was appointed fifth bishop of Lafayette on November 8, 1994.

The founding bishop of Lake Charles, Jude Speyrer, resigned on December 12, 2000, and was replaced on February 22, 2001, by Edward K. Braxton (1944–), who had served as auxiliary bishop of St. Louis, Missouri, since 1995. In the same month, on February 16, 2001, Hughes moved from Baton Rouge when he was appointed coadjutor archbishop of New Orleans; he was replaced later the same year (December 15) by Robert W. Muench (1942–), bishop of Covington, Kentucky since 1996, and previously auxiliary bishop of New Orleans from 1990 to 1996.

Hughes succeeded to New Orleans as its thirteenth archbishop on January 3, 2002, when Francis B. Schulte retired. O'Donnell resigned after eight years as bishop of Lafayette on November 8 of the same year; he was replaced by Lafayette native Jarrell, who had served as bishop of Houma-Thibodeaux since 1992. On August 1, 2003, Jarrell was succeeded by Jacobs, bishop of Alexandria since 1989. Jacobs was succeeded in Alexandria on November 4, 2004, by Mississippi native Ronald P. Herzog (1942–).

In 2005 Lake Charles began a two year period with no bishop, when Braxton was made Bishop of Belleville, Illinois, on March 15, and was not replaced until Lafayette native Glen J. Provost (1949–) was appointed third bishop of Lake Charles on March 6, 2007. In the interim southern Louisiana and Mississippi were devastated by Hurricanes Katrina on August 29, 2005, and Rita on September 24, 2005, which together took 1,843 lives. On December 20, 2006, the founding bishop of Shreveport, William B. Friend, retired after serving in that office since 1986.

Catholic Population. The history of slavery accounts for the large number of African-American Catholics in south Louisiana, with New Orleans having the highest number of African-American Catholics in the United States. The slave trade remained brisk in New Orleans from its founding until the Civil War. Most slave owners in Louisiana were Catholic and were bound by the prescriptions of the *Code Noir*, which demanded that slaves be baptized and instructed in the Catholic religion. The economy of the sugar plantations in South Louisiana depended on slave labor up to the time of the Emancipation Proclamation. No separate churches existed for African Americans until the late nineteenth century. The first one, St. Katherine's, was established in New Orleans in 1895. In 1897 Father Pierre LeBeau began the Josephite apostolate in Louisiana, and since then, more than 100 separate African-American churches and chapels have been established in the state, most of which are administered by religious communities, most notably the Society of the Divine Word and the JOSEPHITES.

National parishes were established in New Orleans shortly after immigrants from France and Germany arrived in the early 1800s, from Ireland in the mid-1800s, from Italy toward the close of the century, and from Lebanon at the beginning of the twentieth. The fall of Saigon in 1975 resulted in the emigration of many Catholic Vietnamese refugees to Louisiana, where they found a hospitable climate and the opportunity to continue working in the fishing industry. Louisiana has the third largest concentration of Vietnamese Catholics, after California and Texas. Since the late 1960s Hispanic Catholics from Mexico, Central and South America, and the Caribbean have reintroduced Spanish settlement to the state, but in much smaller numbers than in neighboring states. The majority of the diocesan clergy in Louisiana are native born and locally educated, in contrast with the situation a few generations earlier, when bishops depended on European and Canadian priests to staff parishes. Just under half of the clergy in the state belong to religious communities, many are from India, Africa, and Asia.

Educational Institutions. The Church in Louisiana has had a stake in education since the 1700s. Presently, New Orleans has one Catholic university and two colleges— XAVIER UNIVERSITY OF LOUISIANA, Holy Cross Col-

lege, and Our Lady of the Lake College in Baton Rouge. Catholic secondary and elementary schools enroll about twenty-two percent of all children in the state from pre-kindergarten to twelfth grade. Slightly less than half of Catholic school-age children are in Catholic institutions. The number of students enrolled at Catholic schools remains constant. The Confraternity of Christian Doctrine (CCD) is responsible for the religious instruction of Catholic children in public and nonsectarian private schools. Each diocese has its own superintendent of schools and its own CCD director.

SEE ALSO AFRICAN AMERICAN CATHOLICS IN THE UNITED STATES (HISTORY OF); ALABAMA, CATHOLIC CHURCH IN; ALEXANDRIA, DIOCESE OF; AMERICAN FEDERATION OF CATHOLIC SOCIETIES; ARKANSAS, CATHOLIC CHURCH IN; BALTIMORE, ARCHDIOCESE OF; BATON ROUGE, DIOCESE OF; CARDINAL NEWMAN SOCIETY; CATHOLIC CHARITIES USA; CATHOLIC YOUTH ORGANIZATION; CENACLE, RELIGIOUS OF THE; EUCHARISTIC CONGRESSES; MARYKNOLL FATHERS AND BROTHERS; MISSISSIPPI, CATHOLIC CHURCH IN; NATIONAL COUNCIL OF CATHOLIC MEN (NCCM); NATIONAL COUNCIL OF CATHOLIC WOMEN (NCCW); OKLAHOMA, CATHOLIC CHURCH IN; POOR CLARES; SACRED HEART BROTHERS; SERRA INTERNATIONAL; SLAVERY, III (HISTORY OF); TE DEUM; TEXAS, CATHOLIC CHURCH IN; TRUSTEEISM; VATICAN COUNCIL I; VATICAN COUNCIL II.

BIBLIOGRAPHY

Additional information can be found in the archives of the Archdiocese of New Orleans, Diocese of Alexandria, Diocese of Baton Rouge, Diocese of Lafayette, Diocese of Shreveport, and St. Louis Cathedral, New Orleans.

Archdiocese of New Orleans Official Web site, available from http://www.arch-no.org/ (accessed September 30, 2008).

Roger Baudier, *The Catholic Church in Louisiana* (New Orleans 1939).

Henry Edward Chambers, *A History of Louisiana: Wilderness, Colony, Province, Territory, State, People*, vol.1 (Chicago 1925)

Celestin M. Chambon, *In and Around the Old St. Louis Cathedral of New Orleans* (New Orleans 1908).

Glenn R. Conrad, ed., *Cross, Crozier, and Crucible: A Volume Celebrating the Bicentennial of a Catholic Diocese in Louisiana* (New Orleans 1993).

Edwin Adams Davis, *Louisiana, the Pelican State* (Baton Rouge, LA 1959).

Diocese of Alexandria Official Web site, available from http://www.diocesealex.org/ (accessed September 30, 2008).

Diocese of Baton Rouge Official Web site, available from http://www.diobr.org/ (accessed September 30, 2008).

Diocese of Lafayette Official Web site, available from http://www.dol-louisiana.org/ (accessed September 30, 2008).

Diocese of Shreveport Official Web site, available from http://www.dioshpt.org/ (accessed September 30, 2008).

Charles L Dufour, ed., *St. Patrick's of New Orleans, 1883–1958: Commemorative Essays for the 125th Anniversary* (New Orleans 1958).

Albert E. Fossier, *New Orleans: The Glamour Period, 1800–1840* (New Orleans 1957).

Marcel Giraud, *Histoire de la Louisiane Française*, vol. 1, Le Regne de Louis XIV,1698–1715; vol. 2, Annes de Transition, 1715–1717 (Paris 1953–1958).

P. J. Kennedy And Sons, *The Official Catholic Directory* (Providence, NJ 2001).

E. Lauvriere, *Histoire de la Louisiane Francaise, 1673–1939* (Paris 1940).

Louisiana Digest, 1809 to Date (St. Paul, MN 1936–).

The St. Louis Cathedral, New Orleans Official Web site, available from http://stlouiscathedral.org/index.htm/ (accessed September 30, 2008).

Thomas Lynn Smith and Homer L. Hitt, *People of Louisiana* (Baton Rouge, LA 1952).

The Official Catholic Directory, 2008 (New Providence, N.J. 2008)

Msgr. Henry Charles Bezou
Archdiocesan Superintendent of Schools
New Orleans, La.

Rev. Mitchell G. Guidry
Pastor, Sacred Heart Church
Baldwin, La.

Rev. Mark S. Raphael
Professor of Church History
Notre Dame Seminary (2009)

LOUISVILLE, ARCHDIOCESE OF

The Archdiocese of Louisville (*Ludovicopolitana*), comprising twenty-four counties in central Kentucky, is the metropolitan see of the states of Kentucky and Tennessee. The Province of Louisville includes the suffragan sees of Covington, Owensboro, and Lexington in Kentucky and the sees of Nashville, Memphis, and Knoxville in Tennessee. Originally created as the Diocese of Bardstown by PIUS VII on April 8, 1808, the see was transferred to Louisville on February 13, 1841, and created an ARCHDIOCESE on December 10, 1937.

When the Diocese of Bardstown transferred its see city to the growing municipality of Louisville in 1841, Benedict Joseph FLAGET (1763–1850), the first Bishop of the West, found three churches in his new hometown: one for English-speaking, one for German, and one for French. As Germans and Irish increased rapidly in numbers in the area, anti–immigrant and anti–Catholic feelings exploded in the Bloody Monday Riots of August 6, 1855, when more than twenty were killed in mob action.

The earlier history of the city had been (and its subsequent history would be) decidedly more ecumenical. When Louisville's first congregation, Saint Louis, (forerunner to today's CATHEDRAL parish) built its primal church in 1811, Protestants made up over half of the contributors. The cornerstone ceremony for the second church building in 1830 was hosted by a Presbyterian congregation. The first resident priest of the parish was Philip Hosten, a Flemish native who died quite young in 1821 as "a victim of his zeal" as his Louisville tombstone reports. He had been nursing his people through the cholera epidemic and succumbed to the disease.

In the years before the Civil War, several traditional aspects of Catholic culture came to the city: a newspaper, *The Catholic Advocate*; the Jesuit Fathers, to found a short-lived school; the XAVERIAN BROTHERS, to make their first American foundation; a large congregation of teaching Ursuline Sisters from Germany; and the Sisters of the Good Shepherd from France, to begin their social works ministry.

Spalding. Flaget was succeeded by his coadjutor, Martin J. SPALDING. Three years after Spalding became the second BISHOP of Louisville in 1850, the Diocese of COVINGTON was erected by separating the eastern part of Kentucky from Louisville. While in Europe that year, Spalding secured from Belgium several priests and a community of Xaverian Brothers, who in 1854 opened a school in Louisville. That year the Saint Vincent DePaul Society was established in Louisville. Spalding introduced the Ursuline nuns in 1858 and the CHRISTIAN BROTHERS in 1860; the FRANCISCANS and the SCHOOL SISTERS OF NOTRE DAME also joined the DIOCESE at his invitation. In his sixteen years as bishop, eight new churches were built in Louisville and twenty-two new parishes erected elsewhere, making a total of eighty-five parishes in the diocese. On May 1, 1858, the *Catholic Guardian* began publication; it suspended publication in July 1862 because of the Civil War. The war years were characterized by a weakening of Know Nothing and other anti–Catholic movements, especially after the sisters of the diocese became active in nursing the soldiers. In 1862 the army closed Saint Joseph College to use the building; Saint Thomas Seminary barely managed to remain open. The war caused an interruption of all progress.

Lavialle. On June 9, 1864, Spalding was transferred to the see of Baltimore; his brother and vicar-general, Benedict J. Spalding, was made administrator until the third bishop, French-born Peter Joseph Lavialle (1819–1867), was consecrated September 24, 1868. The new bishop had been ordained to the priesthood in 1844 and then served successively as secretary to Flaget, superior of the diocesan seminary (1849–1856), and president of Saint Mary's College (1856–1865). During his brief episcopacy, the diocese started six new churches and purchased ground for Louis Cemetery, and a group of Franciscan sisters, formed under the direction of the TRAPPISTS, opened a school at Mount Olivet near Gethsemani. Failing health caused Lavialle's retirement to Nazareth where he died, May 11, 1867; he was buried beside Flaget in the crypt of the cathedral.

McCloskey. On March 3, 1868, William George MC-CLOSKEY, rector of the American College in ROME, was appointed to the vacancy in Louisville and consecrated in Rome May 24, 1868. Four months later, he arrived in his see city for a turbulent episcopate of forty-one years. His first major dispute was with Spalding over the terms of the will of Spalding's brother. Shortly thereafter, some of the older priests had some difficulty with their bishop and turned to Spalding for aid. During these years, many priests left the diocese, led by the bishop's secretary and the chancellor, John Lancaster SPALDING (1840–1916), nephew of bishop Martin John Spalding and later first bishop of Peoria. Moreover, many religious establishments were the objects of episcopal disfavor. McCloskey first suppressed Saint Mary's College. As early as 1869 the ABBOT of Gethsemani complained that the bishop was hostile to the Trappists. In 1898 the School Sisters of Notre Dame withdrew from the diocese, and the Sisters of Saint Francis from Mount Olivet left for Clinton, Iowa, because of trouble with the bishop. Nor were the DOMINICAN SISTERS, the SISTERS OF MERCY, the Ursuline nuns, the SISTERS OF LORETTO, and the men's orders left unvexed.

Despite these difficulties, religious advancement marked the four decades of McCloskey's administration. Six new religious orders came into the diocese: Carmelite Fathers, RESURRECTIONISTS, the Society of Saint Joseph for Foreign Missions, the PASSIONISTS, the Sisters of Mercy, and the LITTLE SISTERS OF THE POOR. In 1870 the seminary was moved from Saint Thomas to a location known as Preston Park in Louisville. It was closed in 1888, reopened in 1902, and closed again at McCloskey's death. An official diocesan organ, the *Record*, was established in February 1879. In the next decade, about fifty priests and twenty-five churches were added to the diocese and similar progress marked the next ten years. Between 1900 and 1909, the year of McCloskey's death, fourteen churches were established or dedicated in Louisville alone, and a like number elsewhere. By 1909 the Catholics of the diocese had increased to 155,000, the number of priests to 201, and there were almost 100 new churches.

O'Donaghue. Denis O'Donaghue, auxiliary bishop of Indianapolis, Indiana, was transferred to Louisville on February 7, 1910, and a month later was enthroned. A year later, the Clerical Aid Society was organized, the orphan boys home was moved from Saint Thomas to Louisville, and the Catholic Orphans Society was organized. Saint Joseph's College was reopened under the Xaverian Brothers. Four new parishes were organized; twenty-one churches built to replace older or smaller ones; nine new schools were established in the city; and eighteen schools were built in country parishes. O'Donaghue's failing health caused the, HOLY SEE to appoint an apostolic administrator (1921) and a coadjutor (1923). The next year O'Donoghue resigned and was given the TITULAR SEE of Lebedus. He died November 7, 1925, and was buried in Saint Louis Cemetery.

The Louisville see was elevated to the status of an archdiocese by the action of Pope PIUS XI on December 10, 1937. The first archbishop was John A. Floersh (1886–1969), noted both for his piety and business acumen. In his administration, the amazing post–World War II building boom occurred, and new institutions and parishes grew rapidly throughout the archdiocese.

Floersh. John A. Floersh, born October 5, 1886, in Nashville, Tennessee, was ordained June 10, 1911, in Saint John Lateran, Rome. After a year in Nashville parishes, he was called to Washington, D.C. to act as secretary at the apostolic delegation. On February 6, 1923, he was named coadjutor of Louisville and was consecrated in Rome on April 8, 1923, succeeding to the see on July 26, 1924. In December 1937, Louisville was made a metropolitan see with Floersh as its first archbishop. He consecrated his chancellor, Francis R. Cotton, on February 23, 1938, as first bishop of Owensboro. Floersh instituted the Catholic School Board and the Office of Catholic Charities. He brought the Carmelite nuns to Louisville and founded several new high schools as well as Bellarmine College, with Monsignor Alfred Horrigan as first president.

For health reasons, Archbishop Floersh attended only the first session of the Second Vatican Council in 1962, while his auxiliary bishop, Charles Garrett Maloney (consecrated on February 2, 1955), was in attendance at all four. Mary Luke Tobin (1908–2006), at the time president of the Sisters of Loretto, was the only American woman to have official status (auditor) at the conciliar sessions. She would remain a major voice in American Catholicism even into the next century. Another figure from the archdiocese, Passionist Father Carroll STUHLMUELLER, was a *peritus* in the years of the Council. Of all the residents of the archdiocese in those years, the most internationally known was Father Louis (Thomas MERTON), MONK of the Abbey of GETHSEMANI. Less than two years after the Council's close, on March 1, 1967, Archbishop Floersh resigned his see. He died June 11, 1968.

McDonough. Thomas Joseph McDonough (born in Philadelphia in 1911) was installed as the second

Cathedral of the Assumption, Louisville, Ken. *Construction was completed on this cathedral in 1852.* © **DAVID DAVIS PHOTOPRODUCTIONS / ALAMY**

archbishop of Louisville on May 2, 1967. His early pastoral letters signaled his encouragement of those engaged in addressing racism, POVERTY, and other social evils. He noted in 1967 (echoing a Merton title) that the Church and the world could not be "disinterested bystanders" amid social brokenness.

McDonough's tenure helped to initiate not only social, but also ecclesiastical and liturgical change, in the light of the Second Vatican Council. He initiated the restored office of permanent DEACON in the archdiocese beginning in 1976. Sometimes the changes of the era were painful—such as the decision to close down the long tradition of the annual Corpus Christi procession involving, in some years, more than 50,000 people at the famed Louisville Churchill Downs. Dwindling attendance caused its suspension after the 1976 event. McDonough announced his resignation in the autumn of 1981, exiting office with the words: "A good bishop today needs big ears and a small mouth" (Duerr 1982). He died on August 4, 1998.

Kelly. Dominican Thomas Cajetan Kelly (born July 14, 1931) had seen long service with the National Conference of Catholic Bishops in Washington before he was installed as the third archbishop of Louisville on February 18, 1982. Among his first tasks was leading diocesan leaders in the articulation of a mission statement. He also oversaw the restoration of the historic downtown Cathedral of the Assumption through the activity of an innovative, inter-faith Cathedral Heritage Foundation (begun in 1985). The Cathedral was renewed not only architecturally but as a lively inner-city parish where LITURGY, the arts, ecumenical understanding, and social service—especially to the urban poor—flourish. Visitors to the venerable church have included Dorothy DAY, Thomas Merton, Joseph Cardinal BERNARDIN, Jesuit Karl RAHNER, historian Martin MARTY, Muhammad Ali, the Dalai Lama, and Nobel Laureate Jewish scholar Elie Wiesel.

Kelly encouraged and supported individuals with special leadership skills. In the last third of the twentieth century, no fewer than nine clerics, laity, and religious of the archdiocese held national presidencies in professional Catholic groups. One, Father Nick Rice, was elected to three separate leadership roles at the national level. At home, Renew and other programs enhanced parochial and personal spiritual life.

In 1988 the creation of the new Diocese of LEXINGTON reduced the geographical area of the Louisville archdiocese to twenty-four counties in central Kentucky. In addition to metropolitan Louisville and the Holy Land counties, this included creative mission programs in southern portions of the diocese where Catholics are few in number. In 2000 the archdiocese had a Catholic population of some 197,000 (about 16% of the total population), served by 124 parishes and missions (*The Official Catholic Directory* 2000, p. 665).

Strategic and parish planning was an important theme from 1995 to 2005 as the archdiocese addressed rapid changes in the areas of demographics, mission, finances, and personnel. From 1989 to 2002, the archdiocese wrote five strategic plans and in 1995 and 2006 tackled the difficult task of parish reorganization in an effort to strengthen mission and ministries to respond to changing demographics and declining numbers of ordained priests. These reorganizations

resulted in the closing or merger of several parishes in areas of declining growth and most recently the creation or expansion of parishes in areas of rapid growth. At the same time several Catholic schools merged or closed in response to demographic changes and financial realities. These planning efforts also led to new initiatives in the areas of social services, evangelization, lay ministry, multicultural ministry, pastoral care, and education/formation.

Beginning in 2002 the archdiocese was sued by victims of sexual abuse by priests and church employees with claims dating back to the 1950s. This crisis climaxed in 2003 when the archdiocese paid $25.7 million to 243 plaintiffs. At this time, the archdiocese appointed a victim assistance coordinator, revised its sexual abuse policies to conform to the United States Conference of Catholic Bishops' Charter for the Protection of Children and Young People, and established a safe environment training program that, to date, has trained more than 14,000 individuals.

In 2007 Archbishop Kelly celebrated twenty-five years as archbishop of Louisville after submitting his resignation to the Holy See on his seventy-fifth birthday in July 2006. His resignation was accepted on June 12, 2007, with the appointment of Joseph E. Kurtz, D.D., bishop of Knoxville, as the ninth bishop of the Archdiocese of Louisville.

Kurtz. As the Archdiocese of Louisville prepared to celebrate its bicentennial in 2008, Archbishop Joseph E. Kurtz, D.D., was installed as archbishop of Louisville on August 15, 2007. Born on August 18, 1946, in Mahanoy City, Pennsylvania, Kurtz served for twenty-seven years in the Diocese of Allentown, Pennsylvania, in charge of social services, diocesan administration, and parish ministry before being appointed as Bishop of Knoxville, Tennessee, in 1999. In November of 2007 Kurtz was elected treasurer of the UNITED STATES CONFERENCE OF CATHOLIC BISHOPS, while he continued to serve on several bishops' committees, most notably the Bishops' Committee on Marriage and Family and the Bishops' Committee for Pro-Life Activities. At the time of Archbishop Kurtz's appointment, the Archdiocese of Louisville hosted a population of 196,000 (about 17% of the total population) with 121 parishes and missions (*The Official Catholic Directory* 2007, p. 717).

SEE ALSO APOSTOLIC DELEGATION IN THE U.S.; BISHOP, AUXILIARY; CARMELITES; CATHOLIC CHARITIES USA; JESUITS; KENTUCKY, CATHOLIC CHURCH IN; KNOW-NOTHINGISM; KNOXVILLE, DIOCESE OF; LEXINGTON, DIOCESE OF; NORTH AMERICAN COLLEGE; OWENSBORO, DIOCESE OF; PASSIONISTS; SEX ABUSE CRISIS;

S_T_. V_INCENT_ _DE_ P_AUL_, S_OCIETY OF_; T_ENNESSEE_, C_ATHOLIC_ C_HURCH IN_; U_RSULINES_; V_ATICAN_ C_OUNCIL_ II.

BIBLIOGRAPHY

The Archdiocese of Louisville Official Web site, available from: http://www.archlou.org (accessed October 30, 2008).

Clyde F. Crews, *An American Holy Land* (Wilmington, Del. 1987).

Joseph Duerr, "An Era of Change: The 15–Year Louisville Pastorate of Archbishop Thomas J. McDonough," *The Record* February 4, 1982.

Columba Fox, *The Life of the Right Reverend John Baptist Mary David, 1761–1841* (New York 1925).

Mary Ramona Mattingly, *The Catholic Church on the Kentucky Frontier, 1785–1812* (Washington, D.C. 1936).

Victor Francis O'Daniel, *A Light of the Church in Kentucky ... Samuel Thomas Wilson, O.P.* (Washington, D.C. 1932).

The Official Catholic Directory, (New Providence, N.J. 2000, 2007).

J. Herman Schauinger, *Cathedrals in the Wilderness* (Milwaukee, Wisc. 1952).

Martin J. Spalding, *Sketches of the Early Catholic Missions of Kentucky, 1787–1827* (Louisville, Ky. 1844).

Ben J. Webb, *The Centenary of Catholicity in Kentucky* (Louisville, Ky. 1884).

Joseph H. Schauinger
Professor of History
College of St. Thomas, St. Paul, Minn.

Rev. Clyde F. Crews OFMConv
Professor of Theology
Bellarmine University, Louisville, Ky.

Cecelia H. Price
Chief Communications Officer
Archdiocese of Louisville (2009)

M

MAGISTERIUM, ASSENT TO THE

The Magisterium is the teaching authority of the Catholic Church. It resides in the Roman PONTIFF and the college of bishops as legitimate successors to St. PETER and the APOSTLES OF JESUS (*Lumen gentium*, 18–25). The word *magisterium* derives from the Latin word *magister* (teacher, master). It finds its scriptural warrant in CHRIST's great commission to the DISCIPLES to teach in his name (Mt 28:20). This teaching authority was exercised very early at the assembly of the apostles and the presbyters in JERUSALEM to determine whether Gentile converts needed to observe the Jewish cultic law (Acts 15:6–29). Assent to magisterial teaching pertains to pronouncements on FAITH AND MORALS. Disciplinary rulings and the liturgical laws of the Church require obedience, a virtue related to but distinct from the assent given to judgments on faith and morals (Sullivan 1983, p. 162).

Early Writings. Letters by popes, such as CLEMENT I (c. AD 96; Denzinger-Hünermann, 101), CORNELIUS (ca. AD 251; Denzinger-Hünermann, 108) and STEPHEN I (c. AD 256; Denzinger-Hünermann, 110) testify to the early exercise of the papal Magisterium in the Church. Likewise, provincial councils—such as those held at Elvira (c. AD 300–303) and Arles (c. 314)—show that groups of bishops assumed authority to pronounce on disciplinary and doctrinal issues (Denzinger-Hünermann, nos. 117–123). At ecumenical councils (e.g., Nicea I, AD 325, and Ephesus I, AD 431), the bishops, in communion with the patriarchs and the Roman Pontiff, assumed authority to teach for the universal Church.

In the early Christian centuries, doctrinal rulings of popes and councils were sometimes challenged, but from a Catholic perspective, teachings of ecumenical councils and the popes were authoritative for the entire Church. The question of levels of assent to magisterial teaching developed gradually within Catholic history. Because the decisions of some synods, such as the so-called Robber Council of EPHESUS, were overturned, the question emerged as to what constituted clear magisterial authority. A Communion with the HOLY SEE of ROME came to be seen as a necessary requirement for universal magisterial authority (cf. Denzinger-Hünermann, nos. 306, 350–351, 365). In the late MIDDLE AGES, however, the Conciliarists placed the authority of a general council over that of the POPE. This ECCLESIOLOGY, however, was rejected at the Council of FLORENCE in 1439 (Denzinger-Hünermann, 1307).

Martin LUTHER upheld the Holy Scripture as the ultimate norm, and he directly challenged the power of the pope and the Church to establish articles of faith and morals (Denzinger-Hünermann, 1477). The Council of TRENT, in 1546, upheld the authority of the Church to judge the "true meaning and interpretation of Holy Scripture" (Denzinger-Hünermann, 1507).

After Trent, it was assumed that faithful Catholics would give firm assent to all magisterial teachings, especially those of the Roman Pontiff. Some Jansenists, however, claimed that it was necessary to give only exterior, not interior, assent to certain magisterial judgments. Pope CLEMENT XI responded with his 1705 constitution, *Vineam Domini Sabaoth*, and he ruled that the previously condemned Jansenist propositions must be rejected as heretical "not only in the mouth but also in the heart" (*non ore solum, sed et corde*; Denzinger-Hünermann, 2390).

Vatican Council I and II. The definition of papal INFALLIBILITY at VATICAN COUNCIL I in 1870 laid out specific requirements for the exercise of solemn *ex cathe-*

dra doctrinal pronouncements by the Roman Pontiff. Such solemn definitions by the pope clearly required definitive assent, but what about teachings of Roman Pontiffs that were not issued in such a solemn *ex cathedra* manner? In his 1950 ENCYCLICAL *Humani generis*, Pope PIUS XII acknowledged that papal encyclicals do not necessarily exercise the supreme teaching authority, but he rejected the view that their teachings do not, therefore, require assent. Moreover, he noted that if the Roman Pontiffs pronounce a judgment on a matter previously under dispute, such a matter, "according to the mind and will of the Pontiffs, can no longer be considered an object of free discussion among theologians" (Denzinger-Hünermann, 3885).

The question of assent to magisterial teaching was directly addressed by the Second Vatican Council (1962–1965) in its *Lumen gentium* (Dogmatic Constitution on the Church), especially in number III, 25. Three possible expressions of magisterial infallibility on matters of faith and morals were affirmed. First, bishops in communion with the pope can proclaim Christ's doctrine infallibly at an ecumenical council by means of solemn definitions. This is called the extraordinary universal Magisterium. Second, bishops in communion with the pope outside of an ecumenical council can teach infallibly when they "agree on one position as definitively to be held" (*in unam sententiam tamquam definitive tenendam conveniunt*; Denzinger-Hünermann, 4149). This is known as the ordinary, universal Magisterium. Third, the Roman Pontiff, the head of the college of bishops, can teach infallibly when, as the supreme shepherd and teacher of all the FAITHFUL, he proclaims a matter of faith and morals by a definitive act for the entire Church. This is called the extraordinary papal Magisterium. Infallible teachings of the universal college of bishops or the Roman Pontiff require the submission of faith (*fidei obsequio*).

What about teachings that are not definitive or infallible? When the college of bishops, in communion with the pope, exercises its ordinary Magisterium in a nondefinitive manner, the faithful are "to accept their teaching and adhere to it with a religious assent of mind" (*religioso animi obsequio adhaerere*; *Lumen gentium*, III, 25; Denzinger-Hünermann, 4149). With regard to ordinary papal teachings, the council notes that this "religious submission of will and intellect" (*hoc vero religiosum voluntatis et intellectus obsequium*) must be shown in a special way to the authentic Magisterium of the Roman Pontiff, even when he is not speaking ex cathedra. Thus, his supreme teaching authority must be acknowledged with reverence (*reverenter agnoscatur*) and the judgments (*sententiis*) made by him "sincerely adhered to according to his manifest mind and will (*sincere adhaereatur, iuxta mentem et voluntatem manifestatam ipsius*)." The pope's mind and will can be known

especially by the character of the documents (*indole documentorum*), the frequent proposition of the same doctrine (*ex frequenti propositione eiusdem doctrinae*), or his manner of speaking (*ex dicendi ratione*).

Controversy and Dissent. Although VATICAN COUNCIL II, in *Lumen gentium* III, 25, spelled out a clear need for religious assent to nondefinitive teachings of the college of bishops and the Roman Pontiff, questions were raised in the years following the council. Many of these questions grew out of a resistance to Pope PAUL VI's 1968 encyclical, *Humanae vitae*. Various theologians claimed a right to dissent from the encyclical's teaching condemning CONTRACEPTION, such as Fr. Charles Curran (teaching then at The CATHOLIC UNIVERSITY OF AMERICA).

In response to this controversy, the U.S. bishops issued a statement titled *Human Life in Our Day*, on November 15, 1968. This statement affirmed the teaching of *Humanae vitae*, but it also discussed the issue of DISSENT from "non-infallible doctrine." The bishops noted that such "non-infallible" teaching "remains binding and carries with it moral certitude, especially when it is addressed to the Universal Church." They went on to say that dissent from the Magisterium is in order "only if the reasons are serious and well-founded, if the manner of the dissent does not question or impugn the teaching authority of the Church and is such as not to give scandal" (National Conference of Catholic Bishops 1969, p. 51).

Some theologians, like Fr. Curran, used this last sentence to justify their dissent from *Humanae vitae*. They believed their reasons for opposing the encyclical were well founded and not a source of scandal or disrespect to magisterial authority. The Congregation for the DOCTRINE OF THE FAITH, however, rejected Fr. Curran's reasoning, and in 1986 his license to teach as a Catholic theologian was withdrawn.

1983 Code of Canon Law. In 1983, Pope JOHN PAUL II approved the revised Code of Canon Law, which contains several canons touching on levels of assent to magisterial teachings. Canon 750.1 states:

> Those things are to be believed by divine and Catholic faith which are contained in the Word of God as it has been written or handed down in tradition, that is, in the single deposit of faith entrusted to the Church, and which are at the same time proposed as divinely revealed either by the solemn Magisterium of the Church, or by its ordinary and universal Magisterium, which in fact is manifested by the common adherence of Christ's faithful under

the guidance of the sacred Magisterium. All are therefore bound to avoid any contrary doctrines.

With regard to nondefinitive or "non-infallible" teachings of the Magisterium, canon 752 of the 1983 Code states that "a religious submission of intellect and will, even if not the assent of faith, is to be paid to the teaching which the Roman Pontiff or the college of bishops enuntiate on faith and morals when they exercise the authentic Magisterium, even if they do not intend to proclaim it with a definitive act." As a result, the Catholic faithful "are to take care to avoid whatever is not in harmony with that teaching."

Other Church Documents. After the promulgation of the 1983 Code of Canon Law, the Church issued several other documents that further clarified the levels of assent to magisterial teaching. These were the 1989 *Profession of Faith and Oath of Fidelity on Assuming an Office* authorized by the Congregation for the Doctrine of the Faith (CDF); the 1990 document of the CDF *Donum veritatis*, Instruction on the Ecclesial Vocation of the Theologian; the 1990 CODE OF CANONS OF THE EASTERN CHURCHES; the 1998 apostolic letter *motu proprio* (of his own initiative) of John Paul II titled *Ad tuendam fidem*; and the CDF's 1998 *Commentary on the Profession of Faith's Concluding Paragraphs*.

Three Levels of Assent. The 1989 *Profession of Faith* expresses three levels of assent. The first and highest level requires firm faith in "each and everything contained in the Symbol of faith" (the Nicene–Constantinopolitan Creed). This highest level of assent also includes "each and everything contained in the Word of God, whether written or handed down in tradition, which the Church, either by a solemn judgment or by the ordinary and universal Magisterium, sets forth to be believed as divinely revealed" (*Ad tuendam fidem* [Pauline Books & Media ed.], p. 27).

In terms of Catholic THEOLOGY, such teachings are based on *primary objects* of infallibility: namely, truths *contained* in the deposit of faith (divinely revealed matters on faith and morals found either explicitly or implicitly in sacred scripture and tradition). According to the 1998 *Commentary*, these teachings are to be believed with the assent of faith (*de fide credenda*) because they are "based directly on the authority of the Word of God." (CDF 1998 *Commentary*, no. 8; in *Ad tuendam fidem* [Pauline Books & Media ed.], p. 18).

Examples of such teachings would be the divinity of Christ, the Marian dogmas of the IMMACULATE CONCEPTION and the ASSUMPTION OF MARY, and the real and substantial presence of Christ in the Eucharist.

The second level of assent states: "I also firmly accept and hold each and everything definitively proposed by the Church regarding teachings on faith and morals." These magisterial judgments relate to secondary objects of infallibility, that is, "those matters without which that deposit [of faith] cannot be rightly preserved and expounded" (*Mysterium ecclesiae*, Denzinger-Hünermann, 4536). Because of the protection of the Magisterium by the Holy Spirit, such definitive judgments on secondary objects of infallibility are *held* (not believed) as belonging (or pertaining) to the deposit of the faith (*de fide tenenda*).

The secondary objects of infallibility are not proposed by the Magisterium as *de fide*, or formally revealed by God, but they have either a historical or logical connection with what has been formally revealed. The Magisterium can confirm these secondary objects as infallible by means of a definitive judgment, which, according to the 1998 *Commentary*, would require "full and irrevocable" assent (CDF, 1998 *Commentary*, no. 8; in *Ad tuendam fidem* [Pauline Books & Media ed.], p. 18).

Such definitive judgments are "based on the Holy Spirit's assistance to the Magisterium and on the Catholic doctrine of the infallibility of the Magisterium" (*Commentary*, 8). The Holy Spirit would not allow the Magisterium to make such definitive judgments on matters pertaining to faith and morals unless the judgments were true. Some examples provided by the CDF *Commentary* are judgments concerning PROSTITUTION and FORNICATION; the solemn canonization of saints; Pope LEO XIII's 1896 declaration on the invalidity of Anglican ordinations; and John Paul II's 1994 definitive judgment on the inability of the Church to ordain women as priests (*Commentary*, 11). These definitive decisions are not proclaimed as divinely revealed (although in the future some of them might be). They are, however, considered infallible by virtue of the Holy Spirit's protection of the Magisterium in making definitive judgments on secondary objects of infallibility.

The third level of assent is expressed by this passage of the Profession of Faith: "Moreover, I adhere with religious submission of will and intellect to the teachings which either the Roman Pontiff or the College of Bishops enunciate when they exercise their authentic Magisterium even if they do not intend to proclaim these teachings by a definitive act." (*Ad tuendam fidem* [Pauline Books & Media ed.], p. 27).

According to the 1990 instruction of the CDF, *Donum veritatis*, such ordinary teachings of the Roman Pontiff or the college of bishops usually involve "some teaching which leads to a better understanding of revelation in matters of faith and morals and to moral directives derived from such teaching" (III, 17).

Magisterial teachings that do not fall under the first two levels of assent fall under this third level. Examples are the criteria for the assessment of the just use of military force (found in the *Catechism of the Catholic Church* [CCC], 2309) and the strict conditions regarding the use of the death penalty set forth by John Paul II in *Evangelium vitae* III, 56 and the CCC 2267. Another example is John Paul II's March 20, 2004, affirmation of the obligation to provide ASSISTED HYDRATION AND NUTRITION, even by tube-feeding, to persistently unconscious patients, so long as the hydration and nutrition is achieving its proper end of sustaining life and alleviating suffering (a teaching confirmed August 1, 2007, by the Congregation for the Doctrine of the Faith).

The third level of assent requires religious submission (*obsequium religiosum*) of will and intellect. The word *obsequium* comes from the Latin verb *obsequi* (to follow or yield to). Thus, *obsequium* refers to an attitude of compliance, deference, consent, obedience, and allegiance to the teaching articulated. This assent is "religious" because it is based on the virtue of "religion," which requires due reverence for God and his representatives. Religious assent is distinct from the assent of faith, but it "is nonetheless an extension of it" (CCC, 892).

Donum veritatis . The 1990 Instruction *Donum veritatis*, by the Congregation for the Doctrine of the Faith, recognized that "divine assistance" is given to the bishops and the Roman Pontiff in exercising their ordinary Magisterium, even when they are not providing a definitive pronouncement (III, 17). This instruction also noted that teachings of the ordinary Magisterium often involve both "solid principles" and "certain contingent and conjectural elements," and sometimes it is only possible over the course of time "to distinguish between what is necessary and what is contingent" (IV, 24). Moreover, Cardinal Joseph RATZINGER, in a lecture on *Donum veritatis*, acknowledged that some magisterial teachings are "not the final word on a given matter" but an exercise of "pastoral prudence, a sort of provisional policy" (Ratzinger 1995, p. 106).

Because judgments of the ordinary Magisterium are not definitive, the CDF admitted that, in some cases, a theologian might have questions or difficulties about a particular magisterial teaching, either with regard to the arguments used or the manner in which the teaching is presented. In such cases, the theologian should make these difficulties known to the magisterial authorities "in an evangelical spirit and with a profound desire to resolve the difficulties" (*Donum veritatis*, IV, 30). The theologian, however, should avoid public expressions of dissent, such as turning to the mass media. In the last analysis, the "willingness to submit loyally to the teaching of the Magisterium on matters per se not infallible must be the rule" (*Donum veritatis*, IV, 24).

A Fourth Level of Assent? Some theologians (e.g., Avery Cardinal DULLES, S.J.) also speak of a fourth level of assent related to prudential judgments or interventions by the Holy See or bishops regarding the application of moral or doctrinal teachings to concrete circumstances (Dulles 1996, pp. 108–111). For example, the Holy See or a group of bishops might criticize a particular military intervention or offer suggestions on policies of immigration, health care, or the penal system. These judgments would require serious consideration, but the ultimate decisions on such public policies would belong "to the prudential judgment of those who have responsibility for the common good" (CCC, 2309). A distinction, though, must be made between public policies that involve intrinsic evils (e.g., ABORTION, EUTHANASIA)—which can never be justified—and prudential applications of moral principles (e.g., the criteria for justified military force in CCC, 2309) that may or may not be justified, depending on the circumstances.

John Paul II and the Second Level. In terms of canon law, John Paul II's apostolic letter *Ad tuendam fidem* (1998) required an addition to canon 750 of the 1983 Latin Code (CIC) and canon 598 of the Code of Canon Law of the Eastern Churches (CCOE). This addition made it clear that the faithful are to firmly accept and hold definitive teachings of the Magisterium (the second level of assent). Consequently, "anyone who rejects propositions which are to be held definitively sets himself against the teaching of the Catholic Church" (CIC, 750.2; CCOE, 598.2). John Paul II likewise ordered additions to canon 1371 of the Latin Code and 1436 of the Eastern Code mandating a just or appropriate penalty for those who obstinately persist in rejecting definitive teachings of the Magisterium. This was a canonical way of enforcing certain magisterial teachings such as the 1994 judgment that the Church lacks the authority to confer priestly ordination on women. Obstinate resistance to these definitive teachings, though, does not fall under the definition of HERESY, which is "the obstinate post–baptismal denial of some truth which must be believed with divine and catholic faith" (CCC, 2089; CIC, 751). According to canon law, heresy is liable to automatic EXCOMMUNICATION (CIC, 1364.1), but obstinate resistance to definitive teachings would usually involve a lesser PUNISHMENT.

In the final analysis, assent to teachings of the Magisterium is based on the belief that the bishops and the Roman Pontiff teach with the authority of Christ and are protected by the Holy Spirit in the fulfillment of their mandate to preach and teach the GOSPEL. An understanding of the levels of assent, however, is necessary for a proper evaluation of magisterial teachings and the authority they command.

SEE ALSO Ad Tuendam Fidem; Catechism of the Catholic Church; Councils, General (Ecumenical), History of; Councils, General (Ecumenical), Theology of; Evangelium Vitae; Ex Cathedra; Humanae Vitae; Humani Generis; Magisterial Documents; Teaching Authority of the Church (Magisterium).

BIBLIOGRAPHY

Congregation for the Doctrine of the Faith, *Commentary on the Profession of Faith's Concluding Paragraphs.* For the text, see *Acta Apostolicae Sedis* 90 (1998): 542–551; *Origins* 28 (1998): 116–119.

Congregation for the Doctrine of the Faith, *Donum veritatis* Instruction on the Ecclesial Vocation of the Theologian (Doctrinal Document, May 24, 1990), available from http://www.vatican.va/roman_curia/congregations/cfaith/documents/rc_con_cfaith_doc_19900524_theologian-vocation_en.html (accessed May 1, 2008).

Congregation for the Doctrine of the Faith, *Mysterium ecclesiae*, Declaration in Defense of the Catholic Doctrine of the Church against Certain Errors of the Present Day. For the text, see *Acta Apostolicae Sedis* 65 (1973): 397–407; *Origins* 3 (1973): 97, 99–100, 110–112.

Congregation for the Doctrine of the Faith, *Profession of Faith and Oath of Fidelity on Assuming an Office to Be Exercised in the Name of the Church.* For the text, see *Acta Apostolicae Sedis* 81 (1989): 104–106; *Origins* 18 (1989): 661, 663.

Heinrich Denzinger and Peter Hünermann. *Enchiridion symbolorum definitionem et declarationem de rebus fidei et morum*, 40th ed. (Freiburg 2005).

Avery Robert Cardinal Dulles, S.J., *The Craft of Theology: From Symbol to System*, new expanded ed. (New York 1995).

Avery Robert Cardinal Dulles, S.J., *Magisterium: Teacher and Guardian of the Faith* (Naples, Fla. 2007).

Pope John Paul II, *Ad tuendam fidem, Motu proprio* By Which Certain Norms Are Inserted Into the *Code of Canon Law* and Into the *Code of Canons of the Eastern Churches* (Apostolic Letter, May 18, 1998), available from http://www.vatican.va/holy_father/john_paul_ii/motu_proprio/documents/hf_jp-ii_motu-proprio_30061998_ad-tuendam-fidem_en.html (accessed May 1, 2008). Also found in print (as cited above) in John Paul II, Apostolic Letter *Motu Proprio, Ad tuendam fidem* [with the 1998 Commentary on the Concluding Formula of the "Professio Fidei" of the Congregation for the Doctrine of the Faith and appendices containing the Profession of Faith and the Oath of Fidelity on Assuming an Office to be Exercised in the Name of the Church] (Boston: Pauline Books & Media, 1998).

National Conference of Catholic Bishops [now United States Conference of Catholic Bishops], *Human Life in Our Day*, U.S. bishops' Pastoral letter on human life in our day, November 15, 1968, with commentary by John B. Sheerin (Glen Rock, N.J., 1969).

Pope Paul VI, *Humanae vitae*, On the Regulation of Birth (Encyclical, July 25, 1968), available from http://www.vatican.va/holy_father/paul_vi/encyclicals/documents/hf_p-vi_enc_25071968_humanae-vitae_en.html (accessed May 2, 2008).

Joseph Ratzinger (Pope Benedict XVI), *The Nature and Mission of Theology: Essays to Orient Theology in Today's Debates*, translated by Adrian Walker (San Francisco 1995).

Francis A. Sullivan, *Magisterium: Teaching Authority in the Catholic Church* (New York 1983).

Vatican Council II, *Lumen gentium*, Dogmatic Constitution on the Church (Constitution, November 21, 1964), available from http://www.vatican.va/archive/hist_councils/ii_vatican_council/index.htm (accessed May 2, 2008).

Larry Witham, *Curran vs. Catholic University: A Study of Authority and Freedom in Conflict* (Riverdale, Md. 1991).

Robert Fastiggi
Professor of Systematic Theology
Sacred Heart Major Seminary, Detroit, Mich. (2009)

MAINE, CATHOLIC CHURCH IN

Maine is unique among New England states in that it alone can trace its Catholic roots back to the era of the earliest European colonization. In 1604 the French established a settlement on an island near the mouth of the St. Croix River. This settlement, Holy Cross, was the first European colony in New England. Though primarily a business venture headed by the Calvinist Pierre du Guast, Sieur de Monts, and Samuel Champlain, it included a Catholic chaplain, Nicholas Aubry. The colony failed to endure the first harsh winter, but its fate was no deterrent to further exploration. In 1613 the JESUITS Peter Biard and Enemond Masse accompanied a colonizing venture of Pierre La Saussaye bound for the Penobscot River (which they had earlier visited in 1611, offering Mass in the vicinity of present-day Bangor), but dense fog forced the ship to land sooner than planned. At Fernald Point near Southwest Harbor on Mount Desert Island they planted their colony of St. Sauveur. They were welcomed by the indigenous people, and prospects for the young colony seemed good, but within two months it had been destroyed by the Englishman Samuel Argall, Admiral of Virginia, who had instructions to frustrate French attempts to colonize the Penobscot region.

The English and French in Acadia. The territory known as Acadia was exchanged nine times by the French and English in subsequent decades. The history of the settlement at the town on Penobscot Bay, now known as Castine, is typical of this instability. The Plymouth Pilgrims had a trading post there by 1629. In 1632 the area reverted to French control, and the Capuchin Franciscans arrived in 1635, establishing the mission of Our Lady of Hope at the site the French called Pentagoet. The cornerstone of a substantial church was laid in 1648, but its existence was fragile. The English regained control of the territory from 1654 to 1667, and the mission collapsed, though the French were once more in charge from 1667 to 1703. Franciscans returned during these years when the post was in the hands of John Vincent d'Abbadie, Baron of Saint-Castin. The baron encouraged pastoral work among the natives, and by his patronage a CHAPEL dedicated to St. Ann was erected for their use on an island in the Penobscot river ("Indian Island"), the first of a succession of chapels at a mission that endures to this day.

More enterprising work among the indigenous peoples was carried out by Father Gabriel Druillettes, S.J., sent to work among the natives of the Kennebec region in 1646. He established a mission to the Abenakis near present-day Augusta and lived among them until 1647. Following a diplomatic mission to the English at Plymouth and Boston in 1650, he again carried out missionary work with the tribes along the Kennebec in the winters of 1651 and 1652, establishing the village of Norridgewock as his headquarters.

Druillettes's work was continued after a lapse of a few decades by his intrepid brother, Jesuit Sebastian RÂLE, who arrived in Norridgewock in 1694. Proficient in native dialects, he worked tirelessly among the Abenakis, catechizing, adjudicating disputes, caring for the sick, and teaching music, all amidst the ongoing political tensions between the English and the French. Norridgewock village was destroyed in a raid by the Massachusetts colony in 1705; another attack followed in 1722, during which the village was again destroyed. Finally, in 1724 an assault was launched during which Râle himself was murdered, and his scalp sent with twenty-six others back to Boston. Many of the surviving Abenakis fled north toward Canada.

The next century, with its ongoing political tensions and reversals, saw little activity by Catholics. Most of the state was included in the ecclesiastical jurisdiction of the diocese of Boston when it was erected in 1808.

Maine Becomes a State. In 1820 the state of Maine was admitted to the Union. At this time there were three centers of Catholic life in the state, which would serve as the building blocks of the Church in Maine: the surviving native peoples, grouped at Indian Island and Pleasant Point (near Eastport); a group of Acadians at Madawaska by the St. John River; and Irish immigrants living near Damariscotta and Whitefield. Thanks to the intervention of some prominent citizens of the latter group, the new state constitution contained no anti–Catholic restrictions, unlike those of Massachusetts (from which the state was carved) and New Hampshire.

By the 1800s only 750 native peoples remained in Maine. Members of the Penobscot tribe were restricted to Indian Island, while Passamaquody lived near Pleasant Point. Three exiled priests from revolutionary France worked among these tribes from 1792 to 1818. One of the three, Jean CHEVERUS, visited both tribes in 1797 and 1798. He was replaced by James ROMAGNÉ, who built a church at Pleasant Point, and labored among the natives till 1818. A learned, pious, affable man, he introduced farming to his flock, and translated a prayer book into the native dialect.

Catholic Population. By 1820 there were about 108 Catholic families living near Damariscotta and Whitefield. Father (later bishop of Boston, 1808–1823) Cheverus first visited the community in 1798 and returned almost every summer from Boston until 1818, using it as a base from which to search the surrounding countryside for isolated Catholics. James Kavanagh and Matthew Cottrill, who had arrived in Newcastle as young Irish immigrants in the early 1790s and had prospered as merchants and shipbuilders, were the leaders of this prosperous district, which boasted its own church, St. Patrick's. This edifice, built in the year 1808, is the oldest extant Catholic church in New England. Kavanagh's son Edward, though preparing for ordination in 1813, turned his attention to his father's failing businesses, later distinguishing himself as a state legislator, congressman (1831–1835), and governor (1843), the first Catholic in New England to hold these latter offices.

Meanwhile, in the far north of Maine, twenty Acadian families, displaced from St. John, New Brunswick, by American Loyalists, had settled near the St. John and Madawaska Rivers. Between 1790 and 1794 they were joined by Acadians from Nova Scotia and about this time asked the BISHOP of Quebec for a priest and church. An influx of new arrivals swelled their numbers to 2,000 by 1831. Most of the Madawaskans were deeply religious Catholics and could boast of a resident priest after 1808. In 1842 the boundary between the United States and Canada was fixed at the St. John River, leaving the Madawaskans divided. Forty days after the treaty was signed, ROME assigned the care of the Catholics in the region to the Diocese of Fredericton, New Brunswick, including St. Bruno's parish on the southern (U.S.) side of the river, which had been established in 1838. In 1860 the Catholics of Maine Madawaska were given over to the care of the Diocese of St. John, New Brunswick. Not until 1870 and the First Vatican Council was Bishop Bacon of the Diocese of PORTLAND given the spiritual care of the Catholics of northern Maine (though the state had been providing education there since 1843).

Irish Catholics in Maine. The earliest Catholic churches in Maine were built where the immigrant Irish settled. Father Dennis Ryan, ordained by Bishop Cheverus in 1817 (the first ordination in New England), spent twenty-five years pastoring, first at Damariscotta and later at Whitefield (where he built a brick church in 1838). He ministered to Catholics from the Kennebec to the Penobscot, including the towns of Bath, Augusta, and Bangor. Already in 1836 there were 1,000 Irish in the latter town, drawn by jobs in the lumber industry. St. Michael's church there was dedicated in 1839. In Augusta, Ryan made do with a converted Unitarian church purchased in 1836, which served till St. Mary's was built in 1847.

Another intrepid Maine pastor was Father Charles French. His assignment was to care for the large numbers of Irish emigrating into Maine and settling along the seacoast. He based his MINISTRY first in Eastport—the immigrant's gateway from New Brunswick—where St. Joseph's was dedicated in 1835. It was from the flock in Eastport that John E. BARRY, the Portland diocese's first native vocation, would hail. French later moved the focus of his pastoral activity to Portland, where St. Dominic's church had been dedicated in 1833. The Catholic population of the largest Maine city was growing, bolstered by a large number of converts including Josue Young, the future bishop of Erie, Pennsylvania.

Growth and Trials. Despite the growing Catholic population, not all communities were as fortunate as Bangor, Eastport, or Portland. A Catholic presence existed in Belfast from 1827, but no permanent church was built until 1894 (a rented hall was used until 1851, and then again from 1870 to 1885). A lack of priests and resources meant that congregations were slow to grow, and loss of FAITH was common. The growing numbers of Irish immigrants, and the squalid conditions of the urban slums in which many were forced to live, moved Bishop Benedict FENWICK of Boston to propose and promote a Catholic immigrant colony in northern Maine. In 1834 the bishop purchased 11,358 acres in northern Maine, and by 1840 about sixty-five families had taken up residence there. Though Benedicta (as it was named) boasted a church, sawmill, and orphanage and was soon a thriving farming town, it never developed sufficiently to support the college and seminary that Fenwick envisioned.

In 1848 Bishop Fenwick's successor in Boston, John Fitzpatrick, obtained two Jesuits from the Maryland province for work in Maine. Father John BAPST, a thirty-five-year-old exiled Swiss, was the first to arrive and the last of his brethren to leave in 1859. Bapst worked for two years at Indian Island north of Bangor. Divisions among the tribe, however, led to his being transferred to Eastport in 1851. By 1852 he had promoted the construction of three new churches (at Oldtown, Waterville, and Ellsworth) and regularly visited thirty-three stations on his mission circuit. In Ellsworth his pastoral work resulted in a number of prominent converts (including a young lady, Mary Agnes Tincker, who became a well-known novelist of the Victorian age), but also stirred up the ire of local Nativists. Incensed by his vocal support for the rights of Catholic children to withdraw from public schools that promoted the King James Bible and egged on by Bapst's obvious foreignness and success as an evangelist, a local mob assaulted, robbed, tarred, and feathered the Jesuit on a visit to Ellsworth in October of 1854. Public sentiment in Bangor and Portland was aroused, and prominent citizens offered him a gold watch to replace one that had been stolen from him and a purse of $500 to aid him in his work. Nonetheless, not all were repentant—the Catholic Church in Ellsworth was burned in 1856.

Bangor and Eastport. Bangor and Eastport were now the centers of the Jesuits' mission. Bangor grew rapidly (Catholics alone numbered 6,000), and in 1856 a new church, St. John's, was dedicated. Though the site chosen for the church was deliberately inconspicuous, given the recent wave of anti–catholicism, the building itself was in the grandest Gothic style and was acclaimed one of the most beautiful churches in New England. Ironically, the very success of the Jesuits in Bangor and down east Maine led to the first bishop of Portland's desire to reclaim St. John's as a diocesan parish. Father Bapst and his fellow Jesuits departed the diocese in 1859 and members of the order did not return for almost a century. They had, however, overseen the construction of seven churches: Waterville, Oldtown, Ellsworth, Winterport, Rockland, Trescott, and Bangor. Churches in Machias and Calais, though started prior to their ministry in Maine, were completed during their watch.

A Diocese for Maine. The Diocese of Portland was established on July 29, 1853 (the same day as Brooklyn and Burlington, Vermont), encompassing the states of Maine and New Hampshire. The first candidate named to fill the see, Henry Coskery of Baltimore, declined the appointment, and so there was delay before David William BACON's (1813–1874) name was announced. A priest of the New York ARCHDIOCESE, he was an energetic pastor and builder in his native Brooklyn before being appointed to Maine. He was consecrated at St. Patrick's Cathedral in New York on April 22, 1855, and installed at St. Dominic's in Portland on May 31. As there were only six priests working in Maine, the bishop's first task was to find clergy; nine new arrivals from Europe and America swelled the rolls by the year end. Bacon was a talented administrator and worked to remedy a number of deficiencies. Land was purchased in Portland for a CATHEDRAL in 1856, and a small chapel was constructed. Tragically, work begun on the main structure in 1866 was destroyed in the great fire that struck the city on July 4 of that year. Spurred on by Bacon, funds for construction were sought once more, and work was resumed in 1868. When dedicated on September 9, 1869, the Cathedral of the Immaculate Conception was declared one of the finest in the country.

No parochial schools greeted Bacon upon his arrival in the diocese, but by the year of his death they numbered twenty, in addition to six private academies. The bishop was aided in his work by the Sisters of NOTRE DAME, who came to Portland to run St. Aloysius school in 1864. Mother Mary Frances Xavier WARDE and four SISTERS OF MERCY arrived in Manchester, New Hampshire, in 1858, and soon opened three houses in Maine, at Bangor (1865), Whitefield (1871), and Portland (1873—replacing the Notre Dame Sisters). After almost twenty years of vigorous labor, the bishop died on November 5, 1874, while in transit to Rome for his AD LIMINA VISIT, his life ended due to a painful bladder ailment that had plagued him throughout his tenure in Portland.

New Arrivals in Maine. On February 12, 1875, James A. HEALY, pastor of St. James Church in Boston, the largest parish in New England, was appointed to the see of Portland. A native of Georgia, Healy and his brothers had been sent north to attend Holy Cross by their father, who realized that their status as sons of a mulatto slave mother was an insurmountable obstacle to their advancement. The Healy sons prospered: James and Sherwood studied for the diocesan priesthood, Patrick joined the Jesuits. Healy's twenty-five years as bishop of Portland were years of growth: in population, churches, priests, schools, and religious. Besides a heavy indebtedness of $110,000, another challenge to the diocese during Healy's tenure was the massive influx of French-Canadians who arrived during the last quarter of the nineteenth century. Facing continual economic distress in Quebec, tens of thousands of these deeply religious migrants came to New England in search of work, bringing with them their strong attachment to "la foi, la langue, et les moeurs" (faith, language, and customs). A few towns in Maine were completely transformed; Biddeford, for example, was eighty percent French-Canadian by the 1880s. Healy was zealous in his efforts to obtain compatriot clergy and religious to serve the newcomers. Ten new communities of religious women entered the diocese at Healy's invitation, as well as the Dominican and Marist priests and brothers, all of them French-speaking. Lewiston was an outstanding Franco-American center, where the Dominican priests staffed the parish, MARIST BROTHERS taught the boys, Daughters of Sion instructed the girls, and Sisters of Charity ran the orphanage and hospital. Healy's undertakings did not blind him to the contentious nature of some of the new arrivals, whom he found to be quite forceful in their demands.

The year 1884 saw the state of New Hampshire removed from the territory of the Diocese of Portland and formed into the Diocese of Manchester. In the same year the Sisters of Mercy in Maine achieved their independence, with Sr. Mary Teresa Pickersgill as superior. Two years later the MARIST FATHERS opened St. Mary's College in Van Buren, the first Catholic college in Maine, enrolling a large number of French-Canadians among its students.

Healy celebrated his seventieth birthday in 1900, his silver jubilee as bishop of Portland. Sadly, his labors for the church in Maine had sapped his strength, and he died on August 5, after feeling unwell for a few days. The *Boston Pilot* eulogized him as "humble, considerate [and] generous." He left behind eighty-six churches, seventy-six diocesan priests, and a Catholic population of approximately 96,400.

Healy was followed in the see of Portland by a rising star, William O'CONNELL, rector of the NORTH AMERICAN COLLEGE in Rome and a native of Lowell, Massachusetts (born 1859). His appointment did not come till 1901, as deliberations at the VATICAN were complicated when Franco-American priests and laity wrote opposing the terna of names forwarded by the consultors and advocating the nomination of a French-speaker. O'Connell was installed on July 4 and brought a flamboyant touch to the diocese (he employed an Italian valet and coachman). As bishop he was highly visible and used public appearances to enhance the self-esteem of Maine Catholics. He was lionized by the Protestant community and Portland society; chosen to deliver a public oration on the death of President McKinley, he was accepted for membership in the exclusive Cumberland Club. Insisting on an intensely personal management style, he scrutinized parish reports, exercising minute oversight of LITURGY and devotions. In 1903 he issued a pastoral on the new wave of immigrants arriving from Eastern Europe and Italy, asking that they be made welcome by the Church in Maine.

An avid traveler (e.g., the winter of 1904 to 1905 was spent in Rome), O'Connell was away on a diplomatic mission to Japan on behalf of the Vatican when word arrived that he had been appointed as coadjutor to Archbishop Williams in Boston. He bid farewell to the Portland diocese on September 9, 1906, and became archbishop of Boston on August 30, 1907, and was made a CARDINAL in 1911.

Work for the Future. Rome lost no time in appointing a new bishop for the diocese of Portland. Louis Walsh (1858–1924) was a priest from Boston, known for his work at the Seminary of St. John and as an administrator of the archdiocesan schools. A dignified, scholarly,

Our Lady Queen of Peace Church, Boothbay, ME. *The windows of this this beautiful church reflect the golden sunset in the scenic harbor town of Boothbay, Maine.* © **TRAVIS ROWAN / ALAMY**

affable man, he was a builder for the future who had a love of Maine's rich history. He restored a monument Bishop Fenwick had erected for Father Râle, celebrated the centenary of St. Patrick's church in Damariscotta in 1908, and honored the 300th anniversary of the Mount Desert mission with commemorations in 1913 (August 6 in Bar Harbor, October 12 in Portland). He founded the Maine Catholic Historical Society in 1908 and promoted the *Maine Catholic Historical Magazine* (1913–1928).

During Walsh's eighteen-year tenure, thirty-six new parishes were founded (four in Portland, three in Lewiston). To deal with the vast number of immigrants, the bishop encouraged pastors to schedule visits of compatriot priests at least a few times a year to assist the foreign-born among their flocks. Such consideration did not prevent him from stirring up dissension in Biddeford over his reorganization of a French parish and measures to curb the activities of ethnic societies.

Walsh was no stranger to political action. He watched the state legislature closely, always a vocal advocate for state aid to what he referred to as his "Catholic Public Schools." His efforts to obtain a portion of the State Public Fund for schools, however, were rejected in 1915. The bishop was also a prominent figure on the national stage, serving as chairman of the Press and Publicity Department of the National Catholic Welfare Conference (NCWC), successfully working to reverse the HOLY SEE's suppression of that organization in 1922. The energy devoted to that cause and his energetic defense of the Church against the attacks of the KU KLUX KLAN in 1922 and 1923 led to the bishop's increasing exhaustion. Walsh died on May 12, 1924, four days after suffering a cerebral hemorrhage.

Connecticut Natives for Maine. The fifth and sixth bishops of Maine were both natives of Waterbury, Connecticut, boyhood friends, and had attended Crosby High School and Holy Cross College. John Gregory Murray (born 1877), ordained after studies in Louvain, was a brilliant administrator of the diocese of Hartford and served as its chancellor and auxiliary bishop. On October 11, 1925, he was installed as bishop of Portland. A friendly and informal man, he continued Walsh's tradition of involvement on the national stage, serving on administrative committees of the NCWC. In Maine he faced a growing number of Catholics in a state whose population growth was modest overall. In 1930 sixty percent of Maine residents lived in rural areas, yet the number of non-Catholic churches was declining rapidly outside the cities. The bishop worried about his flock's vulnerability to the rising tide of INDIFFERENTISM and spoke out against mixed marriages and birth control.

The number of vacationers in Maine increased, however, and these visitors "from away" brought not only a financial windfall for struggling parishes but also edified natives by their faith and devotion. Murray established thirty new parishes, the number of churches rose from 168 to 183, and the number of priests from 172 to 216. Sadly, St. Mary's College in Van Buren closed its doors in 1927, but a Catholic collegiate presence was maintained by St. Joseph's College (for women), opened in Maine in 1915 by the Sisters of Mercy (by the end of the century it became co-ed and move to a suburban site in Standish). Catholics in the diocese were kept informed on Church news more effectively after the appearance of the *Church World*, a diocesan paper that debuted in July of 1930.

Murray responded aggressively to the dislocation occasioned by the Great Depression by committing the diocese to the needs of the poor. He borrowed heavily to maintain the Church's charitable foundations and ordered that relief committees be established in every parish to oversee fundraising for the assistance of the homeless, destitute, and unemployed. His work in Maine was brought to an abrupt conclusion in November of 1931 when he was transferred to the Archdiocese of ST. PAUL, Minnesota. He was hailed by all as a man of compassion who had worked to ease religious prejudice.

His friend Joseph McCarthy (born in 1876) was consecrated on August 24, 1932, the first such ceremony to be carried on radio. A kind and courteous man, he had served both as a seminary teacher and administrator, as well as a parish priest (with many French-Canadians in his congregations). His primary task upon becoming bishop was to deal with a diocesan debt, which had mushroomed during the Depression to dangerous levels, totaling nearly $5 million. He devised a funding plan, approved by Rome in 1935, which authorized a bond issue and scheduled annual payments on the debt. Though initially construction was curtailed, twelve new churches had been built by 1948 and a Catholic hospital erected in Portland in 1940. Even with the restricted finances, the diocese responded to ruinous fires in Ellsworth and Auburn in 1933 with state-wide collections.

The bishop was heartened by the arrival in the diocese of two contemplative communities of nuns, the Adorers of the Precious Blood in Portland, and the Sisters of the BLESSED SACRAMENT in Waterville. The Jesuits returned to the diocese after an absence of eighty-three years to staff Cheverus High in Portland in 1942, and a group of exiled Lithuanian Franciscans were welcomed in 1944, ultimately settling on a beautiful property in Kennebunkport. McCarthy's declining health necessitated the appointment of an auxiliary, Daniel Feeney (a Portland native), on June 22, 1946, the first native son to be elevated to the episcopacy. In July of 1948 Feeney was given administrative control of the diocese and appointed coadjutor in 1952. Bishop McCarthy died in the fall of 1955, the centenary of Bishop Bacon's consecration.

Second Vatican Council and Beyond. Bishop Feeney labored to eradicate diocesean indebtedness and sought to implement the pastoral provisions of the Second Vatican Council. His successor, Peter Gerety, though bishop for only five years (1969–1974), was responsible for a progressive interpretation of the conciliar decrees that reshaped the diocese before his departure for the see of Newark, New Jersey. Bishop Gerety was succeeded by the second native son, Edward O'Leary (1974–1988), who, assisted by his auxiliary Amedee Proulx (1975–1993), sought to guide the church in Maine through an era of declining numbers of clergy and religious. Bishop Joseph Gerry, the former ABBOT of the Benedictine community of St. Anselm's in Manchester, New Hampshire, the third Maine native to shepherd the Portland diocese beginning in 1988, sought to revitalize and renew his flock of some 140 parishes through a varied and active ministry, aided by auxiliary bishop Michael Cote, appointed in 1995, and about 150 active priests and around 400 women religious. In 1997, after an exhaustive consultation process, the sacrament of CONFIRMATION began to be celebrated at the time of FIRST COMMUNION throughout the diocese. In that same year the first group of permanent deacons was ordained. A diocesan Eucharistic Congress held at the Augusta Civic Center to mark the Great Jubilee of the year 2000 drew thousands. In November 2000 voters narrowly defeated an initiative permitting physician-assisted suicide, a measure which the diocese had vigorously opposed. A new facility for St. Dominic Regional High School opened in Auburn in January 2002, realizing a long-held dream of its alumni and supporters.

On February 10, 2004, Pope JOHN PAUL II (pope 1978–2005) accepted the retirement of Bishop Joseph Gerry, O.S.B., who had reached the age limit of seventy-five. The Most Reverend Richard J. Malone, at the time an auxiliary bishop of Boston, was installed as the eleventh bishop of Portland on March 31, 2004. In the spring of 2005 Bishop Malone promulgated a five-year plan for evangelization which involved regionalizing Catholic schools and parish services. Called "Telling Anew the Story of Jesus," this plan was a response to shrinking populations in northern and eastern counties, growing suburban communities in the central and southern counties, a decline in the number of school-aged children throughout the state, and a decline in the number of priests available for service. In the course of the implementation of the plan, a number of parishes merged with neighboring parishes and consolidated staffs and facilities. By July 2008 the number of parishes stood at eighty-seven; most of these parishes retained multiple churches for worship. In the first decade of the new millennium, Catholics comprise some eighteen percent of the total state population.

Conclusion. The Catholic Church in Maine has a rich heritage and has been a vibrant force for evangelization amidst ever-present challenges. Besides those mentioned above, other Maine Catholic notables include Donald Pelotte, S.S.S., bishop of Gallup, New Mexico (the first native American to be ordained a bishop), and politicians such as Emery San Souci, elected governor of Rhode Island in 1920 (the first Franco-American to be elected a governor in New England), Joseph Brennan (governor of Maine, 1979–1987), and Margaret Chase Smith (the first woman to serve in both houses of the U.S. Congress).

SEE ALSO BALTIMORE, ARCHDIOCESE OF; BOSTON, ARCHDIOCESE OF; CATHOLIC CHARITIES USA; DOMINICANS; EUCHARISTIC CONGRESSES; KNOW-NOTHINGISM; MASSACHUSETTS, CATHOLIC CHURCH IN; MISSION AND MISSIONS; MIXED MARRIAGES, PROHIBITION OF; NATIVISM, AMERICAN; NEW HAMPSHIRE, CATHOLIC CHURCH IN; PRAYER BOOKS; SISTERS ADORERS OF THE PRECIOUS BLOOD; VATICAN COUNCIL I; VATICAN COUNCIL II.

BIBLIOGRAPHY

Vincent A. Lapomarda, *The Catholic Church in the Land of the Holy Cross: A History of the Diocese of Portland, Maine* (Strasbourg, France 2003).

Dolores Ann Liptak, R.S.M., "French Canadians Plead for Survivance," in *Immigrants and Their Church* (New York 1989), 160–170.

Robert H. Lord, John E. Sexton, and Edward T. Harrington, *The History of the Archdiocese of Boston in the Various Stages of Its Development, 1604 to 1943*, 3 vols. (New York 1944).

William Leo Lucey, S.J., *The Catholic Church in Maine* (Francestown, N.H. 1957).

Joseph C. Linck
Instructor, Permanent Diaconate Formation Program
Diocese of Bridgeport, Conn.

Msgr. Marc Caron
Chancellor
Roman Catholic Diocese of Portland, Maine (2009)

MARYLAND, CATHOLIC CHURCH IN

One of the thirteen original colonies and seventh to ratify the Constitution of the United States (April 28, 1788), Maryland is situated on the Atlantic seaboard, bounded on the north by Pennsylvania and Delaware, on the east by Delaware and the Atlantic Ocean, on the south by Virginia and West Virginia, and on the west by West Virginia. Annapolis is its capital, and Baltimore, Cumberland, and Hagerstown are the chief industrial centers. In the past, fishing predominated in the Chesapeake Bay area, and farming and mineral processing were important in the state's economy. In recent decades many high technology and other service industry

The Early Church in Maryland. *This 19th-century engraving titled, "First Mass in Maryland,", depicts the fateful event which occurred March 25, 1634.* © **THE GRANGER COLLECTION**

companies that conduct business with the federal government have set up operations in the state to be close to the national capital. Maryland has become the home of numerous information technology companies as well as bioscience firms.

History. The founding of the palatinate and proprietary colony of Maryland (1634), named in honor of Henrietta Maria (1625–1649), queen of CHARLES I, KING OF ENGLAND, was the work of the first Lord Baltimore, George CALVERT, and of his son and heir, Cecil Calvert.

Colonial Period. In the charter signed in 1632 by the second Lord Baltimore, the proprietor was granted broad and generous powers, with provision made also for a representative form of government through an assembly of all freemen. Despite opposition from the Virginia Company and the PURITANS, the expedition, under Leonard Calvert as governor, sailed from Gravesend on the *Ark and the Dove* with 128 persons aboard, the usual oaths being administered. Approximately seventy-two others joined the expedition before the vessels sailed on November 22, 1633, from Cowes on the Isle of Wight. Since the oath contained material objectionable to Catholics, it is likely that many, if not most, of those boarding at Cowes were Catholics. Two JESUITS, Andrew WHITE and John Altham (1589–1640), accompanied the expedition; White's *Relatio itineris* constitutes a prime source for the early history of the colony, which was

founded in March of 1634 at St. Mary's, between the Potomac River and Chesapeake Bay.

From the beginning Calvert insisted on religious tolerance and separation of CHURCH AND STATE; all Christians were welcomed to the colony, and Jews were tacitly admitted. Treaties were made with the Native Americans, and for some years relations with them remained friendly. A problem arose, however, when a large element in Virginia headed by William Claiborne (1600–1677), who had already established trading posts on Kent Island in Chesapeake Bay within Baltimore's jurisdiction, refused to recognize the authority of Maryland. It took two expeditions (1635 and 1638) to subdue the island; but subsequently (1645), when Richard Ingle (1609–1653), posing as a champion of Parliament and the Protestant cause, attacked and terrorized Calvert's colonists, the governor fled for a time to Virginia. White and his Jesuit companions were seized, their property sequestered, and the priests sent in chains to England to stand trial.

After Leonard Calvert reconquered his colony, increasing numbers of Puritans from Virginia sought and obtained refuge in Maryland, settling mainly near Annapolis, then called Providence. The Toleration Act of 1649, titled "An Act Concerning Religion," was designed to protect Catholics and others from the rising Puritan hostility in the colony and in England. In fact, however, it was less liberal than the previous Baltimore religious policy. By 1651 the Puritan element was strong enough to overthrow the authority of Baltimore; and until 1657 the colony, beset by turmoil and invasion, was in the hands of parliamentarians and Puritans. Help came to Cecil Calvert when Oliver CROMWELL questioned the acts of his adherents in Maryland and in 1657 returned the palatinate to Baltimore. When Charles, the heir of Cecil Calvert, became governor in 1660, there were about 12,000 colonists in Maryland, a total that increased to 20,000 during the next ten years. The tobacco economy became established in the whole Chesapeake area, and a few iron furnaces opened, but the main industry was agriculture.

Under Charles, who became the proprietor in 1675 at the death of his father, the colony enjoyed an era of relative peace and prosperity until the REVOLUTION OF 1688 in England. Thereafter, the proprietary government in Maryland was overthrown, and it became a royal colony, with Sir Lionel Copley (d. 1693) as first royal governor (1691). After his arrival in 1692, the assembly abolished the practice of religious toleration and established the Anglican Church, which lasted until the revolution. In 1702 a limited toleration was granted to Dissenters and Quakers. A test act was imposed against Catholics in 1692, and an act of 1704 forbade Catholics to practice their religion. In 1715 and in 1729 laws provided that the Catholic survivor of a marriage should have any children removed from his care for the purpose of Protestant upbringing. In 1718 a severe law forbade to Catholics the franchise and the holding of governmental posts. A law in 1756 provided, among other restrictions, that any property then held by priests should be taken from them; the law provided also for double taxation on all Catholics.

Revolutionary and Post–Revolutionary Years. Charles, Lord Baltimore, died on February 20, 1715, at the age of 85. He was succeeded by his son, Benedict Leonard (1679–1715), who had renounced his faith in favor of ANGLICANISM. When Benedict died April 15, 1715, his son, Charles II (1699–1751), Lord Baltimore, became proprietor under the terms of the original charter, and Maryland ceased to be a royal colony and again became proprietary. The famous boundary dispute between the Lords Baltimore and the Penns involved prolonged litigation and was not settled until the two proprietors engaged Charles Mason and Jeremiah Dixon, who, between 1763 and 1767, determined the line, later named after them. In the stirring times between 1763 and 1775, Maryland played the usual colonial role, repudiating the Stamp Act and passing resolves denouncing taxation without representation and claiming that the Assembly alone could tax the province. The colony took part also in the nonimportation agreement and in the formation of committees of correspondence. Annapolis had its own tea party in October 1774, with the burning of the *Peggy Stewart*. During the administration of the last proprietary governor, Sir Robert Eden (1768–1776), the famous debate took place between Daniel Dulany (1722–1797) and Charles CARROLL of Carrollton over the question of officers' fees. When Carroll, a Catholic, had the better of the argument, not only did he greatly strengthen the popular side but he won sympathy for the Catholic cause.

In June 1774, at the convention at Annapolis, Charles Carroll, along with other delegates, was appointed to the Continental Congress. On June 28, 1776, the Maryland delegation was empowered to vote for independence. They adopted the first state constitution in 1776; section thirty-three of the Bill of Rights stated that all persons professing the Christian religion were equally entitled to protection of LAW. In the war that followed, Maryland regiments fought from Bunker Hill to Yorktown; the "Old Line State" is a fitting description of the military services of the Maryland Line during the revolution. The clashing interests of Maryland and Virginia resulted in the Mount Vernon and Annapolis meetings, which in turn resulted in the great Philadelphia Constitutional Convention (May 1787). One of the signers of this document was a third prominent Daniel CARROLL. Maryland ratified this document and elected Charles Carroll senator from

Maryland. In 1791 Maryland ceded to the U.S. government its present site, the District of Columbia.

While the government of Maryland organized to meet the exigencies of the new republic, the Catholic Church in the former colonies also went through transition. During the years of the revolution, priests of the recently suppressed Society of Jesus continued to minister to the needs of Maryland Catholics as well as those in nearby colonies. Following the conclusion of hostilities with Great Britain, the Catholic Church in the United States needed its own institutions of governance separate from those of the mother country. The first U.S. census of 1790 recorded the total population of Maryland at 319,700 persons. In a letter to the Holy See five years prior to the census, John Carroll had estimated that there were 15,800 Catholics in the state. From 1784 until 1789, Maryland native Father John Carroll served as prefect apostolic for the Church in the United States. In 1789 the Diocese of Baltimore, which encompassed the entire territory of the United States at that time, was erected and Carroll was ordained its first BISHOP the following year.

As the first bishop in the United States, John Carroll had a tremendous impact in shaping the Church in Maryland and in the nation in general. Historian Thomas W. Spalding credited Carroll with establishing throughout the country the "Maryland tradition" as the dominant ethos of church life in the first half of the nineteenth century. This tradition was rooted in the founding of Maryland as a sanctuary of religious tolerance where the state neither supported nor interfered with the operation of any church. Additionally, the Maryland tradition was patriotic and supportive of democratic principles. It also embraced the notion that the establishment of the new nation marked an exceptional moment in the history of the world and that the Catholic Church in the United States needed to adapt operational practices to this American exceptionalism while remaining FAITHFUL to the doctrines and liturgical traditions of the universal Church.

According to this thesis, which is widely held by Church historians, the Maryland tradition gradually lost influence in Church life in the second half of the nineteenth century as massive waves of Catholic immigrants forced the Church to adopt new ways to meet their needs. The Maryland tradition also lost its influence over the life of the Church in the United States as the bishops of Baltimore exercised authority over an ever smaller ecclesiastical jurisdiction.

Civil War Era and Beyond. During the War of 1812, the attack on Fort McHenry in Baltimore harbor inspired Frances Scott Key to write "The Star Spangled Banner." Between 1815 and 1860 the state expanded as a commercial and maritime entity, attracting a large and steady stream of immigrants. In turn a strong nativist sentiment developed, and in 1854 the American party elected a mayor of Baltimore. Nativist power in the state peaked in 1856 as Maryland was the only state carried by former president Millard Fillmore (1800–1874) and the Know Nothing party in the presidential election.

The fateful presidential election of 1860 reflected clearly the divided sentiment of Maryland, a border state. With secession the Maryland position was difficult—growing industrial and commercial ties bound the state to the North and the Union; its large and wealthy tidewater was the home of slavery and agriculture. A Marylander, James Ryder Randall (1839–1908), living in New Orleans, gave the state its song, "Maryland, My Maryland," a consequence of the bloody riots in Baltimore on April 19, 1861. The former slave, renowned abolitionist, and civil rights leader, Frederick Douglass (1818–1895), was born in Maryland.

Harriet Tubman (c. 1820–1913), the intrepid free black woman who led hundreds of slaves to freedom, was also a native of the state. In the state constitution drawn up in 1864, provisions were made to end slavery, for increased representation for Baltimore, and for a state system of education. Following the Civil War the growth of the state paced that of the nation, although after World War II state growth exceeded that of the country. The steel industry, ship building, and aircraft manufacturing contributed heavily to the growth and expansion of the Baltimore area. The expansion of the federal government in Washington during the second half of the twentieth century precipitated rapid population growth in the neighboring Maryland counties. Combined, the Baltimore–Washington corridor is one of the largest metropolitan areas in the country. Improved facilities in transportation and communication have done much to weld the Maryland population as well as its scattered areas into one.

The Washington and Baltimore metropolitan areas with their large populations dominate the politics of the state, and Maryland has become one of the most liberal states in the union. In the last nine presidential elections Maryland was carried six times by the Democratic candidates, who won nationally only four times. Since 1968 Democrats have controlled the governorship all but four years, and only a few Republicans have served in the Maryland delegation in the Congress.

The Catholic Church and other pro-life supporters have been unsuccessful in moving voters to restrict legalized ABORTION. In 1992 the Church was very active in opposing legislation which gave abortion on demand the protection of state law. Despite these efforts the pro-life position was defeated by a 62 to 38 percent margin. Efforts to outlaw partial-birth abortions were defeated in the state assembly in 1999. The National Abortion Rights Action League gave Maryland an *A* on its 2008 report card with only California and Washington state scoring higher on providing abortion services. In such a political environment, it is no surprise that the Church in Maryland, through the Maryland Catholic Conference, has had to fight efforts to legalize EUTHANASIA as well as same-sex marriage.

Ecclesiatical Subdivisions. From the time of its establishment, the see of Baltimore continually experienced the reduction of its territory. The process began in 1808 when Baltimore was elevated to the status of an ARCHDIOCESE and new dioceses were established in Boston, New York, Philadelphia, and Bardstown, (later Louisville) Kentucky. The contraction of the Archdiocese of BALTIMORE not only involved the subtraction of whole states from see authority, it also included the subdivision of Maryland itself as an ecclesiastical jurisdiction. In 1868 the Diocese of WILMINGTON, Delaware was established with the eight Eastern Shore counties of Maryland included in its domain. Then in 1947 the archdiocese surrendered five more Maryland counties as they were united with the District of Columbia to form the Archdiocese of WASHINGTON, D.C.

Between them, the three sees that serve Catholics in the state of Maryland—the Archdiocese of Baltimore, the Archdiocese of Washington, and the Diocese of Wilmington—have had numerous bishops who have served them well. Among them four were given some national prominence. During his forty-six-year tenure as the archbishop of Baltimore, Cardinal James GIBBONS became well known among all Americans for his social grace and amiable ecumenism. His successor, the more combative Archbishop Michael CURLEY, urged the United States government in the 1930s to pressure Mexico to respect the rights of the Church. Curley was also well known in the pre-war years for his support for American isolationism. Cardinal O'Boyle (1896–1987), Archbishop of Washington from 1948 until 1973, gained national prominence for his support of civil rights. He gave the invocation for the 1963 "March on Washington," which was immortalized by Martin Luther King's (1929–1968) "I Have a Dream" speech. Five years later, O'Boyle was once again in the national spotlight for his vigorous response to the public DISSENT occasioned by the ENCYCLICAL *Humanae vitae* which upheld Church teaching regarding the immorality of artificial CONTRACEPTION. Finally, during the firestorm that erupted over the clergy sexual abuse scandal in 2002, Cardinal Theodore McCarrick (1930–) of Washington, who enjoyed unusual favor with the media, emerged as the unofficial spokesman for the American hierarchy.

Saint Mary Seminary, Baltimore, MD. *Founded in 1791 by the Sulpicians, it was the first Roman Catholic seminary in the United States.* © PHILIP SCALIA / ALAMY

Education. From the foundation of Maryland, the Jesuits have been in the forefront of Catholic education in Maryland. Bishop John Carroll's designs and hopes for a college for his diocese were realized when Georgetown opened in what is now part of the District of Columbia in 1791. Four SULPICIANS, including F.C. NAGOT, landed in Baltimore in July 1791, and on October 3, St. Mary's Seminary opened. The Sulpicians opened St. Mary's College in 1799 as a preparatory seminary. This institution closed in 1852 to be succeeded by Loyola College. MOUNT ST. MARY'S COLLEGE AND SEMINARY opened in 1808. For women, the Georgetown Visitation Academy opened in what is now the District of Columbia in 1799 and St. Joseph's College, St. Elizabeth Ann SETON's establishment, opened in 1808 at Emmitsburg. The Christian Brothers opened Rock Hill College, Ellicott City, in 1865. In the course of time additional educational institutions were opened by various congregations, including a college at Woodstock (1867) by the Jesuits for training their own members, Calvert Hall College (1845) and La Salle Institute in Cumberland by the Christian Brothers, and Mount St. Joseph's College by the XAVERIAN BROTHERS. Prominent among the earlier girls' schools are the College of Notre Dame of Maryland (1873), conducted by the School Sisters of Notre Dame, and Mount St. Agnes College (1867), conducted by the SISTERS OF MERCY. The state currently has three Catholic colleges: Mount St. Mary's, Loyola, and Notre Dame of Maryland, which remains a college for women. These three colleges had a total enrollment of 12,024 students in 2008 (*The Official Catholic Directory* 2008, p. 74).

SEE ALSO AUTHORITY, ECCLESIASTICAL; BOSTON, ARCHDIOCESE OF; GEORGETOWN UNIVERSITY; GEORGETOWN VISITATION; HUMANAE VITAE; KNOW-NOTHINGISM; LOUISVILLE, ARCHDIOCESE OF; NATIVISM, AMERICAN; NEW YORK, ARCHDIOCESE OF; PENN, WILLIAM; PHILADELPHIA, ARCHDIOCESE OF; POLITICS, CHURCH AND; SEX ABUSE CRISIS; SLAVERY, III (HISTORY OF); TOLERATION ACTS OF 1639 AND 1649, MARYLAND; WASHINGTON, D.C., ARCHDIOCESE OF; WILMINGTON, DIOCESE OF; WOODSTOCK THEOLOGICAL CENTER.

BIBLIOGRAPHY

Robert Brugger, Cynthia Horsburgh Requardt, Robert I. Cottom, Jr., and Mary Ellen Hayward, *Maryland: A Middle Temperament, 1634–1980* (Baltimore 1996).

Rory T. Conley, *The Truth in Charity: A History of the Archdiocese of Washington* (Strasbourg, France 2001).

Peter K. Guilday, *The Life and Times of John Carroll: Archbishop of Baltimore, 1735–1815*, 2nd ed. (New York 1927).

Annabelle M. Melville, *John Carroll of Baltimore, Founder of the American Catholic Hierarchy* (New York 1955).

The Official Catholic Directory, 2008 (New Providence, N.J. 2008).

Thomas W. Spalding, *The Premier See: A History of the Archdiocese of Baltimore, 1789–1989* (Baltimore 1989).

Richard Walsh and William L. Fox, eds., *Maryland: A History, 1632–1974* (Baltimore 1974).

Rev. John J. Tierney SJ
St. Thomas Seminary
Louisville, Ky.

Rev. Rory T. Conley
Historian
Archdiocese of Washington, D.C. (2009)

MASSACHUSETTS, CATHOLIC CHURCH IN

One of the thirteen original colonies, located in northeastern United States, Massachusetts is bounded on the north by Vermont and New Hampshire, on the east and south by the Atlantic Ocean, on the south by Rhode Island and Connecticut, and on the west by New York. Boston is the capital and principal metropolis of the Commonwealth, the official state designation. Other large cities include Worcester, Springfield, and Cambridge. In 2008 the Catholic population of Massachusetts was 2,709,552, about 44 percent of the total (*The Official Catholic Directory*, 2008 p. 2084). In addition to the Archdiocese of BOSTON (1808), there were three other dioceses: Springfield (1870), Fall River (1904), and Worcester (1950).

Early History. The area was first settled by English religious dissenters. The Pilgrims, or Separatists, under John Carver (1576–1621) and William BRADFORD, founded a colony in Plymouth (1620). The PURITANS, or Congregationalists, led by John Endicott (1588–1665) and John Winthrop (1588–1649), under a charter for the Massachusetts Bay Colony, settled in Salem (1628) and Boston (1630). Hundreds of colonists followed Winthrop during the 1630s, and by the end of the decade the Bay Colony had 25,000 settlers and was the largest English colony in North America.

Calvinism in Colony. The Puritan leaders established a bible commonwealth based on CALVINISM. Congregational Church polity was transferred to the political system, and self-government developed in the towns. "No man shall be admitted to the freedom of this body," declared the General Court, "but such as are members of the [Congregational] church." Those who did not subscribe to Congregationalism were permitted to reside in the Bay Colony, but were not allowed to take an active role in the governance of the colony. Roman

Catholics, however, along with Quakers and Jews, were not permitted in the colony at all. This Bible commonwealth did not survive the seventeenth century, and control of the CONGREGATIONAL CHURCHES was further weakened by the Charter of 1691, ruling that representatives of the general court were to be elected on the basis of property rather than religious affiliation. Nevertheless, the Puritans, with their zeal for religion, intense hostility to the Catholic religion and practices, concern for education, and strict moral attitudes, dominated New England. Massachusetts took the lead in the events that led to the War for Independence, and the Battles of Lexington and Bunker Hill in 1775 marked the beginning of the war. Maine remained a district of Massachusetts until 1820, when it entered the Union under the Missouri Compromise.

Early Catholicism. During the colonial period Catholics avoided Massachusetts, whose laws of 1647 and 1700 forbade Catholic priests to reside in the colony under pain of imprisonment and execution. The approximately 1,200 exiled Acadians assigned (1755–1756) to Massachusetts were scattered among the towns, where they were gradually assimilated or from which they eventually escaped. Thanks largely to an alliance and friendship with France during the War for Independence, Americans became more tolerant of Roman Catholics, and by the time independence was achieved, a small group of French and Irish residents had organized a small congregation and began holding services. Although the new Massachusetts Constitution of 1780 provided a bill of rights guaranteeing "equal protection of the law" to all religious denominations, it required that all state officials swear that they were not subject to the authority of any "foreign prince, person, prelate, state, or potentate." Since Protestants assumed that Catholics were subject to both POPE and PRELATE, this clause automatically excluded them from holding public office in Massachusetts until 1821, when the test was finally removed.

Diocese of Boston. Despite the continued existence of political limitations, the number of Catholics increased in Massachusetts, and in 1808 the Diocese of Boston was established with Frenchman Jean Lefebvre de CHEVERUS as its first BISHOP. The first DIOCESE encompassed all of New England, extending from Buzzards Bay and Nantucket Sound in the south to Maine and the Canadian border in the north. Twelve years later, an estimated 3,850 Catholics lived in New England, including several members of Native American settlements in northern Maine who had been converted earlier by the French and who now came under the jurisdiction of the bishop of Boston. When Benedict Joseph FENWICK succeeded Cheverus as bishop of Boston in 1825, he found

himself in charge of the smallest and weakest of the nine dioceses in the United States at that time. In all New England only eight churches existed, and the larger part of the Catholic population was still restricted to the Boston area. As the result of repressive land policies in the British Isles after the Napoleonic wars, the number of Irish immigrants coming to the United States grew rapidly, so Fenwick had to build several new churches in the city.

The sudden rise in the number of Irish Catholics created considerable anxiety among native Bostonians, who feared the social and economic impact of unskilled workers and resented their religious beliefs. During the summer of 1825, roving gangs of vandals broke windows, damaged furniture, and actually destroyed several small houses in the Irish district. In 1834 a local mob burned down the Ursuline CONVENT in nearby Charlestown, and in 1837 groups of Yankees and Irish residents clashed in downtown Boston in what became known as the Broad Street Riot.

Roman Catholicism also spread to other parts of Massachusetts during this same period. By the mid-1820s, for example, a number of Irish immigrants had moved some forty-five miles north of Boston in search of work at locations along the Merrimack River, where Boston investors were constructing new textile factories. Irish workers from Boston, along with French-speaking Catholic workmen from Canada, soon made up a sizeable portion of the work force in such towns as Lowell and Lawrence, where they dug the canals and constructed the buildings. After acquiring land near the Western Canal, on July 3, 1831, Bishop Fenwick dedicated St. Patrick's Church as further evidence of Catholic expansion. Between 1828 and 1830 he supervised the dedication of churches in Newport and Pawtucket, Rhode Island, and in New Bedford, Massachusetts. To serve a group of Irish glassworkers who had moved to Sandwich, Fenwick had a small frame church constructed in Boston and shipped by water to the Cape Cod town. On June 17, 1830, he dedicated Holy Trinity, the first Catholic church in Connecticut. Meanwhile, he continued to minister to Native American populations at Old Town and Eastport, Maine.

Failing health did not prevent Bishop Fenwick from traveling incessantly during the 1840s. He administered the sacrament of CONFIRMATION in Lowell, dedicated a new church in Fall River, and traveled to Vermont for another new church, then to Providence, Rhode Island, and Bridgeport, Connecticut. In September 1842 he dedicated a new church in Quincy, Massachusetts, and the following month he arrived in Lowell to dedicate St. Peter's Church. In 1842 Fenwick purchased property in Worcester, Massachusetts, for the college he had always dreamed of—the College of the Holy Cross—named after the original church in Boston.

Irish Immigration. Although the Boston diocese lost some 10,000 Catholics when Fenwick detached Connecticut and Rhode Island in 1844, nearly 70,000 still lived in the remaining four states that John Fitzpatrick (1812–1866) took over when he succeeded Fenwick in 1846. Massachusetts alone contained over 50,000 Catholics, with nearly 30,000 in the capital city. "In Boston, we are sadly off for want of churches," complained the new bishop as he proceeded to add churches in the diocese. In August 1846 he dedicated St. Joseph's Church in Roxbury and a short time later saw the completion of Holy Trinity Church for German immigrants in the South End. As the terrible aftereffects of the Great Famine brought additional Irish-Catholic immigrants to the shores of America during the late 1840s, Bishop Fitzpatrick stayed busy creating new parishes and dedicating new churches in other parts of Massachusetts. On the north shore, new pastors were sent to take charge of expanding Catholic populations in Chelsea and Lynn; St. Mary's Church in Salem was made responsible for mission stations in Marblehead, Gloucester, and Ipswich. On the south shore, St. Mary's Church in West Quincy provided a focal point for people in Quincy, Braintree, Weymouth, and Milton as well as for residents of Randolph and Stoughton, for those in Hingham and Cohasset, and for communities as far south as Plymouth. Because of the increase in textile manufacturing, Fall River showed amazing growth, and in August 1840 the Church of St. John the Baptist was constructed to serve the estimated one thousand Catholics in that area. To the west of Boston, things went even more rapidly. Before 1840, not a single church or CHAPEL existed west of Worcester. By the time Fitzpatrick took office in 1846, however, brand new churches had been built at Cabotville, Pittsfield, Northampton, and Springfield. The number of Catholics in the city of Worcester alone had risen to nearly two thousand, and in June of 1846 Fitzpatrick dedicated the Church of St. John the Evangelist.

The region along the Merrimack River had the most dramatic increase in numbers. The expanding textile center attracted many Irish immigrant workers, and by 1841 the Catholic population of Lowell was estimated to have reached 4,000, requiring Bishop Fenwick to add St. Peter's Church in 1842 to the original St. Patrick's Church he had constructed ten years earlier. The nearby textile city of Lawrence also experienced a population explosion, going from fewer than 200 Catholics in 1845 to more than 6,000 by 1848. At this time the jurisdiction of the bishop of Boston included not only the commonwealth of Massachusetts, but also the states of Vermont, New Hampshire, and Maine. Vermont was the most populous of the three, but its 5,000 Catholics were widely dispersed, with few churches and only a handful of priests. Most parishes were concentrated in the extreme northwestern parts of the state near the town of Burlington, where Fenwick had dedicated St. Peter's Church in 1841. In New Hampshire the small number of Catholics received little attention until the Amoskeag Manufacturing Company began its textile operations at Manchester in 1839. After that it became necessary for an itinerant priest to say Mass on a regular basis until the bishop of Boston could work out a more permanent arrangement. With well over 45,000 Catholics, Maine ranked second to Vermont in northern New England, and during the 1830s its growing population resulted in new churches at Dover, Portland, and Eastport. As a result of the sale of valuable timber land, the town of Bangor experienced a speculative boom that attracted about a thousand new Catholics for whom St. Michael's Church was built in 1839. There were also small Catholic communities at Ellsworth, West Mathias, and Lubec, with a small church at Houlton to meet the needs of those who lived close to the Canadian border. In addition to Catholics of European lineage, Bishop Fitzpatrick was also responsible for the Penobscot and Passamaquoddy tribes in the northern regions.

Anti–Immigrant and Anti–Catholic Measures. The continued influx of foreigners into the United States during the late 1840s and 1850s and the success of Catholic prelates in gaining some measure of social and economic benefits for their parishioners convinced many native-born Americans that they had to stem the immigrant tide. In 1852 a number of nativist groups formed the American party—more popularly known as the Know-Nothing party—to prevent further immigration and to keep immigrant Americans in a subservient position. Despite an amazing burst of power in Massachusetts and other northern states during 1854 and 1855, the emergence of the slavery issue caused the party to fail completely in its attempt to nominate a presidential candidate in 1856.

Impact of Civil War. The slavery controversy continued to provoke hostilities between the states of the North and the South, and in November 1860 the election of Republican candidate Abraham Lincoln led to the secession of southern states from the Union. On the morning of April 12, 1861, with the bombardment of Fort Sumter, a federal fort in Charleston Harbor, the Civil War began. With the outbreak of war, Irish Catholics joined the fight to preserve the Union. With the approval of Governor John A. Andrew (1818–1867), Catholic leaders in Boston formed a separate regiment of Irish soldiers. Companies from Boston, joined by military units from Salem, Milford, Marlboro, and Stoughton, banded together to form the 9th Regiment, Massachusetts Voluntary Infantry. In response to the gallant efforts of the "Fighting Ninth," Governor Andrew approved recruitment for a second all-Irish regiment—the 28th—that was sworn into service in December 1861 and became one of the five regiments that made up the Irish Brigade. The impressive PATRIOTISM displayed by Boston Catholics, the heroism of Irish troops on the battlefield, and the support they received from loyal Catholic citizens did much to create a higher level of tolerance throughout the state. Bishop John Fitzpatrick was awarded an honorary degree from Harvard College, Catholic clergymen were permitted to attend patients in public institutions, and Catholic school children were no longer forced to read the Protestant version of the Bible in the public schools.

Diocesan Divisions. Once the Civil War was over, large-scale immigration resumed, and additional Catholic immigrants joined earlier arrivals in spreading across the state of Massachusetts. Following the death of Bishop Fitzpatrick in 1866, his friend Father John J. WILLIAMS took over as bishop and made arrangements for the expanding diocese. As early as 1868 he asked permission from ROME to divide the diocese of Boston. He proposed to separate the five counties of western and central Massachusetts and form them into a new diocese with Springfield as its see city. In 1870 Pope PIUS IX (pope 1846–1878) signed the bull creating the diocese of Springfield. Patrick Thomas O'Reilly (1870–1892), a native of Ireland, was consecrated the first bishop of the new diocese and was succeeded by Thomas Beaven (1892–1920), a native of Springfield. When the diocese was created, nearly 100,000 Catholics lived in the area; that number more than doubled by 1900. At the same time Bishop Williams suggested another diocese to encompass Rhode Island and three counties in southeastern Massachusetts. In 1872 Rome established the diocese of Providence, Rhode Island. It grew so fast that in 1904 the three Massachusetts counties were formed into the diocese of FALL RIVER. In his brief tenure, William Stang, the first bishop of Fall River (1904–1907) wrote three pastoral letters, summoned a diocesan synod and, within two months of its publication, began implementing *Acerbo nimis*, Pope Pius X's instruction on catechesis.

Despite these geographic divisions, the diocese of Boston was still growing at such a remarkable rate that on February 12, 1875, Pope Pius IX approved the transformation of Boston from a diocese into an ARCHDIOCESE, and Bishop John William was elevated to the rank of ARCHBISHOP. The new ecclesiastical province included all the dioceses of New England.

As Catholics increased in numbers during the late 1870s and early 1880s, some moved up from political positions at the local level to more significant places in city, state, and even national government. In 1881, for example, the city of Lawrence chose John Breen as its first Catholic mayor; the following year the city of Lowell elected John J. Donovan as mayor. In 1884 Boston chose Hugh O'Brien as the first Irish-born, Roman Catholic mayor of the city. In 1894 John F. Fitzgerald of Boston's North End was elected to the U.S. House of Representatives from the ninth congressional district, and Joseph F. O'Connell of Dorchester went to Washington from the tenth congressional district. The impoverished conditions of the immigrants during the 1850s, followed by the disruptive years of the Civil War during the 1860s, had caused earlier prelates to go slowly in building Catholic schools. Archbishop John Williams, however, undertook the creation of a parochial school system throughout the archdiocese, and in 1884 reported to the Third Baltimore Council that thirty-five of his parishes had parochial schools, with many more to follow. The two dominant teaching communities in the archdiocese of Boston were the Sisters of NOTRE DAME DE NAMUR, who had arrived in Boston in 1848, and the Sisters of ST. JOSEPH, who arrived in 1873.

New Immigrants. In the late 1880s and early 1890s, the ethnicity of immigrants to Massachusetts changed dramatically. During the early part of the nineteenth century, most immigrants to the United States had come from northern and western Europe. In the late 1880s the bulk of people entering the country came from southern and eastern Europe. Fleeing high taxes, low wages, drought, famine, political oppression, and religious persecution, these new immigrants came to America seeking liberty and opportunity. In the decade between 1900 and 1910, more than 150,000 Italians entered the Bay State, along with some 80,000 Poles and nearly 25,000 Lithuanians. Many newcomers were Roman Catholics who settled in various parts of Massachusetts and who posed challenges to a Church that was overwhelmingly Irish in its clerical personnel and its cultural institutions. Sensitive to the desires of these non-English-speaking groups to have their own Churches, their own priests, sermons in their own languages, and observances of their own religious feast days, Archbishop Williams permitted them as much national expression as possible in their religious observances, while keeping their new churches and their congregations under his episcopal authority.

There had been a small but active German-speaking community in Boston before the Civil War, and in 1872 Archbishop Williams laid the cornerstone to a new Holy Trinity Church that enlarged the original church, constructed in 1844. The number of French-speaking immigrants also expanded after the Civil War, when the numerous textile mills in the Merrimack Valley hired immigrants from Europe as well as from Canada. In 1868 Archbishop Williams recruited French-speaking

OBLATES OF MARY IMMACULATE to staff the first French parish of St. Joseph (later changed to St. Jean Baptiste) in Lowell. To further accommodate Canadian immigrants, the archbishop brought the MARIST FATHERS to Haverhill in the 1870s. Later, after assuming responsibility for St. Anne's parish in Lawrence, the Marists in 1885 purchased a site in the Boston Back Bay for the construction of the Church of Notre Dame des Victoires, popularly known as "the French Church." Archbishop Williams also responded to the arrival, between 1899 and 1910, of more than 45,000 Portuguese immigrants. He brought in several Portuguese-speaking priests to serve their spiritual needs while they lived in the North End of Boston and later to support Portuguese parishes in Cambridge and in Lowell.

By the turn of the century, nearly ten thousand Polish immigrants had settled in the greater Boston area, and in 1894 a Polish-speaking priest named Father John Chmielinski dedicated the church of Our Lady of Czestochowa in the Boston area and also ministered to groups of Polish immigrants in Lowell and Salem. From 1893 to 1918 Archbishop Williams and his successor Archbishop William O'CONNELL sanctioned as many as fifteen Polish parishes, despite occasional efforts by separatist Polish groups to establish independent national churches. During the same period, about one thousand Lithuanian immigrants settled in the South Boston peninsula and were provided with a young Lithuanian priest who established St. Joseph's Church, but whose controversial nature led a number of parishioners to erect a church of their own (St. Peter's). Five other Lithuanian parishes were established in various parts of the archdiocese—in Brockton, Lawrence, Lowell, Cambridge, and Norwood—places where Lithuanian immigrants had gone in search of work. The largest of the new immigrant groups arriving in Massachusetts came from Italy. As early as 1886 the average number of Italian immigrants had already reached 222,000; many of the newcomers settled in Boston. At first they congregated along the waterfront in the North End, where the Italian population grew from 1,000 in 1880 to 7,000 in 1895. As their numbers grew, steps needed to be taken to meet their spiritual needs. In 1876 St. Leonard's Church was constructed in the North End, with Franciscans providing the services; later, the Church of the Sacred Heart was established and placed under the direction of the Missionaries of St. Charles. Both churches developed parochial grammar schools and also provided for the predominantly Italian neighborhood social clubs and religious centers that featured yearly outdoor festivals honoring various PATRON SAINTS.

Twentieth-Century Developments. On February 2, 1907, Bishop Stang of Fall River died; he was succeeded by the Most Reverend Daniel F. Feehan (1907–1934).

Later that same year, after forty-one years of service as fourth bishop and first archbishop of Boston, Archbishop Williams died (August 30) and was succeed by William Henry O'CONNELL, bishop of Portland, Maine. Both Feehan and O'Connell arrived when the Church in Massachusetts was expanding rapidly. At the time of his accession, Archbishop O'Connell assumed responsibility for an archdiocese that covered about 2,500 square miles and served some 850,000 Catholics. The archdiocese contained almost 200 parish churches, had nearly 6,000 priests, and almost 1600 sisters of various religious orders. Fifty thousand students attended church-related schools, from the elementary grades to the college level, and some 70,000 cases a year were being handled by various hospitals and charitable agencies operated by the archdiocese. In addition to the increasing number of parishes in the city of Boston, a series of new churches went up in other parts of the state. From Winthrop and Revere, to Lynnfield, Danvers, and Newburyport, the spires of new churches marked the Catholic movement into north shore areas. The archdiocese stayed busy supplying priests and building churches for new immigrant families moving into the textile centers of Lowell and Lawrence as well as into the neighboring communities of North Andover, Tewksbury, and Dracut. South of Boston, St. John's Church in Quincy was the basis of a network of other churches and mission stations, while new parishes went up in the nearby towns of Braintree, Weymouth, Milton, and Randolph. Along the seashore areas of Hull, Cohasset, and Scituate as well as Plymouth, Kingston, and Duxbury, a number of new churches were constructed, and several temporary missions were converted into parishes. With numerous industries in the Brockton area offering employment for unskilled European immigrants, several large churches went up in Brockton itself and in such nearby towns as Whitman, Bridgewater, and Middleboro. During this same period, the number of non-English-speaking churches also increased. By the time Cardinal O'Connell died in 1944, 29 such churches existed. Many were in French-Canadian communities such as Lowell, Lawrence, Haverhill, Salem, and Beverley; others were in Italian and Polish communities. By 1945 a total of 15 Italian churches had been established in the North End, in east Boston, and in such towns as Revere, Somerville, Everett, Waltham, and Salem. The original 6 Polish churches had expanded to 15 by 1945. During the first 18 months of his episcopacy, O'Connell could point to 31 new parishes, 29 additional priests, 9 more parochial schools, 2 more orphan asylums, and 3 new religious orders of nuns added to those already serving the archdiocese.

In 1944 Richard J. CUSHING succeeded Cardinal O'Connell as archbishop of Boston and found the

The Cathedral of the Holy Cross, Boston, MA. *A small group of parishioners attends Sunday mass at the cathedral.* JOHN MOT-
TERN/GETTY IMAGES

Church in Massachusetts growing at a rate of about 250,000 to 300,000 every five years, with the number of parishes increasing from 325 in 1944 to 396 in 1960. At the time Cushing became archbishop, 4,054 women were serving in 44 female religious orders; by 1960 the number had risen to 5,543, representing 63 orders. In 1944 there were 253 seminarians; by 1960 the figure had jumped to 418. The archdiocese had such a surplus of priests that Cardinal Cushing created a program that sent Boston priests to dioceses in parts of the country like Utah, Louisiana, Colorado, and Wyoming, where serious shortages of clergy existed.

The diocese of Springfield experienced similar growth. The Catholic population had more than doubled since the turn of century. In January 1950 Worcester county, the central section of Massachusetts, was detached from the diocese of Springfield to form a separate diocese. The first bishop of the new Diocese of WORCESTER was John Joseph WRIGHT, formerly an auxiliary bishop in Boston. When Bishop Wright was transferred to Pittsburgh at the beginning of 1959, Bishop Joseph Flanagan was transferred from Norwich, Connecticut, to succeed him. In 1969 the bishops established the Massachusetts Catholic Conference

(MCC) to serve as the official voice of the four Catholic dioceses in the Commonwealth. The MCC identifies pressing needs in areas of welfare, health, education, and civil rights and represents the Church's position on social issues and matters of public policy to government agencies.

By the late 1960s and early 1970s changes throughout the state reflected many of the tensions in the Church and the nation during those disruptive years. Mass attendance declined; the number of parochial schools was substantially reduced; the number of incoming seminarians dropped off dramatically; fewer women were entering religious orders, and more and more parish priests were retiring because of age. In part, many of these statistical changes resulted from demographic shifts in Massachusetts that saw older populations moving out of the cities into the suburbs and the arrival of new immigrants from Latin American countries and many parts of Southeast Asia who settled in urban centers. Cardinal Bernard F. LAW, who became archbishop of Boston in 1984, confronted these changes, as did other bishops in the state, by closing older parishes in depopulated urban districts and by creating new parishes in recently developed suburban areas.

Early Twenty-First-Century Developments. Both as a percentage of the population (from half of the state population) and in political strength and influence, the Catholic Church in the early 2000s had declined since the 1960s. An important factor in the collapse of the Church's prestige was the SEX ABUSE CRISIS. The first significant case in the state was that of James Porter, an ex-priest of the Fall River diocese, who pleaded guilty in 1993 to molesting twenty-eight children. The trial of John Geoghan (c. 1935–2003), however, a defrocked priest of the Archdiocese of Boston and his conviction in January 2002, gained both state and national attention. The revelation during the trial of a larger pattern of sexual abuse by priests, and of malfeasance and deception by the archdiocese, created a firestorm of criticism and protest that eventually led to the resignation of Cardinal Law on December 13, 2002. He was succeeded by Sean Patrick O'Malley (1944–) in July 2003. O'Malley, as bishop of Fall River, had dealt successfully with the aftermath of the Porter case before being sent to Palm Beach, Florida, in 2002, where two consecutive bishops had resigned after sex-abuse scandals. Once in Boston he quickly moved to heal the damage caused by the scandals, both by settling with the victims and by showing real pastoral concern. Despite his successes on a pastoral level, the economic costs of the SCANDAL were such that a new round of parish closings was announced, and the archdiocese was forced to sell substantial amounts of property.

In 2004, by a ruling of the Supreme Judicial Court of Massachusetts, the state became the first U.S. state to permit same-sex marriages. Since then the Catholic bishops in the state have worked consistently to restore traditional marriage through the political process. In 2008 the 1913 marriage law was repealed, thus allowing marriage licenses in Massachusetts to same-sex couples living in other states that do not recognize same-sex marriage.

Institutions of Higher Learning. Founded in 1843 as a liberal arts college for men by the JESUITS, Holy Cross College shares the distinction of being the oldest Catholic college in Massachusetts. Its first graduating class included James Augustine HEALY and his brother Hugh, both freed African-American slaves, while the second graduating class included their brother Patrick, the first African-American to be awarded a Ph.D. James Healy, who was also the valedictorian for the first graduating class, went on to become the first African American to be named bishop when he was appointed bishop of Portland, Maine, in 1875. In addition to Holy Cross College, the Jesuits also administer BOSTON COLLEGE, established in 1863. Other Catholic colleges in the state include Stonehill College in North Easton (sponsored by the Holy Cross Fathers), Emmanuel College in Boston (established in 1919 by the Sisters of Notre Dame de Namur), Regis College in Weston (sponsored by the Sisters of St. Joseph), College of Our Lady of the Elms in Chicopee (sponsored by the Sisters of St. Joseph), Merrimack College in North Andover (established in 1947 by the AUGUSTINIANS), Anna Maria College in Paxton (sponsored by the Sisters of ST. ANNE), and Assumption College in Worcester (sponsored by the Augustinians of the Assumption).

SEE ALSO BALTIMORE, COUNCILS OF; MAINE, CATHOLIC CHURCH IN; KNOW-NOTHINGISM; NATIVISM, AMERICAN; NEW HAMPSHIRE, CATHOLIC CHURCH IN; SLAVERY, III (HISTORY OF); SPRINGFIELD IN MASSACHUSETTS, DIOCESE OF; URSULINES; VERMONT, CATHOLIC CHURCH IN; WORCESTER, DIOCESE OF.

BIBLIOGRAPHY

Francis James Bradley, *Brief History of the Diocese of Fall River, Mass.* (New York 1931).

John G. Deedy, ed., *The Church in Worcester, New England; A Modern Diocese with an Ancient Name* (Worcester, Mass. 1956).

Oscar Handlin, *Boston's Immigrants 1790–1880: A Study in Acculturation*, rev. ed. (Cambridge, Mass. 1959). The best study of the impact of the Irish on Boston.

Marcus Lee Hansen, "The Second Colonization of New England," *The Immigrant in American History*, edited by Arthur M. Schlesinger (Cambridge, Mass. 1940). Corrects some false ideas about the immigrants.

Robert H. Lord, John E. Sexton, and Edward T. Harrington, *History of the Archdiocese of Boston in the Various Stages of Its Development, 1604 to 1943*, 3 vols. (New York 1944; repr. Boston 1945).

Massachusetts Digest Annotated, 1761 to Date (Boston 1933).

Massachusetts General Laws Annotated (St. Paul, Minn. 1958–1959).

J. J. McCoy, "Diocese of Springfield," in *History of the Catholic Church in the New England States*, edited by William Byrne, William A. Lecky, J. J. McCoy, et al. (Boston 1899).

Samuel Eliot Morison, *The Builders of the Bay Colony* (Boston 1930).

Samuel Eliot Morison, *The Intellectual Life of Colonial New England*, 2nd ed. (New York 1956).

Thomas H. O'Connor, *Boston Catholics: A History of the Church and Its People* (Boston 1998).

Arthur J. Riley, *Catholicism in New England to 1788* (Washington, D.C. 1936).

Mary Xaveria Sullivan, *The History of Catholic Secondary Education in the Archdiocese of Boston* (Washington, D.C. 1946).

Leon Edgar Truesdell, *The Canadian Born in the United States* (New Haven, Conn. 1943). Statistics for French Canadians.

William Leo Lucey SJ
Professor of American History and Librarian of Dinand Library
Holy Cross College, Worcester, Mass.

Thomas H. O'Connor
Professor Emeritus of History
Boston College, Chestnut Hill, Mass.

Dom Paschal Scotti OSB
Chairman, Christian Doctrine Department
Portsmouth Abbey School, Portsmouth, R.I. (2009)

METAPHYSICS

From the Greek τὰ μετὰ τὰ φυσικά (what comes after the physical) and the Latin *metaphysica* (after or beyond the physical), the notion of metaphysics can be interchanged with ONTOLOGY, first philosophy, THEOLOGY, and wisdom. Such identity reflects profoundly the imprint of ARISTOTLE even though he does not use the term in his writings. His work known as *Metaphysics* centers on the science (ἐπιστήμη) of being *qua* being (τὸ ὄν ᾗ ὄν) (hence ontology), as well as connecting this science with the study of the divine (hence theology) and with the study of first principles or causes (hence, first philosophy). The association with wisdom (σοφία) is clear through the recognition that the "lover of wisdom" is the "lover of first things."

Taking being *qua* being as the subject of metaphysics, the focus, via traditional Scholastic usage, is on both its material and formal character. In its object understood materially, or in the number of things it studies, metaphysics is all-inclusive, extending to everything and every aspect of whatever is or can exist, whether of a material, sensible, physical nature or of a higher, nonmaterial nature. Nevertheless, metaphysics retains its distinctive point of vision, or object considered formally, inasmuch as it is concerned with things as beings, that is, according to the relation that any thing or aspect of things has to "being itself," rather than to one of the particular aspects treated in the other sciences. The unity of this point of view, centered on what is most fundamental to all reality, enables metaphysics to investigate the way in which the many are interrelated to the one in some form of real unity. Indeed, being and unity can be treated as convertible terms. Further, truth and intelligibility lie in the unity and being of things. Knowledge, then, understood intellectually and metaphysically, is the knowledge of being. And it is this knowledge which constitutes wisdom.

According to Hans Reiner, Aristotle's early disciples coined the term, or more specifically, a pupil Eudemus of Rhodes (third century BC). These Peripatetics, understood as students and followers of Aristotle, applied the title to treatises embodying the science Aristotle called *first philosophy* or *theology*. As such, the treatises dealt with what is separate from matter and so "beyond the sensible." That Aristotle's corpus of writings is ordered such that the physical treatises, or *Physics* precede the metaphysical treatises because of their differing doctrinal content might be considered a reasonable action. However, Johann Buhle's (1763–1821) contention that Andronicus of Rhodes (first century BC) editorially appended or placed these latter treatises with the title *Metaphysics* after the *Physics* for lack of knowing how to classify them appears erroneous. In Reiner's view the use of the name *Metaphysics* by Eudemus of Rhodes, the first editor of Aristotle's works, reflected not only that its study takes up what lies beyond physical things, but also the corresponding Aristotelian concern for the order of learning as proceeding from the sensible order of material beings to the supersensible, or what completely transcends matter. This article considers metaphysics in two parts. The first is concerned with its history, and the second with its identity and treatment as science.

HISTORY OF METAPHYSICS

Metaphysical thought arises from the wonder generated by the tension between the characteristics of things experienced as multiple, individual, contingent, changing, and temporal, on the one hand, and those of truth as one, universal, necessary, unchanging, and eternal, on the other. The history of metaphysics is constituted by man's progression toward a more penetrating mode of vision and the correlative intrinsic and extrinsic principles that enable him to understand both the many-as-constituting-one order of reality and the one truth that underlies its multiple realizations.

Primitive Origins. That man's mind is naturally metaphysical is indicated by the vision of reality as a whole and the concern for explanation manifested in the ancient myths. In Greece these were summarized in the *Theogony* of Hesiod, which portrayed the parts of the universe in the anthropomorphic form of the gods, unifying them in a genetic series and identifying in Eros an active principle for their interrelation. To attain a more precise view of this unity, it was necessary to supersede the anthropomorphic and symbolic form of the myths to attain a more explicit identification of their intellectual content and its source. This step was accomplished in concrete and personal terms by the HEBREWS and in abstract terms by the Hindus and others in the East and by the Greeks in the West.

The Jews, from their earliest history to the Babylonian exile in the sixth century BC, under the tutelage of divine providence, came to see that persons and things, however many, were one in their common dependence on GOD or, more exactly, in their dependence on a common personal God. "I am the first and I am the last;

there is no God but me" [Isaiah 44:6]. This unity in things was paralleled in the intentional order, where individuals by their fundamental response of mind and heart related themselves and their world to God. The repetition of this relation in concrete and personal terms for single types of things ("who made the heavens in wisdom...who spread out the earth upon the waters..."—Psalms 135:5–6) manifests the need for a more abstract thought capable of identifying the proper extension and comprehension of the unifying relation to God.

The Oriental mind, in contrast to the Hebraic mind, carried metaphysical thought to a more deeply abstract level. HINDUISM in its scriptures, the UPANISHADS, expressed a decisive appreciation of unity through the one impersonal SUBSTANCE, BRAHMAN or Ātman, as the intimate reality of all things. However, by an overriding treatment of the world of EXPERIENCE as unreal and an illusion, it turned the search for wisdom into an ascetical and mystical approach of withdrawal from activity. As such, one entered into a rigorous movement toward natural CONTEMPLATION of God as a prelude to reabsorption into Ātman. In the sixth century BC, BUDDHISM, as an offspring of Hinduism, carried on the same inward approach to an even greater extreme. In its initial form of HINAYANA Buddhism, it reduced everything, including the SOUL, to empty PHENOMENA in flux. Deliverance from EXISTENCE involved the teaching that there is no Brahman. Such denial, however, like all negative theologies, took the movement toward a nameless state of supreme affirmation. For the Buddhist this is NIRVĀNA. On a further note, it is not the purpose here to take up the many forms of Hinduism and Buddhism, which qualify to various degrees the preponderant negativity of the world of experience embodied in their respective metaphysical outlooks. Nonetheless, what is clear throughout this oriental mindset is the tendency to eliminate the many or to treat the many as modes of the one through PANTHEISM. Further, regardless of this mindset's treatment of the many, the affirmation of being or unity remains powerfully present.

The primitive origins of metaphysics, emerging as they do out of natural religion, center on what can be called the sacred. Mircea Eliade, in his description of primitive and ancient religions (including Hinduism and Buddhism), identifies the sacred with "unconditioned being" (Eliade, 1969). To carry this further, all things in the world participate in or reflect the sacred. As for those forms of Hindusim and Buddhism that reduce these things to illusions, such reduction does not mean the sacred is eliminated. Rather, as previously seen, the sacred or the divine remains as the "perfect unity."

Greek Philosophy. The Greeks, in initiating their own speculative unification in the sixth century BC, possessed a firm appreciation of the reality of their world and a growing awareness of the value of intellectual clarity. Hence, their first steps in describing this reality were based on the evidence of the external senses and concluded in correlative terms that all was but particular states of water (Thales, c. 640–550) or other similar elements. Even here their concern opened beyond the merely physical to the metaphysical problem of overall unity, as is reflected in Anaximander's (c. 611–546) further reasoning to the boundless as beyond the diverse elements, unborn, all-encompassing, all-governing, and divine. PYTHAGORAS (c. 580–500), in holding all to be numbers, attained a second level of evidence corresponding to the internal senses, that is, to the relation between IMAGINATION and mathematical description. Finally, PARMENIDES arrived at the third, uniquely intellectual and metaphysical appreciation of the real in its own proper term, *being*. For only the path of being is thinkable, and non-being is unthinkable. In this regard, since being could differ only by "not being" and BECOMING is not yet and so is reducible to NONBEING or nothing, Parmenides denied anything other than the one absolutely perfect and unchanging sphere of being. This gave being the meaning of identity or what can be thought, contrasting with the position of HERACLITUS (540–475) that all was becoming. So too this contrast reflected the attainment by GREEK PHILOSOPHY of the properly metaphysical: the real as such. This then shows the clear identifying of the notion of being with the one. In sum, early Greek philosophy stresses the search for the unifying principle that grounds the many which are its manifestations. Even in the case of Parmenides, granted that the realm of the many, and so of becoming, is rejected, he still affirms the world, or κόσμος, as a spherical space filled with indivisible being.

The Presocratic groundwork, having prepared the way for a deeper grasp of the one-many relation, was followed by the golden age of Greek philosophy. PLATO (429–348), ever in the shadow of SOCRATES, concluded in the *Sophist* from the fact of multiple beings to a principle of LIMITATION or nonbeing, that is, of difference, and from the similarity among beings to something one or absolute in which the multiple participate as limited imitations. Present here is the Parmenidean meaning of being as intelligible identity, but also the affirmation of the reality of difference. This is also to say that the philosopher as dialectician knows how to find the one in the many and the many in the one. Indeed he can do so because of the doctrine of PARTICIPATION. In an earlier work, the *Republic*, this doctrine stands out with great clarity. In this regard the Socratic method of dialectic led to the transfer of reality from the multiple to that which the multiple imitate, the transcendent formal unities as Ideas or Forms to be contemplated and hierarchically ordered under the supreme Idea of the

Good or the One. It should be noted that the world of becoming is not an illusion. Rather the many or sensible things by way of participation in the One take on a "semi-real" status. However, the One as source of this sharing would seem to differentiate itself. Such a result would mean that the One could only remain undifferentiated under a pantheistic vision.

Aristotle (384–322) initiated a more active understanding of FORM, based on a realist appreciation of the form of matter in changing things. This led him to forms separated from matter, which were not only objects of contemplation but themselves living, acting, knowing, and ultimately the PURE ACT of thinking, that is, the thinking of thinking thinking (νόησις νοήσεως νόησις). What was called earlier the science of being *qua* being studies all physical or immaterial substances, that is, individual things. Thus it is this science that affirms the reality of sensible things. At the same time, by concentrating on the forms or immaterial principles of material things, Aristotle arrives at ultimate being, which is unchanging, immaterial, and divine. This one being, which is pure act, is the ultimate END (τέλος) of all things. However, Aristotle's insight into being was not sufficient to allow for an adequate understanding of the way in which the highest being could be the cause of the being of the world. In this regard the act of divine being is one of indifference, which simply attracts all beings to the unmoved mover as pure act. Unlike in Plato there is no AGENT cause active in the making of particulars. Yet, since the world of sensible things is eternal and is made up of beings, each of which is an act–potency composition, there must be pure mind (νοῦς), that is, an unmoved mover understood as subsistent thought and so free of POTENCY or matter, which provides the ultimate ground for movement from potency to act. So it is that Aristotle connects the many with the one. The result of pantheism by way of the world's movement toward and need for sharing in pure form or act appears an inevitable outcome. The Parmenidean problem of the one and the many thus remains insoluble in these terms.

Christianity. Christian thought presented the context for a penetrating insight into the ACT of being, which superseded the pantheistic affirmations of the Oriental and Greek minds. Already the Hebraic mind embraced the doctrine of a supremely personal God, whose name is "I am Who am." And further, the Jews possessed the teaching that this one and true God created the world, a notion which included implicitly CREATION *ex nihilo* ("out of nothing"). The philosophical rigor of Christian theology then makes this explicit. As the initial example, attention is given to St. AUGUSTINE (354–430), who in spite of the influence of NEOPLATONISM, founded by PLOTINUS (205–270), powerfully embraces the Christian

affirmation of God as creator. In this regard, all things of the world could not be of God since they would then be equal to God. Nor could there be an eternal existence of matter to which forms would be joined: Otherwise God would have to rely on matter as an aid in making the world and so would not be omnipotent. So it is God created the world *ex nihilo*. In the Scholastic period St. Anselm (1033–1109) refined the notion of *ex nihilo* by making doubly clear that a thing is in no sense created out of nothing taken as its material. Rather, what is created is made *non ex aliquo* (not out of something). St. THOMAS AQUINAS (1224–1274) carries one's understanding further with his teaching that God's ESSENCE is His *esse* (His *to be*, or act of existing). In contrast, the essence of created or finite beings is really distinct from their *esse*. Hence, God's essence is totally different from the essence of every creature since there is no distinction between ESSENCE AND EXISTENCE in God's being; He is simply pure and infinite *to be*. Creation then is in no wise a part of God and yet is caused by God *ex nihilo*. As for the problem of the one and the many, the resolution is now present. The many or finite beings are grounded in and participate in one God as the cause of their being, thereby take their likeness from God, and yet are in no way identified with the One's being. The changing temporal world and its many things thus exist as unique realities but are still contingent upon the one, infinite, unchanging, eternal being. In addition, a further medieval enrichment of metaphysics occurred through the notion of person. The Hebraic tradition had already begun a powerful stress on God as personal. In distinguishing person from nature in the doctrine of the Trinity, Christian thought heightened divine being's character as personal and communal and intensified the created person's reality as *imago Dei*, that is, as image of the Trinity. Regarding the latter point, what stood out was the deepening realization of the analogous participation by the human INTELLECT and WILL in the Trinitarian life of God through the Son as the personified, subsistent (Λόγος) eternally generated from the Father and through the Holy Spirit as the personified, subsistent love eternally proceeding from the Father and the Son.

In conclusion the history of metaphysics in the MIDDLE AGES consists in the major developments made possible by the ongoing penetration of being and evoked by the elaboration of the resultant theologies. These developments were made first on a more Platonic basis by Augustine and his school, with its culmination in St. BONAVENTURE (1231–1274), and then with an increasing addition of the Aristotelian systemization and REALISM by way of Islamic philosophy, culminating in the major syntheses of Aquinas and Bl. John DUNS SCOTUS (c. 1274–1308).

Modern Era. Early modern (fifteenth to eighteenth centuries) and later modern (nineteenth to twenty-first centuries) thought, finding the realistic metaphysics of being of the classical Christian philosophies of the Middle Ages already negated in the conceptualist philosophy of WILLIAM OF OCKHAM (c. 1285–c. 1349) and his followers, proceeded to develop its metaphysics by turning to the human subject as manifested in the *cogito* of R. DESCARTES (1596–1650). For the deleterious results, extending even to the negation of the possibility of metaphysics as a science, *see* METAPHYSICS, VALIDITY OF. Within this context, however, such classical rationalists as B. SPINOZA (1632–1677) and G.W. LEIBNIZ (1646–1727) contributed importantly to working out a logically deductive pattern of ideas. So too the schemata of the critical philosophy of I. KANT (1724–1804) and the dialectical sequences of G.W.F. HEGEL (1770–1831) deepened the understanding of the organic and developing character of reality. Nonetheless, without realistic foundations, these philosophies inevitably progressed from positing that being is met in CONSCIOUSNESS to IDEALISM, which holds that being is consciousness. In addition, the subjective or *a priori* foundation of knowledge as generated by the Cartesian "I think" made problematic the reality of the many or beings of the sensible world. Of note, too, is the irony of British EMPIRICISM, which sought to remedy the rationalist neglect of sense experience and tried to give proper due to sensible things. However, this attempt ended in the pan-phenomenalism of David HUME (1711–1776). It is worth pointing out that Kant, realizing that neither RATIONALISM nor empiricism could arrive at knowledge in the sense of what is universal and necessary, attempted to join sense experience with his *a priori* structures of consciousness. In so doing, he maintained that the *noumena*, or things-in-themselves, are the origin of the matter of SENSATION. Paradoxically, the things-in-themselves remain unknowable. So it is that any claim to knowledge of what is universal and necessary does not reach beyond the PHENOMENA or objects of appearance, which are relative to the constructing powers of consciousness. This leads him then to relegate metaphysics to a regulatory science where the *noumena* of SELF, world, and God are simply ideas of pure reason, which are useful to unify the phenomena of experience. In response to what, in effect, is Kant's rejection of metaphysics, German idealism affirms knowledge of the noumenal reality of the mind or consciousness and culminates in Hegel's Absolute Spirit or Consciousness. And as rooted in this divine Unity, Hegel understands the many of the world, taken both naturally and historically, as finite particularizations and phases in the ABSOLUTE's dialectical unfolding of itself. What results is a dialectical pantheism where the many

are, in effect, modes in the ongoing development of the Absolute. Further, with reference to the self-growing process of the Absolute, in spite of Hegel's ongoing endeavor to preserve the permanence of being as part of the dialectical SYNTHESIS of being-in-and-for-itself, the process cannot escape the dominance of TIME and becoming. Thus, his dialectic renders problematic both the being of the One and, consequently, any real metaphysics.

The nineteenth century after Hegel as well as the entire twentieth century and now twenty-first century in the West are dominated by a philosophical landscape where metaphysics tends to fade into the background of POSITIVISM, MATERIALISM, and NIHILISM. In this regard positivism centers on sense experience and empirical science as the measure of truth, a standard developed programmatically by Auguste COMTE (1798–1857) in his positive/social philosophy and basic in a variant manner to utilitarianism, Darwinism, pragmatism, and LOGICAL POSITIVISM. As for materialism it integrates itself with empirical science through Karl MARX (1818–1883) and Friedrich ENGELS (1820–1895) in dialectical/historical materialism, Ludwig Büchner's (1824–1899) force–matter reality, mind-brain identity (Herbert Feigl [1902–1988] and John Jamieson Carswell Smart [b.1920] as examples), and neo-Darwinism (Daniel Dennett [b. 1942] and Edward Osborne Wilson [b. 1929] as examples). These strict materialists, however, contrast with tempered materialist views like those of Herbert SPENCER (1820–1903; affirmation of an ultimate unknowable force) and John Searle (b. 1932; advocate of the mind's non-reduction to the brain). The reduction of everything to matter, of course, eliminates what is truly metaphysical, that is, beyond the physical. Indeed, this reduction makes no sense when matter is identified with potentiality and has no substance, for example, in the view of Aristotle. Further, empirical science of the later modern period rejects corpuscular substance, the solid matter of classical mechanics, stressing in its place quantized force fields. Under such description, SPACE, time, and energy become materialized and intermeshed with mass. As a result accidentals like QUANTITY, space, time, and relation provide the empirical scientific ground of materialism, a precarious basis indeed since, without the substantial and immaterial foundation of being *qua* being, accidental flux triumphs, leaving an abyss of becoming. Appropriately, attention is now given to Friedrich NIETZSCHE (1844–1900), who declares that being is a "vapor" and becoming pervades everything. In turn this teaching joins his advocacy of nihilism, that is, the nihilating of God and all values. What follows from Nietzsche's descent into the abyss is the loss of intelligibility, since only the permanence of being or unity can provide intelligibility. In sum, positivism, materialism, and nihilism all converge on the path of becoming where nothing ever is.

Around 1900 the philosophical landscape witnessed a striking attempt to fan the flame of being through Edmund HUSSERL (1859–1938). By way of his phenomenological method, he desired to return to the things themselves free of any positivistic and materialistic constraints as well as free of the limits of CONTINGENCY and change. Seeking a description of *pure essences* he sought contact with the intelligibility of being. His notion of *epoche*, that is, "bracketing," could not, however, preclude the incursion of facticity through the presence of temporality. Indeed, for two of his quasi-disciples, Martin HEIDEGGER (1889–1976) and Maurice MERLEAU-PONTY (1908–1961), time as identified with being turns being into a process and assures thereby the triumph of becoming. Further, Heidegger, in his later thought, transforms his philosophy into an aestheticism where the world of ART covers all of reality. In his case the world of art is the world of language, and language in its origin is the very temporalizing process of being. In conjunction with Heidegger's primacy of language, it is well now to draw a larger picture of the critical and even dominant role language plays in much twentieth century thought. The Vienna Circle (begun in 1922), through its logical positivism, rejecting philosophical assertions as meaningless, that is, nonsensical, wanted to limit the truth of all areas to what can be sensed and under the scope of empirical science. As a result, there is no metaphysics, only the privileged position of logic and empirical science. The philosophical task then is to describe the world of facts and assure the logical truth of what is stated. What is seen here is a kind of flight by philosophy into language. And when ordinary language, particularly under the influence of the later thought of Ludwig WITTGENSTEIN (1889–1951), came to dominate British philosophy, thereby supplanting the privileged place of scientific language, the flight expanded. Somewhat parallel to British interests are the Continental developments of STRUCTURALISM, the HERMENEUTICS of Hans-Georg GADAMER (1900–2002), the poststructuralism of Michel Foucault (1926–1984), and the DECONSTRUCTIONISM of Jacques Derrida (1930–2004). In this regard, his thought, arguably the strongest marker of what is called postmodernism (the historical accuracy of this designation is debatable since postmodernism remains in many ways a true child of the modern era), attacks what he calls *logocentrism*, his characterization of Plato and what basically follows throughout the history of Western philosophy. He claims that philosophy is trapped in its own logic and conceptualizations and that this world of its own making governs what is expressed, written, and set forth as truth. For Derrida this constitutes what he maintains is the illusion of logocentrism, which is expressed through the *différance* of language, that is, through the play of difference where the distinctions of terms dissolve into one another endlessly and every word and meaning gives way to other words and meanings. Since nothing is outside language, there is no connection with things. This disengagement with nature and the things themselves, and so with being, carries on dramatically the descent into the Nietzschean abyss. So it is that Derrida's logocentric renderings and flight into language leave behind what is primary in metaphysics, because things and their being are prior to and govern all conceptualization and language. Further, it should be noted that the objects of genuine knowledge are not found in the world of language, images, concepts, and mind. Rather, things are the objects in which such knowledge terminates, and concepts are the medium through which minds grasp things in their being.

To complete the picture of the modern era, an account must be given of the Neoscholasticism that emerged out of the Christian philosophies of realism in the Middle Ages. This movement continues, throughout the entire era, to affirm the many finite beings as rooted in the one divine and infinitely perfect being who is their creator and end. Concerning the early modern period, attention is drawn particularly to three Neoscholastics who are very much a part of the Thomist tradition: the dominicans' CAJETAN (1468–1534), JOHN OF ST. THOMAS (1589–1644), and the Jesuit Francisco SUAREZ (1548–1617). (Thomist referring to a follower of Aquinas, where the latter's thought serves as primary ground for, at least, a major part of the former's philosophy and/or theology. That some Thomists deviate significantly from Aquinas's teaching on certain points is not an uncommon occurrence in any philosophical school)

Cajetan carries on the real distinction of *esse* and essence. However, his knowledge of the being of metaphysics takes place within the context of the three degrees of conceptual ABSTRACTION. On the level of the third degree the mind abstracts from all matter and thereby grasps being itself. As a result his epistemological approach to being itself represents a critical departure from Aquinas's teaching that the being of metaphysics is known through JUDGMENT and separation (concerning these two notions, *see* Thomistic Revolution in Metaphysics below). John of St. Thomas, in turn, upheld the teaching of Cajetan. In addition, his doctrine of *formal sign* whereby this SIGN or *species expressa* plays the role of medium through which the same essence existing outside the mind also intentionally exists in the knower. Suarez, too, viewed Aquinas as his master and endeavored to develop a philosophy and theology consonant with the latter's vision. By contrast, however, to the Dominicans' teaching, Suarez rejected the real distinction of *esse* and essence, embracing an essentialist position, which reflects to varying degrees the influence of Scotus. In the period after this Second Scholasticism, that is, in the eighteenth century, a decline took place in the face of the ENLIGHTENMENT secularism, the impact of modern philosophy, and the suppression of the Jesuit Order. In the latter half of the nineteenth century, a Thomistic revival occurred once again. Of special impetus to this revival was LEO XIII's *Aeterni Patris* (1879). The realism of Thomistic metaphysics now took on a momentum that has lasted into the twenty-first century with sustained vitality, whether through the likes of Réginald GARRIGOU-LAGRANGE's (1877–1964) Dominican THOMISM, Joseph Maréchal, S.J.'s (1878–1944) transcendental Thomism, Jacques MARITAIN's (1882–1973) direct realism, or Étienne GILSON's (1884–1978) existential Thomism.

THE SCIENCE OF METAPHYSICS

The human mind naturally strives to attain a vision of reality as a unified whole. So it is that the history of metaphysics has through the large majority of its past shown an ongoing openness and receptivity of the intellect to the transcendent gift of being. However, the modern era in Western culture has now, for the most part, embraced the triumph of subjectivity and becoming. Indeed, the human DESIRE for intelligibility can be perverted, following Eric Voegelin's description of the deformation of consciousness, into an ego-construction of pseudo-intelligibility or can be kept at the margins of experience, one or other of these cases being present in so much of later modern thought (Voegelin, 1978). In the context of the twenty-first century, there is then a critical and even urgent need to renew the understanding of metaphysics as science since this notion is at the heart of human fulfillment and perfection. In Aristotle's encompassing usage of the term, science ($\epsilon\pi\iota\sigma\tau\eta\mu\eta$) is a much richer, broader term than what the world now generally accepts as its meaning. Indeed, the renewal of its Aristotelian sense is fundamental to restoring a unified vision of all knowledge. Such a vision means genuine (certain) knowledge that grounds all other sciences, even the empirical sciences, and can also be called wisdom ($\sigma o\phi\iota\alpha$). Further, the positivist and empiricist outlooks that dominate twenty-first century philosophical interpretation of what empirical science describes bring into doubt whether empirical science provides any knowledge at all. In contrast Aristotle's notion of science stresses demonstrative knowledge through causes, that is, deductive knowledge based on FIRST PRINCIPLES. Concerning this, in all demonstration the middle term taken universally must appear in at least one of the premises. In turn, it connects the truth in the conclusion with the simpler truths present in the premises. As for grasping first principles (includes both forms of things and the laws of thought), this happens

through the activity of mind ($\nu o\tilde{\nu}\varsigma$), which is the life of wisdom. Hence, the conclusions or more complex truths follow from the premises of simpler truths where the ultimate basis is the simplest truth or first principle, which is divine reality itself. Through inductive inspection of particulars, one breaks through to the wisdom of UNIVERSALS or forms, that is, one seizes them by intellectual INTUITION. Returning to the findings of empirical science, the telling contention of William A. Wallace, O.P., is that the natural sciences give knowledge of specialized details concerning the things of nature (Wallace, 1979). In this regard he provides numerous examples of empirical scientific conclusions concerning the properties of natural things, which are, in fact, demonstrable. This becomes possible when the mathematical description of things is not isolated from the focus on nature. So it is that, following Aristotle and Aquinas, QUANTITY is not just mathematical but can be investigated physically. Whether then dealing with the specialized details of empirical science or with the philosophy of nature, that is, with the more generalized realities of material substance, a real knowledge occurs. This is so because the knowledge of a natural thing's properties is rooted in the substantial forms or universals of the particulars under investigation.

It is well to point out here the full breadth of what constitutes the domain of metaphysics. Concerning this, Aristotle affirms, on the one hand, being *qua* being, that is, being in general, which covers the being of all that is, both material and immaterial (Book Gamma of the *Metaphysics*), and, on the other hand, theology as identified with the study of being *qua* being, that, in his distinction of the theoretical sciences, stresses divine being, which is utterly free of matter and MOTION (Book Epsilon of the *Metaphysics*). However, given these two contrasting descriptions of the subject matter of the science of being *qua* being, Aristotle leaves unresolved the question of what the domain of metaphysics includes and excludes. At any rate only the incorporation of both affirmations can do justice to the unified study of being and so to metaphysics. That is to say, such incorporation assures that metaphysics has solid grounding in the material world, while affirming the immaterial character of forms, the spiritual dimension of the material world, and divine TRANSCENDENCE. Aquinas gives proper due to such a unified study by describing, as John F. Wippel points out, metaphysics' inclusion of things that can exist in matter while remaining immaterial, yet still embrace the stronger sense of what is essentially immaterial, that is, divine being (Wippel 2000). As for the latter, Aquinas's teaching indicates that divine things as such are not the subject of metaphysics, but only receive treatment as the principles or causes of being *qua* being. Knowledge of these principles is not presupposed in the study of being *qua* being but rather is set forth as the end of the investigation.

Thomistic Revolution in Metaphysics. The science of being *qua* being takes on a far-reaching and even radical transformation with Aquinas's real distinction and relation between *esse* and essence. Each finite thing or substance is described as a composition of these two principles. Further, these principles are not two distinct realities, as though the nature or essence and the *esse* come together as separate entities. The *esse* is not added to the essence. Rather the essence is nothing unless actualized by the *esse*. In short there is neither essence nor *esse* unless there is the thing that exists as a single substantial being. In light of the above, something should be said about the historical perspective via its influences on what Aquinas is describing. While the Greeks remain on the quiddative or essentialist level of being, Aristotle's ἐνέργεια or act shows considerable kinship with Aquinas's identity of act with *esse*. In the Hebraic tradition, unlike that of the Greek, an identity between being and *esse* is set forth in God's name as "I am who am" and as *Yahweh* or "He who is." Here being is a verb rather than a noun. As related to Aquinas he clearly identifies what he calls the most proper name of God, that is, "He who is," with *esse*. The influences on Aquinas's grounding of metaphysics in *esse* would be incomplete without one final reference—namely, the teaching of ibn Sīnā (AVICENNA; 980–1037). The latter clearly contributed to this revolutionary focus on being by identifying the essence of necessary being or God with existence, taken here as equivalent to Aquinas's *esse*. Further, for ibn Sīnā, where necessary being causes a finite being to exist, existence is joined to a finite essence or possible being, in the sense, not of a predicamental, but of simply an accessory ACCIDENT. Let it be stated too that in ibn Sīnā's eyes, as pointed out by David B. Burrell, C.S.C., the essence of any possible being when considered alone is indifferent to existence or non-existence (Burrell, 1993). In contrast, for Aquinas, essence should in no wise be understood as indifferent to existence. For *esse* is the only *essential being*, and finite essence of itself is nothing. In this regard, cognitional existences are not essences, and essence is only properly a potency to real existence. Here then ibn Sīnā appears to fall short of a proper understanding of the relation between *esse* and essence. That is to say, for him, given his isolation of essence, there seems to be no sense that the meaning and reality of essence lies in an intrinsic relation to *esse* and so in the ordering of essence as potency to *esse* or the act of existing. However, in the case of Aquinas, the fulfillment of his metaphysical revolution requires such ordering and thereby *esse*'s actualizing of essence, which is nothing without this act.

Further, as previously taken up, Aquinas affirms that God has no composition because his essence is his *esse*. And, in this regard, attention must also be paid to Aquinas's joining God's creation *ex nihilo* along with the Platonic doctrine of participation to his teaching of *esse* as the core and primary metaphysical principle in constituting the reality of things. As for creation *ex nihilo*, it is known through Revelation, but is also, as Aquinas points out, knowable through reason alone. And what Aquinas accentuates, through understanding God as creating the many *ex nihilo* and so as finite realities wholly different from the One who is God, is the total difference in the essences of God and creatures, because God's essence is his *esse*, whereas a creature's essence is distinct from its *esse*. At the same time, as effect of infinite *esse* as cause, finite *esse* participates in God by way of likeness, that is, every effect is related to and so like its cause. In expanding the recognition that the fullness of being must center on *esse*, the ontological primacy of *esse* over essence should be noted. Granted that there is no temporal priority, ontologically essence is identified with potentiality, both materially *via* matter and spiritually *via* form, whereas *esse* is the act of the thing. This transforms Aristotle because, for Aristotle, act is form. As a result there is no essence of an actual thing unless actualized by *esse*. Additionally, *esse* is also a higher perfection since it perfects or actualizes the essence or potential of the thing.

Next, attention is given in Aquinas's revolution in metaphysics to his approach to the knowledge of being, that is, the knowledge of *esse*. In this regard he does not deny the apprehension of a thing's essence through abstraction, but places priority on the "judgment that the thing exists." For it is this *existential judgment* that takes one to the grounding knowledge of being. In Aristotelian fashion, sensible things for Aquinas are the origin of human thought. So it is that perception through the image of the object becomes transformed by an intellectual act of abstraction. What is abstracted from the image through the active power of the intellect is the intelligible content of the sensible thing. In turn the intellect in its passive power conceptualizes the thing's nature or essence. Further, the apprehension of its nature occurs simultaneously with the immediate grasp of the thing's existence in judgment. The intellect thus judges the thing to exist while at the same time knowing what it is conceptually. So too the sensible thing's actual existence is always grasped in composition with that thing; for example, "this stone exists." Let it be noted then that the knowledge of *esse* is not given in the concept of the thing. Rather, *esse* is, as Joseph OWENS, C.Ss.R., points out, seized through judgment in an intuitive act (Owens, 1963). To carry this further, the positive judgment that something exists leads to REFLECTION on the commonality or universality of the particular beings whose existence is experienced. And what follows here, for Aquinas, is the process of *separation* whereby negative judgments reveal what is not temporal, not mobile, not sensible, and so on. As a result, the separation reveals what remains, that is, being qua being, which is common being (*ens commune*). In this regard, what emerges as the subject of metaphysics, being qua being, does not really fit the Scholastic notion of formal object. That is to say, such Scholastic usage falls short in handling being as *esse* because the *esse* of a thing is known immediately through judgment. To state further, there can be no formal abstraction leading to the GENUS of being. Thus, the traditional Scholastic approach of dealing with a metaphysics of essence must open itself to the depth of being, to the metaphysics of *esse* described by Aquinas's revolution.

Elaboration of Common Being. In sum, the subject of metaphysics is not God or a particular kind of being but being-in-general or being beyond the sensible. As already indicated, common being in its conceptualization through separation arises from *esse* present and knowable through judgment in individual instances and so in all sensible beings, which are composite realities of essence and *esse*. As such, reflection on common being allows for various affirmations, including the first principles of being and thought, the demonstration of the existence of God or subsistent being through the requirements of causal principles, and the transcendentals of being. As for the reality status of common being itself, it remains a conceptualization referable to the community of *esse* embodied in each particular instance of the *esse* of individual beings and to the participation of all composite beings *via* their *esse* in subsistent being (*esse subsistens*) or the infinite *esse* of God.

What is called the distinctiveness of common being identifies with being-in-general or immaterial being as separated from what is sensible and so includes for study both the being of sensible things and supersensible being, or being not limited by the sensible order. With the notion of common being there is no restriction to particular types of being, such as, following Aristotle, mobile being in the science of physics, taken as the philosophy of nature, or quantified being in the science of mathematics. To reiterate, the subject of metaphysics is being *qua* being or being itself. Stressing then being itself draws attention to what was present at least implicitly in the reference to Aquinas's metaphysical revolution. That is to say, the concept of common being is expressed through the coming together in each sensible particular of the *what* (or essence), and the *is, to be,* or existence (*esse*) of the thing. In addition, common being as rooted in the judgment of *esse* in each individual instance is conceptualized in the concrete when it signifies the thing that exists, that is, signifies "a being" (*ens*),

which is a composite of essence and *esse*. By contrast, when it is conceptualized in the abstract, common being signifies the act of existing in isolation from the thing. Given then the priority of conceptualization in the concrete, the science of common being or being *qua* being is also the science of "beings *qua* beings." Further, from the foundation and mode of separation of being, the resulting notion is not a univocal least common denominator whose differences have been progressively removed; rather, it actually includes the reality of all such differences precisely as real, even if only implicitly. At the same time, the notion of being is not equivocal, that is, lacking in any common significance in its application to the many different things. On the contrary, the notion of being is analogical; it includes within itself the differences by which beings are really distinct one from another—it is different simply in its application to distinct things, while at the same time it has a certain similarity in its significance when applied to each of them.

After it is seen that the subject of metaphysics is being itself and that its mode is analogical, the first and necessary phase of the science of metaphysics is to identify the properties of its subject, thus unfolding its meaning. These properties, however, cannot be really distinct from being; rather, they express explicitly what is already actual and implicit in any being. Hence, while conceptually distinct from being, they are convertible with being. These properties include unity, truth, goodness, and BEAUTY. By *unity* the metaphysician means that any given being is undivided, whether divisible (such as a rock, a plant, or an animal) or INDIVISIBLE (such as an angel or a human soul), and by implication, distinct from any other being. As for *truth* the metaphysician means that any given being as being is intelligible, that is, able to become present to an intellect, and hence able to serve as the objective ground for anything to be known as it truly is in itself. By the term *good* the metaphysician names the PROPERTY of being that is its ability to benefit or perfect other beings, hence its attractiveness or desirability. As for the property of *beauty*, it draws all of these together, in a certain manner, through calling attention to the integrity, proportion, and resplendent light of being.

In conjunction with these transcendental properties, a realist metaphysician is committed to certain correlative first principles of being and thought. Correlated with transcendental unity are three important such principles. By the principle of CONTRADICTION the metaphysician means that nothing can be and not-be at the same time, considered in the same respect. The principle of EXCLUDED MIDDLE means that there is no third possibility between options that are contradictory opposites. And by the principle of identity, the metaphysician means that a being that remains substantially the same can be re-identified as the same being despite the passage of time or a change of circumstances, so long as its essential features remain. Additionally, the principle of SUFFICIENT REASON, as correlated with the principle of identity, articulates a basic insight about the intelligibility of all reality, namely, that there is an adequate explanation for everything, either in the thing itself, as in the case of God, or in another. To deal with the latter situation, metaphysics offers the correlative principle of CAUSALITY: When some thing does not have an adequate explanation in itself, then the explanation must come from a cause other than itself. Further, realist metaphysics is thoroughly teleological in character, and the principle of FINALITY as embodiment of the good expresses the causal end and purpose of all things.

What is primal, as indicated earlier, in the consideration of the being in sensible things is the *esse* grasped through the ongoing judgments that this thing exists and that some other thing exists, and so on. And what follows is a reflection on the intrinsic principles of a sensible thing, that is, its *esse* and essence as linked to act and potency, MATTER AND FORM, substance and accidents. Additionally, reflection on this make-up of the sensible thing and the existential demands inherent within these principles, and on the supersensible character of common being leads to the notion of *esse subsistens*, that is, pure *esse* that means complete identity of *esse* and essence. To carry further the understanding of sensible being, its limitation discloses the contingency of its *esse*. As a consequence, each sensible thing requires a grounding for its *esse* in an extrinsic principle. The path is then open to reach an efficient first cause that is *esse subsistens*. As a result, various proofs for God's existence can be established, an endeavor carried out, for example, through Aquinas's "five ways." In addition, as previously treated, the resolution of the problem of the one and the many through creation *ex nihilo* is articulated through Aquinas's notion of *esse*. Understood through the ANALOGY of being as *esse*, the many creatures as analogues or effects of the divine causality of *esse subsistens* are like the pure act of existing (positive theology). At the same time created beings as caused *ex nihilo* and through their *esse–essence* real distinction are totally unlike the divine essence (negative theology). Thus, the many finite beings as contingent through their *esse* on the one infinite being participate analogically in *esse subsistens*.

In Praise of Metaphysics. In the natural order of things, metaphysics is the science of sciences. So it is that Aquinas in the "Prologue" to his *Commentary on Aristotle's Metaphysics* considers this science supreme in intellectuality since it possesses a knowledge of first causes. In addition, to possess such knowledge is to know the beginning and end of the universe, which as-

sures a unified science of all being. Further, as the science of being *qua* being, it deals with the most universal principles, and these principles govern every particular science, every kind of being, and every particular being. Thus this science is supreme in universality. Through its intellectuality, metaphysics is also supreme in CERTITUDE, which derives from being *qua* being and from its reasoning processes, as founded and verified in the first and most evident of all principles of demonstration, the principle of contradiction.

To further enhance the praiseworthy character of metaphysics, focus is placed on two contemporary concerns of special note: the notions of person and lived experience. Regarding the first, the integral role of person in the metaphysical constitution of reality was noted in the Hebraic treatment of God and in the Christian stress on the Trinity as well as on the human person as the image of the Trinity. The twenty-first century, in turn, intensifies the role and place of the person as an intrinsic metaphysical principle through such thinkers as St. Teresa Benedicta of the Cross/Edith STEIN (1891–1942), JOHN PAUL II (1920–2005), and W. Norris Clarke, S.J. (b.1915–2008). As for the second concern, PHENOMENOLOGY draws attention to the importance of the lived experience of reality, that is, of direct contact with reality. However, phenomenological description of such contact, when based on thinkers like Husserl and Merleau-Ponty, is set loose from the foundation of being *qua* being. The result is a description caught within the realm of time and so of the accidental. By contrast, metaphysical realism, characterized, in particular, by centering on direct contact with substantial reality, brings the knower to intuition of this reality. What is grasped is the substantial principle of a thing, a contact occurring through Aristotle's abstraction of the substantial act taken as the form of the thing. Describing this contact on the deeper level of the metaphysics of *esse*, what occurs, as stated earlier, is Aquinas's intuition through judgment of the substantial act taken as the *esse* of the thing. Thus each of these direct contacts with substantial reality, in their respective manner and degree, joins the knower with the core of lived experience.

Finally, as the science that is most perfectly universal, intellectual, and certain; metaphysics takes on the character of natural wisdom. Extending even to what most transcends the human mind, metaphysics knows the principles of all being, stands at the culmination of man's knowledge, and serves as the foundation for all the other sciences. Indeed, since it uses other sciences to enlarge its knowledge, its ordering function in their regard is part of the work of wisdom itself.

So it is that the perfection of the knower requires the study of wisdom. For the human soul possesses a nature that can know all things, that is, can take in the perfection of the whole universe. However, there is a higher science that is in the SUPERNATURAL order of things, the science of sacred doctrine. Its subject is God Himself. Hence, sacred doctrine, also understood as sacred theology or the theology of revelation, carries out the study of Divine Wisdom through the pursuit of eternal beatitude. It is fitting here to close with Aquinas's comparison of the quest for natural and supernatural wisdom: "The ultimate perfection which the soul can attain, therefore, is, according to the philosophers, to have delineated in it the entire order and causes of the universe. This they held to be the ultimate end of man. We, however, hold that it consists in the vision of God..." (*De ver.* 2.2).

SEE ALSO AETERNI PATRIS; ANALOGY; ANSELM OF CANTERBURY, ST.; ANTHROPOMORPHISM; ASCETICISM; CARTESIANISM; CHRISTIAN PHILOSOPHY; CONCEPTUALISM; DARWINISM, SOCIAL; DIALECTICS; EFFICIENT CAUSALITY; ENLIGHTENMENT, PHILOSOPHY OF; EPISTEMOLOGY; FINAL CAUSALITY; FINITE BEING; GOD, NAME OF; GOD, PROOFS FOR THE EXISTENCE OF; INTELLIGIBILITY, PRINCIPLE OF; ISLAM; JESUITS; KANTIANISM; LIGHT, METAPHYSICS OF; LOGOS; MATHEMATICS, PHILOSOPHY OF; MATTER, PHILOSOPHY OF; METAPHYSICS, VALIDITY OF; MYSTICISM; MYTH AND MYTHOLOGY; NATURE (IN PHILOSOPHY); NEOSCHOLASTICISM AND NEOTHOMISM; NOUMENA; PERSON (IN PHILOSOPHY); PHENOMENALISM; PROCESS PHILOSOPHY; PROPORTIONALITY, PRINCIPLE OF; PROVIDENCE OF GOD (IN THE BIBLE); SCHOLASTICISM; SOUL, HUMAN; THEOLOGY, NATURAL; THOMISM, TRANSCENDENTAL; TRINITY, HOLY; YAHWEH.

BIBLIOGRAPHY

GENERAL WORKS

Emile Bréhier, *The History of Philosophy*, 7 vols., translated by Joseph Thomas (vol. 1) and Wade Baskin (vols. 2–7) (Chicago 1963–1969).

Anton-Hermann Chroust, "The Origin of 'Metaphysics'," *The Review of Metaphysics* 14 (1961): 601–616.

W. Norris Clarke, S.J., *The One and the Many: A Contemporary Thomistic Metaphysics* (Notre Dame, Ind. 2001).

James Daniel Collins, *A History of Modern European Philosophy* (Milwaukee 1954). Also includes the period from Hegel to the twentieth century.

Frederick Charles Copleston, S.J., *A History of Philosophy*, 9 vols. (New York 1993).

Harald Høffding, *A History of Modern Philosophy: A Sketch of the History of Philosophy from the Close of the Renaissance to Our Own Day*, translated by B.E. Meyer (New York 1955).

Gerald A. McCool, S.J., *From Unity to Pluralism: The Internal Evolution of Thomism* (New York 1992).

Gerald A. McCool, S.J., *The Neo-Thomists* (Milwaukee, Wis. 1994).

Joseph Owens, C.Ss.R., *An Elementary Christian Metaphysics* (Milwaukee, Wis. 1963).

Joseph Owens, *An Interpretation of Existence* (Milwaukee, Wis. 1968).

Hans Reiner, "Entstehung und Ursprüngliche Bedeutung des Namens Metaphysik," *Zeitschrift für Philosophische Forschung* 8 (1954): 210–237.

Richard C. Vitzthum, *Materialism: An Affirmative History and Definition* (Amherst, N.Y. 1995).

William A. Wallace, O.P., *From a Realist Point of View: Essays on the Philosophy of Science*, 2nd ed. (Washington, D.C. 1979).

William A. Wallace, O.P., *The Modeling of Nature: Philosophy of Science and Philosophy of Nature in Synthesis* (Washington, D.C. 1996).

ANCIENT PERIOD (ORIENTALS AND GREEKS)

Primary Works

Aristotle, *Physics*, translated by R.P. Hardie and R.K. Gaye in *The Complete Works of Aristotle: The Revised Oxford Translation* vol. 1, edited by Jonathan Barnes (Princeton, N.J. 1984).

Aristotle, *On the Soul*, translated by J.A. Smith (Princeton, N.J. 1984), available from http://www.greektexts.com/library/Aristotle/On_The_Soul/eng/index.html

Aristotle, *The Metaphysics*, 2 vols., translated and with introduction by Hugh Tredennick (London 1933–1935).

Edwin A. Burtt, ed., *The Teachings of the Compassionate Buddha: Early Discourses, the Dhammapada, and Later Basic Writings* (New York 1955).

Edward Conze, ed. and trans., *Buddhist Texts through the Ages*, edited in collaboration with I.B. Horner, D. Snellgrove, A. Waley (New York 1964).

Kathleen Freeman, *Ancilla to the Pre-Socratic Philosophers: A Complete Translation of the Fragments in Diels, "Fragmente der Vorsokratiker"* (Cambridge, Mass. 1957).

G.S. Kirk, J.E. Raven, and M. Schofield, *The Presocratic Philosophers: A Critical History with a Selection of Texts* (Cambridge, Mass. 1962).

Swami Nikhilananda, trans. and ed., *The Upanishads* (one volume abridgement) (New York 1964).

José Pereira, ed., *Hindu Theology: A Reader*, introduction and notes by Jose Pereira (Garden City, N.Y. 1976).

Plato, *Phaedo*, translated by Hugh Tredennick; *Symposium*, translated by Michael Joyce; *Republic*, translated by Paul Shorey; *Parmenides*, translated by F.M. Cornford; and *Sophist*, translated by F.M. Cornford; all from *The Collected Dialogues of Plato, Including the Letters*, translated by Lane Cooper et al., edited by Edith Hamilton and Huntington Cairns (New York 1961).

Plotinus, *The Enneads*, 6 vols., translated and with preface by A.H. Armstrong (also includes Armstrong's translation of Porphry's "On the Life of Plotinus and the Order of His Books") (Cambridge, Mass. 1966).

Sarvepalli Radhakrishnan and Charles A. Moore, eds., *A Sourcebook in Indian Philosophy* (Princeton, N.J. 1957).

Secondary Works

Edward Conze, *Buddhism: Its Essence and Development* (New York 1951).

Jean Daniélou, *God and the Ways of Knowing* (New York 1957).

Mircea Eliade, *The Sacred and the Profane: The Nature of Religion*, translated by Willard R. Trask (New York 1959).

Mircea Eliade, *Yoga: Immortality and Freedom*, translated by Willard R. Trask (Princeton, N.J. 1969).

John N. Findlay, *Plato: The Written and Unwritten Doctrines* (New York 1974).

Kathleen Freeman, *The Pre-Socratic Philosophers: A Companion to Diels, "Fragmente der Vorsokratiker"* (Oxford, U.K. 1953).

W.K.C. Guthrie, *A History of Greek Philosophy*, 6 vols. (Cambridge, Mass. 1962–1981).

John A. Hardon, S.J., *Religions of the World*, vol. I (Garden City, N.Y. 1963).

G.R.G. Mure, *Aristotle* (Westport, Conn. 1975).

Joseph Owens, C.Ss.R., *The Doctrine of Being in the Aristotelian Metaphysics: A Study in the Greek Background of Mediaeval Thought*, preface by Étienne Gilson (Toronto 1951).

Giovanni Reale, *The Concept of First Philosophy and the Unity of the Metaphysics of Aristotle*, edited and translated by John R. Catan (Albany, N.Y. 1980).

William D. Ross, *Aristotle: A Complete Exposition of His Works & Thought* (Cleveland, Ohio 1959).

Alfred.E. Taylor, *Plato: The Man and His Work* (Cleveland, Ohio 1952).

MEDIEVAL PERIOD (ST. AUGUSTINE TO WILLIAM OF OCKHAM)

Primary Works

St. Anselm, *Anselm of Canterbury: The Major Works*, edited and with an introduction by Brian Davies and G.R. Evans (Oxford, U.K. 1998).

St. Augustine, *Confessions*, translated with introduction and notes by Henry Chadwick (Oxford, U.K. 1991).

St. Augustine, *On Genesis: Two Books on Genesis against the Manichees and On the Literal Interpretation of Genesis, an Unfinished Book*, translated by Roland J. Teske (Washington, D.C. 1991).

St. Augustine, *The Trinity*, translated and with introduction by Edmund Hill, O.P., in *The Works of Saint Augustine: A Translation for the 21st Century*, part 1, vol. 1, edited by John E. Rotelle (Brooklyn, N.Y. 1991).

St. Bonaventure, *Saint Bonaventure's* De Reductione Artium ad Theologiam, translated with commentary and introduction by Sister Emma Therese Healy (Saint Bonaventure, N.Y. 1940).

Ibn Sīnā, *The Metaphysica of Avicenna (ibn Sīnā): A Critical Translation-Commentary and Analysis of the Fundamental Arguments in Avicenna's Metaphysica in the Dānish nāma-i 'Alā'ī (The Book of Scientific Knowledge)*, translated by Parviz Morewedge (New York 1973).

Bl. John Duns Scotus, *Questions on the Metaphysics of Aristotle*, 2 vols., translated by Girard J. Etzkorn and Allan B. Wolter (St. Bonaventure, N.Y. 1997–1998).

St. Thomas Aquinas, *Commentum in Quatuor Libros Sentiarum Magistri Petri Lombardi* in *Opera Omnia*, v. 6 (Parmae 1856).

St. Thomas Aquinas, *On Being and Essence*, translated and with introduction by Armand A. Maurer, CSB (Toronto 1968).

St. Thomas Aquinas, *The Disputed Questions on Truth*, 3 vols., translated by Robert W. Mulligan, S.J. (Questions I–IX); James V. McGlynn, S.J. (Questions X–XX); and Robert W. Schmidt, S.J. (Questions XXI–XXIX) (Albany, N.Y. 1993).

St. Thomas Aquinas, "The Divisions and Methods of the Sciences," questions V and VI of his unfinished *Commentary on Boethius' De Trinitate*, translated and with introduction by Armand Maurer, CSB (Toronto 1963).

St. Thomas Aquinas, *The Power of God (Quaestiones Disputatae de Potentia Dei)*, translated by Father Lawrence Shapcote, O.P. (Westminster, Md. 1952).

St. Thomas Aquinas, *Commentary on Aristotle's Metaphysics*, translated and introduction by John P. Doyle (Notre Dame, Ind. 1995).

St. Thomas Aquinas, *Summa Theologiae: Latin Text and English Translation*, Edition: Blackfriars (London 1964 and on).

William of Ockham, *Ockham: Philosophical Writings*, translated and edited by Philotheus Boehner, OFM (London 1957).

Secondary Works

David B. Burrell, C.S.C., "Aquinas and Islamic and Jewish Thinkers," in *The Cambridge Companion to Aquinas*, edited by Norman Kretzmann and Eleonore Stump (Cambridge, Mass. 1993).

Donald X. Burt, OSA, *Augustine's World: An Introduction to His Speculative Philosophy* (Lanham, Md. 1996).

Cornelio Fabro, *Participation et causalité selon S. Thomas d'Aquin* (Louvain, France 1961).

Joseph de Finance, S.J., *Être et agir dans la philosophie de Saint Thomas*, 2nd ed. (Rome 1960).

L.B. Geiger, "Abstraction et Separation d'après S. Thomas," *Revue des Sciences Philosophiques et Theologiques* 31 (January 1947): 3–40.

Étienne Gilson, *History of Christian Philosophy in the Middle Ages* (New York 1955).

Étienne Gilson, *The Spirit of Mediaeval Philosophy*, translated by A.H.C. Downes (New York 1936).

Mary Beth Ingham and Mechthild Dreyer, *The Philosophical Vision of John Duns Scotus: An Introduction* (Washington, D.C. 2004).

Oliver Leaman, *A Brief Introduction to Islamic Philosophy* (Malden, Mass. 1999).

Gordon Leff, *William of Ockham: The Metamorphosis of Scholastic Discourse* (Manchester, U.K. 1975).

John Marenbon, *Early Medieval Philosophy (480–1150): An Introduction* (London 1983).

Seyyed Hossein Nasr, *Three Muslim Sages: Avicenna, Suhwarardi, ibn 'Arabī* (Delmar, N.Y. 1964).

Joseph Owens, C.Ss.R., *St. Thomas Aquinas on the Existence of God: Collected Papers of Joseph Owens, CSsR*, edited by John R. Catan (Albany, N.Y. 1980).

Eugene Portalie, S.J., *A Guide to the Thought of Saint Augustine*, translated by Ralph J. Bastien, S.J. and with introduction by Vernon J. Bourke (Chicago 1960).

R. W. Schmidt, "L'Emploi de la séparation en métaphysique," *Revue Philosophique de Louvain* 58 (1960): 373–393.

John F. Wippel, *Metaphysical Themes in Thomas Aquinas* (Washington, D.C. 1984).

John F. Wippel, *The Metaphysical Thought of Thomas Aquinas: From Finite Being to Uncreated Being* (Washington, D.C. 2000).

John F. Wippel, *Metaphysical Themes in Thomas Aquinas II* (Washington, D.C. 2007).

EARLY MODERN PERIOD (NEO-SCHOLASTICS TO KANT)

Primary Works

Tommaso de Vio Cajetan, O.P., *Commentary on* Being and Essence: De Ente et Essentia d. *Thomas Aquinatis*, translated by Lottie H. Kendzierski and Francis C. Wade, S.J. (Milwaukee, Wis. 1964).

René Descartes, "Discourse on the Method of Rightly Conducting the Reason and Seeking Truth in the Sciences" and "The Meditations Concerning First Philosophy," translated by Laurence J. Lafleur in *Discourse on Method and Meditations* (New York 1960).

René Descartes, *Principles of Philosophy*, translated by Blair Reynolds (Lewiston, N.Y. 1988).

David Hume, *A Treatise of Human Nature*, edited by L.A. Selby-Bigge (Oxford, U.K. 1978).

John of St. Thomas, O.P., (John Poinsot), *Introduction to the Summa Theologiae of Thomas: The Isagogue of John of St. Thomas*, translated by Ralph McInerny (South Bend, Ind. 2004).

John of St. Thomas, *The Material Logic of John of St. Thomas: Basic Treatises*, translated by Ives R. Simon, John J. Glanville, and G. Donald Hollenhorst and with preface by Jacques Maritain (Chicago 1955).

Immanuel Kant, *Critique of Pure Reason*, translated by Norman Kemp Smith (New York 1965).

Immanuel Kant, *Prolegomena to Any Future Metaphysics*, translated by Lewis W. Beck (New York 1951).

Gottfried Wilhelm Freiherr von Leibniz, *Monadology and Other Philosophical Essays*, translated by Paul Schrecker and Anne Martin Schrecker (New York 1965).

Baruch (Benedict) Spinoza, "On the Improvement of the Understanding" and "The Ethics," translated by R.H.M. Elwes in *Philosophy of Benedict De Spinoza* (New York 1936).

Francisco Suárez, S.J., *Disputationes metaphysicae*, 2 vols., edited by Georg Olms (Hildesheim 1965).

Secondary Works

Lewis White Beck, *Early German Philosophy: Kant and His Predecessors* (Cambridge, Mass.1969).

John Niemeyer Findlay, *Kant and the Transcendental Object: A Hermeneutic Study* (Oxford, U.K. 1981).

Jonathan Francis Bennett, *Locke, Berkeley, Hume: Central Themes* (Oxford, U.K. 1971).

John Cottingham, *Descartes* (Oxford, U.K. 1986).

John Cottingham, *The Rationalists* (Oxford, U.K. 1988)

Alexander Boyce Gibson, *The Philosophy of Descartes* (London 1932).

Étienne Gilson, *The Unity of Philosophical Experience* (San Francisco 1999).

Stephán Körner, *Kant* (New Haven, Conn. 1982).

Norman Kemp Smith, *A Commentary to Kant's "Critique of Pure Reason"* (London 1923).

LATER MODERN PERIOD (HEGEL AND AFTER)

Primary Works

Ludwig Büchner, *Force and Matter, Or Principles of the Natural Order of the Universe: With a System of Morality Based Thereon: A Popular Exposition* (New York 1918).

Mario Bunge, *Scientific Materialism* (Dordrecht, Holland 1981).

William Norris Clarke, S.J., *Person and Being* (Milwaukee, Wis. 1993).

Auguste Comte, *The Positive Philosophy*, translation of *Cours de Philosophie Positive* by Harriet Martineau and with introduction by Abraham S. Blumberg (New York 1974).

Daniel Clement Dennett, *Darwin's Dangerous Idea: Evolution and the Meanings of Life* (New York 1995).

Jacques Derrida, *Of Grammatology*, translated by Gayatri Chakravorty Spivak (Baltimore 1976).

Jacques Derrida, *On the Name*, edited by Thomas Dutoit, translated by David Wood ("Passions: An Oblique Offering"), John P. Leavey, Jr. ("Sauf le nom (Post Scriptum)"), Ian McLeod ("Khora"); (Stanford, Calif. 1995).

Herbert Feigl, *The "Mental" and the "Physical": The Essay and a Postscript* (Minneapolis, Minn. 1967).

Michel Foucault, *The Archaeology of Knowledge*, translated by A.M. Sheridan (New York 1972).

Hans-Georg Gadamer, *Truth and Method*, 2nd ed., translated by Joel Weinsheimer and Donald G. Marshall (New York 1989).

Réginald Garrigou-Lagrange, O.P., *God: His Existence and His Nature: A Thomistic Solution of Certain Agnostic Antinomies*, vols. I and II, translated by Bede Rose, OSB (London: 1934–1936).

Étienne Gilson, *Being and Some Philosophers* (Toronto 1961).

Étienne Gilson, *Thomist Realism and the Critique of Knowledge*, translated by Mark A. Wauck (San Francisco 1986).

Georg Wilhelm Friedrich Hegel, *Phenomenology of Spirit*, translated by A.V. Miller with analysis of text and foreword by J.N. Findlay (Oxford, U.K. 1991).

Georg Wilhelm Friedrich Hegel, *Hegel's Science of Logic*, translated by A.V. Miller with foreword by J.N. Findlay (Atlantic Highlands, N.J. 1989).

Martin Heidegger, *Being and Time*, translated by John Macquarrie and Edward Robinson (New York 1962).

Martin Heidegger, "The Origin of the Work of Art" in *Poetry, Language, Thought*, translated and with introduction by Albert Hofstadter (New York 1971).

Martin Heidegger, *On the Way to Language*, translated by Peter D. Hertz (New York 1971).

Martin Heidegger, *On Time and Being*, translated and with introduction by Joan Stambaugh (New York 1972).

Edmund Husserl, *The Phenomenology of Internal Time–Consciousness*, edited by Martin Heidegger, translated by James S. Churchill, introduction by Calvin O. Schrag (Bloomington, Ind. 1964).

Edmund Husserl, *Ideas: General Introduction to Pure Phenomenology* (includes Husserl's "Preface to the English

Edition"), translated by W.R. Boyce Gibson (New York 1962).

Edmund Husserl, "Philosophy as Rigorous Science" in *Phenomenology and the Crisis of Philosophy*, translated and with introduction by Quentin Lauer, S.J. (New York 1965).

Edmund Husserl, *The Crisis of European Sciences and Transcendental Phenomenology: An Introduction to Phenomenological Philosophy*, translated and with introduction by David Carr (Evanston, Ill. 1970).

John Paul II (Karol Wojtyła), *The Acting Person*, translated by Andrzej Potocki, edited by Anna-Teresa Tymieniecka (Dordrecht, Holland 1979).

Leo XIII, *Aeterni Patris*, On the Restoration of Christian Philosophy (Encyclical, August 1879), available from http://www.vatican.va/holy_father/leo_xiii/encyclicals/documents/hf_l-xiii_enc_04081879_aeterni-patris_en.html (accessed April 3, 2008).

Joseph Maréchal, S.J., *A Maréchal Reader*, translated and edited by Joseph F. Donceel, S.J. (New York 1970).

Jacques Maritain, *Philosophy of Nature* (includes Yves R. Simon's "Maritain's Philosophy of the Sciences"), translated by Imelda C. Byrne (New York 1951).

Jacques Maritain, *Existence and the Existent*, translated by Lewis Galantiere and Gerald B. Phelan (Garden City, N.Y. 1956).

Jacques Maritain, *Distinguish to Unite; or, The Degrees of Knowledge*, translated under supervision of Gerald B. Phelan (New York 1959).

Karl Marx and Friedrich Engels, *Basic Writings on Politics and Philosophy*, edited by Lewis S. Feuer (Garden City, N.Y. 1959).

Maurice Merleau-Ponty, *Phenomenology of Perception*, translated by Colin Smith (London 1962).

Maurice Merleau-Ponty, *The Visible and the Invisible, Followed by Working Notes*, translated by Alphonso Lingis, edited by Claude Lefort (Evanston, Ill. 1968).

John Stuart Mill, *Auguste Comte and Positivism* (Ann Arbor, Mich. 1961).

Friedrich Wilhelm Nietzsche, *Twilight of the Idols* in *Twilight of the Idols; and, The Anti–Christ*, translated and with commentary by R.J. Hollingdale (Baltimore 1968).

Friedrich Wilhelm Nietzsche, *Thus Spoke Zarathustra: A Book for All and None*, translated and with a preface by Walter Kaufmann (New York 1995).

Friedrich Wilhelm Nietzsche, *Beyond Good and Evil: Prelude to a Philosophy of the Future*, translated by Judith Norman, edited by Rolf-Peter Horstmann and Judith Norman (Cambridge, Mass. 2002).

John Searle, *Minds, Brains, and Science* (Cambridge, Mass. 1984).

John Jamieson Carswell Smart, *Philosophy and Scientific Realism* (New York 1963).

Herbert Spencer, *First Principles* (New York 1958).

Edith Stein (St. Teresa Benedicta of the Cross), *Finite and Eternal Being: An Attempt at an Ascent to the Meaning of Being*, translated by Kurt F. Reinhardt (Washington, D.C 2002).

E.O. Wilson, *On Human Nature* (Cambridge, Mass. 1978).

Ludwig Wittgenstein, *Philosophical Investigations*, translated by G.E.M. Anscombe and with introduction by Bertrand Russell (New York 1973).

Ludwig Wittgenstein, *Tractatus logico-philosophicus* translated by C.K. Ogden (London 1981).

Secondary Works

William Desmond, *Hegel's God: A Counterfeit Double?* (Burlington, Vt. 2003).

Étienne Gilson, Thomas Langan, and Armand Maurer, CSB, *Recent Philosophy: Hegel to the Present* (New York 1966).

R. J. Hollingdale, *Nietzsche* (London 1973).

Walter Arnold Kaufmann, *Nietzsche: Philosopher, Psychologist, Antichrist* (New York 1968).

Joseph J. Kockelmans, ed., *Phenomenology: The Philosophy of Edmund Husserl and Its Interpretation* (Garden City, N.Y. 1967).

Quentin Lauer, S.J., *Phenomenology: Its Genesis and Prospect* (New York 1958).

Jean-François Lyotard, *The Postmodern Explained: Correspondence 1982–1985*, edited by Julian Pefanis and Morgan Thomas; translated by Don Barry, Bernadette Maher, Julian Pefanis, et al.; afterword by Wlad Godzich (Minneapolis, Minn. 1993).

Allan Megill, *Prophets of Extremity: Nietzsche, Heidegger, Foucault, Derrida* (Berkeley, Calif. 1985).

George Pitcher, *The Philosophy of Wittgenstein* (Englewood Cliffs, N.J. 1964).

Eric P. Polten, *Critique of the Psycho-Physical Identity Theory: A Refutation of Scientific Materialism and an Establishment of Mind-Matter Dualism by Means of Philosophy and Scientific Method* (The Hague 1973).

A. Seth Pringle-Pattison, *Hegelianism and Personality* (New York 1971).

William J. Richardson, S.J., *Heidegger: Through Phenomenology to Thought*, preface by Martin Heidegger (The Hague 1963).

Walter Terence Stace, *The Philosophy of Hegel: A Systematic Exposition* (New York 1955).

Horace Standish Thayer, *Meaning and Action: A Critical History of Pragmatism* (Indianapolis, Ind. 1968).

Eric Voegelin, *Anamnesis*, translated by Gerhart Niemeyer (Notre Dame, Ind. 1978).

Henry R. West, ed., *The Blackwell Guide to Mill's Utilitarianism* (Oxford, U.K. 2006).

David Wood and Robert Bernasconi, eds., *Derrida and Difference* (Evanston, Ill. 1988).

Rev. George Francis McLean OMI
Associate Professor of Philosophy, The Catholic University of America
Professor of Philosophy, Oblate College, Washington, D.C.

Atherton C. Lowry
Professor and Chair of the Philosophy Department
St. Charles Borromeo Seminary
Wynnewood, Penn. (2009)

METHODOLOGY (PHILOSOPHY)

Method is a "way after" (derived from the Greek μέθοδος from μετά, "after," and ὁδός, "road" or "way"). It is applied both to the process or art of investigation and to the treatise or body of knowledge resulting from investigation. Methodology seeks to determine the principles that guide a mode of inquiry; inasmuch as each science has its own subject matter, each science will have its own proper methodology. The study of philosophical methodology is also known as *metaphilosophy*. Method is used in three distinct but related applications in philosophy: (1) to logic or parts of logic, as inductive or axiomatic methods; (2) to procedures of the sciences, as mathematical or experimental methods; and (3) to modes of philosophizing, as Cartesian or phenomenological methods. In general, philosophical method differs from the methods of other sciences in seeking ultimate principles by means of critical rational analysis of assumptions and dialectical criticism of arguments. In seeking the ultimate principles, differing philosophical commitments result in two distinct methods: The first, more characteristic of Greek and medieval thought, aims to resolve data to the most universal explanatory principles; the second, more typical of modern thought, aims to resolve proposition and concepts into the most simple constituent parts. These principles provide the foundations for further arguments and proofs in philosophical method.

PLATO was the first philosopher to use the term *method*; ARISTOTLE gave it a technical meaning. They both refer to mathematical and medical methods to explain philosophical methods, and later interpretations of method based on their theories influenced and were influenced by developments of method in the arts and sciences. Plato and Aristotle use earlier terms such as way (ὁδός), reason (λόγος), mode (τρόπος), treatment (πραγματεία), and art (τέχνη), in connection with or in the place of method, and those terms continued to be used in later theories.

Greek Thought. In the *Republic* Plato uses "method" to relate DIALECTICS to the five kinds of mathematics. This is the only method that proceeds directly to first principle without hypotheses (*Republic* 533C). Plato's SOCRATES develops his arguments on the analogy of the arts or even of the "method" of hunting (*Soph.* 218D). He distinguishes two processes in dialectic, division (διαίρεσις) and bringing together (συναγωγή), and argues that they are appropriate to RHETORIC, and constitute the art of HIPPOCRATES (*Phaedrus* 266D. 270C).

Aristotle records that Socrates was the first to examine universal definitions and inductive arguments, because he was concerned with the principles of science and with syllogizing (*Meta.* 1078b 17–31). Aristotle raises the question of whether there is one method of inquiry for all subject matters, as syllogistic DEMONSTRATION applies to all proofs. He concludes that there are as many methods as there are subject matters or parts of subject matters, and he frequently divides his scientific treatises into several methods or parts. Aristotle wrote a treatise, now lost, called *Methodics*. Dialectic is a method (*Topica* 100a18), comparable to the methods of rhetoric and medicine (*Topica* 101b 5–6); one of its functions is to discover the principles of all methods or sciences (*Topica* 101b 2–4). Syllogistic demonstration, unlike the method of inquiry, is universal to all proofs. The demonstrative syllogism is "analyzed," first, into the terms or parts that compose it and into other syllogisms, and second, in what was later called the *Posterior Analytics*, into the principles of instruction and proof.

During the Hellenistic period the Stoics, Epicureans, and Academics divided philosophy into physics, ethics, and logic. Under logic they placed the criteria of knowledge and the rules of dialectic and rhetoric. Art was conceived as a skill in proceeding by a way or method, or a canon or rules of judgment, or a calculus or probabilities. Pappus in the fourth century AD states the position, attributed to Euclid, that mathematical inquiry employs two converse methods: analysis (positing what is sought and proceeding to what must be assumed) and synthesis (positing what is assumed and proceeding to what is sought). Galen in the second century AD reviews the methods of all the arts, particularly rhetoric and mathematics, and philosophy, including the theories of Plato, Aristotle, and the Stoics, to clarify the methods of instruction and practice in medicine. He enumerates three methods of instruction: analysis, which begins with the idea of the end; synthesis, which compounds what had been discovered by analysis; and partition (διάλυσις), which breaks definitions into essential parts. The Greek commentators on Aristotle and Plato made use of these distinctions to characterize the methods of philosophers. Ammonius Hermiae found a fourfold method in Plato's dialectic: DIVISION, DEFINITION, demonstration, and ANALYSIS. The four dialectical methods (or three—analysis, division, and reduction to absurdity) are referred to by JOHN PHILOPONUS, JOHN DAMASCENE, Alcinous, and PROCLUS. Alexander of Aphrodisias applied the geometric conception of analysis to Aristotle's *Analytics*, and he distinguishes in Aristotle's method the converse methods of analysis and synthesis.

Roman and Medieval Development. For the Romans, methodological distinctions were distinctions applied to *via* or *ratio* or *ars*; the term *methodus* came into use during the late Middle Ages. CICERO applied two basic distinctions of rhetoric—invention and judgment—to all discursive art (*ratio disserendi*) and attributed their origin to Aristotle. The art of invention is expounded in the *Topics*. The translation of Arabic medical works, including Galen, in the eleventh century, and of the last four books of Aristotle's *Organon*, in the twelfth century, focused discussion of the LIBERAL ARTS on problems of method. In the treatment of *methodus* during the late thirteenth century, analysis and synthesis took the place of *resolutio* and *compositio*.

THOMAS AQUINAS seldom uses *methodus*, but he does distinguish between invention and judgment, and also between resolution and composition. He applies composition and division to the act of the intellect forming propositions, true and false, and invention and judgment to the discursive processes of reason from known to unknown. The process of reason by which the certitude of science is acquired is treated in the judicative part of logic, which Aristotle called *Analytics*: *Prior Analytics* when considering the form or structure of the syllogism; *Posterior Analytics* when considering the matter or content of the syllogism. The processes of reason that fall short of certitude are treated in the inventive part: (1) invention leading, not to judgment, but to conviction or OPINION based on PROBABILITY in the *Topics*; (2) invention leading to suspicion leaning to one side of an opposition in the *Rhetoric*; and (3) invention producing only estimation because of a pleasing representation in the *Poetics* (*In 1 Anal. Post.* 1.4–6). St. Thomas also distinguishes two ways (*viae*) of proceeding to knowledge of the truth (that is, two parts of judicative logic): the mode (*modus*) of resolution, by which one proceeds from composites to simples—that is, from the confused experience known first in nature to explanatory principles—and the way of composition, by which one proceeds from simples to composites, that is, from universal principles to particular facts (*In 2 Meta.* 1.278). The former is the way of discovery; the latter is the way of instruction, or proof.

Renaissance Transition. The method of Aristotelian logic was transformed by the development of terminist logics, Lullian combinatory arts, and dialectical and rhetorical arts of invention. The transformed methods were used in the renewed study of medicine, mathematics, and literature. As a result, the differences between discovery and proof—and the relation of both to analysis and synthesis and to INDUCTION and DEDUCTION—became subjects of interest and controversy. The new arts and encyclopedias and the new logics of the Renaissance were methods. The importance of method in the reform of the arts, sciences, and education is seen in the proliferation of titles such as the *Ratio seu methodus compendio perveniendi ad veram theologiam* of D. ERASMUS

and the *Methodus ad facilem historiarum cognitionem* of J. Bodin.

Giacomo Aconcio, in *De methodo* (1558), treats method as the right way (*recta ratio*) of investigating and transmitting arts and sciences. Three methods are required in inquiry and teaching: the *method of definition* to demonstrate what a thing is, the *method of resolution and composition* to treat causes and effects, and the *method of division* to order parts and wholes. The *De inventione dialectica* (1480) of R. Agricola transfers the Ciceronian division of discourse into invention and judgment, and the priority of invention or topics from rhetoric to dialectic.

Peter RAMUS identifies dialectic with logic, and both with the art of discoursing well (*ars bene disserendi*). He divides logic into two parts, invention and judgment. Invention is achieved by the topics or commonplaces, beginning with causes, as cause is "the first place of invention, the foundation of all science and knowing," and ending with distribution, definition, and description. Judgment is the disposition of the arguments discovered by invention. Ramus argued, therefore, that there is a single method of all the arts and sciences, because method is disposition of arguments proceeding from the more general and prior in nature. Jacob Schegk (1511–1587), a physician and logician, maintained against Ramus that method is a way of knowing, rather than a discoursing, and undertook to show in his *De demonstratione* (1564), using Aristotle and Galen, that analysis or method is the way both of discovery and judgment in science. J. ZABARELLA included four books *De methodis* in his *Logica* (1587), in which, after examining theories of kinds of method, he argues that two, the demonstrative and resolutive, suffice for the investigation of all things.

The Seventeenth Century. The distinctions of methods and the oppositions about methods recur with few changes in philosophic statements of scientific method and its application to philosophy. Francis BACON criticizes the various classifications of method, including the single method and dichotomies of Ramus (*De aug. sci.* 6.2). According to Bacon, the intellectual arts are four: inquiry or invention, examination or judgment, custody or memory, and elocution or transmission—adaptations of four of the traditional five parts of rhetoric: invention, arrangement, expression, memory, and delivery. Bacon makes use of the topics (or places) for invention, and he rejects the syllogism.

René DESCARTES turned to the analysis of ancient geometry and of algebra to set forth an art of invention and a universal mathematics, contrasted to the logic of syllogisms and the art of R. LULL, which provide rules for discoursing about things that one does not know. Analysis is the true way by which a thing is methodically discovered and derived; synthesis proceeds conversely from effect to cause. Descartes concludes, therefore, that analysis is also the best and truest method of teaching.

The *Port Royal Logic*, influenced by the Cartesian method, has four parts, the first three on concepts, judgments, and reasoning, and the fourth on method. Method is the art of disposing well a series of many thoughts for either discovery or proof. The method of discovering truth is called analysis, or the method of resolution, or the method of invention. The method of explaining or proving a known truth is called synthesis, or the method of composition, or the method of doctrine.

The Eighteenth Century. The *Treatise of Human Nature* by D. HUME is announced by its full title as an exercise in method: It is *an Attempt to Introduce the Experimental Method of Reasoning into Moral Subjects*. All reasoning is nothing but a comparison and a discovery of those relations that two or more objects bear to each other. There are two kinds of beliefs: Some are relations of ideas that are based entirely on associations formed within the mind, and some are matters of fact that depend wholly on direct sense experience. Efforts to ascertain causal relations in the traditional sense are methodologically impossible as no necessary connections can be discerned between mere facts, and thus we are left with little certain knowledge of the world.

I. KANT adapted Hume's skeptical method in his construction of a critical philosophy, but he differed from Hume concerning both judgments and methods. He argued that mathematical judgments are synthetic, not analytic as Hume thought, and that mathematics, physics, and ethics are all based on synthetic judgments a priori. In the *Prolegomena* he distinguishes rigorously between the use of analytic and synthetic applied to judgments and applied to method. He uses both the analytical and synthetic methods in his philosophy. In *The Foundations of the Metaphysics of Morals* he says that his method is to proceed analytically from common knowledge to the determination of its supreme principle and then synthetically from the examination of this principle and its sources back to common knowledge, where it finds its application. The structure of the three *Critiques* is synthetic in method and proceeds in logical sequence through a doctrine of elements, containing an analytic and a dialectic, to a doctrine of method.

The Nineteenth Century. During the nineteenth century the methods of transcendental logics and of empirical logics were elaborated; the implications for methods of history, psychology, sociology, and of the theory of evolution were examined; and classifications of the sciences, with special attention to the methods of

the natural sciences and the humanistic sciences, or *Geisteswissenschaften*, were constructed.

G.W.F. HEGEL argued that the Kantian distinction between judgment and method, analytic and synthetic, is unduly abstract. All judgments and all methods are simultaneously analytic and synthetic. The reactions of S.A. KIERKEGAARD and K. MARX to the Hegelian dialectic laid the foundations of the methods of PHENOMENOLOGY and EXISTENTIALISM and of materialistic DIALECTIC.

A. COMTE developed the positivistic method in connection with his inauguration of sociology, expounded an interrelated series of classifications of the sciences, and developed a "subjective synthesis: as a universal system of conceptions proper to humanity." W. DILTHEY devoted himself to a critique of historical reason, which he found lacking in Kant, and to an examination of the principles and methods of the *Geisteswissenschaften*. F. Brentano's psychology "from an empirical standpoint" and W. Wundt's "physiological" psychology, both published in 1874, revolutionized the methods of both psychology and philosophy.

Sir William HAMILTON, who endeavored to combine Kantian and Scottish common-sense philosophies, divided his logic into two parts: stoicheiology, or the doctrine of elements (in which he treats concepts, judgments, and reasoning), and methodology, or the doctrine of method. For Hamilton, method consists of two processes, analysis and synthesis; and logical methodology has three parts: the doctrine of definition, the doctrine of division, and the doctrine of probation.

John Stuart MILL, in his *System of Logic, Ratiocinative and Inductive: Being a Connected View of the Principles of Evidence and the Methods of Scientific Investigation*, devotes one chapter to his "four methods of experimental inquiry," another to the deductive method, and the final book to the methods of the social sciences. His defense of Utilitarianism is a method of examining consequences rather than a priori precepts. Herbert SPENCER applies the conception and method of evolution in the construction of his system of synthetic philosophy.

Another logical innovation of the era proved to be greatly influential for the development of twentieth-century thought. This is the predicate calculus of Gottlob Frege, a purely formal system in which propositions are analyzed by means of quantifying symbols and functional relations. His use of this calculus showed that language could be properly represented in terms of purely logical relations.

The Twentieth Century. Twentieth-century philosophy is dominated by three major schools, each of which represents a different reaction to Kant: American

Pragmatism, Anglo-American analytic philosophy, and Continental philosophy (though, it is to be noted, these geographic labels are not to be taken too literally). The methodological differences between these schools made dialogue among them impossible for much of the century. However, the last two decades of the century saw the schools coming together both in topical concerns and in methods, so that the insights of each approach are increasingly being acknowledged by all philosophers.

PRAGMATISM, the unique American contribution to philosophy, accepts the Kantian notion of an active subject, but reacts against Kantian transcendentalism by grounding philosophical method on a more experiential and scientific foundation. Charles Sanders PEIRCE argues that the way to clarify an idea is to reduce it to the practical effects or expected consequences associated with that idea. Thus, the pragmatic method does not operate according to principles, but rather is determined by consequences; as a result, it is primarily synthetic and pluralistic. William JAMES broadened this to comprise a theory of truth, such that beliefs can be said to be true if they are confirmed by our experience. J. Dewey seeks a "method of inquiry" to avoid the errors revealed by experience in past inquiries. He defines inquiry as "the controlled or directed transformation of an indeterminate situation into one that is so determinate in its constituent distinctions and relations as to convert the elements of the original situation into a unified whole." W.V.O. Quine, rejecting the Kantian distinction between analytic and synthetic judgments and epistemological foundationalism, argues that our knowledge is a "web" of internally coherent beliefs that are pragmatically adjusted as necessary. Richard Rorty extends this critique by attacking philosophy's claim to objective knowledge of principles, instead arguing that knowledge is merely a matter of evolving social practice.

Anglo-American analytic philosophy takes up Kant's close attention to propositions and focuses primarily on the analysis of meaning and language, especially in terms of the symbolic logic developed by Frege in the late nineteenth century. The methods of G.E. Moore and B. RUSSELL were the starting point of the philosophical analysis that ran through logical atomism and LOGICAL POSITIVISM to linguistic analysis. Analytic philosophers ground the meaning of concepts by reducing all propositions to analytic tautologies or those based on direct empirical observation; thus, analysis is predominantly reductive in form, in that principles are not the most universal, but rather the most atomistic foundations of knowledge. They believe that philosophical problems can be dissolved if we properly understand how language carries signification. This project took two main approaches: One, influenced by the early work of Ludwig Wittgenstein and the logical positivism of the Vienna Circle, employs Frege's predicate calculus to analyze

propositions by revealing their elementary logical structure; the second, influenced by the later work of WITTGENSTEIN and J.L. AUSTIN and P.F. Strawson, believed ordinary language had sophisticated principles for analysis embedded within its use, and its philosophy aimed at exploring how those principles guide the complexities of real discourse. For both approaches, the objectives of method applied to language are to determine the conditions of VERIFICATION or the varieties of use and to expose false inferences, spurious questions, and non-sensical assumptions. With Quine's questioning of the analytic-synthetic distinction, the reductive nature of philosophical analysis was moderated.

Continental philosophy finds inspiration in Kant's notion of the constructive role of the human mind in constituting reality. While this tradition takes on many permutations, they are all modifications of phenomenology, whose founder, Edmund HUSSERL, sought to make philosophy a rigorous science. His *Formal and Transcendental Logic*, according to its subtitle, is a *Critique of Logical Understanding*. Taking its beginning from experience of the sciences and logic, the phenomenological method does not consist in deducing, in *erklaren* (mere "explanation by theories"), but rather in *aufklaren* (seeing things as they are). The functions of logic reflect the meanings of *logos*: "speaking," "thinking," and "thing thought." Phenomenological research must cover all three, because formal logic depends on transcendental logic. The unifying element is the notion of intentionality: The world has significance for us in relation to modes of consciousness because we are aware of the world only in terms of some intentional attitude. These various intentional modes of consciousness, as the principles behind our diverse experiences of the world, are revealed in phenomenological analysis of experience. The centrality of subjective consciousness as a methodological principle is developed in different ways by later continental thinkers. Martin HEIDEGGER undertakes to analyze and describe the meanings of individual phenomena. He seeks to free philosophy from dependence on the special sciences and to destroy the misconceptions of traditional philosophies, which have forgotten or distorted and trivialized the insights and truths of earlier thinkers. The question of being must be restated explicitly; and to understand *Sein* one must begin with *Dasein*: The approach to ontology must be made by analysis of experiences such as temporality and of emotions such as concern and dread, because consciousness of being is unavoidably colored by one's historical and cultural contexts. In arguing for the need for hermeneutics, Hans-Georg GADAMER emphasizes the necessary historicity of interpretative contexts, which impedes the discernment of absolutely objective principles. Another movement to develop from this is structuralism, an interdisciplinary approach that aims to analyze large social structures in terms of their smallest constituent elements, which occur according to regular underlying patterns. The notion of the contextual nature of knowledge is carried to its skeptical conclusion in the deconstructionism of Jacques Derrida and other "postmodern" philosophies, in which the meaning of every sign is established only within its changing contexts, thus making stable reference impossible. A creative application of the constructive role of the subject as crucial for philosophical methodology (arising in conjunction with Pragmatist principles) occurred in the development of feminist philosophy, which concentrates on discerning affective and relational principles of knowledge and behavior, as opposed to rational principles favored by traditional Western thought. Finally, a very different and particularly fruitful offshoot of Kant's focus on the subject has been the development of personalism within Roman Catholic thought, especially in the writings of Jacques MARITAIN and Karol WOJTYŁA. For personalism, the experience of the person as a unique transcendent being guides our interpretation of facts of the world and grounds moral arguments in the infinite worth of the individual.

Summation. From the beginning of rational thought, men have speculated about methods, or ways, or modes, or instruments of thinking. The meanings of method have been as diverse as the kinds of philosophies, sciences, arts, beliefs, and problems. During the Renaissance, method became a central problem of philosophy and science, and by the seventeenth century the numerous divisions of method had been all but amalgamated into the distinction between analytic and synthetic. Some important problems were encountered in that reduction: Thus, some philosophers argued that the method of discovery is analytic, others that it is synthetic. During the nineteenth century the differences between classification of the methods of the sciences and arts were subjects of inquiry and controversy: The a priori method was presented as synthetic, as analytic, or as impossible; the a posteriori method was analytic or synthetic of empirical experience. In the twentieth century, the methods of philosophies set them in controversial opposition in regard to the detection of errors, the clarification of meanings, and the establishment of truths. Pragmatism tends to be synthetic; logical positivism, ANALYTICAL PHILOSOPHY, phenomenology, and existentialism tend to be analytic. As the various schools have realized the limitations of overly narrow methodology, they have been able to see more clearly what they have in common; this serves to reduce the misunderstandings and controversies that have developed in contemporary philosophy.

SEE ALSO METHODOLOGY (THEOLOGY); PHILOSOPHY AND SCIENCE; SCHOLASTIC METHOD.

BIBLIOGRAPHY

Michael Beaney, "Analysis," in *The Stanford Encyclopedia of Philosophy*, available from http://plato.stanford.edu (accessed March 3, 2008).

René Descartes, *Discourse on Method and Related Writings*, translated by Desmond M. Clarke (London 1999).

N.W. Gilbert, *Renaissance Concepts of Method* (New York 1969).

Pierre Hadot, *What Is Ancient Philosophy?*, translated by Michael Chase (Cambridge, Mass. 2002).

Pope John Paul II, *Restoring Faith in Reason [Fides et Ratio]* , edited by Laurence Paul Hemming and Susan Frank Parsons, translated by Anthony Meredith and Laurence Paul Hemming (London 2002).

R. McKeon, "Philosophy and the Development of Scientific Methods," *Journal of the History of Ideas* 27 (1966): 3–22.

Jeanne Peijnenburg, "Identity and Difference: A Hundred Years of Analytic Philosophy," *Metaphilosophy* 31 (2000): 365–381.

Nicholas Rescher, *Philosophical Dialectics: An Essay in Metaphilosophy* (Albany, N.Y. 2006).

Robert Sokolowski, "The Method of Philosophy: Making Distinctions," *Review of Metaphysics* 51 (1998): 515–532.

Richard Peter McKeon
Distinguished Service Professor of Philosophy and Greek
University of Chicago

James M. Jacobs
Professor of Philosophy
Notre Dame Seminary, New Orleans, La. (2009)

MIAMI, ARCHDIOCESE OF

When Miami (*Miamiensis*) was established as a DIOCESE on August 13, 1958, its territory consisted of fourteen counties formerly of the diocese of St. Augustine. When the dioceses of Orlando and St. Petersburg were established on June 13, 1968, Miami was made an ARCHDIOCESE with the new dioceses, along with St. Augustine, as its suffragans. In 2001 the Province of Miami included, in addition to the above-named dioceses, St. Petersburg (1975), Pensacola-Tallahassee (1975), Palm Beach (1984), and Venice (1984). The territory of the archdiocese had been reduced to three counties in southern Florida—Broward, Dade, and Monroe—but the Catholic population had grown to 830,969 Catholics, or about twenty percent of the total population of 3.9 million (*The Official Catholic Directory* 2002).

The first bishop, Coleman F. Carroll (1905–1977) of Pittsburgh, Pennsylvania, served as auxiliary in Pittsburgh until his installation as bishop of Miami on October 7, 1958. During the years of his episcopacy

Saint Mary's Catholic Church, Miami, FL. *Priests hold mass beneath an ornate mural inside the church of this predominately Cuban parish.* © PATRICK WARD/CORBIS

(1958–1977), the extraordinary growth in population that had begun after World War II continued in southern Florida. The increase, which reached boom proportions, came as a consequence of the attractive climate, real-estate development for year-round residents in middle income brackets, and an influx of refugees from Cuba. Carroll initiated an extensive series of building projects and pastoral programs to meet the needs of his vastly diverse flock.

Within the first five years he more than doubled the number of parishes, many of which were provided with schools. Bishop Carroll took the initiative in constructing and staffing diocesan high schools, Catholic hospitals, and retreat centers. In 1958 he blessed the new St. John Vianney College Seminary, the first minor seminary on the East Coast south of Baltimore, Maryland, and in 1962 he inaugurated a major seminary, St. Vincent de Paul, opened at Boynton Beach. Early in 1960 Carroll established the *Centro Hispano Catolico* for all Spanish-speaking people in the area; it had day nurseries, a medical clinic, a dental clinic, and arrangements for medical assistance. In addition to housing, food, and clothing, the center provided employment opportunities as well as transportation from Cuba for children and RELIGIOUS at considerable expense to the diocese. He dealt with the issues of race and ethnicity by pushing for steady, if gradual, integration in parishes and schools. To staff the new institutions Carroll brought to the diocese eight religious communities of priests, twenty-five of sisters, and five of brothers.

In September 1976 Bishop Edward A. McCarthy (1918–2005), of PHOENIX, was appointed coadjutor with right of succession, becoming the second archbishop of Miami (1977–1994) when Archbishop Carroll died the following year. The population in Florida continued to grow, and diocesan boundaries were once again realigned in 1984 with the creation of the dioceses of Palm Beach and Venice. McCarthy carried on the pastoral outreach and general policies of his predecessor in trying to help the refugees who flowed into Florida from Cuba and Haiti. Archbishop McCarthy had the honor of welcoming Pope JOHN PAUL II to Miami when the PONTIFF paid his second visit to the United States in September 1987. John Paul addressed large audiences in both English and Spanish and met with a group of prominent Jewish leaders.

When Archbishop McCarthy reached the mandatory age of retirement in 1994, New Orleans-born John C. Favalora (1935–), the bishop of St. Petersburg since 1989, was appointed to succeed him. Like his predecessor, Archbishop Favalora spoke out forcefully for fair treatment of immigrants, especially Haitians. One of his chief priorities was education, in particular providing financial support to keep inner-city Catholic schools open. He also opened two new high schools in 1998,

the first to be built in the archdiocese in twenty-five years. To ensure the long-term financial stability of the archdiocese, the archbishop conducted a Vision 2000 campaign to generate a $75-million endowment to enable the church in Miami to continue its educational and charitable ministries into the twenty-first century. Vision 2000 collected nearly $90 million for the archdiocese. The archbishop, who was one of the U.S. delegates to the Synod for America in 1997, also emphasized missionary activity at the parish and school level, creating an office for that purpose and reviving archdiocesan participation in the Holy Childhood Society.

On its fiftieth anniversary, the archdiocese consisted of 111 parishes and 7 missions in Miami-Dade, Broward, and Monroe counties. More than 790,000 registered Catholics were served by 264 diocesan priests, 98 religious order priests, 143 permanent deacons, 291 women religious, and 49 men religious (*The Official Catholic Directory* 2008).

Catholic institutions of higher learning in the archdiocese include Barry University and St. Thomas University in Miami. Founded as Barry College for women in 1940 by the DOMINICAN SISTERS of Adrian, Michigan, it went co-educational and subsequently attained university status in 1981. St. Thomas University was originally established as Biscayne College by the Augustinian Friars in 1961. It evolved from an all-male college to a coeducational university with a graduate school and became the only accredited Catholic-affiliated LAW school in the Southeastern United States. Since 1988 the University has been under the sponsorship of the Archdiocese of Miami.

SEE ALSO AUGUSTINIANS; BISHOP, AUXILIARY; FRIARS; PITTSBURGH, DIOCESE OF.

BIBLIOGRAPHY

Archdiocese of Miami Official Web site, available from: http://www.miamiarch.org (accessed October 17, 2008).

Fr. Daniel Kubula, *History of the Archdiocese of Miami: 1958–2008* (Miami 2007).

Michael J. McNally, *Catholicism in South Florida, 1868–1968* (Gainesville, Fla. 1982).

Edward A. McCarthy, *Walking Together: Archdiocese of Miami First Synod, 1985–1988* (Miami 1989).

The Official Catholic Directory (New Providence, N.J. 2002, 2008).

Sister Marie Enda Kennedy OP
Dean, St. Thomas Aquinas College
Sparkill, N.Y.

Ana Rodriguez-Soto
Editor, Miami edition
Florida Catholic newspaper (2009)

MICHIGAN, CATHOLIC CHURCH IN

One of the north central states of the United States, admitted to the Union in 1837 as the twenty-sixth state, Michigan is composed of an upper (northern) and a lower (southern) peninsula, which are separated by the Straits of Mackinac, spanned by the great Mackinac Bridge, opened in 1957. Four of the five Great Lakes form a part of the boundary of the peninsulas. Lake Michigan separates the two peninsulas, forming the southern boundary of the upper and the western boundary of the lower. Lansing is the capital, and Detroit is the largest city. In January 2008 the Catholic population of the state of Michigan was 2,216,372 or twenty-two percent of the total population of 10,029,784 (*The Official Catholic Directory* 2008, p. 2085). Michigan is organized into 7 dioceses: the Archdiocese of DETROIT and the 6 suffragan sees: Grand Rapids, Lansing, Marquette, Saginaw, Gaylord, and Kalamazoo. As of 2008, there were 774 parishes and 50 missions served by 981 diocesan priests, 306 religious order priests, 427 permanent deacons, 91 brothers, and 2,505 sisters. The state had two free-standing seminaries, six Catholic colleges or universities, twenty-six Catholic hospitals, forty-one Catholic high schools, and 228 Catholic grade schools (*The Official Catholic Directory* 2008, p. 2085).

Early History. The beginnings of the Catholic Church in Michigan date from the seventeenth century. In the fall of 1641 the French JESUITS Charles Raymbaut (1602–1642) and Isaac Jogues (1607–1646) visited the Chippewa Indians in the area later called Sault Sainte Marie in northern Michigan. Thirty years later, with headquarters at St. Ignatius mission, Jacques MARQUETTE, Gabriel Druillettes (1610–1681), and other Jesuits cared for the area surrounding the Straits of Mackinac that link Lakes Huron and Michigan. By 1679, when Robert Cavelier de LA SALLE and Louis HENNEPIN, O.F.M., explored the St. Joseph River and built a chapel at its mouth on Lake Michigan, priests had visited almost all parts of Michigan. Detroit itself was colonized in 1701 when Antoine Cadillac (1658–1730) arrived from Montreal, Canada, on July 24, bringing with him a Franciscan and a Jesuit. A primitive chapel was built within Cadillac's Fort Ponchartrain, and resident priests served as chaplains. In 1708 construction of a church was begun; the parish register of St. Anne's received its first entry on July 17, 1722, signed by Reverend Bonaventure Liénard. During the following decades Jesuits, including Armand de la Richardie (1686–1758), arrived in Detroit for work among the native people, while the Franciscans continued to minister to the white settlers.

The surrender of Montreal to the British in 1760 marked the influx to Detroit of its first Protestant element—Irish, Scotch, and English traders, soldiers, and merchants. It also presaged a change in ecclesiastical jurisdiction for the missions of the area, which until then had been under the bishop of Quebec, Canada. With the independence of the thirteen English colonies and the establishment of the United States, ROME named John CARROLL prefect apostolic (1784) and then first BISHOP of Baltimore (1789), with authority over all Catholics in the new republic. Detroit raised the American flag in 1796, at about the time that St. Anne's received Reverend Michael Levadoux, the first pastor appointed by an American bishop. Two years later, Levadoux welcomed as assistants two Sulpician confreres, Jean Dilhet and Gabriel RICHARD, the latter succeeding to the pastorate of St. Anne's in 1802. Richard opened a seminary, a school for Native Americans, and an academy for girls. On August 31, 1809, he printed the *Michigan Essay*, probably the only issue of the first paper in Michigan. He was one of the founders (1817) of the University of Michigan, Ann Arbor, and also served as vice-president and professor.

In 1808 the Michigan Territory was assigned to the new Diocese of Bardstown, Kentucky. When Bishop Benedict Joseph FLAGET made his visitation in 1818, he erected six parishes in Detroit and resolved the difficulties that had prevented the erection of a new St. Anne's after the old structure had been leveled in the fire of 1805. Although it was first occupied in 1822, the church was not completed until Christmas 1828. To Bishop Edward Dominic FENWICK, who had been named ordinary of the new Diocese of Cincinnati (1821), with jurisdiction over the Michigan Territory, Richard reported in 1826 that there were 7,000 white Catholics in the territory and about 100 African Americans. They were served by eight priests, including Stephen BADIN at St. Joseph, Samuel MAZZUCHELLI, O.P., at Mackinac Island and Green Bay, and Frederic BARAGA in the northwest sector and the upper peninsula. Although the majority of the Catholics were French settlers or native converts, the Irish were trickling into Wayne and Washtenaw counties, and in 1831 Reverend Patrick O'Kelly (d. 1858) became their pastor in Northfield Township.

Diocese. On March 4, 1827, LEO XII named Detroit a diocese with Richard as its first ordinary, but his nomination was suppressed before the bull erecting the diocese was officially issued (March 20). Apparently, interventions by Father Stephen Badin and Father Frederic Résé gave Rome pause: There was concern about the poor financial resources of the Church in Detroit coupled with the fact that Richard had been imprisoned for defamation of character at one time for excommunicat-

St. Florian's Church, Hamtramck, MI. *Pictured is an aerial shot of the church and surrounding neighborhood.* © JAMES L. AMOS/
CORBIS

ing a local man who had divorced and was living with another woman. This hold on establishing the diocese lasted until Richard's death on September 13, 1832. Within two weeks, Fenwick also was dead, and the Church in Michigan was deprived of the leadership under which it had begun its growth.

Résé. On March 8, 1833, without reference to the action taken by Rome in 1827, GREGORY XVI established Detroit as a diocese for the second time; Frederic Résé of Cincinnati became its first bishop and St. Anne's its first CATHEDRAL. The diocese embraced the present states of Michigan, Wisconsin, Iowa, Minnesota, and the portions of North and South Dakota east of the Mississippi. By 1838 the Michigan population had increased to 170,000; of these, between 20,000 and 24,000 were Catholics; 3,000, converted Native Americans; 8,000, English, Irish, German, and American; and the balance, French. To help care for this flock, Résé had about thirty priests. As administrator of the Diocese of Cincinnati, he brought the POOR CLARES to Detroit in 1833 to establish the first CONVENT and the first school for girls.

In 1835 Most Holy Trinity parish was established for the English-speaking Catholics, primarily the Irish. German immigrants settled in Clinton County in 1836, and within two years a resident priest was assigned to the community that became Westphalia. In Detroit, Reverend Martin KUNDIG was deputed to minister to the German Catholics, especially at the mission that became Assumption Grotto parish. Kundig also organized the Catholic Female Society in 1834 to assume responsibility for the poor and orphans made homeless by the cholera epidemic of 1834. He was appointed the town superintendent of the poor, and he directed the county poor house, the infirmary, and the orphan asylum. The orphan asylum, financed solely by Catholic funds, represented the beginning of organized Catholic charity in Detroit.

Lefevere. Disputes with other bishops, mishandling of his oversight of the Poor Clares of Pittsburgh, a possible drinking problem, and unauthorized fundraising in Europe were reasons for Résé's forced resignation in 1840. He remained bishop of Detroit but spent the rest of his life in Europe, where he died in 1871. Peter Paul LEFEVERE, who had come to the Missouri missions from

Belgium only eight years earlier, was named coadjutor and administrator of Detroit on July 23, 1841, and consecrated on November 22. During his twenty-eight-year episcopate, the diocese grew from a pioneer settlement into a well-structured community capable of further development. The territory originally administered by Résé was divided first by the erection of the Diocese of Dubuque in 1837, then of Milwaukee in 1843. The upper peninsula was made a vicariate in 1853, and Bishop Baraga established his see first at Sault Sainte Marie and then, in 1865, at Marquette.

Under Lefevere, the Detroit Catholic population increased to more than 150,000, the number of priests to eighty-eight, and the number of churches to eighty, with much of the growth across the southern tier of the state, in the Grand Rapids region, and around Saginaw. In 1843 five Sisters of the Holy Cross arrived to establish a school at Bertrand, near St. Joseph. In 1844 the Daughters of Charity began St. Vincent's Select School for girls in Detroit and in 1845 they opened St. Vincent's, which five years later was moved to a new location and renamed St. Mary's, and became the first private hospital in the Northwest Territory to care for the mentally ill. In 1860 they opened St. Joseph's Retreat in present-day Dearborn, the first hospital in Michigan, and the second in the nation to care exclusively for the mentally ill. In 1845, at his parish in Monroe, Reverend Louis Gillet, C.Ss.R., working with Mother Teresa Maxis DUCHEMIN, founded the Sisters, Servants of the IMMACULATE HEART OF MARY, one of the few native sisterhoods in the United States. Lefevere introduced into the diocese two other communities, the Religious of the Sacred Heart in 1851 and the SCHOOL SISTERS OF NOTRE DAME the following year. Also in 1852 four BROTHERS OF THE CHRISTIAN SCHOOLS arrived to teach at St. Mary's. By 1874 approximately thirty-eight parochial schools were operating in the diocese. The first diocesan regulations were issued under Lefevere, who convened the first diocesan synod in 1859.

Progress was made in Catholic journalism with the appearance on July 23, 1842, of the first issue of the *Western Catholic Register,* the first newspaper under Catholic auspices since Richard's short-lived *Michigan Essay.* It was succeeded in 1853 by the *Detroit Catholic Vindicator,* which survived approximately six years. On September 12, 1868, the *Western Catholic* appeared; it was in turn succeeded by the *Western Home Journal* in 1872. Eleven years later the paper was acquired by the diocese and was renamed the *Michigan Catholic.*

The preparatory seminary which Richard and Dilhet had attempted to establish at St. Anne's in 1804 was destroyed by fire. From 1846 to 1854, Lefevere conducted St. Thomas Seminary, probably in his own home, apparently abandoning it in favor of the American College at LOUVAIN which, together with Bishop Martin SPALDING of Louisville, he launched in 1857. Until Sacred Heart Seminary opened in 1919, the only other diocesan seminary was St. Francis in Monroe, which operated from 1886 to 1889. In 1885 the cornerstone was laid for SS. Cyril and Methodius Seminary, Orchard Lake, established to train young men for the service of Polish Catholics throughout the country. A new cathedral, SS. Peter and Paul, had been built in 1848 by Lefevere; he was buried there following his death on March 4, 1869.

Borgess. Caspar Henry BORGESS, chancellor of the Archdiocese of CINCINNATI, Ohio, was installed as third Detroit ordinary on May 8, 1870. The eighteen years of his administration were marked primarily by a consolidation of diocesan gains. The great influx of German and Irish immigrants found national parishes already established. St. Wenceslaus was organized in 1871 for the Bohemians; in the same year, St. Albertus became the first of many parishes to serve the great number of Polish immigrants who flocked to Detroit. St. Aloysius parish in downtown Detroit was established in 1873; it was made the procathedral in 1877, and SS. Peter and Paul was entrusted to the JESUITS, who also opened Detroit College (1877). It became the University of Detroit and in 1963 had the largest student enrollment of any Catholic college or university in the United States. Besides the Jesuits, four other religious communities of men entered the diocese: Franciscans, Capuchins, HOLY GHOST FATHERS, and BASILIANS; the REDEMPTORISTS returned after an absence of a few years. In 1874 the LITTLE SISTERS OF THE POOR arrived to take up their work among the aging. In 1879 the Sisters of St. Felix came from Warsaw, Poland, and three years later established provincial headquarters in Detroit; in 1936 they moved to nearby Livonia.

In the northwest sector of the lower peninsula, lumber and fertile land attracted so many people that between 1869 and 1883 the number of churches increased from thirteen to thirty-two. In May 1882, the HOLY SEE established the Diocese of Grand Rapids containing thirty-nine counties, all but two north of a line from the southern extremity of Saginaw Bay to Lake Michigan. This reduced the Diocese of Detroit to twenty-nine counties, an area of about 18,558 square miles, with eighty-five priests, 100,455 Catholics, and forty-two parochial schools with 9,832 pupils. The Grand Rapids diocese contained about 50,000 Catholics served by about forty priests. Ill health caused Borgess to resign in 1887; three years later he died in Kalamazoo, Michigan, where he was buried in St. Augustine's parish cemetery.

The upper-peninsula Diocese of Marquette, first headed by Bishop Baraga, saw two fellow Slovenians succeed him, Ignatius MRAK (1869–1878) and John VERTIN (1879–1899), both of whom sought to impose order on a very disparate diocese. Frederick Eis, the fourth Bishop of Marquette (1899–1922), held the second diocesean synod (1905). Henry Joseph Richter was the first Bishop of Grand Rapids (1883–1916). He established the initial institutions of this new diocese, including the Seminary of St. Joseph (1909). His coadjutor, Michael Gallagher (1866–1937), ordained in 1915, succeeded him (1916) until being transferred to Detroit in 1918.

Foley. John Samuel Foley (1833–1918) of Baltimore, Maryland, was installed as successor to Borgess on November 25, 1888. During his thirty-year episcopate, the Catholic population increased to 386,000, largely because of the great waves of immigrants who settled principally in Detroit to work in the newly established automobile industry. In 1899 San Francisco, the first parish for Italians, was founded, and soon there were churches for the Slovaks, Lithuanians, Hungarians, and Rumanians, among others. In 1900 St. Patrick's Church was named the cathedral and in 1918 it was retitled SS. Peter and Paul.

Significant developments took place among religious communities. In 1891 the Sisters of ST. JOSEPH were founded in Kalamazoo, Michigan, where they opened Borgess Hospital (1901). The Sisters of St. Dominic, in Michigan since 1877 when they staffed a parish school in Traverse City, chose Adrian, Michigan, as the location of their provincial house (1892) and their motherhouse (1923). In 1910 the Sisters, Servants of the Immaculate Heart of Mary, founded St. Mary's College in Monroe; they renamed it Marygrove in 1925 and two years later transferred it to a new site in Detroit. In 1906 the cloistered DOMINICAN NUNS established a convent, and the Sisters of BON SECOURS their hospital in Detroit. In 1911 the SISTERS OF MERCY opened St. Joseph Mercy Hospital in Ann Arbor. When Foley died on January 5, 1918, the diocese had 318 priests serving 246 churches and missions.

Gallagher. Bishop Michael James Gallagher of Grand Rapids was installed as bishop of Detroit in 1918 and immediately addressed the problems of an expanding, polyglot population. Among the 105 new parishes he began, 33 were for Catholics speaking foreign languages. Parish schools more than doubled in number and enrollment. In 1919 Siena Heights College was established by the DOMINICAN SISTERS in Adrian; and Nazareth College opened in 1924 under the Sisters of St. Joseph. In 1919 Sacred Heart Seminary was founded, with high school and college departments training young

men for the diocesan priesthood; the Gothic structure was ready for use in the fall of 1924. Retreat houses were built for laymen and women. The Diocesan Council of Catholic Men was started. A chancery office and a new St. Aloysius Church in downtown Detroit were erected. Hospitals multiplied: St. Francis, in Hamtramck; Mercywood Sanitarium, in Ann Arbor; St. Joseph's Mercy, in Pontiac; and Mercy, in Monroe. In the 1920s the Dominican Sisters of the Third Order of St. Dominic, Discalced Carmelite Nuns, and the Sylvestrine BENEDICTINES established provincial headquarters in the diocese.

During the 1920s the Catholics of Michigan also struggled to protect their right to send their children to Catholic schools. In 1920 and 1924 they fought a state constitutional amendment that would oblige all children to attend public schools. When Gallagher died in 1937, more than 800 priests were ministering to 602,000 Catholics.

The Diocese of Grand Rapids experienced the same growth as Detroit. Edward Kelly, ordained as an auxiliary Bishop of Detroit in 1911, became the fourth bishop of Grand Rapids in 1919 and built many institutions. He was a leader, along with the Marquette and Detroit bishops, in successfully defeating the 1920 and 1924 anti–Catholic school amendment campaigns. His successor, Joseph Pinten (1926–1940), wisely paid off Kelly's bills, helping the diocese to survive the Depression better than most dioceses. Paul Nussbaum, the bishop of Marquette (1922–1935), served while the upper peninsula experienced a serious post–World War I economic decline, which continued into the twenty-first century. His successor, Joseph Plagens (1935–1940), a Detroit auxiliary bishop, faced the added trial of a burned cathedral.

The state ecclesiastical scene changed on August 3, 1937, when Detroit was made an archdiocese with Grand Rapids and Marquette as suffragan sees. The creation of Lansing the next day and of Saginaw on February 26, 1938, raised the number of suffragans to four. Both new sees were industrial cities that experienced great growth, especially after the Second World War. Their bishops were primarily focused on establishing the institutions of a new diocese. Beginning in the late 1960s, they also experienced the same urban trials that beset Detroit. Marquette struggled on, seeing under Bishop Thomas Noa (1947–1968) a share in the state's post–World War II boom with the erection of many buildings and ecclesial institutions. After the dynamic leadership of Francis HAAS, as the sixth bishop of Grand Rapids (1943–1953), this diocese experienced the steady and competent leadership of several bishops into the early twenty-first century.

The Archdiocese of Detroit, meanwhile, found itself not only a leader in the state hierarchy but a crucial diocese in the Church in the United States. This was more due to the archbishops who held this see than to the diocese itself: Edward MOONEY (1937–1958; CARDINAL in 1946), John DEARDEN (1958–1980; cardinal in 1969), Edmund SZOKA (1980–1990; cardinal in 1988), and Adam MAIDA (1990–; cardinal in 1994).

Two more suffragan sees were created on December 19, 1970—Kalamazoo and Gaylord. The former has a Catholic population that is a very small percentage of the total population. The latter served an increasing resort population.

Catholics in Michigan gained a powerful agent with the establishment of the Michigan Catholic Conference (MCC), which eventually handled insurance, pensions, and investments for the dioceses of Michigan in addition to lobbying State officials on critical moral and social questions. Michigan Catholics successfully defeated a measure which would have allowed physician-assisted suicide in 1998, but twice were defeated in efforts to gain some state financial assistance for their schools (Proposal *C* in 1970 and the Voucher Proposal in 2000). Educational efforts usually accompanied these campaigns. Thus the bishops issued a pastoral letter in 1998 against assisted suicide. And in 2007, the MCC conducted a major educational campaign using compact discs sent to all Catholic households to help them distinguish between immoral embryonic stem-cell research and moral adult stem-cell research. The MCC also conducted two successful 2004 campaigns to override the Catholic governor's vetoes. As a result partial-birth abortion was banned (though this ban was subsequently ruled unconstitutional) and Definition of Marriage legislation was enacted. All the Michigan dioceses in the 1980s implemented policies regarding sexual abuse by priests, requiring cooperation with state authorities and compliance with civil law. Review boards were established in 2002 to receive allegations and the Virtus program to train adults to create safe environments for children was utilized beginning in 2003. The MCC in 2003 fully supported a state law requiring clergy to report immediately any suspicion of child abuse. In April 2007, the Michigan bishops also issued a statement calling for immigration reform legislation.

Demographic changes created many new problems for the Church in Michigan, leading to the closing of many urban schools and parishes and leaving insufficient resources to create sufficient new institutions where Catholics relocated. There was also a steady fall-off in Catholic practice. Evangelization thus came to be seen as a primary focus of Catholic life. In terms of media, this has led to the founding of the Catholic Television Network/Detroit and of numerous Catholic radio stations. In 1999, the Diocese of Lansing premiered

Faith magazine, a glossy monthly sent to all Catholic households. The Grand Rapids diocese has also adopted this format.

During the first decade of the twenty-first century, the Province of Michigan saw a complete changeover in episcopal leadership. Bishop Robert Carlson governed Saginaw (2004–); Bishop Walter Hurley governed Grand Rapids (2005–); Bishop Alexander Sample governed Marquette (2005–); and Bishop Earl Boyea governed Lansing (2008–). Adam Cardinal Maida of Detroit reached retirement age in 2005, while Bishop James Murray of Kalamazoo (1997–) reached that age in 2007, and Bishop Patrick Cooney of Gaylord (1989–), in 2009.

On January 5, 2009, Pope Benedict XVI accepted the resignation of Cardinal Maida, which, following canon law, had been submitted in 2005. He was succeeded by Archbishop Allen H. Vigneron, who, before being named the Bishop of Oakland in 2003, served as an auxiliary bishop of Detroit and Rector of Sacred Heart Major Seminary. Archbishop Vigneron was installed on January 28, 2009, becoming the first archbishop of Detroit ordained as a priest for the Archdiocese. On April 6, 2009, Bishop Murray's resignation was accepted by Pope Benedict XVI. He was succeeded by Bishop Paul Joseph Bradley, a former auxiliary bishop of Pittsburgg, PA, who was installed as the new archbishop of Kalamazoo on June 5, 2009.

SEE ALSO AFRICAN AMERICAN CATHOLICS IN THE UNITED STATES (HISTORY OF); CARMELITES, DISCALCED; CHURCH AND STATE IN THE UNITED STATES (LEGAL HISTORY); DUBUQUE, ARCHDIOCESE OF; EMBRYOLOGY, HUMAN; IOWA, CATHOLIC CHURCH IN; LOUISVILLE, ARCHDIOCESE OF; MILWAUKEE, ARCHDIOCESE OF; MINNESOTA, CATHOLIC CHURCH IN; MISSION AND MISSIONS; NATIONAL COUNCIL OF CATHOLIC MEN (NCCM); NORTH DAKOTA, CATHOLIC CHURCH IN; SEX ABUSE CRISIS; SISTERS OF CHARITY, FEDERATION OF; SOUTH DAKOTA, CATHOLIC CHURCH IN; SULPICIANS; WISCONSIN, CATHOLIC CHURCH IN.

BIBLIOGRAPHY

Gaspar F. Ancona, *Where the Star Came to Rest: Stories of the Catholic People in West Michigan* (Strasbourg, France 2001).

George B. Catlin, *The Story of Detroit* (Detroit 1926).

James K. Jamison, *By Cross and Anchor: The Story of Frederic Baraga on Lake Superior* (Paterson, N.J. 1946).

Peter Leo Johnson, *Stuffed Saddlebags: The Life of Martin Kundig, Priest, 1805–1879* (Milwaukee, Wisc. 1942).

Maxine Kollasch, *A Vision, a Voice, a Presence: A History of the First Forty Years of the Michigan Catholic Conference* (Sterling Heights, Mich. 2005).

J. McGee, *The Catholic Church in the Grand River Valley, 1833–1950* (Grand Rapids, Mich. 1950).

George C. Michalek, *Golden Jubilee: Diocese of Lansing Parish: Historical Sketches* (Lansing, Mich. 1987).

The Official Catholic Directory, 2008 (New Providence, N.J. 2008).

George W. Paré, *The Catholic Church in Detroit, 1701–1888* (Detroit 1951).

Antoine Ivan Rezek, *History of the Diocese of Sault Ste. Marie and Marquette*, 2 vols. (Chicago 1906–1907).

Leslie Woodcock Tentler, *Seasons of Grace: A History of the Catholic Archdiocese of Detroit* (Detroit 1990).

Frank B. Woodford and Albert Hyma, *Gabriel Richard: Frontier Ambassador* (Detroit 1958).

Sister Mary Rosalita Kelly IHM
formerly Professor of History
Marygrove College, Detroit, Mich.

Rt. Rev. Francis Xavier Canfield
Rector and President
Sacred Heart Seminary, Detroit, Mich.

Most Rev. Earl Boyea
Bishop of Lansing, Mich. (2009)

MILITARY SERVICES, USA, ARCHDIOCESE FOR

The Archdiocese for Military Services, USA is responsible for the spiritual and sacramental care, including the maintenance of sacramental records, of Catholics and their families in the United States Armed Forces, including the army, navy, air force, Marine Corps, and Coast Guard, as well as Catholics in Veterans Affairs hospitals and anyone employed by the U.S. government overseas. The ARCHBISHOP for the military services is also recognized by the federal government as the sole endorser for all Catholic priest chaplains who serve these FAITHFUL.

Development of a Military Vicariate. Catholic priests have served American armed forces with distinction since Revolutionary War times. In 1888 the APOSTOLIC SEE granted exclusive competency to the archbishop of New York to designate navy chaplains. After the Spanish American War, a commission of the U.S. bishops, under James Cardinal GIBBONS, was established to recruit priests for the military chaplaincy. At the outbreak of World War I, sixteen priests served in the army, eight in the navy, and a further ten in the National Guard. The need for priests was urgent, so the bishops of America, with significant support from the KNIGHTS OF CO-LUMBUS, formed a National Catholic War Council. By Armistice Day 1919, a total of 1,026 priests were serving with the U.S. armed forces. Most were commissioned officers, but some 165 of those served as civilians paid from funds donated by the Knights of Columbus.

In the United States, as in other countries, the military constituted a vast DIOCESE with no regularly constituted head until Pope BENEDICT XV authorized each country to have an *episcopus castrensis*, or bishop for the military. On November 24, 1917, he appointed Patrick HAYES, an auxiliary bishop of New York, to be "Ordinary of all Catholics who fight in the Army and Navy during the present war." Bishop Hayes organized the new jurisdiction, with headquarters at St. Stephen's Church, New York City, and five regional vicariates. The organization came to be known as the Military Vicariate and its offices as the Military Ordinariate. Special faculties for general absolution, the EUCHARIST, and marriage were among many privileges granted only to military chaplains by the Military Ordinariate.

War was threatening again when Cardinal Hayes died in September 1938. On November 25, 1939, Pope PIUS XII designated Archbishop Francis SPELLMAN, the new ordinary of New York, as military vicar of the United States of America and episcopal administrator for chaplain affairs. The first administrator was Father John O'HARA, C.S.C., president of the University of Notre Dame. O'Hara was later named bishop of Buffalo and afterward CARDINAL archbishop of Philadelphia.

When peacetime conscription was instituted in 1940, Archbishop Spellman and Bishop O'Hara appealed to the American bishops for clergy. By December 8, 1941, 500 priests were on active duty. During World War II, 2,453 priests served as army chaplains and 817 as navy chaplains, of whom 676 died in service. After World War II, as realities dictated an American presence in outposts far from home, the jurisdiction of the Military Ordinary was expanded to include civilians serving the U.S. government overseas. In June 1946 the Veterans Administration program was placed under the canonical jurisdiction of the Military Ordinariate. During the Korean War, with many nations fighting under United Nations auspices, the Holy Father placed all Catholic chaplains in Korea under the American military vicar.

On April 25, 1951, an instruction of the HOLY SEE, *Sollemne semper*, set norms for canonically establishing a permanent vicariate for the apostolate to military personnel. It was made specific for the United States in a subsequent decree, *Mysticam petri naviculam*, of September 8, 1957. This decree formally erected the Military Vicariate and placed it under the archbishop of New York, with the tribunal of the Archdiocese of NEW YORK appointed to hear the cases of its subjects. It operated as a separate office in the New York Chancery, with its own staff and auxiliary bishops. Bishop Terence COOKE succeeded Cardinal Spellman as archbishop of New York and military vicar of the U.S. Armed Services in the spring of 1968. To assist him Bishop Joseph RYAN, who had been bishop of Anchorage, Alaska, was installed as coadjutor archbishop of the Military Vicar in

Catholic Soldiers in Iraq. *Father Durine, a chaplain of the Seventh Marine regiment, leads a Catholic mass in the camp of the 7th Battalion, part of the Marine Corp., in the desert of Iraq, some 150 kilometers north of the town of Nassiriyah.* © OLEG POPOV/ REUTERS/CORBIS

December 1975, and a separate ecclesiastical tribunal was created to attend to the needs of the military.

Creation of the Archdiocese. When Cardinal Cooke died on October 6, 1983, the Holy See determined that the military vicariate should have its own independent status, not as an added role for the archbishop of New York, but with its own full-time ordinary, to function as any other diocese. After a brief interregnum, during which time Archbishop John O'CONNOR of New York served as apostolic ADMINISTRATOR, Archbishop Ryan was named and installed as the first ordinary of the new Archdiocese for Military Services in March 1985. In January 1986 Archbishop Ryan created the administrative headquarters of the newly independent jurisdiction in the Washington, D.C., area. Archbishop Ryan retired in 1991, and the Most Reverend Joseph T. Dimino, who had been auxiliary bishop of the Military Vicar, was appointed the second ordinary for the military services. When Archbishop Dimino retired in 1997, he was succeeded by the Most Reverend Edwin F. O'Brien, an auxiliary bishop of New York. Archbishop O'Brien was later installed as Archbishop of Baltimore on October 1, 2007.

Twenty-First Century. On November 19, 2007, Pope Benedict XVI appointed Archbishop Timothy P. Bro-

glio, a priest of the Diocese of Cleveland, as archbishop of the Military Services. Archbishop Broglio, an Apostolic NUNCIO with the Holy See diplomatic service, was serving as the nuncio to the Dominican Republic and APOSTOLIC DELEGATE to Puerto Rico. Broglio was formally installed as archbishop for the Military Services on January 25, 2008, at the BASILICA of the NATIONAL SHRINE OF THE IMMACULATE CONCEPTION in Washington, D.C.

The archdiocese is the sole endorser (certifier) of Roman Catholic chaplains to the United States government. A ROMAN CATHOLIC priest cannot serve within the United States Military as a priest without the express permission of the archdiocese. As of 2008, 282 Roman Catholic priests were currently endorsed by the archdiocese for active-duty MILITARY SERVICE (Records of Archdiocese for the Military Services, USA). These chaplains serve on loan from their diocese of incardination or religious order/society and are released for a term of military service. Chaplains never become members of the archdiocese; instead, they always remain obedient to their home bishop/religious superiors. The only clergy incardinated into the archdiocese are its archbishop and auxiliary bishops.

Once a priest receives the endorsement and the subsequent faculties of the archdiocese, he becomes a commissioned military officer of the United States. A priest's assignments are provided by the Office of the Chief of Chaplains of each respective branch of the U.S. military.

The archdiocese is also the sole endorser of chaplains for the Veterans Administration hospitals. In 2008, 259 priests were endorsed for service in the Veterans Administration. Approximately 1.4 million Catholic men and women are served by the archdiocese (Records of Archdiocese for the Military Services, USA). To meet the needs of the faithful, the archdiocese had two auxiliary bishops to assist the archbishop in his pastoral duties. Both former chaplains, Bishop Joseph Estabrook (2004–) hailed from the navy, and Bishop Richard Higgins (2004–), from the air force. The archdiocese is currently headquartered in the northeast section of Washington, D.C., adjacent to The CATHOLIC UNIVERSITY OF AMERICA.

The archdiocese receives no funding from the United States government, due to the Establishment Clause of the U.S. Constitution. Rather, the archdiocese is solely funded from the generosity of its chaplains, men and women in uniform, and private benefactors. Unlike a conventional diocese, the archdiocese has no parishes or parish registries. CHAPELS are property of the United States government. Although the archdiocese exercises jurisdiction over the RELIGIOUS EDUCATION program and the celebration of Catholic LITURGY, it maintains no jurisdiction over the physical property of the chapel. Because base/command chapels are United States government property, all records of sacraments performed on U.S. Military installations are maintained by the archdiocese in its Office of Sacramental Records. This starkly contrasts with the model used in conventional parishes, where all sacraments are recorded in the parish registry. By the early 2000s, the archdiocese maintained more than 2.5 million records of sacraments performed on military installations.

General Norms. On April 21, 1986, Pope JOHN PAUL II issued the APOSTOLIC CONSTITUTION *Spirituali militum curae*, effective July 21, which made each military vicariate or ordinariate juridically comparable to a diocese. *Spirituali militum curae* recognized that military people "constitute, as a matter of fact, a particular social body, and because of the special conditions of their way of life, they have need of a concrete and specific form of pastoral assistance." Each ordinariate is headed by a military ordinary, normally a bishop, with all the rights and obligations of a diocesan ordinary, insofar as possible, given the nature and pastoral conditions of the military. Canonically, this ecclesiastical entity is denominated *Ordinariatus militaris seu castrensis*. A local title more suitable to the language of the particular

country being allowable, in the United States the designation is Archdiocese for the Military Services.

The Apostolic Constitution laid down certain general norms valid for all military ordinariates. In addition, each military ordinariate is ruled by its particular statutes as approved by the Apostolic See. The military ordinary, nominated by the POPE, belongs by right to the National Episcopal Conference. His jurisdiction is personal and exercised over all persons pertaining to the ordinariate, wherever they may be; it is ordinary for both the internal and external forums and proper, but cumulative, with the jurisdiction of the diocesan bishop. The areas and places reserved to military personnel fall chiefly under the jurisdiction of the military ordinary and, secondarily, in the absence of a chaplain, under the diocesan bishop. The military ordinary has the right to erect a seminary, to incardinate clerics, and to petition for a proper tribunal.

The following belong to the military ordinariate and come under its jurisdiction: the faithful who are military persons, as well as those who are at the service of the armed forces, provided that they are bound to this by civil laws; all members of their families, spouses, and children, even those who, though independent, live in the same house, as well as relatives and servants also living with them in the same house; those who attend military training schools, or who live or work in military hospitals, homes for the aged, or similar institutions; and all the faithful, both men and women, whether or not they are members of a religious institute, who carry out in a permanent manner a task committed to them by the military ordinary or with his consent. Particular statutes of each ordinariate may further specify the areas of proper subjects.

SEE ALSO MILITARY ORDERS; MILITARY SERVICE.

BIBLIOGRAPHY

Archdiocese for the Military Services, USA, Official Web site, available from: http://www.milarch.org/ (accessed November 30, 2008).

For the text of *Sollemne semper*, see: *Acta Apostolicae Sedis* 43 (1951): 562–565 (Latin).

John Paul II, *Spirituali militum curae*, On the Spiritual Care of the Military (Apostolic Constitution, April 21, 1986), available in Latin from http://www.vatican.va/holy_father/john_paul_ii/apost_constitutions/documents/hf_jp-ii_apc_19860421_spirituali-militum-curae_lt.html (accessed November 12, 2008).

Rev. Thomas J. Connelly
Vice Chancellor
Archdiocese for the Military Services, USA, Washington, D.C.

Rev. Nicholas Halligan OP
Judicial Vicar
Archdiocese for the Military Services, USA, Silver Spring,
Md.

John L. Schlageter
General Counsel
Archdiocese for the Military Services, USA (2009)

MILWAUKEE, ARCHDIOCESE OF

Milwaukee (*Milwauchiensis*) was established as a DIO-CESE on November 28, 1843, and as an ARCHDIOCESE on February 12, 1875. In 2007 it had a population of 678,173 Catholics, thirty percent of the general population of 2,283,410 in ten counties in southeastern Wisconsin, an area of 4,758 square miles (Milwaukee Catholic Press Apostolate 2007). The ecclesiastic Province of Milwaukee includes all the Wisconsin dioceses as its suffragans, namely, Green Bay, La Crosse, Madison, and Superior. From 1843, when Milwaukee was erected as a separate see, it was governed by the following prelates: John Martin HENNI, 1844–1881; Michael HEISS, 1881–1890; Frederic KATZER, 1891–1903; Sebastian Gebhard MESSMER, 1903–1930; Samuel Alphonse STRITCH, 1930–1940; Moses Elias Kiley, 1940–1953; Albert Gregory Meyer, 1953–1958; William Edward Cousins, 1958–1977; Rembert G. Weakland, O.S.B., 1977–2002; and Timothy Michael Dolan, 2002–February 23, 2009, when he was appointed tenth Archbishop of New York.

Early on Wisconsin became a center for Native Americans and a destination for French explorers, of whom the first was Jean Nicolet (1598–1642) who, seeking a route to China, landed at Green Bay in 1634. In the summer of 1661 the first missionary, René Ménard (1605–1661), S.J., entered Wisconsin at the source of the Wisconsin River, and four years later Claude AL-LOUEZ, S.J., built the first church between Bayfield and Washburn. But wars, liquor, traders, the official policy of concentrating the Native Americans near Detroit, and the French government suppression of the JESUITS in 1762 ruined the Jesuit missions. John Baptist Chardon, S.J., remained at Green Bay until 1728, when it too was given up. With the exception of a missionary or two, no priest entered Wisconsin for about a century. Reverend Gabriel RICHARD of Detroit stopped off at Green Bay and started a church building in 1823, which was completed in 1825 by Reverend Vincent Badin, also from Detroit. In 1840 the Wisconsin Territory, including eastern Minnesota, had a Catholic population of 14,600 (of whom 11,000 were Native Americans) out of a total of 40,000. Before the establishment of a diocese

in Wisconsin, it had been visited by several bishops, including Edward FENWICK of Cincinnati, who stopped at Green Bay in 1829 and 1831. In 1838 Frederic Résé (1833–1871) of Detroit paid a visit to La Pointe and Little Chute, and two years later Mathias LORAS's trip from Dubuque, Iowa, included visits at Green Bay, Little Chute, Kenosha, Milwaukee, and Potosi. Charles Auguste de FORBIN-JANSON, a French refugee BISHOP of Nancy and Toul, was offered the temporary administration of the Detroit diocese, but after a tour of inspection in 1840, which touched on Wisconsin, he declined the charge.

Difficult Years. From 1840 to 1870 most settlers in the area came from Germany, Ireland, and Norway. Later, the Poles led (1870–1920), followed by the Swedes (1900–1920), Italians (1900–1910), and other nationalities with lesser numbers. Opposition to the Church took the form of segregation designed to isolate Catholics, especially the foreign-born, and was sponsored in turn by religious sects, Nativists, Know-Nothings, Forty-eighters, Whigs, and Turners. Bishop Henni and his successors had to contend with these external threats, but gradually by the acquisition of property, the organization of parishes, schools, and societies, and a vigorous, informed press, they succeeded in making Catholicism respectable.

Nativist Attacks. In 1844, after a Nativist Gospel-Whig, Reverend John J. Miter (1809–1875), launched an attack against Romanism, charging that the hierarchy was dedicated to the overthrow of the government by control of the Irish vote, Henni's *Facts Against Assertions* (1845) silenced open attacks and offered a basis for respect and understanding. The press attack of Frederic Fratny of the Forty-eighters against the Church as being antagonistic to republican forms of government and intolerant toward personal liberty, principally via its regulation of marriages and burials, was proved a hoax by the Catholic press. Henni recruited F. J. Felsecker for the PROPAGANDA war against the Forty-eighters, and he demonstrated that their press was filled with material fabricated in LUTHER's time. As a result Catholics became more closely organized through societies and much better informed.

Among the other external obstacles to the Church, the problem of religious freedom for inmates of public reformatories and prisons was settled by legislative enactment in 1891, after two decades of conflict. Little encouragement was accorded KNOW-NOTHINGISM in the 1850s, but later the AMERICAN PROTECTIVE ASSOCIATION (APA) developed strength in the state, and about 100 branches were organized. Catholics countered the movement through activities of the Milwaukee Columbian League and in their press, especially the *Catholic*

Citizen. The Edgerton Bible Case brought notice and significance to the question of reading the BIBLE in public schools. In 1891 the state supreme court declared reading the Bible in public schools sectarian instruction and therefore unconstitutional. Reverend James F. Bowe, of Edgerton, whose efforts were financed by funds raised through the columns of the *Catholic Citizen*, received credit for raising the issue. The Bennett Law, enacted in 1889, was a compulsory education act that included provisions for teaching English and going to school in the district of one's residence. Under the leadership of Archbishop Heiss, the bishops of Wisconsin registered an able and effective protest. The Bennett Law became the issue in the gubernatorial election of 1890, and it was repealed in 1891. In the OPINION of Archbishop Katzer, the intelligence and organization of the laity, under the leadership of Humphrey J. Desmond (1858–1932), lawyer, editor, author, and at that time chairman of the education committee in the legislature, were responsible for this reversal.

Thus, with the exception of the Civil War period, outbreaks of hatred marked every decade prior to 1900. In 1853 the visit to Milwaukee of Archbishop Gaetano BEDINI, papal nuncio to Brazil, provided an opportunity for Forty-eighters to express their hatred of the Church, particularly in their press. They planned to hang Bedini in effigy, but were forced to drop the scheme when no Native Americans could be induced to join them. A notable address to Bedini from the Catholic laity did much to silence the opposition. Among the anti–Catholic actions in the 1870s was the CONVENT libel case, which involved defamatory remarks in a Protestant weekly, the *Christian Statesman*, about the NOTRE DAME SISTERS in Milwaukee, remarks that actually comprised a veiled attack on the Catholic school system. The case was tried in circuit court at Milwaukee in February 1875 and ended in a hung jury over the question: Can a corporation be libeled? The affair was settled when the editor retracted his statement. In 1875–1876 hatred for the Catholic Church in the German press and the Milwaukee city council was blamed for blocking a donation of land to the Sisters of Charity for a lying-in hospital and infant asylum. The same sisters engaged in litigation with the city (1890–1900) for damages when Terrace Avenue was extended through their property. Proceedings in the council and feelings elsewhere were marked at times by charges of bigotry, prejudice, and illegality. The city finally paid $5,000 damages and issued a quitclaim deed. In 1897, legislative action that placed a statue of MARQUETTE in the national capitol that produced an outburst of hostility. Positive apologetics in the press and letters by laymen, such as Desmond, to the lawmakers helped to steady the latter. At the end of the nineteenth century, socialism grew locally and nationally. Archbishop Messmer tried to check its effect on labor unions through the Federation of Catholic Societies, the ENCYCLICAL *Rerum novarum* of Pope LEO XIII, and the presentation of lectures by noted speakers.

Messmer was also conscious of the need for a pastoral outreach to the blacks. When Lincoln Charles Valle, a black layman from Chicago, called on Messmer in 1908 to interest him in evangelizing the blacks in Milwaukee, Messmer encouraged the work and lent the assistance of diocesan clergy. The Capuchins took over the work in 1911 and, after the building of St. Benedict the Moor's church, the apostolate began to bear fruit.

Internal Dissension. Besides strife arising from the outside, the Milwaukee diocese experienced trouble from within in the form of trusteeism, Fenianism, and nationalism. Lay trusteeism never became a major problem to Church leaders who employed COMMON SENSE and publicity against it. Henni used indirect methods to curb Fenians by persuading local Irish leaders to eschew all support of this association already condemned by the bishops of Ireland. The choice of a coadjutor for Henni in the last years of the 1870s sparked dissension in the press as well as in correspondence and discussion among the English and German-speaking elements, particularly clerical, in the archdiocese and elsewhere. The appointment of Heiss, though gratifying to Henni, not only disrupted the archdiocese and its UNITY, but had repercussions far beyond Wisconsin, especially by opening up the entire nationalistic question in the United States. By focusing attention on the role of nationality, the debate in ecclesiastical circles awakened a livelier regard for immigrants. The *Kuryer Polski*, a Polish daily of Milwaukee founded in 1888, advocated the creation of Polish dioceses with Polish bishops. For twenty-five years people were embittered by official letters banning the paper and by lawsuits. Finally in 1916 the *Kuryer Polski* lost its case charging the bishops of the Wisconsin province with conspiracy and boycott. The state supreme court decided in favor of the bishops on the grounds of ecclesiastical jurisdiction, which the plaintiff acknowledged.

The need to counter a hostile press and to furnish information gave rise to a German Catholic press. In 1852 the *Seebote* appeared in Milwaukee, followed by the *Columbia* in 1872, and the *Excelsior* in 1883. World War I, and the limitation of immigration after it, presaged the doom of the German press and also the lessening of the appeal of other foreign-language newspapers. The *Star of Bethlehem* (1869) and *Catholic Vindicator* (1870) appeared in English to counter new antagonisms. Both merged in 1878 into the *Catholic Citizen*, which in turn became the *Catholic Herald-Citizen* in 1935. The foregoing papers, particularly the *Catholic Citizen*, which was well informed and edited, may be credited with much of the unity and aggressiveness of the Catholic laity. Beginning in 1885 three successive attempts to publish a Polish paper failed, but the *Kuryer Polski* began its continuous appearance in 1888. To counter its nationalistic LAICISM, a clerical opposition press was started at various times. The *Katolik* (1895) and the *Dziennik Milwaucki* (1899) were short-lived, but the *Nowiny Polskie*, founded in 1907, lasted to 1950, by which time popular interest, as well as income, had waned.

Institutional Growth. Father Martin KUNDIG introduced the first parochial school at Milwaukee in 1842 with lay teachers, and four years later Henni secured the Sisters of Charity from Emmitsburg, Maryland, to do the teaching. Milwaukee's first public school opened in June 1846 in the basement of St. Peter's Cathedral by an arrangement with Henni, who agreed not to teach the catechism during school hours. By the 1850s the needed churches had been built and a supply of priests assured by the new seminary (1856). Nothing was closer to the heart of Henni than parish schools. The DOMINICAN SISTERS of Sinsinawa, founded by Reverend Samuel MAZZUCHELLI, O.P., in 1847, provided a partial fulfillment of Henni's plan to obtain teachers for English-speaking congregations. Mother Karolina GERHARDINGER of the SCHOOL SISTERS OF NOTRE DAME from Bavaria, who had settled in Pennsylvania in 1847, arrived at Milwaukee in 1850. By 1860 her sisters had charge of thirteen diocesan grade schools. They also operated Mount Mary College, established 1872, in Milwaukee.

The Sisters of St. Francis of Assisi arrived in 1849 and undertook their first teaching assignment in 1864 at Jefferson. Founded in 1937 by the Sisters of St. Francis of Assisi for the education of novices and sisters, St. Clare College was renamed Cardinal Stritch College in 1946. In that year, it admitted laywomen and became a women's college. In 1970 Cardinal Stritch College went coeducational, and in 1997 it attained university status.

The School Sisters of St. Francis came to Milwaukee from Baden in 1873, and after some migrating settled there in 1888. In 1963 they taught in forty-four archdiocesan grade schools. German Dominican sisters staffed numerous parish schools in the archdiocese and established a motherhouse at Racine in 1863, where they conducted coeducational Dominican College (1935). The college was closed in the 1970s.

The Sisters of St. Agnes, founded at Barton, Wisconsin, in 1858, to teach in rural district schools and take charge of grade schools, established Marian College for women (1963) in Fond du Lac, Wisconsin. St. Thomas College, opened by Mazzuchelli at Sinsinawa in 1847 and chartered in 1848, had a competent faculty and adequate equipment, but was closed in 1865 because of the death of its founder among other reasons.

Two high schools opened by the Jesuits in Milwaukee had been suppressed by 1872. In 1881 Marquette began as a college; its transformation into a university began in 1907, and its graduate school was organized in 1922. A branch of the Capuchins was organized in 1856 at Mt. Calvary, where St. Lawrence Seminary was started in 1860 and has since graduated many young men destined for the priesthood. Holy Cross Fathers from Notre Dame, Indiana, set up a college at Watertown in 1872, which ceased operation in 1911, when it became a training school for their brothers.

A normal school, started in 1870 to supply lay teachers and organists, was located in St. Francis and is associated with the work of John Singenberger (1848–1924), composer and organist. The Catholic Summer School of the West was organized at Madison in 1895. In 1906 Reverend Henry Hengell (1877–1937) was named chaplain of the Catholic students at the University of Wisconsin, becoming the first to so serve at any secular university in the United States.

The Sisters of Charity from Emmitsburg, Maryland, opened the first hospital on May 15, 1848, in Milwaukee; since 1858 this has become well-known as St. Mary's. In 1963 there were also St. Joseph's Hospital, conducted by Franciscan sisters, and four lesser general hospitals in Milwaukee, as well as ten others within the archdiocese. Special hospitals were conducted by the School Sisters of St. Francis: the Sacred Heart Sanitarium (1893), and its annex for mental cases, St. Mary's Hill (1912). St. Rose's orphanage for girls was started in 1848 and St. Aemilian's for boys in 1849 at the residence of the Sisters of Charity. In 1855 the boys were put under the charge of the Sisters of St. Francis. In 1908, when there were seventeen Polish parishes in the archdiocese, St. Joseph's orphanage opened at Wauwatosa to meet the need for a Polish orphanage. St. Vincent's Infant Asylum, opened in 1877 by the Sisters of Charity to care for foundlings, uncared-for babies, and unwed mothers, ceased operation October 1, 1958, because small children were placed in foster homes. The sisters at once adopted a project to aid girls with emotional problems in a group home. In 1877 the Good Shepherd Sisters came to care for delinquent girls, whereas boys went to an industrial school that was an annex to St. Aemilian's orphanage, probably the earliest predecessor of St. Charles Boys' Home, a protective institution. St. John's School for the Deaf opened in May 1876. A Conference of the Society of ST. VINCENT DE PAUL, formed at Milwaukee in 1849, then lapsed from 1874 to 1908, when it started anew. The LITTLE SISTERS OF THE POOR have been active in serving the destitute and aged since 1876.

Welfare work became more closely organized, beginning with the appointment of a superintendent in 1920. Since its establishment the welfare bureau has arranged the adoption of 3,000 children into Catholic homes. Its other services include family counseling, homemaker guidance, care for unmarried parents, resettlement help, care for children in foster homes, group homes, and child-care institutions. In 1917 Reverend Joseph Hurst established St. Bernard's Workingmen's Home, a refuge for migratory workers, and before it was closed in 1932 it had fed and lodged 200,000 men. The archdiocese also engaged some notable clerical economists in 1910; these included F. J. HAAS and A. J. MUENCH, who won international fame, and P. DIETZ, who influenced labor councils in the American Federation of Labor and ran a school for workers in Milwaukee, mainly to combat socialism. Dietz also led a campaign to legalize parish credit unions in Wisconsin.

Post–War and Post–Conciliar Years. In the years after World War II the archdiocese of Milwaukee had to handle the growth and mobility of the Catholic community. The number of Catholics swelled in proportion to the general population, and many Catholics moved to new suburban developments. Milwaukee-born Albert G. Meyer, installed as archbishop in 1953, addressed the expanding needs of a growing population, establishing new parishes and fostering the growth of the Catholic colleges and universities in the archdiocese. When Meyer succeeded Cardinal Stritch as archbishop of Chicago in 1958, he was succeeded by the Most Reverend William Cousins, the bishop of Peoria. Installed in January 1959 as the eighth archbishop of Milwaukee, Cousins continued Meyer's building program. He attended all the sessions of the Second Vatican Council and moved swiftly to implement its decrees and recommendations. Archbishop Cousins retired when he reached the age of seventy-five in 1977. (He died September 14, 1988.)

Cousins' successor was Rembert G. Weakland, former ABBOT of ST. VINCENT'S ARCHABBEY in Latrobe, Pennsylvania, and abbot primate of the Order of St. Benedict in ROME. Already well known throughout the country as a spokesman for monastic renewal, he transferred his ACTIVISM, tireless ZEAL, and broad vision of the Church in the modern world to Milwaukee when he was installed as archbishop in November 1977. He reorganized the archdiocesan curia, and closed the preparatory seminary built by his predecessor in 1963, turning it into diocesan offices and a retirement home for clergy. In his weekly column in the *Catholic Herald*, the diocesan newspaper, Archbishop Weakland addressed timely topics, sometimes taking controversial positions on social issues, foreign policy, and the role of women in the Church. Under his direction the archdiocese intensi-

fied its pastoral outreach to Hispanics, ministered to Hmong and Laotian refugees, and established the first urban parish for Native Americans.

Weakland met opposition on a number of fronts and for a number of reasons, but none stirred more furor than his plan to remodel the CATHEDRAL. The Cathedral of St. John the Evangelist, consecrated in 1853, had been the focus of controversy before, when in the nineteenth century the German *Zwiebelturm* (onion dome) of the original structure was removed, a gesture that was interpreted as an effort to placate Irish Catholics. In January 1935 a fire completely demolished the interior and the roof, weakened the walls, and destroyed the stained glass windows. The restoration of the cathedral, slowed because of the war, was finally completed just prior to the centennial of the archdiocese in 1943. In the 1960s Archbishop Cousins authorized a new design and reconstruction of the main altar to bring the sanctuary space into conformity with liturgical directives of Vatican II, and in 1977 he initiated a more extensive remodeling. Twenty years later Archbishop Weakland initiated the Cathedral Project, a comprehensive plan to preserve the historical legacy of the Cathedral of St. John the Evangelist and to make the environment and furnishing better serve the spirit of the LITURGY. In addition, the plan called for the property north of the Cathedral church to be developed as a center for social outreach to the poor and homeless. A vocal opposition denounced the Cathedral Project and even won a favorable hearing from the Congregation for DIVINE WORSHIP AND THE DISCIPLINE OF THE SACRAMENTS. Nonetheless, the project went forward and on February 9, 2002, bishops from throughout the state joined the priests of the archdiocese and representatives from each of the parishes in a liturgical celebration dedicating the renovated cathedral. Archbishop Weakland reached mandatory retirement age later in the year.

A New Era. Pope JOHN PAUL II named Timothy M. Dolan the tenth archbishop of the Archdiocese of Milwaukee on June 25, 2002. Archbishop Dolan, a native of St. Louis, came to Milwaukee after serving as an auxiliary bishop in his home diocese for one year. He was installed on August 28, 2002, at the Cathedral of St. John the Evangelist.

In 2004 Archbishop Dolan identified six pastoral priorities for the archdiocese: 1) to develop an interior conversion in the heart of each Catholic and to deepen each one's union with JESUS CHRIST; 2) to strengthen parishes; 3) to foster a sense of vocation; 4) to strengthen Catholic education and FAITH formation; 5) to emphasize the missions of JUSTICE and CHARITY; and 6) to focus on the Biblical VIRTUE of stewardship.

St. John the Evangelist Cathedral, Milwaukee WI. *Pictured is a large crucifix and crown of thorns suspended from the ceiling of the cathedral. Designated as a Milwaukee landmark in 1977, the cathedral is a well-recognized edifice in the city.* © FRANK VETERE / ALAMY

Pope BENEDICT XVI appointed William Patrick Callahan, O.F.M. Conv., auxiliary bishop of Milwaukee on October 30, 2007, marking the first time in its 164–year history that two auxiliary bishops had served the archdiocese. Bishop Callahan, the first Conventual Franciscan to be named a bishop in the United States, joined Auxiliary Bishop Richard J. Sklba, who had served as an auxiliary bishop in Milwaukee since 1979.

On February 23, 2009, Pope Benedict XVI appointed Archbishop Dolan the new archbishop of New York. He was formally installed into his new archdiocese on April 15, 2009.

There are close to 675,000 Catholics in the Archdiocese of Milwaukee, which has experienced considerable growth in suburban and rural areas since the 1980s. In 2007, the archdiocese had 211 parishes and 132 schools (110 elementary, 13 secondary); both numbers declined, as shifting demographics played a role in changes in ministering to the Catholic community (Milwaukee Catholic Press Apostolate 2007). The Hispanic and Hmong Catholic communities, however, experienced substantial growth. In 2007 the archdiocese announced a $105 million fundraising campaign—Faith In Our Future—to support Catholic education and faith formation initiatives.

SEE ALSO AFRICAN AMERICAN CATHOLICS IN THE UNITED STATES (HISTORY OF); AMERICAN FEDERATION OF CATHOLIC SOCIETIES; CHURCH AND STATE IN THE UNITED STATES (LEGAL HISTORY); DETROIT, ARCHDIOCESE OF; LA CROSSE, DIOCESE OF; MISSION AND MISSIONS; NATIVISM, AMERICAN; RERUM NOVARUM; SISTERS OF CHARITY, FEDERATION OF; VATICAN COUNCIL II.

BIBLIOGRAPHY

Archdiocese of Milwaukee Official Web site, available from: http://www.archmil.org (accessed October 17, 2008).

H. Russell Austin, *The Wisconsin Story: The Building of a Vanguard State*, 2nd ed. (Milwaukee, Wisc. 1957).

Steven Avella, *In the Richness of the Earth: A History of the Archdiocese of Milwaukee, 1843–1958* (Milwaukee, Wisc. 2002).

Benjamin Joseph Blied, *The Catholic Story of Wisconsin* (Milwaukee, Wisc. 1948).

Benjamin Joseph Blied, *Three Archbishops of Milwaukee: Michael Heiss (1818–1890), Frederick Katzer (1844–1903), Sebastian Messmer (1847–1930)* (Milwaukee, Wisc. 1955).

Peter Leo Johnson, *Crosier on the Frontier: A Life of John Martin Henni, Archbishop of Milwaukee* (Madison, Wisc. 1959).

Milwaukee Catholic Press Apostolate, *2007 Wisconsin Pastoral Handbook* (Milwaukee, Wisc. 2007).

Leo Rummel, *History of the Catholic Church in Wisconsin* (Madison, Wisc. 1976).

Alfred Steckel, "The Catholic Church in Wisconsin," *Records of the American Catholic Historical Society of Philadelphia* 7 (1896) 225–233; 8 (1897) 20–27.

Paul Wilkes, *The Education of an Archbishop: Travels with Rembert Weakland* (Maryknoll, N.Y. 1992).

Rt Rev. Peter Leo Johnson
Professor of History
St. Francis Seminary, Milwaukee, Wisc.
Editor, *Salesianum*

Kathleen Hohl
Formerly Communications Director
Archdiocese of Milwaukee (2009)

MIND-BODY PROBLEM

In the past fifty years the question of how the mind is related to the body has received even more intense scrutiny than previously. While MATERIALISM still has a prominent place in contemporary PHILOSOPHY, it is no longer the reigning ORTHODOXY—or if it is, dissenters are more visible than they were forty or fifty years ago.

Materialism and substance DUALISM (the idea that mind and body are two different things, two different substances) still have proponents, but both have been subjected to telling criticisms. As a consequence, the idea of a *via media*—a position that is neither materialist nor identifies the person with the mind—has received renewed attention.

As its proponents replied to criticisms, materialism became more complicated. Its basic tenet is the IDENTITY theory, namely, the view that every mental event is *identical with* a material event, such as a brain process. According to this view, one's thought that vertically opposite angles are equal is actually nothing but certain neurons firing in the brain. One problem with this view, however, is that an extraterrestrial intelligent creature might not have neurons but still have the thought about vertically opposite angles. So, it seems that the thought that vertically opposite angles are equal cannot be identical with a certain type of neuron firing.

To overcome this difficulty, materialists have distinguished between type–type identity theory (also called reductive materialism) and token–token identity theory (also called nonreductive materialism). A *type* is a kind; a *token* is an individual. Usually, there are several tokens (individuals) of the same type. So, for example, in the cheer, "Go, go!" there are two words if we count tokens, but only one if we count types. Likewise, the first word is identical with the second (the same *in type*), but *not* identical (considering tokens). So, according to type–type materialism the thought that vertically opposite angles are equal is identical with a certain type of material process, namely, neuron firing. But this will not work, since a creature that has no neurons might have the same thought (also, in the same human being the same neurons might not fire every time one has the thought that vertically opposite angles are equal). So, *token–token materialism* was proposed, and it is still the main competing form of materialism. According to this view, although the thought that vertically opposite angles are equal is not necessarily identical with a certain type of material process, in each case that thought is identical with some material process or other—the thought–token is identical with a material-process token.

A popular form of token–token materialism is *functionalist materialism*. The functionalist observes that many things are classified by the function they perform rather than by the materials they are made of. For example, a cup might be made of porcelain, paper, or Styrofoam, but it is still a cup. The materialist who is a functionalist, then, says that a mental state is characterized by its function within the life of an organism and is identical with some physical process or other, although not always of the same type.

However, contemporary materialism faces serious objections. Functionalist materialism fails to explain abstract thought and free CHOICE. Indeed, functionalism fails even to explain CONSCIOUSNESS itself. For example, the content of consciousness contains colors and not just shades of gray—but the functionalist explanation is oblivious to, say, the differences between gray, red, and blue. Consciousness obviously has a content apart from its functionality (its typical causes and effects), but functionalism, by definition, fails to explain that.

There also are powerful arguments to show that conceptual thought and free choice are nonmaterial actions. The abstractness of conceptual thought and the self-determining character of free choice cannot be accounted for by material structures or laws governing actions of material causes. From this, one can infer that the formal source of this action must also be nonmaterial—that is, there must be an immaterial aspect of the human self.

On the other hand, powerful arguments have also been advanced against substance dualism—the idea that the body is an entity possessed, or inhabited, by the SELF, which is then identified with the mind. The logical difficulties posed by dualistic interactionism have been pressed, and, more important, the dependence of conceptual thought (and volition) on the brain has been even more clearly shown than previously. It has become even clearer than before that thought is not just triggered by sensory and brain processes, but is formally caused (specified) by them. Thus, St. THOMAS AQUINAS's argument that the formal source of conceptual thought and volition, the human soul, is naturally incomplete and that the soul by its nature is a part of the whole human being, and not the human being himself or herself, has been greatly strengthened.

So, the way is opened for a third position between materialism on the one hand and substance-dualism on the other. This is consistent with Catholic teaching, namely, that the human being is body and soul, not just material but also not just a soul. On the one hand, a human being is essentially a physical organism, an animal, but on the other hand, the human being has a spiritual, immortal soul. Both materialism and substance dualism are excluded. Human beings are strange creatures, animals with immortal souls, and FAITH tells us that after death their souls await the resurrection of the body, when the whole human being will again be alive.

The past thirty or forty years have also shown that profoundly important ethical issues are linked to the question of how the mind and the body are related. For example, in the controversy concerning ABORTION, a key issue is the status of the developing human embryo or fetus that is deliberately destroyed by induced abortion. Sometimes it is claimed that a human organism begins to exist at one time but the human person begins to exist only at a later time. This makes no sense if the human person is a particular type of organism. Because a human person is a body-soul composite, a particular type of organism, whenever the human organism begins to exist is the time that the human person begins to exist. And a similar point applies at the end of life: One cannot reasonably claim that the human person has died or passed on even though his or her human organism continues to live, as, for example, in the case of human beings who are persistently unconscious or severely demented.

Further, the fact that human beings have a nonmaterial aspect not produced simply by the interaction of lower material forces is equally important for controversial contemporary moral issues. If human beings were only different in degree and not in kind from other animals, plants, molecules, and so forth, then it would be hard to see any justification for holding that they are the kind of beings to whom we have any serious moral obligation to treat with full moral respect (e.g., to treat as ends and never as mere means). God created man from the dust of the earth, but God also created man in his image and likeness.

SEE ALSO BODY, THEOLOGY OF; IDENTITY, PRINCIPLE OF; PERSON (IN PHILOSOPHY); RESURRECTION OF THE DEAD; SOUL-BODY RELATIONSHIP; SOUL, HUMAN, ORIGIN OF.

BIBLIOGRAPHY

Edward Feser, *The Philosophy of Mind: A Short Introduction* (Oxford, U.K. 2005).

Germain Grisez, *Beyond the New Theism: A Philosophy of Religion* (Notre Dame, Ind. 1975).

William Hasker, *The Emergent Self* (Ithaca, N.Y. 1999).

Patrick Lee and Robert P. George, *Body-Self Dualism in Contemporary Ethics and Politics* (New York 2008).

E. Jonathan Lowe, *An Introduction to the Philosophy of Mind* (New York 2000).

James B. Reichmann, *Evolution, Animal "Rights," and the Environment* (Washington, D.C. 2000).

John R. Searle, *Mind: A Brief Introduction* (New York 2004).

J. J. C. Smart and J. J. Haldane, *Atheism and Theism* (Oxford, U.K. 1996).

William A. Wallace, *The Modeling of Nature: Philosophy of Science and Philosophy of Nature in Synthesis* (Washington, D.C. 1996).

Patrick Lee
Director, Institute of Bioethics
McAleer Professor of Bioethics
Franciscan University of Steubenville (2009)

MINNESOTA, CATHOLIC CHURCH IN

In 2007 the Catholic Church in Minnesota numbered 1,061,696 communicants, about 21 percent of the state population of 5,112,530 (*The Official Catholic Directory* 2008, p. 2087). The history of the Catholic Church in Minnesota falls into three rather distinct chapters. The first chapter encompasses the age of exploration of the upper Midwest during the 1700s, when missionaries accompanied fur traders and explorers along the upper Mississippi River and western Lake Superior. The second chapter focuses on the first years of the Diocese of St. Paul from 1850 to 1877, when the diocese was elevated to archiepiscopal status. The third chapter relates the growth of Catholicism in the state since that time with suffragan sees necessitated by Catholic population growth. St. Cloud, Duluth, and Winona became suffragan sees in 1887, Crookston in 1909, and New Ulm in 1957.

Early History. Daniel Greysolon Duluth, sieur (1636–1710), and Father Louis HENNEPIN arrived in the region in the 1680s. During the early eighteenth century, European explorations, especially from France and England, were launched into the Minnesota region to dominate the lucrative fur industry. Catholic missionaries, French Recollect Fathers, and Jesuit priests, desirous of converting indigenous Ojibway and Sioux and of ministering to scattered settlers around crude forts, accompanied these sorties. They erected chapels near these forts and fur trade entrepots. The early eighteenth century brought Fathers Charles-Michel Mesaiger (d. 1766) and Jean-Pierre Aulneau (1705–1736) to the northern regions of the territory and the JESUITS to an area around Lake Pepin in the south. Chapels were erected at Pembina, Fort St. Charles, Grand Portage, and Fort Beauharnois on Lake Pepin.

In 1818 the U.S. government erected Fort Snelling at the confluence of the Mississippi and Minnesota Rivers, and by 1845 French Canadian and Swiss settlers from the colony of Lord Selkirk (1771–1820) near Pembina in the far north clustered in the area around Fort Snelling, known as the Fort Snelling Reserve. In 1840 a log chapel (St. Peter's) was built in Mendota near the fort, and in 1841 Father Lucien Galtier (1811–c. 1860), a missionary from the Diocese of Dubuque, erected a log CHAPEL on the cliffs above the river port known as "Pig's Eye Landing." Galtier dedicated this chapel to St. Paul, and ultimately the surrounding village took on that name. This crude chapel was the first CATHEDRAL of the Diocese of St. Paul. A large stone marker on the bluff above the river memorializes St. Paul's first cathedral. At this time of missionary activity in the region, Minnesota really belonged to the Diocese of Dubuque and just a small portion in the southeast triangle to the Diocese of Milwaukee.

St. Paul Diocese. A papal decree issued July 19, 1850, created the Diocese of St. Paul and appointed Joseph CRÉTIN (1799–1857), vicar general of Dubuque at the time, as first BISHOP. The DIOCESE extended from Lake Superior to the Missouri River and from Iowa to the Canadian border. Initially, parts of North and South Dakota were included in the St. Paul diocese.

Crétin. Joseph Crétin was from Belley, France, and had come with missionary zeal to the Midwest frontier at the behest of Bishop Jean Mathias Pierre LORAS of Dubuque. Severe challenges faced the new bishop as he came to this outpost facing the Minnesota wilderness. Diocesan church buildings consisted of log structures in St. Paul, Mendota, St. Anthony, and Pembina. His diocesan priests were few: Augustin RAVOUX in Mendota, George Anthony BELCOURT and Albert LACOMBE at Pembina. The Catholic population was scattered. The total population of the entire region was 30,000 Native Americans and 6,000 whites. Of necessity, Crétin was an itinerant bishop. His motto, "All things to all men," exemplified a leadership style of personal sacrifice and SELF-DENIAL that attracted young men to serve in this untamed territory. In 1853, he sent two St. Paul recruits, John IRELAND and Thomas O'GORMAN, to the preparatory seminary of Meximieux and recruited seven seminarians from that region in France to come to St. Paul. A combined church, residence, and school on Wabasha and Sixth Streets became the new cathedral, episcopal see, and seminary for the diocese.

In 1851 Crétin brought the Sisters of ST. JOSEPH of Carondelet from St. Louis to staff a school for girls. St. Joseph's Academy, the first Catholic school in the diocese, was at first located in the old log chapel on the bluff, but later a new building for the academy was erected at Virginia and Nelson (later Marshall) Streets. This building also served as motherhouse and novitiate for these sisters. A Catholic hospital was also erected, and the Sisters of St. Joseph took charge of that institution when a cholera epidemic broke out in the city from 1855 to 1856. These sisters were also administrators of St. Mary's Hospital in Minneapolis for more than one hundred years. They also undertook missionary work among the Winnebago Native Americans in Long Prairie, a project dear to the heart of Bishop Crétin. Financial problems caused the demise of this mission in 1856.

At Crétin's encouragement, numbers of French, Irish, and German immigrants came to the region and took up lands along the Mississippi, Minnesota, and St. Croix Rivers. Prosperous settlements developed throughout the diocese, and the Catholic population increased. In 1853 because the German Catholic population in St. Paul had grown so rapidly, a German parish, the Assumption, was established. German-speaking priests were sought to administer the parish, and in 1856 three BENEDICTINES came from Latrobe, Pennsylvania, to staff the Assumption parish and to help with the growing German population of Stearns County. They settled in St. Cloud, opened St. John's Seminary, and in 1856 moved permanently to Collegeville. This ABBEY became renowned for its leadership in liturgical reform and ecumenical endeavors throughout the development of the Catholic Church in America. Other dedicated religious men and women established regional headquarters in the diocese to assist in the charitable works so needed among the immigrant throngs.

Church Difficulties. Although Catholic immigrants to Minnesota signified tremendous growth in numbers for the Catholic Church in America, cultural differences among these newcomers posed serious problems for Church leaders. Irish prelates dominated the American hierarchy, and other ethnic groups voiced the desire to have bishops over them who were of their cultural background. While the Irish Immigration Society encouraged Irish from the old sod and from congested eastern states to settle in Minnesota, groups of Germans also came from various principalities in Germany. The German language held these disparate groups in cultural unity. For the Germans the retention of their German language remained at the heart of their cultural identity well into the twentieth century. St. Paul's Germans

wanted their language used in WORSHIP, Catechetical instruction, other Church rites, and parochial education. They organized the St. Joseph Aid Society and purchased land in St. Paul for a cemetery for German Catholics. Bishop Thomas L. Grace (1814–1897), successor to Crétin, intervened, and this property became the site of St. Joseph's Orphanage, staffed by Benedictine Sisters. Polish and Italian groups in St. Paul also demanded clergy of their specific nationalities, but Grace opposed this tendency. He wanted all Catholics to be accepted as loyal Americans by the dominant Protestant groups in society. At that time anti–Catholic activities of the Know-Nothing Party still hung heavy over the land, and Grace wanted no action of Catholics in his diocese to fan the fire of hatred generated by this group. *The Northwestern Chronicle* became the official organ of the diocese. In short order the Germans launched *Der Wanderer*, the French began *Le Canadien*, and the Irish began publishing the *Northwest Standard*. Other ethnic papers appeared as newer immigrants found their way into Minnesota. Ethnic parishes with their special church construction and cultural thrust proliferated in both rural and urban Minnesota up to the turn of the century.

Bishop Grace welcomed other groups of religious into the diocese to help with the needs of the growing Catholic community: Sisters of St. Dominic of Sinsinawa in 1865, Sisters of the Good Shepherd in 1868, Christian Brothers in 1871, Sisters of the Visitation in 1873. By 1919 other religious groups were serving in the diocese as well. Among these were SCHOOL SISTERS OF NOTRE DAME, Sisters of CHRISTIAN CHARITY, FRANCISCAN SISTERS from Milwaukee and Toledo, POOR HANDMAIDS OF JESUS CHRIST, and Felician Sisters. The various sisterhoods, providing education for young women beyond the elementary level, truly paved the way for changing feminine thought toward more active roles in society for women.

From the very beginning of the diocese, lay leadership collaborated with the clergy and religious in addressing the needs of the growing Church, especially the needs of the poor. Benevolent societies were founded to provide aid to families in time of exigencies. Economic, political, and social bigotry in the young United States excluded Catholics as recipients of public charities.

Pope PIUS IX's *Syllabus of Errors,* condemning various kinds of religious LIBERALISM, brought a barrage of criticism in the United States against everything Catholic. The Second Council of Baltimore in 1866 affirmed the pope's decree, and Grace, like the other American bishops, pledged to implement the *Syllabus* in the St. Paul diocese. Deaneries were organized to do this. Too ill to attend the First Vatican Council (1869–1870), Grace sent Father John Ireland to represent him. Though unfinished, the council declared the INFAL-

LIBILITY of the POPE in matters of FAITH AND MOR-
ALS, causing more negative reaction against the Catholic
Church among American Protestants. In America this
led to stricter laws demanding separation of CHURCH
AND STATE, particularly when Catholic leaders strove
for financial aid for their struggling parochial schools.
The plea of Catholic parents that they were being doubly
taxed for educating their children according to CON-
SCIENCE was not accepted in American courts. This issue became acute in Minnesota during the 1890s, when
Archbishop Ireland experimented with creative (though
ultimately unsuccessful) plans for obtaining public support for parochial schools.

Despite this controversy, Bishop Grace continued to
champion Catholic education. His endeavors resulted in
the beginnings of Crétin High School in St. Paul and an
attempt to start a Catholic Industrial School on the
property that became the site for the University of St.
Thomas. The industrial school later moved to Swift
County but closed in 1879.

Diocesean Changes. The Catholic population in the
diocese continued to grow, and in 1875 the Vicariate of
Northern Minnesota was established with the Right
Reverend Rupert Seidenbusch (1830–1895), O.S.B.,
consecrated as vicar apostolic of the new territory with a
residence in St. Cloud. That same year John Ireland
became coadjutor to Bishop Grace with the right of
succession. In 1879 the Vicariate of North Dakota was
created with Right Reverend Martin MARTY, O.S.B., its
first bishop. Thus the Diocese of St. Paul became focused
on the southern half of Minnesota. In 1884 Grace
resigned as bishop of the St. Paul diocese in favor of his
coadjutor, John Ireland. The diocese was raised to
archiepiscopal status in 1888 with Ireland the first
ARCHBISHOP. In 1889 five suffragan sees were erected:
Sioux Falls in South Dakota; Fargo in North Dakota;
and Duluth, Winona, and ST. CLOUD in Minnesota.
Although the ARCHDIOCESE at the time comprised both
rural and urban areas, by far the greater population was
concentrated within the Twin Cities of St. Paul and
Minneapolis, with all the attending problems that urban
concentrations imposed on an immigrant Church. Six
priests of the province were at the same time consecrated
as bishops by Ireland in the St. Paul Seminary chapel to
fill these new sees as well as to provide an auxiliary for
Ireland. This auxiliary, John J. Lawler (1862–1948,
bishop 1910), became bishop of Lead, South Dakota, in
1916.

Perhaps more than any other prelate in Minnesota's
history, John Ireland put the Minnesota Catholic Church
in the limelight. Ireland's championship of the Americanization Movement brought him into conflict with
Catholic ethnic leaders in Minnesota, the nation, and
ROME. Ireland demanded that immigrants shed the ways

of the old world in becoming American. This required
them all to adopt English and relinquish foreign
languages in educational instruction, business enterprises,
and liturgical services. Many ethnic groups, particularly
Germans, wanted to retain their old customs and
cultures, especially the use of their native languages.
Ireland feared that the use of foreign tongues would
bring grave criticism on the Catholic Church in America.
St. Paul Germans, affiliated with the St. Raphael Verein
founded by Peter Paul CAHENSLY in 1883 to provide
for the spiritual welfare of foreign language groups,
believed that priests in their national parishes should
teach the truths of the faith in the language of each
particular ethnic group. Ireland and his supporters from
The CATHOLIC UNIVERSITY OF AMERICA insisted that
all newcomers adopt English as their national language.
The St. Raphael's Verein had international support.
Rome refused to take sides in this issue, but the
controversy resulted in a rift between Ireland and ethnic
groups in his archdiocese. Irish clergy blamed German
hierarchy in Cincinnati, Milwaukee, and St. Louis for
attempting to control Catholic affairs in America. The
Americanization Movement also called for new methods
of approaching non-Catholics. Catholic DOCTRINE had
to be adapted to modern times. Ireland's enemies accused him of the HERESY of MODERNISM and contributed to his failure to be named a CARDINAL.

The episcopacies in Minnesota following the death
of Archbishop Ireland in 1918 faced the hardships
imposed on their flocks by two world wars and the Great
Depression in between. Archdiocesan social programs
expanded during these decades. The voice of the local
Church was ever present in addressing rural and urban
problems facing the poor. The work of Minnesota's own
Monsignor John A. RYAN had its impact on local needs
of the working poor as well as on the national social
legislation that marked the 1930s. World Wars I and II
tried the PATRIOTISM of all Americans, and Minnesotan
Catholics responded nobly. Chaplains, nurses, and
soldiers in all branches of the service included many
from the ranks of Minnesota Catholics. The outstanding
Minnesota Catholic event between the wars was the
celebration of the Ninth Eucharistic Congress in the
summer of 1941 in the Twin Cities. As a result of this
demonstration of the Catholic faith, daily exposition of
the Blessed Sacrament was initiated in several diocesan
churches and chapels of religious. This has continued or
been renewed in many parishes throughout the state, in
the form of perpetual adoration or chapels of
convenience.

Later Twentieth-Century Developments. From 1950
to the turn of the century, the Church in Minnesota
faced many of the moral and social issues that challenged other dioceses throughout the country, though in

Catholic Education. *An unidentified girl inspects materials about renewable energy at an Oct. 29, 2006, forum at Pax Christi Catholic Church in Eden Prairie, Minn.* AP IMAGES

somewhat less dramatic form. The population of the state grew to more than 5,000,000, while the Catholic population remained close to 25 percent of the total. About two out of every three Catholics lived in the Twin Cities of Saint Paul and Minneapolis. Faced with a declining number of priests and changes in population, each of the dioceses changed parish structures to accommodate. The rural Diocese of New Ulm in particular became a national leader in the assignment of religious and lay persons to the roles of parish life coordinator.

In the closing decades of the twentieth century, new minority populations joined the Catholics of Minnesota. The Latino population grew in the Twin Cities and in the Crookston diocese in the northwestern part of the state. At the same time, the Twin Cities also became home to a significant Hmong population, a number of whom were Catholic.

Catholic education in the state experienced both successes and setbacks. The state was long noted for one of the best public school systems in the country, but it also had a vibrant system of parochial schools. Several U.S. Supreme Court decisions in the early 1970s, however, undermined a generous system of public support for parochial schools. Both elementary and secondary enrollments declined as a result but rebounded, at least on the secondary level, early in the twenty-first

century. During the same period, Catholic higher education flourished. The University of St. Thomas grew dramatically to become the largest private institution of higher education in the state, while the College of St. Catherine became the largest Catholic women's college in the country. Two Benedictine foundations, St. John's University and the College of St. Benedict, preserved their single-sex status but entered into an unusual and successful collaboration on curriculum and faculty. Both the College of St. Scholastica and St. Mary's University successfully became co-educational.

The Second Vatican Council brought a great many changes to the Catholic Church in the United States and in Minnesota. Although Minnesota was generally spared the more divisive responses to the council, it did experience a decline in vocations to the priesthood and religious life as well as a number of defections from active MINISTRY, including the widely publicized defection of an auxiliary bishop of the archdiocese. At the same time, many more positive results occurred. St. John's University and Abbey had long been an active center of liturgical renewal, and its influences were felt throughout the state. Minnesota also played a leading role in changes in religious education, especially at the elementary and secondary levels. Furthermore, although the number of priests diminished somewhat in the 1970s and 1980s, several Minnesota dioceses enthusiastically supported the permanent diaconate and integrated scores of new deacons into the diocesan clergy.

Twenty-First-Century Developments. During the first decade of the new millennium, all but one of the dioceses of Minnesota (St. Cloud) experienced a change in episcopal leadership. In 2001 Bishop John C. Nienstedt, an auxiliary bishop of the Archdiocese of DETROIT, was named to succeed Bishop Raymond Lucker as ordinary of the Diocese of NEW ULM. Six years later he was named coadjutor archbishop of St. Paul-Minneapolis and succeeded to that see in May 2008. In 2008 John M. LeVoir, a priest of the Archdiocese of ST. PAUL AND MINNEAPOLIS became bishop of New Ulm.

After thirty-one years as ordinary of the Diocese of Crookston, Bishop Victor Balke was succeeded in 2007 by Bishop Michael J. Hoeppner, formerly vicar general of the Diocese of WINONA. In Winona Bishop Bernard Harrington was succeeded in 2008 by Bishop John M. Quinn, formerly an auxiliary bishop of the Archdiocese of Detroit. Also in 2008, Duluth Bishop Dennis M. Schnurr was named coadjutor archbishop of Cincinnati.

In other areas, although common Catholic traditions and shared interests are characteristic of the Church in Minnesota, the third phase of its history is best recounted in connection with the individual dioceses.

SEE ALSO AMERICANISM; BALTIMORE, COUNCILS OF; DUBUQUE, ARCHDIOCESE OF; EUCHARIST, EXPOSITION OF THE; EUCHARISTIC CONGRESSES; FARGO, DIOCESE OF; KNOW-NOTHINGISM; MILWAUKEE, ARCHDIOCESE OF; MISSION AND MISSIONS; SIOUX FALLS, DIOCESE OF; ST. RAPHAEL'S SOCIETY; SYLLABUS OF ERRORS; VATICAN COUNCIL I; VATICAN COUNCIL II.

BIBLIOGRAPHY

Patrick Henry Ahern, ed., *Catholic Heritage in Minnesota, North Dakota, South Dakota* (St. Paul, Minn. 1964).

Archives of the Archdiocese of St. Paul and Minneapolis (St. Paul, Minn.).

Marvin Richard O'Connell, *John Ireland and the American Catholic Church* (St. Paul, Minn. 1988).

The Official Catholic Directory, 2008 (New Providence, N.J. 2008).

Annabelle Raiche and Ann Marie Biermaier, *They Came to Teach: The Story of Sisters Who Taught in Parochial Schools and Their Contributions to Elementary Education in Minnesota* (St. Cloud, Minn. 1994).

James Michael Reardon, *The Catholic Church in the Diocese of St. Paul: From Earliest Origin to Centennial Achievement* (St. Paul, Minn. 1952).

John Christine Wolkersterfer, *You Shall Be My People: A History of the Archdiocese of Saint Paul and Minneapolis* (Strasbourg, France 1999).

Sister John Christine Wolkersterfer CSJ
Professor Emerita of History
The College of St. Catherine, St. Paul, Minn.

Robert G. Kennedy
Professor of Catholic Studies
University of St. Thomas, St. Paul, Minn.

MISSISSIPPI, CATHOLIC CHURCH IN

A state in the southern United States, Mississippi is bounded on the north by Tennessee, on the east by Alabama, on the south by a portion of Louisiana and an arm of the Gulf of Mexico, and on the west by the Pearl River and the Mississippi River, which separates the state from Arkansas and Louisiana. The two Catholic dioceses in the state, Natchez-Jackson (1837, renamed Diocese of JACKSON in 1977) and Biloxi (1977) are suffragan sees of the Archdiocese of Mobile. In April 2008, Bishop Thomas J. Rodi (b. 1948) was named the second ARCHBISHOP of Mobile.

History. In 1540 Hernando de Soto (d. 1542) and his Spanish expedition passed through this region. Several priests accompanied him, but because in a previous attack by Native Americans, they had lost their Mass wine and some utensils, Mass probably was not offered here at that time. The earliest French explorers of the Mississippi River were Louis Jolliet (1645–1700) and Rev. Jacques MARQUETTE in 1673 and René-Robert Cavelier, sieur de la Salle (1643–1687) in 1682. Accompanying the La Salle expedition was Reverend Zenobius Membre (1645–1687), who on Easter Sunday, March 29, near the present site of Fort Adams, celebrated the first Mass on Mississippi soil of which there is a definite record. In 1699 missionaries from the Seminary of Quebec, Canada, descended the Mississippi River to work among the Indians and took up their stations near present-day Natchez. In the same year the French established a temporary settlement in what later became Ocean Springs. In 1717 they founded Natchez and in 1720, Biloxi; other settlements were established soon after. During the latter half of the eighteenth century, Great Britain and Spain in turn dominated this area. When in 1798 Spain withdrew in favor of the United States, the Spanish-trained Irish clergy who had served in the area also withdrew. The Mississippi Territory (including the future Alabama) was then organized. Its government was modeled on the Northwest Ordinance with one major exception, the toleration of slavery. In 1817 Mississippi was admitted to the Union as the twentieth state.

Antebellum Period. Post–territorial Catholic Mississippi was successively part of the Diocese of Baltimore, the proposed (1822) but not implemented vicariate of Alabama and Mississippi, the Diocese of Louisiana, and in 1826 the Diocese of New Orleans. On July 28, 1837, GREGORY XVI established the Diocese of Natchez (later redesignated Jackson) to embrace the whole state of Mississippi. Although the DIOCESE was established on July 28, 1837, almost four years passed before Bishop John Chanche (1795–1852), the first ordinary, was consecrated on March 14, 1841. When he arrived in Mississippi on May 19, he found two sizable Catholic communities at Natchez and Vicksburg, a large number of families and small communities along the Gulf Coast, and an unknown number of families and individuals scattered throughout the state. The state had no Catholic churches or institutions and only two priests.

Mississippi economy, politics, and culture were molded during the 1830s when former Native American lands were opened to settlement. An influx of immigrants quickly followed, and the growing presence of Baptist and Methodist congregations gave the state its predominately Protestant religious profile. Cotton-based agriculture, mainly worked first by black slaves and later by sharecroppers, created a distinctive political, social, and economic society that endured until World War II. Strong regional differences appeared between the planter societies of the river counties and the small farms of the north and the Piney Woods. Simultaneously the race question shaped the future of the state.

Mississippi Catholicism grew both in numbers and organization under the antebellum leadership of Bishops John Chanche (1841–1852), James Oliver Van de Velde, S.J. (1853–1855), and William Henry Elder (1857–1880). By 1861 the diocese numbered about 10,000 Catholics served by a bishop and 18 diocesan priests; 13 parishes with resident priests and 28 mission stations; 15 churches with several more under construction; five parochial schools, two day schools, three boarding schools, and two orphanages staffed by five religious communities and several lay teachers; numerous parish devotional, altar, and charitable societies; and regular parish missions and clerical conferences. Bishop Chanche laid the foundation for an imposing CATHEDRAL that he viewed as "the needed stimulus to the whole mission."

Civil War and Reconstruction. Mississippi was a major battleground during the Civil War. Natchez, Vicksburg, Jackson, Meridian, Okolona, and Corinth were among the Catholic communities that were battle sites or suffered property damage. Catholic church facilities at Jackson were destroyed three times by federal troops. Bishop William Henry Elder was briefly sent into exile in Louisiana in July 1864, when he refused to allow the local federal military commander to dictate specific prayers for Northern civil authorities at Mass.

The war left the state devastated politically, economically, and socially; brought ruin to numerous families whose fathers and sons were killed or disabled; and depleted the already meager resources of Mississippi Catholicism. Mississippi was readmitted to the Union in 1870, but remained under a reconstruction government until 1875. The state was hampered by an undiversified agriculture, the lack of industry, poor education, and a primitive financial system based on merchants. The greatest post–war challenge was the peaceful, productive incorporation of newly freed blacks into Mississippi life. This challenge was met, after a brief reconstruction period, by a political-economic-social structure of sharecropping, segregation, and disenfranchisement that closely mirrored antebellum, slave society.

Bishop Elder worked among the camps for freed blacks outside Natchez during the final years of the war and struggled to find the resources to address the challenge of evangelizing them. By 1884 Mississippi numbered 1,500 African-American Catholics. Bishop Francis Janssens (1881–1887) adopted an approach common in missionary lands—small chapel-schools overseen by priests but staffed by trained African-American catechists. In 1890 Holy Family Parish, the first state parish for African Americans, was established at Natchez. Between 1906 and 1914 seven additional parishes for African Americans were founded at Vicksburg, Pascagoula, Jackson, Meridian, Pass Christian, Greenville, and Biloxi; all were staffed by JOSEPHITES or Divine Word Fathers.

Early Twentieth Century. Despite the upheavals of reconstruction and its aftermath, Mississippi Catholicism took on a new vigor in the late nineteenth and early twentieth centuries under the leadership of Bishops Francis Janssens, Thomas Heslin (1889–1911), and John Gunn, S.M. (1911–1924). More than 250 Catholic communities, many short-lived, existed in the state between 1865 and 1910. The Society for the PROPAGATION OF THE FAITH, the AMERICAN BOARD OF CATHOLIC MISSIONS, the Indian and Colored Missions Fund, and the Catholic Church Extension Society provided a significant part of the financial resources for these communities. The diocese of Jackson continued to receive funding from these sources even into the twenty-first century.

After statehood (1817), a series of broken treaties and government policies of displacement to Native American territory left Mississippi with only 2,300 Native Americans by 1900. Through the initiative of Bishop Francis Janssens, a small, active Catholic Choctaw community, centered in the Philadelphia area, developed in the late nineteenth century and remains a vital part of Mississippi Catholicism. By 1917 more than 28,000 Catholics were scattered across the state in 41 parishes,

Father James Marquette. *Pictured here is the grave of the Jesuit missionary who explored the Mississippi.* WALLACE KIRKLAND/TIME LIFE PICTURES/GETTY IMAGES

69 missions, and 54 stations; 11 percent were African Americans. Forty-two schools and two orphanages had a combined enrollment of 4,736; 29 percent of the students were African Americans; 8 percent, Choctaws.

When Bishop John Gunn arrived in 1911, he set as one of his primary goals to establish chapels throughout the state. With generous aid from the Catholic Church Extension Society, more than twenty-five new churches and chapels were built between 1912 and 1924 alone. With Bishop Gunn's encouragement, the Society of the DIVINE WORD established a seminary to train African-American priests, first at Greenville in 1920 and then at Bay St. Louis in 1921. The first four graduates were ordained in 1934, and several later graduates were among the pioneer twentieth-century African-American bishops, including Harold Perry (1916–1991; New Orleans), Terry J. Steib (b. 1940; St. Louis/Memphis), and Dominic Carmon (b. 1930; New Orleans).

The Gerow Era. Bishop Gunn's successor, Richard O. Gerow (1885–1976), shepherded the Church in Mississippi for more than forty years (1924–1966), during which time the state, like the rest of the country, suffered through the depression of the 1930s, World War II and its aftermath, and later the civil rights movement. When the newly consecrated Bishop Gerow arrived, Catholicism was the third largest religious denomination

in Mississippi, after the Baptists and Methodists. The state had 31,387 Catholics served by 60 priests, but only 42 of the 149 churches and chapels had a resident pastor; 5,829 children were being educated in 41 Catholic schools.

The Church struggled during the 1930s when parishes and other Catholic institutions suffered the harsh effects of the depression. The post–World War II years, however, witnessed the waning of Mississippian insularity and isolation as the state became more industrialized and assimilated into the mainstream of the American economy. They also heralded a period of major administrative change in the Catholic Church in Mississippi. In 1952 Bishop Gerow divided the diocese into nine deaneries, and the following year he moved the bishop's residence and chancery from historic Natchez to Jackson. In 1953 he launched a diocesan newspaper, the *Mississippi Register* (later *Mississippi Today* and then *Mississippi Catholic*) to replace the Natchez edition of *Catholic Action of the South,* a cooperative venture of the Louisiana and Mississippi dioceses. On December 18, 1956, the name of the diocese was changed to Natchez-Jackson.

The most striking changes in Mississippi society took place in the area of race relations. Bishop Gerow had worked quietly and within the existing legal and social structure to expand opportunities among the regional African-American population. He concentrated on establishing parishes and strong schools staffed by sisters in urban areas and acted forcefully against all blatant acts of discrimination in diocesan churches.

The issue of desegregating Catholic schools came to public attention following the 1954 Supreme Court decision, *Brown v. Board of Education.* The violence with which some Mississippians opposed integration, evidenced in the 1963 murder of Medgar Evers (1925–1963), prodded the mild-tempered Bishop Gerow to take a more public and forceful stance. On June 14, he issued a statement that proclaimed a mutual responsibility for Evers's murder and the growing violence and pleaded for a common ground "based on human dignity and the concept of justice under God's law." On August 4, 1964, Gerow, at the urging of auxiliary bishop Joseph Brunini (1909–1996) and Father Bernard LAW (the future CARDINAL archbishop of Boston), ordered the integration of the first grade in all Catholic schools of the diocese. The following year he ordered the integration of all grades.

The Brunini Years. Bishop Gerow was succeed by his auxiliary, Joseph B. Brunini. A native of Vicksburg, Brunini had studied and was ordained to the priesthood in ROME, received a doctorate in canon law from The CATHOLIC UNIVERSITY OF AMERICA in Washington, D.C., and served as a pastor before being ordained as auxiliary bishop in 1957. Bishop Brunini attended the Second Vatican Council (1962–1965). It fell to him to guide Mississippi Catholics through the implementation of integration.

In 1967 Bishop Brunini committed the diocese to full integration of Catholic schools. He established an open, participative style of leadership, fostered lay participation and MINISTRY, expanded the Church's social ministry, led statewide efforts to break down racial barriers, and worked to establish closer bonds with other churches. In his 1969 Christmas HOMILY, Bishop Brunini called for Mississippi religious leaders to speak with a united voice to bring about racial justice and peace. Soon afterwards, the Mississippi Religious Leadership Conference was established with Brunini as the first chairman. The conference became a major voice in the state, urging political leaders to foster education and end segregation and racism throughout the state. Brunini's support encouraged Sister Thea BOWMAN, a Missionary Sister Servant of the Holy Ghost, who served in the diocese from 1961 until her death from cancer in 1990. She became a national voice for change and reconciliation, proclaiming her message in word and song.

During Brunini's tenure, Catholic services to the needy, poor, and elderly rapidly expanded. He actively recruited Irish clergy, formed the Catholic Foundation

in 1973, established new personnel and finance policies, encouraged the establishment of parish councils, and fostered adult education programs. Under Brunini's leadership, the diocese agreed to staff Our Lady of Perpetual Help Parish in Saltillo, Mexico. Although begun as a provincial venture, Brunini and the Catholic people of Mississippi soon adopted, funded, and supplied clergy for the mission.

Diocesan Changes. On March 1, 1977, Pope PAUL VI established a second diocese in Mississippi. The seventeen southern counties were organized into the Diocese of BILOXI. Bishop Joseph L. Howze (b. 1923) was named the first bishop. Later that year, on June 6, 1977, the name of the other diocese was redesignated as the Diocese of Jackson. In 1980 the two Mississippi dioceses became part of the new ecclesiastical Province of Mobile. In 2000 the Biloxi diocesan administration moved to a new Catholic chancery building. On July 2, 2001, Monsignor Thomas J. Rodi, a native New Orleanian and former VICAR GENERAL of the Archdiocese of NEW ORLEANS, was ordained as Biloxi's second bishop. Bishop William R. Houck (b. 1926), who had succeeded Brunini in Jackson in 1984, established spiritual renewal as one of his first priorities.

Between 1950 and 2000 the number of Mississippi Catholics increased from 50,559 to 115,196. By 2000 Catholics numbered about 4.2 percent of the total state population, a significant increase from 2.4 percent a half century earlier. The largest concentrations were on the Gulf Coast, in the capital city of Jackson, and in Vicksburg. While the number of priests increased slightly, the number of RELIGIOUS brothers and sisters serving in the state declined by 15 percent. In 1950 priests constituted 3.5 percent of the Catholic population; brothers and sisters, 8.8 percent; and the laity, 87.7 percent. By 2000 these figures had changed to 1.7 percent, 3.3 percent, and 95 percent respectively.

Between 2001 and 2005 the Catholic Church in Mississippi experienced a change in episcopal leadership. In 2001 Monsignor Thomas J. Rodi, a priest of the Archdiocese of New Orleans, became the second bishop of Biloxi. In 2003 Monsignor Joseph N. Latino (b. 1937), a priest of the Diocese of Houma-Thibodaux, was installed as the bishop of Jackson. In 2005 Monsignor Ronald P. Herzog (b. 1942), a priest of the Diocese of Biloxi, was installed as the bishop of Alexandria in Louisiana.

In 2001, 59 percent of Mississippi Catholics lived in the Diocese of Biloxi. In the sprawling Jackson Diocese, where Catholics numbered less than 2.5 percent of the population, twenty of the seventy-four parishes were without a resident pastor; the diocese also had twenty missions. A Mission and Ministry Planning

Process, begun in 2000 in the Jackson Diocese, addressed the challenge of maintaining viable FAITH communities with a declining number of priests.

Recovery from Katrina. On August 29, 2005, Hurricane Katrina slammed into Louisiana and the Mississippi Gulf Coast causing loss of life, unprecedented destruction, and the largest refugee dislocation in American history. The following two-and-a-half years witnessed a slow recovery and even slower return of population. Katrina damaged 428 of the 433 Biloxi diocesan buildings; 20 percent of the churches and a third of the schools were destroyed or damaged beyond repair. More than 30,000 Gulf Coast residents became refugees throughout the country. Bishop Rodi remained in the area during and after the storm, directing the massive recovery, assisted by donations and volunteers from throughout the country.

In the Diocese of Jackson, Catholic Charities channeled donations and assistance to the refugees. Northern parishes provided assistance to thousands of Louisiana and Gulf Coast refugees. Schools welcomed and assisted refugee students. In Natchez, Assumption Parish became one of a network of faith-based shelters to assist more than 10,000 refugees.

Between 2001 and 2007 the percentage of Catholics in Mississippi declined from 4.2 percent to 3.5 percent, the first such decline in more than 150 years. The reduced numbers were concentrated on the Gulf Coast.

By April 2008 the Diocese of Biloxi had more than fifty repair, renovation, and construction projects completed. Nineteen new buildings had been completed or were under construction. When St. Patrick High School in Gulfport opened in the fall of 2007, it was the first new post–Katrina school in the Texas to Alabama Katrina-Rita area. Despite the continued loss of an estimated 25,000 residents in the three Gulf Coast counties and a significant decline in baptisms, Catholic schools were at 99 percent of pre-Katrina enrollment, the Catholic educational fund drive far surpassed its $14,000,000 goal, and parish collections returned to pre-Katrina levels.

Noteworthy was the return from Baltimore and on January 19, 2008, the re-interment on the grounds of St. Mary Basilica of the body of the first Natchez bishop, John Chanche (1841–1852). William Cardinal KEELER of Baltimore presided.

SEE ALSO ALABAMA, CATHOLIC CHURCH IN; ALEXANDRIA, DIOCESE OF; BALTIMORE, ARCHDIOCESE OF; BAPTISTS; BISHOP, AUXILIARY; CATECHIST; CATHOLIC CHARITIES USA; LOUISIANA, CATHOLIC CHURCH IN; METHODIST CHURCHES; MEXICO (MODERN), THE CATHOLIC CHURCH IN; MOBILE, ARCHDIOCESE OF; RECONCILIATION, MINISTRY OF; SLAVERY, III (HISTORY OF); VATICAN COUNCIL II.

BIBLIOGRAPHY

Cleta Ellington, *Christ, the Living Water: Catholic Church in Mississippi*, edited by Janna Avalon (Jackson, Miss. 1989).

Richard Oliver Gerow, *Catholicity in Mississippi* (Natchez, Miss. 1939).

Michael V. Namorato, *The Catholic Church in Mississippi, 1911–1984: A History* (Westport, Conn. 1998).

Charles E. Nolan, *St. Mary's of Natchez: The History of a Southern Catholic Congregation, 1716–1988*, 2 vols. (Natchez, Miss. 1992)

Charles E. Nolan, *The Catholic Church in Mississippi, 1865–1911* (Lafayette, La. 2002).

James L. Pillar, *The Catholic Church in Mississippi, 1837–1865* (New Orleans 1964).

John Ray Skates, *Mississippi: A Bicentennial History* (New York 1979).

Most Rev. Richard Oliver Gerow
Bishop of the Diocese of Natchez-Jackson, Mississippi

Charles E. Nolan
Retired Archivist, Archdiocese of New Orleans, Long Beach, Miss. (2009)

MISSOURI, CATHOLIC CHURCH IN

Located in the central United States, Missouri is separated from Illinois, Kentucky, and Tennessee by the Mississippi River and is bounded on the north by Iowa; on the west by Nebraska, Kansas, and Oklahoma; and on the south by Arkansas. It was admitted to the Union in 1821 as the twenty-fourth state. The capital is Jefferson City; St. Louis and Kansas City are the largest cities. In 2008 the population of the state was 5,770,436 of whom 757,319, or about thirteen percent, were Catholic (*The Official Catholic Directory* 2008, p. 2088). There are four Catholic dioceses: the Archdiocese of ST. LOUIS and its three suffragan sees—KANSAS CITY-ST. JOSEPH, Springfield-Cape Girardeau, and Jefferson City.

Early History. The expedition of Hernando DeSoto (c. 1496–1542), including a priest, may have passed through Missouri in 1541, and in 1673 the Jesuit Jacques MARQUETTE accompanied the explorer Louis Joliet (1645–1700) down the Mississippi River, briefly visiting territory on the west side of the river. The French presence in the Mississippi Valley increased throughout the seventeenth and eighteenth centuries, due especially to the fur trade, but after the Seven Years' War (1756–1763) France was forced to cede Upper Louisiana to Spain, a transfer that placed the area under the jurisdiction of the Spanish BISHOP of Havana rather than the French bishop of Quebec. Parishes were established at

Ste. Genevieve (1759), St. Louis (1770), New Madrid (1789), Florissant (1790), and St. Charles (1792).

Diocese of Louisiana. In 1818 the Sulpician Bishop Louis William Valentin DUBOURG, a native of Santo Domingo, moved the headquarters of the Diocese of Louisiana from New Orleans to St. Louis. The same year The Congregation of the Mission (VINCENTIANS) founded St. Mary's Seminary at The Barrens (Perryville), an institution that would eventually provide missionaries for areas as far away as Texas and California. In 1823 Flemish JESUITS established at Florissant St. Stanislaus Seminary, from which missionaries were eventually sent across the Great Plains and to the Pacific Northwest. In 1818 St. Rose Philippine DUCHESNE founded a Congregation of the Religious of the Sacred Heart of Jesus at St. Charles and started a Catholic girls' school. Also in 1818 Bishop DuBourg started the St. Louis Academy for boys that was soon entrusted to the Jesuits and evolved into ST. LOUIS UNIVERSITY.

The region relied primarily on French missionaries, although in 1815 Henri Pratte (1788–1822) of Ste. Genevieve became the first native Missourian ordained to the priesthood. As early as 1790 there was an Irish pastor, James (also known as Diego and Jacques) Maxwell, at St. Genevieve, and in the DuBourg era another Irish pastor, Thomas Flynn, at St. Louis.

Diocese of St. Louis. The Italian Vincentian Joseph ROSATI was appointed coadjutor to DuBourg in 1824, and when the Diocese of Louisiana was divided in 1826, DuBourg resigned and went to France, leaving Rosati as the first bishop of St. Louis and administrator (until 1830) of the Diocese of New Orleans. Upon his death in 1843 he was succeeded by an Irish priest from Philadelphia, Peter Richard KENRICK, and in 1847 St. Louis was made an ARCHDIOCESE. Fifteen new parishes were established during the Rosati era. Like those founded in the previous century, all were within a few miles of the Mississippi River, as pastoral and missionary activity tended to follow the Mississippi north and south rather than the Missouri River westward deeper into the state.

The occasional priest who did travel west hurried through Missouri to reach the Indian missions of Kansas. In 1833–1835 Father Benedict Roux became the first resident pastor at Liberty and Westport (later Kansas City), but after his departure the area was served only by visiting Jesuits. Peter Paul LEFEVERE, the future administrator bishop of Detroit, worked for a time in the central part of the state and complained to Rosati about the diocesan neglect of that region.

Early clergy often lamented that their Creole flocks were irreligious and debauched, but beginning in the

The Assumption Catholic Church in Cedron, Mo. *According-ing to a history book written about the Cedron area, the church's origins date to 1838, when Father Ferdinand Helias, also known as the "Apostle of Central Missouri," visited the area and offered mass in a private home.* AP IMAGES

1830s the French character of Missouri rapidly changed through the influx of Irish and Germans. Both groups were numerous in the city of St. Louis. Whereas many Irish spread across the state building railroads to the West, many Germans were farmers, causing old French communities like Ste. Genevieve to become predominantly German. The Germans founded newer communities with names such as Westphalia, Weingarten, and Gildehaus; in 1840 German Catholics founded Deepwater (later Germantown) on the western border of the state.

For a time most of the priests were circuit-riders, visiting settlements that harbored as few as a dozen Catholics and celebrating Mass in private homes, with only the occasional town able to afford a simple frame church or support a resident pastor. The apostle of central Missouri was the Jesuit Ferdinand Helias de Huddeghen, son of a Flemish baron, who made his headquarters at Westphalia and traveled incessantly until his death in 1874.

Into the 1840s the Catholic population of the western part of the state remained predominantly Creole, people who had been attracted to the edge of the Great Plains by the fur trade. In 1845 both Westport and St. Joseph received resident pastors—Bernard Donnelly and James Scanlon, respectively, both of whom were Irish. (Unlike many of his fellow priests, Donnelly, who remained at his post until 1880, had a favorable view of the Creoles.) Strong anti–Catholic sentiment existed everywhere in the state, although less so in St. Louis than elsewhere. In rural areas priests encountered many lapsed Catholics who had fallen away from their FAITH after years of having no contact with a priest.

The institution of slavery existed among Missouri Catholics, including the Jesuits at Florissant and the Vincentians at Perryville. While most Germans were thought to be pro-Union and anti–slavery at the time of the Civil War, most French and Irish were thought to have the opposite loyalty. The circuit-riding priest John J. HOGAN recorded his loathing of the institution but said he was warned that if he made his sentiments known he might suffer mob violence. After the Civil War, however, he was one of a number of clergy who refused to take an oath of allegiance to the Union, for which he was briefly jailed.

Archdiocese of St. Louis. St. Louis was made an archdiocese in 1847. After Rosati its ordinaries have been: Peter Richard Kenrick (1843–1895), an Irish priest from Philadelphia; John J. Kain (1895–1903), bishop of Wheeling, West Virginia; John J. Glennon (1903–1946), coadjutor bishop of Kansas City, Missouri; Joseph E. Ritter (1946–1967), archbishop of Indianapolis; John J. Carberry (1968–1980), bishop of Columbus, Ohio; John L. May (1980–1992), bishop of Mobile, Alabama; Justin F. Rigali (1992–2003); a Vatican official; and Raymond L. Burke (2003–2008), bishop of LaCrosse, Wisconsin. Three St. Louis archbishops were made cardinals— Glennon shorty before his death in 1946, Ritter in 1960, and Carberry in 1969.

Diocese of St. Joseph. In the mid-1850s Father Hogan set out across Missouri to minister to itinerant Irish railroad workers and tried unsuccessfully to establish an Irish Catholic farming community. But Chillicothe was the only town in northern Missouri where he established a permanent parish. While pastor there in 1868, he was named the first bishop of St. Joseph, a DIOCESE of only seven parishes.

Inexplicably, the remainder of western Missouri remained part of the Archdiocese of St. Louis until Kansas City was made a diocese in 1880, with Hogan as its first bishop, but he continued to administer the St. Joseph diocese until 1893. In 1911, eleven northeastern Missouri counties were transferred from St. Louis to St. Joseph.

Hogan's successors at St. Joseph were the Irish-born Maurice F. Burke (1893–1923), bishop of Cheyenne, Wyoming, a noted Dante scholar; Francis Gilfillan (1923–1933), an Irish priest who had been rector of the St. Louis Cathedral; and Charles H. LeBlond (1933–1954), chancellor of the diocese of Cleveland.

Diocese of Kansas City. In 1896 the Irish immigrant Father John Joseph GLENNON became Hogan's coadjutor, but in 1903 Glennon was made ARCHBISHOP of St. Louis. The next year Bishop Thomas F. Lillis (1861–1938) of Leavenworth, Kansas, a former Kansas City priest, became coadjutor, succeeding to the see at Hogan's death in 1913. Lillis died in 1938 and was succeeded the next year by Bishop Edwin V. O'HARA of Great Falls, Montana.

After World War II, perhaps following the lead of Archbishop Joseph E. RITTER of St. Louis, O'Hara ordered the desegregation of the diocesan schools, trained some of his priests and seminarians to engage in street-preaching in largely Protestant rural communities, and began sending priests to serve in Bolivia. He also showed a particular interest in the rural areas, building a number of small, but serviceable, churches.

Diocese of Kansas City-St. Joseph. Following the death of Bishop O'Hara in 1956, Coadjutor Bishop John P. CODY of St. Joseph was named bishop of the newly consolidated Diocese of Kansas City-St. Joseph. When he was transferred to New Orleans in 1961, he was succeeded in turn by Bishop Charles H. Helmsing of Springfield-Cape Girardeau (1961–1977); Bishop John J. Sullivan of Grand Island, Nebraska (1977–1993); Bishop Raymond J. Boland of Birmingham, Alabama (1993–2005); and Monsignor Robert W. Finn, editor of the St. Louis archdiocesan newspaper (coadjutor 2004–2005, ordinary 2005–).

Diocese of Jefferson City. The diocese, whose see city is the state capital, was established in 1956, embracing thirty-eight counties in the northeastern part of the state, taken from St. Louis, Kansas City, and St. Joseph. Its bishops have been Auxiliary Bishop Joseph M. Marling of Kansas City, Missouri, a Precious Blood Father (1956–1969); Monsignor Michael F. McAuliffe of Kansas City-St. Joseph (1969–1997); and Monsignor John R. Gaydos of St. Louis (1997–).

Diocese of Springfield-Cape Girardeau. Established in 1956, this diocese is composed of thirty-nine counties carved out the dioceses of St. Louis and Kansas City. Ordinaries have been Auxiliary Bishop Charles H. Helmsing of St. Louis (1956–1962); Monsignor Ignatius J. Strecker of Wichita, Kansas (1962–1969); two successive directors of ecumenical activities for the United States

Catholic Conference in Washington, Monsignor William W. BAUM (1970–1973) and Monsignor Bernard LAW (1973–1984); Monsignor John E. Leibrecht, a St. Louis priest (1985–2008); and Monsignor Richard Vann Johnston of Knoxville, Tennessee (2008–).

Unusually, the first four ordinaries were all transferred to larger sees—Helmsing as bishop of Kansas City-St. Joseph; Strecker as archbishop of Kansas City, Kansas; Baum as cardinal archbishop of Washington, D.C., and a member of the papal Curia; and Law as cardinal archbishop of Boston.

Religious Orders. The state has been especially rich in the ministrations of religious orders, including Jesuits, Vincentians, MARIANISTS, CHRISTIAN BROTHERS, PASSIONISTS, REDEMPTORISTS, and Franciscans among male orders and Sisters of St. Joseph of Carondolet, SCHOOL SISTERS OF NOTRE DAME, Religious of the Sacred Heart, Daughters of Charity, PRECIOUS BLOOD SISTERS, Mercy Sisters, CARMELITES, URSULINES, Lorettines, and Franciscan Sisters of Mary among female communities.

Until after World War II only one Benedictine monastery existed in Missouri—Conception Abbey at Conception (1865), in the diocese of St. Joseph. The St. Louis Priory (now Abbey) was founded from England in 1956. A Trappist foundation, Our Lady of the Assumption, operates at Ava in the diocese of Springfield-Cape Girardeau. Dominican friars were unknown in Missouri until the Aquinas Institute moved to St. Louis in 1985.

Education. St. Louis University is the oldest institution of higher learning west of the Mississippi; the Jesuits also operate Rockhurst College in Kansas City (1910). The Sisters of Saint Joseph of Carondelet sponsored two colleges, Fontbonne in St. Louis (1923) and Avila in Kansas City (1916), though neither is any longer administered by sisters. St. Louis and Kansas City both have an abundance of Catholic high schools and charitable institutions. Kenrick-Glennon Seminary in St. Louis and Conception Abbey Seminary educate diocesan clergy, whereas the Aquinas Institute trains men for the Dominican priesthood and also has programs for lay ministers.

Religious Culture. With only modest Hispanic migration, Catholic growth in Missouri is also modest. St. Louis tends to be oriented towards the East and the upper Midwest, and about twenty-six percent of the people of the archdiocese are Catholics (thirty percent in the immediate metropolitan area). Jefferson City and Kansas City are oriented more to the Great Plains; each has about ten percent. Springfield-Cape Girardeau, part of the "Bible Belt," has the lowest percentage of Catholics

of any of the Missouri sees, about five percent.

The four dioceses form the Missouri Catholic Conference, which provides moral leadership and advocacy on public policy issues of concern to the Church. The Catholic Church is the largest single denomination in Missouri, followed by Southern BAPTISTS, Missouri Synod Lutherans, and ASSEMBLIES OF GOD, conservative groups which, while not especially ecumenical, have helped give the state a generally conservative moral and religious tone and have forged with Catholics a strong pro-life movement.

The Redemptorists' Liguori publishing house is located near St. Louis. In 1964 Bishop Helmsing provided assistance to staff of his diocesan newspaper who were attempting to start an independent national Catholic publication. The paper, *The National Catholic Reporter*, was a success, but as it developed into an organ of theological DISSENT, Helmsing repudiated his support. The paper continued to be published in Kansas City into the early twenty-first century.

SEE ALSO BAKER, DIOCESE OF; BENEDICTINES; CATHOLIC CHARITIES USA; CHURCH AND STATE; DOMINICANS; IDAHO, CATHOLIC CHURCH IN; MONTANA, CATHOLIC CHURCH IN; NEW ORLEANS, ARCHDIOCESE OF; OREGON, CATHOLIC CHURCH IN; SEX ABUSE CRISIS; SLAVERY, III (HISTORY OF); SULPICIANS; VATICAN COUNCIL I; VATICAN COUNCIL II.

BIBLIOGRAPHY

Timothy M. Dolan, *Some Seed Fell on Good Ground: The Life of Edwin V. O'Hara* (Washington, D.C. 1992).

Gilbert J. Garraghan, S.J., *Catholic Beginnings in Kansas City, Missouri* (Chicago 1920).

John J. Hogan, *On the Mission in Missouri* (Cleveland, Ohio 1892; reprint Glorieta, N.M. 1976).

John J. Hogan, *Fifty Years Ago* (Kansas City, Mo. 1907).

Dorothy Brandt Marra et al., *This Far by Faith: A Popular History of the Catholic People of West and Northwest Missouri*, 2 vols. (Kansas City, Mo. 1992).

The Official Catholic Directory, 2008 (New Providence, N.J. 2008).

John O'Hanlon, *Life and Scenery in Missouri* (Dublin 1890).

John E. Rothensteiner, *History of the Archdiocese of St. Louis*, 2 vols. (St. Louis 1928).

Peter James Rahill
Formerly Editor, The Catholic University of America Press
The Catholic University of America, Washington, D.C.

Patrick Foley
Editor, *Catholic Southwest: A Journal of History and Culture*
Azle, Tex.

James Hitchcock
Professor, Department of History
St. Louis University, St. Louis, Mo. (2009)

MOBILE, ARCHDIOCESE OF

Erected in November 16, 1980, the Province of Mobile (*Mobiliensis*) consists of the states of Alabama and Florida. Formerly suffragan of New Orleans, the archdiocese comprises the lower twenty-eight counties in Alabama and has an area of 22,969 square miles. In 2008 Catholics numbered 67,351 of a total population of 1,680,384 (*The Official Catholic Directory* 2008, p. 802).

Catholic Origins. Catholicism in the region traces its origins to early Spanish and French explorations and permanent settlements at Pensacola, Florida, in 1696 and Mobile, Alabama, in 1702, where a parish was erected on July 20, 1703, with Henry Rolleaux de la Vente as first pastor. The parish registers, virtually intact from 1704, faithfully mirror the unsettled conditions of those early days. Secular and religious priests in turn acted as pastors as the territory passed from French through British into Spanish hands. Ecclesiastical responsibility shifted from Quebec, Canada, to Santiago de Cuba and in 1793 to a mainland DIOCESE with the see at New Orleans. After the Gulf Coast area became part of the United States, the states of Alabama and Florida were erected into a vicariate apostolic in August 1825, and Michael PORTIER was chosen to head the new jurisdiction.

Diocese. Portier developed and ordered religious life in the area, which was raised to a diocese in May 1829, and in 1850 reduced in size. He was notably successful in founding institutions of education and welfare, and by the time of his death in 1859 there were, exclusive of the staff of Spring Hill College, ten priests serving nine parishes and nine mission stations. The Catholic population had grown from about 6,000 to an estimated 10,000, most of it centered in the southern part of the diocese.

John Quinlan (1826–1883) was consecrated as the second BISHOP of Mobile in New Orleans on December 4, 1859. A native of County Cork, Ireland, Quinlan immigrated to the United States in 1844, was ordained for the Diocese of Cincinnati, Ohio, in 1852, and two years later became rector of the diocesan seminary. His early years in the South were spent amid the confusion of the Civil War, and the remainder of his life was devoted to improving the status of the Church through the difficult years that followed. Quinlan secured a supply of clergy from Ireland, repaired the war losses, continued construction on the CATHEDRAL, and increased the number of parishes and mission stations to thirty-six. Resident pastors were placed in the northern part of the diocese for the first time, due largely to the introduction

in 1876 of BENEDICTINES from St. Vincent Abbey (now Archabbey), Latrobe, Pennsylvania. This group formed the nucleus from which St. Bernard Abbey and College later developed. By the time of Quinlan's death his clergy had increased to forty-five, about evenly divided between secular and religious, to care for a Catholic population of about 18,000. The diocese was, at the same time, burdened by crushing financial obligations.

The third bishop, Dominic Manucy (1823–1885), was born in St. Augustine, Florida, and was ordained by Portier in 1850. He was consecrated by Quinlan in 1874 for the vicariate apostolic of Brownsville, Texas, but was transferred to Mobile in March 1884, while yet retaining the administration of his former jurisdiction. Ill health, combined with the difficult situation in Mobile, led Manucy to resign before the year end.

Jeremiah O'Sullivan (1844–1896), a native of Ireland and priest of the Archdiocese of BALTIMORE, Maryland, was consecrated fourth bishop of Mobile on September 20, 1885. Although he was successful in extricating the diocese from its financial difficulties, his years were necessarily characterized more by retrenchment and consolidation than by new gains. He added towers to the cathedral and prepared conditions for later growth throughout the area, but the estimated Catholic population suffered a slight decline.

Edward Patrick ALLEN, who followed Bishop O'Sullivan, was consecrated in Baltimore on May 16, 1897. Prior to that he had been president of Mount St. Mary's College, Emmitsburg, Maryland. During Allen's thirty-year rule, the Catholic population grew to 48,000, while churches and clergy increased threefold. New efforts were made in rural districts, and the Josephite fathers ministered to a large African American population. Much was accomplished in the fields of education and welfare in Mobile through the benefactions of the McGill family of that city.

Growth continued during the administration of Thomas Joseph TOOLEN (1886–1976), consecrated the sixth bishop of Mobile in Baltimore on May 4, 1927. During his episcopate sixty-nine parishes were established and 154 churches built to keep pace with notable gains in urban as well as rural Catholic populations. Of the seventy-seven counties within his jurisdiction, those without churches were reduced from forty-nine to nineteen. Outside the Mobile district, the diocese was divided into three deaneries: North Alabama, centered at Birmingham where, since 1954, St. Paul's Church had been the cocathedral; Central Alabama, the area around Montgomery; and Northwest Florida, dominated by Pensacola. The number of priests had increased three-fold to provide for a like growth in Catholic population.

Social welfare services were efficiently organized under a bureau of Catholic Charities, and the diocesan

St. Margaret Catholic Church, Bayou la Batre, Alabama.
This church holds a yearly "Blessing of the Fleet" celebration to pray for a bountiful harvest for its parishioners. © JEFF GREEN-BERG / ALAMY

school system was annually responsible for the education of more than 25,000 students. Adequate Catholic hospital facilities existed in the major cities, and, beginning in 1934, the diocese had an independent newspaper, *The Catholic Week.* Toolen's success in coping with such growth and the special attention he gave to the needs of African-American Catholics in the area merited him the title of *archbishop ad personam* (1954). In 1968 the Pensacola Deanery was added to the Diocese of St. Augustine. Archbishop Toolen resigned on October 8, 1969, at which time the see was divided into the Diocese of Mobile and the Diocese of Birmingham in Alabama. Toolen died on December 4, 1976.

John C. May (1922–), an auxiliary bishop of Chicago, was installed as the seventh bishop of Mobile on December 10, 1969. He effectively fostered liturgical and standard changes provided for by VATICAN COUN-CIL II and gave renewed emphasis to the Church's social apostolate (housing and health care). May established new parishes, mostly in rural areas, along with a number of missions. The diocese made significant advances in social integration of diocesan organizations and had notable success in the parish at Selma, Alabama. Despite a number of school closings and consolidation, the

diocese established two new elementary units. A diocesan pastoral council formed in 1974, and lay leadership emerged in parish and diocesan structure. The diocese put a program in place for the retirement of lay employees. Ecumenical initiatives bore fruit for direct help to the needy, and a Jewish-Christian dialogue began in Mobile, the longest ongoing such exercise nationwide. In 1979 Bishop May ordained the first class of permanent deacons for the diocese. He was appointed ARCH-BISHOP of St. Louis on January 29, 1980.

On November 16, 1980, Oscar H. Lipscomb (1931–, ordained 1956), a native of Mobile, was consecrated as the first archbishop of Mobile. The new province, erected that same day, consisted of the states of Alabama and Mississippi with Jackson, Biloxi, and Birmingham as suffragan sees. Reported Catholic population grew, but only slightly. Notable decreases occurred in rural areas, but included a Southeast Asian and significant Hispanic presence; an office for Hispanic ministry addresses the latter. Although only one new parish was established, older parishes built permanent or new churches, the result of substantial increases in the Catholic populations. The number of diocesan priests remained stable at fifty-five, with more than average success in the program for priestly formation. In 2008 Catholic high and elementary schools enroll 6,703 students, and other programs for youth RELIGIOUS EDU-CATION counted 4,797 students. Jesuit Spring Hill Col-lege, the oldest in Alabama, had a student body of 1,867 (*The Official Catholic Directory* 2008, p. 815). The social apostolate grew, with new centers in Montgomery, Dot-han, and Robertsdale, and pro-life offices served the Mobile, Montgomery, and Dothan areas.

On November 20, 2005, the annual archdiocesan celebration of the Feast of CHRIST THE KING was also the Silver Jubilee of the episcopal ordination of Archbishop Lipscomb and the establishment of the ecclesial Province of Mobile. After the establishment of the Province of Mobile, the Archdiocese of Mobile saw demographic changes in its Catholic population, with growth in the southeastern part of the archdiocese, as well as on the eastern shore of Mobile Bay. In particular, the Hispanic population, found in all areas of the ecclesial jurisdiction, experienced a rapid increase. Between 2001 and 2004, the historic Cathedral-Basilica of the Immaculate Conception underwent an extensive restoration, and other patrimony of the archdiocese underwent restoration, including the historic St. Joseph's Chapel at Spring Hill College, Mobile (2006), and the historic and structurally beautiful Portier House (2007). In April 2008, Bishop Thomas J. Rodi was named the second archbishop of Mobile.

SEE ALSO ALABAMA, CATHOLIC CHURCH IN; BILOXI, DIOCESE OF; CATHOLIC CHARITIES USA; CINCINNATI, ARCHDIOCESE OF;

FLORIDA, CATHOLIC CHURCH IN; JACKSON, DIOCESE OF; JOSEPHI-
TES; MISSISSIPPI, CATHOLIC CHURCH IN; MOUNT ST. MARY'S
COLLEGE AND SEMINARY; NEW ORLEANS, ARCHDIOCESE OF; ST.
LOUIS, ARCHDIOCESE OF; ST. VINCENT ARCHABBEY.

BIBLIOGRAPHY

Archdiocese of Mobile Official Web site, available from: http://
www.mobilearchdiocese.org/ (accessed October 30, 2008).

M. T. A. Carroll, *A Catholic History of Alabama and the Floridas* (New York 1908).

M. Kenny, *Catholic Culture in Alabama: Centenary Story of
Spring Hill College* (New York 1931).

Reverend Oscar H. Lipscomb, *The Administration of Michael
Portier, Vicar Apostolic of Alabama and the Floridas, 1825–
1829, and First Bishop of Mobile, 1829–1859*. Ph.D. diss.,
The Catholic University of America, Washington, D.C.,
1963.

Reverend Oscar H. Lipscomb, "The Administration of John
Quinlan, Second Bishop of Mobile, 1859–1883." *Records of
the American Catholic Historical Society of Philadelphia* 78
(1967).

Andrew S. Moore, *The South's Tolerable Alien: Roman Catholics
in Alabama and Georgia, 1945–1970* (Baton Rouge, La.
2007).

The Official Catholic Directory (New Providence, N.J. 2008).

Most Rev. Oscar Hugh Lipscomb
Archbishop of Mobile, Ala.

Msgr. Michael L. Farmer
Chancellor
Archdiocese of Mobile, Ala. (2009)

MODERN MEDIA AND THE CHURCH

In 1963, the Second Vatican Council and Pope PAUL VI
issued *Inter Mirifica, A Decree on the Media* (or *Means*)
of Social Communications. In so doing, they declared to
the Church, the laity, and the world the importance of
the mass media and its power to reach and influence the
entire human race. The Church clearly recognized that
the media, when properly used, could be a profound
means for spreading the Gospel and educating the faithful, and *Inter Mirifica* insisted that all Catholics, not just
religious but the laity as well, had both the inherent
right and duty to get involved in the field of
communications. The document went on to state:

> It is, therefore, an inherent right of the Church
> to have at its disposal and to employ any of
> these media insofar as they are necessary or use-
> ful for the instruction of Christians and all its
> efforts for the welfare of souls. It is the duty of
> Pastors to instruct and guide the faithful so

that they, with the help of these same media,
may further the salvation and perfection of
themselves and of the entire human family. In
addition, the laity especially must strive to
instill a human and Christian spirit into these
media, so that they may fully measure up to
the great expectations of mankind to God's
design. (*Inter Mirifica* 1:3)

Although *Inter Mirifica* was issued more than four
decades ago, at a time when the mass media consisted of
films, advertising, television, radio, and print publications, its message is even more pertinent in the twenty-
first century. Indeed, looking back, this document from
VATICAN COUNCIL II seems prophetic, for the ability
to reach all of society has increased dramatically. The
mass media, a term first used in the 1920s and 1930s
following the birth of radio and the expansion of
newspaper circulation, have exploded into an enormous
industry that covers the globe with a myriad of images
via the Internet, radio, cable television, satellites, cellular
phones, and countless other communications technologies that can connect one part of the planet to another
almost instantaneously.

The Development of the Modern Mass Media. In his
2005 Apostolic Letter titled *The Rapid Development*,
JOHN PAUL II referred to the rapid development of
communications technology as a sign of progress. That
progress, in terms of numbers alone, is overwhelming
and difficult to calculate. Statistics from the Central
Intelligence Agency's *The World Factbook 2007* reveal
that in 2007 there were approximately 44,000 AM and
FM radio stations worldwide. These same sources claim
there were more than 21,000 broadcast television stations globally in 2007, excluding multiple cable and
satellite distributors that offer subscribers thousands of
additional choices in news and entertainment
programming.

Undoubtedly, the most significant growth and
outreach can be seen in the Internet. According to a
March 2007 survey by the digital research firm Com-
Score, 747 million people aged fifteen and over were
using the Internet worldwide at that time. This was a 10
percent increase over 2006 data, showing that Marshall
McLuhan's "global village" theory, regarding the media's
impact on the way human beings relate to one another,
has come of age in a much more profound way than
even the well-known media analyst, English professor,
and communications theorist could have ever imagined.
However, one needs to add these numbers to the additional outreach achieved through newspaper and
magazine readership; the usage of cellular phones and
ipods; the sales of CDs, DVDs, and video and computer
games; and the bombardment of additional messages

coming from the advertising and film industries to fully realize the enormous impact the media has, as well as the opportunity it represents.

Church Guidelines for the Media. Early in his pontificate, during a message given to an audience at the United Nations, John Paul II said truth does not pass, change, or go away, but endures. Prior to that powerful statement, in *Inter Mirifica*, the Church had warned of the media's efforts to deny objective truth and use their means for evil instead of good: "The Church recognizes, too, that men can employ these media contrary to the plan of the Creator and to their own loss. Indeed the Church experiences maternal grief at the harm all too often done to society by their evil use" (*Inter Mirifica* i:2). This and other warnings about the growth and impact of the mass media seem prescient to many in the twenty-first century. While the Gospel is certainly being proclaimed from many new media outlets, it is also competing with, and in many cases being drowned out by, destructive messages that promote, endorse, and embrace gratuitous violence, sexual promiscuity, abortion, euthanasia, birth control, pornography, and many other practices that contradict or directly attack the Church's teachings.

Research by such professional organizations as the American Academy of Pediatrics and the American Medical Association, meanwhile, has shown a link between what is being beamed into people's homes every day and the social, physical, spiritual, and psychological ills occurring in society. Since the 1970s, for example, more than one thousand studies have shown a strong correlation between violence in the media and aggressive behavior in children. Yet as the media landscape has grown and changed, the Church has remained constant in its guidelines and instructions regarding proper media usage that, when applied to today's media-saturated culture, can help communications outlets serve as beacons of light in an ever darkening world.

The Church believes that those who work in or use the media must apply norms of morality and adopt a proper moral outlook. As John Paul II stated in *The Media and the Family: A Risk and a Richness*, his Message for the 38th World Communications Day on May 23, 2004, "all communication has a moral dimension." He went on to summarize Church teaching concerning the mass media's role, how to effectively apply the media to one's daily life, and how to promote positive change in the media. He also stressed the responsibility of public authorities in upholding marriage and family for the sake of society and the common good: "Without resorting to censorship, it is imperative that public authorities set in place regulatory policy and procedures to ensure that the media do not act against the good of the family.

Family representatives should be part of this policy-making"(*Media and the Family* 4).

John Paul II also insisted that media consumers, especially Catholic parents, become involved in the process by being good examples with their own media choices, limiting their children's media exposure, and contacting media outlets regarding the quality of their programming and news coverage. He elaborated on this theme by saying:

> This would include planning and scheduling media use, limiting the time children devote to media, making entertainment a family experience, putting some media entirely off limits and periodically excluding all of the media for the sake of other family activities. Above all parents should give good examples to children by their own thoughtful and selective use of media.... Families should be outspoken in telling producers, advertisers, and public authorities, what they like and dislike. (*Media and the Family* 5)

Use of the Media by the Church. Church leaders have embraced modern technology in its varied forms, and they continue to use radio, television, the Internet, and print media to spread the Gospel message. These outlets include the Vatican Television Center, Vatican Radio, the VATICAN WEB SITE, and the Vatican Publishing House. *L'Osservatore Romano* serves as the Vatican daily newspaper, and *Acta Apostolicae Sedis* (Acts of the Holy See) is a monthly periodical that contains public papal documents and other information relating to the Holy See and VATICAN CITY. In 1948 the Church established the Pontifical Council for Social Communications (formerly known as the Pontifical Commission for the Study and Ecclesiastical Evaluation of Films on Religious or Moral Subjects).

In addition to Vatican-operated media outlets, many other examples of Catholic media promote evangelization—or the "new evangelization" spoken of so often by John Paul II—around the world. Catholic radio and TV apostolates, as well as print apostolates, run by either religious orders or the laity, continue to grow. In the United States, these apostolates include the ETERNAL WORD TELEVISION NETWORK (EWTN), EWTN Radio, Ave Maria Radio, Immaculate Heart Radio, the Guadalupe Radio Network, and Catholic Answers, to name just a few. These outlets uphold, affirm, and explain Church teaching through original daily Catholic programming and talk shows, live daily Mass broadcasts, and the recitation of different traditional Catholic prayers, including the Rosary and Divine Mercy Chaplet. As of 2007, some 200 Catholic terrestrial radio stations were on the air in the United States alone, and EWTN, which was begun by Mother Angelica in Birmingham, Alabama, is now the largest religious media organization in the world.

Catholic radio and television stations can also be found on the World Wide Web and satellite radio, giving them a potential outreach in the millions. According to a 2004 survey by the Pew Internet and American Life Project, 64 percent of Internet users claim they use the Internet for religious reasons. According to an online article by David J. Hartline, the author of *The Tide Is Turning Toward Catholicism* (2006), "Catholic Laity are in the forefront of evangelizing and defending the Faith. While there are thousands of Catholic websites that zealously defend the Church, there are but a handful of heterodox or liberal Catholic websites questioning the Church's teachings" (Hartline 2007). In the United States, a variety of orthodox Catholic newspapers and magazines have appeared, including *Our Sunday Visitor*, the *National Catholic Register*, *This Rock*, *Envoy*, and *Faith and Family*.

In a 1975 Apostolic Exhortation, *Evangelii nuntiandi* (*On Evangelization in the Modern World*), Pope Paul VI said "the Church would feel guilty before the Lord if she did not utilize these powerful means." Whether speaking through Catholic or secular media outlets, or instructing the faithful and the entire human race on the proper usage of mass media, the Church is indeed using the powerful means of the media to accomplish the central meaning of its existence, which is fulfilling the Great Commission to "go and make disciples of all nations" (Matt 28:19).

SEE ALSO INTERNET AND THE CHURCH; INTERNET SITES, CATHOLIC; VATICAN WEB SITE.

BIBLIOGRAPHY

Central Intelligence Agency, *The World Factbook 2007* Television Broadcast Stations, available from https://www.cia.gov/library/publications/the-world-factbook/fields/2015.html (accessed March 3, 2008).

Central Intelligence Agency, *The World Factbook 2007*, Radio Broadcast Stations available from https://www.cia.gov/library/publications/the-world-factbook/fields/2013.html (accessed March 3, 2008).

ComScore, "Worldwide Internet Audience Has Grown Ten Percent in Last Year" (Press Release, March 6, 2007), available from http://www.comscore.com/press/release.asp?press=1242 (accessed March 3, 2008).

David Hartline, "The Tide Is Turning Toward Catholicism: The Laity," In *Catholic Exchange*, July 16th, 2007, available from http://www.catholicexchange.com/node/62663 (accessed March 3, 2008).

John Paul II, *The Media and the Family: A Risk and a Richness* (World Communications Day Message, May 23, 2004), available from http://www.vatican.va/holy_father/john_paul_ii/messages/communications/documents/hf_jp-ii_mes_20040124_world-communications-day_en.html (accessed March 3, 2008).

John Paul II, *The Rapid Development*, To Those Responsible for Communications (Apostolic Letter, January 24, 2005) available from http://www.vatican.va/holy_father/john_paul_ii/apost_letters/documents/hf_jp-ii_apl_20050124_il-rapido-sviluppo_en.html (accessed March 3, 2008).

Pew Internet and American Life Project, *Faith Online: 64% of Wired Americans Have Used the Internet for Spiritual or Religious Purposes* By Stewart M. Hoover, Lynn Schofield Clark, and Lee Rainie (Embargoed for publication April 7, 2004), available from http://www.pewinternet.org/pdfs/PIP_Faith_Online_2004.pdf (accessed March 3, 2008).

Paul VI, *Evangelii Nuntiandi*, On Evangelization in the Modern World (Apostolic Exhortation, December 8, 1975), available from http://www.vatican.va/holy_father/paul_vi/apost_exhortations/documents/hf_p-vi_exh_19751208_evangelii-nuntiandi_en.html (accessed March 3, 2008).

Vatican Council II, *Inter Mirifica*, On the Media of the Social Communications (Decree, December 4, 1963), available from http://www.vatican.va/archive/hist_councils/ii_vatican_council/documents/vat-ii_decree_19631204_inter-mirifica_en.html (accessed March 3, 2008).

Teresa Tomeo
Syndicated Catholic Talk Show Host
Catholic Connection/Ave Maria Radio
Detroit, Mich. (2009)

MONTANA, CATHOLIC CHURCH IN

Montana, located in the Rocky Mountain region of the northwest United States, was admitted to the Union as the forty-first state in 1889. The fourth largest state, it is bounded on the north by Canada, on the east by North and South Dakota, on the south by Wyoming and Idaho, and on the west by Idaho. Helena is the capital, and Billings is the largest city. There are two dioceses in the state: the Diocese of Helena (*Helenensis*) and the Diocese of Great Falls-Billings (*Magnocataractensis-Billingensis*), both of which are suffragans of the Metropolitan See of Portland in Oregon. The Diocese of Helena, established in 1884, encompasses the western counties of the state, an area of 51,922 sq. miles; the Diocese of Great Falls, erected 1904 and redesignated in 1980 as the Diocese of Great Falls-Billings, consists of the eastern counties, an area of 94,922 sq. miles.

History. The United States acquired the eastern two-thirds of the region, an extension of the Great Plains, in the Louisiana Purchase. The predominantly mountainous western third, containing the Continental Divide, passed to the United States with the settlement of the

Oregon Question. The state contains numbers of Native American tribes, including the Gros Ventres, Assiniboine, Blackfeet, Flathead, and Crow tribes, located on reservations.

White fur traders of the Canadian Northwest Fur Company entered Montana either in the late eighteenth or early nineteenth century. The first American explorers to enter the region were the members of the Lewis and Clark Expedition (1804–1806), who spent considerable time in the area on both the outbound and return phases of their journey. Montana was an important sphere of activity in the fur-trading era. The Canadian Northwest Company trapped in the western and northwestern sectors of the region, whereas American groups, such as the Missouri Fur Company, the American Fur Company, and the Rocky Mountain Fur Company, ranged over the entire area. After the decline of the fur trade, mining succeeded as the dominant form of economic activity in Montana; later it became energy production (natural gas and oil). Cattle raising and wheat farming are also important.

Missionary Activity. Catholicism was introduced in Montana when Iroquois moved west with Canadian fur traders and settled among the Flatheads of western Montana (1811–1812), giving the latter a basic idea of the Faith. The Flatheads sent four successive expeditions (1831, 1835, 1837, and 1839) to Bishop J. ROSATI of St. Louis, Missouri, to obtain the services of missionaries, but lack of available personnel prevented his providing them with services until 1839. In 1840 Pierre Jean DE SMET went on an exploratory journey among the natives. One year later he returned with fellow Jesuit priests and lay brothers to establish St. Mary's Mission, thus beginning an era of fruitful Jesuit endeavor among the Native Americans and, later, the whites.

Diocesan Development. Montana became a vicariate apostolic in 1883, and in 1884 the HOLY SEE established the Diocese of Helena, coextensive with the entire territory, with John Baptist BRONDEL, BISHOP of Victoria, Vancouver Island, Canada, and vicar apostolic of Montana as its first bishop. Until his death on November 3, 1903, Brondel labored diligently to build the DIOCESE among Native Americans as well as trappers, miners, and other immigrants to the area. When he arrived in 1884, four diocesan priests, twelve religious priests, sixteen churches, four hospitals, two parochial schools, and two schools for Native Americans served a Catholic population of 15,000. By 1903, the last year of his life, 38 diocesan priests, fifteen religious priests, 65 churches, eight hospitals, nine parochial schools, and ten schools for Native Americans served a Catholic population of 50,000.

Diocesan Division. Soon after Brondel's death in 1904, his earlier request for a division of the diocese was granted. The eastern two-thirds of the state became the Diocese of Great Falls. Mathias C. Lenihan (1854–1943), pastor in Marshaltown, Iowa, was consecrated the first bishop of the diocese on September 21, 1904. At that time the diocese had fourteen priests, eleven parishes, two schools, and four Native American missions. When Lenihan retired in 1930, 68 priests, 45 parishes, 88 missions, eleven schools, fifteen Native American missions, four private academies, and eight hospitals cared for a Catholic population of 33,345. In the western section of the state, John P. CARROLL of Dubuque, Iowa, became the second bishop of Helena on December 21, 1904. Given his academic background as president of St. Joseph College (now Loras College) in Dubuque, Iowa, it was not surprising that he made Catholic education a high priority. In addition to five high schools, he founded Mount St. Charles College (now called Carroll College in honor of its founder), which opened in September 1910. Two years earlier Carroll had laid the cornerstone for the magnificent Gothic Cathedral of St. Helena in the see city. It was consecrated on January 3, 1924. Bishop Carroll died on November 4, 1925. During his episcopacy thirty-two new parishes had been erected.

O'Hara. Meanwhile in eastern Montana, Father Edwin V. O'HARA, founder and director of the National Catholic Rural Life Conference and zealous promoter of the CONFRATERNITY OF CHRISTIAN DOCTRINE (CCD) in the United States, was consecrated the second bishop of the Diocese of Great Falls on October 28, 1930. Given the rural nature of the diocese, O'Hara labored to establish the Confraternity of Christian Doctrine program (CCD) locally to meet the religious education needs of children and adults. Working with the SISTERS OF PROVIDENCE and the Ursuline Sisters, O'Hara founded the College of Great Falls in September 1932. In April 1939 O'Hara was named ARCHBISHOP of Kansas City, Missouri.

Finnigan and Hayes. In western Montana, the unexpected death of Bishop Carroll in 1925 left the Diocese of Helena without a bishop until May 22, 1927, when PIUS XI appointed Father George J. Finnigan, C.S.C., provincial of the Congregation of HOLY CROSS at Notre Dame, Indiana, the third bishop of the diocese. He was the first member of his religious congregation in the United States to be consecrated a bishop. Before his death on August 14, 1932, Finnigan established the CCD program throughout the diocese and a diocesan newspaper, *The Register: Western Montana*. On September 23, 1933, Father Ralph Leo Hayes of Pittsburgh, Pennsylvania, was consecrated the fourth bishop of the diocese. His brief time in Helena ended in 1935 when he was appointed rector of the NORTH AMERICAN COLLEGE in ROME.

Condon. In Great Falls, William J. Condon, vicar general of the diocese of Spokane, Washington, was consecrated the third bishop of the diocese on October 18, 1939. Until his retirement on August 17, 1967, the diocese witnessed a period of remarkable growth. Given the difficulty of caring for a diocese with such a vast territory, he requested the Holy See to grant him an auxiliary bishop, and on October 30, 1961, Monsignor Eldon B. Schuster, chancellor of the diocese, rector of the cathedral parish, and the superintendent of schools, was appointed TITULAR BISHOP of Amblada and auxiliary bishop of the Diocese of Great Falls. He was consecrated a bishop on December 21, 1961.

Gilmore. Meanwhile, in the Diocese of Helena, Father Joseph M. Gilmore, born in New York but raised in Montana from the age of five, was consecrated the fifth bishop of Helena on February 29, 1936. To meet the needs of a rapidly growing Catholic population, new and larger facilities were needed, and he immediately began to build and strengthen the institutions of the diocese. Accordingly, a chancery building, twenty churches, and six grade schools and high schools were built. The Cathedral of St. Helena was completely renovated in time for the diamond jubilee of the diocese in 1959. Gilmore's years as bishop were considered by many to be golden building years for the diocese.

Hunthausen. When Gilmore died on April 2, 1962, he was succeeded by Raymond G. Hunthausen, president of Carroll College and a native of Montana. Hunthausen was consecrated the sixth bishop of the diocese on August 30, 1962. From 1962 to 1966 Hunthausen participated in the sessions of the Second Vatican Council, where he met Bishop Angélico Mellotto Mazzardo (1959–1986) of Solalá, Guatemala. Although Guatemala was 90 percent Catholic, Bishop Mellotto's diocese was experiencing a critical shortage of clergy. Soon after the meeting, Hunthausen opened the Diocese of Helena mission in Guatemala. In addition, he labored diligently to implement the decrees of the Second Vatican Council throughout the diocese. The decline in the number of vocations to the priestly and religious life had a dramatic impact on the schools, hospitals, and parishes in the diocese. With schools closing, greater emphasis was placed on the CCD program, which had existed for many years in the rural areas of the diocese. In addition, religious education centers staffed by religious, clergy, and laity were set up throughout the

diocese. Although the changes were painful for many, Hunthausen's willingness to listen and his intense desire to be faithful to the teachings of the Second Vatican Council made the difficult transition possible. He was appointed archbishop of Seattle on February 25, 1975.

Schuster and Murphy. In the Diocese of Great Falls, Auxiliary Bishop Eldon B. Schuster was chosen to succeed Bishop Condon on January 23, 1968. Schuster also took part in the sessions of the Second Vatican Council. His diocese did not escape the depletion in the ranks of the clergy and the closing of many Catholic schools in the ensuing years after Vatican II. When Schuster retired on December 27, 1977, Pope PAUL VI appointed Thomas J. Murphy to be the fifth bishop of Great Falls. A native of Chicago and rector of Our Lady of the Lake Seminary in Mundelein, Illinois, Murphy was consecrated bishop on August 26, 1978. He served the diocese until May 27, 1987, when he was named coadjutor archbishop of Seattle. Faced with serious personnel shortages, Murphy, with the help of his presbyteral council, consolidated parishes and schools. Cluster parishes were formed to care for areas with fewer priests. Women RELIGIOUS were called upon to conduct the day-to-day administration of these parishes. Another significant development was the decision in 1980 to change the name of the diocese to the Diocese of Great Falls-Billings, thus recognizing the importance of the Catholic community in Billings, the largest city in the state.

Later Great Falls-Billings Bishops. Anthony M. Milone, auxiliary bishop of Omaha, Nebraska, was named the sixth bishop of the Diocese of Great Falls-Billings on February 23, 1988. At that time the seventy-three parishes and fifty-six missions in the diocese had only fifty-eight resident pastors. Father Elden F. Curtiss, president-rector of Mount Angel Seminary in St. Benedict, Oregon, was named by the Holy See to succeed Bishop Hunhausen in Helena. He was consecrated the seventh bishop of the diocese on April 28, 1986. For the next seventeen years, Curtiss dealt with a wide range of problems. He chose as his motto a paraphrase of John 17:21, "That we all may be one," and his desire to unify and reconcile a sometimes divided diocesan church was the hallmark of his episcopacy. He presided over a diocesan synod in 1988, the first one held in eighty years. It was announced on May 4, 1993, that Curtiss had been named archbishop of Omaha, and Monsignor Alexander J. Brunett of Detroit, Michigan, was subsequently appointed the eighth bishop of Helena on April 19, 1994, a post he held until he was named archbishop of Seattle, on October 28, 1997. His successor was

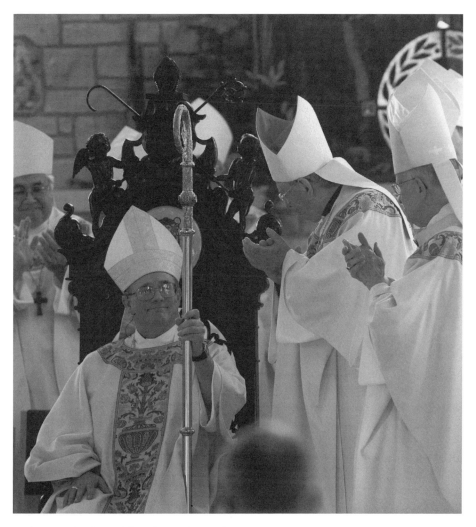

Bishop Michael Warfel. *The newly installed bishop (center) is congratulated by other bishops as he takes his seat on the cathedra and holds the staff of his office as the seventh bishop of the Great Falls-Billings Diocese. Wafel was installed by Archbishop Pietro Sambi, the apostolic nuncio to the United States, on Wednesday, Jan. 16, 2008, at Holy Spirit Catholic Church in Great Falls, Montana.* **AP IMAGES**

Robert C. Morlino, another priest of Detroit, who was consecrated the ninth bishop in the Cathedral of St. Helena on September 21, 1999.

Twenty-First Century. At the beginning of the twenty-first century, approximately 125,000 Catholics lived in Montana, out of a total population of about 815,800 persons. They were served by about 122 active diocesan, extern, and religious priests. The two dioceses served 5 Native American reservations and a total of 124 parishes and 86 missions. Bishops Schuster and Hunthausen established the Montana Catholic Conference on Social Welfare, which in turn led to the formation of Catholic Social Services of Montana and the Montana Catholic Conference.

In the summer of 2003 Bishop Morlino of the Diocese of Helena was appointed bishop of Madison, Wisconsin. On March 23, 2004, Bishop George Thomas, auxiliary bishop of the Archdiocese of SE-ATTLE, was named as his successor. The Diocese of Great Falls-Billings also experienced a change in leadership in 2006 when Bishop Milone retired after eighteen years. He was replaced by Bishop Michael Warfel of Juneau, Alaska, on November 20, 2007.

In February 2008 Bishops Thomas and Warfel issued a joint statement regarding a proposed state constitutional initiative that defined personhood as beginning at the moment of fertilization. In the statement the bishops strongly reaffirmed the Church's position on the protection of human life from the moment of conception. However, they did not believe that this constitutional initiative was the most beneficial venue to pursue the changes necessary to protect the unborn.

Two new Catholic schools opened in Montana during the early 2000s. Great Falls Central Catholic High School reopened in 2001 after having been closed in the mid-1970s. Initially housed at the University of Great Falls, a new school facility was opened in September 2007. On the Blackfeet Indian Reservation, the Diocese of Helena opened the De La Salle Blackfeet School for grades five through eight. De La Salle belongs to a network of schools that serve predominately at-risk populations and are operated by the De La Salle CHRISTIAN BROTHERS.

In the Diocese of Helena, St. Ann's Mission in Somers and St. Catherine's Parish in Bigfork joined to become Pope John Paul II Parish. In Missoula, Pope John XXIII and Holy Family parishes combined to become Blessed Trinity Catholic Community. In the Diocese of Great Falls-Billings, Holy Family Parish, St. Gerard's Parish, and Sts. Peter and Paul Parish in Great Falls combined to form Holy Spirit Parish.

In September 1999 four POOR CLARES arrived in Great Falls to establish a foundation in the Diocese of Great Falls-Billings. A MONASTERY was completed in March 2008.

As of 2008 approximately 104,000 Catholics lived in Montana. They were served by 116 parishes and 92 missions. They were ministered to by 159 priests and 95 women religious (*The Official Catholic Directory* 2008, p. 2088).

SEE ALSO JESUITS; PORTLAND, ARCHDIOCESE OF; URSULINES; VATICAN COUNCIL II.

BIBLIOGRAPHY

Cornelia M. Flaherty, *Go with Haste into the Mountains: A History of the Diocese of Helena* (Helena, Mont. 1984).

William J. Greytak, "The Roman Catholic Dioceses of Montana: An Abbreviated History." In *Religion in Montana: Pathways to the Present*, edited by Lawrence F. Small (Guilford, Conn. l995), 31—84.

Kim Larsen, *From Age to Age: A History of the Catholic Church in Eastern Montana* (Great Falls, Mont. 2003).

The Official Catholic Directory, 2008 (New Providence, N.J. 2008).

Lawrence Benedict Palladino, *Indian and White in the Northwest: A History of Catholicity in Montana* (Baltimore 1984, repr. Lancaster, Pa. 1922).

Wilfred P. Schoenberg, *Jesuits in Montana, 1840–1960* (Portland, Ore. 1960).

Suzanne H. Schrems, "God's Women: Sisters of Charity of Providence and Ursuline Nuns in Montana, 1864–1900," Ph.D. dissertation, University of Oklahoma, 1992.

Thomas Anthony Clinch
Associate Professor of History and Department Head
Carroll College, Helena, Mont.

William J. Greytak
Professor of Modern European History
Carroll College, Helena, Mont.

Connie Erickson
Formerly Historian-Archivist
Diocese of Helena, Mont. (2009)

MORAL THEOLOGY, HISTORY OF (20TH-CENTURY DEVELOPMENTS BEFORE VATICAN II)

Biblical Study. The mid-twentieth-century movements in the Church led to a change in approach and method in the teaching of moral theology, reflected also in subsequent writings. The remarkable increase in interest and work in biblical studies, made possible and encouraged by PIUS XII's encyclical *Divino afflante Spiritu* and important archeological discoveries, brought about a desire among theologians to use a more biblical approach and to rely on scientific biblical exegesis for interpretation of the message of SALVATION. Such a renewal was undoubtedly needed in all branches of theology, but especially in moral theology where so much weight had been attached to philosophical and ethical reasoning and so little to the study of the teaching of the inspired Word of God. The biblical and kerygmatic movements helped much toward a more theological approach to moral theology even apart from the greater and more exact use of scriptural texts. This new approach appeared especially in preaching and actual classroom teaching, and only more slowly in the textbook manuals, especially those that are merely new editions of older works.

More Positive Orientation. One of the effects of the kerygmatic movement was a movement away from the predominantly negative type of presentation that had prevailed in many older manuals. Whole books were written in an attempt to integrate this more positive, more theological, and more biblical approach to moral theology; but by the mid-1960s not much success had been achieved in fully integrated works that would also stand as thorough scientific treatises of the whole of moral theology. It was left more to the living teachers and preachers to exhort their hearers to a fuller response of love to the call of Christ and at the same time to make clear what Christ himself demanded in fulfillment of the Decalogue as a means of showing true love of God.

Some felt that such a positive approach requires a rearrangement of the order as well as the manner of treating moral theology by dividing the matter of special moral theology according to the virtues rather than according to the precepts of the Decalogue, or according to the various relations that human beings have to God, to themselves, and to others (considered both as individuals and collectively in society). But it also proved possible to take a positive approach by giving special emphasis to the virtues within an arrangement that continued to be based on the precepts of the Decalogue. No one arrangement is essential to a positive approach.

Others felt that moral theology should also include a treatment of the ideal response to the call of Christ by intermingling what had been treated separately under the headings of ascetical theology and moral theology, on the ground that every individual Christian should respond on the ascetical plane, wanting to love Christ more and do the better thing always, and yet should know what morality requires.

Influence of Existentialism.

Various philosophical movements such as EXISTENTIALISM, utilitarianism, emotivism, and situation ethics proved to have tremendous influence, for both good and bad. These traditions had a good influence in calling more attention to the personal and subjective factors entering into every real moral decision, and thus assisting in the assessment of the actual moral responsibility in individual real-life situations. They also helped moralists, priests, and counselors in general to be more aware of the many complications of real-life problems and to see that a mere restatement of a universal negative precept of the divine law is not an adequate explanation for many such problems; when possible, help must be given to find alternative solutions that would be morally acceptable.

But existentialism also had a bad influence in a number of ways that called forth warnings and condemnations by Pius XII and the Holy Office in the 1950s. The ATHEISM of the extremists in the movement seems to have led some Christian and even some Catholic writers to leave all consideration of God out of morality and to make morality merely a matter of deciding what best integrates an individual's own personality. Even when God is taken into account, some proponents of a school of thought such as situation ethics tended to make morality into merely a personal dialogue with God in which the individual tries to feel what God would have us do in a given situation, while omitting all consideration of revelation and the teaching authority of the Church. Milder forms of bad influence appeared in writers of the emotivist school of ethics who tended to neglect basic principles and rely more on sentiment and emotion in making moral decisions.

Summary. To sum up the trends prior to the Second Vatican Council: There was a definite effort on the part of most moral theologians to be more theological and biblical, less philosophical and abstract; to be more positive in approach and emphasis, less negative; to treat morality more as a personal response to the divine call, less as something that could be calibrated merely by reflection on human nature. The ideal seemed to lie in a delicate balance of the various elements, without letting the new emphasis entirely eliminate the less important but still necessary elements.

SEE ALSO EXEGESIS, BIBLICAL; KERYGMATIC THEOLOGY; MORAL THEOLOGY; MORAL THEOLOGY, HISTORY OF (TO 700); MORAL THEOLOGY, HISTORY OF (700 TO VATICAN COUNCIL I); MORAL THEOLOGY, HISTORY OF (TRENDS SINCE VATICAN II); MORAL THEOLOGY, METHODOLOGY OF; SITUATION (SITUS).

BIBLIOGRAPHY

F. Böckle, ed., *Moral Problems and Christian Personalism* (New York 1965).

Raymond F. Bulman and Frederick J. Parrella, eds., *From Trent to Vatican II: Historical and Theological Investigations* (New York 2006).

Francis J. Connell, *Outlines of Moral Theology* (Milwaukee 1953).

Charles E. Curran, *The Origins of Moral Theology in the United States: Three Different Approaches* (Washington, D.C. 1997).

John C. Ford and Gerald A. Kelly, *Contemporary Moral Theology*, 2 vols. (Westminster, Md. 1958–1963).

John A. Gallagher, *Time Past, Time Future: An Historical Study of Catholic Moral Theology* (New York 1990).

Gérard Gilleman, *The Primacy of Charity in Moral Theology* (Westminster, Md. 1959).

Bernhard Häring, *Christian Renewal in a Changing World: A New Approach to Moral Theology* (New York 1964).

John Mahoney, *The Making of Moral Theology: A Study of the Roman Catholic Tradition* (New York 1987).

Dominic M. Prümmer, *Handbook of Moral Theology* (New York 1957).

George Weigel, *The Truth of Catholicism: Ten Controversies Explored* (New York 2001).

Rev. Joseph James Farraher SJ
Professor of Moral and Pastoral Theology and Rector of
Alma College, Los Gatos, California
Advocate, Archdiocesan Tribunal of San Francisco

Rev. Joseph W. Koterski SJ
Professor, Department of Philosophy
Fordham University, N.Y. (2009)

MORAL THEOLOGY, HISTORY OF (TRENDS SINCE VATICAN II)

Moral theology has been an arena of vigorous discussion and lively debate throughout the period beginning with VATICAN COUNCIL II (1962–1965). Wholly new questions emerged in such areas as MEDICAL ETHICS and BIOETHICS, and new approaches have been developed for some long-standing questions. Moral theologians during this period have taken divergent stands on proper methodology as well as on substantive questions. Mindful of the Church's need to be a moral teacher ever faithful to CHRIST, the TEACHING AUTHORITY OF THE CHURCH (MAGISTERIUM) has issued a series of important documents on moral matters, including Pope PAUL VI's *Humanae vitae* (1968) and Pope JOHN PAUL II's *Veritatis splendor* (1993) and *Evangelium vitae* (1995).

Vatican Council II. None of the sixteen documents of Vatican II is directed primarily to moral theology or its methodology, but many of its documents touch on this area, especially *Gaudium et spes*, *Dignitatis humanae*, and *Optatam totius*. For a proper understanding of the impact of the council on moral theology, however, one must consider not only the actual conciliar documents but also the renewal of the Church that the council initiated and the way in which the council and its documents have been interpreted. Pope JOHN XXIII's hope for an AGGIORNAMENTO (opening up) has been operative in moral theology as much as anywhere else in the Church.

Each POPE elected since the close of Vatican II (not only John Paul II and Pope BENEDICT XVI but even the briefly reigning Pope JOHN PAUL I) included in their inaugural addresses the intention of implementing the directives of the council. Mindful of the trend to claim "the spirit of Vatican II" for revisionist perspectives on moral theology and other aspects of ecclesial life, John Paul II devoted much of his PAPACY to promoting a sense of the continuity between the pre- and postconciliar periods of the Church's history. His pre-papal book *Sources of Renewal* (1980), written while he served as the cardinal ARCHBISHOP of Krakow, Poland, offers a hermeneutic for the proper understanding of the council. The range of opinions on the proper way to interpret Vatican II is evident in the difference of perspective taken in the five-volume history of the council published by scholars from the so-called School of Bologna (under the direction of Giuseppe Alberigo from 1995 to 2001) when compared with the counterpoint provided by such scholars as Agostino Marchetto (2005). In addition to the historiographical debates about the council's actual proceedings, there is a debate about whether Vatican II should be understood as an event in an open-ended process of ongoing development or as a set of documents that should be regarded as determinative for the governance of the Church and for the direction of theological inquiry, including moral theology, for the foreseeable future.

In addressing the relation of the Church to the world, *Gaudium et spes* stands squarely within the tradition of Catholic social teaching that has been articulated mainly through papal encyclicals. This conciliar document references LEO XIII's *Rerum novarum* (1891), PIUS XI's *Quadragesimo anno* (1931) and *Casti connubii* (1931), and John XXIII's *Mater et magistra* (1961) and *Pacem in terris* (1963). As a preparation for its substantive comments on marriage and family (*Gaudium et spes*, II, 47–51), cultural development (II, 53–62), economics (III, 63–72), politics (IV, 73–76), and war and PEACE (V, 78–87), it develops at length the themes of the inviolable dignity of the human person (I, 12–22), the common good (II, 23–32), authentic and inauthentic notions of freedom and autonomy (III, 33–39), and the difference between justice and social charity (IV, 40–45).

The structure of the argument that *Gaudium et spes* provides is typical of Catholic moral theology in the period after Vatican II: The resolution of ethical problems requires clarity about the principles of MORALITY, and the principles of morality ultimately depend on a certain version of the human person as made in the image of GOD. The distinctive status of human beings among God's creatures bestows an inviolable moral dignity on every person, regardless of age or abilities. The theological basis for the argument is found in a vision of humankind as created in God's likeness, fallen in sin, and redeemed in Christ; the philosophical basis for the argumentation relies on NATURAL LAW REASONING and on PERSONALISM.

Recurrent in the text of *Gaudium et spes* is the assertion of various fundamental human rights. The ENCYCLICAL makes free use of terminology appropriated from modern political PHILOSOPHY but puts this terminology into a religious framework. The conciliar declaration on religious liberty, *Dignitatis humanae*, also employs the language of human rights. Whereas earlier papal statements such as *Quanta cura* (1864) of Pope PIUS IX and *Mirari vos* (1832) of Pope GREGORY XVI condemned the term *religious freedom* when understood in the sense of religious indifferentism, *Dignitatis humanae* asserts that religious freedom is a basic human right needed for seeking the TRUTH about God and for offering proper WORSHIP (*Dignitatis humanae*, 2). Careful analysis of the text does not support the allegation voiced in circles suspicious of Vatican II that this position contradicts earlier magisterial teaching and thereby undermines the legitimacy of the council. The apparent contradiction can be resolved by noting that the term *religious freedom* is being used for quite different things. For example, in the earlier texts the term refers to a slogan in the propaganda of antireligious forces, but in the conciliar text religious freedom describes a condition indispensable in the practice of religion in secular society. Regarding the history of moral theology, the conciliar use of the language of rights in documents such as these modeled a concern with human rights and political structures that would influence much of the moral theology written in the second half of the twentieth century.

The Second Vatican Council's greatest contribution to the methodology of moral theology came, however, in *Optatam totius*, its decree on the training of priests. In the revival of Catholic thought that took the form of NEOSCHOLASTICISM AND NEOTHOMISM after Leo XI-II's *Aeterni Patris* (1890), moral theology had acquired a sound philosophical footing in NATURAL LAW theory. But the textbooks and manuals in use during the first half of the twentieth century seldom used biblical sources except in the presentation of brief proof-texts. *Optatam totius* (V, 17) calls for "the perfecting of moral theology" by a return to the sources of moral knowledge, so that "its scientific presentation should draw more fully on the teaching of holy Scripture and should throw light on the exalted vocation of the faithful in Christ and their obligation to bring forth fruit in charity for the life of the world."

Controversy over Humanae vitae. The organic development of moral theology along the lines envisioned by *Optatam totius* might have proceeded more smoothly had there not been such a sharp reaction to Paul VI's defense of the Church's long-standing condemnation of CONTRACEPTION in *Humanae vitae*. The reaction to this encyclical was not limited to the topic of birth control but quickly expanded to a controversy over moral methodology (Smith 1991, 1993; Odozor, 2003). At issue was a question about whether there is a distinctive Christian morality by reason of something that FAITH adds to the demands of the natural law. The debate has numerous facets: Is there a distinctive "faith ethics" (*Glaubensethik*), or does faith play mainly a parenetic role to motivate moral action? If ETHICS is independent of faith, what are the contours and the limits of this "autonomous ethics"? Does "nature" play any role in disclosing ethical obligations, or does recognition of any role for nature in morality compromise the legitimate claims of human autonomy? There is much evidence of influence on moral theologians from contemporary philosophy, especially through the Kantian and existentialist emphasis on autonomy and their repudiation of natural law thinking as intrinsically heteronomous (in the sense of requiring adherence to a standard prior to human choice). Although dissenters from *Humanae vitae* claimed to be the proponents of personalist values, it has proven to be moralists committed to personalism and to the renewal of moral theology by the unification of

enriched biblical theology and metaphysically informed philosophy who have supported *Humanae vitae* more strongly than those who initially championed "personalist values."

Many of the moral theologians who objected to *Humanae vitae* explained that they did so in the name of personalist values and on rational grounds. Taking their cue from the statements in *Gaudium et spes* that listed the mutual LOVE of spouses and the procreation of offspring as parallel ends of marriage, rather than prioritizing procreation (II, 48–51), they argued that contraception might be helpful, or even necessary, to preserve a marriage or to promote the mutual love of the spouses for one another. Methodologically, they tended to accentuate the role of personal CONSCIENCE in decision-making and to stress autonomy as essential to the dignity of free rational agents. They often dismissed natural law argumentation against contraception as a kind of physicalism excessively dependent on biology for drawing ethical conclusions, and they warned against appeals to the authority of the Church in these matters as "paternalistic" (see Smith 1991, 1993 and Odozer 2003). The rationalistic character of the dissent from *Humanae vitae* in certain respects resembles the very tendencies toward minimalism and legalism in some texts of the manual tradition from before Vatican II and shows little sign of the biblical leavening of moral theology called for by *Optatam totius*.

In the decades following the 1960s, many moral theologians developed positions on other moral questions that manifested a similar independence from magisterial authority and an opposition to natural law reasoning. There were also a number of social movements that emerged from the new ways of viewing moral theology. For instance, in the emphasis placed on "the social Gospel" and the need for solidarity with the poor, some proponents of LIBERATION THEOLOGY often claimed that what the tradition had seen as the obligations of charity were really obligations of justice. Some proponents of this position yoked their espousal of social change to Marxism and communism and conflated oppressive political authority with the moral authority of the Church (see Ellacuría and Sobrino 1993). Likewise, secular movements such as FEMINISM challenged numerous points of traditional Catholicism, including its male priesthood and its defense of heterosexual marriage. Some feminist moral theologians of this period adopted the philosophical strategies of DECONSTRUCTIONISM and postmodernism for the critique of positions that they took to be the arbitrary imposition of repressive structures by patriarchal authorities (see Schüssler-Fiorenza 1996; Miller 1995). The sexual revolution that swept the West found theological voice in some moralists who argued for a change in the Church's positions, not just on contraception but on such topics as remarriage after DIVORCE, HOMOSEXUALITY, and MASTURBATION (see Kosnik 1977; Grabowski 2003).

Proportionalism. The theoretical underpinnings of the revisionist position generally took the form of proportionalism (see Hoose 1987; Kaczor 2002). In fundamental moral theology, this approach was developed by such thinkers as Louis JANSSENS, Bruno Schüller, Josef FUCHS, and Peter Knauer (1935–) in Europe and by Charles Curran and Richard A. MCCORMICK in the United States. Using the distinction between a "classicist mentality" and "historical consciousness" that was popularized by Bernard LONERGAN (1990), the revisionist approach questioned the notion that some acts are intrinsically EVIL and inherently immoral because of the very nature of the action and regardless of the intentions of the agent. Where traditional moral theology has insisted that every deliberate human act must be evaluated in terms of its object (the end of the action), its intention (the end of the agent), and its circumstances (see *Catechism of the Catholic Church*, §1750, §§1756–1757, and *Veritatis splendor*, II, 74), the revisionist position regards an act as "pre-moral" and argues that no type of action can be universally prohibited independently of a reckoning of the consequences in specific circumstances and the particular intentions of specific human beings. For the resolution of such questions, they have promoted the principle of proportionality to argue that "premoral evil" may be done for a proportionate reason. An important source for tracing the history of the development of revisionist moral theology is "Notes on Moral Theology" that have appeared in *Theological Studies*, written for many years by Richard A. McCormick (1981, 1984) and more recently by various other scholars.

One school of thought that has taken issue with this methodological position is the so-called "new natural law theory" associated with Germain Grisez (1983–1997) and John Finnis (1991), among others. Taking the view that the basic human goods are incommensurable and that none of them may ever be violated, these authors argue that there can never be a proportionate reason for acting against a basic human good. In their view the proportionalists have turned moral theology into a religious form of the utilitarian calculation of values. Proponents of more traditional forms of natural law thinking, such as Russell Hittinger (1987, 2003), share this objection to proportionalism, even while disagreeing with the penchant of the new natural law theorists to rely on reason to the exclusion of nature in formulating its moral argumentation. A theological form of virtue ethics (see Melina 2001; Pinckaers 1995; Cessario 1991) has tried to bring balance and perspective to moral theology by stressing the importance of the natural and SUPERNATURAL virtues for a properly ordered moral

life, and theologians such as Paul Quay (1975, 1985) and Bartholomew Kiely (1985) have provided penetrating critiques of proportionalist moral theories by exhibiting their intrinsic contradictions.

Papal Correctives. At various points during this period the papacy has found the revisionist program in moral theology a sufficiently serious challenge to warrant explicit correction. A comprehensive summary of official Catholic teaching on matters of morality can be found in the *Catechism of the Catholic Church*, Part III, "Life in Christ." In addition, there have been many more specific pronouncements, including the 1975 declaration *Persona humana* issued by the Congregation for the DOCTRINE OF THE FAITH, which reaffirmed traditional Catholic teachings on sexual morality, such as the need for marital fidelity and the intrinsic disorder of masturbation. On the question of homosexuality it emphasized a distinction between inclination and activity that is crucial for the proper pastoral care of homosexual persons (VIII).

John Paul II's *Veritatis splendor* (1993) not only addressed questions of the proper methodology for moral theology but also returned attention to the often neglected directive in *Optatam totius* about joining a systematic return to the biblical sources of moral knowledge with a careful use of philosophical argumentation, especially as drawn from natural law theory and personalism, properly understood. The opening chapter of *Veritatis splendor* presents an extensive reflection on the dialogue between Christ and the rich young man (Mt 19), and its final chapter makes use of other biblical texts to encourage a proper moral ordering for one's life by seeking true freedom in Christ. The opening chapter counters a minimalist understanding of morality in terms of law and obligation with the fuller understanding of morality in terms of VIRTUE and perfection. It brings out the interconnection between the first and second tablets of the decalogue (that is, the commandments about serving God and those that deal with respect for other human beings) as well as the indispensability of divine assistance, both for keeping the Ten COMMANDMENTS and for living the sort of life described in the Beatitudes, a prospect that might seem too difficult without the help of the grace of God, with whom "all things are possible" (I, 22, quoting Mt 19:26; see also Pinckaers 1995).

The lengthy second chapter of *Veritatis splendor* takes up four errors that the pope found to be prominent in much modern moral theology. By bringing to bear reflection on such scriptural lessons as the choice between good and evil in the Garden of Eden (Gn 2) and the reminder by St. Paul that it is never licit to do evil that good may come (Rom 3:8), the pope made a careful distinction between authentic and inauthentic presentations of certain crucial moral concepts. First, there is need to distinguish between legitimate and illegitimate forms of autonomy (II, 35–53). Human freedom is not compromised by respecting the moral law but is directed to its true fulfillment and enhanced by the self-mastery that is promoted by the law's guidance.

Second, CONSCIENCE (*Veritatis splendor*, II, 54–64) should not be understood merely in terms of sincere conformity to one's chosen principles but in terms of judgments that need to be made in accord with divine law and natural law. The basic principles of morality are in principle knowable to anyone by the use of reason, for human nature is universal across cultural differences. Because cultures, like individuals, can progress or regress in maturity, however, the divine law accessible through revelation makes clear various important moral truths. The pope emphasized the importance of conscience as the privileged place for dialogue between the individual and God. He also emphasized the need of each person to work at the proper formation of conscience by learning the objective truth about morality. A properly formed conscience will help to protect the human dignity of a life lived according to God's will and to avoid subjective errors about what is morally good and evil that can destroy moral dignity.

Third, moral theologians should not confuse the highly praiseworthy ideal of a free commitment of the whole of one's life to God with the revisionist notion of "fundamental option" understood in the sense of some generic intention that is broad enough to give moral coloration to all subsequent actions (*Veritatis splendor*, II, 65–70). Directed against the notion of a calculation of value by the weighing of pre-moral goods and evils, this portion of the encyclical insists it is always the deliberate choices of a concrete kind of behavior in particular circumstances that will give expression to a fundamental option and thereby realize any such life-orientation that a person wishes to make. The section on mortal and venial sin (II, 69–70) is especially important in light of various challenges to the validity of these concepts in some quarters.

Finally, *Veritatis splendor* reaffirms that proper moral evaluation of human acts needs to make use of the traditional categories, namely, consideration of the "object" of an action (the end to which an action is directed, regardless of the intention of the agent), the "intention" (the end of the agent by virtue of deliberation and choice), and the "circumstances" in which the action occurs (II–III, 71–104). Moral theologians should thus distinguish between proper and improper notions of teleology, so as to give due weight to the consideration of the consequences of action without reducing moral reasoning solely to some form of utilitarian calculation of values. The section on "intrinsic evil" (II, 79–82) cor-

rects the tendency to abandon or falsely interpret the concept of teleology in proportionalist forms of moral theology by rehearsing the list of intrinsically evil acts that is provided in Vatican II's *Gaudium et spes*, I, 27.

The observations of *Veritatis splendor* on fundamental moral theology have been applied to a wide variety of topics. Of special note is John Paul II's *Evangelium vitae* (1995), which again employs the technique of extensive recourse to exegesis and biblical theology in its opening chapters on the story of Cain and Abel (Gn 4) in 7–28. John Paul II uses this and other passages from the Old Testament and the New Testament (29–51) to set the stage for careful explanations of the absolute prohibition on the private use of lethal force against the innocent. Special sections are included on procured ABORTION (58–63) and EUTHANASIA (64–67), and there are carefully nuanced discussions on the relation of law and morality (68–77) as well as on the questions of legitimate self-defense (55) and of CAPITAL PUNISHMENT (56).

There have also been further encyclicals on Catholic social teaching in the wake of *Gaudium et spes*. Paul VI's *Octagesima adveniens* and *Populorum progressio* reinforced the Vatican Council II's teaching that vigorous efforts at cultural and economic development will help to make efforts at evangelization all the more credible. John Paul II's *Laborem exercens* (1981), *Sollicitudo rei socialis* (1987), and *Centesimus annus* (1989) have contributed to the tradition in important ways. They recognize the possibilities for human dignity in honest work and in the forms of participation that come with DEMOCRACY. They also identify some of the challenges to morality that come from a forgetfulness of God and morality in a prosperous consumerist society, including the problems that can arise for the protection of individuals and minorities from majority rule in democratic polities. One of the great themes of both papal and conciliar expressions of Catholic social teaching is that the family is at the heart of society and that personal and social morality are deeply intertwined, not separate spheres that can be treated in isolation.

Sollicitudo rei socialis is especially important for its reminder that authentic human development is not simply a matter of material and economic progress, but also of religious and human formation in the broad sense. It corrects the Marxist charge that belief in God is a source of human alienation by showing that faith in God leads to the fulfillment of the human vocation for self-donation and that union with God is ultimately the answer to the problems of human life. The first encyclical of Benedict XVI, *Deus caritas est* (2005), has also taken up the theme of Catholic social teaching by giving special attention to the intrinsic connection between properly ordered love in personal morality (I, 2–18) and properly ordered social charity (II, 19–39). In this encyclical, as in *Spe salvi* (2007), the pope shows a deeply Augustinian sense of the distinction between what St. augustine called "the two cities" for the proper understanding of the spheres of justice and of charity in moral theology (esp. II, 19–28).

An extremely fruitful approach that is becoming increasingly evident in the most recent writings on Catholic moral theology is the theology of the BODY. Initiated by the weekly addresses John Paul II delivered early in his papacy (John Paul II 2006), the theology of the body has stimulated much speculative and practice work by other thinkers. John Paul II's own contribution includes his extensive reflection on such biblical texts as the story of the creation of Adam and Eve in Genesis, the texts from the Gospel of Matthew on marriage and divorce, the texts from St. Paul on sexuality and the body, and *Humanae vitae*. The philosophical sources for his work include both the contributions of phenomenological REALISM, in the spirit of Max SCHELER and Dietrich von HILDEBRAND, and of THOMISM, with special reliance on the analysis of the HUMAN ACT, moral virtue, and the proper ordering of loves. His development of such concepts as original innocence, the proper role of SHAME, the way in which bodily action expresses the person, and the spousal meaning of the body has been the source of much fruit for moral theology.

In summary, the more rationalist approach of those continuing to pursue the revisionist project in moral theology (see Salzman 1999) has made some of their results hard to distinguish from that of secular ethicians. The most recent works in moral theology that have been produced with stronger connections to the Church's magisterium have profited much from the recent papal and conciliar contributions to moral theology, including work on many contemporary moral problems in which it remains crucial to distinguish carefully between perennially valid moral principles and prudential judgments that are made in the attempts to apply those principles.

SEE ALSO AETERNI PATRIS; BODY, THEOLOGY OF; CASTI CONNUBII; CENTESIMUS ANNUS; COMMON GOOD AND CATHOLIC SOCIAL TEACHING, THE; DEUS CARITAS EST; EVANGELIUM VITAE; HUMANAE VITAE; LABOREM EXERCENS; MATER ET MAGISTRA; NATURAL LAW IN POLITICAL THOUGHT; PACEM IN TERRIS; PERSONALIST ETHICS; POPULORUM PROGRESSIO; QUADRAGESIMO ANNO; RERUM NOVARUM; REVISIONIST THEOLOGY; SOLLICITUDO REI SOCIALIS; TELEOLOGICAL ETHICS; VERITATIS SPLENDOR.

BIBLIOGRAPHY

Giuseppe Alberigo, ed., *Storia del Concilio Vaticano II* [History of Vatican Council II], 5 vols. (Bologna, Italy 1995–2001). English version, *History of Vatican II,* edited by Joseph A. Komonchak, translated by Matthew J. O'Connell (Maryknoll, N.Y. 1995–2006).

T. A. Cavanaugh, *Double-Effect Reasoning: Doing Good and Avoiding Evil* (New York 2006).

Romanus Cessario, *The Moral Virtues and Theological Ethics* (Notre Dame, Ind. 1991).

Charles E. Curran, *Tensions in Moral Theology* (Notre Dame, Ind. 1988).

Charles E. Curran and Richard A. McCormick, eds., *The Distinctiveness of Christian Ethics* (New York 1980).

Charles E. Curran and Richard A. McCormick, eds., *The Historical Development of Fundamental Moral Theology in the United States* (New York 1999).

Joseph A. DiNoia and Romanus Cessario, eds., *Veritatis Splendor and the Renewal of Moral Theology* (Princeton, N.J. 1999).

Ignacio Ellacuría and Jon Sobrino, eds., *Mysterium liberationis: Fundamental Concepts of Liberation Theology* (Maryknoll, N.Y. 1993).

John Finnis, *Moral Absolutes: Tradition, Revision, and Truth* (Washington, D.C. 1991).

Josef Fuchs, *Personal Responsibility and Christian Morality,* translated by William Cleves et al. (Washington, D.C. 1983).

John A. Gallagher, *Time Past, Time Future: An Historical Study of Catholic Moral Theology* (New York 1990).

John S. Grabowski, *Sex and Virtue: An Introduction to Sexual Ethics* (Washington, D.C. 2003).

Germain G. Grisez, *The Way of the Lord Jesus,* 3 vols. (Chicago 1983–1997).

Bernhard Häring, *Free and Faithful in Christ: Moral Theology for Clergy and Laity,* 3 vols. (New York 1978–1981).

Bernhard Häring, *The Law of Christ: Moral Theology for Priests and Laity,* translated by Edwin G. Kaiser (Westminster, Md. 1961).

Kristin E. Heyer, *Prophetic & Public: The Social Witness of U.S. Catholicism* (Washington, D.C. 2006).

Russell Hittinger, *A Critique of the New Natural Law Theory* (Notre Dame, Ind. 1987).

Russell Hittinger, *The First Grace: Rediscovering the Natural Law in a Post–Christian World* (Wilmington, Del. 2003).

Bernard Hoose, *Proportionalism: The American Debate and Its European Roots* (Washington, D.C. 1987).

John Paul II, *Man and Woman He Created Them: A Theology of the Body,* edited and translated by Michael M. Waldstein (Boston 2006).

Christopher R. Kaczor, *Proportionalism and the Natural Law Tradition* (Washington, D.C. 2002).

Bartholomew M. Kiely, "The Impracticality of Proportionalism," *Gregorianum* 66, no. 4 (1985): 655–686.

Peter Knauer, *Handlungsnetze: Über das Grundprinzip der Ethik* (Frankfurt-am-Main, Germany 2002).

Peter Knauer, "The Hermeneutic Function of the Principle of Double Effect," *Natural Law Forum* (now *American Journal of Jurisprudence*) 12 (1967): 132–162.

Anthony Kosnik, ed., *Human Sexuality: New Directions in American Catholic Thought,* A Study Commissioned by the Catholic Theological Society of America (New York 1977).

Bernard J.F. Lonergan, *Method in Theology* (Toronto 1990).

John Mahoney, *The Making of Moral Theology: A Study of the Roman Catholic Tradition* (New York 1987).

Agostino Marchetto, *Il Concilio Ecumenico Vaticano II: Contrappunto per la sua storia* [The Second Vatican Ecumenical Council: A Counterpoint to the History of the Council] (Rome 2005).

David Matzko McCarthy, "Moral Theology" in *The Blackwell Companion to Catholicism*, edited by James J. Buckley, Frederick C. Bauerschmidt, and Trent Pomplun (Malden, Mass. 2007).

Richard A. McCormick, *Notes on Moral Theology: 1965 through 1980*, composed of articles originally appearing in *Theological Studies* (Washington, D.C. 1981).

Richard A. McCormick, *Notes on Moral Theology: 1981 through 1984* (Lanham, Md. 1984).

Livio Melina, *Sharing in Christ's Virtues: For a Renewal of Moral Theology in Light of* Veritatis splendor, translated by William E. May (Washington, D.C. 2001).

Monica Migliorino Miller, ed., *Sexuality and Authority in the Catholic Church* (Scranton, Pa. 1995).

Paulinus Ikechukwu Odozor, *Moral Theology in an Age of Renewal: A Study of the Catholic Tradition since Vatican II* (Notre Dame, Ind. 2003).

Servais Pinckaers, *The Sources of Christian Ethics*, translated from the 3rd ed. by Sr. Mary Thomas Noble (Washington, D.C. 1995).

Paul M. Quay, "The Disvalue of Ontic Evil," *Theological Studies* 46, no. 2 (1985): 262–286.

Paul M. Quay, "Morality by Calculation of Values," *Theology Digest* 23, no. 4 (1975): 347–365.

Todd A. Salzman, ed., *Method and Catholic Moral Theology: The Ongoing Reconstruction* (Omaha, Neb. 1999).

Bruno Schüller, *Wholly Human: Essays on the Theory and Language of Morality*, translated by Peter Heinegg (Washington, D.C. 1986).

Elisabeth Schüssler-Fiorenza, ed., *The Power of Naming: A Concilium Reader in Feminist Liberation Theology* (Maryknoll, N.Y. 1996).

Joseph A. Selling, Franz Böckle, et al., eds., *Personalist Morals: Essays in Honor of Professor Louis Janssens* (Louvain, Belgium 1988).

Janet E. Smith, Humanae Vitae: *A Generation Later* (Washington, D.C. 1991).

Janet E. Smith, ed., *Why Humanae Vitae Was Right: A Reader* (San Francisco 1993).

Karol Wojtyła, *Sources of Renewal: The Implementation of Vatican II*, translated by P. S. Falla (San Francisco 1980).

VATICAN DOCUMENTS

Benedict XVI, *Deus caritas est*, On Christian Love (Encyclical, December 25, 2005), available from http://www.vatican.va/holy_father/benedict_xvi/encyclicals/documents/hf_ben-xvi_enc_20051225_deus-caritas-est-en.html (accessed April 8, 2008).

Catechism of the Catholic Church (Rome 1993), available from http://www.vatican.va/archive/ENG0015/_INDEX.HTM (accessed April 8, 2008).

Congregation for the Doctrine of the Faith, *Persona humana*, On Certain Questions Concerning Sexual Ethics (Declaration, December 29, 1975), available from http://www.vatican.va/roman_curia/congregations/cfaith/documents/rc_con_cfaith_doc_19751229_persona-humana_en.html (accessed April 8, 2008).

John Paul II, *Evangelium vitae*, On the Value and Inviolability of Human Life (Encyclical, March 25, 1995), available from http://www.vatican.va/edocs/ENG0141/_INDEX.HTM (accessed April 8, 2008).

John Paul II, *Veritatis splendor* (Encyclical, August 6, 1993), available from http://www.vatican.va/edocs/ENG0222/_INDEX.HTM (accessed April 8, 2008).

Paul VI, *Humanae vitae*, On the Regulation of Birth (Encyclical, July 25, 1968), available from http://www.vatican.va/holy_father/paul_vi/encyclicals/documents/hf_p-vi_enc_25071968_humanae-vitae_en.html (accessed April 8, 2008).

Vatican Council II, *Dignitatis humanae*, On the Right of the Person and of Communities to Social and Civil Freedom in Matters Religious (Declaration, December 7, 1965), available from http://www.vatican.va/archive/hist_councils/ii_vatican_council/documents/vat-ii_decl_19651207_dignitatis-humanae_en.html (accessed April 8, 2008).

Vatican Council II, *Gaudium et spes*, On the Church in the Modern World (Constitution, December 7, 1965), available from http://www.vatican.va/archive/hist_councils/ii_vatican_council/documents/vat-ii_cons_19651207_gaudium-et-spes_en.html (accessed April 8, 2008).

Vatican Council II, *Optatam totius*, On Priestly Training (Decree, October 28, 1965), available from http://www.vatican.va/archive/hist_councils/ii_vatican_council/documents/vat-ii_decree_19651028_optatam-totius_en.html (accessed April 8, 2008).

Rev. Joseph W. Koterski SJ
Professor, Department of Philosophy
Fordham University, N.Y. (2009)

MUḤAMMAD

Founder of the religion of ISLAM; b. MECCA, ARABIA, c. AD 570; d. MEDINA, Arabia, 632. His life is generally divided into three periods: (1) his early life, the period of about forty years before he received his prophetic call; (2) his first, or Meccan, period as PROPHET of Islam, dating from his first revelations and public appearances declaring his message (about 610) and extending to 622, the date of his flight from Mecca to Medina (known as the HIJRA, or emigration); and (3) his second, or Medinese, period as prophet and statesman, during which he firmly established Islam as a religion and a state, between 622 and his death in 632.

Early Life. Muḥammad's father died before his birth, and at age six he lost his mother. During his earliest years he was entrusted to the care of his paternal grandfather, 'Abd-al-Muṭṭalib (d. 578), and later came under the protection of his paternal uncle Abu Ṭalib. The Hashim clan into which he was born was a part of the Quraysh tribe, then prominent in Mecca. It was in fact among the more important constituents of the Quraysh, although clearly below the two leading families of Makhzum and 'Umayyah. In spite of their social prominence, however, the Hashimites had grown relatively poor just before Muḥammad's birth, and indications are that his early years as an orphan were spent under conditions rather miserable, even for the times. Although later generations would cultivate a biographical tradition marked by edifying narratives such as the famous BAHIRA LEGEND, little reliable information concerning his youth has come down in the ISLAMIC TRADITIONS (ḤADITH). What is certain, however, is that as a young man Muḥammad engaged in commerce and trade, perhaps to the extent of participating in trade caravans to Syria, and that his financial situation improved substantially when, at the age of about 25, he received a marriage proposal from his employer, a rich merchant's widow named Khadijah (c. 595–619). By her he had four daughters who lived to maturity and a son who died in infancy.

Home to a prestigious religious sanctuary, at the heart of which lay the cube-shaped shrine known as the Ka'bah, Mecca was a place of religious pilgrimage for many neighboring tribes. Because of an upset in the old overland trade routes caused by incessant warring between the Byzantine and Persian empires, it had also recently emerged as a bustling and prosperous center of commerce. At the same time, however, by the time of Muḥammad the city seems to have been suffering from a desperate malaise. This was almost certainly brought about in part by rapid economic changes that upset the traditional social equilibrium formerly maintained by the increasingly irrelevant egalitarian tribal values of the Arabian steppe.

Religious Setting. There is little doubt that Muḥammad was well acquainted with the idolatrous beliefs and practices that were commonly adhered to by his tribe, by most of the citizens of Mecca, and by much of Arabia. Also, it is clear that Muḥammad gradually came to be appalled at the absurdities of PAGAN worship and the low level of pagan morals around him—seen, for instance, in the live burial of female infants. The extent of his knowledge of Arabian Jews and Christians during his early years is much more difficult to determine, although it is reasonable to assume that he encountered members of the Abrahamic faiths while working as a

caravanner. Perhaps more significant is the often-advanced argument that Muḥammad was influenced by a small group of men—which may have included his wife's cousin Waraqa ibn Nawfal, identified as having been a Christian hermit—who thought of themselves as *ḥunafa'* (the pure ones) and who favored a monotheism of a somewhat syncretistic nature that tended toward neither JUDAISM nor Christianity. It was perhaps the essential simplicity and the syncretistic quality of the *ḥanif* views that impressed Muḥammad deeply enough to prompt him to withdraw into SOLITUDE more frequently to meditate on them. For this purpose he developed a habit of going up to a cave on *Ḥira'*, a small mountain near the city. There he had an experience that completely changed his own life and profoundly affected the course of human history.

Meccan Period. According to Muslim tradition, it was during one such solitary retreat, in the sacred month of Ramadan in the year 610, that he is reported to have experienced a personal vision of, or encounter with, a spiritual force that commanded him, "Recite!" to which he replied, "What shall I recite?" According to later interpretations concerned with proving him illiterate and thereby establishing more firmly the veracity of the QUR'AN as his confirmatory miracle, he said, "I cannot recite [read]." There followed the revelation of the first part of Qur'an 96 or, according to other versions of the tradition, 68, 74, or 93.

At first, Muḥammad was frightened, incredulous, and unsure of the meaning of this experience. It required persuasion from his wife and close associates before he was convinced that he had actually received a revelation from God. As a basic article of faith, Muslim tradition has maintained that all of the revelations of the Qur'an were delivered to Muḥammad through the medium of the Archangel GABRIEL and that he memorized them, but never wrote them out, for his disciples. Critical scholarship has tended to take the opposite view. In any case, after his first doubts Muḥammad never again questioned that his revelations were in a literal sense the word of God. He seems to have believed, with assistance from the revelations in the Muslim view, that he was not to be considered inspired (let alone divine), but rather the vehicle through whom God and his angel were dictating a final revelation, a redaction of previous revelations whose authenticity he never challenged, to the Arabs and to all mankind. That dictation came in parts—*ayat*, or verses, in Arabic-from a heavenly archetype over a period of some two decades. Muḥammad was both a messenger (*rasul*) and a prophet (*nabi*), indeed the last of the prophets, as the Qur'an itself eventually came to assert.

Early Chapters of the Qur'an. The temper of the earliest chapters (*sura*) of the Qur'an is simple and fiery, strongly eschatological in tone, warning of an impending day of judgment when God will weigh every man's deeds and consign him to either eternal bliss or HELLFIRE. The nature of Muḥammad's message as conveyed is mainly a warning to men of their sins, more particularly to the Meccans against polytheism and social injustice. One supreme God, ALLAH, best understood by most contemporaries as *ilah* (god, with the definite article), whose attributes and statements identified him as the God of the Jews and the Christians, demanded surrender of men's wills to himself (and thus *islam*, submission). He commanded men to heed his ancient call, reform, purify their actions, and unify in faith and mutual brotherhood. No longer was one to act on the whim of vain fancy and tribal custom, but rather to lead a life of moral discipline and pious SOBRIETY. He reminded some (and told most for the first time) that there is an AFTERLIFE in which, after judgment, men will continue forever in a state of punishment or felicity. During these years they clearly were not regarded by Muḥammad and his followers as the basis of a new religion per se but rather as a proof and continuation of the ancient religion of the patriarch Abraham (early second millenium BC) within which the Arabs, too, had a noble destiny as his sons through the line of Abraham's son Ishmael.

Opposition at Mecca. Unfortunately for all concerned, but chiefly for Muḥammad himself, his message and claims were met either with indifference and scoffing or with general, swift, and powerful opposition. The pagan Meccans, including most of Muḥammad's well-to-do relatives, took his vivid warnings very much to heart, but not as he intended. They immediately set about organizing resistance to Muḥammad and planning the elimination of his tiny group of followers, called *muslimun* (Muslims; those who have surrendered). Their reaction was justifiable inasmuch as the growth of a religious community in Mecca with principles such as Muḥammad's constituted not only an affront to ancient Arabian tradition but also a serious threat to the basis of a major source of wealth and prestige for Mecca's leading families, the custodianship of the city's lucrative pilgrimage sanctuary. The cardinal Qur'anic virtue of SOCIAL JUSTICE probably also elicited a negative reaction from a social and economic elite that thrived on the exploitation of the weaker members of Arabian society, of which as an orphan Muḥammad himself certainly had direct, bitter experience. Even worse for Muḥammad, considering the results, was the refusal of neighboring Jews and Christians to recognize in him a true prophet in the line of their common tradition.

Concessions to Paganism. At this point, interesting new material was introduced into the more recent chapters of the Qur'an, much of it seeming to aim at, or conveniently coincide with, coming to terms with the opposition. The Meccans were treated to sermons against trust in wealth, which leads only to PRIDE and hinders man from realizing his dependence upon God. On the other hand, the goddesses (al-Lat, worshipped at Ṭa'if; al-'Uzza, worshipped at Nakhlah; and Manat, whose shrine lay between Mecca and Medina) were acknowledged to be venerable "daughters of Allah" (Qur'an 22. 51) whose CULTS might therefore be expected to continue without hindrance. These devices neither convinced nor placated the Meccans, and Muḥammad was soon to regret such revelations—they were declared Satanic suggestions rather than God's revelation. Ultimately, no small number of verses in the Qur'an were abrogated in this fashion. For the benefit of Jews and Christians, the revelations embarked on fuller statements embodying items in their creeds and references to, even a few tentative narrations of, their Biblical sources. Whether this latter attempt produced more concrete results or merely promised a more fruitful line of development for Islam is impossible to determine. At any rate, it lasted well into the Medinese period.

At the same time, Muḥammad sent about eighty Muslims across the RED SEA to Abyssinia to seek refuge with the Christian negus (sovereign). Surface indications are that the increasing persecution of the Meccans alone prompted this action, but closer scrutiny suggests that Muḥammad may have been troubled over sharp differences within his community. Perhaps he hoped to prevent APOSTASY by entrusting one group with a mission to attempt to win sympathy from the negus and perhaps also the promise of military assistance, or at least the establishment of trade relations. The negus was understandably perplexed but refused the demands of the Quraysh for the forced repatriation of their refractory kinsmen. Some of them did not return to Arabia until seven years after the Hijra.

By 617 Muḥammad was obviously losing ground in Mecca. There were planned attacks and humiliations during his public preaching and severe economic boycotts against his followers. Ghettoized in a small quarter of the city and without means to obtain basic necessities such as food and clothing, about 619 he lost both the stabilizing presence of his wife, Khadijah (perhaps due to the deprivations), and the protective presence of his guardian, Abu Ṭalib, who as chief of the Hashim clan had warded off more violent steps toward destroying Muḥammad. Faced with mounting opposition, Muḥammad seemed to have only a single set of alternatives: to abandon his cause and community altogether or to find a different site in which to settle them. Reports from the Abyssinian diaspora had evidently not raised hopes of possibilities in that direction. Then a highly fortuitous opportunity presented itself.

First Followers at Medina. On occasion Muḥammad had had among his audience in Mecca various tribesmen from other parts of Arabia, and he had already asserted in clear terms that Islam was destined to unify the warring Arab tribes. During the annual pilgrimage of 620, six pilgrims from the agricultural oasis of Yathrib (later renamed Medina) met Muḥammad in Mecca and were so impressed by his personality that in the following year a larger delegation came and invited him to come to the city to serve as an arbitrator among them. Yathrib was home to at least eight strong Arab clans who controlled the oasis, although three Arabized Jewish clans, who owned much of the surrounding agricultural land, also called the city home. Over the past decade, there had been much feuding within the oasis settlement, and as a result its fragile agricultural economy was suffering. In inviting an outside and impartial arbiter with no commercial interests in the city to arbitrate their disputes, the tribal leaders of the city hoped to put an end—once and for all—to the quarrelling that threatened their livelihoods. Muḥammad readily accepted their offer and formalized the invitation with a pact, known as the Pact of al-'Aqaba, which stipulated that the members of the delegation would accept him as a prophet, obey his legislation and instructions, and avoid various types of sinful behavior. Accordingly, arrangements were made for his followers to leave Mecca unobtrusively in small groups and, finally, for his own departure on the heels of an assassination plot hatched by his opponents. On his arrival in the settlement, Muḥammad drew up and ratified an agreement with the native Yathribites, the so-called Constitution of Medina. This agreement stipulated the creation of a federation between the Meccan Muslim emigrants and the Arab tribes of Yathrib, including its three Jewish clans, all of whom vowed to protect one another against common enemies.

Medinese Period. The first day of the Arabian lunar year in which the Hijra took place, July 16, 622, was later chosen as the beginning of the Islamic era. It might at first appear strange that that date was selected in preference to that of Muḥammad's birth or first revelation, but the selection was a natural one after the fact. Islam as an independent religious community in control of its own affairs was born with the Hijra. Scholars have tended to exaggerate somewhat the difference in Muḥammad's character after the Hijra. Difference there was, but far greater was the difference in the community of Islam itself as it was transformed into a self-governing

polity at Medina, a sort of super tribe in which blood ties were subordinated to the kinship of faith.

Results of the Hijra. That transformation did not take place at once. Change was neither rapid nor general at first, for the Hijra had not by any means solved all of Muḥammad's problems. Although this early period of trial in Medina was eased by the fact that so many of the Medinese, later called the *Anṣar* (helpers), accepted Islam, Muḥammad still encountered strong opposition to his presence and his message and was not able to halt the feuding of its tribes immediately. However, Muḥammad took two particular steps at this time aimed at a bold solution to the major problems. First, he integrated as far as possible the *Muhajirun*, the emigrants who had come from Mecca, with the native population of Medina by means of employment, intermarriage, and a system of assumption of fraternal relationship. Then he attempted to win the moral support of the Jewish tribes in and around the city. His optimism on this score was, however, misguided. Most of the Jews of the settlement came to reject his claims to prophethood, a break symbolized early on by a change in the direction of the Muslim PRAYER from JERUSALEM to the Ka'bah in Mecca. At the same time, however, the Hijra represented an axial moment in the history of the nascent Muslim community. The event not only witnessed the creation of a self-governing religious polity that provided a social setting in which to implement the Qur'anic vision; it also marked a decisive rupture with a pagan past in which the old Arab moral universe was replaced by an ethos emphasizing social justice, piety, communal loyalty, and steadfast COMMITMENT to God's will as mediated through his Prophet. This enraged the Meccans as much as it reassured the Muslims of the reality of their divine mandate.

Opening of Hostilities with Mecca. On the political front, as de facto head of the newly constituted Muslim state, Muḥammad proved himself to be a shrewd and eminently practical political leader. For economic and social reasons the venerable Arabian institution of raiding (*ghazw*) was sanctioned, and he ordered or led expeditions against trading caravans and neighboring Bedouin tribes. It seems quite clear that these expeditions were part of a more general strategy whereby Muḥammad hoped to blockade his most formidable enemies, the pagan Meccans, into surrendering to his authority, while impressing the rest of the Arab tribes with the growing force of his unified super tribe in Medina.

In 624 the Muslims won their first major military victory at Badr, outside of Medina. The opposition had been accustomed to attack and assembled an army of approximately 1,000 men. Muḥammad, with a force of only about 300, ambushed the army and greatly elevated Muslim morale and his own position in the eyes of both the enemy and the neutral forces. But the battle of Badr did not secure an unshakable footing for Muḥammad or his followers. In the next year, the Muslims were badly defeated by a Meccan attack at Uḥud, and Muḥammad himself was wounded. Yet the only major Meccan effort against Muḥammad, a siege of Medina in 627 that came to be known as the Battle of the Ditch, ended in failure. Much to the chagrin of the Meccans, this victory further raised the status of Muḥammad and his community in the eyes of the surrounding Bedouin tribes, inevitably strengthening a formidable intertribal confederacy united in their opposition to the Quraysh of Mecca.

The Conquest of Mecca. In 628 Muḥammad announced his intention of coming to Mecca with his followers for the purpose of making the pilgrimage to the Ka'bah. Fearing an attack, the Meccans barred the way of the pilgrims at a place called al-Ḥudaybiyyah, on the outskirts of the city. There, after lengthy negotiations, a treaty was made. Muḥammad agreed not to enter the sacred precincts for a period of one year, but the following year the Meccans were to decamp for three days to allow the Muslims to complete their pilgrimage. In addition, the agreement stipulated that hostilities would be suspended for a period of ten years. In the following year the Muslims made the pilgrimage without incident. Shortly thereafter, however, a Bedouin tribe allied with the Meccans attacked a tribe allied with the Muslims, effectively breaking the truce. Against only token resistance, in 630 Muḥammad entered Mecca and smashed the idols arrayed around the Ka'bah. A few recalcitrants aside, the Meccan aristocracy was quick to offer its allegiance and submit to Islam. The peaceful conquest of the city, which included a general amnesty and a prohibition on looting, was a major victory for Muḥammad. Victory had to be consolidated, however, and, working from Medina, Muḥammad spent much of the remaining two years of his life seeking solutions to the complicated problem of tribal allegiances. His efforts met with considerable success in 631, the Year of Delegations (of Arab tribal shaykhs) of early Islamic historiography.

Consolidation of His Triumphs. Not all of Muḥammad's time was occupied in state-building activities during the Medinese period. The bulk of Qur'anic revelation in these years far outweighs that from Mecca. In these chapters there is little left of the imagery, succinctness, and fire that characterized those associated with the Meccan period. For the most part, they are ponderous relations of Biblical stories and cultic and legislative detail, clearly directed toward the needs of a new com-

munity of faith attempting to organize its social, political, economic, and religious life anew. At Mecca Muḥammad had proclaimed a new religion that was rather bare. At Medina it was clothed and set it up as a community embodying a radical reform of the prevailing Arabian social structure. He succeeded in replacing Arab tribalism with a notion of *ummah*, a community of true believers under God destined for success in this world and a reasonable assurance of felicity in the next.

At the same time, Muḥammad had experienced bitter disappointment in the failure of many Jews and Christians to accept Islam. His relationship with the Jews of Medina was a particularly torturous one, although he was too respectful of the prophetic tradition in which he saw himself—and perhaps too economically canny—to fail to single out the *ahl al-kitab* (people of the Scripture, hence Jews and Christians) from the pagans. Whereas the latter were given little choice, those of the former who were willing to accept Islamic rule could retain their faiths under certain conditions, chief among which was the payment of a type of poll tax (*jizya*) levied in lieu of the statutory alms-tithe (*zakat*) required of those who converted to Islam.

Muḥammad did not return to Mecca to make the pilgrimage in 631. Instead he sent his longtime companion and ardent supporter Abu Bakr (c. 573–634) to proclaim that henceforth pagans were not to participate in the pilgrimage. In the following year Muḥammad made his Farewell Pilgrimage, solely in the company of believing Muslims, defining thenceforth the essential rites and rituals of the annual Muslim pilgrimage (*ḥajj*). A few months later, in 632, after a short illness, Muḥammad died in the lap of his favorite wife, 'A'ishah (614–678), in their home in Medina and was buried on the spot. Abu Bakr succeeded him as his first CALIPH (*khalifah*, successor).

SEE ALSO ISLAMIC ART; ISLAMIC CONFRATERNITIES.

BIBLIOGRAPHY

Tor Andrae, *Mohammed: The Man and His Faith*, translated by Theophil Menzel (New York 1936).

Karen Armstrong, *Muhammad: A Biography of the Prophet* (San Francisco 1992).

Michael Cook, *Muhammad* (Oxford 1983).

Muhammad Ibn Ishâq, *Sîrat Rasûl Allâh* (The Life of Muhammad), translated by Alfred Guillaume (London 1955).

Ibn Kathir, *Life of the Prophet Muḥammed*, translated by Trevor Le Gassick (Reading, U.K. 1998).

Martin Lings, *Muhammad: His Life Based on the Earliest Sources* (New York 1983).

Francis E. Peters, *Muhammad and the Origins of Islam* (Albany, N.Y. 1994).

Maxime Rodinson, *Mohammed*, translated by Anne Carter (New York 1971).

William Montgomery Watt, *Muḥammad at Mecca* (Oxford 1953).

William Montgomery Watt, *Muḥammad at Medina* (Oxford 1956).

William Montgomery Watt, *Muḥammad: The Prophet and Statesman* (London 1961).

William Montgomery Watt, *Muḥammad's Mecca: History in the Qur'an* (Edinburgh, Scotland 1988).

James Kritzeck
Professor of Oriental Languages and History, and Director of the Institute for Higher Religious Studies
University of Notre Dame, Notre Dame, Indiana

Erik S. Ohlander
Assistant Professor, Department of Philosophy
Indiana University–Purdue University, Fort Wayne, Ind.
(2009)

MURPHY, FRANCIS X.

Redemptorist priest, scholar, and journalist; b. Bronx, New York, June 26, 1914; d. Annapolis, Maryland, April 11, 2002.

Francis Xavier Murphy was an American Redemptorist of the Baltimore Province. After attending elementary school at Immaculate Conception Parish, in the Bronx, New York, he went to Mount St. Mary's Seminary, the Redemptorist juvenate in North East, Pennsylvania, and then to Mount St. Alphonsus Seminary, the Redemptorist theologate in Esopus, New York. He professed his vows as a Redemptorist on August 2, 1935, and he was ordained a priest on June 23, 1940.

After ordination, Father Murphy studied at The CATHOLIC UNIVERSITY OF AMERICA in Washington, D.C. from 1941 to 1944, earning M.A. and Ph.D. degrees in medieval history. From 1944 to 1947 he served as the Catholic chaplain to the midshipmen at the U.S. Naval Academy in Annapolis, Maryland. In 1948 he was called to Rome to attend a Redemptorist historical congress, which led into a year spent deepening his appreciation of the SPIRITUALITY and MORAL THEOLOGY of St. ALPHONSUS DE LIGUORI (1696–1787), the founder of the Redemptorist order. From 1951 to 1958 he was a chaplain in the U.S. Army, serving in such places as Korea, Berlin, Orleans, and Paris. He was awarded the Bronze Star for his service on the front lines during the Korean War with the Seventh Infantry Regiment.

After his military service, Father Murphy became a professor of patristic moral theology at the Accademia Alfonsiana in ROME. He served in that post for twelve years, from 1959 to 1971. He was a popular professor who offered a wide range of courses on PATRISTIC THEOLOGY and MISSIOLOGY, and he directed many students in their licentiate and doctoral theses. He was a *peritus* at the Second Vatican Council, serving as an advisor to the Redemptorist bishop Aloysius Willinger of Monterey-Fresno.

A prolific author, Murphy wrote some 24 books and numerous articles on a wide range of themes. During his years in Rome, he also served as staff editor for the *New Catholic Encyclopedia*, focusing on early Christianity and the Byzantine Empire. Of his many writings, Murphy is best known for his "Letters from Vatican City" series, published in the *New Yorker* magazine during the time of VATICAN COUNCIL II and later republished in book form in four separate volumes.

Written under the pseudonym "Xavier Rynne" (after his mother's maiden name), these letters provided witty and provocative "behind the scenes" reporting on the activities of the council. Their unique blend of theological insight, political savvy, and astute insider knowledge made them a landmark in religious journalism. To this day they are greatly valued by Church historians for their insights into the Conciliar period.

Murphy wrote under a pseudonym to protect his sources and his identity, as well as to escape detection (and possible retaliation) by disgruntled Church officials. For years the identity of Xavier Rynne was uncertain. Murphy openly denied having written the letters, and he did not finally admit it until the late 1970s, when he jokingly speculated that a self-seeking competing journalist might "fill the void" and shamelessly take credit for them. Although subject to editorial oversight, the conception, content, and style of the letters were unmistakably his. For this reason, the news profession generally credits him with pioneering a new genre of religious news reporting, one that he often referred to as "theological journalism."

In addition to his teaching at the Accademia Alfonsiana, Murphy also was a visiting professor at Princeton University, Johns Hopkins University, Towson State College, St. Olaf's College in Minnesota, and Union Theological Seminary. When he returned to the United States, he served as rector of Holy Redeemer College in Washington, D.C., and he later became an author-in-residence at St. Mary's Parish in Annapolis, Maryland. Over the years, his scholarly and journalistic activities earned him many local and national awards. Although struck by Parkinson's disease in his later years, he managed to keep an active schedule and was working on his autobiography up until a few months before he succumbed to his final illness. He died on April 11, 2002, at Anne Arundel Medical Center in Annapolis, Maryland, due to complications from surgery for lung cancer. He was 87 years old.

F. X. Murphy was one of the most noted and accomplished Redemptorists of the twentieth century, and he was recognized as such. As a way of highlighting his unique contribution for his Xavier Rynne writings, the author of his obituary in the *London Times* (April 20, 2002) ends with this fitting eulogy: "The heroes of the Second Vatican Council are usually listed as theologians such as Hans Küng, Karl Rahner, Henri de Lubac and Yves Congar. To their names, for his quite different but no less important contribution, should be added that of Francis Murphy."

SEE ALSO REDEMPTORISTS; MODERN MEDIA AND THE CHURCH.

BIBLIOGRAPHY

WORKS BY FRANCIS X. MURPHY

Rufinus of Aquileia (345–410): His Life and Works (Washington, D.C. 1945).

A Monument to St. Jerome (editor, New York 1948).

Peter Speaks through Leo: The Council of Chalcedon, A.D. 451 (Washington, D.C. 1951).

Fighting Admiral: The Story of Dan Callaghan (New York 1952).

Erasmus and His Times, trans. of L. Bouyer's *Autour d'Erasme* (1959).

Pope John XXIII Comes to the Vatican (New York 1959).

Politics and the Early Christian (New York 1967).

Synod, '67: A New Sound in Rome, with Gary MacEoin (Montreal 1968).

Moral Teaching in the Primitive Church (Glen Rock, N.J. 1968).

Constantinople II, 553: Histoire des counciles oeccumeniques (Paris 1974).

John Nepomucene Neumann, Saint (South Hackensack, N.J. 1977).

John Paul II: A Son from Poland, with Norman Shaifer (1978).

The Pilgrim Pope: A Man for All People (South Hackensack, N.J. 1979).

This Church, These Times: The Roman Catholic Church since Vatican II (Chicago 1980).

The Papacy Today (New York 1981).

The Christian Way of Life: Message of the Fathers of the Church (Wilmington, Del. 1986).

Patristic Heritage in the Renaissance and the Modern World, edited by Norman Shaifer and Marie F. Porter (Tappan, N.J. 1990).

WORKS BY XAVIER RYNNE

Letters from Vatican City: First Session (New York 1963).

Letters from Vatican City: Second Session (New York 1964).

Letters from Vatican City: Third Session (New York 1965).

Letters from Vatican City: Fourth Session (New York 1966).

Vatican Council II (New York 1968).

John Paul's Extraordinary Synod (Wilmington, Del. 1986).

WORKS ABOUT FRANCIS X. MURPHY

Dennis J. Billy "Ricordando il Prof. F. X. Murphy C.Ss.R," in *Accademia Alfonsiana: Inaugurazione Anno Accademico 2002–2003* (Rome 2002), 51–54.

Marie Porter and Norman Shaifer, "Francis Xavier Murphy, C.Ss.R., Ph.D.: A Biographical Note," in *Patristic Heritage: In the Renaissance and the Modern World* (Tappan, N.Y. 1990), 229–235.

Rev. Dennis J. Billy CSSR
John Cardinal Krol Chair of Moral Theology
St. Charles Borromeo Seminary (2009)

N

NEBRASKA, CATHOLIC CHURCH IN

Nebraska, a largely agrarian Midwestern state situated near the center of the contiguous forty-eight states, is bounded on the north by South Dakota, on the west by Wyoming, in its southwestern corner by Colorado, and on the south by Kansas. On the east the Missouri River separates the state from Iowa and the northwestern corner of Missouri. The Platte River flows throughout the state from west to east, separating the Diocese of Lincoln in the south from the two sees to the north—the Archdiocese of OMAHA in the northeast and the Diocese of Grand Island in the northwest.

Early Catholic History. Nebraska first fell under Catholic ecclesiastical jurisdiction in 1493 when Spain laid claim to North America. France took control of the area in 1682, putting the region under the authority of the BISHOP of Quebec. Native populations in what would later become Nebraska included the Omaha, Oto, Pawnee, Ponca, and Sioux. The first European Catholics made their appearance in the area in 1720, when Lieutenant Colonel Pedro de Villasur entered with a party of more than 100, including Friar Juan Mingues, a Franciscan chaplain to the group. The Pawnee attacked their camp near the fork of the Platte and the present-day city of North Platte and killed Villasur, Mingues, and many others. French-Canadian brothers Pierre (1704–c. 1751) and Paul Mallet (c. 1706–c. 1753) explored and crossed the region in 1739 in search of a passage to New Mexico. For nearly a century thereafter, francophone fur trading developed in the area, particularly near the confluence of the Platte and the Missouri Rivers close to the future towns of Bellevue and Omaha. Many of the fur traders took native women as brides,

and their offspring were among the first Catholics in the area to be baptized by later missionaries.

Ecclesiastical authority shifted between the Spanish and the French as often as political control changed, until the United States secured the area as part of the Louisiana Purchase in 1803, when the region became the pastoral responsibility of the bishop of Baltimore. The Lewis and Clark expedition, which camped on the west bank of the Missouri near present-day Fort Calhoun in the summer of 1804, opened the region to more intensive fur-trading activities. Among the most prominent and successful of the traders were Manuel Lisa (1772–1820), Lucien Fontanelle, and Peter Sarpy (1805–1865); the latter two befriended and supported missionaries to the region. In 1846 the Mormons on their way to Utah made camp for about a year at Florence, north of present-day Omaha. Ecclesiastically, the region was assigned to the jurisdiction of the bishop of New Orleans in 1815, and then of the bishop of St. Louis in 1827.

In 1827 three JESUITS, Father Felix Verreydt (1798–1883), Brother Andrew Mazelli, and Father Pierre Jean DE SMET, established the St. Joseph Mission in what is now the city of Council Bluffs, Iowa, to minister to the Potowatami. Missionary service to the future Nebraska area commenced when Father de Smet crossed the Missouri River to baptize two Oto infants, Elizabeth Loise and Julia Tayon, in Bellevue on July 6, 1838. These were the first documented baptisms in what later became the state of Nebraska.

Father de Smet's subsequent travels took him in 1851 to the Great Plains Council, which took place thirty-five miles down the Platte from Fort Laramie, Wyoming, just inside the current Nebraska border. The Council gathered about 10,000 Native Americans of various tribes to whom the government had offered indemnity for future white incursions through their territories. Father de Smet performed the first documented Mass in Nebraska at the Council on September 14. Eleven days later, Father de Smet witnessed the first documented Catholic marriage in the area, between Louis Vasquez and Narcissa at Fort Kearney.

Miège. In 1850 Pope PIUS IX established the Vicariate Apostolic of the Territory East of the Rocky Mountains (also known as "of Indian Territory"), which included the present-day states of Nebraska, Kansas, and Oklahoma and those parts of the present-day states of South Dakota, North Dakota, Wyoming, and Colorado that lay between the Missouri River and the Rocky Mountains. Jean Baptist MIÈGE, S.J., appointed vicar apostolic, was consecrated a bishop and began his ministries to the region in 1851. Bishop Miège faced the immense difficulty of administering a huge territory with very few priests. A few offered assistance from the Diocese of Dubuque, and a tiny number of Jesuit missionaries ministered to the western parts of the area. In 1854 the Kansas-Nebraska Act divided the political region into two distinct territories along the fortieth parallel and opened the area to white American settlement, meaning that Bishop Miège had to minister to a growing number of whites as well as the native populations. And in 1855 Congress called for the construction of military and wagon roads westward, with Omaha as the eastern terminus, ensuring the future of the town as a transportation hub.

In August 1856 at Eighth and Harney Streets in Omaha, Bishop Miège and area Catholics dedicated St. Mary's, the first church building of any denomination in the future state of Nebraska. Many non-Catholics contributed to its construction, in part to attract immigration and to raise real estate values in the city. Father Jeremiah TRECY (1824–1888), a priest of the Diocese of Dubuque and an advocate of Catholic colonization efforts, led a group of Irish immigrants into present-day Dakota County to found St. John's City, the first all-Catholic settlement in Nebraska. The colony failed within a few years, largely because of a destructive tornado in 1860. Most of the settlers sought their fortunes as miners in the West, but several relocated to the nearby town of Franklin (later renamed Jackson) or retained their farming claims. Daniel SHEEHAN, ARCHBISHOP of Omaha from 1969 to 1993, descended from one of the original Dakota County families.

In 1855, frustrated by his inability to minister to such a vast region, Bishop Miège asked that a second vicariate be carved out of his territory. The HOLY SEE announced the creation of the Vicariate of Nebraska on February 17, 1857, in a division that coincided with the 1854 political settlement, with the understanding that Bishop Miège would govern both vicariates for the time being. In response to his continued pleas, on January 28, 1859, James Myles O'Gorman (1859–1874), a Trappist MONK from New Melleray Abbey in Dubuque, was named a bishop and first vicar apostolic of Nebraska. The first communities of RELIGIOUS women in the state were the SISTERS OF MERCY, who arrived in 1864, and the BENEDICTINE SISTERS, who came in 1865.

O'Gorman. Bishop O'Gorman established Omaha as his see city and shortly thereafter, on June 25, 1859, ordained the first priest of the vicariate, Father William Kelly. During Bishop O'Gorman's tenure, several factors brought about significant growth in the future state of Nebraska and the town of Omaha. The Civil War closed off other routes west, funneling the traffic through Nebraska to mines in California, the Black Hills, and especially Colorado, where gold had been discovered in 1850. Irish Catholics among the freighters and outfitters bolstered Church numbers in the Omaha area. After the war the Union Pacific built its transcontinental railroad, with Omaha as one of its major centers. Becoming a transportation center also boosted the state agricultural economy. The Irish immigrants attracted by the availability of railroad construction work swelled the state Catholic population. Nebraska gained sufficient population to become the thirty-seventh state on March 1, 1867.

However, Bishop O'Gorman still struggled with the problem of administering such a large area with so few priests. By the end of 1860, Bishop O'Gorman had only four priests and a Jesuit brother to assist him in MINISTRY, and only nine priests in 1864 to minister to an estimated 50,000 Catholics. Bishop O'Gorman oversaw the building of a modest Gothic CATHEDRAL at Ninth and Howard Streets, St. Philomena's, financed in part by Edward and Mary Lucretia CREIGHTON. But because the area Catholics were often too poor to support their clergy or to build churches, Bishop O'Gorman depended significantly on financial support from the Society for the PROPAGATION OF THE FAITH in Lyons, France, as well as the occasional aid of the Leopoldine Society of Vienna and the LUDWIG MISSIONSVEREIN of Munich.

Father Emmanuel Hartig, O.S.B., of the Atchison, Kansas, Benedictine PRIORY was assigned to minister to Catholics in Nebraska City. On July 11, 1862, he dedicated St. Benedict's Church, the oldest standing church in the state of Nebraska. Nebraska City also occasioned the earliest ethnic infighting in the Nebraska Church, as English-speaking Irish Catholics chafed at attending German-speaking services. Such tensions became a greater problem as increased numbers of German immigrants, fleeing the KULTURKAMPF streamed into the area, and waves of aspiring Bohemian farmers entered the state in the 1870s. About one of every eight

Bohemians living in the United States prior to World War I lived in Nebraska. The majority of these, about 5,000 families, resided on farms in Butler, Colfax, Saline, and Saunders counties. Meanwhile, in the 1870s, Irish Catholics established colonies at O'Neill in Holt County and Greeley in Greeley County. John Fitzgerald (d. 1894), a contractor of the Burlington railroad who moved to Lincoln in the early 1870s, established himself as the first millionaire in that city. He financed a CONVENT and an orphanage in Lincoln and drew national attention as president of the American branch of Charles Stewart Parnell's Land League, the Irish National League.

O'Connor. O'Gorman died on July 4, 1874. Father John IRELAND, pastor of the cathedral of St. Paul, Minnesota, was appointed to succeed him on February 12, 1875, but his ordinary, Bishop Thomas Grace of St. Paul, successfully requested that the appointment be revoked so that Ireland could remain in Minnesota and become his coadjutor. At long last, Bishop O'Gorman's successor, James O'Connor, was consecrated as vicar apostolic on August 10, 1876. Bishop O'Connor is especially remembered for having been the spiritual director who guided St. Katharine DREXEL, foundress of the Sisters of the Blessed Sacrament for the Indian and Colored Peoples, to pursue religious life and missionary work. St. Katharine founded St. Augustine's Indian School in Winnebago in Thurston County in 1908. St. Augustine's remains the prime educational facility for Native Americans in Nebraska. In 2000 a delegation of Winnebago students and parishioners attended Drexel's CANONIZATION in ROME. Bishop O'Connor also invited the Jesuits to direct Creighton University, founded in 1878 with the proceeds of a generous bequest of Edward and Mary Lucretia Creighton.

Bishop O'Connor's ecclesiastical territory diminished in geographical size over the course of his episcopate, beginning with the creation of the Vicariate of Dakota in 1880 and the Vicariate of Montana in 1883. Omaha was erected a DIOCESE consisting of the states of Nebraska and Wyoming on October 2, 1885, with Bishop O'Connor as its first ordinary. Soon thereafter, on August 2, 1887, the Holy See also established the Diocese of Cheyenne, consisting of the entire state of Wyoming, and the Diocese of Lincoln, consisting of all of Nebraska south of the Platte River, all of which was territory formerly assigned to Omaha. During this period Italian, Polish, Hungarian, and Ukrainian immigrants joined the Catholic communities in the city of Omaha and in the Nebraska countryside.

Diocese of Lincoln. Thomas Bonacum, the first bishop of the Diocese of Lincoln (1887–1911), inherited 32 priests, 29 parishes, 74 missions, and 23,160 Catholic

FAITHFUL. His successors were J. Henry Tihen (1911–1917), Charles O'Reilly (1918–1923), Francis Beckman (1924–1930), Louis B. Kucera (1930–1957), James V. Casey (1957–1967), Glennon P. Flavin (1967–1992), and Fabian W. Bruskewitz (1992–). On August 18, 1965, the APOSTOLIC DELEGATE, Archbishop Egidio VAGNOZZI, presided at the dedication of the new Lincoln Cathedral of the Risen Christ, of distinctly modern design.

Scannell. Bishop O'Connor died on May 27, 1890, and was succeeded by Richard Scannell (1891–1916), whose episcopate was characterized by the economic struggles of the 1890s, poor health, and the commissioning of St. Cecilia's Cathedral, designed by Thomas Kimball (1862–1934). On October 6, 1907, Bishop Scannell blessed the cornerstone of this Spanish Renaissance structure, which remains one of the ten largest cathedrals in the country. The cathedral was restored in 2000 to reflect Kimball's original designs for the interior.

Dioceasan Division. On March 8, 1912, the Holy See again divided the territory of the Diocese of Omaha, erecting the Diocese of Kearney out of its western portion and appointing James A. Duffy as its first bishop. The Kearney diocese, two-and-a-half times the size of the Omaha diocese, featured approximately 40,000 sparsely populated square miles, including ranch lands, the desolate Sand Hills, and the Scottsbluff National Monument. The assignment of the more populous and prosperous counties of Hall, Howard, Greeley, and Wheeler, on the western edge of the Omaha diocese, however, remained in dispute until May 13, 1916, when these counties were officially transferred to the Kearney diocese. Subsequently, the see city was transferred to Grand Island in Hall County, on April 11, 1917. Bishop Duffy resigned in 1931 and was succeeded by Stanislaus V. Bona (1931–1945), Edward J. Hunkeler (1945–1951), John L. Paschang (1951–1978), and Lawrence J. McNamara (1978–). At the time of his death, at the age of 103, on March 21, 1999, retired Bishop Paschang was the oldest bishop in the world. On December 13, 2004, William J. Dendinger, a priest of the Archdiocese of Omaha and former Air Force chaplain was ordained as the seventh bishop of Grand Island.

Boys Town. In December 1917 Father Edward FLANAGAN, an Irish immigrant priest, housed twelve homeless boys and founded what would later be known as BOYS TOWN. He attracted substantial philanthropic support with his plan to provide homeless and abandoned youth with vocational and academic education under a program of gentle discipline. A building program in the 1920s marked the creation of a large community to the west of Omaha to serve a growing number of young men. During the 1980s and 1990s, the city of Omaha grew around the Boys Town main campus. In 2001 the institution served 2,130 boys and girls and had 18 satellite sites in 15 states serving a total of 35,410 young people. Boys Town began to offer services to girls in 1979, and in August 2000, based upon a referendum of community residents, its name was changed to Girls and Boys Town.

Archdiocese of Omaha. Omaha witnessed a succession of notable ordinaries: Jeremiah HARTY (1916–1927) came to Omaha after thirteen years as archbishop of Manila, and Joseph RUMMEL (1928–1935) later became the archbishop of New Orleans, where he courageously desegregated the Catholic school system in the face of bitter opposition. In September of 1930, during Rummel's episcopate, Omaha hosted the Sixth National Eucharistic Congress, a public gathering of thousands of the local faithful and prelates from across the nation. James Hugh RYAN (1935–1947) was transferred to Omaha following his controversial rectorship of The CATHOLIC UNIVERSITY OF AMERICA, where he had tried to reform and improve the academic programs. During his episcopacy, on August 10, 1945, Omaha was elevated to an ARCHDIOCESE, with Lincoln and Grand Island assigned as its suffragan sees. Archbishop Gerald T. Bergan (1948–1969) presided over a program of copious institutional expansion. Archbishop Daniel Sheehan (1969–1993), a native of the Omaha archdiocese, worked hard to preserve Catholic education while carrying out the decrees of the Second Vatican Council.

In the postconciliar decades, declining birthrates among farm families, the corporatization of agriculture, and the shift of population from rural to urban areas led to smaller rural congregations. Rather than closing parishes, all three dioceses in the state instituted the modern equivalent of clerical circuit-riding whereby a pastor serves up to three parishes or missions.

Growth and Change. In the 1990s economic prosperity in the state brought change to Nebraska Catholicism. In the city of Omaha, the arrival and growth of the communications and agribusiness industries engendered significant suburban expansion. Gigantic megaparishes emerged on the southern and especially the western sides of the metropolitan area to accommodate the abundant growth of Catholic populations there. Lincoln also saw large growth and established two new parishes.

Low unemployment and needy job markets, particularly in the meat-packing industry, led to a boom in the number of Hispanic immigrants entering the state, especially in the latter half of the decade. The state Hispanic population grew from 36,969 in 1990 to 94,425 in 2000 to 130,856 in 2006 (U.S. Census

Bureau, State & County QuickFacts). Although many of these immigrants could be described as migrant workers, an increasing number of Hispanics established roots in the state by purchasing houses or starting small businesses. This created a new ministerial need. In 2002 Bishop Bruskewitz established Cristo Rey Parish for the Hispanic community in Lincoln. As of 2008, twelve parishes in the Archdiocese of Omaha and eight each in the Grand Island and Lincoln dioceses provided Mass in Spanish.

Meanwhile, a growing need arose for Sudanese, Hmong, and Vietnamese ministry. Several Nebraska parishes sponsored refugees in the wake of the Vietnam War and continued immigration swelled their numbers. In 1999 Bishop Bruskewitz established a diocesan congregation of Vietnamese Sisters, the Missionary Sisters of the Blessed Virgin Mary, Queen of Mercy. In 2002 the Vietnamese parish in Lincoln moved to a larger facility as a result of increased population.

The African-American Catholic population in the state has remained small and is largely concentrated at St. Benedict the Moor and Sacred Heart Parishes in Omaha. Father John Markoe, S.J., founded the De-Porres Club at Creighton University in 1947 to work toward racial justice. During the 1950s and 1960s, Archbishop Bergan spoke out in support of equal treatment for African-Americans in education, employment, and housing.

In the post-conciliar period the Diocese of Lincoln garnered an international reputation as a particularly traditional diocese. By the mid-1990s the Diocese of Lincoln was one of only two dioceses in the United States that retained the traditional use of altar boys at Mass. In 1996 Bishop Bruskewitz issued extra-synodal legislation that provided the penalty of automatic EX-COMMUNICATION to individuals who did not renounce their membership in organizations whose principles, policies, or activities were contrary to the mission of the Church or to its Articles of Faith. These forbidden societies include the Masons and their auxiliary organizations, Planned Parenthood, Society of Pius X, Call to Action (in its various forms), Catholics for a Free Choice, and the Hemlock Society.

Religious Communities. Religious communities of men represented in Nebraska include the Jesuits, with communities at Creighton University and Creighton Preparatory School in Omaha; the BENEDICTINES, who run the Mount Michael High School near Elkhorn; and the COLUMBAN FATHERS, whose national headquarters are in Bellevue. Women's congregations include the Sisters of Mercy, who founded the College of St. Mary for women in Omaha in 1923; the DOMINICAN SISTERS; the SERVANTS OF MARY; the POOR CLARES; the

Creighton University. *Father Roc O'Conner holds a mass at St. John's Church on the Creighton University campus in Omaha, Nebraska. Creighton is a Jesuit-run university.* © **ALYSSA SCHUKAR/EPA/CORBIS**

NOTRE DAME SISTERS; the Society of the SACRED HEART, who operated Duchesne College prior to its closing; the Marian Sisters; School Sisters of Christ the King; Benedictine Sisters; Franciscan Apostolic Sisters; Sister Servants of the Holy Spirit of PERPETUAL ADORATION; and the Schoenstatt Sisters of Mary.

In 1997 the Diocese of Lincoln established St. Gregory the Great Seminary in Seward, Nebraska, for college seminarians. It was the first freestanding diocesan seminary to open in the United States in several decades and has seen a steady increase in enrollment since its beginning. In addition to forming seminarians from the Diocese of Lincoln, the seminary has served students from six other dioceses and two religious orders. In 1998 construction began in Denton, Nebraska, on Our Lady of Guadalupe Seminary, the house of formation for English-speaking members of the Priestly Fraternity of St. Peter, a group dedicated to providing the faithful with the extraordinary form of the ROMAN RITE. The seminary was solemnly blessed and dedicated on December 9, 2000. Also in the 1990s, the diocese welcomed a group of Holy Family Sisters of the Needy from Nigeria and a group of Discalced Carmelite Sisters, who established a new MONASTERY in Agnew in 1999. Meanwhile, in the Archdiocese of Omaha, a new community of men and women, the Intercessors of the

Lamb, was granted the canonical status of a public association of the faithful in 1998.

Turn-of-the-Century Developments. In 1985 groundbreaking began in Omaha on the Pope Paul VI Institute for the Study of Human Reproduction. The Institute has gained national and international recognition for its Catholic research and education on matters of human reproduction, especially NATURAL FAMILY PLANNING. On January 9, 1999, lay Catholics in Omaha began broadcasts from radio station KVSS, which featured material from EWTN and St. Joseph Radio as well as local church programming. In 2007 a lay group of Catholics formed KOLB media with the desire to begin a Catholic radio station for Lincoln. In March 2008 KOLB partnered with KVSS of Omaha. Pending FCC approval and the necessary financing, this partnership will form one FM radio station with the potential to reach 1.2 million listeners throughout Eastern Nebraska and parts of Iowa and Missouri.

In 2000 Archbishop Curtiss (1993–) of Omaha, Bishop Bruskewitz (1992–) of Lincoln, and Bishop McNamara (1978–) of Grand Island united successfully to support a proposed "Defense of Marriage" referendum, which established in state law that marriage could only be contracted between a man and a woman. They also voted to ensure that the ecclesiastical Province of Omaha would remain the only province in the nation outside of the East Coast to maintain the traditional day (i.e., forty days after Easter) for the celebration of Ascension Thursday rather than moving it to the subsequent Sunday. In 2005 the three diocesan bishops, through their association as the Nebraska Catholic Conference, issued and disseminated to all parishes in the state a joint pastoral statement, "Affirming the Dignity of the Mentally Ill," on upholding and respecting the inherent dignity of the mentally ill and those with substance abuse disorders or other addiction problems. The bishops' unified efforts reflect a common vision within an increasingly diverse Catholic population in the state of Nebraska.

In addition to Bishop William Dendinger (1965–), several other priests from Nebraska have been ordained as bishops. In 1998 Blase Cupich of Omaha (1975–1998) was ordained bishop of Rapid City, South Dakota. In 1999, Thomas Olmsted of Lincoln (1973–1999) was ordained coadjutor bishop of Wichita, Kansas, subsequently became bishop of Wichita in 2001, and in 2003 was named bishop of Phoenix, Arizona. In 2000 Robert Vasa of Lincoln (1976–1999) was ordained bishop of Baker, Oregon. In 2005 Michael Jackels of Lincoln (1981–2005) was ordained the bishop of Wichita, Kansas.

All three dioceses emphasize a strong Catholic educational system that promotes academic excellence and fidelity to the teachings of the Catholic Church. In 2008 the Archdiocese of Omaha had 28,000 students attending 2 Catholic universities, 60 elementary schools, and 18 high schools. The Diocese of Lincoln had 7,000 students attending 6 high schools and 28 elementary schools. The Diocese of Grand Island had 1,400 students attending 4 high schools and 6 elementary schools (*The Official Catholic Directory* 2008, pp. 504, 683, 949).

At the turn of the century, the University of Nebraska-Lincoln, University of Nebraska–Omaha, and Nebraska Wesleyan University in Lincoln welcomed onto their campuses the Fellowship of Catholic University Students, or FOCUS. FOCUS has had great success in energizing young college students to practice their Catholic faith by promoting small group BIBLE studies, large group leadership training, and one-on-one discipleship.

Total state population in 2008 according to Catholic records: 1,769,457.

Catholic population: 366,894. 20.7 percent of total.

Omaha Catholics: 220,430 out of total: 897,254. 24.6 percent of total.

Lincoln Catholics: 93,989 out of total: 570,875. 16.5 percent of total.

Grand Island Catholics: 52,475 out of total: 301,328.

17.4 percent of total. (*The Official Catholic Directory* 2008, pp. 504, 683, 949)

SEE ALSO BALTIMORE, ARCHDIOCESE OF; CARMELITES, DISCALCED; DUBUQUE, ARCHDIOCESE OF; ETERNAL WORD TELEVISION NETWORK (EWTN); EUCHARISTIC CONGRESSES; LATTER-DAY SAINTS, CHURCH OF JESUS CHRIST OF; LEOPOLDINEN STIFTUNG (LEOPOLDINE SOCIETY); MONTANA, CATHOLIC CHURCH IN; NEW ORLEANS, ARCHDIOCESE OF; NORTH DAKOTA, CATHOLIC CHURCH IN; SOUTH DAKOTA, CATHOLIC CHURCH IN; ST. LOUIS, ARCHDIOCESE OF; TRAPPISTS; VATICAN COUNCIL II; WYOMING, CATHOLIC CHURCH IN.

BIBLIOGRAPHY

Henry W. Casper, S.J., *History of the Catholic Church in Nebraska* (Milwaukee, Wisc. 1960–1966); Vol. I: *The Church on the Northern Plains*, 1960; Vol. II: *The Church on the Fading Frontier*, 1966; Vol. III: *Catholic Chapters in Nebraska Immigration*, 1966.

Sister Loretta Gosen, C.P.P.S., *History of the Catholic Church in the Diocese of Lincoln, Nebraska, 1887–1987* (Lincoln, Neb. 1986).

Sister Katryn Maney, M.S., ed., *History of the Diocese of Lincoln, Nebraska, 1987–2002*, vol. 2 (Lincoln, Neb. 2002).

The Official Catholic Directory, 2008 (New Providence, N.J. 2008).

William E. Ramsey and Betty Dineen Shrier, *A Gentle Shepherd: The Life and Times of Archbishop Daniel E. Sheehan* (Omaha, Neb. 1999).

Stephen Szmrecsanyi, *History of the Catholic Church in Northeast Nebraska: Phenomenal Growth from Scannell to Bergan, 1891–1969* (Omaha, Neb. 1983).

U.S. Census Bureau State & County QuickFacts, available from http://quickfacts.census.gov/qfd/states/31000.html (accessed November 30, 2008).

Anthony S. Weidner
Independant Scholar
Omaha, Neb.

Rev. Daniel Rayer
Chancellor
Diocese of Lincoln, Neb.(2009)

Rev. Nicholas Kipper
St. Patrick's Church
Lincoln, Neb. (2009)

NEOPLATONISM

In the strict sense, Neoplatonism designates the particular form that PLATONISM took in late antiquity, from the third to the sixth centuries after Christ. In a broad sense, it includes the continuous development of Platonism, from its revival in Middle Platonism to its influence on Jewish, Christian, and Islamic thought, extending through the Middle Ages and the Renaissance. Discussed here are the place of Neoplatonism in the history of ancient thought, the history of Neoplatonism, and the relationships between Neoplatonism and Christianity.

Characteristics of Neoplatonism. Neoplatonism exhibits three principal characteristics. First, it is an exegesis of PLATO, especially the *Sophist, Parmenides*, and *Timaeus*. Second, it is a method of spiritual life, moving the soul from being held captive by the sense world to its true freedom in the intelligible and final union with the One. Third, and notably in the successors of PLOTINUS, such as PROCLUS, it is a pagan theology that seeks to counter Christianity both as a philosophy and a religion.

Since the 1970s, scholarship in all areas of Neoplatonism has increased dramatically, ranging from new editions and translations of major figures to specialized studies of the roots, development, and influence of Neoplatonism. Middle Platonism and other philosophical schools, such as STOICISM, contributed to the philosophical language and structures used by the Neoplatonists. While recognizing the differences between Plato and ARISTOTLE, the Neoplatonists do not see them as opposed to one another, but as providing complementary ways to understand the cosmos. Plato's ontology of being and becoming gives the basic hierarchical structure of Neoplatonism, and Aristotle's notion of act and potency is reformulated to explain how the lower levels in the hierarchy can participate in the higher. Aristotle's theory of sensation, memory, and imagination are also put to use in supplementing Plato's account of perception in the *Theaetetus* and in explaining the actual working of Platonic recollection. The emphasis on philosophy as a method of spiritual life, moreover, is illustrated in the Neoplatonic insistence on beginning philosophical reflection with the soul's empirical life. Thus, the system is in fact constructed from the bottom up and not, as some popular presentations used to imply, as a purely rational deduction from the One, which makes it appear abstract and divorced from human life. This concern with human experience also ties the religious dimension of late antiquity into the background of these philosophers and of their essentially religious concerns.

The continuity of Neoplatonism with its immediate past in no way diminishes its original contributions to philosophy, which are most apparent in its desire to make clear what Plato (and to a lesser extent Aristotle) actually held. In this vein, Plotinus is the first to articulate some major philosophical distinctions about the nature of the corporeal as necessitating division into parts and about the incorporeal as involving indivisibility and omnipresence in the case of forms, SOUL,

INTELLECT, and the One, and pure possibility and indefiniteness in the case of matter. These distinctions, in turn, imply a critical use of language, which is based on our experience of the sensible as corporeal and thus must be adjusted radically to accommodate discussion of soul and intellect. Further, in relation to the One, Plotinus formulates what later is known as negative theology, the peculiar way in which predicates can be attributed to God. We thus find in Plotinus a discussion of the divine attributes of UNITY, simplicity, OMNIPRESENCE, goodness, and INFINITY that are basic in medieval and subsequent philosophical theology and MYSTICISM. The medical advances in understanding the nervous system in GALEN and the rich Stoic terminology of sympathy, perception (*antilepsis*), and CONSCIOUSNESS (*synaisthesis* and *parakoulouthesis*) help to fill out the analysis of human knowing inherited from Plato and Aristotle, including for the first time a theory of the unconscious. Plotinus accounts both for the internal unity of the subject as well as the external unity of the sensible cosmos, with sympathy as the fundamental, necessary condition for sensation and other forms of awareness of the sensible cosmos.

Neoplatonism thus transferred the cosmic unity of Stoicism to the Platonic universe. Everything is in all: Each level of the hierarchy of things is contained in and seeks the level above it, capturing the whole of possible reality, but under different formalities. The human body, for example, seeks its soul, which thereby becomes a center of unity for individual experience. The soul makes its ascent by first identifying with the world soul, capturing the unity of the sensible cosmos and its own kinship with the world soul. The soul's ascent continues into the intelligible world, becoming purely itself, "alone" in Plotinus's precise vocabulary. Once the soul has realized its full presence in the intelligible, it is ready for union with the One, leaving all that is alien aside, as he phrases it already in the "Treatise on Beauty." Only after describing this ascent does Plotinus speak of the One as the power of all things, their transcendent cause, totally independent of them and yet also completely omnipresent to them. Similarly, each higher level of the hierarchy of reality is transcendent and not related to what comes from it, though still omnipresent to that lower level. Within each level of reality, however, all the parts are mutually related, forming a unified whole in relation to its more unified source.

History of Neoplatonism. At the beginning of the third century, at ALEXANDRIA, Plotinus pursued the courses of Ammonius Saccas (c. AD 160–c. AD 242), who was the teacher also of ORIGEN, the father of the Church. Plotinus acknowledged the influence of his teacher and later, in Rome, taught "according to the spirit of Ammonius" (*Vita* 14, 15–16). Plotinus uses

Plato to move from the realm of soul to the realm of the intelligible, with Aristotle's divine mind, thought thinking itself, becoming the place for Plato's forms, the principles of life, intelligence, and being. By using Aristotle, Plotinus emphasizes the unity of the intelligible world and, by using Plato, its diversity in the multiplicity of the forms. As Aristotle's categories ground his analysis of sensible experience, so Plato's genera from the *Sophist* are the basis for understanding the nature of the intelligible and its relation to the sensible. In particular, the "otherness" of the *Sophist* becomes not only the form correlated to "sameness," but the fundamental principle for understanding everything other than the One. Otherness, thus, becomes the principle of multiplicity, related to motion and matter and extending from the initial inchoate state of intellect itself to the matter of the sensible cosmos, which is pure potentiality and as such nonexistent and identified with evil.

Souls and intellects are thus many and one without the separation that the sensible involves, a distinction analyzed in terms of a new understanding of the infinite. They are infinite because they are not cut off from one another. Further, as powers that are never exhausted, they are infinite relative to what comes from them. This is easily illustrated by analogy to human activities. For example, the power of speech is infinite in that it is not exhausted by any particular language nor by the innumerable number of languages that exist or could exist. The power of speech, thus, is necessarily in act, giving rise to many languages as potential expressions of its power. The relationship of the power to its instances is nonreciprocal. They depend on it but it does not depend on them. The instances, however, are related reciprocally, the original context for Aristotle's notion of act and potency to explain sensible change. Since intellect is the duality of being and knowing, it cannot be ultimate, which Plotinus reserves for the One. While his doctrine of the One has roots in Plato, the Good beyond being of the *Republic*, and the dialectical discussions of unity in the *Parmenides*, Plotinus is aware that he is doing something that goes beyond Plato and other Greek philosophers of the classical period.

Porphyry's Influence. With PORPHYRY, a disciple of Plotinus and his successor at Rome, a decisive turning point was reached. While preserving the purely Platonic message of his teacher, Porphyry returned to the earlier traditions and held that religious revelations, too, could make the way of salvation known. He is the first known philosopher to comment upon the *Chaldaean Oracles*, a long poem composed during the era of Marcus Aurelius (AD 121–AD 180), supposedly by Julian the Theurgist. This poem pretended to expound a divine revelation that, besides theurgic practices aimed at leading the soul

to the heavenly world, proposed a theological system inspired by Platonism and Pythagoreanism. It taught that after a supreme, transcendent God, endowed with intellect and self-determination, there was a second God, the triad of being, life, and intelligence, and a whole hierarchy of astral divinities. Because of Porphyry's influence, these *Oracles* were to become the bible of Neoplatonism. However, taken literally, their teachings were hardly compatible with the doctrine of Plotinus. The work of Pierre Hadot has been crucial for understanding Porphyry's independence as a philosopher and his role in the increasingly anti–Christian polemic of later pagan Neoplatonism.

Iamblichus and Proclus. All later Neoplatonism can be defined as an attempt to achieve a systematic exegesis of Plotinianism, the *Chaldaean Oracles*, and the *Orphic Hymns*. In opposition to Porphyry, his successors multiplied the intermediary hypostases and the levels of reality to safeguard the transcendence of the One (strongly maintained by Plotinus) by taking account of even the smallest details in the text of the *Oracles*. At the beginning of the fourth century the Syrian, IAMBLICHUS, initiated this new exegetical method in his Platonic commentaries. He regarded the dialogues as inspired texts, needing symbolic interpretation to keep them consistent both with the *Oracles* and *Hymns* and with Plato himself in each dialogue and the corpus as a whole. Although he taught in Syria, after his death (c. 330) the greater part of his disciples formed a group at Pergamum in Mysia. From this school came the writings of Emperor Julian (c. 331–363) and the treatise of Sallustius (c. fourth century AD) titled *On the Gods and the World*). The tradition of Iamblichus seems to have been introduced at Athens during the second half of the fourth century.

At the beginning of the fifth century, Syrianus and Proclus, representatives of this tendency, constructed a vast system that brought Platonism, Chaldaeanism, and ORPHISM into unison. Two basic principles dominate this synthesis. The first is the principle of analogy: While developing the unity represented by the immediately higher level of reality, each level of reality imitates this unity; everything is in all, according to more or less unified modes. The second principle is that of mediation: To imitate transcendent unity, each level of reality is endowed with a ternary structure, which, departing from unity, unfolds itself and goes on to return to unity because of conversion; to become itself, it must leave itself.

In 529, Emperor JUSTINIAN I decided to bring an end to the school at Athens, the last bastion of paganism in the Christian Empire. The head of the school, Damascius (c. 480–c. 550), then took refuge with his disciples near King Chosroes (531–579) in Persia. Damascius was the last great Neoplatonist. His *Questions and Solutions Concerning First Principles* constitutes a profound criticism of Neoplatonism. The ineffable character of the One is pushed to its extreme limit, so that the ABSOLUTE does not have any relation with anything else and can no longer be the PRINCIPLE. By the very claim that the Absolute is utterly unknowable and undefinable, the relation of other things to the Absolute becomes undefinable. With that, the whole metaphysical edifice of Neoplatonism is in danger of crumbling.

Effects in the East and West. If the East was dominated by the tradition of Iamblichus, the Latin West knew only the tradition of Porphyry and Plotinus. This is true of pagan authors—FIRMICUS MATERNUS, MACROBIUS, and Martianus Capella (fl. fourth century-fifth century)—as well as of Christian writers—MARIUS VICTORINUS, AMBROSE, AUGUSTINE, CALCIDIUS, and mamertus CLAUDIANUS. BOETHIUS, who wrote at the beginning of the sixth century, came under the influence of the schools at Athens and Alexandria. Even at Alexandria, the influence of Iamblichus's tradition was disseminated slowly and in moderate form. At the beginning of the fifth century, Hypatia (c. 370–415) and SYNESIUS OF CYRENE knew only Plotinus and Porphyry. Only at a later date did Hierocles of Alexandria (fl. c. 430), Christian apologist and philosopher Hermias, Ammonius (c. 435/445–517/526), Olympiodorus the Younger (c. 495–570), and Simplicius of Cilicia (fl. c. 530) follow the courses given at the school in Athens; furthermore, the Neoplatonism that they professed was always more sober, of a more moral character, and more scientific than that professed by their teachers: Syrianus, Proclus, or Damascius. Moreover, from the sixth century onward, the school became predominantly Aristotelian and Christian.

Neoplatonism and Christianity. From Porphyry to Damascius, Neoplatonism was always anti–Christian. Attacking Christian Gnostics, Porphyry simultaneously combated such specifically Christian notions as that of CREATION. Porphyry and the Emperor Julian wrote treatises against the Christians that provoked refutations from EUSEBIUS OF CAESAREA and CYRIL OF ALEXANDRIA.

From the middle of the fourth century onward, however, Christian thought was strongly influenced by Neoplatonic philosophy and mysticism. In the East, BASIL of Caesarea, GREGORY OF NYSSA, Synesius of Cyrene, and NEMESIUS OF EMESA, and in the West, Marius Victorinus, Ambrose, and Augustine, made abundant use of Plotinus or Porphyry, frequently without citing them. In the fifth century, PSEUDO-DIONYSIUS borrowed his idea of the hierarchical universe from Proclus.

In the East, this direct influence of Neoplatonism persisted throughout the Byzantine period, notably up to Michael Psellus (1018–c. 1078), Michael Italicos (fl. twelfth century), Nicephoros Gregoras (1295–1360), and Gemistos PLETHON. Plethon played a role in restoring Neoplatonism to the West in the course of the Italian Renaissance, at the court of the MEDICI. In the West, from the high period of the Middle Ages onward, Neoplatonism was accepted through the works of Ambrose, Augustine, Boethius, Calcidius, and Macrobius. In the ninth century, JOHN SCOTUS ERIUGENA translated the writings of Pseudo-Dionysius and MAXIMUS THE CONFESSOR and in his *De divisione naturae* combined the Proclean Neoplatonism of Pseudo-Dionysius with the Porphyrian Neoplatonism of Augustine.

Islamic Thought. From the twelfth century onward, Neoplatonism entered the medieval West by another route, namely, that of Islamic philosophy. In fact, the texts of the Greek philosophers had been translated into Syriac by Nestorian Christians at the school of Edessa from 431 to 439, and once they had been propagated in Persia, they were translated into Arabic during the ninth century, after the establishment of Baghdad. Under the influence of these translations, Islamic philosophy included Neoplatonic interpretations of the works of Aristotle. Once it came into Spain during the twelfth century, this philosophy placed Christian thought into renewed contact with Neoplatonism.

From the twelfth century onward, Latin translations from Arabic or Greek gave Christian theologians a direct knowledge of Neoplatonic works, namely, the *Liber de causis* (translated during the twelfth century), the *Theology of Aristotle*, the *Elements of Theology* by Proclus, and Proclus's commentary on the *Parmenides*, translated by WILLIAM OF MOERBEKE in the thirteenth century. Having received a strongly Platonized thought from the Christian tradition, certain theologians of this era, reading these Neoplatonic texts, regarded Platonism as naturally Christian. BONAVENTURE represents a continuation of the Latin tradition of Neoplatonism, with its roots in the works of Augustine. His particular philosophical synthesis develops Neoplatonism as a method of spiritual life. *The Soul's Journey into God* is his most complete expression of this synthesis, using the categories of Neoplatonic thought to expound the mystical experience of FRANCIS OF ASSISI. Indebted to Augustine and Pseudo-Dionysius, Bonaventure recounts the ascent of the soul to God, with Christ as the means and goal of this ascent and with vestiges of the Trinity in all of creation. Bonaventure's Christocentric account of all reality contrasts with the more reserved approach of THOMAS AQUINAS, who adapts the Neoplatonic doctrine of participation to an Aristotelian account of reality, emphasizing the centrality of intellect rather than Bonaventure's emphasis on will.

Later Mysticism. The influence of Neoplatonism reached its apogee, at the end of the thirteenth century, in the writings of certain German Dominicans, all disciples of ALBERT THE GREAT, namely, THEODORIC (DIETRICH) OF FREIBERG, Berthold of Mosburg, NICHOLAS OF STRASSBURG, and Meister ECKHART. Under the influence of this current, mysticism in the Rhine region developed also through the writings of HENRY SUSO, Johannes TAULER, and Jan van RUYSBROECK. This German Neoplatonism was to become one of the sources of modern thought through the work of NICHOLAS OF CUSA, who transformed the metaphysics of Proclus into a method of knowledge that sought an ever-deeper vision of the unity of the universe.

All these Byzantine, Latin, Islamic, or Germanic currents of Neoplatonism were united in the Italian Renaissance, beginning with Cardinal Bessarion (1403–1472) and Marsilio FICINO. Bessarion, a student of Gemistos PLETHON, favored Aristotelianism, but wrote *In Calumniatorem Platonis*, advocating the Byzantine attempts at reconciling Platonism and Aristotelianism. Ficino, his younger contemporary, led the Florentine revival of Platonism. Ficino translated Plato and the Neoplatonists, especially Plotinus. His Latin translation of the *Enneads* is still of great value to scholars and translators. His originality shows in his synthesis of the Italian humanist tradition and the movement of lay piety with the Platonic and Neoplatonic traditions. An example of this can be seen in his revival of interest in Plato's *Phaedrus* and *Symposium*, synthesized with the love described by St. PAUL. Later, Italian humanism produced the great attempts at religious and philosophical unity by Giordano BRUNO and Tommaso CAMPANELLA. During the modern era, the Platonic tradition was to be perpetuated both in England by the CAMBRIDGE PLATONISTS and in George BERKELEY's *Siris* (1744) and in Germany by the IDEALISM of Friedrich SCHELLING and Georg William Friedrich HEGEL.

Evaluation. The encounter between Neoplatonism and Christianity thus conditions the entire history of Western philosophy. During the patristic period, it provided an apt vocabulary for theology. The Trinitarian theology of Marius Victorinus, Basil of Caesarea, Augustine, and Synesius borrowed formulas from Porphyry, enabling it to express the unity of substance in the Trinity of hypostases. The Porphyrian expressions concerning the union of the soul and the body were of equal service in the formulation of the dogma concerning the hypostatic union, that is, a union without confusion of natures. In this regard, Nemesius has been a most valuable witness.

Yet from the patristic era onward, Neoplatonism has had an influence on Christian teachings concerning the spiritual life that is highly controversial. The ancient tradition went from the humanity of Christ to the knowledge of the Father; it took ecclesiastical experience, that is, the effect of the Holy Spirit in the Church, as its point of departure to attain God. Neoplatonism, on the contrary, claimed that it is possible to have immediate and experiential knowledge of the transcendent God. While making the necessary corrections in this matter, St. Augustine and St. Gregory of Nyssa were led to a similar doctrine. From this there would result, in teachings on mysticism, a disequilibrium between the doctrine on union with God and the doctrine on the mediation of the Incarnate Christ. Pushed to the extreme, the danger makes its appearance in such writings as those of Meister Eckhart, who held that "the uncreated spark" of the soul is co-eternal with the Ineffable.

SEE ALSO PHILOSOPHY, HISTORY OF; PORPHYRIAN TREE; THEOLOGY, INFLUENCE OF GREEK PHILOSOPHY ON.

BIBLIOGRAPHY

A. H. Armstrong, *An Introduction to Ancient Philosophy*, 3rd ed. (London 1957).

A. H. Armstrong, ed., *The Cambridge History of Later Greek and Early Medieaval Philosophy* (London 1967).

A. H. Armstrong, trans., *Plotinus: Enneads*, 7 vols. (Cambridge, Mass. 1966–1988).

René Arnou, *Dictionnaire de théologie catholique*, edited by A. Vacant, 15 v. (Paris 1903–1950; Tables générales 1951–) 12.2:2258–2392.

John Bussanich, *The One and Its Relation to Intellect in Plotinus: A Commentary on Selected Texts* (Leiden, Netherlands 1988).

W. Norris Clarke, "The Limitation of Act by Potency: Aristotelianism or Neoplatonism," *The New Scholasticism* 26 (1952) 167–194.

John J. Cleary, ed., *The Perennial Tradition of Neoplatonism* (Leuven, Belgium 1997).

Kevin Corrigan and John D. Turner, eds., *Platonisms: Ancient, Modern, and Postmodern* (Boston; Leiden, Netherlands 2007).

Pierre Paul Courcelle, *Les Lettres grecques en Occident, de Macrobe à Cassiodore*, new rev. ed. (Paris 1948).

Damascius Le Diadoque, *Dubitationes et solutiones de primis principiis*, edited by C. E. Ruelle (Paris 1889).

John Dillon, *The Middle Platonists, 80 B.C. to A.D. 220* (Ithaca, N.Y. 1977).

John M. Dillon, ed. and trans., *Iamblichi Chalcidensis in Platonis dialogos commentariorum fragmenta* (Leiden, Netherlands 1973).

Fondation Hardt, pour l'études de l'antiquité classique, v.5, *Les Sources de Plotin* (Geneva 1960).

E. R. Dodds, trans, *Proclus: The Elements of Theology*, 2nd ed. (Oxford 1963).

Richard Dufour, *Plotinus: A Bibliography, 1950–2000* (Leiden, Netherlands; Boston 2002).

André Jean Festugière, *Contemplation et vie contemplative selon Platon* (Paris 1936).

William D. Geoghegan, *Platonism in Recent Religious Thought* (New York 1958).

Stephen Gersh, *Middle Platonism and Neoplatonism: The Latin Tradition*, 2 vols. (Notre Dame, Ind. 1986).

Lloyd P. Gerson, ed., *The Cambridge Companion to Plotinus* (Cambridge; New York 1996).

Gary M. Gurtler, *Plotinus: The Experience of Unity* (New York 1988).

Pierre Hadot, *Plotin, Porphyre: Études Néoplatoniciennes* (Paris 1999).

Paul Henry, *Plotin et l'Occident: Firmicus Maternus, Marius Victorinus, Saint Augustin et Macrobe.* (Louvain, Belgium 1934).

Jesús Igal, trans., *Plotino: Enéadas*, 3 vols. (Madrid 1982–1998).

Hans Lewy, *Chaldaean Oracles and Theurgy* (Cairo 1956).

Philip Merlan, *From Platonism to Neoplatonism* (The Hague, Netherlands 1953).

Eric D. Perl, *Theophany: The Neoplatonic Philosophy of Dionysius the Areopate* (Albany, N.Y. 2007).

J. M. Rist, *Plotinus: The Road to Reality* (Cambridge 1967).

Léon Robin, *Les Rapports de l'être et de la connaissance d'après Platon* (Paris 1957).

Sallustius, *Concerning the Gods and the Universe*, translated and edited by Arthur Darby Nock (Cambridge, U.K. 1926).

Paul Shorey, *Platonism, Ancient and Modern* (Berkeley, Calif., 1938).

Willy Theiler, *Die Vorbereitung des Neuplatonismus* (Berlin 1930).

Willy Theiler, *Die chaldäischen Orakel und die Hymnen des Synesios* (Halle, Germany 1942).

C. J. de Vogel, "On the Neoplatonic Character of Platonism and the Platonic Character of Neoplatonism," *Mind* 62 (1953) 43–64.

Thomas Whittaker, *The Neo-Platonists: A Study in the History of Hellenism*, 2nd ed. (Cambridge, U.K. 1928).

Pierre Hadot
Director of Studies, École pratique des Hautes Études
(Sciences religieuses)
Chargé de recherches, Centre National de la Recherche
Scientifique

Gary M. Gurtler
Associate Professor of Philosophy
Boston College (2009)

NEVADA, CATHOLIC CHURCH IN

The formal beginning of Roman Catholicism in the territory that eventually became the state of Nevada dates back to August 16, 1860, when Archbishop Joseph Sa-

doc ALEMANY of San Francisco sent the Reverend Hugh GALLAGHER to establish a mission at Carson Valley. Evidence is inconclusive, however, that Franciscan missionary explorers Atanasio Dominguez (c. 1740–c. 1804) and Silvestre de Escalante (1750–1780) passed through the area in 1776 seeking a new route from Santa Fe, New Mexico, to Monterey, California. Another Franciscan, Fray Francisco GARCÉS (1748–1781), following the Colorado River, is credited with having said the first Mass near what became Laughlin, Nevada, that same year.

The whole region was nominally a part of Mexico, but the Mexican government did little to colonize or govern it because it seemingly had little economic value. During the first decades of the 1800s, American trappers and explorers entered the area. The Old Spanish Trail was opened through Las Vegas in the 1830s. In 1848 the Treaty of Guadalupe Hidalgo was signed, and Mexico formally ceded to the United States the territory that included what are now the states of California, Nevada, and Utah as well as most of Arizona and parts of New Mexico, Colorado, and Wyoming.

Thousands of emigrants traveled through the deserts of the Great Basin en route to California, but the first permanent settlements in the Nevada territory date from 1851 when both Mormon Station (Genoa) and Gold Canyon (Dayton) were established. In 1854 Carson County was created in Western Utah territory. By 1857 the residents of Carson County were petitioning the federal government to allow them to create their own government as Nevada Territory. The Nevada Territory was established in 1861, and three years later in 1864 it was admitted to the Union as the thirty-sixth state. Nevada might not have come into existence so soon had it not been for the discovery of silver. The Sierra passes had been explored prior to the Gold Rush, and after 1848 the Humboldt River route, long known to trappers, became a highway for gold seekers journeying to California. Rich silver deposits were discovered during the following decade, leading to the famous Comstock bonanza of 1859.

Shifting Boundaries. In 1866 the eastern boundary of Nevada was moved one degree of longitude east giving Nevada additional territory from Utah. The final change in the state territory came in 1867 when land was taken from Arizona Territory and added to Lincoln County in southern Nevada.

The shifting of political and ecclesiastical boundaries had an impact on Church development. The Nevada territory was a part of the DIOCESE of Sonora, Mexico, until 1840 when it was placed under the jurisdiction of the BISHOP of the Two Californias, GARCIA DIEGO Y MORENO. After occupation by Americans, the territory was brought into the diocesan structure of the United

St. Mary's in the Mountains Catholic Church, Virginia City, Nevada. *This church flourished during the mid-1800s as Irish immigrants settled in the area to help mine the Colmstock Load, a vast deposit of silver and gold ore discovered under Virginia City, Nevada. It is now one of the state's most photographed historic buildings.* **PURESTOCK/GETTY IMAGES**

States. The territory of Upper California, including Nevada, was placed under the jurisdiction of the newly created diocese of Monterey, California. Three years later, in 1853, Nevada was transferred to the Archdiocese of SAN FRANCISCO when Bishop Joseph Sadoc Alemany became the first PRELATE of that new ARCHDIOCESE. During this time the population was sparse and care of souls in this vast territory was of little concern, nor was there any missionary outreach to the somewhat nomadic native peoples who lived in the area. The discovery of the valuable mineral deposits brought about a dramatic change to the territory in general and to the Church.

In 1858, given the increase in numbers of people, Archbishop Alemany sent the brothers Joseph and Hugh Gallagher, the first priests assigned to Carson County. Father Joseph Gallagher (1821–1887) began service in Genoa, Carson City, and Virginia City in 1858 but most likely traveled from Bodie, California. His brother Hugh (1815–1887) later settled in the territory and built churches in the town of Genoa in 1860 and in Carson City and Virginia City, the last directly on the Comstock Lode, center of Nevadan mining riches.

O'Connell and Manogue. In 1860 when the Vicariate Apostolic of Marysville, California, was created, it included Carson County. All the territory from the Pacific Ocean to the western boundary of Utah and north of the thirty-ninth degree of latitude was assigned to the new vicariate apostolic under the jurisdiction of Right Reverend Eugene O'Connell (d. 1891), who was consecrated bishop February 3, 1861. All the territory in Nevada south of the thirty-ninth degree of latitude was left in the care of the Archdiocese of San Francisco. At this time the population of Nevada was centered mostly around the area of Carson County. The division of the territory of the state of Nevada between two ecclesiastical jurisdictions continued for seventy years.

In 1862 Bishop O'Connell sent newly ordained Patrick MANOGUE, a former miner, to serve the Church in Nevada. From the time of his arrival at the end of June 1862 until 1884, when he became the bishop of Grass Valley, Patrick Manogue was the driving force behind the growth of the Catholic Church in northern Nevada. His parish was all of the Nevada territory north of the thirty-ninth parallel, and St. Mary's in the Mountains in Virginia City became the center of Catholic life in Western Nevada. The parish church that Manogue built in 1877 is still in use.

In 1864 with substantial support from Mr. and Mrs. John Mackay, Comstock mine-owners, Manogue constructed a school and orphanage. The Daughters of Charity led by Sister Frederica McGrath came from San Francisco to staff these institutions. In 1875, again with financial support from the Mackay family and the Miners Union, he began construction of a hospital. The Daughters of Charity operated the hospital until 1897, when it was sold to Storey County and the sisters left Virginia City.

Alone at first, and later with the aid of assistants, Manogue ministered to the Catholics in the far-flung mining camps and ranches. Little by little new parishes were cut off from the parish of St. Mary's in the Mountains. Divide and Gold Hill were established in 1863; Austin, 1864; Carson, 1865; Reno, 1871; Eureka, 1872; and so on through the years. Manogue was made coadjutor bishop of the Diocese of Grass Valley, California, in 1881, but he spent a great deal of time in Virginia City until he succeeded to the see in 1884. With the erection of the Diocese of Sacramento (1886), eight counties of the state of Nevada were included in the California diocese.

The rise and fall of the mining camps shaped the early formation of the Church in Nevada. The coming of the railroads stabilized some portions of the population. Among the early immigrants who came into the state were Italians and Basque peoples from the Pyrenees Mountains. Many Italians first came to northern Nevada to work for the railroad but soon purchased land and focused on farming and ranching. Nevada geography lent itself to sheep herding. The Basque people were first brought to Nevada as shepherds, a trade for which they were noted. These two groups along with the Irish, who originally came to the mines, made up the bulk of the early Catholic population of northern Nevada.

Dioceses Reorganized. The southern portion of the state developed more slowly. The territory below the thirty-ninth parallel remained under the jurisdiction of the Archdiocese of San Francisco until 1887, when it was detached and ceded to the Vicariate of Salt Lake. Father Lawrence SCANLAN, whom Archbishop Alemany had sent to establish a parish in Pioche in 1870, was appointed the first vicar apostolic of Utah and Nevada. When Salt Lake City became a diocese in 1891, the ecclesiastical jurisdictions of Nevada were again reorganized. It was more practical to divide the state along a north-south line rather than the previous east-west line. The eastern and southern counties of Elko,

Lander, Eureka, White Pine, Nye, Lincoln, and eventually Clark were attached to Salt Lake. The western counties of Washoe, Humboldt, Storey, Ormsby, Douglas, Churchill, Lyon, Mineral, Esmeralda, and later Pershing were assigned to Sacramento.

By 1871 the little town of Reno located along the banks of the Truckee River had grown sufficiently to support a parish that became the center for the Washoe County Missions. St. Mary's parish included much of northern Nevada up to the Oregon border and parts of eastern California as well. In 1879 a group of Dominican nuns from Delaware opened Mt. St. Mary's Academy for young ladies. It flourished for ten years, but by the turn of the 1890s as the mines failed, it fell on hard times. Two of the sisters stayed in Reno, and as their number grew they opened a small hospital. In 1912 on the advice of Bishop Thomas Grace (1841–1921), they affiliated with the Congregation of the Most Holy Name of Jesus in San Rafael, California. The coming of the sisters from California was a milestone in hospital care in Reno. St. Mary's Hospital received full accreditation in 1922, and in 1930 a more modern facility was built. Earlier, in 1904, the Southern Pacific Railroad had moved their shops and divisional headquarters from Wadsworth to a site four miles east of Reno. The new town of Sparks came into being almost overnight, and the parish of the Immaculate Conception was founded.

An Eventful Year. In 1931 two events occurred that shaped the future of the Church in the state of Nevada, the one directly and the other indirectly. On March 27, 1931, the HOLY SEE detached all the territory within the state of Nevada from the Dioceses of Sacramento and Salt Lake and created the Diocese of Reno. It was the first time the Catholics of the state of Nevada were contained in one ecclesiastical jurisdiction. Reverend Thomas K. Gorman (1892–1980), a priest of the Diocese of Los Angeles, was installed as the first bishop of Reno on August 19, 1931. His new diocese consisted of thirteen priests serving 8,500 Catholics scattered across the 110,540 square miles of the state of Nevada. The creation of the diocese was occasioned almost by chance. The Chicago George Cardinal MUNDELEIN, during a train ride through Nevada en route to San Francisco, asked who served as bishop of this vast expanse. He was astonished to learn that of all the forty-eight states, Nevada was the only one without its own bishop. Upon his return to the Archdiocese of CHICAGO, Cardinal Mundelein took steps to rectify the situation.

From the time of Bishop Patrick Manogue to the formation of the diocese of Reno, the part of Nevada belonging to the diocese of Sacramento had been governed by Bishop Thomas Grace from 1896 to 1921, by Bishop Patrick Keane from 1922 to 1928, and by

Bishop Robert Armstrong from 1929 to 1931. The portion of Nevada within the jurisdiction of Salt Lake had, since the death of Bishop Scanlan in 1915, been governed by Bishop Joseph Glass from 1915 to 1926 and by Bishop MITTY from 1926 to 1931.

Las Vegas. Even as Bishop Gorman began to structure the new Diocese of Reno, another event occurred that radically changed Nevada. In 1931 the Nevada legislature legalized gambling, and the first casino opened on Fremont Street in Las Vegas.

The history of Las Vegas was much like that of other dusty, desert towns in Nevada. Because it had an artesian well, however, it was a regular stop for travelers. Sometime between 1830 and 1848, Vegas (*Meadows*), as shown on the maps, was changed to Las Vegas. Mormon settlers had come to the area in 1855, but they abandoned the valley in 1858. By 1890 railroad developers had decided that this water-rich valley would be a prime location for a railroad stop and town. By 1904 a tent city had sprung up to support the construction of the first railroad grade into Las Vegas. In 1905 the San Pedro, Los Angeles, and Salt Lake Railroad made its inaugural run from California to points east. That same year the Union Pacific auctioned off 1,200 lots in a single day in an area that today is known as Glitter Gulch: Fremont Street in Las Vegas. In 1908 Bishop Scanlan of Salt Lake established St. Joan of Arc Parish, the lone Catholic parish in Las Vegas for the next thirty-four years.

The Las Vegas economy was only slightly effected by the Depression. The construction of Hoover Dam, begun in 1930, gave rise to Boulder City and the parish of St. Andrew (1931). The development of the Union Pacific Railroad and legal gambling ensured a fairly steady stream of income. With World War II the federal government found sites in Nevada attractive for military and other uses. Nellis Air Force Base expanded, and a major titanium plant was built in Henderson. The well-known Area 51, the secret flight-testing base, was in mid-Nevada as was Mercury Test Site, used for atomic weapons. Casinos, though often small and simple, were found in every city, town, and hamlet throughout the state, but it was after World War II that the state began its amazing development.

Dwyer. When Bishop Gorman was transferred to the Diocese of Dallas-Fort Worth as coadjutor bishop in 1952, his successor was Robert J. Dwyer (1908–1976), the RECTOR of the Cathedral of the Madeleine in Salt Lake City. Nevada was experiencing great growth particularly in the Las Vegas area, and Bishop Dwyer continued the task of providing parishes and schools. He convened the first diocesan synod in 1957. In an effort to support the missions and newly developing

parishes and to build schools, he developed the *Frontier of the Faith* newsletter and traveled extensively throughout the country to raise funds. He invited sisters from Ireland, Cuba, and the Philippines to join American religious to staff the schools.

At the time Bishop Dwyer arrived in Nevada the total population was about 160,000 including about 25,000 Catholics. By 1960 the population of the state had risen to slightly more than 285,000, and the Catholic population had more than doubled. Much of the growth occurred in southern Nevada and was indicative of a trend that continued to the end of the century.

Bishop Dwyer was appointed archbishop of Portland, Oregon, in December 1966, and Bishop Joseph Green (1917–), auxiliary bishop in Lansing, Michigan, became the third bishop of Reno. Installed in May of 1967, Bishop Green's main task was implementing the reforms of VATICAN COUNCIL II. He instituted the Catholic Services Appeal to provide support for the necessary diocesan programs that served parishes statewide. He also traveled extensively to encourage vocations to the service of the Church in Nevada and fostered a spirit of ecumenism. Even as the population boomed, Bishop Green maintained a steady focus on renovating and upgrading existing parishes and developing the Church as envisioned by the fathers of Vatican II. A series of illnesses, aggravated by a severe financial crisis, caused Bishop Green to retire in 1974.

McFarland and Walsh. Bishop Norman F. McFarland (1922–1998), auxiliary in San Francisco who first came to Nevada as apostolic ADMINISTRATOR in 1974, was appointed bishop of the Diocese of Reno in February 1976. With the collegial assistance of the American hierarchy, McFarland put the diocese on a firm financial footing. The same year he was appointed bishop of the diocese, McFarland petitioned, and Pope PAUL VI agreed, to redesignate it as the Diocese of Reno-Las Vegas with Guardian Angel Shrine in Las Vegas as the co-cathedral. In the midst of the financial crisis, the growth of the diocese continued unabated.

In August 1987 Bishop Daniel F. Walsh (1937–), auxiliary of San Francisco, succeeded McFarland who had been named bishop of Orange, California. Walsh's installation was celebrated at Guardian Angel Cathedral in Las Vegas, where he also established a chancery office and a residence to be more available to the needs of the Church in southern Nevada, where fifty-eight percent of the Catholic population lived. Las Vegas had become a major destination city for people from all around the world. The thousands of visitors to the mega-resorts and entertainment and convention centers required the services of the Church. Bishop Walsh also put an increased focus on ministry to the Hispanic population in the state.

The need to minister to the Catholic community scattered across 110,540 square miles of desert and the constant travel between Reno and Las Vegas, almost 500 miles apart, taxed the health and stamina of Bishop Walsh as it had Bishop Green. It became increasingly clear that this could not continue. By 1995 the population of Nevada had risen to nearly 1.5 million people with nearly 450,000 Catholics. Recognizing the situation, the Holy See announced on March 21, 1995, the division of the Diocese of Reno-Las Vegas into 2 separate dioceses. The Diocese of Reno consisted of 12 northern counties with 25 parishes and 11 missions. The newly created Diocese of Las Vegas consisted of 5 southern counties with 23 parishes and 8 missions. Bishop Phillip F. Straling (1933–) of San Bernardino, California, was appointed sixth bishop of Reno and Bishop Daniel F. Walsh was appointed first bishop of Las Vegas.

In May 2000 Bishop Daniel Walsh was installed as bishop of Santa Rosa, California. Monsignor Joseph A. Pepe (1942–), a priest of the Archdiocese of PHILADEL-PHIA serving in Santa Fe, was appointed the second bishop of Las Vegas. He was installed at Guardian Angel Cathedral on May 31, 2001. The story of the Church in Nevada in the late twentieth century was a story of growth. The beginning years of the twenty-first century saw a continuation of this pattern. The metropolitan areas experienced extraordinary growth, and even some more rural communities nearby saw major development. Both the Diocese of Las Vegas and the Diocese of Reno faced similar challenges in meeting the needs of this influx of new parishioners.

Population Growth. As was true in the past, the population of Southern Nevada in and around Las Vegas claimed the largest percentage of growth. In 2007 the population of the Las Vegas diocese was 1.83 million people, and the Catholic population was approximately 710,400. With three new parishes added since 1995, twenty-seven parishes served the ever-growing population. Many parishes in the diocese had an extremely large number of families. One of the greatest challenges for the diocese is to obtain land and clergy for future growth. Four of the parishes serve a predominantly Hispanic population. A Vietnamese Catholic community and a Korean Catholic community are also present. Catholic Charities of Southern Nevada assisted more than 500,000 persons in 2007. Bishop Gorman High School, the only Catholic high school in Las Vegas, which opened in 1957, moved to a new site in Southwest Las Vegas. The new facility, situated on thirty-eight acres, opened in 2007 and serves more than 1,200 students. The diocese relies on extern priests to assist in providing ministry to its people. The diocese instituted an Office of Social Justice and began a Permanent Deacon Formation Program.

The northern twelve counties of Nevada, which make up the territory of the Diocese of Reno, also saw accelerated growth between 1998 and 2007, especially along the eastern slope of the Sierra Nevada. In 2008 the population of the Reno diocese was 682,500, and the Catholic population was estimated at 129,675. Twenty-eight parishes and six missions served the diocese (*The Official Catholic Directory* 2008, p. 1111).

Bishop Phillip Straling's request for retirement was accepted on June 21, 2005. Pope BENEDICT XVI appointed Father Randolph Calvo (1950–), a priest of the Archdiocese of San Francisco, as the seventh bishop of Reno. He was ordained bishop and installed on February 17, 2006. Bishop Calvo faced the same challenges as his predecessors; namely, how to maintain a Catholic presence in widely scattered areas of the diocese. Congregations in many communities had outgrown the parish churches, so it was necessary to provide new accommodations.

Construction of new and larger facilities was the focus in the early twenty-first century. Additionally, some of the older facilities of the diocese, including the CATHEDRAL, need to be retrofitted to meet safety standards. Bishop Manogue Catholic High School, founded in 1948, was outgrown, so a new facility was built in South Reno. The new campus, situated on fifty acres, had an enrollment of 650 students in 2008. Programs in both English and Spanish increased to assist parishes in planning, education, leadership training, and adult FAITH formation. Fifteen permanent deacons were ordained in 2006, and another eleven were in formation in 2008. A new program focused on Adult Faith Formation was to be introduced in 2009. Catholic Community Services provided direct service to 380,000 persons in 2007 and provided financial assistance to outlying parishes for their use in outreach programs for the needy. The diocese depends on the assistance of extern and foreign-born priests to meet the needs of the expanding Catholic population.

Despite their small numbers in a heavily unchurched state, Nevada Catholics have been visible and successful in a variety of political, economic, and community endeavors. They have held elective offices on both the state and national levels and have been active in every aspect of the civic life. At the beginning of the twenty-first century the Church's charitable outreach is without equal in the state. In some small communities across Nevada the faith is lived out much as it has been for many years, but the larger cities have an urgent need to assimilate newcomers, which is made more difficult by the shortage of priests. Being without priests is not a new experience in Nevada. In the formative days of the Church, small communities were visited by a priest on an infrequent basis. The laity, assisted by a small cadre of zealous clergy and religious, will be responsible for keeping the faith strong in the years ahead as was so often the case in Nevada history.

SEE ALSO CALIFORNIA, CATHOLIC CHURCH IN; CATHOLIC CHARITIES USA; LOS ANGELES, ARCHDIOCESE OF; MEXICO, COLONIAL; UTAH, CATHOLIC CHURCH IN.

BIBLIOGRAPHY

K. M. Franks, ed., *Strength of Our Roots, Faith of Our Vision: Brief Histories and Biographies of the Dominican Sisters of San Rafael, 1850–2000* (San Rafael, Calif. 2000).

Thomas Kiely Gorman, *Seventy-Five Years of Catholic Life in Nevada* (Reno, Nev. 1935).

Effie Mona Mack and Byrd Wall Sawyer, *Here Is Nevada: A History of the State* (Sparks, Nev. 1965).

The Official Catholic Directory, 2008 (New Providence, N.J. 2008).

U.S. Work Projects Administration, *Historical Records Survey: Inventory of the Church Archives of Nevada; Roman Catholic Church* (Reno, Nev. 1939).

Br. Matthew Cunningham FSR
Chancellor, Diocese of Reno
Reno, Nev. (2009)

NEW HAMPSHIRE, CATHOLIC CHURCH IN

One of the thirteen colonies, New Hampshire was admitted to the Union (1788) as the ninth state. It is bounded on the north by Canada, on the east by Maine and the Atlantic Ocean, on the south by Massachusetts, and on the west by the Connecticut River and Vermont. Concord is the state capital, and Manchester, the largest city, is the episcopal seat of the only DIOCESE in the state. In 2008, 319,269 Catholics comprised about 24 percent of the state population of l.3 million (*The Official Catholic Directory* 2008, p. 745). Manchester is a suffragan see of the Archdiocese of BOSTON.

Early History. Originally a dissenting offshoot of the Massachusetts Bay colony, New Hampshire became a separate royal colony in 1680 and in the aftermath of the Revolutionary War established itself as a sovereign state, always retaining its Protestant bent. Under the revised constitution of 1784, the state imposed a religious test that excluded Catholics from major offices in the state government. The constitution also authorized towns to support "public Protestant teachers of piety, religion, and morality" (art. 6).

Abenaki natives, converted by Jesuit missionaries from Quebec, were the first Catholics of New Hampshire. The first Catholic Masses in New Hampshire were celebrated in July 1694 by a pair of French Jesuit priests who had accompanied a war party that raided a European settlement at Oyster River near Durham. During the colonial wars they were forced back into Maine and eventually into Canada. Beginning with the last decade of the eighteenth century, missionaries, including Francis A. MATIGNON and Jean L. CHEVERUS, stopped in New Hampshire, particularly at Portsmouth, on their way to and from Maine, a far more promising mission field. When Boston became a diocese (1808), Bishop Cheverus was given jurisdiction over all New England, including about 100 Catholics in New Hampshire. In 1816 Virgil BARBER, an Episcopalian minister from Claremont, New Hampshire, entered the Catholic Church with his wife and five children. Later he became a Jesuit, was ordained in 1822, and founded a church and an academy at Claremont, the first Catholic institutions in the state. Financial and family problems forced his removal in 1827, causing the abandonment of about 100 converts, who for the most part lapsed from the Faith.

The first parish was founded at Dover in 1828 by Reverend Charles French; two years later Michael Healy was established as resident pastor. Also serving the area were itinerant missionaries, such as John B. Daly, OFM, who spent nineteen years there. By 1835 there were 387 Catholics, two churches, and two priests in New Hampshire. The number of Catholics in the state remained negligible until the influx of Irish settlers in the wake of the famines of the mid-1840s. Their presence was resented; in 1855 Gov. Ralph Metcalf, elected by the Know-Nothing (nativist) party, made a vigorous anti–Catholic speech to the legislature. But the agitation died down quickly, and the Know-Nothings quietly disappeared as the newly founded Republican Party solidified its ranks for the election of 1860. In 1877 constitutional changes abolished substantially all the religious qualifications for public office.

Diocese of Portland. In 1853 Maine and New Hampshire were separated from the Boston diocese to form the new Diocese of PORTLAND. At the time the only three parishes in New Hampshire were at Dover, Claremont, and Manchester. By 1858 increased immigration led William McDonald, pastor of St. Anne's, Manchester, to invite the SISTERS OF MERCY to open the first Catholic grammar school. From 1863 to 1869 the municipal school board took complete financial responsibility for this institution. After the Civil War, French-Canadian immigration predominated, resulting in the creation in 1871 of the first national parishes, St. Augustin at Manchester and St. Aloysius of Gonzaga at Nashua. In 1884 New Hampshire was split from the Diocese of Portland, Maine, and Manchester became the seat of the new diocese.

Manchester Diocese. After Manchester became a separate diocese in 1884, the Most Reverend Denis M. BRADLEY who, though Irish-born, had grown up in Manchester, was named the first BISHOP (1884–1903). Bradley increased the number of churches, chapels, mission stations, and parish schools. The Catholic population swelled from 45,000 to more than 100,000, the clergy from 40 to 107, and the children in Catholic schools from 3,000 to 12,000. Bradley's successor, John B. Delany, served only twenty-one months before succumbing to appendicitis. He was followed by George A. Guertin (1907–1932), a native of Nashua of French-Canadian descent.

Bishop Guertin, who stressed the building of parochial schools, had to contend with the nationalistic controversies of the 1920s. A segment of the French-Canadian clergy and FAITHFUL opposed certain policies of the bishop as being contrary to their national rights and interests, which led to deep divisions among the clergy. Bishop Guertin, because of his heritage and his position as bishop, found himself squarely in the middle of the controversy. Elsewhere in the state, Polish congregations were experiencing similar conflicts that led to the establishment of the POLISH NATIONAL CATHOLIC CHURCH. The stress of these controversies, plus a nine-month strike at the Amoskeag Mills, the major employer in Manchester, and the onset of the Depression led to Guertin's retirement to a sanitarium in New Jersey in 1931. He died a few months later at the age of sixty-two, and was succeeded by John B. PETERSON (1932–1944), who had been an auxiliary bishop in Boston. The fourth bishop of Manchester proved himself a skilled administrator by guiding the diocese through the Depression and maintaining harmony in the diocese by establishing a balance between English-speaking and non-English-speaking clergy and administrators.

Post–World War II Era. The Catholic Church in New Hampshire experienced considerable growth in the years immediately following World War II. Bishop Matthew F. BRADY (1944–1959) established thirty new parishes, built seventeen churches, and added eleven elementary schools, fourteen convents, five high schools, three homes for the aged, and two large summer camps for children. Early in 1959 the newly elected Pope JOHN XXIII called for an ecumenical council. Bishop Brady, who was suffering from heart problems, did not live to participate. He died on September 20, 1959, and on December 2, Bishop Ernest Primeau was named as his successor.

Bishop Primeau (1960–1974) was known in ROME from his time as rector of the residence for Chicago priests working the curia. During the preparatory period (1960–1962), he was a member of the Commission for the Discipline of the Clergy and Faithful. Later in Rome,

Bishop Primeau played an active role in the council itself, serving as a U.S. representative on the International Committee of Bishops and in the Secretariat for Promoting Christian Unity. Back in New Hampshire Bishop Primeau took steps to implement the directives of the council. He began by convoking a diocesan synod. The first general session opened on November 3, 1965, at Immaculata High School in Manchester, and three years later, the synodal acts were promulgated after a Mass at the CATHEDRAL on June 3, 1968. On the administrative side, the diocese consolidated all of its departments into a new administration building, which was dedicated on August 9, 1964.

Bishop Primeau resigned in January 1974 (died June 15, 1989) and was succeeded the following year by Bishop Odore Gendron (1975–1990). Gendron was a native of Manchester and served as pastor of a number of prominent ethnic French parishes. During this period a shift began in the state Catholic population. As the state ethnic population assimilated, loyalty to ethnic churches decreased. This led to the decline of ethnic parishes in the cities. At the same time, population growth in the southern part of the state, which is less than one hour from Boston, resulted in new parishes being established in southern suburban locations.

Post–Vatican II Era. In the world that followed the Second Vatican Council, changes in the Catholic Church and new opportunities for women in the secular world led to a significant decrease in the number of women religious in the state. In the decade that followed, the loss of these women, many of whom staffed state Catholic schools, led to the consolidation and closure of many schools throughout New Hampshire. By 1990, when Bishop Gendron retired and was replaced by Bishop Leo E. O'Neil (1989–1997), the situation was exacerbated by the declining number of priests available to serve as pastors. Bishop O'Neil began a system of *twinning*, whereby two small parishes share the same pastor. Bishop O'Neil also sought to invigorate older parishes by assigning new immigrant groups to them as a home parish. Two examples are St. Louis Gonzaga Church in Nashua, which had been predominantly French, and St. Anne Church in Manchester, which was Irish. Both churches are now home parishes for Hispanic and Vietnamese Catholics. Other recent immigrant groups include Portuguese, Sudanese, Bosnian, and Croatian.

Upon his death in 1998, Bishop O'Neil was succeeded by Bishop John B. McCormack. McCormack was born and raised in Massachusetts and served both as a pastor and administrator for the Archdiocese of Boston before coming to New Hampshire. Bishop McCormack

La Salette Shrine, near Enfield, New Hampshire. *The shrine commemorates the appearance of Mary, the Virgin Mother of God, to several children in La Salette, France, on September 19, 1846.* © PHIL SCHERMEISTER/CORBIS

oversaw the consolidation of older parishes in the cities and the construction of new ones in the suburbs. For example, in 2000 four parishes in Berlin, an industrial city in the northern part of the state, were combined to create one new parish. At the same time suburban communities in the southeastern part of the state built larger churches or established new parishes.

Bishop McCormack's focus on building up parish life, bolstering Catholic education, especially in Catholic schools, and building a spirit of prayerful support for vocations, especially to the priesthood, diaconate, and CONSECRATED LIFE, resulted in a number of significant changes in the Church.

In 2001 he appointed a Long-Range Planning Commission to work with parishes to maintain vibrant parish life in the face of shifting demographics in the state, to increase the availability of permanent deacons and lay pastoral ministers, and to handle the retirement of the many priests ordained in the post–World War II era. The commission includes laity, religious sisters, and pastors. The bishop asked the commission to establish thirty-one clusters, which encompassed the 130 diocesean parishes and 38 missions. Over a period of three years, each cluster, which consisted of a pastor and two lay liaisons from each parish, met and developed recommendations for how the parishes could serve their faithful with an allocated number of priests by the year 2012. The recommendations, after review by the dean and the commission, were sent to Bishop McCormack. By the end of 2007 he had accepted recommendations from 28 of the 31 clusters. The implementation of these recommendations resulted in the formation of 12 new parishes from the merger of existing parishes. Between 2002 and 2008 the total number of parishes decreased from 130 to 102 and the missions from 38 to 16. Bishop McCormack also approved the construction of 12 new parish churches between 2000 and 2008.

In 2006 Bishop McCormack published the results of a diocesan-wide study and strategic plan for Catholic schools. The superintendent of Catholic schools worked with the Diocesan School Board to implement many of the recommendations contained in the plan. The bishop also placed renewed emphasis on RELIGIOUS EDUCATION and established the Office for Education and Formation of the Laity. In addition to working with parishes on youth religious education, this office established a Lay Ministry Formation program.

Bishop McCormack appointed a priest as director of vocations and priest recruiters to lead the diocesan effort to promote the priesthood to young men and to support those who discern a vocation. The bishop also ordained the largest class of permanent deacons in diocesan history and prepared to reinvigorate the formation program for deacons, a permanent diocesan initiative.

Education. Catholic institutions of higher learning in New Hampshire include St. Anselm's College, founded (1887) in Manchester by the BENEDICTINES (St. Anselm Abbey); Rivier College in Nashua, sponsored by the Sisters of the PRESENTATION OF MARY; Magdalen College, founded in 1973 in Warner; and St. Thomas More College in Merrimack, founded in 1978.

SEE ALSO CONVERTS AND CONVERSION; COUNCILS, GENERAL (ECUMENICAL), HISTORY OF; JESUITS; KNOW-NOTHINGISM; LAITY, FORMATION AND EDUCATION OF; MAINE, CATHOLIC CHURCH IN; MISSION AND MISSIONS; NATIVISM; VATICAN COUNCIL II.

BIBLIOGRAPHY

Robert B. Dishman, *A New Constitution for New Hampshire?* (Durham, N.H. 1956).

Mary St. Laure Kegresse, *A History of Catholic Education in New Hampshire* (Boston 1955).

Robert H. Lord, John E. Sexton, and Edward T. Harrington, *History of the Archdiocese of Boston in the Various Stages of its Development, 1604–1943*, 3 vols. (New York 1944).

New Hampshire Revised Statutes Annotated, 1955 (St. Paul, Minn. 1955).

The Official Catholic Directory, 2008 (New Providence, N.J. 2008).

James Duane Squires, *The Granite State of the United States: A History of New Hampshire from 1623 to the Present*, 4 vols. (New York 1956).

State of New Hampshire, Office of Energy and Planning, 2007 Census Data, available from: http://www.nh.gov/oep/programs/DataCenter/index.htm (accessed October 30, 2008).

West's New Hampshire Digest, 1760 to Date, Covering Cases from State and Federal Courts (St. Paul, Minn. 1951).

Francis Lyons Broderick
Director, United States Peace Corps
Ghana, Africa

Rev. Wilfrid Henry Paradis JCD
Vice Chancellor, Diocese of Manchester, N.H.
Peritus, Vatican Council II

Kathryn Schofield Staub
Director, Diocesan Museum
Manchester, N.H.

Patrick F. McGee Sr.
Director of Planning and Development
Diocese of Manchester, Manchester, N.H. (2009)

NEW JERSEY, CATHOLIC CHURCH IN

A middle Atlantic State bordered by New York, Pennsylvania, Delaware, and the Atlantic Ocean, New Jersey was the third state to join the Union, doing so on December 18, 1787. Known as *The Garden State*, New Jersey is a mix of urban, suburban, and rural areas. Although it is the most densely populated of the states, three-fifths of the land mass remains undeveloped. As of January 1, 2008, according to statistics in *The Official Catholic Directory* (2008), the Catholic population was 3,562,389, or 40.9 percent of the total population of

8,707,112. This Catholic population was divided into 683 Latin rite parishes and 54 Eastern rite parishes. There were 12 Catholic hospitals, 7 Catholic colleges and universities, and 70 high schools operating under Catholic auspices.

Catholic Political and Social Status. Originally settled by Dutch, Swedes, and English, for much of its early history New Jersey was officially anti–Catholic. In 1668 the first general assembly of the Province of East Jersey was held in Elizabeth. William Douglas of Bergen, who had been elected, was refused his seat because, as a Catholic, he was not able to take the required oath.

In 1683 the Catholic King James II appointed an Irish governor of New York, Thomas Dongan (1634–1715), who brought with him a Catholic priest, later to be joined by two more, who occasionally would go to Elizabeth and Woodbridge to administer the sacraments. When James was overthrown, the anti–Catholic sentiment returned. In 1698 the East Jersey Assembly promised religious tolerance, but not for those of the "Romish" religion.

When New Jersey became a royal colony in 1702, Queen Anne (1665–1714) wrote to her representative, Lord Cornbury (1661–1723), that he should give liberty to all "except Papists." Under George II (reigned 1727–1760), an oath was administered to civil and military officers, which contained anti–Catholic sentiments.

In 1738 New Jersey was established as a separate legal entity under Lewis Morris (1671–1746), the first royal governor. In 1758 religious toleration for all "except papists" was reiterated. While New Jersey officially remained anti–Catholic, the ministrations of the JESUITS from Philadelphia were tolerated, although instances of anti–Catholic prejudice still occurred.

The state constitution adopted in 1776 continued the anti–Catholic sentiment. It guaranteed civil rights to all Protestant inhabitants, who alone could hold political office. Due probably to the influx of Catholic immigrants, the revised state constitution, adopted in 1844, removed the prohibition of Catholics holding elective office. But anti–Catholic prejudice did not abate. The rapid growth of the foreign Catholic population caused concern among the mostly Protestant native population, and anti–Catholic sentiment again arose. Nationally, the American Party, whose motto was "America for Americans," grew in popularity. This and other related political parties became popularly known as "Know-Nothings"—a reference to the fact that, when asked questions about their political leanings, they said they knew nothing—and they espoused policies to retard the growth of immigration, especially that of Catholics.

The Know-Nothings were particularly prominent in New Jersey. Anti–Catholic activity culminated in an attack on St. Mary's Catholic Church, a German ethnic parish on William Street in Newark. Tension had built following a fire in the nearby Halsey and Taylor factory, whose workers were mainly Irish and German immigrants, that was ignored by the Protestant fire brigades nearby. The Austrian pastor, the outspoken Benedictine Nicholas Balleis (b. 1808), had over the years alienated many Protestants in the city, especially by his comments about Hungarian freedom fighter (and Protestant) Louis Kossuth (1802–1894). During an Orangemen parade on September 5, 1854, an exchange of words and rocks gave way to a riot that destroyed the church and led to the deaths of two Irishmen, one shot point blank "at the hands of persons unknown," according to the inquest, but who had certainly been shot by one of the marchers, and the other who died, at least officially, from cholera, even though he had a deep sword wound in his neck.

As a result of the Civil War, when many immigrants fought nobly for their adopted country, Catholics slowly began to be accepted socially. A new wave of immigration at the end of the nineteenth and beginning of the twentieth centuries, however, resulted in a new surge of anti–catholicism in the guise of the revived KU KLUX KLAN, particularly in the southern part of the state, during the 1920s.

Over the next few decades the Catholic population increased. By the turn of the twenty-first century, New Jersey ranked third among the states with regard to the Catholic percentage of the population. Seven of New Jersey's nine governors between 1962 and 2006 were Catholic.

The Catholic Population. More Catholics may have lived in colonial New Jersey than has been usually thought, but many of these, because of the lack of priests and churches, intermarried with non-Catholics, and their descendants were lost to the Church. In the early nineteenth century, the pastor of Saint Mary's Episcopal Church in Burlington was a former Jesuit, Charles Wharton. The congregation was ecumenical and included a number of Roman Catholics. Priests from New York visited Catholics in Woodbridge and Elizabeth beginning in 1683.

An early Catholic inhabitant of Trenton was John Tatham, also known as John Gray, a former MONK of the English Benedictine Congregation, who left the monastic life (possibly absconding with some funds in the process) about the time that priests were expelled from London, where he had been serving as a chaplain. He married and settled first in Pennsylvania and then in New Jersey. The inventory of his estate shows that he possessed items for the celebration of the Eucharist. He served on the Council of Proprietors of West Jersey in 1688 and 1689 and as president in 1695.

St. Anthony of Padua Chapel in West Orange, New Jersey. *Rev. Richard Munkelt conducts mass in Latin in the chapel.* ©
SARAH RICE/STAR LEDGER/CORBIS

A Catholic Church was established in Philadelphia in 1729, staffed by the Jesuits. Soon thereafter, Theodore Schneider, S.J., a native of Heidelberg, cared for the spiritual needs of Catholics in New Jersey, especially in Salem County, where a number of Catholics, predominantly from Germany, had settled to work in the glass factories. These trips were taken over by Ferdinand Steinmeyer, who adopted the English name FARMER. Save for a few exceptions, he made twice-yearly trips through New Jersey to visit the communities of Catholics. His mission stations included Ringwood, Basking Ridge, Charlottenburg, Pilesgrove, Cohansey, Long Pond, Mount Hope, Springfield, and other sites in Burlington County, Hunterdon County, and Sussex County. Catholics had come to Ringwood in 1764 to work in the mines. Farmer spent a total of twenty-one years ministering to the scattered Catholics of New Jersey. His registers include Irish, English, German, and French names.

Patrick Colvin, a Catholic, operated a ferry on the Delaware near Trenton and is reputed to have supplied some of the boats that George Washington used to ferry his troops from Pennsylvania on Christmas Eve, 1776, when he was on his way to attack the Hessian troops at Trenton. Some Catholic officers from France who had come to help the cause of the revolution settled at war's end in Madison. They were soon joined by other French Catholics who fled the FRENCH REVOLUTION. Although these Catholics worshiped in the Presbyterian church because of the lack of a Catholic church, they remained staunch Catholics, and their descendants were among the founders of Saint Vincent Martyr Church in Madison.

The first Catholic church was built in Trenton in 1814. The first parish with a resident pastor, however, was Saint John's in Newark, where Gregory Pardow took up residence in 1826.

The 1830s saw an influx of Irish Catholics who came to work on the canals and railroads, the first major expansion of the Catholic population. The Irish Famine of the 1840s and 1850s, and political and religious troubles in Germany, brought even more Catholic immigrants. Italians came in large numbers at the end of the nineteenth century, and many eastern Europeans came in the first quarter of the twentieth century. An example of the tremendous growth by immigration is seen by considering the Poles, who numbered only 748 in the state in 1880, but had grown to 14,000 by 1900. The 1930s saw the arrival of African Americans from the southern United States, leading to the establishment of African-American parishes. Among the more recent Catholic immigrants have been Vietnamese, Koreans, Nigerians, and other West Africans. Over the years, the new immigration led to the establishment of new dioceses and eparchies. The Eparchy of Passaic, embracing those Catholics of the Byzantine-Ruthenian Rite living in New Jersey and eastern Pennsylvania, was established in 1963, with Most Reverend Stephen J. Kocisko as first eparch. The Eparchy of Our Lady of Deliverance of Newark for Syrian-rite Catholics was established in 1995, with Most Reverend Joseph Younan as eparch. As of 2008, Mass was offered in the state in thirty languages. Socially, the Ancient Order of Hibernians, the KNIGHTS OF COLUMBUS, and the Catholic Daughters were joined by the Catholic Sokol of the Polish community and the Knights and Ladies of Peter Claver, a fraternal organization of African-American Catholics.

Pope JOHN PAUL II visited Newark as part of his 1995 pilgrimage to the United States. He participated in a prayer service in Sacred Heart Cathedral, during which he agreed with Archbishop McCarrick that the CATHEDRAL deserved to be a minor BASILICA, and so it became. He also presided at a Mass in Giants Stadium.

Changes Affecting the Church. The population shift from the cities to the suburbs that began in the 1950s led to the restructuring of parishes. As a result of the process, which continued into the early 2000s, a number of parishes, predominantly in the cities, were closed or merged. Of the 28 parishes listed in the city of Trenton (the state capitol) in *The Official Catholic Directory* (2008), 17 were designated as closed. The city of Newark had 27 active parishes, with 11 listed as closed or merged.

Another major event that affected the life of Catholics in the state was the SEX ABUSE CRISIS. Each of the dioceses was affected to some degree by clergy abuse. One of the most egregious cases involved James T. Hanley, pastor of St. Joseph's Church in Mendham. The family of one victim sued the Diocese of Paterson, and a settlement was negotiated, part of which required that neither he nor his family discuss the case publicly. Hanley's successor, Kenneth Lasch, made the case public and became an advocate for those abused by priests. In response to the mandate of the American bishops, each of the dioceses instituted the "Protecting God's Children" program. The Diocese of Metuchen established a review board that includes a member of SNAP (The Survivors' Network of those Abused by Priests). At

St. Joseph's Parish, a stone shaped like a millstone was set up as a memorial to abuse victims. Commissioned by a former parishioner, Bill Crane, who says he was one of those abused by Hanley, it was inspired by JESUS's words as reported in the Gospel of Matthew about anyone who would cause a child to SIN that "it would be better for him to have a great millstone hung around his neck and to be drowned in the depths of the sea." On the legislative level, a LAW was passed that requires church officials to inform legal authorities of suspected cases of abuse, and a "Memorandum of Understanding" regarding the reporting of sexual abuse, between the New Jersey Division of Criminal Justice and the dioceses of the state, was agreed to in 2002.

Education. New Jersey is home to a number of Catholic institutions of higher learning. Seton Hall University, founded in 1856 in Madison as Seton Hall College, and now located in South Orange, is a diocesan university staffed by the priests of the Archdiocese of NEWARK as well as many lay professors. The major seminary for the archdiocese, Immaculate Conception Seminary, serves as the graduate school of THEOLOGY. The minor seminary, Saint Andrew's, is also part of Seton Hall. Redemptoris Mater Missionary Seminary, which trains seminarians of the NEOCATECHUMENAL WAY, also operates under the auspices of the Archdiocese of Newark. Other Catholic colleges in the state include Caldwell College (sponsored by the DOMINICAN SISTERS), St. Peter's College in Jersey City (sponsored by the Jesuits), Georgian Court College in Lakewood (sponsored by the SISTERS OF MERCY), Felician College (sponsored by the Felician Sisters), and the College of St. Elizabeth in Convent Station (sponsored by the Sisters of Charity of St. Elizabeth).

Renew, the program of spiritual enrichment now popular throughout the country, was developed under the inspiration of two priests of the Archdiocese of Newark in 1976. The New Community Corporation, a nationally-known community development corporation spearheaded by Reverend William Linder, a priest of the Archdiocese of Newark, was incorporated in 1968, in the aftermath of the Newark riots.

Each of the Latin-rite dioceses, as well as the Byzantine Eparchy of Passaic, has a diocesan newspaper. Seton Hall University operates a radio station that offers, as part of its general programming, programs devoted to Catholic themes. New Jersey is also home to Paulist Press, one of the largest Catholic publishers in the United States.

Ecclesiastical History. The first bishopric in the United States was established at Baltimore in 1789, with John CARROLL chosen as the first bishop. Other sees were established in 1808, with the northeastern part of New

Jersey (roughly corresponding to the old Province of East Jersey) placed under the jurisdiction of the bishop of New York, and southwestern New Jersey (roughly corresponding to the old Province of West Jersey) placed under the supervision of the bishop of Philadelphia. The tremendous growth of the Catholic population led ROME to establish the Diocese of Newark, encompassing the whole of the state, in 1853. James Roosevelt BAYLEY, a former Episcopalian, and nephew of Mother Seton, was named first bishop.

The fourteen counties of central and southern New Jersey were split from the Diocese of Newark to form the Diocese of Trenton in 1881. Michael J. O'Farrell (1881–1894) of New York was named first bishop. The Diocese of Paterson, comprised of Morris, Passaic, and Sussex counties in the northwest part of the state, was split from the Diocese of Newark in 1937. Thomas H. McLaughlin (1881–1947), auxiliary BISHOP of Newark, was named the first bishop. That same year, the six southernmost counties were split from the Diocese of Trenton to form the Diocese of Camden. Bartholomew Eustace (1887–1956) of New York was named first ordinary. At the same time, Newark was made an archdiocese and the metropolitan see. The state saw one more split, in 1981, when four east central counties were set aside as the Diocese of Metuchen, with Theodore E. McCarrick of New York as first bishop.

SEE ALSO BENEDICTINES, ENGLISH; BYZANTINE THEOLOGY; CATHOLIC DAUGHTERS OF THE AMERICAS; JAMES II, KING OF ENGLAND; KNIGHTS OF PETER CLAVER; KNOW-NOTHINGISM; LATIN RITE; MATTHEW, GOSPEL ACCORDING TO; NEW YORK, ARCHDIOCESE OF; PHILADELPHIA, ARCHDIOCESE OF; SETON, ELIZABETH ANN BAYLEY, ST.

BIBLIOGRAPHY

Christopher Ciccarino, *Seeds of Faith, Branches of Hope: The Archdiocese of Newark, New Jersey* (Strasbourg, France 2003).

Augustine J. Curley, *New Jersey Catholicism: An Annotated Bibliography* (South Orange, N.J. 1999).

Joseph M. Flynn, *The Catholic Church in New Jersey* (Morristown, N.J. 1904).

Charles J. Giglio, *A Glorious Past, a Brilliant Future: The History of the Diocese of Camden* (Strasbourg, France 2002).

Michael Krull, *The History of the Roman Catholic Diocese of Metuchen, New Jersey: Of This We Are All Witnesses: Twenty-fifth Anniversary, 1981–2006* (Strasbourg, France 2006).

Raymond J. Kupke, *Living Stones: A History of the Catholic Church in the Diocese of Paterson* (Clifton, N.J. 1987).

John D. McCormick, *History of the Catholic Church in Trenton in the Nineteenth Century* (South Orange, N.J. 2004).

New Jersey Catholic Historical Records Commission, *The Bishops of Newark, 1855–1978* (South Orange, N.J. 1978).

The Official Catholic Directory (New Providence, N.J. 2008).

Joseph C. Shenrock, ed., *Upon This Rock: A New History of the Diocese of Trenton* (Trenton, N.J. 1993).

Rt. Rev. Joseph H. Brady
Immaculate Conception Seminary
Darlington, N.J.

Rev. Augustine J. Curley
Newark Abbey, Newark, N.J. (2009)

NEW MEXICO, CATHOLIC CHURCH IN

New Mexico, located in the southwestern United States, was admitted to the Union in 1912. Bordered by Arizona on the west, Colorado on the north, Oklahoma and Texas on the east, and the Mexican states of Chihuahua and Sonora on the south, New Mexico is a triadic state—having three geographic areas, three cultures, three flags, three congressional districts, three dioceses. The land area of 121,364 square miles (fifth largest) is roughly divided into the Great Plains in the east, the Rocky Mountains in the center, and a high plateau in the west. The state is bisected by the Rio Grande, known in Spanish times as the Rio Bravo del Norte, which is a major source of irrigation. The largest cities in the state are Albuquerque, a major transportation and commercial hub of the Southwest; Las Cruces, the major city in the southern part of the state; and Santa Fe, the capital.

In 2008 the New Mexico population numbered about 1,984,356 (thirty-sixth largest) of which 43.4 percent claimed Hispanic ancestry (highest proportion in the United States) and 8.9 percent Native American (highest after Alaska and Oklahoma) (U.S. Census Bureau 2008). The Hispanic population ranges from families who have been present in the state for nearly four centuries to recent immigrants. The Native American population includes the Pueblo people, whose historic villages dot the Rio Grande valley, and the Navajos, whose enormous reservation occupies much of northwestern New Mexico into Arizona. The 498,334 Catholics, about 25 percent of the state population, are served by the Archdiocese of SANTA FE and the Dioceses of GALLUP and Las Cruces (*The Official Catholic Directory* 2008, p. 2092). The Province of Santa Fe also includes the Dioceses of Tucson and Phoenix in Arizona.

New Mexico is a study in contrasts. Acoma Pueblo is the oldest occupied town in the United States, dating to perhaps 1,000 years before the English settlement at Jamestown. Santa Fe is the oldest capital city in the country; the Palace of the Governors, the oldest public building; and San Miguel in Santa Fe, the oldest continuously functioning church in the United States. But in the twentieth century, New Mexico ushered in the atomic age. The Manhattan Project, which developed the first atom bomb, was housed at the government laboratories at Los Alamos, and the first bomb was detonated at Trinity Site on the White Sands National Monument near Alamogordo.

The Colonial Period. Early attempts at exploration and evangelization went hand in hand under the Spanish. A Franciscan friar, Marcos de NIZA (c. 1495–1558), assisted by a Moorish survivor of a previous expedition under Cabeza de Vaca, led a small expedition north from Mexico in 1539. The Moor was killed by the inhabitants of Zuni Pueblo, and the friar retreated south. Fueled by the friar's descriptions of Zuni, coupled with legends of the wealthy "seven cities of Cibola," a major expedition was mounted in 1540 under Francisco Vasquez de Coronado (1510–1554). For two years Coronado explored the present American Southwest, wintering twice along the Rio Grande. Although it failed to locate any wealthy cities, Coronado's expedition, wandering from the Grand Canyon to the Kansas plains, added immeasurably to geographic knowledge of the Southwest.

When Coronado withdrew in 1542, several of the FRANCISCANS stayed behind and established a mission on the Rio Grande. All were eventually killed. Fray Juan de PADILLA (c. 1500–1544), the protomartyr of the United States, was probably killed somewhere in western Kansas. Fray JUANA DE LA CRUZ became the first MARTYR of New Mexico. Over the next half century, New Mexico languished in the Spanish colonial empire. Religiously, several Franciscans, moved by both a missionary spirit and a sense of the millennial possibilities, made forays into the area. In political and geographic minds, the area took shape as a frontier against possible southern expansion by the English.

Oñate. Finally in 1598, a serious colonizing expedition was mounted under Don Juan de Oñate (1552–1630). Initially Oñate established his capital at a pueblo called Ohkay Owingeh on the east bank of the Rio Grande, which he christened San Juan de los Caballeros. Two years later the capital was moved to a new settlement named San Gabriel on the west bank of the Rio Grande at its confluence with the Rio Chama. In 1608 Oñate resigned the governorship under pressure and was replaced by Pedro de Peralta (1584–1666). In 1610 Peralta supervised the establishment of a new capital, La Villa Real de la Santa Fe de San Francisco de Asis, some thirty miles southeast of San Gabriel.

The early Franciscan missionaries were members of the Province of the Holy Gospel in Mexico, and, although thinly spread among a growing number of missions, they were, by and large, dedicated missionaries. Nonetheless, the FRIARS were hampered by difficulties of personnel and resources. In addition, the friars'

presentation of Christianity in western European cultural terms often placed them at odds with the neophytes, especially in language, societal relations, and COSMOLOGY.

After the departure of Oñate, the friars moved their headquarters from San Gabriel to the more centrally located pueblo of Santo Domingo. In 1616 New Mexico was designated a semi-autonomous Franciscan *custody* of the Conversion of Saint Paul. Fray Estevan Perea, the first *custos*, reported 11 missions, 20 friars, and some 10,000 Christianized natives. A triennial supply train from Mexico provided for the needs of the missions. Significant among the friars in this period was Fray Alonso de BENAVIDES (c. 1580–1636), appointed *custos* in 1623. He arrived in Santa Fe late in 1625, bearing with him the image of the Blessed Virgin Mary, still venerated in the Santa Fe Cathedral as *La Conquistadora*, Our Lady of Peace, the oldest Marian image in the country. Returning to Spain in 1630, he wrote a "Memorial" to the king and the Franciscan minister general, detailing the state of the province and the missions, and asking for the appointment of a BISHOP for New Mexico.

Pueblo Unrest. Isolated at the very edge of the Spanish colonial empire, the early years of the New Mexico colony were neither prosperous nor peaceful. The colony failed to produce much material wealth either for the colonists or for the governments in Mexico City and Madrid. Often the friars were at odds with the governors over the support of the missions and the treatment of the natives. When the friars and the governors were in agreement, it was often at the expense of the native peoples.

On August 10, 1680, the pent-up rage among the Pueblo people, coupled with several years of agricultural failure, erupted into a full-scale revolt, remarkable for its ferocity and for the UNITY it produced, albeit temporarily, among the pueblos. Under the leadership of a man named Popé (c. 1630–1692) from San Juan Pueblo, the natives mounted a successful offensive despite language barriers. The missions were desecrated, twenty-one friars and four hundred Spaniards were killed, and the rest took shelter at Santa Fe, which soon came under siege. On August 21, under the watchful eyes of the natives, who were glad to see them go, the Spaniards abandoned Santa Fe and trekked south to El Paso, where they remained for the next dozen years.

In 1692, concerned about an unprotected border and about the bad example the revolt presented to other natives, Spain commissioned Don Diego de Vargas (1644–1704) to reconquer the province for Spain. Leading a contingent of friars, soldiers, and colonists north from El Paso, de Vargas re-entered Santa Fe on December 16, 1693. The pueblos were, for the most part, peace-

The San Francisco de Asis Mission Church, Taos, New Mexico. *Built in 1772, it is one of the best known and most photographed churches in the state.* PAUL DAMIEN/GETTY IMAGES

ably restored to Spanish and CHRISTIAN hegemony—but with a difference. The cultural and religious sensibilities of the natives were treated with more RESPECT than previously, and gradually a more authentically New Mexican spirituality emerged from the convergence of cultures. During the next century this spirituality flowered in several areas. Creating the only truly American form of religious architecture, the New Mexicans constructed churches of adobe and woodwork that blended with the landscape. Native *santeros* developed an indigenous religious devotional art, both primitive and highly evocative. In addition, devotional sites, PILGRIMAGES, celebrations, and confraternities, such as *La Fraternidad Piadosa de Nuestro Padre Jesus Nazareno* (better known as the *Penitentes*), evolved that combined aspects of the different cultures in the province.

Diocese of Durango. For almost the entire colonial period, New Mexico theoretically came under the jurisdiction of the vast Diocese of Durango in Mexico, founded in 1620, which was for many years the largest DIOCESE in New Spain. But at a distance of 1,500 miles

from Durango, Santa Fe only experienced an episcopal visitation a handful of times over the course of two Spanish centuries, notably by Bishop Benito Crespo (1673–1737) in 1730. In reality, the Franciscans were in almost exclusive control of the New Mexican church. However, they were not assiduous in developing native vocations in the province, but relied instead on missionaries from Spain and Mexico.

Santiago Roybal (1694–1744), ordained a secular priest in Durango around 1730, was the first in a thin line of native New Mexicans, who, at considerable difficulty, left the province to be educated and ordained in Mexico and then returned to serve as priests in the northern kingdom. Born near present-day San Ildefonso Pueblo, Roybal is presumably the first native of what is now the United States to be ordained a priest. During his priestly ministry he was the bishop's *vicario* in Santa Fe, and he was also the sole non-Franciscan in the province.

Nineteenth Century. The early nineteenth century was, in general, a time of decline for church structures in New Mexico. The emergence of independence movements in various areas of Spanish America diverted funds from the missions, which were still supported by the Spanish crown. Once Mexico achieved independence from Spain in 1821, New Mexico was theoretically no longer as distant from the national government, but the struggling newly independent government was even less generous with remote ecclesiastical outposts and indeed sought money from the Church. In addition, the Mexican Congress ordered all Spanish citizens expelled from the country, so by 1848 all friars had left New Mexico. Nor did the HOLY SEE immediately recognize Mexican independence, which resulted in a standoff over appointments to vacant sees. By 1827 no bishops remained in Mexico; thus, no ordinations occurred.

This combination of a lack of leadership, clergy, and money deeply affected New Mexico, located at the fringe of the newly independent country. At the beginning of the nineteenth century, subsidized provisions were made for twenty-two priests in New Mexico. In the first three decades of the century, Spanish settlements grew more numerous and more widespread, and the population itself grew in size and diversity as trade routes opened up with Missouri to the northeast. At the same time, the bishops in Durango began to secularize the larger Spanish parishes beginning in 1816. But the changes brought by independence were quickly felt, and by 1829 only twelve priests served the province, mostly native New Mexicans, caring for a growing population with dwindling resources. As a result of these conditions, many churches fell into disrepair and ruin, and the sacraments were rarely celebrated in the more remote missions. In many of these missions, the spiritual life was left to the leadership of lay groups, such as the *Penitentes*. Prominent among the New Mexican priests of this era were Juan Felipe Ortiz in Santa Fe, Jose Manuel Gallegos in Albuquerque, and Antonio Jose Martinez in Taos.

In 1832 Durango received a new bishop, Jose Antonio Laureano de Zubiria (1791–1863). Over the next twenty years, he made pastoral visits to New Mexico (in 1833, 1845, and 1850). Zubiria appointed Father Ortiz in Santa Fe as his vicar for the area and authorized Father Martinez in Taos to establish a rudimentary preparatory seminary. Over the next dozen years, twelve young men who had initially been trained at Taos returned to serve as priests in New Mexico, which raised the number of clergy in the province to seventeen by 1851.

Vicariate Apostolic. The Treaty of Guadalupe Hidalgo in 1848, ending the two-year Mexican-American War, brought New Mexico under the aegis of the United States. This change in civil control rather quickly resulted in a change in ecclesiastical government as well. The question of a bishop for New Mexico, which had

been bandied about in Mexico City and Madrid for more than two centuries, was decisively answered by the American bishops in the Seventh Provincial Council of Baltimore in 1849. In addition to asking for new archdioceses and dioceses, the bishops requested a vicariate be established for the vast territory between California and the Rocky Mountains recently acquired from Mexico. Pope PIUS IX responded on July 19, 1850, by establishing the Vicariate Apostolic of New Mexico with the seat at Santa Fe. A few days later the POPE named Jean Baptiste LAMY (1814–1888), a French diocesan priest working in the Cincinnati diocese, as titular bishop of Agathonica and first vicar apostolic. A native of Lempdes in the French Puy-de-Dome, Lamy was serving at Covington, Kentucky, at the time. He was consecrated on November 4, 1850, at Saint Peter in Chains Cathedral in Cincinnati, and, together with Joseph MACHEBEUF, a comrade from France, he arrived in Santa Fe on August 10, 1851.

Lamy. Lamy's new vicariate contained, by his own count, 68,000 Catholics, 8,000 to 9,000 Catholic natives, 26 churches, 40 chapels, and 12 native priests. At its height Lamy's jurisdiction extended to all of New Mexico, Arizona, Colorado, and part of Utah. Lamy's first concern was to build up the Church in New Mexico by means of a more numerous and better educated clergy and through Catholic schools. Lamy recruited the Sisters of LORETTO from Kentucky (1852), the BROTHERS OF THE CHRISTIAN SCHOOLS from France (1859), the Sisters of Charity of Cincinnati (1865), the Jesuit Fathers from Naples (1867), and numerous secular priests and seminarians from France and elsewhere. This growth resulted in subsequent institutional development. The vicariate apostolic was erected as the Diocese of Santa Fe in 1853; Arizona and Colorado were erected as separate vicariates apostolic in 1868 with Machebeuf and another French missionary, Jean Baptiste Salpointe (1825–1898), as first vicars; and Santa Fe was advanced to a metropolitan ARCHDIOCESE in 1875.

Lamy's thirty-five years as bishop in New Mexico were not without difficulties. His struggle with the bishops of Durango over boundaries and jurisdiction went on for two decades. He was disappointed several times in his dealings with the U.S. Bureau of Indian Affairs over education for the natives. And his dealings with the native clergy remained controversial, sometimes resulting in suspension, or, in the case of Father Martinez of Taos, EXCOMMUNICATION. Lamy saw these priests as poorly educated and lacking in clerical discipline. On their part the priests viewed his introduction of European clergy, RELIGIOUS, and customs as disdainful of their own indigenous CULTURE and religiosity. The gradual rise of the walls of Lamy's new French Romanesque CATHEDRAL (1869–1884) around the existing adobe *parroquia* of Santa Fe was perhaps emblematic of their sense of Lamy's supplanting the native FAITH.

As leader of the established Catholic faith of the Spanish inhabitants, but at the same time having been deeply steeped in Catholic European culture and thoroughly Americanized during his decade as a missionary in Ohio and Kentucky, Lamy became an important figure in nineteenth-century New Mexico. He helped the area to mature religiously and to transform its self-understanding from the northern frontier of an old kingdom to part of the great American West. Willa Cather (1873–1947) in her 1927 novel *Death Comes for the Archbishop* memorialized Lamy, and Paul Horgan (1903–1995) wrote of him in his 1975 Pulitzer-prize-winning biography, *Lamy of Santa Fe.*

Twentieth Century. Lamy was followed by a succession of French archbishops: Salpointe (1885–1894), Placide Louis CHAPELLE (1894–1897), Peter Thomas Bourgade (1899–1908), and Jean Baptiste Pitaval (1909–1918). Salpointe prevailed upon Katherine DREXEL to send her Sisters of the BLESSED SACRAMENT to Santa Fe in 1894 to staff St. Catherine's Indian School. In his retirement he wrote a history of the Church in the Southwest, *Soldiers of the Cross,* often used by later historians. While bishop of Tucson, Bourgade reintroduced the Franciscans to New Mexico, inviting the brown-robed friars of the Cincinnati Province (not the blue-robed friars of colonial times) to staff the vast Navajo reservation. When promoted to Santa Fe, Bourgade brought the friars to Pena Blanca in 1900 and gradually from there to many of the ancient pueblos and other parishes in the state. Bourgade also helped found the Catholic Church Extension Society and established St. Joseph's Hospital in Albuquerque.

By 1918, with the outbreak of World War I, the availability of priests from France ended, and, with that in mind, Archbishop Pitaval resigned and suggested that the Holy See name a Franciscan to replace him, because the order might secure much-needed priests for the diocese. In 1919 ROME complied with his request and appointed the pastor of Pena Blanca, Albert T. Daeger, O.F.M. (1919–1932), as ARCHBISHOP. In 1929, after a drought of many years, Archbishop Daeger had the joy of ordaining three New Mexican priests.

Daeger was succeeded by Rudolph A. Gerken (1933–1943), Edwin V. Byrne (1943–1963), and James P. Davis (1964–1974). Gerken had been the first bishop of Amarillo, Texas; Byrne and Davis had previously served as bishops in Puerto Rico. The Byrne years witnessed the tremendous post–war growth in New Mexico, including the establishment of the atomic energy laboratories at Los Alamos. To meet the growth, Catholic colleges developed in Santa Fe and Albuquer-que, and numerous new parishes and schools opened, including sixteen in Albuquerque alone. Byrne fostered native vocations by establishing a minor seminary at Santa Fe. Archbishop Byrne was also instrumental in founding three religious communities: the Servants of the Holy Paraclete, who work with troubled priests; the Handmaids of the Precious Blood, a contemplative community; and the Little Brothers of the Good Shepherd, who care for the destitute. Archbishop Davis presided over the implementation of the Second Vatican Council decrees, and in 1967 moved the archdiocesan headquarters from Santa Fe to Albuquerque.

Diocesan Changes. The growth of the Santa Fe metropolitan province is indicative of the religious, geographical, political, and demographic developments in the Southwest during the 1900s. When Santa Fe was made a metropolitan archdiocese in 1875, it had two suffragans, the vicariates apostolic of Colorado and Arizona, which later evolved into the Dioceses of Denver (1887) and Tucson (1897). A third suffragan was added in 1914, when the Tucson diocese was divided and southern New Mexico and the West Texas Panhandle formed the Diocese of EL PASO. The growth across the Southwest in the early decades of the twentieth century was reflected in a series of ecclesial changes that affected the area from 1936 to 1941. In 1936 Los Angeles, California, was raised to a metropolitan see, and Tucson was placed in this new province. In 1939 northern Arizona was detached from Tucson, northeastern New Mexico was detached from Santa Fe, and a new diocese was established at Gallup. Then in 1941 Denver was made a metropolitan archdiocese and at the same time divided with a new diocese at Pueblo. Thus from 1941 to 1969 Santa Fe had just two suffragans, El Paso and Gallup, and the province included New Mexico, west Texas, and northern Arizona.

In 1969, with territory taken from both Tucson and Gallup, a new diocese was created at Phoenix, Arizona. As a result of this division, Gallup lost most of its Arizona territory with the exception of the Navajo and Hopi reservations. Because three new dioceses were created in southern California in the same decade, both the new diocese at Phoenix and that of Tucson were returned to the Santa Fe province. In 1982 southern New Mexico was detached from El Paso and a new diocese established at Las Cruces. With its territory reduced to the West Texas Panhandle, the El Paso diocese joined the other Texas sees as part of the San Antonio province. This marked the first time since the late sixteenth century that El Paso was not ecclesiastically joined to Santa Fe. Thus in the early twenty-first century Santa Fe province comprised all New Mexico and Arizona, with the four suffragan sees of Gallup, Las Cruces, Phoenix, and Tucson.

In 1974, with the retirement of Archbishop Davis, the archdiocesan vicar general, Robert F. Sanchez, became the tenth archbishop of Santa Fe. A native of Socorro, he was the first New Mexican to head the archdiocese. Sanchez initiated a number of programs to preserve the ancient culture of the archdiocese, especially its churches, and to better integrate the Hispanic, Native American, and Anglo cultures present in the state. From 1992 to 1993 a series of scandals compromised Sanchez's ability to provide leadership for the archdiocese. He resigned in 1993 and was succeeded by Bishop Michael J. Sheehan of Lubbock, Texas. Sheehan successfully led the archdiocese through a time of financial and morale crisis and celebrated his twenty-fifth anniversary of service in 2008.

Threshold of the Third Millennium. At the beginning of the third Christian millennium, the Santa Fe archdiocese spanned fifteen full and part of an additional four counties in northern and eastern New Mexico with 275,955 Catholics in 90 parishes. The Gallup diocese covered four full and four partial counties in western New Mexico, as well as two full and one partial county in northeastern Arizona with 54,258 Catholics in 58 parishes. The territory of Las Cruces diocese consisted of ten southern counties with a Catholic population of 127,370 in 45 parishes.

The first bishop of Gallup was a Franciscan friar, Bernard T. Espelage, O.F.M. (1939–1969). He was succeeded by Jerome J. Hastrich (1969–1990) and Donald E. Pelotte, S.S.S. (1990–). Bishop Pelotte, a member of Maine's Abenaki tribe, became the first Native American bishop in the United States. Bishop Ricardo Ramirez, C.S.B. (1982–) has served the Las Cruces diocese since its inception. In 2003 Gerald Frederick Kicanas succeeded Manuel Duran Moreno (1982–2003) as bishop of the Diocese of Tucson. In 2008, following Bishop Pelotte's resignation, Thomas J. Olmsted, who had served as bishop of the Phoenix diocese (2003–2008), became apostolic administrator of the Gallup diocese. At that time, the Diocese of Gallup served a Catholic population of 58,292, the Diocese of Las Cruces, 132,646; the Diocese of Tucson, 382,123; the Diocese of Phoenix, 644,119; and the Archdiocese of Santa Fe, 307,396 (*The Official Catholic Directory* 2008, pp. 2070, 2091–2092).

Sex Abuse Crisis. From the late 1990s and into the early 2000s, the Church in New Mexico faced great challenges when the SEX ABUSE CRISIS affected the nation. Questions also arose concerning the effectiveness of the SERVANTS OF THE PARACLETE's treatment of priests at Jemez Springs. Some priests who had been sent to the center for sexual abuse problems later worked in or visited nearby communities; others were deemed cured and were reassigned to dioceses around the United States, where some of them again engaged in the same behaviors.

By 2002 the Church in New Mexico had paid more than $30 million to settle 187 lawsuits (Kohn 2002). The Diocese of Tucson filed for bankruptcy protection in 2004, and reorganization was completed in 2005. A portion of Tucson's victim compensation costs were borne by the Diocese of Phoenix, which had been part of the Tucson diocese when some of the abuse occurred. In addition to providing financial compensation, the dioceses established programs to protect children and to offer counseling and support to victims.

Social Services. Begun in 1973 by the New Mexico Conference of Churches (NMCC), The Storehouse, the largest food pantry in New Mexico, ranks in the top 10 percent of food pantries in volume in the United States. During the years 2003 to 2006, The Storehouse increased 178 percent in productivity but experienced a 6 percent decrease in operating expenses. By 2006, it served more than 2.53 million meals (http://www.nmchurches.org/node/66). The following year The Storehouse became independent from the NMCC.

In addition to Offices of Hispanic, Native American, and African-American Ministries, the archdiocesan Office of Social Justice coordinates a variety of programs to support social action, including ministries such as Just-Faith (adult training in compassion and social missions), Respect Life, Peace and Human Development, Elizabeth Ministry (support for women during the childbearing years), Project Rachel (post–abortion healing), and Emergency Social Services.

Religious Communities. Several religious communities are important to the fabric of religious life in New Mexico. The BENEDICTINES have two prominent abbeys—Christ in the Desert at Abiquiu, with its striking church, and Our Lady of Guadalupe at Pecos, with its extensive MINISTRY in the Charismatic Movement. The PREMONSTRATENSIANS, or Norbertines, also have a monastic foundation at Albuquerque at Santa Maria de la Vid Priory. Beginning in 1985, the Franciscans again had their own Southwest jurisdiction in the Province of Our Lady of Guadalupe headquartered in Albuquerque. Among the Franciscan ministries is Father Richard Rohr's Center for Action and Contemplation at Albuquerque. The Conventual Franciscans staff Holy Cross Retreat Center in Mesilla Park in the Las Cruces diocese. The Christian Brothers staff the College of Santa Fe, St. Michael's High School, and the Sangre de Cristo refoundation center for priests and religious at Santa Fe. The Servants of the Holy Paraclete have their headquarters at Jemez Springs, and the AUGUSTINIAN RECOLLECTS have a provincial delegate house in Mesilla.

Women religious have been present in New Mexico since the advent of the Sisters of Loretto in 1856. Originally introduced to open schools and hospitals, sisters from many different congregations serve in parochial, educational, and health-care ministries. New Mexico has cloistered Carmelite monasteries at Santa Fe and Gallup, a POOR CLARES MONASTERY at Roswell, and a Benedictine PRIORY at Blanco (formerly at Abiquiu). The Handmaids of the Precious Blood have their motherhouse and novitiate at Jemez Springs. The Canossian Daughters of Charity have a provincialate at Albuquerque, and the Felician Sisters, at Rio Rancho.

The adobe churches of New Mexico—from Cristo Rey in Santa Fe, the largest adobe structure in the country, to the small village *moradas* of the enitentes—constitute a distinctive and cherished artistic patrimony of the state and a significant architectural contribution to the United States. Among the most-photographed are San Estevan in Acoma Pueblo, San Jose de Gracia in Trampas, San Miguel del Vado in Ribera, San Francisco de Asis in Ranchos de Taos, and the famous pilgrimage *Santuario* of El Senor de Esquipulas in Chimayo.

SEE ALSO BALTIMORE, COUNCILS OF; CARMELITES; CHARISMATIC RENEWAL, CATHOLIC; JESUITS; MARY, BLESSED VIRGIN, ICONOGRAPHY OF; MISSION AND MISSIONS; MISSION IN COLONIAL AMERICA, I (SPANISH MISSIONS); NEOPHYTE; VATICAN COUNCIL II.

BIBLIOGRAPHY

Archdiocese of Santa Fe Official Web site, available from http://www.archdiocesesantafe.org/ (accessed January 19, 2009).

Henry Warner Bowden, "Spanish Missions, Cultural Conflict and the Pueblo Revolt of 1680," *Church History* 44, no. 2 (June 1975), 217–288.

Angelico Chávez, *But Time and Chance: The Story of Padre Martinez of Taos, 1793–1867* (Santa Fe, N.M. 1981).

Angelico Chávez, *My Penitente Land: Reflections on Spanish New Mexico* (Albuquerque, N.M. 1974).

Diocese of Gallup Official Web site, available from http://www.dioceseofgallup.org/ (accessed January 19, 2009).

Diocese of Las Cruces Official Web site, available from http://www.dioceseoflascruces.org/ (accessed January 19, 2009).

Diocese of Phoenix Official Web site, available from http://www.diocesephoenix.org/ (accessed January 19, 2009).

Diocese of Tucson Official Web site, available from http://www.diocesetucson.org/ (accessed January 19, 2009).

Francisco Atanasio Domínguez, *Missions of New Mexico, 1776*, translated by Eleanor B. Adams and Angelico Chávez (Albuquerque, N.M. 1956).

Paul Horgan, *Great River: The Rio Grande in North American History* (New York 1954, repr. Hanover, N.H. 1991).

Paul Horgan, *Lamy of Santa Fe: His Life and Times* (New York 1975).

John L. Kessell, *The Missions of New Mexico since 1776* (Albuquerque, N.M. 1980).

David Kohn, "The Archbishop," *CBS News* (April 21, 2002), available from http://www.cbsnews.com/stories/2002/04/19/60minutes/main506755.shtml (accessed January 19, 2009).

New Mexico Conference of Churches, "The Storehouse," available from http://www.nmchurches.org/node/66 (accessed January 19, 2009).

The Official Catholic Directory (New Providence, N.J. 2008).

John Baptiste Salpointe, *Soldiers of the Cross: Notes on the Ecclesiastical History of New-Mexico, Arizona, and Colorado* (Banning, Calif. 1898).

France Vinton Scholes, *Church and State in New Mexico, 1610–1650* (Albuquerque, N.M. 1937).

France Vinton Scholes, *Troublous Times in New Mexico, 1659–1670* (Albuquerque, N.M. 1942).

Blandina Segale, *At the End of the Santa Fe Trail* (Milwaukee, Wisc. 1948).

Michael J. Sheehan, ed., *Four Hundred Years of Faith: Seeds of Struggle, Harvest of Faith: A History of the Catholic Church in New Mexico* (Santa Fe, N.M. 1998).

Thomas J. Steele, Paul Rhetts, and Barbe Awalt, eds., *Seeds of Struggle/Harvest of Faith: The Papers of the Archdiocese of Santa Fe Catholic Cuarto Centennial Conference on the History of the Catholic Church in New Mexico* (Albuquerque, N.M. 1998).

U.S. Census Bureau, *Annual Population Estimates 2000 to 2008* (July 1, 2008), available from http://www.census.gov/popest/states/NSt-ann-est.html (accessed January 14, 2009).

Msgr. Raymond J. Kupke
Pastor, Holy Family Parish
Florham Park, N.J.

Laurie J. Edwards
Independent Scholar
Reidsville, N.C. (2009)

NEW ORLEANS, ARCHDIOCESE OF

(*Novae Aureliae*) Metropolitan see erected April 25, 1793, as the Diocese of Louisiana and the Floridas by PIUS VI upon the application of King Charles IV (1748–1819) of Spain. The vast territory of the original DIOCESE, except for the area under the jurisdiction of the Diocese of Baltimore, stretched from the Rocky Mountains to the Atlantic and from Canada to the Gulf of Mexico. The territory, detached from the See of Havana, was previously part of the older Diocese of Santiago de Cuba, under whose jurisdiction the Louisiana colony had passed in 1762. Before that date, Quebec had spiritual jurisdiction over French colonial Louisiana. After the 1849 Provincial Council of Baltimore recommended additional ecclesiastical jurisdictions, PIUS IX on July 19, 1850, raised New Orleans to the rank of metropolitan see. The first suffragan dioceses were those of Galveston, Texas; Mobile, Alabama;

Natchez, Mississippi; and Little Rock, Arkansas. By 2001 the province included the Archdiocese of New Orleans and six additional Louisiana dioceses: Alexandria, Baton Rouge, Houma-Thibodaux, Lafayette, Lake Charles, and Shreveport. The ARCHDIOCESE covers 4,208 square miles and includes eight civil parishes (counties), namely, Jefferson, Orleans, Plaquemines, St. Bernard, St. Charles, St. John the Baptist, St. Tammany, and Washington. In 2008 the Catholic population numbered about 384,994 or 36.8 percent of the total population (*The Official Catholic Directory* 2008, p. 855).

Early History. The parish church with the longest uninterrupted history is St. Louis Basilica, whose origin extends practically to the founding of New Orleans in 1718. The first Mass in what is now the archdiocese was offered nearly twenty years earlier, on March 3, 1699, by Reverend Anastase Douay, a Franciscan missionary, with the expedition of Pierre LeMoyne (1661–1706), Sieur d'Iberville, who established the power of France in the Lower Mississippi Valley. On a later expedition to Louisiana with Iberville, the Jesuit Paul du Ru used his fragmentary knowledge of the languages of the Bayagoula, Ouma, and Natchez tribes to prepare a rudimentary catechism for their instruction. By early spring of 1700, du Ru was supervising the construction of a small church in a native village in Iberville parish.

The Council of the Marine in 1717 recommended turning the colony over to John Law's Company of the West and its successor, the Company of the Indies (or Mississippi Company). In accordance with the charter issued by the regent, PHILIP II, Duke of Orleans, religious affairs were included in the activities of the Company of the West from 1717 to 1731. Occasionally priests, known as concession chaplains, were among the personnel assigned to the land grants in the colony. More important than the concessions, however, was the founding of New Orleans as the new capital of the colony by Jean Baptiste LeMoyne (1680–1767), Sieur de Bienville, brother of Iberville, in 1718. The plan for the city, laid by Adrien de Pauger (d. 1726), provided for a church and presbytery. Divine services were held in improvised and inadequate quarters until April 1727, when the first substantial St. Louis parish church was finally completed.

Carmelite, Jesuit, and Capuchin priests labored in the colony during its formative years. The first Capuchins were Bruno de Langres, who arrived in New Orleans towards the end of 1722, and Philibert de Vianden, who took charge of the district from the Chapitoulas, a few miles above the original boundaries of the city, to Pointe Coupée, including Les Allemands, the German Coast, and the intervening concessions. Les Allemands had a CHAPEL, dedicated to St. John, on the west bank of the Mississippi as early as 1724. In April 1723 Bruno was replaced as superior of the Capuchin missions in Louisiana by Raphael de Luxembourg, who was also vicar general of the BISHOP of Quebec. Raphael established, in 1725, the first school for boys in New Orleans, but it lasted only five or six years. Nicolas Ignace de Beaubois, founder of the Jesuit missions in New Orleans, induced the URSULINES of Rouen, France, to establish a military hospital and school for girls. The pioneer group of Ursulines reached New Orleans on August 6, 1727, and began an educational enterprise that continued without interruption into the 2000s. In 1722 the JESUITS, who contributed notably to the spiritual and economic well-being of the area, undertook the spiritual jurisdiction of the native peoples of the colony, a responsibility entrusted to them by Bishop Louis DUPLESSIS-MORNAY of Quebec. Their endeavors were supported in large measure by an extensive indigo and sugar plantation adjacent to New Orleans. In July 1763, while Michael Baudouin (1691–1768) was superior, the Jesuits were dispossessed of their property and banished from Louisiana. Their departure, some ten years before the society was suppressed, seriously hampered and retarded the growth of the Church in colonial Louisiana.

After 1772 Church affairs in New Orleans bore a definite Spanish stamp. Cirilo de Barcelona, chaplain of the Spanish expedition against the British in West Florida, was consecrated auxiliary bishop for the Louisiana colony on March 6, 1785. Shortly before leaving for his consecration in Cuba, he appointed his assistant, Antonio de SEDELLA, temporary pastor of St. Louis. For decades thereafter, Sedella, known as Père Antoine, was the center of controversy in the area.

First Bishops. When the Diocese of Louisiana and the Floridas was created in 1793, Luis Ignacio de PEÑALVER Y CÀRDENAS was consecrated as first ordinary; he arrived in New Orleans on July 17, 1795, marking the beginning of home government in Church affairs. Peñalver noted in a report to the Spanish government that of the 11,000 Catholics in New Orleans, only about 400 performed their Easter duty. He instituted a number of necessary reforms, combated religious indifference and Voltaireanism, and established parishes in such places as the Poste des Avoyelles, Many (Neustra Señora de Guadalupe at Bayou Scie), and Monroe. Meanwhile, the parish church in use since 1727 had been destroyed in the great fire of 1788 and a new structure, the future Cathedral of St. Louis, was completed in 1794. Renovated several times, it was elevated to a minor BASILICA in 1964.

In 1801 Peñalver was transferred to the Archdiocese of Guatemala and jurisdictional quarrels, interdiction, and threats of SCHISM marked the next fifteen years in New Orleans. Père Antoine was at odds with Reverend

Patrick Walsh and Canon Thomas Hassett, who administered the diocese during the episcopal vacancy. The wardens of the CATHEDRAL (*marguilliers*), after assuming control of Church temporalities in 1805, waxed more and more arrogant; and, to complicate matters further, Spain ceded Louisiana back to France, which, in turn, sold it to the United States in 1803. Aware of the territorial transfer, the HOLY SEE decided not to send Bishop-elect Francisco Porro y Peinado to Louisiana, and on September 1, 1805, placed it temporarily under the spiritual supervision of Bishop John CARROLL of Baltimore, Maryland. Carroll in time named the chaplain of the Ursulines, Jean Olivier, his vicar general, but the latter's authority was openly challenged by Père Antoine and the cathedral wardens. Finally, on August 18, 1812, Reverend Louis William DUBOURG, president of Georgetown College and founder of St. Mary's College in Baltimore, was named administrator apostolic by Archbishop Carroll. Dubourg, complying with Andrew Jackson's request, officiated at a TE DEUM in St. Louis Cathedral following the U.S. victory over the British at the Battle of New Orleans on January 8, 1815.

On September 24, 1815, Dubourg was consecrated in ROME, and Louisiana finally had a bishop, after an interregnum of nearly fifteen years. Dubourg, however, remained in Europe for the next two years, enlisting priests and seminarians as well as the services of the Religious of the Sacred Heart and helping to form the organization that eventually became the Pontifical Society for the PROPAGATION OF THE FAITH. Upon arriving in the United States, Dubourg went to St. Louis, Missouri, and returned to New Orleans only in late 1820. The next year he called a synod, attended by twenty priests. On March 25, 1824, Joseph ROSATI, C.M., was consecrated as Dubourg's coadjutor, but he supervised from a distance because he resided in St. Louis. The Sisters of Charity from Emmitsburg, Maryland, arrived to staff the Poydras Asylum in New Orleans. Dubourg resigned in mid-1826 and died in 1833 as archbishop of Besançon, France.

Dubourg's resignation left the lower end of the Mississippi Valley without a resident bishop, which caused disorder that Rosati's annual visits could not completely control. Rosati, appointed bishop of St. Louis in 1827, in time recommended a fellow Vincentian for the See of New Orleans, and Leo Raymond de Neckère (1800–1833) was consecrated in St. Louis Cathedral on June 24, 1830. His regime was brief, for he was stricken with yellow fever and died on September 5, 1833. A few months before on April 21, 1833, he had established the second New Orleans parish, St. Patrick's, to accommodate the Irish immigrants and other English-speaking people of the city. He had also invited to the diocese the Sisters of Our Lady of Mount Carmel from Tours,

France, but they arrived after the bishop's death and settled in Plattenville on Bayou Lafourche.

A remarkable period of Church expansion coincided with the growing importance of New Orleans as a center of commerce and expanding population. The city emerged as fourth largest in the nation; its population increased from 29,737 in 1830 to 102,193 in 1840. The diocese covered the entire state and had a total population approaching 300,000, served by twenty-six churches and twenty-seven priests, when Antoine BLANC became fourth bishop on November 22, 1835.

Blanc. During the twenty-five years Blanc administered the see, the number of churches increased to 73 and priests, to 92. He established Assumption Seminary on Bayou Lafourche, 2 colleges, 9 academies and schools, 4 orphanages, a hospital, and a home for girls. Under the guidance of Etienne Rousselon, vicar general, the Sisters of the HOLY FAMILY were founded in 1842 as a diocesan African-American RELIGIOUS congregation to teach, care for orphans, and tend to the aged of the African-American community. The cause for the canonization of their foundress, Henriette Dehille (1813–1862), was introduced in 1988. Blanc invited five communities of nuns to the diocese: the Sisters Marianites of Holy Cross (1848), the Sisters of ST. JOSEPH of Bourg (1856), the SCHOOL SISTERS OF NOTRE DAME (1856), the Sisters of Our Lady of the GOOD SHEPHERD (1859), and the DOMINICAN SISTERS, who did not arrive from Cabra, Ireland, until four months after his death. The Redemptorist fathers established themselves (1843) in nearby Lafayette, where German, Irish, and French immigrants had settled. The Jesuit fathers opened the College of the Immaculate Conception in 1849 on a plot of ground that had once formed part of the plantation of which they had been defrauded in 1763. The Congregation of HOLY CROSS came (1849) to stabilize St. Mary's Orphan Boys' Home, opened by Adam Kindelon, first pastor of St. Patrick's. Reverend Cyril De la Croix organized the first conference of the Society of ST. VINCENT DE PAUL after a layman, William Blair Lancaster, brought a manual of the society to New Orleans (1852).

Blanc called two diocesan synods and two provincial councils. A long and severe struggle with the church wardens culminated in the withdrawal of the clergy from the cathedral (1843). During the recrudescence of NATIVISM, he was the target of polemics and abuse in the press, but a loyal laity, represented by the Catholic Temperance Society, rallied to his defense. In Blanc's litigation with the wardens, the Louisiana supreme court upheld the position of the bishop (1844). Three years after Blanc became archbishop of New Orleans in 1850, his jurisdiction was reduced about 22,000 square miles by the erection in the upper part of the state of the Diocese of Natchitoches, but the Catholic population of the archdiocese decreased by only 25,000. After his death on June 20, 1860, the archdiocese was administered by Father Rousselon until the arrival of Archbishop-elect Jean Marie ODIN from Galveston, Texas.

Odin. The second archbishop took possession of his see only a few days after the bombardment of Fort Sumter on April 12, 1861. Louisiana had already seceded from the Union and joined the Confederacy. During the Civil War, the archbishop's position was an extremely delicate one, calling for infinite tact and diplomacy. The times grew more trying after the city was occupied by federal troops on May 1, 1862. Union forces wrought considerable damage on Church properties in such places as Pointe Coupée and Donaldsonville, and the war years witnessed a disruption of religious and educational work in Thibodaux, Convent, Plaquemine, Grand Coteau, and elsewhere. Reconstruction was no less trying, but Odin continued, within limitations, the expansion program of his predecessor.

During the archbishop's visit to Europe in 1863 in search of men and money for his diocese, the MARIST FATHERS accepted his invitation to labor in Louisiana. In 1867 the OBLATE SISTERS OF PROVIDENCE, a Baltimore community of African-American nuns, began staffing a home for dependent children. The LITTLE SISTERS OF THE POOR opened their home for the aged poor after a committee of pious women, called Les Dames de la Providence, asked for their help in maintaining a home for the aged founded in 1840. The Brothers of the Sacred Heart came to New Orleans from Mobile, Alabama, in 1869. The archbishop invited the SISTERS OF MERCY, who began visits to the parish prison, city workhouse, boys' house of refuge, and mental hospital in 1869. The first Benedictine CONVENT in the archdiocese opened (1870) in the German national parish of Holy Trinity, New Orleans. The nuns arrived from Covington, Kentucky, and later established a motherhouse in Covington, Lousiana.

After numerous request for assistance, Odin obtained a coadjutor with right of succession, Napoléon Joseph Perché (1805–1883), who had been chaplain of the Ursulines for many years, founder (1842) of the first Catholic newspaper in Louisiana, *Le Propagateur Catholique* (1842), and vicar general of the archdiocese. He was consecrated in St. Louis Cathedral on May 1, 1870, and succeeded to the see when Odin died in France on May 25, 1870.

Perché and Leray. Like his predecessors, Perché invited several communities to the archdiocese: the Sisters of Perpetual Adoration, now known as the SISTERS OF THE MOST HOLY SACRAMENT, who arrived at Waggaman in 1872; the Sisters of CHRISTIAN CHARITY, who established themselves at St. Henry's convent, New

Orleans, in 1873; and the Discalced Carmelite Nuns, who arrived in 1877. In addition, Archbishop Perché approved the founding of a diocesan community, the Sisters of Immaculate Conception, organized on July 11, 1874, in Labadieville with Elvina Vienne as first superior. Soon after his installation as head of the see, Perché inaugurated a costly program of church building, school construction, and parish foundations that contrasted sharply with the record of his predecessor. These expenses, plus financial aid to families impoverished by the Civil War, increased archdiocesan debt to $590,925, of which $257,080 was due European bondholders.

Weakened by age and infirmities and overwhelmed by the tremendous debt, the archbishop asked for a coadjutor. The Holy See appointed François Xavier Leray (1825–1887) of Natchitoches, who became archbishop upon Perché's death on December 27, 1883. Leray's chief concern as coadjutor and as ordinary was reducing archdiocesan debt, so he began few building or expansion programs. The only new community established in the archdiocese was that of the Poor Clare Nuns (1885). Upon his death on September 23, 1887, Leray was succeeded by Francis Janssens (1843–1897), the Dutch-born bishop of Natchez.

Janssens. The new archbishop received the PALLIUM from Cardinal James GIBBONS on May 8, 1889, although he had taken possession of the archdiocese on September 16, 1888. He invited the BENEDICTINES of St. Meinrad's Abbey in Indiana to open a seminary to train priests. Luke Grüwe, O.S.B., established in 1890 what later became St. Joseph's Abbey (St. Benedict, Louisiana), and Janssens dedicated the seminary on September 3, 1891. The archbishop welcomed Mother Frances Xavier CABRINI to New Orleans and encouraged her in 1892 to establish a house primarily to assist Italians, who were migrating in large numbers to the city. In 1893 he asked the Sisters of the Holy Family to care for dependent or neglected African-American boys, and thus started the present Lafon Home for Boys, one of several institutions named for, and supported by, a bequest from the local African-American philanthropist Thomy Lafon (1810–1893).

Janssens was greatly esteemed throughout the archdiocese, which numbered 341,613 in the centennial year of 1893. He encouraged spiritual ministrations to patients at the leprosarium at Carville, Louisiana. When the hurricane of 1893 swept the Louisiana Gulf Coast, Janssens used a small boat to reach the Italian, Spanish, and Malay fishermen in the island settlements to comfort them; he later helped rebuild their homes. He promoted DEVOTION to Our Lady under the title of Prompt Succor. The corporate structure of each parish, as it existed in the early 2000s, was determined in 1894, when each parish was legally incorporated, with the archbishop, the vicar general, the pastor, and two lay directors as board members. Janssens was the first ordinary to promote native vocations on a large scale. His predecessors depended on priests and seminarians from Europe and leaned heavily on religious to staff new parishes. He sponsored the Catholic Winter School, opened parochial schools, and launched a dozen new parishes. Alarmed at the defections from the Faith among the African Americans, he established St. Katherine's (1895) as an African-American parish, but on a temporary basis, because he did not wish to promote racial segregation. He died June 9, 1897, while en route to Europe in the interest of the archdiocese.

Chapelle. Placide Louis CHAPELLE, sixth archbishop of New Orleans, was transferred from Santa Fe, New Mexico, in February 1898. Concerned about the archdiocesan debt, he ordered the annual contribution of 12 percent of the revenues of each parish for five years. This helped in the eventual liquidation of the long-standing debt, but aroused the displeasure of some pastors. Chapelle's relationships with his priests, many of them born and educated in France, were hardly improved by his extended, though necessary, absences as APOSTOLIC DELEGATE extraordinary to Puerto Rico and Cuba, and later as apostolic delegate to the Philippine Islands. He needed an auxiliary, and the pastor of Annunciation Church in New Orleans, Gustave Rouxel (1840–1908), was consecrated on April 9, 1899. In 1898 the archbishop, to economize, withdrew aid from the preparatory seminary at St. Benedict. Yet he opened a theological seminary (1900) in an existing building next to St. Stephen's Church, New Orleans, with Fathers of the Congregation of the Mission as professors. Some twelve parishes and missions were established during Chapelle's regime, and the Dominican fathers began (1903) their MINISTRY in the archdiocese. Chapelle died a victim of yellow fever on August 9, 1905.

Blenk. The next ordinary, James Hubert Blenk (1856–1917), S.M., was well known to the archdiocese long before his appointment on April 20, 1906. He had served as bishop of Puerto Rico, former auditor and secretary to the apostolic delegation to the West Indies, rector of Holy Name of Mary Church, and president of Jefferson College, Convent, Louisiana. Blenk, an ardent promoter of Catholic education, set up in 1908 the first archdiocesan school board and appointed the first superintendent of schools. The preparatory seminary was again placed under the care of the Benedictine fathers of St. Joseph's Abbey (1908), but theological courses were discontinued (1907). Most major seminarians of the archdiocese matriculated at Kenrick Seminary in St. Louis or St. Mary's Seminary in Baltimore or

studied abroad. In September 1904 the Jesuits started a small college in New Orleans, which in 1911 was amalgamated with the College of the Immaculate Conception and became Loyola University. Blenk designated (1908) St. Mary's the normal school for women religious engaged in teaching in the archdiocese. In time St. Mary's Dominican became an accredited Catholic women's college.

French Benedictine nuns, forced in 1906 to leave their country, settled in Ramsay under the guidance of Paul Schaeuble, O.S.B., who had become first ABBOT of St. Joseph's in 1903. The Sisters SERVANTS OF MARY, who left Mexico during the Carranza revolution, found refuge also in the archdiocese and inaugurated (1914) their ministrations among the sick and bedridden in the city. The sisters of the Society of ST. TERESA OF JESUS, likewise refugees from Mexico, began teaching at St. Louis Cathedral School in 1915. That same year, the archbishop urgently requested Mother Katharine DREXEL, foundress of the Sisters of the BLESSED SACRAMENT, to undertake the education of African-American youth in New Orleans. In 1917 the sisters opened a normal school, and the following year the state legislature authorized them to conduct colleges and confer degrees. The sisters launched XAVIER UNIVERSITY OF LOUISIANA in 1925. For further ministration to the African-American population, the archbishop solicited the services of St. Joseph's Society of the SACRED HEART (JOSEPHITES) and the HOLY GHOST FATHERS and assigned six parishes to the former and one to the latter. In 1911 the BROTHERS OF CHRISTIAN SCHOOLS purchased St. Paul's College, Covington, from the Benedictine Fathers. In 1912 the Ursulines, under the supervision of their chaplain, François Racine, moved from their third convent building to a new site on State Street, where ten years later the national SHRINE of Our Lady of Prompt Succor was erected.

Early in his administration, Blenk strengthened lay groups. He organized the State Board of Holy Name Societies in 1906, the Louisiana State Federation of Catholic Societies in 1909, and the Federation of Catholic Societies of Women of Louisiana. He promoted the Catholic Order of Foresters, the KNIGHTS OF COLUMBUS, and the KNIGHTS OF PETER CLAVER. The growth of the population in the archdiocese, especially in southwest Louisiana, made a division expedient. Partition occurred on January 11, 1918, shortly before Archbishop John William Shaw (1863–1934) was promoted to the New Orleans see. Jules Benjamin Jeanmard (1879–1957), administrator of the archdiocese following the death of Blenk on April 15, 1917, was named first bishop of the new Diocese of LAFAYETTE. The area of the archdiocese was reduced by about 11,000 square miles, forty church parishes, and a population of about 300,000.

Shaw. One of Shaw's first actions was to invite the OBLATES OF MARY IMMACULATE, with whom he had worked closely as bishop of San Antonio, Texas, to administer St. Louis Cathedral and take charge of the churches and missions in Livingston parish. In 1919 the Sisters of Charity of the INCARNATE WORD from San Antonio came to teach at St. Francis de Sales parochial school. In 1920 Archbishop Shaw, with his chancellor August J. Bruening, laid plans for a financial campaign to erect a major seminary. With the help of laymen, the campaign realized close to $1 million, and Notre Dame Seminary, staffed by Marist Fathers, became a reality in September 1923. In Baton Rouge the Sisters of St. Francis of Calais opened Our Lady of the Lake Hospital (1923). Franciscan Fathers returned to the archdiocese on July 21, 1925, to oversee the newly established parish of St. Mary of the Angels in the city and the missions of the Lower Coast. The Sisters of the Holy Ghost and Mary Immaculate arrived from San Antonio in September 1926 to teach the African-American children of St. Luke's School in Thibodaux. Shaw encouraged the endeavors of Catharine Bostick and Zoé Grouchy in the establishment of the MISSIONARY SERVANTS OF THE MOST HOLY EUCHARIST of the Third Order of St. Dominic, a community intended for religious instruction of the children in public schools and for social relief work. In 1928 the Society of the DIVINE WORD took over the mission stations along the lower Mississippi River. In 1931 the Jesuits purchased the old Jefferson College in Convent and converted it into Manresa House for laymen's retreats.

Father (later Bishop) Maurice Schexnayder (1895–1981) began Newman Club work in 1929 at Louisiana State University, one-third of whose student body was Catholic. Monsignor Peter M. H. Wynhoven established (1925) Hope Haven for orphaned and abandoned boys, later placed under the Salesian Fathers of St. John Bosco. Opposite Hope Haven, Madonna Manor for small boys replaced St. Mary's and St. Joseph's Orphanages. Wynhoven, in addition to many other assignments, also reorganized the social services and charities of the archdiocese by setting up in 1924 Associated Catholic Charities. In 1922 Shaw convoked the sixth synod, the first in thirty-three years. In 1932, he launched the official diocesan paper, *Catholic Action of the South*, and served as first editor in chief. It replaced the *Morning Star*, published between 1878 and 1930.

Shaw's last years were burdened by problems of the Depression of the 1930s. Some archdiocesan funds were frozen in local banks, and several parishes struggled to meet the high interest due on monies borrowed during the 1920s. Nevertheless thirty-three new parishes opened between 1919 and 1934. After a brief illness Shaw died on November 2, 1934, and Jean Marius Laval (1854–1937), who in 1911 had been consecrated as Blenk's auxiliary, became administrator.

Rummel. Joseph Francis RUMMEL (1876–1965) became the ninth archbishop of New Orleans. He was born in Germany and immigrated to New York City with his parents in 1882. Rummel studied at seminaries in New Hampshire, New York, and Rome, where he was ordained to the priesthood in 1902 and received his S.T.D. (Doctor of Sacred Theology) in 1903. He took an early interest in social problems and led the relief work for Germans. In 1928 he was ordained bishop of Omaha, Nebraska. On March 9, 1935, he was appointed archbishop of New Orleans. He guided the archdiocese during a period of rapid Catholic growth that saw the establishment of forty-eight new parishes and several schools.

The increasing participation of the laity in Church life became more evident during this period. The most tangible evidence was the growth and multiplication of many local units of national organizations such as the CONFRATERNITY OF CHRISTIAN DOCTRINE (CCD) (1935), the Archdiocesan Council of Catholic Women (1936), the Catholic Youth Organization (CYO) (1936), CHRISTIAN FAMILY MOVEMENT (1953), and Young Christian Workers (1954). The most striking example of the changing nature of Louisiana Catholicism during this period was the Eighth National Eucharistic Congress, held in New Orleans on October 17–20, 1938—the first National Eucharistic Congress to be held in the South.

With the bombing of Pearl Harbor on December 7, 1941, the United States became a nation at war. Louisiana Catholics entered wholeheartedly into the conflict. Archbishop Rummel immediately issued "A Nation at War," urging Catholic support for the war effort. Young men and women enlisted, and the local work force reoriented itself to a wartime economy. Catholic parishes, schools, and institutions participated in the many patriotic drives to support the war effort.

After the war, the archdiocese encouraged generous support for relief efforts, worked for a temporary extension of rent control, and established a local resettlement bureau to assist (and sometimes resettle) more than 33,000 displaced persons who entered the United States via New Orleans between 1949 and 1952.

The post–war years were a time of rapid demographic growth and change. In 1945 the Catholic population of the archdiocese was estimated at 385,000. By 1962 the number increased to 630,000. The G.I. bill provided many with opportunities for college educations, better jobs, and new homes. Whole sections of New Orleans and its surrounding areas witnessed rapid development as new home construction boomed.

Undeveloped suburban land rapidly transformed into populated neighborhoods.

In 1935, 43,411 children were being educated in 122 Catholic elementary, secondary, and special schools. Two Catholic universities—Loyola and Xavier—existed in the archdiocese. By 1965 more than 92,600 students were attending 197 Catholic elementary and secondary schools in the Archdiocese of New Orleans and the recently established Diocese of BATON ROUGE. High school programs rapidly expanded; more teachers and principals held degrees and state certification; curricula diversified as science and mathematics programs expanded; and the proportion of lay teachers grew steadily. The guiding force for much of this period was Monsignor Henry C. Bezou (1913–1989), who served as superintendent of archdiocesan schools from 1943 to 1968.

Rummel labored patiently for more than a quarter century to create a community atmosphere conducive to full racial equality; to foster the growth of church organizations, facilities, and activities among African-American Catholics; and eventually to achieve integration of Catholic parishes, schools, organizations, and institutions. In 1939 Xavier University in New Orleans began a Catholic Action School for African Americans. In 1951 the first archdiocesan secondary school for young black males—St. Augustine High School—was established. Many national and local African-American leaders received their secondary education at St. Augustine.

The 1954 Supreme Court decision in *Brown v. the Board of Education of Topeka, Kansas* marked the legal end to segregated public schools. Louisiana, like the other southern states, resisted desegregation. Legislative attempts to prohibit integration, even in Catholic schools, were eventually declared unconstitutional. Archbishop Rummel was the first Catholic bishop in the South to accept African-American students into his minor and major seminaries. On March 15, 1953, his pastoral letter, "Blessed are the Peacemakers," ordered the desegregation of all Catholic parish activities and organizations. He suspended all Catholic services at Jesuit Bend mission (1955–1958) after an African-American priest was prevented from celebrating Mass there. In his pastoral letter of February 11, 1956, he declared racial segregation morally wrong and sinful. He was also influential in preparing and gaining support for the 1958 U.S. Catholic bishops' statement condemning racism. He believed, however, that the process of integration had to proceed slowly to be successful. Not all shared his patience.

Rummel encouraged local clergy to educate their parishioners in SOCIAL JUSTICE issues and consistently supported their efforts to implement social programs. In 1940 the first Southern Catholic Conference on Industrial Problems was held in New Orleans. Rummel vigorously supported the rights of the working class. He publicly opposed the Louisiana right to work laws and actively supported the efforts of Louisiana agricultural workers, particularly sugar cane workers, to organize in the 1950s. He supported the unsuccessful 1953 sugar cane workers' strike.

Rummel turned over administration of the Archdiocese of New Orleans to Archbishop John P. CODY on June 1, 1962. He passed away in New Orleans on November 8, 1964.

Cody. John Patrick Cody (1907–1982), a native and priest of St. Louis, was ordained in Rome in 1931, ministered in the Vatican Secretariate of State and Archdiocese of St. Louis, and served as auxiliary bishop of St. Louis, coadjutor bishop of St. Joseph, Missouri, and bishop of Kansas City-St. Joseph before his appointment as coadjutor archbishop of New Orleans on July 20, 1961. He was named apostolic administrator on June 1, 1962, and became archbishop on November 8, 1964.

Cody oversaw the rapid expansion of parishes and schools; initiated an extensive building program, particularly for high schools; initiated new programs for the needy and handicapped; expanded programs for Catholic students in state universities and colleges; reorganized archdiocesan administration and finances; promoted greater lay participation through the Confraternity of Christian Doctrine and Family Life Bureau; and encouraged closer relations with Protestant and Jewish communities through Operation Understanding. Twenty-five new parishes were established during his brief tenure.

On March 27, 1962, Cody announced the desegregation of all Catholic schools for the 1962–1963 school year. As Monsignor Henry Bezou later recalled, Archbishop Cody "made it clear that neither gradualism nor tokenism could remain the New Orleans policy." The desegregation order unleashed a storm of protest. The Catholic school in Buras was set on fire. A small, vocal group attacked archdiocesan officials in citizen council meetings; mimeographed sheets, newspaper advertisements, and press releases; and staged public demonstrations. Three protesters were eventually excommunicated, not for their outspoken opposition to integration, but for their public disobedience. One, Judge Leander Perez (1891–1969) of Plaquemines parish, was later reconciled. Despite some student withdrawals, Catholic school enrollment steadily increased in the first three years of desegregation.

Cody also implemented the initial reforms of the Second Vatican Council. Changes in liturgical practices, parish administration, lay involvement, and social outreach were soon evident. He also established new archdiocesan offices to assist an increasingly complex ministry: the Vocation Office, the Family Life Office, the Cemeteries Office, and the Building Commission. In 1965 Cody was transferred to Chicago; he died in 1982.

Hannan. Philip Matthew Hannan (1913–), a native of Washington, D.C., was ordained a priest in 1939, became auxiliary bishop of Washington in 1956, and was named eleventh archbishop of New Orleans on September 29, 1965. In the same year, Harold R. Perry (1916–1991), a native of Lake Charles, Louisiana, and former provincial of the Society of the DIVINE WORD, was appointed auxiliary bishop of New Orleans, the first twentieth-century African-American Catholic bishop.

During his episcopate, the archdiocesan social services programs grew at a tremendous rate. Christopher Homes, Inc. was established in 1966 to provide safe and affordable housing. Catholic Charities sponsored a massive refugee resettlement program for the Cubans and Vietnamese. In 1983 Second Harvesters was established to distribute food to the needy. By the late 1980s the archdiocese was the largest single private provider of social services in Louisiana.

Parish expansion continued at a rapid rate. Thirty-one new parishes were established between 1966 and 1988: eight in New Orleans and twenty-three in the seven surrounding civil parishes. Eastern New Orleans, St. Tammany Parish, the west bank of Jefferson Parish, and St. Charles Parish were the centers of Catholic parish growth.

Existing archdiocesan offices were expanded and new offices such as the Office of Black Ministries and Latin American Apostolate were established. The new consultative process was evident in the establishment of an archdiocesan pastoral council, a priests' council, an elected archdiocesan school board, and several other major advisory boards. A series of town hall meetings led to an archdiocesan-wide RENEW program. The Eighth Archdiocesan Synod (1987), culminating seven years of consultation and review, promulgated a new set of policies, procedures, and norms to reflect the new vision of the Church and to "renew the life of the People of God by setting forth regulations accommodated to the needs of the times."

The first archdiocesan formation program for permanent deacons began in 1972; the first class was ordained two years later. By 2001 there were 192 permanent deacons in the archdiocese. Permanent deacons minister in a variety of programs in parishes, prisons, hospitals, the Stella Maris Maritime Center, Ozanam Inn, and Project Lazarus (hospice for AIDS patients), among others.

In 1975, 80,000 attended the HOLY YEAR celebration in the newly built Superdome. In 1984 Vatican Pavilion was part of the Louisiana World Exposition held in New Orleans. On September 12–13, 1987, Pope JOHN PAUL II made his historic visit to the city.

Schulte. Francis Bible Schulte (1926–), a native of Philadelphia, was ordained priest in 1952, ordained auxiliary bishop in 1981, appointed bishop of the Diocese of Wheeling-Charleston, West Virginia, in 1985, and elevated to the twelfth archbishop of New Orleans on February 14, 1989.

Almost immediately, Archbishop Schulte undertook a comprehensive study of archdiocesan schools. The study recommended strengthening the office of superintendent, establishing a strong middle-school program, subsidizing needy schools, making teachers' salaries higher and uniform, standardizing registration and activity fees, and developing a marketing strategy for parochial schools. In 1991 the many archdiocesan ministries, apostolates, programs, and services were reorganized. Six departments—Clergy, Religious, Christian Formation, Community Services, Financial Services, and Pastoral Services—were created to direct and coordinate the ministries of archdiocesan offices and programs. In 1992 a new mission statement emphasized the multicultural composition of the archdiocesan family as well as the Church's commitment to proclaim and embody the Good News of JESUS CHRIST, to build a peaceful kingdom, and to be a servant to all regardless of social condition or religious affiliation.

The rapid expansion of archdiocesan parishes, schools, and social programs; the centralization and growth of administration; and the resultant growth of lay employees placed new financial demands on the archdiocese. In 1989 the archdiocese had a $12 million external debt. In 1990 a finance council of local business leaders was established. Central accounting procedures were standardized. Departmental budgeting, reporting, and accountability were put in place. Regular internal audits of parishes and schools began. A decade later the archdiocesan external debt was eliminated, despite continued, though restrained, expansion.

In 1993 the archdiocesan bicentennial celebration included a special Mass, the publication of a volume of historical essays, an exhibit at the New Orleans Museum of Art, and a capital campaign to establish a $20 million endowment for Notre Dame Seminary, needy Catholic schools, and retired and infirm priests. The campaign surpassed its goal and was the most successful in archdiocesan history.

In 1996 the archdiocese began a five-year parish reevaluation and planning program called Catholic Life: 2000. Each parish undertook a detailed, broad-based self-study, assessing its strengths and weaknesses in wor-

Easter in New Orleans. *Worshipers look on during Easter services at Saint Louis Cathedral on March 23, 2008, in New Orleans, Louisiana.* MARIO TAMA/GETTY IMAGES

ship, word, service, and resources. These were reviewed and coordinated at a deanery and then an archdiocesan level. Catholic Life: 2000 was promulgated in 2001, charting the future of parish revitalization, transformation, and restructuring to better serve the Church and the wider community with available resources.

New Orleans has always been a cosmopolitan city; the archdiocese was no different. African Americans formed the core of city political leadership. More than a dozen Catholic parishes were predominantly African American. Hispanic membership increased in many parishes. The fastest growing archdiocesan immigrant community was the Vietnamese. In 1983 the first Vietnamese parish was established; in 1995 St. Agnes Le Thi Thanh Parish for Southeast Asians was founded in Marrero. By 2001 two national parishes and three missions served the vibrant and fast-growing Vietnamese Catholic community in the archdiocese. In 2001 Hanmaum Korean Catholic Church opened in Metairie.

Twenty-First-Century Developments. Between 2001 and 2008 the eight civil parishes comprising the Archdiocese of New Orleans experienced a change in leadership, the massive destruction and population dislocation following Hurricane Katrina, and a renewed commitment to evangelization and the promotion of racial harmony.

On January 3, 2002, Archbishop Alfred C. Hughes (1932–), the former bishop of Baton Rouge, was appointed archbishop of New Orleans to succeed retiring Archbishop Francis B. Schulte. The previous year Archbishop Hughes had been named coadjutor. Archbishop Hughes indicated evangelization as his highest priority.

Three archdiocesan priests were named to the episcopacy: Monsignor Thomas J. Rodi to Biloxi (2002), Monsignor Roger P. Morin as a New Orleans auxiliary (2003), and Monsignor Dominic Luong to Orange, California (2003). Bishop Luong became the first Vietnamese bishop in the United States. In 2006 Father Sheldon J. Fabre, a priest of the Diocese of Baton Rouge, was named auxiliary bishop of New Orleans.

On July 1, 2001, Blessed Frances Xavier Seelos Parish was established, but five parishes below the French Quarter were closed and consolidated. In August, Henriette Delille School opened as a tuition-free school for inner-city girls. Twenty-three religious communities pledged financial support for the school. The school did not reopen after Hurricane Katrina.

In 2003 the two largest archdiocesan social agencies, the Social Apostolate and Catholic Charities, merged to form Catholic Charities, Archdiocese of New Orleans. In the fall of 2004 Francesco Cardinal Marchisano (1929–) presided at the inauguration of St. Louis Cathedral/Old Ursuline Convent: A Catholic Cultural Heritage Center. In 2005 the archdiocesan phase of the Cause for Canonization of Henriette Delille was completed and sent to the VATICAN. Henriette Delille (1812–1862) founded the Sisters of the Holy Family and became the first African American whose Cause for Canonization was canonically introduced.

On August 29, 2005, Hurricane Katrina slammed into Louisiana and the Mississippi Gulf Coast. More than 1,000 archdiocesan buildings were damaged or destroyed. St. Nicholas of Myra Parish facilities and records, together with Father Arthur Ginart, the pastor, were swept into the Gulf of Mexico. The hurricane occasioned the largest refugee movement in American history.

Immediately after the storm, the archbishop and his staff reassembled in Baton Rouge where Bishop Robert Muench (1942–) made his staff and facilities available. Offices resumed operation, sharing space with their Baton Rouge counterparts. Initial efforts concentrated on locating personnel and parishioners scattered throughout the country and on assessing damages. Daily executive meetings facilitated the slow process of reestablishing archdiocesan ministries. The Office of Catholic Schools initially concentrated on a nationwide effort to find schools for dislocated students.

The first mass after the hurricane was celebrated by candlelight in St. Louis Cathedral in mid-September with mostly military and first responders in attendance. On October 17, Cathedral School reopened in the French Quarter, the first school to reopen in Orleans Parish. The archbishop and his administrative staff returned to New Orleans in late December. Catholic Charities became the conduit through which millions of relief dollars reached those struggling to return and rebuild. An interim pastoral plan permanently closed six parishes and temporarily closed more than twenty others. During the next two and a half years efforts concentrated on the slow process of assisting people, parishes, schools, and institutions rebuild lives and community.

On December 15, 2006, Archbishop Hughes, recalling Archbishop Joseph Rummel's 1956 "The Morality of Racial Segregation," promulgated "Made in the Image and Likeness of God." This pastoral letter on racial harmony addressed the ever-present, unresolved racial undercurrents and mandated steps to address these issues. Among the unresolved issues, the archbishop cited white privilege, generational POVERTY, substandard public education, and a two-tiered healthcare system "extenuated by post–Katrina." The archbishop personally led the action to address these issues.

On January 27, 2007, Cardinal Marchisano returned to inaugurate the delayed Exhibit of the Vatican Mosaic Studio, the first extensive exhibit of the studio ever held outside Rome. The exhibit was a significant contribution to the cultural rebirth of the city.

On April 9, 2008, Archbishop Hughes, following a comprehensive consultation process, announced a new pastoral plan that addressed the changed demographics of the area and the decline in clergy. Three temporarily closed parishes in St. Bernard and Plaquemines Civil Parishes reopened. Twenty-five parishes closed or merged. Four additional parishes became missions, while two others became campus ministry centers. Two years after Katrina, according to statistics in *The Official Catholic Directory, 2008*, the total population declined by twenty-two percent (22%); the number of Catholic households, by twenty-four percent (24%); and Catholic school enrollment, by twenty percent (20%). Among the clergy and vowed religious, the greatest decline was among religious women (48 percent) and religious brothers (32 percent) (*The Official Catholic Directory* 2006; 2008 p. 855). The lack of adequate healthcare prevented many elderly religious men and women from returning to the area.

In promulgating the new pastoral plan, Archbishop Hughes noted that it would result in the loss of some sacred places and significantly reconfigure many sectors of the archdiocese. "All sectors are being asked to share in the sacrifices that it will entail" (Hughes 2008).

SEE ALSO AFRICAN-AMERICAN CATHOLICS IN THE UNITED STATES (HISTORY OF); ALABAMA, CATHOLIC CHURCH IN; ALEXANDRIA, DIOCESE OF; ARKANSAS, CATHOLIC CHURCH IN; BALTIMORE, ARCHDIOCESE OF; BALTIMORE, COUNCILS OF; CANONIZATION OF SAINTS (HISTORY AND PROCEDURE); CARDINAL NEWMAN SOCIETY; CARMELITES; CATECHISMS; CATHOLIC CHARITIES USA; CUBA, THE CATHOLIC CHURCH IN; DEACON; DISCALCED ORDERS; EDUCATION, CATHOLIC (K THROUGH 12) IN THE UNITED STATES; EUCHARISTIC CONGRESSES; EXCOMMUNICATION; FLORIDA, CATHOLIC CHURCH IN; GALVESTON-HOUSTON, ARCHDIOCESE OF; GEORGETOWN UNIVERSITY; LOUISIANA, CATHOLIC CHURCH IN; MISSION AND MISSIONS; MISSISSIPPI, CATHOLIC CHURCH IN; MOBILE, ARCHDIOCESE OF; NATIONAL COUNCIL OF CATHOLIC WOMEN (NCCW); NUN; POOR CLARES; REDEMPTORISTS; SACRED HEART BROTHERS; SALESIANS; ST. MEINRAD ARCHABBEY; TE DEUM; VATICAN COUNCIL II; XAVIER UNIVERSITY OF LOUISIANA.

BIBLIOGRAPHY

Additional information available in the Archives of the Archdiocese of New Orleans.

Archdiocese of New Orleans, *Sacramental Records of the Roman Catholic Church of the Archdiocese of New Orleans, 1718–1825*, vols. 1–7 edited by E. Woods and Charles E. Nolan;

vols. 8–16 by Charles E. Nolan and D. Dupont (New Orleans 1986–2001).

Archdiocese of New Orleans Official Web site, available from: http://www.arch-no.org/ (accessed September 30, 2008).

Roger Baudier, *The Catholic Church in Louisiana* (New Orleans 1939; repr. 1972).

Thomas Becnel, *Labor, Church, and the Sugar Establishment: Louisiana 1887–1976* (Baton Rouge, La. 1980).

Henry C. Bezou, *Metairie: A Tongue of Land to Pasture* (Gretna, La. 1973).

Glenn R. Conrad, ed., *Cross, Crozier and Crucible: A Volume Celebrating the Bicentennial of a Catholic Diocese in Louisiana* (Lafayette, La. 1993).

Michael J. Curley, *Church and State in the Spanish Floridas (1783–1822)* (Washington, D.C. 1940).

Archbishop Alfred C. Hughes, "Advancing the Church's Mission for All," *Clarion Herald*, April 12, 2008, available from http://www.clarionherald.org/pdfs/2008/04_12_08/pastoral/page01.pdf (accessed December 15, 2008).

Annemarie Kasteel, *Francis Janssens, 1843–1897, A Dutch-American Prelate* (Lafayette, La. 1992).

Dolores Egger Labbé, *Jim Crow Comes to Church: The Establishment of Segregated Catholic Parishes in South Louisiana*, 2nd ed. (Lafayette, La. 1971).

Annabelle M. Melville, *Louis William DuBourg: Bishop of Louisiana and the Floridas, Bishop of Montauban, and Archbishop of Besançon, 1766–1833* (Chicago 1986).

Earl F. Niehaus, *The Irish in New Orleans, 1800–1860* (Baton Rouge, La. 1965).

Charles E. Nolan, *A Southern Catholic Heritage*, vol. 1, *Colonial Period, 1704–1813* (New Orleans 1976).

Charles E. Nolan, *A History of the Archdiocese of New Orleans* (Strasbourg, France 2000).

The Official Catholic Directory, 2008 (New Providence, N.J. 2008).

Charles Edwards O'Neill, "Church and State in French Colonial Louisiana: Policy and Politics to 1732" (New Haven, Conn. 1966).

Msgr. Henry Charles Bezou
Archdiocesan Superintendent of Schools
New Orleans, Louisiana

Charles E. Nolan
Retired Archivist, Archdiocese of New Orleans
Long Beach, Miss. (2009)

NEW YORK, ARCHDIOCESE OF

(*Neo-Eboracensis*) Metropolitan see, 4,717 square miles, comprising the boroughs of Manhattan, Bronx, and Richmond, in New York City and the counties of Westchester, Putnam, Dutchess, Rockland, Orange, Sullivan, and Ulster. The DIOCESE was created April 8, 1808; the ARCHDIOCESE, July 19, 1850. The dioceses suffragan to New York included Albany, Brooklyn, Buffalo, Ogdensburg, Rochester, Rockville Centre, and Syracuse. These, along with Newark, Paterson, and part of Trenton, New Jersey, made up the territory of the original see. In the first division (1847), the creation of the Dioceses of Albany and Buffalo cut off the northern and western sections of the state; in the second (1853), the new Sees of Brooklyn and Newark removed Long Island and New Jersey. Since 1861, when the boundary between Albany and New York was readjusted, the limits of the archdiocese, with the exception of the period from 1885 to 1932, when the Bahama Islands were under the jurisdiction of New York, have remained unchanged.

Colonial Period. From the time that Giovanni da Verrazano (c. 1485–c. 1527) discovered New York Bay (1524), the area has had Catholic associations. The explorers Estevan Gomez (c. 1483–1538) and Samuel de Champlain (1537–1635) preceded Henry Hudson (1565–1611) in sailing both the southern and northern waters of the state.

The Dutch. The Dutch settlement of New Amsterdam was only one year old when the Franciscan Joseph d'Aillon, probably the first priest to enter the state, visited the Niagara region (1627). Thereafter JESUITS established missions among the Iroquois. René Goupil (1608–1642) became the first MARTYR within the confines of the state (1642); his companion Isaac Jogues (1607–1646) suffered martyrdom in 1646, with John de Lalande, at Ossernenon (Auriesville). Fathers Claude DABLON and Pierre Chaumonot (1611–1693) built a CHAPEL where Syracuse now stands (1655). Two years later Father Simon Le Moyne (1604–1665) came downriver to minister to a few Catholics, both Dutch and French, in New Amsterdam and probably to offer Mass there on a French ship and in the settlement.

The English. Apart from the converts made by the JESUITS among the indigenous peoples, Kateri TEKAKWITHA being the most famous example (1676), very few Catholics were found in the colony when the Dutch ceded it to the English in 1664. The former, while establishing the Reformed Church, had been mildly tolerant; the latter, especially under the Catholic governor, Thomas Dongan (1683–1688), were for a time even more generous. Dongan's Charter of Liberties and Privileges granted religious freedom, thereby enabling the Jesuits who arrived about this time—Fathers Thomas Harvey (d. 1719), Henry Harrison, and Charles Gage, with two lay brothers to assist them—to celebrate Mass and to set up a short-lived Latin school near the present Trinity Church.

The overthrow of King JAMES II in England and Jacob Leisler's rebellion (May 1689) in New York put an end to such tolerance. Penal laws, similar to those in Britain, thereafter specifically excluded Catholics from the rights of citizenship and banned their priests from the colony under pain of perpetual imprisonment and of death upon escape and recapture. In 1709 the Jesuits were forced to abandon their missions among the Iroquois, and barely a trace of Catholics, native or white, is discernible for the rest of the colonial period. John Ury, a nonjuring Protestant clergyman, suspected of being a Catholic priest and a leader of the "Negro Plot" of 1741, was executed, along with several Spanish Catholic African slaves. A number of exiled French-Acadian Catholics entered New York in 1755 but were scattered through the colony under indenture and soon lost to history as Catholics.

A band of Scottish Catholics settled in the Mohawk Valley (1773) under Father John MacKenna, the first resident priest since Dongan's time. As loyalists they moved to Canada in the course of the American Revolution. Probably as early as 1775 Father Ferdinand FARMER, S.J., began periodic visits to New York City to say Mass secretly for a handful of Catholics in a loft on Water Street. Father de la Motte and other French naval chaplains, one with Washington's troops on the site of the present archdiocesan seminary in Yonkers, celebrated Mass for Catholics of the area during the Revolution. It was not, however, until the state constitution of 1777 guaranteed religious liberty and the British evacuated New York that Father Farmer could openly enter the city in 1784.

Catholic Presence after the Revolution. In October of the same year Charles WHELAN, an Irish Capuchin, arrived in New York, where he began to say Mass in the house of José Roiz Silva, a wealthy Portuguese merchant; Silva's house became the nucleus of a congregation of about 200 Catholics. In the whole state, prefect apostolic John Carroll estimated (1785), there were about 1,500 Catholics. New York was the capital of the republic until 1800, and the small Catholic body was augmented by official representatives of Catholic European powers, in whose houses chaplains also celebrated Mass, and by the few Catholic members of Congress. Led by Hector St. John de Crèvecoeur (1735–1813), the French consul, and taking advantage of a state law of 1784 permitting any religious denomination to organize as a body corporate, they set up The Trustees of the Roman Catholic Church in the City of New York. Crèvecoeur, with $1,000 advanced by Thomas Stoughton, the Spanish consul general, and the latter's business partner, Dominick Lynch, bought the unexpired leases of five lots of the Trinity Church Farm. There, on October 5, 1785, the Spanish ambassador Don Diego de Gardoqui (1735–1798) officiated at the laying of the cornerstone of the mother church of New York, Old St. Peter's, on Barclay Street. In the very method of its establishment, St. Peter's was to be the prototype in a half century of trustee difficulties for the American Church.

With the arrival in late 1785 of another Capuchin, Andrew Nugent, the possibility of abuse in the system became apparent. Nugent, with a group of trustees and parishioners, soon created a faction against Whelan which, despite a hurried visit of Carroll to New York, caused the first SCHISM in the American Church and Whelan's departure from the city. Although Nugent had the satisfaction of opening St. Peter's on November 4, 1786, he in turn antagonized the trustees, and Carroll, who made a second visit to the city in 1787, suspended him. Nugent lost his post through the trustees' legal action and was succeeded by a Dominican, William O'BRIEN. For a decade thereafter O'Brien maintained harmony and collected funds and furnishings for the infant church. In periodic yellow fever epidemics he ministered heroically to victims. In his time a second church, St. Mary's in Albany (1798), was built. St. Peter's free school opened (1800), the first of its kind in New York and the recipient of public funds after 1806. Elizabeth Ann Seton, later foundress of the Sisters of Charity, was received into the Church in 1805.

Diocese. On April 8, 1808, Pope PIUS VII (pope 1800–1823) created the Diocese of New York and appointed Richard Luke Concanen (1747–1810), an Irish Dominican resident in ROME, first BISHOP. Due to the Napoleonic Wars, Concanen never reached his see and died in Naples. In June 1810 the POPE empowered John Carroll, now ARCHBISHOP of Baltimore, to appoint a vicar general for New York. Thus, in October 1808 Anthony KOHLMANN, accompanied by fellow Jesuit Benedict FENWICK, and four scholastics, arrived from Maryland as administrator. Although the two priests found St. Peter's congregation to be composed mainly of Irish-Americans, they preached in French and German as well as in English and soon attracted a numerous flock (14,000). On June 8, 1809, Kohlmann laid the cornerstone of the second church in the city, St. Patrick's, intended as a CATHEDRAL for the first bishop.

In the same year he founded the New York Literary Institution, a college that prospered until the recall of most of the Jesuits to Maryland in 1813. In 1812 three Ursuline nuns from Ireland opened an academy and free school. In 1813 a group of exiled French TRAPPISTS started an orphan asylum in the building vacated by the Literary Institution. Again the promise proved abortive: The Trappists returned to France in 1814, and the URSULINES sailed for Ireland two years later. Meanwhile Kohlmann was recalled to Maryland (1815) two years

Altar of St. Patrick's Cathedral, New York. *Dedicated in 1879, this cathedral is one of the most recognized landmarks in New York City.* © BOB KRIST/CORBIS

after winning, in a celebrated case before the Court of General Sessions, a favorable decision respecting the seal of Confession, which set a precedent in American law. On May 4, 1815, old St. Patrick's Cathedral, Mott Street, was dedicated by Bishop CHEVERUS of Boston.

Connolly. Six months later John CONNOLLY, who had been an Irish Dominican living in Rome at the time he was consecrated second bishop of New York on November 6, 1814, arrived in his see. He found about 15,000 Catholics in a population of 100,000, only three churches, and four priests in a diocese covering all of New York state and the northern half of New Jersey. Compelled to act as bishop, parish priest, and curate, he succeeded in opening another free school in the basement of St. Patrick's (1816). He also introduced Mother Seton's Sisters of Charity to the city (1817), made long visitations of his diocese (1817 and 1820), and established nine additional churches. New York State grew rapidly and became after 1820 the most populous in the Union. Construction of the Erie Canal (1817–1825) attracted thousands of Irish laborers for whom the bishop could not provide priests. He had no seminary and noted sadly what he considered the repugnance of American youth to the ecclesiastical state. His problems multiplied when public aid for church schools ended in 1824 because of alleged misuse of funds by the Bethel Baptist Church corporation. Moreover, he lost probably his ablest assistant when Benedict Fenwick was withdrawn from New York by his Jesuit superiors (1817). He also had strained relations with some of his clergy and especially with the trustees who controlled the churches. Fathers Charles French and Thomas Carbry supported the bishop and were in open opposition to Fathers Peter Malou and William Taylor, who were on the side of the trustees. So acrimonious did the debate become that the trustees sent Taylor to Rome to complain against and possibly to supplant the ordinary. Bishop PLESSIS of Quebec was directed by the cardinal prefect of the Congregation of Propaganda Fide to visit New York (1820) and report on the trouble. The departure from the diocese of the priests who led both factions and the suspension of Malou brought an uneasy peace, but it further depleted the ranks of the clergy.

When Bishop Connolly died on February 6, 1825, the diocese fell to the care of his vicar general, John POWER, who arrived from Ireland in 1819. By his moderation and his ability, Power won the affection of all parties and was expected to succeed to the see. In the twenty-one months of his administration, he reinstated Malou; founded New York's first Catholic newspaper, the *Truth Teller* (1825); built a new orphan asylum under the care of the Sisters of Charity (1826); and dedicated a third church in the city, St. Mary's (1826). The ap-pointment, therefore, of John DUBOIS, president of MOUNT ST. MARY'S COLLEGE AND SEMINARY in Emmitsburg, Maryland, as third bishop in 1826 came as a somewhat unwelcome surprise to the preponderantly Irish congregations in New York. They viewed him as a Frenchman, incapable of fluent English and seemingly, as a former Sulpician, imposed on them by Archbishop MARÉCHAL of Baltimore and the SULPICIANS there. The new bishop's first pastoral letter (July 1827), in which he sought to refute such suspicions, got a cool reception.

John Dubois. In the summer of 1828, when Dubois made a 3,000–mile tour of visitation, only eighteen priests in his vast diocese ministered to a population of nearly 150,000 Catholics. Shortly thereafter (1829), to secure both priests and funds for a seminary, he journeyed to Rome and Paris. Two years later, unsuccessful in recruiting additions to his clergy, but with about $18,000 in financial aid from the Congregation of Propaganda and the Society for the PROPAGATION OF THE FAITH, he laid the cornerstone of a seminary at Nyack, New York (1833). Within slightly more than a year the building was destroyed by fire, uninsured and a total loss. Subsequent attempts to establish a seminary in Brooklyn and in Lafargeville were equally disappointing. The trustees of the cathedral frustrated Dubois's effort (1829) to set up a school for boys under a RELIGIOUS brotherhood, and in 1834 they refused to accept a successor to their pastor, Thomas Levins, whom Dubois had suspended. They even threatened to withhold the bishop's salary.

Anti–Catholicism. Distracted by internal dissension, the Catholics became targets of a renascent bigotry. Already in 1824 the recently introduced Orange Society had provoked an anti–Catholic riot in Greenwich Village. Ten years later in the same neighborhood, men of St. Joseph's Parish guarded by night the work of building their church, and in 1835 armed parishoners prevented a threatened attack on the cathedral. Editorials in the *Protestant*, the *Awful Disclosures* of Maria Monk, William Brownlee's American Protestant Association, and Samuel Morse's Native American Democratic Association all fomented hatred. Bishop Dubois shunned controversy, but his priests were not so reticent. John Power and Felix Varela in the *Truth Teller*, Thomas Levins and Joseph Schneller in the *Weekly Register* and *Catholic Diary*, and Constantine Pise in the *Catholic Expositor* vigorously rebutted the Protestant press. In Philadelphia, Father John Hughes made a public mark in debate with a Presbyterian minister, John Breckenridge.

In 1837 Dubois, debilitated by his struggle with the trustees, by age, and by crippling attacks of rheumatism, accepted the appointment of John HUGHES as his coadjutor, with right of succession, and consecrated him in St. Patrick's Cathedral on January 7, 1838. From the outset the coadjutor proved master of the situation. Long familiar with the abuses of TRUSTEEISM in Philadelphia, he successfully appealed to the congregation of the cathedral against their truculent trustees (1839) and thus dealt the system a blow from which it was never to recover in New York. In the same year Dubois resigned diocesan management to his coadjutor and entered a reluctant retirement. He died on December 20, 1842. Despite the travail of his administration, the Catholic population of his diocese had risen by one-third, the number of clergy had tripled, and churches had increased fourfold. To care for German immigrants, who increased rapidly after 1830, he had welcomed the REDEMPTORISTS into the diocese, encouraged the building of St. Nicholas's Church in the city, and provided Father John Raffeiner as superintendent of the scattered German communities.

Archdiocese. Under Hughes the See of New York, like the city itself, gained preeminence in America. In the two decades after 1840 about seventy percent of the more than four million immigrants to the United States entered through the port of New York. Many of them, Irish and Germans uprooted by famine and revolution, were Catholics who settled in the city or were drawn along the Hudson and Mohawk valleys to the cotton and woolen mills, iron and tanning industries, and construction on the Croton Aqueduct and the Hudson River railroad. In 1851 alone, 221,213 Irish landed in New York.

John Hughes. For the protection of these immigrants, Hughes encouraged the formation of the Irish Emigrant Society, the Emigrant Industrial Savings Bank, and an immigrant commission of the state legislature. He denounced the importation of Irish secret societies, the foreignism of Young Irelanders and their radical press, and the too-swift Americanization advocated by such native converts as Orestes BROWNSON. He fought sectarian proselytism preying upon the immigrants' destitution, and, controversially, Catholic projects to settle them on western lands. They so swelled the population of the diocese that it was split in 1847 by the erection of the Sees of Albany and Buffalo. New York was raised to an archdiocese in 1850 and restricted again in 1853 by the creation of Brooklyn and Newark. Yet at the time of Hughes's death in 1864, the churches and chapels in this now reduced territory outnumbered by more than twenty those for the whole area of 1840, and the number of priests had more than tripled. The archbishop had established St. Joseph's Seminary (1840) and St. John's College (1841), both at Fordham, New York; promoted the founding of the NORTH AMERICAN COLLEGE in Rome (1859); welcomed the opening of Manhattan College, New York City (1853); and planned a provincial seminary at Troy.

Bishop Hughes's reputation as a formidable controversialist, already proved in the Breckenridge debate, was further publicized in sharp and sometimes bitter exchanges with Mayor James Harper, Colonel William Stone, "Kirwan" (the Reverend Nicholas Murray), Horace Greeley, James Gordon Bennett, Senator Lewis Cass, Erastus Brooks, and Orestes BROWNSON. In 1840 the bishop led a campaign to regain for the eight Catholic free schools of New York City a proportionate share of the common school fund. His argument before the Common Council drew attention (as did his endorsement of a slate of candidates favorable to the Catholic claims in the state election of that year) to the injustice of a situation whereby the professedly nonsectarian, but actually Protestant and privately controlled, Public School Society received state funds at the same time that Catholic schools were excluded from such benefit. Two years later the state legislature, by extending the common school system of the rest of the state to the city, spelled the eventual demise of the society. The apparent failure of the Catholics forced them back upon their own meager resources. Led by Hughes, they established thirty-eight new free schools and academies before the end of his episcopate.

The aggressiveness of their bishop, while inspiriting his largely immigrant and hitherto rather supine flock, excited nativist alarm. A mob smashed the windows of the cathedral and of the bishop's house in 1842. Two years later, armed Catholics, with Hughes's encouragement, again defended the cathedral and themselves from a repetition of the nativist riots in Philadelphia. Anti–Catholic sentiment also accounted for the election in 1844 of James Harper (1795–1869) as mayor on the Native American ticket and for the origin in New York in 1852 of the Know-Nothing party. The city, although it fervently greeted the revolutionist Louis Kossuth (1802–1894) in 1851, treated shamefully papal nuncio Archbishop BEDINI two years later. National absorption in the issues leading to the Civil War helped to dissipate prevalent bigotry. Archbishop Hughes, who in 1846 had declined a request of President Polk (1795–1849) that he intercede with the Catholic Mexicans at the outset of the Mexican War, readily accepted in 1861 a commission from his friend William Seward (1801–1872), Secretary of State, and from President Lincoln (1809–1865) to visit Europe and there represent the Union cause. The Catholic laity of New York, largely Irish, while deprecating abolitionism as did their archbishop, contributed impressive numbers and valorous service, particularly in the famous New York 69th Regiment, to the Union forces. Their religious communities, especially the Sisters of Charity and the SISTERS OF MERCY, were among the first nurses of the battlefield. Moreover, it was mainly the personal appeal of the archbishop himself, at the request of Governor Horatio Seymour (1810–1886), that quelled the notorious New York draft riots of 1863.

John Hughes died on January 3, 1864, leaving a well-ordered archdiocese and ecclesiastical province. Improvements had been effected through the legislation of the first two New York diocesan synods (1842, 1848) and three provincial councils (1854, 1860, 1861). Hughes had organized a diocesan chancery (1853), patronized ten new religious communities, and rescued church property from the mismanagement of lay trustees. His flock had increased in numerical strength and by the accession of notable converts in what appeared to be an American counterpart of the OXFORD MOVEMENT. They had an articulate press as represented by Brownson's *Quarterly Review,* the *Freeman's Journal,* the *Metropolitan Record,* and Father Isaac HECKER's *Catholic World.* Archdiocesan charities were advanced by the founding of a pioneer conference of the Society of ST. VINCENT DE PAUL and the opening of St. Vincent's Hospital. A local branch of the Society for the Propagation of the Faith was established. The cornerstone was laid for the boldly conceived new St. Patrick's Cathedral, and the archbishop had been recognized as a figure of national prominence.

John McCloskey. The importance of New York in the nation and in the universal Church received recognition during the next episcopate (1864–1885) in the elevation of its archbishop to the cardinalate. John MCCLOSKEY—a native of New York, consecrated coadjutor to Hughes in 1844, transferred to Albany as its first bishop in 1847, and installed as fifth bishop and second archbishop of New York on August 21, 1864—became America's first prince of the Church in 1875. The ceremonies of INVESTITURE of the new CARDINAL and the dedication, four years later, of the new cathedral received unprecedented publicity, attesting the change in public sentiment toward the Church. This was further evidenced by the election in 1880 of William R. Grace (1832–1904) as first Catholic mayor of the city. The cardinal, unlike his predecessor, mild-mannered and benign, stood as a public figure mainly because of his rank. During his irenic administration the archdiocese experienced more than double the growth in number of churches, clergy, and schools. Significantly, as immigrants raised the Catholic population of towns along the Hudson, fifty-eight of the ninety new churches were built outside New York City. Holy Rosary Mission was founded (1884) to minister to the large proportion of Catholics among the more than six million immigrants who debarked at Castle Garden between 1861 and 1890.

To provide for Catholic Italians, who arrived in steadily increasing numbers after 1880, the first church exclusively for their use was entrusted to the Pallottine Fathers (1884).

The national complexion of the clergy was also changing. Hitherto, although 107 priests had been ordained from St. Joseph's Seminary in Fordham (1840–1861), a major proportion of the New York clergy was recruited in Europe, especially in Ireland. With the opening of St. Joseph's Provincial Seminary in Troy (1864–1896), the 741 priests ordained there for the various dioceses of the ecclesiastical province were almost all native Americans. From 1864 to 1885 approximately sixteen religious communities of priests, sisters, and brothers arrived to assist them. Charitable works increased proportionately, notably the opening of the New York Foundling Hospital under the Sisters of Charity, the first institution of its kind in the United States; the New York Catholic Protectory for delinquent children; Father John DRUMGOOLE's Mission of the Immaculate Virgin for homeless waifs; and a rapid multiplication of conferences of the St. Vincent de Paul Society. Elsewhere signs of confidence and maturity appeared in the founding of Hecker's Catholic Publication Society, P. J. Hickey's popular *Catholic Review,* and John Gilmary SHEA's United States Catholic Historical Society. Although the third and fourth diocesan synods (1868 and 1882) and the fourth provincial council (1883), which the cardinal convoked, did not effect all the executive reorganization and pastoral adaptation necessary in a fast-changing archdiocese, his untroubled administration stands in contrast to those of his predecessor and successor. Enfeebled in his last years, he relied increasingly upon the assistance of a coadjutor archbishop until his death on October 10, 1885.

Corrigan. The coadjutor since 1880, Michael A. CORRIGAN immediately succeeded to the archbishopric. One of his first acts was to convoke the fifth New York diocesan synod (1886), the decrees of which, in twenty titles and 264 numbers, were so thorough and brought such efficiency into diocesan administration and discipline that the four subsequent synods of his episcopate (1889, 1892, 1895, 1898) added little to them. The Catholic population almost doubled during Corrigan's administration (1885–1902). More than five million immigrants entered the country between 1881 and 1890, followed by almost four million in the next decade, the majority now coming from Catholic sections of Europe. As early as 1886 the archbishop, in a report to Rome, noted among the foreign-language-speaking Catholics in New York City some 60,000 Germans, as many Bohemians, 50,000 Italians, 25,000 French, 20,000 Poles, and lesser numbers of French-Canadians,

Spaniards, Greeks, and Lithuanians. By 1902 non-English-speaking Catholics in New York had the services of more than 100 priests of their respective nationalities and more than 50 churches. The Italians alone, the largest group among them, had 50 Italian priests and 20 churches and chapels as well as the ministrations of the recently arrived Pallottine sisters, Mother Cabrini's MISSIONARY SISTERS OF THE SACRED HEART, the Scalabrinian Fathers, and the SALESIANS. The BLESSED SACRAMENT FATHERS came to work among the French-Canadians and the ASSUMPTIONISTS among the Spanish-speaking. During the same period the total number of churches and chapels again more than doubled, as did the number of diocesan and regular clergy. Eight new religious communities of men and sixteen of women began work in the archdiocese. Two of them, the Sisters of the DIVINE COMPASSION and the DOMINICAN SISTERS of St. Rose of Lima, were founded in New York. Despite the severe depression of 1893 to 1896, a model seminary, the new St. Joseph's in Dunwoodie, was built. Corrigan also inaugurated a trend toward specialization in the work of the clergy by establishing the New York apostolate, a CONFRATERNITY OF CHRISTIAN DOCTRINE, a superintendent and an association of diocesan charities, a diocesan superintendent of schools, examining boards for teachers, and school commissioners for the various districts of the archdiocese.

Catholic education was a hotly debated issue. The archbishop had the satisfaction of promulgating in his synod of 1886 the instructions of the Third Plenary Council of Baltimore (1884) on the necessity of parochial schools. He doubled the number of such schools within his own jurisdiction and rallied New York patronage as the main support of a national Catholic summer school (1892). He viewed as harmful to the concept and growing system of Catholic schools such compromise solutions as the Faribault-Stillwater experiments of Archbishop John IRELAND of St. Paul and the POUGHKEEPSIE PLAN in operation in his own archdiocese since 1873. His conservative position on this question and on others such as membership of Catholics in secret societies, Irish nationalism, the Catholic University in Washington, and the prevalence of a heterodox AMERICANISM, led to disagreement with other members of the American hierarchy, particularly Archbishop Ireland, and to an ecclesiastical *cause célèbre* in New York.

Edward MCGLYNN, rector of St. Stephen's Church and long an opponent of separate schools, in 1886 actively associated himself with the mayoral campaign of Henry George (1839–1897), to whose radical land and tax theories he publicly subscribed. Refusing to obey the archbishop's prohibition of such political engagement, McGlynn was repeatedly suspended and eventually removed from St. Stephen's. Subsequently excommunicated for failure to account in Rome for his insubordination and his adherence to the Georgian economic theories, he and his supporters bitterly denounced the archbishop and the Roman authorities. The affair, exploited by a sensational newspaper press, focused unwarranted attention on personalities and detracted from more substantial and positive elements of the New York Church. Despite the furor, the archbishop, characteristically, held to a routine of efficient diocesan administration. He oversaw construction of the seminary in Dunwoodie, completed the spires of his cathedral and projected its Lady Chapel, and planned, before his death on May 5, 1902, a preparatory seminary.

Farley. His successor, John M. FARLEY, auxiliary bishop since 1895, was installed as fourth archbishop of New York on October 5, 1902. Astutely pursuing a policy of conciliation, dramatically emphasized in his returning from Rome in 1904 with the nomination to monsignorial dignity of eight of his priests (an unprecedented number and some of them former partisans of McGlynn), he soon overcame the residue of disunion in the ranks of the clergy. The beginning of monthly days of RECOLLECTION for priests in the same year, the opening of Cathedral College as a preparatory seminary in 1903, and a doubling of the number of priests of religious communities also added vigor and numbers to the clergy, so necessary to cope with a still mounting population. Although before the end of his administration (1918), the trend of older residents away from Manhattan toward Brooklyn and New Jersey had begun, immigration still accounted for a rise of about 200,000 in Catholic population. In a decade (1901–1910) that greeted nearly 9,000,000 immigrants, of whom 1,285,349 came in 1907, the peak year in American immigration history, Italians constituted the largest segment of Catholics. Only a few months after his accession, the archbishop presided at a meeting of his Italian clergy to discuss the problem. Of the slightly more than 100 new churches he established, more than a third were for the care of Italian-Americans. The HOLY GHOST FATHERS began their ministry among the African Americans of Harlem, and in 1912 Mother Drexel's Sisters of the BLESSED SACRAMENT opened their first school for African-American children there.

The era also saw the ebbing of debate over Catholic education. The archbishop, created a cardinal in 1911, strongly supported the rather precarious fortunes of The CATHOLIC UNIVERSITY OF AMERICA, the infant NATIONAL CATHOLIC EDUCATIONAL ASSOCIATION, and the organization of the College of New Rochelle, the first Catholic college for women in the state. While the Catholic population of the archdiocese rose by about twenty percent, church schools and their enrollments doubled in number; two priests were appointed superintendents of parochial schools. Approximately 2,000 Catholic teachers in the public schools were united in an association called The Workers for God and Country. Other signs of vitality appeared in the publication, under the auspices of Dunwoodie Seminary, of the highly respected *New York Review* (1905–1908), the first scientific Catholic theological journal in the United States, and the *Catholic Encyclopedia* (1907–1914), largely under the cardinal's patronage. These years also marked the corporate conversion of the Anglican Friars and Sisters of the Atonement, the beginning of the laymen's retreat movement, and public celebration of the centenary of the diocese. The Lady Chapel of the cathedral was completed and the entire edifice solemnly consecrated. The Catholic Foreign Mission Society of America (Maryknoll) established its headquarters and seminary in the archdiocese, the local Society for the Propagation of the Faith was reconstituted, and contributions to missions rose from a few thousand dollars annually to more than a quarter of a million by 1918. An attempt to coordinate all other charities of the archdiocese in an organization known as the United Catholic Works was arrested by the outbreak of World War I.

Before Cardinal Farley died on September 17, 1918, the U.S. entrance into the war tested the resources of the archdiocese. The cardinal founded the New York Catholic War Council, which sponsored a soldiers' and sailors' club, a women's Catholic patriotic club, and a Catholic hospital for shell-shocked patients. His auxiliary bishop (since 1914), Patrick J. HAYES, was appointed by the Holy See to be bishop ordinary of the U.S. army and navy chaplains (1917). He so effectively recruited and organized the corps of Catholic chaplains that by the end of the war there were 1,523 priests in five vicariates under his jurisdiction. Of the 1,023 Catholic chaplains already commissioned by November 11, 1918, the 87 from New York formed a contingent more than twice as large as that from any other diocese. Bishop Hayes also made personal appeals on behalf of the Liberty Loans and was a director of a KNIGHTS OF CO-LUMBUS drive that raised nearly $5 million for work among servicemen.

Hayes. On March 10, 1919, in the same year that a fellow native of the lower East Side, Alfred E. Smith (1873–1944), became the first elected Catholic governor of the state, the former auxiliary was named to the See of New York as its fifth archbishop. Five years later he received an enthusiastic reception, replete with ticker-tape parade from the Battery, when he returned from Rome a cardinal. During the nineteen years of his administration the Catholic population of the archdio-cese fell from more than 1,250,000 to about 1,000,000. This was the result of the gradual decline in immigration during the 1920s and a sharp drop during the Depression years of the 1930s as well as an accelerated exodus of Catholic families to metropolitan areas beyond his jurisdiction. The number of churches, nevertheless, increased by one-sixth; schools, by one-half; and the clergy, by one-third. Charitable institutions and services had multiplied, often with overlapping and duplication of activity and at the expense of economy and efficiency. Three months after his accession the new archbishop announced a detailed survey of the more than 200 welfare agencies of the archdiocese, and in the following year he coordinated them all under a secretary for charities, at the head of a corporation entitled Catholic Charities of the Archdiocese of New York. The new organization was commended by the New York State Board of Charities (1920) as "the most significant and important event of the year in the field of charitable work." The Catholic Charities of the Archdiocese of New York quickly assumed a position of leadership among private welfare organizations throughout the country and served as a model for other dioceses. Supported by a special gifts committee of the laity and an annual parish appeal that soon netted over $1 million yearly, Catholic Charities successfully met the challenge of the severe financial depression following the stock market collapse of 1929 and earned for its founder the popular title Cardinal of Charity.

Never a dynamic public figure, the cardinal spent the last years of his life in semi-retirement. He did, however, introduce the Catholic Youth Organization to the diocese (1936), patronize the literature committee that bore his name, and promote a Catholic theater movement. The heart ailment which seriously restricted his activities eventually resulted in his death on September 4, 1938.

Spellman. The appointment of Francis J. SPELLMAN, the auxiliary bishop of Boston, as the sixth archbishop of New York on April 15, 1939, shattered two precedents. He was the first archbishop of New York in 100 years who had not been closely associated with his predecessor, and he was a significant figure in the American hierarchy even before his appointment to New York. As a result of his friendship with both Pope PIUS XII and President Franklin D. Roosevelt (1882–1945), as well as his own intelligence, energy, and ambition, Spellman became the most important archbishop of New York since John Hughes and the most influential American PRELATE since James Cardinal GIBBONS. As expected, he received the cardinal's red hat at the first postwar consistory on February 18, 1946.

Once installed as archbishop on September 8, 1939, Spellman quickly modernized and centralized the organizational structure of the archdiocese. He refinanced the diocesan debt of $28 million through bankers in New York and Boston, saving the archdiocese $500,000 per year in interest payments. In short order he introduced a central purchasing agency, a diocesan insurance office, and a diocesan building commission. He also reorganized the chancery office, matrimonial tribunal, and administrative offices of the archdiocese, housing them in an elegant mansion across the street from St. Patrick's Cathedral. Spellman's centralizing policies ended the autonomy that pastors had enjoyed under Hayes. Although Spellman compensated them with a lavish bestowal of papal honors, he deliberately remained an aloof and impersonal figure to his priests. For the day-to-day administration of the archdiocese, he relied heavily on the services of James Francis MCIN-TYRE and later John MAGUIRE, both of whom in turn were appointed coadjutor archbishops without the right of succession.

Spellman played an important role on both the national and international scene. He was instrumental in persuading President Roosevelt to appoint a personal representative to the Holy See on December 23, 1939. Spellman's responsibilities as military vicar for the Armed Forces (an appointment he received on December 11, 1939) increased dramatically following the U.S. entry into World War II. Thereafter the Military Ordinariate became one of the largest dioceses in the world with several million military personnel and their families and some 5,000 full- and part-time chaplains. Throughout the era of the Cold War, Spellman remained an outspoken foe of Communism both at home and abroad. His ecclesiastical influence was further enhanced because New York City was the headquarters of important national agencies such as Catholic Relief Services, the Catholic Committee on Refugees, the Bishops' Resettlement Committee for Refugees, the Catholic Near East Welfare Association, and the Society for the Propagation of the Faith.

The advent of World War II forestalled any large-scale building projects in the archdiocese, but, even before Pearl Harbor, Spellman established two new parishes, installed a new main altar in St. Patrick's Cathedral, relocated the minor seminary, and began a system of diocesan high schools. After the war the archdiocese embarked upon a major expansion of its infrastructure. Between 1939 and 1967 enrollment in Catholic schools almost doubled on the elementary level (to 179,052) and almost tripled on the high school and college levels (to 49,842 and 27,949 respectively). Spellman spent several million dollars renovating St. Joseph's Seminary, adding a new library and gymnasium. Catholic Charities also experienced a major expansion of its 200 member agencies as well as the construction of a dozen new hospitals, homes for the aged, and childcare centers. The New York Foundling Hospital, one of Spellman's favorite charities, was moved to a modern facility, and St. Vincent's Hospital developed into a full-fledged medical center.

After declining during the 1920s and 1930s, the Catholic population of the archdiocese almost doubled during the Spellman years from about 1,000,000 to 1,848,000. Much of the increase was due to the influx after World War II of more than 600,000 Puerto Rican immigrants, who transformed many of the traditional Catholic ethnic neighborhoods into solidly Hispanic enclaves while the older residents joined the flight to the suburbs. To meet this major pastoral challenge, Spellman established an Office of Spanish Catholic Action and made a major commitment of diocesan clergy. By 1961 the archdiocese had over 200 Spanish-speaking priests, and approximately one-third of the parishes provided religious services in Spanish.

Vatican II. After Vatican II (1962–1965), Spellman dutifully implemented the liturgical changes although he deplored them privately as "too many and too soon." He also divided the archdiocese into six vicariates, established an elected Senate of Priests, and agreed to the creation of two experimental parishes headed by a team of priests. One of Spellman's proudest moments occurred on October 4, 1965, when Pope PAUL VI (1963–1978) made a one-day visit to New York City and celebrated Mass in Yankee Stadium before a crowd of 92,000 worshippers. In the fall of 1966 (at the age of seventy-seven) he offered the pope his resignation, but it was refused. During the 1960s the Civil Rights movement and the Vietnam War together with the impact of Vatican II led to a period of unprecedented turmoil for American Catholics. By the time of Spellman's death on December 2, 1967, the successful synthesis of Catholicism and Americanism that he once epitomized no longer seemed adequate to the needs of the day.

Cooke. The appointment on March 8, 1968, of Terence J. COOKE as the seventh archbishop of New York was a surprise to many knowledgeable observers. A native New Yorker only forty-seven years old, Cooke was the youngest of the ten auxiliary bishops and (with the exception of Hughes and Corrigan) the youngest ordinary ever appointed to New York. His selection was widely attributed to the influence of Spellman, with whom he had been closely associated for the previous ten years. Like Spellman, Cooke was also appointed Military Vicar for the Armed Forces (April 4, 1968) and was made a cardinal (April 28, 1969).

Cooke received his baptism of fire on the day of his installation, April 4, 1968, when the assassination of Dr.

Martin Luther King, Jr. (1929–1968), touched off riots throughout the country. That evening Cooke went to Harlem to plead for racial peace. He played little role in national or international affairs, except as chairman of the U.S. Bishops' Committee on Pro-Life Activities, where he worked vigorously to combat ABORTION. However, he concentrated his attention on his own diocese, providing two much-needed skills, managerial ability and pastoral sensitivity. An affable man who preferred conciliation to confrontation, he was also the master of the soft answer that turns away wrath but concedes nothing. A born micro-manager, he used his detailed knowledge of the inner workings of the archdiocese to administer carefully the available financial resources. Critics complained that his financial expertise was not matched by long-term vision, but his non-confrontational style of leadership spared New York the ideological polarization among the clergy that occurred in some other dioceses.

During Cooke's years as archbishop, the population of the archdiocese remained virtually the same, but only because Catholic immigrants, predominantly Hispanic, replaced the dwindling number of middle-class white Catholics. The sacramental statistics indicated an abrupt decline in religious practice. Infant baptisms fell from 50,219 in 1967 to 32,168 in 1984, and church weddings declined from 15,511 to 10,208. For the first time in history a sharp drop occurred in the number of both diocesan priests (from 1,108 to 777) and diocesan seminarians (from 501 to 238). Under Spellman the number of parishes had increased by 34; under Cooke there was a net gain of only 4 parishes. In order to utilize better the diminishing resources, Cooke established the Inter-Parish Finance Commission, which levied a tax on all parishes and then used the income to subsidize the poorer parishes. By 1979 the total funds disbursed amounted to $26 million. As a result only 49 of the 305 parish elementary schools were forced to close despite a massive decline in enrollment (from 179,052 in 1967 to 89,853 in 1984) and the mass exodus of 3,257 of the 4,130 sisters from the classrooms.

Cooke consolidated the administrative offices of the archdiocese in a new Catholic Center on the East Side of Manhattan, established the Office of Pastoral Research, opened the St. John Neumann Residence for seminarians, founded the Archdiocesan Catechetical Institute, and organized the Inner-City Scholarship Fund, which provided subsidies of more than one million dollars per year to minority students (two-thirds of them non-Catholic) in parochial schools. Sensitive to the demographic changes in the archdiocese, he appointed the first African-American and Hispanic auxiliary bishops, created the Office of Black Catholics, and supported the Northeast Center for Hispanics. As Military Vicar he discreetly defended U.S. involvement in the Vietnam War and also continued Spellman's practice of frequent visits to troops overseas.

Not all of the leadership in the archdiocese came from the top. In South Bronx, the poorest Congressional district in the United States, as crime, arson, and the abandonment of buildings engulfed twenty square miles of the borough in the early 1970s, parish priests and religious organized community action groups and sponsored urban renewal projects to stop the decline. Jill Jonnes, the historian of the Bronx, wrote in 1986: "The Catholic Church quietly emerged as the institution most committed to preserving and resurrecting the benighted South Bronx. Not one church or Catholic school was closed." In 1979, when the newly elected Pope JOHN PAUL II made a two-day visit to New York City, he overrode the security concerns of the police and stopped in both Harlem and the South Bronx before celebrating Mass in Yankee Stadium. On August 26, 1983, after a secret eight-year struggle with cancer, Cooke revealed to the public that he was terminally ill. After his death on October 6, 1983, large crowds filed past his bier and attended his funeral in tribute to the inspiring way that he had faced death. The New York *Daily News* commented: "[He] showed us all how to pass from time to eternity with courage and grace."

O'Connor. Cooke's successor was John J. O'CONNOR, a native of Philadelphia, who was appointed the eighth archbishop of New York on January 31, 1984. He had served in the Military Ordinariate as auxiliary bishop to Cooke from 1979 until 1983, when he became the bishop of Scranton. Prior to that, he had spent twenty-seven years as a navy chaplain, rising to Chief of Chaplains with the rank of Rear Admiral. O'Connor was made a cardinal on May 25, 1958. On that same day the Military Ordinariate was separated from New York, ending a personal connection that had existed under the three previous archbishops since 1917.

Despite his sixty-four years, O'Connor adopted a busy schedule that he maintained almost to the end of his sixteen years in New York. He preached virtually every Sunday in St. Patrick's Cathedral and made frequent pastoral visits throughout the archdiocese as well as numerous trips to Rome. Unlike Cooke, he adopted a high profile and signaled his intention to give New York the same national prominence that it had enjoyed under Spellman. Unlike Spellman, however, who relied on personal political and business connections, O'Connor made deft use of his communications skills to influence public opinion through the media. An admirer of the feisty John Hughes, the first archbishop of New York, O'Connor seemed to welcome public confrontation over controversial issues such as abortion. The *New York Times*, often a critic of O'Connor, grudgingly admitted in 1998 that he was "perhaps the one person in New York with a platform to rival that of the mayor" and shortly before his death acknowledged him as "the de facto leader of American Catholics." (*New York Times*, May 31, 1994).

Between 1984 and 2000 the Catholic population of the archdiocese increased from 1,839,000 to 2,407,393, constituting 45 percent of the total population. However, the number of baptisms remained virtually the same, and the number of marriages declined by a quarter. The ethnic, economic, and social diversity of the archdiocese was remarkable. One rural parish in Dutchess County contained 50,000 acres of private land for fox hunting, while in one Bronx parish 58 percent of the people lived below the poverty level. Mass was celebrated in at least twenty-two languages every Sunday with 135 of the 413 parishes providing Mass in Spanish. Hispanic Catholics included not only Puerto Ricans, but also Dominicans, Mexicans, and natives of many Central and South American countries. A new phenomenon was the influx of Asian Catholics from Korea, China, Vietnam, and the Philippines. Immigrants from Albania, Palestine, Portugal, Haiti, and even an increase in immigration from Ireland added to the ethnic mix.

The enrollment in the 303 Catholic elementary and high schools remained steady at around 100,000, with almost half of the students (many of them non-Catholics) coming from minority groups. The archdiocese also remained a major provider of health care and social services with 17 hospitals, 3 health care facilities, 17 homes for the aged, 14 child-caring institutions, and 129 social agencies operated by Catholic Charities. "They provided the best social services that were available," said Mayor Edward Koch (1924–). The staffing of parishes and schools became increasingly difficult because O'Connor in his later years was reluctant to close or consolidate them despite the decline in the number of diocesan priests (from 777 in 1984 to 563 in 2000), teaching sisters (from 873 to 236), and teaching brothers (from 93 to 60). On a more positive note, two new religious communities were founded, the Franciscan Friars of the Renewal and the Sisters of Life, and the number of permanent deacons increased to 310.

O'Connor offered his resignation to the pope upon reaching age seventy-five in 1995, but it was refused. That year Pope John Paul II (pope 1978–2005) made his second visit to New York and celebrated Mass in Central Park with 125,000 people in attendance. In late August 1999 O'Connor underwent surgery for a brain tumor from which he never recovered and died on May 3, 2000.

Egan. The appointment of Edward Egan (1932–) as the ninth archbishop of New York was announced on May 11, 2000, only eight days after the death of Cardinal O'Connor. A native of Oak Park, Illinois, Egan was ordained in Rome as a priest of the Archdiocese of CHICAGO on December 15, 1957. He returned to Rome to earn a doctorate in canon law and later to serve as a judge of the Roman Rota from 1971 until 1985. In that year he was appointed auxiliary bishop of New York where he served as the vicar for education until his appointment as the bishop of Bridgeport on November 8, 1988. He was installed as archbishop of New York in St. Patrick's Cathedral on June 19, 2000, and was made a cardinal on February 21, 2001.

The bloody events of September 11, 2001, made a lasting impact on the people of New York City. On that day Islamist terrorists in two highjacked commercial airplanes attacked the twin towers of the World Trade Center resulting in a loss of almost 3,000 lives. Every parish church held impromptu services and more formal services on September 14, a national day of mourning. Some parishes in New York City and the suburbs suffered the loss of dozens of parishioners and celebrated memorial Masses for victims whose bodies were never recovered. At the cathedral, Archbishop Egan presided over two or three funeral Masses a day for weeks. An estimated 90 percent of the almost 400 police officers and firefighters who lost their lives in the collapse of the twin towers were Catholics. Among them was Father Mychal Judge (1933–2001), O.F.M., the fire department chaplain, who was killed by falling debris while ministering to the dying. For weeks afterwards the crowded churches testified to the searing impact of the atrocity on the souls of all New Yorkers.

Like Spellman in 1939, one of Egan's main priorities was the restoration of the financial condition of the archdiocese, a task that he had already accomplished in the diocese of Bridgeport. In keeping with his goal of reducing the annual operating deficit of more than $20 million, he consolidated the seminary facilities, streamlined the administrative offices of the archdiocese, closed some failing schools, reduced the weekly archdiocesan newspaper to a monthly, and gave clear indication of the need for further economies. By 2002 the annual operating deficit had been eliminated, and by 2007 the last of the archdiocesan debt was liquidated.

In 2006 Egan announced the first comprehensive realignment of parishes in the history of the archdiocese. The plan called for the closure of ten parishes, the merger of ten others, and the establishment of six new parishes. In addition the fate of five other parishes was left undecided depending on a further review, and eleven new churches were to be erected in existing parishes. The plan won general acceptance from clergy and laity alike as a necessary response to the changing demographics of an archdiocese whose boundaries had not been changed in over 150 years.

Papal Visit. *Pope Benedict XVI celebrates Mass at St. Patrick's Cathedral in New York on Saturday, April 19, 2008.* AP IMAGES

The total Catholic population reached 2,554,454 in 2007, reclaiming the lead over both Chicago and Boston, and making New York second only to Los Angeles in number of Catholics. Much of the increase was due to the influx of Catholic immigrants from Latin America and the Caribbean and later from Asia and Africa. By the bicentennial year of 2008, Mass was celebrated every Sunday in thirty-three languages, including Akan, Arabic, Igbo, and Tagalog.

Beginning in 2002 the Catholic Church in the United States was racked by one of the most serious crises in its history with the unfolding of the full dimensions of the SEX ABUSE SCANDAL. A survey commissioned by the U.S. bishops concluded that between 1960 and 2002 four percent of the U.S. Catholic clergy had been accused of the sexual abuse of minors. The comparable figure for the archdiocese of New York was less than one percent. Despite the relatively favorable statistics, the archdiocese did not seek to minimize the gravity of the situation. "Any case of sexual abuse of a minor by a member of the clergy is a tragedy," declared

Egan, who created a Safe Environment Office, formulated a Code of Conduct for the Clergy, and established a review board composed primarily of lay people.

Egan also made a major effort to preserve the troubled Catholic school system. Although enrollment decreased from 227,120 in 1965 to 106,400 in 2007, it increased modestly each year throughout Egan's tenure. Thus the archdiocese of New York directed the largest private school system—religious or secular—in the nation. The archdiocese also made a major commitment to expanding and enhancing the quality of religious instruction for the 108,229 Catholic children in public schools and more than 10,000 catechists were engaged in parish programs.

Communication also received attention. The archdiocesan newspaper, *Catholic New York*, became a bimonthly rather than a monthly publication and had the largest circulation of any diocesan newspaper in the United States. The archdiocese also acquired a channel on Sirius Satellite Radio to carry Catholic programming, twenty-four hours a day, seven days a week, throughout the United States and Canada.

The Catholic Charities of the archdiocese remained the largest private provider of social services in New York State with an annual budget in excess of a half-billion dollars. More than 100 institutions and agencies ran the gamut from the venerable New York Foundling Hospital to newly developed programs to feed the hungry that provide families and individuals with more than 6,000,000 meals a year. In 2007 Catholic Charities assisted 516,093 people, and Catholic hospitals and specialized homes provided care for 1,471,770 patients.

The highlight of the 2008 bicentennial celebration of the archdiocese, which included Masses and receptions in nineteen vicariates, lectures, concerts, and museum exhibits, was a three-day visit to New York by Pope BENEDICT XVI beginning on Friday, April 18, 2008, when he addressed the General Assembly of the United Nations, met with the Jewish community at the Park East Synagogue, and conducted an ecumenical prayer service at St. Joseph's Parish Church in the Yorkville section of Manhattan. The following day the Holy Father celebrated Mass in St. Patrick's Cathedral for the clergy and religious, and then drove to St. Joseph's seminary, Dunwoodie, where he met with and blessed handicapped children and addressed a youth rally of 34,000. On his final day in New York the PONTIFF visited Ground Zero and celebrated Mass at Yankee Stadium for 60,000 people. "Follow faithfully in the footsteps of those who have gone before you," Benedict told the enthusiastic crowd before flying home to Rome.

In accord with canon law, Cardinal Egan submitted his resignation on April 2, 2007, having reached the mandatory retirement age of 75. His retirement was made official a little over two years later on February 23, 2009, when the Archbishop of Milwaukee, Timothy Dolan, was appointed the new head of the Archdiocese of New York. Archbishop Dolan was officially installed as the tenth Archbishop of New ork on April 15, 2009,

SEE ALSO Bahamas, The Catholic Church in the; Baltimore, Archdiocese of; Baltimore, Councils of; Cabrini, Frances Xavier, St.; Catholic Charities USA; Converts and Conversion; Dominicans; Drexel, Katharine Marie, St.; Education, Catholic (K through 12) in the United States; Excommunication; Faribault Plan; Freedom of Religion; Irenicism; Know-Nothingism; Military Services, USA, Archdiocese for; Mission and Missions; Nativism, American; Netherlands Reformed Church; Newark, Archdiocese of; New Jersey, Catholic Church in; North American Martyrs; Nuncio, Apostolic; Pallottines; Secret Societies, Church Policy on; Scalabrinians; Seton, Elizabeth Ann Bayley, St.; Sulpicians; Vatican Council II.

BIBLIOGRAPHY

Archdiocese of New York Official Web site, available from: http://www.ny-archdiocese.org/ (accessed December 2, 2008).

Mary Elizabeth Brown, *Churches, Communities and Children: Italian Immigrants in the Archdiocese of New York, 1880–1945* (Staten Island, N.Y. 1995).

Mary Peter Carthy, *Old St. Patrick's, New York's First Cathedral*, edited by Thomas J. McMahon (New York 1947).

Florence D. Cohalan, *A Popular History of the Archdiocese of New York* (Yonkers, N.Y. 1983).

Robert Emmett Curran, *Michael Augustine Corrigan and the Shaping of Conservative Catholicism in America, 1878–1902* (New York 1978).

Ana María Díaz-Stevens, *Oxcart Catholicism on Fifth Avenue: The Impact of the Puerto Rican Migration upon the Archdiocese of New York* (Notre Dame, Ind. 1993).

Stephen Michael DiGiovanni, *Archbishop Corrigan and the Italian Immigrants* (Huntington, Ind. 1994).

Jay P. Dolan, *The Immigrant Church: New York's Irish and German Catholics, 1815–1865* (Baltimore 1975).

John Murphy Farley, *Memorial of the Most Reverend Michael Augustine Corrigan, D.D., Third Archbishop of New York* (New York 1902).

John Murphy Farley, *The Life of John Cardinal McCloskey: First Prince of the Church in American, 1810–1885* (New York 1918).

Maureen Fitzgerald, *Habits of Compassion: Irish Catholic Nuns and the Origins of New York's Welfare System, 1830–1920* (Urbana, Ill. 2006).

Robert I. Gannon, *The Cardinal Spellman Story* (Garden City, N.Y. 1962).

Benedict J. Groeschel and Terrence L. Weber, *Thy Will Be Done: A Spiritual Portrait of Terence Cardinal Cooke* (Staten Island, N.Y. 1990).

John R. G. Hassard, *Life of the Most Reverend John Hughes, D.D., First Archbishop of New York* (New York 1866).

Historical Records and Studies, 50 vols. (New York 1899–1964).

Jill Jonnes, *We're Still Here: The Rise, Fall, and Resurrection of the South Bronx* (Boston 1986).

Bernadette McCauley, *Who Shall Take Care of Our Sick? Roman Catholic Sisters and the Development of the Catholic Hospitals in New York City* (Baltimore 2005).

Leo Raymond Ryan, *Old St. Peter's, the Mother Church of Catholic New York (1785–1935)* (New York 1935).

Richard Shaw, *Dagger John: The Unquiet Life and Times of Archbishop John Hughes* (New York 1977).

Thomas J. Shelley, *Dunwoodie: The History of St. Joseph's Seminary, Yonkers, New York* (Westminster, Md. 1993).

Thomas J. Shelley, *The History of the Archdiocese of New York* (Strasbourg, France 1999).

Thomas J. Shelley, *The Bicentennial History of the Archdiocese of New York, 1808–2008* (Strasbourg, France 2007).

Thomas J. Shelley, *Empire State Catholics: A History of the Catholic Community in New York State* (Strasbourg, France 2007).

John Talbot Smith, *The Catholic Church in New York*, 2 vols. (New York 1905).

Thomas G. Young, *A New World Rising: The Story of St. Patrick's Cathedral* (New York 2006).

Very Rev. James A. Reynolds
Professor of History
St. Joseph's Seminary, Dunwoodie, Yonkers, N.Y.

Msgr. Thomas J. Shelley
Professor of the History of Christianity
Fordham University, Bronx, N.Y. (2009)

NEW YORK, CATHOLIC CHURCH IN

The eleventh of the original thirteen states to ratify the U.S. constitution (1788), New York is bounded on the north by Lake Ontario, the St. Lawrence River, and Canada; on the east by Vermont, Massachusetts, and Connecticut; on the south by New Jersey, Pennsylvania, and the Atlantic Ocean; and on the west by Pennsylvania, Lake Erie, and the Niagara River. The capital city is Albany; other major cities, in addition to New York City, the most populous metropolitan area, are Buffalo, Rochester, and Syracuse. In 2008 the New York population was 19,926,453, second largest in the nation, of whom 7,166,308, about thirty-six percent, were Catholics (*The Official Catholic Directory* 2008, p. 2093). There were eight dioceses. In addition to the metropolitan see of New York City, they include Albany and Buffalo, Brooklyn and Ogdensburg, Rochester and Rockville Centre, and Syracuse.

Early History. Long before New York became known as the Empire State, it was the home of a mighty confederacy of Native American tribes made up of the Mohawks, Oneidas, Onondagas, Cayugas, and Senecas. This union of tribes was known to the French as the Iroquois and to the English as the Five Nations (later Six when the Tuscaroras joined in 1715). Successful in dominating the other Native American tribes of the area, they also terrorized European settlers and missionaries and exercised an important influence on the colonial history of this area.

The first Europeans to come into contact with the Five Nations were the French, who occasionally sent vessels up the Hudson to trade with the Native Americans after Giovanni da Verrazano (c. 1485–c. 1527), a Florentine in the service of Francis I (1494–1547) of France, discovered in 1524 the river and New York Bay. By July 1609 French efforts to found New France and to spread Christianity had penetrated to Lake Champlain, thereby arousing the hostility of the Iroquois, who

for years thereafter held the balance of power between the English and the French in America.

In September 1609 Henry Hudson (1565–1611), an English mariner employed by the Dutch East India Company to search for a new passage to the East Indies, entered New York harbor in the *Half Moon* and followed the river that bears his name as far north as the present site of Albany. On the basis of this claim, the Dutch colony of New Netherland was founded in 1624, when the first permanent settlers consisting of about thirty families, mostly Walloon, arrived. The population had grown to 200 or more by 1626, when the government of the province was fully established with power vested mainly in a director-general and council. Soon after, Manhattan Island was purchased from the Native Americans for sixty guilders (twenty-four dollars), and Fort Amsterdam was erected at its lower end and the settlement there made the seat of government. Although the charter of 1640 declared that "no other Religion shall be publicly admitted in New Netherland except the Reformed...," these Dutch Calvinists were less virulent in their opposition to Catholicism than their New England brethren. In fact, the Dutch at Fort Orange rescued Isaac Jogues (1607–1646), S.J., from the tortures of the Iroquois and brought him to New Amsterdam in the fall of 1643, where Governor William Kieft (c. 1600–1647) received him kindly. Nevertheless, the paucity of Catholic settlers—Jogues found only two in the town—continued during the entire period of Dutch rule despite the fact that the total population of the province increased from 2,000 to 10,000 between 1653 and 1664.

Colonial Period. New Netherland passed into the hands of the English when, in March 1664, CHARLES II erected it with additional territory into a province and awarded it to his brother, James, Duke of York, who became its lord proprietor. The conquest of the Dutch colony was completed without fighting when, on September 8, Governor Peter Stuyvesant (d. 1672) formally surrendered to the English. This marked the beginning of brighter prospects for Catholic settlement in the province henceforth to be known as New York. The conversion to Catholicism in 1672 of the royal proprietor, the future JAMES II, was soon reflected in the directives he issued for the government of his American domain. In 1682 he appointed a Catholic, Colonel Thomas Dongan (1634–1715), as governor and instructed him to accede to the long-standing demand of the colonists for a representative assembly. When the new governor arrived in New York in August 1683, his party included an English Jesuit, Thomas Harvey (d. 1719), who was later joined by two other priests and two lay brothers of his society.

Dongan, an administrator of considerable ability, lost no time in summoning the assembly that in October

1683 passed the bill of rights that he had proposed. This Charter of Liberties and Privileges, containing a guarantee of FREEDOM OF RELIGION, placed the Catholic governor of New York with Roger WILLIAMS, the CALVERTS, and William PENN as the chief promoters of religious freedom in colonial America. During the remainder of Dongan's term of office, the various denominations had their respective houses of worship, and the little Catholic CHAPEL in Fort James was the first site where Mass was regularly offered in New York by the JESUITS, who ministered to the relatively few Catholic settlers. Dongan planned to counteract the influence of French missionaries by seeking additional English Jesuits to take up work among the Native Americans to the north, an area that he felt rightly belonged to the British crown. But his official career ended before the English Jesuits could carry out the mission.

After the English revolution of 1688 and the accession of William and Mary, the American colonies were thrown into a ferment of excitement. In New York the German-born Calvinist Jacob Leisler (1640–1691) led an armed rebellion in May 1689, which ushered in a reign of terror. The policy of religious toleration in New York was soon replaced with restrictive measures against Catholics; the former Governor Dongan was hunted as a traitor, and the Jesuits were compelled to flee the colony. With the establishment by LAW of the Church of England in four of the leading counties of New York in 1693, the long dark night of penal legislation descended upon the few Catholics who were courageous enough to remain in the province. Although Leisler was removed and executed in 1691, anti–Catholic legislation multiplied under Henry Sloughter (1691–1692), the new governor, and his successors.

An act of 1700 made it a crime for a priest to be found in New York, and anyone who harbored a priest was subject to a fine of 200 pounds. Perhaps no other single incident better illustrates the intensity of colonial anti–Catholic rancor than the reception accorded the Acadians, or French Neutrals, expelled from their homes in 1755 and distributed among the colonies from Massachusetts to Georgia. Of the quota sent to New York, the adults were bound out as indentured servants and the children assigned to Protestant families. Unquestionably this persecution and proscription of Catholics in the colony not only sufficed to keep their numbers from increasing but also discouraged any who might have possessed the faith from announcing the fact. These dismal conditions remained until after the Revolution, and Mass was not celebrated in a public manner until offered by the chaplains of the French troops who were sent to aid the colonies in their struggle. Meanwhile, affairs in the colony generally were concerned chiefly with the defense of the northern frontier and the rising disaffection of the colonists with the English colonial policy.

Revolutionary War. The quickening spirit of rebellion against the political and economic measures of the mother country undoubtedly drew increased strength from the prejudice aroused by the passage of the Quebec Act in June 1774. In colony after colony, pulpit and press warned that the "popery act" that secured for Canada freedom for the exercise of the Catholic religion was a serious menace to colonial Protestantism. The first colonial flag run up in New York in place of the English colors bore on one side the inscription "George III–Rex. and the Liberties of America.—No Popery." It is small wonder, then, that Catholics found their position a difficult one, faced as they were with the dilemma of deciding on which side to cast their lot as the colony moved to make common cause with the revolutionists. On July 9, 1776, the delegates to the New York provincial congress adopted the Declaration of Independence and formally committed the province to the rebel cause. Undoubtedly the Catholic colonists were aware that many of the most vigorous opponents of the British policy of coercion had been the bitterest persecutors of papists. On the other hand, their experience with the British government offered little hope for religious liberty or political and social equality. In the end the greater number of Catholics cast their lot with the revolutionists, and only a few joined the loyalist group. The patriotic part played by American Catholics in the revolutionary struggle and the aid of Catholic France and Spain marked a weakening of the anti–Catholic bias. However, when Congress advised the several states to adopt constitutions, the New York convention meeting for that purpose at Kingston on March 6, 1777, adopted an amendment to the naturalization clause, proposed by John Jay (1745–1829), which effectively excluded foreign-born Roman Catholics from citizenship. Not until 1806 was this offensive clause abrogated. Nevertheless, the period of Catholic proscription was drawing to a close, and when on November 25, 1783, the British forces finally evacuated New York City, Catholics in the city assembled once again for the open celebration of their religion.

Institutional Growth. In the years that followed the War for Independence, and especially in the early nineteenth century, remarkable gains were made in the social and economic fields, the extension of agriculture, the development of manufactures, the growth of commerce and transportation, and the improvement of educational facilities. Companies that acquired land grants from the state encouraged systematic colonization of Iroquois country, drawing settlers from Vermont, Massachusetts, Connecticut, and elsewhere in the state.

The need for laborers to build the great inland waterways, the Erie and the Champlain-Hudson canals, in the time of Governor De Witt Clinton (1817–1821; 1825–1828), brought a flood of immigrants from Ireland, Scotland, England, and Germany. Their descendants settled the towns and cities that grew up along the canals, and in turn drew others into the region. Thus the population of the state grew from 340,120 in 1790 to almost two million in 1830, and there were a goodly number of Catholics among the new immigrants, notably the Irish.

When Baltimore was raised to the status of an archbishopric in 1808, New York was one of the new suffragan sees. Its territory included all of New York state and the upper half of New Jersey. The first division of the DIOCESE was made in 1847 when the northern and western sections of the state were cut off to create the dioceses of Albany and Buffalo. Bishop John MCCLOSKEY, then coadjutor bishop in New York, became the first BISHOP of Albany from 1847 to 1864, when he returned to New York City as ARCHBISHOP. The Reverend John TIMON, superior of the Congregation of the Mission (VICENTIANS) and sometime missionary in Texas, was named the first bishop of Buffalo. In 1850 Pope PIUS IX made New York a metropolitan see and named Bishop John HUGHES as the first archbishop. Boston, Hartford, Albany, and Buffalo were its suffragans. Two more dioceses were carved out of the archdiocese of New York in 1853, Brooklyn and Newark, New Jersey. The Reverend John LOUGHLIN was named the first bishop of Brooklyn, and the Reverend James Roosevelt BAYLEY (a nephew of Elizabeth Bayley SETON), the first bishop of Newark (and later, the eighth archbishop of Baltimore). The diocese of Rochester was separated from Albany in 1868 with Bishop Bernard J. MCQUAID as the first ordinary. Four years later in 1872 Ogdensburg was made a diocese. About the time that Syracuse was made a diocese in 1886, the Bahama Islands were placed under New York jurisdiction because access was thought to be easier than from Charleston, South Carolina, which formerly had jurisdiction. The diocesan structure of the state of New York remained unchanged from 1886 until 1957, when Rockville Centre was separated from Brooklyn.

For much of the nineteenth century, the Church in New York depended on priests from Europe to staff the national parishes that were being established to serve different ethnic groups, but early on the bishops of New York endeavored to establish their own seminary. Bishop DUBOIS built a seminary at Nyack-on-Hudson in 1833, but it burned down as it was ready to open. After several other abortive attempts, Bishop John Hughes opened St. John's Seminary in 1841 at Fordham, then a village outside the city. In 1864 the students were moved to St. Joseph's Provincial Seminary in Troy, New York. Before it closed in 1896 it educated more than 700 priests. The poor living conditions at the Troy seminary caused Bishop McQuaid to open St. Bernard's Seminary in Rochester in 1893, and in 1896 Archbishop CORRIGAN established St. Joseph's Seminary in the Dunwoodie section of Yonkers. The Dunwoodie seminary gained a reputation as an intellectual center of American Catholicism. From 1905 to 1908 its faculty were major contributors to the *New York Review*, the leading Catholic theological publication in the country, and to the *Catholic Encyclopedia* (1907–1912).

Immigration picked up momentum after the Civil War. Beginning in the 1880s immigrants from Italy and Slavic lands came in increasing numbers. By the turn of the century, an estimated 400,000 immigrants lived in the archdiocese of New York alone, and Buffalo had a number of large Polish parishes. French-Canadians emigrated from Quebec to settle in upstate New York around Cohoes and Plattsburg. But the flood of immigrants also stirred a new wave of anti–Catholic bigotry. In the 1850s Archbishop John Hughes openly confronted the Know-Nothing movement so that it did not have the impact in New York that it had elsewhere in the country. In 1855 the state legislature passed a statute that prohibited Catholic bishops from holding title to property in trust for the churches and ecclesiastical institutions, but it was quietly repealed after the Civil War began. Later in the century, however, the National League for the Protection of American Interests (NLPAI) made an effort to deny government funds to Catholic schools and charitable institutions.

The legacy of the NLPAI continued. Several city and state investigative committees submitted Catholic social agencies to close scrutiny in the years before World War I. In 1916 the bishops organized the New York Catholic Conference, the first such organization in the United States to provide a forum for the exchange of information between dioceses on social issues and matters of concern to the Church. The conference enabled the dioceses of the state to present a unified position with regard to existing legislation and public policy. After the war Archbishop Patrick J. HAYES (1919–1938) reorganized Catholic Charities and set professional standards for social welfare that were widely imitated by other dioceses.

Despite restrictive laws in the 1920s, immigration continued during the years between World War I and World War II. As Catholics increased in numbers they came more and more to exercise political influence and public policy. Alfred E. Smith (1873–1944), the first Catholic presidential nominee of a major party, was known for his efforts to bring about reforms during his four terms as governor of New York (1919–1920; 1923–1928). Catholic social agencies collaborated in welfare

Papal Visit. *Pope Benedict XVI greets Catholic faithful as he exits the altar after conducing Mass on April 20, 2008, at Yankee Stadium in New York.* JULIE JACOBSON/AFP/GETTY IMAGES

programs during the depression, and individual Catholics like Dorothy DAY and John LAFARGE were prophetic voices speaking against war and racial discrimination.

In the wake of World War II, the Church experienced many changes. An influx of Puerto Ricans arrived in the city of New York. The GI Bill created a whole new clientele for colleges and universities, and thus caused Catholic institutions to expand both physical plants and academic programs. The growth of the suburbs, at the expense of the size, economy, and social make-up of the urban centers, had an impact on the Church in the cities. As the urban congregations dwindled in size and number, dioceses were forced to build new parishes and schools in the suburbs. The diocese of Rockville Centre was an example of the change. The Catholic population, predominantly white middle class, almost tripled between the time it was split off from the diocese in Brooklyn in 1957 to 2008, growing from 497,000 to 1.4 million (*The Official Catholic Directory* 2008, p. 2093).

Catholic Education. Alongside the free elementary schools, provided as early as 1633 during the period of Dutch control, and higher education that had its beginning with the founding of King's College (Columbia) in 1754, the Church gradually developed an extensive network of elementary schools, high schools, and colleges. At the beginning of the twenty-first century, twenty-nine Catholic universities and colleges existed in the state, many of which were located in the metropolitan region of New York City. Jesuit-run Fordham University (1841) was the first Catholic institution for higher education in New York, and the College of New Rochelle (established 1904 by the URSULINES) was the first Catholic college for women chartered in the state. Other prominent Catholic universities in the state include ST. BONAVENTURE UNIVERSITY (sponsored by the Franciscans); St. John's University in Jamaica, New York, and Niagara University (both sponsored by the Vincentians); Manhattan College in the Bronx (sponsored by the De La Salle Brothers); Iona College in New

Rochelle (sponsored by the IRISH CHRISTIAN BROTH-ERS); and Canisius College in Buffalo (sponsored by the Jesuits).

The Twenty-First Century. In the bicentennial year of the establishment of the diocese of New York on April 8, 1808, Empire State Catholics faced many of the same pastoral challenges as other Catholics in the old industrial cities of the Northeast and Midwest that had once been the thriving heartland of American Catholicism.

In 2007 New York state still contained three of the largest dioceses in the United States, the archdiocese of New York (2,554,454) and the dioceses of Brooklyn (1,561,638) and Rockville Centre (1,396,723), which together accounted for three-quarters (74%) of the Catholic population of the state. By contrast the five dioceses that comprised forty-eight of the fifty-two upstate counties all experienced a decrease in their Catholic population as a result of stagnant demographic growth (1.1% in the 1990s, comparable to North Dakota and West Virginia), the exodus of young people, and long-term economic decline. The change was most notable in the diocese of Buffalo, where the Catholic population declined from 913,640 in 1965 to 692,215 in 2007. The decrease in the Catholic population in upstate New York would have been even greater except for the influx of Hispanic immigrants, especially from Mexico, and lesser numbers of Catholic immigrants from Asia, Africa, and Eastern Europe.

As a result of these population changes, the dioceses of Buffalo, Rochester, and Syracuse announced plans to close or merge a quarter of their parishes, reducing the number from 590 in 2005 to 440 in 2007. A steep decline in the number of priests throughout the state also occurred, from 7,404 diocesan and religious priests in 1965 to 4,186 in 2007. The shortage of clergy was especially acute in the diocese of Ogdensburg, the largest diocese in area in the state, where the number of parishes without resident pastors increased from one in 1965 to forty-one of 109 parishes in 2007, leaving many pastors responsible for two parishes (*The Official Catholic Directory* 1965, 2005, 2007).

In the forty years after the close of Vatican II, Catholic elementary and high schools suffered a catastrophic loss of more than two-thirds of their enrollment, from 788,985 students in 1965 to 231,806 students in 2008, with almost half of the remaining students (92,697) in schools in the archdiocese of New York (*The Official Catholic Directory* 2008, p. 2093). The backbone of the Catholic educational system had always been the teaching sisters, but they dwindled from 15,027 in 1965 to 637 in 2008, less than five percent of their former numbers. On a happier note, 412,556 public school children received religious instruction in 2008. However, sacramental practice did not keep pace

with the growth of the Catholic population. Baptisms decreased by almost two-thirds from 210,937 in 1965 to 78,868 in 2008. Marriages declined by more than two-thirds, from 58,778 in 1965 to 18,443 in 2008 (*The Official Catholic Directory* 2008, p. 2093).

Skyrocketing costs and the inefficiency of small hospitals reduced the number of Catholic hospitals virtually by half, from sixty-one in 1965 to thirty in 2008. Nonetheless, they cared for 5,221,841 patients in 2008. Likewise Catholic Charities in the eight dioceses continued to perform an indispensable function as providers of social services, assisting 1,936,325 people in 2008 (*The Official Catholic Directory* 2008, p. 2093). Catholic health care institutions were among the first to respond to the state call for dedicated units to care for AIDS patients. Governor Mario Cuomo (1932–) said in January 1990: "They were the first and they do the most. It's an inspiration to the community." (*Catholic New York* January 11, 1990).

Another encouraging development was the increase in the number of permanent deacons to 1,273. However, in the year 2007 only eighteen men were ordained to the diocesan priesthood to serve a Catholic community of more than 7 million (*The Official Catholic Directory* 2007, p. 2073). In 2008, 28 men were ordained (*The Official Catholic Directory* 2008, p. 2093). Even more ominous for the future was the fact that there were only 159 diocesan seminarians. International priests, especially those from India, Nigeria, and the Philippines, became indispensable in maintaining pastoral services in many parishes.

In 2008 Catholics remained the largest religious community in the state with 7,166,308 people or thirty-seven percent of the total population (*The Official Catholic Directory* 2008, p. 2093). On the organizational level the Catholic Church in New York was better prepared than ever before to speak with one voice on major public issues as a result of the formation of the New York State Catholic Conference, which represented the Church's position on such issues as education, right-to-life, health care, and criminal justice.

SEE ALSO BALTIMORE, ARCHDIOCESE OF; CATHOLIC CHARITIES USA; KNOW-NOTHINGISM; MISSION AND MISSIONS; NETHERLANDS REFORMED CHURCH; NEWARK, ARCHDIOCESE OF; NEW YORK, ARCHDIOCESE OF; NORTH AMERICAN MARTYRS; QUEBEC ACT OF 1774; VATICAN COUNCIL II.

BIBLIOGRAPHY

James R. Bayley, *Brief Sketch of the Early History of the Catholic Church on the Island of New York* (New York 1853; repr., 1870).

Martin Joseph Becker, *A History of Catholic Life in the Diocese of Albany, 1609–1864* (New York 1975).

Margaret Carthy, *A Cathedral of Suitable Magnificence: St. Patrick's Cathedral, New York* (Wilmington, Del. 1984).

Catholic New York January 11, 1990.

Joseph Coen, Patrick J. McNamara, and Peter I. Vaccari, *Diocese of Immigrants: The Brooklyn Catholic Experience, 1853–2003* (Strasbourg, France 2004).

Florence D. Cohalan, *A Popular History of the Archdiocese of New York* (Yonkers, N.Y. 1983).

Jay P. Dolan, *The Immigrant Church: New York's Irish and German Catholics, 1815–1865* (Baltimore 1975).

Joan de Lourdes Leonard, *Richly Blessed: The Diocese of Rockville Centre, 1957–1990* (Rockville Centre, N.Y. 1991).

Robert F. McNamara, *The Diocese of Rochester, 1868–1993*, 2nd ed. (Rochester, N.Y. 1998).

David J. O'Brien, *Faith and Friendship: Catholicism in the Diocese of Syracuse, 1886–1986* (Syracuse, N.Y. 1987).

The Official Catholic Directory (New Providence, N.J. 1965, 2005, 2007, 2008).

John Kean Sharp, *History of the Diocese of Brooklyn, 1853–1953*, 2 vols. (New York 1954).

Richard Shaw, *Dagger John: The Unquiet Life and Times of Archbishop John Hughes of New York* (New York 1977).

Thomas J. Shelley, *Dunwoodie: The History of St. Joseph's Seminary, Yonkers, New York* (Westminster, Md. 1993).

Thomas J. Shelley, *The Bicentennial History of the Archdiocese of New York, 1808–2008* (Strasbourg, France 2007).

Thomas J. Shelley, *Empire State Catholics: A History of the Catholic Community in New York State* (Strasbourg, France 2007).

Mary Christine Taylor, *A History of the Foundations of Catholicism in Northern New York* (New York 1976).

J. David Valaik, *Celebrating God's Life in Us: The Catholic Diocese of Buffalo, 1847–1997* (Buffalo, N.Y. 1997).

Mother Mary Peter Carthy OSU
Staff Editor for American Church History, New Catholic Encyclopedia, The Catholic University of America, Washington, D.C.
Professor of History, College of New Rochelle
New Rochelle, N.Y.

Msgr. Thomas J. Shelley
Professor of the History of Christianity
Fordham University, Bronx, N.Y. (2009)

NEWARK, ARCHDIOCESE OF

During the colonial period there were few Catholics in New Jersey. The colony was openly hostile to "popish recusants." Most Catholics were found in the Elizabeth and Woodbridge areas of northern New Jersey. In southern New Jersey, German Catholics settled around the glass-blowing factories near Salem. The first recorded Mass and Baptism took place in 1743, when a priest from St. Joseph's in Philadelphia, Reverend Theodore Schneider, S.J., visited the glass works. In the latter years of the eighteenth century, Catholics in northern New Jersey were served by the circuit-riding Reverend Ferdinand FARMER, S.J.

New Jersey was a center of several battles during the American Revolution. In the camp at Morristown, the Spanish agent, Don Juan de Miralles, died on April 28, 1780. His funeral, conducted by Father Seraphin Bandol, chaplain of the French Minister, was attended by General Washington.

After the establishment of the Diocese of Baltimore in 1789, New Jersey Catholics were served by priests from New York and Philadelphia. In 1808, when the Dioceses of New York and Philadelphia were established, the northeastern part of the state was designated part of the New York DIOCESE, and the southwestern portion part of the Diocese of Philadelphia. Although the number of Catholics grew, it was only in 1844 that a new state constitution removed the prohibition against Catholics holding public office in New Jersey.

Bayley (1853–1872). The Diocese of Newark (*Novarcensis*) was established by Pope PIUS IX on July 29, 1853, in the apostolic letter *Apostolici ministerii*. At its founding, it included the entire state of New Jersey. In 1853 approximately thirty thousand Catholics lived in the new diocese, most of them in the northeastern part of the state. There were thirty-three churches served by thirty priests, few institutions, and no parish schools (Kupke 1983, p. 1036).

The Great Hunger, caused by the potato famine of the 1840s in Ireland, and the disruptions in Germany after the revolutions of 1848 impelled many Irish and Germans to emigrate. New Jersey was then and remains today a major center of immigration in the United States. The growth of the Catholic population due to immigration spurred the creation of the diocese, and the majority of the Catholics at the time were of Irish and German background, although there were some others as well.

The new BISHOP was James Roosevelt BAYLEY, scion of the prominent Bayley and Roosevelt families of New York. He had been a pastor in the Episcopal Church prior to his conversion in 1842. Catholic education and priestly vocations were a major priority for Bayley. In 1856 he established Seton Hall College in Madison with Bernard MCQUAID, later bishop of Rochester, as president. Bayley named the new institution after his aunt, St. Elizabeth Ann Bayley SETON. Among the first trustees of the college was Orestes A. BROWNSON. In 1860 the college moved to South Orange and expanded to include Immaculate Conception Seminary.

In 1857 a group of Benedictine Sisters arrived from Pennsylvania, and in the following year Bayley sent five women to train with the Sisters of Charity. This led to the establishment of the Sisters of Charity of St.

Elizabeth, a community dedicated to Catholic education. In addition, the Sisters of ST. JOSEPH and of St. Dominic came to the diocese.

Throughout his episcopate, Bayley was bedeviled by financial concerns and received significant support from the Association for the Propagation of the Faith of Lyons, France, and the Leopoldine Society of Vienna. The possible sale of Seton Hall to the CHRISTIAN BROTHERS was averted only by the intervention of Father Michael Augustine CORRIGAN and his brothers who provided a line of credit to ensure the payment of the college debts. In 1872 Bayley left Newark to become archbishop of Baltimore. He died in Newark in 1877.

Corrigan (1873–1880). Bayley was succeeded by Michael Augustine Corrigan, a priest of the diocese. At thirty-four years of age, Corrigan was the youngest bishop in the United States. Corrigan, one of the first class of students at the NORTH AMERICAN COLLEGE, was ordained a priest in 1863. He served as director of the seminary at Seton Hall from 1864 and as president of the college from 1868. Even after his consecration as bishop, he continued to serve as college president.

Like Bayley, he was bedeviled by financial problems. The Panic of 1873 threw diocesan and parish finances into turmoil. Under Corrigan's leadership, the massive debt of St. John's Church in Orange was settled with the assistance of Father Winand WIGGER. A stickler for detail and minutiae, Corrigan's administration was characterized by unceasing efforts to bring the diocese into conformity with the regulations of the Baltimore Councils.

In addition to establishing parishes and schools, Corrigan directed the establishment of Catholic protectories, one for boys and one for girls, when the state homes for troubled youth forced them to attend Protestant services and refused them access to Catholic Mass. In 1878 the JESUITS founded St. Peter's College in Jersey City. This institution evolved into St. Peter's College and St. Peter's Preparatory School. In 1880 Corrigan was named coadjutor archbishop of New York, and in 1885 he succeeded to the see.

The state of New Jersey was growing and was changing. Industry was concentrated in the northern counties, with the area around Newark being the most heavily industrialized. Farming remained the major occupation in the central and southern parts of the state. The bishops of the Province of New York recommended dividing the diocese to create a new diocese in Trenton, the state capital. The new diocese consisted of the southern fourteen counties of New Jersey, leaving the remaining seven to Newark.

Wigger (1881–1901). The appointment of Winand Michael Wigger as third bishop of Newark was unexpected. The bishops of the province had recommended Wigger as the first bishop of the new Diocese of Trenton. They recommended Michael Joseph O'Farrell for bishop of Newark. To the consternation of Archbishop Corrigan of New York and Bishop McQuaid of Rochester, the names were reversed in ROME. Both were suspicious of a German plot to give the larger see to a German-American.

Ordained for the diocese of Newark in 1865 after studies at Brignole-Sale Seminary in Genoa, Wigger was fluent in English, German, Italian, and French. In spite of his German background, he was generally well received by the predominantly Irish clergy in Newark. During a time of conflicts among the German-speaking immigrant population, Wigger tried to foster unity, while recognizing the needs of all immigrant populations.

Wigger attended the Third Plenary Council of Baltimore in 1884, accompanied by several Newark priests who served as theological experts. Among them was Reverend Januarius DE CONCILIO, one of the major authors of the BALTIMORE CATECHISM that set the standard of RELIGIOUS EDUCATION for almost a century.

During the Americanist controversy, Wigger was staunchly conservative and non-compromising. This was evident in his support of parochial schools. He engaged in a lengthy dispute over the school question with Rev. Patrick CORRIGAN, pastor of Our Lady of Grace Parish in Hoboken, New Jersey. He even threatened to excommunicate parents who sent their children to non-Catholic schools. His attempts to secure state support for Catholic schools failed.

In the last years of the nineteenth century, the ethnic composition of the Diocese of Newark changed as large numbers of Italian, German, Polish, and central and eastern European peoples settled in the area. In 1900 almost 432,000 of the New Jersey population were foreign-born; by 1910 this had swelled to more than 658,000; by 1920, to almost 739,000. To accommodate the pastoral needs of these new ethnic groups, numerous national parishes were established (*Sadliers' Catholic Directory, Almanac, and Ordo* 1878; Wilson et al. 1950).

In 1898, Wigger broke ground for the Cathedral of the Sacred Heart. At the time, the estimated cost of the building was one million dollars. This figure multiplied many times before the dedication of the CATHEDRAL in 1954. At the time of his death in 1901, just two years short of the fiftieth anniversary of the diocese, almost 300,000 Catholics were served by 256 priests in 153 parishes in the Diocese of Newark. Since the diocese had been established in 1853, the Catholic population of New Jersey had grown from about 30,000 to 362,000 (Beck 1962, p. 31).

O'Connor (1901–1927). Wigger's successor, John J. O'CONNOR, a priest of the diocese, had served as rector of Immaculate Conception Seminary and as vicar general of the diocese. His time as bishop coincided almost exactly with the first quarter of the twentieth century. During that period the diocese of Newark absorbed thousands of immigrants. This was recognized at the banquet celebrating the Golden Jubilee of the diocese in 1903, when a toast was offered "To the Immigrants of Today," in which the piety, the accomplishments, and the generosity of the Irish, German, Italian, Poles, and Slavic immigrants were equally praised. The wave of immigrants was slowed by World War I and then brought to a trickle by the anti–immigration laws of the 1920s.

The Diocese of Newark welcomed religious communities to an extraordinary extent. In the early twentieth century nearly one out of four parishes was staffed by religious communities of men. They included Jesuits, PASSIONISTS, BENEDICTINES, CARMELITES, DOMINICANS, SALESIANS, and the Pious Society of the Missions. Religious communities of men and women staffed parochial elementary and high schools, orphanages and protectories, homes for the aged and the blind, and Catholic hospitals. Among them were the Christian Brothers, ALEXIAN BROTHERS, and XAVERIAN BROTHERS. Women's congregations included the Sisters of Charity (Convent Station), Sisters of St. Benedict, SISTERS OF CHRISTIAN CHARITY, sisters of ST. FRANCIS, Sisters of Charity (Gray Nuns), Dominican Sisters of the Perpetual Rosary, Sisters of St. Dominic, Sisters of St. Francis, Sisters of the Poor of St. Francis, Sisters of the Good Shepherd, Sisters of St. Joseph, SCHOOL SISTERS OF NOTRE DAME, Sisters of ST. JOSEPH OF PEACE, LITTLE SISTERS OF THE POOR, Felician Sisters, Sisters of the Sorrowful Mother, Pallotine Sisters of Charity, MISSIONARY SISTERS OF THE SACRED HEART, Daughters of Our Lady of Help, the Franciscan Sisters of the Immaculate Conception, and the Sisters of ST. JOHN THE BAPTIST. The Sisters of Charity of St. Elizabeth had moved into higher education; they opened the College of St. Elizabeth in Morristown in 1899 and graduated their first class in 1903. In spite of the growth of Catholic education, large numbers of students remained in the public school system. To provide for better religious education, the diocese established the CONFRATERNITY OF CHRISTIAN DOCTRINE (CCD).

To provide priests for the growing diocese, O'Connor purchased a 1,400–acre estate in the Darlington section of Mahwah. The seminary moved to Mahwah from Seton Hall in April 1927. O'Connor died less than one month later.

Walsh (1928–1937). In 1928 Thomas Joseph Walsh, ordained a priest of the Diocese of Buffalo and formerly bishop of Trenton, was installed as bishop of Newark in the uncompleted Cathedral of the Sacred Heart. The diocesan focus on education continued. Seton Hall College and the diocesan high schools received accreditation from regional accrediting agencies. In 1939 the Dominican Sisters opened Caldwell College. Originally a women's college, it became co-educational in 1986. The campus of Seton Hall was expanded, and in 1951 it was raised to the status of a university. The number of parochial schools continued to increase. Walsh directed new parishes to build schools before constructing churches. This resulted in many temporary auditorium-churches that continued to serve into the twenty-first century.

Walsh was sensitive to racial and ethnic minorities. He established three national parishes for African-American Catholics and a parish for the small number of Spanish and Portuguese immigrants, most of whom came from the Canary Islands and the Azores. The Religious Sisters Filippini, whom Walsh had brought to Trenton, followed him to Newark and focused on the Italian apostolate.

The Great Depression stimulated significant growth in the activities of Catholic Charities and the Mount Carmel Guild, an organization established by Walsh. From 1935 to 1941 the Mount Carmel Guild kitchens for the poor served more than two million meals. It also provided shelters for the homeless and collected, reconditioned, and distributed clothing and furniture to the poor.

Diocese Divided. The counties of Morris, Passaic, and Sussex formed the new Diocese of Paterson. Newark was raised to the rank of ARCHDIOCESE and retained the counties of Hudson, Essex, Bergen, and Union, with a Catholic population of 645,000. Embracing only 511 square miles, it is the smallest archdioceseal territory in the United States. The only see that is smaller is the Diocese of Brooklyn.

Shortly after the division of the diocese, the new buildings of Immaculate Conception Seminary opened. They were erected at a cost of more than two million dollars, a not inconsiderable feat of fundraising during the Depression. Shortly before his death in 1952, Walsh inaugurated the archdiocesan newspaper, *The Advocate*. As the twentieth century reached midpoint, slightly more than one million Catholics were served by 864 diocesan and religious priests in 210 parishes in the Archdiocese of Newark (*The Official Catholic Directory* 1953).

Boland (1953–1974). In 1953 Walsh was succeeded by Thomas A. Boland, former rector of the archdiocesan seminary and bishop of Paterson. The following year, the Cathedral of the Sacred Heart, begun over a half-century earlier, was completed and consecrated.

The archdiocese was changing. Its major cities, Newark, Jersey City, and Elizabeth, had been losing population to the suburbs since the 1930s. This migration accelerated in the post–World War II years and had mixed results for the archdiocese. On the one hand, it signaled an unparalleled expansion of parishes and schools in the suburban areas of the archdiocese. On the other, city parishes were depopulated and carried on with ever-shrinking resources. The small area of the archdiocese meant that many Catholics moving to the suburbs settled outside its boundaries in neighboring dioceses and farther.

At the same time the racial and ethnic composition of the population changed. The 1950s witnessed the arrival of tens of thousands of Puerto Rican immigrants. Most settled in the cities. As a result of the Castro revolution in 1959, large numbers of Cuban refugees settled in the archdiocese, particularly in Union City.

In the 1960s the archdiocese embarked on a development campaign to raise funds for the construction of regional high schools and other institutions. Approximately twenty-four million dollars was raised. However, the cost of the schools alone exceeded thirty-two million dollars. This shortfall and increasing debt caused great difficulties in the following decades.

The late 1960s were tumultuous for all America. Race riots in Newark and neighboring cities hastened the flight from the cities and weakened the already destabilized city parishes. In 1968, twenty Newark priests working in the inner cities accused the Church and the archdiocese of institutionalized racism.

The departure of teaching sisters and brothers caused the cost of Catholic education to skyrocket and the decline of parochial education began. Counter to this trend, Catholic higher education expanded. In 1967, the Felician Sisters received accreditation for Felician College in Lodi.

By the end of the twentieth century, few religious sisters and brothers remained in Catholic elementary and high schools. Catholic education became a lay apostolate. The departure of many priests from the ministry, including several prominent priests from the seminary faculty and the archdiocesan administration, was a cause of pain and discouragement, as it was throughout the nation.

Boland attended the Second Vatican Council, and afterward he directed the liturgical renewal and implemented other structural changes, the most significant of which were the establishment of Parish Councils and the Senate of Priests. In 1971, at the age of seventy-five, Boland submitted his resignation. It was accepted three years later in 1974. At the end of his tenure, the Catholic population of the archdiocese had reached 1,520,000, almost three times the population of

1938, when the diocese was split (*The Official Catholic Directory* 1939, 1975). Archbishop Boland died in 1979.

Gerety (1974–1986). Peter Leo Gerety, bishop of Portland, Maine, succeeded Boland. Ordained in Paris in 1939, Gerety founded and served almost a quarter-century in St. Martin de Porres, an African-American parish in the inner city of New Haven, Connecticut. He was named coadjutor bishop of Portland in 1966 and succeeded to the see in 1969.

Shortly after his arrival in Newark in 1974, Archbishop Gerety became aware of a massive archdiocesan debt, both internal and external. He quickly took measures to rein in spending, thereby reducing and eliminating many offices and services. He also initiated an annual fundraising campaign. The changing economic demographics of the diocese and the failure of the capital campaign of the 1960s to achieve its stated goals hampered efforts to raise funds. However, by 1983, the debt was liquidated.

A major pastoral initiative of the Gerety period was RENEW, a parish based program of spiritual and pastoral renewal based upon reflection on scripture and the documents of the Second Vatican Council. RENEW expanded to many dioceses in the United States and throughout the world. In 1976 the archdiocese was an active participant in the national CALL TO ACTION CONFERENCE. The conference aroused enthusiastic participation throughout the archdiocese. Among other pastoral initiatives was the "Father's Embrace," a program of penance services that included general absolution. Responding to concern expressed by the HOLY SEE, this program was ended after a short time.

Gerety oversaw several reorganizations of the archdiocesan structure and policies. In an effort to encourage SUBSIDIARITY, the archdiocese was divided into four episcopal vicariates corresponding to each of the counties and subdivided into twenty-five deaneries. The tenure of pastors was limited to two six-year terms, and all archdiocesan appointments had term limits of various durations.

In 1984 Archbishop Gerety sold the property of Immaculate Conception Seminary, and the seminary moved to and affiliated with Seton Hall University in South Orange, New Jersey. At the time this was a controversial move, but the affiliation over time worked well and resulted in mutual satisfaction.

As a result of the 1965 Hart-Cellar Immigration Reform Act, the archdiocese of Newark experienced major demographic changes. The already established pattern of suburbanization continued. The traditional European ethnic parishes declined in numbers and vitality. The number of Catholics in urban areas decreased. Much of this decline, due to migration out of the archdiocese, was made up for by new immigrants. Although some of the new immigration was European, chiefly from Portugal and Poland, the majority of Catholic immigrants were from Latin America, the Caribbean, and Asia, particularly the Philippines, Korea, and Vietnam. Not surprisingly, the number of ethnic-specific apostolates continued to grow.

While religious communities declined and some withdrew from the care of parishes and schools, the MISSIONARIES OF CHARITY opened a mission in Newark. In addition, religious communities of men such as the Vocationist Fathers and the Adorno Fathers were received into the archdiocese, and OPUS DEI opened a house near Seton Hall University.

McCarrick (1986–2000). Gerety retired in 1986 and was succeeded by Theodore E. McCarrick. McCarrick, a priest of the Archdiocese of NEW YORK, had served as secretary to Cardinals SPELLMAN and COOKE and as the president of the Catholic University of Puerto Rico. He came to Newark after five years as the founding bishop of the adjoining Diocese of Metuchen. Recognizing the extraordinary growth of the Hispanic presence in the archdiocese, he implemented a pastoral plan for Hispanic MINISTRY. He also opened an Office of Evangelization to serve the increasingly diverse linguistic and cultural groups within the archdiocese.

In 1990 McCarrick opened Redemptoris Mater Archdiocesan Missionary Seminary of the NEOCATECHUMENAL WAY. He also introduced Neocatechumenal communities into several parishes of the archdiocese. After McCarrick was named superior of the mission *sui juris* of the Turks and Caicos Islands in 1998, he entrusted this mission to priests ordained for the Neocatechumenal Way.

In 1993 the tenth synod of the archdiocese was held at Seton Hall University. The last synod had taken place in 1941. Unlike previous synods that included only clergy, the 1993 synod was made up of representatives of laity and clergy. Among its outcomes was a call for more involvement by young people with the Church.

In October 1995 Pope JOHN PAUL II (pope 1978–2005) visited Newark and presided at Evening Prayer in The Cathedral of the Sacred Heart. President and Mrs. William J. Clinton attended the service, marking the first time in United States history that a president and a pope were at the same church service. After the Evening Prayer service, Pope John Paul II told Archbishop McCarrick that he would designate the cathedral a minor BASILICA, the only one in New Jersey.

During the visit, the pope celebrated Mass at Giants Stadium in a tremendous downpour. Despite the rain, the crowd stayed. The pope was impressed, stating a few weeks later that "The strong faith, united with hope, of the church of New Jersey was meaningfully expressed … at Giants Stadium where not even the driving rain so badly needed in that state could dampen the enthusiasm and devotion of those present."

On November 21, 2000, Archbishop McCarrick was named Archbishop of Washington and was elevated to the College of Cardinals the following year.

Throughout the second half of the twentieth century, ethnic, economic, social, and demographic forces had a great impact on the archdiocese. At the beginning of the twenty-first century, more than 1,300,000 Catholics were served by 961 diocesan and religious priests in 235 parishes (*The Official Catholic Directory* 2001).

Myers (2001–). John J. Myers came to Newark from Peoria, Illinois, where he had served as coadjutor bishop from 1987 to 1990 and as bishop after 1990. Installed just over a month after the September 11, 2001, terrorist attacks on the World Trade Center and the Pentagon, Myers presided at several very emotional memorial Masses, including a Mass for deceased Port Authority police and personnel that filled the cathedral to overflowing.

The economic slowdown of the early twenty-first century resulted in the emergence of financial problems in the archdiocese. It became necessary to reallocate archdiocesan programs and services. The strain of maintaining parishes, schools, and institutions created for an earlier age led the archdiocese to evaluate all of its pastoral activities through a program called "New Energies." As a result of the consultations that were part of this program, several schools and parishes merged and some closed. To preserve the religious and cultural heritage of the archdiocese, Myers established a Commission for the Ecclesiastical Patrimony to oversee within the archdiocese the transfer or sale of religious artifacts. The archdiocese also sold its three hospitals to Catholic Health East Corporation, which continues to maintain a presence of Catholic healthcare in the city of Newark.

In the early years of the twenty-first century, the archdiocese of Newark addressed pastoral challenges common to most major urban sees. Changing ethnic and demographic patterns demanded new pastoral responses. The Catholic population in 2008 was nearly forty percent Latino. In addition to the Puerto Rican, Cuban, and Dominican population, new arrivals came from Colombia, El Salvador, Mexico, and Peru. Immigrants from Haiti and Brazil added to the diversity. The Korean and Filipino communities also continued to increase. Unlike their immigrant predecessors, who settled together in rather clearly defined urban centers, the new immigration spread throughout the archdiocese

Elevation of a New Archbishop. *Archbishop John J. Myers sits in the ornate cathedral chair signifying his elevation to head of the Roman Catholic Newark Diocese during his installation at the Cathedral Basilica of the Sacred Heart in Newark, N.J., Tuesday, Oct. 9, 2001. Myers, who was the bishop of Peoria, Ill., reaffirmed traditional Roman Catholic doctrine during his installation.* AP IM-AGES

in both urban and suburban areas. As a result, whereas some parishes serve a specific ethnic group, many serve a continually changing multi-ethnic community.

Since its foundation in 1853, the Archdiocese of Newark has shrunk in geographic terms, but its population has greatly expanded. In its early years its diversity was based on many European ethnicities. In the early twenty-first century its ethnic, racial, and cultural diversity makes it a microcosm of the universal Church.

SEE ALSO BALTIMORE, ARCHDIOCESE OF; BALTIMORE, COUNCILS OF; BENEDICTINE NUNS AND SISTERS; CATHOLIC CHARITIES USA; CONVERTS AND CONVERSION; EPISCOPAL CHURCH, U.S.; EXCOMMUNICATION; LEOPOLDINEN STIFTUNG (LEOPOLDINE SOCIETY); NEW JERSEY, CATHOLIC CHURCH IN; PHILADELPHIA, ARCHDIOCESE OF; PROPAGATION OF THE FAITH, SOCIETY FOR THE.

BIBLIOGRAPHY

Henry G.J. Beck, *The Centennial History of Immaculate Conception Seminary, Darlington, N.J.* (1962)

The Catholic Directory and Almanac (New York 1901).

Christopher Ciccarino, *Seeds of Faith, Branches of Hope: The Archdiocese of Newark, New Jersey* (Strasbourg, France 2003).

Joseph M. Flynn, *The Catholic Church in New Jersey* (New York 1904).

Raymond Kupke, "Catholic Church in New Jersey," in *The Encyclopedia of American Catholic History* (Collegeville, Minn. 1997).

Raymond Kupke, "The Church in New Jersey," in *The Encyclopedia of American Cahtolic History*, edited by Michael Glazier and Thomas Shelley (Collegeville, Minn. 1983).

New Jersey Catholic Historical Records Commission, *The Bishops of Newark, 1853–1978: The First 125 Years of the Archdiocese of Newark as Seen through the Lives and Administrations of the Seven Men Who Have Been Its Leaders* (South Orange, N.J. 1978).

The Official Catholic Directory (New Providence, N.J. 1926, 1939, 1951, 1953, 1975, 2001, 2007).

Sadliers' Catholic Directory, Almanac, and Ordo (New York 1878).

Harold F. Wilson et al., *Outline History of New Jersey* (New Brunswick, N.J. 1950).

Rev. Msgr. Robert J. Wister
Associate Professor, Church History
Immaculate Conception Seminary School of Theology,
Seton Hall University (2009)

NORTH CAROLINA, CATHOLIC CHURCH IN

One of the thirteen original states of the United States, North Carolina was inhabited primarily by Tuscarora, Catawba, and Cherokee people when the first attempts at colonization by English settlers began in the 1580s. It is located on the Atlantic seaboard between Virginia and South Carolina and is bordered on the west by Tennessee. Charles II granted a charter for the territory lying between Virginia and Florida, running west to the "South Seas," to eight "absolute lords proprietors" in 1663. North Carolina was established as a separate royal colony in 1729. In addition to the English, smaller groups of Scottish, Irish, Welsh, German, Swiss, and French settled there. African Americans, both slave and free, became a significant minority as the colony grew in population, and labor-intensive crops of rice, cotton, and tobacco formed an important sector of the economy.

Early Catholic History. Although evidence shows that Hernando de Soto (c. 1497–1542) passed through the territory during his explorations of 1539 to 1543 and a few historians speculate that some of the first colonists at Roanoke Island in the 1580s were Catholic recusants from England, the first explicit mention of Catholic residents in the colony was made by John Brickell (*The Natural History of North-Carolina*) in 1737. No official toleration of Catholicism occurred in the colony until after independence, and much of the population, though Protestant, was unchurched. According to the diary of Bishop John ENGLAND of Charleston, South Carolina, in 1821 only about 150 adults in a statewide population of nearly 650,000 were Catholic (Lewis 1997, pp. 1056–1057; U.S. Census Bureau 2002). The first priest on record as having resided in the state (1784–1790) was a native of Ireland, Patrick Cleary, who originally came to settle his brother's estate in New Bern.

Dr. Thomas BURKE of Hillsboro, elected a member of the first Provincial Congress in 1775 and later of the Continental Congress, was a Catholic. In 1781 he became the state governor, though the North Carolina Constitution of 1776 contained a test oath, barring from public office those who denied the existence of GOD or "the truth of the Protestant Religion." This provision stood until 1836. The most famous Catholic legislator and jurist of the period was William J. GASTON of New Bern (1778–1844), who was also the first student to enroll at Georgetown College in 1791. As early as 1823 Bishop England sought Gaston's assistance in eliminating the offensive test oath, and in the Convention of 1835, Gaston, who by that time was a state supreme court justice, contributed to the effort

which eventually resulted in substituting the word "Christian" for "Protestant."

John England, a native of Ireland, was named BISHOP of the DIOCESE of Charleston, South Carolina, in 1820. At that time the diocese included both North and South Carolina as well as Georgia. By the time of his death in 1842, only four Catholic churches could be found in the state—in Washington, Fayetteville, Raleigh, and New Bern—each with small congregations. The number of adult converts was small, but it included both free blacks and slaves, who worshipped together with whites when a priest was present. England himself preached throughout the state, often using courthouses and Protestant churches as venues. In addition, he promulgated a Constitution of the Diocese of Charleston, which established elected representatives of the several congregations to govern the local Church and to meet in state- and diocesan-wide conventions. His successors in office quickly abandoned the system he had established.

Anti–Catholicism. The spirit of tolerance in the state dissipated during the antebellum period, which saw the rise of the Nativist and anti–Catholic Know-Nothing movement. Public lectures denouncing Catholicism and the 1852 conversion to Catholicism of Levi Silliman IVES (1797–1867), the second Episcopal bishop of North Carolina, contributed to religious tensions and prejudice. An exception to this trend was the invitation of the 1856 University of North Carolina graduating class to Archbishop John J. HUGHES of New York to speak at their commencement. Unable to do so that year, he was again invited and gave the address at graduation in 1860.

Vicariate of North Carolina. Pope PIUS IX established the Vicariate Apostolic of North Carolina on March 3, 1868, and he named James GIBBONS of Baltimore (1834–1921) its first vicar apostolic. Three priests assisted Gibbons to serve the estimated 700 Catholics present throughout the state. When Gibbons was named bishop of Richmond in 1872, he retained responsibility for the vicariate until 1877, when he became coadjutor ARCHBISHOP of Baltimore with the right of succession. During his administration of the vicariate, the number of Catholics in North Carolina surpassed one thousand. In addition, the SISTERS OF MERCY from Charleston were established at Wilmington in 1869, and Benedictine monks from Latrobe, Pennsylvania, founded a MONASTERY (and later a college) at Garibaldi (later Belmont), North Carolina, in 1876.

John J. KEANE, who succeeded Gibbons as bishop of Richmond in 1878, also inherited the responsibility for the administration of the Vicariate of North Carolina. Mark S. Gross, the vicar general, refused the

St. Paul's Roman Catholic Church, New Bern, North Carolina. *Pictured here as it stood c. 1950, this church is the oldest Catholic church in North Carolina.* THE LIBRARY OF CONGRESS

appointment as vicar apostolic in 1880, and Henry P. Northrop (1842–1916), a native of Charleston, was then consecrated a bishop for the vicariate in 1882. The following year Northrop was named bishop of Charleston and, like Gibbons before him, was responsible until 1887 for the administration of the Church in North Carolina while also resident bishop of a diocese.

The fourth vicar to be appointed was the first ABBOT of Maryhelp Abbey in Belmont, Leo M. HAID, O.S.B. (1849–1924), who was ordained a bishop by Gibbons in 1888. In 1891 nine counties, which included the city of Charlotte for a period of fifty years, were assigned to the pastoral care of the abbey. During Haid's tenure, a motherhouse of the Sisters of Mercy was established in Belmont (1892); an orphanage, named Nazareth, was founded outside of Raleigh (1897); and many churches were built. Father Thomas F. PRICE (1860–1919), a native of Wilmington, North Carolina, and in 1911 a cofounder of the Catholic Foreign Mission Society of America (Maryknoll), had been ordained in 1886. Authorized by Haid to function as an itinerant preacher in 1896, Price established a base at the orphanage, where in 1901 he founded the Regina Apostolorum, an association of secular clergy whose goal was to

evangelize North Carolina and foster vocations to the priesthood there. He also founded and edited *Truth* (1897), a national monthly magazine with more than 17,000 subscribers by 1905.

New Jurisdiction Established. PIUS X, by a papal bull of June 8, 1910, erected the *abbatia nullius diocesis* of Belmont, assigning eight counties from the vicariate to the new jurisdiction. Haid, now ABBOT ordinary of Belmont, remained both abbot and vicar apostolic until his death in 1924. Although the monastic community found the arrangement reasonable, as it provided for its own security as well as the financial and pastoral stability of the vicariate, the secular clergy, including Price, strongly objected to the arrangement, especially the provision that the monastic chapter had the right to nominate all future vicars apostolic of North Carolina, so they petitioned the HOLY SEE for the establishment of a regular diocese within the state.

Diocese of Raleigh. Only after Haid's death was the Diocese of RALEIGH erected by papal decree on December 12, 1924, leaving the *abbatia nullius diocesis* of Belmont with its unique status, as given in 1910. In 1944 seven of its eight counties were transferred to the jurisdiction of the bishop of Raleigh, and in 1960 Gaston County, with the exception of the monastery property, was incorporated into the Diocese of Raleigh. Finally, in 1977 the *abbatia nullius diocesis* was suppressed by papal decree at the request of the U.S. hierarchy.

William J. Hafey (1888–1954), a priest from Baltimore, was consecrated as the first bishop of Raleigh and took possession of his see in 1925. He led a small and largely scattered Catholic population, which had relatively little social, cultural, or political influence in the state. He made an intense and somewhat successful effort to secure the assistance of RELIGIOUS men and women to support his pastoral efforts. By the time he was transferred to the Diocese of Scranton in 1937, the number of religious priests working had increased from 8 to 26 and the number of sisters from 84 to 199. The total number of churches had also increased from 61 to 91, and the number of "stations" where Mass was at least occasionally celebrated, including private homes, grew from 60 to 154. The Catholic population rose from a little more than 6,000 to over 10,000 people during a time of little immigration into the state (*The Official Catholic Directory* 1926, p. 625; 1937, p. 481). Efforts were made for the evangelization and conversion of the African-American population, especially by some of the religious congregations of men, who had been recruited for this work, with some small successes.

When Eugene J. McGuinness (1889–1957), a priest of Philadelphia who had been working with the Catholic Church Extension Society, was named the second bishop of Raleigh in 1937, he continued much of the pastoral direction of his predecessor, and the number of religious priests serving in the diocese rose to 59. The number of secular clergy climbed as well, from only 23 in 1925, to 53 in 1937, and to 83 in 1944, the year in which McGuinness was made bishop of Oklahoma City and Tulsa (*The Official Catholic Directory* 1926, p. 625; 1937, p. 481; 1944, p. 615). The Catholic population experienced a modest rise during those years, to nearly 13,000 as conversions continued and national wartime mobilization brought greater numbers of military personnel and their families into the state.

The first southern-born bishop of the diocese was Vincent S. Waters (1904–1974), a native of Roanoke, Virginia, who served as ordinary from 1945 until his death in 1974. With dedicated zeal he continued in the footsteps of his two predecessors, seeking to strengthen the institutional presence of the Church throughout the state. In addition, he boldly addressed the question of racial discrimination in an era of heated controversy. In May 1953 he issued a pastoral letter condemning the SIN of racism and calling for the end of all racial barriers in Catholic institutions within the diocese. He implemented his directive by closing the "black" church and

school in Newton Grove and ordering the integration of the larger "white" church and school, a move that was widely regarded as prophetic by progressive voices, nationally and beyond, but largely decried locally. The process continued slowly, in most cases by closing churches and schools in African-American communities, through the 1960s.

Waters also established a diocesan paper, the *North Carolina Catholic*, as well as the North Carolina Laymen's Association, and he sought to extend the CONFRATERNITY OF CHRISTIAN DOCTRINE (CCD), using the most contemporary teaching techniques, into all corners of the diocese. In the wake of the Second Vatican Council, having attended all the sessions, he embarked on a series of lectures and conferences, to which he invited nationally known theologians and pastors to educate clergy and laity on the teachings of the council. He soon encountered much opposition from some clergy and religious, however, who thought that he was impeding the pace of needed pastoral and liturgical reforms. Several members of the diocesan clergy sent a petition to the Holy See seeking his removal.

Diocese of Charlotte. Tensions eased somewhat when ROME established the Diocese of CHARLOTTE in November 1971, separating the forty-six counties of western North Carolina from the Raleigh Diocese and naming the well-liked diocesan priest Michael J. Begley (1909–2002) its first bishop. The new diocese was made part of the Province of Atlanta, as was the Diocese of Raleigh when the former was created in 1962. Begley served from 1972 until his retirement in 1984, during a period of rapid population growth within the state and in Catholic Church membership. The immigration was largely from the northern states, fueled by an expanding economy, and was experienced also in the eastern part of the state. Beginning in the 1970s and continuing throughout the following decade, another wave of immigration, bringing tens of thousands of Mexican and Central American laborers into the state, created a new pastoral reality for both dioceses, which slowly received an organized response in the form of special ministries.

The Diocese of Charlotte developed its own identity under the leadership of its second bishop, John F. Donoghue (1928–), who established a separate diocesan newspaper, the *Catholic News and Herald*. This former chancellor of the Archdiocese of WASHINGTON, D.C., was appointed the ordinary for Charlotte in 1984 and remained there until he was made archbishop of Atlanta in 1993. He was succeeded in 1994 by another Washingtonian, Auxiliary Bishop William F. Curlin (1927–). At the beginning of the new millennium, the diocese counted more than 120,000 Catholics in its jurisdiction, served by 134 active priests, both secular and religious. The number of sisters involved in ministry declined from 249 in 1972 to 134, including those retired and infirm, in 2000 (*The Official Catholic Directory* 1972, p. 159; 2000, p. 213).

Church Growth. In 1975 F. Joseph Gossman (1930–), an auxiliary bishop of Baltimore, took possession of the Diocese of Raleigh, committing himself to what he described as a collegial style of governance and to the ECUMENICAL MOVEMENT. Within twenty-five years the population of the diocese climbed dramatically to more than 150,000 registered Catholics, a figure which often did not include the number of Hispanic Catholics actually present. The number of religious communities who initiated a presence in the diocese also rose sharply. In 1975 14 men religious from 7 congregations served in the diocese; by 2000 there were 54 from 10 different communities. With regard to women religious, the number of congregations active also increased in that same time from 16 to 28, but the total number of sisters working declined from 137 to 86, 10 of whom had been appointed "pastoral administrators" of parishes. The number of active diocesan priests during this quarter century failed to keep pace with the increased Catholic population, growing only by 5, from 53 to 58 men (*The Official Catholic Directory* 1975, p. 703; 2000, p. 1014).

Dramatic growth continued to characterize both the general and the Catholic population of North Carolina in the first years of the twenty-first century. The Raleigh and Charlotte metropolitan areas were identified among the fastest growing regions in the nation. Each of the dioceses reported nearly 200,000 registered parishioners and noted that these numbers did not reflect many of the Hispanic Catholics who continued to immigrate into the state. By 2005 more than 600,000 Hispanics, both documented and undocumented, comprised approximately seven percent of the general population (Kasarda and Johnson 2006, p. i). An increase in anti–immigrant sentiment made the undocumented Hispanic presence a pastoral concern within both dioceses.

By 2008 the Diocese of Raleigh reported more than 1,700 lay employees and 39 permanent deacons in addition to the 59 active diocesan and 49 religious priests, while the number of women religious, 50, continued its striking decline (*The Official Catholic Directory* 2008, p. 1101). The Diocese of Charlotte counted 56 active diocesan and 52 religious priests, a total decline of 26 from the year 2000. There were also 108 deacons, but the number of women religious, including retirees, declined to 118 (*The Official Catholic Directory* 2008, p. 235).

Moreover, both dioceses witnessed a generational change in leadership: Charlotte in 2003, with the ordina-

tion of its fourth ordinary, forty-six-year-old native-son Peter J. Jugis (1957–), J.C.D.; and Raleigh in 2006, with the appointment of forty-nine-year-old Michael F. Burbidge (1957–), D. Ed., former seminary rector and auxiliary bishop of Philadelphia, as the fifth bishop of the diocese. Together, both bishops embarked on a unified effort to educate Catholics as well as the state legislature, with regard to Catholic teaching on stem cell research and immigration issues. In addition, both dioceses placed a renewed emphasis on recruiting vocations to the priesthood and on establishing a vigorous liturgical life in conformity with the rites of the universal Church.

SEE ALSO AFRICAN-AMERICAN CATHOLICS IN THE UNITED STATES (HISTORY OF); ATLANTA, ARCHDIOCESE OF; BENEDICTINES; CATHOLIC CHARITIES USA; CHARLES II, KING OF ENGLAND; CONVERTS AND CONVERSION; GEORGETOWN UNIVERSITY; GEORGIA, CATHOLIC CHURCH IN; KNOW-NOTHINGISM; MONK; NATIVISM, AMERICAN; SOUTH CAROLINA, CATHOLIC CHURCH IN; TOLERANCE; VATICAN COUNCIL II.

BIBLIOGRAPHY

Paschal Baumstein, *My Lord of Belmont: A Biography of Leo Haid* (Belmont, N.C. 1985).

Paschal Baumstein, "A Conflict of Miters: The Diverse Polities and Cathedral Abbey of Bishop Leo Haid," *Word and Spirit* 14, (1992): 76–95.

John Brickell, *The Natural History of North Carolina* (Dublin 1737; repr. Murfreesboro, N.C. 1968).

John D. Kasarda and James H. Johnson Jr., "The Economic Impact of the Hispanic Population on the State of North Carolina," Frank Hawkins Kenan Institute of Private Enterprise Kenan-Flagler Business School (Chapel Hill, N.C. 2006).

Gerald Lewis, "North Carolina, Catholic Church in," in *The Encyclopedia of American Catholic History*, edited by Michael Glazier and Thomas J. Shelley (Collegeville, Minn. 1997), 1056–1057.

The Official Catholic Directory (New Providence, N.J. 1926, 1937, 1944, 1972, 1975, 2000, 2008).

William F. Powers, *Tar Heel Catholics: A History of Catholicism in North Carolina* (Lanham, Md. 2003).

Joseph Herman Schauinger, *William Gaston, Carolinian* (Milwaukee, Wisc. 1949).

U.S. Census Bureau, "Table 48. North Carolina–Race and Hispanic Origin: 1790 to 1990" (2002), available from http://www.census.gov/population/www/documentation/twps0056/tab48.pdf (accessed November 16, 2008).

Stephen C. Worsley, "Catholicism in Antebellum North Carolina," *North Carolina Historical Review* 60, no. 4 (October 1983): 399–430.

Rev. James F. Garneau
Mount Olive College
Mount Olive, N.C. (2009)

NORTH DAKOTA, CATHOLIC CHURCH IN

Exactly when Roman Catholicism entered the Dakotas is difficult to determine, but the Catholic population has continued to grow steadily. As of 2008 the ROMAN CATHOLIC population stood at 146,153, or roughly 22.7 percent of the total population of the state (641,551), in the two Dioceses of Bismarck and FARGO, both suffragan sees of the Archdiocese of ST. PAUL AND MINNEAPOLIS, Minnesota (*The Official Catholic Directory* 2008, p. 2094).

French trappers and fur traders, ostensibly Catholic, had been trading with the native peoples of North Dakota—the Arikaras, the Mandans, and the Hidatsa—since the mid-eighteenth century, but no evidence indicates that they made a concerted effort to evangelize the local tribes. The first Frenchmen the North Dakota natives met were from the expedition of Sieur Pierre Gaultier de Varennes de La Verendrye (1685–1749), a hero of the War of Spanish Succession, in late autumn 1738. "On the morning of the 28th we arrived at the place indicated as a rendezvous for the Mandan, who arrived in the evening, one chief with 30 men and four Assiniboin," La Verendrye recorded in November 1738. "I confess I was greatly surprised, as I expected to see people quite different from the other savages according to the stories that had been told us. They did not differ from the Assiniboin, being naked except for a garment of buffalo skin carelessly worn without any breechcloth. I knew then that there was a large discount to be taken off all that had been told me." La Verendrye failed to find the Northwest Passage to the Pacific, but he put the northern Missouri River and North Dakota on the French map.

Early Catholic History. The first documented Roman Catholic presence for missionary purposes came in the summer of 1818 with the arrival of Father Severe Dumoulin at the fur trading post of Pembina, now the extreme northeast corner of North Dakota. Fearing the effect of the restless and rootless fur trappers, the bishop of Quebec, Joseph O. PLESSIS, sent Dumoulin and Father Joseph Norbert PROVENCHER, who set up a mission at Fort Douglas (later St. Boniface). The population of Pembina was composed of nearly 350 indigenous peoples and Métis (peoples of mixed Native American and European descent, mostly from Chippewa, Cree, and Assiniboin families). As the bishop had suspected, the fur trappers sold alcohol freely to the native peoples, and it adversely affected the social structures and stability of the native cultures. Though unable to stop the flow of alcohol, the two priests did what they could to ameliorate the damage. In 1819 Dumoulin baptized 30 Native Americans. During his five years at Pembina, he

baptized an additional 364 persons and married nearly 70 couples. Dumoulin also established a school, teaching the native and Métis children to read and write French and Latin. The priest also said daily Mass (sometimes preaching in Ojibwa) and gave religious instruction to the children. Under the leadership of Dumoulin, the Métis had an awakening as a new type of people. Economically, the peoples of Pembina prospered as farmers by selling their produce to the Hudson's Bay Company (HBC). Though the Métis predominated in the area, the population continued the traditional buffalo hunt every summer and fall, shortly after the respective plantings and harvests. Usually, a priest traveled with them, enforcing the SABBATH as well as ensuring that the poorer hunters had as much chance to capture the buffalo as the better hunters.

In 1823, under orders from the U.S. government, Major Stephen H. Long (1784–1864) surveyed the U.S.-Canadian border. The new survey line ran through the northern end of Pembina, so most of it lay in U.S. territory. The British, noting Father Dumoulin's ability to attract large numbers of indigenous peoples to Pembina, feared the Americans might use the native and Métis population and the community as a base of operations against the Canadians, and so they forced the community to resettle north of the new border. The forced resettlement disrupted community life, and the population of Pembina dispersed. By 1836 Pembina was completely deserted. Upset and frustrated by the geopolitical developments and the disruption of his mission, Dumoulin departed for Quebec.

Missionary Endeavors. Despite Dumoulin's departure, other priests attempted to evangelize the region. The most prominent was Father George A. BELCOURT, who in 1848 established a new mission at Pembina. Unlike Dumoulin, who had been driven back to Canada by the British government, Belcourt was exiled from Canada when he demanded that the Hudson's Bay Company give up its monopoly on the fur trade. The priest fought for the HBC to allow the non-HBC indigenous peoples to compete in a free and open market, which he considered just. The free traders lost, and, as their leader, Belcourt found himself living in the Dakotas. His new mission at Pembina consisted of a log church, a large garden, and a rectory. After a serious flood in 1851, Belcourt moved the mission to Walhalla, roughly 30 miles west of Pembina. There, the Métis and the natives created a thriving agricultural community, despite frequent attacks by the Sioux. Belcourt impressed the native peoples with his fluency in a variety of Algonquian languages. With the aid of the Sisters of the Propagation of the Faith, Belcourt also started an excellent school.

Interior of the Chapel at Annunciation Priory, Bismarck. This Benedictine priory was established in 1878 by four Sisters from St. Benedict's Priory in St. Joseph, Minnesota. © G. E. KIDDER SMITH/CORBIS

Other individual priests made their marks as well. One of the most famous missionaries to visit North Dakota was the Jesuit Father Peter John DE SMET (1801–1873). Though most of the Native Americans in the Dakotas greatly revered and sought the wisdom of de Smet, he spent more of his energies among the indigenous peoples of the Pacific Northwest. Fearless and carrying no weapons of self-defense, just his BRE-VIARY and flag of the Blessed Virgin MARY, de Smet remains one of the only missionaries to have walked through the Dakotas unharmed. He attempted several times to establish a chain of Jesuit missions along the upper Missouri, but the U.S. government never consented.

At Fort Totten, Sister Mary Clapin and the Sisters of Charity established a school in 1874. As one of the chaplains at the fort, Father Jerome Hunt translated a hymnal, a prayer book, a history of the BIBLE, and a catechism into Lakota. In 1876 a Benedictine from St. Meinrad's in southern Indiana, Father Martin MARTY, established a mission at Fort Yates. Three years later, Pope LEO XIII declared all of Dakota Territory a vicariate and named Father Marty the first BISHOP.

First Bishop. When North Dakota became a state in late 1889, Pope Leo XIII established the region as a single diocese, naming John Shanley, a priest of Irish descent, the first diocesan bishop. Roughly 31,000 North Dakotans were Roman Catholic at the time. His twenty-year reign saw considerable growth and prosperity among the Catholic population. The number and diversity of immigrants distinguished North Dakota from every other state in the Union. In 1890 almost 43 percent of its population was foreign-born. Ten years later that percentage had only dropped to 35.4 percent. At the turn of the century, Norwegians or the children of Norwegians accounted for nearly 23 percent of the population; Germans, 10.1 percent; Canadians, 9.7 percent; and Germans from Russia, 7.5 percent. While most of the Norwegians were Lutheran, many of the Germans and Germans from Russia were Roman Catholic. Each ethnic group maintained allegiance to cultural patterns and traditions, and Bishop Shanley had to handle the situation delicately. To placate the more easy-going Germans from Russia, for example, Shanley recruited Swiss BENEDICTINES, whom the Germans from Russia greatly respected. They feared, however, true Germans, whom they saw as harsh and oppressive. Frequently, priests preached in a variety of languages, including Bohemian, German, and Polish. The tradition of speaking central and eastern European languages in the area continued during the Cold War when clerical refugees from Communist Europe fled to the United States.

Diocesan Division. Though homesteading reached its zenith in 1906, more than 250,000 pioneers migrated to the state between 1898 and 1915. When Bishop Shanley passed away in 1909, the HOLY SEE divided North Dakota into two dioceses, the Diocese of Bismarck and the Diocese of Fargo, reflecting the continued population growth in the state. The POPE appointed a popular Benedictine, Vincent WEHRLE, as bishop of the former, and an Irishman, James O'Reilly (1855–1934), as head of the latter. Between 1910 and 1939 Bishop Wehrle presided over substantial growth in the DIOCESE and fought socialism in all of its varieties, especially during the tumultuous 1920s and 1930s. Using the papal encyclicals *Aeterni Patris* and *Rerum novarum*, Wehrle especially objected to and sought to attenuate the power of the radical Non-Partisan League of North Dakota, which attempted to overturn the state constitution and implement a socialist regime in 1916 and 1917. Studious and pensive, Bishop O'Reilly also oversaw significant growth in the church during his reign. His successor in 1935 was the impressive Aloisius MUENCH of Milwaukee. In 1946, Muench became the Holy Father's personal envoy to postwar West Germany and was created a CARDINAL by JOHN XXIII in 1959. Other bishops in the Diocese of Bismarck have been Vincent J. Ryan (1940–1951), Lambert A. Hoch (1952–1956), Hilary B. Hacker (1956–1982), John F. Kinney (1982–1995), and Paul A. Zipfel (1996–). Other bishops in the Diocese of Fargo have been Leo F. Dworschak (1947–1970), Justin A. Driscoll (1970–1984), James D. Sullivan (1985–2002), and Samuel J. Aquila (2002–).

The population growth North Dakota experienced in the early 1900s shifted to a marked population decline by the year 2000. Not only did the population dramatically decline, it was also aging. Young adults were leaving smaller communities for larger ones within or outside of the state.

Diocese of Fargo. In the Diocese of Fargo, Bishop Aquila's "Pastoral Letter on Parish Life" issued in July 2003 called upon each parish to conduct a one-year evaluation of parish life, which included meetings at the parish and diocesan levels. In August 2004 the pastoral letter titled "Bringing New Life to Our Faith Communities" announced that twenty-four parishes would be consolidated in 2005 and 2006, with the possibility of an ad-

ditional nine by 2010. Some parishes were designated as CHAPELS that could be used for special celebrations. The status of all parishes would be reviewed every five years. Construction of a new West Fargo parish was also recommended, further indication of the population shift from rural communities to North Dakota cities. As of 2008, 136 parishes were served by 154 priests. Catholics in the diocese numbered 85,570, making up 22 percent of the total population of 381,251 encompassed by the diocese (*The Official Catholic Directory* 2008, p. 449).

Diocese of Bismarck. In 2003 Bishop Paul Zipfel expanded the existing diocesan policies relating to sexual misconduct of clerics and lay people serving in the Diocese of Bismarck. The manual *Establishing Bonds of Trust* included many of the provisions adopted by the UNITED STATES CONFERENCE OF CATHOLIC BISHOPS in its charter in 2005. In 2006 Bishop Zipfel announced the hope that the Diocese of Bismarck would become a stewardship diocese by 2010, the year of its centennial celebration. The diocese made steady progress in this regard.

In 2007, responding to the shifting population in the Diocese of Bismarck, which comprises twenty-three counties in western North Dakota, Bishop Zipfel began a three-year program of pastoral planning to assist parishes in dealing with the changing demographics. In 1960 the diocese had a total of 132 churches, with 87 resident priests. In 2008 these numbers dropped to a total of 99 churches, with 44 resident priests. In 2008 the 60,583 Catholics in the diocese were part of a total diocesan population estimated at 260,300 (*The Official Catholic Directory* 2008, p. 120).

SEE ALSO AETERNI PATRIS; CATECHISMS; JESUITS; LUTHERANISM; MISSION AND MISSIONS; PRAYER BOOKS; RERUM NOVARUM; SEX ABUSE CRISIS.

BIBLIOGRAPHY

John Logan Allen, ed., *A Continent Defined* (Lincoln, Neb. 1997).

Robert C. Carriker, *Father Peter John de Smet: Jesuit in the West* (Norman, Okla. 1995).

William Goetzmann and Glyndwr Williams, *The Atlas of North American Exploration: From the Norse Voyages to the Race to the Pole* (New York 1992).

Janet Daley Lysengen and Ann M. Rathke, eds., *The Centennial Anthology of North Dakota History: Journal of the Northern Plains* (Bismarck, N.D. 1996).

Howard R. Lamar, ed., *The New Encyclopedia of the American West* (New Haven, Conn. 1998).

Frederick C. Luebke, ed., *European Immigrants in the American West: Community Histories* (Albuquerque, N.M. 1998).

Walter Nugent, *Into the West: The Story of Its People* (New York 1999).

The Official Catholic Directory, 2008 (New Providence, N.J. 2008).

Elwyn B. Robinson, *History of North Dakota* (Lincoln, Neb. 1966, repr. 1982).

Bradley Birzer
Assistant Professor of History
Hillsdale College, Hillsdale, Mich.

Tanya R. Watterud
Director of Communications, Diocese of Fargo, N.D.
Editor, *New Earth* (2009)

Rev. Mr. Joel Melarvie
Chancellor
Diocese of Bismarck, N.D. (2009)

O

OHIO, CATHOLIC CHURCH IN

The first state formed from the Northwest Territory, Ohio was admitted into the Union in 1803. Its prehistoric inhabitants were the Hopewell, also known as the Mound Builders because of their earthen mounds used for burial and, perhaps, ritual practices. Many of these burial grounds and other unusual earthworks are still preserved in the state, the most noteworthy being the Great Serpent Mound near Hillsboro, Ohio. The Seneca from Canada, Michigan, and New York also constituted a strong presence in Ohio as they followed the Allegheny and Ohio Rivers on long hunting forays in the winter months. The Miami and Wyandotte were also significant tribes within the geographical boundaries of the state.

Early Catholicism in Ohio. Catholicism came to the territory with French explorers and missionaries who entered Ohio through Lake Erie and the Ohio River, but the first permanent settlement in Ohio was not established until 1788 at Marietta. From there the state grew rapidly. By 1800 the population exceeded 45,000, most of these coming from the eastern seaboard and Kentucky. Ethnically and religiously they were Protestant Ulster Irish accompanied later by a significant German immigration from Pennsylvania. Few of these early settlers were Catholic, but there was a group of French Catholics in Gallia County who founded the city of Gallipolis on the Ohio River in the southeastern region of the state. Father Peter Joseph Didier, O.S.B., worked among these Catholics as early as 1791, but seems to have left in discouragement after a few years of hardship and failure.

Until 1785 the entire region was included in the jurisdiction of the Diocese of Quebec. The French JESU-ITS made several missionary journeys in the old territory and founded early missions. None of these became permanent, however, and Ohio remained mission territory into the nineteenth century. In 1789 the Diocese of Baltimore was established in the new republic, and Ohio became part of the first U.S. see.

About 1802 a small group of settlers from near the Maryland-Pennsylvania border moved into Somerset, Pennsylvania, and then went on to found a small community of Catholics called Somerset in southeastern Ohio. Mostly of Alsatian extraction and led by a devout Catholic, Jacob Dittoe (1760–1826), they petitioned Bishop John CARROLL for priests to serve this new settlement. Jacob Dittoe, in fact, had written to Carroll twice, in 1805 and 1808, requesting priests for the isolated Catholic settlements of Ohio. It was not until 1818, after the founding of the Diocese of Bardstown in 1810 and the establishment of the Dominican Friars near Springfield, Kentucky, by Edward FENWICK, O.P. (1768–1832), that the first permanent parish in Ohio was founded. Fenwick and his nephew, Nicholas Young, O.P., came across the village of Somerset on one of their many missionary travels and authorized the construction of a church for the settlement. According to local lore, Father Fenwick heard an ax being wielded in the forest and veered from his route to discover the source of the sound. He found Dittoe at work clearing land (Brennan 1968). Eventually, the DOMINICANS were given 320 acres of cleared farmland, and Somerset became an important center for the FRIARS. In 1830 the DOMINICAN SISTERS from Washington County, Kentucky, opened a girls' academy in Somerset. St. Joseph in Somerset remained an education and formation center for the eastern province of the Dominican Fathers until 1968. The priory remained standing until 1976. The Dominican Sisters moved to St. Mary of the Springs in

Columbus in 1868 after a disastrous fire in 1866 and have maintained the old St. Mary of the Springs College and Academy as Ohio Dominican College.

Edward Fenwick. On June 19, 1824, LEO XII (pope 1823–1829) responded to the expanding Catholic population in Ohio and created the Diocese of Cincinnati with Edward Fenwick as its first BISHOP. The bishop of Bardstown, Benedict FLAGET, consecrated Fenwick in St. Rose Church, Washington County, Kentucky, on January 14, 1822. Fenwick had immediate problems when he transferred his residence from the outskirts of Cincinnati to a location in the city on Sycamore Street. The laity challenged the merging of diocesan and Dominican property and brought the dispute before the Congregation for the PROPAGATION OF THE FAITH. The congregation ordered a separation of diocesan and Dominican property and in 1828 established the policy that diocesan property was to be held by Fenwick in the name of the diocese and willed to his successor in the See of Cincinnati. This arrangement spread throughout the Northwest Territory and kept TRUSTEEISM from becoming a major problem for the Church in these states.

Fenwick was not only a residential bishop but also an active missionary. He traveled extensively throughout Ohio. Fenwick was born of a large landholding family in Maryland and had joined the English province of the Dominicans in Belgium. He returned to Europe on fundraising missions and was aided by Pope Leo XII's support in collecting significant funds in Belgium, Holland, and England. During his absence, from 1823 to 1825, a new episcopal residence was constructed and a cathedral completed and dedicated on December 17, 1826. Fenwick opened a theological seminary, St. Aloysius, in May 1829. Fenwick's intense labors and travels left him in poor health. He petitioned for a coadjutor, but died on a missionary journey in Wooster, Ohio, on September 26, 1832, before one was appointed.

John Baptist Purcell. On May 12, 1833, Pope GREGORY XVI (pope 1831–1846) named John Baptist PURCELL (1800–1883) as the second bishop of Cincinnati. Purcell had completed his studies for the priesthood at St. Sulpice in Paris and was ordained by the archbishop of Paris before returning as professor and president of Mount St. Mary's in Emmitsburg, Maryland. He was consecrated in Baltimore on October 13, 1833. Purcell's half century in office as bishop and later ARCHBISHOP of Cincinnati was a period of enormous growth and expansion of the Church in the state of Ohio. He was a learned and expansive man with a flair for the dramatic.

During the early years of Purcell's reign, a significant social change was underway in Cincinnati. The Catholic population was transformed from an Irish Catholic community into a predominantly German Catholic Church with a minimum of ethnic tensions. Purcell, in contrast to the situation in many other urban areas of the country, managed the transition with little conflict. This was unique in the American Church, as newer ethnic groups often clashed with the increasingly numerous Irish-American hierarchy.

Purcell's European experience gave him inroads into the Church in Europe, where he received both financial assistance and personnel for his rapidly growing missionary diocese. A participant in the first Vatican Council, he initially opposed papal INFALLIBILITY. Nevertheless, he accepted the conciliar definition and, while remaining seemingly intellectually unconvinced, offered his obedience to the Church and, personally, to Pope PIUS IX (pope 1846–1878). Edward FITZGERALD, a priest of the Archdiocese of CINCINNATI who became bishop of Little Rock, Arkansas, in 1867 along with Luigi Riccio (1817–1860), bishop of Caizzo, voted against the definition of papal infallibility, though he too publicly acquiesced.

Purcell allowed great freedom to the German congregations in Cincinnati and accepted a moderate form of trusteeism for the German parishes. Because of the earlier arrangement between the Irish Catholics and Bishop Fenwick, the actual ownership of the German parishes remained in the hands of the local bishop. The extreme forms of trusteeism, therefore, were not experienced in Cincinnati. Purcell, however, was careful not to extend this form of local government to the Irish congregations of Cincinnati. He accepted the assistance of the Tirolean province of the Franciscan Fathers, centered in Innsbruck, Austria, to work with the German population in the city of Cincinnati. He also secured the services of the Precious Blood Fathers and Brothers, under the leadership of Father Francis de Sales BRUNNER, to serve the rural German population of northwestern Ohio. Both of these religious communities became separate provinces centered in the diocese, the Franciscans in Cincinnati and the Precious Blood Fathers in Carthagena, Ohio.

Archdiocese of Cincinnati. In 1850 Pope Pius IX raised Cincinnati, along with New York and New Orleans, to the status of an archdiocese, and Purcell became the first archbishop of the new province of Ohio. One of his goals was to open a seminary to provide the necessary education for those called to the priesthood. After several attempts he undertook the construction of a facility west of the city on Price Hill. The new seminary opened in 1851 as Mount St. Mary's of the West. The name was reminiscent of his days as rector of Mount St. Mary's in Maryland. In 1924 the seminary was moved to Norwood, Ohio, and in the early 1980s to its present location on the eastside of Cincinnati. Religious sisters also came to serve the expanding Catholic population of the state. St. Elizabeth Ann SETON's Sisters of Charity had arrived from Emmitsburg in 1829 and undertook educational and charitable works throughout the diocese. When their congregation affiliated with the French Daughters of Charity, the sisters in Cincinnati chose to become a separate canonical community known as the Sisters of Charity of Cincinnati. In 1920 they established their College of Mount St. Joseph's on the Ohio. Among the many notable women of the congregation, Sister Blandina Segale (1850–1941) has a special place in the folklore of the American West as friend and teacher of Billy the Kid. In 1830, when Bishop Fenwick brought four Dominican Sisters from Kentucky to open a school in Somerset, they included Sister Benvin Sansbury (d. 1873), the sister of Sister Angela Sansbury (d. 1839), the first Dominican Sister professed in the United States. In 1839 Bishop Purcell obtained the services of the Sisters of NOTRE DAME, while visiting their motherhouse in Namur, Belgium, and in 1840 eight NOTRE DAME SISTERS opened a school for girls at St. Xavier's Parish in Cincinnati. In 1865, the sisters opened a school for Holy Cross and St. Patrick's parishes in Columbus.

The remarkable growth of the numbers of religious communities of women in the nineteenth century worked to the great benefit of the Church in Ohio. By mid-century the SISTERS OF MERCY from Kinsale, Ireland; the FRANCISCAN SISTERS of Stella Niagara, New York; the URSULINES; the Sisters of the Holy Humility of Mary; Sisters of ST. JOSEPH; the Good Shepherd Sisters; and many other congregations had come to serve the expanding Catholic population of the state. They worked not only in Cincinnati and the other early Catholic settlements but also among the Catholics moving into the Ohio River valley; the industrially developing cities of Youngstown, Cleveland, Steubenville, and Toledo; and the German farmlands of northwest Ohio. The Sisters of the Precious Blood were an important part of the rural German communities of northwestern Ohio. Along with the Precious Blood Fathers, they were the most significant religious presence throughout that part of the state. Purcell's reign ended, sadly, in SCANDAL and personal tragedy. His brother and chancellor, Father Edward Purcell, had tried to provide a safe banking service for the Catholics of Cincinnati and was successful during some of the financial crises of the mid-nineteenth century. During the Panic of 1877–1878, however, there was a run on Purcell's financial holdings, and the funds to respond to the demands were simply not available. In fact, only a third of the funds demanded were available. The legal battles were not resolved until 1905, when investors received a settlement based on their initial investments.

Archbishop Purcell publicly acknowledged the terrible situation and offered his resignation to Pope LEO XIII (pope 1878–1903). The POPE allowed Purcell to retain the title of archbishop, but Purcell retired, with his brother, to the Ursuline convent in St. Martin, Ohio. He died there, after suffering a series of strokes, on July 4, 1883. He was succeeded by the bishop of Natchez, Mississippi, William Henry ELDER, who faced the task of managing a financially shattered archdiocese, while maintaining the growth and strength of the Catholic Church in the aftermath of disillusionment, anger, and loss of faith. The situation was so widely known and so severe that Bishops Edward FITZGERALD of Little Rock, Arkansas, and Bernard MCQUAID of Rochester, New York, had both refused the appointment to Cincinnati. Elder turned out to be an excellent choice. He was learned and cultured and a good reconciler of divergent opinions and conflicting movements. He held the position for twenty-four years and died October 31, 1904. The courts dealt with the Purcell financial scandal during Elder's entire time as archbishop.

In addition to the strong European immigrant communities, there were also African-American Catholics in Ohio in the nineteenth century. Daniel Rudd (1854–1903), who had been born a slave in Bardstown, Kentucky, published a black Catholic weekly newspaper, the *American Catholic Tribune*, starting in the late 1880s. He began publication in Springfield, Ohio, where he had migrated in order to attend high school, but eventually published the newspaper in Cincinnati, and then in Detroit, until the late 1890s. He was confident that the Catholic Church possessed the means, through its teaching and its structure, to overcome all forms of racism in the nation. Rudd was a principal organizer of the five black Catholic lay congresses, whose delegates were elected by parishes across the country, that were held between 1889 and 1894, including one in Cincinnati (1890). There was a continuing attraction for American blacks to convert to Catholicism through the mid-twentieth century. In several small southern Ohio cities, blacks were not welcome to pursue high school education in the public schools, and so many converted to Catholicism in order to attend Catholic high schools. Chillicothe, Ohio, the first state capital, experienced this phenomenon, and families such as the Menefees, Mitchells, and Hairstons remain an important part of the black Catholic population of southern Ohio.

Creation of Dioceses. The Cincinnati jurisdiction had been divided twice during the reign of Archbishop Purcell. In 1847 Pope Pius IX created the Diocese of Cleveland, comprising the entire northern section of Ohio. The first bishop, Louis Amadeus Rappe (1801–

1877), had come to America with three other French priests, John Baptist LAMY, Joseph MACHEBEUF, and Louis de Groesbriand (1816–1899), all of whom had been recruited for the American missions by Archbishop Purcell. Lamy first went to Danville, Ohio, then known as Sapp Settlement, and served as a missionary priest in central Ohio, founding St. Vincent parish in Mt. Vernon, Ohio, and St. Francis de Sales in Newark, Ohio, before being named the archbishop of Santa Fe. He remains a significant figure in American literature as the archbishop in Willa Cather's *Death Comes for the Archbishop*. Groesbriand went on to become the bishop of Burlington, Vermont, and Machebeuf the bishop of the Diocese of Epiphany, later known as Denver.

Rappe had only one permanent church in his new diocese, St. Mary on the Flats. Within five years, he had built a new CATHEDRAL dedicated to St. John the Evangelist. The Catholic population grew rapidly, and several synods were held to guide the growing Church. Rappe faced great ethnic tensions when waves of immigration broke over the new diocese. The results were less fortuitous for Rappe in Cleveland than for Purcell in Cincinnati. Various ethnic groups in the new diocese were in great conflict with each other and the bishop. Rappe became increasingly disheartened by the intense conflict, and when he submitted his resignation to Pope Pius IX in 1870 while attending the Vatican Council, his enemies in Cleveland used the occasion to accuse him of scandalous behavior. The local newspaper, *The Leader*, took up the story, and Rappe was vilified throughout the city. No truth was ever ascertained concerning the charges of confessional solicitation, but Rappe happily took up missionary work in the Diocese of Burlington among the French-speaking population of northern New York and Vermont. He died on Grand Island in Lake Champlain in 1877 and was buried in the cathedral at Cleveland. On March 3, 1868, Cincinnati was further divided by the creation of the Diocese of COLUMBUS. Sylvester Rosecrans (1862–1868), brother of the Civil War General William Rosecrans (1819–1898) and auxiliary bishop of Cincinnati, was appointed the first bishop of Columbus. Rosecrans converted to Catholicism while a student at Kenyon College in Gambier, Ohio. As a consequence of his conversion he had to withdraw from Kenyon, then an Episcopalian men's college founded by the Protestant Episcopal Bishop Philander Chase (1775–1852) in 1824. By the time Rosecrans became bishop, Columbus had some 40,000 Catholics. Somerset, Ohio, site of the first permanent Catholic church in the state, was in the new diocese and remained under the Dominicans, who had been there since 1818 and who remained responsible for the church in Somerset into the year 2008. Rosecrans built a new cathedral for Columbus, wishing to choose neither the Irish church, St. Patrick's, nor the German

church, Holy Cross (formerly St. Remigius parish), for his cathedral. He dedicated the new St. Joseph Cathedral on October 20, 1878, and died the following day. He was succeeded by John Watterson (1844–1899), president of Mount St. Mary's in Emmitsburg, Maryland.

Watterson paid off the cathedral debt, but by expanding the number of parishes and schools, he left the diocese heavily in debt. There was some consideration of suppressing the new diocese for financial reasons, but Watterson's death and the arrival of the financially adept former Cincinnati chancellor, Henry Moeller (1849–1925), ensured the continued existence of the Columbus diocese. In 1904 James J. Hartley (1853–1944) was appointed bishop of Columbus. He reigned until 1944 and continued the expansion and building of the institutions which spread and supported the faith. In 1923 he opened a local seminary dedicated to St. Charles BORROMEO, which remained in operation until 1969. In the early 2000s it served as the only Catholic boys' high school in Columbus.

Twentieth Century and Beyond. During the early twentieth century, the industrial cities of Ohio grew so rapidly that new dioceses had to be created. In 1910 Toledo became a diocese. The first three bishops of Toledo moved on to other sees: Joseph SCHREMBS to Cleveland, Samuel STRITCH to Chicago, and Karl Alter (1885–1977) to Cincinnati. The Toledo Cathedral of the Queen of the Most Holy Rosary was planned by Bishop Schrembs, begun by Bishop Stritch, and completed in 1940 by Bishop Alter. It is the finest example of Spanish plateresque architecture in the country. Toledo, like the other Ohio industrial cities, was challenged to care for the great waves of immigrants pouring in from eastern and southern Europe. During the Second World War, the wartime economy with its demand for steel and other materials needed for the war effort provided ample opportunity for numerous Catholic immigrants to find work in the Ohio industrial belt. Two new dioceses were erected during these years of rapid wartime expansion: Youngstown, with James McFadden as bishop (1943–1952), in 1943 and Steubenville, with John King Mussio as bishop (1945–1977), in 1944. Schools, hospitals, colleges, and charitable institutions proliferated throughout the state. The sacrifice and hard work of religious sisters maintained most of these institutions.

Higher Education. Ohio became a center for Catholic higher education. Major colleges and universities were founded and sustained by religious congregations of men and women. The University of DAYTON was founded in 1850 by the Marianist Fathers and Brothers, who still provide the leadership of the university. The

Parish Closings. *Parishioners attend services at St. Stephen Roman Catholic Church in Cleveland, Ohio, recently. Regional church committees in Cleveland are recommending that at least two dozen city parishes in the Cleveland Catholic Diocese be closed. At St. Stephen, a national historic landmark on the West Side, some members are trying to save the building, even if they can't save the parish. Not only is it an architectural and historic landmark, it is also an important ethnic parish, being the last to hold masses in German.* AP IMAGES

largest Catholic university in Ohio, it draws students from across the United States and abroad. The Marian Institute of the university has the largest Marian library in the world and grants pontifical degrees in Marian THEOLOGY through its affiliation with the Marianum University in Rome.

Xavier University in Cincinnati and John Carroll University in Cleveland were founded by the Society of Jesus in 1831 and 1886, respectively. These Jesuit universities have provided the Catholic population of Ohio with the Jesuit educational tradition for well over a century and a half. Today they face the same Catholic identity issues that most Catholic colleges and universities face, but still maintain a significant number of priests and scholastics in administration and on the teaching faculty.

The Ursuline Sisters of Toledo and Cleveland were leaders in Catholic higher education for women in northern Ohio, as were the Sisters of Mercy in Toledo and the Holy Humility of Mary Sisters in Cleveland.

The College of Mount St. Joseph on the Ohio River, founded by the Sisters of Charity of Cincinnati, has been a mainstay of Catholic women's education in the Archdiocese of Cincinnati. The funds for the establishment and development of these institutions and other institutions owned and operated by communities of women religious throughout the state and the country were acquired through the ability and skill of the sisters themselves, giving further testimony to the extraordinary ability and resourcefulness of American women religious. Few women in American society during the nineteenth and early part of the twentieth centuries had such opportunities to develop and use their education and natural abilities in such public and professional ways. As the decline in vocations to the religious life accelerated and the costs of operation increased greatly, many of the smaller Catholic colleges merged, closed, or secularized. Nevertheless, many remained and continue to provide educational opportunities for the people of Ohio and across the country.

Franciscan University. *This small Catholic college, pictured above during the celebration of Noontime mass, is well-known for its fidelity to the teachings of the Church.* TONY TOMSIC//TIME LIFE PICTURES/GETTY IMAGES

A unique phenomenon in Catholic higher education in Ohio is the Franciscan University of Steubenville. Founded in 1946 as the College of Steubenville by the Sacred Heart Province of the Third Order Regular of St. Francis with the cooperation of Bishop John King Mussio, the university floundered for many years until Father Michael Scanlan (1931–), T.O.R., was elected president in 1974. He led the university into the Charismatic movement and beyond. By the time Scanlan retired as president in 2000, after twenty-six years of service, the university had gained a national reputation by placing a strong emphasis on orthodoxy and youthful enthusiasm and had won recognition as a source of church renewal and youth retreats.

Ohio is also the home of The Pontifical College JOSEPHINUM, a seminary that offers undergraduate, pretheology, and theology degree programs. Founded originally as St. Joseph's Orphan Home in Pomeroy, Ohio, by German born Father Joseph J. Jessing (1836–1899), the institution became incorporated as a seminary in Columbus in 1888. Jessing sought to provide free SEMINARY EDUCATION for poor German boys to serve the needs of the German immigrant population of the United States, and at the founder's initiative the seminary came under pontifical jurisdiction in 1892. With the Apostolic NUNCIO to the United States as the chancellor and also the ordinary of the Josephinum, the seminary holds the unusual position of being the only such institution for the education of students for the priesthood outside of Italy. The state is also home to

three diocesan seminaries: Mount St. Mary's of the West in Cincinnati as well as Borromeo and St. Mary Seminaries in Cleveland.

National and State Contributions. The hierarchy of Ohio has played a major role in the life of the Church of the United States. Cardinal Joseph BERNARDIN, as general secretary of the National Catholic Welfare Conference (NCWC), was instrumental in founding the United States Catholic Conference and the National Conference of Catholic Bishops (NCCB). He served there as general secretary and president. In 1972 he was named archbishop of Cincinnati and remained there until 1982, when he was transferred to the Archdiocese of CHICAGO. Bishop James Malone (1920–2000), bishop of Youngstown from 1966 to 1995, was also active in the NCWC and the NCCB, serving as its president from 1984 to 1986. Archbishop Daniel Pilarczyk (1974–1982) of Cincinnati and Bishop Anthony Pilla (1932–) of Cleveland have also served as presidents of the conference, from 1990 to 1992, and from 1996 to 1998, respectively.

In addition to Cardinal Bernardin, Bishop Samuel Stritch of Toledo (1921–1930) also became CARDINAL archbishop of Chicago. Bishop John J. Carberry of Columbus (1965–1968) went on to become the cardinal archbishop of St. Louis. Bishop James Hickey of Cleveland (1974–1980) became the cardinal archbishop of Washington, and Auxiliary Bishop John Krol of Cleveland (1953–1961) became the cardinal archbishop of Philadelphia. Other Ohio bishops have also had a significant impact on the life of the national Church. Most notable among these were Archbishops John T. McNicholas of Cincinnati (1925–1950) and Karl J. Alter, also of Cincinnati (1950–1969). Joseph Schrembs, bishop of Cleveland (1921–1945), and Edward F. Hoban, also bishop of Cleveland (1945–1966), were both awarded the personal title of archbishop in recognition of their leadership roles within the Church in the United States.

The bishops of Ohio collaborate in the work of the Church through the Ohio Catholic Conference. Founded in 1945 under the presidency of Archbishop McNicholas, it was known as the Ohio Catholic Welfare Conference. In 1967, in conformity with the change in the National Catholic Welfare Conference, it changed its name to the Ohio Catholic Conference. Meetings are usually held twice a year in Columbus under the presidency of the archbishop of Cincinnati. The conference identifies itself as "the official representative of the Catholic Church in public matters affecting the Church and the general welfare of the citizens of Ohio." It focuses on educational and health issues as well as social concerns, and it lobbies the state legislature on issues pertaining to Catholic interests and those of the general well being of Ohio citizens. In addition the Conference provides facilitation, coordination, and joint programming for diocesan groups involved in various church ministries.

The policies and activities of the conference are governed by a board of directors. The board is comprised of all ROMAN RITE bishops exercising jurisdiction within the Province of Cincinnati, which consists of the state of Ohio. Also, the bishops of three Eastern Catholic jurisdictions, whose headquarters are located in Ohio, are members of the board. The archbishop of Cincinnati, as head of the Province of Cincinnati, acts as chairman of the board. Meetings are usually held four times a year in Columbus.

Assistance for Children. One of the most successful accomplishments on the legislative front has been the approval of various educational programs designed to help students attending chartered nonpublic schools. These programs began in 1966 with the passage of the Fair Bus Bill that provides transportation services for all children regardless of the school they attend. In 1967, followed by various amendments over the course of the next forty years, the legislature approved a program that provides textbooks, instructional materials and equipment, computer hardware and software, and various specialized services such as speech and hearing and psychological services for the benefit of students attending chartered nonpublic schools. In 1982 the Administrative Cost Reimbursement Program was approved.

This program is unique because it provides a direct reimbursement to nonpublic schools for the expenses incurred in meeting various state and federal mandates.

During the legislative session beginning in 1995, the Ohio General Assembly passed legislation providing connectivity to the Internet for nonpublic school children. The legislature also approved the Cleveland Scholarship and Tutoring Program, which provides scholarships for students attending a Cleveland municipal school to attend a chartered nonpublic school within the district. The Cleveland program was challenged by various groups, but was eventually declared constitutional by the United States Supreme Court in 2002.

In 2006 the Educational Choice Scholarship Program was approved by the Ohio General Assembly. Students attending public school buildings in Academic Watch or Academic Emergency are eligible for a scholarship to attend a chartered nonpublic school. During the past forty years the Ohio General Assembly has provided over $4,500,000,000 for students attending chartered nonpublic schools. Ohio leads the country in providing this type of assistance.

In June 2002 the National Conference of Catholic Bishops approved the Charter for the Protection of Children and Young People. One of the requirements of the charter calls for the establishment of Victim Assistance Coordinators in every diocese throughout the country. These persons are charged with helping survivors of childhood sexual abuse receive counseling and other related services. Many survivors expressed concern about returning to the Church for help. In response to this, the bishops of Ohio, through the conference, established a counseling assistance fund, independent of the Church, to help adult survivors of childhood sexual abuse receive counseling or similar mental health services. The program extended from November 2006 until mid-May 2008.

Conclusion. The Catholic Church in Ohio rests on the institutions, leadership, and labor of earlier leaders—clerical, religious, and lay. From Jacob Dittoe of Somerset to the German trustees of Cincinnati to the newer forms of public presence, the FAITHFUL have built and sustained a strong community of believers. The Church in Ohio has positioned itself well to face the challenges of its next century.

SEE ALSO African American Catholics in the United States (History of); Baltimore, Archdiocese of; Association of Catholic Colleges and Universities; Charismatic Renewal, Catholic; Converts and Conversion; Franciscans, Third Order Regular; Marian Fathers; Mission and Missions; Mount St. Mary's College and Seminary; Sex Abuse Crisis; United States Conference of Catholic Bishops (USCCB); Vatican Council I; Vatican Council II.

BIBLIOGRAPHY

Robert Edward Brennan, O.P., *Cradle of the Faith in Ohio* (Somerset, Ohio 1968).

Francis F. Brown, *A History of the Roman Catholic Diocese of Steubenville, Ohio*, vol. I.: *The Mussio Years, 1945–1977* (Lewiston 1994).

James J. Hartley, ed., *A History of the Diocese of Columbus*, 2 vols. (Columbus, Ohio 1918–1943); also see The Catholic Record Society, 197 East Gay St., Columbus, Ohio 43215.

M. Edmund Hussey, *A History of the Archdiocese of Cincinnati* (Strasbourg, France 2000).

Michael J. Hynes, *History of the Diocese of Cleveland: Origin and Growth (1847–1952)* (Cleveland, Ohio 1953).

Lawrence A. Mossing, *History of the Diocese of Toledo*, 9 vols. (Fremont, Ohio 1983).

Frank P. Lane
The Pontifical College Josephinum
Columbus, Ohio

Timothy V. Luckhaupt
Executive Director
Catholic Conference of Ohio (1988–2007) (2009)

OKLAHOMA, CATHOLIC CHURCH IN

Located in the southwestern United States, Oklahoma was admitted to the Union in 1907 as the forty-sixth state. It is bounded on the north by Kansas and Colorado, on the east by Missouri and Arkansas, on the south by the Red River and Texas, and on the west by New Mexico and the Texas Panhandle.

History. The area, traversed by Coronado (c. 1510–1554) in the sixteenth century and explored by the Spanish and French in the seventeenth and eighteenth centuries, became the property of the United States through the Louisiana Purchase of 1803. Federal policy very early designated it as a permanent home for the resettlement of various Native American tribes, and the Five Civilized Tribes of the southeastern United States were moved there (1830–1845). Virtually the whole area was originally apportioned to these groups, but their tribal districts were later reduced, in part because of their support for the Confederacy during the Civil War. Many other tribes were then relocated within what became known as Indian Territory. One unassigned portion near the center, the Oklahoma Territory, was opened to white settlement during the famous run of April 22, 1889. Meanwhile the U.S. government directed the native peoples to give up tribal title to their reservation lands and to take allotments as individuals. The resulting "surplus" lands were opened to whites between 1891 and 1906. This made it possible for the Twin Territories to be granted statehood on November 16, 1907.

In Oklahoma, a traditional stronghold of white Protestant culture, residents of foreign birth were few before the twentieth century. The Southern BAPTISTS constitute the most numerous church group; the Methodists, Presbyterians, Church of Christ, and Disciples of Christ have sizable memberships. Numerous evangelical sects are very active, but the Jewish and Muslim populations are minimal. In 2008 the state had a population of 3,725,676, and Catholics numbered 175,006, or about 4 percent of the total state population (*The Official Catholic Directory* 2008, p. 2096).

Missionary Activity. Although FRIARS and priests had accompanied the Coronado and De Soto (c. 1497–1542) expeditions when they passed through the region in 1541 and 1542, no Catholic missionary activity was seen again until 1830, when the Jesuit Charles VAN QUICKENBORNE offered Mass at three sites in the northeast portion of the present state. Nominally under the BISHOP of St. Louis, Missouri, from 1826 to 1843, this vast country was visited occasionally by JESUITS from the Osage Mission in St. Paul, Kansas, who ministered to the army camps and native tribes. When the Diocese of LITTLE ROCK, Arkansas, was erected in 1843, Oklahoma was included within its original boundaries. Priests from Fort Smith, Arkansas, made regular missionary tours through the western extension of the DIOCESE.

Of the many tribes in the Oklahoma territory during the nineteenth century, only two were predominantly Catholic, the Osage and Potowatomi. The first Catholic church in Indian Territory was built in 1872 at Atoka, Choctaw Nation, by Reverend Michael Smyth (1872–1880) of Fort Smith, but he attended it irregularly. Permanent missionary activity began in 1875 with the arrival of French BENEDICTINES from the Abbey of Pierre-que-Vire. Dom Isidore ROBOT, who briefly took up residence in Atoka, was appointed the first prefect apostolic of the Indian Territory in 1876. (This was the only prefecture apostolic ever established in a region that was then part of the United States.) Among the Potowatomi, Robot founded Sacred Heart Mission, termed "the cradle of Catholicity in Oklahoma," and built boarding schools for boys and girls, the latter in the care of SISTERS OF MERCY from Lacon, Illinois. He was named an ABBOT *honoris causa* by Pope LEO XIII in 1879.

First Bishops. The Benedictine prefecture under Robot and his successor, Ignatius Jean (1887–1916), continued until 1891, when the first bishop, Theophile Meerschaert (1847–1924), a Belgian-born priest working in Mississippi, took over the administration of the Twin

St. Joseph Cathedral, Oklahoma City, Oklahoma. *Monuments to the people who died in the Oklahoma City bombing are seen in the foreground.* © KRAUS MARK/CORBIS SYGMA

Territories. Although Meerschaert's title at first was vicar apostolic of the Indian Territory (1891–1905), in fact the Church was too late to do much effective evangelization of Native Americans, who were too disheartened to respond to the white man's religion. The growth of the Church in Oklahoma came with the arrival of Irish railroad workers, Italian and Polish coal miners, and German farmers.

The seat of the vicariate was located at Guthrie, the territorial capital, following the land run of 1889, but in 1905 when the vicariate was elevated to diocesan rank and styled the Diocese of Oklahoma, Bishop Meerschaert moved the see city to Oklahoma City, which shortly thereafter became the state capital. Including his time as vicar apostolic, Bishop Meerschaert served in Oklahoma for almost thirty-three years (1891–1924). Under Meerschaert the diocese experienced rapid growth in the number of churches and missions and a large increase in priests and sisters.

One incident that occurred during Meerschaert's episcopate had lasting significance on the national scene. In 1917 the state legislature passed the so-called Bone-Dry Law, which forbade the import of alcoholic spirits into Oklahoma. Manufacture of wine and liquor within the state boundaries was already forbidden by the Oklahoma constitution. The diocese went to court, charging infringement of religion, and the state supreme court upheld the complaint in 1918. Ironically, this paved the way for national Prohibition, once the precedent for an exception on religious grounds was established in the Oklahoma case.

Twentieth-Century Developments. When Meerschaert died in 1924, he was succeeded by Francis Clement KELLEY (1924–1948). Bishop Kelley recognized the growing importance of Tulsa to the life of the state and the Church in Oklahoma and took steps to have the diocese redesignated as the Diocese of Oklahoma and Tulsa in 1930. Kelley's successor was his close friend, Bishop Eugene J. McGuinness (1948–1957), who had served as coadjutor with right of succession since 1944. McGuinness in turn was succeeded by an Oklahoman, the pastor of the co-cathedral in Tulsa, Victor J. Reed (1958–1971). Shortly before his sudden death Bishop Reed had initiated discussions about dividing the diocese. Bishop John R. Quinn, his successor, carried the effort forward. In December 1972 ROME created a new ecclesiastical province. The metropolitan see was the Archdiocese of OKLAHOMA CITY, with Quinn as the first ARCHBISHOP (1972–1977). The suffragan sees were the Diocese of TULSA with Monsignor Bernard J. Ganter, chancellor of the Galveston-Houston diocese, as the first bishop (1972–1977), and the Diocese of Little Rock, Arkansas, which was transferred from the Province of New Orleans.

Charles A. Salatka (1977–1991) succeeded Quinn as archbishop of Oklahoma City. The following year Pope PAUL VI appointed Eusebius Joseph Beltran as bishop of the Tulsa diocese. Beltran served in that capacity until 1992, when he replaced Archbishop Salatka, who was retiring. One of Beltran's first acts in his new position was to organize opposition to a proposed ABORTION law. Beltran was replaced in the Diocese of Tulsa by Edward James Slattery (1993–). In Bishop Slattery's second pastoral letter, "The Suffering Faces of the Poor Are the Suffering Face of Christ," he spoke out against U.S. immigration laws and vowed to go to prison, if need be, for aiding all who are poor and suffering, regardless of their citizenship status.

Twenty-First-Century Developments. In 2001 the Church in Oklahoma ended its thirty-seven-year commitment to provide priests to the Micatokla Mission Santiago Atitlan, Guatemala. Begun in 1964, the Church's mission efforts had sent three priests to Central America. The first, Father Ramon Carlin, served for four years. In 1968 he was followed by Father Stanley Rother, who was murdered in 1981. Rother's replacement did not arrive until 1983. Father Thomas McSherry then worked at the mission for seventeen years until the Latin American Church had sufficient staff to run the mission.

In 2007 the Archdiocese of Oklahoma City undertook the cause for BEATIFICATION of Father Stanley Rother (1935–1981), the Oklahoma priest who was shot at the Guatemala mission. Because the Central American church could not afford to pursue the cause, Archbishop Beltran requested permission to transfer the jurisdiction to Oklahoma.

In 2008 the Diocese of Tulsa, which serves 31 counties in eastern Oklahoma, had 61,000 faithful, 78 parishes, 13 schools with approximately 5,000 students, and a biweekly newspaper, the *Eastern Oklahoma Catholic* (Diocese of Tulsa 2008). The *Sooner Catholic*, the biweekly paper of the Archdiocese of Oklahoma, provides information on the 3 counties of the ARCHDIOCESE, which in 2008 had 115,506 faithful, 70 parishes, 22 schools and 1 university with a total of 5,183 students, and was served by 118 priests and 126 religious (*The Official Catholic Directory* 2008, p. 943).

SEE ALSO ARKANSAS, CATHOLIC CHURCH IN; CHRISTIAN CHURCH (DISCIPLES OF CHRIST); EVANGELICAL CHURCH; ISLAM; JUDAISM; METHODIST CHURCHES; MISSION AND MISSIONS; NEW ORLEANS, ARCHDIOCESE OF; PRESBYTERIANISM; ST. LOUIS, ARCHDIOCESE OF; UNITED CHURCH OF CHRIST.

BIBLIOGRAPHY

Archdiocese of Oklahoma City Official Web site, available from: http://www.catharchdioceseokc.org/ (accessed November 20, 2008).

Archdiocese of Oklahoma City, *Sooner Catholic Online*, archdiocesan biweekly newspaper available from http://www.catharchdioceseokc.org/sooner/index.htm (accessed November 19, 2008).

Thomas Elton Brown, *Bible-Belt Catholicism: A History of the Roman Catholic Church in Oklahoma, 1905–1945*, vol. 33 (New York 1977).

Diocese of Tulsa Official Web site, available from: http://www.dioceseoftulsa.org/ (accessed November 20, 2008).

Grant Foreman, *A History of Oklahoma* (Norman, Okla. 1942).

Roy Gittinger, *The Formation of the State of Oklahoma, 1803–1906* (Norman, Okla. 1939).

Edwin C. McReynolds, *Oklahoma: A History of the Sooner State* (Norman, Okla. 1954).

Theophile Meerschaert, *Diary of a Frontier Bishop: The Journals of Theophile Meerschaert*, edited and annotated by James D. White (Tulsa, Okla. 1994).

The Official Catholic Directory, 2008 (New Providence, N.J. 2008).

Oklahoma Catholic Churches, available from http://www.oklahomacatholicchurches.org/ (accessed November 19, 2008).

Oklahoma Digest, 1890 to Date (St. Paul, Minn. 1934–).

Oklahoma Historical Society, *Encyclopedia of Oklahoma History and Culture: Catholic Church*, available from http://digital.library.okstate.edu/encyclopedia/entries/C/CA072.html (accessed November 19, 2008).

Oklahoma Statutes Annotated: Uniform Commercial Code, 1961, 3 vols. (St. Paul, Minn. 1961).

Sister M. Ursula Thomas, O.S.B., *The Catholic Church on the Oklahoma Frontier, 1824–1907* (St. Louis, Mo. 1938).

James D. White, *Getting Sense: The Osages and Their Missionaries* (Tulsa, Okla. 1997).

James D. White, *This Far by Faith, 1875–2000: 125 Years of Catholic Life in Oklahoma* (Strasbourg, France 2001).

Rev. Joseph Francis Murphy OSB
Chairman of the Department of History and Dean of Men, St. Gregory's College
Pastor, St. Benedict's Church, Shawnee, Okla.

William Charles Garthoeffner
Chancery Office
Oklahoma City, Okla.

Rev. James D. White
Historian
Diocese of Tulsa, Oklahoma

Laurie J. Edwards
Independent Scholar
Reidsville, N.C. (2009)

OKLAHOMA CITY, ARCHDIOCESE OF

By reason of a bull of Pope PAUL VI (December 13, 1972), the Diocese of Oklahoma City and Tulsa was divided, and Oklahoma City (*Oklahomapolitana*) was designated the metropolitan see (February 6, 1973). The state of Oklahoma had been established as a vicariate apostolic in 1891 and as a DIOCESE in 1905, with Oklahoma City as the diocesan seat. In 1930 the see was redesignated the Diocese of Oklahoma City and Tulsa. At the time that the Archdiocese of Oklahoma City was established (February 1971), Tulsa was made a diocese, and together with the Diocese of LITTLE ROCK, Arkansas, it became suffragan to the new ARCHDIOCESE. At this time Catholics numbered about 65,000 in a total population of 1.5 million; in 2001 the population of the area increased to 2.2 million and the number of Catholics to 98,000. In 2007 the Archdiocese of Oklahoma was the metropolitan see for the suffragan dioceses of Little Rock, Arkansas, and of Tulsa, Oklahoma. The archdiocese is 42,470 square miles in size and is comprised of forty-six counties. There are 70 parishes plus 44 missions. As of 2007, the Catholic population of the archdiocese was 115,506, about 5 percent of the total population of the area (2,125,676) (*The Official Catholic Directory* 2008, p. 943).

When the Diocese of Little Rock, Arkansas, was erected in 1843, it included the Indian Territory (now Oklahoma). Priests from Fort Smith, Arkansas, made regular missionary tours through the western part of the diocese. In 1872, through the efforts of Father Michael Smyth, the first Catholic church in Oklahoma was built at Atoka, then the terminus of the Missouri, Kansas, and Texas railroad. Three years later, Bishop Edward FITZGERALD of Little Rock assigned the whole Indian Territory to the Benedictine Isidore ROBOT, the first priest to take up permanent residence in Oklahoma. On July 9, 1876, PIUX IX established the territory as a prefecture apostolic and named Robot its first prefect. When Robot resigned in 1886, he was succeeded by another Benedictine, Ignatius Jean (1886–1890).

Diocesan Development. After the opening of a large portion of the area to white settlers in 1889, the HOLY SEE raised Oklahoma to the status of a vicariate apostolic on May 29, 1891, and appointed Theophile Meerschaert (1847–1924), then vicar general of the Diocese of Natchez, Mississippi, as vicar apostolic with episcopal rank.

Forty-four years old at the time of his appointment, Meerschaert served in Oklahoma for thirty-two years. A period of rapid growth in the number of churches and missions was accompanied by a large increase in the ranks of the clergy and RELIGIOUS. Meerschaert despaired of attracting American vocations and chose instead to bring in priests and seminarians from Europe, particularly from his native Belgium. Originally his seat was at Guthrie, the territorial capital following the Land Run, but on August 17, 1905, the Diocese of Oklahoma was erected and the bishop's headquarters was moved to the rapidly growing town of Oklahoma City, which became the state capital in 1910, three years after Oklahoma achieved statehood.

Bishop Meerschaert died in 1924 and was succeeded by Monsignor Francis Clement KELLEY, founder and president of the Catholic Church Extension Society. One of the most illustrious churchmen to work in Oklahoma, he was the author of seventeen books on a wide variety of subjects. As BISHOP he managed the Church's transition from a predominately rural population to an urban one. He opened parishes in Oklahoma City and Tulsa and suppressed several dozen marginal country parishes across the state. He recognized the growing importance of Tulsa to diocesan life. Early in his episcopate he considered moving the episcopal seat there, but in 1930 he settled for a redesignation, the Diocese of Oklahoma City and Tulsa, and named the Church of the Holy Family (built in 1914) in Tulsa as the co-cathedral.

During the Depression, Kelley kept the diocese financially solvent through publishing and by giving retreats and lectures around the country. (He was jokingly known as the bishop *from* Oklahoma.) Although his first years were marked by energetic efforts at expansion, the economic crisis of the 1930s made further initiatives inadvisable. Kelley ordained the first two Oklahoma-born diocesan priests in 1928. Relatively few ordinations followed in succeeding years, but Kelley nevertheless promoted postgraduate studies in ROME and Louvain. This led to several innovations, such as street preaching, and the introduction of the Young Christian Worker and Christian Family movements, begun in Belgium under Joseph Cardijn. The first American unit of the Young Christian Workers was at Ponca City, Oklahoma.

In 1942 Kelley suffered a series of strokes, after which he was a semi-invalid until his death in 1948. In 1944 Rome appointed as apostolic administrator Bishop Eugene J. McGuinness, until then the bishop of Raleigh, North Carolina. McGuinness led the Oklahoma church during the expansive postwar years and opened many new hospitals, parishes, and schools. He also campaigned forcefully for vocations. "You have given me your money," he would tell parishioners, "now give me your blood!" The result was an astounding increase among seminarians and religious women. Kelley had begun a junior seminary in 1928, but by the time it was ready to open, he had no funds to operate it. McGuinness

Little Flower Catholic Church, Oklahoma City, Oklahoma. *Parishiners crowd the church during Mass on Sunday, April 3, 2005, a day following the death of Pope John Paul II.* AP IMAGES

established a temporary institution near Oklahoma City, then made plans for a permanent complex, which opened in 1958, a few months after his death. When the bishop began his episcopate in Oklahoma, there were eleven seminarians. Within a few years of the new seminary's inauguration, it had an enrollment of 128.

On December 5, 1957, Monsignor Victor J. Reed (1905–1971), rector of Holy Family Co-Cathedral in Tulsa, was appointed auxiliary bishop of the diocese. Soon afterward, on December 27, Bishop McGuinness suffered a fatal heart attack. The Holy See appointed Reed to succeed him, and he was consecrated as the fourth diocesan ordinary on March 5, 1958.

The defining issues for Reed's episcopate were the Second Vatican Council and the war in Vietnam. Bishop Kelley had bequeathed a rich intellectual heritage, and one result was that Catholics in Oklahoma were better prepared for the changes that ensued from the Council. In 1966 St. Gregory's in Shawnee was the scene of the first diocesan council held in the United States following Vatican II. At the same time, Bishop Reed was assailed from two fronts within the diocese. On the one hand were those enraged by what they viewed as the Church's betrayal of its traditions, while on the other were priests

and sisters who were disenchanted with the bishop because they were looking for change beyond what he could authorize. A sudden drop in vocations obliged him to close McGuinness's seminary after only ten years in operation. The manifold pressures may have contributed to his sudden death on September 8, 1971, at the age of 65.

Diocesan Changes. At the time he died, Reed had already begun meetings with a view to dividing the diocese. His successor, Bishop John R. Quinn (1929–), the former auxiliary of San Diego, California, carried this effort forward, with the result that on December 19, 1972, Rome announced the creation of the Archdiocese of Oklahoma City, the establishment of the Diocese of Tulsa, and the combining of these two with the Diocese of Little Rock to form a new ecclesiastical province. Quinn was named the first ARCHBISHOP.

Even before the diocese was divided, Quinn had to resolve a difficult situation involving *experimental parishes* in Oklahoma City and Tulsa. He requested an evaluation from the Center for Applied Research in the Apostolate (CARA) of Washington, D.C. Informed that the two parishes were not serving the purposes for which they were formed, he terminated both communities. Another of his accomplishments was in 1974 to resurrect the diocesan newspaper, which had been discontinued, as *The Sooner Catholic*. Subsequently, it went on to receive many awards for excellence from the Catholic Press Association.

When Archbishop Quinn was named archbishop of San Francisco early in 1977, he was replaced in Oklahoma by Archbishop Charles A. Salatka (1918–2003), the former bishop of Marquette, Mississippi. Consecrated as auxiliary bishop of Grand Rapids in 1962, Salatka was among the youngest bishops at Vatican II. At his retirement thirty years later, he was the eldest surviving bishop to have seen service at the Council. In his fifteen years in Oklahoma City, he consolidated the archdiocese's fiscal holdings and developed its outreach to an expanding Hispanic population. Bishop Eusebius J. Beltran (1934–), who had served as bishop of the Tulsa diocese since 1978, was named to succeed Archbishop Salatka when the latter retired in 1992. Archbishop Beltran took office on January 22, 1993. He continued the initiatives of his predecessor toward Hispanics, while extending the archdiocese's outreach toward youth.

Archbishop Eusebius J. Beltran continued his emphasis on service to the poor, needy, and helpless. From his first days in office, Archbishop Beltran worked tirelessly to protect the unborn through his active opposition to ABORTION, through the establishment of an annual archdiocesan Sanctity of Life Mass, and through leading PRAYER vigils. He frequently raised his voice on the death penalty, including his "Call for a Moratorium on the Death Penalty" (June 2000). Archbishop Beltran actively encouraged the development of archdiocesan programs to assist victims of domestic violence. He issued two Pastoral Letters that call for an end to domestic violence (2006 and 2007) and participated in numerous state and local forums on this subject. In 2007 he and his Council of Priests publicly called for the repeal of anti–immigration legislation enacted by the Oklahoma legislature. With the support of the archbishop, the archdiocese built a retirement center to provide assisted and independent living for the elderly, and through Catholic Charities he developed housing throughout the archdiocese for low- and moderate-income elderly and families.

Archbishop Beltran encouraged programs for the youth and children of the archdiocese. In 2000 a camp for the youth of the archdiocese, Our Lady of Guadalupe Catholic Camp, was built to provide a faith experience of God in nature. Archbishop Beltran also initiated an aggressive campaign through the Archdiocesan Foundation to provide affordable Catholic education to the children of the archdiocese.

In 2005, Archbishop Beltran led the Catholics of Oklahoma in a centennial celebration of the Catholic Church in Oklahoma that culminated in a Mass concelebrated by seventeen bishops and 105 priests and attended by over 14,000 Catholics from throughout Oklahoma and elsewhere. In 2007, the Cause for the Beatification of Father Stanley Rother, who was murdered in Guatemala in 1981, was opened.

Archbishop Beltran's spiritual guidance touches countless people. He fosters a spirit of community and dedication to MINISTRY, and his dedication to SOCIAL JUSTICE for all persons inspires many and sets an example for all.

SEE ALSO APOSTOLIC SEE; BEATIFICATION; BENEDICTINES; BISHOP, AUXILIARY; CATHOLIC CHARITIES USA; CHRISTIAN FAMILY MOVEMENT; OKLAHOMA, CATHOLIC CHURCH IN; SAN FRANCISCO, ARCHDIOCESE OF; TRADITION (IN THEOLOGY); TULSA, DIOCESE OF; VATICAN COUNCIL II.

BIBLIOGRAPHY

Archdiocese of Oklahoma City Offical Web site, available from http://www.catharchdioceseokc.org/ (acccessed October 30, 2008).

"Homilies of Archbishop Beltran," Sooner Catholic Online, *The Sooner Catholic Newspaper*, available from http://www.catharchdioceseokc.org/sooner/Past%20Homilies.htm (accessed October 30, 2008).

Sooner Catholic Online, *The Sooner Catholic Newspaper*, available from http://www.catharchdioceseokc.org/sooner/index.htm (accessed October 30, 2008).

M. U. Thomas, *The Catholic Church on the Oklahoma Frontier, 1824–1907* (St. Louis, Mo. 1938; Univ. microfilms 1940).

James D. White, *This Far by Faith: 125 Years of Catholic Life in Oklahoma, 1875–2000* (Strasbourg, France 2001).

James D. White, *Roman and Oklahoman, A Centennial History of the Archdiocese of Oklahoma City* (Strasbourg, France 2004).

William Charles Garthoeffner
Chancery Office
Oklahoma City, Okla.

Rev. James D. White
Historian
Diocese of Tulsa, Okla.

Loutitia Denison Eason
Chancellor
Archdiocese of Oklahoma City (2009)

OMAHA, ARCHDIOCESE OF

Erected as the vicariate apostolic of Nebraska on January 9, 1857, Omaha (*Omahensis*) was designated a DIOCESE on October 2, 1885, and an ARCHDIOCESE on August 7, 1945, with suffragan sees at Grand Island and

Lincoln, Nebraska. In 2008 its territory included twenty-three northeast Nebraska counties and an area of approximately 14,051 square miles. That same year Catholics numbered about 230,000 in a total population estimated at 900,000 (Archdiocese of Omaha Pastoral Report 2007, p. 117; U.S. Census Bureau 2000).

Early History. A destructive tornado cut short a Catholic settlement made at St. John's City in Dakota County in 1856 by Rev. Jeremiah F. TRECY of Dubuque, Iowa, after four years. The first church in the Nebraska Territory was built by Catholics in Omaha. St. Mary's Church was dedicated in August 1856. Within a year, Father William Edmonds of the Diocese of Dubuque said the first Mass in Omaha.

When the first vicar apostolic, James M. O'Gorman (1814–1874), PRIOR of the Trappist MONASTERY at New Melleray, Iowa, arrived in Nebraska on June 3, 1859, he found several hundred Catholic families, principally in Omaha and along the Missouri River. O'Gorman brought in the SISTERS OF MERCY (1864) and the Benedictine Sisters (1865), which laid the foundations for a continuous history of Catholic education. He built a modest CATHEDRAL with money collected in the East and from workers constructing the Union Pacific and Burlington railroads. When he died in 1874, in addition to the BENEDICTINES who had been laboring in southeastern Nebraska, O'Gorman had admitted approximately thirty secular priests, of whom about eighteen continued to serve with some degree of permanence in the vicariate.

Two years later James O'Connor (1823–1890) of Pittsburgh, Pennsylvania, was appointed second vicar apostolic and was consecrated on August 20, 1876. He continued O'Gorman's work, launching the Sisters of Mercy on a program of secondary education and entrusting Creighton College (later University), built with a gift from the estate of Edward CREIGHTON, to the JESUITS. The BISHOP also introduced the POOR CLARES to Omaha, where, with financial assistance from John A. Creighton, they built their first permanent foundation in the United States; invited the Religious of the Sacred Heart to establish an academy, the now-defunct Duchesne College; and requested the Poor Sisters of St. Francis Seraph to inaugurate their extensive system of hospitals. Moreover, O'Connor personally supervised widespread Catholic colonization in the state, notably of the Irish in Greeley County in the 1880s. He showed his solicitude for other national groups that were similarly attracted by cheap farmland or railroad employment by bringing the Franciscans and a group of Jesuits from Central Europe into the vicariate to work among the Bohemians and Poles. In addition, he directed the proliferation of parishes and schools that followed the heavy immigration. Many Omaha parishes founded under Bishop O'Connor's administration remained vibrant into the twenty-first century.

Diocese. When the Diocese of Omaha, consisting of the states of Nebraska and Wyoming, was erected in 1885, O'Connor was appointed its first bishop. Among O'Connor's achievements was his spiritual direction of St. Katharine DREXEL, foundress of the Sisters of the BLESSED SACRAMENT. In Thurston County, Nebraska, in 1908, she founded St. Augustine's Indian School in Winnebago, a ministry that endured into the twenty-first century.

In 1887 the Omaha diocese was further reduced when all of Nebraska south of the Platte River was established as the Diocese of Lincoln. Wyoming, with its see at Cheyenne, became a distinct diocese. Under the watch of O'Connor and his immediate successors, the diocese, and especially the city of Omaha, welcomed Italian, Polish, Hungarian, and Ukrainian immigrants. O'Connor died in 1890 and was succeeded by Bishop Richard Scannell (1845–1916), who was transferred to Omaha from Concordia, Kansas, on January 30, 1891.

By temperament a scholarly recluse, Scannell nevertheless carried forward the work of building new churches and schools. The House of the Good Shepherd opened a home for girls in Omaha. In 1907, following Scannell's decision to raze the old cathedral, the cornerstone was laid for a new edifice in Spanish Renaissance style that took more than fifty years to complete. St. Cecilia's Cathedral was consecrated in 1959; it contains an array of liturgical art including Albin Polasek's (1879–1965) bronze *Crucifixus* on the high altar, his bronze STATIONS OF THE CROSS, and wood sculptures. It was renovated extensively in 2000, in part to reflect Thomas Rogers Kimball's (1862–1934) original designs for the ceiling. In 1912 the central and western counties of the state lying north of the Platte River were erected into a distinct diocese; the see, originally at Kearney, was transferred in 1917 to Grand Island following the annexation of four populous western counties from the Omaha diocese.

After Bishop Scannell's death in 1916, Jer HARTY of St. Louis, Missouri, former ARCHBISHOP of Manila, Philippine Islands, succeeded to the See of Omaha. Ill health marked the greater part of his eleven years there, preventing Harty from accomplishing any aggressive programs. Nevertheless, he did introduce new organization, diocesan in scope, and during his administration and with his encouragement, the world-renowned institution of BOYS TOWN, a community founded to assist homeless and abandoned youth, was started by Rev. Edward FLANAGAN in 1917. Boys Town, renamed Girls and Boys Town in 2000 to reflect the growing female population, continues to attract large numbers of visitors to its campus in West Omaha.

Catholic Education. *St. John's Catholic church is seen beyond a banner on the campus of Creighton University, in Omaha, Nebraska. Creighton is a Jesuit-run institution.* **AP IMAGES**

On May 29, 1928, Joseph RUMMEL, a New York priest, was consecrated to succeed Harty, who died on October 29, 1927. During his tenure, Bishop Rummel organized the Bishop's Committee of the Laity. His intention was to convert the committee into a semi-permanent fundraising organization. But the Depression thwarted many of Rummel's plans. Circumstances forced him to divert funds from a successful campaign in 1930, intended to finance diocesan expansion, to relief work among the FAITHFUL. During Rummel's episcopate, Omaha hosted the Sixth National Eucharistic Congress in September 1930. When Rummel was transferred to the Archdiocese of NEW ORLEANS, Louisiana, in 1935, Bishop James Hugh RYAN, RECTOR of The CATHOLIC UNIVERSITY OF AMERICA in Washington, D.C., took his place. World War II similarly neutralized many of Ryan's efforts.

Archdiocese. Under Bishop Ryan, the growth of the Church in Nebraksa was recognized when, in 1945, Omaha was raised to an archdiocese. Ryan died in 1947, and Gerald T. Bergan of Des Moines, Iowa, under whom the archdiocese experienced phenomenal development, took his place. Archbishop Bergan was known as the "building bishop." During his twenty-one years as head of the archdiocese, the total cost of church-related construction amounted to well over $100 million and included a home for the aged and a now-defunct minor seminary. Twenty-three RELIGIOUS orders of women with a total of 805 sisters, assisted by 562 lay teachers, taught elementary and secondary school. Between 1950 and 1960, the number of students enrolled in Catholic elementary schools almost doubled, and the number enrolled in secondary schools grew by approximately fifty percent (Casper 1960–1966).

Bergan's auxiliary, Daniel Sheehan (1917–2000), named archbishop of Omaha in 1969, endeavored to sustain the diocesan commitment to education in the years following the Second Vatican Council until his retirement in 1993. A native of Emerson, Nebraska, he was the first native son of the archdiocese to hold the office of archbishop of Omaha. Archbishop Sheehan earned a national reputation for his support of Catholic education. During his tenure, the archdiocese was a front-runner in developing methods for the support of Catholic education. Many of the archdiocesean schools have endowments and tuition-support programs to help needy youth attend elementary and secondary Catholic schools.

Archbishop Sheehan's successor, Elden Curtiss (1932–), focused on maintaining the relatively high number of archdiocesan seminarians, averaging seven ordinations to the priesthood per year throughout the 1990s. He directed a successful fundraising campaign to provide a retirement home for priests, camp facilities for area youth, tuition relief for students at Catholic high schools, seminary endowment, archdiocesan centers for adult and youth activities, and archdiocesan ministry needs. He also presided over the first synod in seventy years. In addition, the Catholic education system grew significantly under his leadership. As of 2008 nearly 26,000 students attended two Catholic universities, sixty elementary schools, and eighteen high schools, including the St. Peter Claver Cristo Rey High School, established to serve low-income students from families with no prior college attendance. Archbishop Curtiss also convened a Catholic Schools Symposium in 2008 to address pertinent education issues.

In the 1990s and early 2000s, agribusiness, communication industries, and suburban expansion led to the growth of megaparishes; these emerged on the southern and western sides of the metropolitan area. Hispanic immigrants, attracted by jobs in the meatpacking and other industries, created a new ministerial need. Ministries to Vietnamese, Hmong, and Sudanese refugee populations also grew at the close of the twentieth and beginning of the twenty-first centuries.

Jesuits, who direct Creighton University, Creighton Preparatory School, and Jesuit Middle School in Omaha; Benedictines, who serve Mount Michael High School near Elkhorn; and the COLUMBAN FATHERS, whose national headquarters are in Bellevue, are among the significant communities of men religious represented in the archdiocese. The Sisters of Mercy, who founded the College of St. Mary for women in Omaha in 1923; the SERVANTS OF MARY; the Poor Clares; the NOTRE DAME SISTERS; and the Society of the SACRED HEART, who operated Duchesne College prior to its closing and maintain Duchesne High School, are among the women religious serving northeast Nebraska.

SEE ALSO BENEDICTINE NUNS AND SISTERS; EDUCATION, CATHOLIC (K THROUGH 12) IN THE UNITED STATES; EUCHARISTIC CONGRESSES; IOWA, CATHOLIC CHURCH IN; NEBRASKA, CATHOLIC CHURCH IN; TRAPPISTS; VATICAN COUNCIL II; WYOMING, CATHOLIC CHURCH IN.

BIBLIOGRAPHY

Archdiocese of Omaha Official Web site, available from: http://www.archomaha.org (accessed October 17, 2008).

Archives, Archdiocese of Omaha.

Henry W. Casper, *History of the Catholic Church in Nebraska*, 3 vols. (Milwaukee, Wisc. 1960–1966).

Sister Loretta Gosen, C.P.P.S., *History of the Catholic Church in the Diocese of Lincoln, Nebraska, 1887–1987* (Lincoln, Neb. 1986).

William E. Ramsey and Betty Dineen Shrier, *A Gentle Shepherd: The Life and Times of Archbishop Daniel E. Sheehan* (Omaha, Neb. 1999).

Stephen Szmrecsanyi, *History of the Catholic Church in Northeast Nebraska: Phenomenal Growth from Scannell to Bergan, 1891–1969* (Omaha, Neb. 1983).

U.S. Census Bureau, *United States Census 2000*, available from: http://www.census.gov/main/www/cen2000.html (accessed October 17, 2008).

Henry W. Casper SJ
Professor of History
Marquette University, Milwaukee, Wis.

S. Anthony Weidner
Independant Scholar
Omaha, Neb.

Rev. Timothy F. McNeil
Vice-Chancellor
Catholic Archdiocese of Omaha (2009)

OREGON, CATHOLIC CHURCH IN

Oregon lies on the shores of the Pacific Ocean, surrounded by Washington, Idaho, Nevada, and California. Originally part of the Oregon Country, Oregon became a territory in 1849 and a state in 1859. Salem is the capital, and Portland the most populous city. Ecclesiastically, the state is divided, with the Archdiocese of PORTLAND (until 1928, Oregon City) in the western part of the state, covering 29,717 square miles, and the Diocese of BAKER (until 1952 Diocese of Baker City) on the eastern side, covering 66,826 square miles. Although Catholics are the largest single religious group in Oregon, they are a distinct minority in the total population. In 2008 Catholics in Oregon numbered 442,137, about thirteen percent of the state population of 3.4 million (*The Official Catholic Directory* 2008 p. 2096).

Early History. Jointly occupied by Great Britain and the United States between 1818 and 1846, Oregon was the home of explorers and fur traders, most of whom were in the service of the Hudson's Bay Company. The Catholic French Canadians, former employees of the company, who during the 1820s and 1830s settled in the Willamette Valley south of the Columbia River in the area called French Prairie, desired priests to serve them. At the suggestion of Dr. John McLoughlin (1784–1857), the company director at Fort Vancouver, they petitioned Monsignor Joseph PROVENCHER, vicar apostolic of the Red River Country in Canada, for Catholic missionaries, and on February 28, 1836, the HOLY SEE placed the Oregon Country under his care. Unable to accept, Provencher forwarded the petition to the BISHOP of Quebec, and on April 17, 1838, Francis Norbert BLANCHET was named vicar-general to the ordinary of Quebec with jurisdiction over the vast Oregon territory. At the same time, another young priest of Quebec, Modeste Demers (1809–1871), was appointed to assist Blanchet.

The two priests arrived at Fort Vancouver on November 24, 1838, and began their missionary activities among the French Canadians and Native Americans. Pioneers at French Prairie had already constructed a small log church in 1836. Blanchet celebrated the first Mass there on January 6, 1839, after blessing it under the title of St. Paul the Apostle. This mission was Blanchet's most important one and served as his headquarters during the formative years. Other missions established by Blanchet and Demers were Fort Vancouver, Cowlitz, Oregon City, and Fort Nesqually. In 1842 the missionaries were joined by two priests from Quebec, Anthony Langlois and John Bolduc, who labored for several years in Oregon.

Almost simultaneous with these beginnings was the activity of Pierre J. DE SMET, S.J., among the Native Americans in the Rocky Mountain area and the far eastern part of the Oregon Country. After his initial appearance there in 1840, he returned to St. Louis, Missouri, to obtain help for the western missions. He then set out again for Oregon and arrived at Fort Vancouver on June 8, 1842, where he was welcomed by Blanchet and Demers. During De Smet's short stay at Vancouver, the three priests carefully surveyed the entire mission situation of the Pacific Northwest. They decided that great possibilities existed, but many coworkers, supplies, and finances were necessary. They further resolved to petition the bishops of Quebec, St. Louis, and Baltimore for the establishment of the hierarchy in Oregon country. De Smet, chosen to go East and then to Europe to procure all the help possible, departed on June 30, 1842.

Beginning in 1842, a tide of American immigration flowed toward Oregon from the eastern states, increasing the population so rapidly between 1843 and 1845 that McLoughlin (who had become a Catholic in 1842) petitioned the bishop of Quebec to obtain English-speaking and American priests for Oregon. When a shortage of American priests prohibited this, it was left to European missionaries to care for Oregon. Meanwhile, De Smet reached Europe, recruited a small band of priests and nuns, and returned to Fort Vancouver in August of 1844 with five JESUITS and six Sisters of NOTRE DAME DE NAMUR. St. Francis Xavier Mission was established as Jesuit headquarters near the Willamette River adjacent to St. Paul, and the sisters opened schools at St. Paul and Oregon City.

First Ordinary, 1846–1880. When the entire Oregon territory was erected a vicariate apostolic on December

1, 1843, Blanchet was named vicar, but word did not reach him until November 1844. The bishop-elect then departed for Montreal, where he was consecrated on July 25, 1845. Hoping to obtain more missionary help for Oregon, Blanchet spent the next years in Europe, seeking personnel and funds. During this time, he persuaded the Holy See to erect his vicariate into an ecclesiastical province, and on July 24, 1846, the Archdiocese of Oregon City and two suffragan sees, Walla Walla and Vancouver Island, were established. The creation of the second U.S. ecclesiastical province at this time and in this particular place was considered by some to be premature and unwise.

The new ARCHBISHOP returned to his see in August 1847 with funds collected in Europe and with twenty-one missionaries, including eight priests and seven sisters. The future was promising, for the Native American missions were prospering and heavy American immigration to the area had prompted expansion of facilities at St. Paul, Oregon City, and other missions. During the next decades, however, governmental interference in the Native American missions, incessant wars with the tribes, and unfounded accusations against Catholic missionaries, nearly ruined the mission work among the natives. Moreover, the discovery of gold in California prompted a mass exodus southward, including a majority of the Catholics who had been living in St. Paul and Oregon City. French Prairie almost became a ghost parish. The Jesuits and the Sisters of Notre Dame de Namur terminated their diocesan endeavors and went south, where the need was greater. The clergy dwindled to seven. New settlers were largely non-Catholic, and debts from the building expansion crippled the see for several years.

In the mid-1850s the situation improved somewhat when the archbishop's personal tour of South America for financial help aided in reducing the debt. The Sisters of the HOLY NAMES OF JESUS AND MARY arrived in 1859 from Montreal and reestablished Catholic education. European volunteers increased the ranks of the clergy, and the city of Portland grew. New Catholic immigrants strengthened the parish of the Immaculate Conception, founded by Reverend James Croke in 1851, and it became the center of the struggling archdiocese. In 1862 Blanchet transferred his episcopal residence from Oregon City to Portland. Immaculate Conception became the pro-cathedral, and remained such until 1928, when it became the CATHEDRAL with the change in seat of the archdiocese. John F. Fierens succeeded Croke as rector, and Portland Catholicity made noteworthy progress during his thirty-year pastorate. The diocesan newspaper, *Catholic Sentinel*, began in 1869. More Catholic schools opened, several Catholic societies were founded in the 1870s, and St. Vincent Hospital was established in 1875.

The size of the archdiocese was reduced considerably on March 3, 1868, when the Holy See created the Vicariate of Idaho, making the eastern boundary of Oregon the boundary of the archdiocese. In 1878 increasing disability led Blanchet to accept a coadjutor, Bishop Charles SEGHERS of Vancouver Island. In 1880 Blanchet resigned his see, and three years later he died in Portland, after sixty-four years in the priesthood.

Seghers and Gross. Seghers succeeded to the see on December 20, 1880, but directed its affairs for only a short time. He resigned in 1884 to return to Vancouver Island. In his brief term, however, he made many missionary journeys in Oregon and helped the BENEDICTINES establish an abbey at Mount Angel. On February 1, 1885, Bishop William GROSS, C.Ss.R., of Savannah, Georgia, succeeded Archbishop Seghers.

In his thirteen years as metropolitan, Gross directed many efforts of Catholic expansion, especially in education. In 1886 he founded the Sisters of St. Mary for teaching in diocesan schools. Before his death on November 4, 1898, he had succeeded in bringing to the archdiocese additional RELIGIOUS help, including the Christian Brothers, DOMINICAN SISTERS, SISTERS OF MERCY, and Sisters of the Good Shepherd. He directed the relocation in 1898 of St. Mary's Pro-cathedral from the business section of Portland to a site in a residential area.

Twentieth-Century Developments. Alexander Christie (1848–1925), of Vancouver Island, was appointed February 12, 1899, as fourth archbishop of Oregon City. His twenty-five-year episcopate coincided with a revival of commerce and immigration in Oregon, and he met the challenge of increased population by establishing new parishes, churches, schools, and other institutions. Significant among these was Columbia University, later renamed the University of Portland, which opened in 1901. Another boundary change of the archdiocese came in 1903 when the Diocese of Baker City was erected with jurisdiction over Oregon territory east of the Cascade Mountains. Bishop Charles J. O'Reilly (1860–1923) was appointed the first bishop of the newly constituted diocese (1903–1919). Christie's last years were marked by the controversy over the OREGON SCHOOL CASE, involving a state law of 1922 designed to force all children up to age sixteen to attend public schools. The archbishop died on April 6, 1925, the same year in which the U.S. Supreme Court declared the law unconstitutional.

On April 30, 1926, Edward D. Howard (1877–1983), auxiliary bishop in Davenport, Iowa, was ap-

Cathedral of St. Francis De Sales in Baker, Oregon. *The cathedral at Christmas (2008).* FR. JULIAN CASSAR

pointed to succeed Christie. Since parishes, population, and religious and educational institutions had increased greatly during the period from 1875 to 1925, the new archbishop dedicated himself to organization and consolidation of diocesan functions. Although Archbishop Blanchet had moved the episcopal residence to Portland in 1862, the diocese was still known officially as the Archdiocese of Oregon City. During the time of Archbishop Howard, it became officially designated as the Archdiocese of Portland. He supervised the erection of chancery offices; established new parishes; promoted the liturgical movement; centralized the school system under a superintendent's office; created the Catholic Charities organization to coordinate all social and charitable works; established new schools, notably Central Catholic High School in Portland; developed the catechetical ministry through the CONFRATERNITY OF CHRISTIAN DOCTRINE (CCD); and made a concerted effort to encourage vocations to the priesthood. Howard's administration was marked by a threefold increase in the Catholic population from 61,036 in 1927 to 186,560 in 1961, with the number of clergy increasing from 174 to 430, and the addition of twenty-three parishes (*The Official Catholic Directory* 1927, p. 137; 1961, p. 219).

The Baker diocese was served by Bishops Joseph F. McGrath (1919–1950), Leo F. Fahey, coadjutor (1948–1950), and Francis P. Leipzig (1950–1971). In Eastern Oregon the Catholic population increased from 7,030 in 1927 to 21,528 in 1961. Clergy increased from twenty-four to fifty-four, and the number of parishes and missions increased from fifty-four to sixty-one (*The Official Catholic Directory* 1927, p. 213; 1961, p. 314).

In 1966, at the age of eighty-nine, Archbishop Howard retired from the see of Portland (he died at the age of 105). Howard had attended all the sessions of the Second Vatican Council, but he left to his successors the task of implementing the reforms. Some of the resistance that they encountered in the Archdiocese of Portland was also felt in the Diocese of Baker. The two dioceses collaborated in a number of endeavors, and in the 1970s they formed the Oregon Catholic Conference as a Catholic public policy organization for the state.

Archbishop Howard was succeeded by Archbishop Robert Joseph Dwyer (1966–1974). A former Catholic newspaper editor, he frequently wrote for the CATHOLIC SENTINEL. Archbishop Cornelius M. Power served from 1974 to 1986. He ordained the first two auxiliary bishops in Oregon and renewed the annual fundraising campaign. In the Baker diocese, Bishop Thomas J. Connolly (1971–1999) worked diligently on creative and effective catechetical programs for children and adults. Archbishop William J. Levada (1986–1995) laid the groundwork for celebrating the sesquicentennial of the archdiocese and for the renovation of St. Mary's Cathedral. Archbishop Francis E. George, O.M.I. (1996–1997), served ten months before being appointed to Chicago. Archbishop John G. Vlazny (1997–) had the difficult task of dealing with decades-old clergy sexual abuse issues, and led the Archdiocese into and out of Chapter 11 bankruptcy protection. Bishop Robert F. Vasa (2000–) presided over the centennial celebration of the Diocese of Baker in 2003.

Education. Catholic education in Oregon had its beginnings on October 17, 1843, at St. Joseph's College, a boys' school in St. Paul. The next year the Sisters of Notre Dame de Namur started a girls' school in St. Paul and later in Oregon City. Loss of population and teachers during the Gold Rush forced the discontinuance of all Catholic schools by 1853. Archbishop Blanchet personally went to Quebec in 1859 to recruit twelve volunteers from the Sisters of the Holy Names. With the advent of new religious groups in Portland during the Gross, Christie, and Howard administrations, both elementary and secondary schools increased. Catholic education developed more slowly and differently in the Baker diocese because of the vast area and scattered population. The diocese relied more on parish RELIGIOUS EDUCATION programs than on Catholic schools, although Baker still maintained Catholic schools in larger population areas.

The number of students in Catholic schools peaked in Oregon in 1964. Eighteen high schools served 5,598 students, and seventy-seven elementary schools served 24,042 students. By 1994, eight Catholic high schools in Oregon served 3,552 students, and forty-five elementary schools served 9,286 students. By 2004, the downward trend reversed with ten high schools that served 5,088 students and forty-six elementary schools that serve 9,744 students (*The Official Catholic Directory* 1964, pp. 236, 327; 1994, p. 1954; 2004, p. 2038).

Catholic higher education began when Gross convinced the Benedictine monks to open Mount Angel College in 1887 and a seminary in 1889. The college was discontinued in 1946, but Mount Angel Seminary continued to serve diocesan and religious communities. The Holy Names school, St. Mary's Academy and College in Portland, was empowered to grant degrees in 1893 and became the first liberal arts college for women in the Northwest. In 1910 the school moved to a location near Lake Oswego and in 1930 was renamed Maryhurst College. Closed in 1974, the college reopened that fall as a private, nontraditional, coeducational college for adults and became a university in 1998. Columbia University opened in 1901 as a boys' prep school, and in 1902 the Holy Cross priests bought the campus. Fully collegiate in 1927, the institution became the University of Portland in 1935. The school became coeducational in 1951.

SEE ALSO BALTIMORE, ARCHDIOCESE OF; CATHOLIC CHARITIES USA; IDAHO, CATHOLIC CHURCH IN; LITURGICAL MOVEMENT, I: CATHOLIC; MISSION AND MISSIONS; PAUL, APOSTLE, ST.; SEX ABUSE CRISIS; ST. LOUIS, ARCHDIOCESE OF; VATICAN COUNCIL II.

BIBLIOGRAPHY

Clarence B. Bagley, ed., *Early Catholic Missions in Old Oregon*, 2 vols. (Seattle 1932).

W. B. Bauman, *Catholic Contributions to Oregon History* (Mt. Angel, Ore. 1959).

The Catholic University of America, *Studies in American Church History*, vol. 31, (New York 1940).

Sister Letitia Mary Lyons, *Francis Norbert Blanchet and the Founding of the Oregon Missions, 1838–1848* (Washington, D.C. 1940).

The Official Catholic Directory, (New Providence, N.J. 1927, 1961, 1964, 1994, 2004).

Edwin Vincent O'Hara, *Pioneer Catholic History of Oregon*, 4th ed. (Paterson, N.J. 1939).

Francis Michael Campbell
Principal
Regis High School, Stayton, Ore.

Patricia Brandt
Retired Professor (Reference Librarian)
Oregon State University, Corvalis

Melvin P. (Bud) Bunce
Director of Communications
Archdiocese of Portland, Ore. (2009)

P

PENNSYLVANIA, CATHOLIC CHURCH IN

The second of the original thirteen states to ratify the U.S. constitution on December 12, 1787, Pennsylvania is bordered by the Delaware River that separates it from New Jersey on the east; it also shares borders with Delaware and Maryland on the south, West Virginia on the southwest, Ohio on the west, New York on the north, and about forty miles of Lake Erie shore at the northwest corner. More than eighty percent of the population lives in metropolitan areas. Philadelphia is the largest city, followed in size by Pittsburgh, Erie, and Allentown. Harrisburg is the capital.

The eight dioceses in Pennsylvania comprise the ecclesiastical Province of Philadelphia, anchored in the eastern end of the state by the metropolitan see of Philadelphia and in the west by Pittsburgh. These two oldest dioceses in Pennsylvania also have the largest population of Catholics in the state, both by numbers and by percentage—Philadelphia with approximately 1,400,000 FAITHFUL and Pittsburgh with 747,085, each about 38 percent of total residents of the dioceses (*The Official Catholic Directory* 2008, pp. 2098–2099). Though both dioceses are centered in large metropolitan areas they have very different characters; it has often been said that the Midwest begins in western Pennsylvania, whereas Philadelphia has an atmosphere of established Catholicity that it shares with other East Coast sees such as New York and Boston. In the middle of the state, the Diocese of Harrisburg, centered in the rural agricultural counties of the Susquehanna valley, comprises the lowest percentage of Catholics in the state, with 247,492 faithful out of a total population of 2,027,835 (12%) (*The Official Catholic Directory* 2008, p. 2097). The other dioceses are Allentown, Altoona-Johnstown, Erie, Greensburg, and Scranton. In 2008 about 3.5 million Catholics lived throughout the state, about 28 percent of the total population of a little more than 12 million (*The Official Catholic Directory* 2008, p. 2098).

Colonial Times. William PENN embarked on a unique experiment in religious liberty in his colony of Pennsylvania. As Sally Schwartz observed: ldquo;Other colonies experienced migration of German and Scotch-Irish peoples to their frontiers, but conceded only the privilege of toleration to newcomers, not the right of freedom of conscience. Only in Pennsylvania was there no "establishment" to dispense or withhold favors" (Schwartz 1987, p. 292). Catholics benefited more than most from this freedom of CONSCIENCE. Though barred by the provisions of the Test Oath (1693–1775) from officeholding and the exercise of the franchise, Catholics enjoyed greater opportunities for WORSHIP and the practice of their FAITH in Penn's colony than in any of the other original thirteen colonies.

When, in 1708, news of Catholic activity in the province reached the ears of Governor Logan (1674–1751), he complained to Penn of the "scandal of the Mass." The proprietor responded by warning Logan to watch for an anti–Catholic backlash. None ensued, and indeed Jesuit missionaries regularly traveled north into Pennsylvania from their farm at Bohemia Manor on the Maryland eastern shore. Sources indicate that priests were routine visitors at the Wilcox farm in Ivy Mills near Chester and were certainly celebrating the Eucharist there by 1720. In 1729 Father Joseph Greaton (1680–1753) was living in Philadelphia, celebrating the Mass in private homes, and the year 1732 saw his purchase of a plot of land off Walnut Street, where by 1734 he had erected a small CHAPEL and residence, frequented by a congregation of about forty persons (mostly German). St. Joseph's was one of the first places of public Catholic worship in the colonies.

In 1741 two German JESUITS arrived to care for the sizable number of Catholics who were migrating to southeastern and southcentral Pennsylvania. William Wappeler (b. 1711) found about 300 Catholics in Lancaster, and soon established three mission stations at Conewago (where a chapel serving Catholics from nearby Maryland had already been founded in 1730), Codorus Creek (near York, where a chapel was built in 1750), and Lancaster itself (Wappeler purchased land there in 1742 for a church later known as "old St. Mary's"). Theodore Schneider (b. 1703), a former university professor from Heidelberg, was the other missionary who disembarked in 1741; he traveled to Berks county and set up his headquarters on a farm that Greaton had purchased at Goshenhoppen (present-day Bally, named in honor of a famous nineteenth-century pastor). From there he and his successors attended to congregations in Reading (where a meetinghouse existed by 1753), Lebanon, Pottsville (which boasted a wood church in 1827), Bethlehem, Easton (the mother church of the Lehigh Valley was erected there in 1836), Sunbury, and Williamsport.

A census of Catholics in Pennsylvania in 1757 enumerated 1,365 communicants, of whom 948 were Germans and 416, Irish. About forty percent of the Catholic population was centered in Philadelphia, Chester, and Bucks counties. The increasing number of Catholics in the city of Philadelphia required the erection of a new church; St. Mary's was completed in 1763, its congregation made up mostly of Irish. The city was well served by priests such as Ferdinand FARMER, S.J., who cared for the needy of the city but also immersed himself in its INTELLECTUAL LIFE, serving as a trustee of the fledgling University of Pennsylvania. A zealous pastor, who made missionary journeys throughout Pennsylvania and New Jersey, he was mourned at his death in 1786 as a "father of his people and friend of civilized humanity."

Western Pennsylvania, unlike the east, traces its Catholic roots to France. Father Joseph Bonnecamps, S.J., accompanying a military expedition, offered Mass in what would become Westmoreland county in 1749. The first site of public Catholic worship in the area was at the Chapel of the Assumption of the Blessed Virgin Mary of the Beautiful River, located in Fort Duquesne, at the confluence of the Allegheny and Monongahela rivers (Pittsburgh). The chapel, which functioned until its destruction four years later by British forces, was served by Father Denis Baron, and his extant baptismal register serves as an eloquent testimony to his pastoral labors.

Just as the British victory in western Pennsylvania brought an end to Father Baron's work, so the French and Indian War (1754–1763) saw heightened anti–Catholic tensions in the eastern half of the state. News of General Braddock's defeat in 1755 touched off mob violence in Philadelphia, and St. Joseph's church was only saved from destruction by the intervention of a group of Quakers. In that same year in Goshenhoppen, a Corpus Christi procession was mistaken by neighbors for a military drill, and the Berks County justices wrote to Governor Morris (c. 1700–1764) in alarm. Yet Catholics retained their liberties throughout this period, and by the time of the War for Independence many of them supported the colonials, though Clifton's Regiment, a company of 180 men from St. Mary's church, did fight on behalf of the British. St. Mary's, though, could also boast of a number of prominent patriots, including Stephen Moylan (1734–1811, a merchant and aide-de-camp to Washington), Thomas Fitzsimmons (1741–1811), a financial backer of the colonial cause and Congressional delegate), and Commodore John BARRY (1745–1803, honored as the "father of the American Navy"). The church of St. Mary's itself played a role in the birth of the new nation, serving as the setting for a number of liturgical celebrations attended by members of Congress and foreign dignitaries, including a TE DEUM on July 4, 1779, and a service of thanksgiving for the victory at Yorktown on November 4, 1781.

Philadelphia Diocese and Turmoil. The new state constitution granted all the rights of citizens to Catholics in Pennsylvania, and as the eighteenth century waned their numbers continued to increase. John CARROLL, the newly appointed BISHOP of Baltimore, estimated in 1790 that there were 7,000 Catholics in Pennsylvania, 2,000 of them living in Philadelphia and its environs. Finding clergy to care for them was a challenge (an outstanding young immigrant priest, Lorenz Grässel, died during the great Yellow Fever epidemic of 1793, soon after being named as Carroll's coadjutor). New churches were also needed, especially in Philadelphia. In 1789 the German Religious Society of Roman Catholics, under the guidance of Fathers John and Peter Heilbron, built Holy Trinity Church. This premier national Church was the first of many to seek autonomy in its choice of pastors and internal governance (leading to years of ecclesial strife). St. Augustine's Church was begun in 1796 by newly arrived Irish AUGUSTINIANS, and soon, thanks to the generosity of its subscribers (including George Washington), ranked as the largest church in the city.

The rapidly expanding Catholic population in the young nation moved Bishop Carroll to request a division of his DIOCESE. Among the four sees formed from Baltimore was Philadelphia, which comprised at its establishment not only the states of Pennsylvania and Delaware, but also western and southern New Jersey. An Irish Franciscan, Michael EGAN (who had labored at St. Mary's since 1803), was named the first bishop of Philadelphia on April 8, 1808—Carroll's only choice for that office. Though a fine preacher and a conscientious pastor, Egan was not possessed of a strong constitution, and his peaceable and pious nature was not equal to the conflicts that developed with the trustees of St. Mary's (which had become the new CATHEDRAL). The contentious nature of the two Harolds, the Dominican William and his uncle James, priests of the cathedral, only exacerbated conflicts Egan had with the trustees over financial matters and personnel. Upon Egan's death in July of 1814, ecclesiastical affairs in Philadelphia had reached an impasse.

Following Egan's demise the see was vacant for six years. The War of 1812 and its aftermath hampered communications, and French and Irish factions in the United States and on the Continent feuded over the appointment. Both Louis de Barth (the administrator of the see, resident in Conewago), and Ambrose MARÉCHAL (future ARCHBISHOP of Baltimore) refused the nomination; finally Henry CONWELL, an Irishman from Armagh, arrived in the city in November of 1820, having received the appointment the previous year (ROME had given him his choice of Madras or Philadelphia).

Conwell was not a happy choice. He was seventy-three by the time he arrived in Philadelphia and was an obstinate, vain man, lacking the leadership needed by the diocese. The bishop's lack of skill in the pulpit only added to the prestige of William HOGAN, a flamboyant but troubled young priest, who soon boasted a following among St. Mary's congregants. The parish was divided—many of the trustees sided with Hogan—and both men were sued in court. A bloody riot even broke out on April 9, 1822. Rome was moved by the struggle to weigh in on the proper role of church trustees, and following the letter *Non sine magno* of PIUS VII in August 1822, Hogan's influence waned.

Troubles flared up again in 1826, after the bishop agreed to a pact with the trustees of St. Mary's regulating pastoral appointments. Three of the lay leaders claimed that the deal gave them the authority to veto episcopal appointments. William Harold, now serving as Conwell's vicar general, denounced the bishop's actions, whereupon the latter removed him from his post, only to see his cause taken up by the trustees. Rome criticized the terms of the pact, and Conwell was summoned to Rome. Suffering from the onset of senility, he fled from Rome after giving a report of his actions and headed back to Philadelphia. In response to this bizarre turn of events and prompted by the pleas of the American bishops, Rome appointed Francis Patrick KENRICK as Conwell's coadjutor and entrusted the administration of the diocese to his care. He was consecrated on June 6, 1830, and arrived in Philadelphia on July 7.

Kenrick, both a scholar and administrator, possessing gracious manners and steely determination, acted to bring order to the diocese, which was in a deplorable state. He placed St. Mary's under INTERDICT until such time as the trustees renounced the right of naming pastors (which they soon did) and brought in John HUGHES to supervise the construction of a new church, St. John the Evangelist, that would have no trustees. Though hampered by the hostile meddling of Bishop Conwell, Kenrick made great strides in the diocese. A synod was held in 1832 (whose pastoral provisions were soon copied by many U.S. bishops), a seminary was begun, and a newspaper, the *Catholic Herald*, was founded. Heroic charitable assistance was offered during the cholera epidemic of the same year, most notably by the SISTERS OF CHARITY. Parishes were established to meet the needs of the thousands of immigrants streaming into the diocese, which numbered 100,000 souls by 1832, yet possessed only 38 priests. So great was the pastoral burden that in 1835 Kenrick petitioned to have a new diocese erected in Pittsburgh. Though Rome put off a decision for eight years, finally on August 11, 1843, the Diocese of PITTSBURGH was established, comprising 21,000 square miles of territory and 45,000 Catholics. Michael O'CONNOR, formerly rector of St. Charles Seminary in Philadelphia, was named the first bishop.

Western Pennsylvania Growth. During the time that the Church in Philadelphia was in turmoil, the rest of the state boasted a growing number of Catholics. A band of the faithful from Goshenhoppen had migrated to Westmoreland county, and in 1789 Father Theodore Brouwers joined them to provide for their pastoral needs. Brouwers purchased a 300–acre farm, Sportsman's Hall, near present-day Latrobe, and willed it before his death in 1790 to his successor. The sad escapades of a rogue fortune-hunting priest would cloud much of the following decade, but finally Father Peter Heilbron (who had earlier served at Holy Trinity in Philadelphia) arrived to take up residence at the hall (a small cabin) and minister to the Catholics living throughout western Pennsylvania.

Demetrius GALLITZIN, who joined Heilbron, became known as the Apostle of the Alleghenies. The son of a Russian count and a German princess, Gallitzin completed his seminary studies in Baltimore and was sent by Bishop Carroll to care for Catholics living in the region of Magurie's Settlement (now known as Loretto), where he founded a church and school. From there he traveled for miles on horseback (and sleigh in old age) seeking out Catholics and ministering to their spiritual needs.

When Bishop O'Connor arrived in Pittsburgh, he found St. Patrick's Church, which had been built in

1811 by the first pastor of the city, William O'BRIEN. His successor, Charles MAGUIRE, had begun the second Pittsburgh Catholic church, St. Paul's, in 1820, which upon completion was the largest in the country. It was an obvious and impressive choice for O'Connor's cathedral church. The diocese was, however, in dire need of clergy and RELIGIOUS; while the bishop was in Europe for his consecration, he sought assistance in Ireland. He acquired eight seminarians from Maynooth, and the newly established Sisters of Mercy promised their support and sent seven members to western Pennsylvania where they opened St. Xavier's Academy in 1844 and Mercy Hospital in 1846 (displacing the Sisters of Charity who had operated similar institutions in the city since 1835). The community increased rapidly from this humble beginning and established foundations in Philadelphia, Erie, and Scranton.

Attracted by the plight of German immigrants in the United States, the Bavarian Benedictine Boniface WIMMER and a band of companions arrived in the diocese in 1846 from the Abbey of St. Michael in Metten. Though their plans called for them to settle at Carrolltown, not far from Loretto, they found the land unsuited for farming, and Bishop O'Connor enticed them to Latrobe with the promise of the Sportsman's Hall property. There they founded St. Vincent's Priory (later Archabbey), the first Benedictine MONASTERY in the country and soon they were staffing parishes and missions throughout western Pennsylvania as well as an academy, college, and seminary.

Though he feuded with the headstrong ABBOT over the free education of his seminarians and the MONK's brewery, O'Connor knew what a blessing the community was to his young diocese. Soon he welcomed another religious family, the PASSIONISTS, who sent a pioneer group of three priests and a brother to establish a foundation in Birmingham (the south side of the city) in 1852.

Rise of Nativism. The waves of Catholic immigrants flooding into the country in the 1840s aroused the fear of earlier immigrant groups. These Nativists sought to counteract the influence of the "Catholic menace" through political action and violent intimidation. The Protestant Association of Pittsburgh, for example, planned in 1850 to set fire to Mercy Hospital, which was saved only by the bishop's vigilance in ordering the facility to be guarded day and night. That same year, though, saw O'Connor arrested by the Nativist mayor of the city, who was ironically governing the city from his own prison cell.

More deadly tribulations occurred in Philadelphia, where Nativists were roused to action by the resistance Catholics offered to their children's use of the King James Bible in public schools and their exposure to an-

ti–Catholic materials in the school curriculum. Exacerbated by urban unemployment and ethnic strife, riots broke out in the Kensington section of the city in May 1844, during which two Catholic churches were burned (including St. Augustine's and its extensive library). Two months later, following reports that St. Philip Neri Church was being used to stockpile arms, a pitched battle ensued between a Nativtist mob and the state militia that had been ordered to guard the church. The violence claimed twenty lives, and more than 100 people were injured before order was restored.

Given the hostility that immigrants faced, proposals were made to found rural colonies, where Catholics could live unmolested by prejudice. German families from Philadelphia and Baltimore, who arrived on December 8, 1842, established one such community (a settlement on 35,000 acres of land) in Elk County, northwestern Pennsylvania, and named their village St. Mary's. Though the first harsh winters tested the determination of the colonizers and the REDEMP-TORISTS who had initially backed the project turned it over to the BENEDICTINES from St. Vincent's, in time the community flourished and developed mills and other small industries.

Despite the hostile climate for Catholic immigrants, the number of faithful in the diocese of Philadelphia increased. The pastoral care of his flock was always Bishop Kenrick's first priority, and the arrival of new communities of religious women enabled the diocese to continue its MINISTRY. The Sisters of ST. JOSEPH were established in the city in 1847 and soon were running St. Joseph's Hospital (the first Catholic hospital in Philadelphia, established in 1849), a boy's orphanage, an asylum for widows, and a private academy. They were joined in their service to the Church by the SCHOOL SISTERS OF NOTRE DAME (1848), the Good Shepherd Sisters (1849), and the VISITATION NUNS (1850). The Augustinians had recovered from the loss of their church during the Nativist troubles and embarked on a college, Villanova, founded in 1842; the Jesuits, not to be outdone, opened St. Joseph's College in 1851. The bishop, concerned not only with the spiritual but also economic welfare of his people, founded a diocesan bank in 1848. Finally, before his departure in 1851 to become archbishop of Baltimore, he had the satisfaction of purchasing land at 18th and Race Streets, on which a magnificent cathedral, modeled on the church of San Carlo al Corso in Rome, was later built. The diocese he left behind numbered some 170,000 Catholics, 101 priests, and 92 churches.

Philadelphia's Saintly Bishop. Upon his arrival in Baltimore, Kenrick found himself impressed by a quiet, humble Redemptorist then in residence in the city. Kenrick made a habit of making his confession to this priest, and when the time came for him to submit to Rome the name of his successor in Philadelphia, Father John NEUMANN's name was second on the list drawn up by the suffragans of the Baltimore province (only his foreignness—Neumann was from Bohemia—prevented him from officially occupying the first place, but Kenrick made it clear he was his personal choice). Neumann himself was horrified, but obediently submitted to the divine will, and was consecrated on March 28, 1852. He chose as his motto: "Passion of Christ, Strengthen Me."

Neumann had come to the United States in 1836 as a seminarian and was ordained for the Diocese of New York. After a few years of pastoral work, he entered the Redemptorist community and, after professing his vows (the first in the country to do so), labored energetically in Baltimore and in St. Philomena's parish in Pittsburgh. He brought with him to Philadelphia a uniquely personal approach, spending much of his time in pastoral visitation; by September he had visited half the parishes in the diocese. The bishop referred to the promotion of Catholic parochial schools as his key project. Only a year after the establishment of a diocesan board of education in 1852, the number of children in diocesan parish schools had risen from 500 to 5,000. To help in the evangelization of his ever-increasing flock, Neumann founded parishes; established the first diocesan-wide FORTY HOURS DEVOTION in the United States (1853); assisted in the foundation of a religious community of women, the Sisters of the Third Order of St. Francis (1855); and welcomed a second community, the Sisters, Servants of the IMMACULATE HEART OF MARY, to the diocese in 1858.

Neumann was a paradox, beloved for his piety but criticized by some within and without his diocese for his foreignness and discomfort with Philadelphia society. As the diocese grew (in 1855 it already numbered 145 churches, the largest in the United States), Neumann proposed its division at the Eighth Provincial Council of Baltimore; he suggested that Pottsville be named the cathedral city of the new territory and volunteered himself as the bishop of this more rural see. Some prelates, including O'Connor of Pittsburgh, urged Rome to accept Neumann's offer, but in 1857 it was decided that the diocese would remain as it was, but that Neumann would be given a coadjutor. James Frederic Wood (1857–1883), a financial genius possessed of a more urbane character, was the choice, and he set himself at once to the task of straightening out the diocesan books. In this he was successful, yet his role as diocesan administrator remained nebulous while Neumann lived, even as the latter continued to long for a poorer, less cosmopolitan see. His strength sapped by pastoral labors, the saintly bishop of Philadelphia collapsed on the street on January 5, 1860. He was beatified in 1863 and canonized in 1977.

New Pennsylvania Dioceses. Bishop Wood finally came into his own as bishop of Philadelphia, yet even as he came out of the shadow of his godly predecessor, he earned the nickname "the Shadow," by remaining a quiet, reserved man. As an administrator, though, he guided the diocese with a vigorous and steady hand. The long anticipated Cathedral of Saints Peter and Paul, whose construction had been a long-standing burden to diocesan finances, was dedicated on November 20, 1864, even as the bishop announced plans for a new seminary building in the suburbs at Overbrook ("Wood's Folly"). As the number of Catholic faithful increased, Wood returned to the division of the diocese. Acting on the recommendations of the Second Plenary Council of Baltimore (1866) and Wood's own proposals made to PIUS IX while on a visit to Rome in 1867, the HOLY SEE announced a major revision of diocesan boundaries, erecting three new sees on March 3, 1868. The Diocese of WILMINGTON was created, removing the state of Delaware from the jurisdiction of the bishop of Philadelphia (southern New Jersey had previously been reassigned to Newark in 1853). Bishop William O'Hara (1868–1899) was given charge of the Diocese of Scranton, which was formed from ten counties in northeastern Pennsylvania. Catholic roots here stretched back not only to the pastoral work of Father Jeremiah Flynn, who as recently as 1825 had cared for Catholics throughout the whole region, but also to a settlement in Bradford County aptly named *French Azilum*, whose fifty dwellings and chapel awaited the arrival in 1793 of a band of royalist exiles that was to have been led by Queen Marie Antoinette herself. The Diocese of Harrisburg was created from eighteen counties in the central section of the state, where Jeremiah F. Shanahan (1859–1886) was named bishop. Bishop Wood was relieved by this redistribution of his pastoral responsibilities and no doubt honored when he became archbishop of Philadelphia—the diocese had been raised to the dignity of a metropolitan see in March of 1875. Sadly, the last decade of his life was plagued by illness until his death on June 20, 1883.

By the time the Province of Philadelphia was created, it included not only the dioceses mentioned above, but also Erie, which had been created by Pope Pius IX on April 29, 1853, from thirteen northwestern Pennsylvania counties soon after the recommendation of the Fifth Provincial of Baltimore (1852). Its first bishop was Michael O'Connor, who was transferred by his request from Pittsburgh, but who returned to Pittsburgh seven months later following outspoken and vehement pleas from his former clergy and faithful. The second Erie bishop was the Maine convert Josue Moody Young

(1853–1866), who was followed by Tobias Mullen. During the latter's tenure of three decades (1868–1899) the Catholic population of the diocese increased four-fold, and the number of parishes tripled.

Bishop O'Connor's return to Pittsburgh was not long-lived. For many years the former seminary professor had struggled with a call to the Society of Jesus. Though counseled by the POPE against following this aspiration at the time of his consecration as bishop, O'Connor decided to pursue his dream in 1860 and resigned as bishop of Pittsburgh. Another seminary instructor from St. Charles in Philadelphia, the Spanish Vincentian Michael DOMENEC, succeeded him. Domenec's task as bishop was complicated by financial difficulties, conflicts with numerous religious in his diocese, a restive clergy, and the financial intrigues of Father John Hickey, the rector of St. Paul's Cathedral. In response Domenec recommended in 1875 that the diocese of Pittsburgh be divided and proposed his own name for the newly created see. Accordingly, in January of 1876 Rome created the Diocese of Allegheny City (only across the Allegheny River from the city of Pittsburgh), appointed Domenec its bishop, and named John Tuigg (formerly pastor of St. John's Church in Altoona) as his successor. Tuigg was shocked as he slowly discovered not only the level of indebtedness of many diocesan parishes, but also that diocesan boundaries had been redrawn so that the bulk of the financial (as well as other) problems were located in his, and not Domenec's, see. Following a local audit of diocesan records, the bishop requested the intervention of the Holy See. Bishop Domenec was called to Rome, and, unable to adequately respond to the evidence presented by Tuigg's representatives, was asked to submit his resignation as bishop of Allegheny City. The dioceses were subsequently reunited by Rome, while Bishop Domenec, his health weakened by his ordeal, died in January of 1878 in his native Spain.

The see of Pittsburgh, thus reunited, saw its population continually increase as thousands of immigrants flocked to western Pennsylvania. Bishop Phelan (1889–1904) first requested the division of the diocese in a meeting with Archbishop RYAN of Philadelphia in 1899, and, when a petition of the province's bishops met with no response from Rome, they repeated their entreaty in February of 1901. This latter petition met with a favorable response, and eight counties were united to form the see of Altoona. Eugene A. Garvey (a Scranton priest; 1901–1920) was chosen as the first diocesan bishop. More than half a century later, the see city was twinned with its neighbor to the west to become the diocese of Altoona-Johnstown.

Challenges of an Immigrant Church. The face of the Catholic Church in Pennsylvania continued to be altered by the tens of thousands of immigrants who arrived in its dioceses throughout the second half of the nineteenth century, drawn by promises of employment in the burgeoning state coal mines, steel mills, oil rigs, and garment factories. Many of these new arrivals hailed from central and eastern Europe and longed for an experience of the Church similar to that in their native lands. Pennsylvania bishops responded by creating ethnic or national parishes, some (e.g., St. Joseph's Slovak Church in Scranton or St. Nicholas Croatian in Pittsburgh) were the first of their kind in the nation. Religious communities also sprang up to care for particular ethnic communities, such as Daughters of St. Cyril and Methodius in 1909.

Almost half a million Eastern Rite Greek Catholics had arrived in the United States by the beginning of the First World War, and they presented a unique challenge in Pennsylvania. As early as 1884 a group of Ukrainians had settled in the town of Shenandoah and had asked the archbishop of Lviv for a pastor. A priest, Father Ivan Volansky (1857–1926), arrived to care for the community and celebrated the first LITURGY on December 19 of that same year. Other parishes were established in Freeland (1886) and Hazelton (1887). As occurred elsewhere in America when Greek and LATIN RITE Catholics came into contact, Volansky encountered opposition because of his marital status (he had a wife) and unfamiliar ways. Within five years, at the urging of the American hierarchy, he was recalled to the Ukraine.

In 1890, at the request of many U.S. bishops, Rome restricted Eastern rite clergy in the United States to celibates or widowers and placed them under the jurisdiction of Latin rite bishops. A bishop for the Greek Catholics, Soter Ortynsky (1866–1916), was not appointed until 1907, and not until 1914 in the decree *Cum episcopo* did Rome grant him full ordinary jurisdiction and independence from local bishops. Ortynsky based his EXARCHY (diocese) in Philadelphia. Following his death in 1916 and responding to tensions between Greek Catholics from Galicia (Ukrainians) and Greek Catholics from Hungary/Trans-Carpathia (Rusyns), Rome appointed two administrators, one for each nationality. On May 20, 1924, a bishop for each group was named by the Holy See, Constantine Bohachevsky (1884–1961) for the Ukrainians and Basil Takach (1879–1948) for the Rusyns. Both were consecrated in Rome in June; Bohachevsky became bishop of Philadelphia (with pastoral charge of all Ukrainians in America), and Takach, bishop of Pittsburgh (with pastoral charge of all Byzantine-rite Catholics from Transcarpathia, Slovakia, Hungary, and Yugoslavia). In 1958 Philadelphia was raised to an archeparchy (with Stamford, Con-

The Immigrant Church. *Saint Colman Catholic Church sits along a busy street in Ardmore, Pennsylvania. It is one of many churches nestled in northeast Pennsylvania that were once filled with factory workers, mill workers, and coal miners closely connected to their European roots.* AP IMAGES

necticut, as a suffragan), whereas Pittsburgh became a metropolitan see in 1963 (with the addition of Passaic, New Jersey).

Many Greek Catholics joined the Orthodox Church during the decades of their contentious relationship with the Latin rite hierarchy. Similar struggles occurred between the bishops and other ethnic groups who aggressively, and at times stubbornly, advanced their demands. These cases often resulted in misunderstanding, enmity, or worse as in the case of the Polish National Church. In 1897 a group of Polish Catholics in Scranton had completed construction of Sacred Heart Church and asked Bishop O'Hara for control of the property. When he refused, as required by church law, the congregation of 250 families, led by their priest Father Francis Hodur (1866–1953), built a new church and refused to hand over the title to the property. O'Hara threatened sanctions, and the assembly was ultimately excommunicated, their appeals to Rome having been rejected. Hodur and many of his flock remained adamant, though, and ultimately joined with similarly disaffected Polish Catholics from other dioceses to form a synod and elected Hodur as bishop of the POLISH NATIONAL CATHOLIC CHURCH, which distinguished itself from the Roman Church by its use of Polish in the

liturgy, a married clergy, and lay control of CHURCH PROPERTY.

The growth of secret societies, often formed to protect the rights of unskilled laborers working in Pennsylvanian heavy industries, presented another challenge to the Church. Terence Powderly, a Catholic from Scranton, was the charismatic leader (1879–1893) of the KNIGHTS OF LABOR, the first national union. Unlike the Molly Maguires, miners who used violence in their struggle against the mine owners and operators, Powderly sought arbitration through peaceful means and worked to conform the rituals and practices of the Knights to Catholic teaching. Working tirelessly in close consultation with Bishop O'Hara, Archbishop Ryan, and others in the hierarchy, Powderly received Catholic Church approval for his organization in 1887, though by then its decline had already begun.

Prominent Pennsylvania Catholics. Catholics in Pennsylvania were not only laborers in heavy industry, however. Priests such as the historian Peter GUILDAY (1884–1947) and Herman HEUSER (1851–1932), editor of the *American Ecclesiastical Review*, were acclaimed in academic circles, while Maurice Francis Egan (1852–1924) and Agnes Repplier (1855–1950) were popular literary figures. In the field of medicine, Catholics pointed with pride to such physicians as John M. Keating (1852–1893), a respected pediatrician; the surgeon Ernest Leplace (1861–1924); and Lawrence F. Flick (1856–1938), a leader in the fight against tuberculosis. Nicola A. Montani (1880–1948), the choirmaster of St. John the Evangelist Church in Philadelphia, was known to Catholics across the country for his work in restoring GREGORIAN CHANT to the liturgy and for his authoritative St. Gregory Hymnal (1920). Charles G. Fenwick (1880–1973), an expert in international law, was a dedicated activist in the Peace Movement of the 1920s and 1930s.

The Church in Pennsylvania benefited as well from the material success that rewarded the labors of a number of her members. Nicholas (1838–1930) and Genevieve Garvan (d. 1938) Brady gave large sums of money to Catholic causes and built an impressive novitiate for the Maryland province of the Society of Jesus at Wernersville. Charles Michael Schawb (1862–1939), who rose from engineer at Andrew Carnegie's Braddock works to president of U.S. Steel, donated lavishly to Church-related institutions, including the Franciscan College of Loretto. Other Pennsylvania Catholic millionaires included Martin Maloney and John J. Sullivan, both of whom used their wealth to support the Church, and who were honored in turn with various awards and papal knighthoods.

One outstanding heiress who desired no earthly honors was Katherine DREXEL (1858–1955). Born into a wealthy banking family, which moved in the upper echelons of Philadelphia society, Katherine nonetheless was taught from her youth the importance of sharing the family's wealth with those in need (every week she joined her mother and sisters in distributing food and clothes to the poor who came to their house). As a young woman, Katherine responded to the call of the Third Plenary Council of Baltimore to aid African-American and Native-American missions, but was taken aback when Pope LEO XIII suggested she found her own congregation of missionary religious. That, however, is precisely what she did, and after a novitiate with the Sisters of Mercy in Pittsburgh, she established the Sisters of the BLESSED SACRAMENT for Indians and Colored People in 1891. Traveling across the country with her sisters, she used her substantial fortune (twelve million dollars by the time of her death) to build churches and schools and even a college (Xavier University in New Orleans). St. Katherine Drexel was beatified in 1988 and canonized in 2000.

The generosity of the Catholic laity made possible the founding of numerous colleges across the state, most notably those for women, run by ever-expanding orders of religious sisters, including Marywood (1915) and College Misericordia (1924) in Scranton diocese; Villa Maria (1925) and Mercyhurst (1926) in Erie; Seton Hill (1918) and Mount Mercy [Carlow] (1929) in Pittsburgh; and Immaculata (1920), Rosemont (1921), and Chestnut Hill (1924) in the Archdiocese of PHILADELPHIA.

The Twentieth Century. Philadelphia was fortunate to have a steady hand guiding it for much of the first half of the twentieth century. Dennis DOUGHERTY, "God's Bricklayer," served as archbishop from 1918 to 1951, working with ZEAL and determination to found 112 parishes, 145 schools, 4 colleges, and 12 hospitals, while personally ordaining more than 2,000 priests to serve the needs of his ever-growing ARCHDIOCESE. A formal and demanding administrator, Doughterty was in 1921 the first Pennsylvanian named a member of the college of cardinals. Erie also was blessed with an ordinary of considerable longevity in John Mark Gannon, who served the diocese as bishop from 1920 to 1966. Known for his vigorous work in founding parishes, schools, and even a college, Gannon was honored with the personal title of archbishop in 1953.

Pittsburgh also had a long-lived bishop in Hugh Boyle, whose tenure lasted from 1921 to 1950. As the city continued to grow, so did the diocese, which soon ranked as the eighth largest in the country. Most of this growth was the result of Pittsburgh's booming steel industry, which did not always receive praise from the Church for its labor practices. In fact, Pittsburgh priests and members of the Catholic Radical Alliance such as George Barry O'Toole, Carl Hensler, and Charles Owen Rice were vocal critics of management and enthusiastic supporters of organized labor. The message of the Alliance helped to form Catholics such as Philip Murray, Patrick Fagan, and John Kane, who all became prominent union organizers in the steel and mining industry.

The diocese's postwar population growth soon provided an argument for a further division, and in May of 1951 four of Pittsburgh's eastern counties were united to form the Diocese of Greensburg. The first bishop was Hugh L. Lamb (1951–1959) of the Archdiocese of Philadelphia, which itself was facing a rapidly expanding population. In 1961 Bishop Joseph McShea (1961–1991), who was serving as the administrator in the wake of the death of Cardinal O'Hara (1952–1960), recommended to Rome that a new diocese be erected in either Bethlehem or Allentown. He was pleased by Rome's announcement on February 15 that a new Diocese of Allentown was to be created, but surprised by the news that he would be going there as the first bishop. The same momentous day saw the appointment of John KROL as the new archbishop of Philadelphia. Krol served as an undersecretary at the Second Vatican Council as well as a member of the Central Coordinating Committee. The newly appointed bishop of Pittsburgh, John J. WRIGHT, also distinguished himself as a member of the council's preparatory commission and worked to draft the celebrated chapter on the laity in the Constitution on the Church (*Lumen gentium*). Wright was subsequently named a CARDINAL and prefect of the Congregation of the Clergy in Rome. Krol too was named a cardinal in 1967 and remained in Philadelphia to guide the post–Vatican II church with a firmness and authority till his retirement in 1988, when he was succeeded by Anthony Bevilacqua (1987–1991), the bishop of Pittsburgh.

A number of Catholic dioceses in Pennsylvania faced the challenge of shrinking numbers of clergy as the century drew to a close, and many looked to the reorganization of their parishes as a means not only of ensuring a more effective distribution of priests, but also of revitalizing the faith. Pittsburgh, under the guidance of Bishop Donald Wuerl (1988–2006), took the lead in this initiative.

Serving as a helpful resource to the Church in Pennsylvania in the years following the Second Vatican Council was the Pennsylvania Catholic Conference. Formed in 1960 (as the Pennsylvania Catholic Welfare Committee) with constitutional lawyer William Bentley Ball as general counsel and executive director, the Conference was established to, in its own words "give witness to spiritual values in public affairs and ... provide an agency for corporate Catholic service to the statewide community." It formulates policy positions, speaks on behalf of the Church before state government, and works to educate the public about Catholic teaching on MORALITY, education, and human and civil rights. Most notable, perhaps, was the conference's advocacy on behalf of the Pennsylvania Abortion Control Act of 1989, which led to the U.S. Supreme Court's decision in *Planned Parenthood v. Casey*. After the act went into effect in 1994, the number of abortions statewide fell fourteen percent. The conference was also an outspoken champion of civil rights and seasonal farm workers' rights, educational services for non-public school students, and the right of nonprofit charitable organizations to tax-exempt status. In 2008 the Catholic population was approximately 3.5 million, or 28.7 percent of all Pennsylvanians. The dioceses of Philadelphia and Pittsburgh had the highest concentration of Catholics, at 38 percent; Harrisburg, the lowest, at 12 percent (*The Official Catholic Directory* 2008, pp. 2097–2098).

The New Millennium. In the new millennium, the Catholic Church in Pennsylvania faces challenges both within and outside the Church. Changing demographics prompted many parishes and schools to close, particularly in the Dioceses of Allentown, Greensburg, and Scranton. Yet Pennsylvania Catholics remain significant, numbering 3.7 million people. The aging population and new immigrants from diverse cultures have affected the Church population.

In 2001, revelations about child sex abuse by clergy sent shockwaves throughout the Church. In response the Pennsylvania bishops renewed their commitment to victims and strengthened protections for children in the Church today. In compliance with the 2002 *Charter for the Protection of Children and Young People*, every diocese in Pennsylvania has a zero-tolerance policy for sex abuse and extensive child protection programs.

Through the Pennsylvania Catholic Conference (PCC), the Pennsylvania bishops issued a number of pastoral statements on policy issues ranging from the death penalty to embryonic stem cell research and same sex marriage. They also issued statements about the Sacrament of PENANCE and the Holy EUCHARIST. In response to changes in state law in 2006, the bishops updated their living will and health care power-of-attorney form and added a helpful booklet to guide Catholics through end-of-life decisions. The PCC continues to represent the Church in Harrisburg on issues such as the dignity of the human person, morality, health, welfare, education, and others. In 2000 PCC was instrumental in passing the Religious Freedom Protection Act, the only state law of its kind. In 2001 the Church led the initiative for the Educational Improvement Tax Credit (EITC) program, a groundbreaking school choice initiative that allows tax credits to businesses that contribute to scholarship organizations. In 2007 PCC defeated attacks on religious liberty that would force Catholic hospitals to administer emergency CONTRACEPTION. The Church also committed to ongoing efforts to pass the Pennsylvania Marriage Protection Amendment.

SEE ALSO ABORTION; BALTIMORE, ARCHDIOCESE OF; BALTIMORE, COUNCILS OF; BEATIFICATION; BENEDICTINES; BYZANTINE CHRISTIANITY; CANONIZATION OF SAINTS (HISTORY AND PROCEDURE); CAPITAL PUNISHMENT; CONSCIENCE, FREEDOM OF; CONVERTS AND CONVERSION; DELAWARE, CATHOLIC CHURCH IN; EMBRYOLOGY, HUMAN; EXCOMMUNICATION; FREEDOM OF RELIGION; FRIENDS, RELIGIOUS SOCIETY OF; GREEK CATHOLIC CHURCH (EASTERN CATHOLIC); HAROLD, WILLIAM VINCENT; MAYNOOTH, ST. PATRICK'S COLLEGE; MISSION AND MISSIONS; NATIVISM, AMERICAN; NEW JERSEY, CATHOLIC CHURCH IN; NEWARK, ARCHDIOCESE OF; ORTHODOX CHURCH IN AMERICA (OCA); SANCTION; SECRET SOCIETIES, CHURCH POLICY ON; SEMINARY EDUCATION; SEX ABUSE CRISIS; ST. VINCENT ARCHABBEY; TRUSTEEISM; UKRAINIAN CATHOLIC CHURCH (EASTERN CATHOLIC); VATICAN COUNCIL II; VILLANOVA UNIVERSITY; VINCENTIANS; XAVIER UNIVERSITY OF LOUISIANA.

BIBLIOGRAPHY

James F. Connelly, *The History of the Archdiocese of Philadelphia* (Philadelphia 1976).

Wayland F. Dunaway, *A History of Pennsylvania*, 2nd ed. (Englewood Cliffs, N.J. 1948).

Leo Gregory Fink, *Old Jesuit Trails in Penn's Forest: The Romance of Catholicity Told in the Footprints of the Pioneer Missionaries of Eastern Pennsylvania* (New York 1933).

John P. Gallagher, *A Century of History: The Diocese of Scranton, 1868–1968* (Scranton, Pa. 1968).

Francis A. Glenn, *Shepherds of the Faith, 1843–1993: A Brief History of the Bishops of the Catholic Diocese of Pittsburgh* (Pittsburgh, Pa. 1993).

The Official Catholic Directory, 2008 (New Providence, N.J. 2008).

Pennsylvania Historical and Museum Commission, *Bibliography of Pennsylvania*, compiled by Norman B. Wilkinson, edited by S. K. Stevens and Donald H. Kent, 2nd ed. (Harrisburg, Pa. 1957).

Sally Schwartz, *"A Mixed Multitude": The Struggle for Toleration in Colonial Pennsylvania* (New York 1987).

Joseph C. Linck
Instructor, Permanent Diaconate Formation Program
Diocese of Bridgeport, Conn.

Amy B. Hill
Director of Communications
Pennsylvania Catholic Conference (2009)

PERSISTENT VEGETATIVE STATE

The term *persistent vegetative state* (PVS) was first coined in 1972 by the neurosurgeon Bryan Jennett of Glasgow University and the neurologist Fred Plum of Cornell University. It is the commonly accepted term used to describe a particular form of unconsciousness resulting from a severe traumatic (e.g., blunt trauma to the head) or nontraumatic (e.g., anoxia due to heart attack) brain injury. Defined in the *New England Journal of Medicine* as "a clinical condition of complete unawareness of the self and the environment, accompanied by sleep-wake cycles with either complete or partial preservation of hypothalamic and brain-stem autonomic functions," the characteristic mark of PVS is its pattern of wakefulness without awareness (Multi-Society Task Force on PVS, "Medical Aspects of the Persistent Vegetative State, Part I," 1994, p. 1500).

Based upon clinical study, seven criteria are necessary to accurately diagnose PVS:

1. The patient exhibits no evidence of awareness of self or the surrounding environment, including a complete incapacity to interact with other people.

2. The patient demonstrates no evidence of any sustained, reproducible, purposeful, or voluntary behavioral responses to any visual, auditory, tactile or noxious stimulation.

3. The patient shows no evidence of language comprehension or expression.

4. The patient exhibits intermittent wakefulness, demonstrated by the presence of sleep-wake cycles.

5. The patient possesses sufficiently preserved hypothalamic and brain-stem autonomic functions, making survival possible with medical and nursing care.

6. The patient has bladder and bowel incontinence.

7. The patient possesses some preserved cranial-nerve reflexes, including the papillary, corneal, gag, and spinal reflexes.

PVS vs Brain Death. Compared with patients suffering true BRAIN DEATH, patients in the PVS retain a functional brain stem and hypothalamic activity, but they exhibit little or no higher-brain activity. They are not immobile or silent: they move their limbs without apparent purpose or intent, they smile, grimace, shed tears, grunt, groan, and, in certain circumstances, even scream. They also retain the ability to swallow, grasp, yawn, blink, and visually pursue objects for a few seconds, although they do not normally fixate upon moving objects or purposefully track them for more than a few seconds. A major medical study undertaken by the Multi-Society Task Force on PVS in 1994 indicated that approximately ten to twenty-five thousand adults suffer from PVS in the United States. However, due to the high mortality rate, the overwhelming majority of these patients do not survive longer than three years.

The medical community remains divided on the potentialities and capacities of patients in the PVS, although not sharply so. A small but respected minority of medical professionals claims that some patients in the PVS can, in fact, exhibit purposeful movements (e.g., retreat from painful stimuli), sounds, and emotional expressions. The Multi-Society Task Force on PVS strongly advised caution in this regard, however, stating that the potential for false-positive misinterpretations is high. Similarly, while some medical professionals believe that patients in the PVS might retain the capacity to experience pain and suffering, the majority disagree. Because patients in the PVS are, by definition, unaware of themselves or their environment, the vast majority of medical professionals consider an experience of pain and suffering to be an impossibility for them.

Assertions of certainty aside, however, an accurate diagnosis of the PVS can be difficult to establish, and instances of misdiagnosis do occur. Medical professionals are required to determine if the various sounds and movements exhibited by patients in the PVS are based upon some level of cognitive awareness or if they merely represent reflex actions that derive from a severely dam-

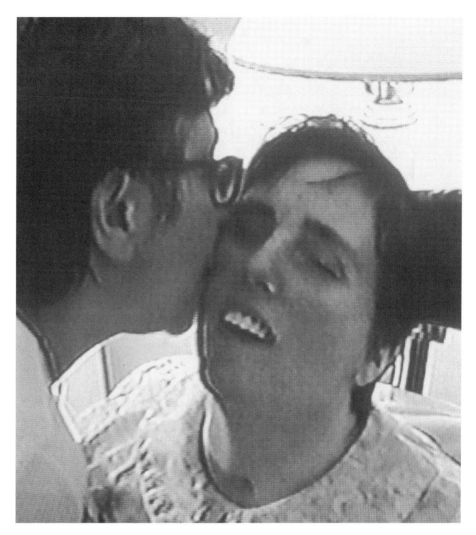

The Case of Terri Schiavo. *Terri Schiavo, right, gets a kiss from her mother, Mary Schindler, in this Aug. 11, 2001, image taken from a videotape and released by the Schindler family on Tuesday, Oct. 14, 2003, in Pinellas Park, Fla. Schiavo had been in a persistant vegetative state for 15 years following a heart attack. After a lengthy legal battle, the courts decided to honor the request of her husband, Michael Schiavo, to have her feeding tube removed. She died of dehydration on March 31, 2005.* AP IMAGES/THW SCHINDLER FAMILY/ THE TERRI SCHINDLER-SCHIAVO FOUNDATION

aged brain. Even considering the advanced state of medical science today, positive proof of the presence or absence of consciousness in a seriously injured person cannot be definitively obtained.

Modern Health Care and Medical Ethics. Although medical science was aware of the PVS condition for many years, the encounter between modern health care and ethical decision-making on this issue did not occur until 1975, when a case involving a twenty-one-year-old New Jersey woman named Karen Ann Quinlan made headlines. On April 15, 1975, Ms. Quinlan stopped breathing after consuming alcohol in combination with the tranquilizer Valium. Although her life was saved, she never regained consciousness and eventually descended into a persistent vegetative state. The subsequent legal battle that led to the removal of the mechanical ventilator sustaining her life became the opening salvo in one of the most hotly contested medical-moral issues of the twentieth century. End-of-life questions regarding the decision to keep or remove a mechanical ventilator eventually gave way to the moral decision to provide or withdraw the assisted delivery of nourishment and hydration, which in turn evolved into deeper questions regarding the right to die. While this is no longer as intense an ethical question in secular circles in the twenty-first century, the issue continues to be a serious concern in some circles, particularly within the Catholic Church.

Once it became apparent that persistently unconscious patients can survive indefinitely without a mechanical ventilator if they are provided with ASSISTED NUTRITION AND HYDRATION (ANH), the ethical focus shifted to whether the provision of ANH constituted a moral option or a moral obligation. Major legal battles waged throughout the 1980s consistently ruled that ANH constituted a medical treatment that could be legally and ethically refused. Among these cases were those of Clarence Herbert (1983), Claire Conroy (1985), and Paul Brophy (1986). By most accounts, the question was conclusively settled in the 1990 U.S. Supreme Court case (*Cruzan v. Director, Missouri Department of Health*) involving a twenty-five-year-old Missouri woman named Nancy Cruzan who survived in a persistent vegetative state for seven years following an automobile accident in January 1983. The final ruling of the Court classified ANH as a medical treatment that no patient was legally obliged to accept.

Catholic Ethical Debate. Within the realm of Catholic MEDICAL ETHICS, the level of care owed to patients in the PVS has become a source of vigorous debate and theological division. One school of thought within the Church has argued that patients in the PVS are, in fact, dying patients who lack the necessary cognitive-affective ability to pursue the spiritual goals of life. Consequently, although such patients remain human beings, the provision of ANH constitutes an extraordinary, and optional, means of preserving life that a patient can morally refuse. Conversely, other theologians have contended that the life of PVS patients remains an intrinsic good of the person that can be easily preserved through the delivery of ANH. In this sense, ANH constitutes a benefit to persistently unconscious patients because it preserves the person's life by utilizing a means that is not excessively burdensome, painful, inconvenient, or expensive.

Since the aftermath of the *Cruzan* case, the overwhelming trend among the Catholic hierarchy and the Vatican has been toward the latter interpretation, while a majority of Catholic theologians have argued in favor of the former position. In Directive 58 of the *Ethical and Religious Directives for Catholic Health Care Services* (*ERD*), the bishops of the United States endorsed an instruction that stated, "there should be a presumption in favor of providing nutrition and hydration to all patients, including patients who require medically assisted nutrition and hydration, as long as this is of sufficient benefit to outweigh the burdens involved to the patient." While pertinent statements of the *ERD* are accepted by Catholics on both sides of the debate,

significant ambiguities remain regarding their practical application to patients in the PVS.

John Paul II on PVS. The 2004 contribution of Pope JOHN PAUL II, in his allocution *Life-Sustaining Treatments and the Vegetative State: Scientific Advances and Ethical Dilemmas*, constitute the latest magisterial attempt to address the care of patients in the PVS. In the document, the Holy Father declared that "the administration of water and food, even when provided by artificial means, always represents a *natural means* of preserving life and not a *medical act*. Its use, furthermore, should be considered, in principle, *ordinary* and *proportionate*, and as such morally obligatory." While this statement remains a source of vigorous debate within the Catholic community, the allocution does constitute an authoritative teaching given by the Church's highest moral authority. As such, ANH should be seriously and prayerfully considered for those suffering in a persistent vegetative state, as well as for other seriously debilitated patients who can benefit from its use.

In addition, the Congregation for the DOCTRINE OF THE FAITH, on August 1, 2007, issued *Responses to Certain Questions of the United States Conference of Catholic Bishops Concerning Artificial Nutrition and Hydration*. This congregation affirmed what John Paul II taught in March of 2004.

SEE ALSO BIOETHICS; BRAIN DEATH; ETHICS; MORAL THEOLOGY; MORALITY; SELF, THE.

BIBLIOGRAPHY

American Academy of Neurology, "Position of the American Academy of Neurology on Certain Aspects of the Care and Management of the Persistent Vegetative State Patient," *Neurology* 39 (1989): 125–126.

American Academy of Neurology, "*Practice Parameters: Assessment and Management of Patients in the Persistent Vegetative State*, A Report of the Quality Standards Subcommittee of the American Academy of Neurology," *Neurology* 45 (1995) 1015–1018.

James L. Bernat, *Ethical Issues in Neurology* (Boston 1994).

Bryan Jennett, *The Vegetative State: Medical Facts, Ethical and Legal Dilemmas* (Cambridge, U.K. 2002).

Bryan Jennett and Fred Plum, "Persistent Vegetative State after Brain Damage: A Syndrome in Search of a Name," *Lancet* 1, no. 7753 (April 1, 1972): 734–737.

Multi-Society Task Force on PVS, "Medical Aspects of the Persistent Vegetative State, Part I," *New England Journal of Medicine* 330, no. 21 (1994): 1499–1508.

Multi-Society Task Force on PVS, "Medical Aspects of the Persistent Vegetative State, Part II," *New England Journal of Medicine* 330, no. 22 (1994): 1572–1579.

National Conference of Catholic Bishops, "Nutrition and Hydration: Moral and Pastoral Reflections," *Origins* 21, no. 44 (1992): 705–712.

Pope John Paul II, "To the Participants in the International

Congress on 'Life-Sustaining Treatments and the Vegetative State: Scientific Advances and Ethical Dilemmas'" (Speech, March 20, 2004), available in Italian from *L'Osservatore Romano*, Anno CXLIV(67) Sabato-Domenica, 20–21 Marzo, 2004; available in English from *L'Osservatore Romano* English Edition 13 (March 31, 2004); Also available from http://www.vatican.va/holy_father/john_paul_ii/speeches/2004/march/documents/hf_jp-ii_spe_20040320_congress-fiamc_en.html (accessed March 3, 2008).

United States Conference of Catholic Bishops, *Ethical and Religious Directives for Catholic Health Care Services* (Washington, D.C. 2004), available from www.usccb.org/bishops/directives.shtml (accessed March 3, 2008).

Donald E. Henke
Assistant Professor of Moral Theology
Kenrick-Glennon Seminary, St. Louis, Missouri (2009)

PHILADELPHIA, ARCHDIOCESE OF

The Archdiocese of Philadelphia (Philadelphiensis) comprises the city and county of Philadelphia and the counties of Bucks, Chester, Delaware, and Montgomery, an area of 2,182 square miles in the southeastern part of Pennsylvania. In 2008, there were 1,460,758 Catholics, representing 38 percent of the general population of 3,885,395 (*The Official Catholic Directory* 2008, p. 1011).

Early History. William PENN's colony, founded in 1682 as a "holy experiment" by which "all persons living in this Province shall in no way be molested or prejudiced in their religious persuasion or practice or in matter of faith or worship," became a refuge for persecuted Catholics (Artical 35, *Frame of Government of Pennsylvania* 1682).

First Catholics. There were Catholics in the Philadelphia area from the beginning of its colonization. The first governor of what is now Pennsylvania, Anthony Brockholes, was a Catholic. Perhaps the first Catholic resident of "Penn's Province" was a servant of Daniel Pastorius, the founder of Germantown. One of the richest men of the time was J. Gray (alias John Tatham), a Catholic from London who had extensive holdings in New Jersey and in Bucks County. JESUITS traveling between Maryland and New York stopped at his residences to celebrate Mass. The Jesuits also visited the home of the wealthy Frenchman Daniel Debuc (d. 1693). There is a record of Mass being celebrated publicly in Philadelphia in 1707. Repeated complaints were made to London

about this "Popish Mass," but Penn's "Great Law" protected the religious freedom of the Catholics.

In 1720 Joseph Greaton, S.J. (d. 1753), was given charge of the Catholics in Pennsylvania. He made his headquarters in Maryland but regularly traveled from Bohemia Manor to Concord, Chester County, Conewago, Lancaster, Philadelphia, and back. Greaton decided to reside permanently in Philadelphia, and in 1733 he purchased land and built the first Catholic church in that city, St. Joseph's, which had about 40 parishioners. A year later the governor questioned the right of Catholics to have this public chapel, but he was overruled by the city council. In March 1741 Greaton received an assistant, Henry Neale, S.J. (d. May 5, 1748), and the services of two priests from Germany to minister to the German Catholics in Pennsylvania. Father William Wappeler resided at Conewago; Father Theodore Schneider at Goshenhoppen (the present parish of Bally, near Reading). Both also ministered to the Germans in Philadelphia. Financial support for the Church in Pennsylvania was given by Sir John James of London, who set up a fund of £4,000, called the Sir John James Fund.

When Greaton retired to Bohemia Manor in 1749, English-born Robert Harding, S.J. (1701–1772) succeeded him. Eight years later Harding reported that in Pennsylvania there were 1,365 Catholics (from 12 years of age) who received the Sacraments; 378 of them were living in Philadelphia.

During the French and Indian War the loyalty of the Catholics was questioned; there was a move to keep all papists out of the Philadelphia militia, but it was unsuccessful. Harding purchased ground for another church and cemetery, and St. Mary's was opened in 1763. It became the parish church of Philadelphia, with Harding as pastor; St. Joseph's remained a chapel. The German Jesuit known in the colony as Father Ferdinand FARMER (d. 1786) came from Lancaster to assist Harding in Philadelphia, but he also continued ministering to the German Catholics in Pennsylvania, New Jersey, and New York. In 1772 Robert MOLYNEUX, S.J., succeeded Harding as pastor.

Revolutionary Era. During the American Revolution, many of St. Mary's parishioners were leaders of the colonial forces. One exception occurred when General Richard Howe (1726–1799) withdrew from Philadelphia in the summer of 1778, taking with him a Roman Catholic battalion of about 180 men, with Col. Alfred Clifton of St. Mary's parish in charge. In general, however, the Catholics of Philadelphia fought bravely for the Revolution. After the French entered the war, St. Mary's Church became the outstanding Catholic church of the colonies. On September 7, 1777, members of the Continental Congress attended the REQUIEM MASS of

General du Coudray. They were again present on July 4, 1779, for the first public religious commemoration of the Declaration of Independence. On November 4, 1781, the Congress met with General George Washington at a Solemn Mass of Thanksgiving for victory over the British. On February 22, 1800, the Congress met at St. Mary's for a memorial service for President Washington.

After the war, Molyneux built the first parish school in Philadelphia at St. Mary's, in May 1782. The practice of charging pew rent was introduced to offset some of the cost. In October 1785 John CARROLL, then prefect apostolic, administered the Sacrament of CONFIRMATION for the first time in Philadelphia. When Farmer died one year later, his funeral was attended by the members of the American Philosophical Society, the professors and trustees of the University of Pennsylvania, and a large number of non-Catholics. Molyneux retired and was succeeded by the Reverend Francis Beeston, S.J., who built the rectory for St. Joseph's. By 1790 there were an estimated 2,000 Catholics in Philadelphia. Five years later Holy Trinity Church for German Catholics was completed, and Father John Heilbron was assigned as pastor. Carroll had reluctantly consented to the erection of this national parish, warning the parishioners against a feeling of separatism and denying them the right to name their own pastors. Meanwhile, a large number of destitute persons from the West Indies arrived in Philadelphia during the spring and summer of 1793, bringing the yellow fever mosquito with them. An epidemic ensued, causing about one-half of the inhabitants to flee Philadelphia, which became a quarantined city. All the priests of St. Mary's died from the fever, among them Father Lorenz GRASSEL, who had been chosen as coadjutor to Bishop Carroll, with residence in Philadelphia.

Early Trusteeism. In December 1793 the Reverend Leonard NEALE was appointed pastor of St. Mary's and coadjutor to Carroll. Because of trouble in Europe, the bulls did not arrive until 1800. The appointment in 1796 of Father John Goetz as Heilbron's assistant marked the beginning of TRUSTEEISM at Holy Trinity. Heilbron was forced to retire to St. Joseph's, where he conducted services for the loyal Germans. Although Goetz was suspended, he persisted in his opposition and was joined by Father William Elling, who came to Holy Trinity from Reading to teach in the school that the trustees were forming. At length, Carroll, in February 1797, was constrained to publicly excommunicate both Goetz and Elling. There was a falling out among the schismatics. Four months later, Goetz was forced to resign, and the trustees made Elling pastor. When the trustees tried to make common cause with another group of German schismatics in Baltimore, Carroll came to

Philadelphia in 1798. A court case ensued during which the trustees argued that Carroll was bishop of other nationalities, but not of the Germans. The case reached ROME, and the HOLY SEE backed Carroll against the trustees. But it was not until 1802 that Elling, the trustees, and the parishioners of Holy Trinity, which had been put under INTERDICT, publicly recanted. Their abjuration was taken by Thomas Matthew CARR, O.S.A., the vicar-general.

Under Carr, the Irish AUGUSTINIANS began another parish in 1796. But it was not until 1801 that St. Augustine's, called the largest church in Philadelphia, was dedicated. President Washington, Commodore John BARRY, and Stephen Girard were among the largest contributors. When the trustees of St. Mary's petitioned Carroll to send them a pastor capable of preserving the dignity of what they called the leading church in the United States, he appointed Michael EGAN, O.S.F., who had been stationed at Lancaster, and gave him Father John Rossiter as assistant.

Diocese of Philadelphia. On April 8, 1808, Egan was appointed bishop of the new Diocese of Philadelphia, which included the states of Pennsylvania and Delaware as well as the western and southern parts of New Jersey, to a border slightly south of Barnegat Bay. St. Mary's was selected as the cathedral. Napoleonic difficulties in Europe prevented the bulls from arriving until 1810, so during the interval Egan remained at St. Mary's as Carroll's vicar-general.

Michael Egan. At its beginning the Diocese of Philadelphia had 16 churches attended by 11 priests, who ministered to 30,000 Catholics. Unfortunately, the trustee problem at St. Mary's marred the new bishop's administration from the beginning. In 1808 Egan accepted William HAROLD, an Irish Dominican, as a priest of the diocese and in 1810 made him his vicar-general. The next year Father James Harold, an uncle of William Harold, was accepted into the diocese. Trouble, instigated by the Harolds, then developed between the bishop and the trustees of St. Mary's. Although the Harolds returned to Ireland and a schism was averted, the trustees of St. Mary's had acquired such ill fame that it was five years before a successor was named after Egan's death on July 22, 1814. John Baptist Mary DAVID, later Bishop of Bardstown, Kentucky; Ambrose MARÉCHAL, future ARCHBISHOP of Baltimore; and Louis De Barth, pastor of Conewago, all refused the Diocese of Philadelphia. During the interval, De Barth was the administrator of the diocese. Finally Henry CONWELL (1748–1842), vicar-general of Armagh, Ireland, was nominated. Having been consecrated in London by Bishop William POYNTER on September 24, 1820, he arrived in Philadelphia on November 25.

Henry Conwell. The most urgent problem awaiting Conwell was the case of William HOGAN, a priest from Albany, New York, whom the administrator had admitted into the diocese without proper credentials and who preached a sermon against Conwell in the bishop's presence within a week after he took possession of the see. This was the beginning of a schism that is known as Hoganism. At Conwell's invitation, William Harold returned to Philadelphia in November 1821 and allied himself with Father Ryan (former rector of the College of Corpo Santo in Lisbon, Portugal) in defense of Conwell against Hogan and his followers. Defeated and disgraced, Hogan left Philadelphia in August 1824, but the trustees of St. Mary's continued to fight against their bishop. Finally, on October 9, 1826, Conwell signed the notorious pact with the trustees giving them the right to veto his appointment of their pastors. This pact was rejected by the Congregation of the Propaganda, and the rejection was approved by Pope LEO XII on May 6, 1827. Further trouble ensued when Harold, who had been appointed pastor of St. Mary's and vicar-general, was suspended by Conwell on April 3, 1827. There were appeals to Rome and to the U.S. government. Finally, the aged Conwell was summoned to Rome; Harold and Ryan were transferred from the diocese, and the Holy See named Francis Patrick KENRICK (1796–1863) coadjutor with right of succession. Conwell returned unexpectedly to the United States and gave many anxious moments to Kenrick and to the Holy See until his death in 1842 at age 94.

Francis Patrick Kenrick. On June 6, 1830, Kenrick was consecrated in the Cathedral of St. Joseph at Bardstown, Kentucky. He arrived in Philadelphia on July 7 of that year, but it was not until August 1831 that Pope GREGORY XVI approved the brief that entrusted all ecclesiastical jurisdiction to Kenrick alone. The trustee problem at St. Mary's continued until Kenrick closed the church and the cemetery on April 16, 1831. The greatest problem confronting him was the lack of priests, so in June 1832 he opened the diocesan seminary of St. Charles BORROMEO, which obtained a state charter six years later. During the first three years of his administration, Kenrick doubled the number of churches. St. John the Evangelist Church, built by Father (later Bishop) John Joseph HUGHES before he was transferred to New York (1838), was dedicated April 8, 1832 (it became the cathedral in 1838). Next, St. John the Baptist, Manayunk, was dedicated, with Father Thomas Gegan as first pastor. On April 8, 1833, the cornerstone of St. Michael's in Kensington was laid, with Father Terence J. Donoghue as founding pastor. By 1832 the diocese numbered 100,000 Catholics, 38 priests, and 50 churches.

When the cholera epidemic devastated Philadelphia in 1832, the Sisters of Charity at St. Joseph's and St. John's Orphan Asylums gave heroic nursing service to the victims. Michael HURLEY, O.S.A., pastor of St. Augustine's, turned his school and CONVENT into a hospital where 367 patients were treated. In the following year the city council passed a formal resolution of gratitude and gave a purse to the Sisters of Charity. Parochial expansion characterized these years; St. Francis Xavier parish was founded for the Fairmount district and St. Patrick's for the Schuylkill suburb (1839). The following year St. Philip Neri's parish was established in the Southwark district, with Father John P. Dunn as pastor. In 1842 the Redemptorist Fathers were given the new parish of St. Peter's, which was built for the Germans in Kensington. In 1843 St. Paul's was founded in the Moyamensing section, and St. Stephen's parish was founded in Nicetown near a spot where the early missionaries had celebrated the first Masses in Philadelphia.

When the western portion of Pennsylvania became the Diocese of Pittsburgh (1843), Philadelphia was left with 58 churches, 7 missions, 43 priests, and a Catholic population of 100,000. Despite the bitter NATIVISM of these years, which erupted in the 1844 riots in Philadelphia, and the burning of two churches, Kenrick continued to direct the steady progress of his diocese. On November 16, 1848, St. Anne's, founded in Port Richmond, was dedicated by Father Francis X. Gartland, later Bishop of Savannah, Georgia. On September 28, 1845, Bishop de la Hailandière of Vincennes, Indiana, laid the cornerstone for St. Joachim's Church in the Frankford district. On June 29, 1846, Bishop Kenrick issued a pastoral letter announcing his determination to build a cathedral. It was to be modeled after San Carlo al Corso in Rome, with Napoleon Lebrun as its architect. Other foundations included the Church of the Assumption (1848), with Charles I. H. Carter, a convert and later vicar-general of the diocese, as pastor; St. Dominic's (1849) in the far north suburb of Holmesburg; the parish of St. James (1850) in West Philadelphia; and St. Malachy's Church, the cornerstone of which was blessed on May 25, 1850. Before its completion Kenrick transferred to the Metropolitan See of Baltimore. The suburb of Germantown received its parish when St. Vincent de Paul's was founded on July 13, 1851, and placed under the care of the Vincentian Fathers, who conducted the seminary. The first pastor was Father Michael DOMENEC, later bishop of Pittsburgh.

Kenrick also opened the first Catholic hospital in Philadelphia, St. Joseph's, staffed by the Sisters of St. Joseph, in June 1849. Educational facilities were expanded with the arrival in March 1846 of the Sacred Heart nuns to conduct a private school for girls, and of the Sisters of St. Joseph, who came the following year. In 1850 the Christian Brothers arrived to teach the boys in the Assumption parochial school. Two colleges for men were established as well: Villanova (Augustinians) in 1842 and St. Joseph's (Jesuits) in 1851. When Kenrick left in 1851 to assume his new duties as archbishop of Baltimore, Philadelphia had 92 churches, 8 chapels, 101 priests, 43 seminarians, 2 colleges, 6 academies for girls, 7 charitable institutions, and 170,000 Catholics.

John Neumann. John Nepomucene NEUMANN, the fourth bishop of Philadelphia, was consecrated on March 28, 1852. He had immigrated to the United States from Bohemia in 1836; was ordained for the Diocese of New York on June 25, 1836; and was the first Redemptorist to be professed in America (1842). During his episcopate, Neumann constantly pressed for parochial schools. He was unsuccessful in his relations with the trustees of Holy Trinity, but he undermined their influence when he established the parish of St. Alphonsus (1852) for German-speaking Catholics. In the same year he established St. Mary Magdalen de Pazzi, the first parish for Italian-speaking Catholics. He also introduced the FORTY HOURS DEVOTION in the diocese at St. Philip Neri's Church.

In 1853 the New Jersey section of the diocese was taken to form part of the Diocese of Newark, leaving Philadelphia with 121 churches, 32 missions, 119 priests, and 175,000 Catholics. On April 26, 1857, Neumann received as coadjutor with right of succession, James Frederick Wood, to whom was committed the work of completing the cathedral. Wood succeeded to the see upon Neumann's death on January 5, 1860. Neumann's cause was introduced in Rome in 1897, and on October 13, 1963, Pope PAUL VI beatified him. He was canonized by Paul VI on June 19, 1977; his feast day is January 5.

James Frederick Wood. The fifth bishop had been baptized a Unitarian but was received into the Catholic Church in 1838 and the next year was sent to Rome to study at the Propaganda College. Wood was ordained in Rome on March 25, 1844, and returned to Cincinnati, Ohio, where he served as curate at the cathedral and pastor of St. Patrick's Church until his consecration on April 26, 1857. His thorough knowledge of the financial world was one of the reasons for his appointment to Philadelphia. In the first year of his administration, Wood established the parishes of the Annunciation in South Philadelphia and All Saints, Bridesburg. His cathedral was nearing completion, but because of the Civil War, he was not able to sing the first Mass there until November 20, 1864. On December 8, 1865, he announced the purchase of 100 acres at Overbrook

(which some people called "Wood's Folly") as the site for a seminary. By 1871 this seminary had 128 students.

During a visit to Rome in 1867, Wood petitioned for the erection of two dioceses. On March 3, 1868, the new dioceses of Harrisburg, Scranton, and Wilmington were founded, leaving Philadelphia with 93 churches, 67 missions, 157 priests, 42 parochial schools, 491 sisters, and a Catholic population of 200,000. Wood was prominent at the Second Plenary Council of Baltimore and attended VATICAN COUNCIL I (1869–1870), but ill health forced his early return from Rome. He was unanimously appointed treasurer of the episcopal board of the new NORTH AMERICAN COLLEGE in Rome. On October 15, 1873, he solemnly consecrated the diocese to the Sacred Heart of Jesus.

Archdiocese of Philadelphia. In 1875 Philadelphia became the metropolitan see for the state of Pennsylvania, with Wood as archbishop. Although in poor health, Wood went to Rome in 1877 for the golden jubilee of Pope PIUS IX's episcopate. On May 23, 1880, he presided over the first provincial council of Philadelphia. When he died, he left 127 churches, 53 chapels, and 58 parochial schools.

Patrick J. Ryan. The see was vacant for one year until Rome appointed St. Louis's coadjutor, Bishop Patrick J. RYAN, second archbishop of Philadelphia. Ryan, often referred to as the Bossuet of the American Church and perhaps the outstanding pulpit orator of his day, took formal possession of Philadelphia on August 20, 1884. Under his care the archdiocese was provided with such charitable institutions as St. Joseph's Protectory for Girls, Norristown; St. Vincent's Home and Hospital, Philadelphia; St. Francis Vocational School, Eddington; and the Philadelphia Protectory for Boys, near Phoenixville. In 1890 Cahill High School for Boys (later called Roman Catholic High School), Philadelphia, was opened as the first free central Catholic high school in the United States. In 1908 Ryan announced that a free central high school for girls (later called the John W. Hallahan Catholic Girls' High School) was opened, but he died before its completion in September 1912. A leading figure in the development of Philadelphia's Catholic school system was the diocesan superintendent of schools, Philip McDevitt, later bishop of Harrisburg.

Ryan took paternal interest in the founding of the motherhouse of the Sisters of the Blessed Sacrament for Indians and Colored People, whose founder, Mother Katharine DREXEL, dedicated her life and her fortune to the salvation of African Americans and Native Americans. At his death on February 11, 1911, Ryan was succeeded by Edmond Francis PRENDERGAST, who had been consecrated auxiliary bishop to Ryan on February 24, 1897.

Edmond Francis Prendergast. The third archbishop, Edmond Francis Prendergast, directed the building of many new institutions: Misericordia Hospital, the Chapel of Divine Love, the Archbishop Ryan Memorial Institute for the Deaf, St. Edmond's Home for Crippled Children, the West Philadelphia Catholic High School for Boys, and the Archbishop Ryan Memorial Library at the seminary. He also renovated the cathedral. He died in Philadelphia on February 26, 1918, and was succeeded by Bishop Dennis DOUGHERTY of Buffalo, New York, the first native son to be appointed the archbishop of Philadelphia.

Dennis Dougherty. Archbishop Dennis Dougherty was enthroned by Cardinal James GIBBONS on July 10, 1918. During his 33–year administration, 112 parishes, 145 parochial schools, 53 Catholic high schools, 4 Catholic colleges, 12 hospitals, and 11 homes for the aged were established. He consecrated 15 bishops and ordained over 2,000 priests. On March 7, 1921, Pope BENEDICT XV made him a cardinal priest. He died at his residence on the 61st anniversary of his ordination and was buried in the crypt of the Cathedral of Saints Peter and Paul. At that time the archdiocese had 1,896 priests (1,224 diocesan), 401 parishes, 9 chapels, 62 missions, 6,825 sisters, 7 colleges, 35 parochial and diocesan high schools, 21 private high schools, 330 parochial elementary schools, 20 private elementary schools, and 1,114,122 Catholics.

John F. O'Hara. On November 28, 1951, John F. O'HARA, former bishop of Buffalo, was appointed the ninth ordinary of Philadelphia and was solemnly installed on January 9, 1952. Although O'Hara was never in good health, his episcopate in Philadelphia was active and vigorous. Embarking on a bold and imaginative program to expand education facilities, he created 30 parishes, opened 55 new parish schools, and improved about 300 others. Fourteen new high schools were built, including Cardinal Dougherty High School, with a capacity of 6,000 students. He was also actively interested in the education of the mentally retarded. He continued the unique system of financing Catholic education in the archdiocese, under which the pastors of the students, not the students themselves, are responsible for their tuition. On November 16, 1958, he was named cardinal priest by Pope JOHN XXIII. Two years later on August 28, he died in his see city; his remains were interred in Sacred Heart Church at the University of Notre Dame, South Bend, Indiana. After his death the archdiocese was further divided when the Diocese of Allentown was established on January 28, 1961, with Joseph McShea, former auxiliary bishop of Philadelphia and administrator of the archdiocese, as first bishop.

The counties of Philadelphia, Bucks, Chester, Delaware, and Montgomery were left to Philadelphia.

John Joseph Krol. On February 11, 1961, John Joseph KROL, former auxiliary bishop of Cleveland, Ohio, was nominated archbishop of Philadelphia; he was installed on March 22. Born in Cleveland, Krol was ordained on February 20, 1937, and served as chancellor of the Cleveland diocese. He was appointed auxiliary bishop of Cleveland and vicar-general on July 11, 1953, and was consecrated September 2.

In the wake of VATICAN COUNCIL II, Philadelphia was caught up in the dramatic changes in church life, as well as in America's societal changes. If the city escaped some of the unrest that sprang from the civil rights movement, it was in no small measure attributable to the success of the newly created Archbishop's Commission on Human Relations, which helped bring the different factions together.

A first English-language Mass was celebrated November 29, 1964; new rituals, increased roles for the laity, and the reinstitution of the permanent diaconate came in timely fashion. However, introduction of Saturday evening Mass was delayed until 1983, when it was mandated for the entire American Church. Krol had opposed the change, but on some other issues he was quite open; for example, the Philadelphia archbishop was vocal in his support of disarmament and opposition to nuclear weapons. On June 26, 1967, he was created cardinal, along with another Philadelphian, Francis BRENNAN, dean of the Holy Roman Rota.

In 1976, the Bicentennial Year, Philadelphia hosted the 41st International Eucharistic Congress. Among the dignitaries who attended were MOTHER TERESA OF CALCUTTA, Dorothy DAY, Archbishop Fulton J. SHEEN, Cesar CHAVEZ, Dom Helder CAMARA, and U.S. President Gerald Ford. Pope Paul VI was absent for health reasons, but almost unnoticed among the host of prelates attending was the future POPE, JOHN PAUL II, Poland's Cardinal Karol Wojtyła, who had received his red hat with Krol and who had become a fast friend.

In 1977 Philadelphians traveled to Rome for the canonization of their fourth bishop, John Neumann, as America's first male saint. The cause had begun under Cardinal Dougherty, then languished until it was given new life by Krol, with beatification in 1963. Under his administration too, the cause for Mother Katharine Drexel was also begun and seen through the critical early stages.

After the death of Paul VI and the brief pontificate of JOHN PAUL I (1978), Krol was able to participate in the 1978 election of Cardinal Wojtyła as John Paul II. The new pope visited Philadelphia as part of an American tour the following October, and his Mass on

Cathedral-Basilica of Saints Peter and Paul, Philadelphia, PA. *In 1976, Pope Paul VI raised the Cathedral of Saints Peter and Paul to the status of a basilica after the grand cathedral hosted the 41st International Eucharistic Congress.* **WILLIAM THOMAS CAIN/GETTY IMAGES**

Logan Square facing the cathedral attracted more than a million people of all faiths. On December 8, 1987, Cardinal Krol, then 77 and in poor health, announced his retirement.

Anthony J. Bevilacqua. On February 11, 1988, Anthony Joseph BEVILACQUA was installed as archbishop of Philadelphia at the Cathedral Basilica of Saints Peter and Paul. Ordained a priest for the Diocese of Brooklyn, New York, on June 11, 1949, and possessing degrees in both canon and civil law, he was ordained as an auxiliary bishop for Brooklyn on July 24, 1980, and was named 10th Bishop of Pittsburgh on October 7, 1983, before his appointment to the Archdiocese of Philadelphia.

As archbishop of Philadelphia, one of his first priorities was a reorganization of the archdiocesan administration to a system of regional vicariates overseeing the parishes and secretariats to administer the diocesan offices. This established a chain of command that freed the archbishop from much of the administrative detail, affording more time for pastoral care. An early pleasant duty for Bevilacqua was that of leading a pilgrimage to

Rome for the November 20, 1988, beatification of Mother Katharine Drexel, the Philadelphia-born heiress who had renounced her wealth to found the Sisters of the BLESSED SACRAMENT, a congregation devoted to the evangelization and care of Native Americans and African Americans.

A major challenge in Philadelphia—as elsewhere— was problems associated with shifts in Catholic population from the core city to the suburbs, along with skyrocketing costs that were driving students away from the archdiocese's vaunted parochial school system. During Bevilacqua's administration, it was decided after exhaustive study that some underutilized churches would close or be twinned with another parish, as would some schools. In certain cases the closed parishes were replaced by evangelization centers, which were charged with reintroducing the Church to the affected region. The archdiocesan high schools were a special problem; in 1992 consultants recommended drastic reduction in the number of schools. Through aggressive fundraising and elimination of restrictive territorial admission policies, most of the schools were saved; tuition increases were

Archbishop Justin Rigali. *Newly installed Archbishop of Philadelphia Justin Rigali greets members of the Philadelphia diocese during a mass held on October 7, 2003, in Philadelphia, Pennsylvania.* WILLIAM THOMAS CAIN/GETTY IMAGES

reduced to affordable levels and enrollment stabilized. Parishes also underwent self-studies and were formed into clusters, which enabled group cooperation and joint programs.

Bevilacqua, who was elevated to the College of Cardinals on June 28, 1991, fostered the spirituality of his archdiocese through a nine-year renewal leading up to the Jubilee Year 2000. As part of the renewal, a Bless Me hot line was inaugurated in 1997 on telephone and Internet, resulting in thousands of inquiries from people who wished to be reconciled with the Church or counseled by a priest. Ecumenism and interfaith relations were also encouraged during the Bevilacqua years, with special outreach to Philadelphia's Jewish community. Seminary formation was also enhanced in 1991 through the addition of a separate Spirituality Year away from St. Charles Borromeo Seminary, Overbrook, at Mary Immaculate Seminary in Northampton, Pennsylvania, which was acquired from the Vincentians for this purpose. A shortage of Spanish-speaking clergy was partly addressed in 1999 through the adoption of a parish in Arecibo, Puerto Rico, where Philadelphia priests and seminarians could become accustomed to the special needs of Hispanic Catholics. In that same year a Spanish-language radio program was launched by the archdiocese. With the October 1, 2000, canonization of Mother Katharine Drexel, Philadelphia had the unusual distinction, at least at the time, of being the only diocese

in the United States with two canonized saints. Her feast day is March 3.

Justin Francis Rigali. Bevilacqua's resignation due to his age was accepted in July 2003, when he was appointed archbishop emeritus and apostolic administrator. At the same time, Justin Francis Rigali was appointed the eighth archbishop of Philadelphia. Rigali, who had spent many years in the service of the Holy See, and more than nine years as archbishop of St. Louis, was installed on October 7, 2003. He was elevated to the College of Cardinals on October 21, 2003.

Immigration continued to have an impact on the archdiocese at the beginning of the twenty-first century, albeit from more diverse countries of origin than in previous generations. In addition to existing "national" parishes for descendants of European immigrants, Rigali established Holy Angels Parish, Philadelphia (founded 1900), as the archdiocese's first personal parish for Korean-speaking Catholics in 2006. The archdiocesan Office for Pastoral Care of Migrants and Refugees coordinated official apostolates to more than twenty ethnic and language groups, and the Vicar for Hispanic Catholics provided social and pastoral service to Spanish-speaking parishioners and large numbers of migrant workers, particularly through the Misión Santa Maria, Madre de Dios (founded 1992).

As of 2008, 617 diocesan priests (144 retired) and 368 religious priests served a Catholic population of 1.46 million (more than 37% of the total population) in 270 parishes. More than 187,000 children, youth, and young adults received religious instruction in schools and parish programs, many conducted by the nearly 3,000 religious women and more than 100 religious brothers present in the archdiocese (*The Official Catholic Directory* 2008, p. 1011).

A forty-month investigation conducted by the district attorney of the City of Philadelphia resulted in a more than 600–page Grand Jury report released on September 21, 2005, alleging sexual abuse of minors by 63 diocesan priests since 1950. No criminal charges were filed against the archdiocese or the priests, all of whom had either died or been removed from ministry by the time the report was issued. Bevilacqua had established a Safe Environment Office in June 2002, with responsibility for assisting victims of sexual abuse by archdiocesan clergy and employees. Rigali continued to address the situation through such programs as Witness to the Sorrow (September 15, 2006), in which several victims of abuse addressed archdiocesan priests and seminarians.

Changing demographics led Rigali to consolidate some parishes in urban areas while establishing new ones in suburban counties. A major initiative was announced in January 2008 to build two new state-of-the-art high schools in parts of Montgomery and Bucks counties that were experiencing rapid growth. Rigali spoke out on various moral issues of local and national importance, most notably successfully calling for the rescinding of a city council resolution declaring Philadelphia a Pro-Choice City in June 2007.

SEE ALSO AFRICAN AMERICAN CATHOLICS IN THE UNITED STATES (HISTORY OF); CARDINALS OF THE CATHOLIC CHURCH; EDUCATION, CATHOLIC (HIGHER) IN THE UNITED STATES; EDUCATION, CATHOLIC (K THROUGH 12) IN THE UNITED STATES; FREEDOM OF RELIGION; PENN'S CHARTER OF LIBERTIES; PENNSYLVANIA, CATHOLIC CHURCH IN.

BIBLIOGRAPHY

Archdiocese of Philadelphia Official Web site, available from: http://archphila.org/home.php (accessed October 17, 2008).

Philip G. Bochanski, ed., *Our Faith-Filled Heritage: The Archdiocese of Philadelphia, 1808–2008* (Strasbourg, France 2007). Spanish edition, *Nuestra Herencia Llena de Fe: La Iglesia de Filadelfia, 1808–2008.*

James F. Connelly, ed., *The History of the Archdiocese of Philadelphia* (Philadelphia 1976).

Thomas J. Donaghy, *Philadelphia's Finest: A History of Education in the Catholic Archdiocese, 1692–1970* (Philadelphia 1972).

Michael I. J. Griffin, ed., *American Catholic Historical Researches* (Philadelphia 1887–). Archives, Archdiocese of Philadelphia.

Joseph L. J. Kirlin, *Catholicity in Philadelphia from the Earliest Missionaries down to the Present Time* (Philadelphia 1909).

Frame of Government of Pennsylvania (May 5, 1682), available from: http://avalon.law.yale.edu/17th_century/pa04.asp (Accessed October 22, 2008).

Daniel T. Mahoney, *Historical Sketches of the Catholic Churches and Institutions of Philadelphia* (Philadelphia 1895).

Hugh J. Nolan, "The Most Reverend Francis Patrick Kenrick, Third Bishop of Philadelphia, 1830–1851," in *Studies in American Church History*, The Catholic University of America (Washington, D.C. 1948), 37.

George Edward O'Donnell, *St. Charles Seminary, Overbrook,* vol. 2 (Philadelphia 1943–1953).

The Official Catholic Directory, 2008 (New Providence, N.J. 2008).

James Francis Connelly
Professor of History
St. Charles Seminary, Philadelphia, Pa.

Louis Baldwin
Staff Writer
The Catholic Standard & Times, Pittsburgh, Pa.

Rev. Philip G. Bochanski CO
The Oratory, Philadelphia, Pa. (2009)

PHILOSOPHY OF NATURE

The philosophy of nature is a vast and complex field, owing to its long history (beginning in ancient Greece) and its intersection with the revolutions in physics in the seventeenth century and in biology in the nineteenth century through the work of DARWIN. Traditionally, those working in this discipline have been involved in an attempt to define what is meant by the term "nature." However, the growth and power of modern natural science, beginning in the seventeenth century, has virtually displaced the philosophy of nature, which is now often regarded as a marginal, antiquarian pursuit without a mission of serious worth. Accordingly, three main aspects of the philosophy of nature will be explored here: (1) the premodern philosophy of nature; (2) the impact of modern natural science; and (3) the mission of the field in the twenty-first century. Unfortunately, the need for brevity precludes discussion of many topics of great value and intrinsic interest.

The Premodern Philosophy of Nature. Work in this area really began with the physical and biological works of ARISTOTLE. Late Greek, Jewish, Islamic, and Medieval Christian thinkers then supplied an immense body of commentaries on these works, extending into the seventeenth century. The main subject matter of the premodern philosophy of nature was material beings (in contrast to mathematical and immaterial beings); that is, it dealt with bodies—with the various kinds of bodies, with their interrelated patterns of change and stability, and with the causes and principles that account for them. The relative lack of attention to light, the other great source of agency in nature, is an unfortunate but understandable defect of premodern natural philosophy.

The endeavor to synthesize the Aristotelian idea of an eternal and finite cosmos with the biblical doctrine of temporal creation by an infinite being provided an underlying motivation for the work of the commentators. These individuals also brought the philosophy of nature into a relationship with a METAPHYSICS of created and uncreated being that goes beyond Aristotle's first unmoved mover and first intellect. Of the commentators, Albertus Magnus (ALBERT THE GREAT) and THOMAS AQUINAS are of special importance for the Catholic intellectual tradition.

It is important to understand why Aristotle is regarded as the founder of the philosophy of nature. Aristotle provided a new departure from Platonic idealism, which could not envision a *science* of changing objects, and pre-Socratic MATERIALISM, which did not have an adequate sense of *form*. In Platonic teaching, only the immaterial and unchanging Ideas can be objects of genuine science (*epistêmê*). The material, and thus changeable, beings (both natural and artificial) perceived by the senses cannot be objects of science, but only of opinion and myth (Plato 1964, pp. 745, 1161, 1176–1177). The intelligible Ideas are separate from the sensible individuals, and they alone are immutable. Thus, they alone can provide an adequately stable source for genuine *knowledge*, in the strict sense of the word. There is, accordingly, no natural science (*epistêmê physikê*)—and in particular, no biology—in the Platonic dialogues, for specific physical objects and living beings are constantly subject to change, and thus not stable enough for scientific knowledge.

The pre-Socratic materialists (the first physicists) typically attempted to account for the behavior of the many kinds or forms of visible bodies by reducing them to a few kinds of tiny, invisible material parts—such as the eternal and unbreakable atoms of DEMOCRITUS (c. 460–370 BC). In this reductionist type of physics, a natural whole (e.g., a squirrel) is understood to be an aggregate of parts (atoms), each of which is what it is independently of the whole, like bricks in a wall or gears in a clock. As such, the natural whole possesses no special or intrinsic unity. There is no source of its being that belongs to the whole, as such, that is irreducible to the parts, or that makes the parts, taken together, be what they are. Further, the natural whole can be understood by studying the parts in isolation, and then reaggregating them to compose the whole, as if the whole were simply the sum of the parts, like an artifact.

Thus, as Aquinas reports, "the ancient physicists ... held that the natural forms [e.g., squirrel form] were accidents [because the parts happen (*accidunt*) to be arranged in a certain way but could be arranged otherwise], as the forms of artificial things are" (Aquinas 1963, p. 11). In particular, no special reasons are given for the most striking aspect of living things—that they reproduce in a regular way according to their kind or species, and thus contain within them the source of their own production in a way that artifacts do not. In this view, living things must be ultimately reducible to their material parts, without any need to consider the wholes they make up, as if living things could be understood the way an artifact is understood.

But for Aristotle, whose thinking stays close to the phenomena, living things self-evidently display themselves as integrated wholes possessing species-typical structures and functions for which no materialist account could be fully adequate. Therefore, in addition to matter, one must grant the reality of another principle at work in natural, and especially in living things—namely, form (*eidos*), which is (unlike a Platonic Idea) intimately internal to the body it informs (Aristotle 1995, p. 51). It is the squirrel-form that is responsible for the specific unity and behavior of squirrels. Squirrel-matter is of course necessary, but it is not sufficient to explain the phenomena: "nature is two fold, and is both form and matter ... natural things will be neither without matter nor determined by their matter.... [Indeed] the form is nature to a higher degree than the matter" (Aristotle 1995, pp. 51–52).

But the form of a natural whole is not simply static—it is active and at work (*energeia*), in the good operation of the formed substance, such as in the tendency toward health and healing, the self-maintaining and self-reconstituting life processes characteristic of every living thing. Further, each species has distinctive capacities and activities (e.g., dogs bark, cats meow) that distinguish it from others, and whose exercise is good for it. Thus, "if the eye were an animal, its vision would be its soul [the form of an organic being]" (Aristotle 2001, p. 83). The perceiving animal strives to preserve itself as a perceiving being, not just a reproducing, or (as might be said today) gene-projecting, being. This is because its specific activity is not only good for it but pleasant: "what is appropriate by nature to each being is best and most pleasant for each" (Aristotle 2002, p. 193), for "nature does nothing in vain" (Aristotle 1984, p. 37).

Aquinas sums it up succinctly: "The soul and other natural forms are not per se subject to motion ... they are moreover the perfections of mutable things" (Aquinas 1986, p. 31). The cosmos is understood as an order of natural kinds or species, each having its proper operation or end (telos) that is by nature good for it, and taken together, all these species ultimately point to and are dependent on the pure actuality of the first unmoved mover, the first intellect, God (Aristotle 1999, pp. 241–242). Thus, Aristotle—famously or infamously—raises the banner of formal and final causality in nature: the irreducibility of wholes to parts, and the specific ends to which natural beings are intrinsically directed.

Implicit in this account of the universe is the notion of grades of being between what *is* most fully (and is thus wholly without matter, beyond divisibility and change) and what *is* least of all (primary matter thus without form, which cannot exist on its own but must be posited as an ultimate principle of all changeable beings). These changeable beings accordingly lie between pure act and primary matter. Every such composite (form–matter) being is able, by virtue of its matter, to be other than it now is, in some respect; that is, it is potentially something other than what it now is. By virtue of its form, every such composite being is partly active and able to induce change in both itself and in other bodies. The actuality of the potentialities of composite (form–matter) beings is physical motion (*kinêsis*). By contrast, mathematical objects do not possess matter, so they are not subject to physical motion *per se*, but only to motion *per accidens*, that is, by being *in* something that *is* moved *per se*. Therefore, for the premodern philosophy of nature, a purely mathematical physics, one without essentially qualitative notions of action and passion, may be *applicable* to nature, but it cannot be *adequate* to nature, because it knows not of POTENCY AND ACT. ("Essentially qualitative notions of action and passion" means simply that things such as PLEASURE and pain do not possess mathematical features, in contrast to things such as mass and gravitational attraction.)

These three—form, end, and actuality–potentiality (a pair that must be thought of together)—are the most fundamental terms in the Aristotelian and Thomistic understanding of nature. They were also the main targets of the seventeenth-century attack on that tradition by early-modern philosophy in the name of the new, non-teleological, mathematical, and experimental physics. The greatest victory of the Scientific Revolution is represented by classical physics, which includes mechanics, electromagnetism, thermodynamics, and relativity. This mathematical type of physics is a remarkably fruitful and powerful body of theory, one attended by a self-confident and thoroughly mathematical world conception, which was then shaken to its foundations by the quantum revolution of the early twentieth century—a development that remains to be fully digested philosophically (nature has surprises).

Let us now consider the meaning of early-modern philosophy and the version of science to which it gave birth. Darwinian biology, although not mathematical

and occurring almost two centuries later, is included here because it shares with modern classical physics what could be called "anti–formism," or the thesis that Aristotelian forms are not principles and causes, but rather products and effects of something prior to form (which accords with biblical teaching that God created the visible kinds or forms of beings), and, most importantly, that they are such *per accidens*; that is, the forms or species of things do not exist according to a purpose or design, but only by chance and necessity (as contemporary Darwinism maintains).

Modern Natural Science. The impact of natural science on the premodern philosophy of nature is to be found especially in the works of BACON, DESCARTES, and Newton. (GALILEO is a special case and would require a separate treatment.) The most salient points of natural science in this regard are: (1) the rejection of forms and ends in favor of laws of nature, and (2) the rejection of act and potency in favor of a mathematical conception of all physical change. The great extent to which laws of nature can be mathematically expressed unifies these two components.

A law of nature—as proposed by Bacon and Descartes, and as realized paradigmatically in Newton's law of universal gravitation—expresses a relation between various properties of bodies (e.g., mass, m) that are common to all species or kinds of bodies, both natural and artificial, living and nonliving, and celestial and terrestrial. Such common properties are therefore not species-typical (e.g., dogs bark, cats meow, characteristics traditionally understood to flow from the Aristotelian natural form of the dog and cat); on the contrary, they are universal across all bodies simply (e.g., all have mass). Most strikingly, the mathematical laws into whose algebraic expression these properties enter (e.g., the equation for gravitational force, $F = -GMm/R^2$) make known new possibilities for the human prediction, control, manipulation, and alteration of natural phenomena (e.g., humanly controlled space flight, or the production of information-bearing electromagnetic radiation). The possibility of such results undermines both the traditional primacy of Aristotelian form and the distinction between the natural and the artificial. Bacon's *New Organon* is prophetic for the new physics:

> When man contemplates nature working freely, he meets with different species of things, of animals, of plants, of minerals; whence he readily passes into the opinion that there are in nature certain primary forms which nature endeavors to educe.... Which [opinion] ... tend[s] wholly to the unfair circumscription of human power.... [I]n nature nothing really exists besides individual bodies [true particles, II.8] perform-

ing pure individual acts according to law.... [W]hosoever is acquainted with [laws of nature] embraces the unity of nature in materials the most unlike, and is able therefore to detect and bring to light things never yet done, and such as neither the vicissitudes of nature, nor industry in experimenting, nor accident itself, would ever have brought into act. (Bacon 1960, pp. 63, 86, 122, 129)

A magnet and living flesh exemplify "materials the most unlike." Magnetic resonance imaging in medical diagnostics today exemplifies "things never yet done," and thus testifies to the truth—partial but remarkable—of Bacon's prescient vision. (By "industry in experimenting," Bacon means experimentation unguided by his own method.)

Laws of nature were unknown to the ancient (pre-Socratic) atomists. Thus, mastery of nature was not a theme of their science. Here is Descartes:

In place of that speculative philosophy that is taught in the schools, we can find a practical one, by which ... we could ... make ourselves like masters and possessors of nature.... All the variety in matter, all the diversity of its forms, depends on motion.... The only principles which I accept, or require, in physics are those of geometry and pure mathematics; these principles explain all natural phenomena. (Descartes 1985, pp. 142–143, 232, 247)

Descartes describes his cosmology in "proto-Darwinian" terms:

[The] nature [of all purely material things, which includes animals] is much easier to conceive if we see them develop little by little in this way [under Descartes's laws of nature] than if we consider them only as entirely completed. (Descartes 1985, pp. 133–134)

Thus, if one considers things such as bees and flowers in their completed forms (as Aristotle and the medievals tended to do), Descartes believes this will lead to the erroneous opinion that they are the result of an intention, plan, or design. Rather, all the species of things now present on the surface of the earth must, according to Descartes, be thought to have come to be "as by accident" from simpler antecedent elements (Descartes 1985, p. 93). The denial of natural ends entails a broad freedom for experimentation on the (merely accidental) forms of bodies.

Although Descartes's laws of nature are largely false (geometrical optics is the only piece of his physics that survives), Newton's laws of motion are solidly warranted

and basic to the training of every physicist today. In regard to the particular class of gravitational phenomena, Newton's physics fulfills Bacon's prescription for a proper "law of nature" and inspires the universal forces-and-particles model, a conception that captured the imagination and belief of physicists for over two centuries:

I derive from the celestial phenomena the forces of gravity with which bodies tend to the sun and the several planets. Then from these forces ... I deduce the motions of the planets, the comets, the moon, and the sea. I wish we could derive the rest of the phenomena of Nature by the same kind of reasoning from mechanical principles, for I am induced by many reasons to suspect that they may all depend upon certain forces by which the particles of bodies, by some causes hitherto unknown, are either mutually impelled towards one another, and cohere ... or are repelled and recede.... These forces being unknown, philosophers have hitherto attempted the search of Nature in vain. (Newton 1962a, p. xviii)

This is a reductionist program for future research in physics: One must view every body as if it were a solar system writ small, or a system of particles interacting by forces, for "nature is exceedingly simple and conformable to herself. Whatever reasoning holds for greater motions [e.g., of planets] should hold for lesser ones [of particles] as well" (Newton 1962b, p. 333). Note, however, that Newton's assertion is incompatible with quantum physics.

In reading the above excerpts from Bacon, Descartes, and Newton, one must be attentive to the words *nothing* and *all* ("nothing really exists besides [particles]," "All the variety in matter, all the diversity of its forms," "All ... the rest of the phenomena of nature)". Here one can clearly see universal philosophic claims about nature inspired by particular scientific results. The particular results are sound, even spectacular (e.g., geometrical optics, Newton's gravitational theory), but the ascent to the universal claim is unwarranted. Correction of this common error of generalization is an important mission of the modern philosophy of nature.

Finally, we come to Darwin, whose science, although not mathematical, is, again, anti–formist, in the sense discussed above. In *The Origin of Species*, Darwin wrote, "We shall have to treat species in the same manner as those naturalists treat genera, who admit that genera are merely artificial combinations made for convenience. This may not be a cheering prospect; but we shall at least be free from the vain search for the undiscovered and undiscoverable essence of the term species" (Darwin 1958, p. 447).

In this view, the visible species in the biosphere are accidental products of a general process (of random variation and natural selection for reproductive fitness) aimed at no particular outcome, at no particular order of plants, animals, and human beings. As such, Darwinism stands in notorious contention with biblical teaching on divine creation, as well as any metaphysics of mind as ultimate principle of the universe (e.g., Plato, Aristotle). Now the natural form or species that is most important, whose essence most demands to be understood and rightly disposed, is the human species. Thus, the philosophy of nature necessarily makes contact with philosophical anthropology, as well as with metaphysics and THEOLOGY.

Modern Philosophy of Nature In the twenty-first century, the mission of the philosophy of nature is, very broadly, twofold: (1) to critique modern science, and (2) to rethink (which includes recovery of) the premodern tradition. Let us begin from our present position: The expansion of human power to change the forms of things is a hallmark of modernity. This power brings benefits to humanity that no one should minimize, but it also creates a problem. As Leon Kass puts it, "everything is in principle open to intervention; because all is alterable, nothing is deemed either respectably natural or unwelcomely unnatural" (Kass 1985, p. 11).

Does the problem that Kass describes arise because of the way nature really is? Or does it arise because of misinterpretation of natural science? In fact, both propositions are partly true. Nature is less Aristotelian and more malleable than Aristotle and Aquinas thought, and this indeed poses burdensome ethical problems. But there is also misinterpretation of the implications of natural science through unwarranted extrapolation of particular results, as noted above. A critique of science requires determining what science truly says about nature and human nature, as well as what it does not say. One must therefore assess the legitimate range, and the resulting limitations, of science. Carrying out this important task requires expertise in both philosophy of nature and a relevant specialty in the natural sciences. In the early twenty-first century, however, few possess this double qualification, and educating students so that they have it is a desideratum for education, especially Catholic education.

For the philosophical comprehension of modern science, two items are especially conspicuous today: The long-standing conceptual puzzles of quantum physics (see Greenstein and Zajonc 1997, pp. 131–150, 157–162, 181–185) and the debate over evolutionary biology. Regarding EVOLUTION, the open question is whether random variation and natural selection are exclusively adequate to explain all living phenomena. If they are only partially adequate, they need to share the stage with other principles, such as some intelligent guidance or nonrandom direction of the causal steps that produce the variation that can then be subject to natural selection.

Rethinking and revitalizing the premodern tradition means returning to the primary sources to recover a philosophically adequate account of body, motion, and causality—thus to recover notions of form and end, of act and potency. It is a lamentable fact that discourse in America during the twentieth and early twenty-first centuries has been dominated by zealous and opposed proponents of scientism and biblical literalism. The middle way—philosophy—has had no audible public voice. The philosophy of nature and, more generally, the Catholic intellectual tradition, can play a role in the endeavor to remedy this defect.

Last but not least, the philosophy of nature must confront the basic difference between Aristotle's eternal cosmos of unchanging forms and the modern universe—namely, that all nature has a history. From the BIG BANG to the formation of galaxies, the ignition of the sun and the genesis of life on earth, all that one now sees in the universe did not exist at one time. The history of the universe is characterized by the coming into being of new structures whose complexity and performance cannot be adequately understood in terms of simpler antecedent parts. Accounting for such phenomena of emergence poses a challenge to natural science, the philosophy of nature, and metaphysics. To say "God did it" is proper to religious faith, but—as St. Augustine shows in exemplary fashion—the human mind is by its very nature led to ask, "*Quomodo autem fecisti caelum et terram?*" (But how didst Thou make the heaven and the earth?) [Augustine 1974, p. 257].

SEE ALSO NATURE (IN PHILOSOPHY); NATURE (IN THEOLOGY); PLATO; SCIENCE (IN ANTIQUITY); SCIENCE (IN THE RENAISSANCE); SCIENCE (SCIENTIA).

BIBLIOGRAPHY

ON THE PREMODERN PHILOSOPHY OF NATURE AND ITS MODERN RECOVERY

Aristotle, *The Physics, On the Soul, Metaphysics, Nicomachean Ethics*, and *Politics*; in *Aristotle*, The Loeb Classical Library (Cambridge, Mass. 1970), Vols. IV–V, VIII, XVII–XVIII, XIX, XXI. Of the English translations, those of Joe Sachs—*The Physics* (New Brunswick, N.J. 1995), *On the Soul* (Santa Fe, N.M. 2001), *Metaphysics* (Santa Fe, N.M. 1999), and *Nicomachean Ethics* (Newburyport, Mass. 2002)—are noteworthy for their fidelity to the meaning of Aristotle's Greek, and especially valuable for the introductory essay to each translation. See also Carnes Lord's version of *Politics* (Chicago 1984).

Augustine, *Confessions*, translated by R. S. Pine-Coffin (Harmondsworth, Middlesex, England 1974).

Thomas Aquinas, *In octo libros physicorum Aristotelis exposito* (Turin, Italy 1965); published in English as *Commentary on*

Aristotle's Physics, translated by Richard J. Blackwell, Richard J. Spath, and Edmund Thirlkel (New Haven, Conn. 1963).

Thomas Aquinas, *The Division and Methods of the Sciences*, translated by Armand Maurer (Toronto 1986).

Louis DeBroglie, *Physics and Microphysics* (New York 1955).

Charles De Koninck, *The Hollow Universe* (Quebec City, Canada 1964).

Kurt Goldstein, *The Organism: A Holistic Approach to Biology Derived from Pathological Data in Man* (New York 2000; originally published 1939).

Richard F. Hassing, ed., *Final Causality in Nature and Human Affairs* (Washington, D.C. 1997).

Werner Heisenberg, *Physics and Beyond*, translated by Arnold J. Pomerans (New York 1971).

Hans Jonas, *The Phenomenon of Life* (Evanston, Ill. 2001; originally published 1979).

Institute for the Study of Nature Official Web site, available from http://www.isnature.org (accessed March 31, 2008).

Leon R. Kass, *Toward a More Natural Science* (New York 1985).

Leon R. Kass, "The Permanent Limitations of Biology," in *Life, Liberty, and the Defense of Dignity* (San Francisco 2002).

Leon R. Kass, "Science, Religion, and the Human Future," *Commentary*, April 2007, 36–48.

Jacob Klein, "Aristotle, an Introduction" and "On the Nature of Nature," in *Lectures and Essays by Jacob Klein*, edited by Robert B. Williamson and Elliott Zuckerman (Annapolis, Md. 1985).

Jacque Maritain, *Philosophy of Nature* (New York 1951).

Plato, *The Collected Dialogues*, edited by Edith Hamilton and Huntington Cairns (New York 1964).

Kurt Riezler, *Physics and Reality* (New Haven, Conn. 1940).

Vincent E. Smith, *The Science of Nature, An Introduction* (Milwaukee, Wis. 1966).

William A. Wallace, *The Modeling of Nature* (Washington, D.C. 1996).

ON THE IMPACT OF MODERN NATURAL SCIENCE

Francis Bacon, *The New Organon*, edited by Fulton H. Anderson (New York 1960; originally published 1620).

Charles Darwin, *The Origin of Species* (New York 1958; originally published 1859).

Descartes, *Discourse on Method, The World*, and *Principles of Philosophy*; in *The Philosophical Writings of Descartes*, translated by John Cottingham, Robert Stoothoff, and Dugald Murdoch (Cambridge, U.K. 1985), Vol. 1.

George Greenstein and Arthur G. Zajonc, *The Quantum Challenge: Modern Research on the Foundations of Quantum Mechanics* (Sudbury, Mass. 1997).

Martin Heidegger, *What is a Thing?* Translated by W. B. Barton, Jr., and Vera Deutsch (Chicago 1967).

Richard Kennington, *On Modern Origins: Essays in Early Modern Philosophy*, edited by Pamela Kraus and Frank Hunt (Lanham, Md. 2004).

Ernst Mayr, *One Long Argument: Charles Darwin and the Genesis of Modern Evolutionary Thought* (Cambridge, Mass. 1991).

Isaac Newton, *The Mathematical Principles of Natural Philosophy*, translated by Andrew Motte and Florian Cajori (New York 1962a; originally published in 1729).

Isaac Newton, "Unpublished Conclusion of the *Principia*," in *Unpublished Scientific Papers of Isaac Newton*, edited by A. R. and M. B. Hall, (Cambridge, U.K. 1962b).

Richard F. Hassing
Associate Professor of Philosophy
The Catholic University of America (2009)

POLITICS, CHURCH AND

The Church's basic view about politics was set forth by Christ himself in the Gospels: "Render unto Caesar the things that are Caesar's, and render unto God the things that are God's" (Matthew 22:21–22). In other words, politics and the state have a natural, necessary, inevitable place in human existence, which concerns preeminently man's temporal well-being. As Saint AUGUSTINE of Hippo put it, the city is needed to insure concord. Still, some in the early Church, such as ORIGEN, counseled Christians to keep their distance from politics because it was dominated by pagans and focused on the things of this world. To the contrary, Augustine stressed men's civic responsibilities and, effectively, saw Christianity reinforcing patriotism by making obedience to civil authority—so long as it did not contravene God's law—a religious obligation. Saint Augustine's view was echoed strongly almost 1,600 years later by Pope JOHN PAUL II when he told the Robert Schuman Foundation for the Cooperation of European Christian Democrats: "The complaints often made against political activity don't justify an attitude of disengaged skepticism on a Catholic's part who has the duty, rather, of taking responsibility for society's well-being" (November 7, 2003).

Church Statements from the Nineteenth to the Twenty-First Century. In the nineteenth century, Pope LEO XIII taught about the role of both citizen and statesman. He said that the natural law enjoins men to love and defend their homeland. He also stated that civil laws should be obeyed and even revered, even though God's laws take precedence over them. He also pointed out that the virtues of obedience and abstinence shaped by religion make better citizens. He insisted that rulers govern as God does, with as perfect justice and charity as possible. He understood that rulers must act prudently, but must also have courage and not surrender basic moral principles or compromise God's law.

In the twentieth century, Pope PIUS XII anticipated both the Second Vatican Council and Pope John Paul II in his teaching about the Church's role in politics and the rights and obligations of citizens. Pius, like previous popes, made clear the Church's right and duty to speak out when the state acts tyrannically, violates the legitimate rights of its people, or infringes upon her rightful prerogatives. He also insisted that, while the Church should stay aloof from partisan politics, she would not be silent about politicians who worked against religion and the Church. He admonished all who have the right to vote in elections to do so, and insisted that the person who "abstains, especially out of cowardice, commits a grave sin, a mortal fault" (Address to the Delegates of the International Conference on Emigration, October 17, 1951).

Gaudium et spes from Vatican II (1965, #75–76) ties in the obligation of political participation with the common good: "Every citizen ought to be mindful of his right and his duty to promote the common good by using his vote." It makes it incumbent upon the state to recognize, protect, and foster such participation. Citizen participation comes with a warning, however: Citizens should not put too much power in the hands of public authorities or make excessive demands on them. Citizens themselves, families, and social groups cannot surrender their social responsibilities to government (which John Paul II emphatically restates in the encyclical *Centesimus annus* [1991, #48–49]). Christian citizens are urged to be examples to the broader political community, showing (among other things) dedication to the common good and respect for their fellow men. The encyclical nudges them toward moderation and appropriate compromise in saying that they "should recognize the legitimacy of differing points of view about the organization of worldly affairs." The community needs to provide "civil and political education" so that citizens can properly play their role in public affairs. Regarding the Church, *Gaudium et spes* says that she "is not identified with any political community," nor tied to any particular type of political order. While she will not interfere with the state's role, she cannot be completely uninvolved with it. She will "pass moral judgments even in matters relating to politics, whenever the fundamental rights of man or the salvation of souls requires it." She also expects the state not to interfere with her salvific work.

In *Christifideles laici* (1988, #42), John Paul II emphasizes that all have a right and duty to participate in public life, in different capacities as suited to each. Echoing Vatican II, he states that politics as a profession is a noble undertaking if one understands it as a life of service. John Paul deepens the meaning of politics as the

pursuit of the common good within a spirit of justice by saying that it seeks to forge solidarity, which he defines as "*a firm and persevering determination* to commit oneself to the *common good*." Politics rightly understood seeks to extend this solidarity even beyond the borders of one's own nation, to the entire world. With this focus on solidarity, the particular "fruit" of politics—as it ought to be pursued—is peace.

Laity, Clergy, and Religious in Politics. Vatican II said that the "renewal of the temporal order" is the "distinctive task" of the laity (*Apostolicam actuositatem*, 1965, #7). It mentions politics, of course, as one important aspect of this. Faithful and well-formed Catholics should not hesitate to enter politics. The CONGREGATION FOR THE DOCTRINE OF THE FAITH's 2002 *Doctrinal Note on Some Questions Regarding the Participation of Catholics in Political Life* (#1) specifically holds that, "By fulfilling their civic duties, *guided by a Christian conscience*, in conformity with its values, the lay faithful exercise their proper task of infusing the temporal order with Christian values, all the while respecting the nature and rightful autonomy of that order." The Church's encouragement of political involvement is an expression of the society of participation that is stressed by John Paul II in such encyclicals as *Centesimus annus*, and in line with the recommendation of different social encyclicals for worker participation in workplace decision-making in the economic order.

Following this stress on politics being the particular province of the laity, in 1980 John Paul II ordered all priests to withdraw from electoral politics. The most prominent priest serving as an elected official in the United States at the time was Father Robert DRINAN, SJ, Democratic Representative from Massachusetts. He complied with the pope's order, although he continued political efforts in non-elective capacities with such organizations as the Americans for Democratic Action. Drinan had become controversial because of his support for legalized abortion. Father Robert Cornell, the only other priest ever to serve as a voting member of Congress (1975–1979), also bowed out of the 1980 race to regain his Wisconsin seat. John Paul's order was in the spirit of the 1967 Synod of Bishops' statement *Ultimis temporibus*, which called for priests to be excluded from leadership or "active militancy" on behalf of a political party except in exceptional circumstances.

While the HOLY SEE has not imposed a similar prohibition on religious in political office, in 1981 the Sacred Congregation for Religious and Secular Institutes addressed this question in the document *Le scelte evangeliche*. While all citizens should be involved in politics in the broad sense of working to improve the "dynamic organization" of society, identification of religious with a political ideology or party could result

John Paul II: Upholding Moral Truth in the Public Realm. *President Bill Clinton greets Pope John Paul II during ceremonies on their arrival at Newark International Airport in Newark, N.J., Oct. 4, 1995. Air Force One is seen in the background left. During his trip the Pope preached against materialism and sought to strengthen the Church in America.* AP IMAGES

in their "losing their identity as religious and as Christian apostles" (#11–12). Hence, this type of political activity for them should be the exception and not the rule.

Moral Imperatives for Catholics in Political Life. Since the 1970s, the Church's statements on politics have increasingly been concerned about instructing Catholic citizens and politicians about their moral obligations when making decisions about certain public questions. This has reflected the entry into the political arena of issues that involve basic principles of Christian morality on such questions as respect for human life and dignity that may not be compromised. More fundamentally, since these principles are also part of the natural law and not merely sectarian, the Church rightfully can advocate their adoption by the broader political community. For example, the Sacred Congregation for the Doctrine of the Faith's *Declaration on Procured Abortion* (1974) implicitly admonished legislators to not legalize abortion since that would signal that the state was, effectively, authorizing or approving it. It also instructed citizens that they may not take part in public

propaganda campaigns for abortion legalization, and neither citizens nor legislators may vote for it. In its 1994 document on *Ethical and Pastoral Dimensions of Population Trends*, the Pontifical Council for the Family insisted that governments should have policies that help the family regarding work, taxation, housing, and education. The rights of married couples to procreate without state interference must also be protected. In his social encyclicals *Sollicitudo rei socialis* (1987) and *Centesimus annus*, John Paul II condemned coercive population control campaigns carried out both by national governments and internationally.

The Congregation for the Doctrine of the Faith's *Doctrinal Note on Some Questions Regarding the Participation of Catholics in Political Life* states clearly that, "a well-formed Christian conscience does not permit one to vote for a political program or an individual law which contradicts the fundamental contents of faith and morals" (#4). It insists that each Catholic has a responsibility, which cannot be delegated to others, to work for the common good. It emphasizes that Catholics have a particular responsibility to witness in the public arena on such questions as: abortion; euthanasia; the rights of parents and the family; the evils of divorce, cohabitation, drug abuse, and prostitution; protection of the young; religious liberty; an economy that promotes justice and solidarity; and peace. It enjoins Catholics to take account of practical considerations and the complexities involved in the latter two areas and to avoid slipping into secular approaches to them. It underscores that Catholics are not promoting "confessional values" or threatening the rightful "autonomy of the temporal order" in promoting Catholic teaching on the above; the "ethical precepts are rooted in human nature itself and belong to the natural moral law" (#5). To allow such matters to be consigned to the realm of personal choice would not be a "legitimate pluralism," but "moral anarchy." This contrasts with the complete freedom the Church permits to Catholics in shaping their views on "contingent questions" (#6). Both Catholic citizens and public officials must understand, however, that they cannot live separate lives in the public and private/spiritual realms.

Statements by the U.S. Hierarchy and Developments in Other Countries. Statements have also come forth from the U.S. hierarchy about the moral obligations of both citizens and public officials. In 1976, for example, the U.S. bishops issued a statement on "Political Responsibility," in which they lamented the low voter turnout in elections and urged all citizens to register to vote, become informed on issues, become "involved in the party or campaign of their choice, and to vote freely according to their consciences" (#1–2).

In 2004, the U.S. Conference of Catholic Bishops issued *Faithful Citizenship: A Catholic Call to Political Responsibility*. The document, as would be expected, echoes many of the themes of magisterial and other Holy See documents from the particular standpoint of the American situation. The bishops say that "faithful citizenship" requires Catholics to approach their civic responsibilities from the standpoint of their faith formation, and to bring their moral convictions into the public arena. They stress to their flock that Catholics can legitimately disagree about the specific applications of the Church's teachings. They make it very clear that the Church is not of the nature of an interest group—which is such a common feature in American politics—and does not endorse candidates or line up with political ideologies or parties. The Church has a responsibility, however, to assess how well *all* the candidates, policies, parties, and platforms uphold the dignity of the human person and further the common good. The Church has a right and responsibility to make her teaching known and to help shape Catholic understanding about the moral questions present in the public domain. As far as the responsibilities of Catholics as citizens are concerned,

the bishops say they may not support political initiatives at variance with faith and morals, should not focus just on individual aspects of Catholic social teaching apart from the rest, should carefully judge candidates and policies in light of the faith, and should work to build a culture of life. The document singles out broad issues that are "moral priorities for public life": protecting human life, protecting family life, pursuing economic justice, and promoting global solidarity. It also addresses specific issues and public policy proposals that were currently being debated under each of these categories.

Individual U.S. bishops have also issued statements about Catholics and politics. In 2004, Archbishops Raymond Leo Burke (St. Louis) and Charles J. Chaput (Denver) made noteworthy pronouncements. Burke provided particular directives regarding Catholics' voting decisions. A Catholic may not vote for a candidate who supports without limit immoral practices such as abortion and embryonic stem-cell research, but may—in some circumstances—support a candidate who is more qualified in such support. Chaput said that believers have a positive responsibility to advance public morality in the political arena; to fail to do so is "not tolerance but cowardice." He explained that America's founding fathers believed that the state was not exempt from moral judgment and criticism from religious authorities and their adherents. There are no grounds for removing religion from public debate.

Many of the same public moral issues the U.S. hierarchy is confronting are also a current preoccupation of the Church in many other countries. For example, in Italy the Church has strongly opposed the Italian government's attempt to give financial, inheritance, and "next of kin" rights to cohabiting heterosexual couples and same-sex couples. In Poland, the Church has joined the government in resisting the attempts by the European Union to pressure the country to permit legalized abortion, homosexual rights, and same-sex marriage. In the United Kingdom, the Church has been speaking up against abortion and same-sex marriage in the name of the natural law, and is opposing a new law that will require its adoption agencies to place children with same-sex couples. The Church campaigned against the legalization of same-sex marriage in the federal parliament in Canada, and one of its bishops was legally threatened for calling for the de-legalization of homosexual practices. In Brazil, the Church is resisting government moves to legalize abortion and promote explicit sex education. The cardinal-archbishop of Mexico City, with Pope BENEDICT XVI's support, excommunicated the city's mayor after he signed a bill legalizing abortion.

In summation, the Church has made consistently clear that: She has the right and duty to speak up for moral truth in the public realm; her public efforts will focus on preserving natural law principles and her rightful freedoms, and she will not interfere in matters where there can be legitimate disagreement; political activity must seek to promote the common good; citizens have a moral obligation to participate in politics although they will have different roles; political activity—especially on a professional level—is the particular role of the laity; and citizen voting and official decision-making must be shaped by sound morality.

SEE ALSO CENTESIMUS ANNUS; CHRISTIFIDELES LAICI; CHURCH AND STATE; CHURCH AND STATE IN THE UNITED STATES (LEGAL HISTORY); COMMON GOOD; NATURAL LAW IN POLITICAL THOUGHT; POLITICAL THEOLOGY; SOLIDARITY.

BIBLIOGRAPHY

Congregation for the Doctrine of the Faith, *Doctrinal Note on Some Questions Regarding the Participation of Catholics in Political Life* (Rome 2002); Also available from http://www.vatican.va/roman_curia/congregations/cfaith/documents/rc_con_cfaith_doc_20021124_politica_en.html (accessed August 26, 2008).

John Paul II, *Christifideles laici*, On the Vocation and the Mission of the Lay Faithful in the Church and in the World (Apostolic Exhortation, December 30, 1988) (Santiago, Chile 1988); Also available from http://www.vatican.va/holy_father/john_paul_ii/apost_exhortations/documents/hf_jp-ii_exh_30121988_christifideles-laici_en.html (accessed August 26, 2008).

Leo XIII, *Diuturnum illud*, On the Origin of Civil Power (Encyclical, June 29, 1881) (Rome 1881); Also available from http://www.vatican.va/holy_father/leo_xiii/encyclicals/documents/hf_l-xiii_enc_29061881_diuturnum_en.html (accessed August 26, 2008).

Sacred Congregation for Religious and Secular Institutes, *Le scelte evangeliche* (Rome 1981).

Synod of Bishops, *Ultimis temporibus* (Rome 1967).

U.S. Conference of Catholic Bishops, *Faithful Citizenship: A Catholic Call to Political Responsibility* (Washington, D.C. 2003).

Vatican Council II, *Apostolicam actuositatem*, On the Apostolate of the Laity (Decree, November 18, 1965) (Rome 1965); Also available from http://www.vatican.va/archive/hist_councils/ii_vatican_council/documents/vat-ii_decree_19651118_apostolicam-actuositatem_en.html (accessed August 26, 2008).

Vatican Council II, *Gaudium et spes*, On the Church in the Modern World (Pastoral Constitution, December 7, 1965) (Rome 1965); Also available from http://www.vatican.va/archive/hist_councils/ii_vatican_council/documents/vat-ii_cons_19651207_gaudium-et-spes_en.html (accessed August 29, 2008).

Stephen M. Krason
Professor of Political Science and Legal Studies
Franciscan University of Steubenville (2009)

POPES, LIST OF

This list of popes is taken from *Annuario Pontificio* for 2008, and it reflects the results of the most recent historical research. For the first two centuries of the Christian era the dates of the pontificates are not secure, and until the middle of the eleventh century there often remain doubts as to the precise day and month. The *Annuario* has formatted this list so that "two or three dates at the beginning of the pontificate indicate the election, ordination and coronation from which pontiffs were accustomed to calculate their pontificates." The last date reflects the POPE's death, deposition, or resignation. When dates of consecutive pontiffs overlap, it is often because the validity of a papal election was disputed, and it is difficult to determine the party that has the legitimate claim, "which, existing de facto, assures the legitimate and unbroken continuation of the successors of St. Peter" (*Annuario Pontificio* 2008, p. 12*). The names in square brackets are those of antipopes.

The liturgical books and HAGIOGRAPHY of the Church consider as martyrs all popes before Sylvester I (314–335) and as saints those from Sylvester I to Felix IV (526–530), inclusive. There are two exceptions: Liberius (352–366) and Anastasius II (496–498).

Throughout the almost 2,000–year history of the PAPACY, anomalies have arisen in regard to the sequential numbers given to popes who have had or chose certain names. ANTIPOPE Felix (355–366) was erroneously confused with St. Felix, a Roman martyr and was given a place in the list of Roman pontiffs as Felix II. Thus the next two legitimate popes who were named Felix have been called Felix III (483–492) and Felix IV (526–530), instead of Felix II and Felix III. An antipope of the fifteenth century took the name Felix V (1439–1449).

A Roman priest named Stephen was chosen pope after the death of Zacharias (741–752), but he lived for only four days after his election and died before his consecration, which, according to the canon law of the time, was the true beginning of a pontificate. A pope is now considered to be pope from the time of his election, so Stephen should today be counted as a legitimate pope, and this unusual circumstance has added confusion to the numbering system. To make the matter more complex, the man who followed him to the throne of St. Peter was also called Stephen. He now is given the name and number Stephen II (III) by the *Annuario Pontificio*. The same accommodation is made for all other popes named Stephen.

The most dramatic skewering of papal numbers concerns the name John. The pontificate of John XIV (983–984) was erroneously attributed to two men with the same name. In addition, Antipope John XVI (997–

998) has had his pontificate counted in the numbering system of legitimate popes. When Romanus of Tusculum was elected pope in 1024, he took the number XVIII, his rightful number, but he was designated in documents recorded a little later as John XX. By the thirteenth century this corrupted numbering had been everywhere accepted, so the next Pope John, Peter of Spain, took the name John XXI on his accession in 1276. Subsequently, Romanus of Tusculum's number was changed to John XIX (1024–1032), but because Peter of Spain remained John XXI (1276–1277), there is no Pope John XX listed in the *Annuario Pontificio*. All this explains what the *Annuario* calls "the strange nomenclature" that can be found in the BASILICA of St. Paul's Outside the Walls in ROME, where portraits of all the popes line the walls. Captions read "John XVI or XVII," "John XVII or XVIII," "John XVIII or XIX or XX," and so forth.

Simon of Brie became Martin IV (1281–1285) upon his election by placing Marinus I (882–884) and Marinus II (942–946) as well as Martin I (649–655) among the Martins. Oddo of Colonna took the name Martin V in 1417. An antipope, Ottaviano of Monticello, called himself Victor IV (1159–1164) instead of Victor V. He did so, the *Annuario* speculates, because a previous antipope, Victor IV (1138), reigned only two months before spontaneously submitting to Innocent II. Thus he was not counted when Ottaviano of Monticello assumed the name of Victor. Both are listed in *Annuario Pontificio* as Antipope Victor IV. Antipope Benedict X seems to have been included in the numbering of the legitimate popes named Benedict. Finally, Alexander VI (1492–1503) should have become Alexander V, a name that had been assumed in 1409 by an antipope created by the Council of PISA during the Great SCHISM.

In this edition of *New Catholic Encyclopedia* there is a separate article on every pope and antipope, which contains the important biographical and historical material relating to each individual.

St. Peter, 64 or 67

St. Linus, 68–79

St. Anacletus (Cletus), 80–92

St. Clement I, 92–99 (or 68–76)

St. Evaristus, 99 or 96–108

St. Alexander I, 108 or 109–116 or 119

St. Sixtus I, 117 or 119–126 or 128

St. Telesphorus, 127 or 128–137 or 138

St. Hyginus, 138–142 or 149

St. Pius I, 142 or 146–157 or 161

St. Anicetus, 150 or 157–153 or 168

St. Soter, 162 or 168–170 or 177

St. Eleutherius, 171 or 177–185 or 193

St. Victor I, 186 or 189–197 or 201

St. Zephyrinus, 198–217 or 218

St. Callistus I, 218–222

[St. Hippolytus, 217–235]

St. Urban I, 222–230

St. Pontianus, July 21, 230–September 28, 235

St. Anterus, November 21, 235–January 3, 236

St. Fabian, 236–January 20, 250

St. Cornelius, March 6 or 13, 251–June 253

[Novatian, 251]

St. Lucius I, June or July, 253–March 5, 254

St. Stephen I, March 12, 254–August 2, 257

St. Sixtus II, August 30, 257–August 6, 258

St. Dionysius, July 22, 259–December 26, 268

St. Felix I, January 5, 269–December 30, 274

St. Eutychian, January 4, 275–December 7, 283

St. Gaius (Caius), December 17, 283–April 22, 296

St. Marcellinus, June 30, 296–October 25, 304

St. Marcellus I, 306–January 16, 309 (His pontificate could have started in 307 or 308 and ended in 308 or 310.)

St. Eusebius, April 18, 309–August 17, 309 (His pontificate could have ended in 308 or 310.)

St. Miltiades, July 2, 311–January 10, 314

St. Silvester I, January 31, 314–December 31, 335

St. Mark, January 18, 336–October 7, 336

St. Julius I, February 6, 337–April 12, 352

Liberius, May 17, 352–September 24, 366

[Felix II, 355–November 22, 365]

St. Damasus I, October 1, 366–December 11, 384

[Ursinus, September 24, 366–367]

St. Siricius, December 15, 22, or 29, 384–November 26, 399

St. Anastasius I, November 27, 399–December 19, 401

St. Innocent I, December 22, 401–March 12, 417

St. Zosimus, March 18, 417–December 26, 418

St. Boniface I, December 28, December 29, 418–September 4, 422

[Eulalius, December 27, December 29, 418–April 3, 419]

St. Celestine I, September 10, 422–July 27, 432

St. Sixtus III, July 31, 432–August 19, 440

St. Leo I (The Great), September 29, 440–November 10, 461

St. Hilary, November 19, 461–February 29, 468

St. Simplicius, March 3, 468–March 10, 483

St. Felix III (II), March 13, 483–February 25 or March 1, 492

St. Gelasius I, March 1, 492–November 21, 496

Anastasius II, November 24, 496–November 19, 498

St. Symmachus, November 22, 498–July 19, 514

[Lawrence, November 22, 498–499, 502–506]

St. Hormisdas, July 20, 514–August 6, 523

St. John I, August 13, 523–May 18, 526

St. Felix IV (III), July 12, 526–September 20 or 22, 530

Boniface II, September 20 or 22, 530–October 17, 532

[Dioscorus, September 20 or 22, 530–October 14, 530 (Possibly a legitimate pope. See his biography.)]

John II, December 31, 532, January 2, 533–May 8, 535

St. Agapetus I, May 13, 535–April 22, 536

St. Silverius, June 8, 536–537

Vigilius, March 29, 537–June 7, 555

Pelagius I, April 16, 556–March 4, 561

John III, July 17, 561–July 13, 574

Benedict I, June 2, 575–July 30, 579

Pelagius II, November 26, 579–February 7, 590

St. Gregory I (The Great), September 3, 590–March 12, 604

Sabinian, March, September 13, 604–February 22, 606

Boniface III, February 19, 607–November 10, 607

St. Boniface IV, August 25, 608–May 8, 615

St. Deusdedit I (Adeodatus I), October 19, 615–November 8, 618

Boniface V, December 23, 619–October 23, 625

Honorius I, October 27, 625–October 12, 638

Severinus, October 638, May 28, 640–August 2, 640

John IV, August, December 24, 640–October 12, 642

Theodore I, October 12, November 24, 642–May 14, 649

St. Martin I, July 5, 649–September 16, 655

St. Eugene I, August 10, 654–June 2, 657

St. Vitalian, July 30, 657–January 27, 672

Adeodatus II (Deusdedit II), April 11, 672–June 16, 676

Donus, November 2, 676–April 11, 678

St. Agatho, June 27, 678–January 10, 681

St. Leo II, January 681, August 17, 682–July 3, 683

St. Benedict II, June 26, 684–May 8, 685

John V, July 23, 685–August 2, 686

Conon, October 23, 686–September 21, 687

[Theodore, 687]

[Paschal, 687]

St. Sergius I, December 15, 687–September 7, 701

John VI, October 30, 701–January 11, 705

John VII, March 1, 705–October 18, 707

Sisinnius, January 15, 708–February 4, 708

Constantine, March 25, 708–April 9, 715

St. Gregory II, May 19, 715–February 11, 731

St. Gregory III, March 18, 731–November 28 741

St. Zachary, December 3, 741–March 15, 752

Stephen II (III), March 26, 752–April 26, 757

St. Paul I, April, May 29, 757–June 28, 767

[Constantine, June 28, July 5, 767–July 30 768]

[Philip, July 31, 768]

Stephen III (IV), August 1, August 7, 768–January 24, 772

Adrian I, February 1, February 9, 772–December 25, 795

St. Leo III, December 26, December 27, 795–June 12, 816

Stephen IV (V), June 22, 816–January 24, 817

St. Paschal I, January 25, 817–February–May 824

Eugene II, February–May 824–August 827

Valentine, August 827–September 827

Gregory IV, September 827, March 29, 828–January 25, 844

[John, January 25, 844]

Sergius II, January 25, 844–January 27, 847

St. Leo IV, January, April 10, 847–July 17, 855

Benedict III, July, September 29, 855–April 17, 858

[Anastasius (The Librarian), September 21–24, 855]

St. Nicholas I (The Great), April 24, 858–November 13, 867

Adrian II, December 14, 867–November or December 872

John VIII, December 14, 872–December 16, 882

Marinus I, December 882–May 15, 884

St. Adrian III, May 17, 884–August or September 885

Stephen V (VI), September 885–September 14, 891

Formosus, October 6, 891–April 4, 896

Boniface VI, April 11, 896–April 26, 896

Stephen VI (VII), May or June 896–July or August 897

Romanus, July or August 897–November 897

Theodore II, December 897–December 897 or January 898

John IX, December 897 or January 898–January–May 900

Benedict IV, January–May 900–July 903

Leo V, July 903–September 903

[Christopher, September 903–January 904]

Sergius III, January 29, 904–April 14, 911

Anastasius III, June or September 911–June or August or October 913

Lando, July or November 913–March 914

John X, March or April 914–May or June 928

Leo VI, May or June 928–December 928 or January 929

Stephen VII (VIII), January 929–February 931

John XI, March 931–January 936

Leo VII, January 936–July 13, 939

Stephen VIII (IX), July 14, 939–October 942

Marinus II, October 30, November, 942–May 946

Agapetus II, May 10, 946–December 955

John XII, December 16, 955–May 14, 964

Leo VIII, December 4, December 6, 963–March 965

Benedict V, May 964–July 4, 964 or 965

John XIII, October 1, 965–November 6, 972

Benedict VI, December 972, January 19, 973–July 974

[Boniface VII, June–July 974; then August 984–July 20, 985]

Benedict VII, October 974–July 10, 983

John XIV, November or December 983–August 20, 984

John XV, August 985–March 996

Gregory V, May 3, 996–February or March 999

[John XVI, February or March 997–May 998]

Silvester II, April 2, 999–May 12, 1003

John XVII, May 16, 1003–November 6, 1003

John XVIII, December 25, 1003–June or July 1009

Sergius IV, July 31, 1009–May 12, 1012

Benedict VIII, May 18, 1012–April 9, 1024

[Gregory, May–December 1012]

John XIX, April 19, 1024–1032

Benedict IX, August or September 1032–September 1044

Silvester III, January 13 or 20, 1045–March 1045

Benedict IX (for second time), March 10, 1045–May 1, 1045

Gregory VI, May 1, 1045–December 20, 1046

Clement II, December 24, 1046–October 9, 1047

Benedict IX (for the third time), October 1047–July 1048

Damasus II, July 17, 1048–August 9, 1048

St. Leo IX, February 2, February 12, 1049–April 19, 1054

Victor II, April 13, 1055–July 28, 1057

Stephen IX (X), August 2, August 3, 1057–March 29, 1058

[Benedict X, April 5, 1058–January 1059]

Nicholas II, December 1058, January 24, 1059–July 27, 1061

Alexander II, September 30, October 1, 1061–April 21, 1073

[Honorius II, October 28, 1061–May 31, 1064]

St. Gregory VII, April 22, June 30, 1073–May 25, 1085

[Clement III, June 25, 1080, March 24, 1084–September 8, 1100]

Bl. Victor III, May 24, 1086, May 9 1087–September 16, 1087

Bl. Urban II, March 12, 1088–July 29, 1099

Paschal II, August 13, August 14, 1099–January 21, 1118

[Theodoric, 1100]

[Albert, 1101]

[Silvester IV, November 18, 1105–April 12 or 13, 1111]

Gelasius II, January 24, March 10, 1118–January 28, 1119

[Gregory VIII, March 10, 1118–April 22, 1121]

Callistus II, February 2, February 9, 1119–December 13 or 14, 1124

Honorius II, December 15, December 21, 1124–February 13 or 14, 1130

[Celestine II, December 1124]

Innocent II, February 14, February 23, 1130–September 24, 1143

[Anacletus II, February 14, February 23, 1130–January 25, 1138]

[Victor IV, March 1138–May 29, 1138]

Celestine II, September 26, October 3, 1143–March 8, 1144

Lucius II, March 12, 1144–February 15, 1145

Bl. Eugene III, February 15, February 18, 1145–July 8, 1153

Anastasius IV, July 12, 1153–December 3, 1154

Adrian IV, December 4, December 5, 1154–September 1, 1159

Alexander III, September 7, September 20, 1159–August 30, 1181

[Victor IV, September 7, October 4, 1159–April 20, 1164]

[Paschal III, April 22, April 26, 1164–September 20, 1168]

[Callistus III, September 1168–August 29, 1178]

[Innocent III, September 29, 1179–January 1180]

Lucius III, September 1, September 6, 1181–November 25, 1185

Urban III, November 25, December 1, 1185–October 20, 1187

Gregory VIII, October 21, October 25, 1187–December 17, 1187

Clement III, December 19, December 20, 1187–March 1191

Celestine III, April 10, April 14, 1191–January 8, 1198

Innocent III, January 8, February 22, 1198–July 16, 1216

Honorius III, July 18, July 24, 1216–March 18, 1227

Gregory IX, March 19, March 21, 1227–August 22, 1241

Celestine IV, October 25, October 28, 1241–November 10, 1241

Innocent IV, June 25, June 28, 1243–December 7, 1254

Alexander IV, December 12, December 20, 1254–May 25, 1261

Urban IV, August 29, September 4, 1261–October 2, 1264

Clement IV, February 5, February 22, 1265–November 29, 1268

Bl. Gregory X, September 1, 1271, March 27, 1272–January 10, 1276

Bl. Innocent V, January 21, February 22, 1276–June 22, 1276

Adrian V, July 11, 1276–August 18, 1276

John XXI, September 16, September 20, 1276–May 20, 1277

Nicholas III, November 25, December 26, 1277–August 22, 1280

Martin IV, February 22, March 23, 1281–March 29, 1285

Honorius IV, April 2, May 20, 1285–April 3, 1287

Nicholas IV, February 22, 1288–April 4, 1292

St. Celestine V, July 5, August 29, 1294–December 13, 1294

Boniface VIII, December 24, 1294, January 23, 1295–October 11, 1303

Bl. Benedict XI, October 22, October 27, 1303–July 7, 1304

Clement V, June 5, November 14, 1305–April 20, 1314

John XXII, August 7, September 5, 1316–December 4, 1334

[Nicholas V, May 12, May 22, 1328–August 25, 1330]

Benedict XII, December 20, 1334, January 8, 1335–April 25, 1342

Clement VI, May 7, May 19, 1342–December 6, 1352

Innocent VI, December 18, December 30, 1352–September 12, 1362

Bl. Urban V, September 28, November 6, 1362–December 19, 1370

Gregory XI, December 30, 1370, January 3, 1371–March 26, 1378

Urban VI, April 8, April 18, 1378–October 15, 1389

Boniface IX, November 2, November 9, 1389–October 1, 1404

Innocent VII, October 17, November 11, 1404–November 6, 1406

Gregory XII, November 30, December 19, 1406–July 4, 1415

[Clement VII, September 20, October 31, 1378–September 16, 1394]

[Benedict XIII, September 28, October 11, 1394–November 29, 1422 or May 23, 1423]

[Alexander V, June 26, July 7, 1409–May 3, 1410]

[John XXIII, May 17, May 25, 1410–May 29, 1415]

Martin V, November 11, November 21, 1417–February 20, 1431

Eugene IV, March 3, March 11, 1431–February 23, 1447

[Felix V, November 5, 1439, July 24, 1440–April 7, 1449]

Nicholas V, March 6, March 19, 1447–March 24, 1455

Callistus III, April 8, April 20, 1455–August 6, 1458

Pius II, August 19, September 3, 1458–August 14, 1464

Paul II, August 30, September 16, 1464–July 26, 1471

Sixtus IV, August 1, August 9, August 25, 1471–August 12, 1484

Innocent VIII, August 29, September 12, 1484–July 25, 1492

Alexander VI, August 11, August 26, 1492–August 18, 1503

Pius III, September 22, October 1 (consecrated), October 8, 1503–October 18, 1503

Julius II, November 1, November 26, 1503–February 21, 1513

Leo X, March 11, March 19, 1513–December 1, 1521

Adrian VI, January 9, August 31, 1522–September 14, 1523

Clement VII, November 19, November 26, 1523–September 25, 1534

Paul III, October 13, November 3, 1534–November 10, 1549

Julius III, February 7, February 22, 1550–March 23, 1555

Marcellus II, April 9, April 10, 1555–May 1, 1555

Paul IV, May 23, May 26, 1555–August 18, 1559

Pius IV, December 26, 1559, January 6, 1560–December 9, 1565

St. Pius V, January 7, January 17, 1566–May 1, 1572

Gregory XIII, May 13, May 25, 1572–April 10, 1585

Sixtus V, April 24, May 1, 1585–August 27, 1590

Urban VII, September 15, 1590–September 27, 1590

Gregory XIV, December 5, December 8, 1590–October 16, 1591

Innocent IX, October 29, November 3, 1591–December 30, 1591

Clement VIII, January 30, February 9, 1592–March 3, 1605

Leo XI, April 1, April 10, 1605–April 27, 1605

Paul V, May 16, May 29, 1605–January 28, 1621

Gregory XV, February 9, February 14, 1621–July 8, 1623

Urban VIII, August 6, September 29, 1623–July 29, 1644

Innocent X, September 15, October 4, 1644–January 7, 1655

Alexander VII, April 7, April 18, 1655–May 22, 1667

Clement IX, June 20, June 26, 1667–December 9, 1669

Clement X, April 29, May 11, 1670–July 22, 1676

Bl. Innocent XI, September 21, October 4, 1676–August 12, 1689

Alexander VIII, October 6, October 16, 1689–February 1, 1691

Innocent XII, July 12, July 15, 1691–September 27, 1700

Clement XI, November 23, November 30, December 8, 1700–March 19, 1721

Innocent XIII, May 8, May 18, 1721–March 7, 1724

Benedict XIII, May 29, June 4, 1724–February 21, 1730

Clement XII, July 12, July 16, 1730–February 6, 1740

Benedict XIV, August 17, August 22, 1740–May 3, 1758

Clement XIII, July 6, July 16, 1758–February 2, 1769

Clement XIV, May 19, May 28, June 4, 1769–September 22, 1774

Pius VI, February 15, February 22, 1775–August 29, 1799

Pius VII, March 14, March 21, 1800–August 20, 1823

Leo XII, September 28, October 5, 1823–February 10, 1829

Pius VIII, March 31, April 5, 1829–November 30, 1830

Gregory XVI, February 2, February 6, 1831–June 1, 1846

Pius IX, June 16, June 21, 1846–February 7, 1878

Leo XIII, February 20, March 3, 1878–July 20, 1903

St. Pius X, August 4, August 9, 1903–August 20, 1914

Benedict XV, September 3, September 6, 1914–January 22, 1922

Pius XI, February 6, February 12, 1922–February 10, 1939

Pius XII, March 2, March 12, 1939–October 9, 1958

John XXIII, October 28, November 4, 1958–June 3, 1963

Paul VI, June 21, June 30, 1963–August 6, 1978

John Paul I, August 26, September 3, 1978–September 28, 1978

John Paul II, October 16, October 22, 1978–April 2, 2005

Benedict XVI, April 24, 2005–

SEE ALSO ANNUARIO PONTIFICIO; CONSECRATED LIFE (CANON LAW); PONTIFF; POPES, ELECTION OF; POPES, NAMES OF.

BIBLIOGRAPHY

Erich Ludwig Eduard Caspar, *Geschichte des Papsttums von den Anfängen bis zur Höhe der Weltherrschaft*, 2 vols. (Tübingen 1930–1933).

Louis Marie Olivier Duchesne, ed., *Le Liber pontificalis*, edited by (Paris 1886–1892).

Gerhart B. Ladner, *Die Papstbildnisse des Altertums und des Mittelalters*, vol. 1 (Vatican City 1941).

Henri Leclercq, *Dictionnaire d'archéologie chrétienne et de liturgie*, ed. Fernand Cabrol, Henri Leclercq, and H. I. Marrou (Paris 1907–1953), 13.1:1111–1345.

A. Mercati, "The New List of the Popes," *Mediaeval Studies* 9 (1947): 71–80.

Ludwig Pastor, *The History of the Popes from the Close of the Middle Ages*, 40 vols. (London-St. Louis 1938–1961).

Franz Xaver Seppelt, *Geschichte der Päpste von den Anfängen bis zur Mitte des zwanzigsten Jahrhunderts* (Munich 1954–1959).

*Much of the information in this article is taken from the notes that accompany the list of popes in the *Annuario Pontificio* (2008), 7–20.

Thomas Edward Carson
Editor, Gale Publishing
Lecturer in History and Humanities, Wayne State University, Detroit, Michigan

Douglas A. Dentino
Editor, Cengage Learning (2009)

PORTLAND, ARCHDIOCESE OF

The metropolitan see of Portland (*Portlandensis*) was erected as a vicariate apostolic on December 1, 1843, and created the Archdiocese of Oregon City on July 24, 1846; its name was changed to the Archdiocese of Portland, Oregon, on September 26, 1928. It comprises 29,717 square miles in western Oregon, from the Cascade Mountains to the Pacific Ocean between California and the Columbia River, with a total population in 2007 of 3,141,515, including 400,440 Catholics (*The Official Catholic Directory* 2007, p. 1055). The metropolitan province of Portland includes the Dioceses of Baker in Oregon, Boise in Idaho, and Great Falls-Billings and Helena in Montana.

Early History. When Oregon country was jointly occupied by Great Britain and the United States (1818–1846), it was the home of native peoples, explorers, and fur traders. Gradually the Hudson's Bay Company, under the guidance of Dr. John McLoughlin (1784–1857) at Fort Vancouver, dominated the territory. French Canadians, mostly Catholics, and fur trappers settled in the Willamette Valley near St. Paul around 1830, and in 1834 they sent a letter to Bishop Joseph PROVENCHER of Red River, Canada, begging for priests. The bishop arranged to bring the Columbia area into his vicariate and eventually responded to the settlers' requests. In anticipation of the arrival of priests, the French Canadians built a log church on French Prairie in 1836, the first Catholic church in Oregon.

Blanchet. The ARCHBISHOP of Quebec selected Francis Norbert BLANCHET (1795–1883) to be vicar general of the Columbia Mission on April 17, 1838. On May 3, 1838, Father Blanchet left Montreal for Red River, where Father Modeste Demers (1809–1871) joined him. The two missionaries reached Fort Vancouver on November 24, 1838. Soon after their arrival Blanchet visited the log church on French Prairie and celebrated the first Mass in what became the state of Oregon and dedicated the chapel to St. Paul the Apostle on January 6, 1839.

Pierre DE SMET, S.J., working in the Rocky Mountains, learned of the priests in the Northwest, and in 1842 he came to Fort Vancouver and St. Paul Mission to discuss the future of the mission with Blanchet and Demers. On their own initiative, the three men laid out a plan for the development of the church in Oregon country. De Smet left for Europe to secure personnel; Demers went to New Caledonia (now British Columbia) to expand the missions to native tribes; and Blanchet continued to serve the existing missions, writing to church authorities urging support for the plan.

In August 1844, De Smet returned to Oregon with a party of five JESUITS and six Sisters of NOTRE DAME DE NAMUR. Meanwhile, Blanchet's letters influenced the decision to elevate the Columbia Mission to a vicariate on December 1, 1843. When the news reached Oregon on November 22, 1844, Francis Blanchet reluctantly accepted the nomination as BISHOP of the Vicariate of Philadelphia (later changed to Drasa). Blanchet journeyed to Montreal, where he was consecrated bishop on July 25, 1845, and from there he sailed for Europe to gather personnel and financial support. Assisted by Vatican insiders, Blanchet convinced the HOLY SEE to establish the ecclesiastical Province of Oregon City in Oregon country; it had two suffragan bishops, a bishop of Walla Walla and a bishop of Vancouver Island. On June 18, 1846, the U.S. Senate ratified the treaty bringing Oregon into the Union. On July 24, 1846, Oregon City became the second ARCHDIOCESE in the United States.

Blanchet's triumphal return to St. Paul on August 26, 1847, with a group of twenty-one, including eight priests and seven more sisters, inspired a flurry of ecclesiastical activity. In December 1848, Archbishop Blanchet officially moved to Oregon City, the seat of his see. Following the Whitman Massacre in 1848, during which the Cayuse tribe killed fourteen people at the Protestant mission, Catholics were blamed for inciting the massacre, and widespread anti–catholicism ensued. Along with the debts from building and the departure of much of the male population to the California Gold Rush (1848–1855), the archdiocese struggled to avoid bankruptcy. The desperate archbishop made a successful two-year trip to South America to raise funds.

The Oregon Donation Land Law of 1850 drew population to the territory. Although few of the newcomers were Catholics, the Church slowly recovered and established new parishes. Oregon City, however, failed to develop, and in 1862 Blanchet transferred his episcopal residence to Portland. In 1851 the Reverend James Croke had established the parish of the Immaculate Conception, and the church that he built became the pro-cathedral. Twelve Sisters of the Holy Names came from Quebec to revive Catholic education in Oregon in 1859. They soon had schools throughout the state and by 1871 had a novitiate in Portland. Catholic lay societies grew, particularly in Portland. With the assistance of the St. Vincent de Paul Society, the Sisters of Providence opened St. Vincent's Hospital in Portland in 1875.

While Blanchet was in ROME attending the first Vatican Council (1868–1870), a Portland group established a newspaper, *The Catholic Sentinel*, which is still in existence. Blanchet used the paper to battle inequities in Grant's Peace Policy, which turned supervision of native reservations over to religious groups, most often Protestant ones.

Establishment of the Vicariate of Idaho in 1868 reduced the size of the archdiocese, but the resignation of its bishop in 1876 forced Blanchet to take over its administration once again. The aging Blanchet tried for some time to resign. Charles John SEGHERS, bishop of Vancouver Island, became his coadjutor in 1878. After he arrived in Portland in July of 1879, Blanchet retired in 1880 and died on June 18, 1883.

Early Archbishops. Bishop Seghers (1837–1886) left Vancouver Island reluctantly. While waiting for acceptance of Blanchet's retirement, Seghers toured the archdiocese, visiting places no priest had ever been before. A consummate missionary, Seghers paid special attention to the native peoples. During the Seghers administration the BENEDICTINES came to Oregon and established an abbey at Mount Angel, and Benedictine Sisters took up educational work. The archdiocese was consolidated within the state boundaries when vicars apostolic were named for Idaho and Montana. While at a meeting in Rome, Seghers resigned from Portland to return as bishop to the Diocese of Vancouver Island. He was killed by a crazed assistant on November 28, 1886, while on a missionary trip to Alaska.

William Hickley GROSS, bishop of Savannah, became third archbishop of Oregon City on February 1, 1885. He was the first American-born archbishop of Oregon City, the first American-born bishop in the West, and the first member of a RELIGIOUS congregation, the REDEMPTORISTS, to become an archbishop in Oregon. One of his first acts was to dedicate the second Cathedral of the Immaculate Conception in Portland, begun in 1878. By 1894 this building had been replaced by a temporary CATHEDRAL elsewhere because the area around the second cathedral had become commercial.

Gross attracted many new religious communities to the state. Not content with importing nuns, he created his own congregation, now known as the Sisters of ST. MARY OF OREGON. During this period the Church grew rapidly, added new parishes, and dramatically expanded the parochial school system. With Gross's encouragement and support, the Benedictines founded Mount Angel College (1887) and a seminary (1889) at their abbey. Social work advanced with the arrival of several congregations of sisters, who opened institutions to serve various needy groups. Eastern Oregon parishes also grew during this period, with additional parishes, schools, and a Catholic hospital in Baker City.

Archbishop Gross died suddenly in Baltimore on November 14, 1898, and was buried there. Again the Diocese of Vancouver Island provided an archbishop when Bishop Alexander Christie (1848–1925) became the fourth archbishop of Oregon City in February of 1899. The archdiocese was deeply in debt, but the population was growing and more varied than before. In 1903 the archdiocese shrank to its current size, with the establishment of the Diocese of Baker City in the eastern part of the state.

Later Archbishops. Archbishop Christie purchased a former Methodist college in Portland in 1901 to found a school, originally named Columbia University. In 1902 Holy Cross priests and brothers took over the institution, which became the University of Portland. Anti–Catholicism, led by the KU KLUX KLAN, played an important role in Oregon affairs in Christie's time. In 1922 the state legislature passed the Oregon School Bill intended to force all children up to the age of sixteen to attend public schools. Designed to close parochial schools, it lead to the famous OREGON SCHOOL CASE. The Sisters of the Holy Names challenged the LAW and won. The state in turn appealed to the U.S. Supreme Court, which declared the law unconstitutional in 1925. Christie organized the Catholic Truth Society, which joined the KNIGHTS OF COLUMBUS in fighting for Catholic rights. Beginning in 1909, visits from chapel cars, sponsored by the Catholic Church Extension Society, led many towns to build churches. A chapel car was a converted railroad car built to serve as a small church. When the train stopped in an isolated community, a priest would say Mass in the portable chapel. Archbishop Christie proposed a new edifice to replace the building that had served as a temporary cathedral, but as his dream for a new cathedral was about to be realized, he died on April 6, 1925.

His replacement was a former teacher and college president from Iowa, Edward Daniel Howard (1877–

1983), destined to serve for more than forty-two years, from 1924 to 1966. Howard immediately transferred the archdiocese from Oregon City to Portland, which was officially effected in 1928. With the archdiocese near bankruptcy, Howard consolidated financing and set up a chancery office. The Catholic Truth Society (today the Oregon Catholic Press) began publishing weekly missals that were distributed all over the country. Social work was coordinated under Catholic Charities as was education, under the superintendent of education. The archbishop supported the CATHOLIC ACTION movement and was deeply involved in social welfare problems, for which he received numerous awards. He also encouraged apostolates for racial minorities. One of his special projects was the development of a diocesan-supported Central Catholic High School in Portland to encourage candidates for the priesthood. Archbishop Howard was the oldest archbishop from the United States at Vatican II. He implemented changes and allowed innovations, starting a priests' senate and encouraging ecumenical programs. In 1966 he resigned at the age of eighty-nine, and died at the age of 105.

Robert Joseph Dwyer (1908–1976), bishop of Reno, succeeded Howard. Having been a newspaper editor, he continued to write erudite, articulate columns for the *Catholic Sentinel*. While church programs and activities increased in the post–Vatican II era, the loss of priests and nuns contributed to school closures. Conflicts over Vatican II changes caused turmoil. Dwyer set up a business manager for the archdiocese and established a formal budget and standard accounting practices. He created a vicariate for the Spanish-speaking and encouraged inner-city social work. The Maronite rite came to the state, the permanent diaconate was reinstituted, and Newman centers at colleges and universities expanded. Failing health forced Dwyer's resignation in 1974.

The first native northwesterner to become archbishop of Portland was Cornelius Michael Power (1913–1997). Former bishop of Yakima, he was appointed as seventh archbishop of Portland on January 22, 1974. Continuing the work of Archbishop Dwyer, he organized the archdiocesean bureaucracy using a business model. Rome appointed two auxiliary bishops, Paul Waldschmidt, C.S.C., and Kenneth Steiner to assist him. Power divided the archdiocese into area vicariates, established a Southeast Asian vicariate, and welcomed the Byzantine Rite to the area. He retired in 1986.

Installed as eighth archbishop of Portland on September 22, 1986, William Joseph Levada (1936–), supported lay ministry, ecumenism, and social programs. He reorganized Catholic Charities and carried on a successful campaign to provide a retirement home for priests. Catholic school enrollment again grew. In 1993 the archdiocese formed a political action committee that carried on a vigorous, but ultimately unsuccessful,

Filing for Chapter 11. *Archdiocese of Portland Archbishop John Vlazny speaks during a press conference in Portland, Ore., Tuesday, July 6, 2004. Vlazny announced that the Portland Archdiocese would file for Chapter 11 bankruptcy.* AP IMAGES

campaign against the Oregon assisted-suicide bill. Under the leadership of Archbishop Levada, renovation work began on St. Mary's Cathedral of the Immaculate Conception in 1995. Originally dedicated in February 1926, the $6.5 renovation included saving the STAINED GLASS windows—some of which date back to the 1850s. The nine Emil Jacques murals, completed in 1936, were cleaned and renewed. The cathedral was rededicated on February 14, 1996. Levada left in 1995 to become archbishop of San Francisco. In May 2005 Pope BENEDICT XVI appointed Archbishop Levada prefect of the Congregation for the DOCTRINE OF THE FAITH. Levada was created a CARDINAL on May 24, 2006.

For only the second time, a member of a religious community became archbishop of Portland when Francis Eugene George, O.M.I. (1937–), who had been bishop of Yakima, came to Portland in 1996. He presided over the sesquicentennial celebration of the archdiocese on July 24, 1996. His was the shortest administration of any Portland archbishop, not quite one year, before he was named archbishop of Chicago in 1997. He was created a cardinal on February 21, 1998.

The Most Reverend John George Vlazny (1937–), bishop of Winona, was appointed on October 28, 1997, to succeed him. The archdiocese celebrated the second millennium of Christianity with a Eucharist 2000 Mass at the Portland Memorial Coliseum that 10,000 people attended. Four parishes in the north section of Portland were consolidated into Holy Cross parish, and a new

parish dedicated to St. Juan Diego was created in Washington County. Three elementary schools closed; however, an elementary school, a middle school, and high school opened. During the ten year period from 1997 to 2007, the Catholic population increased by more than forty percent. In 2007 Catholics in the archdiocese were served by 153 diocesan Priests, 167 religious order priests, 90 religious brothers, 475 religious sisters, and 37 permanent deacons (*The Official Catholic Directory* 2007, p. 1055).

Archbishop Vlazny served during one of the most difficult times in archdiocesan history. The clergy sex abuse scandal came to light in 2000. By 2004 the archdiocese had paid out $53 million in settlements on more than 100 claims. Faced with many more claims, Archbishop Vlazny filed for Chapter 11 Bankruptcy on July 6, 2004—the first diocese in the United States to file for bankruptcy. The archdiocese emerged from bankruptcy on September 28, 2007. The evangelization mission of the Church continued throughout this challenging time.

SEE ALSO BAKER, DIOCESE OF; BENEDICTINE NUNS AND SISTERS; CATHOLIC CHARITIES USA; CHURCH AND STATE; IDAHO, CATHOLIC CHURCH IN; MISSION AND MISSIONS; MONTANA, CATHOLIC CHURCH IN; OREGON, CATHOLIC CHURCH IN; SEX ABUSE CRISIS; ST. VINCENT DE PAUL, SOCIETY OF; VATICAN COUNCIL I; VATICAN COUNCIL II.

BIBLIOGRAPHY

Archdiocese of Portland Official Web site, available from: http:// www.archdpdx.org (accessed October 17, 2008).

Patricia Brandt and Lillian A. Pereyra, *Adapting in Eden: Oregon's Catholic Minority, 1838–1986* (Pullman, Wash. 2002).

John R. Laidlaw, *The Catholic Church in Oregon and the Work of Its Archbishops* (Smithtown, N.Y. 1977).

Sister Letitia Mary Lyons, *Francis Norbert Blanchet and the Founding of the Oregon Missions, 1838–1848* (Washington, D.C. 1940).

The Official Catholic Directory, 2007 (New Providence, N.J. 2007).

Edwin Vincent O'Hara, *Pioneer Catholic History of Oregon*, 4th ed. (Paterson, N.J. 1939).

Wilfred P. Schoenberg, *A History of the Catholic Church in the Pacific Northwest, 1743–1983* (Washington, D.C. 1987).

Mary Jo Tully, *Archdiocese of Portland in Oregon, 150th Anniversary, 1846–1996* (Strasbourg, France 1996).

Patricia Brandt
Retired Professor (Reference Librarian)
Oregon State University, Corvalis, Ore.

Melvin P. (Bud) Bunce
Director of Communications
Archdiocese of Portland, Ore. (2009)

PSYCHOLOGY (CONTEMPORARY)

Roman Catholicism and psychology have had a complex, and at times conflicted, history. At the turn of the twentieth century, a "new psychology" of experimentalism emerged that separated itself from both PHILOSOPHY and THEOLOGY. This movement was followed shortly by the psychoanalytical psychology of Sigmund FREUD. Due to Freud's ATHEISM and philosophical DETERMINISM, a great deal of animosity developed between psychology and religion, including Roman Catholicism. In response to these developments, early Catholic psychologists, such as Edward PACE (1861–1938) and Thomas Verner MOORE (1877–1969) at The CATHOLIC UNIVERSITY OF AMERICA, promoted a neoscholastic psychology, which they envisioned as being an empirical psychology with a SOUL.

In other clinical circles Catholic mental-health clinicians emerged, including Sr. Annette Walters (1911–1978), Dr. Francis Braceland (1900–1985), and Dr. Leo Bartemeier (1895–1982). These three became recognized leaders in the fields of psychology, psychiatry, and psychoanalysis, respectively. Their clinical leadership fostered greater dialogue and understanding between psychology and Catholicism. Institutions at such places as ST. LOUIS UNIVERSITY, Fordham University, and Loyola University of Chicago developed reputable psychology programs that were soon accredited by the American Psychological Association. As a result, these universities produced Catholic clinicians, educators, and experimentalists for psychology's emerging fields.

Led by Fr. William Bier, S.J. (1911–1980), the American Catholic Psychological Association was founded in 1947. This organization served as an important instrument to "bring psychology to Catholics and to bring a Catholic viewpoint into psychology" (Bier 1975, p. 4). The St. John's Summer Institute in Collegeville, Minnesota, became a vital vehicle for this goal. From 1954 to 1973 dozens of the leading psychologists, psychiatrists, and even psychoanalysts came together at St. John's to educate clergy and religious alike. Moreover, the address that Pope PIUS XII gave to participants at the 1953 International Congress of Psychotherapy and Clinical Psychology served as an impetus to both the Summer Institute and the opening of a dialogue between Catholicism and clinical psychology.

Catholic Institutional Appropriation of Psychology. By the time of the Second Vatican Council, and its spirit of *aggiornamento*, Church authorities had a more collaborative relationship with clinical psychology. From this collaboration sprang a new emphasis upon "experience" as a category of Catholic thought. One example of such an emphasis on "experience" may be seen in the way the council document, *Gaudium et spes*, led the Church's canon lawyers to consider the sacrament of marriage as having the twofold purpose of fostering a mature partnership between a man and a woman for life (*Consortium vitae*) in addition to the procreation of children. This dual purpose had implications for marriage tribunals in cases where one or both partners were not developmentally mature (i.e., psychologically) to enter into such a partnership. Consequently annulments based on psychological facts became more readily accessible. Controversy, however, continues around how to best incorporate developmental factors into the dissolution of the marital bond.

In response to the increased mental-health demands and increases in government and private funding during the years following the council, psychology departments opened and expanded in Catholic colleges and universities, and an increasing number of priests and religious were trained in clinical psychology and pastoral counseling. It became commonplace for those applying to seminaries and religious life to undergo a series of psychological tests and interviews. Ongoing and midlife formation programs for priests and religious were encouraged, with many of them having a psychological emphasis. At the same time, pastoral programs in dioceses, parishes, schools, and retreat centers began using the methods and understandings advocated by psychologists in initiating and deepening programs for those considering marriage, those already married, and those who had experienced separation, DIVORCE, or the death of a spouse.

Most of the conflict between Catholicism and the clinical psychologies had subsided by the mid-1970s. In contrast to their previous aversions, the attitude of Church authorities gradually became more open to the possible uses of psychological findings and theories in tending to their flocks. For example, Catholic parishes, schools, and retreat centers began adapting psychological insights, strategies, and tests for their own purposes. Some writers, however, cautioned that this new attitude was too accommodating in its appropriation of psychology.

Phillip Rieff, in his seminal work, *The Triumph of the Therapeutic* (1965), issued an early caution about the dangers of appropriating too much psychology. The Catholic author and psychologist Paul Vitz, at New York University, also warned against this tendency in his book *Psychology As Religion* (1977). Vitz, for example, found problematic the humanistic psychological writings of Erich Fromm, Carl ROGERS, Abraham Maslow, and Rollo May. For Vitz such writers glorified the SELF to the extent that they had a tendency to make psychology a religion.

Conversely, pastoral counseling and spiritual direction programs at Catholic universities have shown, by means of more integrated pastoral training and supervised applications, that psychology can be appropriated within the framework of Catholic thought and values. Such institutions have included Duquesne University, Loyola University of Chicago, Fordham University, Creighton University, Loyola College of Maryland, Boston College, Iona College, Seattle University, and Neumann College.

Integration of Psychology and Spirituality. Since the closing of the Second Vatican Council, former hostilities between psychologists and Church authorities have all but disappeared. Indeed, the Catholic psychologists have demonstrated ways in which psychological concepts can promote psychological as well as moral development. Important psychospiritual integrative steps were made through the writings of such luminaries as Charles A. Curran (1913–1978) and Eugene Kennedy at Loyola University of Chicago, as well as Adrian van Kaam and Susan Muto at Duquesne University. Initially, these writings focused on the psychological and spiritual formation of priests and religious. By the mid-1970s, however, with the increased interest of the laity in spiritual direction and spiritual literature, a new wave of psychospiritual literature had emerged.

The Dutch priest and psychologist Henri NOUWEN (1932–1996) was the most notable writer in this respect. Having received training in pastoral psychology at the Menninger Clinic, Nouwen, through his more than forty books and innumerable articles and presentations, was able to combine sound psychological insights and spiritual wisdom in a way that could be easily understood by his audience.

Indian Jesuit and psychologist Anthony DeMello (1931–1987), although not as prolific a writer as Nouwen, proved himself to be another popular Catholic psychospiritual writer. Combining the popular wisdom of India with the clinical training he received as a graduate student at Loyola University of Chicago, DeMello's books and videos were provocative and profound. His writings and tapes have been especially used within retreat settings. It should be noted, however, that while the books he published when he was alive were accepted by Church authorities, some of the writings transcribed at his retreats and published posthumously have been criticized.

Servite sister and psychologist Joyce Rupp has in recent decades been arguably the most popular American Catholic psychospiritual writer. By means of her religious and clinical training, Rupp's writings have proved to be particularly successful in the areas of bereavement and midlife transitions.

Beginning in the 1970s a movement emerged at many Catholic retreat centers that incorporated psychological understandings into spirituality. Insights gleaned from the writings of Carl Jung and Carl Rogers were especially utilized. One example of this psychospiritual integration occurred at the Jesuit Spiritual Center for Spiritual Growth in Wernersville, Pennsylvania. Since the early 1970s, Ignatian spirituality training programs at the Jesuit Spiritual Center, initially coordinated by Fr. George Schemel, S.J., and Sr. Judith Roemer, have incorporated Jungian insights about archetypes, symbols, and the unconscious. Moreover, midlife spiritual programs given by the psychologists Sr. Ann Brennan and Sr. Janice Brewi have been similarly influenced by Jungian concepts.

Besides Catholic clergy and religious writers, a growing number of laymen and laywomen have emerged as popular psychospiritual writers. They include Robert Wicks, a clinical psychologist and university professor. Wicks has written more than thirty books and made numerous public presentations in dioceses throughout the United States and abroad. Among his notable topics have been the influences of psychological factors such as stress as they relate to an individual's ministry. During this period another leading psychospiritual author with a Catholic formative background has been Thomas Moore. Combining his experience of twelve years as a Catholic monk with his psychotherapeutic training, Moore's *Care of the Soul* (1992) reached the best-seller list. The clinical psychologists Carolyn Gratton and Fran Ferder have also made important contributions to psychospiritual literature.

Priest, psychologist, and television host Fr. Benedict Groeschel, C.F.R., has incorporated his clinical training into his sacramental perspectives. His writings indicate the importance of blending a healthy psychology into the formation of one's faith. At the same time, Groeschel has criticized a tendency among some psychospiritual authors of having lost touch with the traditions of Catholic spiritual devotions and practices for the purpose of promoting psychological growth. It seems that for Groeschel psychology should be in the service of the Church's traditions in theology, and not vice versa.

Another significant Catholic author whose writings have served to establish the field of spiritual direction has been the clinical psychologist Fr. William Barry, S.J. Barry's book, *The Practice of Spiritual Direction* (1980), coauthored with his Jesuit colleague William Connelly, is the seminal work in the fledging field of spiritual direction. Drawing on some of the key principles of psychotherapy, the book provides a means whereby principles pertaining to psychotherapy can inform avenues of spiritual direction. In addition, Barry has served as the editor of the quarterly magazine, *Human Development*. Founded in 1980 by the psychiatrist Fr.

James Gill, S.J., M.D. (1925–2003), this periodical has provided its audience with a look at current psychological trends related to religious growth and leadership.

While not practicing psychologists, other popular Catholic spiritual writers have incorporated many psychological insights into their writings. These include George Aschenbrenner, Maureen Conroy, Richard Rohr, and Ronald Rolheiser.

Religion and Personality Theorists. The ancient and perennial issues of faith and reason are reflected in the contemporary quest to integrate psychology and Catholic thought. Expressed traditionally in the Thomistic axiom *gratia perficit naturam* (grace perfects nature), the axiom has achieved particular relevance in the thought of psychiatrist and psychoanalyst Fr. William Meissner, S.J. Since 1961 he has published a series of articles and numerous books suggesting how the axiom can be incorporated within a psychoanalytical framework. For example, in *Ignatius of Loyola: The Psychology of a Saint* (1990) Meissner discusses the psychological conditions whereby God's grace influenced and inspired the psychic structure of Ignatius.

In her seminal work, *The Birth of the Living God* (1979), Catholic psychoanalyst Ann Marie Rizzuto employed the psychoanalytic developmental theory of Donald Winnicott to overturn Freud's dictum that religious belief is an illusion. Winnicott, a leading British psychoanalyst, clinically argued that illusion is a necessary ingredient for a child's journey to maturity. His position enabled Rizzuto to posit that a child's early image of God emerges out of a healthy sense of illusion. Meanwhile Catholic psychoanalyst Joanne M. Greer has promoted both psychoanalytical religious research and quantitative measures of the psychology of religion.

In the area of moral and religious education, the developmental psychologies of Lawrence Kohlberg, Jane Loevinger, James W. Fowler, and Robert Kegan have been especially influential. Their influence may be found in the pastoral psychological writings of Elizabeth Leibert, who has incorporated the use of developmental theories into spiritual formation and practices.

Empirical Psychospiritual Research. A growing number of articles, books, and journals are being published about the psychology of religion that have relevance to Catholics. Professional associations such as the American Psychological Association, the American Counseling Association, and the American Association of Pastoral Counselors have, through their respective publications, disseminated pertinent findings by psychologists of religion, pastoral counselors, and religious-minded psychologists to their respective professional audiences. For instance, the research of Kenneth

Pargament about religious factors used in coping, Harold Koenig concerning spiritual factors in aging, and Crystal Park pertaining to variables of religion and meaning-making frameworks in coping have led to flourishing streams of psychospiritual research. Research in this area includes Michael Donohue's social-psychological research on sexual abstinence, Ralph Piedmont's psychometrical work on spiritual transcendence scales, and Nichole Murray-Swank's work on images of God.

Meanwhile, a new force in psychology known as "positive psychology" has ushered in a new stream of psychospiritual literature. Psychologists Martin Seligman, Mihaly Czikszentmihalyi, Robert Emmons, and Christopher Peterson, whose research has been funded generously by the Templeton Foundation, have been some of the major proponents of such psychological research focused upon positive factors in the human personality. As a result, psychologists have engaged in extensive studies on quasi-religious variables such as GRATITUDE, HOPE, OPTIMISM, and VIRTUE. Important contributions within the Catholic community from the positive psychology perspective have been made by Joseph Ciarrocchi on virtue and Fr. Charles Shelton, S.J., on gratitude.

Critical Moral Issues. By far the most significant interactions between psychology and Catholicism have revolved around the crisis of clerical sexual abuse. In addition to the moral and legal ramifications of sexual abuse, Church authorities have turned to psychologists and psychiatrists for advice about prevention and treatment. Since the 1970s, various areas of clinical psychology and psychiatry have evolved in their understanding of post–traumatic stress disorder and in the diagnosis and treatment of PEDOPHILIA and ephebophilia (sexual attraction to post–pubescent adolescents). As a result, standards for deciding about prevention and treatment went through several stages and culminated in the Dallas resolutions of the UNITED STATES CONFERENCE OF CATHOLIC BISHOPS in 2002. These resolutions responded to the six areas of concern to which they were mandated to respond:

(1) Dealing effectively with priests who sexually abuse minors and others;

(2) assisting victims/survivors;

(3) addressing morale of bishops and priests;

(4) screening candidates for ministry;

(5) assisting bishops in assessing possible reassignment; and

(6) regarding church employees and volunteers. (U.S. Conference of Catholic Bishops, "USCCB Efforts

to Combat Clergy Sexual Abuse Against Minors: A Chronology 1982–2006")

The clinical writings of Len Sperry, Thomas Plante, Paul McHugh, Br. Sean Sammon, and Fr. Gerald McGlone, in addition to the clinical leadership of Sr. Donna Markham at Southdown Institute, Ontario, Canada, and Fr. Stephen Rossetti at St. Luke's Institute in Tacoma Park, Maryland, have been influential in establishing more effective church standards for diagnosis, prevention, and treatment.

Finally, in addition to the psychological issues raised by the moral concerns surrounding abortion, addiction, martial infidelity, and divorce, there has been a growing interest in the psychological effects of genetic engineering. The writings of individuals such as Patrick McNamara, a professor of neurology at the Boston University School of Medicine, suggest that future psychological research will have important insights to contribute to the Church's pastoral approach to biological and social genetics. Future interactions between the psychological disciplines and Catholicism will no doubt involve the psychological ramifications of genetics as they pertain to moral concerns and decision-making.

SEE ALSO AGGIORNAMENTO; HOMOSEXUALITY, REPARATIVE THERAPY FOR; JUNG, CARL GUSTAV; MARRIAGE LEGISLATION (CANON LAW); MORAL THEOLOGY; MORALITY; PSYCHOLOGY (CLASSICAL); PSYCHOTHERAPY; SEX ABUSE CRISIS; SPIRITUAL THEOLOGY; THOMISM.

BIBLIOGRAPHY
William C. Bier, S.J., "PIRi-Bridge between the ACPA and APA," presidential address to Psychologists Interested in Religious Issues: Division 36 of the American Psychological Association, August 30, 1975, 4.

Joseph Ciarrocchi, "Introduction to Special Section on Positive Psychology." *Research in the Social Study of Religion* 18 (2007): 97.

Mihaly Csikszentmihalyi and Isabella Selega Csikszentmihalyi, eds. *A Life Worth Living: Contributions to Positive Psychology* (New York 2006).

C. Kevin Gillespie, *Psychology and American Catholicism: From Confession to Therapy?* (New York 2001).

Benedict Groeschel, *Stumbling Blocks or Stepping Stones: Spiritual Answers to Psychological Questions* (New York 1987).

Robert Kugelmann, "Neoscholastic Psychology Revisited." *History of Psychology* 8, no 2 (2005): 131–175.

Elizabeth Liebert, *Changing Life Patterns: Adult Development in Spiritual Direction*(St. Louis, Mo. 2000).

William W. Meissner, *Ignatius of Loyola: The Psychology of a Saint* (New Haven, Conn. 1990).

Pope Pius XII, "Psychotherapy and Religion: An Address to the Fifth International Congress of Psychotherapy and Clinical Psychology," *Catholic Mind* (July 1953): 435.

Phillip Reiff, *The Triumph of the Therapeutic* (Chicago 1965).

Ana Marie Rizzuto, *The Birth of the Living God* (Chicago 1979).

Charles Shelton, "Gratitude: Considerations from a Moral Perspective," in *The Psychology of Gratitude*, edited by Robert Emmons and Michael E. McCullough (New York 2004), 257–281.

U.S. Conference of Catholic Bishops, "USCCB Efforts to Combat Clergy Sexual Abuse against Minors: A Chronology 1982–2006," available from http://www.usccb.org/comm/combatefforts.shtml (accessed March 3, 2008).

Paul C. Vitz, *Psychology As Religion: The Cult of Self-Worship* (Grand Rapids, Mich. 1977).

Robert W. Wicks, *The Resilient Clinician* (New York 2006).

Rev. C. Kevin Gillespie SJ
Associate Professor of Pastoral Counseling
Loyola College (2009)

PSYCHOTHERAPY

PSYCHOTHERAPY is a planned process of using psychological theory and practice to assist individuals, couples, and families to modify dysfunctional feelings, thoughts, and behaviors. While a fairly wide array of clinical theories exist, in actual practice a handful of approaches dominate the field. Each approach has its own view of human PERSONALITY, psychological health and pathology, approach to assessment and intervention, therapists' roles, and explanations for change. Marital, family, and parenting issues are among the most frequent presenting problems in psychotherapists' offices.

Marital and Family Therapy. Two marital therapies stand out as especially effective. Emotionally Focused Marital Therapy views marital conflict as a result of failed emotional connection and broken attachment bonds, so it seeks to create a safe environment for partners to share and respond with increased vulnerability. Integrative Couple Therapy assists partners in distinguishing changeable from unchangeable dimensions of the relationship and in bringing acceptance to the former and negotiation to the latter. This unique approach reminds one of the Serenity Prayer.

Bowen Family Systems Theory helps individuals, couples, and families explore the intergenerational transmission of anxiety and defensive reactions. Therapy makes use of the genogram, a clinical version of a family tree, and the timeline to explore constricting relational patterns, to develop insight into their dynamics, and to create new and free responses to current reality. Bowenian approaches have proven quite useful in religious formation work and clinical pastoral education contexts and in understanding relational struggles in parish, school, and religious community contexts.

Internal Family Systems Therapy (IFS) is an exciting new approach to balancing interpersonal and intrapsychic dimensions of counseling. IFS views personality as complex, consisting of many parts, and governed by a central self, which is also referred to as SOUL. Persons and relationships do not function optimally when parts are out of balance and self-leadership is compromised. The approach resonates with Thomas Merton's understanding of True and False Selves. For Merton, true self is a person's best self, one's center, where a person is most alive and also most in touch with God. False selves are those parts of the self that distract and/or preoccupy a person in ways that are less than life-giving.

Traditional Therapy. Among the more traditional and frequently practiced approaches are the following: Psychoanalytic (includes Self-Psychology), Object Relations Theory, and Attachment Theory. These approaches pay particular attention to the role of early parent–infant/child relationships as they influence current psychological functioning. Therapy is especially attentive to the transference and counter-transference dynamics between therapist and client. That is, people carry old emotional models of themselves, their relationships, and the world into current interactions with the expectation that the present will unfold like the past.

Rogerian Person-Centered approaches tend to be more "here-and-now" focused and emphasize a person's growth potential. Therapist empathy, warmth, and positive regard are essential. Gestalt Therapy is process-oriented and seeks to bring clients into a here-and-now awareness of the emotional and relational dimensions of their lives.

Cognitive and Behavioral approaches assist the client in modifying negative, dysfunctional belief and behavioral systems respectively. Clients are taught to monitor and challenge constraining BELIEFS, unrealistic expectations, and faulty attributions as well as to increase desirable or decrease undesirable behaviors.

Innovative Approaches. An integrative revolution describes the blending of the best of approaches across traditions. For example, cognitive and behavioral are often now a single approach. Rogerian empathy, warmth, and positive regard are considered foundational to most approaches. Therapy increasingly pays attention to the whole person and seeks to balance interpersonal with intrapsychic; feeling, thinking and behavior; past, present, and future; and strengths with symptoms.

Spirituality is drawing increasing attention across a variety of clinical contexts. Clients want to explore their values and search for meaning and a sense of vocation; they hunger for something more than material well-being. They want to explore the place of PRAYER and MEDITATION in their lives, to know about and practice forgiveness, and to retrieve and/or construct the ritual dimensions of their lives.

Related to the growing interest in the spiritual is the new field of Positive Psychology. This approach emphasizes identifying and utilizing one's core values and strengths; practicing gratitude and service; enhancing positive emotions, HOPE, and OPTIMISM; and building HAPPINESS. This is a significant shift from psychology's long-term preoccupation with pathology and a mental illness model of patients.

Research about the body and the brain is having a tremendous influence on psychotherapy practice. Findings about human reactivity—how people are hard wired for fight-flight reactions, how perceptions narrow with increased reactivity, and how important it is to develop emotional skillfulness (awareness, expressiveness, empathy, calming, and soothing)—are feeding back directly to practice.

Therapy approaches are increasingly sensitive to gender, culture, and ethnic influences. Culture often constrains healthy male and female development, emotional expressiveness, healthy interdependence, and expression of intimacy. The selves people construct according to the "cultural narrative" are most often not life-giving.

In conclusion, psychotherapy is a diverse practice intent on participating in the natural desire to live happy, joyous, and free lives by understanding and managing constraining forces and by increasingly identifying with the life-giving forces. Psychotherapy and spiritual/religious practice are increasingly viewed as complementary partners in assisting humans to respond to the joys and sufferings presented by life.

SEE ALSO MERTON, THOMAS; PSYCHOLOGY (CLASSICAL); PSYCHOLOGY (CONTEMPORARY); SELF, THE.

BIBLIOGRAPHY

Dan Baker and Cameron Stauth, *What Happy People Know: How the New Science of Happiness Can Change Your Life for the Better* (Stuttgart, Germany 2004).

Alan S. Gurman and Stanley B. Messer, eds. *Essential Psychotherapies: Theory and Practice* (New York 2003).

Neil S. Jacobson and Andrew Christensen, *Acceptance and Change in Couple Therapy: A Therapist's Guide to Transforming Relationships* (New York 1996).

Susan M. Johnson, *The Practice of Emotionally Focused Marital Therapy: Creating Connection* (New York 1996).

Michael P. Nichols and Richard C. Schwartz, *Family Therapy: Concepts and Methods* (New York 2005).

P. Scott Richards and Allen E. Bergin, *A Spiritual Strategy for Counseling and Psychotherapy* (Washington, D.C. 1997).

Richard C. Schwartz, *Internal Family Systems Therapy* (New York 1995).

Martin E. P. Seligman, *Authentic Happiness: Using the New Positive Psychology to Realize Your Potential for Lasting Fulfillment* (New York 2004).

Len Sperry and Edward P. Shafranske, *Spiritually Oriented Psychotherapy* (Washington, D.C. 2005).

Froma Walsh, ed. *Spiritual Resources in Family Therapy* (New York 1999).

Paul Giblin
Associate Professor of Pastoral Counseling and Graduate
Program Director, MA Pastoral Counseling Program
Loyola University Chicago (2009)

R

RELIGION, PHILOSOPHY OF

The philosophy of religion is not intended as a replacement for religion or religious FAITH but instead seeks to determine the human intellect's capacity to arrive on its own at knowledge of GOD and related matters, such as the existence of God, the divine nature, the problem of EVIL, God and MORALITY, religious pluralism, miracles, the nature of religious belief, and the relation between religion and SCIENCE. Catholic DOCTRINE sees no antagonism between faith and REASON; indeed, each depends on the other. For example, the First Vatican Council proclaimed that "God, the first principle and last end of all things can be known with certainty from the created world by the natural light of human reason." The New Testament supports this, for St. Paul teaches in Romans that from a knowledge of the visible things of the created world, we can arrive at a knowledge of the invisible things of the uncreated world.

Philosophy and Theology. The most recent statement of the Church on this topic is JOHN PAUL II's ENCYCLICAL, *Faith and Reason* (1998). There he writes that "reason and faith cannot be separated without diminishing the capacity of men and women to know themselves, the world and God in an appropriate way." Divine revelation gives answers to those questions that cannot be grasped by unaided human reason and are known by faith alone, such as God's creation of the universe from nothing, the divinity of CHRIST, and divine grace. In addition, revelation presents truths that, although accessible in themselves to reason, might have escaped its notice; for example, the concept of God as free and personal as well as the creator of the world. This concept has exerted an enormous influence in the progress of philosophical thinking, particularly with regard to the philosophy of BEING.

Philosophy, in turn, contributes to THEOLOGY because the latter needs concepts and reasoning to unfold the implications of divine revelation and thus "to confirm the intelligibility and universal truth of its claims." When philosophy places itself at the service of religion in this way, it is subservient to the Church's Magisterium insofar as it then functions as a tool of theology. In the domain of natural reason, however, philosophy is autonomous, as it must remain faithful to its own principles and methods. Nevertheless, its commitment to seek TRUTH in the natural order implies an openness to truth *as such*, which is to say, to SUPERNATURAL truth as well. Although incapable of justifying the articles of religious faith, philosophy can nevertheless demonstrate the reasonableness of revealed doctrine and the need for religious faith. Perhaps the most remarkable of all attempts by philosophy to justify Christianity as the true religion is *Of True Religion*, written by St. AUGUSTINE of Hippo (354–430).

Faith and Reason. With regard to the relation between faith and reason, contemporary philosophers, notably Alvin Plantinga (1997), William P. Alston (1991), and Nicholas Wolterstorff (1995), have challenged the regnant view that, because religious belief cannot be justified by rational thought, such belief is unreasonable. They insist, on the contrary, that the evidentialist requirement for justification of a proposition is unduly constrictive. For example, it is rational to believe that God exists even if his existence cannot be shown to be true either by appealing to empirical evidence or by showing that the statement, "God exists," is a self-evident truth. This approach relies on an internal system of epistemology, which holds that religious belief derives its plausibility from a web of other plausible beliefs. So, although it is impossible to demonstrate that material things exist, personal experience, both past and present, lead one to affirm the truth of their existence. Equally, a rich spiritual interior life along with a sense of fulfillment lead one to accept beliefs in and about God as true: that God is all-powerful, all-knowing, all-good, and all-loving; and that he has providential concern for his creation and intervenes in the personal lives of men and women.

This approach has revolutionized the philosophy of religion by ablating the lines of demarcation between rational justification and religious belief, thereby broadening the range of topics deemed worthy of philosophical inquiry to include miracles, religious experience, fideism, the trinity, the incarnation, sin, divine providence, prayer, and revelation. But the bedrock of the philosophy of religion is constituted by the traditional topics of investigation, starting with the question of God's existence.

The Existence of God. With regard to the question of God's existence, the philosophy of religion assesses arguments for and against the capacity of natural knowledge—knowledge based on instruments of reason: the evidence of human experience in the world and logical argument—to arrive at a knowledge of God's existence. The traditional arguments in favor of arriving at the existence of God by means of unaided reason are the *Ontological Argument* of St. Anselm (1033–1109) and the *Five Ways* of St. THOMAS AQUINAS (c. 1225–1274). The traditional arguments against proving God's existence are generally variations of David HUME's (1711–1776) denial that experience reveals any necessary connection between events and Immanuel KANT's (1724–1804) claim that unaided reason cannot rise above sensible experience. Historically, the most common reason offered for ATHEISM is based on the experience of evil in the world.

Divine Nature of God. Regarding the divine nature, is God infinite or finite? Absolutely perfect or not? Does he know the future? Is human FREE WILL compatible with God's OMNISCIENCE and OMNIPOTENCE? PROCESS PHILOSOPHY, as defended by Alfred North WHITEHEAD (1861–1947), would avoid such problems by challenging classical theism with a conception of a God that can change. Because he is not perfect, but rather moves toward perfection, God is neither omnipotent nor omniscient.

The classical view of St. Augustine and St. Thomas Aquinas denies the defensibility of a changeable God. Crucial to an understanding of the divine nature and attributes is the question of God's relation to the world. Is

he identical with the world (PANTHEISM)? Is he inextricably involved in the world and thus incapable of transcending it (IMMANENTISM)? If God is transcendent and thus not part of, or bound by, the world, does he therefore have no knowledge of or concern or capacity for intervention in the world (DEISM)? Can a transcendent God (theism) have a personal knowledge of and providential care for the world (Augustine, Aquinas)?

Another project of the philosophy of religion is to discover what terms can correctly be applied to God. The doctrine of a transcendent God poses problems of conceptualizing him. For if he is not any part of the universe, how do terms derived from human experience in the world apply to him? For example, can the term *being* be applied to God and everything else if it has the same meaning in each case? If so, then one is forced to accept either pantheism or AGNOSTICISM: pantheism because a univocal use of *being* means that there can only be one being, and thus God and the world would be identical; or agnosticism because if *being* applies to humans, it cannot at the same time apply to a transcendent God, who is, by definition, beyond all human experience. Thus knowledge of God is impossible, and all other terms traditionally applied to him—person, all-love, all-good, all-knowing, all-powerful, Father—have only metaphorical meaning.

Aquinas and those who subscribe to his thought respond to this challenge by resorting to the doctrine of the ANALOGY of being: A concept can have a single meaning and still apply to diverse things in a manner that preserves their respective differences. This is because concepts—such as being, GOOD, truth, and BEAUTY—are transcendental in that they are not limited by categorical boundaries and thus apply to everything that is, even if beyond human experience and knowledge. If the sufficient reason for the existence of contingent beings (creatures) necessitates the existence of an absolutely necessary being who is absolutely perfect, it follows that this being must be absolutely self-sufficient, must be existence itself, and thus must be infinite in being, personhood, knowledge, power, goodness, and LOVE.

Divine Creation. The most important question regarding God's relation to the world and thus regarding the divine nature is the question of creation. Is the universe eternal or was it created in TIME? If God created the universe, did he do so freely (Augustine, Aquinas); or was its existence necessitated by his nature as ARISTOTLE (384–322 BC), AVICENNA (AD 980–1037), and SPINOZA (1632–1677) maintained?

Problem of Evil. The problem of evil receives attention in the philosophy of religion for the following reasons: If God created the world, does that mean that he is the cause of evil? If not, does it mean that he tolerates evil?

In either case, especially in the former, evil in the world must be reconciled with the claim that God is all-perfect and thus all-good. The classical answer was introduced by Augustine and amplified by Aquinas. To say that a thing is evil or has suffered an evil is to say that it has deteriorated in some way, as when one has gone blind. Since blindness is the absence of sight in a being that by its nature has vision, it is a privation and thus a (natural) evil. In contrast, potatoes are sightless by nature, and thus their absence of sight is not an evil. A being possessing free will who chooses actions that turn him or her from God suffers moral evil insofar as they produce a privation in his or her spiritual and moral self. Because evil is a privation, it follows that God is not the cause of evil. God created all things, but, as the absence of a due good, evil is, metaphysically speaking, non-being. It remains to ask why, if God is all-knowing, all-good, and all-powerful, does he permit evil. But the existence of a being with those attributes is not incompatible with evil in the world, for it is conceivable that the supremely perfect being would have the wisest of reasons for the permission of evil. Moreover, the creation of beings possessing free will allows the possibility of evil choices.

But here philosophy's account of moral evil ends and theology's begins. Divine revelation teaches that human acts cannot fully be understood without the doctrine of grace, sanctifying and actual. Similarly, granted that the problem of natural evil—for example, famine, pestilence, along with other forms of pain and suffering—can properly be investigated by philosophy, it must ultimately be addressed within the context of the doctrine of ORIGINAL SIN, which is the province of theology. Philosophy's dependence on theology for its proper understanding of such topics expands its horizons in two ways, as John Paul II noted. First, the theological VIRTUE of faith frees reason from PRESUMPTION, the characteristic failing of the philosopher, instilling in its place the virtue of HUMILITY. This virtue encourages the philosopher to address problems that challenge resolution if revealed data are excluded from consideration. Such problems include the scandal of evil and suffering, the personal nature of God, the meaning of life, and its foundation, the radical metaphysical question, why is there something rather than nothing?

SEE ALSO Anselm of Canterbury, St.; Christian Philosophy; God in Philosophy; God, Proofs for the Existence of; Infinity of God; Intervention, Divine; Nature (in Philosophy); Nature (in Theology); Paul, Apostle, St.; Perfection, Ontological; Philosophy and Science; Pluralism, Philosophical; Religion and Morality; Religion, Sociology of; Religion, Virtue of; Religions, Comparative Study of; Romans, Epistle to the; Vatican Council I.

BIBLIOGRAPHY

William P. Alston, *Perceiving God: The Epistemology of Religious Experience* (Ithaca, N.Y. 1991).

St. Augustine, *Of True Religion*, translated by J. H. S. Burleigh (Chicago1959).

Brian Davies, O.P., ed., *Philosophy of Religion: A Guide to the Subject* (Washington, D.C. 1998).

Brian Davies, O.P., ed., *Philosophy of Religion: A Guide and Anthology* (Oxford, U.K. 2000).

John Paul II, *Faith and Reason* (Boston 1998).

Jacques Maritain, *Approaches to God* (New York 1954).

Alvin Plantinga, "Reformed Epistemology," in *A Companion to the Philosophy of Religion*, edited by Philip L. Quinn and Charles Taliaferro (Cambridge, Mass. 1997), 383–392.

Louis P. Pojman, ed., *Philosophy of Religion: An Anthology* (Belmont, Calif. 1987).

Brendan Sweetman, *Religion: Key Concepts in Philosophy* (New York 2007).

Richard Swinburne, *The Existence of God* (Oxford, U.K. 2004).

Raymond Dennehy
Professor, Philosophy Department
University of San Francisco (2009)

REPRODUCTIVE TECHNOLOGY

Reproductive technology is a term that generally describes treatment for infertility. Infertility may be defined as the inability of a couple to conceive after one year of sexual intercourse uninhibited by any chemical, surgical, or barrier methods of birth control. It is estimated that 7 percent of married couples in the United States in which the woman is of childbearing age are infertile, and that one in six couples experience infertility worldwide.

Assisted Reproductive Technology (ART) is the technical term used to designate a specific type of reproductive technology for which data is periodically collected on a worldwide basis. The Centers for Disease Prevention and Control (CDC) defines ART as: "All treatments or procedures that involve surgically removing eggs from a woman's ovaries and combining the eggs with sperm to help a woman become pregnant. The types of ART are in vitro fertilization (IVF), gamete intrafallopian transfer (GIFT), and zygote intrafallopian transfer (ZIFT)" (United States Department of Health and Human Services, p. 503). This definition and a similar one from the World Health Organization exclude technologies that only manipulate sperm (intrauterine insemination

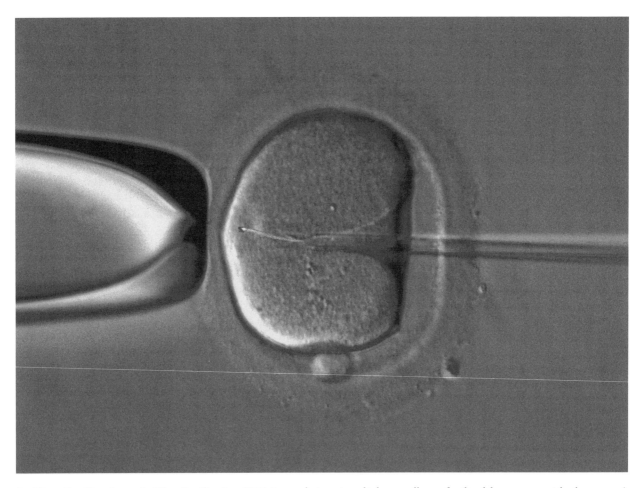

In Vitro Fertilization. *In Vitro Fertilization (IVF) is a technique in which egg cells are fertilized by sperm outside the woman's womb (in vitro). A single sperm is injected directly into the egg using Intracytoplasmic Sperm Injection (ICSI).* © DAVID GREGS / ALAMY

[IUI]) or only stimulate egg production (ovarian stimulation).

Fertilization using the IVF technique can take place either by placing egg and sperm in a culture medium or by directly injecting a sperm into an egg. This latter method is called Intracytoplasmic Sperm Injection (ICSI). In either case fertilization takes place outside the woman's body by the actions of third parties. Human embryos resulting from these procedures are transferred into the woman's uterus. GIFT uses a laparoscopic procedure to transfer eggs and sperm into the woman's fallopian tube. ZIFT engenders human embryos using IVF and then places them in the woman's fallopian tube using a laparoscopic procedure. ART cycles may use non-donor or donor eggs, sperm, or human embryos, any of which may never have been frozen or may have been previously frozen and then thawed for the procedure. Depending upon applicable law in different countries, the number of embryos transferred during ART cycles can number from one to five or more.

The European Society of Human Reproduction & Embryology (ESHRE; 2006) has estimated that as of 2002 the total number of ART treatment cycles per year worldwide was one million, and that more than three million babies have been born as the result of ART since the first baby in 1978. ESHRE reported that worldwide the pregnancy rate, delivery rate, and newborn rate (live birth) per initiated ART cycle using "fresh" (unfrozen) human embryos was 25.1 percent, 18.5 percent, and 22.9 percent respectively (2006). There are large variations in the success rates among different countries. For example, the CDC reported that in the United States in 2004 the overall rate for pregnancies per ART cycle was 33.7 percent and the rate for live births per cycle was 27.7 percent (2006).

Roman Catholic Moral Teaching. The fullest exposition of Catholic teaching on reproductive technologies is contained in *Donum vitae* from the Congregation for the Doctrine of the Faith (1987). Catholic teaching on reproductive technologies rests on a foundation of three moral criteria: (1) as with science and technology in general, reproductive technologies must always serve the good of the human person; (2) these technologies must respect the primary and fundamental right to life; and (3) use of these technologies must be conditioned by the body-soul unity of the human person, which places a specific moral responsibility to use the procreative powers as a gift from God.

Central to the good of the human embryo is the fact that it is a self-directing and self-integrating actual, unified human individual with a human nature. This fact about the human embryo means that it must be respected as a person who has fundamental rights, "among which in the first place is the inviolable right of every innocent human being to life" (*Donum vitae*, I, 1). One reason why ART procedures are gravely immoral is because they destroy or risk the life of an embryo.

The moral evaluation of ART procedures themselves in Catholic teaching focuses on the use of the procreative powers. The bodies of the man and woman are not mere complexes of tissues, organs, and physiological systems. The human person exists as a composite unity of body and spiritual soul. This body-soul unity of the human person reaches to the conjugal act and informs it both with procreative and unitive meanings that are inseparable and fulfilled only in and through each other. This means that human life may be engendered only through the conjugal act of spouses. Moreover, the child who is engendered has a moral right to be born as the fruit of a conjugal act between mother and father. Given the centrality of the conjugal act to the engendering of new life, *Donum vitae* teaches: "If the technical means facilitates the conjugal act or helps it to reach its natural objective, it can be morally acceptable. If on the other hand, the procedure were to replace the conjugal act, it is morally illicit" (II, B, 6). Catholic teaching does not reject reproductive technologies in principle nor does it oppose procedures for their artificiality, but prohibits only those that supplant the conjugal act or subject the human embryo to instrumentalization and manipulation.

A routine aspect of ART procedures is the cryopreservation and storage of human embryos for possible use in future procedures. This practice has resulted in hundreds of thousands of frozen embryos worldwide. A question arises as to whether it is morally acceptable to rescue frozen embryos, who would otherwise be discarded or given over to research, by means of transferring them for gestation and adoption. Theologians and ethicists who are in favor of embryo adoption have made two different arguments. According to one view, embryo transfer under these conditions is justified only if the child is permanently adopted by the gestational mother and her husband. Another view is that rescue is morally acceptable by either single or married women, whether they adopt the child themselves or put the child up for adoption by others. For both positions the procreative and unitive goods of marriage are not violated because the embryo has already been conceived. Moreover, it is claimed that magisterial statements on the fate of frozen human embryos are restricted to the research context. Those who are opposed to embryo adoption argue that magisterial statements do prohibit human embryo adoption, and that pregnancy under these circumstances violates the exclusivity of the marriage bond. In particular, husband and wife do not become mother and father through each other, because embryo transfer represents a nonconjugal impregnation of the woman. To date there are no magisterial pronouncements that settle the issue of embryo adoption.

SEE ALSO Bioethics; Cloning; Ectopic Pregnancy; Embryology, Human; In Vitro Fertilization; Magisterial Documents; Magisterium, Assent to the; Philosophy and Science.

BIBLIOGRAPHY

Mark H. Beers, ed. *The Merck Manual*, 18th ed. (Whitehouse Station, N.J. 2006).

Thomas V. Berg, and Edward J. Furton, eds. *Human Embryo Adoption: Biotechnology, Marriage, and the Right to Life* (Philadelphia 2007).

Peter J. Cataldo, "Catholic Teaching on Reproductive Technologies," in *Catholic Health Care Ethics: A Manual for Ethics Committees*, edited by P. J. Cataldo and A. S. Moraczewski, OP (Boston 2001).

Catechism of the Catholic Church, 2nd edition (Vatican City 1997).

Congregation for the Doctrine of the Faith, *Instruction on Respect for Human Life in Its Origin and on the Dignity of Procreation* (Vatican City 1987). For the text of *Donum vitae*, see: *Acta Apostolicae Sedis* 80 (1988) 70–102 (Latin); *Origins* 16 (March 19, 1987) (English).

European Society of Human Reproduction & Embryology, "World Report on ART (Assisted Reproductive Technology) Fact Sheet, June 11, 2007," available from http://www.eshre.com/emc.asp?pageId=807 / (accessed March 3, 2008).

D. I. Hoffman et al, "Cryopreserved Embryos in the United States and Their Availability for Research," *Fertility and Sterility* 79 (5, 2003): 1063–1069.

Human Fertilisation & Embryology Authority, *A Long Term Analysis of the HFEA Register Data (1991–2006)* (London 2006).

John Paul II, *Evangelium vitae* (Vatican City 1995). For the text of *Evangelium vitae*, see: *Acta Apostolicae Sedis* 87 (1995) 401–522 (Latin); *Origins* 24 (1995): 659–730 (English).

John Paul II. *Familiaris consortio* (Vatican City 1981). For the text of *Familiaris consortio*, see: *Acta Apostolicae Sedis* 74 (1982): 81–191 (Latin); Origins 11 (1981) (English).

United States Department of Health and Human Services, Centers for Disease Control and Prevention, *2004 Assisted Reproductive Technology Success Rates: National Summary and Fertility Clinic Reports* (Atlanta, Ga. 2006).

A. M. Waters, J. H. Dean, and E. A. Sullivan, *Assisted Reproduction Technology in Australia and New Zealand 2003* (Sidney 2006).

Peter J. Cataldo
Ethics Consultant
The National Catholic Bioethics Center
Philadelphia, Penn. (2009)

RHODE ISLAND, CATHOLIC CHURCH IN

Rhode Island is the smallest state in the United States (1,212 square miles) and the eighth smallest in population (est. 1,079,189). It is the most Catholic of states, however, with an estimated 645,713 Catholics making up 60 percent of its population.

Early History. Founded by Roger WILLIAMS (1603–1683) as an enclave of religious tolerance and confirmed as such by the royal charter of 1663, Rhode Island became a haven for every sort of religious dissenter, even a few Catholics. However, by a statute of the General Assembly in 1719, not removed until 1783, Catholics were excluded from full citizenship. The first public Mass said in Rhode Island was at Newport in 1780 for the funeral of the commander of the French fleet sent to help the colonists in the War of Independence.

Rhode Island was first under the jurisdiction of Bishop CARROLL of Baltimore and then under the bishops of Boston, first Jean CHEVERUS (1808–1823) and then Benedict FENWICK (1825–1844). In 1844 the Vermont-born convert, William Barber Tyler, was created the first bishop of Hartford (which included all of Connecticut and Rhode Island) with his CATHEDRAL and residence at Rhode Island's capital of Providence. With Tyler's death in 1849, Irish-born Bernard O'REILLY became the second bishop, but his ship was lost at sea on a return trip from Europe in 1856. Francis P. MC-FARLAND, a native-born son of Irish immigrants, became the third bishop of Hartford in 1858. When in 1872 the DIOCESE of Providence was created, it included all of Rhode Island and, until 1904, southeastern Massachusetts. Thomas F. Hendricken (1827–1886), a zealous Irish-born priest who had once dreamed of being a missionary in Asia, was its first bishop.

Catholic Immigration. Until the 1820s Catholics were few and far between, with priests making periodic trips to the scattered Catholic population. The first permanent church in Rhode Island, now St. Mary's, was founded in Newport in 1828; the second, also St. Mary's, was erected in 1829 in Pawtucket; and in 1837 the parish of SS. Peter and Paul, which would become the cathedral, was established in Providence. The growth of the Church was primarily due to the transformation of the state from a mercantile and agrarian economy to one based primarily on manufacturing in metals and textiles and the need for cheap labor to maintain it. Rhode Island was a leader in the American industrial revolution (the first mechanized textile mill in the nation opened just north of Providence in 1790), and the factories and mills of Providence and the Blackstone and Pawtuxet river valleys in the northern half of the state drew mostly Catholic immigrants in great numbers, with the Irish being the first and largest group.

The influx of the Irish, which would become a flood in the late 1840s, led to a transformation of the population of the state so that the Irish made up nearly three out of every eight people by 1865. This led to the growth of anti–immigrant and anti–Catholic feeling. The constitution of 1843, by retaining property requirements for voting by naturalized foreign-born citizens while removing them for the native-born, was designed to disfranchise Irish Catholics. In the 1855 elections, the nativist Know-Nothings swept the state, winning five of every seven votes. Their anti–Catholicism seems to have been based primarily on religious and cultural issues, lacking the economic aspect that was so important, for example, in Massachusetts. The Know-Nothings were soon eclipsed by the newly born Republican party which, while eschewing the Know-Nothings' anti–Catholic sentiments, absorbed most of their supporters. Whereas the old English stock became the pillar of the Republican party, the Irish became wedded to the Democratic party. In 1888 the Bourn Amendment was passed by referendum. While it removed the property qualification for naturalized foreign-born citizens to vote in state and national elections, it included a clause that required ownership of $134 in real or personal property for voting on all financial questions and in most municipal elections. By then the Republicans saw the virtue of using newer immigrants, particularly the French Canadians, as a counter to the Democratic Irish. While the first Catholic governor was the Irish Democrat James H. Higgins (1906), the second was the French Canadian Republican Aram J. Pothier (1908). While the sectarian violence that was seen in other places never occurred in Rhode Island, the divisions were deep and long-lasting, and anti–Catholic bigotry continued well into the next century.

The demands of the Civil War led to an expansion of mills and factories and the need for workers to fill them. This was the beginning of the next great immigration, the French Canadians. The trickle of French Canadians before the war became a flood so that between 1860 and 1910 over 35,000 came to Rhode Island, and by 1930 an estimated 57,000 had arrived. The city of

Woonsocket, which was 70 percent French Canadian by 1930, became the "Quebec of New England." Like the Irish both in the firmness of their Catholicism and their nationalism and in their fusion of the two, the French Canadians created their own national parishes, schools, and organizations to preserve their language and culture. However, they did not get along well with the Irish, who considered them a threat to their jobs (the French Canadians were dubbed *the Chinese of the East* for their willingness to work long hours at low wages), or with the Irish-dominated Church, which pushed for much greater centralization and Americanization. *La surviv-ance*, the *survival* or maintenance of French Canadian culture, was the pillar of their communities and a continual point of contention.

Other major Catholic immigrant groups followed: from the late 1880s, the Italians; and from 1900, Poles and Lithuanians. The Portuguese long had a presence in the state, especially from the whaling days, but in the 1870s, and particularly after 1890, they came in great numbers. The Portuguese were divided by their place of origin: the Azores, Cape Verdes, and mainland Portugal. Syrians (Melkite and Maronite) and Ruthenians also immigrated to the state, though in much smaller numbers. National parishes were created for all these groups. The enactment of the national origins quota system (1924) and the decline of the mills (from 1923) led to a great decrease in immigration. In the late twentieth and early twenty-first century, however, there was some Catholic immigration (though not to the high degree of the earlier groups) from the Portuguese islands, Latin America, and, to a lesser extent, Southeast Asia. Except for the Portuguese from Cape Verdes, for whom a national parish was created in 1979, these groups were cared for within already existing parishes.

Growth of the Church. In its early years Rhode Island was a missionary country and depended on the financial support of foreign missionary societies and on priests from Ireland. By the late 1860s the Church was able to maintain itself, to start building churches and schools on its own, and to find vocations among its members. This was less true for the newer immigrant groups, and finding priests for them was often difficult and a source of friction. Even if priests could be found who spoke their language, national pride or cultural differences could get in the way. Although Catholics were at the bottom of the social ladder and the overwhelming majority of Catholics were laborers whose jobs depended on the vagaries of the business cycle, some had prospered and had become professionals and businessmen. The growing wealth and security of the Church was manifested by Bishop Hendricken's construction of a magnificent new cathedral in 1878. Although not consecrated until 1889, its first Mass was for Hendricken's funeral in 1886. Another manifestation of stability was Hendricken's founding of the *Weekly Visitor* in 1875, which eventually became the diocesan newspaper under the name the *Providence Visitor*. In 1993 a Spanish edition of the *Providence Visitor* was introduced, and in 2007 the paper was redesigned and renamed the *Rhode Island Catholic*.

The death of Hendricken led to the appointment of Matthew Harkins (1845–1921), a second-generation Irish American, whom ARCHBISHOP John IRELAND once called "my ideal type of bishop." He was a learned and able Boston priest, under whose tenure the diocese experienced phenomenal growth. On his arrival there were thirty-nine parishes and sixty-three diocesan priests in Rhode Island, and when he gave up the administration of the diocese in 1919 to his coadjutor, Bishop William A. Hickey (1869–1933), there were an additional sixty-two parishes (a majority of them national parishes) and 207 diocesan priests, all but one of whom were ordained during his episcopacy. He also created an extensive system of charitable institutions, among them St. Joseph's Hospital in 1892 in Providence. Harkins was careful to include French Canadians and Italians in diocesan offices and, to better serve the non-English speaking FAITHFUL, he brought in the Scalabrini Fathers, the MARIST FATHERS, the HOLY GHOST FATHERS, and the Missionaries of the Sacred Heart. The Brothers of the Sacred Heart and twenty different congregations of women religious entered the state, joining the SISTERS OF MERCY, the Society of the Sacred Heart, the URSULINES, the RELIGIOUS OF JESUS AND MARY, and the Christian Brothers in the work of education. Following the decrees of the Third Plenary Council of Baltimore (1884), which mandated parochial schools, Harkins created a diocesan school board and pushed for the construction of schools wherever feasible. By 1921 there were forty-one parish schools, three academies for young men, and five for young ladies. As the capstone of this educational system, Harkins wished to create a Catholic college. The JESUITS had taken on a parish in Providence (1876) in the hope that they would eventually open a college, but when they left the state in 1899, Harkins had to look elsewhere. Eventually the Dominican friars agreed to staff such a college, and in 1919 Providence College opened with seventy-one students. It has become a flourishing coeducational school, still run by the DOMINICANS, of over 4,800 students (undergraduate and graduate) on a 105–acre campus in the city of Providence. Harkins also cared for the educational quality of his priests. He raised the standards for accepting young men as seminarians and sent many of his young priests for further studies to universities in Europe and America. He was an early supporter of The Catholic University of America, in Washington, D.C., and became a trustee in 1903.

Among the other orders that entered the diocese at this time were the TRAPPISTS (1900) and the BENEDICTINES (1919). The Trappists moved from Nova Scotia to Lonsdale onto land donated by Harkins but moved to Spencer, Massachusetts, after their MONASTERY burned down in 1949. The Benedictines of Portsmouth PRIORY (raised to an abbey in 1969) have remained and direct a flourishing, coeducational preparatory school, opened in 1926. Harkins had studied with the English Benedictines for a year in the English College at Douai, France, before training with the SULPICIANS in Paris. When Leonard Sargent, a convert priest on his way to join an English abbey, broached the subject of founding a Benedictine house in the state, Harkins was enthusiastic and, when Sargent returned, Harkins not only gave him permission to set up a house at Portsmouth but also supplied $5,000 to make the foundation possible.

Increase in Educational Institutions. At Harkins's death, his coadjutor, Hickey, immediately became the ordinary, and although some sixteen parishes were created during his tenure, he gave greater emphasis to the consolidation and improvement of already existing institutions. He was extremely active, however, in the area of education, creating fourteen parish schools and expanding the size of already existing schools. He also reorganized the establishing and funding of the high schools. He was an aggressive fundraiser, raising a million dollars for his high school fund and vast sums for diocesan charitable institutions in his centralized annual Catholic Charity Fund Appeal. With the beginning of the Great Depression, Hickey speeded up church construction work to provide jobs and, in order to relieve immediate needs for food and clothing, he directed that branches of the St. Vincent de Paul Society be established in every parish.

Hickey's centralization of Catholic high schools and their funding led to a rebellion of the ultranationalists among the French Canadians, led by Elphège Daignault (1879–1937) of Woonsocket, who saw it as a threat to their separate way of life. In 1924 they began a French-language newspaper, *La Sentinelle*, to promote their views. In 1925 they appealed to ROME against Hickey's "illegal assessment" of parish funds. When their petition was denied, they appealed in 1927 to the civil courts (unsuccessfully) and began a boycott of all contributions to the Church. In February 1928 Hickey declared that boycotters would be denied the sacraments. All those who had signed the appeal to the civil courts were excommunicated by Pope PIUS XI in April 1928, and *La Sentinelle* was put on the Index. The controversy gained national attention and led to much bitterness and divi-

sion in the French Canadian community. Within a year all of those excommunicated had capitulated, and the conflict was over.

Rise of Catholic Political Power. The 1930s were a turning point for Rhode Island Catholics, for it marked their ascent to political power. From the 1850s until the 1930s, the state had been dominated by a Yankee Republican oligarchy supported by wealthy businessmen and rural voters. The 1920s was a period of disenchantment among French Canadians and Italians toward the Republicans. While partly due to economic decline and to the negative Republican reaction to the major strikes of the decade, it was primarily due to the revival of nativism. This nativism was seen in the rise of the avowedly anti–Catholic KU KLUX KLAN (even in Rhode Island), in the immigration restriction laws of 1921 and 1924, and in the Peck Act passed by the Republican General Assembly in 1922, which required that instruction in all basic subjects be taught in English in all private schools. The Peck Act angered the French Canadians because of its direct attack on the integrity of their culture, and the rest of the Catholic body saw the removal of the supervision of private schools from local communities to the state Board of Education as an attack on local autonomy and religious freedom. The law was never enforced, and it was repealed in 1925. The presidential election of 1928 was the political "coming of age" for Catholics in the state. The Catholic Al Smith (1873–1944) was only the second Democrat to have carried the state since the founding of the Republican party. But the voting showed a polarized electorate, with Smith doing very badly in the Yankee areas and extremely well in the Catholic ethnic ones. Also, there was a substantially larger turnout in the Catholic ethnic districts. In 1928 the restrictive property qualifications for voting in city council elections were also removed. While the Great Depression and New Deal continued the political transformation of the state, it was not until the "Bloodless Revolution" of 1935, when the Democratic administration forced through the General Assembly a massive reorganization of the state government, that the structures that kept the Yankee minority in power were removed. In the elections of 1936 the triumph of the Catholic ethnics was made complete.

Expansion of Infrastructure. Francis P. KEOUGH (1890–1961), a priest of Hartford, was made bishop at Hickey's death in 1933 and remained until he was made archbishop of Baltimore in 1947. When he arrived there were 328,528 Catholics, 270 diocesan priests, and 95 religious priests; and when he left there were 427,364 Catholics, 344 diocesan priests, and 145 religious priests. In his time fifteen new parishes, four high schools, and

Installation of Bishop Thomas Tobin. *Priests form a procession as they depart the Cathedral of Saints Peter & Paul, in Providence, R.I., following the installation of Thomas Tobin as bishop of the diocese of Providence on Tuesday, May 31, 2005.* AP IMAGES

fourteen elementary schools were founded. In 1939 he founded a minor seminary in Warwick Neck, and in 1947 the Sisters of Mercy founded Salve Regina College in Newport, now a successful coeducational university of some 2,600 students (undergraduate and graduate).

Russell J. McVinney (1898–1971) was named the fifth bishop of Providence in 1948—the first Rhode Island native to hold that position. The first part of his tenure witnessed a period of remarkable growth, with the construction of twenty-eight parishes and forty schools, especially in the suburbs and the growing rural areas of the state. The school system reached its peak at this time with 106 out of 154 parishes having a parish school. The expansion in education, however, led to the need for lay teachers and tuition payments for the first time. He opened a new hospital, Our Lady of FATIMA, in 1954; a diocesan retreat house at Narragansett in 1952; and a youth retreat center at Peace Dale in 1954. He also expanded the seminary and founded a diocesan congregation of Sisters, Sisters of Our Lady of Providence (1955), and a society of diocesan brothers, Brothers of Our Lady of Providence (1959).

A Time of Social Change. The final decade of McVinney's tenure was as tumultuous and painful as the first part was stable and prosperous. It coincided with the profound social changes of the 1960s and early 1970s as well as the Civil Rights Revolution, the Vietnam War and its protests, and the changes occasioned by the Second Vatican Council. Even before this, with the decline of ethnic enclaves and the movement to the suburbs, Catholics had become far more assimilated to American middle-class life and its mores. Bishop McVinney, although essentially politically and religiously conservative, took a leading role in the movement for political and economic rights of minorities and the poor and was a strong advocate of the Fair Housing laws passed by the General Assembly in 1965. He also dutifully implemented the changes following the Council. In this period a profound decline in religious and priestly vocations began, with many religious leaving their orders (the Sisters of Our Lady of Providence were dissolved at this time) and even many priests leaving the active ministry. Among those leaving was McVinney's auxiliary since 1964, Bishop Bernard M. Kelly, who resigned on June 14, 1971. Two months later McVinney died, and in December 1971 Louis E. Gelineau (b. 1928), the vicar general of the Diocese of Burlington, Vermont, was appointed bishop.

Bishop Gelineau reorganized the administrative structures of the diocese to emphasize the pastoral dimension of his office, to increase participation of the clergy and people in its running, and to develop strategic planning. The decline in Mass attendance and in priestly and religious vocations continued, as did resignations

from the priesthood and religious life. With the decline in numbers of teaching religious, more lay faculty had to be hired, and schools became much more expensive. From 1968 schools started to close: some sixty-five elementary schools and twelve high schools either closed or merged with other schools. Enrollments continued to decline until 1980 when the first increase appeared since 1963. The seminary also experienced declining enrollment: In 1989 the high school seminary closed, and in 1975 the college seminary began sending its students to Providence College; the college seminary itself moved to Providence in 1983. While a few new parishes were established, changing demographics also led to the merging of some: In the late 1990s a number of parishes merged in Warwick, Central Falls, and Woonsocket; and in 2003, in Centreville and Arctic. Over a three-year period (1995–1998), the highly successful Vision of Hope Campaign raised more than forty million dollars for diocesan initiatives. In 1995 Bishop Robert E. Mulvee (b. 1930), bishop of Wilmington, Delaware, was appointed coadjutor, and in 1997, with the retirement of Bishop Gelineau, he became the seventh bishop of Providence.

The Twenty-First Century. In 2005 Bishop Thomas J. Tobin (b. 1948), bishop of Youngstown, Ohio, became the eighth bishop of Providence. As of January 1, 2007, the diocese had 150 parishes, 5 missions, 287 diocesan priests (of which 175 are active in the diocese and 8 are active outside), 124 religious priests, 16 extern priests, 106 permanent deacons, 513 sisters, 100 brothers, 12 Catholic high schools, 44 Catholic elementary schools, and 1 Catholic hospital (Our Lady of Fatima Hospital and the old St. Joseph's Hospital are parts of the St. Joseph Health Services of Rhode Island).

SEE ALSO BALTIMORE, ARCHDIOCESE OF; BALTIMORE, COUNCILS OF; BENEDICTINES, ENGLISH; CATHOLIC UNIVERSITY OF AMERICA, THE; EXCOMMUNICATION; BOSTON, ARCHDIOCESE OF; HARTFORD, ARCHDIOCESE OF; INDEX OF PROHIBITED BOOKS; KNOW-NOTHINGISM; MARONITE CHURCH; MELKITE GREEK CATHOLIC CHURCH; RELIGIOUS (MEN AND WOMEN); SACRED HEART BROTHERS; ST. VINCENT DE PAUL, SOCIETY OF; VATICAN COUNCIL II.

BIBLIOGRAPHY

Patrick T. Conley and Matthew J. Smith, *Catholicism in Rhode Island: The Formative Era* (Providence, R.I. 1976).

Robert W. Hayman, *Catholicism in Rhode Island and the Diocese of Providence, 1780–1886* (Providence, R.I. 1982).

Robert W. Hayman, *Catholicism in Rhode Island and the Diocese of Providence, 1886–1921* (Providence, R.I. 1995).

Richard Sherman Sorrell, "The Sentinelle Affair (1924–1929) and Militant *Survivance*: The Franco-American Experience in

Woonsocket, Rhode Island" (Ph.D. diss., State University of New York at Buffalo, 1975).

Evelyn Savidge Sterne, *Ballots and Bibles: Ethnic Politics and the Catholic Church in Providence* (Ithaca, N.Y. 2004).

Dom Paschal Scotti
Chairman, Christian Doctrine Department
Portsmouth Abbey School
Portsmouth, R.I. (2009)

S

SACRAMENTALS

Sacramentals are sacred signs established by the Church to render HOLY the various circumstances of life. Such signs can take the form of rites, prayers, or objects outside those seven rites properly called sacraments. Sacramentals resemble the sacraments inasmuch as they signify effects—chiefly, although not exclusively, an increase in HOLINESS obtained through the INTERCESSION of the Church. Sacramentals dispose those who use them to receive the principal effect of the sacraments. Unlike the sacraments, the number of which is fixed at seven, sacramentals include a wide variety of rites, prayers, and religious objects. The number of sacramentals may be increased or decreased as the Church deems fit.

History of Definition. It was only with PETER LOMBARD in the twelfth century that the term *sacrament* began to be restricted to the seven rites of baptism, CONFIRMATION or chrismation, EUCHARIST, penance, ANOINTING of the sick, holy order, and matrimony. Prior to this DEFINITION, no strict distinction obtained between what now are regarded as sacramentals and the seven sacraments. HUGH OF SAINT-VICTOR (1066–1141), for example, in the generation before Peter Lombard, included the blessing of salt and water, the reception of ashes, the benediction and distribution of palms, and many other similar rites among the sacraments in his treatise *De sacramentis christianae fidei* (1134). As scholastic THEOLOGY refined the term *sacrament* to refer to perceptible signs instituted by CHRIST to give sanctifying GRACE, those sacred actions and objects instituted by the Church rather than by Christ came to be called *sacramentals*.

The *Compendium of the Catechism of the Catholic Church* (2005) presents the most succinct and most recent official definition of sacramentals:

> These are sacred signs instituted by the Church to sanctify different circumstances of life. They include a prayer accompanied by the sign of the cross and other signs. Among the sacramentals which occupy an important place are: blessings, which are the praise of God and a prayer to obtain his gifts, the consecration of persons and the dedication of things for the worship of God. (CCCC 2005, Question 351)

Comparison to Sacraments. Like the sacraments, sacramentals constitute part of the sacred LITURGY or official WORSHIP offered to God by the Church. Their status as official public prayer, then, excels in dignity and efficacy that of private devotions or personal acts of individual piety. Sacramentals moreover enjoy the power of the Church's own impetration or priestly intercession with God. Hence exorcisms (whether of catechumens or of ergoumens, that is, victims of demonic possession), Christian funerals, the blessing of an ABBOT or an ABBESS, the blessing of the oils, and the consecration of sacred chrism on HOLY THURSDAY all qualify as sacramentals instituted by the Church to sanctify the Christian FAITHFUL on various occasions.

The Second Vatican Council mandated a revision of the sacramentals both to heighten the active, intelligent, and fruitful participation of the lay faithful and to render more clearly the meaning of the effects that, as signs, the sacramentals actually signify (Constitution on the Sacred Liturgy *Sacrosanctum concilium* 1963, nn. 62, 79). Accordingly, the various rites and blessings contained in the *Rituale romanum* (1952) underwent considerable changes, so that many of the titles or parts of the *Rituale* were reorganized and redistributed over several separate books. These include the *Ordo exsequiarum*, *De benedictionibus*, *De exorcismis*, and the Rite of Blessing an Abbot or an Abbess. The process of revising the entire *Rituale* concluded only in 2002 with the promulgation of the Rite of Exorcism.

Effects of Sacramentals. Indeed even in their effects and efficaciousness, sacramentals differ from the seven sacraments. Because the sacramentals encompass a wide variety of rites, their effects are rather numerous. These are for the most part primarily spiritual, although sacramentals may well play a role in, for instance, restoring health or protecting the life of blessed or consecrated persons. Whereas other temporal benefits also may accrue from the celebration of the sacramentals, their chief purpose as signs of Christ's paschal MYSTERY remains the growth in holiness of those who use them. Hence the blessings of fields and crops, the prayers for good harvests and for protection against natural disasters or adverse weather, aim not just to alleviate distress, but also to encourage growth in grace because of deliverance from spiritual and temporal harm.

The effect of sacramentals is somewhat different from that of the sacraments. Whereas the sacraments cause the grace signified *ex opere operato*, that is, the work itself is accomplished validly by the use of due matter and form, the Church's prayer in the sacramentals works *ex opere operantis ecclesiae*. This means that in the sacramentals the Church, as the bride and the MYSTICAL BODY OF CHRIST, uses the power of Christ's priesthood to offer an objectively holy prayer that always pleases God. The objective quality of this kind of prayer excels the more subjective nature of those petitions motivated by individual devotion of Church members, even when offered in common.

The great value of the sacramentals, then, resides in the power they derive from the Church's intercession, of which they are signs. In other words, the sacramentals, like the sacraments, have their effect independent of the subjective dispositions of the ministers and recipients. Hence, blessings take effect even when the ministers or recipients are not duly disposed to receive the sanctifying gifts of grace that they communicate.

Correct Use of Sacramentals. After Vatican II (1962–1965), debate ensued concerning whether the term *sacramental* could legitimately be applied to an object. Also disputed was whether ceremonies within the celebration of Mass and the other sacraments but beyond the specific actions performed *in persona Christi capitis* can be construed as sacramentals. Although the 1917 Code of Canon Law (canon 1144) included *things* as well as

ritual *actions* (*res aut actiones*) in its definition of sacramentals, *Sacrosanctum concilium* 60 avoided any reference to blessed objects as sacramentals. The liturgical constitution instead referred only to signs (*sacramentalia sunt signa sacra*). This led to a tendency evident even in official liturgical books of blessing to frame blessings almost exclusively in terms of people who occupy certain places or who use various objects (e.g., crucifixes, holy water, statues, rosaries, medals, SCAPULARS) rather than the dwellings, spaces, or articles of devotion themselves.

Some pastoral liturgists fear that a disproportionate regard for blessed objects may approach SUPERSTITION, perhaps bordering even on IDOLATRY: "Too often in the past, blessed objects have taken on a quasi-magical importance, as if they possessed more significance than, for example, the celebration of the eucharist" (Smolarski 2003, p. 86). Consequently, the current *Book of Blessings* (1989) stresses the active role of the faithful and discourages the mere signing of an article or place with only the sign of the CROSS: "The outward signs of blessing, and particularly the sign of the cross, are in themselves forms of preaching the GOSPEL and of expressing FAITH. But to ensure active participation in the celebration and to guard against any danger of superstition, it is ordinarily not permissible to impart the blessing of any article or place merely through a sign of blessing and without either the word of God or any sort of prayer being spoken" (20). This restriction, however, was not applied by the 2003 edition of the *General Instruction of the Roman Missal* in the blessing of INCENSE during Mass: "The priest, having put incense into the thurible, blesses it with the sign of the Cross, without saying anything" (277). More consistency may be achieved in subsequent editions of the liturgical books. In any case, it is undeniable that the Church has always blessed objects and still does bless objects as well as people and places, setting them aside for the worship of God. Some, like incense and the medal of St. Benedict, even serve as a demonifuge. Inasmuch as these blessed objects benefit those who use them reverently in the service of God and for an increase in the likeness to Christ, they may correctly be termed *sacramentals*. Nevertheless, that term now is applied primarily and more frequently to the blessing or action performed in conjunction with the Church's impetratory power.

Since the Church aims through the sacramentals to dispose the faithful to the principal effects of the sacraments, it is worth considering how certain ceremonies surrounding and resembling the actual rites of the seven sacraments can legitimately rank as sacramentals. Those related to baptism include the blessing of Easter water at the Paschal Vigil and the blessing of holy water at other times; such rites of the CATECHUMENATE and baptism as signs of the cross, exorcisms, anointings, the imposition of hands, and the bestowal of the white garment and the candle. Likewise connected with baptism are religious profession and the consecration of virgins. The sacramental chiefly related to confirmation is the consecration of chrism on Holy Thursday. The main sacramental associated with penance is the blessing and distribution of ashes on Ash Wednesday.

All sacramentals, together with everything that constitutes the Church's life and mission, relate to the Eucharist. This is clearly signified by the celebration of so many sacramentals within the Mass: the blessing of both the oil of the catechumens and the oil of the sick, plus the consecration of the chrism on Holy Thursday; the blessing, distribution, and procession of palms on Palm Sunday; the blessing and procession of candles on CANDLEMAS; and the various blessings and ceremonies of the EASTER VIGIL as well as other celebrations that take place during Mass. Religious profession, too, constitutes a sacramental that according to Vatican II ought to take place within Mass.

The consecration of chrism belongs also to the sacrament of orders, as do the blessings of an abbot and the dedication of a church. The sacramentals most closely related to matrimony are the nuptial blessing and the blessing of the wedding rings, but the various blessings of women before and after childbirth, the blessing of a betrothal or an engagement, and the blessing of the home are also connected to marriage. Linked to the anointing of the sick are blessings for the faithful at different phases of sickness, the commendation of a departing soul, and the FUNERAL RITES, including BURIAL.

Similar to, but less than the sacraments, the sacramentals nonetheless enjoy an efficacy more powerful than strictly private prayer. As such, they play a distinct role in the economy of SALVATION, rendering holy various situations in life and directing those who use them to a deeper participation in divine worship and in the holiness of God.

Inclusive Interpretation. By means of the motu proprio *Summorum pontificum* (2007) and its attendant letter *Con grande fiducia*, Pope BENEDICT XVI removed any restrictions pertaining to the LITURGICAL BOOKS OF THE ROMAN RITE in vigor up to 1962. Indeed as early as 2006 the Congregation for DIVINE WORSHIP AND THE DISCIPLINE OF THE SACRAMENTS, with the collaboration of the Congregation for the DOCTRINE OF THE FAITH and with the approval of Pope JOHN PAUL II, granted permission to exorcists to use the rite of exorcisms provided in Title XII of the 1952 Roman Ritual. The wider and more generous use of the blessings and other rites contained in the earlier liturgical books means that in accordance with the hermeneutic of continuity, whereby current rites and practices of the Church are to be understood and applied in harmony with the long-standing TRADITION of the Church, future theological

discussion of the nature and use of sacramentals must take into account the definition of sacramentals furnished by the Council of TRENT and the 1917 Code of Canon Law. The definition given in this entry echoes the explanation of sacramentals in *Sacrosanctum concilium*, the 1983 Code of CANON LAW, and the CATECHISM OF THE CATHOLIC CHURCH. It likewise allows an interpretation inclusive of the wider tradition pertaining to the Church's teaching on the nature and application of sacramentals.

SEE ALSO ANOINTING OF THE SICK, II: LITURGY OF; ASHES, LITURGICAL USE OF; BAPTISM, SACRAMENT OF; BLESSINGS, LITURGICAL; CANDLES; CANON LAW, HISTORY OF; CRUCIFIX; DEVOTIONS, POPULAR; DISPOSITION; EX OPERE OPERANTIS; EX OPERE OPERATO; EXORCISM; HOLY OILS; HOLY ORDERS; IMPOSITION OF HANDS; MATRIMONY, SACRAMENT OF; MEDALS, RELIGIOUS; PENANCE, SACRAMENT OF; PROFESSION OF FAITH; ROSARY; SACRAMENTS, ARTICLES ON; SIGN; SUMMORUM PONTIFICUM; VATICAN COUNCIL II; WATER, LITURGICAL USE OF.

BIBLIOGRAPHY

Benedict XVI, *Summorum pontificum*, Of the Supreme Pontiffs (Apostolic Letter, July 7, 2007), available from http://www.vatican.va/archive/ENG1104/_INDEX.HTM (accessed November 6, 2008).

Catechism of the Catholic Church, 2nd. ed. (Vatican City 1997).

Compendium of the Catechism of the Catholic Church (Vatican City 2005).

Irénée Henri Dalmais, *Introduction to the Liturgy*, translated by Roger Capel (Baltimore 1961).

International Commission on English in the Liturgy, ed., *Book of Blessings* (Collegeville, Minn. 1989).

Hugh of Saint-Victor, *On the Sacraments of the Christian Faith (De sacramentis Christianae fidei)* translated by Roy J. Deferrari (Cambridge, Mass. 1951).

John Paul II, *Code of Canon Law* (January 25, 1983), available from http://www.vatican.va/archive/ENG1104/_INDEX.HTM (accessed November 6, 2008).

Pierre Jounel, "Blessings," in *The Church at Prayer III: The Sacraments*, edited by A.-G. Martimort, translated by M. J. O'Connell (Collegeville, Minn. 1987), 263–284.

A. Michel, *Dictionnaire de Théologie Catholique*, ed. A. Vacant et al., 15 vols. (Paris 1903–1950; Tables générales 1951–), 14.1:465–482.

John H. Miller, *Fundamentals of the Liturgy* (Notre Dame, Ind. 1960), 427–433.

John H. Miller, *Signs of Transformation in Christ* (Englewood Cliffs, N.J. 1963).

Paul VI, *Sacrosanctum concilium*, On the Sacred Liturgy (Constitution, December 4, 1963), available from http://www.vatican.va/archive/hist_councils/ii_vatican_council/documents/vat-ii_const_19631204_sacrosanctum-concilium_en.html (accessed November 6, 2008).

Rituale Romanum, editio prima iuxta typicam Vaticanam (New York 1952).

Dennis C. Smolarski, *Q&A: Seasons, Sacraments and Sacramentals* (Chicago 2003).

United States Catholic Conference, Inc., *General Instruction of the Roman Missal* (Washington, D.C. 2003).

Cipriano. Vagaggini, *Theological Dimensions of the Liturgy: A General Treatise on the Theology of the Liturgy* , translated by L. J. Doyle and W. A. Jurgens (Collegeville, Minn. 1959).

Rev. John R. Quinn
Professor of Classical Languages and Theology and
President, St. Francis College, Minor Seminary
Diocese of San Diego, El Cajon, Calif.

Rev. Neil J. Roy
University of Notre Dame
Notre Dame, Ind. (2009)

SAN ANTONIO, ARCHDIOCESE OF

(*Santi Antonii*) Metropolitan see embracing 23,180 square miles in the state of Texas. The DIOCESE was established on September 8, 1874; the ARCHDIOCESE on August 3, 1926. The suffragans include the Texas dioceses: Amarillo, Lubbock, Fort Worth, Dallas, El Paso, San Angelo, and Laredo. In 2008, Catholics in the archdiocese numbered 687,788, about one-third of the total population of 2,171,851 (*The Official Catholic Directory*, 2008). This change was due to the creation of the Archdiocese of Galveston which took seven dioceses, including itself, away from the Archdiocese of San Antonio.

Early History. San Antonio was a little-known village in 1691, when the chaplain of a Spanish expedition, Damian Massenet, O.F.M., camped on that site and gave it the name of the day's saint, ANTHONY OF PADUA. The first settlement was made and the first mission founded, "San Antonio de Valero" (the Alamo), in 1718. By 1731 the Franciscans had established four other missions in the vicinity: La Purisima Concepción, San Juan Capistrano, San Francisco de la Espada, and San José; this last was made illustrious by the ministry of Fray Antonio MARGIL. The small settlement, increased by fifteen Canary Island families, organized the first city government in Texas in 1731. The colonists immediately provided for the building of a church and the support of a parish priest. Under Spanish rule a very clear distinction existed between a mission and a parish church. The mission was devoted entirely to the care of the Native Americans, while the Spanish colonists were organized into regular parishes. Thus, the first parish in Texas, and for many years the only one, was the old San Fernando Church of San Antonio, founded in 1731. The original dome and sanctuary form part of the present CATHE-DRAL, while the rest has been rebuilt and replaced several times. The grandiose plan of the mission churches never worked out in San Antonio and after a few years was almost entirely abandoned as the Native Americans moved away. San Fernando likewise suffered as, in turn, Mexico waged war against the mother country and Texas revolted against Mexico.

During these years of revolution, the Texas and San Antonio Catholics were practically abandoned. The achievement of Texas independence (1836) left them nominally under the jurisdiction of the BISHOP of Monterey, who had no English-speaking clergy to serve the American settlers. The Catholics of San Antonio, represented by John McMullen, petitioned the closest (600 miles) American bishop, Anthony BLANC of New Orleans, for priests to keep the scattered flock together. The HOLY SEE had already been apprised of the plight of the FAITHFUL in Texas and had also asked Blanc to investigate. In 1838, at Blanc's request, John TIMON, provincial of the VINCENTIANS, made a reconnaissance tour of the young republic. There he estimated the population at 1,500 with fifty American Catholics carelessly attended by two clerics of the old regime. The first Vincentians arrived in the spring of 1839, and later that year when Timon was appointed prefect apostolic of Texas, he sent John Mary ODIN, C.M., as vice prefect. Odin landed at Port Lavaca on July 12, 1840, and immediately proceeded to San Antonio where he formally appointed his Spanish companion Miguel Calvo, C.M., pastor of San Fernando. Gradually the haphazard conditions of the Church in San Antonio improved, as instanced by Odin's decree that church bells would be rung henceforth only to summon the faithful to services instead of the former practice of ringing them to announce horse races, cockfights, public dances, and the burial of non-Catholics. In late September, Odin visited the old missions and made plans to establish clear title to them for the Church. Three months later, with the help of the French chargé d'affaires, Alphonse de Saligny, he obtained from the legislature the restoration to the "chief pastor and his successors" of all former Spanish and Mexican CHURCH PROPERTY, including that of the Alamo and all other San Antonio missions.

Odin was named vicar apostolic of Texas on July 16, 1841, and was consecrated in New Orleans on March 6, 1842. On May 4, 1847, on the recommendation of the Sixth Provincial Council of Baltimore (1846), ROME raised the vicariate to the Diocese of Galveston and appointed Odin the first ordinary and suffragan of New Orleans. At that time ten churches were in actual use, served by six Vincentians and four secular priests. In 1847, Odin appointed resident pastors for St. Louis in Castroville and for the German settlements of Fredericksburg (1848) and New Braunfels (1849). Ursuline Academy opened in 1851, and the next year the Brothers of Mary started a school for boys in the city. When San Fernando became too small for the growing population, St. Mary's opened in early 1857 and remained a landmark in the heart of the city until 1923, when it was torn down and rebuilt after a disastrous flood. Claude Dubuis (1817–1895), who was in charge of both congregations when Odin was promoted to New Orleans (1860), succeeded his compatriot as second bishop of Galveston and was consecrated by Odin in their home diocese of Lyons, France.

In 1868 Dubuis blessed the new St. Michael's Church (Polish) in San Antonio and laid the cornerstone of St. Joseph's (German). The Poles and the Czechs meanwhile had built churches and even schools in many of their settlements south and east of the city. The closing years of the 1860s were notable for the arrival of religious communities destined to play an important role in the fields of education and charity in San Antonio.

Among them were the SISTERS OF DIVINE PROVIDENCE, who arrived at Castroville in 1868, and the Sisters of Charity of the INCARNATE WORD, at San Antonio in 1869. Both congregations provided higher education for women and staffed many elementary and secondary schools and hospitals. The second diocesan synod met in December 1868 for the purpose of reorganizing the constantly expanding diocese. Although the synod was held in two sections—Galveston for the east, San Antonio for the west and south—busy pastors of scattered communities could not absent themselves for long, so only half of the eighty Dubuis secular and religious priests were in attendance. Four chancellors were named for Galveston, San Antonio, Brownsville, and Laredo, foreshadowing the impending partition of the huge diocese.

Diocese. When in 1874 the Holy See created the Diocese of San Antonio and the vicariate apostolic of Brownsville (later the dioceses of Corpus Christi and Brownsville), Anthony D. Pellicer, a native of Florida, was consecrated December 8, 1874, for San Antonio, where he found about 12,000 Catholics in the city and 40,000 in the diocese. St. Mary's became the episcopal residence and chancery office for Pellicer, whose jurisdiction covered all counties between the Colorado and Nueces Rivers and extended as far west as El Paso and New Mexico, about 90,000 square miles (this remained without significant change until the creation of the Diocese of EL PASO in 1914). Frequent long journeys over the vast area, not reached by railroads until 1877, and the hardships of pioneer life undermined the health of the bishop, who died on April 14, 1880. At that time 47,000 Catholics in the diocese were served by forty-five priests and fifty churches. From 1876 to 1880, the Mexican JESUITS accepted students for the priesthood in their short-lived Guadalupe College at Seguin.

The next two ordinaries, John Claude Neraz (1881–1894) and John Anthony Forest (1895–1911), had spent all their priestly lives in the diocese. Neraz was pastor of San Fernando, and Forest had had a long and distinguished missionary career at Hallettsville, Lavaca County. They were the last representatives of the French secular priests who came to the United States in the nineteenth century and who laid the foundation of the Church in Texas. They seldom exercised their ministry among their own countrymen, but learned English and tried to master the language of the Mexicans and even those of the various other European immigrants to the area. In 1884 Neraz invited the OBLATES OF MARY IMMACULATE to take over St. Mary's parish and the mission district of the western part of the diocese. From 1884 to 1890 he accepted the additional burden of administering the affairs of the vicariate apostolic of Brownsville. By 1894, the Brothers of Mary had completed the first building of St. Louis College in the western outskirts of the city, later the main campus of St. Mary's University.

Under Bishop Forest the Catholic population increased from 66,000 to almost 100,000, and many missions and stations developed into self-sustaining parishes, some of them even able to build and maintain parochial schools. Forest laid the cornerstone of the new motherhouse of the Sisters of Divine Providence at Our Lady of the Lake (1895) and that of the Sisters of Charity of the Incarnate Word at Brackenridge Park (1899). In 1903 he blessed the new St. Anthony's Theological Seminary, operated by the oblate fathers, and sent some of his own seminarians there during the following decade. The death of Forest marked the end of the missionary period in the greater part of the diocese. He was succeeded in 1911 by his coadjutor, John William Shaw, who in turn was promoted to New Orleans in January 1918. Both Shaw and his successor, Arthur Jerome Drossaerts (1918–1940), sponsored charitable works on behalf of refugees from Mexico, especially members of the hierarchy. They successfully met the challenge of a growing population with many new churches and schools. Shaw founded the first diocesan seminary (1915) in the former episcopal residence and chancery on Dwyer Avenue. Bishop Drossaerts later moved it to a more suitable location next to Mission Concepción (1920). Closely associated with Shaw was his chancellor, William W. Hume, who served as first rector of the seminary and began the restoration of the four famous missions south of San Antonio.

Archdiocese. On August 3, 1926, when San Antonio was raised to metropolitan rank, Drossaerts became the first ARCHBISHOP. The new province included all of Texas and the state of Oklahoma, with the exception of the Diocese of El Paso. Its suffragans were Galveston,

Dallas, Corpus Christi, Oklahoma City, and Amarillo, to which Austin was added in 1947 and San Angelo in 1961. Although by 1908 the United States as a whole had ceased to be a frontier mission, outside aid was still vital to the preservation and spread of the Faith in many sections of the South and West. The archdiocese, unable to raise enough priests for its own needs, was indebted to the Irish and other clergy. In addition, the original Diocese of Galveston received from the Lyons Council of the Propagation of the Faith a total of $309,646 between 1846 and 1901, a sum larger than was granted to any other diocese in the United States. Between 1874 and 1918 San Antonio itself received $34,000 from the same source. The help extended by the Catholic Church Extension Society enabled the dioceses of Texas to care for the thousands of Spanish-speaking Catholics who came from Mexico during the troubled years of the Mexican persecution. By 1950 it had contributed to the Archdiocese of San Antonio alone the sum of $392,388 (not counting $138,446 in Mass stipends) for buildings, furnishings, and priests' support. Also, the AMERICAN BOARD OF CATHOLIC MISSIONS gave the archdiocese $307,925 from 1925 to 1951, and the Commission for Catholic Missions Among the Colored and Indians contributed $156,750 during the period from 1887 to 1951 (Castaneda 1936–1958, vol. 7, pp. 196–197).

Growth and New Developments. Under the leadership of Archbishop Robert E. LUCEY, who succeeded to the see in 1941, a CONFRATERNITY OF CHRISTIAN DOCTRINE (CCD) program was instituted in all the parishes of the archdiocese. A Catholic Welfare bureau was established as the church agency to coordinate Catholic social work; a Catholic Action Office was organized and extensive restoration of the Old Spanish Missions was begun. Although the *Southern Messenger* had been published for more than fifty years by the Menger family and was the official paper of the diocese, Lucey founded the *Alamo Register* as the official Catholic paper. The *Messenger* remained as the official paper for other dioceses in Texas. In 1957 the *Messenger* merged with the *Register* to form the *Alamo Messenger* and its companion in Spanish, *La Voz*.

The archdiocese also provided permanent headquarters for the Bishop's Committee for the Spanish Speaking to promote SOCIAL JUSTICE among Spanish-speaking peoples in the Southwest and among the migratory farm workers in the North. Lucey combined a social LIBERALISM with an ecclesiastical conservatism. He led the state in a successful racial integration of parochial schools in 1954, three years before the federally mandated integration of the public schools. With social activists such as Father Sherrill Smith, he spotlighted farmworker problems in Texas. In 1966 Lucey brought three federally funded POVERTY programs to San Antonio.

Lucey took part in Vatican II and implemented some of the council's recommended liturgical changes, but he refused to resign after reaching the age of seventy-five, as prescribed by Vatican II rules. In 1968 some fifty-one diocesan priests petitioned Pope PAUL VI for Lucey's retirement. The resulting conflict between Lucey and his clergy resulted in the departure of about one-third of the clergy and most of the seminarians. Rome intervened and appointed Bishop Francis Furey of San Diego as his successor. Furey actively promoted the lay movement with the use of the extraordinary ministers of the Eucharist and led the country in the promotion of the permanent diaconate. He picked as his auxiliary Patrick F. Flores, the first Mexican American to become a bishop (and the third to become archbishop). He began a pension plan for the priests and lay finance boards. The diocesan paper was reorganized under the name *Today's Catholic*.

In 1972, with Father Virgil Elizondo and Bishop Flores, Furey oversaw the establishment of the Mexican American Cultural Center on the campus of Assumption Seminary. His achievements were many: the establishment of eleven new parishes, maintenance and promotion of a strong anti–abortion stance, active promotion of labor rights, support of the Citizens Organized for Political Service (COPS) program, and strong leadership of his growing Hispanic flock.

A year after the death of Archbishop Furey on April 23, 1979, Bishop Patrick Flores of El Paso became the fourth archbisop of San Antonio. In June 1981, Archbishop Flores laid out his vision for the archdiocese in a document called *A New Pentecost*, calling for action in five areas: (1) a call to ministry, stressing the role of the lay ministry; (2) parish development, focusing on office parish development to educate leaders and work along with COPS; (3) preference for persons with special needs, developing new programs for the poor, elderly, and handicapped; (4) reorganization of diocesan structures to focus on service and give increased attention to the needs of the rural areas of the diocese; and (5) initiation of the Emmaus program for priestly development.

An important highlight of the episcopate of Archbishop Flores was the visit of Pope JOHN PAUL II to San Antonio on September 13, 1987. The pope spent twenty-two hours in the city and made three major speeches.

Other significant developments included the convocation of a synod in 1994 to plan for the future direction of the archdiocese; the introduction of new programs for the spiritual needs of prison inmates, pregnant adolescents, the homeless, abused children, and

Installation of Archbishop-elect Jose Gomez. *Archbishop Patrick Flores, front center, and Archbishop-elect Jose Gomez, center right, during Mass of Installation for Gomez as the Archbishop of San Antonio, at San Fernando Cathedral on February 15, 2005, in San Antonio, Texas.* © KIN MAN HUI/SAN ANTONIO EXPRESS/ZUMA/CORBIS

battered women; the encouragement of lay participation through programs such as RENEW; the establishment of a diocesan television station (the only diocesan-operated station in the United States), providing 24–hour broadcasting; and the erection of new dioceses. The Victoria diocese was formed from nine eastern counties of the archdiocese and counties from Corpus Christi and Galveston-Houston. Bishop Grahmann became the first bishop. In 2000 four western counties were detached from the archdiocese and added to some from Corpus Christi to form the new diocese of Laredo.

The NEWMAN APOSTOLATE expanded to all the non-Catholic colleges and universities in the archdiocese. BOYS TOWN of Nebraska established two facilities in the archdiocese to care for runaway and abandoned youth and to provide family counseling. In 1982 the Catholic Consultation center was established to provide psychological screening for seminarians and religious as well as mental health programs. This subsequently expanded to include laity of all faiths. The Catholic Youth Organization provides recreation and sports for hundreds of thousands of youth throughout the archdiocese as well as an annual youth congress and other youth programs.

In June 2000 Archbishop Flores was kidnapped and held for eight hours, and others on his staff were trapped in the situation. The event was broadcast around the world. The kidnapper wanted Flores to intervene with authorities to restore his papers so he could get employment and support his family. He previously had been deported on drug charges. The bishop convinced him to surrender peacefully. On December 29, 2005, Pope BENEDICT XVI accepted the retirement of Archbishop Patrick Flores and appointed Bishop Jose H. Gomez as the fifth archbishop of San Antonio. At the same time the province of Texas was split, and Galveston-Houston was raised to the rank of archdiocese.

The Cathedral of San Fernando underwent a total renovation and restoration. The highlight is the twenty-four-foot gold altar of repose. All the auxiliary buildings were completed in 2003. The SHRINE of the Little Flower, also known as Our Lady of Mount Carmel and St. Therese, was raised to the rank of a BASILICA in 1999. The shrine of St. PADRE PIO was completed in December 2007.

A $15 million addition to Assumption Seminary, built to house sixty additional seminarians, was completed in the fall of 2007. To comply with the bishops' committee request, the Office of Victim Assistance and Safe Environment was created. The archdiocese provided a large amount of aid to its sister diocese of Tegucigalpa, Honduras, following hurricane Mitch in 1998 and to others in 2005. San Antonio

Catholic Radio began broadcasting in 2007 with one station in English and another in Spanish.

SEE ALSO BALTIMORE, COUNCILS OF; GALVESTON-HOUSTON, ARCHDIOCESE OF; MEXICO, COLONIAL; MISSION AND MISSIONS; NEW ORLEANS, ARCHDIOCESE OF; OKLAHOMA CITY, ARCHDIOCESE OF; OKLAHOMA, CATHOLIC CHURCH IN; TEXAS, CATHOLIC CHURCH IN; VATICAN COUNCIL II.

BIBLIOGRAPHY

Archdiocese of San Antonio, Diamond Jubilee, 1874–1949 (San Antonio, Tex. 1948). Although a commemorative album, this is a better-than-average illustrated record of the foundation and growth of all the parishes and institutions of the archdiocese.

Archives (Catholic), Austin, Texas.

Archives, University of Notre Dame.

Ralph Bayard, *Lone-Star Vanguard: The Catholic Re-occupation of Texas, 1838–1848* (St. Louis, Mo. 1945).

Bony, *Vie de Mgr. Jean-Marie Odin: Missionaire Lazariste, Archevêque de la Nouvelle-Orléans* (Paris 1896).

Saul E. Bronder, *Social Justice and Church Authority: The Public Life of Archbishop Robert E. Lucey* (Philadelphia 1982).

Carlos E. Castañeda, *Our Catholic Heritage in Texas, 1519–1936*, 7 vols., edited by Paul J. Foik (Austin, Tex. 1936–1958).

Sister Mary Angela Fitzmorris, *Four Decades of Catholicism in Texas, 1820–1860* (Washington, D.C. 1926).

Leo Vincent Jacks, *Claude Dubuis: Bishop of Galveston* (St. Louis, Mo. 1946).

Steve Landregan, *Catholic Texans: Our Family Album* (Strasbourg, France 2003).

Martin McMurtrey, *Mariachi Bishop: The Life Story of Patrick Flores* (San Antonio, Tex. 1987).

The Official Catholic Directory (New Providence, N.J. 2008).

P. F. Parisot and C. F. Smith, *History of the Catholic Church in the Diocese of San Antonio* (San Antonio, Tex. 1897).

Stephen A. Privett, *Robert E. Lucey: Evangelization and Catechesis among Hispanic Catholics* (Ann Arbor, Mich. 1985).

Franklin C. Williams, Jr., *Lone Star Bishops: The Roman Catholic Hierarchy in Texas* (Waco, Tex. 1997; Supplement 2003).

Rev. Bernard Doyon OMI
Professor of Philosophy, History, and Liturgical Music
Oblate College of the Southwest, San Antonio, Tex.

Br. Edward J. Loch SM
Archivist, Archdiocese of San Antonio
San Antonio, Tex. (2009)

SAN FRANCISCO, ARCHDIOCESE OF

Metropolitan see, established July 29, 1853, the Archdiocese of San Francisco (*Sancti Francisci*) embraces the California counties of San Francisco, Marin, and San Mateo, an area of 1,012 square miles. In 2008 the ARCHDIOCESE numbered some 382,500 Catholics in a total population of 1,698,282, about twenty-three percent (*The Official Catholic Directory* 2008, p. 1276). The ecclesiastic Province of San Francisco includes northern California and the states of Nevada, Utah, and Hawaii. Its suffragan sees are the Dioceses of Sacramento (established May 28, 1886), Oakland (February 21, 1962), Santa Rosa (February 21, 1962), Stockton (February 21, 1962), and San Jose (January 27, 1981) in California; Salt Lake City in Utah (January 27, 1891); RENO (March 27, 1931) and LAS VEGAS (March 21, 1995) in Nevada; and Honolulu, Hawaii (September 10, 1941).

Early History. Explorers such as Juan Rodriguez Cabrillo (1542), Sir Francis Drake (1572), and Sebastian Vizcaino (1602–1603) visited what is now northern California but actual colonization did not begin until late in the eighteenth century. In 1769 Gaspar de Portola's party began the actual Spanish penetration of modern California; his soldiers and the Franciscans under Junípero SERRA founded San Diego. Almost immediately Portola, Father Juan Crespi (1721–1782), and a detachment of soldiers marched north in an effort to find the Monterey Bay described by Cabrillo and Vizcaino. Crespi's diary gives an excellent account of this exploration in which the party, failing to recognize the open roadstead of Monterey as the sheltered Cabrillo port, continued on to discover San Francisco Bay. On November 1, 1769, the expedition's scout, Sergeant José de Ortega, became the first white man to see this almost landlocked bay that Crespi described as "a very large and fine harbor, such that not only all the navy of our Most Catholic Majesty, but those of all Europe could take shelter in it." From November 6 to 11 the explorers made their base of operations beneath a giant redwood (the *palo alto*) that has given its name to the adjacent university city and that can be seen from nearby St. Patrick's Archdiocesan Seminary, Menlo Park.

In 1770, when the DOMINICANS took over the missions in Baja California of modern Mexico, Father Francisco PALÓU, later the founder of the Mission Dolores in San Francisco, was released to join his fellow Mallorcans, Serra and Crespi, in the new Franciscan mission field of Alta California. In 1772 Crespi and Lieutenant Pedro Fages returned north, exploring along the east shore, or *contra costa*, of San Francisco Bay. They were the first white men to pass through the area where the large population centers of Hayward, San Leandro, Oakland, Berkeley, Richmond, Martinez, and central Contra Costa County later developed. From Mount Diablo they discovered the great Central Valley and its rivers.

In 1774 hopes for the extensive colonization of Alta California soared when Juan Bautista Anza (1736–1788) of Mexico opened up a land route from Sonora in Mexico to San Gabriel Mission near modern Los Angeles. The first San Franciscan colonists traveled along this new route. On August 1, 1775, Juan Manuel Ayala (1745–1797) successsfully brought the galleon *San Carlos* through the mile-wide entrance into San Francisco Bay; on September 29 Anza and the Franciscan Pedro Font (1738–1781), a Catalan, led the original San Francisco colonists from their homes in Sonora and Sinoloa on the first stage of a 1,600–mile trek to the new site at the Bay of St. Francis. The contingent began with 240 persons and reached San Gabriel on January 4, 1776, with 244. At Monterey, Anza and Font left the colonists behind while they pushed on to select the actual sites for the mission and presidio on San Francisco Bay.

In 1774 Palóu, while exploring with Rivera, had recommended establishing a mission near modern Palo Alto on San Francisquito Creek. But Anza and Font chose sites on the tip of the peninsula, with the presidio near the harbor entrance and the mission beneath the shelter of the Twin Peaks. When on March 29, 1776, both agreed on the new mission site, they called it *Arroyo de los Dolores* because it was the Friday of Sorrows. They also recommended the establishment of a future mission in San Mateo. The actual foundation of the colony in San Francisco was made by Lieutenant José Joaquin Moraga (1745–1785), Anza's aide, and by Father Palóu, while Anza and Font left for Sonora, never to return to California.

Under their new leaders Palóu and Moraga, the San Francisco colonists reached the Arroyo de los Dolores on June 29, 1776. Mass was celebrated in the presidio for the first time on July 28. The presidio was formally dedicated on September 17, and the new mission CHAPEL was blessed on October 3. Other Franciscan missions within the present limits of the archdiocese include Santa Clara and San Rafael; the first Mass at Santa Clara was celebrated by Father Tomas de la Pena on January 12, 1777. Later that year the first California town, as distinguished from missions and military installations, was established by colonists from San Francisco and named San José, but the proximity of that pueblo to the mission was not a source of consolation to the missionaries of Santa Clara.

On June 11, 1797, Father Fermin Francisco de Lasuen (1736–1803), Serra's successor, founded Mission San José de Guadalupe, the first church in Alameda County (now the Diocese of Oakland). The first Mass at the *asistencia* of San Rafael Arcangel, which was to serve as a branch of Mission Dolores, was celebrated on December 14, 1817. Subsequently San Rafael became a mission, but this first foundation north of San Francisco

Bay was established too late in the California mission period to prosper. The only California mission opened during the Mexican period was Mission San Francisco Solano, founded on July 4, 1823, in Sonoma (now the Diocese of Santa Rosa). This northernmost of the missions was hampered from the start in that unsettled time of revolution and SECULARIZATION.

When on July 17, 1781, Yuma tribespeople wiped out the Spanish settlements along the Sonora border, the plan to colonize California by land expeditions was abandoned, leaving Alta California with the prospect of inadequate manpower. By 1820 there were only 3,270 non-Native Americans in all that territory. In 1811 all aid from Spain to the California establishments ceased because of the revolutionary situation in Mexico; from then until 1834 the missions sustained both their own works and that of the civil authority. In April 1822 California recognized the new regime in Mexico, and on November 22 Luis Argüello (1784–1830), a native Californian, was appointed governor of the territory north to Oregon and east to the Rocky Mountains. On January 7, 1824, news reached Monterey that the new empire of Mexico had become a republic, and on March 26, 1825, California was officially declared a territory of the Mexican Republic. Eight years later the Mexican government decreed that the friars should be replaced with secular priests and their possessions put under civil control. On August 9, 1834, the California assembly published the law of secularization of the missions. A year later the property of fifteen of the twenty-one missions had been secularized. In 1836 the Mexican government recommended that a DIOCESE of the two Californias be formed. It agreed to contribute for its support $6,000 annually, plus maintained the right to administer the PIOUS FUND. Unfortunately, when the diocese was formed in 1840, this support was not given. Meanwhile, the native Californians began to resist the Mexican government, whose policies toward the missions eventually led to the breakdown of the system so carefully prepared by the Franciscans.

First Bishop. The first California BISHOP, the Zacatecan friar Francisco GARCIA DIEGO Y MORENO, was consecrated on October 4, 1840, for a see to be established at San Diego. However, when he found that town too small to support him, he moved to Santa Barbara on June 10, 1842. On June 29 he ordained Miguel Gomez there; this was the first ordination ceremony in California. Father Gonzales Rubio (1804–1875), who played an important role after Diego's death, moved down from Mission San José to be his secretary. At that same time President Santa Anna (c. 1794–1876) of Mexico took over the Pious Fund to finance his new regime, with the promise that he would pay the diocese six percent annually on the capital. Meanwhile the new

bishop was without support. Although he founded a seminary at Santa Inés Mission in 1844, the shortage of clergy remained acute. The Mission Dolores in San Francisco was without a priest from 1839 to 1846, because General Mariano Vallejo (1807–1890) in Sonoma insulted the bishop and any priest who attempted to serve that area. Diego died on April 30, 1846. Four days later Pio Pico (1801–1894), leader of the Spanish-speaking Californians, in disregard of the restrictions of the Mexican government, began to sell the last mission properties.

American Period. A new force entered the field when war broke out between the United States and Mexico on May 13, 1846, and a group of Americans ran up the Bear Flag in Sonoma (June 14) in revolt against the Mexican government and started the short-lived Republic of California. On July 7 the American flag was flown in Monterey, and two days later it was raised in San Francisco. In 1847 the Church in California was saved from complete extinction after General Stephen W. Kearney (1794–1848) assumed charge of the state civil government and made Monterey his capital. On March 22 he issued a proclamation that the missions of Santa Clara, San José, Santa Cruz, and Santa Ines were to remain in the hands of the priests until such time as a proper tribunal could study the cases. This strong action held off both California despoilers and Yankee squatters and paved the way for the 1854 decision of the government land commission that confirmed Archbishop Joseph Alemany's claim to parts of the mission property. Kearney's military successors, Colonel Richard Mason and General Bennett Riley, maintained this same position and even removed Yankee squatters from mission buildings.

On January 30, 1847, the name San Francisco was given to the little town then numbering 375 whites, 34 Native Americans, 40 Sandwich Islanders, and 10 African Americans. In addition there was a young Spanish-speaking secular priest, Prudencio Santillan, newly appointed to the Mission Dolores. With the conclusion of the Mexican War in 1848, California was ceded to the United States and steps were taken to set up a constitutional government there. In November 1849 Peter Burnett (1807–1895), a Catholic convert from Tennessee, was elected the first civilian American governor, and San José was chosen as the first capital. During this same year over 80,000 gold seekers came into a California that had but 15,000 white inhabitants a year earlier. On February 18, 1850, the new legislature created the twenty-seven original counties of the state, and on September 9 California officially became a state.

During this period of transition the affairs of the Church in California were in the hands of the Zacatecan Franciscan José María Gonzales Rubio, who had been named administrator of the see of the two Californias after Diego's death. He protested the rapacity of the native Californians, obtained the protection of the American military governors, kept the small seminary in Santa Ines open, assigned his few priests as effectively as he could, and sought clerical assistance from other areas. His appeal to the Congregation of the Sacred Hearts (Picpus Fathers) brought help from their missions in the Sandwich Islands and in Valparaiso, Chile. In December 1848 Father John Baptist BROUILLET, a French Canadian then serving as vicar general of the Diocese of Walla-Walla in the Oregon Territory, arrived in San Francisco to visit those who had left the North for Californian gold fields. Moved by the grave need in San Francisco, he built the first Catholic church in the old Yankee settlement of Yerba Buena and named it St. Francis. With Rubio's encouragement, he wrote to Oregon for help.

Brouillet remained only a year in the new settlement but was joined by another French Canadian, Anthony Langlois, who arrived on July 19, 1849, en route to Missouri, and remained to work at St. Francis during this critical time. After Brouillet returned to his Oregon post in December 1849, he was replaced by the JESUITS Michael ACCOLTI and John NOBILI, who had come from that territory in response to Brouillet's letter. These two recruits played a notable role in the ecclesiastical development of northern California, including the establishment of Santa Clara University and the University of San Francisco. In 1850 Santillan left the Mission Dolores to return to Mexico, but in midyear James Croke (d. 1889), an Irish priest on his way from Paris to the Oregon missions, reached San Francisco just when cholera broke out. He stayed to help and was the only English-speaking priest there when Alemany, the new bishop, arrived on December 6. Subsequently Croke went on to Oregon but returned later to become the pastor of the first Catholic Church in Oakland, vicar general, founder of St. Mary's College (then in San Francisco), and manager of St. Vincent's orphanage, San Rafael.

Joseph Sadoc Alemany. In May 1849 the Seventh Provincial Council of Baltimore submitted three names to ROME for bishop of the Californias, and Charles Pius Montgomery, O.P., of Zanesville, Ohio, was chosen by PIUS IX (pope 1846–1878) in November of that year. When Montgomery's refusal of this assignment reached Rome in the spring of 1850, the pope appointed Joseph Sadoc ALEMANY, U.S. provincial of the Dominicans, who was then in Rome to attend a chapter meeting. Alemany was consecrated in Rome on June 30 and returned to the United States with Francis VILARRASA, O.P., who established the Dominican Order in California, and the Belgian Sister M. Goemare, O.P., the first

Catholic sister for the new state. In New York Alemany accepted for service in his new diocese John Maginnis, who had been ordained in 1823 and who subsequently became the first pastor of St. Patrick's Church, San Francisco, founder of the first parochial school in the city, and director of the orphan asylum that the Daughters of Charity staffed in 1852.

When Bishop Alemany arrived in San Francisco by ship on December 6, 1850, and offered Mass in St. Francis of Assisi Church, San Francisco had an estimated 20,000 people. The entire state had only twenty-four churches open, and twenty-two of these were either old mission or pueblo churches. The other two were St. Francis in San Francisco, and St. Rose in Sacramento. The latter was built in 1850 by Peter Augustine Anderson, O.P., who had served with the new bishop in the eastern field, but who died of cholera just before Alemany arrived in California. Anderson was succeeded shortly after his death by John Ingoldsby of Chicago, Illinois, who was probably the first priest to penetrate into the active mining region in northern California. For all California, Alemany had twelve diocesan priests, seven aging Franciscans left from the earlier period, seven French Picpus priests from the missions of Valparaiso and the Sandwich Islands, a Dominican who had transferred from Baja California to Monterey, and a Jesuit (Accolti had returned to Oregon to become provincial). This shortage was further complicated by the fact that Alemany's jurisdiction included, until December 21, 1851, Baja California, although protests of the Mexican government made this responsibility a purely technical one.

On February 4, 1851, Alemany transferred his residence from Santa Barbara to Monterey, where the royal chapel of the presidio served as his CATHEDRAL. There also Vilarrasa and Mother Goemare established their Dominican communities. Concepción Argüello received the Dominican habit from the bishop on April 11, 1851, and became the first native Californian to enter a religious community for women. In that same year the Sisters of NOTRE DAME DE NAMUR entered the state and on August 14 opened in San José the first foundation of religious women within the present confines of the Archdiocese of San Francisco. In December John Nobili established at the Santa Clara Mission a school that later became the University of Santa Clara. During the year Eugene O'Connell (1815–1891), later bishop of Grass Valley (Sacramento after 1886), came from All Hallows in Ireland to direct the struggling diocesan seminary at Santa Ines.

On March 19, 1852, Alemany held the first synod of his new diocese; it treated the rights of the Church to the mission properties, parish and diocesan support, and the laws of Christian marriage. Shortly thereafter Alemany left for the First Plenary Council of Baltimore.

While in the East he persuaded the Daughters of Charity of St. Vincent de Paul at Emmitsburg, Maryland, to accept a mission in San Francisco. Two of the pioneer band died of fever while crossing the Isthmus of Panama en route to California, but the remaining sisters established the first CONVENT in San Francisco. They not only took over the orphans whom Father Maginnis of St. Patrick's Church was sheltering, but also taught in the parish school there. Another recruit for the California mission was Father Hugh GALLAGHER, who had served as theologian to Bishop Michael O'CONNOR of Pittsburgh, Pennsylvania, at the council. Gallagher volunteered to work for a year in the West, but remained there for the rest of his life and played a major role in bringing the Presentation Nuns and the SISTERS OF MERCY to San Francisco in 1854. On November 21, 1852, Eugene O'Connell was assigned to Mission Dolores, where the diocesan seminary was reestablished. On December 26 John Quinn, a seminarian from St. Patrick's, Carlow, Ireland, was ordained at St. Francis Church in the first ordination ceremony in San Francisco.

Archdiocese. On July 29, 1853, Alemany became ARCHBISHOP of San Francisco, a see that included all of California from the southern boundary of the Pueblo of San José to the Oregon border, together with all the territory north of the Colorado River and west of the Rocky Mountains. At the same time Bishop Thaddeus AMAT, C.M., was appointed to the Diocese of Monterey, with residence in Santa Barbara. When the archdiocese was formed, 22 priests and 25 churches served approximately 50,000 Catholics. Outside San Francisco only 13 churches had resident pastors, and 10 of these were in the mining regions of northern California. The 3 nonmining-area churches outside the see city were St. Joseph, San José; St. Rose, Sacramento; and St. Mary, Stockton. While St. Mary's Cathedral was being built for its dedication in 1854, St. Francis Church served as a temporary cathedral.

The struggling archdiocese received help with the arrival in 1854 of five Presentation Nuns on November 13 and eight Sisters of Mercy on December 8. With the earlier arrivals, these sisters established schools, hospitals, and works of charity—despite the violence that led to the formation of the Vigilantes; the regular cholera outbreaks; the disappointments; the bigotry of the Know-Nothings, who carried the 1856 elections; and dire financial need. In 1868 the Holy Names Sisters arrived to open the first Catholic school in Oakland, and the DOMINICAN SISTERS from Holy Cross Convent, Brooklyn, New York, followed in 1876. In distant Utah, still part of the archdiocese in 1875, the Holy Cross Sisters reached Salt Lake City. During Alemany's episcopacy the Ursuline sisters established their school in

Santa Rosa in 1880, and the Sisters of St. Joseph of Carondelet established theirs in Oakland in 1883. The first brothers arrived in 1868 when the devoted sons of St. John Baptist DE LA SALLE took over St. Mary's College, which had been operated by diocesan priests since 1863. In 1884 the Brothers of Mary reached Stockton.

The sprawling archdiocese was first divided when the Vicariate of Marysville was formed in 1861 to include all of California north of the thirty-ninth parallel. Although the Diocese of Sacramento eventually developed from the Marysville vicariate, the archdiocese retained Sacramento, Yolo, El Dorado, Amador, Calaveras, Tuolumne, Alpine, Mono, and Mariposa counties until 1886. Alemany strengthened Church administration through the diocesan synod of 1862 and the provincial councils of 1874 and 1882. In 1877 the *Monitor*, which had been founded in 1858, was made the official paper of all the dioceses in the Province of San Francisco. In 1872, under the direction of Monsignor John J. Prendergast, vicar general of the archdiocese between 1874 and 1914, Elizabeth Armer, foundress of the Holy Family Sisters, began her work with neglected children. In 1878, in response to Alemany's request, Bishop William ELDER of Natchez, Mississippi, was appointed to aid Alemany, but an outbreak of yellow fever in Mississippi forced him to ask for a delay. In 1880 he was sent as coadjutor to Cincinnati, Ohio, and a disappointed Alemany renewed his appeal for assistance. In 1883 Patrick W. RIORDAN of St. James Church, Chicago, was named coadjutor of the San Francisco archdiocese; he was consecrated on September 16.

Patrick W. Riordan. LEO XIII (pope 1878–1903) accepted Alemany's resignation on March 27, 1884, but the act did not become effective until December 28. In the interval the archbishop attended the Third Plenary Council of Baltimore, where he served as chairman of the commission of bishops to report on the expediency of a uniform catechism (the famous BALTIMORE CATECHISM). When, on December 28, 1884, Riordan succeeded to the see, there was a Catholic population of 120,000, served by 156 priests in 133 churches and chapels. Two years later the next territorial change in the Archdiocese of San Francisco took place when the Diocese of Grass Valley, formerly the Vicariate of Marysville, was changed to the Diocese of Sacramento. At this time certain counties south of the thirty-ninth parallel, including Sacramento and Yolo, were transferred to the new see. Another change took place when the vicariate apostolic of Utah was formed on January 25, 1887.

During Riordan's episcopacy, the solid foundations of the archdiocese were further strengthened despite the impact of the Spanish-American War and the tragic 1906 earthquake and fire. More religious communities of men and women arrived to share in the work of the pioneers. The new St. Mary's Cathedral was solemnly dedicated on January 11, 1891. In 1892 the *Monitor* was taken over by the archdiocese as owner and publisher. On September 20, 1898, St. Patrick's Seminary, Menlo Park, opened with the Sulpician priests in charge. Encouraged by the Council of Baltimore, parochial schools increased rapidly. Prior to this period all but a handful of schools had been academies or community operated, but toward the end of the nineteenth century the parish school became dominant. Riordan established a board of diocesan education and in 1894 introduced the annual convention of teaching orders. Father Peter C. YORKE (1864–1925) was active at this time not only in arranging programs but also in writing his widely used textbooks of religion (1896). In 1899 John J. Cantwell, later archbishop of Los Angeles, began the Newman Club for Catholic students at the University of California at Berkeley.

Public matters also claimed the attention of Archbishop Riordan. In 1894 he named Yorke as editor of the *Monitor*, with a commission to combat the wave of bigotry stirred up by the AMERICAN PROTECTIVE ASSOCIATION. In 1900 Riordan led a successful campaign to free the churches in California from the burden of state taxation, and two years later he represented the hierarchy of California before the International Court at The Hague in their successful prosecution of justice in the Pious Fund case. By 1903, when the archdiocese was celebrating its fiftieth year, there were 250,000 Catholics, in contrast to the 40,000 throughout all northern California in 1853. They were served by 271 priests in 148 churches and missions. Riordan's request for a coadjutor was answered on March 27, 1903, when George Montgomery (1847–1907), bishop of Monterey-Los Angeles, was appointed titular archbishop of Osimo and coadjutor with right of succession.

On April 18, 1906, while Riordan was in the East, northern California was struck by a severe earthquake that was followed in San Francisco by a calamitous fire. Twelve parishes, with all their facilities, were wiped out by the fire, along with St. Mary's and Mary's Help Hospitals, two colleges and three academies, three day homes for children, the home for the aged poor, and the Youths' Directory for homeless boys. In the unburned part of the city, two other churches were destroyed and three were damaged, while elsewhere in the diocese a number of buildings, including the new St. Patrick's Seminary, were severely shaken. During this disaster more than 300,000 people left the city. Oakland, which had about 66,000 people in 1900, grew to more than 276,000 in 1907. Although San Francisco rapidly rebuilt after this tragedy, the strain was too much for Montgomery, who died on January 10, 1907, and Riordan again

petitioned Rome for a coadjutor. Rome did not believe that the time was opportune for a coadjutor but on December 24, 1908, named Denis J. O'Connell (1849–1927), former rector of the NORTH AMERICAN COLLEGE in Rome and of The CATHOLIC UNIVERSITY OF AMERICA, Washington, D.C., as auxiliary to Riordan. When, on January 16, 1912, O'Connell was transferred to the Diocese of Richmond, Virginia, the archbishop again appealed for a coadjutor; on October 22, 1912, Edward J. HANNA of Rochester, New York, was appointed TITULAR BISHOP of Titopolis and auxiliary of San Francisco.

Edward J. Hanna. Riordan's death on December 27, 1914, ended his thirty-one-year episcopacy, and Hanna succeeded to the see. He was installed on July 28, 1915, as third ordinary by Archbishop John Bonzano, APOSTOLIC DELEGATE. He gave immediate attention to diocesan administration; appointed John J. Cantwell (1874–1947) as his vicar general; established a matrimonial court under the direction of the eminent canonist Henri Ayrinhac, SS; and strengthened Catholic education by appointing Reverend Ralph Hunt as first superintendent of diocesan schools (1915). The archbishop also directed the formation of a teachers' scholastic council to advise about texts and courses of study (1916) and of a teachers' institute (1916); he appealed for, and received, city health services in the schools (1916). Moreover, he sponsored a one-week summer school (1916), the first four-week summer school in the archdiocese (1918), the national convention of the Catholic Education Association (1918), and the opening of new schools on all levels.

Hanna's prominent role in the National Catholic War Council of the bishops during World War I resulted in his election as the first chairman of the administrative council of the postwar National Catholic Welfare Conference. He also took a leading part in the effort to lift the burden of taxation from orphanages (1920), cemeteries (1926), and nonprofit elementary and secondary schools (1933). Through Hanna's civic activities the Church achieved a position in public life that did much to offset the unfortunate efforts of the KU KLUX KLAN and other similar groups of the post–World War I period. During this era of war, boom, and depression, the main chapel of St. Patrick's Seminary was completed (1918); St. Joseph's College, Mountain View, the archdiocesan minor seminary, opened (1924); the College of Notre Dame was transferred from San José to Belmont (1923); St. Mary's College moved its site from Oakland to Contra Costa County (1928); San Francisco College for Women opened at the Lone Mountain location (1930); the Convent of the Good Shepherd came into being (1932); and the Catholic Youth Organization was established (1933). Interest in the foreign-born resulted

St. Ignatius Church, San Francisco. *Pictured here is an aerial view of St. Ignatius Church lit at twilight. The church is located on the Jesuit-run campus of the University of San Francisco.* © **DANITA DELIMONT / ALAMY**

in the formation of the Italian Catholic Federation (1924), St. Mary's Chinese School (1921), and Morning Star Japanese School (1930). In 1922 the creation of the Diocese of Monterey-Fresno slightly altered the southern boundary of the archdiocese; the new line followed existing counties.

John J. Mitty. To assist him in meeting the demands of the growing archdiocese, Hanna received as his coadjutor, on January 29, 1932, John J. MITTY, who had been appointed bishop of Salt Lake City, Utah, on June 21, 1926, while serving as pastor of St. Luke's Church, New York City. Hanna resigned on March 2, 1935, and died in Rome on July 10, 1944. Mitty, after succeeding to the see on March 2, 1935, presided over the second diocesan synod (1936), which produced a complete set of statutes governing the activities of the various departments in the archdiocese. In June 1936 Los Angeles, a suffragan of San Francisco, was raised to an archdiocese, and California became the first state with two distinct ecclesiastical provinces. During World War II, when San Francisco became the major port of embarkation to the Pacific theater of war, the archdiocese generously assisted

military personnel and their dependents; thirty-five diocesan priests and fifty-four religious from the archdiocese served in the chaplain corps.

In the postwar period the spectacular growth of the Far West was reflected in the increase of population in the archdiocese. It led to an extension of social services, youth activities, the CONFRATERNITY OF CHRISTIAN DOCTRINE (CCD), and specialized CATHOLIC ACTION to an unprecedented degree. New elementary schools and new high schools were opened, and each of the seven Catholic four-year colleges in the archdiocese expanded both in buildings and in programs. In 1952 and 1958 campaigns to free private, nonprofit schools from the burden of taxation were vigorously and successfully prosecuted in the archdiocese. In 1955 a new chancery building, housing the archbishop's office, the diocesan curia, the *Monitor*, the department of education, and the Confraternity of Christian Doctrine was constructed adjacent to the Mission Dolores. Wider participation in Catholic Action characterized these years, making possible the Family Rosary Crusade, which culminated in a public rally attended by an estimated

The Cathedral of St. Mary of the Assumption, San Francisco. *Pictured here is an aerial view of the uniquely designed cathedral.* © AERIAL ARCHIVES / ALAMY

500,000 people in the polo field of Golden Gate Park on October 7, 1961. Eight days after this great public PRAYER, Archbishop Mitty died at St. Patrick's Seminary, Menlo Park.

Joseph T. McGucken. On February 19, 1962, Joseph T. McGucken (1902–1983), bishop of Sacramento, was appointed fifth archbishop of San Francisco, and his solemn installation in St. Mary's Cathedral took place on April 3, 1962. McGucken, born in Los Angeles and a former student at St. Patrick's Seminary, Menlo Park, and the North American College, Rome, was the first native Californian to be named to the see. With his appointment Rome announced also the formation of the three dioceses of Oakland, Santa Rosa, and Stockton, thus downsizing the territory, population, and number of institutions in the San Francisco Archdiocese. The destruction of St. Mary's Cathedral by fire, on September 7, 1962, marred the first year of McGucken's episcopacy. The loss spurred a generous response when the archbishop launched a successful building drive to replace the cathedral (despite some protests), construct new high schools and a home for the aged, and expand the archdiocesan seminary. McGucken played an active role

in VATICAN COUNCIL II, particularly as episcopal moderator of the American press panel. Even while Vatican II was still in session, he established social action committees in every parish and encouraged the renewal called for by the council. In 1972 priests of the archdiocese threatened a strike in the face of McGucken's opposition and successfully agitated for a priest association.

John R. Quinn. When McGucken retired in 1977, the Most Reverend John R. Quinn, archbishop of Oklahoma City, was transferred to San Francisco as his successor. Quinn oversaw the increasing ethnic-cultural diversification of the archdiocese, resulting from huge influxes of Mexican migrant laborers and their families, Vietnamese refugees, and other Asian immigrants. A high point of his episcopacy was Pope JOHN PAUL II's visit to San Francisco in 1987. At the same time, Quinn had to grapple with worsening archdiocesan finances. In response, he proposed a new archdiocesan pastoral plan, reorganized archdiocesan structures, initiated opportunities for lay ministries, established innovative youth and other service and outreach programs, and set up a school for training laity for leadership and ministry roles. His attempts to rein in the growing archdiocesan deficit generated much controversy when he attempted to close ten inner-city parishes and consolidate their dwindling congregations, including the oldest parish church, St. Francis.

William J. Levada. When Quinn submitted his resignation in 1995, he was succeeded by the Most Reverend William J. Levada (1936–). Levada was archbishop of Portland, Oregon, from 1983 to 1995, when he was transferred to San Francisco as coadjutor archbishop to Quinn. On December 27, 1995, Levada succeeded Quinn as archbishop. Two weeks earlier they had co-signed a joint Archdiocesan Pastoral Plan to address the new realities of the church in the twenty-first century. One of the most controversial aspects of the plan, the closure of ten parishes, met with some protest. In light of these protests, Levada re-opened several of the churches for alternative uses, such as St. Francis, which became the National Shrine of St. Francis of Assisi in 1999. Many of the older urban parishes that were not closed needed to retrofit their buildings as a result of the severe new city building codes on unreinforced masonry buildings. Expenses for retrofitting totaled well over $100 million. (The need to retrofit so many buildings is what prompted the closing of parishes.)

The influx of immigrants continued apace, most notably from Asia and Latin America. By 2000 nearly one of every four Catholics in the archdiocese was of Filipino descent. In San Francisco, the Chinese became the largest ethnic group in the city, surpassing even Caucasians. To the elation of the Chinese, Monsignor Ignatius Wang (1934–), a native of Beijing, was elevated to auxiliary bishop on December 13, 2002, making him the first bishop of Chinese and Asian origin in the history of the United States Catholic Church.

Since the 1970s San Francisco had emerged as a center of gay and lesbian culture and population, a reality that created tensions with the Catholic community. Issues such as domestic partners' legislation, same-sex marriages, and the right of gay couples to adopt conflicted with the traditional teaching of the Catholic Church on sexual issues and marriage. Conversely, the Church was one of the main providers of hospice care to men and women suffering from HIV/AIDS, and Most Holy Redeemer parish in the Castro district served a predominantly gay and lesbian congregation.

On February 12, 1999, as a result of the efforts of its director of communications, Maury Healy, the archdiocese began a new weekly newspaper, *Catholic San Francisco*, replacing *The Monitor*, which had ceased publication in 1984. Daniel Morris-Young was the first editor.

On May 13, 2005, Archbishop Levada was named prefect of the Vatican Congregation for the DOCTRINE OF THE FAITH, replacing Cardinal Joseph Ratzinger, who had become Pope BENEDICT XVI. Levada was the first U.S. bishop to hold this office. He became a CARDINAL in February 2006. Succeeding Levada in December 2005 was Archbishop George Niederauer (1936–), originally from the archdiocese of Los Angeles, who had served as bishop of Salt Lake City since 1994.

On December 23, 2005, Randolph R. Calvo (1950–), a native of Guam, pastor of Our Lady of Mount Carmel in Redwood City, was appointed bishop of Reno. Bishop John Wester (1950–), who had served as an auxiliary bishop since 1998, and had briefly served as archdiocesan administrator following Levada's departure for Rome, was appointed bishop of Salt Lake City in January 2007.

Catholic Institutions of Higher Learning. These include the Jesuit-run University of San Francisco, the College of Notre Dame in Belmont (sponsored by the Sisters of Notre Dame de Namur), and the Dominican College of San Rafael (sponsored by the Dominican Sisters). Of these, the University of San Francisco is the oldest and largest, established 1855 as St. Ignatius College for men. Upon attaining university status in 1930, it was renamed University of San Francisco. It became coeducational in 1964.

SEE ALSO BALTIMORE, COUNCILS OF; CALIFORNIA, CATHOLIC CHURCH IN; CARDINAL NEWMAN SOCIETY; HAWAII, CATHOLIC CHURCH IN; HOSPICE MOVEMENT; KNOW-NOTHINGISM; MARRIAGE LEGISLATION (CANON LAW); MEXICO, COLONIAL; MISSION AND MISSIONS; MISSION HISTORY, I: CATHOLIC; NATIONAL CATHOLIC EDUCATIONAL ASSOCIATION (NCEA); NEVADA, CATHOLIC CHURCH IN; SULPICIANS; URSULINES; UTAH, CATHOLIC CHURCH IN.

BIBLIOGRAPHY

Archdiocese of San Francisco Official Web site, available from: http://www.sfarchdiocese.org/ (accessed October 2, 2008).

Archdiocesan Archives, San Francisco, including the diary of Bishop Diegoy Moreno, continued by Archbishop Alemany.

Archives, University of Santa Clara, including the diary of Father Langlois. Spanish and Mexican archives in the University of California.

Alessandro Baccari, Jr., Vincenza Scarpaci, Gabriel Zavattaro, et al., *Saints Peter and Paul Church: The Chronicles of "the Italian Cathedral" of the West, 1884–1984* (San Francisco 1985).

John A. Berger, *The Franciscan Missions of California* (Garden City, N.Y. 1948).

Joseph Stanislaus Brusher, *Consecrated Thunderbolt: A Life of Father Peter C. Yorke of San Francisco* (Hawthorne, N.J. 1973).

Jeffrey M. Burns, *A History of the Archdiocese of San Francisco*, 3 vols. (Strasbourg, France 1999–2001).

Jeffrey M. Burns, ed., *Catholic San Francisco: Sesquicentennial Essays* (Menlo Park, Calif. 2005).

The California Historical Society papers. Dominicana files (St. Dominic's Priory, San Francisco), available from http://www.californiahistoricalsociety.org/collections/index.html (accessed October 2, 2008).

Peter Thomas Conmy and Jeffrey M. Burns, "The Mexican Catholic Community in California," in *Mexican Americans and the Catholic Church, 1900–1965*, edited by Jay P. Dolan and Gilberto M. Hinojosa (Notre Dame, Ind. 1994).

Juan Crespi, *Fray Juan Crespi, Missionary Explorer on the Pacific Coast, 1769–1774*, edited by Herbert Eugene Bolton (Berkeley, Calif. 1927).

Bernard Cornelius Cronin, *Father Yorke and the Labor Movement in San Francisco, 1900–1910* (Washington, D.C. 1943).

Pedro Font, *Font's Complete Diary: A Chronicle of the Founding of San Francisco*, translated and edited by Herbert Eugene Bolton (Berkeley, Calif. 1933).

James P. Gaffey *Citizen of No Mean City: Archbishop Patrick Riordan of San Francisco, 1841–1914* (Wilmington, Del. 1976).

James P. Gaffey *Men of Menlo: Transformation of an American Seminary* (Washington, D.C. 1992).

Maynard J. Geiger, *The Life and Times of Fray Junípero Serra, O.F.M.; Or, The Man Who Never Turned Back, 1713–1784: A Biography*, 2 vols. (Washington, D.C. 1959).

Richard Gribble, *Catholicism and the San Francisco Labor Movement, 1896–1921* (San Francisco 1993).

Richard Gribble, C.S.C., *An Archbishop for the People: The Life of Edward J. Hanna* (Mahwah, N.J. 2006).

John Bernard McGloin, *California's First Archbishop: The Life of Joseph Sadoc Alemany, 1814–1888* (New York 1966).

John Bernard McGloin, *Jesuits by the Golden Gate* (San Francisco, 1972).

The Official Catholic Directory, 2008 (New Providence, N.J. 2008).

Francisco Palóu, *Life of Fray Junípero Serra*, translated and annotated by Maynard J. Geiger (Washington, D.C. 1955).

San Francisco Monitor Special Centennial Issue, September 4, 1953.

Henry L. Walsh, *Hallowed Were the Gold Dust Trails: The Story of Pioneer Priests of Northern California* (Santa Clara, Calif. 1946).

Francis J. Weber, *A Biographical Sketch of the Right Reverend Francisco Garcia Diego y Moreno, First Bishop of the Californias, 1785–1846* (Los Angeles 1961).

Rt. Rev. John Thomas Foudy
Superintendent of Schools, Archdiocese of San Francisco;
Director, Confraternity of Christian Doctrine
Archdiocesan Consultor
Pastor of St. Agnes Church, San Francisco, Calif.

Jeffrey M. Burns
Archivist
Archdiocese of San Francisco (2009)

SANTA FE, ARCHDIOCESE OF

Metropolitan see comprising an area of 61,142 square miles in the state of New Mexico, the Archdiocese of Santa Fe (*Sanctae Fidei*) was established as a vicariate apostolic in 1850, a DIOCESE in 1853, and an ARCHDIOCESE in 1875. Originally it covered New Mexico, Arizona, and Colorado, but after the creation of the Vicariates of Arizona and Colorado in 1868, it was confined to New Mexico, minus the southernmost counties bordering on Texas and Mexico; these counties, as part of the Gadsden Purchase, were first in the Arizona vicariate (later the Diocese of Tucson), then in the Diocese of EL PASO, Texas, created in 1914. With the erection of the Diocese of GALLUP in 1939 and the Diocese of Las Cruces in 1982, the archdiocese was further restricted to the eastern and north central part of the state. The suffragan sees are Tucson and Phoenix in Arizona and Gallup and Las Cruces in New Mexico. In 2008 the Catholic population of the Archdiocese of Santa Fe numbered approximately 23 percent of the total population, distributed among 93 parishes and 216 active missions (*The Official Catholic Directory* 2008, p. 1295).

Early Period. The history of New Mexico began with the Native American people who have been in the area more than 10,000 years. By the 1500s the people now called the Pueblo Indians lived in the Rio Grande Valley and in areas throughout New Mexico in settled villages. Navajo and Apache Indians also migrated into the area of the greater Southwest. Fray Marcos de NIZA, a Franciscan priest, discovered New Mexico in 1539. The Coronado expedition explored it from 1540 to 1542 with the double purpose of extending the Spanish Empire and propagating the Faith. No "golden cities" were found to justify immediate colonization, but two Franciscans remained to start a rudimentary mission; subsequently Fray Juan de PADILLA was killed by Native Americans on the Great Plains, whereas Fray Luis de Ubeda, a lay brother left at the pueblo of Pecos, was slain by his charges. Some forty years later, three FRIARS, Augustin Rodriguez, Francisco LÒPEZ, and Juan de Santa Maria, were sent by the viceroy on another exploratory mission. Unscrupulous soldiers accompanying them foiled their purposes, and Tigua tribes people of the middle Rio Grande Valley killed the trio. But in 1598 a permanent colony was established at last under Governor Juan de Oñate (1552–1626), while a sizable missionary band ministered to the pueblos.

By 1610 the Villa of Santa Fe (*Holy Faith*) was established as a permanent capital, the only Spanish town in that century. Like other towns called Santa Fe in Spanish America, it was named after the royal military camp near Granada, where Ferdinand and Isabella dealt the final defeat to the Moors in Spain. The original patronal title of the parish church was Our Lady of the Assumption, which in the next decade became that of the Conception. Enshrined in it was a statue of the Assumption, brought by Fray Alonso de BENAVIDES in 1625; it gathered lasting fame as *La Conquistadora*, the Queen of the Kingdom of New Mexico and its Villa of Santa Fe. The CHAPEL of San Miguel served the indigenous Mexicans brought along by the Spaniards. The mission enterprise, called the Custody of the Conversion of St. Paul, began most auspiciously, having within a short time more than thirty churches, ranging from the northernmost pueblo of Taos near the present Colorado border down to the pueblo of Guadalupe del Paso, now the city of Juárez in Mexico. Several of these missions lay well east of the Rio Grande basin, touching on the Great Plains, while as many more stretched westward to the Hopi pueblos in what is now northeastern Arizona. Each of these great mission establishments was built by the Native Americans under the guidance of the Franciscans.

However, grave opposition developed among the ruling medicine men, particularly when it was deemed necessary to destroy their idolatrous ceremonial chambers and suppress their immoral secret dances; this and the interference of certain Spanish officials brought on troubles that ended in a giant holocaust. Posing for years as the spokesman for the Great Spirit, *Po-he-yemu*, a mulatto former slave hiding in Taos, united the various pueblo leaders into inciting the great Pueblo Revolt of 1680, which produced twenty-one Franciscan martyrs in a single day. Santa Fe was sacked, Our Lady's church destroyed completely, and San Miguel chapel partially. The colonists fought their way out, fleeing south to Guadalupe del Paso where they remained exiled for thirteen years. Late in December 1693 they and the missionaries returned in what is called the DeVargas reconquest. They had saved *La Conquistadora* from destruction and kept up her CULT during exile and the reconquest of Santa Fe. For about a year Mass was celebrated in the palace of the governors, until Governor DeVargas (c. 1643–1704) built a temporary church of St. Francis in 1695. Further political troubles and Native American campaigns prevented the rebuilding of the original parish and SHRINE of Our Lady as the governor had publicly vowed. These were finally built on the site of the old parish (1714–1717), but the title of the temporary church was carried over to the new structure, thus making St. Francis of Assisi the permanent parish and town patron.

Gradually most of the missions were reestablished, and the Spanish people spread out in new towns with their own chapels. However, the new century proved disastrous to both the colonists and their Pueblo neighbors, for by 1800 long periods of drought and continual invasions had seriously impoverished the people. Spain, a rapidly waning power, had been unable to help. Nor could Mexico do much, even after its separation from Spain in 1821, due to the hundreds of miles of arid wilderness that separated New Mexico from the rest of Spanish America. Life there was not only precarious, but also devoid, for the most part, of educational opportunities and even material necessities when, in 1846, the United States took over New Mexico and the surrounding Southwest.

Ecclesiastical Jurisdiction. Although jurisdiction was claimed by the bishops of Mexico, Guadalajara, and Durango, the Franciscan Custody had acted as an independent mission for more than a century. In 1730 Bishop Benito Crespo (1673–1737) of Durango exercised effective jurisdiction when he appointed a secular priest, Santiago Roybal, who had been born in New Mexico in 1694 or 1695, as his vicar in Santa Fe. The Franciscans continued in charge of all mission and parish work, which declined due to economic circumstances and conflict with Native Americans as well as a dearth of missionary replacements from their motherhouse in Mexico City. In 1798 the BISHOP of Durango secularized the parish of Santa Fe and other large towns, but few of the diocesan priests stayed for long. Several native New Mexicans were ordained after 1800, but these and the last few aging friars were unable to meet the demands of so vast and impoverished a region. Mexican independence from Spain in 1821 aggravated the situation by removing Spanish-born missionaries. By the time the United States took over, the ancient Franciscan missions were crumbling fast; the descendants of the Spanish colonists, for the most part illiterate, had kept the faith ardently alive but sadly marred by ignorance; and the Pueblo peoples, never fully Christianized, had merely covered their PAGAN beliefs with the outward signs of Catholicity.

Soon after New Mexico was made part of the United States in 1846, the American hierarchy petitioned the HOLY SEE for a bishop in the Great Southwest. Historic Santa Fe was selected as the see city, and John Baptist LAMY, named bishop, arrived there late in 1851.

Lamy. The new bishop chose St. Francis as patron of the diocese, and the old parish church of St. Francis became the CATHEDRAL. Finding a mere handful of priests, some of whom resented him as an intruder, Lamy not only brought numbers of French clergy to serve his vast territory but soon ordained some native candidates and founded a seminary. Priests were also sent to the faraway populated areas of Tucson and Denver. The lack of educational facilities was remedied by the introduction of RELIGIOUS teachers. In 1853 the

Kentucky Sisters of LORETTO founded Our Lady of Light Academy in Santa Fe and later opened schools at Taos, Mora, Las Vegas, Albuquerque, Bernalillo, Socorro, and Las Cruces. In 1859 the French CHRISTIAN BROTHERS founded St. Michael's in Santa Fe, then subsequently opened other schools at Las Vegas, Mora, and Bernalillo. By 1865 the Cincinnati Sisters of Charity had founded St. Vincent's Hospital and Orphanage in the capital, followed by an academy and two parish schools in Albuquerque. In 1867 the bishop welcomed a group of Neapolitan JESUITS who, through their printing of *La Revista Catolica* in Las Vegas and by preaching throughout the territory, helped to save the FAITHFUL from the many Protestant proselytizers who poured in with the coming of the railroad. In 1869 a new stone cathedral replaced the old adobe church—keeping intact, however, the ancient Conquistadora SHRINE as its Lady Chapel. In 1875 Santa Fe was erected a metropolitan with Tucson and Denver as suffragan dioceses. Lamy resigned in 1885 and died three years later.

Salpointe, Chapelle, and Bourgade. John Baptist Salpointe (1825–1898), coadjutor since 1884, succeeded to the see on July 18, 1885, and devoted much of his time and effort in behalf of education for the Native Americans. St. Catherine's Indian School, under the direction of the Sisters of the Blessed Sacrament for Indians and Colored People, was opened in Santa Fe. Salpointe's term was marked also by difficulties with the *Penitentes*, a flagellant society, which flared up in opposition to diocesan regulations. He resigned on January 7, 1894, and retired to Banning, California, where he wrote his *Soldiers of the Cross*, a source history of the pioneer American Church in the Southwest. His successor was Placide Louis CHAPELLE, coadjutor since 1891, who became third ARCHBISHOP of Santa Fe on January 7, 1894, but was transferred to New Orleans in 1897. During his brief term the Leavenworth Sisters of Charity founded St. Anthony's Hospital at Las Vegas. His successor was Peter Bourgade (1845–1908), who had served as vicar apostolic of Arizona and, since 1897, as first bishop of Tucson, before his transfer to Santa Fe on January 7, 1899.

As bishop of Tucson, Bourgade had induced the Cincinnati Franciscans to open missions among the Navajos; as archbishop he reintroduced them to some of the ancient Pueblo missions of New Mexico and to the whole northwest section of the state, which eventually passed into the Gallup diocese. The Franciscans founded the first parishes in the southeast part of New Mexico. Bourgade also took a leading part in founding the Catholic Church Extension Society. The Lafayette FRANCISCAN SISTERS opened mission schools in areas served by the Franciscan fathers. The Charity Sisters from Santa Fe founded St. Joseph Hospital and a school of nursing in Albuquerque, whereas the Sisters of the Sorrowful Mother established St. Mary's Hospital in Roswell. By 1908 forty-five parishes with 340 mission chapels existed in the archdiocese, denoting a marked increase in the population as well as definite economic progress. This progress, however, had not caught up with that of other parts of the nation where large industry and extensive agriculture helped dioceses to develop much more rapidly.

Later Archbishops. Bourgade died in 1908 and on January 3, 1909, was succeeded by John Baptist Pitaval (1858–1928), who had been his auxiliary since 1902. Pitaval introduced the OBLATE Fathers of Texas to the extensive Springer parish, while the Franciscan Sisters founded St. Anthony's Orphanage for boys in Albuquerque. New Mexico became a state in 1912. Three years later Pitaval dedicated a fine bronze statue of Archbishop Lamy in front of the cathedral; the first state governor and other major officials took part in the ceremonies. Resigning in February 1918 because of ill health, Pitaval was succeeded by Albert T. Daeger (1872–1932), O.F.M., who was consecrated on May 7, 1919, thus marking the end of a continuous line of French archbishops. Since the recruiting of clergy from France had ceased during the war, the new archbishop faced a serious dearth of priests. Lamy's original seminary had closed with his death; Daeger tried to start one at Las Vegas, but it also was short-lived. Meanwhile, the Holy Family Fathers from Spain took over the large Santa Cruz area, while the Servite Fathers from Chicago were given that of Belen. The Franciscans returned to the cathedral after a century, at the urging of Monsignor A. Fourchegu, vicar general since 1895, who personally financed the cathedral debt and purchased the major furnishings. Archbishop Daeger also received the vows of the first missionary catechists of OUR LADY OF VICTORY, founded in Indiana, for work in his archdiocese. He died on December 2, 1932, and was succeeded the following summer by Rudolph Aloysius Gerken (1887–1943), first bishop of Amarillo.

After his installation in Santa Fe on August 23, 1933, Gerken organized archdiocesan administration along more modern lines. He established a seminary in Albuquerque, opened new parishes and schools throughout the state, and introduced new religious communities. The archbishop personally supervised the preparation of the historic Montezuma Hotel near Las Vegas as a major seminary, which the U.S. and Mexican hierarchy founded in 1937 for seminarians from persecuted Mexico. The very first Presidium of the LEGION OF MARY in America was established at Raton. The Franciscan Sisters in Albuquerque opened a teachers' college, the DOMINICAN SISTERS established Nazareth Sanatorium at Alameda, and Holy Family Sisters took over a

St. Francis of Assisi Cathedral. *Dedicated in 1886, this cathedral combines Adobe, Ro-manesque, and Modern architectural styles.* © KIM KARPELES / ALAMY

new hospital in Taos. Archbishop Gerken died on March 2, 1943, and was succeeded by Edwin Vincent Byrne (1891–1963), who had served as first bishop of Ponce, Puerto Rico, and then bishop of San Juan there, before his transfer to Santa Fe on June 15, 1943.

The war and its aftermath brought enormous changes to New Mexico as a consequence of the permanent military and atomic installations there, which spurred other industries and brought in many new Catholic families to swell the increasing native population. The need for more parishes with schools was successfully met as these increased from five to twenty-one in Albuquerque alone. The diocesan seminary, transferred to Santa Fe under the title of the IMMACULATE HEART OF MARY, grew steadily in students and facilities and warranted the addition of a philosophy department in 1962. As a result native ordinations also increased steadily. Old St. Michael's in Santa Fe was established (1947) as a four-year liberal arts college, as was the College of St. Joseph on the Rio Grande in Albuquerque. One of the best-equipped New-man Centers in the nation was established at the University of New Mexico under the Dominican Fathers; two branch universities at Las Vegas and Portales also have active Newman Centers. Two local foundations, which in a few years spread far beyond the archdiocese, were the Servants of the Holy Paraclete (1952) and the Little Brothers of the Good Shepherd (1951).

When Byrne died on July 25, 1963, his successor was Archbishop James Peter Davis (1904–1988), who

was transferred from San Juan, Puerto Rico, and installed in Santa Fe on February 25, 1964. Archbishop Davis had attended sessions of VATICAN COUNCIL II and led the archdiocese through the early changes and renewal programs promulgated by the council. To conform to the new liturgical norms, he began renovations at St. Francis Cathedral, beginning with the sanctuary. Parts of earlier church structures from 1717, 1806, and 1895 were razed to accommodate the changes in the cathedral, including the addition of a new BLESSED SACRAMENT chapel. Many of the changes and renovations were criticized because they did not complement the soft Ro-manesque look of Archbishop Lamy's original building. More recent renovations that included the addition of New Mexican-style *santero* art under the direction of Archbishop Sanchez and Archbishop Sheehan conformed with the style of the long Catholic tradition of New Mexico. In 2001 a full immersion baptismal font was added in the central portion of the nave.

Archbishop Davis restored the diaconate and ordained the first deacons for the archdiocese in 1972. The Archdiocese of Santa Fe joined the interdenomina-tional Council of Churches that led to the establishment of the archdiocesan Office of Ecumenical Affairs in 1979. Davis relocated the archdiocesan administrative offices from the see city to the larger, and more centrally located, city of Albuquerque in 1967.

One of the most lasting programs of Archbishop Davis was the institution of official PILGRIMAGES in the archdiocese that led to the establishment of the historic

Santuário de CHIMAYÓ as the official archdiocesan pilgrimage site in 1979. This site has been known since prehistoric times as a place of spiritual and physical healing. Regular pilgrimage to the Santuário began after World War II when survivors of the Bataan Death March (1942) made a pilgrimage in thanksgiving for their safe return to New Mexico.

Archbishop Davis retired in 1974 and passed away in Albuquerque on March 4, 1988. Prior to his retirement, Archbishop Davis, other priests, and lay people from New Mexico recommended that the next Archbishop of Santa Fe be someone from among the native-born Hispanic priests in the archdiocese. One of those recommended was Father Robert Fortune Sanchez (1934–), born and raised in Socorro, New Mexico, and a priest of the archdiocese since his ordination in 1959. Father Sanchez had served as teacher and assistant principal at St. Pius High School as well as assistant pastor of Annunciation Parish in Albuquerque. He also attended The CATHOLIC UNIVERSITY OF AMERICA in Washington, D.C., for special studies in CANON LAW. When he returned from Washington, he was appointed pastor of the combined parishes of St. Joseph/Holy Family in the remote northeastern portion of the state. In 1971 he was appointed pastor of the historic parish of San Felipe de Neri in Albuquerque, and Archbishop Davis appointed him vicar general of the archdiocese on May 1, 1974. He was serving the archdiocese in these positions when he was named the tenth archbishop of Santa Fe in 1974.

Sanchez and Sheehan. Archbishop Sanchez's installation brought great joy to the people of the archdiocese, not only because he was a native New Mexican but because of his strong dedication and pastoral leadership. He established formal programs to assist and meet the pastoral needs of Hispanics, Native Americans, and other U.S. immigrant groups. Among these outreach programs are the archdiocesan newspaper, the *People of God*, established in 1982 and distributed by parishes to thousands of Catholics in the archdiocese, and the weekly televised Mass seen on one of the local channels that reaches many homebound Catholics. Efforts to increase Native American spirituality and participation in LITURGY were advanced in 1974 when the archbishop celebrated the first Native American liturgy in the Cathedral of St. Francis. Native rituals such as PRAYERS, blessings, and ceremonial dances were for the first time held in the cathedral.

The archbishop's love for New Mexico, its people, and its history—especially the role the Church played in this history—led him to establish the Archbishop's Commission for the Preservation of Historic New Mexico Churches in 1987. The commission developed guidelines for any renovations or preservation efforts planned by parishes and missions. During this period many New Mexico churches, including the Santuário de Chimayó, San Jose de Gracia in Las Trampas, and San Francisco de Assisi in Ranchos de Taos, were designated as National Historic Landmarks and listed on the State Register of Cultural Properties and the National Register of Historic Places.

Another institution in the archdiocese, Via Coeli (Heaven's Way), a MINISTRY to priests troubled by addictions and other problems, became the focus of much criticism and notoriety in the 1980s. The therapeutic program at the center sponsored by the SERVANTS OF THE PARACLETE was one of the first to offer specialized treatment for the clergy. Dioceses and religious orders from across the country sent priests to the center located at Jemez Springs for treatment of addictions and problems of various kinds, including PEDOPHILIA. A number of priests were rehabilitated and returned to the active ministry in their home dioceses; some stayed to work in New Mexico, and some relapsed. This last group created serious problems for the archdiocese and the archbishops of Santa Fe. The allegations, the legal costs, and the monetary compensations paid to the victims and their families damaged the morale of the archdiocese and brought it to the brink of bankruptcy. These problems along with charges of sexual misconduct with women brought against Archbishop Sanchez led to his resignation in 1993. Subsequently, the Servants of the Paraclete closed the therapeutic program at Jemez Springs and concentrated instead on retreats and spiritual renewal.

On April 6, 1993, the Most Reverend Michael J. Sheehan (1939–), serving as the first bishop of Lubbock at that time, was named as apostolic administrator of the Archdiocese of Santa Fe. He was appointed the eleventh archbishop of Santa Fe on August 17 and installed on September 21, 1993. His leadership and pastoral guidance helped the archdiocese and its people through this most difficult period. His immediate concern and love for the Archdiocese of Santa Fe and its people was evident by his involvement in programs and the long traditions of the Church of New Mexico. Archbishop Sheehan brought a new sense of trust to the archdiocese by working closely with clergy, religious, and lay people. Ministries and programs of the archdiocese were given a new sense of hope for the future by his promise to serve the people of the archdiocese with all his energy and with all his heart. During the first years of his episcopate, Archbishop Sheehan visited many parishes and missions of the archdiocese, including the Native American parishes and missions. He had a processional CROSS depicting a Native American CHRIST made, and presented one as a gift to each of the Pueblo parishes and missions. He also involved the native peoples in Church plans for the commemoration of the

400th anniversary of the formal establishment of New Mexico in 1998. All who participated in Church events during this yearlong observance considered them extremely successful because of their sensitive and accurate interpretation of historic events involving Native American peoples and their culture and traditions. The archbishop's command of the Spanish language and its inclusion in liturgy as well as his love for and participation in longstanding Hispanic and Native American traditions truly symbolize his commitment to the people of the Archdiocese of Santa Fe.

Administratively, offices of the archdiocese were given a greater sense of their role in the pastoral ministry of the Church and were brought up to more professional standards. The archdiocesan museum, a dream of Archbishop Sanchez, was completed, opened, and blessed by Archbishop Sheehan in October 1993. The success of the Catholic Foundation, established in 1991, was made a priority, and by 2007 the foundation had assets of more than $41 million. The Annual Catholic Appeal (ACA) Foundation, founded as Faith in Action in 1983 as an annual archdiocesan-wide appeal to support the pastoral, educational, evangelical, and developmental needs of the archdiocese as well as the universal Church, donated nearly $50 million to support the mission of the archdiocese. Through the rebate feature of the ACA, all the parishes of the archdiocese share in millions of dollars returned for local use. The Office of Lay Personnel Services, later Human Resources, ensures that rights and benefits are provided for all employees of the archdiocese. The finance division of the archdiocese oversees all financial dealings, and profits from the sale of land on a site previously occupied by St. Pius High School made it possible for the Archdiocese of Santa Fe to be debt free.

Pastoral ministries of the archdiocese, including offices of Evangelization, Family Life, Formation for Christian Service, and Pastoral Outreach, are directed by committed individuals who initiate and plan programs. The youth office promotes its ministry through the yearly Youth Conference, established in 1979, where the youth of the archdiocese are invited to come together for prayer, REFLECTION, and discussion of youth-related issues. The Catholic schools of the archdiocese are also of great importance to Archbishop Sheehan and the Archdiocese of Santa Fe. The Archbishop's School Fund Dinner, established in 1978, provides much-needed funds for school programs and scholarships for students who are not able to afford the tuition. A new school, the Santo Niño Regional Catholic School, replaced St. Francis of Assisi and Cristo Rey Catholic Schools in Santa Fe in 2006 and joined the other fifteen Catholic schools in the archdiocese. Archbishop Sheehan successfully led the archdiocese through the RENEW program, a spiritual process that nourishes spiritual growth of

Catholics. Its goals were the teaching of and witness to the Word of God, the building of a vibrant faith community, and the promotion of justice. He was also very committed to the commemoration of the anniversary of Christ's birth, the JUBILEE YEAR, beginning on Christmas Eve 1999. Catholics were encouraged to visit Jubilee churches of the archdiocese and to attend the Eucharistic Congress held during the jubilee year on September 23, 2000, planned and sponsored by the archdiocesan office of WORSHIP. Archbishop Sheehan also saw to the conservation of the artwork in the Santuário de Chimayó, begun in 1999 and which continued and was finished in 2004. He also administered the preservation of many historic churches and attended the rededication of many of them, including the beautiful church in the remote Mora area called Monte Aplanado. Archbishop Sheehan was also instrumental in sending a special collection to the survivors and parishes of Hurricana Katrina in 2005. He installed thirty-one new clergy to the archdiocese, settled clergy problems, and restored the trust of the community in the Church. In 2008 Catholic radio began in the archdiocese, giving a new opportunity for evangelization and adult formation in the faith.

In 2000 Archbishop Sheehan appointed secular clergy to St. Francis Cathedral, ending Franciscan administration started in 1920. Since that time the cathedral has improved, not only in the number of parishioners, but also by its dedication to its renovation. It was elevated to the status of BASILICA in 2005. Since that time, a redevelopment program has enhanced the area surrounding it. The repairs to the exterior stone of the cathedral basilica of St. Francis of Assisi will be completed by the time the Archdiocese of Santa Fe celebrates the 400th anniversary of the city of the Holy Faith in 2010.

SEE ALSO ARIZONA, CATHOLIC CHURCH IN; BLESSINGS, LITURGICAL; CARDINAL NEWMAN SOCIETY; CATECHIST; COLORADO, CATHOLIC CHURCH IN; FLAGELLATION; MARTYR; MISSION AND MISSIONS; NEW MEXICO, CATHOLIC CHURCH IN; SECULARIZATION; SERVITES; TEXAS, CATHOLIC CHURCH IN; WORLD COUNCIL OF CHURCHES.

BIBLIOGRAPHY

Archdiocese of Santa Fe Official Web site, available from: http://www.archdiocesesantafe.org/ (accessed February 5, 2009).

Archdiocese of Santa Fe, *People of God*, monthly archdiocesan newspaper.

Archdiocese of Santa Fe, *Lamy Memorial: Centenary of the Archdiocese of Santa Fe, 1850–1950* (Santa Fe, N.Mex. 1950).

Archdiocese of Santa Fe, *Archives of the Archdiocese of Santa Fe, 1678–1900*, compiled by Angélico Chávez (Washington, D.C. 1957).

Angélico Chávez, *The Old Faith and Old Glory: Story of the Church in New Mexico since the American Occupation, 1846–*

1946 (Santa Fe, N.Mex. 1946).

Francisco Atanasio Dominguez, *The Missions of New Mexico, 1776*, translated by Eleanor B. Adams and Angélico Chávez (Albuquerque, N.Mex. 1956).

The Official Catholic Directory (New Providence, N.J. 2008).

Jean Baptiste Salpointe, *Soldiers of the Cross: Notes on the Ecclesiastical History of New Mexico, Arizona, and Colorado* (Banning, Calif. 1898).

Michael J. Sheehan, ed., *Four Hundred Years of Faith: Seeds of Struggle, Harvest of Faith: A History of the Catholic Church in New Mexico* (Santa Fe, N.Mex. 1998).

Rev. Angelico Chavez OFM
St. Joseph Church
Cerillos, N.Mex.

Marina Ochoa
Archivist, Archdiocese of Santa Fe
Santa Fe, N.Mex. (2009)

SCOPES TRIAL

In the first decades of the twentieth century, populist political movements passed laws against the teaching of human EVOLUTION in public schools in several states of the United States. One such law led to the now famous confrontation of Clarence Darrow (1857–1938) and William Jennings Bryan (1860–1925) in the *Scopes* "monkey trial" in Dayton, Tennessee, in 1925.

The iconic *Scopes* trial is one of the most misunderstood of the well-recognized episodes of American history, thanks largely to the great popular success of a supposed retelling of the story by the play (and subsequent motion picture) *Inherit the Wind*, which purports to be a dramatization of the *Scopes* trial. In reality, the story told in *Inherit the Wind* is almost entirely mythical, a morality play about the supposed bigoted close-mindedness of small-town Christians that has almost nothing in common with the fascinating facts of the "monkey trial." This gap has created misunderstandings in the public mind regarding the history of the teaching of evolution, public education, and the interaction between Christians and the broader culture around these topics.

By the 1920s "molecules to man" evolutionary theories (usually in straight Darwinian form but sometimes in more teleological variants) were regnant in mainstream academic biology. As a result, evolutionary theory was a central theme in high school and college biology textbooks. Although it is likely that large parts of the populace did not believe comprehensive evolutionary theories, the mere presence of narrowly scientific claims regarding the origin and development of life on earth (including the development of humankind) would probably not have resulted in sufficient public ire to bring about any laws regarding the teaching of evolution. It was the nonscientific claims often coupled with evolutionary theory that led to the confrontations of the 1920s.

The principal motivation behind the "anti–evolution" laws in Tennessee and elsewhere during that period was not to promote a literalist Biblical understanding of CREATION and/or biology. Instead, the primary purpose of the laws was to ban the teaching in public schools of materialistic accounts of the origin of humankind, as well as to combat the growing influence of the EUGENICS movement, which at the time was closely tied to evolutionary science. For example, the state-approved textbook at issue in the "monkey trial" was George William Hunter's *Civic Biology*, a frankly racist and eugenicist "science" text that taught the superiority of the white race over "lower" forms of human life and the need for humans to control their evolutionary destiny by selective breeding and population control. Tennessee's "Butler Act," for example, clearly reflects that focus. While the language of the preamble is broad ("An Act prohibiting the teaching of the Evolution Theory"), the substantive provision Section 1—the part of the law that created a legally binding rule—banned only the teaching of *human* evolution. Section 1 banned in any Tennessee public school the teaching of "any theory that denies the Story of the Divine Creation of man as taught in the Bible, and teaches instead that man has descended from a lower order of animals" (For the text of the Butler Act, See: http://www.law.umkc.edu/faculty/projects/ftrials/scopes/tennstat.htm) Violation of the law was a misdemeanor, punishable only by fine.

Other major elements of the true story of the *Scopes* trial will come as a surprise to viewers of *Inherit the Wind*. First, the Tennessee law at issue in the *Scopes* trial was clearly symbolic: Every single state-approved biology textbook of that time taught evolutionary theory, including human evolution from "lower" animals. It was impossible to teach high school biology in Tennessee using a state-approved textbook without violating the law. There were no changes to those textbooks under consideration before the case arose, nor any evidence that prosecutions were being contemplated for using the state-approved textbooks.

Second, the prosecution of Scopes was an entirely friendly affair that arose only because the American Civil Liberties Union (ACLU), from its New York headquarters, actively sought out possible victims of the new Tennessee law. The ACLU ran advertisements in Tennessee newspapers offering free legal defense to anyone prosecuted under the law. One of those advertisements gave some leading citizens of Dayton, Tennessee, the idea of "putting their town on the map" by making

The Adversaries. *Clarence Darrow (l) and William Jennings Bryan (r), seated at a courtroom table; a crowd of onlookers is gathered in background, Dayton, Tennessee, 1925.* AP IMAGES

it the location of a show trial sure to garner national attention. Their plans suffered an initial setback when the regular high school biology teacher, a family man, was unwilling to take the risk of a criminal prosecution, even one undertaken for local fun and profit—and even though the local schemers promised to pay any fine that might ensue. The plan was saved, however, when the townspeople discovered John Scopes (1900–1970), the physical education teacher and *substitute* biology teacher, who confessed in his autobiography that he had never taught anything about evolution in his few days in the biology classroom. Far from a persecuted rationalist hero, Scopes was a willing "victim" in a perfectly friendly, staged event.

As to their plan for publicity, the town leaders succeeded beyond their wildest dreams. The prosecution made headlines around the world. Yet the result was by no means all fun and games. As the case progressed and an astounding media circus spiraled out of control, powerful divisions emerged across the nation between an elite secular culture that condemned the Tennessee law and a populist Christian culture that supported it.

At the climax of the trial, in a highly unusual agreement by lawyers to take the witness stand on behalf of their clients, defense attorney Darrow first cross-examined the assistant prosecutor, Bryan, by most accounts making Bryan look foolish. Darrow, who had

evolutionist beliefs, then made a motion conceding his client's guilt, thus avoiding a promised reciprocal cross-examination by Bryan. The judge had no choice but to convict Scopes. The conviction was overturned on appeal on a procedural technicality, and as a result the constitutional establishment clause question was not addressed until decades later.

Nevertheless, following the Scopes controversy, high school textbook publishers cautiously minimized discussion of evolution, as well as accompanying materials on eugenics. The result was the miseducation of more than a generation of high school students concerning the major organizing theory behind much of modern biology, including population genetics, zoology, and paleontology. When *Sputnik's* orbit in 1957 provoked an outcry for improving science education in the United States, new biology textbooks resumed explicit teaching of Darwinian evolutionary theory, this time without the eugenics overlay.

While the anti–evolutionists won the battle, they clearly lost the war of public opinion. As Edward Larson shows in an impressive work of historiography at the end of his book *Summer for the Gods*, thanks to tendentious media coverage at the time—and even more so subsequent retellings of the story of the trial in popular writings, history books, and text books—within little more than a decade the general public developed a perception of the *Scopes* trial much like the mythical confrontation portrayed in *Inherit the Wind*, a confrontation between narrow-minded, small-town religionists and the benign forces of enlightenment and scientific progress that must ultimately carry the day. In reaction, Fundamentalist Christians further retreated from mainstream culture, establishing their own colleges and universities and developing a parallel, BIBLE-oriented, intellectual culture that continues to the present day.

SEE ALSO CREATIONISM; DARWIN, CHARLES ROBERT; FUNDAMENTAL-ISM; INTELLIGENT DESIGN; LIFE, ORIGIN OF; MORALITY PLAYS; PHILOSOPHY OF NATURE.

BIBLIOGRAPHY

Edward J. Larson, *Summer for the Gods: The Scopes Trial and America's Continuing Debate over Science and Religion* (Cambridge, Mass. 1998). (This is a Pulitzer Prize-winning history of the *Scopes* trial, written by a historian and lawyer.)

The Monkey Trial, available from http://www.themonkeytrial.com (accessed March 2, 2009). (This is a good popularization of the true story, although obviously sympathetic to the Christian perspective on the case. The facts [condensed from Larson's book and the trial transcript] are contrasted with the movie *Inherit the Wind*; many clips from the movie are included).

Mark Ryland
President and Senior Fellow
Institute for the Study of Nature, Washington, D.C.
(2009)

SEATTLE, ARCHDIOCESE OF

Metropolitan see in the state of Washington, bounded by the Canadian border on the north, the Columbia River on the south, and extending from the crest of the Cascades on the east to the Pacific Ocean, an area of 24,834 square miles. In 2008 there were 577,400 Catholics in a total population of 5,064,500 (*The Official Catholic Directory* 2008, p. 1325). It was erected May 31, 1850, as the Diocese of Nesqually but was renamed the Diocese of Seattle (*Seattlensis*) on September 11, 1907; it became an ARCHDIOCESE on June 23, 1951, and the metropolitan see of the Seattle Province with the dioceses of Spokane and Yakima as its suffragan sees.

First Missionaries. The Catholic history began with the arrival at Fort Vancouver on November 24, 1838, of two missionary priests, Francis Norbert BLANCHET and Modeste Demers (1809–1871), who had been sent from the Diocese of Quebec, Canada, in answer to the repeated requests of the Canadian and Iroquois employ-

ees of the Hudson's Bay Company. Blanchet, vicar general of the new mission, which numbered twenty-six Catholics, Canadians, and Iroquois, celebrated Mass there for the first time. Within a short time Demers learned the Chinook language, instructed the native residents, translated the most important PRAYERS, and composed hymns. From Vancouver, Blanchet visited the Catholics at Cowlitz, where several delegations of Native Americans came to hear and see the Blackgown. To instruct the native peoples, Blanchet hit upon a singularly effective device called the *Catholic Ladder*. Taking a flat board, he drew forty marks to represent the forty centuries before CHRIST. With thirty-three points, he indicated the thirty-three years of Christ's life. A CROSS recalled the REDEMPTION. Eighteen marks and thirty-nine points represented the years since the birth of Christ. At either side of this symbolic outline of Church history, the missionary graphically represented important CHRISTIAN doctrines. The use of the Catholic ladder spread widely and rapidly.

Demers followed the route of the hunters and trappers, visiting settlements and stopping at Nesqually, Walla Walla, and Colville. Within a few years the chief factor of the company, James Douglas (1803–1877), permitted the missionaries to make foundations south of the Columbia. In 1842 Pierre Jean DE SMET, S.J., arrived at Vancouver from the northeast section of the Oregon Territory, where he had been sent by the BISHOP of St. Louis, Missouri, to work among the native peoples. At a conference of the missionaries, de Smet was chosen to enlist additional workers in St. Louis and Belgium and to bring to the attention of ecclesiastical authorities the need for a bishop in Oregon country. His mission succeeded: De Smet returned to Oregon with more helpers, and on December 1, 1843, the Oregon mission was made a vicariate apostolic with Blanchet as vicar apostolic.

After his consecration in Montreal, Canada, on July 25, 1845, Blanchet sailed for Europe to enlist assistance for his vicariate and to lay its needs before the HOLY SEE. On July 24, 1846, PIUS IX named him ARCHBISHOP of the new Province of Oregon City; his brother Augustine Magloire Alexander Blanchet (1797–1887) was appointed bishop of the newly established Diocese of Walla Walla, and Father Demers was named bishop of Vancouver Island.

Blanchet. Augustine Blanchet, the first and only bishop of Walla Walla, who in 1850 became the first bishop of Nesqually, was born near St. Pierre Riviere du Sud, Canada. He was ordained on June 3, 1821, became a canon of the Cathedral of St. James in Montreal, and was consecrated bishop of Walla Walla on September 27, 1846. When he left Canada, he had with him only one priest for his new jurisdiction, John BROUILLET, but four others, OBLATES OF MARY IMMACULATE, joined him later. In the northeastern part of the DIOCESE five JESUITS worked among the native populations. Shortly after Blanchet's arrival in his diocese—which included eastern Washington and eastern Oregon, the state of Idaho, that portion of Montana west of the Rockies, and the northwest corner of Wyoming—the Protestant missionary Dr. Marcus Whitman (1802–1847) was murdered on November 29, 1847. Because of the hostilities resulting from this crime and its punishment, the presence of non-natives at Walla Walla and its vicinity was forbidden, so the bishop established his headquarters at the Dalles.

In 1850, after the bishop had petitioned the Holy See to move his headquarters to Fort Nesqually near Vancouver, ROME officially made the territory of Nesqually a diocese. This region, until 1850 subject to the Archdiocese of Oregon City, included the territory west of the Cascade Mountains and north of the Columbia. When appointed bishop of Nesqually, Blanchet established his CATHEDRAL at Vancouver, where it remained until 1907. Among those who worked under him for the welfare of the diocese were Fathers John Brouillet, Charles Marie Pandosy (1824–1891), and Eugene Casimer Chirouse (1821–1892), and the Sisters of Charity of Providence. The first Mass was said in the city of Seattle in 1852 by Bishop Demers. In 1853 the Diocese of Walla Walla was suppressed, and Nesqually acquired that part of its territory west of the Rockies and north of the Columbia and the forty-sixth degree of latitude. In 1868 the creation of the Vicariate Apostolic of Idaho further reduced the area of the diocese, confining it to the limits of the state of Washington. When Blanchet resigned in 1879 he was named TITULAR BISHOP of Ibara; he died February 25, 1887.

Junger and O'Dea. Blanchet's successor, Aegidius Junger (1879–1895), who had served the diocese since ordination, was consecrated on October 28, 1879. An earnest worker, fluent in English, French, and German, the new bishop directed the diocese well during a period when Washington became a state and the Catholic population increased from 12,000 to 30,000. To care for parishes and missions, the bishop sought the help of Jesuits, REDEMPTORISTS, and BENEDICTINES. The Sisters of the Holy Names, DOMINICAN SISTERS, Good Shepherd Sisters, and FRANCISCAN SISTERS undertook the direction of new schools in various parts of the diocese. The Brothers of Our Lady of Lourdes staffed a school in Seattle. Under Junger 60 new churches, including a cathedral, were built, and 15 parish schools, 2 schools for Native Americans, and 3 colleges begun.

Junger died on December 26, 1895, and Edward John O'Dea (1896–1932) was consecrated at Vancouver,

Washington, on September 8, 1896. The problems facing the young bishop were enormous; among these were heavy debts on the cathedral and diocese and a great financial depression throughout the country. The pastors and their people generously cooperated with the bishop to meet the financial problem. In response to the bishop's appeal to other dioceses throughout the country and in Europe for priests for his ever-increasing flock, volunteers arrived, many of them from Ireland.

When the first years of the twentieth century moved the center of state activities to Seattle, Bishop O'Dea found it increasingly difficult to administer the diocese from Vancouver. Accordingly, he made Seattle the cathedral city, built St. James Cathedral, dedicated it on December 22, 1907, and announced the official change in title of the diocese from Nesqually to Seattle. A few years later the increasing population of eastern Washington impelled O'Dea to recommend to Rome the establishment of a new diocese in that part of the state, and on December 17, 1913, the Diocese of Spokane was created. The line of division, north and south, nearly coincided with the 120th meridian and the north and south course of the Columbia River. In 1928 the bishop established a seminary in Seattle under the SULPICIANS, a project the bishops of the province had approved in 1917. The first students were admitted to the new St. Edward's Seminary on September 15, 1931. O'Dea survived the completion of his work only a year and died on December 25, 1932. During his tenure the number of Catholics in the diocese had increased from about 42,000 to 100,000, diocesan priests from 40 to 113, the regular clergy from 29 to 123, and churches from 42 to 90.

Shaughnessy and Connolly. On July 1, 1933, Pius XI appointed Gerald SHAUGHNESSY, S.M., bishop of Seattle. Without delay, he set about strengthening the financial structure of the diocese. He also sought and obtained priests from other sections of the country and from Europe and founded the SERRA INTERNATIONAL for help in recruiting and supporting seminarians. The years of Shaughnessy's administration were important for the consolidation and organization of diocesan affairs rather than for the multiplication of buildings. He suffered a serious cerebral hemorrhage in 1945 and, after several years of enforced inactivity, died on May 18, 1950.

In February 1948, upon Shaughnessy's petition, Rome appointed Bishop Thomas A. Connolly (1950–1975), auxiliary of San Francisco, as coadjutor bishop of Seattle with the right of succession. Connolly, once chancellor of the archdiocese of San Francisco and pastor of the historic Mission Dolores parish there, had been consecrated in San Francisco on August 24, 1939. Soon after his arrival in Seattle, he made plans for celebrating the centenary of the diocese. Missions were preached in all parishes as part of the spiritual program, and work on the renovation of the cathedral was begun. A pilgrimage, led by Bishop Connolly, journeyed to Rome to unite the jubilee of Seattle with that of the Universal Church. On September 14, 1950, Amleto CICOGNANI, then APOSTOLIC DELEGATE to the United States, celebrated the centennial Mass of thanksgiving in the presence of the largest gathering of the hierarchy the Pacific Northwest had yet seen.

The next year, Pope PIUS XII created a new ecclesiastical province in the Northwest (June 23, 1951). Seattle became the metropolitan see of the new province and Connolly, the first archbishop. At the same time Pius XII created the Diocese of Yakima from parts of Spokane and of Seattle and appointed the Most Reverend Joseph P. Dougherty, chancellor in Seattle, as ordinary of the new suffragan see. During the next few years, it became more and more difficult for Archbishop Connolly to perform all episcopal functions and attend to the multiplying details of administration. In 1956 Rome appointed Thomas E. Gill (1908–1973), rector of St. James Cathedral and archdiocesan director of Catholic Charities, as auxiliary bishop of Seattle.

To provide the laity with retreat facilities all year round, Connolly constructed two retreat houses. Numerous educational institutions of the archdiocese were established also under Connolly's direction, among them Blanchet High School, Seattle (1955), and the major seminary of St. Thomas the Apostle, Kenmore (1958). The first, a coinstructional school for 1,500 students, is directed by priests of the archdiocese, assisted by sisters of various communities and by lay teachers. The new seminary building was dedicated on April 14, 1959, by Cardinal James MCINTYRE of Los Angeles, California; the first students had been received the preceding September. Connolly's record of accomplishment included the establishment of twenty-six parishes, thirty schools, and an extensive building program.

Hunthausen and Murphy. Connolly retired because of age, and on February 25, 1975, Raymond G. Hunthausen (1975–1991) became the second archbishop of Seattle. As bishop of Great Falls, Montana, Hunthausen was the youngest bishop in attendance at the Second Vatican Council. Inspired by the ecclesiology of Vatican II, he moved to instill in the archdiocese a vision of the local church as a communion of communions (parishes). He promoted formation of the laity, engaged extensively in ecumenical conversation, and participated in tax resistance as a protest against nuclear weapons. His commitment to peace, including nuclear disarmament, garnered international attention. It inspired many inside and outside the Church, and evoked opposition in a state with a heavy military presence. In the 1980s the

Holy See investigated allegations of liturgical and doctrinal irregularities in the archdiocese. Chicago-born Thomas J. Murphy (1932–1997), who had been bishop of Great Falls since 1978, was appointed coadjutor archbishop in 1987 and became third archbishop of Seattle when Archbishop Hunthausen retired in 1991.

After Archbishop Murphy died of leukemia in June 1997, Bishop Alexander J. Brunett (1930–), since 1994 the bishop of Helena, was installed as his successor. Archbishop Brunett committed himself to the participative leadership style of his two predecessors and to fostering collaboration among the parishes and other agencies of the archdioceses.

Brunett. Alexander J. Brunett (1934–), a priest of the Archdiocese of Detroit, was appointed archbishop of Seattle on October 28, 1997. Brunett was born January 17, 1934, in Detroit, the second of fourteen children of Cecelia and Raymond Brunett. He completed his studies in Rome and was ordained a priest on July 13, 1958, by Cardinal Luigi Traglia (1895–1977), the vicar of Rome. He served in archdiocesan parishes and did college chaplaincy work at the University of Michigan-Ann Arbor. He was even pastor for a time of the Shrine of the Little Flower in Royal Oak, Michigan, made famous by Father Charles COUGHLIN, the Radio Priest of the 1930s. He was for a time academic dean of St. John's Provincial Seminary in Plymouth, Michigan. He holds degrees in THEOLOGY and education and did post–graduate work in ecumenical studies in Jerusalem, Paris, and Radolfzell, Germany. Throughout his MINISTRY, he placed special emphasis on ecumenical affairs. From 1973 to 1991 he was the director of the Division of Interreligious Affairs of the Archdiocese of Detroit and from 1974 to 1981 he was president of the National Association of Diocesan Ecumenical Officers. Made a monsignor in 1990, he was appointed bishop of Helena, Montana, in 1994 and consecrated on June 6, 1994. On October 28, 1997, he was selected by Pope JOHN PAUL II to succeed the late Archbishop Thomas Murphy.

In 1999 there were 508,000 Catholics in the archdiocese, which had 199 diocesan priests, 135 religious order priests, 86 deacons, 33 RELIGIOUS brothers, 650 sisters, and 138 parishes. In 2005 the Catholic population had risen to 570,000 and the number of parishes to 142. The number of priests (religious and diocesan) had gone down to 274, the number of sisters to 450, and brothers to 18. The number of permanent deacons grew to 104 (*The Official Catholic Directory* 1999). Brunett ordained three auxiliary bishops: George Thomas (1950–), whom he consecrated in 2000 (and who was later transferred to the See of Helena); Joseph Jude Tyson (1957–), and Eusebio Elizondo (1954–), M.Sp.S, who received episcopal orders on June 6, 2005.

Church Outreach. *The Most Reverend Alexander J. Brunett, Archbishop of Seattle, blesses La Casa de San Juan Diego in Woodland, a complex offering housing for farmworker families. The Archbishop is assisted by Joshua Monge, 11, of Woodland, an altar server at St. Philip Catholic Church in Woodland, and by Kay Lagreid, of Seattle, the master of ceremonies for the program (the blessing and opening), who is also the director of communicaitons for Catholic Community Services of Western Washington and for the Archdicesan Housing Authority.* AP IMAGES

The consecration of Bishop Elizondo, a native of Mexico, and Bishop Tyson, who is multilingual, highlighted the growing presence of Hispanic/Latino Catholics in the Archdiocese of Seattle. Father Michael Holland began offering Spanish Masses in the churches and migrant camps of the Skagit Valley in the late 1970s. In 2002 the archdiocese hired a new director for its Hispanic/Latino Ministry Office. In 2005 Elizondo became the episcopal vicar for Hispanic Ministry and a pastoral plan, "From Guests to Hosts: Pastoral Priorities for the Ecclesial Integration of Hispanics," laid down objectives and strategies to meet the needs of this fast-growing demographic of Seattle Catholic life.

Concern for the plight of mostly Hispanic agricultural workers led to the creation of an affordable farm-worker family housing project, *La Casa de Padre Miguel,* in Mount Vernon in 1998. This was the first of seven farm-worker housing sites that provide shelter for 1,150 people. Brunett and the bishops of the region have taken a strong stand against raids for undocumented persons in churches and during religious ceremonies.

Asian Catholics, a significant demographic in the West, have received important recognition. Korean Catholics opened churches in Seattle in 2002 and 2006 respectively. Father Phuong Hoang was appointed vicar for Vietnamese Ministry. Native American Catholics began an annual gathering in 2003, and in 2006 the

archdiocese played host to the national Tekakwitha Conference, which drew Native American Catholics from around the country. Recruitment for the priest-hood and the permanent diaconate seeks to add bilingual and bicultural candidates for ordained ministry. A number of extern priests from Africa, Germany, India, Korea, the Philippines, Samoa, and Spain have tempo-rarily joined the ranks of the Seattle clergy. Brunett ordained thirty-three men to the priesthood between 1997 and 2007.

The archdiocese added three new parishes in 2003. Brunett placed a high priority on expanding Catholic education. Three new elementary schools opened between 1997 and 2007. St. Elizabeth Anne Seton Catholic high school in Ridgefield represented an important expansion of Catholic secondary education in Southwestern Washington. Another archdiocesan high school in the South Sound region was established in 2005.

The Archdiocese of Seattle has faced the array of challenges typical of western dioceses. The state of Washington has a very high percentage of population that claims no religious affiliation. In the Archdiocese of Seattle there are nearly 600,000 Catholics out of a total population of nearly five million. Among the various ways in which the Catholic Church has reached out to this diverse population has been through an active social ministry. The homeless, a highly visible reality in many western cities, have challenged Catholic Charities and local parishes. Through Catholic Community Services and the Archdiocesan Housing Authority, the archdiocese has sponsored Harrington House, a transitional residence for homeless pregnant women or women with young children.

Likewise, under the leadership of Father Michael Ryan, the historic St. James Cathedral underwent substantial renovations in 1994 that not only enhanced the beauty of the physical space but also accentuated the role of the cathedral as a social and cultural center for the city of Seattle. A highly active core of parishioners and staff have sustained its excellent musical ministries as well as its ties with the diverse and religiously heterogeneous larger community. Emblazoned on the inner dome of the cathedral are the words: "I am among you as one who serves." St. James's multiple ministries, and its music, art, and buoyant liturgies have made it an important bridge to the community at large and a model for other cathedral communities in the United States.

School ministry accentuated the positive efforts of the Archdiocese of Seattle on matters concerning children and teens. In 2002 the dark cloud of sexual abuse of children broke over the Catholic community in the United States. Seattle Catholics, laity, priests, religious, deacons, and bishops sadly acknowledged the depth of the problem and the need for restitution of victims and preventive action to make sure it did not reoccur. As of 2007 the archdiocese reported that it had provided pastoral care and settlements to more than 200 victims of child sexual abuse. The cost for these settlements, attorneys fees, and counseling fees totaled nearly $27 million. Brunett himself met with forty victims to apologize and provide pastoral support. Safe environment programs were mandated for each parish, and a staff person was dedicated to insure compliance with the mandates of the Dallas Charter and the requirements of local law enforcement. Although the sexual abuse scandal has not yet run its course, the actions of Pope BENEDICT XVI, who openly addressed the scandal and met victims in a private meeting during a 2008 visit to the United States, may constitute a turning point.

Seattle's changes in the years 1997 to 2007 reflect not only the inner dynamics of the unique history and culture of this see, but also the transformation of the larger Church culture during the pontificates of Pope John Paul II (1978–2005) and Pope Benedict XVI (2005–). Both pontiffs continued to pursue an active engagement with the modern world but also sought to bring order to areas of church life that some perceived had gone astray in the aftermath of Vatican II.

SEE ALSO CATHOLIC CHARITIES USA; IDAHO, CATHOLIC CHURCH IN; LAITY, FORMATION AND EDUCATION OF; MISSION AND MIS-SIONS; MONTANA, CATHOLIC CHURCH IN; OREGON, CATHOLIC CHURCH IN; PILGRIMAGES, ROMAN; SEX ABUSE CRISIS; VATICAN COUNCIL II; WASHINGTON, CATHOLIC CHURCH IN; WYOMING, CATHOLIC CHURCH IN.

BIBLIOGRAPHY

Archdiocese of Seattle Official Web site, available from: http://www.seattlearch.org/ (accessed December 9, 2008).

David M. Buerge and Junius Rochester, *Roots and Branches: The Religious Heritage of Washington State* (Seattle 1988).

P. O'Connell Killen, "The Geography of a Minority Religion: Roman Catholicism in the Pacific Northwest," *U.S. Catholic Historian* 18, no. 3 (Summer 2000): 51–72.

The Official Catholic Directory (New Providence, N.J. 1999, 2008).

Wilfred P. Schoenberg, *A History of the Catholic Church in the Pacific Northwest, 1743–1983* (Washington, D.C. 1987).

Carlos A. Schwantes, *The Pacific Northwest: An Interpretive History* (Lincoln, Neb. 1996).

Christine M. Taylor, ed., *Abundance of Grace: A History of the Archdiocese of Seattle 1850–2000* (Strasbourg, France 2000).

Rev. John McCorkle SS
Instructor in Church History and Librarian
St. Thomas Seminary, Kenmore, Wash.

Rev. Steven M. Avella
Professor of History
Marquette University, Milwaukee, Wis. (2009)

SEX ABUSE CRISIS

Beginning in January 2002 news articles and the official response of the Boston Archdiocese regarding allegations of Father John Geoghan's sexual abuse of children introduced the phrase "sex abuse crisis" to describe the Catholic Church's response to sexual abuse by clergy in the United States.

While the public and the secular media became aware of some clergy's actions in 2002, more than two decades earlier the U.S. Catholic bishops, clergy, and lay leaders had begun a systematic examination of sexual abuse by church workers. In 1984 allegations of sexual abuse by Father Gilbert Gauthe of Lafayette, Louisiana, launched discussions among some church leaders, including staff of the United States Catholic Conference (USCC) (now the U.S. Conference of Catholic Bishops). By 1985 the national staff recommended that dioceses and archdioceses consider five steps in responding to allegations of abuse:

(1) Remove the alleged offender from active ministry;

(2) Refer the alleged offender to professional evaluation;

(3) Respond pastorally and immediately to the victim and their family;

(4) Make efforts to protect the confidentiality of the claim;

(5) Comply with civil law requirements.

These five elements became known as The Five Principles and were part of a public statement released by the National Conference of Catholic Bishops at their June 1992 general meeting.

Other church leaders responded to the issue. Perhaps most notable was the work of the Committee on Priestly Life and Ministry that developed training for clergy and the work of seminary rectors and other seminary leadership to develop psychosexual formation for seminarians based on modern psychological theories.

In 1993 ongoing discussions with the HOLY SEE resulted in a meeting and a letter from Pope JOHN PAUL II to the U.S. bishops which condemned child abuse and announced the formation of a joint study commission to address the bishops' concerns regarding how canon law addressed the behavior of abusive priests. The following year at the June general meeting of the U.S. bishops, an ad hoc committee on sexual abuse was formed. The committee asked experts from the medical and psychological fields for advice on how to address the issue of sexual abuse by clergy.

In November 1994 the committee issued "Restoring Trust, Vol. I," a review of 157 diocesan policies that addressed clergy sexual abuse of minors, the description of ten treatment centers in addition to a number of resources for serving victims, parish communities, and offenders. "Restoring Trust, Vol. II" and "Restoring Trust, Vol. III" followed in 1995 and 1996, respectively, with additional resources and information for diocesan bishops and their staffs.

Meanwhile, staff from the USCC and U.S. bishops began meeting with VATICAN officials and church leaders from other English-speaking conferences to discuss this issue. These meetings began in 1996 and continue through 2008.

Professional Response and Research. To develop their policies and procedures the U.S. bishops and their staff relied on psychologists, law enforcement officials, and other experts who have dealt with sexual abusers. Over the years, as more research was made available, medical professionals and law enforcement agencies have changed how they respond to sexual abusers.

In the 1950s the Federal Bureau of Investigation developed a program to prevent sexual abuse of children. It focused on strangers, abductions, and protecting innocent children. But as it became clear that the majority of sexual abuse was perpetrated by someone the child knew and trusted—such as a family member or close friend—civil entities in the United States began passing child-abuse reporting laws in the 1960s. Discussion at that time often focused around whether family privacy was being violated by someone reporting sexual abuse to the police.

The *Diagnostic and Statistical Manual of Mental Disorders* (Third Edition), issued in 1980, distinguished between someone who was sexually attracted to pre-pubescent minors and someone attracted to post–pubescent minors. Initially, it was recommended that someone who was sexually attracted to any minor, no matter what the age range, could respond to treatment. Church leaders would send a clergy to treatment and then be advised that he could return to active ministry, even if that meant close contact with minors. By the 1990s medical professionals were reporting low success rates for the treatment of someone with a sexual attraction to pre-pubescent minors and expressed concern regarding the perpetrator's access to children.

The Boston Scandal. While reports of sexual abuse by clergy had been surfacing for years, the case of Father John Geoghan captured the public's interest in an unprecedented way. The official response of the Boston Archdiocese, especially that of Cardinal Bernard Law (archbishop of Boston), became the focus of many media outlets. Massachusetts Attorney General Thomas F. Reilly pressed to obtain church documents in order to resolve cases brought forward by alleged victims in the opening months of 2002.

Cardinal Law submitted his resignation as archbishop to Pope JOHN PAUL II on December 13, 2002. Because of the publicity generated regarding the cases in Boston, other victims felt comfortable coming forward to publicly accuse their abusers, leading to the resignations of bishops, priests, deacons, and lay leaders.

Although the U.S. bishops have taken strong measures to prevent the sexual abuse of minors in the future, some dioceses and archdioceses continue to endure the cost of large financial settlements for past offenses. As of 2007 it was estimated that $2.5 billion had been spent nationwide on legal claims and victims' needs.

The Bishops' Response. The intense media exposure and public response resulted in the U.S. bishops seeking, and receiving, affirmation from ROME for their efforts. In late April 2002 all of the U.S. cardinals met with Pope John Paul II, who spoke strongly on the issue: "The abuse which has caused this crisis is by every standard wrong and rightly considered a crime by society; it is also an appalling sin in the eyes of God," he told the cardinals. "People need to know that there is no place in the priesthood and religious life for those who would harm the young."

The June 12 to 14, 2002, meeting of the U.S. bishops in Dallas became a focal point for public outrage and media speculation. The bishops announced that the meeting would be dedicated entirely to addressing the issues of clergy sexual abusers and the church leaders' response to the abuse.

The meeting resulted in the approval of a "Charter for the Protection of Children and Young People," in which the bishops wrote:

> We commit ourselves to a pastoral outreach to repair the breach with those who have suffered sexual abuse and with all the people of the Church. We renew our determination to provide safety and protection for children and young people in our church ministries and institutions. We pledge ourselves to act in a way that manifests our accountability to God, to his people, and to one another in this grave matter. We commit ourselves to do all we can to heal the trauma that victims/survivors and their families are suffering and the wound that the whole Church is experiencing. We acknowledge our need to be in dialogue with all Catholics, especially victims and parents, around this issue. By these actions, we want to demonstrate to the wider community that we comprehend the gravity of the sexual abuse of minors. ("Charter for the Protection of Children and Young People," 2002)

The charter reiterated what had been previously recommended by the National Conference of Catholic Bishops concerning the promotion of healing and reconciliation for victims and survivors, cooperation with civil authorities, and removal of offenders from active ministry. It also expanded on the work done previously by bishops and other church leaders, calling for everyone wishing to serve minors—whether lay or clergy—to be trained in what constitutes a safe environment for children, and to undergo an evaluation of their criminal history.

The charter also called for every bishop to consult with a review board comprised of independent lay experts in regard to all allegations of sexual abuse of minors by clergy in their DIOCESE, and for the establishment of a national Office of Child and Youth Protection and a National Review Board. It stated that dioceses would report any accusation of sexual abuse of a minor to civil authorities; that dioceses would have a victims' assistance coordinator and a communications policy that reflects a commitment to transparency and openness; and that dioceses would not enter into confidentiality agreements, except at the insistence of a victim. It also resulted in what was described as a zero-tolerance policy: The bishops agreed that only one instance of abuse was enough to remove a priest or deacon from ministry.

A document titled "Essential Norms for Diocesan/Eparchial Policies Dealing with Allegations of Sexual Abuse of Minors by Priests or Deacons" was also approved and provided guidelines for canonical processes in removing clergy from their ministerial role. It received *recognitio* from the HOLY SEE in 2002. That recognition was renewed in 2005.

National Effort. In approving the "Charter for the Protection of Children and Young People" the U.S. bishops agreed to hold each other accountable to its principles by submitting their diocese to audits by independent entities and by cooperating with the National Review Board in studies to determine the scope and nature of abuse among Catholic clergy. It may be the first time in the history of the Catholic Church in the United States that the bishops entered into such a comprehensive and collaborative effort.

As a result the John Jay College of Criminal Justice in New York City was contracted to gather information on sexual abuse by Roman Catholic clergy in the United States from 1950 through 2002. The study was released in late February 2004. It reported that about four percent (4,392) of priests and deacons who served from 1950 through 2002 were accused of abusing 10,667 minors. Experts confirmed that this percentage was similar to that found in other child-serving professions such as teaching, counseling, and coaching.

Of the 4,392 priests, 149 (3.5%) were allegedly responsible for abusing 2,960 victims, 26 percent of all alleged victims. Most of the accused priests (56%) were reported to have one victim; almost 27 percent were accused of two or three victims, and nearly 14 percent were alleged to have abused four to nine victims.

Most of the priests (68%) with allegations of abuse were ordained between 1950 and 1979. A slightly higher—although statistically insignificant—percentage of diocesan priests over priests in religious orders were accused of abuse.

About one half (51%) of alleged victims were between the ages of 11 and 14; 27 percent were between ages 15 and 17; 16 percent between ages 8 and 10; and 6 percent were under age 7. The victims were disproportionately male: 81 percent male and 19 percent female.

The Center for Applied Research in the Apostolate (CARA), based at Georgetown University in Washington, D.C., was also commissioned to conduct annual surveys on new allegations of abuse. Surveys completed in 2004, 2005, and 2006 indicate that the number of new allegations declined over the three years and that approximately 75 percent of all incidents occurred between 1960 and 1984. In November 2005 the U.S. bishops and the National Review Board engaged John Jay College and Fordham University to conduct a study that focused on the reason for that trend along with other circumstances and factors related to the overall issue of child abuse by clergy.

SEE ALSO BOSTON, ARCHDIOCESE OF; CHILD SEXUAL ABUSE; MODERN MEDIA AND THE CHURCH; UNITED STATES CONFERENCE OF CATHOLIC BISHOPS (USCCB).

BIBLIOGRAPHY

Monica Applewhite, "Putting Abuse in Context," *America* 195, no. 8 (September 25, 2006).

Agostino Bono, "National Sex Abuse Study Holds Insights on Causes, Prevention," *Catholic News Service* (February 23, 2004), available from http://georgiabulletin.org/world/2004/02/23/Us-2/ (accessed March 13, 2008).

Chuck Colbert, "Pressure over Abuse Cases Mounts," *National Catholic Reporter* (March 15, 2002), available from http://natcath.org/NCR_Online/archives2/2002a/031502/031502i.htm (accessed February 17, 2008).

John Paul II, "Address of John Paul II to the Cardinals of the United States" (April 23, 2002), available from http://www.vatican.va/holy_father/john_paul_ii/speeches/2002/april/documents/hf_jp-ii_spe_20020423_usa-cardinals_en.html (accessed February 17, 2008).

Gerald W. Lynch, et al, "The Nature and Scope of the Problem of Sexual Abuse of Minors by Catholic Priests and Deacons in the United States: A Research Study Conducted by the John Jay College of Criminal Justice" (Washington, D.C. 2004).

Office of Media Relations, U.S. Conference of Catholic Bishops, "Efforts to Combat Clergy Sexual Abuse against Minors: A Chronology, 1982–2006" available from http://www.usccb.org/comm/combatefforts.shtml (accessed February 17, 2008).

Office of Media Relations, U.S. Conference of Catholic Bishops, "Restoring Trust: Response to Clergy Sexual Abuse," available from http://www.usccb.org/comm/restoretrust.shtml (accessed February 18, 2008).

U.S. Conference of Catholic Bishops, "Essential Norms for Diocesan/Eparchial Policies Dealing with Allegations of Sexual Abuse of Minors by Priests or Deacons" (June 2002, rev. ed., June 2005), available from http://www.usccb.org/bishops/norms.shtml (accessed February 18, 2008).

U.S. Conference of Catholic Bishops, "Charter for the Protection of Children and Young People" (June 2005), available from http://www.usccb.org/ocyp/charter.shtml (accessed February 18, 2008).

Most Rev. Gregory M. Aymond
Roman Catholic Bishop of Austin, Texas
Chair, Committee for the Protection of Children and Young People, U.S. Conference of Catholic Bishops (2009)

Helen Luebbering Osman
Executive Secretary of Communications
U.S. Conference of Catholic Bishops (2009)

SOUTH CAROLINA, CATHOLIC CHURCH IN

The Diocese of Charleston began the twenty-first century under the leadership of Robert J. Baker (b. 1944), who was appointed as the twelfth bishop of the DIOCESE on July 13, 1999, by Pope JOHN PAUL II. Baker was consecrated in Charleston on September 29, 1999, and installed in the Cathedral of Saint John the Baptist. The diocese, established by Pope PIUS VII on July 11, 1820, comprises the land area of the entire state and with Richmond, Virginia, was the first diocese created in the South.

In 2008 the diocese included about 183,356 Catholics, representing 4 percent of the state population. The diocese was served by 125 active priests (of whom 38 were members of religious orders), 101 permanent deacons, and 157 religious brothers and sisters serving in 92 parishes, 23 missions, and 1 pastoral center. The diocese sponsors 3 hospitals, 7 social service centers, a retirement center, 28 parochial schools, and 2 high schools (*The Official Catholic Directory* 2008, p. 227).

History. The first act of christian worship in what is now South Carolina was probably a Mass celebrated by Catholic priests accompanying the explorations of Lucas de Ayllon (d. 1526) and Hernando de Soto (d. 1542) through the area in the first half of the sixteenth century, but it was not until more than 250 years later that the Church developed in the region. The English crown gave eight lords proprietors a charter in the seventeenth century to develop the colony of Carolina. Charleston, the see city of the diocese, was settled in 1670 when the first English colonists arrived with their slaves from Barbados. The English, reflecting European political divisions, adopted a policy prohibiting the immigration of Catholics and all manifestations of their religion. The Carolina royal governor observed in 1770 that there was religious freedom for everyone in the colony "except Papists." The Church took root in the state only after the success of the American Revolution, during which the Church of England was disestablished. An Italian priest celebrated the first Mass in Charleston in 1788 as he was passing through the city on a ship bound for South America.

Matthew Ryan was the first priest assigned to minister to the small Catholic population in Charleston. Bishop John CARROLL of Baltimore, the first ecclesiastical superior in the emerging nation, sent the Irish priest to Charleston in 1788. The fledgling congregation acquired a building on Hasell Street in 1789 and established Saint Mary's Church. Charleston was an important seaport on the southern Atlantic coast, and the number of Catholics increased as the city grew with immigration from Ireland and other European nations.

French Catholics arrived in Charleston from the Caribbean after a slave revolution in Haiti led to the flight of many residents from Haiti and Santo Domingo. Among them were two daughters of Admiral le comte de Grasse (1722–1788), a French naval hero of the American Revolution. Both girls died in Charleston in 1799 and their bodies were laid to rest in Saint Mary's churchyard.

The Gallagher Years. Simon Felix GALLAGHER, an Irish priest with a degree from the University of PARIS, came to Saint Mary's in 1793. Gallagher was an important figure in the Charleston community as well as at Saint Mary's during the thirty years he lived in the city. He was a member of the faculty of the College of Charleston and served as its president on two occasions. He founded a school called the Athenian Academy and was a founder of an association of Irishmen called the Hibernian Society that is still in existence.

Both Gallagher and the congregation at Saint Mary's were often embroiled in conflicts with the ecclesiastical authority. The congregational disputes reflected the republican disposition of the young nation and a desire for independence from outside control. Bishop Carroll received frequent complaints from Charleston Catholics about Gallagher's personal behavior. Carroll warned Gallagher on more than one occasion about using inappropriate language during services and for celebrating Mass in an inebriated condition.

The congregation at Saint Mary's decided that it wished to have a voice in the selection of bishops chosen to serve in Charleston as well as elsewhere in America. When its proposals to have a veto power over the selection of bishops were thwarted, the congregation attempted to recruit a bishop of its own liking from among Old Catholic separatists or from one of the Eastern Orthodox Churches to establish an "Independent Catholick Church" in America. The mission was unsuccessful, but problems continued until closer ecclesiastical supervision could be established.

Many priests came to America from France to escape the FRENCH REVOLUTION. Their immigration resulted in a disproportionately large number of French clergy in the American church. Disputes arose within the Church as many Catholics of Irish origin thought that too many French clerics were appointed to positions of authority. The tension was heightened in South Carolina where the Church was predominately Irish from the earliest days, but where there was also a significant French Catholic population.

Carroll, now ARCHBISHOP of Baltimore, sent a French priest to Charleston in about 1810 to assist Gallagher. Joseph Picot Limoelan de la CLORIVIÈRE had been a royalist officer at the beginning of the French Revolution and was forced to leave France. When he returned to France after the Revolution, Clorivière was implicated in a plot to assassinate Napoleon Bonaparte. He escaped execution for his involvement in the affair only because his uncle, the head of the Society of Jesus in France, arranged his secret emigration to America. Clorivière arrived in Baltimore, attended Saint Mary's Seminary, was ordained to the priesthood, and was assigned to Saint Mary's in Charleston. He was not acceptable to Gallagher or to many in the congregation, which led to further fragmentation of the parish, and Saint Mary's was placed under an INTERDICT by Carroll's successor, Archbishop Leonard NEALE of Baltimore, in 1817.

Diocese of Charleston. The Diocese of Charleston was created on June 20, 1820, and John ENGLAND, a native of Cork, Ireland, was nominated its first bishop. England was consecrated in Ireland on September 1, and arrived in Charleston on December 30 with his sister, Joanna Monica England, and a priest, Denis Corkery. The first Mass celebrated by a bishop of Charleston occurred at Saint Mary's Church on December 31, 1820.

The newly erected Diocese of Charleston comprised three states, North Carolina, South Carolina, and Georgia, and covered 142,000 square miles that contained no more than five churches and less than 400 Catholics. Bishop England wasted no time establishing a coherent diocesan organization. He established the Cathedral of Saint Finbar on Broad Street in Charleston, giving it the same name as that of his home parish in Cork. The bishop opened a seminary, Saint John the Baptist, adjacent to the CATHEDRAL, and its first student was Andrew BYRNE, who later became the first bishop of Little Rock, Arkansas. England established the *United States Catholic Miscellany*, the first Catholic publication of general circulation in the nation. He wrote a constitution for the diocese that enabled lay people to participate in the affairs of church governance through state and diocesan conventions of elected representatives. The bishop and his sister, Joanna, were instrumental in founding a religious order for women known as the Sisters of Charity of Our Lady of Mercy, and he invited a community of Ursuline nuns to Charleston, where they founded a non-sectarian school that was perhaps the first such school in the state. England founded schools in Charleston for slaves, free blacks, and mulattos to promote education among the African-American population. Saint Peter's Church, established in Columbia, the capital city, was one of the first parishes in the midlands of the state. It was dedicated by England on December 12, 1830. Churches were established wherever there were Catholics to support them as the population moved farther into other parts of the state. The Church was firmly established in South Carolina by the time Bishop England's ministry ended with his death at age 56 in 1842. From his first days in America, he had preached a message of tolerance among all people, and worked to make Catholicism acceptable in the emerging nation. He appreciated American DEMOCRACY and endeavored to present it as compatible with the Catholic FAITH. The essentially Irish character of the Church that emerged in the diocese continued until well into the twentieth century.

Ignatius A. Reynolds (1798–1855) became the second bishop of the diocese. A native of Bardstown, Kentucky, Reynolds was consecrated in Cincinnati and arrived in Charleston on April 3, 1844. Under Reynolds's leadership the diocese expanded beyond the city of Charleston as more Catholics settled in the region. He raised funds to pay debts incurred by Bishop England and built a new cathedral, which was consecrated in 1854. The Sisters of Charity of Our Lady of Mercy prospered and opened a hospital in Charleston in 1852. Schools were opened in Columbia, where Saint Joseph's Church was established in 1854. The diocese was reduced in territorial size when the Diocese of SAVANNAH, including the entire state of Georgia, was erected in 1850. Reynolds served until his death on March 6, 1855.

The Lynch Era. A local priest, Patrick Neison LYNCH, became the diocesan administrator upon the death of Reynolds and was soon appointed the third bishop of the diocese. Born in Ireland, Lynch became the first bishop consecrated in the diocese. Bishop Lynch's episcopate was engulfed by the disruption and turmoil of the Civil War that began when South Carolina seceded from the Union on December 20, 1860.

A devastating fire struck the city of Charleston on December 11, 1861, which added to the wartime destruction. The Charleston fire destroyed the cathedral, the bishop's residence, the Catholic Institute Hall, the seminary library, and an orphanage near the cathedral. The separation from the Union brought about the change of the name of the *U.S. Catholic Miscellany* to the *Charleston Catholic Miscellany*, and its last edition was published on December 14, 1861, three days after the fire. The population of the city was endangered and church property damaged by hostile shelling during a siege by northern forces from 1863 to 1865. The Ursuline CONVENT in Columbia was severely damaged by fire in 1865. Several Sisters of Our Lady of Mercy joined the war effort as nurses supporting the Confederate Army. During the war, the westward expansion of the diocese continued as more Catholics settled the Carolina back-country.

Lynch became an advocate for the Confederate cause and, like some of the other southern bishops, was a slave owner. He defended the institution of slavery and justified its existence on moral grounds; he felt that to sustain it the Catholic Church should see to the proper treatment and education of slaves. Jefferson Davis (1808–1889), the president of the Confederacy, asked Lynch to represent the rebellious southern government on a diplomatic mission to the HOLY SEE. The bishop agreed to undertake the assignment and arrived in ROME in June 1864 as a Special Commissioner of the Confederate States of America to the States of the Church to seek Pope PIUS IX's diplomatic recognition of the Confederate government. Lynch had an audience with the POPE and presented his credentials as minister of the Confederate States, but his petition evidently did not proceed beyond that point. He was unable to return to the diocese because he was declared *persona non grata* by the United States government. Lynch was pardoned by President Andrew Johnson (1808–1875) after taking an oath of allegiance to the United States before the ambassador in Paris on October 14, 1865, thus enabling him to return to South Carolina. The bishop returned to the diocese to find much destruction and the need for substantial funds for rebuilding the fabric of the Church and the community.

A vicariate apostolic was established for North Carolina in 1868, separating it from the Diocese of Charleston and relieving Bishop Lynch of further responsibilities there. Lynch spent much of his time during Reconstruction away from the diocese raising funds in the North for rebuilding. He also developed ideas and plans for the assimilation of former slaves into the Church and society. Economic stability was not achieved in the South until many years after the Civil War, and much needed to be done to restore the spirit of the people and church property when Lynch's episcopate ended upon his death on February 26, 1882.

Northrop's Episcopate. The period between Lynch's death and World War I was one of steady growth and progress in the diocese. Henry P. Northrop, the only native of the city of Charleston to be named bishop of the diocese, became the fourth bishop on March 11, 1883. He had been serving in North Carolina as the vicar apostolic. A time of religious and minority intolerance followed the Civil War. The Reconstruction era brought with it the establishment of such organizations as the KU KLUX KLAN and the enactment of Jim Crow laws throughout the region. The Catholic Church unfortunately became the target of more than its share of vitriolic language and behavior. In addition, a severe earthquake hit Charleston in 1886. It caused damage to church property in the city and surrounding area, requiring renewed fundraising efforts to repair the damage.

A synod of the diocese, the first since the time of Bishop England, was called in 1887 and attended by sixteen priests. A new wave of immigrants from predominantly Catholic European countries and from Lebanon led to a sharp increase in the number of communicants in the diocese around the turn of the twentieth century. The Lebanese brought the Maronite Rite with them, but they were soon largely assimilated into the LATIN RITE Catholic population. The demography of the diocese shifted with the new immigration from one of traditional Irish dominance to one with broader cultural diversity. There were about 9,000 Catholics in South Carolina at the turn of the century, and many improvements were made in the fabric of the diocese as the economic hardships of the Reconstruction era subsided. A cathedral school was opened in 1887, and new churches were established across the diocese to accommodate the increasing numbers of Catholics.

Northrop's episcopate, the longest in the history of the diocese, was marked by steady progress in the development of diocesan institutions. Saint Angela's Academy opened in Aiken in 1900, a branch of the KNIGHTS OF COLUMBUS was organized in Charleston in 1902, the Holy Name Society was established, and Bishop England High School was founded in 1915. James Cardinal GIBBONS, the ARCHBISHOP of Baltimore, celebrated a Mass of dedication on April 14, 1907, for the reconstructed cathedral on the twenty-fifth anniversary of Bishop Northrop's consecration. And in about 1910, a new motherhouse for the Sisters of Charity of Our Lady of Mercy began operation at Queen and Legare Streets in Charleston.

Northrop's death came on June 17, 1916. He was succeeded by William T. Russell of Washington, D.C. Installed on March 22, 1917, Russell continued the development of mission work throughout the diocese and blessed many new parishes. Saint Francis Xavier Hospital was organized in Charleston, where the bishop died in 1927.

The Walsh Years. Russell's successor was Emmet Michael Walsh, a much beloved native son of the diocese who came from Atlanta and was installed as the sixth bishop of Charleston on September 22, 1927. Walsh served in Charleston until his appointment as coadjutor bishop of the Diocese of Youngstown, Ohio, in 1949. Catholic hospitals were established in Charleston, Greenville, Rock Hill, York, Columbia, and Dillon. Bishop Walsh founded a Council of Catholic Women, a Council of Catholic Men, and a Catholic Youth Council. Camps for children were organized, and a parish for African Americans was begun in Columbia.

Bishop Walsh developed an innovative program for the development of new church buildings. A priest at Belmont Abbey in North Carolina developed a standard church building design that provided the diocese with simple, dignified church buildings of wooden frames on brick pillars with cedar shingles on the outside walls. These simple buildings were designed to include all the necessary furnishings and fixtures down to the curtains for the confessionals. The standard design made it possible to construct identical buildings any place in the diocese where a church was needed at low cost in a minimal time. At least twelve of these structures were put into service, including church buildings at Myrtle Beach, Union, Dillon, Bennettsville, Bishopville, and Saint Patrick's in Columbia.

Mepkin Abbey was established in the diocese in 1949 by the Order of Cistercians of the Strict Observance (Trappist). Clare Booth Luce (1903–1987) and her husband, Henry Luce (1898–1967), whose bodies lie at rest on the abbey grounds, gave the order 3,000 acres of land for the abbey in Berkeley County, just north of Charleston. The first monks arrived at Mepkin in the fall of 1949 under the leadership of Dom Anthony Chassagne. The leadership of Abbot Francis Kline (1990–2006) continued the tradition of making the abbey and its monastic community an important part of the life of the local diocese.

Later Bishops. From the departure of Bishop Walsh in 1949 until 1963, three bishops were appointed to the see of Charleston, and all were later transferred elsewhere. John J. RUSSELL was installed in 1950 and appointed bishop of Richmond, Virginia, in 1958; Paul J. HALLINAN was installed in 1958 and became archbishop of the new Province of Atlanta in 1962; Francis F. Reh (1911–1994) was installed in 1962 and became rector of the NORTH AMERICAN COLLEGE in Rome in 1963.

Joseph L. BERNARDIN, a native of Columbia, was ordained in the Charleston cathedral in 1953 and became Bishop Russell's secretary. He served as a priest in the diocese for fourteen years after his ordination until his appointment as auxiliary BISHOP of Atlanta. A distinguished son of the diocese, Bernardin later served as general secretary to the National Conference of Catholic Bishops and CARDINAL archbishop of Chicago.

A new publication, the *Catholic Banner*, was inaugurated in 1951 to provide a newspaper for the diocese for the first time in many years. In 1959 the motherhouse of the Sisters of Charity of Our Lady of Mercy moved to a new site on James Island, overlooking Charleston Harbor, and Cardinal Newman High School was dedicated in Columbia in 1961. Upon the departure of Bishop Reh in 1963, Joseph L. Bernardin became the diocesan administrator until the installation of Ernest L. Unterkoefler (1917–1993) as the tenth bishop of the diocese on February 22, 1964.

Cathedral of St. John the Baptist, Charleston, South Carolina. *The recessional leaves the cathedral following a memorial mass for Pope John Paul II on Friday, April 8, 2005.* AP IMAGES

The episcopate of Unterkoefler was marked by a strong voice from the Church on matters of racial justice and social concerns. Unterkoefler courageously led public civil rights marches in the diocese in the 1960s to demonstrate the commitment of the Church to the achievement of SOCIAL JUSTICE for everyone in America. He also strongly supported ecumenical activities with other Christian bodies.

David B. Thompson (b. 1923) became the eleventh bishop of the diocese in 1990 and promptly set about the task of improving the Catholic school system. He also took steps to insure a racial balance in all the educational institutions of the diocese. The name of the diocesan newspaper was changed to the *New Catholic Miscellany* to honor Bishop England's founding of the first general publication for Catholics in the nation.

The church in South Carolina was racially segregated until the mid-1960s. There were several parishes in the diocese, Saint Patrick's in Charleston, Saint Martin de Porres in Columbia, Saint James at Ritter, and others that specifically served the African-American Catholic population. Immaculate Conception in Charleston was a high school for African-American students. Under the leadership of Unterkoefler the parishes, schools, and other diocesan institutions were successfully desegregated.

Bishop Thompson convened a synod in 1995, called the Synod of Charleston, to plan and empower the participation of lay people in the work of the Church. The Synod, involving lay people and clergy, led to the renewal of participation by lay people in the parishes of the diocese as lectors, cantors, Eucharistic ministers, and pastoral associates. It also encouraged the development of new RELIGIOUS EDUCATION and peace and justice programs.

Vatican II and Beyond. The cultural diversity of the Church in South Carolina continued to broaden as the American population became more mobile in the twentieth century. By the end of the millennium the Irish dominance of the Church in earlier times had given way to a Catholic population reflecting the attributes of the rich cultural heritage of America. These changes along with the reforms of the Second Vatican Council placed the Diocese of Charleston in the mainstream of American Catholicism.

The deep roots of Catholicism in South Carolina led to the healthy growth of the church in the first decade of the twenty-first century. The growth represented not only an increase in the institutions serving the diocese, but also healthy improvements in the quality of the spiritual life of the people. Important changes occurred in the diocese. After leading the Diocese of Charleston for nearly eight years, Bishop Robert J. Baker, who succeeded Bishop Thompson in 1999, was appointed bishop of Birmingham, Alabama, by Pope BENEDICT XVI on August 14, 2007. Monsignor Martin T. Laughlin, a longtime priest of the diocese, was elected and appointed administrator of the diocese on October 3, 2007, the day after Bishop Baker's installation at Birmingham.

Bishop Baker's episcopacy was marked by two principle themes: the need for daily prayer among all the FAITHFUL, and the need for education about the Catholic faith. These themes were inculcated by dedicating each year in the new millennium to a special program throughout the diocese to emphasize prayer, reconciliation, evangelization, the ROSARY, stewardship, and the family. The bishop was an outspoken opponent of ABORTION; he supported public efforts to outlaw it and admonished Catholic politicians to work for such a ban.

The first years of the twenty-first century brought a steady increase in the number of new parishes and missions and growth in most of the established places of worship. Of particular significance was a canonical decree in March 2006 establishing a SHRINE to Mary, Our Lady of South Carolina, under the auspices of the diocese. Funds were raised for structural improvements to the Cathedral of St. John the Baptist that included the addition of a steeple to replace one destroyed by fire in the nineteenth century. New ministries were developed to spiritually nurture the ever-growing number of Latino immigrants. Programs were established for training the clergy of the diocese in the use of the Spanish language. The diocese moved into the twenty-first century as a unified community of many diverse cultures with the

goal of providing a steadfast and deeply rooted witness of faith to everyone.

SEE ALSO CISTERCIANS; EASTERN CHURCHES; GEORGIA, CATHOLIC CHURCH IN; MARONITE CHURCH; NAPOLEON I; NATIONAL COUNCIL OF CATHOLIC MEN (NCCM); NATIONAL COUNCIL OF CATHOLIC WOMEN (NCCW); NORTH CAROLINA, CATHOLIC CHURCH IN; OLD CATHOLICS; SLAVERY, III (HISTORY OF); TRAPPISTS; UNITED STATES CONFERENCE OF CATHOLIC BISHOPS (USCCB); URSULINES; VATICAN COUNCIL II; VIRGINIA, CATHOLIC CHURCH IN.

BIBLIOGRAPHY

The Rev. Scott James-Allen Buchanan, "Catholicism in the Carolinas and Georgia: 1670–1820" (Thesis, Pontificiae Univertatis Gregorianae 1998).

Diocese of Charleston Official Web site, available from: http://www.catholic-doc.org (accessed November 2, 2008).

John Geaney, executive producer, and Gonzalo Accame, producer/director, *Fire Tried Gold: A Documentary History of Catholics in South Carolina* (Kensington, Md. 2000), film.

Peter Guilday, *The Life and Times of John England, First Bishop of Charleston (1786–1842)*, 2 vols. (New York 1927).

Richard C. Madden, *Catholics in South Carolina: A Record* (Lanham, Md. 1985).

Jeremiah Joseph O'Connell, *Catholicity in the Carolinas and Georgia* (New York 1879).

The Official Catholic Directory, 2008 (New Providence, N.J. 2008).

Thomas Tisdale, *A Lady of the High Hills: Natalie Delage Sumter* (Columbia, S.C. 2001).

Thomas Tisdale
Independent Writer
Charleston, S.C. (2009)

SOUTH DAKOTA, CATHOLIC CHURCH IN

South Dakota, a state on the northern plains, extends over 77,000 square miles and borders Iowa, Minnesota, North Dakota, Wyoming, Montana, and Nebraska. 153,357 (about 20.5%) of the more than 751,364 residents are Catholic (*The Official Catholic Directory* 2008, p. 2100). These include many first- or second-generation Americans of German-Russian and Irish ancestry as well as a scattering of people of Czech, Polish, French, and Scandinavian descent. About half of the Native Americans living on the eight reservations and in the larger towns are Catholic.

The Missouri River divides South Dakota into an East River and a West River region with a DIOCESE in each, namely Sioux Falls and Rapid City. The more populated Sioux Falls diocese numbered 126,196

Catholics in 2008 (*The Official Catholic Directory* 2008, p. 1346). The West River diocese had 27,161 (*The Official Catholic Directory* 2008, p. 1107). These dioceses are suffragan sees of the Archdiocese of ST. PAUL-MINNEAPOLIS. Both dioceses coordinated efforts to influence legislation to end abortions, casino and video gambling, and the death penalty. Each diocese posted its sexual abuse policy on its Web site and mandated videos or materials related to abuse for all teachers and other personnel ministering in the dioceses. Although the state is not populous, a vibrant Catholic presence is apparent almost everywhere one travels across South Dakota. Catholic church buildings, educational institutions, hospitals, and spiritual as well as social and medical services are in evidence.

History. Although many eighteenth-century Catholic French-Canadian fur trappers and traders took Native American wives, it was in the nineteenth century that the Belgian Jesuit missionary, Pierre Jean DE SMET, first baptized natives and whites in what was then known as Dakota Territory, later divided and admitted to the Union in 1889 as North and South Dakota. De Smet, based in St. Louis, earlier spread the GOSPEL to the native tribes and mediated their disputes, thereby earning their respect and love as well as the appellation *Blackrobe*. The Sioux later called his most prominent successor, Martin MARTY, *Blackrobe Lean Chief*, because of his spare physique. Marty, a Swiss-born Benedictine ABBOT of St. Meinrad's, arrived in the Territory in 1876 shortly after the Battle of Little Big Horn occurred just across the western border. Bishop Marty traveled to confer with Sitting Bull in his Canadian refuge after Custer's fall and also a time or two later, before the death of this prominent Hunkpapa Lakota holy man at Standing Rock reservation in 1890. Although interested in CHRISTIANITY and grateful for the education the Church was giving the Lakota children, the tribal chief never converted, because it meant rejecting one of his two wives.

Marty was a renowned circuit-riding missionary. In 1879 Pope LEO XIII appointed him vicar apostolic for the territory and titular BISHOP. Marty organized the spotty, small church communities into parishes and authorized and supervised the erection of church buildings and other missions on the reservations. He recruited monks from Conception and St. Meinrad's abbeys, German refugee JESUITS, and other diocesan and religious order priests and brothers to assist him in the ministry. In 1949 St. Meinrad's founded Blue Cloud Abbey near Marvin, South Dakota, to enable the monks ministering to the Native Americans to have a base closer than Indiana. Because of the paucity of members, however, the abbey withdrew from reservation ministry. Jesuits, Sacred Heart Fathers from Hales Corners, Wisconsin,

priests from other orders, and diocesan clergy continued the Native American ministry.

Bishop Marty also brought Swiss and German Benedictine Sisters from Maryville, Missouri, to the Indian missions in the territory, then to Zell, and finally to Yankton, where their motherhouse remains. He recruited Presentation sisters from Ireland. They worked first in Fargo, North Dakota, after brief ministries in South Dakota, but were then successfully urged by the Irish Father Robert Haire to found a motherhouse in Aberdeen, South Dakota, where they still minister. Both religious orders have colleges (Mount Marty sponsored by the BENEDICTINES in Yankton and Presentation by the sisters in Aberdeen) and several hospitals. The two major motherhouses also co-sponsor Avera Health, an organization that manages numerous medical entities in the Dakotas and neighboring states. Other smaller motherhouses include the Franciscans in Mitchell, Benedictines in Rapid City and Watertown, Oblates of the Blessed Sacrament at Marty Mission, contemplative CARMELITES in Alexandria, and Perpetual Adoration Sisters of the Blessed Sacrament in Sioux Falls. Historically, members of over fifty religious communities of women have ministered in the state. Women RELIGIOUS still sponsor or staff eleven hospitals; dozens of parish, reservation, and private Catholic elementary and high schools; some diocesan offices; and the Catholic colleges, Presentation and Mount Marty.

Bishop Marty resided in Yankton, the earliest capital of Dakota Territory, but in 1889 on appointment as the first bishop of South Dakota after its admission to the Union, he chose Sioux Falls as his diocesan see. A year before his death in 1896, Marty, for reasons of health, was transferred to the St. Cloud diocese. In 1902 the Sioux Falls diocese was divided. Lead, a Black Hills town, became the see city until 1930 when it was transferred to Rapid City. The major Indian reservations then came under the jurisdiction of that diocese, including the Rosebud and Pine Ridge Reservations, where, in Sioux history, Wounded Knee (1890) is second in importance only to Custer's Last Stand (1876).

Sioux Falls Diocese. Bishop Marty's successors were Bishops Thomas O'Gorman consecrated in 1896; Bernard Mahony consecrated in 1922; William O. Brady consecrated in 1939; Lambert Hoch consecrated in 1956; Paul Dudley consecrated in 1977; Robert Carlson consecrated in 1995; and Paul Swain was consecrated in 2006. According to *The Official Catholic Directory*, in 2008 more than 100 active and retired priests served 126,196 Catholics in 150 parishes (p. 1346). Four small rural churches closed between 2002 to 2008. As of 2008, more than 1,700 children and adults were baptized annually. The needy were served in sixteen social service centers. Approximately 4,000 students attended twenty

Silent Night. *Moonrise above Our Lady of Victory Catholic Church, Plainview, South Dakota.* JOEL SARTORE/GETTY IMAGES

elementary schools, 916 matriculated at three high schools, and more than 2,000 attended the Catholic colleges in Aberdeen and Yankton. Our Lady of Guadalupe, established in 1996, ministers to the Spanish-speaking Catholics in Sioux Falls. The diocese ordained twelve priests and seven permanent deacons between 2000 and June 2008.

Rapid City Diocese. In 1998 Bishop Blase Cupich succeeded to the bishopric of Rapid City. The first bishop in the city of Lead was John Stariha consecrated in 1902. His successors were Bishops Joseph Busch consecrated in 1910; John J. Lawler consecrated in (1916–1948), who moved the see city to Rapid City; Leo Dworschak consecrated in 1946; William T. McCarty consecrated in 1948; Harold J. Dimmerling consecrated in 1969; and Charles J. Chaput consecrated in 1988, who in 1997 became archbishop of Denver. According to *The Official Catholic Directory, 2008*, in 2008 48 diocesan and religious as well as 11 retired priests and 25 permanent deacons ministered to more than 27,161 Catholics on the reservations and in 88 parishes (p. 1107). Only 26 of these had resident pastors; 25 permanent deacons, 3 religious brothers, and 50 women from religious communities assisted them.

Special efforts were made to serve the large Catholic Native American population. In the early 2000s a Lakota Sioux woman directed the Office of Native Concerns and acted as liaison between the Native American communities and the diocese. She also headed the diocesan office of the Pontifical Mission Society. The Sioux Spiritual Center at Howes increased its number of retreats for Native Americans and is the site of an annual conference that draws Native American participants from all over the United States. St. Isaac Jogues Church and Mother Butler Center in Rapid City minister to the large Native American population there. Native American rituals and ART appear in some churches and buildings in Rapid City and on the reservations. Incorporating the Lakota reverence for nature, the Standing Rock Reservation parish church at Kenel, which replaced an earlier one destroyed by lightning, has a huge tree trunk as the main altar. Uprooted from the family farm of a priest of the diocese, it was given by the owners for this purpose.

In the centennial year (2002), after a gap of fifty years, Bishop Cupich convened a twenty-first-century collegial synod with broad delegate participation. It addressed the concerns of the local, regional, and diocesan entities and eventually, after years of processing, established goals for each of these. An outstanding colored pictorial review of the diocese, including photos of every parish, with a history written by a Benedictine nun from Rapid City, was published to commemorate the diocesan centennial.

SEE ALSO CONVERTS AND CONVERSION; RAPID CITY, DIOCESE OF; SIOUX FALLS, DIOCESE OF.

BIBLIOGRAPHY

M. Claudia Duratschek, *The Beginnings of Catholicism in South Dakota* (Washington, D.C. 1943).

M. Claudia Duratschek, *Crusading along Sioux Trails: A History of the Catholic Indian Missions of South Dakota* (St. Meinrad, Ind. 1947).

M. Claudia Duratschek, *Builders of God's Kingdom: The History of the Catholic Indian Church in South Dakota* (Yankton, S.D. 1985).

Robert F. Karolevetz, *Bishop Martin Marty: "The Black Robe Lean Chief"* (Yankton, S.D. 1980).

Robert F. Karolevetz, *With Faith, Hope, and Tenacity: The First One Hundred Years of the Catholic Diocese of Sioux Falls, 1889–1989* (Mission Hill, S.D. 1989).

Ann Kessler, "First Catholic Bishop of Dakota: The Black Robe Lean Chief," in *South Dakota Leaders*, edited by Herbert T. Hoover and Larry J. Zimmerman (Vermillion, S.D. 1989).

Ann Kessler, *Benedictine Men and Women of Courage: Roots and History* (Yankton, S.D. 1996).

The Official Catholic Directory, 2008 (New Providence, N.J. 2008).

Eleanor Solon, *We Walk by Faith: The Growth of the Faith in Western South Dakota* (Strasbourg, France 2002).

Sister Ann Kessler OSB
Professor Emerita
Mount Marty College, Yankton, S.D. (2009)

SPE SALVI

Spe salvi is the second ENCYCLICAL of the pontificate of Pope BENEDICT XVI. Issued on November 30, 2007, it follows Pope Benedict's first encyclical, *Deus caritas est*, dated December 25, 2005. The title of *Spe salvi* comes from the Latin of Romans 8:24, "*Spe salvi facti sumus*" (in HOPE we are saved). Since hope is one of the three theological virtues (along with FAITH and LOVE), the encyclical, in many respects, follows logically from Pope Benedict XVI's initial encyclical on Christian love.

The theme of Christian hope reflects Pope Benedict XVI's abiding interest in ESCHATOLOGY (THEOLOGY of the last things). In 1977 he published a book in German that was later translated into English (1988) as *Eschatology: Death and Eternal Life* (CUA Press) and

republished in a second edition (2007). In this book, as in *Spe salvi*, the pope distinguishes the false hopes of LIBERALISM and Marxism as compared to Christian hope, which always has an eschatological dimension focused on the future life and the return of CHRIST in glory.

Spe salvi has a total of fifty sections, which is more than the forty-two of *Deus caritas est*. In the opening sections the Holy Father shows the close connection between faith and hope. Citing 1 Peter 3:15 ("always be ready to give an answer concerning the *logos*—the meaning and reason—of your hope"), he notes that hope, in many respects, is equivalent to faith (n. 2). Christian hope overcomes the despair of those who grieve because they have no hope (cf. 1 Thess 4:13), and it is not only "informative" but also "performative." Hope "makes things happen and is life-changing" (n. 2). Referring to the Greek and Latin of Hebrews 11:1 ("Faith is the substance [*hypostasis/substantia*] of things hoped for, the proof [*elenchos/argumentum*] of things not seen"), Pope Benedict, like St. THOMAS AQUINAS, maintains that hope refers to "a stable disposition of the spirit, through which eternal life takes root in us and reason is led to consent to what it does not see" (n. 7). Thus, hope implies the presence in Christians of what is hoped for, and, along with faith, it "shapes our life in a new way" (n. 10).

Spe salvi not only discusses hope in a theological sense; it also provides some historical examples of hope's transforming power. Among these examples is St. Josephine BAKHITA (c. 1869–1947), who was canonized in 2000. Living as a slave in Sudan and suffering multiple beatings, she found hope in the Lord after being purchased for the Italian counsel and brought to Italy. After her conversion to Christ and liberation from slavery, she learned that the supreme Lord of the universe, unlike her previous "masters," loved and cared for her (cf. n. 3). Thus, the Christian faith gave her hope and meaning in life.

Another example of Christian hope is the Vietnamese Cardinal Nguyen Van Thuan (1928–2002), a prisoner for thirteen years (1975–1988), with nine spent in solitary confinement. The prayers of the Church supplied him with hope throughout his confinement (n. 34). The Vietnamese MARTYR Paul Le-Bao Tinh (d. 1857) is likewise mentioned in *Spe salvi*, as someone sustained by Christian hope even in the "hell" of a concentration camp (n. 37).

The encyclical touches a wide range of questions related to Christian hope. It disputes the claim that Christian hope is individualistic (n.13–15). It traces the transmutation of Christian hope in the modern age toward a faith in human progress (n. 16–18). It discusses the rational faith of KANT and the revolutionary hope of

Marxism (20–21). Citing twentieth-century thinkers such as Theodor W. Adorno (1903–1969), the Holy Father points out the dangers of separating human progress from ETHICS, FREEDOM, and human dignity (22–23).

Pope Benedict XVI highlights the true shape of Christian hope (24–31): "It is not science that redeems man: man is redeemed by love" (26). "Man's great, true hope which holds firm in spite of all disappointments can only be God…" (27). "We must avoid replacing the Biblical hope in the Kingdom of God with hope in the kingdom of man" (30). In Jesus, the world discovers hope by seeing God with a human face (31).

The latter parts of the encyclical supply "settings" for learning and practicing hope. First, PRAYER is presented as a school of hope (n. 32–34). Prayer provides hope because God listens when no one else seems to listen (32). Citing St. AUGUSTINE, the Holy Father observes that prayer is an exercise of the heart, and there is the need to cleanse the heart of vinegar to have it filled with the honey of God's goodness and tenderness (33).

Then Pope Benedict XVI discusses hope grounded in "action and suffering for the kingdom" (35–40). He notes that the KINGDOM OF GOD cannot be built by human efforts because it is a gift. Christians need to avoid both frustration and fanaticism in their work on earth for the Kingdom (36). Recognizing suffering as part of human EXISTENCE, the PONTIFF teaches that the endurance of suffering can be a "journey of hope" (38). God's desire to suffer with and for humankind provides the consolation of His compassionate love. The lives of the martyrs show that "the capacity to suffer for the sake of truth is the true measure of humanity" (39). All of the FAITHFUL can share in the spirit of the martyrs by offering up their daily hardships (40).

The final setting of hope is eschatological JUDGMENT (41–48). Christ is the hope of the innocent who suffer, because only God can establish JUSTICE beyond this life (43). Eschatological hope is rooted in God for "a world without God is a world without hope" (cf. Eph 2:12; n. 44). Only God can create justice. Faith gives Christians the certainty that He does so. The image of the "Last Judgment" is not primarily an image of terror, but an image of hope, because for the faithful it is "the decisive image of hope" (44).

Pope Benedict XVI discusses judgment after DEATH with a particular focus on PURGATORY. He mentions the Jewish understanding of intermediate state (45) and St. Paul's reference to being saved "as through fire" (1 Cor 3:12–15). For Pope Benedict, however, the fire of purgatory is a "blessed pain." It is "the holy power of [God's] love" that "sears through us like a flame," and "the pain of love becomes our salvation and our joy"

(47). Duration in purgatory remains a mystery since it deals with "the heart's time" (47). Both the Christian East and the West uphold belief in the prayers of the living for the souls in purgatory, a belief grounded in the solidarity of communion and love (48).

The encyclical ends by pointing to Mary as the star of hope (49–50). She is like a star of hope in the dark and stormy voyage of life (49), just as she was a source of faith and hope, "even in the darkness of Holy Saturday" (50).

SEE ALSO CONVERTS AND CONVERSION; DEAD, PRAYERS FOR THE; DEUS CARITAS EST; FAITH, HOPE, AND CHARITY, SS.; FIRE OF JUDGMENT; HOPE (IN THE BIBLE); HOPE OF SALVATION (IN THE BIBLE); MAGISTERIAL DOCUMENTS; MAGISTERIUM, ASSENT TO THE; MARY, BLESSED VIRGIN, ARTICLES ON; PAUL, APOSTLE, ST.; SLAVERY, III (HISTORY OF); THEOLOGY OF HOPE.

BIBLIOGRAPHY

Benedict XVI, *Spe salvi*, On Christian Hope (Encyclical, November 30, 2007), available from http://www.vatican.va/holy_father/benedict_xvi/encyclicals/documents/hf_ben-xvi_enc_20071130_spe-salvi_en.html (accessed July 1, 2008).

Ratzinger, Joseph, *Eschatology, Death, and Eternal Life*, 2nd ed., translated by Michael Waldstein, translation edited by Aidan Nichols (Washington, D.C. 2007).

Robert L. Fastiggi
Professor of Systematic Theology
Sacred Heart Major Seminary, Detroit, Mich. (2009)

ST. LOUIS, ARCHDIOCESE OF

Metropolitan see, comprising 5,968 square miles in the east central part of Missouri. The DIOCESE (*S. Ludovici*) was established July 14, 1826; the ARCHDIOCESE, July 20, 1847. The suffragan sees include the dioceses of Jefferson City, Kansas City-St. Joseph, and Springfield-Cape Girardeau, all in Missouri. In 2008 the archdiocese numbered 476,477 Catholics in a total population of 2,205,007 (*The Official Catholic Directory* 2008, p. 1186).

Early History. The west bank of the Mississippi River, which eventually formed the eastern boundary of the see of St. Louis, was probably first seen by Europeans in 1683, when Louis Joliet (1645–1700) and the Jesuit Jacques MARQUETTE passed on their voyage of discovery. French fur traders and settlers followed, accompanied by missionaries whose evangelization of the Native Americans was of only limited success. (Holy Family parish in Cahokia, Illinois, across the river from St. Louis, began in this way and claims to be the oldest continuous parish in the United States.) Rich deposits of lead also attracted miners to Missouri, but the suppression of the Society of Jesus in the French domains in 1763 left the area with few priests.

In 1763 and 1764 Pierre Laclede Liguest (1729–1778) and Auguste Chouteau (1750–1829) started a trading post just south of the confluence of the Missouri and Mississippi rivers, which Laclede named St. Louis, after the patron of the reigning French monarch. However, unknown to those founders, France had just ceded Louisiana to Spain, putting the French settlement under Spanish rule for the remainder of the century.

The first baptism recorded in St. Louis, by the ex-Jesuit Sebastian MEURIN, was in 1766, and a log cabin church was blessed in 1770. Capuchin Father Bernard de Limpach (d. 1796) was the first resident pastor. During the Revolution, Father Pierre GIBAULT, who divided his time between Cahokia and St. Louis, was instrumental in persuading his parishioners to support the American cause.

The first bishop of Louisiana and the Floridas was the Dominican Luis PENALVER Y CARDENAS. However, after France once again acquired the Louisiana Territory, before selling it to the United States, he was sent to Guatemala and not replaced. With the hoisting of the stars and stripes in St. Louis in 1804, an influx of Americans diluted the French presence.

DuBourg (1818–1826). Shortly after the outbreak of the War of 1812, Archbishop John CARROLL of Baltimore dispatched the Sulpician Louis William Valentin DUBOURG, a native of Santo Domingo, to the Louisiana Territory as administrator. However, finding his few priests reluctant to acknowledge his authority, he went to ROME in 1815, where PIUS VII named him BISHOP of Louisiana and assigned the Congregation of the Mission (VINCENTIANS) to help him. The diocese in effect then had two see cities, New Orleans and St. Louis.

DuBourg arrived in St. Louis in 1818 and began a number of enterprises: a brick CATHEDRAL; a seminary at the Barrens near Perryville, south of St. Louis, under the direction of the Vincentians; a Catholic girls' school at St. Charles, a few miles northwest of St. Louis, under Religious of the Sacred Heart led by St. Rose Philippine Duchesne; and the St. Louis Academy for boys.

In 1824 the saintly Vincentian Joseph ROSATI was named coadjutor bishop and consecrated by DuBourg at Donaldsonville, Louisiana. Two years later, discouraged by opposition that persisted in New Orleans, DuBourg left for Europe, where he resigned his see and was appointed bishop of Montauban, France, and, shortly before his death in 1833, archbishop of Besançon.

Rosati (1827–1843). When the Diocese of Louisiana was divided in 1826, Rosati was named first bishop of St. Louis, but continued to administer New Orleans until 1830. His jurisdiction extended from the southern boundary of Arkansas to the Great Lakes and from the Mississippi River to the Rocky Mountains, including half the state of Illinois, a vast territory from which nearly forty other dioceses were eventually carved out.

In 1823 the JESUITS founded a novitiate, St. Stanislaus, at Florissant, northwest of St. Louis, and a few years later were entrusted with the boys' academy, which developed into ST. LOUIS UNIVERSITY. In 1828 the Sisters of Charity from Emmitsburg, Maryland, founded a hospital in St. Louis. The DuBourg cathedral had never been completed, primarily because of lack of funds, but a more ambitious stone structure in the Federal style (now the Basilica of St. Louis King of France, popularly known as the Old Cathedral) was consecrated in 1834.

Because of a shortage of personnel, only sporadic attempts were made to convert the Native Americans, but in 1840 Rosati authorized the Jesuit Pierre Jean DE SMET to embark on the journeys that eventually made him one of the most famous of missionaries. St. Louis was the origin of numerous missionary efforts, such as those of the Vincentians in Texas, and it provided bishops for places as far away as Toronto and Los Angeles.

In 1841 Rosati visited Rome, where he was named APOSTOLIC DELEGATE to Haiti. Before leaving the United States he had consecrated a Philadelphia priest, the Dubliner Peter Richard KENRICK, as his coadjutor, and Kenrick succeeded Rosati on the latter's death in Rome, September 25, 1843. St. Louis was elevated to an archbishopric, the third in the country, in 1847, and soon after the boundaries of the see were reduced to the state of Missouri.

Kenrick (1843–1895). Kenrick faced immediate financial problems upon his arrival in St. Louis, which he overcame, as Rosati had done, partly through appeals to Europe. But among the Irish was St. Louis's first millionaire, John Mullanphy (1758–1833), and the Mullanphy fortune benefited the Church in a number of ways. For a time Kenrick also acted as a banker for his people, thereby keeping their savings secure and making money available to the Church. In 1845 the first American conference of the St. Vincent De Paul Society was established at the Cathedral.

St. Louis in 1800 had been an almost entirely Catholic city but, paradoxically, as the proportion of non-Catholics increased dramatically, and as the French character of the city was gradually obliterated, the actual number of Catholics increased equally dramatically after 1840, because of immigration. (Catholics have never been outsiders in the local communities of New Orleans and St. Louis like they have been in most other major American cities.)

Most of the immigrants were Irish and Germans, and for the remainder of the century the city operated under a dual system of separate parishes for the two groups, often only a few blocks apart, each group under its own vicar general. The first Bohemian parish in the United States, St. John Nepomuk, was established in St. Louis in 1854, but only a handful of parishes existed for the small number of Southern and Eastern Europeans who immigrated later in the century. German Catholics in particular were found in the rural areas, especially in the old towns south of St. Louis and the newer settlements along the Missouri River. Missouri produced native-born clergy as early as 1815 but until the end of the century still depended heavily on priests from Europe.

St. Louis was a national center of German Catholicism, partly through the *Pastoral Blatt* newspaper edited by Father William Faerber. Some German priests joined in national expressions of complaint at being discriminated against by Irish bishops. (A St. Louis priest of Irish ancestry, David S. Phelan (1841–1915), edited an equally outspoken journal, *The Western Watchman*.) St. Louis German clergy also made positive intellectual contributions to the Church, through Faerber's widely used catechism, Innocent Wapelhorst's work on LITURGY, and Fredrick G. HOLWECK's research on HAGIOGRAPHY and hymnography.

During the Civil War, Kenrick, who owned a slave and was sympathetic to the South, prudently kept silent. But when Missouri after the war sought to impose an oath on all clergymen (that they had never supported the Confederacy), the archbishop ordered his priests not to conform, and the case of Father John A. Cummings was carried to the U.S. Supreme Court, which voided the oath.

At the First Vatican Council (1869–1870), Kenrick opposed the definition of papal INFALLIBILITY. Afterwards he announced his acceptance, but then went into virtual seclusion, while his coadjutor bishop, Patrick J. RYAN, handled the external affairs of the archdiocese until being named archbishop of Philadelphia in 1884. Despite his age Kenrick then resumed all episcopal functions and in 1891 was the first man to complete fifty years as a bishop in the United States.

His last years were marred by conflict. In 1893 he tried to get his vicar general, Philip P. Brady, appointed coadjutor, only to face an open rebellion of his priests. The VATICAN then named the Virginia-born Bishop John Joseph Kain (1841–1903) of Wheeling, West Virginia, as coadjutor, but Kenrick ignored him, forcing Kain to go to the civil courts to get control of the

archdiocese. Kenrick resigned in 1895 and died the following year.

Kain (1895–1903). Kain's major accomplishment was the establishment of Kenrick Seminary, which he entrusted to the Vincentians. Recognizing that his health was failing, he requested a coadjutor, and on April 27, 1903, Coadjutor Bishop John Joseph GLENNON of Kansas City, Missouri, an Irishman, was appointed. Kain then departed for Baltimore, where he died October 13, 1903.

Glennon (1903–1946). Glennon's first major project was the erection of a new cathedral, a magnificent Romanesque-Byzantine structure that opened in 1914, followed by a new suburban seminary campus two years later.

Catholic education was especially strong in St. Louis. In addition to St. Louis University, there were three Catholic colleges for women (Maryville, Fontbonne, and Webster). Almost all parishes had grammar schools, several had high schools as well, and there were eventually fifteen high schools run by religious orders and another dozen under archdiocesan auspices.

The title "the Rome of the West" was sometimes bestowed on St. Louis because of the large number of religious communities working in the archdiocese, many of whom had their novitiates and provincial headquarters there: more than thirty communities of men, notably Jesuits, Vincentians, MARIANISTS, Christian Brothers, and Franciscans, and more than fifty of women, especially the Sisters of St. Joseph of Carondolet, the SCHOOL SISTERS OF NOTRE DAME, the Religious of the Sacred Heart, the Daughters of Charity, the PRECIOUS BLOOD SISTERS, and the Franciscan Sisters of Mary.

St. Louis was also a center of Catholic health care, and eventually had ten hospitals and numerous orphanages and retirement homes. The Catholic Hospital Association long had its national headquarters in the city, while St. Louis University had one of the few Catholic medical and dental schools.

St. Louis priests continued to play major roles in Catholic life nationally, including Monsignor Martin B. Hellriegel (1890–1981) in the liturgical movement, Monsignor George J. Hildner in the National Catholic Rural Life Conference, and the Jesuit author and preacher Daniel A. LORD.

Glennon was named a CARDINAL by Pope PIUS XII at the end of 1945, at the age of 83. The following March he traveled to Rome for the ceremony, but died in Ireland before he could return to the United States.

Ritter (1946–1967). On July 20, 1946, Archbishop Joseph Elmer RITTER of Indianapolis, a native of

The Cathedral-Basilica of Saint Louis, St. Louis, Missouri. *Pope John Paul II holds a prayer service at the cathedral on January 27, 1999.* CHARLES ARCHAMBAULT/GETTY IMAGES

Indiana, was named St. Louis's fourth archbishop. Not long after his arrival, Ritter announced that archdiocesan schools would no longer be racially segregated, at a time when St. Louis public schools remained so. The decree provoked open opposition, which collapsed after the archbishop threatened ecclesiastical sanctions against the resisters. He also in effect abolished ethnic parishes by assigning pastors who were not of the relevant ethnic background, a policy that was reversed by his successors.

Ritter expanded, centralized, and professionalized the archdiocesan bureaucracy and its finances. He also added specialized offices for its various missions and started an annual fund-raising campaign that financed the rapid expansion of parishes and other institutions. The archdiocese had always been notably generous in its support of missions and in 1956 became the first U.S. diocese to undertake a foreign mission itself, when three volunteer priests were dispatched to La Paz, Bolivia. Many more followed over the next half century.

Also in 1956 the establishment of two new dioceses left only the ten counties surrounding the city of St. Louis as archdiocesan territory. Like all large cities, St. Louis saw a major exodus of its population to the suburbs after World War II, and the archdiocese kept pace with the move, starting an average of one new high school and four new parishes each year through the 1950s.

Ritter was named a cardinal at the end of 1960 and played an important role in the Second Vatican Council of 1962–1965, where he was considered a leading progressive. The liturgical movement was strong in St. Louis, and Ritter in 1964 presided at the first authorized vernacular Mass in the United States, celebrated by Hellriegel in a St. Louis convention center. He was also notable for his support of racial equality and ecumenism. He died in 1967.

Carberry (1968–1979). Bishop John Joseph Carberry of Columbus, Ohio, a Brooklyn priest, was named archbishop of St. Louis by Pope Paul VI on February 17, 1968, and was created cardinal the next year. He was elected vice-president of the American bishops in 1976.

In 1973 he established the first archdiocesan pro-life committee in the United States, and he remained alert to theological dissent, firmly upholding disputed church teachings and encouraging Marian piety. Meanwhile, however, the decline of religious vocations closed many parish schools and some high schools and virtually brought an end to the establishment of new parishes. Carberry retired in 1979 but lived until 1998.

May (1980–1992). John Lawrence May, a Chicago priest who was bishop of Mobile, Alabama, was appointed archbishop of St. Louis on January 24, 1980, and served as president of the National Conference of Catholic Bishops from 1986 to 1989. Considered liberal, he set the tone of his administration when, shortly after his installation, he visited the site of an ABORTION clinic and forbade pro-lifers to engage in civil disobedience, indicating that he valued ecumenical and community relations highly. He resigned because of ill health late in 1992 and died in March 1994.

Rigali (1994–2003). After an unusual delay, Archbishop Justin Francis Rigali, a native of Los Angeles who was serving as Secretary of the Congregation of Bishops and Secretary of the College of Cardinals in Rome, was appointed archbishop of St. Louis on January 25, 1994. Rigali greatly strengthened archdiocesan finances and encouraged Eucharistic piety, reviving Corpus Christi processions and urging Eucharistic adoration in the parishes. He publicly opposed St. Louis University's sale of its hospital to a secular, for-profit corporation, and after the Vincentians withdrew from Kenrick-Glennon Seminary, he revitalized it with archdiocesan clergy. The highlight of Rigali's tenure was the 1999 visit of Pope JOHN PAUL II to St. Louis, the only visit to a single diocese of the United States during his pontificate. Rigali was appointed archbishop of Philadelphia in July 2003 and named cardinal a few months later.

Burke (2003–). On December 2, 2003, Pope John Paul II appointed Bishop Raymond Leo Burke, a Wisconsin native who was bishop of his home diocese of LaCrosse, to be the eighth archbishop of St. Louis. A noted canon lawyer, Burke almost immediately moved against canonical and doctrinal irregularities. He excommunicated the trustees of a historically Polish parish that retained legal title to its property, in violation of Canon Law, and he urged that communion be denied to Catholic politicians who supported legal abortion. He also instituted canonical procedures against two women who had been ordained to the priesthood in a ceremony in a St. Louis synagogue. In addition to his ardent pro-life commitment, he was a strong promoter of devotion to the Sacred Heart and of Our Lady of Guadalupe and successfully encouraged vocations to the priesthood.

Although the process began under Rigali, it was largely left to Burke to implement the closing of parishes, because of the priest shortage, closings that made possible the establishment of new parishes in the outer suburbs where most Catholics had come to reside.

In July 2006, he was appointed by Pope BENEDICT XVI as a member of the Supreme Tribunal of the Apostolic Signatura, the highest court in the Catholic church, and in July 2008, he became the first American named to head the Signatura and therefore ceased to be archbishop of St. Louis.

Although the archdiocese of St. Louis continued to experience modest growth, over five decades it lost size relative to some other dioceses, so that by 1980 it had ceased to be considered a cardinalatial see.

SEE ALSO BOLIVIA, THE CATHOLIC CHURCH IN; CHURCH PROPERTY; CONVERTS AND CONVERSION; ILLINOIS, CATHOLIC CHURCH IN; KANSAS CITY–ST. JOSEPH, DIOCESE OF; LITURGICAL MOVEMENT, I: CATHOLIC; LOUISIANA, CATHOLIC CHURCH IN; MISSION AND MISSIONS; MISSOURI, CATHOLIC CHURCH IN; NEW ORLEANS, ARCHDIOCESE OF; SACRED HEART, DEVOTION TO; ST. VINCENT DE PAUL, SOCIETY OF; SULPICIANS; UNITED STATES CONFERENCE OF CATHOLIC BISHOPS (USCCB); VATICAN COUNCIL I; VATICAN COUNCIL II.

BIBLIOGRAPHY

Archdiocese of St. Louis Official Web site, available from: http://www.archstl.org/ (accessed October 17, 2008).

Timothy Michael Dolan, *Archdiocese of St. Louis: Three Centuries of Catholicism, 1700–2000* (Strasbourg, France 2001).

Frederick Easterly, *The Life of the Rt. Rev. Joseph Rosati, C.M., First Bishop of St. Louis, 1789–1843* (Washington, D.C. 1942).

William B. Faherty, *Dream by the River: Two Centuries of St. Louis Catholicism, 1766–1980* (St. Louis 1971).

Annabelle M. Melville, *Louis William DuBourg: Bishop of Louisiana and the Floridas, Bishop of Montauban, and Archbishop of Besançon, 1766–1833*, 2 vols. (Chicago 1986).

The Official Catholic Directory, 2008 (New Providence, N.J. 2008).

Peter J. Rahill, *Catholic Beginnings of St. Louis* (St. Louis 1964).

John E. Rothensteiner, *History of the Archdiocese of St. Louis*, 2 vols. (St. Louis 1928).

Nicholas A. Schneider, *The Life of John Cardinal Glennon, Archbishop of St. Louis* (Liguori, Mo. 1971).

Paul C. Schulte, *The Catholic Heritage of Saint Louis: A History of the Old Cathedral Parish, St. Louis, Mo.* (St. Louis 1934).

Mary Constance Smith, *Our Pastors in Calvary: Biographical Sketches of Parish Priests of St. Louis, 1854–1924* (St. Louis 1924).

James Hitchcock
Professor, Department of History
St. Louis University, St. Louis, Mo. (2009)

ST. PAUL AND MINNEAPOLIS, ARCHDIOCESE OF

The DIOCESE of St. Paul was established on July 19, 1850. Initially, the diocese was bounded by Iowa on the south, Canada on the north, Wisconsin on the east, and the Missouri and White Earth Rivers in the Dakotas on the west. It became an ARCHDIOCESE in 1888, and in 1966 Pope PAUL VI redesignated it as the Archdiocese of St. Paul and Minneapolis (*Archiodioecesis Paulopolitana et Minneapolitana*). The other dioceses in Minnesota as well as the dioceses of North and South Dakota are its suffragan sees.

Early Catholic History. The city of St. Paul grew up around and was named after the log CHAPEL that Father Lucien Galtier (1811–1866) dedicated to St. Paul in 1841, and wherein French-born Joseph CRETIN was installed as the first BISHOP of the diocese on July 2, 1851. He immediately set about constructing a new CATHEDRAL. Cretin had served in the Diocese of Dubuque before coming to St. Paul. Arriving with two priests and three seminarians, he opened a mission for the Native Americans at Blue Earth and established a parish near the Falls of St. Anthony, thus opening the first Catholic Church and parish school in what would become Minneapolis. Conversions of Chippewa and Sioux natives in northern parts of the diocese were helped by JESUITS around Grand Portage and by the veteran missionary Francis PIERZ, who came to the diocese in 1852 and established a mission near Brainerd.

Cretin ceded the original log chapel to the Sisters of ST. JOSEPH, whom he had invited into the region to teach young girls. This chapel became the original St. Joseph's Academy and also served as the original St. Joseph's Hospital when the sisters were called on to minister to the sick during the cholera epidemic of 1855. Cretin authorized new churches to be built in Wabasha, Chaska, Hastings, Maryburg, Credit River, New Prague, Winona, Lake City, and Derrynane. By the end of Cretin's administration, 29 churches and 35 stations with about 20 priests attended a Catholic population of about 50,000. The diocese had a Catholic Temperance Society, a St. Vincent de Paul Society, a Society of the Living Rosary, and a Confraternity of the Sacred Heart of Mary. Bishop Cretin died on February 22, 1857, and was buried in Calvary Cemetery, which he had blessed in 1856. Augustin RAVOUX, the vicar general, administered the diocese until a new bishop was appointed two years later. Ravoux served as vicar general of the diocese until 1892, when poor health demanded retirement. He died in 1906 and is remembered for the services he rendered to the thirty-eight condemned Sioux after the infamous Sioux Uprising in 1862.

Grace. Thomas Langdon Grace (1814–1897), O.P., a native of South Carolina, known for his administrative skills and his commitment to Catholic education, was named the second bishop of St. Paul on July 29, 1859. He devised a constitution for the diocese, stipulating directives for celebrating the Eucharist, erecting parish buildings, teaching children the rudiments of Catholicism, and keeping parish records. Grace's mettle was tested during the Civil War (1861–1865), when, because of his Southern roots, his loyalty was questioned. He sent the young Father John Ireland to serve as chaplain for the Northern forces in battles fought on Southern soil. Upon his return to the diocese, Ireland became Grace's secretary. The Sioux Uprising of 1862 further tested his diplomatic skills. His correspondence with the Bureau of Indian Affairs in Washington fell upon deaf ears.

Grace championed Catholic education, inviting various groups of teaching RELIGIOUS to address this need. He established many new ethnic parishes and, to ward off the slander against the Catholic Church by the Know-Nothing Party, was an advocate of the Catholic press, making *The Northwestern Chronicle* the official organ of the diocese. He is also credited with organizing deaneries in the diocese to implement the directives of the Second Council of Baltimore. Grace resigned in 1884 and died in 1897, leaving a legacy of significant attainments. During his capable administration, the Catholic population of the state rose to about 130,000 with a presbyterate of 147: 119 diocesan and 28 regular clergy. The diocese had 195 churches and 51 stations, 29 seminarians, 6 religious communities of men, 14 religious communities of women, 2 hospitals, 5 asylums, and 10 academies and boarding schools for young women. The diocese boasted 7 St. Vincent de Paul Conferences, Total Abstinence Societies in many communities, and ROSARY societies, sodalities, and confraternities of the Sacred Heart in most parishes.

Ireland. John IRELAND, a native of Ireland and immigrant to Minnesota, had been sent to France to study for the priesthood by Bishop Cretin. He was ordained in 1861, served briefly as a curate in the cathedral parish and then as a military chaplain. After the war he was appointed RECTOR of the cathedral and was made Cretin's representative at VATICAN COUNCIL I, which the ordinary of St. Paul did not attend. Ireland was also a vigorous proponent of the Catholic Total Abstinence Society and became a nationally known speaker in its cause. Originally designated vicar apostolic of Nebraska, Grace succeeded in having the nomination revoked, and Ireland was named his coadjutor with right of succession in 1875. Ireland succeeded to the see in 1884 upon Grace's resignation. In the thirty-four years of his episcopacy, he was one of the most prominent prelates in America.

Ireland's confidence that the constitutional guarantee of FREEDOM OF RELIGION benefitted the Church and his strong conviction that immigrants should assimilate identified him with the Americanist HERESY. Some of Ireland's American opponents encouraged this association in the minds of Roman authorities. It is entirely consistent that, together with Cardinal James GIBBONS, Bishops Denis O'CONNELL, John J. KEANE, and others, Ireland strongly identified himself and attempted to identify the Catholic Church in the United States with patriotic and democratic sensibilities.

These postures later proved useful to Leo XIII, who in 1892 sent Ireland as his envoy to France to bolster support for the PONTIFF's new policy of RALLIEMENT to the Republic. Ireland opposed the efforts of the German lay leader Peter Paul CAHENSLY to establish special ecclesiastical jurisdictions and appointments for German, Italian, and other immigrants in the United States. Ireland is often blamed for alienating thousands of Eastern Rite Catholics to the Orthodox Churches because of his Americanizing convictions and his unwillingness to recognize the jurisdiction and validity of their immigrant priests. Closely associated with many major political figures, both local and national, Ireland was often a supporter of and an influential figure within Republican Party politics. He was unable, however, to deter the course toward war with Spain in 1898, the diplomatic mission the HOLY SEE had entrusted to him. He was more successful in his efforts to negotiate a settlement between the Holy See and the United States with regard to FRIARS' lands in the Philippine Islands in the wake of the war. Notwithstanding his political involvements, Ireland also supported the KNIGHTS OF LABOR and endorsed Gibbons's efforts to prevent a papal condemnation of the organization. He was also an outstanding leader in the fight against racial discrimination within the Church and society.

Ireland was always passionately concerned about education. He was notable, for example, for crafting in Faribault and Stillwater an arrangement with public school authorities to provide material support for parochial schools. By these agreements, local school boards leased parochial school buildings during the day and hired teachers (most of whom were women religious). In return Ireland agreed that only secular subjects would be taught during the normal school day; RELIGIOUS EDUCATION was provided outside of the usual school hours. The plans were bold (though not unprecedented) for the time and might well have provided significant benefits to all parties. However, a number of people on both sides were unhappy with what they perceived to be, in the one case, unreasonable public support for RELIGION and in the other, a danger-

ous accommodation with public education. After a short time, the critics prevailed, and the experiments were abandoned.

Other initiatives were more successful. In 1885 he opened the St. Thomas Aquinas Seminary on land he had purchased west of St. Paul near the Mississippi River. Though the early years were quite difficult, the institution survived to become the College, and later the University, of St. Thomas. In 1894, with the assistance of a $500,000 gift from railroad entrepreneur James J. Hill (1838–1916), he opened St. Paul Seminary. Ireland was also a strong advocate for the establishment of The CATHOLIC UNIVERSITY OF AMERICA in Washington, D.C., and he remained a supporter of the institution throughout his life.

St. Paul was made an archiepiscopal see in 1888, and Ireland was its first ARCHBISHOP. His influence within the newly created province and throughout the region, and his strong personality, caused him to be known as "The Patriarch of the West," as well as "the consecrated blizzard of the northwest." It was often rumored that he would be created a CARDINAL, but the appointment to the Sacred College was never made, despite the efforts of his friends. He died on September 25, 1918.

Dowling. Ireland's successor in office, Austin DOWLING, a native of New York City, was ordained for the Diocese of Providence, Rhode Island, in 1891, following studies at The Catholic University of America. He taught church history at St. John's Seminary in Brighton, Massachusetts, served as editor of the *Providence Visitor*, and was named rector of the cathedral church. He was consecrated the first bishop of Des Moines, Iowa, in 1912 and was translated to St. Paul in 1919. He was instrumental in the establishment of the National Catholic Welfare Conference and was elected to its first administrative board. Locally, he firmly established offices of Catholic Charities in the archdiocese and advanced the cause of Catholic education through fundraising and establishing educational institutions, including a diocesan teachers college for sisters and lay teachers (1925). Dowling published scholarly works and lectured throughout his episcopacy. He died in 1930.

Murray. John Gregory Murray (1877–1956), former auxiliary bishop of Hartford and bishop of Portland (Maine), was installed as third archbishop of St. Paul on January 27, 1931. In marked contrast to the style of his predecessor, Murray often rode the trolleys or walked in the downtown area of the capital city. His concern for the downtrodden prompted him to organize a crusade of charitable giving to support those in need regardless of CREED or color. In November 1935 he opened the Catholic Labor School for members of labor unions.

The Cathedral of St. Paul, St. Paul, Minnesota. *The first liturgy held in this cathedral was on Palm Sunday, March 28, 1915.*

The school offered classes in Catholic social teaching, economics, parliamentary procedures, and labor law. Priest-teachers became well acquainted with labor leaders and were frequently called on as arbitrators in industrial disputes in the region.

Murray encouraged the certification of teaching sisters at the diocesan teachers' college. He organized the CONFRATERNITY OF CHRISTIAN DOCTRINE (CCD) and study clubs to train teachers for instructing Catholic youth attending public schools during the "release periods" permitted by Law. The Confraternity of Christian Doctrine also sponsored the formation of the Catholic Choral Club under Reverend Francis A. Missia and the opening of Catholic Youth Centers in St. Paul and Minneapolis.

Murray attacked the prevalent evils of socialism, communism, ANARCHISM, EUGENICS, and birth control, forbidding Catholics to become members of societies supporting birth control and sterilization. When Cardinal Eugenio Pacelli (later Pope PIUS XII) arrived in St. Paul in 1936 on an unofficial visit to the United States, he encountered a flourishing parochial life within the archdiocese. Moreover, when the ninth National Eucharistic Congress was held in the Twin Cities on June 22–26, 1941, hundreds of thousands of participants came. During World War II, when many priests and laity were called into armed services abroad and women replaced men in defense plants, family life became strained. To meet the crisis, Murray formed the Diocesan Bureau of Charities, the Family Guild, and an Archdiocesan Prayer Front for Peace.

In response to regional immigration, Murray opened a new parochial school for African-American Catholics in St. Peter Claver parish. In the years following World War II, the archdiocese established fifty-nine new parishes to meet the needs of the growing Catholic population. However, Murray did not anticipate the movement of young Catholic families to the suburbs, and many of the new urban parishes failed to grow to a viable size. Propelled by the baby boom, enrollment in grade schools increased, and additional Catholic high schools were in demand. The SCHOOL SISTERS OF NOTRE DAME opened St. Agnes Parish High School and the Sisters of Charity of the Blessed Virgin Mary staffed Our Lady of Peace Academy. Several small parish high schools also opened in rural areas. Enrollment in the two Catholic colleges in the Twin Cities tripled, and seminary enrollment grew.

A Newman Center and chapel near the University of Minnesota in Minneapolis was erected in 1953. Murray also oversaw the establishment of four retreat houses, two homes for the aged, and a home for incurable cancer patients. He authorized an independent PRIORY of the Sisters of St. Benedict to be erected in St. Paul (1948)

and established a major seminary of the Conventual Franciscan Fathers in Chaska (1951). James J. Byrne (1908–1996) was appointed auxiliary bishop in 1947. When Byrne became bishop of Boise, Idaho, in 1956, Bishop William O. Brady (1899–1961) of Sioux Falls, South Dakota, was appointed coadjutor archbishop with right of succession. Archbishop Murray died on October 11, 1956, and was buried in Resurrection Cemetery in Mendota Heights.

Brady. Archbishop Brady oversaw seventeen counties in Minnesota, which numbered more than 434,000 Catholics. In 1957 the Diocese of New Ulm was carved from this territory, and Alphonse Schladweiler (1902–1996) appointed its first bishop. At the same time Leonard Cowley (1913–1973) was named an auxiliary bishop to assist Brady. Brady was a vibrant and forward-looking decision-maker. When freeway construction displaced many in his cathedral parish, he worked with the St. Paul Housing Redevelopment Authority to assist in family relocation. During the Cold War he made the archdiocese an active participant in civil defense functions. The birth of baby boomers, suburban sprawl, the debate over birth control, and the drug culture were all addressed in the revised *Catholic Bulletin*. Brady also encouraged the expansion of the *Catholic Digest* into Europe. This periodical, published in St. Paul under the leadership of Reverend Louis Gales, reached a circulation of almost 900,000 in 1958. Brady furthered the work of women's groups and promoted the extension of lay volunteers for the Home Missions and PAPAL VOLUNTEERS FOR LATIN AMERICA (PAVLA). He encouraged the organization of parish-based cells of Young Christian Workers. He also seized the opportunity of more affluent times to undertake the major completion of the interior of the dome of the cathedral, to erect a new chancery office, and to launch a campaign for building needed Catholic high schools.

Brady had a particular interest in the LITURGY. His leadership encouraged the implementation of the new ritual of HOLY WEEK approved by Pope Pius XII throughout the archdiocese. As a member of a special liturgical committee of the UNITED STATES CONFERENCE OF CATHOLIC BISHOPS, he championed using the vernacular in administrating the sacraments and in all liturgical rites. During a flight to Rome while working on a pre-conciliar liturgical commission, Archbishop Brady suffered a heart attack and died in Rome on October 1, 1961.

Binz. Leo Binz (1900–1979), archbishop of Dubuque, became archbishop of St. Paul in 1962. The early years of his episcopacy were absorbed with the Second Vatican Council and the challenges of managing the change that it provoked. Though criticized by some both inside and outside the Church for not embracing new ideas rapidly enough, Binz did implement many reforms authorized by the VATICAN. He authorized the first Cursillo in the archdiocese in 1968, continued the May Day Rosary processions, and strove unsuccessfully to elevate the rosary to a place alongside the Divine Office as an official PRAYER of the Church. Prompted by the growth of the Twin Cities metropolitan area, the archdiocese was redesignated the Archdiocese of St. Paul and Minneapolis in 1966. At that time the Basilica of St. Mary in Minneapolis, the first BASILICA in America, was designated the co-cathedral of the archdiocese.

During these same years, the commitment to Catholic education in the archdiocese remained strong. By the early 1970s a set of U.S. Supreme Court decisions had made unconstitutional various arrangements for public support of parochial elementary and secondary education. As a consequence, tuition at these schools in Minnesota increased dramatically and enrollment declined. A new position, director of religious education, appeared in many parishes to address the needs of Catholic students in public schools.

Catholic Charities expanded during the 1960s, addressing the needs of the marginalized. The CHRISTIAN FAMILY MOVEMENT and the Rural Life Conference addressed the family life problems in rural areas of the archdiocese. Concerns for the rights of the working class in the state were championed by clergy of the archdiocese, especially by Monsignor Francis J. Gilligan, who spoke for the archdiocese at religion and labor meetings and often acted as arbiter in settling many local labor-management disputes. Minnesota Citizens Concerned for Life was a strong citizen lobby against ABORTION legislation and abortion clinics in the state. Care for retarded children, long given in Faribault, saw new programs in the metropolitan Catholic hospitals and a new facility in St. Paul.

The Catholic Interracial Council provided grants for minorities to attend Catholic schools. Parishes, through the Black Catholics Concerned program, worked to obliterate discrimination, and the archdiocese supported the St. Paul NAACP in its struggle for equal justice for African Americans in Minnesota. The work of Sister Giovanni, SSND, with the Hispanic community on St. Paul's West Side, focused attention on the needs of that minority in the archdiocese as well as the state. In 1967 the archdiocese sponsored four PAVLA volunteers for work in Latin America. Eventually, large numbers of refugees from Vietnam and Laos in the Twin Cities necessitated new ministries.

Byrne. Troubled by diabetes and other health problems, Binz requested that a coadjutor be appointed. His request was granted when Leo C. Byrne (1908–1974) was appointed coadjutor archbishop *cum iure successionis*

in 1967. Not long after, much of the day-to-day work of the archdiocese was entrusted to Byrne. A champion of the Second Vatican Council, Byrne was an advocate of a married deacons program for the archdiocese. He collaborated with the Joint Religious Legislative Coalition in its work for SOCIAL JUSTICE and established the Board of Investment Ethics to review the archdiocesan portfolio. The code drawn up by this board was the most comprehensive of any U.S. diocese. Byrne also encouraged workers to organize their own unions. He supported St. Mary's Hospital treatment center for alcoholics and established a policy to address alcohol and drug abuse among clergy and religious. An advocate of the aged, he also planned a retirement home for archdiocesan priests. To involve laity more directly in local church affairs, he set up the Archdiocesan Pastoral Council in 1972 to act as an advisory group. When the American Indian Movement moved its headquarters to Minneapolis and a flood of new immigrants added to the homeless poor in the urban areas, the Priests' Senate, with Byrne's approval, organized an Inner-City Urban Ministry to help with housing concerns in the Twin Cities. In 1971 Raymond Lucker (1927–2001) and John Roach (1921–2003) were consecrated auxiliary bishops for the archdiocese.

The papal ENCYCLICAL *Humanae vitae* caused the greatest controversy of Byrne's episcopacy. When more than seventy priests of the archdiocese publicly dissented from the encyclical, he demanded his priests' OBEDIENCE and support of the Church's teaching. Although *Humanae vitae* received strong support in many quarters of the archdiocese, notably the Council of Catholic Men and the Council of Catholic Women, dissatisfaction with the encyclical prompted Auxiliary Bishop James Shannon (1921–2003) to resign his appointment and seek to leave the priesthood. A number of priests and religious subsequently followed his example, creating personnel problems for Catholic parishes and service institutions under archdiocesan auspices. When the U.S. Supreme Court issued the *Roe v. Wade* decision in 1973, a NATURAL FAMILY PLANNING program was established as one means of counteracting the massive influx of birth control and pro-abortion literature that flooded the area.

Archbishop Byrne organized an Ecumenical Commission, which included clergy, laity, and men and women religious. Byrne worked with leaders of other faiths and formed closer ties with Jewish leaders in the area. Many groups within the state were working hard for ecumenism, but he was hesitant to join the Minnesota Council of Churches, fearing their aggressive approach.

Byrne died suddenly on October 21, 1974, never having become ordinary of the archdiocese. He left behind a reputation for commitment to social justice, reconciliation, and valuing human life. Archbishop Binz returned to administer the archdiocese until a new archbishop could be appointed.

Roach. In 1975 John Roach was the second native son to become archbishop. As rector of the preparatory seminary Nazareth Hall, he oversaw its closing and the establishment of St. John Vianney Seminary at the College of St. Thomas. Regarding the Second Vatican Council as the most significant event in the twentieth century, he approached renewal and revitalization of the Church in his archdiocese with optimism and vision. As president of the National Conference of Catholic Bishops (NCCB; 1980–1983), he supported collegiality and mutuality within all structures of the Church and was responsible for the bishops' pastoral letter, The CHALLENGE OF PEACE (1983). He supported the Detroit Call to Action program of 1976. A believer in delegating AUTHORITY, Roach called on clergy and laity within the local Church to address issues through various archdiocesan commissions. He championed the cause of ecumenism at the local and national levels. He appointed a special Commission on Women and named many women to serve on archdiocesan boards and commissions. New religious groups, such as the Brothers of Peace, were welcomed into the archdiocese. The growing demands of episcopal leadership in the archdiocese prompted Roach to ask for auxiliary bishops. Bishops Paul Dudley; John Kinney; Richard Hamm, M.M.; William Bullock; Robert Carlson; Joseph Charron, C.P.P.S.; and Lawrence Welsh were all consecrated during Roach's episcopacy. All but Bishop Welsh, who died in 1999, were called to serve as ordinaries of other dioceses.

New immigrant groups moved into the archdiocese in the 1970s and 1980s. Hmong were notably served at St. Mary's in Lowertown St. Paul, and Vietnamese in north Minneapolis made St. Joseph's Church their parish church. By 1978 Hispanics were scattered throughout the archdiocese. Roach called for lay and religious leaders to help these newcomers assimilate into American culture. Roach strove for better relations between Catholics and Jews in the archdiocese and throughout the universal Church. In August 1987 he represented the NCCB at a meeting in Rome to establish a commission to draw up an official Catholic statement on the Holocaust.

During his administration the Catholic Education Center influenced in 1978 the passage of a Minnesota state law that mandated public service to handicapped children within non-public schools within the state. Roach acceded to the urging of many priests, religious, and laity to establish an AIDS ministry in the archdiocese. During the Roach years, Catholic Charities grew into the largest non-governmental social service agency in the metropolitan area. To address the growing needs of the aging, Catholic Elder Care was opened in northeast Minneapolis with archdiocesan support. Roach led the archdiocese in a campaign of prayer to fight the atrocities against human rights committed abroad, especially the killing of religious and lay missionaries in Latin America and Africa. He used his influence as president of the NCCB to draw the attention of Congress to these matters. Prodded by lay leaders in the archdiocese, Roach supported the establishment of the Minnesota Center for Medical and Legal Aspects of Torture to provide services for victims of human rights violations seeking asylum in the United States. The Archdiocesan Urban Affairs Commission endorsed the Nuclear Freeze Campaign, urging Congress to press for negotiations between the United States and the U.S.S.R. for nuclear arms reduction. When the problems of farmers escalated during the 1980s, Roach, as leader of the National Catholic Rural Life Conference, lobbied Congress for laws protecting farmers.

Flynn. On February 22, 1994, Bishop Harry J. Flynn (1933–) of Lafayette, Louisiana, was appointed coadjutor archbishop of St. Paul and Minneapolis. He assumed full responsibilities in 1995 upon Roach's retirement. Flynn's new see covered 12 counties and included 222 parishes and more than 40 archdiocesan agencies serving a variety of ministries. His weekly column in the official organ of the archdiocese, which he renamed *The Catholic Spirit*, emphasized the ongoing presence of CHRIST in the work of His Church. A staunch supporter of the pro-life movement, he also spoke out against CAPITAL PUNISHMENT. He strongly encouraged an active role for the laity. Because of the shifting areas of population growth in the metropolitan area, Flynn called on his flock to support the merging of some parishes and the founding of others. Under his leadership, the Cathedral of St. Paul, constructed by Archbishop John Ireland and opened in 1915, underwent extensive exterior renovation in 2002.

The year 2000 marked the sesquicentennial of the Archdiocese of St. Paul and Minneapolis with many special celebrations. At that time, according to *The Official Catholic Directory, 2000,* the Catholic population of the archdiocese numbered 759,662 in a total population of 2,792,064. There were 342 diocesan priests, 158 religious priests, 171 permanent deacons, 50 brothers, 1,094 sisters, and 563 lay ministers. There were 222 parishes, 3 Catholic hospitals, 4 homes for the aged, 5 centers for social services, 3 colleges and universities, 9 Catholic high schools, and 89 Catholic elementary schools. The schools were staffed mainly by laity. In 2008 the Catholic population of the archdiocese numbered 623,000 in a total population of 3,015,000. There were 338 diocesan priests, 90 religious priests,

217 permanent deacons, 49 brothers, 878 sisters, and 467 lay ministers. There were 218 parishes, 4 Catholic hospitals, 8 homes for the aged, 17 centers for social services, 3 colleges and universities, 10 Catholic high schools, and 96 Catholic elementary schools (*The Official Catholic Directory* 2008, p. 1207). The schools were staffed mainly by laity.

In early 1999 auxiliary bishop Lawrence Welsh (1935–1999) died after a long illness. That same year, Father Frederic Campbell (1943–) was consecrated an auxiliary bishop for the archdiocese. He was translated to Columbus, Ohio, as ordinary in 2004. Monsignor Richard Pates (1943–) was appointed auxiliary bishop in 2001 and subsequently translated to Des Moines, Iowa, as ordinary in 2008. In April 2007, in anticipation of Archbishop Flynn's retirement, Bishop John Nienstedt (1947–) of New Ulm was appointed coadjutor archbishop, succeeding to the see in May 2008.

SEE ALSO AMERICANISM; BALTIMORE, COUNCILS OF; CARDINAL NEWMAN SOCIETY; CATHOLIC CHARITIES USA; CONVERTS AND CONVERSION; CURSILLO MOVEMENT; DUBUQUE, ARCHDIOCESE OF; EDUCATION, CATHOLIC (K THROUGH 12) IN THE UNITED STATES; EUCHARISTIC CONGRESSES; HUMANAE VITAE; KNOW-NOTHINGISM; MINNESOTA, CATHOLIC CHURCH IN; MISSION AND MISSIONS; NATIONAL COUNCIL OF CATHOLIC MEN (NCCM); NATIONAL COUNCIL OF CATHOLIC WOMEN (NCCW); NORTH DAKOTA, CATHOLIC CHURCH IN; ORTHODOX AND ORIENTAL ORTHODOX CHURCHES; PAUL, APOSTLE, ST.; SOUTH DAKOTA, CATHOLIC CHURCH IN; ST. VINCENT DE PAUL, SOCIETY OF; TEMPERANCE MOVEMENTS; VATICAN COUNCIL II.

BIBLIOGRAPHY

Additional information can be found in the Archives of the Archdiocese of St. Paul and Minneapolis, St. Paul, Minn.

Patrick Henry Ahern, ed., *Catholic Heritage in Minnesota, North Dakota, South Dakota* (St. Paul, Minn. 1964).

Archdiocese of St. Paul and Minneapolis Official Web site, available from http://www.archspm.org/ (accessed October 31, 2008).

Marvin R. O'Connell, *John Ireland and the American Catholic Church* (St. Paul, Minn. 1988).

The Official Catholic Directory (New Providence, N.J. 2000, 2008).

Annabelle Raiche and Ann Marie Biermaier, *They Came to Teach: The Story of Sisters Who Taught in Parochial Schools and Their Contributions to Elementary Education in Minnesota* (St. Cloud, Minn. 1994).

James Michael Reardon, *The Catholic Church in the Diocese of St. Paul* (St. Paul, Minn. 1952).

John Christine Wolkerstorfer, *You Shall Be My People: A History of the Catholic Archdiocese of St. Paul and Minneapolis* (Strasbourg, France 1999).

Sister John Christine Wolkerstorfer CSJ
Professor Emerita of History
The College of St. Catherine, St. Paul, Minn.

Robert G. Kennedy
Professor of Catholic Studies
University of St Thomas, St. Paul Minn. (2009)

SUMMORUM PONTIFICUM

Summorum Pontificum is a *motu proprio*, a papal document issued on the initiative of Pope BENEDICT XVI on July 7, 2007, granting generous permission for the celebration of Mass according to the typical edition of the Roman MISSAL of 1962, as well as for the celebration of the sacraments of BAPTISM, CONFIRMATION, MATRIMONY, PENANCE, and the ANOINTING OF THE SICK and the use of the Roman BREVIARY according to the liturgical books in force in 1962. The *Summorum Pontificum*, which constitutes universal law for the ROMAN RITE, was accompanied by an explanatory letter addressed to the bishops of the Church by Pope Benedict XVI (*AAS* 99 (2007) 795–799). It was preceded by the indult *Quattuor abhinc annos* of October 3, 1984, which granted the use of the 1962 Roman Missal under strict conditions and by the late Pope JOHN PAUL II's *motu proprio Ecclesia Dei* of July 2, 1988, which invited the bishops of the world to make "a wide and generous application of the directives" (*Ecclesia Dei* 6 c.) contained in the original indult.

Summorum Pontificum marks a new stage in the postconciliar liturgical life of the Roman Rite by establishing the availability of the prior typical edition of the Roman Missal as a universal LAW. The earlier two documents had not promulgated a new law, but simply made an exception to what was laid down in Pope PAUL VI's APOSTOLIC CONSTITUTION *Missale Romanum* of April 3, 1969, which promulgated his new missal and made it obligatory for the entire Roman Rite. Paul VI, in *Missale Romanum*, stated, "It is our will that these decisions and ordinances should be firm and effective now and in the future, notwithstanding any Constitutions and Apostolic Ordinances made by our predecessors, and all other decrees including those deserving of special mention, no matter of what kind." He did not thereby abrogate the former missal but left open the possibility of its use by priests who found difficulty in adjusting to the new missal, allowing them to celebrate according to the 1962 Roman Missal, but without a congregation. The primary innovation of *Summorum Pontificum* is that all priests who are capable of doing so are free to celebrate Mass according to the Roman Missal of 1962 in private, without seeking special permission, and that the public celebration of this Mass no longer requires the explicit permission of the local bishop, but depends on the discernment of the local pastor.

The Roman Missal of 1962 was the direct lineal successor of the Roman Missal promulgated by Pope St. PIUS V with his Apostolic Constitution *Quo Primum*, of July 1, 1570, in compliance with the decrees of the Council of TRENT. Emendations of this missal had been published by subsequent pontiffs in the course of the centuries with the introduction of new feasts, new liturgical formularies, and the alteration of rubrics governing the ritual actions for the celebration of the Mass, but the fundamental form of the missal had remained intact. Hence, the name Tridentine, referring to the Council of Trent, was given to this missal in all of its various editions from 1570 to 1962.

Pope Paul VI was obviously convinced that, just as the Council of Trent had mandated a liturgical reform, which at that time required the work of experts to establish a standard uniform missal for use throughout the entire Roman Rite, so *Sacrosanctum Concilium*, the Constitution on the Liturgy issued by the Second Vatican Council on December 4, 1963, also required the promulgation of a new missal in line with the reform of the sacred liturgy that it mandated. In recent years there has been mounting debate about whether, or to what extent, the missal of Pope Paul VI exceeded the reforms the Second Vatican Council had requested. One of the most consistent critics in this regard was Cardinal Joseph RATZINGER (Pope Benedict XVI), who wrote, "One of the weaknesses of the postconciliar liturgical reform can doubtless be traced to the armchair strategy of academics, drawing up things on paper which, in fact, would presuppose years of organic growth" (1986, p. 81). He was clearly referring to the work of the CONSILIUM, which was responsible for preparing new editions of the missal of Pope Paul VI and of the other liturgical books. He consistently argued in favor of the "organic" development of the Roman liturgy, which had taken place over the course of millennia, rather than the reform by means of academicians and liturgists in committee.

At the time of the promulgation of the missal of Paul VI and subsequently, many liturgical experts took the occasion to insist on the differences between the Tridentine and the postconciliar missals. Pope Benedict XVI has made the "hermeneutic of continuity" a hallmark of his pontificate ("Address to the Roman Curia Offering Them His Christmas Greetings," December 22, 2005), and thus insists on the continuity of the two missals and how "the two Forms of the usage of the Roman Rite can be mutually enriching" (*Summorum Pontificum* accompanying Apostolic Letter, July 7, 2007). His making available the classic liturgical forms as "the extraordinary form of the Roman Rite" is, in effect, not only a generous provision for the faithful who desire it, but also a very important measure that can bring about

Latin Tridentine Mass. *Monsignor Ignacio Barreiro Carambula celebrates the Latin Tridentine mass in St. Giuseppe a Capo le Case church in central Rome. Pope Benedict XVI published a decree allowing greater use of mass in Latin, signalling a bid to heal a decades-old split in the Roman Catholic Church.* **ALBERTO PIZZOLI//AFP/GETTY IMAGES**

the eventual "organic liturgical development" that he wishes to promote.

Groups such as the *Una Voce* International Federation, which have been pleading for "a wide and generous application of the directives" contained in the original indult, were delighted with the publication of *Summorum Pontificum*, as were many others who see the free availability of the 1962 Roman Missal as an indispensable point of reference for the return to a greater sense of the sacred and the continuity of the tradition in the Roman Rite. Of course, those who have effectively identified with what Pope Benedict XVI has described as "a hermeneutic of discontinuity and rupture" ("Address to the Roman Curia Offering Them His Christmas Greetings," December 22, 2005), among whom there are a number of bishops and liturgists, seem determined to block the concrete application of the provisions of the *motu proprio*. The extent to which this provision may provide a bridge for the Society of St. PIUS X to return to full communion with the Church remains to be determined.

SEE ALSO LITURGICAL BOOKS OF THE ROMAN RITE; LITURGICAL RITES; MASSES; RITUAL, ROMAN; TRIDENTINE MASS.

BIBLIOGRAPHY

Klaus Gamber, *The Reform of the Roman Liturgy: Its Problems and Background* (Fort Collins, Colo. 1993).

George Neumayr, "*Summorum Pontificum*: It Marks a New Era of Liturgical Seriousness," *Catholic World Report* (August/September 2007): 1.

Joseph Cardinal Ratzinger, *The Feast of Faith* (San Francisco 1986).

Joseph Cardinal Ratzinger, *Salt of the Earth* (San Francisco 1997), 174–177.

Joseph Cardinal Ratzinger, *The Spirit of the Liturgy* (San Francisco 2000).

Joseph Cardinal Ratzinger and Vittorio Messori, *The Ratzinger Report: An Exclusive Interview on the State of the Church* (San Francisco 1985), 119–134.

Alcuin Reid, *The Organic Development of the Liturgy: The Principles of Liturgical Form and Their Relation to the Twentieth-Century Liturgical Movement Prior to the Second Vatican Council* (San Francisco 2005).

Andrea Tornielli, "'Not a Rejection of the Council': Interview with the President of the Pontifical Commission *Ecclesia Dei*, Cardinal Castrillón Hoyos," *Inside the Vatican* (August/September 2007): 31.

SACRED CONGREGATION OF RITES

Congregation for Divine Worship, "*Quattuor abhinc annos*, Oct. 3, 1984," *L'Osservatore Romano*, English edition (October 22, 1984): 9. For the text, see *Acta Apostolicae Sedis* 76 (1984): 1088–1089.

Second Vatican Council, "*Inter oecumenici*, Sept. 26, 1964," in *The Conciliar and Post Conciliar Documents: Vatican Council II*, edited by Austin Flannery, rev. ed. (Boston 1992), 45–56.

Second Vatican Council, "*Tres abhinc annos*, May 4, 1967," in *The Conciliar and Post Conciliar Documents: Vatican Council II*, edited by Austin Flannery, rev. ed. (Boston 1992), 98–99.

PAPAL DOCUMENTS

Benedict XVI, "Address to the Roman Curia Offering Them His Christmas Greetings" (Speech, December 22, 2005), available from http://www.vatican.va/holy_father/benedict_xvi/speeches/2005/december/documents/hf_ben_xvi_spe_20051222_roman-curia_en.html (accessed March 3, 2008).

Benedict XVI, *Summorum Pontificum*, *Motu proprio* on the Missal of Blessed John XXIII (Apostolic Letter, July 7, 2007), *L'Osservatore Romano*, English edition (July 11, 2007): 8–9; *Acta Apostolicae Sedis* 99 (2007) 777–781.

John Paul II, *Ecclesia Dei*, *Motu proprio* (Apostolic Letter, July 2, 1988), available from http://www.vatican.va/holy_father/john_paul_ii/motu_proprio/documents/hf_jp-ii_motu-proprio_02071988_ecclesia-dei_en.html (accessed March 3, 2008).

Paul VI, *Missale romanum*, On the New Roman Missal (Apostolic Constitution, April 3, 1969), available from http://www.vatican.va/holy_father/paul_vi/apost_constitutions/documents/hf_p-vi_apc_19690403_missale-romanum_en.html (accessed March 3, 2008).

Msgr. Arthur B. Calkins
Official, Pontifical Commission "Ecclesia Dei"
Vatican City State (2009)

T

TENNESSEE, CATHOLIC CHURCH IN

A south central state bordered by Kentucky, Virginia, North Carolina, Georgia, Oklahoma, Mississippi, Arkansas, and Missouri, Tennessee is regionally divided into eastern, western, and central areas, with Nashville as its capital and Memphis as its largest city. The state comprises three dioceses: Nashville, Memphis, and Knoxville, all suffragans of the Metropolitan See of Louisville, Kentucky. As of 2008 Catholics comprised approximately 4 percent of the total state population (*The Official Catholic Directory* 2008, p. 2100).

History. Catholics came to Tennessee not too long after Europeans began to settle in North America, but they were few, and they left no enduring impressions. *The Final Report of the United States De Soto Commission*, prepared on behalf of the U.S. government in 1939, concluded that Spaniard Hernando de Soto (c. 1497–1542) and his party entered what became Tennessee on June 1, 1540, during their exploration of much of the Southeast. Although the 1540 route cannot be determined with any certainty, the *Final Report* situates the Spanish in the area that was later to be Polk, Bradley, Hamilton, and Marion counties, the extreme southeastern corner of present-day Tennessee. Later, the Spanish moved into what is now Alabama before again entering the far southwestern corner of Tennessee. In this corner, near the site of present-day Memphis, they discovered what they called *El Rio del Santo Espiritu*, "The River of the Holy Spirit," now known as the Mississippi River. Accompanying De Soto were twelve priests. Presumably one of these priests celebrated Mass for the first time on Tennessee soil when the band was in southeastern

Tennessee. They founded no missions; they came and went without leaving a trace in the region.

More than a century and a third passed before Catholics again were recorded in the Tennessee area. In 1673 the French expedition including Louis Joliet (1645–1700) and the Jesuit, Père Jacques MARQUETTE, traveled southward on the river that they dedicated to the IMMACULATE CONCEPTION (the Mississippi). Marquette's journal recalls the group's pause at Chickasaw Bluffs, where Memphis later was located. He met natives of the area who told him that they had encountered other Europeans, and that these Europeans gave them what must have been rosaries and pictures of the saints. Once more, no missions or continuing Catholic presence were established.

Other French explorers, including priests, passed along the Mississippi River. The French founded Fort Prud'homme on the site of present-day Memphis in 1682. It later was called Fort Assumption, but it was not a missionary center. French fur traders ventured from time to time into Middle Tennessee at Salt Lick, a place on the Cumberland River where Nashville now stands. They, too, came and went, except Timothe de Monbreun (1747–1826), a Catholic and one of the founders of the city. He built a permanent home where present-day Nashville stands, and he lived there for many years. His son, William, was the first Caucasian born in what now is Middle Tennessee.

Nashville, at first called Nashborough, was formed as a community on December 25, 1780, when two groups, one coming overland, the other on the Cumberland River, arrived from North Carolina and Virginia. At least one Catholic, Hugh Rogan (1747–1813), who had fled the British domination of Ireland, accompanied these expeditions. Rogan eventually settled in Sumner

County, where he and his wife remained faithful Catholics.

Tennessee Statehood. The American Revolution eventually led to statehood for Tennessee on June 1, 1796, following a long and bloody struggle. When Tennessee became the sixteenth state, the people elected John Sevier (1745–1815) as their first governor. Sevier was a great-grandnephew of St. Francis XAVIER, although the new governor himself was born in North America and descended from the Huguenot branch of the saint's family. In 1799 Sevier offered Father Stephen BADIN, whom he had met, enough land to settle 100 Catholic families, but Bishop John CARROLL declined the offer.

The first report of Catholics in any number in Tennessee occurred in a letter, dated 1800, from Father Badin to Archbishop John Carroll. It stated that 100 Catholic families lived in Hawkins County in the northeastern corner of the state. The letter also noted that a Catholic Frenchman, James Dardis (d. 1846), lived in the household of U.S. Senator William Blount (1749–1800), whose home still stands as a historical shrine in downtown Knoxville. Although these Catholics had been recorded, quite possibly there were others because Irish names appear in places in old records; nevertheless, the Catholic population of Tennessee was tiny. But, it gradually grew and was served by visiting priests. Father Badin visited Knoxville again in 1808 and preached four times in the State House. He returned in 1810 and spoke in the Court House about the Catholic belief in the resurrection of Jesus.

The Catholic population of Nashville swelled when a sizeable group of Irish laborers came to the city to build a bridge across the Cumberland River. Their exact number is unknown, but the group was large enough in size and determination to appeal to Bishop Benedict Joseph FLAGET, S.S., in Bardstown, Kentucky, for a priest to serve them. The priest who came in 1820 was Father Robert Abell. He eventually built the first Catholic church in Tennessee, named in honor of the Holy Rosary, and situated about 100 yards from the site where the state capitol now stands, on land donated by the Grand Master of Nashville Masons. In 1821 Bishop Flaget visited Nashville. Timothe de Monbreun received him. He also was entertained by Felix Grundy (1777–1840), later a U.S. senator and attorney general, and by a Presbyterian minister. Other Catholics in Tennessee seldom saw a priest, however, and the Church had no presence outside Nashville.

Diocese of Nashville. On July 28, 1837, in response to an appeal by the American bishops, Pope GREGORY XVI founded three new dioceses in the United States: Dubuque, Iowa; Natchez, Mississippi; and Nashville. The new See of Nashville received jurisdiction over the entire state of Tennessee. At the same time the POPE named Father Richard Pius Miles (1837–1860), the Dominican provincial general in America, as the first BISHOP. Ordained a bishop in Bardstown, Kentucky, on September 16, 1838, Miles was installed in Father Abell's little church in Nashville on the following October 15. He faced a daunting challenge. The Nashville CATHEDRAL was the only Catholic church in Tennessee, and the bishop himself was the only priest.

During the next twenty-two years, Bishop Miles met the challenge and created a Catholic presence, which in some instances still exists. Soon after arriving in Nashville, he began a tour of the state, looking for Catholics. He estimated that only 300 Catholics were among the population, enumerated in the 1830 U.S. Census at 682,000. On one trip to Jonesborough, in Washington County, in upper East Tennessee, he met the Aiken family. A son of this family, John F. Aiken, later entered the JESUITS in Maryland and was ordained a priest in 1844. He was the first Tennessean to be ordained. The bishop's first concern was to secure priests. He recruited priests from elsewhere in the United States, but he relied heavily on priests of his own order. At one time, most priests in Tennessee were DOMINICANS. These Dominicans founded the first parish in Memphis, St. Peter's, in 1840. Among the parishes founded by Miles, active parishes still exist in Chapel Hill, Chattanooga, Clarksville, Gallatin, McEwen, Memphis, and Nashville.

In 1843 the State General Assembly finally and permanently fixed the capital in Nashville. Located on the Cumberland River and already incorporated for sixty-three years, Nashville was also the largest city in Tennessee. Wishing to make a mark in the city as well as to serve its increasing numbers of Catholics, Bishop Miles dedicated a new cathedral on October 31, 1844, in honor of the Seven Dolors of the Blessed Virgin Mary. It came to be known simply as St. Mary's. Historians dispute as to who drew the plans, although most think it was Adolphus Heiman (1809–1862), a Prussian immigrant. In any case the new cathedral, imposing in size for its time, and chaste and simple in its Grecian lines, instantly won citywide attention and admiration.

The Sisters of Charity of Nazareth, Kentucky, arrived in Nashville in 1841 and opened a school for girls, a hospital, and an orphanage. These sisters soon formed themselves as a new, independent congregation, the Sisters of Charity of Nashville. Into their number in 1852 came Julia Voorvoart, from a Nashville family, the first woman in Tennessee to profess vows as a NUN. In 1851 DOMINICAN SISTERS from St. Catherine, Kentucky, a community Miles had helped to found, along with other Dominican Sisters from St. Mary's Convent, Somerset, Ohio, arrived in Memphis. At the beginning

St. Mary's Cathedral. *Begun in 1844, this cathedral was designed by the famed architect, William Strickland, soon after his arrival in Nashville, Tennessee. A simple, well-proportioned Greek Revival edifice, it is said to have been considered by Strickland to be his best ecclesiastical design. The tomb of Bishop Richard P. Miles, who was largely responsible for the erection of the cathedral, lies beneath its high altar. Father Abram Ryan, the "Poet Priest of the South," served as its assistant pastor from 1864 to 1865.* THE LIBRARY OF CONGRESS

of the new millennium, the Kentucky Dominican presence continued in Memphis.

Anti–Catholicism. Bishop Miles founded St. Joseph's Seminary and established a congregation of male RELIGIOUS, the Brothers of St. Patrick, though neither endeavor survived. When Miles first came to Tennessee, Catholics were more often a curiosity than the object of derision. Andrew Jackson (1767–1845) even attended Mass in Nashville. Things changed somewhat with the development of the Know-Nothing movement. When the Know-Nothings mounted a campaign for governor in 1854, the Catholics found for themselves a champion they had not expected, Andrew Johnson (1808–1875), former mayor of Greeneville and a congressman. In blistering language, he attacked the Know-Nothing bigotry against Catholics and won. He went on to become a U.S. senator, military governor of Tennessee, vice president, president, and later a U.S. senator again. He sent his children to Catholic schools, his daughter

and daughter-in-law became Catholics, and he attended Mass regularly, giving generously to build the first Catholic church in Greeneville.

Slavery and Secession. In 1850 Nashville was the scene of a convention of delegates from the fifteen slaveholding states to discuss slavery. Tempers already were high. No action was taken, but clouds were gathering. Like most dioceses where slavery was considerable, the Diocese of Nashville paid virtually no attention to African Americans. However, old records show that slaves at times were baptized. Still, it must be assumed that Bishop Miles had no strong feelings against slavery. In fact, when the Civil War began, the DIOCESE itself owned four slaves. Bishop Miles did not live to see the war. His health failed as the 1850s ended. He asked the HOLY SEE for a coadjutor, and on March 15, 1859, Pope PIUS XI named another Dominican, Father James Whelan (1859–1878), a native of Ireland, as the coadjutor bishop of Nashville. Whelan succeeded Miles when the elder bishop died on February 20, 1860.

At about the same time, the Sisters of Charity of Nashville moved to Leavenworth, Kansas, to form a new community. But, their absence was filled by more Dominican Sisters from Ohio, who opened St. Cecilia Academy in Nashville. It was the only school the federal authorities allowed to remain open during the wartime occupation of Nashville. Though long since in other buildings, the academy, the parent of Aquinas College, still exists, and the sisters formed their own congregation, the Dominican Sisters of St. Cecilia.

As events climaxed in the spring of 1861, Tennessee at first voted to remain in the Union. Later, Abraham Lincoln's call for troops to suppress the rebellion begun at Fort Sumter in the Charleston harbor turned the tables. Before formally receiving a request, the Confederate Congress admitted Tennessee to the Confederacy. In June 1861 the people voted overwhelmingly to secede, though the vote varied from region to region. In East Tennessee, secession failed, and some there tried to form a new state, as occurred with West Virginia when it split from Virginia. But in Middle and West Tennessee, the vote to secede was heavy. The war was hard on Tennessee. More battles were fought on its soil than in any other state except Virginia. Thousands died. Many fought for the Union, though the majority fought for the Confederacy.

Among the dead was Father Emmeran Bliemel (1831–1864), a Confederate, once pastor of Assumption Church in Nashville, the only chaplain on either side to be killed in action. St. Mary's Cathedral was taken by the U.S. Army and used as a hospital and then a stable. Sts. Peter and Paul's Church in Chattanooga also was seized for military use. For reasons unknown, Bishop Whelan resigned in 1863, before the war ended. Whether true or not, he had been thought to be a Union sympathizer, and in Nashville, where secession had carried seven to one, this made him very unpopular. When the war ended, men loyal to the Union, generally from East Tennessee, quickly took control of the state government. Under their direction and with dispatch, they moved Tennessee back into the Union. Reconstruction, therefore, did not pose all the difficulties it did elsewhere in the South, but it still remained a difficult period.

Feehan. Father Patrick Augustine FEEHAN, a native of Ireland who was then a pastor in St. Louis, was named the third bishop of Nashville in 1865. Bishop Feehan soon faced a much more insidious problem than a depressed, postwar economy. Cholera struck Chattanooga, Memphis, and Nashville, but yellow fever in Chattanooga and especially Memphis was particularly devastating. By this time Memphis had a considerable Catholic population with several churches and schools. The city suffered a mighty blow; thousands died in the epidemics. But, Catholic nuns, many of whom died in caring for the stricken, won a respect for the Church that endured. For generations the City of Memphis allowed Catholic nuns to ride its streetcars and buses free of charge as a gesture of appreciation.

The loss of nuns and priests to these diseases was great, but Bishop Feehan found replacements. The diocese grew in numbers and in institutional presence. In 1871 the CHRISTIAN BROTHERS opened a school for boys in Memphis that eventually became Christian Brothers University. Four years later the Sisters of the Good Shepherd established a refuge for troubled girls in Memphis. The SISTERS OF MERCY also came and became a major source of teachers and, later, nurses in the Tennessee Catholic schools and hospitals. Despite reconstruction and the epidemics, the Church made strides.

The See of Nashville again fell vacant when on September 10, 1880, Pope LEO XIII named Bishop Feehan the first ARCHBISHOP of Chicago. His replacement, Joseph Rademacher, a priest from the Diocese of Fort Wayne, Indiana, was appointed on April 3, 1883. Bishop Rademacher was in Nashville only ten years, then he returned to Fort Wayne in 1893 as its bishop. Still, the number of Catholic people and institutions grew during his tenure. Succeeding Bishop Rademacher was Father Thomas S. Byrne, a seminary rector in the Archdiocese of CINCINNATI. Named on July 15, 1893, Bishop Byrne left a deep mark on Tennessee Catholicity.

Byrne. Byrne was an innovator; he had a vision, and he could press his vision through to reality. He encouraged Mother (Saint) Katharine DREXEL in founding facilities for African Americans in Jackson, Memphis, and Nashville. He invited LITTLE SISTERS OF THE POOR to open a home for the elderly in Nashville. He asked the Daughters of Charity to establish a Catholic hospital in Nashville. He formed mission centers in Harriman, Winchester, and Johnson City. He built parishes and schools across the state. The FRANCISCAN SISTERS of Lafayette, Indiana, opened St. Joseph's Hospital in Memphis in 1899. He mingled with the great and influential, making friends for the Church. He stressed native vocations, and the response was considerable. Four of his priests became bishops, including the future Samuel Cardinal STRITCH. He always regarded as the crown of his tenure the Cathedral of the Incarnation, completed in 1914. Of strict Romanesque BASILICA style, the cathedral is one of the largest and most imposing of the city churches. When he died in 1923, negotiations were in progress with the Jesuits to build a college and with the Brothers of Mary to open a high school in

Nashville. Neither project developed, but high hopes were typical of the Byrne era.

Smith and Adrian. Alphonse J. Smith, a priest of Indianapolis, was appointed the next ordinary on December 24, 1923, by Pope PIUS XI. Bishop Smith suffered from two disadvantages: his poor health and the Great Depression. Nevertheless under his leadership the Church of Tennessee grew. In 1929 he opened Father Ryan High School for boys in Nashville. The school was named in honor of Father Abram RYAN, the unofficial poet laureate of the South during and after the Civil War. In 1931 the Sisters of Mercy founded St. Mary's Hospital in Knoxville, and the POOR CLARES established a MONASTERY in Memphis. After only a relatively short time in office, Bishop Smith died suddenly on December 16, 1935.

His successor, William L. Adrian, a priest of Davenport, Iowa, served the diocese for an unprecedented thirty years (1936–1966). Bishop Adrian founded a weekly diocesan newspaper, the *Tennessee Register*, and organized lay groups. In the years following World War II, he led the largest Catholic building campaign in Tennessee history, opening sixty-five churches, five secondary schools, and thirty-three elementary schools across the state. At his behest, the Sisters of Charity of Nazareth opened a hospital in Chattanooga, and the Sisters of NOTRE DAME of Cleveland, Ohio, founded St. Mary's Hospital in Humboldt. More than 100 priests, almost all of them native Tennesseans, were ordained.

Changing Times. By the time Pope PAUL VI accepted Bishop Adrian's resignation in 1966, the full impact of the 1954 U.S. Supreme Court decision, *Brown v. Topeka Board of Education*, that ended school desegregation had reverberated throughout Tennessee. It fell to Bishop Joseph A. Durick to deal with these momentous, and at times violent, changes. Auxiliary bishop of Mobile-Birmingham, Alabama, Durick was named Bishop Adrian's coadjutor on December 5, 1963. Not only did he help to implement the decisions of the second Vatican Council and forcefully end racial separation throughout the diocese, but he also made himself, and the Church, the most obvious moral voices in an area still only minimally Catholic. Durick was able to undertake this role in great measure because of the strong institutional presence of the Church in the Tennessee cities and because he took full advantage of a new day in communications, ecumenism, mobility, and outlook in America.

The Catholic Church in Tennessee reached a milestone on January 6, 1971, when the Diocese of Memphis formally came into being. A new diocese for West Tennessee had been discussed for many years. Cre-

ated by Pope Paul VI, the new diocese had a Virginia priest, Monsignor Carroll T. Dozier, as its first bishop. Bishop Dozier, who served until his retirement in 1978, in general continued the Durick policies, but in his own special style. He spoke against the Vietnam War and reiterated opposition to racism. As with Durick, admirers saw in him a PROPHET; others were less delighted.

Following the retirement of Bishop Dozier, Auxiliary Bishop (later Cardinal) J. Francis STAFFORD of Baltimore was appointed to Memphis by the Holy See. Although in Memphis for only a short time (1982–1986) before going to Denver as its archbishop, Stafford kept the spotlight on the Church's position on racism. JOHN PAUL II named Benedictine Daniel M. Buechlein, the rector of ST. MEINRAD ARCHABBEY seminary in Indiana, to succeed Stafford in 1986. Like Stafford, Buechlein too did not stay long in Memphis; he moved to Indianapolis as archbishop in 1992. Terry J. Stieb, S.V.D., an auxiliary bishop of St. Louis, was appointed to Memphis in 1993.

In Nashville, Bishop Durick retired in March 1975, and Pope Paul VI appointed Monsignor James D. Niedergeses, a native of Lawrenceburg, Tennessee, the ninth bishop of Nashville. Bishop Niedergeses attempted to steady the diocese after the turmoil of the preceding decade, and he built facilities to serve the growing Catholic population, especially in the small cities. This growth significantly contributed to Pope John Paul II's establishment on September 8, 1988, of the new Diocese of Knoxville. Anthony J. O'Connell, a priest of the Diocese of Jefferson City, Missouri, and a native of County Clare, Ireland, was named its first bishop in 1988. Bishop O'Connell not only formed a diocesan structure, but his personality proved to be the adhesive holding together a vibrant Catholic community. When O'Connell was appointed bishop of Palm Beach in 1999, he was succeeded by Monsignor Joseph E. Kurtz of the Diocese of Allentown, a native of Pennsylvania, as the second bishop of Knoxville.

In 1992 Pope John Paul II accepted the resignation of Bishop Niedergeses of Nashville, who had reached the retirement age, and Auxiliary Bishop Edward U. Kmiec of Trenton, a native of New Jersey, became the tenth bishop of Nashville. Bishop Kmiec's achievements included the development of a long-range diocesan strategic plan, a development plan for the diocesan system, a reinstitution of the permanent diaconate, and a program of nurturing vocations to the priesthood.

Post–World War II population growth in the state was significant and caused an increase in the Catholic population as well. Before 1980, 99 percent of the Catholics were white Americans. In the late 1970s a significant number of Hispanics immigrated to Tennessee, and, by the turn of the new century, they constituted more than one-third of the total state Catholic population. The Catholic demographic growth in Tennessee from 1970 to 2000 was greatest in the Nashville diocese, to a lesser degree in Knoxville, and mostly unchanged in Memphis. The number of Hispanic Catholics in the Nashville diocese alone in 2000 was reported as more than 50,000. African Americans comprise about 1 percent of the Catholic population. A small, but growing, Vietnamese Catholic presence is also found in the state.

Twenty-First-Century Developments. The Tennessee population continued to grow as the twenty-first century began. Overall, the state economy remained good. New industries were started, and businesses moved to Tennessee from elsewhere. From 2000 to 2008 the number of persons identifying themselves as Catholics in the Diocese of Nashville increased by 12.6 percent, in the Diocese of Memphis by 15.8 percent, and in the Diocese of Knoxville by 33.7 percent. Much of this increase was the result of immigration into the state by Americans from other places within the United States. Immigrants also arrived from abroad, among them many Spanish-speaking people, mainly from Latin America. Across Tennessee, new parishes were established, existing facilities were expanded, and ministries dedicated specifically to various language or ethnic groups were formed, at times in places that had previously seen little Catholic presence.

Enrollment in Christian Brothers University in Memphis and Aquinas College in Nashville, the two Catholic colleges in the state, and in Catholic elementary and secondary schools grew by 26.4 percent. New schools were built, and existing schools were enlarged. Among the three dioceses, the number of seminarians almost doubled between 2000 and 2008.

Early in the new century, accusations of child sex abuse by Catholic priests, often widely reported by the media, emerged across the state. One former priest of the Nashville diocese was convicted of sexually molesting youth and sent to prison. Out-of-court settlements required the outlay of millions of dollars to victims of abuse. As of 2008 accusations continued to be made, and litigation was still pending.

On August 12, 2004, Bishop Kmiec of Nashville was transferred to Buffalo. Chosen to succeed him was a Nashville native and priest of the Nashville diocese, Father David R. Choby, who was installed on February 27, 2006. Bishop Kurtz of Knoxville was appointed archbishop of Louisville on June 12, 2007.

SEE ALSO DUBUQUE, ARCHDIOCESE OF; ECUMENICAL MOVEMENT; HUGUENOTS; KNOXVILLE, DIOCESE OF; LOUISVILLE, ARCHDIOCESE OF; RESURRECTION OF CHRIST; ROSARY; SAINTS AND BEATI; SEX ABUSE CRISIS; SLAVERY, III (HISTORY OF); VATICAN COUNCIL II.

BIBLIOGRAPHY

Owen Francis Campion, "A History of the Diocese of Nashville" (BA thesis, in collection of the Tennessee State Library and Archives, Nashville, Tenn. 1962).

George J. Flanigen, ed., *Catholicity in Tennessee; A Sketch of Catholic Activities in the State, 1541–1937* (Nashville, Tenn. 1937).

Mary Loyola Fox, *A Return of Love: The Story of the Sisters of Mercy in Tennessee, 1866–1966* (Milwaukee, Wis. 1966).

Julia Gilmore, *Come North! The Life-Story of Mother Xavier Ross, Foundress of the Sisters of Charity of Leavenworth* (New York 1951).

Sister Mary de Lourdes Gohmann, *Political Nativism in Tennessee* (Washington, D.C. 1938).

Rose M. Masserano, *The Nashville Dominicans: A History of the Congregation of Saint Cecilia* (Roslyn Heights, N.Y. 1985).

Anna Blanche McGill, *The Sisters of Charity of Nazareth, Kentucky* (New York 1917).

Joel William McGraw, Milton J. Guthrie, and Josephine King, *Between the Rivers: The Catholic Heritage of West Tennessee* (Nashville, Tenn. 1996).

Herman A. Norton, *Religion in Tennessee: 1777–1945* (Knoxville, Tenn. 1981).

Victor Francis O'Daniel, *The Father of the Church in Tennessee, or the Life, Times, and Character of the Right Reverend Richard Pius Miles, O.P.* (New York 1926).

Denis Alphonsus Quinn, *Heroes and Heroines of Memphis* (Providence, R.I. 1887).

Thomas Stritch, *The Catholic Church in Tennessee: The Sesquicentennial Story* (Nashville, Tenn. 1987).

Msgr. Owen F. Campion
Associate Publisher, *Our Sunday Visitor*
Huntington, Ind. (2009)

TEXAS, CATHOLIC CHURCH IN

After Alaska, Texas is the largest state in the United States. It embraces an area of 267,339 square miles, divided into 254 counties. The state's boundaries, for the most part, are natural features: the Rio Grande on the west and south, the Gulf of Mexico shoreline and the Sabine River on the east, the Red River covering much of the north. The Panhandle, separating Texas from New Mexico and Oklahoma, is delimited by straight lines established through various agreements. Texas can be divided generally into four natural regions stretching in irregular belts from north to south: the eastern Texas plains, an area of extensive timberlands and rich agricultural soil that supports cotton, corn, sugarcane, and the raising of dairy cattle; the Texas prairies, a fertile, grassy strip that is the most populous region of the state; the middle Texas province, which was the original cattle range of Texas; and the arid western high plains. Almost 80 percent of the people of Texas live in urban areas. Houston is the largest city in the state, and Austin is the state capital. Other large metropolitan areas include Dallas, San Antonio, El Paso, and Fort Worth.

In 2008, the ROMAN CATHOLIC population of Texas was 6,586,240, approximately 25 percent of the state's population (*The Official Catholic Directory* 2008, p. 2103). The ecclesiastical structure of the state includes two archdioceses, those of SAN ANTONIO and GALVESTON-HOUSTON, and thirteen suffragan dioceses. San Antonio was established as a DIOCESE in 1874 and was made an ARCHDIOCESE in 1926. Galveston-Houston was originally created as the Diocese of Galveston in 1847. On December 29, 2004, Pope JOHN PAUL II elevated the diocese, by then the Diocese of Galveston-Houston, to the status of a metropolitan archdiocese. Today the thirteen suffragan dioceses are Dallas (1890), Corpus Christi (1912), El Paso (1914), Amarillo (1926), Austin (1948), San Angelo (1961), Brownsville (1965), Beaumont (1966), Fort Worth (1969), Victoria (1982), Lubbock (1983), Tyler (1986), and Laredo (2000). Austin, Beaumont, Brownsville, Corpus Christi, Tyler, and Victoria are now suffragan sees of Galveston-Houston, and Amarillo, Dallas, El Paso, Fort Worth, Laredo, Lubbock, and San Angelo are suffragan sees of San Antonio. Most Reverend Jose H. Gomez was installed as ARCHBISHOP of San Antonio on February 15, 2005, and Archbishop Daniel DiNardo, named as Texas's first CARDINAL, has been archbishop of Galveston-Houston since 2006.

Early Missions. The Apache, Comanche, and other indigenous tribes inhabited the area when the Spaniards established their first settlement in 1682, near present-day El Paso del Norte. The Spanish colonization of Texas, as part of northern New Spain, included the foundation of thirty-six Franciscan missions between 1683 and 1794. In addition to the first mission established at Isleta near El Paso del Norte, the FRIARS built a half dozen missions in eastern Texas. They began with Mission San Francisco de los Tejas, which Fray Damian Massanet founded in 1690. A second cluster was founded in the vicinity of Matagorda Bay, inland from the Gulf of Mexico, and a third centered on what would become San Antonio de Bexar. The latter included Mission San Antonio de Valero, built in 1718 under the direction of Fray Antonio de San Buena-Ventura y Olivares; the mission would later be known as the Alamo. Other missions in the San Antonio de Bexar group were Mission San Jose y San Miguel de Aguayo, erected in 1720, and three missions built in 1731: Nuestra Senora de la Concepcion, San Juan Capistrano, and San Francisco de la Espada.

For well over a century the missionaries, among whom Antonio MARGIL de Jesus was the best known, labored on the frontier and at various areas in the interior of Texas. The Spanish authorities had originally planned to convert each mission into a parish church, with secular priests manning them individually after a few years. The Franciscan priests, it was thought, would move on to serve missions in other locales, starting the missions process anew. However, the missions system was gradually abandoned, and SECULARIZATION—converting the missions into diocesan parishes—was undertaken between 1794 and approximately 1830. Although Texas was opened to immigrant colonies, both under the Spanish later in their governmental control and under the new Mexican government beginning in September 1821, all colonists were required to be Roman Catholics. Stephen F. Austin and other impresarios brought in numerous colonists from the United States who willingly accepted nominal membership in the Church, among them Sam Houston. However, there were never enough priests during that time to serve the needs of practicing Catholics, much less nominal ones.

Catholic Life in the Nineteenth Century. When Texas became an independent republic in 1836, the Catholics of the new political entity remained under the ecclesiastical jurisdiction of the bishop of Linares (later Monterrey), Mexico, Jose Maria de Jesus Belaunzaran y Urena. Bishop Anthony BLANC of New Orleans, Louisiana, desiring a clear hierarchical authority for the Republic of Texas, asked the Congregation for the PROPAGATION OF THE FAITH to study the situation. Father John TIMON, C.M., who was visitor (superior) of the VINCENTIANS in America, was sent to Texas in late 1838 to investigate. With the cooperation of Bishop Blanc, a prefecture APOSTOLIC was established for Texas, and Timon was named prefect apostolic. He then sent another Vincentian, missionary from France, Father Jean-Marie Odin, C.M., as vice prefect apostolic, to revive the Catholic faith in Texas. Odin arrived in Texas, accompanied by three Spanish Vincentians, on July 13, 1840. Thus began the rebuilding of Catholic life in Texas. In 1842, Odin was consecrated a bishop to head a separate Vicariate Apostolic of Texas. He served the Texas Catholics from 1842 until the spring of 1861, when he was transferred to New Orleans as that metropolitan see's second archbishop. Until then, however, he continued to labor to build up the Catholic presence in what was to become the state of Texas on December 29, 1845. Meanwhile, in 1847 Texas was elevated to the ecclesiastical status of a diocese, and Father Odin was named bishop of Galveston.

Mission Señora de la Purísima Concepción, San Antonio, Texas. *Known as the "nest preserves" of the Texas missions, it was designated as a National Historic Landmark in 1970.* THE LIBRARY OF CONGRESS

Bishop ODIN had to revive much of old Catholic Texas. For example, he reclaimed missions land from the government of Texas and worked among Catholic Hispanics and indigenous peoples as well as Irish, Germans, Czechs, and others who had settled in the land. Subsequently he labored among the Belgians, French, Swiss, and the first Polish to settle permanently in the United States, at Panna Maria (Virgin Mary in Polish) in 1854 under the leadership of Father Leopold Moczygemba, a Conventual Franciscan.

As the Church continued to flourish, further administrative developments emerged. In 1874 a second diocese was established, in San Antonio, and Father Anthony Pellicer was consecrated the first bishop of that city. In response to the needs of the Catholic population in north central Texas, the Diocese of Dallas was organized in 1890. The first bishop, Thomas F. Brennan, resigned after a short term (1891–1892), and

Bishop Edward Joseph Dunn succeeded him. Dunn served from 1893 to 1910. In south Texas, where many people of Hispanic heritage lived and where the OBLATES OF MARY IMMACULATE served in a large number of parishes, the Diocese of Corpus Christi was erected in 1912. West Texas grew rapidly, and the Diocese of EL PASO was founded in 1914. At the time, El Paso included territory in southern New Mexico. It thus remained a suffragan of the Archdiocese of SANTA FE until 1982.

Catholic Life in the Twentieth Century. As the twentieth century advanced, the Church recognized a need for a general ecclesiastical reorganization to better serve the needs of Texas Catholics. On August 3, 1926, Pope PIUS XI raised the Diocese of San Antonio to an archdiocese and erected a new diocese in Amarillo. In 1948 the Diocese of Austin was organized for the

Hurricane Katrina. *Three women evacuated due to Hurricane Katrina sit on bedding, September 7, 2005, at the Vietnamese St. Catherine's Catholic convent in Houston, Texas.* **STAN HONDA/AFP/GETTY IMAGES**

Catholics of central Texas. Galveston, the first diocese in Texas, was in 1959 redesignated as the Diocese of Galveston-Houston, recognizing that Houston had grown to become one of the most populous cities in the United States. In 1953 the Diocese of Dallas was redesignated as the Diocese of Dallas-Fort Worth, only to be renamed the Diocese of Dallas in 1969 when Fort

Worth erected a separate diocese. Meanwhile, San Angelo, in west central Texas, was made an episcopal see in 1961. The Vicariate Apostolic of Beaumont, established in 1874 and later subsumed into the Diocese of Corpus Christi, was made a diocese in 1966.

As the Roman Catholic population of Texas continued to increase, more new dioceses were created in the years after VATICAN COUNCIL II: Victoria in 1982, Lubbock in 1983, Tyler in 1986, and Laredo in 2000. In 1964 the bishops established the Texas Catholic Conference to provide a forum in which the dioceses of the state, through the bishops' gatherings, could exchange information and coordinate their activities regarding government policy and legislation on social issues and other matters of concern to the Church.

In the wake of Vatican II, during a time of social change and the continued growth of the Catholic population, the Church experimented with various new aspects of Catholic life and ministries in Texas. After the Vietnam War, new communities of Vietnamese Catholics made it necessary to build Vietnamese parishes in many locales. Most parishes organized programs for the permanent diaconate, and nearly all promoted the training of lay ministries. From these came the growth of such movements as the Catholic CHARISMATIC RENEWAL, MARRIAGE ENCOUNTER, and the CURSILLO MOVEMENT. The latter began in Spain and had its U.S. origins in Texas. Laity and clergy alike made concerted efforts to maintain the best of the Hispanic legacy of Texas. In the 1970s such advocacy groups as the Padres, an organization of Mexican American priests, and Las Hermanas, an organization made up chiefly of women religious, labored for the advancement of Hispanics. Their efforts and the endeavors of similar groups led to the appointments of bishops with Hispanic ancestry. Bishop Patricio F. Flores, the first Mexican American bishop in the nation, was consecrated for the Diocese of El Paso in 1978 and was named to the Archdiocese of San Antonio the following year.

Regarding Catholic historical studies, the Texas Catholic Historical Society, originally founded in the 1920s, was reorganized in 1976, with Professor Karl M. Schmitt of The University of Texas at Austin as its president. The university founded the United States' only regional Catholic historical scholarly journal in 1988, *The Journal of Texas Catholic History and Culture*, known today as *Catholic Southwest: A Journal of History and Culture*. This journal has won many national awards since it began publishing.

Education. Believing that Catholic schools were significant in putting the Church on a solid foundation in Texas, as early as 1847 Bishop Odin brought URSULINES from New Orleans to Galveston to open a school. In 1851 another community of Ursulines was established in San Antonio. From those two foundations the Ursuline schools expanded to different Texas locations. Many other religious communities of women joined them in the work of education, including the Congregation of the Incarnate Word, the Sisters of the Incarnate Word, the SISTERS OF DIVINE PROVIDENCE, the Sacred Heart Sisters, the DOMINICAN SISTERS, and

the Sisters of the Holy Ghost and Mary Immaculate (founded by Sister Mary Margaret Healy-Murphy, who conducted schools for African-American students). In 1964 there were approximately seventy communities of religious women in Texas, most of them involved in teaching. To educate the boys in San Antonio, Bishop Odin secured the services of the Society of Mary. It opened St. Mary's Institute in 1852 and from that beginning has developed schools, colleges, and universities throughout the state. In 2008 Texas had 370 Catholic elementary schools, 52 secondary schools, and 9 colleges or universities under Catholic auspices (*The Official Catholic Directory* 2008, p. 2103). In many parts of the state, bilingual clergy and teachers were indispensable for Catholics of Mexican descent, a population that forms the largest minority in Texas. A special Catholic council was organized to provide for the religious, social, economic, educational, and cultural advancement of Mexican Americans. In 1945 that council was given status by the bishops of the Southwest when they formed their own bishops' committee for the Spanish-speaking. Among its other tasks, the bishops' committee undertook the monitoring of the socioeconomic conditions of migrant workers, urging remedial legislation and providing opportunities for migrant children.

SEE ALSO EDUCATION, CATHOLIC (HIGHER) IN THE UNITED STATES; EDUCATION, CATHOLIC (K THROUGH 12) IN THE UNITED STATES; MEXICO, COLONIAL; MISSION AND MISSIONS; MISSION IN COLONIAL AMERICA, I (SPANISH MISSIONS).

BIBLIOGRAPHY

Felix D. Almaraz, Jr., *Knight without Armor: Carlos Eduardo Castaneda, 1896–1958* (College Station, Tex. 1999).

Felix D. Almaraz, Jr., "The Legacy of Columbus: Spanish Mission Policy in Texas," *Journal of Texas Catholic History and Culture* 3 (1992): 17–36.

Ralph F. Bayard, *Lone-Star Vanguard: The Catholic Re-Occupation of Texas, 1838–1848* (St. Louis 1945).

Carlos Eduardo Castaneda, *Our Catholic Heritage in Texas, 1519–1936*, 7 vols. (Austin, Tex. 1936–1958).

Bernard Doyon, *The Cavalry of Christ on the Rio Grande, 1849–1883* (Milwaukee, Wis. 1956).

Patrick Foley, "Jean-Marie Odin, C.M., Missionary Bishop Extraordinaire of Texas," *Journal of Texas Catholic History and Culture* 1 (March 1990): 42–60.

Patrick Foley, "The Historic Catholic Cultural Base of the American Southwest: The Spanish and the Irish," *Catholic Southwest: A Journal of History and Culture* 17 (2006): 35–48.

Marion A. Habig, *San Antonio's Mission San Jose: State and National Historic Site, 1720–1968* (San Antonio, Tex. 1968).

Sheila Hackett, *Dominican Women in Texas: From Ohio to Galveston and Beyond* (Houston, Tex. 1986).

Mary Loyola Hegarty, *Serving with Gladness: The Origin and History of the Congregation of the Sisters of Charity of the Incarnate Word, Houston, Texas* (Milwaukee, Wis. 1967).

Timothy M. Matovina, *Guadalupe and Her Faithful: Latino Catholics in San Antonio from Colonial Origins to the Present* (Baltimore 2005).

James Talmadge Moore, *Through Fire and Flood: The Catholic Church in Frontier Texas, 1836–1900* (College Station, Tex. 1992).

James Talmadge Moore, *Acts of Faith: The Catholic Church in Texas, 1900–1950* (College Station, Tex. 2002).

The Official Catholic Directory, 2008 (New Providence, N.J. 2008).

Rev. Joseph W. Schmitz SM
Vice President and Dean of Faculties
St. Mary's University, San Antonio, Texas

Rev. Giles G. Carie OFM Conv
Associate Judge, Marriage Tribunal
Diocese of El Paso, El Paso, Texas

Patrick Foley
Professor Emeritus, History, Tarrant County College
Fort Worth, Texas
Adjunct Professor of History
Columbia College of Missouri (2009)

U

UNITED NATIONS AND THE PAPACY

During the course of the twentieth century, the popes—from LEO XIII (1878–1903) to JOHN PAUL II (1978–2005)—abandoned the political and diplomatic isolationism of PIUS IX (1846–1878) and assumed an increasingly active internationalist stance. This change contributed to the establishment of the Permanent Observer Mission of the Holy See to the United Nations in 1964.

Because the United Nations was formed during the pontificate of PIUS XII (1939–1958), some observers have concentrated on his attitude toward the organization, convinced that his view of the UN was influenced by the close relationship between the VATICAN and the United States following President Franklin Delano Roosevelt's appointment of a personal representative to the HOLY SEE in 1940. While this was certainly an important influence, so was the long-standing call on the part of the transnational Church for an alternative to the idea of a "balance of power" in the world and the waging of war to resolve international issues. In fact, a number of religious, diplomatic, and ideological factors combined to determine the position of the universal Church in relation to the United Nations and its predecessor, the League of Nations.

The Papacy and the League of Nations. Although many of the principles advocated by the League of Nations, and later adopted by the United Nations, mirrored positions of the Catholic Church and centuries-old Christian traditions, there were obstacles to the Church's participation in an international community organized on the basis of independent sovereign states. The creation of VATICAN CITY in 1929 provided the

Holy See with the opportunity to enter the concert of powers, giving it, in the eyes of some observers, a stronger position than it had at the time of the formation of the League of Nations in 1920.

The PAPACY, however, pointed out that some confused the Holy See with Vatican City. The latter's recognition as a sovereign body made it, theoretically at least, equal to other states, despite its small territory and population and the peculiarities of its organization and action. The Church, on the other hand, insisted that admission and recognition be granted to the Holy See, the supreme organ of government of the Catholic Church. This difference in perception influenced the Holy See's attitude toward both the League of Nations and the United Nations, as well as its participation in international conferences. Nonetheless, the papacy, beginning with Leo XIII, recognized the need for the Church to make its voice heard in international affairs.

Pope Leo XIII was supportive of the International Peace Conference convoked at the Hague in May 1899, at the initiative of Nicholas II (1894–1917) of Russia. The limitation of armaments and the pacific settlement of international disputes were on the agenda, and the czar dispatched an invitation to the pope to take part. The host, Queen Wilhelmina of Holland, also sought the cooperation of the pope, but both failed to consult the Italian government, whose conflict with the papacy over the ROMAN QUESTION remained an open wound. Italy therefore opposed papal participation at the conference, and the Italian Foreign Office prevailed upon the Russians and Dutch to withdraw the invitation. The pope warned that efforts at peace would be undermined if the Church were excluded from civil society. Yet despite the slight instigated by the Italians, Leo reassured Queen Wilhelmina that the papacy would continue to work for peace among nations, and he approved of the Permanent Court of Arbitration that emerged from the Conference.

Although Pope BENEDICT XV (1914–1922) shared Leo's view that humanity could not rely solely on secular means and institutions, it is not true that he was hostile to the projected League of Nations sponsored by President Woodrow Wilson. Pinpointing the inability of the present international configuration to peacefully resolve conflicts, he proposed an alternative as early as 1914. In his encyclical *Ad beatissimi apostolorum* (*Appealing for Peace*), promulgated in November 1914, Benedict appealed to the nations of the world to find some other means of resolving differences. He also implored the world powers to adhere to existing international law until some new structure to deal with conflicts emerged. Benedict believed that both the violation of laws and the recourse to arms contributed to the carnage of World War I, and he prayed that a new code would assure a more tranquil future.

In his peace note of August 1917, Benedict called for the institution of universal arbitration as a substitute for armed conflict. Subsequently, the papal secretary of state, Cardinal Pietro GASPARRI, clarified and elaborated upon the pope's peace proposal, focusing on Benedict's call for a new order that would include "the suppression, by common accord, of [...]compulsory military service; the constitution of a Court of Arbitration for the solution of international questions; and lastly, for the prevention of infractions [...] the establishment of a universal boycott" (Koenig 1943, pp. 238–239). In his encyclical of May 1920, *Pacem, Dei munus pulcherrimum* (*On Peace and Christian Reconciliation*), Benedict was even more forceful in expressing his support for the League of Nations that President Wilson had proposed. Rather than engineering or even gloating over the American failure to enter the organization, as some suspected, Benedict regretted both this turn of events and the subsequent lack of leadership shown by the League.

This sentiment was shared by his successor, Achille Ratti, who assumed the papacy as PIUS XI in 1922. In his first encyclical, *Ubi arcano Dei consilio* (*On the Peace of Christ in the Kingdom of Christ*), promulgated on December 23, 1922, Pius lamented that the nations of the world had failed to establish a true peace following the conclusion of the Great War. In the summer of 1923, when John Eppstein, an officer of the League of Nations, proposed that diplomatic relations be established between the League's Council and the Vatican, Cardinal Gasparri outlined the papal position. Foreshadowing the later papal reaction to the United Nations, Gasparri noted, "the Holy See would be at the disposal of the League for matters within its competence; that is to say, for the elucidation of questions of principle in regard to morality and public international law, and also to give help to the League's relief work, where its [the Holy

See's] intervention would be of value to suffering peoples" (Koenig 1943, p. 365). Although not a member of the League, the Vatican remained supportive of its mission for peace and charity.

The Vatican position towards the League was further elaborated by the LATERAN PACTS that the Vatican signed with Italy in 1929. Article 24 of the Treaty of Conciliation stipulated, "With regard to the sovereignty pertaining to it in the field of international relations, the Holy See declares that it wishes to remain, and will remain, extraneous to all temporal disputes between nations, and to international congresses convoked for the settlement of such disputes, unless the contending parties make a joint appeal to its mission of peace" (Clough and Saladino 1968, p. 477).

Pius XII Seeks a New International Order. Pius XII, who assumed the papal tiara on the eve of World War II, also favored negotiation and arbitration to resolve international tensions. His sense of urgency was partly fueled by the outbreak of war in early September 1939. His disappointment was reflected in his first encyclical letter, issued in October 1939, *Summi pontificatus* (*On the Limitation of the Authority of the State*). The Pope decried the lack of morality in international relations and invoked an alternative approach. In a letter to the new minister from Haiti, in November 1939, Pius returned to this theme and, following Benedict XV, called for a fruitful international organization that would secure the reciprocal independence of small and large nations alike, while also safeguarding the liberty of all. Pius repeated his call for a new system of international relations in his Christmas message of 1939, in which he invoked international institutions for preserving the peace. Subsequent Christmas messages continued this call.

In 1942, President Franklin D. Roosevelt referred to the twenty-six nations at war with the Axis Powers as the "United Nations," and he suggested this be the name of a new international organization to replace the League of Nations. From August to October 1944, when delegates from the United States, Great Britain, the Soviet Union, and China met in Washington to outline plans for the new organization, Pius proved supportive. In fact, in his Christmas message of 1944, Pius deemed the formation of a new international organization for the preservation of the peace to be essential.

Pius XII and United Nations. When the United Nations officially came into existence in October 1945, Pius approved of its general aims, just as Benedict had earlier approved of the aims of the League of Nations. In Chapter I, Article 1, the UN Charter listed four purposes:

(1) To maintain international peace and security, and to take collective measures to do so;

(2) to develop friendly relations among nations based on the principle of equal rights and justice;

(3) to achieve international cooperation in solving international problems of an economic, social, cultural or humanitarian character, and in promoting respect for human rights and fundamental freedom for all without distinction of race, sex, language, or religion; and

(4) to serve as a center for harmonizing the actions of nations in the attainment of these goals.

To be sure, the pope had some reservations about the UN's two-tier organization, which differentiated the Great Powers in the Security Council from the general membership in the General Assembly. The veto power accorded the Soviet Union was also a cause for concern. Nonetheless, Pius perceived the organization to be the best hope for world peace and order. In his Christmas message of 1948, Pius provided the doctrinal basis for papal support of the United Nations, asserting that the Church had long maintained that the nations of the world constituted a community, and he rejected the notion of absolute state sovereignty. He hoped the UN would resolve the problem of PALESTINE and work to avert war in the Middle East. He repeated his hopes and support in his Christmas message of 1951.

Also in 1951, following the suggestion of Giovanni Montini (the future PAUL VI), Pius appointed Angelo Roncalli (the future Pope JOHN XXIII), as the Vatican's first Permanent Observer to UNESCO in Paris. He did not, however, accept the Permanent Observer status that was accorded to any state that belonged to one or more of the United Nations' specific agencies. In part, this hesitation stemmed from differences over the nature of papal participation in the organization; that is, over the question of whether Vatican City or the Holy See would be represented. This was later resolved by an exchange of letters, in which it was agreed that the representation at the UN would, as the Pope insisted, be accorded to the Holy See.

John XXIII and United Nations. Roncalli proved equally supportive of the United Nations when he became Pope John XXIII in 1958. He recognized it's the organization's role in perceiving the world as a family of nations, and in inculcating mutual trust and respect among them. He also applauded its work in assisting refugees and confronting the economic and social problems that burdened mankind. He elaborated his position before the Tenth International Conference of the UN Food and Agricultural Organization in November 1959, at which he praised the organization's efforts in the global campaign against hunger. In his eighth and last encyclical, *Pacem in terris* (*Peace on Earth*) of 1963, Pope John devoted a number of paragraphs to the inter-relationship between individual nations and the world community, particularly commending the work of the United Nations. He considered the emergence of the UN to be an important step in the political and juridical organization of the world community, and he praised its role as the guardian of human rights. Finally, he wrote that he believed the organization would increasingly become the arbiter of international disputes and the preserver of the peace worldwide.

Paul VI and United Nations. John's successor, Paul VI (1963–1978), had long been among the staunchest supporters in the Vatican of the UN, and he praised the organization's goals and efforts soon after he became pope. In July 1963, shortly after his election, Paul received an official visit from U Thant, the UN Secretary General. Paul expressed his esteem for the United Nations, comparing its temporal universality with the spiritual universality of the church:

> In recent years, the voice of the Popes, Our Predecessors, was among the first to augur the formation of a body such as that of which you, Mister U Thant, guide the activities. In his own time, Pope Benedict the Fifteenth desired it; its fundamental criteria were traced with happy foresight by Pope Pius the Twelfth in his Christmas message of nineteen hundred and thirty-nine, and that of September, nineteen hundred and forty-four; then its importance was underlined and its increasingly perfect functioning was encouraged by Pope John the Twenty-third in his last Encyclical Letter, *Pacem in terris*, the text of which, bearing the autograph signature of the Pontiff, was consigned to you, Mister Secretary, by Cardinal Suenens. (*Address of Pope Paul VI to the Secretary General of the United Nations*, July 11, 1963)

This verbal support was followed by concrete action when the pontiff appointed a Permanent Observer to the United Nations in 1964. Under the terms of the agreement, the Holy See's Permanent Observer status allows it to participate in General Assembly debates, have its communications circulated as official Assembly documents, and cosponsor resolutions and matters affecting it. From the first, Pope Paul seconded the organization's quest for disarmament and its campaign against hunger, and agreed to address the UN General Assembly—the first pope to do so—on the occasion of the organization's twentieth anniversary.

On October 4, 1965, as he left for New York, Paul explained that his aim was to encourage, strengthen and bless the efforts that people of good will were making to

John Paul II and the United Nations. *Pope John Paul II addresses the 50th session of the United Nations General Assembly on Oct. 5, 1995. Among other topics, his speech touched on his concern for the stuggles of the family in the modern world.* © RICK MAIMAN/SYGMA/CORBIS

safeguard, guarantee, and promote peace. His message was a simple one, delivered with humility and love for all peoples: "no more war, war never again." Perceiving the UN as an engine of world peace, he compared its role in the temporal order to the Church's role in the spiritual realm. Paul's support of the United Nations continued throughout his pontificate, and in 1970 he sent a message of support and praise for its (1948) Charter of Human Rights on the twenty-fifth anniversary of the organization (*Acta Apostolicae Sedis*, vol. 62, pp. 683–687). That same year (1970) he applauded the United Nations for initiating a nuclear nonproliferation treaty. Subsequently, he received its Secretary General, Kurt Waldheim, in Rome, in 1972 and 1977.

John Paul II and United Nations. JOHN PAUL II (1978–2005) proved to be no less supportive of the United Nations than his predecessors. Early in October 1979, he addressed the UN in New York—the second pope to do so—and cited the special bond that linked the Apostolic See to the United Nations, especially their common effort for peace and unity. This pledge of papal

support was later repeated when John Paul received Waldheim's successor, Javier Perez de Cuellar, in 1982, and again in the pope's message to the organization in 1985 on the occasion of its fortieth anniversary. A similar message of support was transmitted in 1989 to commemorate the twenty-fifth anniversary of the Permanent Mission of the Holy See to the United Nations. In the early 1990s, in response to the reports of atrocities in Bosnia-Herzegovina, John Paul invoked the intervention of the United Nations, citing its moral authority to do so.

Papal approval of the UN was expressed again in October 1995, when John Paul spoke before the General Assembly a second time, in commemoration of the fiftieth anniversary of its foundation. During this address, John Paul acknowledged the organization's contribution to the promotion of harmony and solidarity among the world's peoples and nations. He assured the member states that they had the complete support of the Holy See in the work of promoting justice, building peace, and ensuring that human rights and dignity would be respected worldwide. Acknowledging that the

Church did not promote any specific political or economic program, he stressed that it spoke to the heart of mankind and magnified the voice of human conscience, reminding humanity that the human person had perforce to be the true focus of all social, political, and economic activity. The pope concluded by asserting that the dedicated work of the United Nations represented a promising sign that the new millennium would witness a reflowering of a true humanity of compassion and solidarity between peoples and nations.

Despite this overwhelming and constant papal support for the United Nations, the papacy has not sought full membership in the organization. Perhaps this is because it has not wanted to be embroiled in political and economic conflicts not related to its spiritual mission, or perhaps because it has not wanted to apply for membership as a state. This hesitation to apply for full membership has not hindered its discussion and participation on those religious and moral issues that impinge upon its universal spiritual mission. In the wake of the September 2001 attacks in Washington, D.C., and New York City, John Paul II favored a United Nations action, under the auspices of its then Secretary General, Kofi Annan, rather than an American unilateralist action. The papal stance, as well as that of others, persuaded Washington to present its case against Iraq before the United Nations.

Benedict XVI and United Nations. John Paul's successor, BENEDICT XVI, has continued the papacy's approval of the United Nations' humanitarian and pacific policies, and in November 2007 he accepted an invitation to visit UN headquarters in New York in April 2008. In September 2005 he dispatched his secretary of state, Cardinal Angelo SODANO (b. 1927), to participate in the United Nations World Summit, held in New York. Sodano urged the participants to fulfill their previous commitments to help the poor, the sick, and the hungry. In September of the following year, the Vatican used the stage of the United Nations to ease the strain created by Pope Benedict's remarks on MUHAMMAD and ISLAM. The Vatican's recourse to the UN to defuse this tension was appreciated by most states, which by and large have viewed the Vatican's participation in the organization positively. Thus, the campaign of a small minority to terminate the Vatican's Permanent Observer status has found neither sympathy nor support among the institution's 192 members. In fact, at the end of 2006, the U.S. Congress passed legislation according the Vatican the privileges and immunities enjoyed by the diplomatic missions of the UN member states.

SEE ALSO COLD WAR AND THE PAPACY; ECONOMIC JUSTICE FOR ALL; EUROPEAN UNION AND THE PAPACY; NATURAL LAW IN POLITICAL THOUGHT; LEAGUE OF NATIONS AND THE PAPACY; PACEM IN TERRIS; SUMMI PONTIFICATUS; UNITED STATES RELATIONS WITH THE PAPACY.

BIBLIOGRAPHY

Kola Bakare, *Glimpses into International Relations: From the Holy Alliance to the United Nations System* (Lagos, Nigeria 2002).

Mats Berdal and Spyros Economides, eds. *United Nations Interventionism, 1991–2004*, rev. ed. (New York 2007).

Hyginus Eugene Cardinale, *The Holy See and the International Order* (Toronto 1974).

Simon Chesterman, ed., *Secretary or General?: The UN Secretary General in World Politics* (New York 2007).

Shepard B. Clough and Salvatore Saladino (eds), *A History of Modern Italy: Documents, Readings, and Commentary* (N.Y.: Columbia University Press, 1968).

Frank J. Coppa, *The Modern Papacy since 1789* (New York 1998).

Jacques Fomerand, *Historical Dictionary of the United Nations* (Lanham, Md. 2007).

Edward J. Gratsch, *The Holy See and the United Nations, 1945–1995* (New York 1997).

J. Derek Holmes, *The Papacy in the Modern World* (New York 1981).

Paul M. Kennedy, *The Parliament of Man: The Past, Present, and Future of the United Nations* (New York 2006).

Peter C. Kent and John F. Pollard, eds. *Papal Diplomacy in the Modern Age* (Westport, Conn. 1994).

Harry C. Koenig, ed., *Principles for Peace: Selections from Papal Documents from Leo XIII to Pius XII* (Washington, D.C. 1943).

Hans van Mangoldt et al., eds. *The United Nations System and its Predecessors* (New York 1997).

Frank J. Coppa
Professor of History
St. John's University, N.Y. (2009)

UNITED STATES RELATIONS WITH THE PAPACY

Contact between the PAPACY and the United States commenced at the time of the formation of the Union. As early as 1784, following the Treaty of Paris, which confirmed the independence of the United States, the papal nuncio in Paris informed the American peace commissioners that the Papal States had agreed to open the ports of Civitavecchia and Ancona to the vessels of the new nation. The U.S. government did not respond, however, until the Italian Giovanni Sartori, who was involved in Mediterranean trade and in correspondence with Robert Morris, superintendent of finance during the American Revolution, suggested that it would be in the interest of the United States to have a consul in ROME to protect the nation's growing trade and assist Americans who visited Italy. In the interim, Pope PIUS VI (1775–1799) named John CARROLL as provisional apostolic delegate in 1784; in 1789, he was named bishop of Baltimore, making him the nation's first bishop. In 1797 Sartori was commissioned the first of eleven consuls to represent American interests in Rome. The need for such a consul disappeared with the collapse of the temporal power of the VATICAN in 1870.

Sartori remained in office until he was replaced by the Roman lawyer Felix Cicognani in 1823, and for several years he was both the U.S. consul to Rome and consul general of the Papal States in America. During Cicognani's consulate (1823–1837), trade reciprocity was established between the two governments, although this did not lead to increased commercial intercourse between the two states. As the number of American visitors to Rome grew, so did the demand for a consul of American birth. Early in 1837 the U.S. State Department commissioned George W. Greene of Rhode Island, the grandson of Nathanael Greene of Revolutionary War fame, as Cicognani's successor. In July 1845 Greene was succeeded by Nicholas Brown of New York.

The Establishment of Full Diplomatic Relations.

Giovanni Maria Mastai-Ferretti was elected to the papacy as PIUS IX in June 1846, and he followed a reformist course that reversed the conservatism of his predecessor, GREGORY XVI (1831–1846). This change excited the imagination of liberal Americans, who pressed for the establishment of full diplomatic representation at the papal court. This sentiment was reinforced by a demonstration held at the Broadway Tabernacle in New York City on November 19, 1847. An address given by Horace Greeley at this event was forwarded to Pius IX via the American consul. In return, the pope sent a collection of Raphael's engravings and some coins minted under the new pontificate as a gift to the United States.

Despite some bitter opposition, the U.S. Congress, which was overwhelmingly Protestant, supported President James Polk's recommendation for a chargé d'affaires to the Papal States. Moved by the prospect of the commercial and political union of the peninsula under the leadership of the pope, and by the U.S. involvement in a war with Catholic Mexico (which was denounced by some U.S. Catholics), Congress viewed diplomatic relations with the Vatican in a more positive light. In April 1848, Jacob L. Martin, the secretary to the American legation in Paris, was commissioned to the new office. From the first, the chargé was instructed to devote his efforts exclusively to civil relations between the Papal States and the United States, and to refrain from any interference in ecclesiastical issues relating to

the United States, or any other part of the world.

The establishment of diplomatic relations between the largely Protestant United States and the center of Catholicism was a result of the goodwill enjoyed by Pius IX at the beginning of his reign. The relations thus established were to continue for the next twenty years without interruption, despite the fears of some that this would provide undue advantage to Catholics at the expense of the Protestant denominations. Martin arrived in Rome early in August 1848, but in less than a month he was stricken and died of fever. He was succeeded by Louis Cass Jr., who remained until 1858 and whose position was raised to the rank of minister resident in 1854. During his tenure, Monsignor Gaetano BEDINI visited Washington and broached the question of the appointment of a papal nuncio to the United States, but he was not encouraged in this endeavor by the American government or people.

At the time, antipapal demonstrations erupted in a number of American cities, fueled by anti–Catholicism and the conservative policies pursued by Rome following the collapse of the Roman Republic and the papal restoration of 1849. Nonetheless, Bedini, spurred by the problems of the Church in the United States, including the enormous diocesan and parochial debts and the "excessive" independence of the clergy, as well as the American annexation of Texas, New Mexico, Arizona, and California, which contained large numbers of Catholics, called for the establishment of a nunciature in the United States. He also called for the establishment of a national college for training the American clergy in Rome. Neither suggestion was immediately implemented, however.

Papal Policy during the American Civil War.

John P. Stockton represented the United States in Rome during the unification period (1858–1861), which saw the Kingdom of Italy absorb substantial portions of the Papal States. When Rufus King succeeded him in 1861, both the United States and the Papal States were threatened with upheaval, for that year witnessed the Confederate attack on Fort Sumter and the proclamation of the Kingdom of Italy. These were difficult days for both the papacy and the American Republic, as the Italians attempted to complete their unification by acquiring the Eternal City, while Union forces fought to suppress the rebellion that threatened the future of the United States.

The American secretary of state, William H. Seward, promised that the United States would not interfere in the domestic crisis of the Papal States, expecting them to do likewise with respect to the Civil War. King did not venture to Rome, however, but instead accepted a commission as brigadier general in the Union army. Alexander W. Randall was appointed to fill the vacancy as a stopgap, but he remained in Rome for only a year (1861–1862), and his successor, Richard M. Blatchford, also served for only a year (1862–1863). Finally, Rufus King was reappointed to the post and served from October 1863 until the official end of the diplomatic mission in 1867.

Problems persisted for both the Vatican and the Union. Secretary of State William Seward, aware that the Holy Father exercised an important influence over the three million Catholics in the divided nation, sent Archbishop John HUGHES of New York to Britain, France, and the Vatican. Upon his arrival in the Eternal City, Hughes championed the cause of the North and warned of Confederate designs on Mexico and other Catholic countries of the Caribbean. The Confederacy likewise appreciated the moral importance of the Vatican, and Father John BANNON, a Confederate agent to Ireland, urged his secretary of state, Judah P. Benjamin, to try to enlist the support of the pope, who might then influence the attitude of the Catholic governments of France, Spain, Portugal, Austria, and Bavaria.

Desirous for peace, the Holy See addressed letters to the archbishops of New York and New Orleans in October 1862, encouraging them to make efforts to establish a reconciliation between North and South. In November, Pope Pius IX discreetly proposed to the American minister that papal mediation would prove less troublesome than involving the major European powers, which had political agendas of their own, but the U.S. government was not disposed to accept Rome's mediation offer. Meanwhile, Bishop Martin J. SPALD-ING of Louisville, Kentucky, sent the Vatican a report critical of the Lincoln government, and in September 1863 President Jefferson Davis commissioned A. Dudley Mann as his special envoy to the Papal States. Mann secured audiences with both Cardinal Giacomo AN-TONELLI, the papal secretary of state, and with the pope himself, but he raised neither the question of papal mediation nor recognition of the Confederacy.

Although Pius addressed a letter to Jefferson Davis, the president of the Confederate States of America, papal officials attached no significance to the title, and An-tonelli denied all rumors of Rome's recognition of the Confederacy. The secretary of state informed the resident minister, Rufus King, of the United States that the pope, as head of the Universal Church, had written to Davis in the interests of peace and humanity, but without any political or diplomatic design. Nonetheless, the Confederacy persisted in its diplomatic maneuvering, and in the spring of 1864 it appointed Bishop Patrick LYNCH of Charleston as the Confederate commissioner to the Papal States, with the mission of securing papal recognition. Lynch was received at the Vatican only in his episcopal capacity, however, rather than as an accredited representative of the Confederacy.

Termination of Relations. Despite the friendly attitude of the Vatican to the U.S. government, in 1867 the American mission to Rome came to an official end when Congress refused to continue the appropriation for its existence. The pretext for this congressional action was that the papal government had ordered the relocation of American Protestant Church outside the walls of Rome. Other factors influenced the closing of this mission, however, including religious bigotry, conflicts between the president and Congress, and American support for the Italian acquisition of Rome for the capital of the Italian Kingdom. Legally, by removing funding, the action of Congress left the mission in existence but unable to function. No explanation was ever provided to the papal government, and the papal consulate in the United States was never officially terminated. This would later play a positive role when the mission was restored in the latter part of the twentieth century. For over seventy years, however, there were to be no formal diplomatic relations between the Vatican and Washington.

The Establishment of an Apostolic Delegation. In the last years of Pius IX's pontificate, the need for a papal representative in the United States was raised again. In light of the ANTI–CATHOLIC sentiment in the nation, which remained widespread, it was considered best to appoint an apostolic delegate, or a personal representative of the pope to the faithful, clergy, and laity, rather than a official representative to the civil or national government. The appointment of an apostolic delegate was discussed at a meeting of the Congregation de Propaganda Fide in January 1877, and in 1878 Bishop George Conroy of Ireland was dispatched as provisional apostolic delegate to Canada, though his mission included an examination of developments in the United States. In his report to Rome, Conroy advised appointing a permanent apostolic delegate to the United States, despite the opposition in the country and the clergy. This proposal was not acted upon at that time, however.

In 1883, Pope LEO XIII (1878–1903) named Bishop Luigi Sepiaccias his apostolic delegate to the Third Plenary Council of Baltimore, and three years later Monsignor Germano Straniero was sent to the United States to bring the red hat to Cardinal James GIBBONS and assess developments there. By this time the United States had acquired sufficient importance to warrant Leo's political interest and a place in his international policies. In 1889 Archbishop Francesco SATOLLI represented Leo at the ceremonies marking the centennial of the United States Catholic hierarchy and the inauguration of The CATHOLIC UNIVERSITY OF AMERICA in Washington, D.C. During the course of his visit, he was assured by officials of the U.S. government that they had no opposition to the creation of a permanent apostolic delegation, and in 1893 such a delegation was established, with Satolli named apostolic delegate.

Despite the fact that Satolli was not accorded any rank or status within the diplomatic corps assigned to the country, at the direction of Cardinal Mariano RAMPOLLA DEL TINDARO, the papal secretary of state, he engaged in correspondence between Mexico, Guatemala, and the Holy See, and in many ways acted as a virtual nuncio. The success of this approach led to the establishment of similar delegations in Canada, Newfoundland, and Mexico over the next decade.

When it seemed that war might break out between the United States and Spain over Cuba, the Spanish ambassador appealed for Vatican mediation. Cardinal Rompolla del Tindaro commissioned John IRELAND to intercede with the administration of William McKinley (1897–1901) as Washington prepared for war. McKinley's conditions were that Spain must grant an armistice, negotiate with the Cuban insurgents, and, if no solution were found within six months, permit the United States to arbitrate a settlement. Pressed by Leo, the Spanish cabinet proclaimed a suspension of hostilities, but this was not sufficient for the American Congress, which pressured the president to intervene at once by establishing an independent government in Cuba.

Leo was disappointed with this turn of events. Archbishop Ireland had encouraged him to utilize his prestige in Madrid to secure the Spanish concession of an armistice, but this had failed to satisfy the Americans, who declared war in spite of this concession. Yet another Vatican failure to exert influence over American policy took place during the Mexican Revolution of 1915, when President Woodrow Wilson ignored the pope's advice to remain neutral in the conflict between Francisco "Pancho" Villa and Venustiano Carranza. Instead, he recognized the latter, who continued to persecute the Church.

The Papacy and the United States during World War I. Other disappointments followed the eruption of World War I, which led Pope BENEDICT XV (1914–1922) to issue a number of appeals for peace, most notably his peace proposal of 1917. His intervention was not well received either by the Allies or the Central Powers, both of which suspected Vatican complicity with the other side. Indeed, the U.S. secretary of state, Robert Lansing, considered the papal peace proposal to be inspired by the enemy. This suspicion contributed to American opposition to the Vatican effort to establish diplomatic relations with China in the summer of 1918. Rome's attempt to appoint a nuncio to Peking was frustrated by the U.S. State Department, which deemed such relations unnecessary and argued that no republic in the Northern Hemisphere maintained diplomatic relations with the Vatican.

Despite this American hostility to papal initiatives, Pope Benedict supported President Woodrow Wilson's "fourteen points," a program very similar to his own, as the basis for negotiation for an end to the war. Indeed, Father Joseph McMahon, director of the Cathedral Library in New York City, addressing the CATHOLIC LIBRARY ASSOCIATION in New York, proclaimed that the president's peace terms were almost identical to Benedict's, and that only the bias against Catholicism and its head prevented this from being perceived in the United States. Likewise, Pope Benedict also supported Wilson's League of Nations, and in his Easter Message to the United States he seconded his call for a new organization of peoples and nations. On January 4, 1919, the pope met with President Wilson, who thus became the first chief executive of the United States to be received by a pope. Although there were rumors that the Vatican wished to interject itself into the peace process at Versailles, these stories proved to be unfounded.

Benedict did dispatch Monsignor Bonaventura Cerretti to Versailles, but this was done to safeguard the position of the missions in the former German colonies rather than to interject the Vatican into the peacemaking process. These papal efforts on behalf of the missions were seconded by Wilson and the American representatives. During the 1920s, American church officials importuned the U.S. government to attempt to influence the Mexicans to cease their persecution of the Church. These contacts were unofficial, however, for from 1867 to 1939 there were no formal relations between the Vatican and the United States.

Franklin Delano Roosevelt's Personal Representative to the Vatican. Following his inauguration in 1933, President Franklin Delano Roosevelt established ad hoc contacts with Rome. Eugenio Pacelli, the secretary of state under PIUS XI (1922–1939), relied on Francis SPELLMAN, the auxiliary bishop of Boston, as one of his chief contacts in the U.S. hierarchy. Thus, in 1936, when Pacelli visited the United States, Spellman arranged for him to meet Roosevelt at Hyde Park, where they discussed the prospect of resuming diplomatic relations. Roosevelt also maintained close contacts with Cardinal George MUNDELEIN, the archbishop of Chicago, who likewise sought closer relations between the United States and the Vatican. Throughout the 1930s, rumors that the president would soon establish formal diplomatic relations with the Vatican provoked protests, including the objections of Reverend Edward W. Schramm, the editor of the *Lutheran Standard*, who demanded a denial.

When Pacelli became Pope PIUS XII (1939–1958) early in 1939, Roosevelt dispatched Joseph Kennedy, the ambassador to Great Britain, as the special representative of the United States to the papal coronation, which prompted protests from the United Lutheran Church in America and the Southern Baptist Convention. Despite the outcry, the prospect of an outbreak of hostilities in Europe prompted Roosevelt to proceed with his plan of establishing some form of diplomatic relationship with the Vatican in order to take advantage of its unique and substantial input in European affairs. On December 24, 1939, in his Christmas letter to Pius XII, Roosevelt announced his intention, with Vatican approval, of dispatching a personal representative to the Holy See. The fact that his agent, the businessman Myron TAYLOR, was an Episcopalian, helped blunt the expected Protestant opposition. Taylor was also sufficiently wealthy to finance the enterprise himself. This was an important consideration because the president did not wish to provoke Congress by seeking an appropriation. Finally, Roosevelt learned from Spellman, who had replaced Cardinal Patrick Hayes as archbishop of New York, that Taylor had the approval of the pope.

Although Taylor's post was deemed temporary, he remained at it for ten years, assisted by Harold H. Tittmann Jr. Among other things, he was able to enlist the aid of the Vatican in supporting the Lend Lease program of aid to the Soviet Union. The Vatican also acted as an intermediary between the Americans and the governments of Italy following the fall of MUSSOLINI. It is possible that Pius XII may have been "silent" regarding Soviet repression because of Allied, and more specifically American, pressure. However, Taylor proved unable to prevent the Holy See from establishing diplomatic relations with Imperial Japan in 1942, during the course of World War II. The Vatican also disapproved of the American recourse to atomic bombs.

After the war, the Division of Southern European Affairs within the U.S. State Department suggested that the president's personal representative to the Vatican was no longer a necessary position. It argued that it was no longer justifiable in terms of its original aims of pursuing parallel peace efforts prior to the war and using the Vatican as an observation post during the conflict. Tittmann disagreed, however, and he recommended the establishment of a permanent U.S. diplomatic mission to the Vatican, citing the common aims of the Vatican and the United States in the postwar period, the advantages of continued contact with the forty or so states with representation to the Vatican, and the favorable impact of such a mission on Latin America. The Vatican and the United States also seemed to share similar concerns about the future of Eastern Europe and the prospect of a communist victory in Italy. For these and other reasons, President Harry S. Truman, who succeeded Roosevelt in 1945, reappointed Taylor as his personal representative to the pope.

When Taylor informed the president of his impending resignation, effective January 1950, Truman explored the possibility of a regular diplomatic appointment. In October 1951 he announced the nomination of General Mark W. Clark as ambassador to Vatican City. This attempt proved abortive, however, in part because Truman misjudged the depth of anti–Catholic feeling in the country. In 1952, therefore, following widespread criticism and indignation, Clark withdrew his name from consideration. Following his withdrawal some eighteen years elapsed—covering the presidencies of Dwight D. Eisenhower, John F. Kennedy, and Lyndon B. Johnson—with neither an official nor an unofficial representative accredited to the Vatican, the pope, or the Holy See. President Kennedy (1961–1963), the first Catholic president of the United States, feared the divisive impact of an appointment, whether official or unofficial, to the Vatican. He did meet with Pope PAUL VI (1963–1978) in 1963, when he was told of the Vatican's reservations about the war in Vietnam. Just before Christmas 1967, President Lyndon B. Johnson paid an unexpected visit to Paul VI on his return from a visit to American troops in Vietnam, perhaps hoping to avoid a papal condemnation of American action in Vietnam. It was through the Vatican's intervention that the Paris Peace Talks were opened in the spring of 1968.

In 1969, President Richard M. Nixon (1969–1974) restored the office of "personal representative" to the pope, appointing Henry Cabot Lodge, a former ambassador to the United Nations, Vietnam, and Germany, to the post. Lodge assumed his responsibilities in 1970 and served for the remainder of Nixon's term. The wisdom of having a representative at the Vatican was shared by President Jimmy Carter (1977–1981), who appointed David Walters as his envoy. Walters served for one year and was followed by Robert F. Wagner, the former mayor of New York City. Among other things, Wagner devoted his efforts to the problems of rescuing the hostages held at the American embassy in Iran. In October 1979, JOHN PAUL II visited the United States. Shortly after his election, President Ronald Reagan (1981–1989) named his longtime friend and associate William A. Wilson of California to the position of personal representative to the pope, and he received more State Department support in this than any of his predecessors had. Wilson arrived in Rome early in 1981.

The Reopening of Formal Diplomatic Relations.

President Reagan met with Pope John Paul II (1978–2005) in June 1982, and it is believed that the two discussed the difficulties confronting the SOLIDARITY movement in Poland, Soviet domination of Eastern Europe, and how to bring this domination to an end peacefully. Reagan's national security advisor, William Clark, favored close collaboration between the Vatican and Washington and sought the opening of formal

John Paul II and the U.S. Presidents. *Pope John Paul II points to Lake Albano accompanied by President Bush, during their first meeting at the Pontiff's summer residence in Castel Gandolfo near Rome in this July 23, 2001, photo. Five American presidents in a row eagerly sought audiences with Pope John Paul II, even when the pontiff expressed strong opposition to some of their policies, such as President Clinton's support for abortion rights and President Bush's invasion of Iraq. All five who occupied the White House during John Paul II's 26-year papacy—Carter, Reagan, George H. W. Bush, Clinton and George W. Bush—visited the Vatican.* AP IMAGES

diplomatic relations with the Holy See. On January 10, 1984, following assurances of strong bipartisan and ecumenical support for establishing such relations, along with the advice and support of the Reverend Billy Graham, President Reagan announced that Wilson, who had been serving as his personal envoy, would be appointed ambassador to the Holy See. The Senate confirmed his appointment by an overwhelming vote, and his successor, Frank Shakespeare, was approved by the unanimous vote of the U.S. Senate in 1986. Unanimous support was also accorded to both Thomas Patrick Melady, President George H. W. Bush's ambassador, in 1989, and the former mayor of Boston Raymond Flynn, who Clinton appointed to the post in 1993. In November 1991, John Paul II had an hourlong talk with President George H. W. Bush, and in June 1994 he met with President William Jefferson Clinton (1993–2001).

Since the 1980s, American-Vatican relations have focused on four principle areas: human rights, religious freedom, political pluralism and humanitarian issues. At the end of 1989, Mikhail Gorbachev, then head of the Soviet Union, had an historic meeting with John Paul II, who called for the guarantees of human rights and religious freedom in the vast territories governed by the Soviets. In 1989, POLAND became the first of the Communist countries to re-establish diplomatic relations with the Holy See. The Pope also provided both moral and material support for Lech Walesa and his Solidarity movement at this time, as did the United States. The Vatican, no less than the United States, played a key role in the transformation of Poland from a Communist to a democratic state, and subsequently, through its organizational network, it spearheaded the impetus for freedom in the other Eastern European countries.

The mutual concern that the Holy See and Washington had for the deprivation of human rights in Poland

and Eastern Europe provided the basis for their close cooperation throughout the 1980s and played a part in the collapse of Communism, first in Poland, and then later in Czechoslovakia, Hungary, Rumania, Bulgaria, and the Baltic States, and finally in the end of the Cold War. This was acknowledged by President Bush's visit to the Pope in November 1991.

In 1993 the United States pressed the Vatican to open formal diplomatic relations with ISRAEL. With American encouragement, the Holy See and Israel established diplomatic links at the end of 1993. However, the Vatican and Washington have not always been in agreement on the Middle East. The Vatican opposed the war launched by the first President Bush against Iraq in early 1991, calling for a diplomatic rather than a military solution to the dispute in the Middle East. Later, in 2003, John Paul II urged the second President Bush not to go to war in Iraq, again to no avail.

Differences also emerged between the Vatican and Washington regarding the "Third World," particularly in the areas of population control and fiscal and economic policy. This was evident at the 1995 Cairo Conference on Population and Development, when the Holy See opposed the contraceptive policy advocated by the United States and other Western powers. BENEDICT XVI (2005–), like all his postwar predecessors, has questioned the American policy of nuclear deterrence and the recourse to military measures rather than relying on diplomacy to resolve differences. Rome has also assumed a less confrontational stance toward Castro's Cuba than has the United States.

Still, relations between the two have generally been good, and neither the Vatican nor Washington has seriously challenged the value of continuing full diplomatic relations. At the end of 2005, Pope Benedict XVI named Archbishop Pietro SAMBI to replace the retiring Archbishop Gabriel Montalvo, who had served as nuncio in Washington since 1998. Later, in June 2007, President Bush had a long talk with Pope Benedict on the situation in the Middle East, problems in Africa and Latin America, and the status of American-Russian relations.

SEE ALSO CANADA, THE CATHOLIC CHURCH IN; CHURCH AND STATE IN THE UNITED STATES (LEGAL HISTORY); COLD WAR AND PAPACY; EUROPEAN UNION AND THE PAPACY; ITALY, THE CATHOLIC CHURCH IN; LEAGUE OF NATIONS AND THE PAPACY; NATURAL LAW IN POLITICAL THOUGHT; NATURAL LAW IN POLITICAL THOUGHT; LEAGUE OF NATIONS AND THE PAPACY; PACEM IN TERRIS; SUMMI PONTIFICATUS; UNITED STATES RELATIONS WITH THE PAPACY.

BIBLIOGRAPHY

David J. Alvarez, "The Papacy in the Diplomacy of the American Civil War," *Catholic Historical Review* 69, no. 2 (1983): 227–248.

Daniel G. Babis and Anthony J. Maceli, *A United States Ambassador to the Vatican* (New York 1952).

John S. Conway, "Myron C. Taylor's Mission to the Vatican 1940–1950," *Church History* 44, no. 1 (March 1975) 85–99.

Ennio di Nolfo, *Vaticano e Stati Uniti, 1939–1952* (Milan 1978).

George Q. Flynn, "Franklin Roosevelt and the Vatican: The Myron Taylor Appointment," *Catholic Historical Review* 58, no. 2 (1972): 171–194.

Gerald P. Fogarty, "Vatican-American Relations: Cooperation or Conspiracy," *America* 166, no. 12 (1992): 289–293.

Peter C. Kent and John F. Pollard, eds., *Papal Diplomacy in the Modern Age* (Westport, Conn. 1994).

Thomas Patrick Melady, *The Ambassador's Story: The United States and the Vatican in World Affairs* (Huntington, Ind. 1994).

Thomas Patrick Melady, "U.S.–Vatican Relations," *Ambassadors Review* (spring 1996): 29–33.

Jim Nicholson, *The United States and the Holy See: The Long Road* (Rome 2002).

Bernard J. O'Connor, *Papal Diplomacy: John Paul II and the Culture of Peace* (South Bend, Ind. 2005).

John Offner, "Washington Mission: Archbishop Ireland on the Eve of the Spanish-American War," *Catholic Historical Review* 73, no.4 (1987): 562–574.

Leo Francis Stock, ed., *United States Ministers to the Papal States: Instructions and Despatches, 1848–1868* (Washington, D.C. 1933).

Leo Francis Stock, ed., *Consular Relations between the United States and the Papal States: Instructions and Despatches* (Washington, D.C. 1945).

Harry Truman, *Correspondence between President Truman and Pope Pius XII*, Introduction by Myron C. Taylor (New York 1952).

David Woolner and R. G. Kurial, eds., *FDR, the Vatican, and the Roman Catholic Church in America, 1933–1945* (New York 2003).

Frank J. Coppa
Professor of History
St. John's University, N.Y. (2009)

UTAH, CATHOLIC CHURCH IN

Utah Catholicism emerged out of harsh frontier conditions. Its early history is marked by struggle in the midst of POVERTY and isolation. Against a background of mountains and valleys, the Catholic FAITHFUL of Utah, sustained by the distant Archdiocese of SAN FRANCISCO, took on the hardy spirit and personal courage often associated with the American West.

Early History. Utah, bordered by Idaho, Wyoming, Colorado (north and east), New Mexico, Arizona, and Nevada (south and west) encompassed 84,990 square miles of western land marked by the extremes of desert and mountain environments. Long before political boundaries were drawn, native tribes, including the Ute, Southern Paiute, Gosiute, Shoshone, and Navajo, ranged widely across the area, claiming it as their homeland. In 1776 the Ute tribes were among those who welcomed the Spanish explorers, Padre Fray Francisco Atanasio Dominguez (c. 1740–c. 1804) and Padre Fray Silvestre Velez de Escalante (c. 1750–1780) on their expedition in search of a route from Santa Fe, New Mexico, to Monterey, California. Escalante kept a daily journal that describes this historical survey of early western America. Utah state historians retraced the trek in 1976 and created an official Dominguez and Escalante Trail marking the padres' route at camp sites they named along the way. These included the area known as Escalante State Park, San Rafael River in eastern Utah and Santa Clara to the south, and the Virgin River in Zion Canyon. Defining place names perpetuates the memory of the Catholic roots of Utah.

In the early 1800s an onslaught of traders and trappers blazed trails across the intermountain West for about thirty years. Catholic names again appeared on landmarks and trading posts when mountain men from Santa Fe and later from St. Louis and the Great Lakes entered the fur trade in Utah. The city of Ogden today bears the name of Peter Skene Ogden (d. 1854), a French Canadian and chief trader of the Hudson's Bay Fur Company. He explored the Great Salt Lake, led expeditions into Snake River country between 1824 and 1830, and lived for a time near Weber River. Hunter and guide, Étienne Provost (1785–1850), also of French Canadian birth, camped in the Salt Lake Valley during 1824 and 1825 and is believed to be one of the first non-Native Americans to visit the Great Salt Lake. The fleeting presence of these rugged adventurers left a Catholic footprint on the Utah landscape.

In 1847 the arrival into Utah territory of the first representatives of the Church of Jesus Christ of LATTER-DAY SAINTS followed escalating clashes with neighbors in Nauvoo, Illinois, and the murder of church-founder Joseph SMITH. The Mormons, as they refer to themselves, intended to establish an entirely self-sufficient THEOCRACY until the war of 1848, when the United States acquired Mexican land through the Treaty of Guadalupe Hidalgo. However, in a tightly woven communal lifestyle, the Mormons successfully pursued their social and political goals. Catholic travelers joined the stream of miners, merchants, and pioneers flowing across the western United States toward the gold fields and new settlements of the far West. In 1853 Pope PIUS IX established the Archdiocese of San Francisco with jurisdiction extending eastward to the Colorado River and appointed Bishop Joseph Sadoc ALEMANY (previ-

ously BISHOP of Monterey in 1850) as first ARCHBISHOP of the new ARCHDIOCESE. The United States Congress had set the boundaries of Utah Territory in 1850, and thus the Utah wilderness was included under the ecclesiastical responsibility of Archbishop Alemany.

Aware of the growing numbers of settlers in Utah, Archbishop Alemany sent Father Edward Kelly in 1866 from San Francisco to anchor the Church in Salt Lake City. With the help of Catholic residents of the area, Father Kelly bought a small piece of property in a Mormon neighborhood and remodeled the small adobe building on the site. Five years later Father Patrick Walsh replaced the adobe CHAPEL with a new church named in honor of St. MARY MAGDALENE. In 1873 Archbishop Alemany appointed Father Lawrence SCANLAN to an area embracing not only the entire Utah Territory but also 72,667 square miles containing seven counties in eastern Nevada. In March 27, 1931, the size of Scanlan's jurisdiction in the Diocese of Salt Lake, originally created in 1891, was reduced. By APOSTOLIC CONSTITUTION, the HOLY SEE detached jurisdiction of the southern and western counties of Elko, Lander, Eureka, White Pine, Nye, Lincoln, and Clark from Utah to create the new Diocese of RENO. For the first time the boundaries of the Diocese of Salt Lake coincided with the boundaries of the state of Utah.

Upon young Father Scanlan's arrival, ninety Catholics lived in Salt Lake and Ogden combined. His extensive travels throughout his parish on horseback, by stagecoach, and later by rail took on a mantle of heroism. Slowly developing into the quintessential frontier priest, he built churches and schools in Ogden, Silver Reef, Park City, and Eureka. In later years he founded a parish in Bingham Canyon, one in Tooele, and one in Helper, Carbon County. He opened three parishes in Salt Lake City as well as Kearns-St. Ann Orphanage and Judge Mercy Hospital there. A skillful and compassionate diplomat, he focused on the spiritual needs of his growing congregation and did not join those who fervently denounced the Mormon practice of polygamy. Each of Bishop Scanlan's successor bishops in the Salt Lake City diocese has maintained a peaceful coexistence with the Mormon Church.

Named vicar bishop in 1886, Father Scanlan was appointed bishop of the newly created Diocese of Salt Lake in 1891. Having purchased the property in 1890, he laid the CATHEDRAL cornerstone on July 23, 1900. Cardinal James GIBBONS came from New York on August 15, 1909, to dedicate the great structure drawn out of the wilderness by Bishop Scanlan and his flock. When Bishop Scanlan died in 1915, he was buried in a tomb beneath the high altar of his cathedral. Except for minor alterations, the sturdy exterior shell of the cathedral stands almost exactly as he constructed it, though he left the interior with minimal decoration. In

Cathedral of the Madeleine in Salt Lake City. Father El-liott performs Holy Mass as the Pope's health continues to fail on April 1, 2005, at the cathedral. AP IMAGES

an interior renovation of 1920, Bishop Joseph S. Glass (1915–1926), successor to Bishop Scanlan, brought artists, woodcarvers, and muralists from throughout the United States to create a magnificent interior and renamed the church the Cathedral of the Madeleine. Seventy years later in 1994 Bishop William K. Weigand (1980–1993), seventh diocesan bishop, directed a stunning restoration of the entire Bishop Glass interior in centennial celebration of the founding of the diocese in 1891. The restoration generated fresh vitality into the cathedral's existing Good Samaritan program for the poor and established the first annual Madeleine Festival of the Arts and Humanities, an ongoing service to the intellectual and artistic life of the civic community. The renowned elementary Madeleine Choir School, founded in the cathedral basement in 1990, continues its unique academic program with specialization in the disciplines of music and LITURGY on a spacious campus across First Avenue from the cathedral. The children have sung in ROME before Pope JOHN PAUL II, and with the Utah Symphony and the Tabernacle Choir, bringing recognition to the Church's patrimony of sacred music. The Cathedral of the Madeleine remains a cultural center as well as a place of WORSHIP, honored as a historical treasure by people of all faiths in Utah.

Religious Men and Women. Whenever possible Archbishop Alemany sent priests to assist Father Scanlan and his lifelong associate, Father Denis Kiely, as they ministered to their extensive flock. By 1900 the national Wiltzius Directory reported sixteen priests assigned to the diocese, ten of them secular and six in religious orders. Rural Catholic families in outlying areas gathered to welcome the occasional visiting priest into their homes. Though often exhausted after long and perilous travel, these priests would celebrated Mass and brought sacramental ministry. Isolated stations, seldom visited by priests, gradually developed into larger communities called missions that, as the population increased, became parishes. The ranks of priests caring for the growing Utah church were gradually bolstered by native Utah priests, priests incardinated from other dioceses, and men in religious orders. The MARIST FATHERS administered All Hallows College in Salt Lake City from 1889 to 1918. Paulist Fathers from Scarsdale, New York, served in diocesan parishes beignning in 1938 and in later years at St. Paul Chapel in downtown Salt Lake City until 1988. BLESSED SACRAMENT FATHERS cared for parishes from 1981 to 2002. DOMINICANS, JESUITS, OBLATES OF ST. FRANCIS DE SALES, and Apostolic Life Community Priests from Tanzania are among religious order priest active in the Catholic community in 2008. According to the 2008–2009 diocesan directory published by the Diocese of Salt Lake City, they number 80 priests caring for 50 parishes and 18 missions. In 1947 Bishop Duane G. Hunt (1937–1960), fifth diocesan bishop, invited the Trappist monks of Gethsemani, Kentucky, to settle in Huntsvillle, Utah, where they remain.

The permanent diaconate further encouraged and assisted the clergy. Bishop Joseph Lennox Federal (1960–1980), successor to Bishop Hunt, had attended the Second Vatican Council of 1962 through 1965 in Rome, the historic assemblage that brought liturgical renewal to the universal Catholic Church. In the Salt Lake diocese Bishop Federal implemented the norms recommended by the council and in 1974 established the permanent diaconate. He initiated a curriculum of extensive training for deacons and their wives and ordained the first class of deacons on December 26, 1976. By 2008 forty ordained deacons and their wives enriched many parishes, missions, and stations to which they had been assigned.

As dedicated nurses, educators, missionaries, administrators, and contemplatives the sisters of various orders complement and supplement the work of the clergy. The first two sisters arrived in 1875 from the Congregation of the Sisters of the HOLY CROSS at St. Mary, Indiana, in response to Father Scanlan's request of Father Edward Sorin, founder of Notre Dame University and director general of the American Sisters of the Holy Cross. During the Bishop Scanlan era more than sixty Holy Cross Sisters followed to assist in building the schools, hospitals, and orphanages in the early Church in Utah. Records in the sisters' archives name 1,374 different Holy Cross sisters who served in this diocese over the past 132 years. Their Holy Cross Hospital established in 1875 provided 118 years of health care to patients of all faiths. When it was sold in 1994, the sisters created Holy Cross Ministries to accelerate their broadened service to the poor, refugees, and immigrants. Likewise in 1943 the Benedictine Sisters of St. Joseph, Minnesota, arrived in Ogden to administer St. Benedict Hospital for the next fifty-one years, at which time the hospital was sold. Some of the sisters then returned to the newly named Ogden Regional Medical Center, whereas others supported the extensive charitable programs of the St. Benedict Foundation. In 1999 the ORDER formed an independent PRIORY in Ogden at Mount Benedict Monastery. Bishop Hunt invited the Sisters of Charity of the INCARNATE WORD to open St. Joseph Villa in 1947 for the elderly and infirm, where they continue today to provide excellent elder care in Utah. In 1952 Bishop Hunt brought to Salt Lake City the CARMELITE SISTERS, who live cloistered lives committed to contemplative PRAYER. Franciscan Sisters of Atonement came in 1946 from Graymoor, New York, for education and parish work and maintain a presence still at West Jordan. Similarly, the Daughters of Charity taught schools in the

Cathedral of the Madeleine in Salt Lake City. *The original construction of the cathedral was completed in 1909, but the building was substantially renovated and rededicated in 1993.* CATHEDRAL OF THE MADELEINE

diocese beginning in 1926 and remain associated with the care of children and families. OUR LADY OF VICTORY MISSIONARY SISTERS from Victory Noll, Indiana, undertook over fifty years of missionary and ethnic ministries throughout the diocese beginning in 1939. This ongoing procession of religious orders of women through the years strengthens and supports the Catholic FAITH of Utah.

Laity. The early Catholic community formed a casual collection of miners, railroad men, merchants, farmers, shopkeepers, and their families. Included here were soldiers at Fort Douglas military encampment east of Salt Lake City. The names of some few who struck it rich in the mines are preserved at the base of STAINED GLASS windows in the Cathedral of the Madeleine and other parish churches or schools—Judge Memorial School (originally constructed in 1910 and occupied as a hospital), Cosgriff Memorial Elementary School, 1957, and the beautifully restored Kearns-St. Ann School (built in 1900 as an orphanage). Gradually, the wealthy, middle class, and poor blended in a cohesive pioneer community, all united in the universal Church of their ancient faith. In 1935 José Prudenzio Gonzales exemplified that faith when he and his Hispanic neighbors in the remote agricultural community of Monticello, San Juan County, built St. Joseph Church by hand, out of large coal cinders discarded by the nearby industrial ovens. Modern representatives of that same faith are Lady Irene Sweeney along with Sam and Aline Skaggs and their family, generous benefactors who reflect the spirit of Christian CHARITY.

The *Intermountain Catholic* was an offshoot of the former *Colorado Catholic*. The Utah newspaper started in October 1899 to improve communication between clergy and laity and to report on diocesan organizations and events. Its pages recount how thirty-seven men became charter members in 1901 of Council 602 of the KNIGHTS OF COLUMBUS, the first council west of the Rockies. The Catholic Womans League and the Diocesan Council of Catholic Women first met in 1916 and 1928 respectively, both with spiritual and civic goals that actively endure. The League of the Sacred Heart (1899) and the LEGION OF MARY (1939) function regularly. St. Jude Parish, Maronite Rite for Lebanese Catholics (1972), the Ancient Order of Hibernians, the Guadalupana Society, the Basque Club, and the Italian American Civic League express the growing cultural diversity of Utah. Catholic Community Services represents one of the most vital diocesan organizations. Formally founded by Bishop Hunt as Catholic Charities in 1945, the organization continues to serve needy persons, irrespective of race or creed. Its early services of family assistance, adoptions, foster care, and small monetary allotments for transients expanded over the years. Renamed Catholic Community Services in 1981, the program added St. Vincent de Paul Dining Room in 1987 and Weigand Day Center, dedicated in 1996 by Bishop George Niederauer (b. 1936; 1994–2005), eighth bishop of the diocese. Housing for the homeless and children was made available, along with substance abuse treatment programs, refugee resettlement, and immigration services, including legal aid, all of which receive unprecedented interfaith support, including that from the Mormon Church. On July 12, 2007, Bishop John C. Wester (1950–) blessed the new complex in downtown Salt Lake City, where many of these services are centered.

After 1990 Hispanic immigration gradually escalated so that the population of the diocese approached 300,000 in 2008. While in some areas of the country, churches were closed and expansion put on hold, in Utah new parishes, schools, and missions were opened. Areas once known only as Mormon enclaves now have Catholic missions or churches. In 2006 the parish of St. Andrew opened in Riverton to serve South Jordan, Daybreak, and the surrounding communities. The AL-SAM Foundation of Sam and Aline Skaggs provided funds for the St. Andrew Parish school. The Skaggs family also made possible the Skaggs Catholic Center in Draper, Utah, where Juan Diego Catholic High School, one of the finest schools in the United States, was dedicated in 1999. St. John the Baptist Parish and Middle and Elementary Schools, with state-of-the-art labs, libraries, technology centers, and athletic facilities also opened in the Skaggs Center that year. The Skaggs have contributed to expansion and renovation of other diocesan schools, and have provided scholarship funding to ensure the presence of minority and poor youngsters in Catholic schools.

The diocese continually expands. In Provo, Utah, a burgeoning congregation had long overgrown its deteriorated 1936 building. In 2003 the parish moved to a larger site in nearby Orem, where some 2,000 parishioners, many of whom are Hispanic, built an expansive parish center to serve until a new church can be constructed. In northern Utah at Tremonton, a major addition made in 2007 enlarged Santa Ana Mission in Brigham City, cared for by St. Henry Parish. St. Thomas Aquinas Church and parish center were constructed in 2006 at a new location in Hyde Park on the outskirts of Logan to replace the outgrown 1957 facility. In 2004 the declining population in Richfield, Utah, required moving St. Elizabeth Parish from its original 1947 site to a more heavily populated location in Central Valley, Utah.

When the Olympic Winter Games arrived in February 2002, President George Bush came to Salt Lake City to address a gathering of world heads of state. Monsignors Robert J. Bussen and J. Terrence Fitzgerald, chosen from among nine hundred outstanding citizens, served as torchbearers in the 2002 Olympic Torch Relay and carried the Olympic flame in metropolitan Salt Lake City. But the highlight of the decade came on March 14, 2007, when Bishop John C. Wester, appointed by Pope BENEDICT XVI as ninth diocesan bishop, was installed in the Cathedral of the Madeleine. The new bishop was enthusiastically welcomed throughout the diocese. In November 2007, Bishop Wester was named chairman of the UNITED STATES CONFERENCE OF CATHOLIC BISHOPS (USCCB) Committee on Migration and often writes and speaks on this issue.

SEE ALSO CATHOLIC CHARITIES USA; CONTEMPLATIVE LIFE; MONK; NEVADA, CATHOLIC CHURCH IN; PAULISTS; TRAPPISTS; VATICAN COUNCIL II.

BIBLIOGRAPHY

Robert Joseph Dwyer, *The Gentile Comes to Utah: A Study in*

Religious and Social Conflict, 1862–1890 (Washington, D.C. 1941).

Diocese of Salt Lake City, *Directory, Catholic Diocese of Salt Lake City* (Salt Lake City 2008–2009).

J. Terrence Fitzgerald, P.A., *The Sisters of the Holy Cross in Utah, 1875–2008: Paper Presented at Holy Cross History Association Conference, 2008* (Salt Lake City, 2008).

J. Terrence Fitzgerald and Bernice Maher Mooney, *Catholic Utah at the Turn of the Century, 1988–2002* (Salt Lake City 2003).

Anne M. Butler
Editor, *Western Historical Quarterly*
Trustee Professor of History, Utah State University
Logan, Ut.

Msgr. J. Terrence Fitzgerald PA
Vicar General
Diocese of Salt Lake City, Ut. (2009)

Bernice Maher Mooney
Archivist Emeritus
Diocese of Salt Lake City, Ut. (2009)

V

VERMONT, CATHOLIC CHURCH IN

The history of Catholicism in Vermont began in July 1609 with the arrival of Samuel de Champlain, who named the land for its green mountains (*Voilà les monts verts!*). The Church developed slowly, through three phases. The early period of evangelization and missionary activity planted the seed and set down roots. Catholicism in Vermont came of age with the establishment of the DIOCESE of Burlington in 1853. The third, contemporary, phase began after about 1965 with efforts to implement the renewal of VATICAN COUNCIL II.

Evangelization and Missionary Activity. The year before Champlain arrived in Vermont, the explorer had engaged the Society of Jesus to evangelize the Native Americans in the new lands, but the JESUITS did not arrive until the year after his death. One of them was St. Isaac Jogues (1607–1646), who passed through Vermont on at least four journeys between New York and Quebec in the years before his martyrdom. Among his stops as a captive was a little island on Lake Champlain where he was tortured and where later Jesuit missionaries offered Mass.

Before Sieur de La Motte constructed a fort on the island that bears his name, Jesuit Simon Le Moyne crossed through Vermont on a diplomatic journey between Quebec and New York in September 1654, and Pierre Raffeix stopped at the Shrine of St. Anne on the Isle La Motte in May 1666. Charles Albanel joined Raffeix there in September of that year in hearing confessions and saying Mass. And in the summer of 1667, Jesuits Jacques Bruyas, Jacques Frémin (1628–1691), and Jean Pierron ministered to some 300 soldiers on the island near the time of the Feast of St. Anne. Of these, Frémin, famous for converting 10,000 Native Americans, was among the founders of the Isle La Motte.

During this time, Vermont was under the jurisdiction of Blessed François de Montmorency LAVAL (1623–1708), vicar apostolic to New France, who had arrived in North America in the summer of 1659. In 1668, before he became the bishop of Quebec (1674), Laval was the first prelate to visit the Shrine of St. Anne. The apostolate among the Native Americans in Laval's diocese was appointed to the Jesuits.

A letter written by Jesuit Jean Pierron on October 10, 1682, provides evidence that Jesuits cared for the Abenakis at their various missions. They crisscrossed Vermont to help the Native Americans before the fall of Quebec in 1763 and until the suppression of the Society of Jesus in 1773. The association of the Jesuits with the Abenakis was known to New Englanders who raided their mission site on the Connecticut River. The Jesuit church on the St. Francis River in Canada was desecrated by Rogers Rangers in 1759. In 1816 a farmer in West Charleston, Vermont, discovered its candelabra, and about 1838 another Vermonter recovered, near the mouth of Lake Magog, a gilded image taken from that church.

On September 26, 1992, the Order of Alhambra—a Catholic fraternal organization that had caravans at Rutland in 1912 and at Burlington in 1946 and was devoted to marking historical sites—dedicated a plaque at Our Lady of Perpetual Help Church in Bradford to commemorate the old mission at Koes, near what is now Newbury, which was destroyed early in the eighteenth century.

Thereafter, missionary activities centered at what is now Swanton, where the Jesuits had constructed their first church in Vermont. When the state celebrated its tercentenary, the people of Swanton dedicated a large

St. Anne's Shrine in Isle La Motte, Vermont. *Vermont's only Roman Catholic shrine, it was the location of the state's first Catholic Mass, held there in 1666. In this photo Lake Champlain can be seen behind one of the Stations of the Cross.* AP IMAGES

granite shaft commemorating the site of that church on Missisquoi Bay. Peter Kalm, a Swiss naturalist, provided further evidence when, just before the mid-eighteenth century, he found the Jesuits in areas now known as Alburg, Chimney Point, and Ferrisburg. Through such contacts, the Jesuits taught the Abenakis the essentials of religion and of European culture.

John Carroll. When John Carroll (1736–1815), who had visited Vermont in 1776, became the first American bishop in 1789, a Catholic community of French Canadians was flourishing. Like other New England states, Vermont discriminated against Catholics, but it repealed these measures in 1793. Although Vermont was the only state in New England that Carroll did not visit as its bishop, he was influential in placing it in the new Diocese of Boston, established in 1808.

Jean Lefebvre de Cheverus. Jean Louis Lefebvre de CHEVERUS (1768–1836), first bishop of Boston, who visited Vermont only on a trip to Montreal in 1821, left the care of Vermonters to the bishop of Quebec. When

Quebec was elevated to an archiepiscopal see in 1815, Joseph-Octave PLESSIS (1763–1825), the great-grandson of Thomas French, a DEACON of the Congregational Church in colonial Deerfield, Massachusetts, was instrumental in having Father François-Antoine MATIGNON (1753–1818), a Boston priest, set up a mission in Burlington, with its 100 Catholics, in 1815.

Some remarkable converts to Catholicism emerged during the nineteenth century. In 1807, Frances "Fanny" Margaret ALLEN (1784–1819), daughter of hero Ethan Allen, became a Catholic and later the first woman of Vermont to become a nun. In 1818, Daniel Barber (1756–1834), an Episcopal minister who served Vermont from the border area of Claremont, New Hampshire, was accepted into the Catholic Church by Cheverus. Later, Barber's son, Virgil (1782–1847), who had converted in 1816 and was ordained a Jesuit priest on December 3, 1822, established the first Catholic church and school near the site of his father's former church. One of its students was William B. Tyler (1806–1849), a native of Derby, who became the first Catholic bishop of Hartford, Connecticut, in 1844.

Benedict Joseph Fenwick. Benedict Joseph Fenwick (1782–1846), to whom Virgil Barber had brought his reservations about his FAITH, became the bishop of Boston in 1825. On Barber's suggestion, the bishop climbed Mount Ascutney on June 5, 1826, in search of an appropriate site for a college, but Fenwick did not find it suitable. Although Barber won converts, the English-speaking Catholics of Vermont had no resident priest when he left Claremont in 1828. The faithful had to depend on James FITTON (1805–1881), renowned in New England, until Fenwick sent Jeremiah O'CALLAGHAN (d. 1861), a priest from county Kerry in Ireland, to Burlington as its first resident priest in 1830. With Bennington and Middlebury, Burlington, which numbered about a thousand Catholics, was one of three largest Catholic cities in the state.

Jeremiah O'Callaghan. Under O'Callaghan, called the Apostle of Vermont, the Church grew for 25 years. When Fenwick dedicated St. Mary's in Burlington, on September 9, 1832, it was the city's first Catholic church. It was built on land donated by Colonel Archibald W. Hyde (1786–1847), a Protestant who eventually became a Catholic. Meanwhile, O'Callaghan had expanded the Church into other areas, such as Vergennes, where the home of Mrs. Daniel Nichols (Mary Ann Booth) was the center of Catholic worship and where both Fenwick and O'Callaghan offered Mass. St. Peter's, the church later constructed in that town, did not open until 1854.

Like other Catholic priests in New England, O'Callaghan encountered anti–Catholics, who set fire to

St. Mary's in Burlington on May 9, 1838. The church was destroyed, but worship continued. On October 31, 1841, Fenwick dedicated a new church, St. Peter's, on the corner of Cherry and St. Paul streets. Before two more years passed, Catholics in Vermont numbered close to 5,000; the district covering Swanton, St. Albans, and Fairfield had a total of about 2,000 Catholics when Fenwick went there for confirmations with his brother, George, on October 5, 1841. In Swanton, a brick church constructed on land donated by James McNally was completed in 1847. O'Callaghan's efforts led to the expansion of Catholicism into Bennington, Montpelier, Rutland, and Shelburne.

In addition to O'Callaghan, John B. Daly (d. 1870), a Franciscan who became famous as the president of the Catholic Total Abstinence Society in Vermont, served the Church. In 1837, Daly was appointed resident priest in the area of Rutland and Middlebury to lighten O'Callaghan's burdens in the lower half of the state. Although Fitton had visited the Castleton area in 1828, Fenwick did not open a church there until 1836, in what became the parish of St. John the Baptist, with about 150 Catholics. Daly opened a church in Middlebury in 1840; it was later called Assumption Parish.

Perhaps the most famous convert in Vermont's history was Orestes Augustus BROWNSON (1803–1876), a native of Stockbridge. Moving from one set of beliefs to another, he had also served as a Universalist minister in Rutland, Windsor, and Windham. It was to John B. Fitzpatrick (1812–1866), his coadjutor, that Bishop Fenwick entrusted Brownson for instructions in the Catholic faith. This intellectual ended his religious wanderings by becoming a Catholic on October 20, 1844.

John B. Fitzpatrick. At Bellows Falls, Fitzpatrick, a faithful successor to Fenwick, faced hostility against Catholics when Methodists refused them the use of their church. Accompanied by Jesuits George Fenwick and Samuel A. Mulledy, the bishop settled for a pine grove on the west side of town, where he conducted a confirmation ceremony on September 4, 1846, with a thousand people, including some Protestants who witnessed the episcopal visitation.

During Fitzpatrick's time, the first Mass was offered in Brattleboro, on August 15, 1848. This took place when Father Joseph Coolidge Shaw (1821–1851), a Jesuit priest who came from a prominent Boston family, was spending time in the area taking the water cure for his troubled leg. While the medicinal baths were producing their healing effects, Shaw offered Mass in a place called the Wood Farm, where Catholics later built a shed for Sunday Mass.

Under Fitzpatrick, two parishes were established in Vermont: Immaculate Conception in St. Albans in 1847 and St. Augustine's in Montpelier in 1850. General De-

witt Clinton Clarke (1812–1870), a convert and a state legislator, left the senate to attend Mass at St. Augustine's. His letter of November 3, 1850, is the first record of Mass there. In Fitzpatrick's first year as bishop of Boston, William Henry Hoyt (1813–1883), an Episcopal minister, converted to Catholicism and eventually became a Catholic priest. Around this time, Francis Patrick KENRICK (1797–1863), Catholic archbishop of Baltimore, was vindicating the Catholic faith against Vermont's Episcopal bishop John Henry Hopkins, Sr. (1792–1868).

Given the proximity of French-speaking Catholics in Vermont to Canada, Fenwick had entrusted them to the care of Abbé Pierre-Marie Mignault (1784–1868) from Chambly, Canada. Mignault, who was memorialized in the old parish of Notre Dame des Victoires in St. Johnsbury, ministered to those parishioners from the early 1820s until a new see was established at Burlington on July 29, 1853.

Establishment of the Diocese of Burlington. Catholicism in Vermont had come of age with the appointment of Louis De GOESBRIAND (1816–1899) as the first bishop of Burlington. A native of Saint-Urbain, France, he had been the vicar general in the Diocese of Cleveland, Ohio, and began his new diocese with about 20,000 Catholics, 10 churches, and 5 priests. Following De Goesbriand's installation, priests from Ireland and France were accepted into the diocese, so there were at least 50 priests by the end of his episcopate. They helped to expand De Goesbriand's diocese with at least 30 new parishes as Catholics continued to come to the state to build its public works, construct its railroads, excavate its quarries, till its farmlands, and operate its factories.

In 1890, the Catholic population numbered 45,000, of which at least 33,000 were of French-Canadian background. Some of the increase was due to conversions like those, before the Civil War, of the three daughters (Helen, Debbie, and Anna) of Bradley Barlow (1814–1889), one of the most prominent citizens in St. Albans. Yet the growth was due more to the foreign-speaking Catholics for whom De Goesbriand, not unlike other Catholic bishops, opened up more national parishes in addition to St. Joseph's in Burlington, which dates to 1850 and is today the oldest Franco-American parish in New England.

When Bishop De Goesbriand died on November 23, 1899, he was the oldest American bishop and had participated in the councils of Baltimore and in VATICAN COUNCIL I. With his retirement in 1893 to the orphanage that the Sisters of Charity had opened in 1854, his diocese came under John Stephen Michaud (1843–1908).

John Stephen Michaud. A native of Vermont and of Canadian and Irish ancestry, Michaud reflected the ethnic composition of the majority of the Catholic population and became the first Catholic bishop to receive an honorary degree from the University of Vermont.

The diocese had grown to almost a hundred parishes and missions under Michaud, with an equal number of priests, diocesan and religious. In 1898, the KNIGHTS OF COLUMBUS founded their first council in the state with Bennington Council No. 307, and in 1899 Michaud welcomed to Vermont the Society of St. Edmund, which opened St. Michael's College in Winooski in 1904. Of his achievements, the establishment of Fanny Allen Hospital at Winooski Park was important in showing the strength of Catholic social action in Vermont.

Beyond Native Americans, Canadian Americans, and Irish Americans, Catholicism grew because of other immigrants who came to Vermont near the turn of the century. If they did not come to work on the railroads or farmlands, they were in the quarries and or the woolen mills of the state. The Italians, coming in the last decade of the nineteenth century, were concentrated around Barre, where carvers and stonecutters helped to increase the granite and marble industry. Polish immigrants at the beginning of the twentieth century settled around West Rutland, where, in November 1904, they started the Church of St. Stanislaus KOSTKA under the leadership of Father Valentin Michulka (d. 1969), their pastor for more than a half century.

Joseph J. Rice. A native of Leicester, Massachusetts, Joseph J. Rice (1871–1938) was ordained as the third bishop of Burlington on April 14, 1910. While caring for the diocese, he was responsible for De Goesbriand Memorial Hospital, which Rice placed under the Religious Hospitalers of St. Joseph in 1923. Rice showed himself a leader in education by opening three high schools and by welcoming the Sisters of Mercy, who opened Trinity College in 1925. At that time bigotry manifested itself in Montpelier when, on November 21, 1925, the KU KLUX KLAN burned a cross on the steps of St. Augustine's Church.

Matthew F. Brady. Rice's successor in 1938 was Matthew Francis BRADY (1893–1959), a native of Waterbury, Connecticut, who strengthened the substructure of the diocese. Interested in the young people, he organized branches of the Boy Scouts and the Catholic Youth. His tenure also saw the construction of about a dozen new churches, at least half in such towns as Fairfax, Gilman, North Troy, Orleans, and South Burlington, which had never had such parishes.

Edward F. Ryan. With Bishop Brady's transfer to Manchester in 1944, Ryan (1879–1956), a native of Lynn, Massachusetts, became Burlington's fifth Catholic bishop in 1945, having served as a chaplain in World War II. Noteworthy during his tenure were the establishment of the first Carthusian monastery in the United States near Whitingham (later at Arlington) in 1951; the Benedictine Priory at Weston in 1953; and the College of St. Joseph the Provider by the Sisters of St. Joseph, in Rutland in 1954. Responsible for almost two dozen new churches, Ryan also raised the people's consciousness of the importance of the Catholic press, especially by giving the diocese its own weekly newspaper, the *Vermont Catholic Tribune*, in 1956. He showed the Church's ongoing concern for the welfare of the youth by providing a camp and a school for boys in the Burlington area.

Ryan also established Blessed Sacrament Church in Stowe. A native son of Stowe, Joseph Brother DUTTON (1843–1931), who converted to Catholicism in 1883 after serving in the Civil War, spent the rest of his life as a Sacred Hearts Brother, carrying on the work of Father Damien (1840–1889), known as the Apostle of Molokai. More famous was Maria von Trapp (1905–1987), whose life inspired the film *The Sound of Music* in 1959. She made Stowe a tourist attraction with the 800–acre farm the Trapp Family purchased as a music camp in 1942.

Renewal and Reaction to the Second Vatican Council. Robert F. Joyce (1896–1990), a native of Proctor who succeeded Ryan in 1957, directed the renewal of the Catholic Church in an era inaugurated by VATICAN COUNCIL II in 1962. A model for him in handling the reforms was Bernard J. Flanagan (1908–1998), also a native of Proctor, and the second bishop of Worcester (1959–1983) in Massachusetts. In 1958, Bishop Joyce completed Rice Memorial High School, begun by his predecessor and, in the next year, he set up Our Lady of Fatima in Wilmington, a parish that serves the ski area of Mount Snow. By sponsoring the PAPAL VOLUNTEERS FOR LATIN AMERICA and reorganizing services for teaching religion and for children with disabilities, the Catholic Church was reaching out under Joyce. Indicative of the maturity of Catholicism was the elevation of Walter H. Cleary of Newport as the state's chief justice, in 1958.

John A. Marshall. A native of Worcester, Massachusetts, John A. Marshall (1928–1994) was the state's seventh Catholic bishop, from 1971 to 1991, before he was transferred to Springfield, Massachusetts. Coming to grips with new problems that confronted bishops after the Second Vatican Council, the Church was forced to undergo retrenchment with a loss of vocations and the decline in church attendance. Consequently, the only parish founded was that of Our Lady of the Mountains in Shelburne in 1979. Paradoxically, the public face of Catholicism became more evident during Marshall's tenure. Thomas P. Salmon became the first Catholic to be elected governor of Vermont in 1972, and, two years later, Patrick Leahy became the first Catholic to be elected a U.S. senator. But this coming-of-age of Catholics was not without its problems. A more active laity dealt with moral issues, as in the concern raised by CATHOLICS FOR A FREE CHOICE, chartered in 1989, with their first issue of the newsletter *Pro Conscience* published in Middlebury.

Kenneth A. Angell. On November 9, 1992, Kenneth A. Angell (b. 1930), a native of Providence, Rhode Island, was installed as Burlington's eighth bishop. Having served for almost twenty years as an auxiliary bishop in Providence, he was familiar with the workings of a diocese and encountered challenges in the lack of priests and the decline of attendance. These challenges forced a consolidation of such parishes as Sacred Heart and St. Francis de Sales in Bennington, as well as St. Cecilia and St. Frances Cabrini in Washington. Our Lady of the Lake in St. Albans was closed. For St. Francis de Sales, which began in 1830 and had a Gothic church constructed from the stone of Vermont's native quarries dating to 1889, the change was not easy.

Although his problems concerning the relation of the political order to the moral order were no different from those of most New England bishops, Angell was the first to cope with state legislation that, on July 1, 2000, created civil unions, which extended the benefits, protections, and responsibilities of marriage to same-gender couples.

As the horror of September 11, 2001, unfolded, Bishop Angell learned that his younger brother David and his wife, Lynn, were among the nearly 3,000 victims of the terrorist attacks on America. Bishop Angell offered Mass on September 13 and asked all those assembled to pray for the victims, the nation, and the perpetrators.

By 2004, there were six priests under the age of 40 ministering in the diocese. Bishop Angell implemented a process by which parish representatives would work and pray together to identify the needs of their communities, evaluate the vitality of the parish, and offer solutions to the crisis.

Salvatore R. Matano. On March 3, 2005, it was announced at the Apostolic Nunciature in Washington, D.C., that a member of the staff, Msgr. Salvatore R. Matano (1946–), had been named coadjutor bishop of the Roman Catholic Diocese of Burlington by Pope JOHN PAUL II (a coadjutor bishop has the right of succession). Ordained to the priesthood on December 17, 1971, the Rhode Island native had served in Washington, D.C., at the Apostolic Nunciature from 1991 to 1992. He returned to the Providence Diocese to become vicar general and Moderator of the Curia in 1992, resuming his post at the Apostolic Nunciature in Washington in 2000.

Ordained to the Episcopacy on April 19, 2005, Matano became the ninth bishop of Burlington on November 9, 2005, on the retirement of Bishop Angell. Focusing immediately on the pastoral needs of his parishioners, Bishop Matano promulgated a diocesan pastoral plan to address the reduced number of priests available to lead parish life and to administer the Sacraments. The bishop sought priestly assistance from religious orders and other dioceses. Bishop Matano undertook initiatives relative to the sacramental life of the diocese, Catholic schools, religious education programs, Level III health care facilities, and the care of temporalities.

Like dioceses throughout the United States during this time, the Diocese of Burlington was confronted with addressing past incidents of clerical misconduct—some accusations over forty years old. The diocese sought to attain justice and reconciliation for victims while being responsible to all Vermont Catholics, as well as to establish safe environments for all people.

The state population in 2008 was recorded at 620,000 residents, with 118,000 being Roman Catholic. The Diocese of Burlington recorded 91 active religious and diocesan priests, 46 permanent deacons, and 153 sisters ministering in 80 parishes and 44 missions. The diocese included 12 elementary schools, 2 high schools, and a catechetical system with an estimated 1,100 lay teachers instructing almost 11,000 students. With its special centers for social services and homes for the aged, the Diocese of Burlington assisted almost 10,302 Vermonters in 2008 (*The Official Catholic Directory* 2008, p. 210).

Under the leadership of Bishop Matano, the Diocese of Burlington focused on educating Catholics about the teachings of the faith. It also worked to cultivate vocations to the priesthood and religious life and to strengthen lay leadership through a Lay Apostolate Formation Program. Through these efforts the diocese ensured a solid foundation for the future and sought to meet the spiritual, pastoral, and sacramental needs of a people of deep faith, whose love for God, His Church, and their sisters and brothers in the Lord has been and always will be a beacon of hope in the Green Mountain State.

SEE ALSO BENEDICTINE ABBEYS AND PRIORIES IN THE U.S.; CARTHUSIANS; NUNCIO, APOSTOLIC.

BIBLIOGRAPHY

J. N. Couture, *The Catholic Clergy of Vermont* [typewritten manuscript] (St. Michael's College, Winooski, Vt. 1964).

Vincent A. Lapomarda, *The Jesuit Heritage in New England* (Worcester, Mass. 1977).

William L. Lucey, "The Diocese of Burlington, Vermont," *Records of the American Catholic Historical Society of Philadelphia* 64, no. 3 (September 1953): 123–154, and no. 4 (December 1953): 213–235.

V. B. Maloney and J. K. Durick, eds., *1853–1953: One Hundred Years of Achievement by the Catholic Church in the Diocese of Burlington, Vermont* (Lowell, Mass. 1953).

J. S. Michaud, "The Diocese of Burlington," in W. Byrne et al., *History of the Catholic Church in the New England States*, 2 vols. (Boston 1899), 2:465–587.

Maudean Neill, *Fiery Crosses in the Green Mountains: The Story of the Ku Klux Klan in Vermont* (Randolph Center, Vt. 1989).

The Official Catholic Directory, 2008 (New Providence, N.J. 2008).

Francis Xavier Talbot, *Saint among Savages: The Life of Isaac Jogues* (New York 1935).

Rev. Vincent Anthony Lapomarda SJ
Coordinator, Holocaust Collection
Department of History
College of the Holy Cross, Worcester, Mass.

Patricia Gore
Editor, *Vermont Catholic Tribune*
Burlington, Vt. (2009)

Rev. John J. McDermott JCL
Chancellor and Moderator of the Curia
Diocese of Burlington, Burlington, Vt. (2009)

VIRGINIA, CATHOLIC CHURCH IN

The first of the thirteen colonies and one of the four commonwealths in the United States, Virginia is bordered on the north by Maryland and West Virginia, on the south by North Carolina and Tennessee, on the east by Maryland and the Atlantic Ocean, and on the west by Kentucky and West Virginia. Richmond is the capital and Norfolk the largest city. The two Catholic dioceses in Virginia, Richmond (1820) and Arlington (1974), are suffragan of the Archdiocese of BALTIMORE.

Early History. Colonial Virginia was not a friendly place for Catholics. In 1570 eight Spanish JESUITS from Florida established a mission near the future Jamestown, but were betrayed by their Native American guide and massacred. When the Virginia colony was founded at Jamestown in 1607, its charter from James I stated: "We should be loath that any person should be permitted to pass, that we suspected to affect the superstitions of the Church of Rome" (Hening 1823, vol. 1, pp. 268–269). Nominally, the Church of England was officially established. In 1634 hostility toward Catholicism increased with the settlement of Maryland under Catholic auspices. In 1642 Virginia enacted laws banning priests and prohibiting the exercise of Catholicism. Despite these restrictions, in 1651 Giles Brent, a Catholic, and his family, moved from Maryland and settled in Stafford County, between the Potomac and Rappahannaock Rivers. Throughout the colonial period the Brents remained loyal to the Church, and some held public office. Two sisters of John CARROLL, the future BISHOP, married Brents. In 1784 Carroll was named superior of the American mission. In his first report to the Congregation of Propaganda Fide, the missionary arm of the POPE, he stated that "there are not more than 200 [Catholics] in Virginia who are visited four or five times a year by a priest" (Ellis 1986, vol. 1, p. 448).

In 1789 Carroll was named the first bishop of Baltimore with jurisdiction over the entire nation, including Virginia; in 1808 he was named ARCHBISHOP. By the 1790s Catholics had settled in Alexandria, part of the District of Columbia until 1846, and in Norfolk. In 1791 Jean DUBOIS said Mass for a small congregation in Norfolk, but then moved to Richmond where he taught school for more than a year and established friendships with leading Protestants, including Patrick Henry (1736–1799). Once in Richmond, he received a request from Colonel John Fitzgerald, George Washington's aide-de-camp, to say Mass in Alexandria from time to time. While he never visited Alexandria, he did go at Carroll's request to Emmitsburg, Maryland, where he was one of the founders of Mount St. Mary's College before becoming the third bishop of New York. The church in Alexandria was then served—and owned—by former Jesuits, suppressed as an order in 1773 and restored in the United States in 1805.

By 1817 lay TRUSTEEISM had arisen in Norfolk. Though most of the congregation were Irish, a Portuguese physician, Oliviera Fernandez, was their leader. In a series of long, learned, and tedious broadsides, he rejected the authority of Father James Lucas, appointed to Norfolk by Archbishop Leonard NEALE, Carroll's successor, and refused to accept the jurisdiction of Carroll's second successor, the French-born Archbishop Ambrose MARÉCHAL. He argued that the trustees were the heirs to the PATRONATO REAL and that, just as the pope signed a concordat with a king in a MONARCHY allowing him to appoint bishops and pastors, he should sign one with the people in a DEMOCRACY—arguments that could scarcely be persuasive in ROME, which had witnessed the devastating effects on the Church of the

FRENCH REVOLUTION and its form of democracy. Sending a delegation to Rome, Oliviera Fernandez claimed there was no pastor, and then called Thomas Carbry (d. 1829), O.P., to take charge of the church he had built. What exacerbated trusteeism was a Virginia law prohibiting the incorporation of church property, which was therefore held either by lay trustees or by the priest or bishop in his own name—a situation that continued to cause confusion well into the twentieth century.

In 1820, contrary to Maréchal's advice, propaganda established the Diocese of Richmond, which comprised all of Virginia, including the present state of West Virginia, but excluded Alexandria, still subject to the Archdiocese of Baltimore. The first bishop, Patrick Kelly (1779–1829), came from Ireland, but received an icy welcome from Maréchal in Baltimore. In Norfolk, Kelly mollified the trustees, but then removed Father Lucas's faculties. Without ever getting to Richmond, he remained in Norfolk and supported himself by teaching school. After less than a year, he returned to Ireland to become the bishop of Waterford and Lismore. The Diocese of Richmond now fell under the administration of the Archbishop of Baltimore.

In September 1822 Kelly submitted his final report to Propaganda. Out of a total Virginia population of over a million, he wrote, there were about 1,000 Catholics, served by five priests in three principal regions: Norfolk, Richmond, and the northwestern section around Martinsburg and Harpers Ferry. The congregations in each region developed in different ways. Norfolk, a seaport, remained the principal Catholic center as Irish immigrants arrived to work there and in the shipyard at nearby Portsmouth, which soon became a separate parish. For some time, a priest from Norfolk also journeyed to Richmond, where the original Catholic congregation was comprised of several wealthy Frenchmen. One Catholic citizen, Joseph Gallego (d. 1818), left to the congregation a sum of money and land for a church. Because of Virginia laws, the bequest remained in litigation for many years.

The Catholic congregation in Richmond gained stability only with the arrival in 1832 of Father Timothy O'Brien. Determined to make the Catholic presence visible in the city, he built St. Peter's Church, near the capitol. In 1834 he also succeeded in having the Sisters (later named the Daughters) of Charity open St. Joseph's orphanage and, later, a school, the first of numerous institutions the order would staff in Virginia. Richmond lay at the beginning of the James River and Kanawah Canal, which soon drew Irish and later German laborers. O'Brien used the canal to travel to Lynchburg, which had a resident priest by the 1840s. Lynchburg gradually became a center from which priests rode circuit and founded parishes in Wytheville in the west and in Lexington and Staunton in the Shenandoah Valley. Mar-

tinsburg, a small farming town, had a small Catholic congregation by 1794, but it then evolved into first a center for the C&O canal and then for the B&O railroad. It also served as the headquarters for priests riding circuit to Harpers Ferry, Winchester in the northern Shenandoah Valley, and Bath (now Berkeley Springs, West Virginia).

Early Bishops. In 1841 Richard Vincent Whelan (1809–1874), the pastor in Martinsburg, became the second bishop of Richmond. In his see city he opened a short-lived seminary, but, in 1846, he moved to Wheeling, where he unsuccessfully attempted to have the Jesuits open a college. To gain priests for his poor diocese, he begged from other dioceses and then became the first southern bishop to recruit from All Hallows College, outside of Dublin. Irish priests were soon working with Irish immigrant laborers on the railroads, particularly around Harpers Ferry and the Shenandoah Valley.

In 1851 at Whelan's request, the HOLY SEE established the new Diocese of Wheeling for the section of Virginia west of the Allegheny Mountains and transferred Whelan there. John McGill (1809–1872), a priest of Louisville, then became the third bishop of Richmond. Within a week of arriving, he had a dispute with Father O'Brien, who held property in his own name until its debt was paid. After nineteen years of service, O'Brien left Richmond. Unlike the North, Virginia never attracted large numbers of immigrants. Many of the Irish who came to Richmond and Norfolk in the 1830s belonged to the merchant or professional classes. A smaller number of Germans also settled in Richmond, where in 1848 they founded the only strictly national parish in the diocese. Austrian Jesuits, who had fled to the United States from the revolution of 1848, had charge of it until 1860, when BENEDICTINES from Latrobe took over.

In the 1830s and 1840s there were also significant conversions, including the three daughters, wife, and son of Governor John R. Floyd Sr. These converts and the Irish middle class helped gain acceptance for the Church with the Virginia Protestant establishment. During the 1850s, therefore, while the North was wracked with NATIVISM and KNOW-NOTHINGISM, the Church in Virginia was largely spared the tumult, except in the western part of the state and the port areas around Norfolk. In 1855, moreover, Catholics were heroic during the yellow fever epidemic in Norfolk and Portsmouth and won Protestant admiration. Father Matthew O'Keefe of St. Patrick's Church in Norfolk formed a pact with a Protestant minister to remain in the city and, if either died, the other would conduct the funeral. O'Keefe was twice stricken by the fever, but recovered; years later, he did bury his Protestant friend. The DAUGHTERS OF

CHARITY, already operating a school and orphanage in Norfolk, now began nursing the victims. The following year they opened St. Vincent's Hospital (now De Paul Medical Center), the result of a bequest of Anne Behan Plum Herron, a wealthy Irish immigrant who died while nursing the victims. Yet, such Catholic heroism did not completely overcome Protestant prejudice. At midnight on December 7, 1856, arsonists burned O'Keefe's church. O'Keefe made almost weekly trips to the Northeast to raise money for a new church, which was dedicated in 1858 as St. Mary of the Immaculate Conception. In 1991 it was elevated to the rank of a minor BASILICA, the only one in Virginia.

One price of accommodation to the predominantly Protestant culture was that Virginia Catholics, though few were slave owners, opposed abolition. They supported the Confederate cause and many served in the army. Both McGill in Richmond and Whelan in Wheeling supported secession, but, whereas McGill's see city became the capital of the Confederacy, Whelan found himself in the capital of West Virginia which seceded from Virginia. The diocesan boundaries now crossed state lines.

After the war McGill was still plagued with a shortage of priests. To supplement his own clergy diminished by death or departures from the diocese, he recruited from the American College at LOUVAIN. One of his first recruits was Francis Janssens (1843–1897), who, after service in Virginia, was successively bishop of Natchez and archbishop of New Orleans. Another Louvain recruit was Augustine VAN DE VYVER, who became bishop of Richmond and recruited both his nephew and great nephew from Louvain for the diocese. In 1866 Sisters of the Visitation arrived in Richmond from Baltimore to open Monte Maria Monastery and Academy for girls. They later closed the school and later still moved to a more rural location.

As Reconstuction ended in Virginia in 1870, service in the Confederate Army provided the credentials for Catholics to assume prominent positions. In 1870, Anthony J. Keiley, born of Irish parents in New Jersey, but raised in Petersburg, became mayor of Richmond, served for many years as the President of the Irish Catholic Benevolent Union, and later became a judge of the international court in Cairo. James Dooley (1841–1922), son of an Irish merchant in Richmond, served in the state legislature, became a millionaire through railroad and land speculation, and, at his death in 1921, left three million dollars for St. Joseph's Villa to replace the existing orphanage for girls run by the Daughters of Charity in Richmond. Others in high office also had Catholic connections. John W. Johnston (1818–1889) served two terms in the U.S. Senate. His wife, Niketti Floyd, was a convert and their children were all Catholic.

In 1872 McGill died. James GIBBONS, the fourth bishop of Richmond, was a Baltimore native who in 1868 was appointed the first vicar apostolic of North Carolina, jurisdiction over which he and his successor in Richmond retained until 1881. In 1875 Gibbons thwarted the efforts of Bishop John J. Kain (1841–1903) of Wheeling, a Martinsburg native, to have Rome realign the dioceses of Wheeling and Richmond to coincide with the new state lines, for, he said, this would take away the area around Martinsburg, then the most prosperous section of his diocese. Gibbons also initiated work among the freed African Americans, few of whom were Catholic.

In 1877, Gibbons became coadjutor archbishop of Baltimore and was named a CARDINAL in 1886. John J. KEANE, the fifth bishop, was Irish-born, the first foreign-born bishop of Richmond since Kelly, and had served as a pastor in Washington, D.C. Influenced by Isaac HECKER, the founder of the PAULISTS, he sought to nourish the spiritual development of his clergy through semi-annual conferences and monthly regional meetings; he also promoted parish missions for the laity. In the 1880s the southern Shenandoah Valley experienced the greatest Catholic development. In 1882 Roanoke had been founded as a railroad center, but by 1892 it had a school and orphanage staffed by the Sisters of Charity of Nazareth. Moreover, in 1883 the JOSEPHITES opened their first parish for African Americans in Richmond. In 1888 Keane was named the first rector of The CATHOLIC UNIVERSITY OF AMERICA, established by the Third Plenary Council in 1884.

The succession to Keane was fraught with the undertones of ethnic tension characteristic of the American Church elsewhere. Van de Vyver, then the vicar general, was the first choice of both the Richmond priests eligible to nominate and the bishops of the province of Baltimore, but Gibbons sought to gain the appointment of Denis J. O'CONNELL, a priest of Richmond, who had been named rector of the American College in Rome in 1885 and who appeared only on the bishops' list. After Pope LEO III rejected O'Connell's appointment because of his service in Rome, Gibbons and Keane tried to prevent the appointment of van de Vyver, who was, however, named bishop in 1889.

In the 1890s, Gibbons, Keane, and O'Connell, together with Archbishop John IRELAND of St. Paul, took leading roles in the controversies that divided the hierarchy and in the crisis of AMERICANISM, condemned in 1899, but van de Vyver remained aloof and concentrated on the internal development of the diocese. During his episcopate the Josephites expanded their work with African Americans to Norfolk, Lynchburg, and Alexandria. In addition, Louise D. Morrell and her sister, Saint Katherine DREXEL, in 1895 and 1896, respectively, opened high schools for African-American boys and girls

St. Ann's Church. *Pictured is the interior altar on March 10, 1950.* THE LIBRARY OF CONGRESS

at Rock Castle. The diocese also received another major benefaction from Mr. and Mrs. Thomas Fortune Ryan, who built the Cathedral of the Sacred Heart, dedicated in 1906. When van de Vyver died in 1911, O'Connell, then auxiliary BISHOP of San Francisco, was finally named to Richmond.

Twentieth-Century Developments. World War I brought the first major increase in the state Catholic population as the U.S. Navy established the Norfolk Naval Operating Station, and the government located other installations in Northern Virginia. The end of the war temporarily stifled Catholic growth in Virginia, as the United States retreated into isolationism, but these two regions were poised for the growth that followed World War II, when the United States became a superpower. In the early 1920s, however, anti–catholicism also had a resurgence, but the old style of Virginia Catholic accommodation with the political establishment initially held fast. In 1920 O'Connell advised against forming a Catholic Laymen's Association, similar to those in other states, because friendly Protestant legislators had prevented the passage of such bills as CONVENT inspection laws. But in 1924 the KU KLUX KLAN launched a vociferous but unsuccessful campaign

against the reelection of the incumbent state treasurer, John Purcell, a Catholic. In 1925, in what would later be called ecumenism, the Episcopal Diocese of Virginia donated land to the Catholics to build a church at Baileys Crossroads in northern Virginia. But the Al Smith (1873–1944) campaign of 1928 evoked more anti–Catholicism, after which the diocese formed a Laymen's League to defend Catholic rights.

Forced by ill health to resign in 1925, O'Connell died the following year. His successor, Andrew J. Brennan (1877–1956), formerly auxiliary bishop of Scranton, restructured the diocese along the lines of those in the North. The Bureau of Catholic Charities, which had begun in 1922, was expanded. In 1931, St. Joseph's Villa, a model orphanage for girls made possible by Dooley's bequest, opened with a vast display of the Catholic presence in Virginia. Brennan planned the event just before the annual bishops' meeting in Washington, D.C., so as many bishops as possible could attend. But the Depression placed a greater burden on Brennan. In 1934 he suffered a massive stroke that left him unable to speak. In 1935 Peter Leo Ireton (1882–1958), a priest of Baltimore, became coadjutor bishop and, in 1945, succeeded as ordinary when Brennan formally resigned; Brennan died in 1956. While Ireton left much of the diocesan administration to a series of able chancellors, he followed Brennan in modeling his diocese on the larger ones in the North. He actively promoted the Conference of Jews and Christians—later renamed the Conference of Christians and Jews—and established several urban parishes for African Americans. World War II and the postwar years ushered in the period of greatest growth in Catholic population.

In 1936 Ireton reported that the native Virginians moving out of the state far outnumbered those who had moved in. A decade later the situation had changed. Northern Virginia, long a rural outpost of the diocese, rapidly developed into a suburb of Washington, D.C. By 1941 one-sixth of the Virginia Catholic population was in the area, a percentage that would rapidly increase. In the Norfolk area, military expansion and new housing turned Virginia Beach into one of the largest cities in the state. What canals and railroads had been in the nineteenth and early twentieth century, the automobile became in the postwar years. Interstates and highways determined the location of new suburban parishes.

Ireton died in 1958 and was succeeded by John RUSSELL, the bishop of Charleston and a native of Baltimore. Under Russell, the diocese realized a long-time dream and opened St. John Vianney minor seminary in 1961, only to have it close a decade later. In the name of integration, Russell closed many of the African-American parishes Ireton had opened. He actively participated in VATICAN COUNCIL II and immediately sought to implement its decrees. He estab-

Passion Play. *Parishioners from St. Anthony's Roman Catholic Church reenacting the crucifixion of Christ.* KAREN KASMAUSKI/NATIONAL GEOGRAPHIC/GETTY IMAGES

lished an ecumenical commission, the second in the United States, and promoted racial justice. Although only one Virginia priest took part in the March on Selma in 1965, Russell defended the participants. At his retirement in 1973, Walter F. Sullivan (b. 1928), the auxiliary bishop, was appointed administrator. In 1974 Sullivan became the bishop, and, a short time later, the new diocese of Arlington, consisting of twenty-one counties in northern Virginia, was established. Thomas Welch was the first bishop; in 1983 he was transferred to Allentown and was replaced in Arlington by John R. Keating (1934–1998), who died in 1998. In 1999 Paul Loverde (b. 1940), former bishop of Ogdensburg, became the third bishop of Arlington. Those counties of West Virginia that had belonged to the Richmond diocese were transferred to Wheeling, while the counties of southwest Virginia, formerly in Wheeling, and the counties on the Delmarva Peninsula, formerly belonging to the Diocese of Wilmington, were ceded to Richmond. As a result, the dioceses of both Richmond and Arlington coincide with the state boundaries.

Twenty-First-Century Developments. In September 2003 Pope JOHN PAUL II accepted Bishop Sullivan's resignation and appointed Cardinal William KEELER, archbishop of Baltimore, as apostolic administrator of the diocese of Richmond. In March 2004, Francis X. DiLorenzo (b. 1942), a native of Philadelphia, former auxiliary bishop of Scranton, and at that time bishop of Honolulu, was named the new bishop of Richmond. In 2005 Loverde and DiLorenzo formed the Virginia

Catholic Conference to coordinate the activities of the two dioceses within the state. The conference maintains its office in Richmond near the state capitol.

In the fall of 2006 the two bishops issued a joint pastoral letter calling for support of a state constitutional amendment defining marriage as a union between one man and one woman. They also addressed the question of stem-cell research on human embryos. Reflecting the growing immigration to Virginia, both of these pastorals were issued in English and Spanish. In April 2007 the two bishops issued a joint pastoral against the death penalty, a contentious issue in a state where the rate of executions is second only to that of Texas. Their letter also appeared on the opinion page of the *Washington Post*. Later in the year they wrote a pastoral on civic responsibility in the coming elections for the legislature, largely reflecting the positions taken by the national hierarchy.

One of the most dramatic changes in Virginia Catholicism was the election in November 2005 of Timothy M. Kaine as governor. He had served two terms as mayor of Richmond and had been elected lieutenant governor in 2001. He was the first Catholic to run for the highest state office—Virginia is the only state that prohibits governors from a second consecutive term. During the campaign, his personal opposition to CAPITAL PUNISHMENT, based on his Catholic faith, became the principal issue, and he had to promise to uphold the law of the state, a position he maintained during his tenure in office.

In 2008 the Catholic population of the Diocese of Arlington was 413,360 out of 2,763,057 and that of the Diocese of Richmond was 228,704 out of 4,923,801 for a total of roughly 642,064 Catholics in a total population of 7,686,858 (*The Official Catholic Directory* 2008, p. 2104). Much of the increase in the Catholic population of both dioceses is due to Hispanic immigration.

SEE ALSO CATHOLIC CHARITIES USA; CONVERTS AND CONVERSION; EMBRYOLOGY, HUMAN; MOUNT ST. MARY'S COLLEGE AND SEMINARY; NORTH CAROLINA, CATHOLIC CHURCH IN; SLAVERY, III (HISTORY OF); WEST VIRGINIA, CATHOLIC CHURCH IN.

BIBLIOGRAPHY
James H. Bailey, *A History of the Diocese of Richmond: The Formative Years* (Richmond, Va. 1956).

John Tracy Ellis, ed., *Documents of American Catholic History*, 3 vols. (Collegeville, Minn. 1986), 1:148.

Gerald P. Fogarty, S.J., *Commonwealth Catholicism: A History of the Catholic Church in Virginia* (Notre Dame, Ind. 2001).

William W. Hening, *The Statutes-at-large, Being a Collection of All the Laws of Virginia (1619–1792)*, 7 vols. (New York 1823), 1:268–269.

The Official Catholic Directory, 2008 (New Providence, N.J. 2008).

Rev. Gerald P. Fogarty SJ
William R. Kenan, Jr., Professor of Religious Studies and History
University of Virginia (2009)

WASHINGTON, CATHOLIC CHURCH IN

Bounded by British Columbia, including Vancouver Island on the north, the Pacific Ocean on the west, Oregon on the south, and Idaho on the east; the *Evergreen State* was admitted to the Union on November 11, 1889, as the forty-second state. Originally part of the Oregon Territory, Washington Territory was separated from it in March 1853 and reduced to its current boundaries with the formation of the Idaho Territory in 1863. U.S. census estimates for 2006 put the population of Washington at 6,395,798, the majority of whom are of European descent. Twenty-two percent of the total state population is made up of the following ethnic communities: Hispanic/Latino, 9.1 percent; Asians, 6.6 percent; Blacks/African Americans, 3.6 percent; Native Americans and Alaska Natives, 1.6 percent; and Native Hawaiians and other Pacific Islanders, 0.5 percent. Most of the population resides on Puget Sound from Everett to Olympia. To the east the population centers are Spokane, Yakima, and the Tri-Cities area of Richland, Pasco, and Kennewick.

Washington is among the least churched and most religiously diverse states in the United States. Religious organizations claim slightly more than thirty percent of the state population. Twenty-five percent of adults in Washington do not identify with any religious community. Approximately fifteen percent attend church on any given weekend. Catholics comprise about thirteen percent of the state population, followed by Lutherans (3.6%), Latter-Day Saints (3.1%), United Methodists (1.8%) and ASSEMBLIES OF GOD (1.7%) (Killen and Silk 2004, pp. 25–40; North American Religion Atlas; Jones et al. 2002, p. 40). The Catholic Church is the largest religious body in a state where all social institutions are relatively weak. Geographic space, high population mobility, the absence of large, stable ethnic communities, fluid class lines, and limited personnel and financial resources have created a context where committed Catholics from all parts of the Americas, Asia, and Europe have worked to build and sustain their Church. There are three dioceses: In addition to the Archdiocese of SEATTLE (DIOCESE, 1907; ARCHDIOCESE, 1951), the metropolitan see, there are its suffragan sees of Spokane (1914) and Yakima (1951).

Catholic Presence. On July 14, 1775, a Franciscan priest with the Spanish Heceta and Bodega y Cuandra expedition erected a cross at present day Point Grenville. Permanent Catholic presence began with the French-Canadian Métis (persons of mixed French-Canadian and Native American descent) and Native Americans involved in the fur trade in Oregon country. Even before trappers-turned-farmers petitioned Bishop Joseph Signay (1778–1850) of Quebec for priests in 1834, they had secured a separate Catholic cemetery at the Hudson's Bay Company's Fort Vancouver. In November 1838, two French-Canadian priests, Francis Norbert BLANCHET (1795–1883 [1843–1880]) and Modeste Demers (1809–1871) arrived. They immediately began pastoral work among the French and Métis and engaged in evangelistic work among Native Americans, using the *Catholic Ladder*, a pictorial representation of SALVATION HISTORY. They appointed Native Americans and other lay catechists to lead emerging Catholic communities in PRAYER and provide basic instruction. By 1842, Father John Baptiste Bolduc (1818–1889) had arrived, and JESUITS from St. Louis, most notably Pierre DE SMET, S.J. (1801–1873), were active in the eastern portion of the region.

The region changed rapidly between 1840 and 1880. In 1843, Pope GREGORY XVI erected an apostolic vicariate that included the area from the Pacific to the Rockies and Russian Alaska to California. In 1846, less than six weeks after the United States took control of the land below the forty-ninth parallel as a result of the Oregon Treaty, the apostolic vicariate was elevated to the Ecclesiastical Province of Oregon City, the second in the United States. Blanchet was appointed to the metropolitan see, Modeste Demers to the diocese of Vancouver Island, and the archbishop's brother, Augustin Magliore Blanchet (1797–1887 [1846–1879]), to the diocese of Walla Walla, the first diocese in what was to become the state of Washington. The entire province had 6,000 Catholics, over 5,000 of whom were Native Americans. One of the 5,000 was Chief Seattle (1786–1866) of the Suquamish and Duwamish tribes of Puget Sound, after whom the city of Seattle was named. Bishop Augustin Magliore Blanchet traveled to Walla Walla over the Oregon Trail in 1847, accompanied by his vicar general, John Baptist Abraham BROUILLET (1813–1884), and members of the OBLATES OF MARY IMMACULATE. Brouillet, a tireless advocate for Native Americans, became the first director of the Catholic Bureau of Indian Affairs in the 1880s. Fathers Eugene Casimir Chirouse, O.M.I. (1821–1892), and Charles Pandosy, O.M.I. (1824–1891), the first priests ordained in Washington, spent most of their active ministries among Native Americans in the state.

Blanchet arrived at Fort Walla Walla in September 1847. In November the Whitman Massacre occurred, sparking the Cayuse War, exacerbating tensions between Catholic and Protestant missionaries, and forcing closure of the Walla Walla mission. The California Gold Rush emptied much of the Euro-American population from the region. In 1850 Blanchet was transferred from Walla Walla to the newly erected Diocese of Nesqually, with Vancouver as the see city. In 1853 Walla Walla was suppressed, and the Washington territory came under the jurisdiction of Nesqually.

Blanchet depended on the Societies for the Propagation of the Faith in Lyons and Paris and the Leopoldine Society in Vienna for financial support and on Montreal for personnel. In 1856 Mother Joseph of the Sacred Heart (1823–1902), who became known as the first architect of the Pacific Northwest, and four other SISTERS OF PROVIDENCE began work in health care and education. By 1864, thirty-one Providence Sisters, five Jesuits, two Oblate missionaries, and seven diocesan priests served in the diocese. Though Irish and German Catholic populations grew steadily, the Church in Washington retained a French Canadian, Métis, and Native American orientation into the 1880s.

Institutional Growth. The construction of the transcontinental railroad brought Irish and Chinese laborers to Washington. Once it had been completed in 1883, the state became a destination point for immigrants. Between 1880 and 1895, the Euro-American population of the diocese increased from 75,000 to nearly 400,000; the Catholic population, from 12,000 to 30,000. Churches and public chapels increased from 22 to 46, diocesan clergy from 15 to 37, and RELIGIOUS priests, including Jesuits, BENEDICTINES, and REDEMPTORISTS, to 20. Women religious increased from 60 to 286 (Blanchet; Taylor 2000, pp. 29–32). Sisters of Providence and Sisters of the HOLY NAMES OF JESUS AND MARY from Montreal predominated, but many other communities served in the state over the next 150 years, among them Benedictines, Sisters of St. Francis of Philadelphia, and Sisters of St. Dominic.

Bishop Augustin Blanchet resigned in 1879. His successor, Aegidius Junger (1879–1895), was a Belgian who had served the diocese since his ordination in 1864. Like Blanchet, Junger was a missionary bishop oriented toward and dependent on Quebec and Europe. The third bishop, Edward J. O'Dea (1896–1932), the first westerner raised to the episcopacy, transformed Nesqually from an immigrant, frontier missionary diocese to a diocese of the U.S. Catholic Church, the Diocese of Seattle. During his long tenure, the state population quadrupled from nearly 400,000 to 1,600,000. He led the diocese through the turmoil that ensued after the Panic of 1893, the economic disruption of the 1898 Alaska Gold Rush, massive immigration, World War I, anti–Catholic agitation in the 1920s, and the beginnings of the Great Depression. O'Dea moved his see from Vancouver to Seattle in 1903, began construction of a CATHEDRAL in 1905, and at the dedication of the cathedral in 1907 announced the name change of the diocese from Nesqually to Seattle.

Increases in population generated a need for more educational and health care institutions. In 1891, the Jesuits began Seattle College, which became one of the first coeducational colleges in the United States. German Benedictines established St. Martin's College in Lacey in 1895. Between 1903 and 1915 Mother (later Saint) Frances Xavier CABRINI (1850–1917) and the MISSION-ARY SISTERS OF THE SACRED HEART came to Puget Sound to minister to Italian immigrants with an orphanage, a school, and a hospital. An official diocesan newspaper, *The Catholic Northwest Progress*, appeared in 1911.

Lay organizations aimed at spiritual growth, support of the Church, mutual support, and social activities burgeoned between 1880 and 1932 and included expanded altar societies, the Young Men's Institute (1890s), the KNIGHTS OF COLUMBUS (1902), the

Young Ladies' Institute (1905), the Holy Name Society (1909), and CATHOLIC DAUGHTERS OF THE AMERICAS (1910). In the 1920s the diocesan Council of Catholic Women supported the Newman Club at the University of Washington. The Society of ST. VINCENT DE PAUL officially organized in January 1920, successor to the Immaculate Conception Association of Charity, has been active in Seattle since 1893. The NATIONAL COUNCIL OF CATHOLIC MEN (NCCM) provided monetary support for the Catholic Filipino Club in Seattle. The Knights of Columbus began the laymen's retreat in 1918. A women's retreat movement followed in the 1920s. By 1930 the Holy Angels Society, Boys Sanctuary, Children of St. Mary, Sodality of Mary, and League of the Sacred Heart were present in Washington. Annual parish missions were a regular feature. In 1934 Catholic businessmen founded the Serra Club to provide spiritual and financial assistance for priestly vocations.

Even as Catholics participated in the progressive agenda of the 1920s through work in social welfare, including the Catholic Social Betterment League, they faced increasing nativist hostility during the post–World War I years. It reached a peak in 1924 when the KU KLUX KLAN supported initiative No. 49, designed to eliminate private schools. The initiative was defeated, in large part because prominent Catholic laymen, such as William Pigott (1860–1929), helped organize a religiously ecumenical, civic, and business-oriented OPPOSITION to it.

Maryknoll priests and sisters arrived in the state in 1920 to work among the growing Asian population on Puget Sound, especially Japanese and Filipinos. The mission grew out of a proposal in 1916 by a nucleus of Seattle Japanese Catholics, two of whom, Mr. Akashi and Mr. Hirata, traced their Catholicism back to the Nagasaki martyrs. Sisters Teresa and Gemma opened a kindergarten for Japanese children. By 1925 Our Lady Queen of Martyrs Parish was a thriving Japanese-Filipino national parish that carried on a vibrant, intercultural ministry until the internment of the Japanese in 1942. Maryknoll Father Leopold H. Tibesar, pastor from 1935, accompanied parishioners to the camps.

Spokane Diocese. Late in 1913, on O'Dea's recommendation, ROME created a new diocese, Spokane, that encompassed half the territory of the state. Augustine Schinner was appointed the first bishop (1914–1925). He was succeeded by Charles D. White (1926–1954), followed by Bernard J. Topel (1955–1978), and Lawrence Welsh (1978–1990). William S. Skylstad succeeded Welsh in 1990. He served a term as president of the UNITED STATES CONFERENCE OF CATHOLIC BISHOPS (USCCB) beginning in 2004.

Catholicism in Spokane was rooted in the efforts of Jesuits, including de Smet, Joseph Joset (1810–1910),

and Joseph S. CATALDO (1837–1928), as well as diocesan priests Toussaint Mesplie (1824–1895), Emile Kauten (d. 1912), and Peter Poaps (d. 1890). The Sisters of Providence and Sisters of the Holy Names early had established educational and healthcare ministries to Native Americans and Euro-Americans there. Jesuits also worked with Native Americans; in 1887 they established Gonzaga College in Spokane. The Sisters of the Holy Names opened a college, later Fort Wright College, in 1907. It operated until 1981. Bishop White Seminary was built in 1956.

The Seattle Province. After Pearl Harbor was bombed on December 7, 1941, Seattle's Bishop Gerald SHAUGHNESSY, S.M. (1933–1950), spoke out publicly against hatred of Japanese and Japanese Americans, the first western bishop to do so. Washington dioceses cooperated in the war effort through establishing clubs for soldiers and war workers, curtailing building projects, and adjusting liturgies to comply with dim-out regulations.

The war brought tens of thousands of soldiers, workers, and their families into the state. Among them were large numbers of African Americans taking advantage of access to industrial and clerical jobs that opened to them during the labor shortage created by the war. Some were from families with centuries-long histories as Catholics. After the war, the KNIGHTS OF PETER CLAVER and Ladies Auxiliary became the major African American Catholic parish organization in the state. Bishop Thomas J. Connolly (1950–1975) of Seattle established the St. Peter Claver Interracial Center to provide social services to the growing African-American community. He also worked actively for open housing during the 1960s. Black lay Catholics such as Clayton Pitrie and Walter Hubbard (1924–2007) became leaders in the state and nationally with the National Black Catholic Lay Caucus. In the 1970s the first two African American priests in the state were ordained, Fathers Joseph McGowan (1940–), S.J., and John CORNELIUS.

Yakima Diocese. Washington's Hispanic/Latino population began growing rapidly beginning in the 1930s, with people who lost their farms in Colorado during the Great Depression seeking work. The influx of population caused by the construction of the Grand Coulee Dam, the Columbia Basin irrigation project, and the war effort transformed all of eastern Washington, especially the Yakima Valley and Tri-Cities. In response, Bishop Connolly proposed another diocese. Yakima was erected in June 1951; this area had a Catholic presence dating back to the 1850s with ministry by the Jesuits, Oblates, Sisters of Providence, and Sisters of St. Dominic. The new bishop, Joseph P. Dougherty (1951–

St. Aloysius Church, Spokane, Washington. *Located close to the campus of Jesuit-run Gonzaga University, the church, like the university, is named after St. Aloysius Gonzaga.* © **ANDRE JENNY / ALAMY**

1969), quickly began building churches, schools, social services, and an extensive ministry to Spanish-speaking Catholics. Continued growth through the rest of the century made Hispanics a major presence throughout the state. By the beginning of the twenty-first century, one-half of the Catholic population in the diocese of Yakima was Hispanic/Latino.

Bishop Dougherty renewed Catholic ministry at the Yakima Indian Reservation mission, one of the oldest in the state and elevated it to the status of parish with a resident pastor in 1958. In 1981 Heritage College, successor to the Holy Names Sisters' Fort Wright College, opened, serving primarily Native American and Hispanic populations. Cornelius M. Power (1969–1974) succeeded Dougherty, to be followed by Nicholas E. Walsh (1974–1976) and William S. Skylstad (1977–1988). Skylstad's successor was Francis E. George, O.M.I. (1990–1996), who was followed by Carlos J. Sevilla, S.J. (1996–).

Seattle Archdiocese. Seattle became an archdiocese in 1951 amidst the post–war boom. CONFRATERNITY OF CHRISTIAN DOCTRINE (CCD), present in the state since

the 1930s, expanded to serve Catholic students in public schools. Adults joined CATHOLIC ACTION and discussion clubs. Seattle became the third diocese in the nation to have a Knights of Columbus Religious Information Bureau, operated under the guidance of William Treacy (1919–), a diocesan priest who came to Seattle from Ireland in 1945. The archdiocese opened St. Thomas Seminary, which was staffed by the SULPICIANS and operated until 1977. The Catholic Youth Organization facilitated athletics, camping, and other programs for adolescents. Catholic Charities broadened its focus to include housing and a range of social services for the poor, the elderly, and ethnic minorities. Refugee programs were initiated for Hungarians and Koreans in the 1950s, Southeast Asians in the 1960s, and Central Americans in the 1980s.

Vatican II and Beyond. In 1962 the Catholic Church in Washington was institutionally stable and successful. That year the Archdiocese of Seattle hosted the forty-seventh annual LITURGICAL CONFERENCE, its contribution to the Seattle World's Fair. Among the liturgical leaders in attendance was Monsignor Hans A. REIN-

HOLD (1897–1968), who had been incardinated in the Archdiocese of Seattle and later served as curate and pastor (1944–1956) in Sunnyside in the diocese of Yakima.

In the wake of VATICAN COUNCIL II, the archdiocese participated in an ecumenical discussion program on KOMO television, *Challenge*. For over a decade its 300,000 weekly viewers saw Father William Treacy in conversation with Rabbi Raphael Levine (1901–1985) and a Protestant minister.

Seattle University and the archdiocese initiated new education and training programs for catechists and lay leaders. Across the state, parish councils were formed, liturgical renewal initiated, SOCIAL JUSTICE ministries expanded, and pastoral ministries oriented toward diverse ethnic populations. New lay organizations formed, focused around professional, liturgical, educational, and justice issues. Father James Dunning (1937–1995) of Seattle gained national prominence as head of the North American Forum on the Catechumenate.

In 1970 the Washington State Catholic Conference was established to provide a more effective public voice for the Catholic Church in the state on public policy issues. Archbishop Connolly retired in 1975 (d. April 18, 1991) and was succeeded by Raymond G. Hunthausen (1975–1991), bishop of Helena, Montana. Hunthausen had attended all the sessions of Vatican Council II (1962–1965). In Seattle he emphasized peace and justice and full implementation of the reforms of the council, especially expanding lay participation and leadership. Archbishop Hunthausen engaged in tax protest in opposition to the nuclear arms race, an act that alienated some and confirmed his status as a prophetic leader for others. His tax resistance, coupled with a Vatican investigation of his ministry, gained international attention. As a result of the investigation, some of his ministerial powers were transferred to Auxiliary Bishop Donald W. Wuerl in 1986. Those powers were restored to the archbishop in 1987. Bishop Wuerl was transferred in 1987, and shortly after, Bishop Thomas J. Murphy of Great Falls-Billings, Montana, was named coadjutor archbishop of Seattle. In 1988 the Archdiocese of Seattle transformed Catholic Charities into Catholic Community Services of Western Washington to provide better social services to the poor and elderly.

Hunthausen retired in 1991, and Murphy succeeded him. Archbishop Murphy's episcopacy (1991–1997) was cut short by leukemia. Alex J. Brunett (1930–) became archbishop of Seattle in 1997, after serving as bishop of Helena, Montana, beginning in 1994. The Reverend George L. Thomas was appointed auxiliary BISHOP of Seattle on November 19, 1999. Bishop Thomas was moved to Helena in 2004, and in 2005 Eusebio Elizondo and Joseph Tyson became auxiliary bishops.

During the 1990s the number of lay church professionals increased across the state as the number of priests and vowed religious declined. Seattle University and the archdiocese cooperatively established the Institute for Theological Studies, now part of the School of Theology and Ministry, to train pastoral ministers for the church in western Washington. Gonzaga University expanded its pastoral education offerings for the eastern part of the state. Women's religious communities extended current or initiated new ministries in spirituality and social justice as ways of sustaining and expanding their presence and witness. The Church continued to welcome immigrants, engage in pastoral care, and struggle with issues of justice in a state economically influenced by globalization, species extinction, growing income disparity, and other problems.

At the beginning of the twenty-first century, the state episcopacy cooperated with archbishops and bishops in Oregon, Idaho, Montana, and British Columbia on a joint pastoral letter, "The Columbia River Watershed: Caring for Creation and the Common Good" (2001). Since its promulgation the letter has spurred bishops in other parts of North America to consider care of the environment, particularly water, as a major pastoral issue.

While the Church has continued to make major contributions to people in the state through its work in education, housing, and social welfare, public attention has focused primarily on the sexual abuse scandals. Seattle, Spokane, and Yakima all have paid out settlements to victims of sexual abuse, as has the Oregon Province of the Society of Jesus. The Diocese of Spokane declared bankruptcy in 2004. Tensions between the bishops and laity of Spokane and Yakima over the handling of accused personnel, litigation, and payments are affecting the life of parishes and the dioceses. The Archdiocese of Seattle has experienced less visible tension over these issues. Voice of the Faithful and Survivors Network of Those Abused by Priests (SNAP) are active across the state. The sexual abuse scandals have absorbed attention and resources. They also have eroded the credibility of the bishops as moral teachers in the minds of many within the church and in the wider community.

In recent decades the bishops of Washington State have emphasized evangelization; protection of the vulnerable, including children, the elderly, the poor and immigrants; the importance of family life; renewed devotion to the Eucharist; and the need to increase vocations to the priesthood and religious life. A renewed emphasis on Catholic education at the K–12 level also is apparent. Archbishop Brunett's pastoral letters, "Gift of Marriage" (2005) and "Bread of Hope" (2005) reflect these foci. The bishops also emphasize the full implementation of the "General Instruction of the Roman Missal," an occasion of tension in some parishes.

Priests from Asia, Africa, and Latin America are helping to meet the clergy shortage, bringing new cross-cultural contacts to a state that has been marked throughout its history by successive waves of immigration. Growing numbers of priests have responsibility for multiple parishes. The bishops avoid closing or merging FAITH communities as much as possible. Demographic trends, however, are clear, and Catholic communities increasingly rely on lay parish administrators and lay pastoral ministers, both professional and volunteer. The vitality of the Church in Washington State and its capacity to carry forward its extensive social service, health-care, spiritual, educational, and social service ministries depends on a growing and maturing collaboration among clergy, religious, and laity.

SEE ALSO CATECHIST; CATECHUMENATE; CATHOLIC CHARITIES USA; EUCHARISTIC DEVOTION; LATTER-DAY SAINTS, CHURCH OF JESUS CHRIST OF; LEOPOLDINEN STIFTUNG (LEOPOLDINE SOCIETY); LUTHERAN CHURCHES IN NORTH AMERICA; MARYKNOLL FATHERS AND BROTHERS; MARYKNOLL SISTERS; METHODIST CHURCHES; NATIONAL COUNCIL OF CATHOLIC WOMEN (NCCW); NATIVISM (AMERICAN); PROPAGATION OF THE FAITH, SOCIETY FOR THE; SERRA INTERNATIONAL; SEX ABUSE CRISIS.

BIBLIOGRAPHY

Bishop Augustin Magloire Blanchet. *Letter Books*, Archives, Archdiocese of Seattle.

David M. Buerge and Junius Rochester, *Roots and Branches: The Religious Heritage of Washington State* (Seattle 1988).

Madeline Duntley, "Japanese and Filipino Together: The Transethnic Vision of Our Lady Queen of Martyrs Parish," *U.S. Catholic Historian* 18, no. 1 (Winter 2000): 74–98.

Robert E. Ficken and Charles P. LeWarne, *Washington: A Centennial History* (Seattle 1988).

Dale E. Jones et al. *Religious Congregations and Membership in the United States, 2000* (Nashville, Tenn. 2002).

Patricia O'Connell Killen, "The Geography of a Minority Religion: Roman Catholicism in the Pacific Northwest," *U.S. Catholic Historian* 18, no. 3 (Summer 2000): 51–72.

Patricia O'Connell Killen and Mark Silk, eds., *Religion and Public Life in the Pacific Northwest: The None Zone* (Walnut Creek, Calif. 2004).

W. J. Metz, *Washington: History of the Catholic Church in the State*, Archives, Archdiocese of Seattle.

North American Religion Atlas, available from: http://www.religionatlas.org (accessed October 17, 2008).

Wilfred P. Schoenberg, *A History of the Catholic Church in the Pacific Northwest, 1743–1983* (Washington, D.C. 1987).

Carlos Arnaldo Schwantes, *The Pacific Northwest: An Interpretive History* (Lincoln, Ne. 1996).

Christine M. Taylor, ed., *Abundance of Grace: The History of the Archdiocese of Seattle, 1850–2000* (Strasbourg, France 2000).

Patricia O'Connell Killen
Professor of Religion
Pacific Lutheran University, Tacoma, Wash. (2009)

WASHINGTON, D.C., ARCHDIOCESE OF

The ARCHDIOCESE of Washington, D.C. (*Washingtonensis*), was erected by PIUS XII (1939–1958) on July 22, 1939, and united with the Archdiocese of BALTIMORE, Maryland, on equal status, under Michael J. CURLEY, tenth ARCHBISHOP of Baltimore, whose title was changed to archbishop of Baltimore and Washington. On November 27, 1947, the Federal District of Columbia and Montgomery, Prince Georges, St. Mary's, Calvert, and Charles counties of the state of Maryland, an area of 2,104 square miles, were separated from the See of Baltimore and their administration entrusted to Patrick A. O'BOYLE (1896–1987) as archbishop of Washington. Similar to approximately forty other archiepiscopal sees, Washington, D.C., until 1965, had no metropolitan jurisdiction over suffragan sees. However, in 1965, it was given metropolitan status, with the prelature *nullius* of the Virgin Islands as a suffragan see.

Catholic Beginnings. In St. Mary's County on March 25, 1634, the original settlers of colonial Maryland landed from the *Ark and the Dove*, under the leadership of Leonard CALVERT, brother of the lord proprietor, Cecilius Calvert, second baron of Baltimore. Accompanying this group of approximately 150 Englishmen, the majority of whom were Protestants, were three English JESUITS, Fathers Andrew WHITE and John Altham and Brother Thomas Gervase. From the Jesuit headquarters in St. Mary's City, the first colonial capital, came an unbroken succession of priests from whose number the first BISHOP of the United States, John CARROLL, was chosen 155 years later. There, too, the general assembly of the colony, composed of both Catholic and Protestant members, enacted in April of 1649 the famous act of religious toleration, unique in the English-speaking world of that time. The act stated that no one "professing to believe in Jesus Christ, shall from henceforth bee any waies troubled, Molested or discountenanced for or in respect of his or her religion nor in the free exercise thereof within this Province ..." (Ellis 1987, p. 116). After the Protestant triumph in England in 1688, however, Maryland Catholics were subjected to a discriminatory penal code that stayed in effect for the better part of a century. Following the American Revolution a radical change ensued, and on November 11, 1776, the Maryland assembly adopted a Declaration of Rights that guaranteed religious liberty, giving Maryland Catholics a new start.

The federal district and the five counties of Maryland, which constitute the archdiocese, have shared in the rule of the archbishops of Baltimore, who, beginning with Carroll, numbered men such as Francis Patrick KENRICK (1851–1863), Martin John SPALDING (1864–1872), James Roosevelt BAYLEY (1872–1877), and James GIBBONS (1877–1921). With the rise of the United States to a world power in the late nineteenth century, attention focused on its national capital, and the suggestion was made that, in keeping with its dignity, it should be made an episcopal see. Gibbons, who was strongly opposed to the separation of Washington from Baltimore, made a trip to ROME in May 1914, expressly to prevent the rumored separation. However, he was ready to second the suggestion of Giovanni Bonzano, APOSTOLIC DELEGATE to the United States, that the name of Washington be added to that of Baltimore in the title of the see. Gibbons had been dead eighteen years before the HOLY SEE took the first step by erecting the Archdiocese of Washington and putting it under the administration of the same PRELATE who ruled the Archdiocese of Baltimore. The complete separation of the two sees occurred six months after the death of Archbishop Curley, Gibbons's successor.

Independent Jurisdiction. Patrick A. O'Boyle, a priest of the Archdiocese of NEW YORK, was installed as the second archbishop of Washington at St. Matthew's Cathedral on January 21, 1948. During his twenty-five-year tenure, the archdiocese experienced tremendous growth. The size of its Catholic population more than doubled, reaching a total of 389,000 in 1973. The number of Catholic institutions also greatly increased, with the number of parishes growing by fifty percent (to 122) at the time of O'Boyle's retirement.

Under O'Boyle events in the Archdiocese of Washington became the focus of media attention. The first of these events was the successful integration of archdiocesean parishes and schools prior to the Supreme Court decision of 1954 striking down racial segregation. In recognition of his efforts as a progressive leader in the area of race relations as well as of his other accomplishments, O'Boyle was elevated to the College of Cardinals in 1967. The following year, the archdiocese became the focus of worldwide attention when Cardinal O'Boyle withdrew the ministerial faculties of numerous priests who publicly opposed Pope PAUL VI's ENCYCLICAL *Humane vitae.* Cardinal O'Boyle retired in 1973 and died in 1987.

William W. BAUM, bishop of the Diocese of Springfield-Cape Girardeau and a national voice on ecumenism, was consecrated the third archbishop of Washington in May of 1973 and created a CARDINAL in 1976. Six more parishes were established in the archdiocese during Baum's tenure to meet the needs of the ever-expanding Washington suburbs, and new organizations were established to minister to African-American and Hispanic Catholics. One of the highlights

of Cardinal Baum's service as archbishop of Washington was the historic visit of Pope JOHN PAUL II to the national capital in the fall of 1979. The following year the same POPE named Cardinal Baum prefect of the Congregation for Catholic Education. At the time of Cardinal Baum's departure for Rome, the Catholic population of the archdiocese had reached 396,000.

The fourth archbishop of Washington, James A. HICKEY, formerly bishop of Cleveland, was installed on August 5, 1980, and elected to the College of Cardinals in 1988. During Cardinal Hickey's twenty-year tenure, the Archdiocese of Washington met new challenges posed by the changing demographics of the region. The suburbanization of once rural areas necessitated the erection of new parishes in the Maryland counties, with the total number of parishes reaching 141 in the year 2000. Concurrently, the declining population of the city of Washington required a consolidation of its Catholic elementary and secondary schools. The arrival of thousands of Catholic immigrants from the Caribbean, Asia, and especially Latin America, beginning in the 1980s, brought racial and ethnic diversity to the local Church, along with pastoral challenges.

On January 3, 2001, Archbishop Theodore E. McCarrick (1930–) of Newark was installed as the fifth archbishop of Washington. Shortly thereafter, on February 21, 2001, he too was elevated to the College of Cardinals. During his tenure as Archbishop of Washington, Cardinal McCarrick promoted vocations to the priesthood and RELIGIOUS life. These efforts reached fruition. In 2006 McCarrick ordained twelve men to the priesthood, the largest ordination class in the archdiocese in more than thirty years. In 2008 the archdiocese had seventy-three men studying for the priesthood. About one-third of these men were affiliated with the NEOCATECHUMENAL WAY. Cardinal McCarrick introduced this lay movement founded in Spain into the archdiocese, and it sponsors PRAYER groups in several parishes. McCarrick opened the Redemptoris Mater Seminary in 2001 specifically for seminarians from the Neocatechumenal Way. Priests from the "Way" come from all over the world; most are fluent in Spanish, a great benefit in meeting the increasing need for ministry to Hispanics in the archdiocese. Cardinal McCarrick was also successful in recruiting several religious orders to minister to its increasingly diverse population.

In addition to his work for the local church, Cardinal McCarrick was involved in the international efforts of the church. His interactions with political leaders and diplomats resulted in his being the first archbishop of Washington to be well known in the national media. McCarrick's good relations with the press as well as the wise policies of his predecessor, Cardinal Hickey, spared the archdiocese much of the turmoil that surrounded the clergy sexual abuse scandal

Papal Visit. *Clergy and members of the Catholic Church inside a confession tent, before Pope Benedict XVI celebrated a Mass at Nationals Park in Washington, D.C.* © BROOKS KRAFT/CORBIS

that engulfed the church nationally. In July 2005, having reached the canonical age for retirement, Cardinal McCarrick submitted his resignation to Pope BENEDICT XVI, who formally accepted it in April 2006.

The sixth archbishop of Washington, Donald W. Wuerl (1940–), was installed in June 2006. Prior to his appointment to Washington, Archbishop Wuerl served as the bishop of Pittsburgh for eighteen years. Throughout his priesthood Wuerl showed a great interest in catechesis and published the well-received catechism, *The Teaching of Christ.* Archbishop Wuerl was also much involved in the publication of the United States Catechism for Adults, produced by the UNITED STATES CONFERENCE OF CATHOLIC BISHOPS (USCCB) in 2006.

After his arrival in Washington, Archbishop Wuerl developed new strategies to meet the pastoral and financial needs of the archdiocese. One necessary, but painful, measure Wuerl initiated in 2007 was consolidating Catholic elementary schools in the city of Washington. Declining enrollments and rising costs forced the conversion of seven parochial schools to privately operated, value-based charter schools. This

novel arrangement allowed these schools to serve the intercity community with the assistance of public funding not available to church-run schools.

A happier development in the first years of Archbishop Wuerl's tenure was Pope Benedict's visit to Washington for two days in April 2008. This was the second visit by a pope to the national capital; Pope John Paul II made the journey in 1979. The Pope's visit included a Mass at the new stadium of the Washington Nationals. The pope was welcomed by an archdiocese of 140 parishes and approximately 580,000 Catholics (*The Official Catholic Directory* 2008, p. 1462).

The archdiocese of Washington has a unique place within the Catholic Church in America, being home to numerous national Catholic institutions. Among these are the United States Conference of Catholic Bishops, the Archdiocese of the Military Services, The CATHOLIC UNIVERSITY OF AMERICA (1887), Trinity College (1897), GEORGETOWN UNIVERSITY (1789), Mt. St. Sepulchre (the Franciscan MONASTERY, 1899), and the BASILICA of the NATIONAL SHRINE OF THE IMMACULATE CONCEPTION. The archdiocese is also honored to be the residence of the apostolic NUNCIO to the United States.

SEE ALSO CATECHISMS; MARYLAND, CATHOLIC CHURCH IN; MILITARY SERVICES, USA, ARCHDIOCESE FOR; SEX ABUSE CRISIS; TOLERATION ACTS OF 1639 AND 1649, MARYLAND.

BIBLIOGRAPHY

Archdiocese of Washington, D.C. Official Web site, available from: http://www.adw.org/(accessed October 17, 2008).

Rory T. Conley, *The Truth in Charity: A History of the Archdiocese of Washington* (Paris 2001).

John Tracy Ellis, ed., *Documents of American Catholic History* (Wilmington, Del. 1987).

Morris J. MacGregor, *A Parish for the Federal City: St. Patrick's in Washington, 1794–1994* (Washington, D.C. 1994).

Morris J. MacGregor, *Steadfast in Faith: The Life of Patrick Cardinal O'Boyle* (Washington, D.C. 2006).

The Official Catholic Directory, 2008 (New Providence, N.J. 2008)

Thomas W. Spalding, *The Premier See: A History of the Archdiocese of Baltimore, 1789–1989* (Baltimore, Md. 1989).

William W. Warner, *At Peace with All Their Neighbors: Catholics and Catholicism in the National Capital 1787–1860* (Washington, D.C. 1994).

An additional source of information on the archdiocese is The Catholic Historical Society of Washington, which was established in 1976.

Rt. Rev. John T. Ellis
Professor of Church History
University of San Francisco
San Francisco, Calif.

Rev. Rory T. Conley
Historian
Archdiocese of Washington, D.C. (2009)

WEST VIRGINIA, CATHOLIC CHURCH IN

The first significant Catholic presence in West Virginia occurred in the years immediately following the American Revolution. The pioneer Catholic families are believed to have settled in the lower Shenandoah Valley, a region of West Virginia known as the Eastern Panhandle. Although Catholics had been settling on the Maryland/Pennsylvania side of the border of what was then western Virginia since the first part of the eighteenth century, few had crossed over into the lower Shenandoah Valley. The initial reluctance of Catholics to settle in Virginia was directly related to the anti–Catholic laws enacted there during colonial times, when the practice of their religion was declared illegal and behavior toward Catholics was openly hostile. Catholic advance into Virginia began after the state legislature with the 1786 Act for Establishing Religious Freedom removed the restrictions on the religion. Priests from Maryland and Pennsylvania visited the Catholics who had settled in the Eastern Panhandle during these initial years. A letter written by Reverend Denis Cahill in 1795 tells of the conditions he encountered in western Virginia. Based in Hagerstown, Maryland, Cahill traveled into western Virginia, getting as far as Cumberland, Maryland—a distance of some seventy miles. He ministered to the Catholic families he encountered, organizing them into formal missions and initiating the building of churches. He reported finding Catholics throughout the Eastern Panhandle, including the towns of Harper's Ferry, Martinsburg, and Shepherdstown.

The Eastern Panhandle remained the center of Catholic activity until the second decade of the nineteenth century, when a small community was formed in the city of Wheeling, located in the region of western Virginia known as the Northern Panhandle. Although a Catholic presence had been established there in the early part of the nineteenth century, their numbers were not large enough to form a parish until an influx of immigrants arrived around 1818. Many of these immigrants were Irish laborers who had worked on the National Road project. They were soon joined by a number of Germans who were drawn to the city for its opportunities in skill-based trades. With the exception of the Catholic communities in the Eastern Panhandle and the Northern Panhandle, western Virginia was described at this time as an "unorganized spiritual wilderness." In Preston County a small community of German immigrants had settled near what is now Howesville, built a church for the families to worship in, and arranged for a priest to come and visit them. Their experience, however, remained the exception. Most Catholics who settled in western Virginia during this period arrived on their own and settled at great distances from one another. Religious communities such as the JESUITS and REDEMPTORISTS sent missionaries into this region, attempting to locate the Catholic families that had settled there. Priests from neighboring dioceses also traveled into western Virginia to say Mass and minister to the Catholic families, but their numbers were too few to visit the region regularly.

The turning point in the history of Catholicism in western Virginia came with the arrival of the Baltimore and Ohio Railroad project in the mid-1840s. Just as the National Road project brought Catholics to the Northern Panhandle, so the B&O Railroad brought Catholics to the undeveloped interior region of western Virginia. Stretching from Cumberland, Maryland, to Wheeling, Virginia, the locations of Catholic families in this territory can be easily established. The laborers and their families founded new communities along the path of the railroad. The affordable prices of western Virginia land persuaded many laborers to give up their itinerant lives and begin anew as farmers.

Establishment of the Diocese of Wheeling. Encouraged by the increase in the number of Catholics settling in western Virginia as well as the promising future of the region, Bishop Richard V. Whelan (1809–1874) of Richmond, Virginia, petitioned the HOLY SEE for the creation of a new DIOCESE. Until that time the Catholics of western Virginia had been under the spiritual care of the Diocese of Richmond, which encompassed the entire state of Virginia. On July 19, 1850, Pope PIUS IX established the Diocese of Wheeling, naming Whelan its first ordinary. At the time there were just four churches within its borders—St. James, Wheeling; St. Patrick, Weston; St. Mary, Wytheville; St. John, Summersville—one CHAPEL (the German Settlement in Preston County); and a Catholic population of about five thousand. The Allegheny Mountains formed the initial boundaries of the new diocese. At its founding in 1850, the diocese had both a different name and different borders from those it possesses in the twenty-first century. The eight counties of the Eastern Panhandle remained with the Diocese of Richmond, and seventeen-and-a-half counties of southwestern Virginia constituted the Diocese of Wheeling. The outbreak of the Civil War and the creation of the new state of West Virginia in 1863 meant that diocesan and state boundaries were distinct from one another for more than 100 years. It was not until a 1974 decree, promulgated by Pope PAUL VI, that the diocesan borders were realigned to accord with those of the state. The seventeen-and-a-half counties in Virginia that had initially been part of the diocese were transferred to the Diocese of Richmond, and the eight counties of the Eastern Panhandle were incorporated into the Diocese of Wheeling. The name of the diocese was also redesignated at this time to the Diocese of Wheeling-Charleston.

As was true for much of the U.S. Catholic Church, West Virginia had an immigrant Church. At the time the diocese was founded in 1850, many immigrants were Irish and German and had been brought into the region as laborers on public and private works projects of the nineteenth century. Others were attracted by the affordable land and the prospects of Wheeling as a vital commercial center. Within fifty years, when the diocese experienced its largest influx of immigrants, the Irish and Germans were outnumbered by immigrants from Russia, Italy, and the Austro-Hungarian Empire, the majority of whom were employed as unskilled laborers in the emerging industries of the age: coal, steel, oil, natural gas, and timber.

Bishops of the Mountain State. During his episcopacy in the diocese, Bishop Whelan was devoted to building the Catholic Church in West Virginia. At his death in 1874, the diocese consisted of 46 churches, 7 chapels, 9 schools, 1 seminary, and 1 hospital and had 31 priests, 109 women religious, and a Catholic population estimated at 18,000.

Bishop John J. Kain (1840–1903) was appointed to succeed Bishop Whelan in 1875. Bishop Kain's years in the diocese were devoted to meeting the needs of the newly arrived immigrants who came in search of labor in West Virginia mines and factories. He continued his predecessor's efforts of constructing churches and schools and remained in Wheeling until his appointment as ARCHBISHOP of St. Louis in 1893.

Patrick J. Donahue (1849–1922) was bishop of the diocese during its greatest period of growth. In the twenty-eight years he served as bishop, the Catholic population more than tripled, rising from approximately 20,000 when he was appointed bishop in 1894 to more than 62,000 at his death in 1922. Much of this growth took place in the decade between 1900 and 1910 when the Catholic population increased by more than 20,000, and half of the nearly 150 parishes and missions that were founded during Bishop Donahue's episcopacy were established. To serve the growing Catholic population, Donahue invited religious communities to send priests, brothers, and sisters to serve, some of which continue to maintain a presence in the diocese, including the MARIST FATHERS, the Sisters of Our Lady of Charity, the Ursuline Sisters, the DOMINICAN SISTERS, and the Sisters of the POOR CHILD JESUS. He also appealed to the missionary colleges in Ireland to send priests, and he made several trips to Europe to recruit priests who could speak the native languages of the immigrants who were arriving in the diocese. By 1922 the number of priests serving in the diocese had more than tripled, increasing from 36 to 115, and the number of women religious had more than doubled from 143 to 340.

In 1922 Bishop John J. Swint (1879–1962), who was appointed auxiliary bishop earlier that year, succeeded Bishop Donahue. Bishop Swint, a native of Pickens, West Virginia, in Randolph County was the son of immigrants who were among the first Catholics to settle in central West Virginia. He came to office during the period of "brick-and-mortar Catholicism"—a time when the attention of the Catholic community turned from meeting the immediate needs of arriving immigrants to establishing an institutional infrastructure to serve them. When Bishop Swint died on November 23, 1962, he had been bishop of the diocese for forty years. During this period the Catholic population had almost doubled, from more than 62,000 Catholics in 1922 to nearly 110,000. He devoted much of his energy to meeting the material needs of the Catholics in the diocese by building churches and schools and promoting the development of the Catholic healthcare system and social outreach programs. Under his leadership, a new CATHE-DRAL, close to 100 churches, 1 college, 52 elementary and high schools, and 5 hospitals had been established. In recognition of Bishop Swint's contributions to the development of the Catholic Church in West Virginia, Pope PIUS XII conferred upon him the title of *archbishop ad personam.*

Bishop Joseph H. Hodges (1911–1985) succeeded Archbishop Swint as the fifth bishop of the diocese in 1962. His participation in the Second Vatican Council proved to be a defining moment in his life and led to his becoming a major source of renewal and reform for the diocese. He dedicated his episcopacy to implementing the reforms of the council, which encompassed all aspects of Church life and led to new initiatives in the areas of SOCIAL JUSTICE, evangelization, and ecumenism. He was a leader in the state ECUMENICAL MOVEMENT and an advocate for social justice for all West Virginians. He was a driving force behind "The Land Is Home to Me," the 1975 pastoral letter issued jointly by the Roman Catholic bishops of Appalachia that addressed the issues of economic and political powerlessness among the people of the region. During his episcopacy Bishop Hodges also established the four diocesan pastoral centers—Bishop Hodges Pastoral Center in Huttonsville, Blessed John XXIII Pastoral Center in Charleston, Paul VI Pastoral Center in Wheeling, and Priest Field Pastoral Center in Kearneysville. The centers serve as places for all parishes throughout the diocese to gather and host an array of workshops, retreats, and other events. Hodges died on January 27, 1985, after serving as bishop of the diocese for twenty-three years.

In 1985 Bishop Francis B. Schulte (1926–) succeeded Bishop Hodges to become the sixth bishop of the diocese. During Bishop Schulte's episcopacy, the diocesan Catholic Charities underwent reorganization, making it a separate legal entity from the diocese. This reorganization allowed Catholic Charities greater access to state contracts and a broader presence in the state. Bishop Schulte also co-signed the economic pastoral letter "Justice for All" with Episcopal Bishop Robert Atkinson of the Episcopal Diocese of West Virginia. In 1987 St. Joseph Preparatory School in Vienna, the only remaining high school seminary in the diocese, closed due to declining enrollment, marking the end of the high school seminary era. In 1988 Bishop Schulte was appointed the twelfth archbishop of the Diocese of New Orleans, Louisiana, and was ordained in 1989. In 2002 Archbishop Schulte became the archbishop emeritus of the Diocese of New Orleans, having reached the age of retirement.

Bishop Bernard W. Schmitt (1928–) succeeded Bishop Schulte to become the seventh bishop of the diocese in 1989. Under the guidance of Bishop Schmitt, the diocese amalgamated and closed a number of parishes, built new churches and schools in burgeoning areas, and changed the diocesan offices, restructuring services and parishes to better serve diocesan needs. Bishop Schmitt was also the author of several pastoral letters, the first of which was on the family. He authored pastoral letters on each of the seven sacraments—"Do This in Remembrance of Me," "Born of Water and Spirit," "Confirmed in the Faith," "God's Gift of Shepherds for His Flock," "Manifesting God's Covenant of Love," "Turn Away from Sin and Be Faithful to the Gospel," "The Saving Mystery of God," and "The Eucharist: Our Communion & Our Mission," a second letter on the EUCHARIST. He was also among the signatories of "At Home in the Web of Life" and the resigning of "This Land Is Home to Me" on the fifteenth anniversary of the the original signing. In 2003 Bishop Schmitt dedicated the West Virginia Catholic Heritage Center in Wheeling—later named the Bishop Bernard W. Schmitt Catholic Heritage Center in honor of his commitment to the Catholic history of West Virginia—which provides a repository for diocesan artifacts and history. Also, under Bishop Schmitt the Cathedral of St. Joseph in Wheeling underwent extensive renovations, many of which improved functionality and others that made permanent the temporary renovations done according to the Second Vatican Council. The permanent diaconate program, originally established under Bishop Hodges following the Second Vatican Council, was reestablished.

Following the retirement of Bishop Schmitt, Bishop Michael J. Bransfield (1943–), who formerly served as the rector of the Basilica of the NATIONAL SHRINE OF THE IMMACULATE CONCEPTION in Washington, D.C., began his episcopacy in 2005. Bishop Bransfield expressed his concern for Wheeling Hospital, the only remaining diocesan-owned and –operated hospital in the state, and implemented many changes to assure its good financial standing and longevity. Continuing his focus on health and well-being, Bishop Bransfield promulgated his first pastoral letter "A Church That Heals" in 2006, encouraging Catholics in West Virginia to be responsible stewards of health and challenging Catholic communities to work toward better health conditions and practices. In the first years of Bishop Bransfield's episcopacy, three priests were elevated to the title prelate of honor—Monsignor P. Edward Sadie in 2005, Monsignor Frederick P. Annie in 2006, and Monsignor Samuel S. Sacus in 2008; eight individuals received the Pro Ecclesia et Pontifice Medal from Pope BENEDICT XVI, and two individuals were named knights of the

Pontifical Equestrian Order of St. Gregory the Great by Pope Benedict XVI.

Twenty-First-Century Developments. In 1997 the governance of the diocese changed as the fourteen deaneries—Wheeling, Weirton, Fairmont, Parkersburg, Clarksburg, Martinsburg, Weston, Beckley, Bluefield, Elkins, Charleston, Huntington, Keyser, and Logan—were reorganized into seven vicariates—Wheeling, Charleston, Beckley, Clarksburg, Martinsburg, Parkersburg, and Weston. This restructuring occurred because the deaneries covered areas that were too small, whereas the larger vicariate structure provided a more critical mass of churches, better representation of Catholics throughout West Virginia, and allowed for the centralization of diocesan services. In each vicariate, a pastoral services liaison, a faith formation consultant, and a regional director of Catholic Charities West Virginia, along with the VICAR FORANE, work to provide for the specific needs of their vicariate and address Church needs as they arise.

In June 2000 the diocese held the ninth diocesan synod, "On a Journey Together"—the first diocesan synod held since 1933. During the synod Catholics from throughout the state gathered in Wheeling to set goals and charted a new course for the Diocese of Wheeling-Charleston. More than 800 Catholics gathered in the see city for the establishment of the diocesan mission statement and the signing of the primary synodal documents "Our Ministry and Our Communion: Celebrated, Believed, and Lived," "Called and Sent by Name," "The Church: Wise Teacher and Youthful Preacher," and "The Church in Society and the Society of Church."

The first diocesan Eucharistic Congress was held at the Charleston Civic Center in June 2003. Catholics from throughout the state gathered to learn about social justice, EUCHARISTIC DEVOTION, music in LITURGY, and other Church topics. The Eucharistic Congress also provided the opportunity for Catholics from throughout the state to gather for Mass together, proving to be the largest gathering of Catholics in West Virginia history.

In compliance with "The Charter for the Protection of Children and Young People," the diocese established the Office of Safe Environment in 2003. This office is staffed full time and provides screening, awareness programs, and sexual abuse prevention training programs to assure the safety of children throughout churches and Catholic schools in West Virginia. Each year the Office of Safe Environment spends more than $80,000 on programs in Catholic schools, training sessions for diocesan employees, background checks, and other expenses.

The Diocese of Wheeling-Charleston faces many challenges, ranging from the provision of services throughout the state when the main offices are located in the northernmost area to the pastoring of parishes. As fewer and fewer priests serve in the diocese, staffing parishes and sustaining small parish communities become difficult challenges. In most cases parishes are either amalgamated or a single priest serves multiple parishes, which can be difficult as the priest must spend more time traveling than he spends with the parish communities he serves. The need for priests also creates pressure for a shorter learning period for new priests, which may give them less on-the-job training and have an impact on pastoral care. In responding to the needs of parishes throughout the state, the diocese has welcomed priests from countries throughout the world—many of whom have come from Ireland, India, Africa, and countries throughout eastern Europe—which can present some cultural and language challenges. In 2007, to address the declining number of active priests, the age of retirement for priests was raised from sixty-five to seventy.

Contributions of Religious Orders. The arrival of the first religious preceded the founding of the diocese. The Sisters of the Visitation came to Wheeling in 1848 to open an academy for young women at the invitation of Bishop Whelan. Wheeling Female Academy, later known as Mount de Chantal Visitation Academy, opened April 10, 1848, with thirty students enrolled. It was the first of three academies established by the order in the diocese, which also included De Sales Heights Academy, Parkersburg, and Villa Maria Academy, Abingdon, later Wytheville. Originally located near the Cathedral of St. Joseph, the academy and CONVENT relocated outside Wheeling in 1865. Following the 2007–2008 school year, Mount de Chantal, the only remaining Visitation academy in the diocese, closed after 160 years due to rising operation costs and declining enrollment. The Sisters of the Visitation also established St. Joseph's Benevolent School for the children of St. James Parish in Wheeling in 1848. The school, now Wheeling Catholic Elementary School, continues to serve the children of inner-city Wheeling.

The Capuchin Friars were the first male religious order to serve the diocese. Bishop Kain invited the FRIARS to administer the diocesan German parish St. Alphonsus in Wheeling in 1884. Through their work at St. Alphonsus, the Capuchins established an important apostolate among the German community and ministered to German-speaking immigrants throughout the Northern Panhandle. In 1900 they expanded their mission by taking over Sacred Heart Parish in Charleston, currently the Co-Cathedral of the Sacred Heart, and the missions in the Kanawha Valley for which it was responsible. In the early twenty-first century, the parishes that stand as witness to their labors include St. Francis of Assisi Parish in St. Albans, Christ the King Parish in

Ordination and Installation of a New Bishop. *The Most Rev. Michael J. Bransfield lies prostrate in front of the altar during his ordination and installation as the eighth Roman Catholic bishop of West Virginia during services at St. Joseph Cathedral in Wheeling, West Virginiaon on Feb. 22, 2005.* **AP IMAGES**

Dunbar, and Our Lady of the Hills Parish in Elkview. Although the order has withdrawn from both the Co-Cathedral of the Sacred Heart and St. Alphonsus, it continues to administer St. Anthony Parish in Charleston, which now serves as the main residence of the friars in southern West Virginia.

The Marist Fathers are another religious community with longstanding service in the diocese. Bishop Donahue first invited them in 1898 to administer the newly founded St. Michael Parish in Wheeling. Their MINISTRY soon expanded when they agreed to take responsibility for the diocesan parishes and missions in central West Virginia. Holy Rosary Parish in Buckhannon, St. Anne Parish in Webster Springs, and Holy Family Parish in Richwood are among the parishes the Marist Fathers founded in the diocese. They continue to serve in Wheeling and central West Virginia.

The Marist Fathers were also responsible for bringing the PALLOTTINE MISSIONARY SISTERS into the diocese in 1912. Together they built and staffed the first Catholic schools and hospitals in central West Virginia. The hospitals at Richwood and Buckhannon were the first of four established by the Pallottine Missionary Sisters in the diocese. The sisters expanded their ministry in 1923, establishing St. Mary's Hospital in Huntington. They also maintained their commitment to education when they arrived in Huntington by staffing parish schools in the southern region of the diocese. Bishop Donahue in 1899 invited the Sisters of Our Lady of Charity of Refuge, a Canadian congregation of women religious now known as the North American Union of the Sisters of OUR LADY OF CHARITY, to establish a community in Wheeling. The sisters founded Good Shepherd Home for Young Ladies in Wheeling to care for young women who were at risk or in need of financial and emotional support. Over its history Good Shepherd Home took in more than ten thousand young women from across the state and surrounding communities without regard to religious affiliation. Our Lady of the Valley School, as Good Shepherd came to be known, closed in 1972. The sisters transferred the property to the diocese, and the building was converted into Good Shepherd Home for the Aged through a financial bequest from Clara Welty. The sisters continue to maintain a presence at the home.

In 1955 the Society of Jesus accepted Archbishop John J. Swint's invitation to administer Wheeling College, now Wheeling Jesuit University—the only Catholic institution of higher learning in West Virginia. Wheeling College was established as a coeducational liberal arts college in the Jesuit tradition. It is located on sixty acres of property that was purchased by the diocese from the Sisters of the Visitation of Mount de Chantal Visitation Academy in Wheeling. Ground was broken for the first building November 23, 1953, and the college was dedicated two years later on October 23, 1955 and ninety students were enrolled in its first class. The diocese financed the construction of the first three college buildings, which were named after the three bishops most closely associated with its founding—Bishop Richard V. Whelan, Bishop Patrick J. Donahue, and Bishop John J. Swint. The first women's dormitory, completed in 1959, was dedicated to Sara Tracy in recognition of her significant contributions to the college. At Wheeling Jesuit University, the Jesuit traditions of educational excellence and service to others have guided all of its programs. The university has an enrollment of close to 1,900 students and offers more than thirty majors, five graduate programs, and one doctoral program. Since 1995 *U.S. News & World Report* has ranked Wheeling Jesuit University among the top institutions in its "Best Master's Universities in the South" category. The university is also home of the Robert C. Byrd National Technology Transfer Center, the Erma Ora Byrd Center for Educational Technologies, the NASA-sponsored Classroom of the Future, a Challenger Learning Center, and the Clifford M. Lewis, S.J., Appalachian Institute.

Other religious congregations that have made significant contributions in West Virginia include the Sisters of Divine Providence, Sisters Auxiliaries of the Apostolate, Daughters of Charity, Ursuline Sisters, Dominican Sisters, Capuchin Franciscans, Passionist Fathers, GLENMARY HOME MISSIONERS fathers, and many other religious orders of men and women.

Sisters of St. Joseph of Wheeling. In 1853 concern over the staffing and administration of Wheeling Hospital, founded by Bishop Whelan and Dr. Simon Hullihen in 1850, brought a second religious order to the diocese. In 1952 Bishop Whelan had petitioned the SISTERS OF ST. JOSEPH of Carondelet, Missouri, to found a convent in the diocese. Their decision to accept his invitation had tremendous implications for the development of the diocese. Shortly after their arrival, the Sisters of St. Joseph expanded their ministry to include education and social ministries. Over the course of their history in the diocese, the sisters have administered 4 hospitals—Wheeling Hospital, St. Mary Hospital in Clarksburg, St. Joseph Hospital in Parkersburg, and St. Francis Hospital in Charleston—2 orphanages; more than 60 parish schools; and numerous catechism and social outreach programs. An effort to reorganize the governance of the Sisters of St. Joseph of Carondelet in the United States led the members of the Wheeling convent to establish an independent motherhouse in 1860 and to call themselves the Sisters of St. Joseph of Wheeling, the only religious order incorporated in the diocese. Membership in the community peaked in the

1960s with close to 300 sisters. At the end of the twentieth century, however, the community was comprised of approximately 100 sisters. In April 2007 the Sisters of St. Joseph in Wheeling and 6 other Sisters of St. Joseph congregations joined to form the Congregation of St. Joseph, thus ending the 154–year ministry of the Sisters of St. Joseph of Wheeling. As a new congregation, the sisters continue to provide services in Wheeling and in each congregation's original location, while allowing the opportunity to extend the sisters' mission of service.

Catholic Contributions in West Virginia. Catholics of West Virginia have made tremendous contributions to the communities in which they live. They have been engaged in many charitable activities, including the establishment of hospitals and orphanages to care for the most vulnerable members of society. The diocese has become the second largest provider of social services in the state, operating 16 programs, ranging from disaster and emergency relief to pregnancy and parenting classes, with offices established in every region of the state. The Catholic school system in West Virginia, which includes 8 high schools and 27 elementary schools in addition to a number of preschool and daycare programs, began in 1838 and is the largest privately run school system in the state. It provides education in the Catholic tradition for all students in a nurturing, Christ-centered environment.

From Wheeling Hospital, the first hospital founded in West Virginia, to the Children's Health Care Clinic in Pineville, the Catholic healthcare system has benefited tens of thousands of state citizens and has provided the people of West Virginia not only with quality healthcare for the past 150 years, but with a ministry of healing rooted in Catholic tradition that embraces the spiritual values of compassion, hospitality, and reverence for the sanctity of human life.

SEE ALSO CATHOLIC CHARITIES USA; EUCHARISTIC CONGRESSES; PASSIONISTS; SEX ABUSE CRISIS; URSULINES; VATICAN COUNCIL II.

BIBLIOGRAPHY

M. B. Bradley et al., "State Summary, Table 3: Churches and Church Membership by State and Denomination, 1990," in *Churches and Church Membership in the U.S., 1990* (Atlanta, Ga. 1992) p. 35.

Tricia T. Pyne
Historian and Archivist
Diocese of Wheeling-Charleston, Wheeling, W.Va.

D. F. Kratzer
Assistant Editor, *The Catholic Spirit*
Diocese of Wheeling-Charleston (2009)

WISCONSIN, CATHOLIC CHURCH IN

The development of Catholic life in the state of Wisconsin shares the characteristics of the emergence of organized Catholic life in other areas of the upper Midwest. Indeed, its distinctive identity is coextensive with the emergence of the larger patterns of social and economic development in this region of the United States.

First Contacts. Wisconsin was Indian territory before the arrival of Europeans. Chippewa, Menominee, Ho-Chunk, Sauk, Fox, and Miami all laid claim to parts of the land. Europeans patrolled the shores of Lake Michigan in search of water routes to the West. But French fur traders first established trading posts at Green Bay in the east and Prairie du Chien on the west, among other places. These traders came down the Fox River from Green Bay, portaged to the Wisconsin River, and traveled southwest to the Mississippi. Catholic missionaries, mostly JESUITS, used these same routes to spread the Catholic FAITH to the Indians. The majority of settlement took place south of this Fox/Wisconsin axis, which ran diagonally down the state.

French explorer Jean Nicolet (1598–1642) was the first European to enter Wisconsin in 1634. In 1656 French fur traders began operations around Lake Superior. In 1660 Jesuit missionary Rene Menard (1605–1661) began his MINISTRY among the Huron Indians who had fled to Wisconsin. Menard perished in the wilderness and was replaced in October 1665 by a fellow Jesuit, Father Claude Jean ALLOUEZ. At Chequamegon Bay on Lake Superior, Allouez established a CHAPEL a few miles east of present-day Ashland, Wisconsin. In 1669 Allouez opened a mission at present-day Oconto on Green Bay and in 1670, a mission chapel at DePere. Two other missions were established at river intersections to take advantage of these well-traveled fur-trading sites. Successive Jesuit fathers, including Fathers Claude DABLON and Jacques MARQUETTE, penetrated more deeply into the Wisconsin interior.

During this period of initial contact, Jesuit missionaries achieved varying degrees of success with the Indian tribes and the resident French Canadians at Green Bay and Prairie du Chien. Religious development in the region suffered a severe setback in 1682 with the eruption of Indian hostilities. Later, the reconcentration policies of French governor Antoine Cadillac (1658–1730) also had a negative impact on Catholic ministerial efforts. The simmering rivalry between England and France over control of the North American interior exploded in the French and Indian War of 1756–1763. France's loss of the region further marginalized missionary efforts in the Wisconsin area. By 1728 only one solitary priest, John Baptist CHARDON, S.J., remained in Green Bay. The suppression of the Society of Jesus in 1763 dealt an additional blow to the development of the Church in this region. From 1728 until 1823, the remnant of Wisconsin Catholics (converted Indians and French-Canadian traders) received only the occasional ministry of itinerant priests.

Territorial/Early Statehood Period (1820–1870). Wisconsin was transferred to British control after the French and Indian War in 1763. The United States gained the territory in 1783 after the American Revolution. In 1787 the American Confederation congress laid down a pattern of governance for the area by terms of the Northwest Ordinance. Wisconsin was created as a territory in 1836 and entered the federal union in 1848.

Even before Wisconsin statehood, the federal government established three strategic forts along its critical waterways in 1816: Fort Crawford at Prairie du Chien, Fort Winnebago at Portage, and Fort Howard at Green Bay. The government also extinguished Indian claims and built military roads that facilitated internal development.

Critical as well to Wisconsin growth was the development of its local economy. Wisconsin's fertile farmlands and desirable lakefront harbors were not easily accessible until the Erie Canal opened in 1825. The advent of quick and inexpensive lake travel, coupled with the availability of choice sections of Wisconsin land set off a rush of settlement that brought hundreds of Catholics to the region in the 1830s and 1840s. In addition to a thriving lead industry in the southwestern corner of the state, the Wisconsin economy flourished with grain farming, dairying, and lumbering. Lake commerce gave a tremendous boost to commercial agriculture.

Ecclesiastically, Wisconsin began under the jurisdiction of the Diocese of Quebec and remained under its control even after France was expelled from the region in 1763. In 1791 the area was formally transferred to the new See of Baltimore. In 1808 it came under the direction of the newly created Diocese of Bardstown, Kentucky. Bardstown's first bishop, Benedict Joseph FLAGET, actually visited Wisconsin. After this solitary trip he impressed on Roman officials that it was too far for him to ever go again. In 1821 Wisconsin was transferred to the See of Cincinnati and in 1833 was placed under the jurisdiction of the newly created Diocese of Detroit.

Various itinerant priests visited the territory and ministered to the remaining French-speaking Catholics at either Prairie du Chien or Green Bay. In 1816 Trappist Marie Joseph Dunand organized the Prairie du Chien Catholics into a congregation. Father Gabriel RI-

CHARD, a missionary from Michigan, visited Green Bay in 1823 and again in 1826. He noted on one of these trips that 1,224 Catholics lived in Green Bay and an additional 720 in Prairie du Chien. Richard laid plans for a church in Green Bay to replace one that had burned in 1687. In 1825 another wandering missionary, Vincent Badin, visited Wisconsin settlements. While the territory was under the jurisdiction of the Diocese of Cincinnati, Dominican bishop Edward FENWICK inspected Catholic churches and conducted a mission.

Mazzuchelli. By 1830 the Wisconsin territory had grown, and the numbers of Catholics clamoring for stable priestly ministration and regular WORSHIP surged. In 1831 one of the most famous Wisconsin missionaries, Dominican Samuel Charles MAZZUCHELLI, arrived in the state from the upper peninsula of Michigan. Energetic and peripatetic, Mazzuchelli began his work in Wisconsin at Green Bay, where he constructed a church and worked with local Indians. In 1834 he moved to Galena, Illinois, the heart of the lead-mining region. Upon his return to Wisconsin in 1844, he established a number of parishes in the southwestern corner of the state, a college for Catholic men, and a native sisterhood of DOMINICAN SISTERS, which still exists at Sinsinawa Mound. Until his death in 1864, Mazzuchelli was an important force for Catholic development in Wisconsin and he is currently under consideration for BEATIFICATION.

Mazzuchelli was typical of the priests that came to Wisconsin in this early period. Not only was he an agent of spiritual ministry, but also through his associations with land speculators and local politicians, he exercised an influence beyond the realm of the sanctuary and the SACRISTY. During the territorial period and early statehood, the boundaries between CHURCH AND STATE were not as sharply drawn as they would be later. Even non-Catholic lay figures, such as future territorial governor James Doty (1799–1865), regarded the Church as an important element of social order in Wisconsin and noted its presence as a selling point to those interested in moving there.

Diocese of Wisconsin. When Wisconsin was formally organized as a territory in 1836, the sale of federal lands proceeded rapidly. The new onslaught of people who arrived in the 1840s migrated to the chain of attractive cities that grew up around the shore of Lake Michigan. These included Southport (later Kenosha), Racine, and Milwaukee, the latter destined to become the population hub of the state and the leader in Catholic life.

Milwaukee's prominence as the leading city on the lake and the source of population made it a logical center for Catholic growth. The Detroit priest Florimond Bonduel (1799–1861) offered the first Mass in the city in 1833. Land for a small chapel for the tiny Catholic community was donated by one of the city founders, the French-Canadian Solomon Juneau (1793–1856). Increasing numbers of priests worked in the scattered centers of Catholic population along the lake and in the agricultural hinterland. One of these, Martin KUNDIG, a native of Switzerland, was ordained to serve in Cincinnati and Detroit; he eventually migrated to Milwaukee and quickly recognized the potential of the city as a center for Catholic life. He effectively propagandized for the city and the territory, writing letters to eastern newspapers describing robust parochial growth and recounting the wonders of the region. Kundig's salesmanship bore fruit in 1842, when the bishops of the Fifth Provincial Council of Baltimore petitioned ROME to establish a new DIOCESE in Wisconsin. At the time of the petition, estimates indicate nearly 7,000 Catholics were scattered throughout the state. On November 28, 1843, by the bull *In Suprema Militantis*, Pope GREGORY XVI erected the Diocese of Wisconsin with Milwaukee as its see city. He appointed the Swiss-born priest of the Archdiocese of CINCINNATI, John Martin HENNI, as its first BISHOP.

Henni. Henni was born in Switzerland in 1805 and, together with Kundig, had been ordained for the Diocese of Cincinnati in 1828. In Cincinnati he devoted himself to the pastoral needs of the growing number of Germans migrating to the state. He received episcopal consecration on March 19, 1844, and arrived in Milwaukee in company with Father Michael HEISS on May 5, 1844. Henni's reputation as an apostle to the Germans certainly played a role in attracting many German-speaking Catholics to the state. In 1848 Wisconsin entered the federal union.

Henni toured his huge diocese, which comprised the entire state of Wisconsin and a small portion of present-day Minnesota east of the Mississippi. He traveled to the shores of Lake Superior, where Father Frederic BARAGA had restarted the mission on the shores of Lake Superior, abandoned long ago by Allouez. He visited Indian villages, prospering farming communities, and the growing cities of the lake coast. Many places were still in a primitive state of development. But in the counties abutting the busy Lake Michigan, he discovered church-building occurring in Oak Creek, Racine, Kenosha, Burlington, Brighton, Geneva, and Yorkville. By 1853 the Catholic population had grown to 100,000, and the number of priests serving had risen from 19 in 1843 to 64.

Henni also sampled the ethnic diversity of his Catholic flock. There were still old French-Canadian settlers, various Catholic Indians, colonies of Dutch and Belgian Catholics in and around Green Bay, and a small,

but vibrant, Irish community. But to his (and their) delight, he found large numbers of German-speakers, who established Wisconsin's place on the famed *German triangle* of the Midwest together with St. Louis and Cincinnati. But despite this diversity and the growing number of English-speaking Catholics, Henni and his successors Michael Heiss (1881–1890) and Frederick X. KATZER (1890–1903) insisted on maintaining the strong Teutonic flavor of Wisconsin Catholicism. All of the early bishops encouraged the foundation of German-language parishes and parochial schools. To support these endeavors Henni sought and received funds from missionary societies in France, Austria, and Bavaria. Ministering to German Catholics was a key priority for him.

German Catholics were anxious to create their own national institutions. Henni settled down near the first Catholic church of St. Peter in Milwaukee and laid plans to build a new CATHEDRAL. With funds raised from begging tours, he eventually built St. John the Evangelist Cathedral. A mixture of ethnic groups dominated the cathedral church. In 1846 a group of German-speakers formed St. Mary's Church, the first German-ethnic Church in Milwaukee. Located a few blocks west of the cathedral, it became the hub of German Catholic life and the mother Church for a number of German congregations in the city. Parochial expansion in the nineteenth century was tied to ethnicity. Until the 1920s most parishes were formed for ethnic groups or were English-speaking. Reflecting neighborhood residence patterns, rival churches were often located within blocks of each other. Kenosha's first two churches, for example, were for Germans and Irish respectively. Milwaukee had three German parishes by mid-century, while the Cathedral served the English-speaking.

An additional boost to German ambitions was the creation of a seminary for German-speaking priests. Henni built such a seminary and dedicated it to the scholarly bishop of Geneva, St. FRANCIS DE SALES. The Salesianum, as it was known throughout the region, opened its doors in 1856 and was headed by Bavarian Father Michael Heiss. St. Francis quickly acquired a national reputation as a seminary for German-speaking youth. It also was the major supplier of priests for the dioceses of Wisconsin and the upper Midwest until the 1980s.

Religious Orders. With his fellow German Catholics, Henni placed a high priority on parochial schools and recruited RELIGIOUS women from the German-speaking areas of Europe to teach in them. Mother Caroline Friess (1824–1892) and the SCHOOL SISTERS OF NOTRE DAME arrived in 1850 in Milwaukee, where they established their motherhouse. The School Sisters became one of the most powerful influences in Catholic education in the city of Milwaukee as well as in Prairie du Chien. The School Sisters of St. Francis, whose members fanned out across the Midwest, also established their general headquarters in Milwaukee in 1871. Dominican Sisters from Regensburg, Germany, under Mother Benedicta Bauer (d. 1865) established themselves in Racine and opened an academy named for St. CATHERINE OF SIENA in 1864. A group of Franciscan tertiaries, which eventually evolved into a religious order, associated themselves with the care of the diocesan seminary and were indeed the original owners of the land on which it would sit. A split in this community in 1871 created the Franciscan Sisters of Perpetual Adoration, who became prominent in La Crosse.

German religious communities found a favorable reception in Wisconsin. In St. Nazianz, a small farming village north of Milwaukee, Father Ambrose Oschwald (1801–1873) attempted to create a Catholic communitarian society in the 1850s. The failure of this endeavor brought the lands into the hands of the Society of the Divine Savior (Salvatorian Fathers) and the Sisters of the DIVINE SAVIOR in 1895. In 1896 the Salvatorian Fathers opened a MONASTERY at the site. Associated with the first St. Nazianz project were the Franciscan Sisters of Charity, who established themselves in Manitowoc. Capuchin Franciscan Friars began their work in 1857 and opened a seminary at Mount Calvary, Wisconsin, in 1860. The Society of Jesus (Jesuits) settled first in Milwaukee and then resumed work in Wisconsin in 1849. In 1879 they took over a boys academy in Prairie du Chien, founded by the CHRISTIAN BROTHERS, and renamed it for St. Edmund CAMPION.

The emphasis on German-speaking ministry did not mean that the pastoral needs of English speakers were neglected. The Daughters of Charity, an American community, opened one of the first hospitals in Milwaukee. The Sinsinawa DOMINICANS, founded by Father Samuel Mazzuchelli, also taught in the parochial schools of English-speaking parishes.

Catholic Church and Society. Interreligious rivalry existed not only with evangelical groups, but even more with numerous German Lutherans who matched the Catholics church for church. Relatively minor Nativist disturbances broke out in the city in the mid-1850s abetted by local Whigs who feared the potential political power of the largely immigrant flock and their affiliation with the Democrats. Despite some harsh words, bitter editorials in the anti–Catholic press, and occasional catcalls and pranks against priests and sisters, anti–Catholic Nativism never seriously affected the mission and identity of the Catholic Church in Wisconsin.

An informal symbiosis existed between Church and civil society for much of the nineteenth century in Wisconsin. In many parts of the state, Catholics dominated public school boards and could easily shape school policies to their liking. Religious sisters even taught in public schools. Catholic social welfare institutions served the general public. The first Catholic hospital in Milwaukee staffed by the Daughters of Charity also housed the Milwaukee County sick poor until the county built their own facilities in 1861. In 1845 Wisconsin's first public school opened in the basement of St. Mark's Catholic Church in Kenosha.

New Dioceses. As early as his venture of 1844, Henni realized that the broad expanse of his diocese would be too much for one man. In the 1850s the creation of the Diocese of St. Paul took away some of the territory in the northwest. In 1868 two new dioceses were created in Wisconsin. The diocese of Green Bay was established on March 3, 1868, with Austrian-born Joseph Melcher (1806–1873), a priest of the Diocese of St. Louis, as its first bishop. To the southwest, La Crosse, founded in 1841, was chosen as a see city, and Henni's close friend and associate Michael Heiss was selected as its first bishop. In 1875 Milwaukee was raised to metropolitan status, and Henni named ARCHBISHOP. The development of La Crosse and Green Bay dioceses proceeded much more slowly than Milwaukee. Both had vaster and less-populated areas in which to minister.

Catholicism in the Industrial Era (1870–1945). A decisive shift in the development of Catholic life in Wisconsin came about when the economic base of the area shifted dramatically from commercial agriculture to industrial production. The prominence of Wisconsin as a grain-, dairy-, and lumber-producing state had been well established by mid-century. Significant changes in the Wisconsin economy began before the Civil War with the advent of the railroad. By 1857 rail expansion linked Milwaukee with Prairie du Chien. The Wisconsin rail lines increased their mileage and, through consolidation of smaller lines, increased their efficiency.

The railroad also linked Wisconsin more securely to the emerging Midwestern industrial economy. Industrial manufacturing came to the Milwaukee suburb of Bay View in the early 1870s and then to the other cities along the lakeshore: Kenosha, Racine, and Sheboygan. Manufacturing soon replaced farming and shipping as major industries, and Wisconsin became known for a variety of industrially processed products (most notably beer) and also for a respectable line of manufactured goods—small engines, hardware, and earthenware. More and more Wisconsinites earned their living in factories, breweries, and processing plants. They swelled the population of the cities where they worked. Industrialism brought about great changes in society as people moved to urban centers and adapted to the demands of factory work. Many of the Catholics in the state held jobs in this industrial work force. Others found service jobs that were dependent on the industrial economy.

Catholics responded to the growth of the cities with new parishes and schools for their swelling numbers. As the size of industrial dioceses grew, they relied more and more on the organizational techniques of big businesses—bureaucracy, record-keeping, and middle-level management—to coordinate all facets of Church organization. With the blessing of Roman authorities, bishops of the state centralized administrative authority into their own hands and those of a hand-picked diocesan bureaucracy.

During the period 1870 to 1890, the Church underwent rapid growth. The Catholic population in Milwaukee went from 155,000 to 280,000, La Crosse increased from about 40,000 to 67,000, and Green Bay grew from 50,000 to 100,000. Even the underpopulated northern reaches of the state experienced the effects of industrial possibilities. Millionaire John D. Rockefeller (1839–1937) laid plans to turn the distant city of Superior into a major shipping depot on the Great Lakes and to locate some heavy industry in the area. In 1905 the HOLY SEE created the Diocese of Superior out of the eighteen northernmost counties of the state and appointed a Milwaukee priest, Augustine Schinner (1863–1937), as its first bishop.

Ethnic Tensions and Peace. Ethnic tensions between German-speaking and English-speaking Catholics flared in Milwaukee over the succession to the ailing Henni. The aged prelate's choice for coadjutor had been his old friend Heiss, who intended to perpetuate Henni's devotion to the German cause. English-speaking priests vigorously opposed the nomination and succeeded in stalling it for two years until 1880. German-speaking bishops continued to be appointed to the Sees of La Crosse and Green Bay into the twentieth century.

The national reputation of Milwaukee, and by extension Wisconsin, in the latter years of the nineteenth century was as a bastion of Germanic conservatism. A Milwaukee priest, Peter ABBELEN, presented a petition to Pope LEO XIII (the Abbelen Memorial) in 1886 demanding better treatment of Germans in America. Indeed, Wisconsin bishops in general played an important role in opposing the so-called Americanizers in the U.S. hierarchy. Moreover, the active efforts of German speakers in the state (including Lutherans) were successfully deployed in repealing the Bennett Law in 1890, which attempted to curtail the use of foreign languages in schools.

But German hegemony did not last. Industrial work attracted scores of Southern and Eastern immigrants. Polish Catholics, who appeared in greater numbers after 1880, came mostly from the German-dominated area of the former Polish state. Large numbers lived in urban areas, but some also settled in rural areas. Close to 200,000 first- and second-generation Poles may have lived in Wisconsin by 1900. The first Milwaukee Polish-ethnic congregation, St. Stanislaus, opened its doors in 1866. From this nucleus the Polish community expanded rapidly on the south side of the city, dotting the urban landscape with numerous churches and schools.

Bohemians, already on the scene since the 1860s, settled mainly in Racine. A Bohemian parish opened in Milwaukee in 1865 and in Racine, in 1897. Slovaks arrived in statistically measurable numbers in the late nineteenth century, adding to the medley of parishes in most cities. Between 1900 and 1910 the Wisconsin Italian community grew significantly in Milwaukee, Racine, Kenosha, Madison, and Beloit.

For all these newcomers, the ethnic urban parish became a mainstay of their religious identity. The domes and steeples of these churches rose against the skyline of virtually every major city of Wisconsin, some of them, like the majestic St. Josaphat's Basilica in Milwaukee, of truly mammoth proportions. The ethnic Church served not only as a spiritual center, but also offered an array of social services to ease the strains of urban life. German parishes had intricate networks of organizations (*vereinen*) organized according to age and gender. Polish Church life expended much energy on the issue of Poland's restoration as an independent country. Italian Catholics in Kenosha, Racine, Beloit, and Milwaukee replicated devotions from the *mezzogiorno* and withstood pressures to build Catholic schools, which they distrusted.

German Catholic leaders held the reins of power well into the twentieth century, and ethnic tension flared once again, this time from Polish Catholics. Like the English-speaking dissidents of the previous generation, they demanded representation in the Wisconsin hierarchy based on their numbers and the intensity of their Catholicism. These demands, fanned by the writing of Polish Catholic layman Michael Kruszka (1860–1918) on the pages of his newspaper *Kuryer Polski* as well in as the heated pulpit oratory of his half-brother priest, Wenceslaus Kruszka (1868–1937), clashed violently with the authority of the final German-speaking bishop of Milwaukee, Sebastian G. MESSMER (1904–1930), and nearly created a SCHISM within the large Polish-Catholic community. Milwaukee had one Polish-speaking auxiliary bishop, Michigan priest Edward Kozlowski (1914–1915), who lived only a year after his consecration. Messmer tried to placate Poles with the appointment of the multi-lingual Bishop Joseph KOUDELKA, a Bohemian. However, the Poles disliked and would not accept him, and Messmer came to distrust him and had him sent to far-off Superior. Later,

Chicago pastor Paul Peter Rhode (1871–1945) was sent to Green Bay; this began a series of Polish bishops that lasted in that see until the appointment of Robert Banks (bishop, 1990–2003) of Boston in 1990.

Eventually, the hegemony of German Catholics in Wisconsin began to wane by the late nineteenth century. In the 1890s, German Catholic school lessons became bilingual as did parish services, especially devotions, confessions, and sermons. By World War I anti–German feelings gave the bishops of the state the necessary cover to curtail German-language services, religious instruction, and record keeping. Ultimately, immigration in the twenties undercut the perpetuation of ethnicity in Wisconsin. Intermarriage and the Americanizing effects of schooling and public media (radio and movies) decreased ethnic differences.

The steady growth of the urban churches continued. Moreover, the number of priests increased apace as well. From 1870 to 1890, the numbers of priests serving in the three Wisconsin dioceses rose from 197 to 432 (diocesan and religious). The number of Catholics in the state rose at the same time from approximately 250,000 to nearly 450,000. From 1910 to 1940 the number of priests in the four dioceses of the state rose from 837 (diocesan and religious) to 1,494. The number of Catholics for the same period spiraled from 532,217 to 828,140. Catholics in Wisconsin broke the one million mark in 1960, when they recorded more than 1.2 million adherents. The heaviest concentrations of Catholics continued to be in the eastern dioceses of Milwaukee and Green Bay. Madison and La Crosse kept a slower pace, and Superior, its early hopes of becoming a major port on Lake Superior and an industrial center dashed early in the century, always lagged at well under 100,000 Catholics.

Centralized and Romanized. The reorganization of Catholic life in the dioceses of Wisconsin took the form of greater episcopal centralization and the reconfiguration of Catholic identity based on doctrinal distinction rather than ethnicity. Under the direction of Sebastian Messmer (1904–1930) and his successors in Milwaukee, Samuel A. STRITCH (1930–1940) and Moses Elias Kiley (1940–1953), diocesan administration was increasingly centralized and authoritarian. The episcopal residence moved to a stately mansion on the most prestigious street in Milwaukee. Bishops in all dioceses created centrally directed social welfare agencies and school departments, each headed by specially trained priests who functioned as mid-level managers of these large and complex institutions. The diocesan seminary shed its status as a provincial, and even regional, institution and focused its attention on candidates from Milwaukee. Most of these reforms were sanctioned by a new Code of Canon Law which became operative in 1918.

In La Crosse, auxiliary bishop William J. Griffin (1935–1944) spearheaded these efforts. Griffin, a Chicago priest, had been sent in 1935 to aid his old friend and fellow Chicagoan, the elderly and ailing Alexander McGavick (1921–1948). After McGavick outlived his auxiliary and another bishop with the rank of coadjutor, John Patrick Treacy (1946–1964) stepped in. A priest of Cleveland, Treacy was an indefatigable builder and a strong authoritarian. He succeeded McGavick in 1946 and built a minor seminary, which opened in 1951, and a new cathedral, which was dedicated in 1962. In Green Bay, Bishop Paul P. Rhode (1915–1945) implemented reforms in diocesan life. He appointed a school superintendent in 1917 and in 1928 created a unified school department under the direction of Edward J. Wiestenberger, Ph.D. In 1918 he created a diocesan social welfare bureau to coordinate child welfare efforts.

The paucity of clergy and Catholics in the Diocese of Superior kept bureaucratization at a slower pace, but even this diocese experienced a brief boomlet of expansion in the twenties, which culminated in Bishop Joseph Gabriel Pinten's (1921–1926) construction of a magnificent cathedral. Unfortunately, the economic collapse of the region during the Depression left a terrible burden of debt, under which the diocese struggled until the return of prosperity during the Second World War.

Impact of Catholic Action Movements. The twenties and thirties saw the emergence of new Catholic organizations of lay men and women under the banner of CATHOLIC ACTION. Urged by Popes PIUS X and PIUS XI, these groups were designed to engage the laity in "the apostolate of the hierarchy." In Wisconsin, Catholic Action became a part of the agenda of the Holy Name Society, the Sodality Movement, and the local chapters of the National Conferences of Catholic Men and Women. In Milwaukee the Holy Name, under the leadership of layman Leo Dohn, enrolled hundreds of men in behalf of popular crusades against public profanity, developed adult education programs, and enlisted hundreds of Catholic professionals in a speaker's bureau. Bishop Rhode began the Holy Name in his diocese in 1922, and a group developed in La Crosse as well. At the urging of the National Catholic Welfare Conference, diverse organizations associated themselves with local councils of Catholic Women. Katherine Williams, an attorney who went on to head the NATIONAL COUNCIL OF CATHOLIC WOMEN, organized the one in Milwaukee. La Crosse began its diocesan council in 1934. These women's groups not only performed charitable works, such as providing housing for single, working women in cities and catechetical instruction for children not enrolled in parochial schools, but also kept a vigilant eye on local and state government, especially on legislation that might affect Catholic interests.

Catholic Youth Activities became a leitmotiv of the career of Auxiliary Bishop William Griffin of La Crosse, who in 1930 adapted the successful model of the Catholic Youth Organization of his native Chicago to the youth needs of the diocese. Milwaukee Catholic athletic programs began under the auspices of the Holy Name and prospered under the direction of layman Peter Murphy. Griffin also pressed for the development of the Sodality in the diocese and made Jesuit Daniel LORD, a regular visitor to the diocese for speaking engagements, its national leader.

One additional Catholic Action group that developed in all the Wisconsin dioceses in the thirties was a branch of the Catholic Rural Life Conference (Milwaukee 1935, La Crosse 1936), promoted by Bishop Edwin Vincent O'HARA of Great Falls. Devoted to the spiritual and educational needs of rural Catholics, it enjoyed great success in the agricultural areas. All Wisconsin dioceses also created branches of the CONFRATERNITY OF CHRISTIAN DOCTRINE in the 1940s. These groups developed programs of RELIGIOUS EDUCATION for children who did not attend parochial schools.

The Catholic Press. The Catholic press flourished during the middle years of the twentieth century, building on older traditions. Catholic journalism had begun in Wisconsin at the behest of Henni who launched *Der Seebote*, a German-language paper in the 1850s. *Die Columbia* was its successor. English-language publications came and went until layman Humphrey J. Desmond (1858–1932) took over as head of *The Catholic Citizen* in 1891. Desmond's career as a Catholic journalist propelled him to the leadership of an impressive chain of Catholic publications. In 1922 Archbishop Messmer of Milwaukee began an official diocesan weekly, called *The Catholic Herald*, to compete with the lay-controlled *Citizen*. The two merged in 1935 and *The Catholic Herald-Citizen* became the dominant Catholic newspaper in the state, spinning off special editions for the dioceses of Superior and Madison. It was renamed *The Catholic Herald* in the eighties. Green Bay began *The Green Bay Register* in 1956, and La Crosse affiliated with the nationwide *Register* chain in 1935. In 1958 it began its own freestanding paper, *The Times-Review*.

The Great Depression hit the economy of Wisconsin gradually, coming into full force in the latter part of 1931. Milwaukee, Racine, Kenosha, Fond du Lac, and other industrialized regions of the state were severely affected. Catholic social welfare agencies, such as the Society of ST. VINCENT DE PAUL, tried to plug the dike of economic collapse, but were overwhelmed, especially in hard-hit Milwaukee, by requests for assistance. Each diocesan administration adopted economies. In Milwaukee Archbishop Samuel Stritch (1930–1940) refused to purchase land for a new major

seminary and delayed plans to rebuild the cathedral that had been gutted by fire in early 1935. In La Crosse Bishop McGavick forbade a subscription drive by the publisher of *The Catholic Daily Tribune* citing "the financial condition of our parishes" and ordered the debt-encumbered parishes of the diocese to retire their outstanding liabilities. Halting the drain of diocesan finances and seeking to avert the financial collapse of the parishes and charities preoccupied the bishops of Depression-era Wisconsin. Stritch inaugurated a special fund-appeal to assist faltering diocesan agencies. The bishop of Superior, Theodore Revermann (1926–1941), tried to pay off the huge debt left by his predecessor for the cathedral.

Wisconsin Catholics entered the ranks of discussion on the causes of the Depression. Of significant note were the writings and activities of two priests: Aloysius MUENCH (1889–1962), who wrote on social issues and publicly challenged Father Charles COUGHLIN's monetary theories, and Francis HAS (1889–1953), who served as a prominent labor mediator and advisor to the Roosevelt administration.

Catholic Higher Education. At this time an emphasis was placed on Catholic higher education. Already in the nineteenth century, Henni had opened Holy Family Catholic Normal School behind the diocesan seminary (later renamed *Pio Nono*). This institution developed a national reputation as a center for training Church musicians under the leadership of layman John Singenberger (1848–1924). Henni's desire to have a Catholic college in Wisconsin was fulfilled in 1881 (the year of his death), when the Jesuits opened Marquette College. In 1893 St. Norbert's College in DePere under the direction of the Canons Regular of Premontre opened its doors. Higher education for Catholic laywomen in the state was made possible when St. Mary's College in Prairie du Chien opened under the auspices of the School Sisters of Notre Dame. In 1928 this college moved to Milwaukee and was renamed Mount Mary.

Catholic higher education for women religious advanced considerably in the twentieth century. With the passage of teacher certification laws and the imposition of standards on schools who wished to send students to the state university, communities of sisters were compelled to upgrade their teaching training programs. Several communities began college programs at their motherhouses. Already in 1885 the Franciscan Sisters of Christian Charity had begun a normal school that reached a four-year status in 1939. In the thirties as well, the Franciscan Sisters of Penance and Charity in St. Francis opened St. Clare's College (later renamed Cardinal Stritch) in 1932, while the Agnesian Sisters of Fond du Lac opened Marian College in 1936, and the Dominican Sisters of Racine had commenced St. Albertus College (later Dominican College) a year earlier. After desultory efforts to unite with Marquette University, the School Sisters of St. Francis opened St. Joseph's Teaching College (later Alverno) in 1936. In 1937 the Franciscans of La Crosse changed the name of their junior college to Viterbo College.

Catholics attending the University of Wisconsin were not left unattended. In 1908 Archbishop Messmer founded a successful campus chaplaincy in Madison and staffed it with priests of high academic caliber, such as the aforementioned Aloysius Muench, who later became a seminary rector, bishop of Fargo, North Dakota, and apostolic NUNCIO to Germany.

The onset of the war and the return of prosperity to the nation ushered in new changes for the conditions of Catholic life in Wisconsin. By 1945 the Church had come through its early foundational period and had become a prominent and visible urban presence.

Expansion, Suburbia, and Transition (1945–). The dominant motif of this period was one of rapid expansion and a quickening of Catholic life, which seemed to some, a renaissance of Catholic life and culture in Wisconsin. The period after 1965 (the close of VATICAN COUNCIL II) to the early twenty-first century was marked by the reformist spirit of Vatican II, but it was also a time of social and cultural upheaval in American society. National turmoil over American involvement in Vietnam, the advance of the Civil Rights Movement for African Americans and others who also claimed to have been victims of discrimination, and the Watergate scandals that toppled the presidency of Richard M. Nixon (1913–1994), all created a level of ferment, anger, and turmoil in Wisconsin Catholicism. A conservative reaction began in the 1970s and especially in the 1980s as two strong-willed figures, American president Ronald Reagan (1911–2004) and Pope JOHN PAUL II, assumed control of state and Church respectively. Their leadership set the tone for the remainder of the twentieth century.

Postwar Population Growth. The birthrate explosion among Catholics led to unprecedented expansion of existing facilities, especially schools, in all dioceses. Postwar growth led to the creation of the fifth Wisconsin diocese in 1946, headquartered at Madison with Milwaukee priest William Patrick O'Connor as its first bishop. Milwaukee added thirty new parishes in the decade of the fifties; Green Bay, ten; La Crosse, nine; Madison, one; and Superior, twelve. Expansions of existing facilities also reflected the burgeoning growth. Total Catholic population in the decade broke the million mark as it moved from 934,048 to 1,256,147. Everywhere, building, expansion, and Catholic vitality seemed evident.

The Catholic high school was one beneficiary of this era of growth. Although Catholic secondary schools existed before World War II, their number and size increased dramatically after the war. Religious orders and dioceses invested millions of dollars in new buildings and programs for Catholic teens, hoping to keep them faithful to the Church, especially as a sometimes threatening youth culture vied for their hearts during the 1950s and 1960s. Thanks to the G.I. Bill (1944), Catholic colleges experienced tremendous expansion, and many of the sisters' colleges formed in the thirties evolved into four-year institutions that welcomed laywomen to their student bodies.

The advent of suburbanization brought another dynamic to Catholic life in and around the Wisconsin urban areas. As freeways and inexpensive housing lured more and more city dwellers to new suburban subdivisions, the long dominant urban church surrounded by a school and a large hall nestled in a working class neighborhood faded. Much of the tremendous parochial expansion in Milwaukee was in suburban areas of the diocese. The newly built interstate system cut through most big cities of the state, removing houses, neighborhoods, and even churches and other religious institutions. In Milwaukee it cut through the heavily Polish neighborhoods of the south side and caused the destruction of one of the older German parishes in the diocese. Parish memberships fell in areas in and around freeways, but at the same time parishes founded at the perimeter of the city were often inundated with new members, school enrollments, and demands for services.

Wisconsin seminaries also expanded to meet a vocation boom that packed houses of formation, novitiates, and religious houses all over the state with eager new recruits. In the forties, Milwaukee Archbishop Moses E. Kiley (1940–1953) already had separated the high school and junior college programs from the major seminary. But by the early fifties, the old seminary building was so crowded that students had to be turned away. In 1956 a major expansion of the seminary was undertaken, and it opened in time for the centennial celebration. On adjacent property the archdiocese built a magnificent new high school and college seminary that opened its doors in 1962.

Fearing that their students would be excluded from the burgeoning seminaries of the archdiocese, La Crosse under John P. Treacy and Green Bay under Stanislaus Bona (1945–1967) and William P. O'Connor (1946–1967) of Madison all built their own minor seminaries. Religious orders such as the Capuchins, Salvatorians, REDEMPTORISTS, PALLOTTINES, and CISTERCIANS also ran seminaries for their candidates. Ordination classes were large for every diocese. Archbishop Albert G. MEYER (1953–1958) of Milwaukee ordained more than fifty at one memorable ceremony in 1955.

Race and Urban Life. Yet another major postwar phenomenon was the advent of large numbers of African Americans to the urban areas of Wisconsin. Milwaukee saw its black population double between 1950 and 1960. Racine, Madison, and Beloit all saw tremendous increases in African Americans. Efforts to minister to African-American Catholics had begun in Milwaukee in 1908 when a lay couple, Lincoln and Julia Valle, opened a chapel dedicated to St. BENEDICT THE MOOR in Milwaukee. This endeavor, eventually taken over by the Capuchins, became an important hub of African-American Catholicism in Wisconsin. A church was built at Tenth and State for African-American Catholics, and the school continued to grow, with both day and boarding facilities. The school soon acquired the old Marquette Academy and ran a successful boarding school for African-American youth until the fifties.

The impact of African-American migration, especially heavy in the fifties and sixties, changed the face of Catholic life in the urban centers of Wisconsin, where the majority of Catholics lived. The north side of Milwaukee, once heavily German and dominated by fifteen predominantly German parishes, soon dwindled in Catholic population, which required fifteen parishes to consolidate to two in the summer of 1994. The downtown Racine area, once dotted with a myriad of ethnic churches, also saw the numbers attending Mass and attending once-thriving Catholic schools dwindle.

Although parishes in the heavily African-American sections of cities faded, other urban areas flourished with the arrival of new Catholic immigrants. Hispanic Catholics, largely of Mexican descent, began arriving in Milwaukee in the twenties to work at local tanneries. Through the efforts of layman Frank Gross and the KNIGHTS OF COLUMBUS, the spiritual needs of Mexican Catholics were met by various Spanish-speaking priests. In the 1920s Gross founded a chapel for their ministry in an old telephone office on the south side of Milwaukee. Later Hispanic Catholics took over the old Holy Trinity Church on the south side. From this church Hispanic Catholics moved steadily into some of the old Polish parishes on the south side of Milwaukee. A similar dynamic took place in all urbanized areas of Wisconsin as the number of Hispanics, mostly Mexicans, grew significantly in the last decades of the twentieth century.

Implementation of Vatican II. The impact of Vatican II on Wisconsin was largely favorable. All the bishops of the state attended the council. William E. Cousins of Milwaukee (1958–1977), George Hammes of Superior (1960–1985), and later Cletus F. O'Donnell (1967–1992) of Madison and Aloysius Wycislo (1968–1983) of Green Bay returned home to implement reforms. Changes in liturgical practice, architecture, and the enhanced role of the laity in divine services marked the most dramatic and visible changes brought about by the Council in the Advent of 1964. Vernacular masses, the use of popular musical idioms (especially folk music), and a stronger emphasis on hearing and responding to sacred Scripture were well accepted by most Catholics. Many places downplayed the devotionalism and extra-liturgical practice that had once been a hallmark of Catholic life. Pope PAUL VI's directive in 1967 restored the permanent diaconate to the Church. This rank of HOLY ORDERS had once been a distinct ministry in the Church, dedicated to liturgical service and the care of the poor. It had fallen into disuse in the West, and only men destined for the priesthood received it. The revived permanent diaconate was now open to married men, who would assist priests and bishops in the various ministries of the Church. Formation programs prepared the men and their wives for this new rank. In 1975 Milwaukee ordained some of the first deacons in Wisconsin. All Wisconsin dioceses, with the exception of Madison, had permanent diaconate programs in place during the 1970s and 1980s. The ministry continued to thrive into the twenty-first century.

Changes in Religious Roles. Another major transition that affected Wisconsin Catholics in the postconciliar period was the changing role of priests and sisters. Priestly formation changed decisively shortly after the council with the introduction of new theological curricula in the seminaries and a loosening of some of the strict discipline that shaped the lives of young seminarians. Catholic seminaries also began to admit lay men and women to their theological programs, and seminary practices were updated to meet new academic standards as well as an enhanced understanding of the psychological issues involved in embracing a life of celibacy. Religious orders of men and women also renewed their practices in the light of Vatican II. Many religious sisters modified or dropped their religious habits—the most visible outward sign of their community identity. Sisters engaged in other ministries besides education and nursing—some sought pastoral or counseling work and chaplaincies. Both seminaries and religious communities lost membership in the 1960s and 1970s, and huge motherhouses (some of them built on the eve of Vatican II) had vacant wings that had been built for novices and junior members. Many religious communities decreased their ambitious institutional expansion of the postwar era. Fewer and fewer priests, brothers, and sisters were found on the faculties of schools or working in social welfare or health-care institutions.

Priests and religious became more vocal in the post-conciliar years, and Wisconsin bishops were occasionally embroiled in disputes with some of their clerics. Many young men left the priesthood, and fewer and fewer entered St. Francis Seminary—by this time the seminary for the whole state of Wisconsin. Priests wore secular clothes, imitated some of the behavior of the local counterculture (beards and long hair), and insisted on living a much looser form of clerical life than the pastors who mentored them. Some of them publicly dissented from Church teachings on the issues of celibacy and the role of women. A few were vocal in their opposition to Pope Paul VI's ENCYCLICAL *Humanae vitae* (1968), which upheld traditional Church teaching on the immorality of artificial contraception.

Social Activism. More priests engaged in active witness to the value of the GOSPEL in the public sphere. Many became actively engaged with the national Civil Rights Movement and showed their support by marching with demonstrators. Milwaukee Father James Groppi (1930–1985) became the symbol of this new clerical activism. Born to a south side Italian family, young James Groppi was ordained a priest in 1958 and, while serving as an assistant pastor at St. Boniface Church on the north side of Milwaukee, in an African-American neighborhood, he took a leading role in the open-housing marches in the city in 1965. He soon became an acknowledged leader of efforts for racial justice in the heavily segregated city of Milwaukee, and, even as he pressed local and state government—and the local Church—to become more engaged in the racial issue, he also used his influence to quell racial disturbances that wracked Milwaukee in 1968 after the death of Martin Luther King Jr. (1929–1968). Groppi's activities won him support and acclaim from many Catholics but also seriously alienated others. Among his sharpest critics were the police chief Harold Brier, who accused Groppi of stirring up trouble, and Milwaukee's Catholic mayor Henry Maier (1917–1994), who frequently criticized Groppi's tactics in the press. Groppi eventually resigned the priesthood and married, but his work for SOCIAL JUSTICE—and also the strong feelings he engendered—lasted long after he was no longer a visible presence. Few other priests or religious in Wisconsin were quite as vocal or confrontative as Groppi, but many admired him and supported his efforts.

The commitment of women religious to social issues was even more dramatic; members of many congregations became active in advocacy for the poor and homeless and used their corporate investments to challenge the practices of the companies in whom they invested. Many Wisconsin motherhouses were declared nuclear-free zones in the eighties as a protest against the military build-up of the Reagan years. Even more lay and religious women in Wisconsin were influenced by Catholic feminist thought and practice and demanded a greater share in the leadership and governance of the Church. By the end of the millennium, women held key positions of chancellor in some Wisconsin dioceses, and lay and women religious administered priestless parishes in Green Bay, Milwaukee, and Superior.

The decades of the 1980s and 1990s were markedly affected by a conservative resurgence in both Church and state. The election of Pope John Paul II in 1978 and the election of Ronald Reagan in 1980 saw the elevation of two charismatic and popular, but traditional, leaders to high office. Pope John Paul was particularly intent on reining in some of the excesses of the postconciliar era and restoring a sense of direction and purpose to Catholicism. He imposed a strict discipline on dissenting theologians and insisted on bishops who were loyal and obedient to the Holy See. His international travels, including several trips to America, cemented the loyalty of millions. His long pontificate gave him a chance to totally remake the hierarchy of the United States and Wisconsin.

Weakland. Wisconsin was slow to respond to the changes from the VATICAN during the long pontificate of Pope John Paul (1978–2005). The bishops of the state, Cletus O'Donnell of Madison, Frederick Freking of La Crosse, George Hammes of Superior (later succeeded by Raphael Fliss), and Aloysius Wycislo of Green Bay, were all rather supportive of ecclesial reform. The leading Catholic figure in the state, Archbishop Rembert G. Weakland (1977–2002), was appointed to Milwaukee to succeed Archbishop William Cousins. The urban and scholarly Weakland hailed from Pennsylvania, where he had been archabbot of St. Vincent's Abbey in Latrobe. Since 1966 he had been abbot general of the Benedictine Confederation and stationed in Rome. Weakland thoroughly embraced the precepts of Vatican II and reshaped diocesan patterns to reflect his emphasis on collegiality and engagement with wider society. Weakland convened a synod of the diocese in 1987 called "Walking Together" that attempted to maximize the active participation of all archdiocesan Catholics in planning for the future. Sensitive to the rising demands of some that women be ordained to the diaconate and priesthood, Weakland attempted to give women a major voice in the affairs of the diocese; he appointed Dr. Barbara Ann Cusack as his chancellor, Maureen Gallagher as his delegate for parishes, and Ethel Ginthof as editor of the Catholic newspaper.

Weakland's first impulse in governance or in public controversy was to listen to all sides of a debate. For Wisconsin Catholics the ABORTION issue was one of many that created division and controversy. Like all other Catholic prelates, Weakland deplored the *Roe v. Wade* decision of 1973, which allowed states to permit abortions up to the first trimester. But in seeking the best way to curtail the practice—even among Catholic

St. Joan of Arc Chapel. *Renee DeBruin of Milwaukee, Wisconsin, prays for the ailing Pope John Paul II on April, 1, 2005, at the St. Joan of Arc Chapel on the Marquette University Campus in Milwaukee.* DARREN HAUCK/GETTY IMAGES

women—he chose not to engage in denunciations but listened to women, who could speak to this issue in a way men could not. Enlisting the help of Dr. Mary Feeley of St. Francis Seminary, he set up a series of listening sessions and called Catholic women to honestly discuss the issue. These sessions earned him the ire of some Catholics, who accused Weakland of condoning abortion by not denouncing it. Vatican intervention from Apostolic Nuncio Pio Laghi stopped the sessions. Weakland often felt the brunt of conservative Catholic anger. Many did not like his participation in the writing of *Economic Justice for All* (1985), a pastoral on the American economy commissioned by the U.S. bishops that at times was critical of the capitalist system. Others disliked his unwillingness to discipline priests who did not follow liturgical rules. Weakland's effort to renovate his cathedral also engendered heated public controversy. Weakland's last years were clouded by the shadow of the priest SEX ABUSE CRISIS. A number of Milwaukee priests, living and deceased, were credibly accused of misconduct with minors and removed from ministry. Similar actions were taken in all other Wisconsin dioceses. Efforts were made to reach out to victims and

steps were taken to insure such misconduct would never happen again. The reputation of the Church suffered greatly. In 2002 Weakland turned seventy-five and submitted his letter of resignation to the Holy See in April. In May 2002 revelations of an improper relationship with a young man and the transfer of archdiocesan funds as a payoff for the man's silence quickly terminated his episcopate. In August 2002 he was succeeded by the jovial, fifty-two-year-old Timothy Dolan. A priest of the Archdiocese of St. Louis, a former rectory of the Pontifical North American College in Rome, and an auxiliary bishop for not even a year, Dolan assumed the duties of Archbishop of Milwaukee on August 28, 2002.

On February 23, 2009, Pope Benedict XVI appointed Archbishop Dolan the new archbishop of New York. He was formally installed into his new archdiocese on April 15, 2009.

Other Hierarchical Changes. Cletus F. O'Donnell, bishop since 1967, was succeeded in 1993 by William Bullock, the former bishop of Des Moines. Bullock's retirement in 2003 brought Robert Morlino, the former bishop of Helena, to the diocese. In Superior, George

Hammes retired in 1985 and was replaced by Milwaukee priest Raphael Fliss. Fliss retired in 2007 and was replaced by Peter Christiansen, a Minneapolis priest, in 2007. In La Crosse, Bishop Freking (1964–1983) resigned the see, and local diocesan priest Bishop John Paul succeeded him in 1983, then in turn handed it over to Monsignor Raymond Burke, another native of the diocese, in 1994. Burke's tenure witnessed his rise as a major figure in the American hierarchy, particularly with his insistence on withholding Holy Communion from pro-choice politicians. Burke was transferred to St. Louis in 2003 and was succeeded by Chicago auxiliary Jerome Listecki in 2004. Green Bay was served by Aloysius Wycislo, who retired in 1983. His successor was Bishop Adam MAIDA, a canon and civil lawyer from the Pittsburgh chancery, who headed the diocese until 1990, when he was transferred to Detroit; he later was admitted to the Sacred College of Cardinals. Bishop Robert Banks of Boston arrived in 1990 and governed the diocese until 2003. He was succeeded by another son of the Pittsburgh diocese, Bishop David Zubik, who was in office for four years and then returned to Pittsburgh in 2007. Bishop David Ricken, formerly bishop of Cheyenne, Wyoming, took over in 2008.

SEE ALSO AFRICAN-AMERICAN CATHOLICS IN THE UNITED STATES (HISTORY OF); BALTIMORE, ARCHDIOCESE OF; BALTIMORE, COUNCILS OF; BENEDICTINES; DETROIT, ARCHDIOCESE OF; ECONOMIC JUSTICE FOR ALL; FEMINISM; HUMANAE VITAE; LA CROSSE, DIOCESE OF; LAITY, FORMATION AND EDUCATION OF; MINNESOTA, CATHOLIC CHURCH IN; MISSION HISTORY, I: CATHOLIC; NATIONAL COUNCIL OF CATHOLIC MEN (NCCM); NATIVISM, AMERICAN; SALVATORIANS; ST. LOUIS, ARCHDIOCESE OF; ST. PAUL AND MINNEAPOLIS, ARCHDIOCESE OF; TRAPPISTS.

BIBLIOGRAPHY

Steven M. Avella, ed., *Milwaukee Catholicism: Essays on Church and Community* (Milwaukee, Wis. 1991).

Steven M. Avella, *In the Richness of the Earth: A History of the Archdiocese of Milwaukee* (Milwaukee, Wis. 2002).

Gerald Edward Fisher, *Dusk Is My Dawn: The First Hundred Years of the Diocese of La Crosse, 1868–1968* (La Crosse, Wis. 1969).

Peter Leo Johnson, *Crosier on the Frontier: A Life of John Martin Henni, Archbishop of Milwaukee* (Madison, Wis. 1959).

Anthony J. Kuzniewski, *Faith and Fatherland: The Polish Church War in Wisconsin, 1896–1918* (Notre Dame, Ind. 1980).

M. Mileta Ludwig, *Right-Hand Glove Uplifted: A Biography of Michael Heiss* (New York 1968).

Pope Paul VI, *Humanae vitae*, On the Regulation of Birth (Encyclical, July 25, 1968), available from http://www.vatican.va/holy_father/paul_vi/encyclicals/documents/hf_p-vi_enc_25071968_humanae-vitae_en.html (accessed on February 3, 2009).

Leo Rummel, *History of the Catholic Church in Wisconsin* (Madison, Wis. 1976).

United States Conference of Catholic Bishops, *Economic Justice for All* (Pastoral Letter, 1986), available from http://www.osjspm.org/economic_justice_for_all.aspx (accessed February 3, 2009).

Rev. Steven M. Avella
Professor of History
Marquette University, Milwaukee, Wis. (2009)

WYOMING, CATHOLIC CHURCH IN

Wyoming is an Algonquin word for *basin*, an apt name for a high, dry, and windy country of wide-open sagebrush plains with grand vistas of broken mountain ranges. The American historian Hubert Bancroft preferred *Fontana*, as a parallel to *Montana*, to name a region that is the source of so many rivers (Bancroft 1890, p. 756). The landscape of Wyoming is big: "tremendious" (sic), to use the descriptive word of explorers Lewis and Clark (Louis 2002, [*passim*]); in the words of the psalmist, its "mountains leap like rams" (Ps 114:4) "and the rivers clap their hands" (Ps 98:8). Straddling the Continental Divide, the region was part of three annexations to the United States: the Louisiana purchase (1803), the Oregon country (1846), and the Mexican cession (1848). These three names reflect historic European claims defined by the major western watersheds: the Missouri-Mississippi, the Snake-Columbia, and the Green-Colorado. In Wyoming the Rocky Mountains break up into several distinct ranges providing two easy passages through the mountains, either by way of the Oregon-California Trail over the easy grade of the well-watered South Pass, or by way of the more direct Overland Trail through the arid Great Divide Basin, the route later followed by the transcontinental Union Pacific.

Before 1867 Wyoming was *terra incognita*, having neither definite name nor political organization. The Territory of Wyoming was organized in 1868 with the newly founded city of Cheyenne as the capital of an area of about 100,000 square miles and a population that had grown to only a little over half a million by 2008, and thus is a region of big spaces and few people, or as Governor Mike Sullivan (1987–1995) quipped, "Wyoming is like a small town with very long streets." In 1869 the first Wyoming Territorial Legislature granted suffrage to women, the first government in the world to give women the right to vote and hold elective office, hence the state motto, "Equal Rights." Despite this significant pioneer development, historian Bancroft commented: "The political history of Wyoming, fortunately for its happiness, is unmarked by any striking events." The creation in 1872 of the first national park, Yellowstone, brought national notice to the region, and in 1890 Wyoming was admitted to the Union as the forty-fourth state. Soon after, the United States Census Bureau declared the frontier closed.

Early Catholic History. On July 5, 1840, the Jesuit Pierre-Jean DE SMET had "the consolation of celebrating the holy sacrifice of the Mass," the first documented Eucharist in what became Wyoming. De Smet, who came from St. Louis with the American Fur Company's expedition to the Rendezvous on the Green River near present-day Daniel, was traveling to the Flathead Nation in answer to their request for *Blackrobes*, perhaps inspired by Catholic Iroquois who had drifted west. The Flathead delegation, with some Nez Percé and Shoshone mountain men and traders, made up the congregation. De Smet wrote,

> It was a spectacle truly moving to the heart of a missionary, to behold an assembly composed of so many different nations, who all assisted at our holy mysteries with great satisfaction. The Canadians sang hymns in French and Latin, and the Indians in their native tongue. It was truly a Catholic worship;...This place has been called since that time, by the French Canadians, *la Prairie de la Messe.* (de Smet 1905, I, 262)

In 1850, Wyoming east of the Continental Divide was included in the vicariate apostolic of the Indian Territory; west of the Divide remained a practically inaccessible part of the province of Oregon City (established 1846). The first vicar apostolic was a Jesuit, John Baptist MIÈGE (1850–1859), a Savoyard newly arrived from ROME, who established his residence in Leavenworth, Kansas. In consultation with De Smet, he worked to divide the vicariate, which was unmanageable because of its size. Accordingly, in 1857 the Sacred Congregation for the PROPAGATION OF THE FAITH created the vicariate apostolic of Nebraska, which included all of Wyoming. The first vicar apostolic was James Miles O'Gorman (1859–1874), O.C.S.O., born in Ireland and PRIOR of the Trappist MONASTERY of New Melleray founded in 1849 near Dubuque. O'Gorman established his residence in Omaha, the starting point of the Union Pacific Railroad. In 1867 O'Gorman established the first parish in Wyoming, a parish that included the whole length of the state along the railroad extending about 500 miles from Sidney, Nebraska, to the Wasatch Mountains in Utah. When the railroad was completed in 1869, O'Gorman took the train and became the first Catholic BISHOP to visit Wyoming. Two railroad-town parishes with resident pastors,

Cheyenne (1868) and Laramie (1872), and a hospital in Laramie founded by the Sisters of Charity of Leavenworth were established in O'Gorman's time.

James O'Connor, a native of Ireland and a priest of Philadelphia, was second vicar apostolic of Nebraska (1875–1885) and first bishop of Omaha (1885–1890). In 1877 O'Connor made a three-month visitation of Wyoming Catholic communities in towns fathered by railroads and mines, typically in a boom-and-bust pattern, where populations suddenly appeared and sporadically vanished. Six parishes were founded in O'Connor's time: Evanston (1878), Rawlins (1879), Lander (1882), Green River (1884), and Buffalo (1885), with Sheridan (1885) as a mission.

In 1884 the Society of Jesus founded St. Stephen's Indian Mission for the Northern Arapaho on the Wind River Reservation. By 1923 St. Stephen's parochial missions covered all of the Wind River Basin and served from time to time Lander, Riverton, Hudson, Shoshoni, Pilot Butte-Morton-Kinnear, Wind River, Mill Creek, and Dubois. On the reservation itself, Fort Washakie and Ethete remained missions of St. Stephen's. Through 2001 about sixty JESUITS, three or four at a time, came from several provinces of the Society of Jesus in turn: the German province (Buffalo, N.Y., 1884–1886), a Missouri province (St. Louis, 1886–1891), an Italian province (California Rocky Mountain Mission, 1891–1912), another Missouri province (St. Louis, 1912–1992), and then a Wisconsin province (Milwaukee, after 1992). St. Stephen's Indian School was first staffed by the Sisters of Charity of Leavenworth (1888–1890), then by the Sisters of ST. JOSEPH of Concordia, Kansas (1891–1892), and finally by the FRANCISCAN SISTERS of Philadelphia (since 1892). St. Katharine DREXEL visited St. Stephen's and was a considerable benefactress of the mission in the early days.

Religious orders continued to play a significant role in the Wyoming Catholic Church. Seventeen communities of religious women have served in active ministry, the Sisters of Charity of Leavenworth providing the largest number (479) since 1875. Benedictine nuns of Perpetual Adoration from Clyde, Missouri (originally from Maria-Rickenbach near Engleberg, Switzerland), founded a monastery in Wyoming in 1983. In 2003 a Discalced Carmelite monastery for men was established near Powell.

Cheyenne Diocese Established. The Diocese of Cheyenne (*Cheyennensis*), erected by LEO XIII on August 2, 1887, included the state of Wyoming along with Yellowstone National Park, and was suffragan first of St. Louis, then of Dubuque from 1893, and finally of the newly created metropolitan province of Denver in 1941.

Wyoming Catholic College, Lander, Wyoming. *Pictured here are students from the college in a classroom competition trying to help their teammates with guessing the correct Latin word on the chalkboard.* AP IMAGES

First Bishops. Maurice Francis Burke, born in Ireland and a priest of Chicago, was appointed the first bishop of Cheyenne (1887–1893). Upon his arrival in Wyoming, Burke found a DIOCESE about the size of Great Britain with four diocesan priests, eight churches, twenty-eight missions, and about 7,500 widely scattered Catholics. A Jesuit priest and brother resided with about one hundred FAITHFUL at St. Stephen's Indian Mission. Twenty-one religious women served there: Sisters of the Holy Child Jesus, who conducted an academy and school in Cheyenne (closed in 1933), and Sisters of Charity of Leavenworth, who briefly staffed a hospital and school in Laramie. Burke faced attacks against the Catholic Church by members of the AMERICAN PROTECTIVE ASSOCIATION (Know-Nothings) whose hostile acts eventually obliged the Sisters of Charity to leave Laramie (1895). Two parishes were founded in Burke's time, both for new coal mining towns, Rock Springs (1888) and Newcastle (1890). After taking stock of the vast territory, Burke quickly concluded that the erection of the diocese had been premature and petitioned Rome to suppress it. Consonant with the opposition of the

bishops of the surrounding dioceses, Rome rejected his petition and transferred him to the see of St. Joseph in Missouri (1893–1923).

Thomas Mathias Lenihan, born in Ireland and a priest of Dubuque, second bishop of Cheyenne (1897–1901), was appointed Burke's successor after almost four years. But Lenihan's poor health, exacerbated by the high altitude and dryness of Wyoming, severely restricted his activity and finally compelled him to return to Iowa. Only two parishes, Wheatland (1898) and Kemmerer (1901), were established in Lenihan's time. Hugh Cummiskey, pastor of St. Laurence O'Toole in Laramie, served as administrator of the diocese during the two interregna (1893–1897; 1901–1902).

Keane. James John Keane, third bishop of Cheyenne (1902–1911), raised in Minnesota and a priest of St. Paul, came to Wyoming at a time when economic conditions were rapidly improving after a decade of depression. Population increased by sixty percent between 1900 and 1910. Immigration, attracted by newly opened irrigated lands, was made possible by the construction of dams and the introduction of new methods of dry farming.

The increase in coal and iron mining, timber cutting, and oil and natural gas exploration of the vast reserves also contributed to the growth of population. These immigrants were mainly from Ireland and later from the Austrian Empire. Keane undertook the task of bringing order to the diocesan administration and incorporating the diocese according to the laws of the state of Wyoming. Pastors were instructed to incorporate their parishes and to have a board of directors, which included the bishop, the vicar general, the pastor, and two lay trustees. Keane was grateful for the help that he and the priests received from the American Mission Board. Soon after its foundation in 1905, Keane appealed to the Catholic Church Extension Society, which became a generous and never failing channel of funds that benefited the Wyoming Church. Keane directed the building of a CATHEDRAL and residence in Cheyenne; he laid the cornerstone of the cathedral on July 7, 1907. In Keane's time, the following parishes were established: Casper (1903), Torrington and Thermopolis (1906), Douglas (1907), Riverton (1908), Powell (1910), and a second parish for the Slavs in Rock Springs (1911). In 1911 Keane was named ARCHBISHOP of Dubuque (1911–1929).

The Order of Minors Conventual (O.M.C.) or, after 1945, Order of Friars Minor Conventual (O.F.M.Conv.), called *Black Franciscans* because of the color of their habit, came to Wyoming in 1909 at Keane's invitation. These FRIARS came from their nearby mission at Broken Bow, Nebraska, and belonged to the province of the Immaculate Conception (New York) until 1926, then to the province of Our Lady of Consolation (Indiana). On December 15, 1911, Keane formally entrusted the Franciscans with the spiritual care of the parish of St. James in Douglas, together with churches and missions, founded and to be founded in four counties of eastern Wyoming along the North Platte River—Converse, Niobrara, Goshen, and Platte—an area of more than 11,000 square miles, about one-tenth of the state, making it one of the largest territorial parishes in the United States. Three or four friars at a time lived at St. James Friary in Douglas and cared for thirteen missions serving ranchers, farmers, miners, and oil-field workers. Before they went to parishes as resident pastors, the friars normally took the train to the following missions: Lusk, Keeline, Van Tassel, Manville, Lance Creek, and Flattop to the east; Glenrock to the west; and Glendo, Hartville-Sunrise, Guernsey, Torrington, and Wheatland as well as Chugwater (a *blue moon* mission attended on the fifth Sundays of the month) to the south. The Franciscans also briefly maintained a monthly mission to the new Salt Creek oilfield community at Lavoye, now Midwest, in Natrona County (1923–1926). After a half-century of the service of forty-nine friars, the Conventual Franciscans withdrew from Wyoming and formally relinquished their remaining churches in 1960, with the exception of Wheatland, which they kept until 1970.

McGovern and Newell. Patrick Aloysius McGovern, the austere and formidable fourth bishop of Cheyenne (1912–1951), "hegemonist of the hierarchy" as he called himself, was a native and a priest of Omaha. McGovern held two diocesan synods, one at the beginning of his administration (1913) to introduce himself to the priests and one at the end (1948) to introduce the new coadjutor, Hubert Newell. A further purpose of both synods, which included only priests, was to provide for the orderly government of clergy and the people by strengthening ecclesiastical discipline. At the 1913 synod McGovern promulgated the decrees of the plenary COUNCILS OF BALTIMORE and the statutes of the first synod of the Diocese of Omaha to place the governance of the diocese on a regular juridical foundation. Similarly, the 1948 synod passed regulations regarding the duties of priests, administration of sacraments, conduct of LITURGY, preaching and giving instruction, and the care of temporalities, to be in accord with the 1917 Code of Canon Law. Parishes founded in McGovern's time were Pine Bluffs (1913), Greybull (1919), Monarch (1924), Gillette (1926), a second parish for Latinos in Cheyenne (1929), Pinedale (1940), Cody (1942), Worland (1949), and Superior (1949). The Monarch parish was moved to Ranchester (1955) when the coal mines around Monarch closed. An orphan himself, raised by his grandparents, McGovern was very much concerned about the plight of orphans in Wyoming, and worked tirelessly to establish St. Joseph's Children's Home (1930), eventually welcoming the Franciscan Sisters of Milwaukee (1939) to care for the children there. In 1941 McGovern published an authoritative *History of the Diocese of Cheyenne*, compiled from first-hand accounts written by pastors after 1925.

Hubert Michael Newell, native and a priest of Denver, fifth bishop of Cheyenne (1951–1978), was appointed coadjutor bishop of Cheyenne with right of succession on August 2, 1947, and formally took the office of ordinary at the death of his predecessor. Newell began publication of the *Wyoming Catholic Register* (April 11, 1952). In 1953 he persuaded the ladies of the long-existing altar and ROSARY societies to form the Wyoming Council of Catholic Women, a chapter of the national organization, with similar aims and functions as the KNIGHTS OF COLUMBUS. Also in 1953 Newell divided the diocese into five deaneries centered at Cheyenne, Rock Springs, Thermopolis, Sheridan, and Casper. New parishes were founded: two more in Casper (1954 and 1963) and one more each in Cheyenne (1957), Jackson (1955), Saratoga (1960), and Sundance (1966). Guernsey (1969) was founded for the parishioners who moved from Hartville-Sunrise because the iron mine had closed. Mission chapels were established in Hanna and Medicine Bow. Newell established St. Paul's Newman Center (1957) in Laramie and initiated the Catholic Youth Organization (CYO), which held its first state convention in 1959. Newell attended all the sessions of VATICAN COUNCIL II, convened by Pope JOHN XXIII in 1962. After the council Newell quickly implemented the prescribed liturgical, sanctuary, and other church structural changes, and in 1974 he began commissioning men and women as extraordinary ministers of Holy Communion. In 1972 the newly founded diocesan presbyteral council, seconded by the priests' senate, recommended that all pastors be required to retire at age seventy-five, a recommendation that ended the half-century era when pastors remained in the same place for life. At the same time the tenure of pastors and assistants was limited to six years with the option for another six-year term. St. Joseph Society was organized to provide pensions for retired priests. Married permanent deacons began to appear in the 1970s. Newell set up an advisory diocesan pastoral council and a board of Catholic education, the members of both elected on the deanery level. Hubert Joseph Hart came to Cheyenne as auxiliary bishop in 1976, and in 1978 Newell resigned as ordinary, remaining apostolic ADMINISTRATOR until a successor was named. Newell retired to serve at St. Joseph's Orphanage, where he died in 1987.

Hart and Ricken. Joseph Hart, born in Missouri and a priest of Kansas City-St. Joseph, was installed as the sixth bishop of Cheyenne (1978–2001). During Hart's regime the CYO flourished. He continued the post–Vatican II process of using lay administrators and of encouraging lay consultative bodies. After 1980 Hart saw to the establishment of parish pastoral councils and, after 1985, diocesan and parish finance councils. In 1993, after a preparatory three-year spiritual-renewal program, the laity of Wyoming were invited to participate in the third diocesan synod where Hart challenged the participants "to dance out to the edge of possibility" in finding problems and solving them together in an ongoing process. Following the directives of Vatican II, old churches were remodeled and new churches were built to accommodate populations that came following energy booms in oil and coal and the opening of power plants. After Newell, no new parishes were founded in Wyoming, although the two parishes in Rock Springs were combined into one in 1998 under the title of Holy Spirit Catholic Community. In answer to Hart's petition for a successor, John PAUL II on January 6, 2000, ordained David Laurin Ricken, born in Kansas and a priest of Pueblo, coadjutor of Cheyenne with right of succession. On September 26, 2001, Ricken became seventh bishop of Cheyenne (2001–2008).

The burgeoning Latino immigration was the most significant trend affecting the ethnic composition of the Catholic population in Wyoming. Religious vocations in the Wyoming Church paralleled Church trends throughout the industrialized world. After 1965 the number of priests and religious women steadily declined. The diocese of Cheyenne had recruited priests from outside from the beginning, first from Europe, then from the eastern United States and from religious orders. In the 1990s recruitment shifted to Africa, Asia, and South America. Ricken ordained seven priests and ten deacons for the diocese (2000–2008). To help parishes affected by the declining number of priests, in 2007 Ricken established a one-time, five-year permanent DEACON training program administered by the diocese and facilitated in academic formation by ST. MEINRAD ARCHABBEY, with candidates meeting monthly in Casper for instruction. In 2008 a house of discernment was founded in Laramie to foster and test vocations. As part of a pastoral plan, Ricken instituted a stewardship program to mobilize the time, talent, and treasure of the people through lay stewardship committees in the thirty-six parishes and forty-two missions of the diocese.

Ricken actively supported parochial education by clarifying elementary catechetical goals and personally approving instructional texts, by lowering the age for CONFIRMATION to spread the GRACE of the sacrament earlier and more widely among teens, and by expanding youth ministry programs. He promoted the preservation and construction of parochial schools, opening the John Paul II parochial school in Gillette in 2007. This brought the total of diocesan parochial schools to seven in 2008. Ricken resonated with a current of a popular hunger to preserve a distinctive Catholic cultural identity seemingly lost in a secularized post–modern world since Vatican II. He responded to this challenge by encouraging the restoration of popular DEVOTIONS, especially Eucharistic adoration and PILGRIMAGES, and by permitting attempts to revive the TRIDENTINE MASS as allowed by BENEDICT XVI. Inspired by the initial success of a two-week summer School of Catholic Thought and after three years of planning, Ricken convoked the new Wyoming Catholic College in Lander on September 3, 2007. Then on July 9, 2008, Benedict XVI named Ricken bishop of Green Bay, Wisconsin. The college of consultors elected the vicar general, Fr Michael Carr, diocesan administrator.

SEE ALSO BALTIMORE, COUNCILS OF; BENEDICTINE NUNS AND SISTERS; CANON LAW, HISTORY OF; CARMELITES, DISCALCED; DENVER, ARCHDIOCESE OF; DISCERNMENT, SPIRITUAL; DUBUQUE, ARCHDIOCESE OF; KNOW-NOTHINGISM; MISSION AND MISSIONS; NATIONAL COUNCIL OF CATHOLIC WOMEN (NCCW); NEBRASKA, CATHOLIC CHURCH IN; OREGON, CATHOLIC CHURCH IN; ST. LOUIS, ARCHDIOCESE OF; TRAPPISTS; UTAH, CATHOLIC CHURCH IN.

BIBLIOGRAPHY

Hubert Howe Bancroft, *History of Nevada, Colorado, and Wyoming, 1540–1888* (San Francisco 1890).

Gloria S. Carlson, *A Brief History of the Diocese of Cheyenne* (Cheyenne, Wyo. 1993).

Henry W. Casper, S.J., *History of the Catholic Church in Nebraska*, 2 vols. (Milwaukee, Wisc. 1960, 1966).

Pierre-Jean de Smet, S.J., *Life, Letters and Travels of Father Pierre-Jean de Smet, S.J., 1801–1873*, edited and annotated by Hiram Martin Chittenden and Alfred Talbot Richardson (New York 1905).

Diocese of Cheyenne, *History of the Catholic Church in Wyoming*, available from http://www.dioceseofcheyenne.org/history/index.html (accessed October 31, 2008).

Mark Junge, compiler, *Wyoming: A Pictorial History* (Norfolk, Va. 1989, repr. 2004).

Meriwether Louis, *The Journals of the Lewis and Clark Expedition*, 13 vols., edited by Gary E. Moulton (Lincoln, Neb. 2002).

Patrick A. McGovern, ed., *History of the Diocese of Cheyenne* (Cheyenne, Wyo. 1941).

W. E. Mullen, "Wyoming," in *The Catholic Encyclopedia* (New York 1912).

H. M. Newell, "Diocese of Cheyenne," in *New Catholic Encyclopedia* (New York 1964).

Rev. Jan Joseph Santich
Pastor, St. Patrick Church
Wheatland, Wyo. (2009)

INDEX

H

I

Sacrosanctum concilium, (Constitution of the Sacred Liturgy, (Vatican Council II), 1:151, 2:758, 809

Sacus, Samuel S., 2:861

Sadie, P. Edward, 2:861

Safeguarding the Children program, 2:503

Sailer, Johann Michael, 1:60

St. Aloysius Church (Spokane, WA), 2:*854*

St. Anne's Shrine (Isle La Motte, VT), 2:*840*

St. Ann's Church (VA), 2:*847*

St. Anthony of Padua Chapel (West Orange, NJ), 2:*631*

St. Augustine (FL), 1:337–339, *340, 341*

St. Benedict Center (Boston, MA), 1:243

St. Benedict's Church (Honaunau, HI), 1:*386*

St. Catherine of Siena Institute (Colorado Springs, CO), 1:149

St. Cecilia's Cathedral (Omaha, NE), 2:694

Saint Christopher's Catholic Church (Willow, AK), 1:*22*

Saint Colman Catholic Church (Ardmore, PA), 2:*707*

Saint Cyr, Irenaeus, 1:418

Saint Fidelis Friary (Victoria, KS), 2:471

St. Florian's Church (Hamtramck, MI), 2:*562*

St. Francis of Assisi (Web site), 1:438

St. Francis of Assisi Cathedral (Santa Fe), 2:*776, 777, 778*

St. Ignatius Church (San Francisco, CA), 2:*770*

St. Joan of Arc Chapel (Milwaukee, WI), 2:*875*

St. John the Evangelist Cathedral (Milwaukee, WI), 2:*573*

St. John Vianney Theological Seminary (Denver, CO), 1:149, 215

St. John's Catholic Church (Omaha, NE), 2:*695*

St. John's College (Fordham, NY), 2:480, 664

St. John's Summer Institute (Collegeville, MN), 2:739

St. Joseph (MS), Diocese of, 2:586

St. Joseph Cathedral (Oklahoma City, OK), 2:*689*

Saint Leonard's Church (Boston, MA), 1:*91*

St. Louis (MO), Archdiocese of, 2:586, **797–802,** *800*

St. Louis (MO), Diocese of, 2:585–586, 797, 798

St. Louis Basilica (New Orleans), 2:640

St. Margaret Catholic Church (Bayou la Batre, AL), 2:*589*

St. Mary's Cathedral (Nashville, TN), 2:812, *813, 814*

St. Mary's Cathedral -Basilica of the Assumption (Covington, KY), 2:*479*

St. Mary's Cathedral Basilica (Galveston, TX), 1:*350*

St. Mary's Cathedral of the Immaculate Conception (Portland, OR), 2:738

St. Mary's Catholic Church (Miami, FL), 2:*558*

St. Mary's in the Mountains Church (Virginia City, NV), 2:*622*

St. Mary's Seminary (Baltimore, MD), 1:57–58, 2:*533*

St. Michael Church (Pensacola, FL), 1:*342*

St. Michael's Catholic Church (Chicago, IL), 1:*128*

St. Palais, Maurice de (bp.), 1:418

St. Patrick's Cathedral (New York, NY), 2:651, *651,* 652, 653, 657

St. Paul (MN), Diocese of, 2:576–578, 802–803, 868

St. Paul and Minneapolis (MN), Archdiocese of, 2:580, 677, 794, **802–808,** *804*

St. Paul and Minneapolis (MN), Diocese of, 2:579, 580

St. Paul's Roman Catholic Church (New Bern, NC), 2:*674*

St. Petersburg (FL), Diocese of, 1:343

St. Stephen Roman Catholic Church (Cleveland, OH), 2:*685*

St. Therese Church (Boston, MA), 1:*95*

Saint Therese of Lisieux (Web site), 1:438

St. Thomas Aquinas (Web site), 1:438

St. Thomas Syro-Malabar Catholic Diocese, 1:408

Saints, 1:437–438, 2:729
See also specific saints

Sakharov, Andrei, 2:455

Salatka, Charles (abp.), 2:690, 693

Salesians, 1:415

Saligny, Alphonse de, 2:760

Sallustius, 2:618

Salmon, Anthony, 2:478

Salpingectomy, 1:253–254

Salpingostomy, 1:253–254

Salpointe, Jean Baptiste (abp. of Santa Fe), 1:37, 147, 2:637, 638, 775

Salt Lake City (UT), Diocese of, 2:623, 834–835, *835,* 836, *836,* 837

Saltarelli, Michael (bp.), 1:*208*

Saltationism, 1:315

Salvation, 1:233–236, 287

Salvifici doloris (apostolic letter, John Paul II), 2:461

Sambi, Pietro (abp.), 2:833

Same-sex marriage, 1:114, 2:532, 540, 772, 843

Samoans, 2:492

San Antonio (TX), Archdiocese of, 2:**760–764,** *763,* 817–818, *818,* 820

San Diego (CA), Diocese of, 2:494

San Francisco (CA)
Diocese of, 1:108
earthquake of 1906, 2:769
same-sex marriage, 1:114

San Francisco (CA), Archdiocese of, 1:106, 107, 2:**764–773,** *770, 771*
establishment, 2:493, 497
Nevada, 2:623
Utah, 2:833, 834

San Francisco de Asis Mission Church (Taos, NM), 2:*635*

San Gabriel Mission (Los Angeles, CA), 2:493

San Souci, Emery, 2:529

San Xavier Del Bac Mission (Tucson, AZ), 1:*36*

Sanchez, Robert F. (abp. of Santa Fe), 2:639, 776, 777, 778

ISBN-13: 978-1-4144-7528-8
ISBN-10: 1-4144-7528-4

90000

9 781414 475288